D1369650

DUN & BRADSTREET/ GALE GROUP

Industry Handbook

1521-6640

DUN & BRADSTREET/ GALE GROUP

Industry Handbook

Construction and Agriculture

Jennifer Zielinski, Editor

GALE GROUP

Detroit
San Francisco
London
Boston
Woodbridge, CT

Jennifer Zielinski, *Editor*
Erin E. Braun, *Managing Editor*

Wendy Blurton, *Buyer*
Dorothy Maki, *Manufacturing Manager*

Cynthia Baldwin, *Product Design Manager*
Michelle DiMercurio, *Senior Art Director*

ISBN 0-7876-3771-8
ISBN 0-7876-4909-0 (5 volume set)

Printed in the United States of America

CONTENTS

INTRODUCTION

This section presents a general introduction to the contents of *Dun & Bradstreet/Gale Industry Handbook: Construction and Agriculture*. In addition to presenting information on the book's contents, sources, organization, indices, and appendix, special explanations are provided for (1) the statistical tables and the projections used for some years of data and (2) the industry norms and ratios used in the Dun & Bradstreet, Inc. data. Information for contacting the editors completes the introduction.

Dun & Bradstreet/Gale Industry Handbook: Construction and Agriculture is a timely compilation of information on companies, associations, consultants, trade publications, and trade shows participating in or supporting these two industries. Recent statistics from corporate and government sources highlight financial, employment, and other trends. Descriptive materials are included on major industry issues (Foreword), industry history and trends (Industry Overview) and on recent mergers and acquisitions (Mergers & Acquisitions). Overall, *Construction and Agriculture* provides an up-to-date and comprehensive guide to these industries for all—the analyst, investor, planner, marketeer, benchmarker, student, or interested member of the public.

CONTENTS AND SOURCES

Construction and Agriculture is divided into two parts, with Part I featuring *Construction* and Part II featuring *Agriculture*. Each part has the same structure but different content.

Part I - Construction covers 27 industries and *Part II - Agriculture* covers 32 industries as defined in the Standard Industrial Classification (SIC) system. The SIC system is presently undergoing a major revision, with SIC codes in the process of being replaced by North American Industry Classification System (NAICS) codes. This book is still organized by SIC code because most data providers still use the "old" system. However, an SIC to NAICS and a NAICS to SIC conversion table is provided in the appendix. Data provided in *Construction and Agriculture*, shown here in chapter order, include the following categories—

Description and Context. The Foreword presents an expert view of each industry at the beginning of each part. In each part, Chapter 1 features an overview of the industry, including its history, important participants, current trends, and future directions.

Statistics. Chapter 2 presents federal government statistics and projections from 1987 to 1998. These data include establishments, employment, compensation, revenues, and ratios. Data in this chapter are drawn from the most recent edition of *Agriculture, Mining, and Construction USA*.

Company Information. Chapter 3 shows financial norms and ratios for 1996, 1997 and 1998. A full discussion of norms and ratios is presented, below, under the heading **Industry Norms and Ratios**. Chapter 4 presents company capsules for leading participants in each industry in directory format, including company name, parent, address, telephone, sales, employment, company type, SIC classification, description, and name and title of the leading company officer. Chapter 5 shows companies in rank order, first by sales volume and then by employment. The data in Chapters 3-5 in each part were prepared by and are shown by special arrangement with Dun & Bradstreet, Inc. Chapter 6 presents a summary of recent merger and acquisition activity in each industry.

Association Data. Chapter 7 presents a listing of domestic and international associations directly involved in each industry or in support of their activities. Information provided includes name of the organization, electronic access (url and/or e-mail), address, contact person, telephone and fax number, and a full description of the organization's activities, including such categories as founding date, membership, staff. Data shown are adapted from Gale's *Encyclopedia of Associations*.

Consultants. Information on industry consultants is shown in Chapter 8, adapted from Gale's *Consultants and Consulting Organizations Directory*. Categories shown include the name of the organization, e-mail and/or url for electronic access, address, leading officer, telephone and fax numbers, and a full description, including founding date and staff.

Trade Information Sources. Chapter 9 features publications offering trade information for each of the industries covered. The entries are adapted from Gale's *Encyclopedia of Business Information Sources* and include name of the book, periodical, or database, publisher, electronic contact (e-mail, url), complete address, telephone and fax numbers, and a description.

Trade Show Information. Chapter 10 presents information needed by all those planning to visit or to participate in trade shows for the construction or agriculture sectors. Data are drawn from Gale's *Trade Shows Worldwide*. Entries include the name of the show, sponsoring organization, electronic access (e-mail, url), address, telephone and fax numbers, and a description including such categories as frequency of the event, audience, and principal exhibits.

ORGANIZATION

Construction and Agriculture is divided into two parts and organized by chapter. A common Master Index, Geographical Index, and an SIC Index follow Part II. The Appendix presents an SIC to NAICS and a NAICS to SIC lookup guide. Each chapter in each part begins with a brief description of contents and formats (if required). Additional explanatory materials are provided in this Introduction to *Chapter 2, Industry Statistics & Performance Indicators* (see **Statistics and Projections**, below) and *Chapter 3, Financial Norms and Ratios* (see **Industry Norms and Ratios**, below). The formats of these chapters are the same in both parts.

Chapter 1   Industry Overview
Chapter 2   Industry Statistics & Performance
            Indicators
Chapter 3   Financial Norms and Ratios
Chapter 4   Company Directory
Chapter 5   Rankings and Companies
Chapter 6   Mergers & Acquisitions
Chapter 7   Associations
Chapter 8   Consultants
Chapter 9   Trade Information Sources
Chapter 10 Trade Shows

INDEXES AND APPENDIX

Construction and Agriculture features three indexes. Each index provides combined coverage of Parts I and II. The **Master Index** shows company, organization, topical terms, and personal names in alphabetical order, with page references. Also included, in alphabetical order, are industry names followed by SIC codes in parentheses. The **Geographical Company Index** shows companies arranged by state and then in alphabetical order, with page references to each part's Chapter 4. The **Company Index by SIC** presents the Chapter 4 company information arranged numerically by SIC codes.

The Appendix, **SIC/NAICS Conversion Guide**, is a two part look-up facility featuring SIC to NAICS con-

versions in the first part and NAICS to SIC conversions in the second part. The first part is organized by SIC codes in ascending order; the second part is sorted by NAICS codes in ascending order.

STATISTICS AND PROJECTIONS

The tables presented in each part's Chapter 2 are drawn from federal government sources. Federal surveys are comprehensive and accurate, but they are published at some significant delay from the time of data collection. For this reason, projections were used to show data for more recent or future years in the tables in Chapter 2. In this section, terminology used in government data sources is briefly explained and the methods used in making the projections are outlined.

Terminology. Federal data make use of two terms subject to some misunderstanding. These are *establishments* and *value of shipments*.

- **Establishments** are physical locations where economic activity takes place. The establishment count for an industry is rarely the same as a census of the number of *companies* participating. There are typically more establishments than companies in an industry: many companies have multiple locations.

- **Value of Shipments** includes all products shipped from a plant, including primary and secondary products, transfers of goods to another plant, miscellaneous receipts (including contact work and work not related to the SIC at all), sales of scrap, and sales of purchased and resold products. Value of shipments, therefore, includes more than is normally associated with the concept of industry *sales*. The government makes a distinction between value of shipments and value of *product* shipments. In some SICs, the two values are very close (with value of shipments typically slightly higher). In others, there is a significant spread between the two.

Projections. The projections shown in the tables of Chapter 2 are footnoted to indicate that values are estimates. Projections are based on a curve-fitting algorithm using the least-squares method. In essence, the algorithm calculates a trend line for the data using existing data points (survey data). The trend line is the best "straight" line that can be laid over the existing points. Once the trend line has been established, it can be extended into the future. Estimated values, therefore, are points on the extended trend line indicated by past information.

INDUSTRY NORMS AND RATIOS

For each industry, as denoted by SIC, two tables are presented in each part's Chapter 3. The first, entitled **D&B Industry Norms**, presents financial norms for that industry. The second, entitled **D&B Key Business Ratios**, presents ratios. In what follows, each type of table is explained in some detail.

INDUSTRY NORMS

This table shows data for the years 1996-1998. Each table is entitled *D&B Industry Norms* followed by the SIC code and industry name of the industry featured. Next to each year, in parenthesis, is shown the number of companies in the sample used. The "typical" balance-sheet figures are in the first column and the "common-size" balance-sheet figures (in percent) are in the second.

The Common-Size Financial Statement. The common-size balance-sheet and income statement present each item of the financial statement (e.g., *Cash*) as a percentage of its respective aggregate total (e.g., *Total Assets*). Common-size percentages are computed for all statement items for each company in the industry sample. An average for each item is then calculated and presented as the industry norm. This enables the analyst to examine the current composition of assets, liabilities and sales of a particular industry.

The Typical Financial Statement. The typical balance-sheet figures are the result of translating the common-size percentages into dollar figures. They permit, for example, a quick check of the relative size of assets and liabilities between one's own company and that company's own line of business.

Typical values are computed as follows: after the common-size percentages have been calculated for the sample, the actual financial statements are sorted by both total assets and total sales, with the median, or

mid-point figure in both of these groups serving as the "typical" amount. Next, the typical balance-sheet and income statement dollar figures are computed by multiplying the item totals by the common-size percentages.

For example, if the median *Total Assets* for an SIC category is $669,599 and the common-size figure for *Cash* is 9.2 percent, then multiplying the two produces a cash figure of $61,603 for the typical balance sheet (669,559 x 0.092).

KEY BUSINESS RATIOS

This table shows data for the years 1996-1998. For each year, data are provided for the upper quartile, median, and lower quartile of the sample, providing the analyst with an even more refined set of figures. These ratios cover critical areas of business performance with indicators of solvency, efficiency and profitability.

The data serve as the basis for a profound and well-documented insight into all aspects of performance for anyone interested in the financial workings of business—executives and managers, credit executives, bankers, lenders, investors, academicians and students. An explanation of the ratios follows.

In the ratio tables shown, the figures are broken down into the median, upper, and lower quartiles. The *median* is the midpoint of all companies in the sample. The *upper* quartile shows the midpoint of the upper half, the *lower* quartile the midpoint of the lower half of the total sample.

Upper quartile figures are not always the highest numerical value, nor are lower quartile figures always the lowest numerical value. The quartile listings reflect *judgmental ranking*, thus the upper quartile represents the best condition for any given ratio and is not necessarily the highest numerical value. For example, a low numerical value is *better* for such ratios as Total Liabilities-to-Net Worth or Collection Period, indicating low liabilities and rapid collection of receivables.

Each of the 14 ratios is calculated individually for every company in the sample. These individual figures are then sorted for each ratio according to condition (best to worst). The value that falls in the middle of this series becomes the median (or mid-point) for that ratio in that line of business. The figure halfway between the median and the best condition of the series becomes the upper quartile; and the number halfway between the median and the least favorable condition of the series is the lower quartile.

In a statistical sense, each median is considered the *typical* ratio figure for a concern in a given category.

SOLVENCY RATIOS

Quick Ratio

$$\frac{Cash + Accounts\ Receivable}{Current\ Liabilities}$$

The Quick Ratio is computed by dividing cash plus accounts receivable by total current liabilities. Current liabilities are all the liabilities that fall due within one year. This ratio reveals the protection afforded short-term creditors in cash or near-cash assets. It shows the number of dollars of liquid assets available to cover each dollar of current debt. Any time this ratio is as much as 1 to 1 (1.0) the business is said to be in a liquid condition. The larger the ratio the greater the liquidity.

Current Ratio

$$\frac{Current\ Assets}{Current\ Liabilities}$$

Total current assets are divided by total current liabilities. Current assets include cash, accounts and notes receivable (less reserves for bad debts), advances on inventories, merchandise inventories and marketable securities. This ratio measures the degree to which current assets cover current liabilities. The higher the ratio the more assurance exists that the retirement of current liabilities can be made. The current ratio measures the margin of safety available to cover any possible shrinkage in the value of current assets. Normally a ratio of 2 to 1 (2.0) or better is considered good.

Current Liabilities to Net Worth

$$\frac{Current\ Liabilities}{Net\ Worth}$$

Current Liabilities to Net Worth is derived by dividing current liabilities by net worth. This contrasts the funds that creditors are risking temporarily with the funds permanently invested by the owners. The smaller the net worth and the larger the liabilities, the less security is afforded the creditors. Care should be exercised when selling any firm with current liabilities exceeding two-thirds (66.6 percent) of net worth.

Current Liabilities to Inventory

$$\frac{Current\ Liabilities}{Inventory}$$

Dividing current liabilities by inventory yields another indication of the extent to which the business relies on funds from disposal of unsold inventories to meet its debts. This ratio combines with Net Sales to Inventory to indicate how management controls inventory. It is possible to have decreasing liquidity while maintaining consistent sales-to-inventory ratios. Large increases in sales with corresponding increases in inventory levels can cause an inappropriate rise in current liabilities if growth isn't managed wisely.

Total Liabilities to Net Worth

$$\frac{Total\ Liabilities}{Net\ Worth}$$

This ratio is obtained by dividing total current plus long-term and deferred liabilities by net worth. The effect of long-term (funded) debt on a business can be determined by comparing this ratio with Current Liabilities to Net Worth. The difference will pinpoint the relative size of long-term debt, which, if sizable, can burden a firm with substantial interest charges. In general, total liabilities should not exceed net worth (100 percent) since in such cases creditors have more at stake than owners.

Fixed Assets to Net Worth

Fixed Assets

—————

Net Worth

Fixed assets are divided by net worth. The proportion of net worth that consists of fixed assets will vary greatly from industry to industry, but generally a smaller proportion is desirable. A high ratio is unfavorable because heavy investment in fixed assets indicates that either the concern has a low net working capital and is overtrading or has utilized large funded debt to supplement working capital. Also, the larger the fixed assets, the bigger the annual depreciation charge that must be deducted from the income statement. Normally, fixed assets above 75 percent of net worth indicate possible over-investment and should be examined with care.

EFFICIENCY RATIOS

Collection Period

Accounts Receivable

—————

Sales x 365

Accounts receivable are divided by sales and then multiplied by 365 days to obtain this figure. The quality of the receivables of a company can be determined by this relationship when compared with selling terms and industry norms. In some industries where credit sales are not the normal way of doing business, the percentage of cash sales should be taken into consideration. Generally, where most sales are for credit, any collection period more than one-third over normal selling terms (40.0 for 30-day terms) is indicative of some slow-turning receivables. When comparing the collection period of one concern with that of another, allowances should be made for possible variations in selling terms.

Sales to Inventory

Sales

————

Inventory

Obtained by dividing annual net sales by inventory. Inventory control is a prime management objective since poor controls allow inventories to become costly to store, obsolete, or insufficient to meet demands. The sales-to-inventory relationship is a guide to the rapidity at which merchandise is being moved and the effect on the flow of funds into the business. This ratio varies widely between lines of business, and a company's figure is only meaningful when compared with industry norms. Individual figures that are outside either the upper or lower quartiles for a given industry should be examined with care. Although low figures are usually the biggest problem, as they indicate excessively high inventories, extremely high turnovers might reflect insufficient merchandise to meet customer demand and result in lost sales.

Asset to Sales

Total Assets

—————

Net Sales

Assets to sales are calculated by dividing total assets by annual net sales. This ratio ties in sales and the total investment that is used to generate those sales. While figures vary greatly from industry to industry, by comparing a company's ratio with industry norms it can be determined whether a firm is overtrading (handling an excessive volume of sales in relation to investment) or undertrading (not generating sufficient sales to warrant the assets invested). Abnormally low percentages (above the upper quartile) can indicate overtrading which may lead to financial difficulties if not corrected. Extremely high percentages (below the lower quartile) can be the result of overly conservative or poor sales management, indicating a more aggressive sales policy may need to be followed.

Sales to Net Working Capital

Sales

―――

Net Working Capital

Net sales are divided by net working capital (net working capital is current assets minus current liabilities). This relationship indicates whether a company is overtrading or conversely carrying more liquid assets than needed for its volume. Each industry can vary substantially and it is necessary to compare a company with its peers to see if it is either overtrading on its available funds or being overly conservative. Companies with substantial sales gains often reach a level where their working capital becomes strained. Even if they maintain an adequate total investment for the volume being generated (Assets to Sales), that investment may be so centered in fixed assets or other noncurrent items that it will be difficult to continue meeting all current obligations without additional investment or reducing sales.

Accounts Payable to Sales

Accounts Payable

―――

Annual Net Sales

Computed by dividing accounts payable by annual net sales. This ratio measures how the company is paying its suppliers in relation to the volume being transacted. An increasing percentage, or one larger than the industry norm, indicates the firm may be using suppliers to help finance operations. This ratio is especially important to short-term creditors since a high percentage could indicate potential problems in paying vendors.

PROFITABILITY RATIOS

Return on Sales (Profit Margin)

Net Profit After Taxes

―――

Annual Net Sales

Obtained by dividing net profit after taxes by annual net sales. This reveals the profits earned per dollar of sales and therefore measures the efficiency of the operation. Return must be adequate for the firm to be able to achieve satisfactory profits for its owners. This ratio is an indicator of the firm's ability to withstand adverse conditions such as falling prices, rising costs and declining sales.

Return on Assets

Net Profit After Taxes

―――

Total Assets

Net profit after taxes divided by total assets. This ratio is the key indicator of profitability for a firm. It matches operating profits with the assets available to earn a return. Companies efficiently using their assets will have a relatively high return while less well-run businesses will be relatively low.

Return on Net Worth (Return on Equity)

Net Profit After Taxes

―――

Net Worth

Obtained by dividing net profit after tax by net worth. This ratio is used to analyze the ability of the firm's management to realize an adequate return on the capital invested by the owners of the firm. Tendency is to look increasingly to this ratio as a final criterion of profitability. Generally, a relationship of at least 10 percent is regarded as a desirable objective for providing dividends plus funds for future growth.

USING INDUSTRY NORMS FOR FINANCIAL ANALYSIS

The principal purpose of financial analysis is to identify irregularities that require explanations to completely understand an industry's or company's current status and future potential. Comparing the industry norms with the figures of specific companies (comparative analysis) can identify these irregularities. D&B's Industry Norms are specifically formatted to accommodate this analysis.

Relative Position

Common-size and typical balance sheets provide an excellent picture of the makeup of the industry's assets and liabilities. Are assets concentrated in inventories or accounts receivable? Are payables to the trade or bank loans more important as a method for financing operations? The answers to these and other important questions are clearly shown by the Industry Norms, its common-size balance sheet approach and is then further crystallized by the typical balance sheets.

Financial Ratio Trends

Key Business Ratio changes indicate trends in the important relationships between key financial items, such as the relationship between Net Profits and Net Sales (a common indicator of profitability). Ratios that reflect short and long-term liquidity, efficiency in managing assets and controlling debt, and different measures of profitability are all included in the Key Business Ratios sections of the Industry Norms.

Comparative Analysis

Comparing a company with its peers is a reliable method for evaluating financial status. The key to this technique is the composition of the peer group and the timeliness of the data. The D&B Industry Norms are unique in scope for sample size and in level of detail.

Sample Size

The number of firms in the sample must be representative or they will be unduly influenced by irregular figures from relatively few companies. The more than one million companies used as a basis for the Industry

Norms allow for more than adequate sample sizes in most cases.

Key Business Ratios Analysis

Valuable insights into an industry's performance can be obtained by equating two related statement items in the form of a financial ratio. For really effective ratio analysis, the items compared must be meaningful and the comparison should reflect the combined effort of two potentially diverse trends. While dozens of different ratios can be computed from financial statements, the fourteen included in the Industry Norms and Key Business Ratio books are those most commonly used and were rated as the most significant as shown in a survey of financial analysts. Many of the other ratios in existence are variations on these fourteen.

The 14 Key Business Ratios are categorized into three major groups:

Solvency, or liquidity, measurements are significant in evaluating a company's ability to meet short and long-term obligations. These figures are of prime interest to credit managers of commercial companies and financial institutions.

Efficiency ratios indicate how effectively a company uses and controls its assets. This is critical information for evaluating how a company is managed. Studying these ratios is useful for credit, marketing and investment purposes.

Profitability ratios show how successfully a business is earning a return to its owners. Those interested in mergers and acquisitions consider this key data for selecting candidates.

Recent research efforts have revealed that the use of financial analysis (via Industry Norms) is very useful in several functional areas. To follow are only a few of the more widely used applications of this unique data.

Credit

Industry Norm data has proven to be an invaluable tool in determining minimum acceptable standards for risk. The credit worthiness of an existing or potential account is immediately visible by ranking its solvency status and comparing its solvency trends to that of the industry. Short term solvency gauges, such as the quick and current ratios, are ideal indicators when evaluating an account. Balance sheet comparisons supplement this qualification by allowing a comparison of the make-up of current assets and liability items. Moreover, leverage ratios such as current liability to net worth and total liability to net worth provide valuable benchmarks to spot potential problem accounts while profitability and collection period figures provide cash flow comparisons for an overall evaluation of accounts.

In addition to evaluating individual accounts against industry standards, internal credit policies also benefit from Industry Norm data. Are receivables growing at an excessive rate as compared to the industry? If so, how does your firm's collections stack up to the industry?

Finance

Here exists a unique opportunity for financial executives to rank their firm, or their firm's subsidiaries and divisions, against its peers. Determine the efficiency of management via ratio quartile breakdowns which provides you the opportunity to pinpoint your firm's profitability position versus the industry. For example, are returns on sales and gross profit margins comparatively low thereby indicating that pricing per unit may be too low or that the cost of goods is unnecessarily high?

In much the same way, matching the firm's growth and efficiency trends to that of the industry reveals conditions which prove to be vital in projecting budgets. If asset expansion exceeds the industry standard while asset utilization (as indicated by the asset to sales ratio) is sub par, should growth be slowed?

Investment executives have also utilized this diverse information when identifying optimal investment opportunities. By uncovering which industries exhibit the strongest sales growth while maintaining adequate returns, risk is minimized.

Corporate Planning

Corporate plans, competitive strategies and merger & acquisition decisions dictate a comprehensive analysis of the industry in question. Industry Norm data provides invaluable information in scrutinizing the perfor-

mance of today's highly competitive, and sometimes unstable, markets. Does the liquidity of an industry provide a sufficient cushion to endure the recent record-high interest levels or is it too volatile to risk an entry? Are the profitability and equity conditions of an acquisition candidate among the best in the industry thereby qualifying it as an ideal acquisition target?

Industry Norm data provide these all-important benchmarks for setting strategic goals and measuring overall corporate performance.

Marketing and Sales

Attaining an in-depth knowledge of a potential or existing customer base is a key factor when developing successful marketing strategies and sales projections. Industry Norm data provide a competitive edge when determining market potential and market candidates. Identify those industries that meet or exceed your qualifications and take it one step further by focusing in on the specific region or size category that exhibits the greatest potential. For example, isolate the industries which have experienced the strongest growth trends in sales and inventory turnover and then fine tune marketing and sales strategies by identifying the particular segment which is the most attractive (such as firms with assets of $1 million or more).

This information can also be used in a different context by examining the industries of existing accounts. If an account's industry shows signs of faltering profitability and stagnating sales, should precautionary measures be taken? Will the next sale be profitable for your company or will it be written-off? Industry Norm data assist in answering these and many other important questions.

COMMENTS AND SUGGESTIONS

Comments on or suggestions for improvement of the usefulness, format, and coverage of *Dun & Bradstreet/ Gale Industry Handbook* are always welcome. Although every effort is made to maintain accuracy, errors may occasionally occur; the editors will be grateful if these are called to their attention. Please contact—

Editors
Dun & Bradstreet/Gale Industry Handbook
27500 Drake Rd.
Farmington Hills, MI 48331-3535
248-699-GALE

PART I
CONSTRUCTION

THE CONSTRUCTION INDUSTRY:
PRESENT TRENDS AND FUTURE FORECASTS

Matt R. Wall, Ph.D., AIC, CPC

Lacking clairvoyance, no one can predict with certainty what future events or trends are likely to take place in the construction industry. However, it is possible to discern current trends that should continue and may even assume increasing importance in the future. Thus, it is possible to make some predictions of what the future will hold, with a reasonable likelihood of the predictions ultimately being fulfilled.

STAKEHOLDERS IN THE CONSTRUCTION INDUSTRY

Stakeholders in the construction industry extend far beyond the industry itself. To be sure, construction contractors, subcontractors, designers, suppliers, consultants, peripheral firms and their employees are all stakeholders in the construction industry. Beyond the obvious, however, are the developers and users of built space: those industries, firms and entities (including government) that require construction or modification of their facilities to provide necessary services or remain competitive within their own markets, enter new markets, provide space for others or take advantage of emerging trends. This includes owners, tenants and other occupants. The opportunities these entities present for marketing purposes are enormous.

THE CONSTRUCTION INDUSTRY DEFINED

The construction industry is unlike many other industries in that it is quite horizontally fragmented and generally highly localized. It does not have a "Big Three" nor a "Big Ten," but more like a "Top 500" or "Top 1,000" firms-and in some parts of the industry (residential, for instance) a "Top 10,000" firms. To a lesser extent, the same holds true for the suppliers, designers, consultants and other types of firms that support the construction industry.

Many larger construction firms are national and/or international in focus, but the vast majority operate in a certain region or even a single community. This adds to the breadth of the construction industry.

The construction industry encompasses a wide variety of construction categories, which are usually divided into such sectors as:

Highway/Heavy (or Engineering) Construction: Roads, airfields, dams, tunnels, marine facilities and the like.

Industrial: Factories, process plants, warehouses.

Residential: Homes and multi-family housing (apartments and condominiums).

Commercial: Office, retail and other such space.

Specialty: Unique projects that may not be covered by one of the above categories or that may straddle two or more categories.

Broadly defined, the industry includes not only the firms engaged in construction as contractors or subcontractors, but also the design firms, consultants, suppliers and other types of firms that support the industry. Many manufacturers of construction materials and products also service other industries, such as automotive, aerospace or computers.

Federal, state and local governmental agencies are not considered part of the industry *per se,* but they most certainly have a high degree of influence on and control over what takes place, as well as where, how, when, under what conditions and, often, whether or not construction takes place at all.

Much construction is highly localized due to local history, contractor or client familiarity with materials or construction approaches, market distribution patterns or contractor location. Because of this, there are often subtleties that vary from state to state or even between regions within a state. These can have a critical impact on local construction costs or schedules. For example, the San Francisco Bay area has historically been highly unionized, so most large commercial projects there are "union built." In Los Angeles, on the other hand, the union presence is not as strong; plus, Los Angeles has a larger supply of low-cost construction laborers. Little wonder that, except for federally-funded projects where "prevailing wages" are mandated by the Davis-Bacon Act, a far lower percentage of projects in Los Angeles are "union built." Additionally, because of traditions that have developed over the years, there are also differences in business practices and the "pace of living" between the two areas.

In another example of localized industry conditions, most basement foundations in Milwaukee are constructed of concrete block because the area has enjoyed a tradition of masonry contractors. However, there are fewer masonry contractors in Madison, which is only 80 miles to the west, and so their efforts generate more profit by working on fireplaces and masonry veneer. As a result, most foundations in Madison are of poured concrete.

COMPETITION WITHIN THE CONSTRUCTION INDUSTRY

In a classic economic sense, most construction in the United States has all the hallmarks of a competitive industry in that, while there may be some dominant players, no one firm or handful of firms has ever dominated the industry nationwide. Thus, there is considerable competition within the construction industry, particularly in sectors that do not have high capital requirements, such as much residential and light commercial construction. This competition is intensified by firms attempting to diversify into different construction markets or geographical areas.

Because of the high degree of industry fragmentation and the localized nature of most construction projects, many firms interested in competing in new markets or locales attempt to reduce their risk by teaming up with experienced local firms. Significant exceptions to this include those construction sectors that inherently require a high degree of capitalization or contain other formidable barriers to entry and are thus not subject to intense competition. Typical examples of this include land development in areas with stringent development requirements (such as along the California coast), road building, and marine construction.

THE CONSTRUCTION INDUSTRY AND GLOBAL TRENDS

A decade or so ago there was consternation that Asian or European firms might attempt to enter and dominate construction markets in the United States. To be sure, there have been some outright purchases of U.S. construction firms by foreign companies, but most instances of foreign entry into the domestic market have merely involved joint ventures with U.S. construction firms. The feared "foreign invasion" has not materialized to any great extent.

It is unknown whether this is a natural occurrence or whether such factors as the European Economic Union or the Asian financial crises have delayed the "invasion." Only time will tell, but it seems safe to assume for the moment that any "invasion" will be delayed for years, if it comes at all. From a management standpoint, foreign firms entering the U.S. market will have to overcome substantial cultural hurdles, if nothing else.

"Globalization," or the moving of jobs from the United States to lower wage nations south of the border or overseas, is hardly likely to take place in the construction industry because of the obvious fact that the laborers are needed at the project site. Going the other way, however, there is a significant presence of U.S. construction firms in foreign markets. Typical projects are generally limited to design, engineering and construction management services using indigenous labor. Primary areas of involvement include developing regions, particularly in the Middle East and Far East.

Even there, U.S. firms compete with firms from Japan, the United Kingdom, France, Germany and Australia, many of which enjoy the advantages of substantial government subsidies or project financing assistance that are not available to U.S. firms. U.S. firms are able to compete successfully because of their reputation for better project controls and the ability to bring a project in on time and within budget.

Given the differences in wage structures, regardless of any productivity differentials, most expansion by North American firms into foreign markets is likely to be limited to design services, construction management and construction expertise rather than actual construction activities. One possible exception to this would be construction firms that enjoy a monopoly in a very technical niche market, such as in constructing facilities for the petroleum industry.

WALL STREET AND THE CONSTRUCTION INDUSTRY

Hundreds of construction firms are publicly traded, as are firms manufacturing or processing basic construction materials, equipment, supplies or services. The fluctuations of their stocks take the pulse of the industry and its segments and often reflect what stock market analysts predict will be happening to the industry in the near term. What is most important to the construction industry, however, is the matter of money supply and interest rates. These two factors have direct and indirect effects on the industry. Examples of direct effects are the impact of interest rates on the cost of financed or leased construction equipment. The indirect effects are more substantial. Money availability and interest rates control, and often dictate, the decisions of developers, investors and lenders to build, expand or hold off on construction activity. These decisions collectively have massive consequential effects, either generating construction starts and activity or slowing them down.

One cannot disregard the fact that the construction industry competes for funds with all other parties in national and global financial markets. To the degree that "glamour stocks" like high tech or Internet stocks attract investments, these dollars are unavailable to meet the nation's needs for economic investment or expansion into real estate developments or infrastructure that could translate into construction activity. On the other hand, thanks to Wall Street the construction industry is not impacted as greatly by high interest rates and a tight money supply as it was in the past. Twenty years ago, construction in general and homebuilding in particular tended to precede general economic activity, either up or down, in response to changes in interest rates and money supply. A slight rise in interest rates would send housing starts tumbling and since the funds available for lending were limited, money might not be available at any price. The market slowdown was exacerbated by home-buyer reluctance to accept higher mortgage interest rates.

Today, thanks to a secondary mortgage market, mortgage-backed securities and the like, funds are available to finance new land development projects and expansions. Borrower psychology has changed, too. Buyers no longer balk at buying homes because of high interest rates, knowing they can refinance when rates come down. Also, there is a wider variety of loans available today—short term, long term, fixed rate, adjustable rate, etc. The effect of all this has been to reduce the sensitivity of construction starts to inter-

est rates, and hence the money supply is not as critical a factor as it once was.

GOVERNMENT FUNDING AND THE CONSTRUCTION INDUSTRY

Increases or decreases in government funding or loan guarantee programs can have a substantial impact on the construction industry. During past years of ballooning budget deficits, government funding was often reduced or curtailed in order to balance the budget (whereas in a prior era funding was increased in order to stimulate the economy). An example of this was the federal government's action in the early 1990s to use the federal motor fuel taxes collected for the highway trust fund to reduce the deficit, rather than spending those funds on highway construction and repairs. This had a disastrous effect on the highway/heavy construction sector. Now, with budget surpluses being projected for the early decades of the new millennium, the federal government has released more highway trust fund dollars and this has stimulated construction activity in that sector.

Whenever the federal government makes low-cost disaster loans to rebuild after hurricanes, floods, earthquakes or other disasters, this has a sizeable and immediate positive effect on the construction industry. It is not possible to predict when disasters will occur, but we know that whenever they do, the construction industry will experience an up-tick. The January, 1994, Northridge Earthquake illustrates this point. During all of 1993 the California economy was in the doldrums, reeling from defense industry cutbacks, while the national economy was on the upswing. The earthquake caused billions of dollars to pour into the Southern California economy through the construction sector. These funds were provided by the Federal Emergency Management Agency, by insurers who paid off covered earthquake losses and by individuals and businesses who dipped into their own pockets, received low-interest government loans or borrowed from conventional sources in order to rebuild their homes and businesses. California's construction industry rebounded almost instantly, followed by the state economy in general, and both have remained in high gear since.

In summary, direct construction spending by federal, state, county and local governments is immediately translated into construction activity, jobs and profits. This is true regardless of the project in question, be it transportation-related, constructing new government buildings, upgrading or repairing schools or the like. Likewise, any government program that guarantees loans or encourages spending for building or upgrading facilities will soon increase construction activity. And, if projected budget surpluses materialize, lawmakers at all levels will find it hard to resist the temptation to spend it. That bodes well for the construction industry, although one may wonder if this would have an inflationary effect on the economy. Historically, whenever inflation occurs the U.S. Federal Reserve raises interest rates in order to curb inflation. This has a dampening effect on the construction industry as fewer prospective buyers qualify for loans, thus reducing demand for new construction.

EMERGING TECHNOLOGY AND THE CONSTRUCTION INDUSTRY

The construction industry is likely to receive much more in benefits from emerging technology than it is likely to be changed by that technology. There will be some changes in materials, equipment, management techniques and communications, as discussed below, but the construction industry is not likely to be affected by technological advances any more than the business community as a whole, except in those areas in which the construction industry may be lagging.

For example, fiber optics, high-speed digital transmissions and other improvements in communications technology will accelerate the speed of business communications, including in the construction industry, but the industry's adaptation of general technological advances may well come in incremental form over time. Most important for now is the market opportunity this emerging technology presents to construction firms capable of building the facilities and installing the networks required for high tech industries to operate.

On the other hand, because of the rapidity of technological advancement and the expansion of technology in general, there are likely to be market opportunities for new firms or specialty contractors in specific high-tech market niches. These firms must be small or agile enough to adapt to advances in technology. Major con-

struction firms are likely to team up with these specialty contractors as needed, just as they have teamed up with subcontractors for decades.

Emerging trends in computer systems and software applications hold the promise of making construction management more effective through improved scheduling, tracking, communications and management techniques. An area where this may leap to the forefront is the application of Internet technology and information retrieval for solving construction problems and making project operations more efficient. (Internet technology is discussed later under Construction Communications Trends.) Some larger industrial and commercial construction firms have made advances in applications of Internet technology and information retrieval to improve management performance through web-based communications and a dynamic knowledge base. The idea is to improve decision-making by having better and more relevant information available to management. As this concept gains general acceptance, it is likely to pervade the entire construction industry over the next decade or so.

CURRENT CONSTRUCTION MATERIALS TRENDS

The vast majority of construction projects over the next several decades will continue to use today's basic materials: concrete, steel, glass, masonry and wood. There will, however, be important improvements to these materials, with concrete being just a typical example.

Although concrete as a construction material goes back to ancient Roman times, modern concrete is largely a product of the early twentieth century. There have been monumental advances in concrete technology (particularly admixtures and improved aggregates) over the past few decades, and this trend is accelerating. Practical field design strengths are several times what they were only 20 years ago. And, deformed fiberglass reinforcing bars are now available to replace deformed steel reinforcing bars in applications where rust or corrosion could be a serious problem. Glass fiber reinforced concrete was a new technology a few decades ago; now it is commonplace. The French are experimenting with high-strength concrete for bridges that is nearly as strong as steel, using glass fibers as reinforcing and without any steel reinforcing.

Similar improvements are taking place with light gauge steel framing, engineered wood products, aluminum and glass window-walls, waterproofing membranes, interior finishes, mechanical systems and other materials and supplies. These advancements may not seem huge when they first appear, but the pace of improvement is continuous, and over time the total advancement will probably be profound.

Today, most residential roofs are trussed and most doors are pre-hung, the reverse of what they were three decades ago. As skilled construction labor becomes harder to find at any price, the response will be more factory-built components or pre-assembly of components by materials suppliers.

Factory-built construction has always touted the promise of lower cost to the consumer, and it usually is. Such homes are now called modular and not "pre-fab," as the latter has negative marketing connotations. Will modulars or "factory built" houses take over the market because they are cheaper? Not likely, for several reasons. High transportation costs limit the marketing radius of the plants. Many consumers don't like the look of modulars, with their tell-tale low roof slopes and short overhangs necessary for road clearances. Last, but most important, one should not forget the stark economic fact that many "factory" operations are unable to survive severe economic downturns.

NEW CONSTRUCTION MATERIALS TRENDS

The construction industry has been wrongfully accused of being slow to embrace new technology in materials and techniques, when the blame has been largely due to delays in securing product acceptance or approval by governmental agencies at state, county and local levels. This problem is not likely to go away, and acceptance delays will probably continue to hamstring many promising materials.

Currently there are three building codes in the U.S. (Uniform Building Code, Southern Building Code, and the National Building Code), plus one in Canada. These are all slated to be replaced by a forthcoming In-

ternational Building Code (IBC), but the process will take time. It will be several years before the IBC is adopted at the local level, uniformly across the nation. Building codes are promulgated by code organizations having members from building departments, manufacturers and contractors. Thus, the codes represent a compromise among various competing interests. Furthermore, states, counties and cities are free to make codes more stringent, and most do. The packet of California's changes to the current 1997 Uniform Building Code is larger than the code itself.

Construction products can be specifically approved by the code organization, approved by the administration agency (building department, usually) or certified by an accredited, independent testing laboratory. Given all this, one can see that the task of having a new product "meet code" can be daunting.

There have been negative experiences with such new products as aluminum residential wiring, which caused numerous electrical fires, and flexible polybutylene piping, which was easy to install but later sprung leaks at the joints. Thus, the slow pace of product approval does have some justification. Even though there is a trend towards streamlining the product approval process, "instant approval" of revolutionary products is not likely to happen in the near future.

There are also numerous new construction materials that have not "taken off" for various reasons, including consumer or contractor resistance, lack of code acceptance and lack of marketing savvy by the supplier. To some extent, supplier attempts to control the market for their products have contributed to the problem. In the future, developers of "open" systems that go nationwide through liberal licensing agreements should fare much better than those from system developers who try to keep their products proprietary. For instance, several residential construction systems using Styrofoam "Lincoln-logs" or "Lego-blocks" have been patented over the last 25 years. None has gained wide acceptance, and some have bankrupted their inventors and investors. The inventor who has a manufacturer like Dow or Boise-Cascade make the product and then have it distributed by Home Depot or Builders Square is far more likely to be successful.

CONSTRUCTION EQUIPMENT TRENDS

With construction equipment, as with construction materials, the tried and true keeps getting better and new products are always being developed. Larger items of equipment are becoming more user-friendly through the addition of micro-processors and computerized controls. Even though the newer machines are more expensive, when the cost is expressed in terms of output productivity the "in-place" cost per cubic yard or per ton moved declines. This trend should continue for the foreseeable future.

For hand tools, cordless tools continue to be lighter, more compact and more powerful, with positive effects on productivity and worker safety. Worker safety and health will become more of a factor in equipment design, as explained below.

Numerous tools and machinery items are becoming increasingly automated or semi-automated with resulting increases in worker productivity, such as with concrete slip-forming or screeding machines, self-adjusting laser levels, and gang drills. Marketing and servicing of these high-tech tools may create market niches for numerous start-up firms.

Within the construction materials and supply industry, new nationwide supply chains like Home Depot and Builders Square cater to *both* consumers and contractors. This trend is likely to continue for items that can be distributed nationally. Because of their volume purchasing discounts, these chains are often able to sell products and tools at prices lower than many local lumber yards can buy them for. That does not bode well for local lumber yards and hardware stores. However, some local merchants may be able to successfully compete against the large chains by offering a wider selection, unique items or personal service.

CONSTRUCTION SAFETY TRENDS

Due to a combination of legislation, regulation and litigation, project safety has become a major management component of any construction project, with no reversal of this trend in sight. There will continue to be opportunities for safety consultants and purveyors of canned safety programs to assist contractors who cannot afford to hire full-time professionals.

Safety equipment will continue to become smaller, lighter and easier to use. Some of it may become less expensive as manufacturer research and development costs are recovered. Along with this, ergonomic design will be applied to more items to enhance productivity and prevent repetitive stress injuries.

New safety equipment is being developed for hazards never before successfully addressed. For instance, until recently the iron workers union and contractor associations jointly resisted OSHA proposals requiring fall protection (lanyards and harnesses) for iron workers doing steel erection work. The reason for the resistance was simple: the lanyards could easily snag, throwing the worker off-balance and causing a fall that, though non-fatal, might be injurious. Now, an overhead wire that a short lanyard can be snapped onto is being used by numerous contractors, resulting in fewer falls and lower workers compensation premiums.

CONSTRUCTION MANAGEMENT AND ORGANIZATIONAL TRENDS

Look for continued improvements in computer software designed to simplify project estimating and scheduling or provide more powerful performance. Similarly, construction management documentation and information retrieval software and systems will continue to evolve and improve. Industry management is likely to embrace new computer analysis tools for making decisions, such as subcontractor evaluation and selection for a given project based on performances by various contractors on other similar projects.

A PREDICTED CRISIS IN CONSTRUCTION LABOR AVAILABILITY

The Construction Industry Institute (CII), a collaboration of academics and construction firms, predicts a quickly-approaching crisis in construction labor availability caused by two converging trends. First, many construction workers are leaving the industry by age

40 because of the physical demands of their jobs on their aging bodies. Second, construction work is perceived by much of the public as being dangerous, noisy, dirty and not appealing as a career. With so many leaving and so few entering the industry, the CII predicts labor availability will become a serious problem for most sectors of the construction industry.

Numerous trade and labor organizations have attempted to introduce construction as a career option to the K-12 educational system. Elementary school classes routinely visit fire and police stations, but they seldom if ever visit construction sites; thus, children just don't think about construction as a career choice.

Labor organizations have attempted to recruit workers to maintain membership, but it has been said that they have not maximized their efforts for fear of increasing the supply of workers to the point where wages could be adversely affected. Given the law of supply and demand, that fear is understandable. Prevailing wages are required on union jobs but newcomers start at lower apprentice wages, which are typically half the journeyman's rate with the gap being closed over three to five years. For non-union jobs, newcomers often start at minimum wage with higher wages occurring when skills and productivity increase.

Several contractor associations have developed programs to attract young adults to construction careers, and some government "welfare to work" programs are trying to promote their clients to employers in the construction industry as a source of labor. And finally, attitudes are changing in regard to the historical negative stereotyping against women—women are now being actively recruited as workers and as managers in the construction industry.

While there has been moderate success in attracting new workers, the results have not been sufficiently positive at this point to stem the tide of workers leaving the building trades.

CONSTRUCTION COMMUNICATIONS TRENDS

There has been a substantial increase in the amount of paperwork required during the construction process over the past two decades or so. Much of it has been

mandated by liability considerations, but governmental reporting requirements and project owner desires have also contributed to the situation. As a result, documentation and document retrieval have received management attention as never before, and this trend is likely to continue.

The use of fax machines and overnight delivery services are commonplace in construction these days. Two recent developments involving the Internet are resulting in better and faster communications. These are web-enabled project management and electronic mail (e-mail).

Many management teams are using web pages as the external communications exchange medium for their construction projects and for internal communications within their companies. The advantage is that information is disseminated immediately. Requests for information are processed and logged in minutes, with answers received in hours or days as opposed to weeks. Furthermore, everyone on the team is accessible and available to answer questions. Electronic mail is certainly faster than the postal service and it avoids the busy signals that fax machines often encounter. It proves very useful for the immediate distribution of updates to plans and specifications.

Communicating via the Internet will increase in use and importance in the construction industry, and this improved communications holds the promise of improved construction management efficiency and better final construction projects for owners.

LEGISLATION, REGULATION AND LITIGATION IN THE CONSTRUCTION INDUSTRY

Construction projects are increasingly running afoul of laws and regulations designed to address pollution problems at permanent facilities that, given the temporary nature of the construction process, perhaps should be waived or lightened during the construction period.

As water and air quality mandates are tightened nationwide, construction operations are more likely to be affected in the future. For instance, a few years back California's Air Quality Control Board proposed regulations for engines that would have had the practical effect of shutting down all road construction in the state. The future bodes more of such regulations.

The litigation explosion, more pronounced in some regions than in others, is affecting the industry through higher liability insurance rates. In some cases this has resulted in management decisions being dictated by legal risks instead of by what makes good construction and economic sense. A continuation of this trend portends production and efficiency problems for the industry as management is increasingly distracted by litigation.

INDIRECT GOVERNMENT INFLUENCE ON THE CONSTRUCTION INDUSTRY

Government mandates and regulation profoundly impact other sectors of the economy—automotive and electric power generation to name two. This, in turn, affects the construction industry whenever these impacts influence owner or investor decisions to increase or decrease the rate of that industry's facilities construction. The net effect of governmental influence may well be to increase the level of construction in response to retiring or replacing existing facilities that are no longer efficient or environmentally sound.

AN EYE ON THE FUTURE

Change has always been with us. Those individuals and firms who have reacted well to change in the past are likely to survive the changes of the future. Key to survival is a willingness to challenge the old ways of doing things and adapt new technologies to the needs and goals. The changes coming at us are not to be feared. Rather, they are to be viewed as opportunities to be seized and harnessed.

The future will present more golden opportunities to be seized and challenges to be accepted than we have ever seen before. The "good old days" are gone, if they ever existed at all. The "good new days" are ahead of us, for those who can recognize the opportunities that change brings. Remember: what some people call "luck" is really opportunity meeting with preparation.

—Matt R. Wall, Ph.D., AIC, CPC

Professor, Construction Management Department
California Polytechnic State University
San Luis Obispo, California 93407

Matt Wall has over 20 years experience in residential, commercial and governmental construction. He is a licensed contractor and a construction consultant, and he serves as an expert witness, mediator and arbitrator on construction-related disputes. Matt teaches construction management courses at Cal Poly, where he is a tenured full professor. His academic background includes BS and MBA degrees from the University of Wisconsin, Madison, and a Ph.D. in Civil Engineering from Texas A&M University. Matt has conducted numerous construction- and management-related seminars and training programs for several construction firms and associations both nationally and abroad. He can be reached at 805/543-5335.

INDUSTRY OVERVIEW

This chapter presents a comprehensive overview of the Construction industry. Major topics covered include an Industry Snapshot, Organization and Structure, Background and Development, Pioneers in the Industry, Current Conditions and Future Projections, Industry Leaders, Work Force, North America and the World, and Research and Technology. A suggested list for further reading, including web sites to visit, completes the chapter. Additional company information is presented in Chapter 6 - Mergers & Acquisitions.

Industry Snapshot

The construction industry entails the erection of structures, such as houses, other buildings, bridges, and highways, as well as their infrastructure, from electrical systems to decorative elements. Construction is a highly regulated industry and is subject to regional and local requirements and zoning specifications. Within the U.S. and between other countries, these regulations are typically non-standardized and are frequently contradictory. As more construction companies expand geographically, even globally, industry associations and government agencies are working to devise and implement standards to facilitate this growth.

Construction is among the most fragmented of industries. Builders range from very small operations that employ only a handful of permanent positions and outsource most of the work to independent subcontractors, to large corporations that consist of teams of in-house staff that cover every aspect of a complex construction project. Regardless, construction workers engaged in a project cover a wide array of specialized tradespeople. These trades require a high degree of skill and knowledge that is acquired through both formal training and on-the-job experience.

Specifically, the construction industry encompasses these 27 SICs (Standard Industrial Classification codes): **1521: General Contractors—Single-Family Houses**; **1522: General Contractors—Residential Buildings, Other Than Single-Family**, such as apartment buildings, dormitories, and hotels; **1531: Operative Builders**, those who construct dwellings for sale on their own account rather than as contractors; **1541: General Contractors—Industrial Buildings and Warehouses**; **1542: General Contractors—Nonresidential Buildings, Other Than Industrial Buildings and Warehouses**, including administration buildings, churches, fire stations, mausoleums, office buildings, restaurants, shopping centers, and stadiums; **1611: Highway and Street Construction, Except Elevated Highways**; **1622: Bridge, Tunnel, and Elevated Highway Construction**; **1623: Water, Sewer, Pipeline, and Communications and Power Line Construction**; **1629: Heavy Construction, Not Elsewhere Classified**, including canals, dams, docks, golf courses, light and power plants, oil refineries, railroads, sewage treatment plants, and subways; **1711: Plumbing, Heating, and Air-Conditioning**; **1721:**

Painting and Paper Hanging; **1731: Electrical Work**; **1741: Masonry, Stone Setting, and Other Stone Work**; **1742: Plastering, Drywall, Acoustical, and Insulation Work**; **1743: Terrazzo, Tile, Marble, and Mosaic Work**; **1751: Carpentry Work**; **1752: Floor Laying and Other Floor Work, Not Elsewhere Classified**, such as carpet laying, hardwood flooring, and linoleum installation; **1761: Roofing, Siding, and Sheet Metal Work**; **1771: Concrete Work**, such as asphalting, blacktopping, and grouting, as well as parking lot and sidewalk construction; **1781: Water Well Drilling**; **1791: Structural Steel Erection**; **1793: Glass and Glazing Work**; **1794: Excavation Work**; **1795: Wrecking and Demolition Work**; **1796: Installation or Erection of Building Equipment, Not Elsewhere Classified**, including the installation of conveyor systems, elevators, incinerators, and revolving doors; **1799: Special Trade Contractors, Not Elsewhere Classified**, such as artificial turf installation, fence construction, fireproofing, grave excavation, house moving, ornamental metalwork, swimming pool construction, and weather stripping; and **7353: Heavy Construction Equipment Rental and Leasing**.

Organization and Structure

The construction industry is highly decentralized. That is, it is comprised of a loose configuration of specialists who are employed at various stages in the process to perform a specific task.

Unless the future owner of the building has already obtained the site on which it is to be constructed, the builder begins the construction process by purchasing a piece of land, called a lot. The builder then readies the site by obtaining the necessary regulatory approval and by arranging for the construction of roads, sewers, and utilities to service the property.

Government building codes enact requirements to preserve public safety and health. They prescribe load limitations as well as the placement and height of the structure relative to the buildings around it. They also specify electrical system and plumbing requirements. In public or non-residential buildings, building codes also specify additional life-safety requirements regarding stairways, elevators, emergency lighting, and fire protection materials and systems.

Some builders operate on a small enough scale that they can act as the project's architect and engineer as well. Larger building companies, however, usually hire such professionals to act as their on-site agents. The primary function of architects and engineers is to design and execute the construction of a structure that not only conforms to the owner's or builder's specifications, but also complies with zoning, building code, and public health regulations.

General contractors submit bids for a construction job to the architect, engineer, or builder. Contractors are selected based on those bids and their reputation for quality work. These general contractors, in turn, usually receive bids for specific aspects of the job from independent subcontractors that are skilled in such trades as plumbing, electrical, or structural work. Generally, contractors own or lease all the equipment and tools needed for the job and a portion of that expense is usually incorporated into their bid.

Materials for the job are obtained by the builder. Large building companies purchase materials through a centralized purchasing unit, taking advantage of quantity discounts by purchasing enough materials for use in multiple jobs.

Upon completion of the construction project, including its review by state and local building code inspectors, the building is ready for sale. Many commercial buildings and some houses are built specifically for a particular buyer, in which case the builder does not have to begin the process of selling it. Other residential and commercial buildings are constructed before a buyer is identified and the builder must then begin soliciting potential buyers.

Many builders employ a sales force for selling new buildings. They may also encourage real estate agents to promote the property. Large builders often use model homes as sales tools for showcasing their handiwork in the best possible light. These models are impeccably furnished and landscaped and may contain features that are available at an extra cost to the buyer, such as fireplaces, vaulted ceilings, and state-of-the-art kitchens.

Background and Development

The history of construction dates far back into the prehistory of humans. It almost certainly extends beyond the earliest archaeological record of construction, which dates to about 12,000 B.C. These first shelters were temporary tent-like structures appropriate for nomadic hunter-gatherers.

The agricultural revolution, which took place around 10,000 B.C., gave rise to more permanent dwellings. The earliest of these structures were found in the Middle East and Europe, where remains of clay and stone buildings have been excavated. These areas also provide evidence of composite building, a system utilizing a combination of clay and wood. With the wattle-and-daub method, sticks were staked into the ground, bound together by vegetable fibers, and plastered with wet clay.

Around 3,000 B.C., the firing of clay bricks developed as an extension of the technique of firing clay pottery. Soon thereafter, the Egyptians developed stone-cutting technology, which they applied in the construction of temples and pyramids. So advanced were the building and engineering skills of the Egyptians that the Pyramids of Giza remained the world's tallest manmade structures until the 19th century.

The ancient Romans invented the first mortar, a mixture of sand, lime, and water. Over time the recipe was fine-tuned, culminating in the development of the first cement by Joseph Aspdin in late-18th-century Britain.

The ancient Romans also used metals in the structure of their buildings and they utilized lead in their plumbing systems. They built a system of aqueducts that carried water not only to public fountains, where many people collected their water supply, but also into public and private buildings. Only in the 19th century would this ancient system be surpassed by improvements in plumbing.

Stone construction was utilized in ninth-century Europe for the widespread construction of churches and cathedrals. This so-called "cathedral crusade" lasted for five centuries, at which point the use of fired brick was revived.

The Industrial Revolution introduced new building materials along with the demand for new types of structures. Large-scale production of iron gave rise to the development of machinery, which in turn produced new building products. In 1784 Henry Cort developed the puddling process for making wrought iron. This achievement was followed by the industrial production of cast iron, glass, and bricks.

Timber mills developed in North America were capable of producing standard-dimension lumber by the 1820s. The incorporation of lumber in construction was facilitated by the development of machine-made nails in the following decade.

Thomas Young developed the Elastic Theory of Structures in 1807, making prediction of structural performance accurate. Building professionals at this time were becoming increasingly specialized. Societies for design professionals came into being, including the Institution of Civil Engineers (1818) and the American Institute of Architects (1857). The Illinois Architects Act of 1897 called for the government to issue licenses for building design professionals. Meanwhile, governments began specifying municipal and national building codes.

Steel and electricity emerged as the new tools of the building trade around 1880. First produced for railroad rails, steel quickly found use in building structures such as the Eiffel Tower (1889). Chicago's population density spurred a demand for increasingly tall buildings and steel was the material of choice for these structures. William Le Baron Jenney was the architect and engineer behind the first skyscraper, the 10-story Home Insurance Company Building erected in 1885.

The internal service and support systems of buildings are also a part of the construction industry. Steam-powered roped elevators, developed in the late-1850s, were outmoded in 1889 when George #Westinghouse developed elevators powered by electric motor. Steam and hot-water heating systems also arose in the late 19th century. They were incorporated into Willis H. Carrier's heating and cooling devices in 1922. Six years later Carrier first introduced air-conditioning in an office building. Electric lighting went through successive improvements in the 19th and 20th centuries, culminating in that modern-day office building staple, the fluorescent lamp, in 1938.

Pioneers in the Industry

Willis H. Carrier

Willis H. Carrier brought relief to millions of inhabitants of stifling, hot buildings with his invention of the air-conditioner. Born in 1876, this New York native was no stranger to the oppressive heat and humidity of summertime. Yet it wasn't for the comfort of humans that he began work into the theories of air-conditioning. Rather, he became interested in it as a method of cooling down overheated working conditions and machinery.

After graduating from Cornell University, Carrier took a job as an engineer at Buffalo Forge Co., a heating company. He was soon promoted to chief of experimental engineering. Carrier designed the first system to control humidity in 1902. This was in response to a plea from a printer whose colors kept bleeding due to the heat. Four years later he tackled the problem of heat at a cotton mill and received a patent for an "Apparatus for Treating Air." Carrier joined with several former Buffalo Forge engineers to establish the Carrier Engineering Corp. in 1915.

The first centrifugal air-conditioning machine was unveiled in 1922 at a New Jersey theater. Demand for these systems expanded quickly throughout the U.S., first in commercial settings and in the homes of the wealthy. After World War II air-conditioning became accessible to the general public. At the time of his death in 1950, Carrier held more than 80 patents on the conditioning of air.

Henry Cort

Henry Cort revolutionized the British iron industry by developing a method of producing wrought iron. After serving in the Royal Navy for 10 years, Cort purchased an ironworks in 1775. He soon invented a method of producing iron bars through the use of grooved rollers rather than the expensive and time-consuming processes of hammering or cutting.

Cort followed up this invention with the development of a process for converting pig iron into wrought iron. This so-called puddling process, patented in 1784, involved the stirring of molten pig iron in a reverbatory furnace until the circulating air removed the carbon from the iron, producing a loop of pure metal. The combination of Cort's two inventions enabled Britain to quadruple its production of iron in only 20 years.

Despite his great contribution to the economic growth of Britain, Cort died nearly destitute. His patents were taken from him and his company was forced into bankruptcy when the government learned that his partner had invested stolen funds into the business. Cort was granted a modest pension, however, and passed away in London in 1800.

William Le Baron Jenney

The structures of William Le Baron Jenney were monuments to the heights of construction technology in their day. Jenny invented the skyscraper, the first of which was completed in 1885 in Chicago; the 10-story Home Insurance Company Building, which incorporated a steel and iron skeleton, was the first to utilize steel as a structural component.

Jenney was trained as an architect in Paris and later taught architecture at the University of Michigan. Meanwhile, he worked as an architect in Chicago for nearly 40 years, during which time he designed such buildings for the city as the Leiter Building (1879) and the Ludington Building (1891). The Manhattan Building, completed in 1890, is considered to be the world's first 16-story building and was the first to specifically incorporate windbracing into its design.

Thomas Young

Thomas Young was a jack of all scientific trades and a master of many of them. Born in 1773, he established a medical practice in London in 1799. Among his varied accomplishments are discovery of the cause of astigmatism, experiments that established the wave nature of light, the development of the Young-Helmholtz three-color theory pertaining to the eye's perception of color, and deciphering the texts of the Rosetta Stone.

In 1907 he began work on measuring molecules, the surface tension of liquids, and elasticity. The latter pursuit resulted in the development of the coefficient of elasticity, Young's modulus, which contributed much to the construction industry as it allowed for the accurate prediction of structural performance. Young died in 1829 at the age of 56.

Current Conditions and Future Projections

Manufactured Housing

While manufactured housing is classified as a manufacturing industry and not part of the construction industry, it will be discussed briefly here due to its significance in the residential housing market. Once the laughing stock of the residential market, manufactured housing may wind up having the last laugh. These factory-built homes, which had suffered from a poor quality image for many years, have benefited from recent improvements in quality. By 1999 manufactured homes represented nearly one-third of all new housing in the U.S.

Unlike traditional housing, manufactured homes are built in assembly-line fashion at factories. After assembly, they are moved either as a whole or in sections to a lot, where they are mounted on temporary or permanent foundations. Manufactured housing offers several advantages over site-built homes, including mobility and relative affordability.

Champion Enterprises, Inc. is the dominant player in the U.S. manufactured housing industry. It was founded in 1953 and by the mid-1960s it had emerged as one of the nation's market leaders. Part of the company's success was attributed to its vertical integration, as it manufactured every component of its homes, from structural to decorative elements. In the early 1990s Champion Enterprises purchased Redman Industries, which boosted Champion from the nation's number-two position to the top of the industry. In 1998 its operations in 28 states and Canada earned $94.2 million on revenues of $2.2 billion.

Building to Conserve Energy and the Environment

A number of new construction techniques were introduced by the late 1990s to create more energy efficient, environmentally friendly buildings. Initially, the techniques involved were slightly more expensive than traditional methods, but as the cost of lumber continues to rise and the techniques become more familiar to builders, costs for the new methods are expected to become more competitive. Moreover, energy savings level the playing field in terms of long-term costs.

Recycled plastic is a key ingredient in several techniques. Rastra is a system that combines recycled polystyrene and cement to form thick, lightweight, and insulative modules. A second technique involves structural insulated panels, which are insulated, load-bearing modules made of expanded polystyrene foam pressed between two sheets of oriented strand board, a synthetic wood product. In a third system, insulated concrete forms—made of polystyrene and filled with cement—are reinforced with bars to create insulated, load-bearing walls to which siding or wallboard can be attached.

Other techniques use natural or recyclable products. Straw bales are cheap, renewable resources that can be stacked within a load-bearing structural framework and then covered with sprayed cement and coated with plaster to form insulated wall and ceiling surfaces. Soil, a plentiful resource that has been used as a building material for centuries, has been re-introduced in "rammed-earth" structures, in which a mix of soil, cement, and water is sprayed against structural forms and grids. Finally, steel frames, which are 100% recyclable, provide a number of advantages over traditional wood framing, including resistance to insects, fire, and earthquakes.

International Building Codes

The movement toward national building codes for the U.S. began in the early 1990s. Industry associations embarked on the creation and implementation of standard codes to replace the varying and sometimes contradictory regional codes. Under the multiple code system, small building companies wishing to expand geographically are hindered by the amount of resources necessary to become educated in the different codes, and large construction companies that operate across geographic regions sometimes have to employ specialists or consultants who are well-versed in the differences between codes.

The International Code Council (ICC) was formed in 1994 by three organizations: Building Officials and Code Administrators International, the International Conference of Building Officials, and the Southern Building Code Congress International. Its mission is to develop the International Building Code—standard regulations that encompass building, mechanical, plumbing, fire, and other construction-related codes.

The member groups of the ICC were scheduled to vote on the final draft of the International Building Code in September, 1999.

Remodeling on the Rise

The U.S. is experiencing a home remodeling surge that is expected to continue into the new millennium. According to the May, 1999, issue of *American Demographics*, Americans spent $120 billion in 1997 and the same amount in 1998 to repair and remodel their homes. The National Association of Home Builders predicts that figure will increase three to five percent in each of the following five years. A February, 1999, issue of *U.S. News & World Report* projects an even greater expenditure for remodeling in 1999—an all-time annual high of $175 billion.

A number of factors are behind this remodeling boom. About half of all American homes are over 30 years old, about five years older than the typical life-span of such expensive features as roofs, furnaces, and kitchen cabinets. These maintenance expenses account for only one-third of the home improvement picture, though.

Consumer confidence plays a large role in the trend. A secure employment market, low interest rates, a healthy stock market, and an increase in disposable income have prompted many Americans to undertake pricey home improvement and remodeling projects.

Another contributing factor is the desire for convenience brought about by new technologies, such as automatic toilet bowl cleaners and home fax machines and computer systems. Some of these may require electrical, plumbing, or structural modifications to be carried out by construction contractors.

Non-Residential Construction Remains Low

The same market forces that are fueling the home remodeling boom are also driving new residential construction. New-home sales reached an all-time high of 880,000 homes in 1998, according to a January, 1999, issue of *Business Week*. The National Association of Home Builders predicted that 1999 would be another strong year, but it was not expected to surpass the performance of the previous year.

Unfortunately, the forces driving residential construction have not spilled over into the non-residential sector. Industrial-building construction was expected to remain depressed in 1999 due to decreased production levels and the competitive pressures that prompt plant closures and workforce reductions. The commercial industry, too, was likely to remain cautious, as the success of retail and hotel activity depends on the capriciousness of consumer spending.

The only bright spot in the non-residential segment is office construction. After being burned by overbuilding and the recession in the 1980s, office developers had been reluctant to embark on new ventures. As a result, office vacancy rates fell steadily during the early 1990s, putting office space at a premium. The ensuing rise in lease prices has made the market once again attractive for new office building construction.

Industry Leaders

Bechtel Group, Inc.

Founded in 1898 by Warren Bechtel, this firm had become the largest construction company in the western U.S. by 1925 and held the rank of the second-largest heavy construction enterprise in the U.S. by 1998. The company has its roots in railroad, oil, and power construction.

After making a name for itself at home through such projects as the Hoover Dam and the San Francisco Bay Bridge, Bechtel expanded internationally. By the end of the 1950s it had operations on six continents.

The company continued to extend its reach across industrial sectors as well. It worked on pipelines, power plants, transportation projects, and mining ventures. Bechtel constructed the entire city of Jubail, Saudi Arabia in 1976. It was also involved in the cleanup of the nuclear accidents at Three Mile Island in 1979 and Chernobyl in 1986, located in the U.S. and the Ukraine, respectively.

Major projects the company was involved in during the 1990s included the extinguishing of Kuwait's oil well fires during the Gulf War, the construction of the Channel Tunnel linking England and France, and the establishment of Mexico's first private power plant. Bechtel's revenues reached $12.6 billion in 1998.

Bouygues S.A.

Bouygues S.A., one of Europe's largest construction companies, was founded in Paris in 1952 as a building specialist. By 1965 it had expanded into civil engineering and public works construction and had established regional construction subsidiaries throughout France. In the early 1970s Bouygues began obtaining large projects, including that of the Parc des Princes Stadium and the Paris Convention Centre. In 1981 the firm was contracted to build the University of Riyadh; at one million square meters, it was the world's largest building project.

Diversification began in the mid-1970s. The company established Bouygues Offshore, an oil and gas contractor, in 1974. In 1987 it purchased a 25% interest in TF1, a leading French television channel. Bouygues released the award-winning movie, *The Piano*, in 1993, followed by *Secrets and Lies* in 1996. In 1998 Bouygues Telecom, France's third-largest cellular phone group, secured its one-millionth customer.

In 1998 Bouygues S.A. was comprised of two principal segments, Construction and Services. As a whole, the company operated in 80 countries and generated a total turnover of FrF 99.6 billion (15.18 billion euro). The Construction sector encompassed three major businesses: the Building and Civil Works business, which the company projected would generate turnover of FrF 32.7 billion (4.98 billion euro) in 1999; and the Roads and Property sectors, which were forecasted to draw FrF 31.3 billion (4.77 billion euro) and FrF 4.9 billion (0.74 billion euro) in 1999, respectively.

Centex Corp.

With revenues of $5.2 billion in 1998, Centex Corp. is the leading residential construction company in the U.S. It was founded in 1950 as a home constructor based in Dallas, and by 1960 it had erected 25,000 houses.

During the 1960s Centex diversified into construction products and commercial construction. It expanded its reach into mortgage banking and petroleum during the following decade. Centex's industrial and geographic diversification enabled it to survive the collapse of the Texas real estate market in the late 1980s.

Centex acquired a majority interest in Cavco Industries in 1997, marking its foray into the manufactured homes sector. The company added to those operations the next year by purchasing AAA Homes, which sold manufactured homes in 12 U.S. states as well as Canada and Japan. By 1999 Centex was building 12,000 homes annually and operating in 20 states.

EMCOR Group, Inc.

EMCOR, short for Electrical Mechanical Corp., is one of the world's largest specialty construction groups. This Connecticut-based firm was founded in 1887 as the Jamaica Water Supply Company, servicing regions of New York. It continued to grow throughout the nineteenth century and into the twentieth.

The firm was acquired in 1966 by Jamaica Water and Utilities, which then embarked on a diversification program. In the 1970s and 1980s it expanded into mechanical and electrical contracting, as well as such far-flung interests as telecommunications and computer resale. This over-diversification made the company vulnerable to fluctuations in various markets and in 1994 the firm, then known as JWP, filed for bankruptcy.

The company emerged from Chapter 11 protection later that year as EMCOR and regained profitability in 1996. It again took to making acquisitions to achieve growth, this time focusing on firms in line with its core construction operations. EMCOR earned net income of $12.3 million on revenues of $2.2 billion in 1998.

Fluor Corp.

This California-based firm is the nation's leader in heavy industrial construction. Established in 1912 by Simon Fluor, the company soon became involved in oil- and gas-related construction and in 1930 it began building pipelines in Texas. The firm continued to make strides in the energy construction sector through the 1970s.

Fluor purchased Daniel International, a large construction company, in 1977, followed by St. Joe Minerals four years later. The 1980s, however, brought a decline in the call for oil and gas work and as a consequence Fluor posted a $573 million loss in 1985. The company recovered through a program of workforce reduction, divestiture of commodity-based interests, acquisition of construction firms, and the forging of international joint ventures. By the late 1990s Fluor was the industry's largest U.S. firm, with 1998 revenues of $13.5 billion.

Work Force

For most construction trades, the demand for skilled tradespeople is expected to outpace the supply of such workers. Since most jobs are physically strenuous, the need for younger workers to succeed older specialists is fairly constant. Moreover, this demand is heightened by a somewhat reduced number of young people entering the industry, many of whom are reluctant to enter into a career with such demanding working conditions.

The pool of capable youths entering the industry is further drained by an alarming level of illiteracy among applicants. Although the work entailed is largely physical it is also highly precise, requiring skills in mathematics and blueprint reading and the ability to follow written and verbal directions. Workers with an education in drafting and physics are considered highly valuable.

Educational and training requirements vary in duration and necessity, but most trades follow a similar program. Apprenticeships are on-the-job training programs that combine classroom work with hands-on experience. Not only does the apprentice receive this training at no charge, he or she usually receives an hourly wage that increases in increments as the apprentice advances through the program. After successfully completing training and acquiring a number of years of experience in the trade, a worker receives the informal title of journeyworker, meaning skilled employee.

Workers are often at the mercy of weather conditions. Inclement weather that prevents a full day of work also prevents a full day's pay. Such lulls are usually short-term and the worker doesn't have to remain idle for long. In the case of longer term lapses in employment, such as layoffs or other pressures arising from economic fluctuations in the industry, unionized workers can seek other jobs from their union office. Non-union workers generally acquire a new job through referral or newspaper advertisements.

Wages vary widely by geographic region, the type of trade, and the current demand for such crafts. Wage rates are also dependent upon whether or not the worker is a union member and the worker's level of experience. In general, however, pay is greatest in the northeast and southwest Pacific areas of the U.S.; it is typically lowest in the nation's southeast and south-central regions. Still, the average hourly wage for construction workers is among the highest of all skilled workers.

Construction work, regardless of the nature of the project, falls into three general categories: structural, mechanical, and finishing. Unless otherwise indicated, the employment figures in the job descriptions which follow pertain to the U.S. only and were obtained from the *1998-99 Occupational Outlook Handbook*, published by the U.S. Bureau of Labor Statistics.

Structural

Bricklayers and Stonemasons: These closely-related trades focus on the construction of floors, walls, and other structural features. Bricklayers primarily use brick and concrete block, while stonemasons utilize natural-cut stone (such as marble, granite, and limestone) or artificial stone (including concrete and marble chips).

About 30% of the 142,000 bricklayers and stonemasons that held jobs in 1996 were self-employed, often specializing in small jobs such as patios and fireplaces. The remaining 70% held positions with trade, building, or general contractors. Some workers are members of the International Union of Bricklayers and Allied Craftsmen.

Carpenters: Carpentry consists of two basic types: rough and finish. Rough carpentry involves the construction of the wood framework, such as subfloors, partitions, and floor joists, as well as the temporary structures used to protect drying concrete at the site. Finish carpentry entails such elements as molding, paneling, cabinets, doors, stairways, and floors.

Some carpenters are well versed in both types and are highly valued for this versatility and expertise. Such skills not only position the carpenter to advance quickly through the trade, but also provide the opportunity to choose from a variety of available jobs. This is especially handy during times of economic downturn or other extended periods of unemployment in the industry.

Residential housing accounts for two-thirds of all carpentry work, with commercial sites comprising the remainder. In 1996 carpenters held 996,000 jobs in the U.S., representing the largest group of construction workers. About 60% of those carpenters were employed by contractors and builders with the balance being self-employed. Some carpenters belong to the United Brotherhood of Carpenters and Joiners of America.

Concrete Masons: Concrete masons are employed in a wide range of construction jobs, from small jobs like laying patios to large projects like dams and highways. Regardless of the scale of the project, concrete masons set and align the forms for holding the concrete, which is a mixture of cement, sand, gravel, and water. They pour the concrete, spread it evenly, level it, set joints in it to prevent cracking, and retrowel it to create a smooth, textured, or pebble finish.

Of the 130,000 concrete masons employed in 1996, only about 10% were self-employed. Most worked for concrete contractors or general contractors involved in the construction of highways, bridges, shopping centers, and large public or commercial buildings. Many concrete masons are members of the Operative Plasterers' and Cement Masons' International Association of the United States and Canada.

Construction Inspectors: Inspectors are involved in key phases of the construction project to ensure that building codes, zoning regulations, and contract specifications are met. Before the foundation is poured they inspect the condition of the soil and the position of footers and piers. After periodic inspections throughout the project's duration, inspectors give the completed structure a thorough examination before the structure can be put to use. During the construction process, the construction inspector must inform the general contractor of any problem or potential problem. He can issue a work-stop order, particularly in the case of government projects, if corrections are not made in a timely manner.

Construction inspectors must have years of practical experience in a particular specialty, such as electrical work. Increasingly, supplemental college training, such as an associate's degree in construction technology, is becoming a job requirement.

Insulation Workers: This trade involves the installation of insulation into new or renovated buildings, as well as the removal of older types of insulation such as asbestos. Insulation takes a variety of forms and may be either solid or spray-on.

Unlike many other construction trades, insulation work is not physically strenuous. Since the craftspeople must sometimes work in precarious positions, coordination is more important than physical strength. Training is typically informal and is acquired relatively quickly through on-the-job experience. Still, formal training and apprenticeship programs are available and are even necessary for the authorization to remove asbestos, a cancer-causing substance.

Turnover in this trade is high, leaving plenty of demand for entry-level workers. Many insulation workers belong to the International Association of Heat and Frost Insulators and Asbestos Workers.

Material Moving Equipment Operators: This occupation encompasses operators of machinery that move construction materials, soil, manufactured products, or other heavy materials. Equipment includes cranes, towers, excavation and loading machines, graders, dozers, scrapers, hoists, winches, industrial trucks, and tractors.

Of the 1,097,000 material moving equipment operators employed in 1996, 30% worked in the manufacturing industry. The second-largest proportion—25%—were employed in construction and mining. The construction sector is expected to drive growth in the occupation overall through the year 2006 due to increased spending on America's highways, bridges, and dams.

Training for the occupation is typically obtained through practical experience on the job. Some operators in the construction industry, however, are required to participate in three-year formal apprenticeship programs.

Roofers: Roofers install and, more often than not, repair roofs on residential, industrial, and commercial buildings. Depending on the type of building and the pitch, or slope, of the roof, roofing materials may include a combination of tar, asphalt, gravel, rubber, thermoplastic, and metal, as well as shingles made of a variety of substances.

This trade is one of the most physically demanding in the construction industry. It also has the highest incidence of work-related injuries. Working literally at the highest point of the building, roofers are subject to slips and falls from a loss of balance or from a slick surface caused by rain or snow. Most work is concentrated in the summer months, but because a leaky roof usually reveals itself only in inclement weather, the roofer cannot restrict his time on the job to sunny, dry days.

About 138,000 roofers were employed in 1996. The demand for roofers is expected to remain high since the toll of the occupation prompts a high turnover rate. Most roofers work for roofing contractors, although about 30% are self-employed. Many roofers are members of the United Union of Roofers, Waterproofers, and Allied Workers.

Structural Steel Workers and Ironworkers: These tradespeople work in the industrial and commercial sectors. They are employed by general contractors, bridge and dam construction firms, public utilities, and government agencies. They erect and fasten the metal framework that supports buildings, bridges, highways, sewers, power transmission towers, and other structures. They use cranes and other hoisting equipment and devices to build or dismantle the framework, manually position beams and girders into place, and secure them with bolts, rivets, or welds.

Job conditions are sometimes dangerous, as the sites are often at considerable heights and are made slippery by wet weather. To reduce the risk of injury, most workers use such safety devices as belts, scaffolding, and nets.

Structural steel workers and ironworkers held approximately 770,000 jobs in 1996. Many belonged to the International Association of Bridge, Structural, Ornamental and Reinforcing Iron Workers.

Mechanical

Electricians: In 1996 about 575,000 electricians were employed in the U.S. but only about two-thirds of that number worked in the construction industry. The remainder were maintenance electricians specializing in residential, industrial, or commercial fields in a variety of different industries. The International Brotherhood of Electrical Workers is a popular union for construction electricians.

Construction electricians install the electrical systems in new buildings. They follow blueprints that indicate the placement of circuits, outlets, load centers, and panel boards. Because electrical work is regulated by the government, electricians must be cognizant of and comply with the National Electric Code as well as state and local building codes.

Heating, Ventilation and Air-Conditioning (HVAC) Mechanics: These technicians follow blueprints to install the systems that control the temperature, humidity, and air quality in all types of buildings. Equipment varies by type and size, from wall-unit air-conditioning to large refrigeration units for food processing facilities. Heating equipment includes furnaces, steam boilers, and heat pumps. HVAC mechanics typically specialize in either installation or maintenance and repair.

About 256,000 HVAC mechanics were employed in 1996. Half of that total worked for heating and cooling contractors, and about one out of seven were self-employed. Only about 15% of HVAC workers belonged to a union, such as the Sheet Metal Workers' International Association or the United Association of Journeymen and Apprentices of the Plumbing and Pipefitting Industry of the United States and Canada.

Plumbers and Pipefitters: Plumbers and pipefitters install and repair systems that carry water, natural gas, and waste to and from residential, industrial, commercial, and public buildings. Plumbers specialize in water, waste disposal, drainage, and gas systems, while pipefitters generally focus on pipe systems for such industries as manufacturing and power generation, as well as for the heating and cooling of buildings.

About 60% of the 389,000 plumbers and pipefitters employed in 1996 worked in the construction industry with the remainder engaged in maintenance work for a variety of other industries. Licensing for these occupations varies between communities, but most entail some form of examination of the applicant's knowl-

edge of the trade. Many of these workers belong to the United Association of Journeymen and Apprentices of the Plumbing and Pipefitting Industry of the United States and Canada.

Sheetmetal Workers: This trade involves the fabrication, installation, and maintenance of a range of building parts made from metal sheets. Such components include duct systems, roofs, siding, gutters, and skylights. While some parts are crafted at the construction site, most are made in the worker's shop.

Sheetmetal workers are unique in the construction industry in that very few are self-employed. About 75% work for heating, ventilation, and air conditioning (HVAC) or plumbing contractors, while the remainder typically work for general or specialty trade contractors. The total number of sheetmetal workers reached 110,000 in 1996. Many belong to the Sheet Metal Workers' International Association.

Finishing

Carpet Installers: Carpet installers measure, cut, and install carpeting in most types of buildings. The carpeting may be held in place by tackless strips, which is used in residential rooms; staples, for such specialty upholstery work as stairways; or glue, for commercial areas.

In 1996 approximately 64,000 carpet installers were employed in the U.S. About 60% of that total were self-employed; others worked for flooring contractors or floor covering retailers.

Drywall Mechanics and Lathers: These trades entail the finishing of interior walls and ceilings. Drywall mechanics fasten large panels of drywall to the structural framework, tape the panels together, and smooth the seams to ready them for paint or wall covering treatments. Lathers, a small segment of this trade, apply metal or gypsum lath as a framework for the application of plaster.

About 133,000 drywall mechanics and lathers were employed in 1996; approximately 30% were self-employed. They may be members of the International Brotherhood of Painters and Allied Trades or of the United Brotherhood of Carpenters and Joiners of America.

Glaziers: Glaziers cut and install glass and glass substitutes for various elements in a building, including windows, doors, skylights, storefront windows, mirrors, shower doors, display cases, and other architectural features. As with sheetmetal workers, glaziers usually cut and prepare their material at a shop, although it is sometimes necessary to cut the pieces manually at the job site.

About 36,000 glaziers were employed in the U.S. in 1996. Although some worked for retail glass establishments most were employed by specialty or general contractors. The National Glass Association offers written examination to demonstrate competence in this craft. The International Brotherhood of Painters and Allied Trades represents the interests of members of this trade.

Painters and Paperhangers: Painters apply paint, stain, varnish, and others sealants to the interior of buildings for decoration and to the exterior for protection from the elements. Paperhangers adhere wall coverings made of paper, vinyl, or fabric to interior walls and ceilings for a decorative finish. Although each trade employs different skills, they both include the preparation of the wall surface to receive the decorative material.

According to *Exploring Careers in the Construction Industry*, about 572,000 painters and paperhangers were employed in the U.S. in 1990; painters outnumbered paperhangers by far. About 40% were self-employed while others worked for construction contractors or organizations that own large buildings, such as apartment complexes, schools, and hospitals. Many belong to the International Brotherhood of Painters and Allied Trades.

Plasterers: These workers apply plaster primarily to interior walls, although some jobs entail exterior work as insulation or decoration. Plaster has undergone a recent resurgence in demand due to its durability, fire-resistant and soundproof qualities, and its relatively affordable price.

Plasterers held approximately 32,000 positions in the U.S. in 1996. About 20% were self-employed, and most worked for independent construction contractors. Many were members of the Operative Plasterers' and

Cement Masons' International Association of the United States and Canada.

Tilesetters: These workers apply tile, marble, and terrazzo to interior and exterior floors and walls. Tile is particularly popular since it is not only decorative but also durable, waterproof, and easy to clean. Outdoor tilework may consist of patio floors or swimming pools. Indoor work includes floors, tubs and showers, and countertops.

About 29,000 tilesetters were employed in 1996. Nearly half were self-employed while others worked for tilesetting contractors. Some members of the trade belong to the International Union of Bricklayers and Allied Craftsmen or the United Brotherhood of Carpenters and Joiners of America.

North America and the World

The global marketplace is providing business and growth opportunities in many industries, including construction. A number of factors contribute to this environment, including the collapse of communism in eastern Europe, privatization of formerly government-controlled enterprises, and the enactment of legislation in countries with emerging economies to encourage foreign investment.

Asia, once the most fertile market for construction ventures, was dealt a serious blow by an economic crisis in the late 1990s. This region appeared to be on the road to recovery by the approach of the new century, yet analysts expected that full recovery would not be experienced for several years. Still, opportunities are expected to arise steadily. The January, 1999, issue of *Constructor* reported that Asia's interest rates dropped, currencies were rebounding, and foreign exchange reserves were larger than they were in 1993.

Latin America remains a ripe market for foreign contractors. It escaped the brunt of the Asian financial crisis and has enacted legislation encouraging private investment. This region is the site of several of 1998's largest construction projects, including the $2.7 billion Cerro Negro oil project in Venezuela and the $2.5 billion Cadareyta oil project in Mexico.

Europe continues to provide opportunities for foreign investors, yet the continent is still lacking a homogeneous construction industry. The move toward a single European market has made great strides, but construction standards are still regulated nationally. The Single European Act of 1987 called for the European Commission to remove national trade barriers in order to open up competition across borders, yet progress in the construction industry toward that unity has been slow. The March, 1999, issue of *Constructor* estimates that cross-border construction activity in Europe accounts for no more than one or two percent of European contract work.

However, the year 2002 is expected to mark the enactment of the European standard for the licensing of European construction firms. Likewise, so-called "Eurocodes" for the standardization of design codes, construction codes, and product standards are expected to be laid down shortly after the turn of the century.

Research and Technology

The single greatest technological force steering innovation in the construction industry is the Internet. The inexpensive and rapid communication afforded by the Internet has, in a relatively short timeframe, become incorporated into virtually every industry, and construction is no exception. Its growth and acceptance in that field, however, has not been as rapid as in other industries, providing a testament to the reputation of the U.S. construction industry as conservative and resistant to change.

To be sure, the industry has, for some time, employed computers for various tasks. Such applications include computer-aided design, computer models to test a design's structural resistance to wind and earthquakes, and the study of field methodology to determine the best practices for curtailing equipment maintenance expenses.

Only in the latter half of the 1990s, however, has the construction industry begun embracing the Internet as an efficient and effective means of communication. Internet-based information sharing between the disparate workers involved in a project is more timely and inexpensive than through traditional paper and postal routes. Workers receive expedient notification of changes, resulting in fewer errors arising from miscommunication.

E-commerce is also finding an application in the industry. The National Association of Home Builders operates a Web site that connects builders to customers by showcasing floor plans and models and by providing links to the Web sites of thousands of participating builders.

BidCom Inc. offers technology that incorporates many of the Internet's best applications for the construction industry. Its in-Site service converts such paper-based documents as blueprints, purchase orders, and work permits into computer-readable formats. It then posts them over a secure Internet location that is accessible to everyone involved in the project—owners, architects, general contractors, subcontractors, and suppliers. Through this medium, workers are kept apprised of changes to designs or work schedules, contractors can file and share field reports, and owners can track the status of the entire project. BidCom also has plans to enable contractors to place orders for supplies via an e-commerce feature.

A September, 1998, issue of *InformationWeek* summarized the use of the Internet, and information technology (IT) in general, among U.S. construction and engineering firms. About 64% utilized the World Wide Web to provide customer service or to sell products or services. About one percent of the budgets of the 500 largest companies was reserved for IT and about two percent of total revenues were derived from electronic business. The breakdown of IT budgets was thus: salaries accounted for 33%, new products and technology accounted for 14%, electronic business for 13%, and research and development for eight percent. Other IT costs included Year 2000 tasks, IT services and outsourcing, and maintenance and administration.

Further Reading

"Bechtel Timeline." Available from http://www.bechtel.com/aboutbech/timeline.html

Bryson, R.L. *Contracting in All 50 States*. Carlsbad, California: Craftsman Book Company, 1998.

"Centex Investor Relations Home/Profile." Available from http://199.230.26.96/ctx

Champion Enterprises, Inc. 1998 Annual Report. Available from http://www.corporate-ir.net

Clark, Kim. "Home Remakers." *U.S. News & World Report,* 15 February 1999.

"Construction." *Britannica CD 98 Multimedia Edition, 1994-1998.* Encyclopedia Britannica, Inc.

"Construction Sector." Available from http://www.bouygues.fr/version_anglaise/construction/construction.htm

"EMCOR Investors' Overview." Available from http://www.emcorgroup.com/

Fluor Corporation 1998 Annual Report. Available from http://www.fluor.com/investor/inv_frm.htm

"Going Global." *Constructor,* January 1999.

"History of Bouygues." Available from http://www.bouygues.fr/version_anglaise/groupe/groupe.htm

"Homebuilding." *Standard & Poor's Industry Surveys.* New York: Standard & Poor's, 1998.

Ivins, Molly. "King of Cool." *Time,* 7 December 1998.

Lang, Laura. "Will You Be Ready for the International Building Code?" *Nation's Cities Weekly,* 9 February 1998.

Levin, Rich. "Constructive Computing—Construction and Engineering Firms Use IT to Make Monumental Projects Seem Ordinary." *InformationWeek,* 14 September 1998.

Lyle, Elizabeth Stewart. *Careers in the Construction Industry.* New York: The Rosen Publishing Group, 1995.

"Still Hammering Away." *Business Week,* 18 January 1999.

U.S. Bureau of Labor Statistics. *1998-99 Occupational Outlook Handbook.*

U.S. Department of Commerce. *International Construction Review.* Available from http://www.ita.doc.gov/forestprod/construction/11.htm

"U.S. Versus European Construction Industry." *Constructor,* March 1999.

Warner, Melanie. "BidCom." *Fortune,* 5 July 1999.

Whiteley, Peter O. "Building Tomorrow's Home." *Sunset,* May 1998.

Yamamoto, Kaori. "Up on the Roof." *American Demographics,* May 1999.

INDUSTRY STATISTICS & PERFORMANCE INDICATORS

This chapter presents statistical information on the Construction industry. This view of the industry is through the lens of federal statistics. All the data shown are drawn from government sources, including the 100 percent surveys of the Economic Census and the partial surveys of services and other industries conducted annually by the U.S. Department of Commerce. Tables include general statistics, indices of change, and selected ratios.

SIC 1521 - SINGLE-FAMILY HOUSING CONSTRUCTION: GENERAL STATISTICS

Year	Estab-lish-ments	Employment		Payroll ($ mil)		Costs ($ mil)		Revenues ($ mil)	
		Total	Constr. workers	Total	Worker payroll	Total	Cost of materials	All sources	Construc-tion
1977	100,993	437,681	382,806	3,736.4	3,066.0	14,593.3	8,013.2	21,890.3	21,292.7
1982	72,115	309,614	253,457	3,606.3	2,749.0	12,252.6	6,357.3	20,129.1	19,646.4
1987	90,378	396,291	307,305	6,272.2	4,342.9	25,135.6	12,863.5	40,105.3	39,098.1
1988	93,568	397,772	305,059	6,461.5	4,443.5	26,426.1	13,547.3	41,824.2	40,842.4
1989	96,871	399,260	302,829	6,656.6	4,546.4	27,782.9	14,267.5	43,616.8	42,664.6
1990	100,290	400,752	300,615	6,857.6	4,651.6	29,209.4	15,025.9	45,486.2	44,568.0
1991	103,830	402,250	298,417	7,064.6	4,759.3	30,709.1	15,824.7	47,435.7	46,556.3
1992	107,495	403,754	296,236	7,277.9	4,869.5	32,285.8	16,665.9	49,468.8	48,633.3
1993	111,289	405,263	294,071	7,497.6	4,982.2	33,943.5	17,551.8	51,589.1	50,803.0
1994	115,218	406,778	291,921	7,724.0	5,097.5	35,686.3	18,484.8	53,800.2	53,069.5
1995	119,284	408,299	289,787	7,957.2	5,215.6	37,518.6	19,467.5	56,106.1	55,437.1
1996	123,495	409,825	287,669	8,197.4	5,336.3	39,444.9	20,502.3	58,510.8	57,910.4
1997	127,854	411,358	285,566	8,444.9	5,459.8	41,470.1	21,592.2	61,018.6	60,493.9
1998	132,367	412,895	283,478	8,699.8	5,586.2	43,599.4	22,740.0	63,633.9	63,192.8

Source: Economic Census of the United States, 1977, 1982, 1987 and 1992. Data for other years are estimates based on the compounded annual growth/decline rates between 1987 and 1992. Footnoted items (1) are from the *County Business Patterns* for the years indicated. Extracted from *Agriculture, Mining, and Construction USA*, Gale, 1998.

SIC 1521 - SINGLE-FAMILY HOUSING CONSTRUCTION: INDICES OF CHANGE

Year	Estab-lish-ments	Employment		Payroll ($ mil)		Costs ($ mil)		Revenues ($ mil)	
		Total	Constr. workers	Total	Worker payroll	Total	Cost of materials	All sources	Construc-tion
1977	94.0	108.4	129.2	51.3	63.0	45.2	48.1	44.3	43.8
1982	67.1	76.7	85.6	49.6	56.5	38.0	38.1	40.7	40.4
1987	84.1	98.2	103.7	86.2	89.2	77.9	77.2	81.1	80.4
1992	100.0	100.0	100.0	100.0	100.0	100.0	100.0	100.0	100.0

Source: Same as General Statistics but excluding estimates. The values shown reflect change from the base year, 1992. Values above 100 mean greater than 1992, values below 100 mean less than 1992, and a value of 100 in the 1987-91 or 1993-98 period means same as 1992.

SIC 1521 - SINGLE-FAMILY HOUSING CONSTRUCTION: SELECTED RATIOS

For 1992	Avg. of All Sector	Analyzed Industry	Index
Employees per establishment	8.1	3.8	46
Construction workers per establishment	6.3	2.8	44
Payroll per establishment	205,515	67,704	33
Payroll per employee	25,219	18,026	71
Payroll per construction worker	23,093	16,438	71
Costs per establishment	531,494	300,347	57
Costs per employee	65,220	79,964	123
Costs per construction worker	84,663	108,987	129
Materials as % of costs	52.18	51.62	99
Costs as % of revenues	56.48	65.26	116
Costs as % of construction revenues	57.64	66.39	115
Value added per establishment	409,562	159,849	39
Value added per employee	50,258	42,558	85
Value added per construction worker	65,240	58,004	89
Revenues per establishment	941,057	460,197	49
Revenues per employee	115,478	122,522	106
Revenues per construction worker	149,904	166,991	111
CR as % of total revenues	97.98	98.31	100
Net CR as % of CR	74.06	69.21	93
Investment per establishment	13,794	4,296	31
Investment per employee	1,693	1,144	68
Investment per construction worker	2,197	1,559	71

Source: Same as General Statistics. The 'Average of Sector' column represents the average of all construction industries. The Index shows the relationship between the Average and the Analyzed Industry. For example, 100 means that they are equal; 500 that the Analyzed Industry is five times the average; 50 means that the Analyzed Industry is half the national average. The abbreviation 'CR' stands for 'construction revenues'; 'na' is used to show that data are 'not available'. Net CR is revenue less work that has been contracted out.

SIC 1522 - RESIDENTIAL CONSTRUCTION, N.E.C.: GENERAL STATISTICS

Year	Estab-lish-ments	Employment		Payroll ($ mil)		Costs ($ mil)		Revenues ($ mil)	
		Total	Constr. workers	Total	Worker payroll	Total	Cost of materials	All sources	Construc-tion
1977	4,775	55,589	45,707	646.4	484.9	3,370.2	1,084.4	4,514.7	4,442.1
1982	7,464	62,702	50,089	1,077.5	759.6	6,002.7	1,659.6	7,953.3	7,846.1
1987	8,143	81,708	61,245	1,751.7	1,130.3	9,934.4	2,796.3	13,593.0	13,315.5
1988	7,782	73,706	54,794	1,613.2	1,032.1	8,826.6	2,597.0	12,211.5	11,975.5
1989	7,436	66,487	49,023	1,485.7	942.5	7,842.3	2,412.0	10,970.4	10,770.4
1990	7,107	59,975	43,860	1,368.3	860.6	6,967.7	2,240.1	9,855.5	9,686.5
1991	6,791	54,102	39,240	1,260.2	785.9	6,190.7	2,080.5	8,853.8	8,711.7
1992	6,490	48,803	35,107	1,160.6	717.6	5,500.3	1,932.3	7,954.0	7,835.0
1993	6,202	44,023	31,409	1,068.8	655.3	4,887.0	1,794.6	7,145.6	7,046.5
1994	5,927	39,712	28,101	984.4	598.3	4,342.0	1,666.7	6,419.4	6,337.3
1995	5,664	35,822	25,141	906.6	546.4	3,857.8	1,548.0	5,767.0	5,699.6
1996	5,413	32,314	22,493	834.9	498.9	3,427.6	1,437.7	5,180.9	5,126.0
1997	5,173	29,149	20,124	768.9	455.6	3,045.3	1,335.2	4,654.3	4,610.1
1998	4,943	26,294	18,005	708.1	416.0	2,705.7	1,240.1	4,181.3	4,146.2

Source: Economic Census of the United States, 1977, 1982, 1987 and 1992. Data for other years are estimates based on the compounded annual growth/decline rates between 1987 and 1992. Footnoted items (1) are from the County Business Patterns for the years indicated. Extracted from Agriculture, Mining, and Construction USA, Gale, 1998.

SIC 1522 - RESIDENTIAL CONSTRUCTION, N.E.C.: INDICES OF CHANGE

Year	Estab-lish-ments	Employment		Payroll ($ mil)		Costs ($ mil)		Revenues ($ mil)	
		Total	Constr. workers	Total	Worker payroll	Total	Cost of materials	All sources	Construc-tion
1977	73.6	113.9	130.2	55.7	67.6	61.3	56.1	56.8	56.7
1982	115.0	128.5	142.7	92.8	105.9	109.1	85.9	100.0	100.1
1987	125.5	167.4	174.5	150.9	157.5	180.6	144.7	170.9	170.0
1992	100.0	100.0	100.0	100.0	100.0	100.0	100.0	100.0	100.0

Source: Same as General Statistics but excluding estimates. The values shown reflect change from the base year, 1992. Values above 100 mean greater than 1992, values below 100 mean less than 1992, and a value of 100 in the 1987-91 or 1993-98 period means same as 1992.

SIC 1522 - RESIDENTIAL CONSTRUCTION, N.E.C.: SELECTED RATIOS

For 1992	Avg. of All Sector	Analyzed Industry	Index
Employees per establishment	8.1	7.5	93
Construction workers per establishment	6.3	5.4	86
Payroll per establishment	205,515	178,823	87
Payroll per employee	25,219	23,781	94
Payroll per construction worker	23,093	20,440	89
Costs per establishment	531,494	847,510	159
Costs per employee	65,220	112,705	173
Costs per construction worker	84,663	156,674	185
Materials as % of costs	52.18	35.13	67
Costs as % of revenues	56.48	69.15	122
Costs as % of construction revenues	57.64	70.20	122
Value added per establishment	409,562	378,069	92
Value added per employee	50,258	50,277	100
Value added per construction worker	65,240	69,891	107
Revenues per establishment	941,057	1,225,579	130
Revenues per employee	115,478	162,982	141
Revenues per construction worker	149,904	226,565	151
CR as % of total revenues	97.98	98.50	101
Net CR as % of CR	74.06	55.37	75
Investment per establishment	13,794	7,959	58
Investment per employee	1,693	1,058	63
Investment per construction worker	2,197	1,471	67

Source: Same as General Statistics. The 'Average of Sector' column represents the average of all construction industries. The Index shows the relationship between the Average and the Analyzed Industry. For example, 100 means that they are equal; 500 that the Analyzed Industry is five times the average; 50 means that the Analyzed Industry is half the national average. The abbreviation 'CR' stands for 'construction revenues'; 'na' is used to show that data are 'not available'. Net CR is revenue less work that has been contracted out.

SIC 1531 - OPERATIVE BUILDERS: GENERAL STATISTICS

Year	Estab-lish-ments	Employment		Payroll ($ mil)		Costs ($ mil)		Revenues ($ mil)	
		Total	Constr. workers	Total	Worker payroll	Total	Cost of materials	All sources	Construc-tion
1977	23,477	173,819	109,702	2,026.1	1,053.4	15,056.7	5,639.8	22,918.0	19,812.3
1982	14,053	107,635	53,212	1,873.8	709.7	10,542.5	3,613.9	18,084.6	15,607.4
1987	20,766	168,940	79,502	4,385.0	1,478.3	35,274.3	12,773.2	57,474.0	48,959.8
1988	12,388[1]	141,717[1]	72,370	4,092.2[1]	1,379.2	34,338.9	12,769.7	55,000.9	48,052.4
1989	11,252[1]	131,378[1]	65,879	3,797.7[1]	1,286.7	33,428.3	12,766.1	52,634.2	47,161.9
1990	10,396[1]	120,522[1]	59,969	3,415.0[1]	1,200.5	32,541.9	12,762.5	50,369.3	46,287.8
1991	9,279[1]	88,691[1]	54,590	2,638.0[1]	1,120.0	31,679.0	12,759.0	48,201.9	45,430.0
1992	16,989	114,194	49,693	3,358.8	1,044.9	30,839.0	12,755.4	46,127.7	44,588.0
1993	11,225[1]	96,686[1]	45,235	3,175.0[1]	974.9	30,021.2	12,751.8	44,142.8	43,761.7
1994	15,678	97,635	41,178	3,019.0	909.5	29,225.1	12,748.3	42,243.3	42,950.7
1995	15,061	90,280	37,484	2,862.2	848.5	28,450.1	12,744.7	40,425.6	42,154.6
1996	14,468	83,478	34,122	2,713.6	791.7	27,695.7	12,741.1	38,686.0	41,373.4
1997	13,899	77,189	31,061	2,572.7	738.6	26,961.3	12,737.6	37,021.3	40,606.6
1998	13,352	71,373	28,275	2,439.1	689.1	26,246.4	12,734.0	35,428.3	39,854.1

Source: Economic Census of the United States, 1977, 1982, 1987 and 1992. Data for other years are estimates based on the compounded annual growth/decline rates between 1987 and 1992. Footnoted items (1) are from the County Business Patterns for the years indicated. Extracted from Agriculture, Mining, and Construction USA, Gale, 1998.

SIC 1531 - OPERATIVE BUILDERS: INDICES OF CHANGE

Year	Estab-lish-ments	Employment		Payroll ($ mil)		Costs ($ mil)		Revenues ($ mil)	
		Total	Constr. workers	Total	Worker payroll	Total	Cost of materials	All sources	Construc-tion
1977	138.2	152.2	220.8	60.3	100.8	48.8	44.2	49.7	44.4
1982	82.7	94.3	107.1	55.8	67.9	34.2	28.3	39.2	35.0
1987	122.2	147.9	160.0	130.6	141.5	114.4	100.1	124.6	109.8
1992	100.0	100.0	100.0	100.0	100.0	100.0	100.0	100.0	100.0

Source: Same as General Statistics but excluding estimates. The values shown reflect change from the base year, 1992. Values above 100 mean greater than 1992, values below 100 mean less than 1992, and a value of 100 in the 1987-91 or 1993-98 period means same as 1992.

SIC 1531 - OPERATIVE BUILDERS: SELECTED RATIOS

For 1992	Avg. of All Sector	Analyzed Industry	Index
Employees per establishment	8.1	6.7	83
Construction workers per establishment	6.3	2.9	46
Payroll per establishment	205,515	197,702	96
Payroll per employee	25,219	29,413	117
Payroll per construction worker	23,093	21,028	91
Costs per establishment	531,494	1,815,231	342
Costs per employee	65,220	270,058	414
Costs per construction worker	84,663	620,589	733
Materials as % of costs	52.18	41.36	79
Costs as % of revenues	56.48	66.86	118
Costs as % of construction revenues	57.64	69.16	120
Value added per establishment	409,562	899,921	220
Value added per employee	50,258	133,884	266
Value added per construction worker	65,240	307,664	472
Revenues per establishment	941,057	2,715,152	289
Revenues per employee	115,478	403,942	350
Revenues per construction worker	149,904	928,254	619
CR as % of total revenues	97.98	96.66	99
Net CR as % of CR	74.06	60.20	81
Investment per establishment	13,794	13,905	101
Investment per employee	1,693	2,069	122
Investment per construction worker	2,197	4,754	216

Source: Same as General Statistics. The 'Average of Sector' column represents the average of all construction industries. The Index shows the relationship between the Average and the Analyzed Industry. For example, 100 means that they are equal; 500 that the Analyzed Industry is five times the average; 50 means that the Analyzed Industry is half the national average. The abbreviation 'CR' stands for 'construction revenues'; 'na' is used to show that data are 'not available'. Net CR is revenue less work that has been contracted out.

SIC 1541 - INDUSTRIAL BUILDINGS AND WAREHOUSES: GENERAL STATISTICS

Year	Estab-lish-ments	Employment		Payroll ($ mil)		Costs ($ mil)		Revenues ($ mil)	
		Total	Constr. workers	Total	Worker payroll	Total	Cost of materials	All sources	Construc-tion
1977	8,259	202,070	170,787	2,852.8	2,247.2	8,805.6	3,377.5	13,063.1	12,855.5
1982	7,435	153,821	121,517	3,231.0	2,344.1	12,352.2	3,680.8	18,107.9	17,834.7
1987	7,014	143,001	110,785	3,618.9	2,496.9	15,435.1	4,897.5	22,316.9	21,461.6
1988	7,145	138,749	106,759	3,589.9	2,458.3	15,254.7	4,873.0	22,045.2	21,283.5
1989	7,278	134,624	102,880	3,561.2	2,420.3	15,076.3	4,848.7	21,776.9	21,106.9
1990	7,414	130,622	99,142	3,532.7	2,382.9	14,900.1	4,824.4	21,511.9	20,931.7
1991	7,552	126,738	95,540	3,504.4	2,346.0	14,725.9	4,800.3	21,250.1	20,758.1
1992	7,693	122,970	92,068	3,476.4	2,309.8	14,553.7	4,776.3	20,991.4	20,585.8
1993	7,836	119,241	88,723	3,448.6	2,274.0	14,383.6	4,752.5	20,735.9	20,415.0
1994	7,983	115,767	85,499	3,421.0	2,238.9	14,215.4	4,728.7	20,483.6	20,245.6
1995	8,132	112,325	82,392	3,393.6	2,204.3	14,049.2	4,705.1	20,234.3	20,077.6
1996	8,283	108,985	79,398	3,366.5	2,170.2	13,884.9	4,681.6	19,988.0	19,911.0
1997	8,438	105,745	76,513	3,339.5	2,136.6	13,722.6	4,658.2	19,744.7	19,745.8
1998	8,595	102,601	73,733	3,312.8	2,103.6	13,562.2	4,634.9	19,504.4	19,581.9

Source: Economic Census of the United States, 1977, 1982, 1987 and 1992. Data for other years are estimates based on the compounded annual growth/decline rates between 1987 and 1992. Footnoted items (1) are from the County Business Patterns for the years indicated. Extracted from Agriculture, Mining, and Construction USA, Gale, 1998.

SIC 1541 - INDUSTRIAL BUILDINGS AND WAREHOUSES: INDICES OF CHANGE

Year	Estab-lish-ments	Employment		Payroll ($ mil)		Costs ($ mil)		Revenues ($ mil)	
		Total	Constr. workers	Total	Worker payroll	Total	Cost of materials	All sources	Construc-tion
1977	107.4	164.3	185.5	82.1	97.3	60.5	70.7	62.2	62.4
1982	96.6	125.1	132.0	92.9	101.5	84.9	77.1	86.3	86.6
1987	91.2	116.3	120.3	104.1	108.1	106.1	102.5	106.3	104.3
1992	100.0	100.0	100.0	100.0	100.0	100.0	100.0	100.0	100.0

Source: Same as General Statistics but excluding estimates. The values shown reflect change from the base year, 1992. Values above 100 mean greater than 1992, values below 100 mean less than 1992, and a value of 100 in the 1987-91 or 1993-98 period means same as 1992.

SIC 1541 - INDUSTRIAL BUILDINGS AND WAREHOUSES: SELECTED RATIOS

For 1992	Avg. of All Sector	Analyzed Industry	Index
Employees per establishment	8.1	16.0	197
Construction workers per establishment	6.3	12.0	190
Payroll per establishment	205,515	451,891	220
Payroll per employee	25,219	28,270	112
Payroll per construction worker	23,093	25,088	109
Costs per establishment	531,494	1,891,811	356
Costs per employee	65,220	118,352	181
Costs per construction worker	84,663	158,076	187
Materials as % of costs	52.18	32.82	63
Costs as % of revenues	56.48	69.33	123
Costs as % of construction revenues	57.64	70.70	123
Value added per establishment	409,562	836,830	204
Value added per employee	50,258	52,352	104
Value added per construction worker	65,240	69,924	107
Revenues per establishment	941,057	2,728,641	290
Revenues per employee	115,478	170,704	148
Revenues per construction worker	149,904	227,999	152
CR as % of total revenues	97.98	98.07	100
Net CR as % of CR	74.06	53.28	72
Investment per establishment	13,794	19,466	141
Investment per employee	1,693	1,218	72
Investment per construction worker	2,197	1,627	74

Source: Same as General Statistics. The 'Average of Sector' column represents the average of all construction industries. The Index shows the relationship between the Average and the Analyzed Industry. For example, 100 means that they are equal; 500 that the Analyzed Industry is five times the average; 50 means that the Analyzed Industry is half the national average. The abbreviation 'CR' stands for 'construction revenues'; 'na' is used to show that data are 'not available'. Net CR is revenue less work that has been contracted out.

SIC 1542 - NONRESIDENTIAL CONSTRUCTION, N.E.C.: GENERAL STATISTICS

Year	Estab-lish-ments	Employment		Payroll ($ mil)		Costs ($ mil)		Revenues ($ mil)	
		Total	Constr. workers	Total	Worker payroll	Total	Cost of materials	All sources	Construc-tion
1977	18,467	311,588	254,360	4,274.9	3,189.8	20,288.1	5,716.5	27,400.4	27,137.8
1982	22,112	359,856	278,193	7,260.0	5,084.7	40,312.5	9,222.0	52,824.9	52,304.6
1987	31,337	488,480	366,871	11,842.7	7,755.9	66,868.3	15,985.0	91,699.0	89,793.4
1988	31,011	471,005	349,035	11,835.0	7,637.8	68,225.5	16,381.1	92,483.5	90,616.9
1989	30,688	454,156	332,067	11,827.2	7,521.4	69,610.3	16,787.1	93,274.7	91,447.9
1990	30,368	437,909	315,923	11,819.5	7,406.9	71,023.2	17,203.1	94,072.7	92,286.5
1991	30,052	422,243	300,564	11,811.7	7,294.1	72,464.8	17,629.4	94,877.5	93,132.8
1992	29,739	407,138	285,952	11,804.0	7,182.9	73,935.6	18,066.2	95,689.2	93,986.8
1993	29,429	392,573	272,050	11,796.2	7,073.5	75,436.3	18,513.9	96,507.9	94,848.7
1994	29,123	378,529	258,824	11,788.5	6,965.8	76,967.4	18,972.7	97,333.5	95,718.5
1995	28,820	364,988	246,241	11,780.8	6,859.7	78,529.6	19,442.9	98,166.2	96,596.3
1996	28,519	351,931	234,270	11,773.1	6,755.2	80,123.6	19,924.7	99,006.1	97,482.1
1997	28,222	339,341	222,881	11,765.4	6,652.3	81,749.8	20,418.5	99,853.1	98,376.1
1998	27,929	327,202	212,045	11,757.6	6,551.0	83,409.1	20,924.5	100,707.4	99,278.2

Source: Economic Census of the United States, 1977, 1982, 1987 and 1992. Data for other years are estimates based on the compounded annual growth/decline rates between 1987 and 1992. Footnoted items (1) are from the *County Business Patterns* for the years indicated. Extracted from *Agriculture, Mining, and Construction USA*, Gale, 1998.

SIC 1542 - NONRESIDENTIAL CONSTRUCTION, N.E.C.: INDICES OF CHANGE

Year	Estab-lish-ments	Employment		Payroll ($ mil)		Costs ($ mil)		Revenues ($ mil)	
		Total	Constr. workers	Total	Worker payroll	Total	Cost of materials	All sources	Construc-tion
1977	62.1	76.5	89.0	36.2	44.4	27.4	31.6	28.6	28.9
1982	74.4	88.4	97.3	61.5	70.8	54.5	51.0	55.2	55.7
1987	105.4	120.0	128.3	100.3	108.0	90.4	88.5	95.8	95.5
1992	100.0	100.0	100.0	100.0	100.0	100.0	100.0	100.0	100.0

Source: Same as General Statistics but excluding estimates. The values shown reflect change from the base year, 1992. Values above 100 mean greater than 1992, values below 100 mean less than 1992, and a value of 100 in the 1987-91 or 1993-98 period means same as 1992.

SIC 1542 - NONRESIDENTIAL CONSTRUCTION, N.E.C.: SELECTED RATIOS

For 1992	Avg. of All Sector	Analyzed Industry	Index
Employees per establishment	8.1	13.7	169
Construction workers per establishment	6.3	9.6	153
Payroll per establishment	205,515	396,919	193
Payroll per employee	25,219	28,993	115
Payroll per construction worker	23,093	25,119	109
Costs per establishment	531,494	2,486,150	468
Costs per employee	65,220	181,598	278
Costs per construction worker	84,663	258,559	305
Materials as % of costs	52.18	24.44	47
Costs as % of revenues	56.48	77.27	137
Costs as % of construction revenues	57.64	78.67	136
Value added per establishment	409,562	731,484	179
Value added per employee	50,258	53,431	106
Value added per construction worker	65,240	76,074	117
Revenues per establishment	941,057	3,217,634	342
Revenues per employee	115,478	235,029	204
Revenues per construction worker	149,904	334,634	223
CR as % of total revenues	97.98	98.22	100
Net CR as % of CR	74.06	41.40	56
Investment per establishment	13,794	18,267	132
Investment per employee	1,693	1,334	79
Investment per construction worker	2,197	1,900	86

Source: Same as General Statistics. The 'Average of Sector' column represents the average of all construction industries. The Index shows the relationship between the Average and the Analyzed Industry. For example, 100 means that they are equal; 500 that the Analyzed Industry is five times the average; 50 means that the Analyzed Industry is half the national average. The abbreviation 'CR' stands for 'construction revenues'; 'na' is used to show that data are 'not available'. Net CR is revenue less work that has been contracted out.

SIC 1611 - HIGHWAY AND STREET CONSTRUCTION: GENERAL STATISTICS

Year	Estab-lish-ments	Employment		Payroll ($ mil)		Costs ($ mil)		Revenues ($ mil)	
		Total	Constr. workers	Total	Worker payroll	Total	Cost of materials	All sources	Construc-tion
1977	11,748	267,917	232,810	3,595.8	2,927.2	7,979.7	4,917.8	15,620.9	15,021.2
1982	10,111	212,610	180,303	3,989.2	3,138.4	10,401.9	6,304.5	19,035.2	18,157.4
1987	10,986	284,380	239,111	7,041.1	5,397.2	18,408.4	11,067.1	35,528.0	34,161.4
1988	8,780[1]	221,544[1]	233,240	7,274.1[1]	5,409.0	18,888.1	11,295.2	35,748.8	34,392.3
1989	8,345[1]	206,420[1]	227,512	7,320.5[1]	5,420.9	19,380.3	11,528.0	35,971.0	34,624.8
1990	8,476[1]	215,161[1]	221,926	7,564.3[1]	5,432.8	19,885.3	11,765.7	36,194.6	34,858.8
1991	8,563[1]	194,597[1]	216,477	7,044.3[1]	5,444.7	20,403.5	12,008.2	36,419.5	35,094.4
1992	10,090	257,356	211,161	7,357.7	5,456.7	20,935.2	12,255.7	36,645.8	35,331.6
1993	9,833[1]	194,476[1]	205,976	7,671.2[1]	5,468.6	21,480.7	12,508.3	36,873.6	35,570.4
1994	9,752	247,280	200,918	7,488.3	5,480.7	22,040.5	12,766.1	37,102.7	35,810.8
1995	9,588	242,390	195,985	7,554.5	5,492.7	22,614.8	13,029.3	37,333.3	36,052.9
1996	9,426	237,598	191,172	7,621.2	5,504.7	23,204.1	13,297.8	37,565.3	36,296.5
1997	9,267	232,900	186,478	7,688.6	5,516.8	23,808.8	13,572.0	37,798.8	36,541.9
1998	9,111	228,295	181,899	7,756.5	5,528.9	24,429.2	13,851.7	38,033.7	36,788.9

Source: Economic Census of the United States, 1977, 1982, 1987 and 1992. Data for other years are estimates based on the compounded annual growth/decline rates between 1987 and 1992. Footnoted items (1) are from the *County Business Patterns* for the years indicated. Extracted from *Agriculture, Mining, and Construction USA*, Gale, 1998.

SIC 1611 - HIGHWAY AND STREET CONSTRUCTION: INDICES OF CHANGE

Year	Estab-lish-ments	Employment		Payroll ($ mil)		Costs ($ mil)		Revenues ($ mil)	
		Total	Constr. workers	Total	Worker payroll	Total	Cost of materials	All sources	Construc-tion
1977	116.4	104.1	110.3	48.9	53.6	38.1	40.1	42.6	42.5
1982	100.2	82.6	85.4	54.2	57.5	49.7	51.4	51.9	51.4
1987	108.9	110.5	113.2	95.7	98.9	87.9	90.3	96.9	96.7
1992	100.0	100.0	100.0	100.0	100.0	100.0	100.0	100.0	100.0

Source: Same as General Statistics but excluding estimates. The values shown reflect change from the base year, 1992. Values above 100 mean greater than 1992, values below 100 mean less than 1992, and a value of 100 in the 1987-91 or 1993-98 period means same as 1992.

SIC 1611 - HIGHWAY AND STREET CONSTRUCTION: SELECTED RATIOS

For 1992	Avg. of All Sector	Analyzed Industry	Index
Employees per establishment	8.1	25.5	315
Construction workers per establishment	6.3	20.9	332
Payroll per establishment	205,515	729,209	355
Payroll per employee	25,219	28,590	113
Payroll per construction worker	23,093	25,841	112
Costs per establishment	531,494	2,074,844	390
Costs per employee	65,220	81,347	125
Costs per construction worker	84,663	99,143	117
Materials as % of costs	52.18	58.54	112
Costs as % of revenues	56.48	57.13	101
Costs as % of construction revenues	57.64	59.25	103
Value added per establishment	409,562	1,557,052	380
Value added per employee	50,258	61,046	121
Value added per construction worker	65,240	74,401	114
Revenues per establishment	941,057	3,631,896	386
Revenues per employee	115,478	142,394	123
Revenues per construction worker	149,904	173,545	116
CR as % of total revenues	97.98	96.41	98
Net CR as % of CR	74.06	78.86	106
Investment per establishment	13,794	127,012	921
Investment per employee	1,693	4,980	294
Investment per construction worker	2,197	6,069	276

Source: Same as General Statistics. The 'Average of Sector' column represents the average of all construction industries. The Index shows the relationship between the Average and the Analyzed Industry. For example, 100 means that they are equal; 500 that the Analyzed Industry is five times the average; 50 means that the Analyzed Industry is half the national average. The abbreviation 'CR' stands for 'construction revenues'; 'na' is used to show that data are 'not available'. Net CR is revenue less work that has been contracted out.

SIC 1622 - BRIDGE, TUNNEL, AND ELEVATED HIGHWAY: GENERAL STATISTICS

| Year | Estab-lish-ments | Employment | | Payroll ($ mil) | | Costs ($ mil) | | Revenues ($ mil) | |
		Total	Constr. workers	Total	Worker payroll	Total	Cost of materials	All sources	Construc-tion
1977	979	38,093	33,187	535.9	438.7	1,308.1	846.6	2,270.8	2,247.3
1982	999	37,581	32,473	815.5	664.9	2,080.8	1,319.2	3,549.2	3,503.9
1987	1,159	47,494	40,092	1,191.8	909.9	3,149.0	1,767.1	5,579.4	5,480.9
1988	1,134	46,710	39,263	1,245.4	949.4	3,337.1	1,849.3	5,885.5	5,788.0
1989	1,110	45,939	38,452	1,301.6	990.6	3,536.4	1,935.4	6,208.3	6,112.3
1990	1,087	45,180	37,657	1,360.2	1,033.6	3,747.6	2,025.5	6,548.8	6,454.7
1991	1,064	44,435	36,878	1,421.5	1,078.4	3,971.4	2,119.7	6,908.0	6,816.4
1992	1,041	43,701	36,116	1,485.6	1,125.2	4,208.6	2,218.4	7,286.9	7,198.3
1993	1,019	42,980	35,369	1,552.4	1,174.0	4,460.0	2,321.7	7,686.6	7,601.6
1994	997	42,270	34,638	1,622.3	1,225.0	4,726.4	2,429.7	8,108.3	8,027.5
1995	976	41,572	33,922	1,695.4	1,278.1	5,008.7	2,542.8	8,553.0	8,477.2
1996	955	40,886	33,221	1,771.8	1,333.6	5,307.8	2,661.2	9,022.2	8,952.2
1997	935	40,211	32,534	1,851.6	1,391.4	5,624.9	2,785.0	9,517.0	9,453.7
1998	915	39,547	31,862	1,935.0	1,451.8	5,960.8	2,914.7	10,039.0	9,983.4

Source: Economic Census of the United States, 1977, 1982, 1987 and 1992. Data for other years are estimates based on the compounded annual growth/decline rates between 1987 and 1992. Footnoted items (1) are from the *County Business Patterns* for the years indicated. Extracted from *Agriculture, Mining, and Construction USA*, Gale, 1998.

SIC 1622 - BRIDGE, TUNNEL, AND ELEVATED HIGHWAY: INDICES OF CHANGE

| Year | Estab-lish-ments | Employment | | Payroll ($ mil) | | Costs ($ mil) | | Revenues ($ mil) | |
		Total	Constr. workers	Total	Worker payroll	Total	Cost of materials	All sources	Construc-tion
1977	94.0	87.2	91.9	36.1	39.0	31.1	38.2	31.2	31.2
1982	96.0	86.0	89.9	54.9	59.1	49.4	59.5	48.7	48.7
1987	111.3	108.7	111.0	80.2	80.9	74.8	79.7	76.6	76.1
1992	100.0	100.0	100.0	100.0	100.0	100.0	100.0	100.0	100.0

Source: Same as General Statistics but excluding estimates. The values shown reflect change from the base year, 1992. Values above 100 mean greater than 1992, values below 100 mean less than 1992, and a value of 100 in the 1987-91 or 1993-98 period means same as 1992.

SIC 1622 - BRIDGE, TUNNEL, AND ELEVATED HIGHWAY: SELECTED RATIOS

For 1992	Avg. of All Sector	Analyzed Industry	Index
Employees per establishment	8.1	42.0	518
Construction workers per establishment	6.3	34.7	551
Payroll per establishment	205,515	1,426,985	694
Payroll per employee	25,219	33,992	135
Payroll per construction worker	23,093	31,155	135
Costs per establishment	531,494	4,042,872	761
Costs per employee	65,220	96,305	148
Costs per construction worker	84,663	116,531	138
Materials as % of costs	52.18	52.71	101
Costs as % of revenues	56.48	57.76	102
Costs as % of construction revenues	57.64	58.47	101
Value added per establishment	409,562	2,957,066	722
Value added per employee	50,258	70,440	140
Value added per construction worker	65,240	85,234	131
Revenues per establishment	941,057	6,999,939	744
Revenues per employee	115,478	166,745	144
Revenues per construction worker	149,904	201,765	135
CR as % of total revenues	97.98	98.78	101
Net CR as % of CR	74.06	73.85	100
Investment per establishment	13,794	149,052	1,081
Investment per employee	1,693	3,551	210
Investment per construction worker	2,197	4,296	196

Source: Same as General Statistics. The 'Average of Sector' column represents the average of all construction industries. The Index shows the relationship between the Average and the Analyzed Industry. For example, 100 means that they are equal; 500 that the Analyzed Industry is five times the average; 50 means that the Analyzed Industry is half the national average. The abbreviation 'CR' stands for 'construction revenues'; 'na' is used to show that data are 'not available'. Net CR is revenue less work that has been contracted out.

SIC 1623 - WATER, SEWER, AND UTILITY LINES: GENERAL STATISTICS

Year	Estab-lish-ments	Employment		Payroll ($ mil)		Costs ($ mil)		Revenues ($ mil)	
		Total	Constr. workers	Total	Worker payroll	Total	Cost of materials	All sources	Construc-tion
1977	10,227	198,354	173,093	2,837.3	2,347.5	4,030.8	2,798.4	9,553.5	9,361.1
1982	9,413	186,674	160,473	3,576.3	2,906.8	5,123.6	3,189.9	12,129.0	11,952.8
1987	9,919	197,632	165,879	4,513.3	3,427.7	7,165.2	4,734.1	17,255.0	17,010.0
1988	9,981	196,951	164,708	4,716.4	3,578.7	7,448.1	4,875.8	17,847.8	17,605.8
1989	10,043	196,273	163,545	4,928.6	3,736.4	7,742.1	5,021.7	18,461.0	18,222.5
1990	10,106	195,597	162,390	5,150.4	3,901.0	8,047.8	5,171.9	19,095.2	18,860.7
1991	10,169	194,923	161,243	5,382.2	4,072.8	8,365.5	5,326.7	19,751.2	19,521.3
1992	10,233	194,252	160,105	5,624.4	4,252.2	8,695.7	5,486.1	20,429.8	20,205.0
1993	10,297	193,583	158,975	5,877.5	4,439.6	9,039.0	5,650.2	21,131.6	20,912.7
1994	10,361	192,916	157,852	6,141.9	4,635.2	9,395.8	5,819.3	21,857.6	21,645.2
1995	10,426	192,252	156,738	6,418.3	4,839.3	9,766.7	5,993.4	22,608.5	22,403.3
1996	10,491	191,590	155,631	6,707.1	5,052.5	10,152.3	6,172.7	23,385.3	23,188.0
1997	10,557	190,930	154,532	7,009.0	5,275.1	10,553.1	6,357.4	24,188.7	24,000.2
1998	10,623	190,272	153,441	7,324.4	5,507.5	10,969.7	6,547.6	25,019.7	24,840.8

Source: Economic Census of the United States, 1977, 1982, 1987 and 1992. Data for other years are estimates based on the compounded annual growth/decline rates between 1987 and 1992. Footnoted items (1) are from the *County Business Patterns* for the years indicated. Extracted from *Agriculture, Mining, and Construction USA*, Gale, 1998.

SIC 1623 - WATER, SEWER, AND UTILITY LINES: INDICES OF CHANGE

Year	Estab-lish-ments	Employment		Payroll ($ mil)		Costs ($ mil)		Revenues ($ mil)	
		Total	Constr. workers	Total	Worker payroll	Total	Cost of materials	All sources	Construc-tion
1977	99.9	102.1	108.1	50.4	55.2	46.4	51.0	46.8	46.3
1982	92.0	96.1	100.2	63.6	68.4	58.9	58.1	59.4	59.2
1987	96.9	101.7	103.6	80.2	80.6	82.4	86.3	84.5	84.2
1992	100.0	100.0	100.0	100.0	100.0	100.0	100.0	100.0	100.0

Source: Same as General Statistics but excluding estimates. The values shown reflect change from the base year, 1992. Values above 100 mean greater than 1992, values below 100 mean less than 1992, and a value of 100 in the 1987-91 or 1993-98 period means same as 1992.

SIC 1623 - WATER, SEWER, AND UTILITY LINES: SELECTED RATIOS

For 1992	Avg. of All Sector	Analyzed Industry	Index
Employees per establishment	8.1	19.0	234
Construction workers per establishment	6.3	15.6	248
Payroll per establishment	205,515	549,631	267
Payroll per employee	25,219	28,954	115
Payroll per construction worker	23,093	26,559	115
Costs per establishment	531,494	849,770	160
Costs per employee	65,220	44,765	69
Costs per construction worker	84,663	54,312	64
Materials as % of costs	52.18	63.09	121
Costs as % of revenues	56.48	42.56	75
Costs as % of construction revenues	57.64	43.04	75
Value added per establishment	409,562	1,146,688	280
Value added per employee	50,258	60,406	120
Value added per construction worker	65,240	73,290	112
Revenues per establishment	941,057	1,996,458	212
Revenues per employee	115,478	105,171	91
Revenues per construction worker	149,904	127,602	85
CR as % of total revenues	97.98	98.90	101
Net CR as % of CR	74.06	87.04	118
Investment per establishment	13,794	74,808	542
Investment per employee	1,693	3,941	233
Investment per construction worker	2,197	4,781	218

Source: Same as General Statistics. The 'Average of Sector' column represents the average of all construction industries. The Index shows the relationship between the Average and the Analyzed Industry. For example, 100 means that they are equal; 500 that the Analyzed Industry is five times the average; 50 means that the Analyzed Industry is half the national average. The abbreviation 'CR' stands for 'construction revenues'; 'na' is used to show that data are 'not available'. Net CR is revenue less work that has been contracted out.

SIC 1629 - HEAVY CONSTRUCTION, N.E.C.: GENERAL STATISTICS

Year	Estab-lish-ments	Employment		Payroll ($ mil)		Costs ($ mil)		Revenues ($ mil)	
		Total	Constr. workers	Total	Worker payroll	Total	Cost of materials	All sources	Construc-tion
1977	8,342	412,719	318,375	7,298.3	5,274.1	10,835.9	6,353.7	23,282.5	21,624.0
1982	7,662	415,199	329,475	11,062.7	8,649.4	17,357.3	9,452.4	36,310.2	33,657.5
1987	14,532	297,618	238,204	7,662.0	5,726.5	12,009.5	6,949.6	27,310.1	25,633.0
1988	14,780	298,906	238,567	7,958.0	5,924.5	12,642.0	7,263.3	28,561.2	26,934.6
1989	15,033	300,199	238,930	8,265.4	6,129.4	13,307.9	7,591.2	29,869.7	28,302.3
1990	15,289	301,498	239,294	8,584.7	6,341.4	14,008.8	7,933.8	31,238.0	29,739.5
1991	15,550	302,803	239,659	8,916.3	6,560.7	14,746.7	8,292.0	32,669.1	31,249.7
1992	15,816	304,113	240,024	9,260.7	6,787.6	15,523.4	8,666.3	34,165.7	32,836.5
1993	16,086	305,429	240,390	9,618.4	7,022.4	16,341.0	9,057.5	35,730.8	34,504.0
1994	16,361	306,751	240,756	9,990.0	7,265.2	17,201.7	9,466.3	37,367.7	36,256.1
1995	16,640	308,078	241,123	10,375.9	7,516.5	18,107.7	9,893.6	39,079.5	38,097.1
1996	16,924	309,411	241,490	10,776.7	7,776.4	19,061.4	10,340.3	40,869.8	40,031.7
1997	17,213	310,750	241,858	11,193.0	8,045.4	20,065.4	10,807.0	42,742.1	42,064.5
1998	17,507	312,094	242,226	11,625.4	8,323.6	21,122.2	11,294.9	44,700.1	44,200.5

Source: Economic Census of the United States, 1977, 1982, 1987 and 1992. Data for other years are estimates based on the compounded annual growth/decline rates between 1987 and 1992. Footnoted items (1) are from the County Business Patterns for the years indicated. Extracted from Agriculture, Mining, and Construction USA, Gale, 1998.

SIC 1629 - HEAVY CONSTRUCTION, N.E.C.: INDICES OF CHANGE

Year	Estab-lish-ments	Employment		Payroll ($ mil)		Costs ($ mil)		Revenues ($ mil)	
		Total	Constr. workers	Total	Worker payroll	Total	Cost of materials	All sources	Construc-tion
1977	52.7	135.7	132.6	78.8	77.7	69.8	73.3	68.1	65.9
1982	48.4	136.5	137.3	119.5	127.4	111.8	109.1	106.3	102.5
1987	91.9	97.9	99.2	82.7	84.4	77.4	80.2	79.9	78.1
1992	100.0	100.0	100.0	100.0	100.0	100.0	100.0	100.0	100.0

Source: Same as General Statistics but excluding estimates. The values shown reflect change from the base year, 1992. Values above 100 mean greater than 1992, values below 100 mean less than 1992, and a value of 100 in the 1987-91 or 1993-98 period means same as 1992.

SIC 1629 - HEAVY CONSTRUCTION, N.E.C.: SELECTED RATIOS

For 1992	Avg. of All Sector	Analyzed Industry	Index
Employees per establishment	8.1	19.2	237
Construction workers per establishment	6.3	15.2	241
Payroll per establishment	205,515	585,528	285
Payroll per employee	25,219	30,452	121
Payroll per construction worker	23,093	28,279	122
Costs per establishment	531,494	981,498	185
Costs per employee	65,220	51,045	78
Costs per construction worker	84,663	64,674	76
Materials as % of costs	52.18	55.83	107
Costs as % of revenues	56.48	45.44	80
Costs as % of construction revenues	57.64	47.27	82
Value added per establishment	409,562	1,178,698	288
Value added per employee	50,258	61,301	122
Value added per construction worker	65,240	77,668	119
Revenues per establishment	941,057	2,160,196	230
Revenues per employee	115,478	112,345	97
Revenues per construction worker	149,904	142,343	95
CR as % of total revenues	97.98	96.11	98
Net CR as % of CR	74.06	81.49	110
Investment per establishment	13,794	55,871	405
Investment per employee	1,693	2,906	172
Investment per construction worker	2,197	3,682	168

Source: Same as General Statistics. The 'Average of Sector' column represents the average of all construction industries. The Index shows the relationship between the Average and the Analyzed Industry. For example, 100 means that they are equal; 500 that the Analyzed Industry is five times the average; 50 means that the Analyzed Industry is half the national average. The abbreviation 'CR' stands for 'construction revenues'; 'na' is used to show that data are 'not available'. Net CR is revenue less work that has been contracted out.

SIC 1711 - PLUMBING, HEATING, AND AIR CONDITIONING: GENERAL STATISTICS

Year	Estab- lish- ments	Employment		Payroll ($ mil)		Costs ($ mil)		Revenues ($ mil)	
		Total	Constr. workers	Total	Worker payroll	Total	Cost of materials	All sources	Construc- tion
1977	56,435	458,687	368,993	6,414.0	5,024.7	10,750.1	8,495.3	21,431.2	21,072.1
1982	60,243	512,004	397,548	9,860.7	7,476.8	16,559.9	12,165.6	33,521.4	32,661.3
1987	69,566	617,333	470,793	14,329.8	10,310.6	24,307.9	18,556.1	50,219.7	49,503.3
1988	67,926[1]	612,262[1]	467,615	15,434.0[1]	10,589.3	25,047.2	19,046.4	51,628.1	50,901.9
1989	70,663[1]	641,201[1]	464,459	16,529.2[1]	10,875.4	25,809.1	19,549.7	53,076.0	52,339.9
1990	71,791[1]	645,154[1]	461,324	16,934.8[1]	11,169.4	26,594.1	20,066.4	54,564.5	53,818.6
1991	72,047[1]	592,670[1]	458,210	16,213.1[1]	11,471.2	27,403.0	20,596.6	56,094.8	55,339.0
1992	75,395	612,516	455,117	16,613.2	11,781.2	28,236.5	21,140.9	57,668.0	56,902.4
1993	77,162[1]	608,668[1]	452,045	17,542.1[1]	12,099.6	29,095.3	21,699.6	59,285.3	58,510.0
1994	77,861	610,600	448,994	17,625.4	12,426.6	29,980.3	22,273.0	60,948.0	60,163.0
1995	79,124	609,644	445,963	18,154.4	12,762.4	30,892.2	22,861.6	62,657.3	61,862.6
1996	80,408	608,689	442,953	18,699.3	13,107.3	31,831.8	23,465.7	64,414.5	63,610.3
1997	81,712	607,737	439,963	19,260.5	13,461.6	32,800.0	24,085.8	66,221.0	65,407.4
1998	83,038	606,785	436,993	19,838.6	13,825.4	33,797.6	24,722.3	68,078.2	67,255.2

Source: Economic Census of the United States, 1977, 1982, 1987 and 1992. Data for other years are estimates based on the compounded annual growth/decline rates between 1987 and 1992. Footnoted items (1) are from the *County Business Patterns* for the years indicated. Extracted from *Agriculture, Mining, and Construction USA*, Gale, 1998.

SIC 1711 - PLUMBING, HEATING, AND AIR CONDITIONING: INDICES OF CHANGE

Year	Estab- lish- ments	Employment		Payroll ($ mil)		Costs ($ mil)		Revenues ($ mil)	
		Total	Constr. workers	Total	Worker payroll	Total	Cost of materials	All sources	Construc- tion
1977	74.9	74.9	81.1	38.6	42.6	38.1	40.2	37.2	37.0
1982	79.9	83.6	87.4	59.4	63.5	58.6	57.5	58.1	57.4
1987	92.3	100.8	103.4	86.3	87.5	86.1	87.8	87.1	87.0
1992	100.0	100.0	100.0	100.0	100.0	100.0	100.0	100.0	100.0

Source: Same as General Statistics but excluding estimates. The values shown reflect change from the base year, 1992. Values above 100 mean greater than 1992, values below 100 mean less than 1992, and a value of 100 in the 1987-91 or 1993-98 period means same as 1992.

SIC 1711 - PLUMBING, HEATING, AND AIR CONDITIONING: SELECTED RATIOS

For 1992	Avg. of All Sector	Analyzed Industry	Index
Employees per establishment	8.1	8.1	100
Construction workers per establishment	6.3	6.0	96
Payroll per establishment	205,515	220,349	107
Payroll per employee	25,219	27,123	108
Payroll per construction worker	23,093	25,886	112
Costs per establishment	531,494	374,514	70
Costs per employee	65,220	46,099	71
Costs per construction worker	84,663	62,042	73
Materials as % of costs	52.18	74.87	143
Costs as % of revenues	56.48	48.96	87
Costs as % of construction revenues	57.64	49.62	86
Value added per establishment	409,562	390,364	95
Value added per employee	50,258	48,050	96
Value added per construction worker	65,240	64,668	99
Revenues per establishment	941,057	764,878	81
Revenues per employee	115,478	94,149	82
Revenues per construction worker	149,904	126,710	85
CR as % of total revenues	97.98	98.67	101
Net CR as % of CR	74.06	89.20	120
Investment per establishment	13,794	10,003	73
Investment per employee	1,693	1,231	73
Investment per construction worker	2,197	1,657	75

Source: Same as General Statistics. The 'Average of Sector' column represents the average of all construction industries. The Index shows the relationship between the Average and the Analyzed Industry. For example, 100 means that they are equal; 500 that the Analyzed Industry is five times the average; 50 means that the Analyzed Industry is half the national average. The abbreviation 'CR' stands for 'construction revenues'; 'na' is used to show that data are 'not available'. Net CR is revenue less work that has been contracted out.

SIC 1721 - PAINTING AND PAPER HANGING: GENERAL STATISTICS

Year	Estab-lish-ments	Employment		Payroll ($ mil)		Costs ($ mil)		Revenues ($ mil)	
		Total	Constr. workers	Total	Worker payroll	Total	Cost of materials	All sources	Construc-tion
1977	27,369	133,106	121,288	1,361.5	1,191.1	843.3	652.4	3,205.3	3,171.1
1982	24,779	136,130	121,353	1,875.7	1,589.4	1,328.2	958.5	4,688.1	4,652.2
1987	29,867	169,968	145,385	2,978.6	2,386.2	2,311.5	1,641.6	8,028.0	7,953.3
1988	27,625[1]	155,290[1]	143,548	3,082.5[1]	2,402.8	2,416.3	1,725.9	8,165.5	8,095.5
1989	29,439[1]	160,845[1]	141,733	3,211.2[1]	2,419.5	2,525.8	1,814.5	8,305.5	8,240.1
1990	29,393[1]	164,917[1]	139,942	3,321.5[1]	2,436.3	2,640.2	1,907.6	8,447.8	8,387.4
1991	29,715[1]	146,417[1]	138,173	3,092.9[1]	2,453.2	2,759.9	2,005.6	8,592.5	8,537.3
1992	31,920	162,587	136,427	3,164.1	2,470.2	2,885.0	2,108.5	8,739.8	8,689.8
1993	33,542[1]	155,813[1]	134,703	3,405.5[1]	2,487.4	3,015.7	2,216.8	8,889.5	8,845.1
1994	32,780	159,725	133,000	3,241.5	2,504.7	3,152.4	2,330.6	9,041.9	9,003.2
1995	33,219	158,313	131,319	3,280.9	2,522.1	3,295.3	2,450.2	9,196.8	9,164.1
1996	33,664	156,914	129,660	3,320.7	2,539.6	3,444.7	2,576.0	9,354.4	9,327.8
1997	34,114	155,527	128,021	3,361.1	2,557.3	3,600.8	2,708.3	9,514.7	9,494.5
1998	34,571	154,152	126,403	3,402.0	2,575.0	3,764.0	2,847.3	9,677.7	9,664.2

Source: Economic Census of the United States, 1977, 1982, 1987 and 1992. Data for other years are estimates based on the compounded annual growth/decline rates between 1987 and 1992. Footnoted items (1) are from the *County Business Patterns* for the years indicated. Extracted from *Agriculture, Mining, and Construction USA*, Gale, 1998.

SIC 1721 - PAINTING AND PAPER HANGING: INDICES OF CHANGE

Year	Estab-lish-ments	Employment		Payroll ($ mil)		Costs ($ mil)		Revenues ($ mil)	
		Total	Constr. workers	Total	Worker payroll	Total	Cost of materials	All sources	Construc-tion
1977	85.7	81.9	88.9	43.0	48.2	29.2	30.9	36.7	36.5
1982	77.6	83.7	89.0	59.3	64.3	46.0	45.5	53.6	53.5
1987	93.6	104.5	106.6	94.1	96.6	80.1	77.9	91.9	91.5
1992	100.0	100.0	100.0	100.0	100.0	100.0	100.0	100.0	100.0

Source: Same as General Statistics but excluding estimates. The values shown reflect change from the base year, 1992. Values above 100 mean greater than 1992, values below 100 mean less than 1992, and a value of 100 in the 1987-91 or 1993-98 period means same as 1992.

SIC 1721 - PAINTING AND PAPER HANGING: SELECTED RATIOS

For 1992	Avg. of All Sector	Analyzed Industry	Index
Employees per establishment	8.1	5.1	63
Construction workers per establishment	6.3	4.3	68
Payroll per establishment	205,515	99,125	48
Payroll per employee	25,219	19,461	77
Payroll per construction worker	23,093	18,107	78
Costs per establishment	531,494	90,382	17
Costs per employee	65,220	17,744	27
Costs per construction worker	84,663	21,147	25
Materials as % of costs	52.18	73.09	140
Costs as % of revenues	56.48	33.01	58
Costs as % of construction revenues	57.64	33.20	58
Value added per establishment	409,562	183,420	45
Value added per employee	50,258	36,010	72
Value added per construction worker	65,240	42,915	66
Revenues per establishment	941,057	273,802	29
Revenues per employee	115,478	53,754	47
Revenues per construction worker	149,904	64,062	43
CR as % of total revenues	97.98	99.43	101
Net CR as % of CR	74.06	93.15	126
Investment per establishment	13,794	4,540	33
Investment per employee	1,693	891	53
Investment per construction worker	2,197	1,062	48

Source: Same as General Statistics. The 'Average of Sector' column represents the average of all construction industries. The Index shows the relationship between the Average and the Analyzed Industry. For example, 100 means that they are equal; 500 that the Analyzed Industry is five times the average; 50 means that the Analyzed Industry is half the national average. The abbreviation 'CR' stands for 'construction revenues'; 'na' is used to show that data are 'not available'. Net CR is revenue less work that has been contracted out.

SIC 1731 - ELECTRICAL WORK: GENERAL STATISTICS

Year	Estab-lish-ments	Employment		Payroll ($ mil)		Costs ($ mil)		Revenues ($ mil)	
		Total	Constr. workers	Total	Worker payroll	Total	Cost of materials	All sources	Construc-tion
1977	36,764	356,591	296,946	5,482.5	4,496.7	5,733.4	5,240.0	14,481.8	14,221.3
1982	39,563	434,764	351,894	9,106.6	7,346.5	11,318.5	10,234.6	26,441.1	25,948.5
1987	49,436	509,309	405,982	12,663.5	9,622.0	14,458.7	12,788.5	36,275.3	35,838.2
1988	49,144[1]	518,989[1]	400,447	13,931.4[1]	9,704.0	14,965.8	13,184.1	37,124.9	36,681.8
1989	52,127[1]	522,019[1]	394,988	14,165.2[1]	9,786.6	15,490.8	13,592.0	37,994.4	37,545.2
1990	52,201[1]	528,603[1]	389,603	14,628.9[1]	9,870.0	16,034.2	14,012.4	38,884.3	38,429.0
1991	52,928[1]	490,747[1]	384,291	13,919.6[1]	9,954.1	16,596.6	14,445.9	39,795.0	39,333.6
1992	54,022	487,072	379,052	13,623.8	10,038.9	17,178.7	14,892.8	40,727.0	40,259.4
1993	56,406[1]	485,806[1]	373,884	14,576.5[1]	10,124.4	17,781.3	15,353.5	41,680.9	41,207.1
1994	55,973	478,451	368,787	14,028.0	10,210.6	18,405.0	15,828.4	42,657.1	42,177.0
1995	56,975	474,199	363,759	14,234.6	10,297.6	19,050.6	16,318.1	43,656.2	43,169.8
1996	57,995	469,984	358,800	14,444.2	10,385.3	19,718.9	16,822.9	44,678.7	44,185.9
1997	59,033	465,806	353,908	14,656.9	10,473.8	20,410.5	17,343.3	45,725.2	45,226.0
1998	60,090	461,665	349,083	14,872.8	10,563.0	21,126.5	17,879.8	46,796.1	46,290.6

Source: Economic Census of the United States, 1977, 1982, 1987 and 1992. Data for other years are estimates based on the compounded annual growth/decline rates between 1987 and 1992. Footnoted items (1) are from the County Business Patterns for the years indicated. Extracted from Agriculture, Mining, and Construction USA, Gale, 1998.

SIC 1731 - ELECTRICAL WORK: INDICES OF CHANGE

Year	Estab-lish-ments	Employment		Payroll ($ mil)		Costs ($ mil)		Revenues ($ mil)	
		Total	Constr. workers	Total	Worker payroll	Total	Cost of materials	All sources	Construc-tion
1977	68.1	73.2	78.3	40.2	44.8	33.4	35.2	35.6	35.3
1982	73.2	89.3	92.8	66.8	73.2	65.9	68.7	64.9	64.5
1987	91.5	104.6	107.1	93.0	95.8	84.2	85.9	89.1	89.0
1992	100.0	100.0	100.0	100.0	100.0	100.0	100.0	100.0	100.0

Source: Same as General Statistics but excluding estimates. The values shown reflect change from the base year, 1992. Values above 100 mean greater than 1992, values below 100 mean less than 1992, and a value of 100 in the 1987-91 or 1993-98 period means same as 1992.

SIC 1731 - ELECTRICAL WORK: SELECTED RATIOS

For 1992	Avg. of All Sector	Analyzed Industry	Index
Employees per establishment	8.1	9.0	111
Construction workers per establishment	6.3	7.0	111
Payroll per establishment	205,515	252,190	123
Payroll per employee	25,219	27,971	111
Payroll per construction worker	23,093	26,484	115
Costs per establishment	531,494	317,995	60
Costs per employee	65,220	35,269	54
Costs per construction worker	84,663	45,320	54
Materials as % of costs	52.18	86.69	166
Costs as % of revenues	56.48	42.18	75
Costs as % of construction revenues	57.64	42.67	74
Value added per establishment	409,562	435,902	106
Value added per employee	50,258	48,347	96
Value added per construction worker	65,240	62,124	95
Revenues per establishment	941,057	753,897	80
Revenues per employee	115,478	83,616	72
Revenues per construction worker	149,904	107,444	72
CR as % of total revenues	97.98	98.85	101
Net CR as % of CR	74.06	95.73	129
Investment per establishment	13,794	9,407	68
Investment per employee	1,693	1,043	62
Investment per construction worker	2,197	1,341	61

Source: Same as General Statistics. The 'Average of Sector' column represents the average of all construction industries. The Index shows the relationship between the Average and the Analyzed Industry. For example, 100 means that they are equal; 500 that the Analyzed Industry is five times the average; 50 means that the Analyzed Industry is half the national average. The abbreviation 'CR' stands for 'construction revenues'; 'na' is used to show that data are 'not available'. Net CR is revenue less work that has been contracted out.

SIC 1741 - MASONRY AND OTHER STONEWORK: GENERAL STATISTICS

Year	Estab-lish-ments	Employment		Payroll ($ mil)		Costs ($ mil)		Revenues ($ mil)	
		Total	Constr. workers	Total	Worker payroll	Total	Cost of materials	All sources	Construc-tion
1977	24,815	152,167	142,797	1,493.2	1,350.3	1,388.4	1,219.6	3,805.1	3,775.4
1982	20,188	120,600	109,576	1,550.8	1,344.2	1,665.4	1,353.2	4,332.6	4,269.4
1987	23,284	168,978	150,308	2,947.0	2,461.6	3,302.8	2,715.4	8,778.6	8,714.2
1988	21,590[1]	161,459[1]	145,954	3,116.3[1]	2,442.3	3,312.8	2,711.8	8,722.0	8,662.3
1989	21,974[1]	166,667[1]	141,726	3,163.7[1]	2,423.1	3,322.9	2,708.2	8,665.8	8,610.7
1990	21,572[1]	168,297[1]	137,620	3,119.5[1]	2,404.0	3,332.9	2,704.6	8,609.9	8,559.5
1991	20,923[1]	136,446[1]	133,633	2,685.8[1]	2,385.1	3,343.0	2,701.1	8,554.4	8,508.5
1992	22,637	147,892	129,762	2,882.5	2,366.4	3,353.1	2,697.5	8,499.3	8,457.9
1993	23,013[1]	144,106[1]	126,003	2,997.6[1]	2,347.8	3,363.3	2,693.9	8,444.5	8,407.5
1994	22,383	140,214	122,353	2,857.1	2,329.3	3,373.4	2,690.4	8,390.0	8,357.5
1995	22,257	136,525	118,808	2,844.5	2,311.0	3,383.6	2,686.8	8,335.9	8,307.7
1996	22,132	132,934	115,367	2,832.0	2,292.9	3,393.9	2,683.3	8,282.2	8,258.3
1997	22,008	129,437	112,024	2,819.5	2,274.8	3,404.2	2,679.7	8,228.8	8,209.1
1998	21,884	126,032	108,779	2,807.0	2,257.0	3,414.5	2,676.2	8,175.8	8,160.2

Source: Economic Census of the United States, 1977, 1982, 1987 and 1992. Data for other years are estimates based on the compounded annual growth/decline rates between 1987 and 1992. Footnoted items (1) are from the *County Business Patterns* for the years indicated. Extracted from *Agriculture, Mining, and Construction USA*, Gale, 1998.

SIC 1741 - MASONRY AND OTHER STONEWORK: INDICES OF CHANGE

Year	Estab-lish-ments	Employment		Payroll ($ mil)		Costs ($ mil)		Revenues ($ mil)	
		Total	Constr. workers	Total	Worker payroll	Total	Cost of materials	All sources	Construc-tion
1977	109.6	102.9	110.0	51.8	57.1	41.4	45.2	44.8	44.6
1982	89.2	81.5	84.4	53.8	56.8	49.7	50.2	51.0	50.5
1987	102.9	114.3	115.8	102.2	104.0	98.5	100.7	103.3	103.0
1992	100.0	100.0	100.0	100.0	100.0	100.0	100.0	100.0	100.0

Source: Same as General Statistics but excluding estimates. The values shown reflect change from the base year, 1992. Values above 100 mean greater than 1992, values below 100 mean less than 1992, and a value of 100 in the 1987-91 or 1993-98 period means same as 1992.

SIC 1741 - MASONRY AND OTHER STONEWORK: SELECTED RATIOS

For 1992	Avg. of All Sector	Analyzed Industry	Index
Employees per establishment	8.1	6.5	81
Construction workers per establishment	6.3	5.7	91
Payroll per establishment	205,515	127,337	62
Payroll per employee	25,219	19,491	77
Payroll per construction worker	23,093	18,236	79
Costs per establishment	531,494	148,125	28
Costs per employee	65,220	22,673	35
Costs per construction worker	84,663	25,841	31
Materials as % of costs	52.18	80.45	154
Costs as % of revenues	56.48	39.45	70
Costs as % of construction revenues	57.64	39.64	69
Value added per establishment	409,562	227,333	56
Value added per employee	50,258	34,797	69
Value added per construction worker	65,240	39,658	61
Revenues per establishment	941,057	375,458	40
Revenues per employee	115,478	57,469	50
Revenues per construction worker	149,904	65,499	44
CR as % of total revenues	97.98	99.51	102
Net CR as % of CR	74.06	94.07	127
Investment per establishment	13,794	5,981	43
Investment per employee	1,693	916	54
Investment per construction worker	2,197	1,043	47

Source: Same as General Statistics. The 'Average of Sector' column represents the average of all construction industries. The Index shows the relationship between the Average and the Analyzed Industry. For example, 100 means that they are equal; 500 that the Analyzed Industry is five times the average; 50 means that the Analyzed Industry is half the national average. The abbreviation 'CR' stands for 'construction revenues'; 'na' is used to show that data are 'not available'. Net CR is revenue less work that has been contracted out.

SIC 1742 - PLASTERING, DRY WALL, AND INSULATION: GENERAL STATISTICS

Year	Estab-lish-ments	Employment		Payroll ($ mil)		Costs ($ mil)		Revenues ($ mil)	
		Total	Constr. workers	Total	Worker payroll	Total	Cost of materials	All sources	Construc-tion
1977	16,745	180,326	158,479	2,261.9	1,900.7	2,635.4	2,311.0	6,265.6	6,057.5
1982	16,382	199,790	171,511	3,572.6	2,930.0	4,196.4	3,417.3	10,205.7	9,847.5
1987	17,809	253,563	217,392	5,484.8	4,347.9	7,003.2	5,521.0	16,750.8	16,426.8
1988	15,414[1]	244,967[1]	207,796	5,624.3[1]	4,238.1	6,808.9	5,337.2	16,212.6	15,922.6
1989	16,106[1]	253,564[1]	198,624	5,920.9[1]	4,131.0	6,620.0	5,159.5	15,691.7	15,433.9
1990	16,005[1]	255,043[1]	189,856	5,751.6[1]	4,026.7	6,436.3	4,987.7	15,187.6	14,960.1
1991	16,233[1]	208,144[1]	181,476	4,915.1[1]	3,924.9	6,257.7	4,821.6	14,699.6	14,500.9
1992	18,648	206,670	173,465	4,910.1	3,825.8	6,084.1	4,661.0	14,227.3	14,055.8
1993	18,903[1]	203,435[1]	165,808	5,020.8[1]	3,729.1	5,915.3	4,505.8	13,770.2	13,624.3
1994	18,995	190,438	158,489	4,697.4	3,634.9	5,751.2	4,355.8	13,327.8	13,206.1
1995	19,170	182,807	151,493	4,594.6	3,543.1	5,591.7	4,210.7	12,899.6	12,800.7
1996	19,348	175,481	144,806	4,494.0	3,453.6	5,436.5	4,070.5	12,485.1	12,407.8
1997	19,527	168,449	138,414	4,395.6	3,366.3	5,285.7	3,935.0	12,084.0	12,026.9
1998	19,707	161,699	132,304	4,299.3	3,281.3	5,139.1	3,804.0	11,695.7	11,657.8

Source: Economic Census of the United States, 1977, 1982, 1987 and 1992. Data for other years are estimates based on the compounded annual growth/decline rates between 1987 and 1992. Footnoted items (1) are from the *County Business Patterns* for the years indicated. Extracted from *Agriculture, Mining, and Construction USA*, Gale, 1998.

SIC 1742 - PLASTERING, DRY WALL, AND INSULATION: INDICES OF CHANGE

Year	Estab-lish-ments	Employment		Payroll ($ mil)		Costs ($ mil)		Revenues ($ mil)	
		Total	Constr. workers	Total	Worker payroll	Total	Cost of materials	All sources	Construc-tion
1977	89.8	87.3	91.4	46.1	49.7	43.3	49.6	44.0	43.1
1982	87.8	96.7	98.9	72.8	76.6	69.0	73.3	71.7	70.1
1987	95.5	122.7	125.3	111.7	113.6	115.1	118.5	117.7	116.9
1992	100.0	100.0	100.0	100.0	100.0	100.0	100.0	100.0	100.0

Source: Same as General Statistics but excluding estimates. The values shown reflect change from the base year, 1992. Values above 100 mean greater than 1992, values below 100 mean less than 1992, and a value of 100 in the 1987-91 or 1993-98 period means same as 1992.

SIC 1742 - PLASTERING, DRY WALL, AND INSULATION: SELECTED RATIOS

For 1992	Avg. of All Sector	Analyzed Industry	Index
Employees per establishment	8.1	11.1	137
Construction workers per establishment	6.3	9.3	148
Payroll per establishment	205,515	263,303	128
Payroll per employee	25,219	23,758	94
Payroll per construction worker	23,093	22,055	96
Costs per establishment	531,494	326,262	61
Costs per employee	65,220	29,439	45
Costs per construction worker	84,663	35,074	41
Materials as % of costs	52.18	76.61	147
Costs as % of revenues	56.48	42.76	76
Costs as % of construction revenues	57.64	43.29	75
Value added per establishment	409,562	436,678	107
Value added per employee	50,258	39,402	78
Value added per construction worker	65,240	46,944	72
Revenues per establishment	941,057	762,940	81
Revenues per employee	115,478	68,841	60
Revenues per construction worker	149,904	82,018	55
CR as % of total revenues	97.98	98.79	101
Net CR as % of CR	74.06	91.24	123
Investment per establishment	13,794	7,593	55
Investment per employee	1,693	685	40
Investment per construction worker	2,197	816	37

Source: Same as General Statistics. The 'Average of Sector' column represents the average of all construction industries. The Index shows the relationship between the Average and the Analyzed Industry. For example, 100 means that they are equal; 500 that the Analyzed Industry is five times the average; 50 means that the Analyzed Industry is half the national average. The abbreviation 'CR' stands for 'construction revenues'; 'na' is used to show that data are 'not available'. Net CR is revenue less work that has been contracted out.

SIC 1743 - TERRAZZO, TILE, MARBLE, AND MOSAIC WORK: GENERAL STATISTICS

| Year | Estab-lish-ments | Employment | | Payroll ($ mil) | | Costs ($ mil) | | Revenues ($ mil) | |
		Total	Constr. workers	Total	Worker payroll	Total	Cost of materials	All sources	Construc-tion
1977	3,891	22,324	19,084	255.5	207.6	345.7	315.9	788.7	766.1
1982	3,890	25,434	21,695	384.0	306.3	544.8	487.7	1,210.9	1,190.6
1987	5,089	34,420	27,908	734.0	554.1	998.1	871.9	2,315.7	2,271.6
1988	4,178[1]	30,764[1]	27,712	727.8[1]	556.9	1,022.1	890.2	2,348.0	2,304.1
1989	4,049[1]	30,915[1]	27,517	760.3[1]	559.7	1,046.6	908.8	2,380.8	2,337.0
1990	4,541[1]	33,109[1]	27,324	790.6[1]	562.5	1,071.7	927.8	2,414.0	2,370.4
1991	4,491[1]	28,641[1]	27,132	665.1[1]	565.4	1,097.5	947.2	2,447.7	2,404.3
1992	6,499	34,012	26,941	774.8	568.2	1,123.8	967.0	2,481.8	2,438.6
1993	5,849[1]	30,291[1]	26,752	707.6[1]	571.1	1,150.8	987.2	2,516.5	2,473.5
1994	7,167	33,850	26,564	791.7	573.9	1,178.5	1,007.8	2,551.6	2,508.9
1995	7,526	33,770	26,377	800.4	576.8	1,206.8	1,028.9	2,587.2	2,544.7
1996	7,903	33,689	26,192	809.1	579.7	1,235.7	1,050.4	2,623.3	2,581.1
1997	8,300	33,609	26,008	817.9	582.6	1,265.4	1,072.4	2,659.9	2,618.0
1998	8,716	33,529	25,825	826.8	585.6	1,295.8	1,094.8	2,697.0	2,655.4

Source: Economic Census of the United States, 1977, 1982, 1987 and 1992. Data for other years are estimates based on the compounded annual growth/decline rates between 1987 and 1992. Footnoted items (1) are from the County Business Patterns for the years indicated. Extracted from Agriculture, Mining, and Construction USA, Gale, 1998.

SIC 1743 - TERRAZZO, TILE, MARBLE, AND MOSAIC WORK: INDICES OF CHANGE

| Year | Estab-lish-ments | Employment | | Payroll ($ mil) | | Costs ($ mil) | | Revenues ($ mil) | |
		Total	Constr. workers	Total	Worker payroll	Total	Cost of materials	All sources	Construc-tion
1977	59.9	65.6	70.8	33.0	36.5	30.8	32.7	31.8	31.4
1982	59.9	74.8	80.5	49.6	53.9	48.5	50.4	48.8	48.8
1987	78.3	101.2	103.6	94.7	97.5	88.8	90.2	93.3	93.1
1992	100.0	100.0	100.0	100.0	100.0	100.0	100.0	100.0	100.0

Source: Same as General Statistics but excluding estimates. The values shown reflect change from the base year, 1992. Values above 100 mean greater than 1992, values below 100 mean less than 1992, and a value of 100 in the 1987-91 or 1993-98 period means same as 1992.

SIC 1743 - TERRAZZO, TILE, MARBLE, AND MOSAIC WORK: SELECTED RATIOS

For 1992	Avg. of All Sector	Analyzed Industry	Index
Employees per establishment	8.1	5.2	65
Construction workers per establishment	6.3	4.1	66
Payroll per establishment	205,515	119,216	58
Payroll per employee	25,219	22,780	90
Payroll per construction worker	23,093	21,091	91
Costs per establishment	531,494	172,924	33
Costs per employee	65,220	33,042	51
Costs per construction worker	84,663	41,714	49
Materials as % of costs	52.18	86.04	165
Costs as % of revenues	56.48	45.28	80
Costs as % of construction revenues	57.64	46.08	80
Value added per establishment	409,562	208,958	51
Value added per employee	50,258	39,928	79
Value added per construction worker	65,240	50,407	77
Revenues per establishment	941,057	381,881	41
Revenues per employee	115,478	72,970	63
Revenues per construction worker	149,904	92,122	61
CR as % of total revenues	97.98	98.26	100
Net CR as % of CR	74.06	95.24	129
Investment per establishment	13,794	4,223	31
Investment per employee	1,693	807	48
Investment per construction worker	2,197	1,019	46

Source: Same as General Statistics. The 'Average of Sector' column represents the average of all construction industries. The Index shows the relationship between the Average and the Analyzed Industry. For example, 100 means that they are equal; 500 that the Analyzed Industry is five times the average; 50 means that the Analyzed Industry is half the national average. The abbreviation 'CR' stands for 'construction revenues'; 'na' is used to show that data are 'not available'. Net CR is revenue less work that has been contracted out.

SIC 1751 - CARPENTRY WORK: GENERAL STATISTICS

Year	Estab-lish-ments	Employment		Payroll ($ mil)		Costs ($ mil)		Revenues ($ mil)	
		Total	Constr. workers	Total	Worker payroll	Total	Cost of materials	All sources	Construc-tion
1977	24,388	124,646	114,673	1,202.2	1,060.7	1,563.9	1,231.1	3,647.0	3,597.2
1982	30,765	132,543	116,973	1,612.0	1,352.2	2,583.5	1,771.6	5,512.2	5,451.2
1987	36,009	190,431	164,191	3,272.2	2,609.9	5,374.6	3,997.5	11,452.2	11,243.9
1988	29,840[1]	171,895[1]	160,247	3,186.9[1]	2,624.4	5,542.9	4,102.3	11,751.7	11,548.6
1989	28,175[1]	172,021[1]	156,397	3,301.7[1]	2,639.0	5,716.5	4,209.7	12,059.1	11,861.5
1990	29,267[1]	171,123[1]	152,640	3,156.5[1]	2,653.6	5,895.6	4,320.0	12,374.6	12,183.0
1991	27,946[1]	133,059[1]	148,973	2,710.4[1]	2,668.3	6,080.3	4,433.2	12,698.3	12,513.2
1992	38,210	177,601	145,394	3,488.8	2,683.1	6,270.7	4,549.4	13,030.5	12,852.3
1993	36,177[1]	166,813[1]	141,901	3,518.6[1]	2,698.0	6,467.2	4,668.6	13,371.3	13,200.6
1994	39,128	172,714	138,492	3,579.5	2,713.0	6,669.8	4,790.9	13,721.1	13,558.3
1995	39,595	170,322	135,165	3,625.7	2,728.0	6,878.7	4,916.4	14,080.0	13,925.8
1996	40,067	167,962	131,918	3,672.4	2,743.2	7,094.2	5,045.2	14,448.3	14,303.2
1997	40,546	165,635	128,749	3,719.8	2,758.4	7,316.4	5,177.4	14,826.3	14,690.8
1998	41,029	163,341	125,656	3,767.8	2,773.7	7,545.6	5,313.1	15,214.1	15,088.9

Source: Economic Census of the United States, 1977, 1982, 1987 and 1992. Data for other years are estimates based on the compounded annual growth/decline rates between 1987 and 1992. Footnoted items (1) are from the County Business Patterns for the years indicated. Extracted from Agriculture, Mining, and Construction USA, Gale, 1998.

SIC 1751 - CARPENTRY WORK: INDICES OF CHANGE

Year	Estab-lish-ments	Employment		Payroll ($ mil)		Costs ($ mil)		Revenues ($ mil)	
		Total	Constr. workers	Total	Worker payroll	Total	Cost of materials	All sources	Construc-tion
1977	63.8	70.2	78.9	34.5	39.5	24.9	27.1	28.0	28.0
1982	80.5	74.6	80.5	46.2	50.4	41.2	38.9	42.3	42.4
1987	94.2	107.2	112.9	93.8	97.3	85.7	87.9	87.9	87.5
1992	100.0	100.0	100.0	100.0	100.0	100.0	100.0	100.0	100.0

Source: Same as General Statistics but excluding estimates. The values shown reflect change from the base year, 1992. Values above 100 mean greater than 1992, values below 100 mean less than 1992, and a value of 100 in the 1987-91 or 1993-98 period means same as 1992.

SIC 1751 - CARPENTRY WORK: SELECTED RATIOS

For 1992	Avg. of All Sector	Analyzed Industry	Index
Employees per establishment	8.1	4.6	57
Construction workers per establishment	6.3	3.8	60
Payroll per establishment	205,515	91,307	44
Payroll per employee	25,219	19,644	78
Payroll per construction worker	23,093	18,454	80
Costs per establishment	531,494	164,113	31
Costs per employee	65,220	35,308	54
Costs per construction worker	84,663	43,129	51
Materials as % of costs	52.18	72.55	139
Costs as % of revenues	56.48	48.12	85
Costs as % of construction revenues	57.64	48.79	85
Value added per establishment	409,562	176,909	43
Value added per employee	50,258	38,061	76
Value added per construction worker	65,240	46,492	71
Revenues per establishment	941,057	341,022	36
Revenues per employee	115,478	73,369	64
Revenues per construction worker	149,904	89,622	60
CR as % of total revenues	97.98	98.63	101
Net CR as % of CR	74.06	88.19	119
Investment per establishment	13,794	4,059	29
Investment per employee	1,693	873	52
Investment per construction worker	2,197	1,067	49

Source: Same as General Statistics. The 'Average of Sector' column represents the average of all construction industries. The Index shows the relationship between the Average and the Analyzed Industry. For example, 100 means that they are equal; 500 that the Analyzed Industry is five times the average; 50 means that the Analyzed Industry is half the national average. The abbreviation 'CR' stands for 'construction revenues'; 'na' is used to show that data are 'not available'. Net CR is revenue less work that has been contracted out.

SIC 1752 - FLOOR LAYING AND FLOOR WORK, N.E.C.: GENERAL STATISTICS

Year	Estab-lish-ments	Employment		Payroll ($ mil)		Costs ($ mil)		Revenues ($ mil)	
		Total	Constr. workers	Total	Worker payroll	Total	Cost of materials	All sources	Construc-tion
1977	8,969	40,990	33,724	453.1	352.2	850.2	749.8	1,673.9	1,616.9
1982	6,673	32,349	25,410	496.8	364.2	940.8	806.9	1,854.1	1,793.8
1987	8,174	44,579	34,666	906.2	645.5	1,891.7	1,548.3	3,772.0	3,651.4
1988	7,440[1]	44,465[1]	35,013	956.6[1]	660.4	1,979.8	1,614.7	3,914.6	3,794.9
1989	7,439[1]	45,882[1]	35,363	1,003.6[1]	675.6	2,072.0	1,683.8	4,062.6	3,944.0
1990	8,172[1]	47,256[1]	35,716	1,035.8[1]	691.3	2,168.5	1,755.9	4,216.2	4,099.0
1991	8,286[1]	43,581[1]	36,073	961.0[1]	707.2	2,269.6	1,831.2	4,375.6	4,260.1
1992	10,196	48,948	36,434	1,065.2	723.6	2,375.3	1,909.6	4,541.1	4,427.5
1993	10,357[1]	48,367[1]	36,798	1,094.9[1]	740.3	2,485.9	1,991.4	4,712.7	4,601.5
1994	11,139	50,813	37,166	1,136.3	757.4	2,601.8	2,076.7	4,890.9	4,782.3
1995	11,642	51,772	37,538	1,173.6	774.9	2,723.0	2,165.6	5,075.9	4,970.3
1996	12,168	52,750	37,913	1,212.2	792.8	2,849.8	2,258.4	5,267.8	5,165.6
1997	12,718	53,745	38,292	1,252.0	811.1	2,982.6	2,355.1	5,467.0	5,368.6
1998	13,293	54,760	38,675	1,293.2	829.8	3,121.5	2,456.0	5,673.7	5,579.5

Source: Economic Census of the United States, 1977, 1982, 1987 and 1992. Data for other years are estimates based on the compounded annual growth/decline rates between 1987 and 1992. Footnoted items (1) are from the _County Business Patterns_ for the years indicated. Extracted from _Agriculture, Mining, and Construction USA_, Gale, 1998.

SIC 1752 - FLOOR LAYING AND FLOOR WORK, N.E.C.: INDICES OF CHANGE

Year	Estab-lish-ments	Employment		Payroll ($ mil)		Costs ($ mil)		Revenues ($ mil)	
		Total	Constr. workers	Total	Worker payroll	Total	Cost of materials	All sources	Construc-tion
1977	88.0	83.7	92.6	42.5	48.7	35.8	39.3	36.9	36.5
1982	65.4	66.1	69.7	46.6	50.3	39.6	42.3	40.8	40.5
1987	80.2	91.1	95.1	85.1	89.2	79.6	81.1	83.1	82.5
1992	100.0	100.0	100.0	100.0	100.0	100.0	100.0	100.0	100.0

Source: Same as General Statistics but excluding estimates. The values shown reflect change from the base year, 1992. Values above 100 mean greater than 1992, values below 100 mean less than 1992, and a value of 100 in the 1987-91 or 1993-98 period means same as 1992.

SIC 1752 - FLOOR LAYING AND FLOOR WORK, N.E.C.: SELECTED RATIOS

For 1992	Avg. of All Sector	Analyzed Industry	Index
Employees per establishment	8.1	4.8	59
Construction workers per establishment	6.3	3.6	57
Payroll per establishment	205,515	104,467	51
Payroll per employee	25,219	21,761	86
Payroll per construction worker	23,093	19,859	86
Costs per establishment	531,494	232,963	44
Costs per employee	65,220	48,527	74
Costs per construction worker	84,663	65,194	77
Materials as % of costs	52.18	80.39	154
Costs as % of revenues	56.48	52.31	93
Costs as % of construction revenues	57.64	53.65	93
Value added per establishment	409,562	212,413	52
Value added per employee	50,258	44,246	88
Value added per construction worker	65,240	59,443	91
Revenues per establishment	941,057	445,376	47
Revenues per employee	115,478	92,773	80
Revenues per construction worker	149,904	124,638	83
CR as % of total revenues	97.98	97.50	100
Net CR as % of CR	74.06	91.08	123
Investment per establishment	13,794	4,533	33
Investment per employee	1,693	944	56
Investment per construction worker	2,197	1,269	58

Source: Same as General Statistics. The 'Average of Sector' column represents the average of all construction industries. The Index shows the relationship between the Average and the Analyzed Industry. For example, 100 means that they are equal; 500 that the Analyzed Industry is five times the average; 50 means that the Analyzed Industry is half the national average. The abbreviation 'CR' stands for 'construction revenues'; 'na' is used to show that data are 'not available'. Net CR is revenue less work that has been contracted out.

SIC 1761 - ROOFING, SIDING, AND SHEET METAL WORK: GENERAL STATISTICS

Year	Estab-lish-ments	Employment		Payroll ($ mil)		Costs ($ mil)		Revenues ($ mil)	
		Total	Constr. workers	Total	Worker payroll	Total	Cost of materials	All sources	Construc-tion
1977	20,577	171,931	146,307	1,967.8	1,555.3	2,900.3	2,535.6	6,320.7	6,200.4
1982	21,152	191,489	158,901	3,034.8	2,320.7	4,573.7	3,848.6	10,033.5	9,836.5
1987	25,673	231,137	186,916	4,313.7	3,111.0	6,734.5	5,637.2	15,258.9	15,027.8
1988	22,598[1]	212,204[1]	183,136	4,410.5[1]	3,134.4	6,982.4	5,812.7	15,587.6	15,364.4
1989	22,978[1]	210,564[1]	179,432	4,496.6[1]	3,158.0	7,239.4	5,993.7	15,923.3	15,708.6
1990	23,200[1]	216,752[1]	175,803	4,631.7[1]	3,181.8	7,505.9	6,180.3	16,266.3	16,060.4
1991	23,564[1]	194,514[1]	172,248	4,315.7[1]	3,205.8	7,782.2	6,372.8	16,616.7	16,420.2
1992	27,569	215,545	168,764	4,622.5	3,230.0	8,068.6	6,571.2	16,974.6	16,788.0
1993	27,881[1]	214,062[1]	165,351	4,923.8[1]	3,254.3	8,365.6	6,775.8	17,340.2	17,164.0
1994	28,366	209,607	162,007	4,752.1	3,278.8	8,673.6	6,986.8	17,713.8	17,548.5
1995	28,773	206,699	158,730	4,818.3	3,303.5	8,992.9	7,204.3	18,095.3	17,941.6
1996	29,186	203,832	155,520	4,885.4	3,328.4	9,323.9	7,428.6	18,485.1	18,343.4
1997	29,605	201,005	152,375	4,953.4	3,353.5	9,667.1	7,659.9	18,883.2	18,754.3
1998	30,030	198,217	149,293	5,022.4	3,378.7	10,023.0	7,898.4	19,290.0	19,174.4

Source: Economic Census of the United States, 1977, 1982, 1987 and 1992. Data for other years are estimates based on the compounded annual growth/decline rates between 1987 and 1992. Footnoted items (1) are from the *County Business Patterns* for the years indicated. Extracted from *Agriculture, Mining, and Construction USA*, Gale, 1998.

SIC 1761 - ROOFING, SIDING, AND SHEET METAL WORK: INDICES OF CHANGE

Year	Estab-lish-ments	Employment		Payroll ($ mil)		Costs ($ mil)		Revenues ($ mil)	
		Total	Constr. workers	Total	Worker payroll	Total	Cost of materials	All sources	Construc-tion
1977	74.6	79.8	86.7	42.6	48.2	35.9	38.6	37.2	36.9
1982	76.7	88.8	94.2	65.7	71.8	56.7	58.6	59.1	58.6
1987	93.1	107.2	110.8	93.3	96.3	83.5	85.8	89.9	89.5
1992	100.0	100.0	100.0	100.0	100.0	100.0	100.0	100.0	100.0

Source: Same as General Statistics but excluding estimates. The values shown reflect change from the base year, 1992. Values above 100 mean greater than 1992, values below 100 mean less than 1992, and a value of 100 in the 1987-91 or 1993-98 period means same as 1992.

SIC 1761 - ROOFING, SIDING, AND SHEET METAL WORK: SELECTED RATIOS

For 1992	Avg. of All Sector	Analyzed Industry	Index
Employees per establishment	8.1	7.8	97
Construction workers per establishment	6.3	6.1	97
Payroll per establishment	205,515	167,671	82
Payroll per employee	25,219	21,446	85
Payroll per construction worker	23,093	19,139	83
Costs per establishment	531,494	292,671	55
Costs per employee	65,220	37,434	57
Costs per construction worker	84,663	47,810	56
Materials as % of costs	52.18	81.44	156
Costs as % of revenues	56.48	47.53	84
Costs as % of construction revenues	57.64	48.06	83
Value added per establishment	409,562	323,043	79
Value added per employee	50,258	41,318	82
Value added per construction worker	65,240	52,772	81
Revenues per establishment	941,057	615,714	65
Revenues per employee	115,478	78,752	68
Revenues per construction worker	149,904	100,582	67
CR as % of total revenues	97.98	98.90	101
Net CR as % of CR	74.06	92.86	125
Investment per establishment	13,794	8,441	61
Investment per employee	1,693	1,080	64
Investment per construction worker	2,197	1,379	63

Source: Same as General Statistics. The 'Average of Sector' column represents the average of all construction industries. The Index shows the relationship between the Average and the Analyzed Industry. For example, 100 means that they are equal; 500 that the Analyzed Industry is five times the average; 50 means that the Analyzed Industry is half the national average. The abbreviation 'CR' stands for 'construction revenues'; 'na' is used to show that data are 'not available'. Net CR is revenue less work that has been contracted out.

SIC 1771 - CONCRETE WORK: GENERAL STATISTICS

Year	Estab-lish-ments	Employment		Payroll ($ mil)		Costs ($ mil)		Revenues ($ mil)	
		Total	Constr. workers	Total	Worker payroll	Total	Cost of materials	All sources	Construc-tion
1977	16,974	118,116	107,085	1,209.9	1,042.6	1,924.0	1,595.7	4,151.9	4,097.3
1982	19,986	157,241	137,832	2,309.8	1,901.6	3,885.2	2,878.2	8,376.8	8,207.0
1987	23,422	218,194	186,840	4,174.6	3,278.1	6,769.0	5,243.0	15,212.0	15,055.7
1988	20,812[1]	189,434[1]	181,303	4,425.0[1]	3,240.2	6,793.6	5,250.8	15,086.8	14,926.9
1989	20,333[1]	193,024[1]	175,931	4,504.5[1]	3,202.7	6,818.3	5,258.6	14,962.6	14,799.3
1990	21,496[1]	198,241[1]	170,718	4,551.7[1]	3,165.7	6,843.1	5,266.4	14,839.4	14,672.8
1991	21,212[1]	164,947[1]	165,659	3,989.4[1]	3,129.1	6,868.0	5,274.3	14,717.2	14,547.3
1992	26,123	192,539	160,750	4,038.0	3,093.0	6,892.9	5,282.1	14,596.0	14,422.9
1993	25,835[1]	182,049[1]	155,987	4,422.4[1]	3,057.2	6,918.0	5,290.0	14,475.9	14,299.6
1994	27,289	183,142	151,364	3,984.7	3,021.9	6,943.1	5,297.9	14,356.7	14,177.3
1995	27,891	178,618	146,879	3,958.3	2,987.0	6,968.3	5,305.8	14,238.5	14,056.1
1996	28,506	174,205	142,527	3,932.0	2,952.5	6,993.6	5,313.7	14,121.2	13,935.9
1997	29,135	169,900	138,303	3,906.0	2,918.4	7,019.1	5,321.6	14,005.0	13,816.7
1998	29,778	165,703	134,205	3,880.1	2,884.6	7,044.6	5,329.5	13,889.7	13,698.6

Source: Economic Census of the United States, 1977, 1982, 1987 and 1992. Data for other years are estimates based on the compounded annual growth/decline rates between 1987 and 1992. Footnoted items (1) are from the *County Business Patterns* for the years indicated. Extracted from *Agriculture, Mining, and Construction USA*, Gale, 1998.

SIC 1771 - CONCRETE WORK: INDICES OF CHANGE

Year	Estab-lish-ments	Employment		Payroll ($ mil)		Costs ($ mil)		Revenues ($ mil)	
		Total	Constr. workers	Total	Worker payroll	Total	Cost of materials	All sources	Construc-tion
1977	65.0	61.3	66.6	30.0	33.7	27.9	30.2	28.4	28.4
1982	76.5	81.7	85.7	57.2	61.5	56.4	54.5	57.4	56.9
1987	89.7	113.3	116.2	103.4	106.0	98.2	99.3	104.2	104.4
1992	100.0	100.0	100.0	100.0	100.0	100.0	100.0	100.0	100.0

Source: Same as General Statistics but excluding estimates. The values shown reflect change from the base year, 1992. Values above 100 mean greater than 1992, values below 100 mean less than 1992, and a value of 100 in the 1987-91 or 1993-98 period means same as 1992.

SIC 1771 - CONCRETE WORK: SELECTED RATIOS

For 1992	Avg. of All Sector	Analyzed Industry	Index
Employees per establishment	8.1	7.4	91
Construction workers per establishment	6.3	6.2	98
Payroll per establishment	205,515	154,578	75
Payroll per employee	25,219	20,973	83
Payroll per construction worker	23,093	19,241	83
Costs per establishment	531,494	263,864	50
Costs per employee	65,220	35,800	55
Costs per construction worker	84,663	42,880	51
Materials as % of costs	52.18	76.63	147
Costs as % of revenues	56.48	47.22	84
Costs as % of construction revenues	57.64	47.79	83
Value added per establishment	409,562	294,879	72
Value added per employee	50,258	40,008	80
Value added per construction worker	65,240	47,920	73
Revenues per establishment	941,057	558,743	59
Revenues per employee	115,478	75,808	66
Revenues per construction worker	149,904	90,800	61
CR as % of total revenues	97.98	98.81	101
Net CR as % of CR	74.06	91.38	123
Investment per establishment	13,794	12,641	92
Investment per employee	1,693	1,715	101
Investment per construction worker	2,197	2,054	93

Source: Same as General Statistics. The 'Average of Sector' column represents the average of all construction industries. The Index shows the relationship between the Average and the Analyzed Industry. For example, 100 means that they are equal; 500 that the Analyzed Industry is five times the average; 50 means that the Analyzed Industry is half the national average. The abbreviation 'CR' stands for 'construction revenues'; 'na' is used to show that data are 'not available'. Net CR is revenue less work that has been contracted out.

SIC 1781 - WATER WELL DRILLING: GENERAL STATISTICS

Year	Estab-lish-ments	Employment		Payroll ($ mil)		Costs ($ mil)		Revenues ($ mil)	
		Total	Constr. workers	Total	Worker payroll	Total	Cost of materials	All sources	Construc-tion
1977	4,305	22,352	18,720	237.0	188.3	489.5	435.4	1,118.3	1,090.4
1982	3,551	17,153	13,703	249.0	190.2	454.2	374.0	1,031.7	1,013.9
1987	3,414	17,598	13,628	335.2	248.5	588.7	495.7	1,368.3	1,330.1
1988	3,194[1]	17,717[1]	13,833	378.9[1]	261.8	619.0	520.2	1,437.6	1,401.4
1989	3,069[1]	17,910[1]	14,041	399.1[1]	275.8	650.8	545.8	1,510.3	1,476.6
1990	3,261[1]	18,128[1]	14,252	425.5[1]	290.6	684.3	572.7	1,586.7	1,555.9
1991	3,359[1]	18,170[1]	14,466	433.9[1]	306.2	719.5	600.9	1,667.0	1,639.4
1992	3,638	19,346	14,683	443.6	322.6	756.5	630.5	1,751.3	1,727.4
1993	3,661[1]	18,680[1]	14,904	462.9[1]	339.9	795.4	661.5	1,839.9	1,820.1
1994	3,732	20,093	15,128	496.3	358.1	836.3	694.1	1,933.0	1,917.7
1995	3,779	20,477	15,355	524.9	377.3	879.3	728.3	2,030.7	2,020.6
1996	3,828	20,869	15,586	555.2	397.5	924.5	764.2	2,133.5	2,129.1
1997	3,877	21,268	15,820	587.2	418.8	972.0	801.8	2,241.4	2,243.3
1998	3,926	21,674	16,057	621.1	441.2	1,022.0	841.3	2,354.8	2,363.7

Source: Economic Census of the United States, 1977, 1982, 1987 and 1992. Data for other years are estimates based on the compounded annual growth/decline rates between 1987 and 1992. Footnoted items (1) are from the *County Business Patterns* for the years indicated. Extracted from *Agriculture, Mining, and Construction USA*, Gale, 1998.

SIC 1781 - WATER WELL DRILLING: INDICES OF CHANGE

Year	Estab-lish-ments	Employment		Payroll ($ mil)		Costs ($ mil)		Revenues ($ mil)	
		Total	Constr. workers	Total	Worker payroll	Total	Cost of materials	All sources	Construc-tion
1977	118.3	115.5	127.5	53.4	58.4	64.7	69.1	63.9	63.1
1982	97.6	88.7	93.3	56.1	58.9	60.0	59.3	58.9	58.7
1987	93.8	91.0	92.8	75.6	77.0	77.8	78.6	78.1	77.0
1992	100.0	100.0	100.0	100.0	100.0	100.0	100.0	100.0	100.0

Source: Same as General Statistics but excluding estimates. The values shown reflect change from the base year, 1992. Values above 100 mean greater than 1992, values below 100 mean less than 1992, and a value of 100 in the 1987-91 or 1993-98 period means same as 1992.

SIC 1781 - WATER WELL DRILLING: SELECTED RATIOS

For 1992	Avg. of All Sector	Analyzed Industry	Index
Employees per establishment	8.1	5.3	66
Construction workers per establishment	6.3	4.0	64
Payroll per establishment	205,515	121,946	59
Payroll per employee	25,219	22,932	91
Payroll per construction worker	23,093	21,971	95
Costs per establishment	531,494	207,937	39
Costs per employee	65,220	39,102	60
Costs per construction worker	84,663	51,521	61
Materials as % of costs	52.18	83.34	160
Costs as % of revenues	56.48	43.20	76
Costs as % of construction revenues	57.64	43.79	76
Value added per establishment	409,562	273,451	67
Value added per employee	50,258	51,422	102
Value added per construction worker	65,240	67,753	104
Revenues per establishment	941,057	481,388	51
Revenues per employee	115,478	90,525	78
Revenues per construction worker	149,904	119,273	80
CR as % of total revenues	97.98	98.63	101
Net CR as % of CR	74.06	97.03	131
Investment per establishment	13,794	19,104	138
Investment per employee	1,693	3,593	212
Investment per construction worker	2,197	4,733	215

Source: Same as General Statistics. The 'Average of Sector' column represents the average of all construction industries. The Index shows the relationship between the Average and the Analyzed Industry. For example, 100 means that they are equal; 500 that the Analyzed Industry is five times the average; 50 means that the Analyzed Industry is half the national average. The abbreviation 'CR' stands for 'construction revenues'; 'na' is used to show that data are 'not available'. Net CR is revenue less work that has been contracted out.

SIC 1791 - STRUCTURAL STEEL ERECTION: GENERAL STATISTICS

Year	Estab-lish-ments	Employment		Payroll ($ mil)		Costs ($ mil)		Revenues ($ mil)	
		Total	Constr. workers	Total	Worker payroll	Total	Cost of materials	All sources	Construc-tion
1977	2,592	47,166	40,911	673.8	556.5	698.0	574.8	1,882.4	1,803.3
1982	3,705	61,588	52,645	1,291.2	1,056.1	1,273.6	903.5	3,649.8	3,540.7
1987	4,017	65,348	54,729	1,594.0	1,231.6	1,750.5	1,318.1	5,003.9	4,862.7
1988	3,415[1]	61,208[1]	53,119	1,628.6[1]	1,230.7	1,810.9	1,358.5	5,021.9	4,880.4
1989	3,209[1]	62,571[1]	51,556	1,737.1[1]	1,229.7	1,873.3	1,400.2	5,040.0	4,898.2
1990	3,356[1]	60,697[1]	50,039	1,736.6[1]	1,228.8	1,937.8	1,443.1	5,058.2	4,916.1
1991	3,308[1]	55,351[1]	48,567	1,540.7[1]	1,227.8	2,004.6	1,487.3	5,076.4	4,934.0
1992	3,792	57,986	47,138	1,628.9	1,226.9	2,073.7	1,532.9	5,094.7	4,952.0
1993	3,947[1]	57,837[1]	45,751	1,673.5[1]	1,226.0	2,145.2	1,579.9	5,113.1	4,970.1
1994	3,706	55,279	44,405	1,643.1	1,225.0	2,219.1	1,628.3	5,131.5	4,988.2
1995	3,663	53,973	43,099	1,650.2	1,224.1	2,295.6	1,678.2	5,150.0	5,006.5
1996	3,621	52,698	41,831	1,657.4	1,223.1	2,374.7	1,729.6	5,168.5	5,024.7
1997	3,580	51,453	40,600	1,664.6	1,222.2	2,456.5	1,782.6	5,187.2	5,043.1
1998	3,539	50,238	39,405	1,671.8	1,221.2	2,541.2	1,837.3	5,205.9	5,061.5

Source: Economic Census of the United States, 1977, 1982, 1987 and 1992. Data for other years are estimates based on the compounded annual growth/decline rates between 1987 and 1992. Footnoted items (1) are from the *County Business Patterns* for the years indicated. Extracted from *Agriculture, Mining, and Construction USA*, Gale, 1998.

SIC 1791 - STRUCTURAL STEEL ERECTION: INDICES OF CHANGE

Year	Estab-lish-ments	Employment		Payroll ($ mil)		Costs ($ mil)		Revenues ($ mil)	
		Total	Constr. workers	Total	Worker payroll	Total	Cost of materials	All sources	Construc-tion
1977	68.4	81.3	86.8	41.4	45.4	33.7	37.5	36.9	36.4
1982	97.7	106.2	111.7	79.3	86.1	61.4	58.9	71.6	71.5
1987	105.9	112.7	116.1	97.9	100.4	84.4	86.0	98.2	98.2
1992	100.0	100.0	100.0	100.0	100.0	100.0	100.0	100.0	100.0

Source: Same as General Statistics but excluding estimates. The values shown reflect change from the base year, 1992. Values above 100 mean greater than 1992, values below 100 mean less than 1992, and a value of 100 in the 1987-91 or 1993-98 period means same as 1992.

SIC 1791 - STRUCTURAL STEEL ERECTION: SELECTED RATIOS

For 1992	Avg. of All Sector	Analyzed Industry	Index
Employees per establishment	8.1	15.3	189
Construction workers per establishment	6.3	12.4	197
Payroll per establishment	205,515	429,563	209
Payroll per employee	25,219	28,091	111
Payroll per construction worker	23,093	26,028	113
Costs per establishment	531,494	546,865	103
Costs per employee	65,220	35,762	55
Costs per construction worker	84,663	43,992	52
Materials as % of costs	52.18	73.92	142
Costs as % of revenues	56.48	40.70	72
Costs as % of construction revenues	57.64	41.88	73
Value added per establishment	409,562	796,675	195
Value added per employee	50,258	52,099	104
Value added per construction worker	65,240	64,088	98
Revenues per establishment	941,057	1,343,540	143
Revenues per employee	115,478	87,861	76
Revenues per construction worker	149,904	108,081	72
CR as % of total revenues	97.98	97.20	99
Net CR as % of CR	74.06	90.60	122
Investment per establishment	13,794	20,375	148
Investment per employee	1,693	1,332	79
Investment per construction worker	2,197	1,639	75

Source: Same as General Statistics. The 'Average of Sector' column represents the average of all construction industries. The Index shows the relationship between the Average and the Analyzed Industry. For example, 100 means that they are equal; 500 that the Analyzed Industry is five times the average; 50 means that the Analyzed Industry is half the national average. The abbreviation 'CR' stands for 'construction revenues'; 'na' is used to show that data are 'not available'. Net CR is revenue less work that has been contracted out.

SIC 1793 - GLASS AND GLAZING WORK: GENERAL STATISTICS

Year	Estab-lish-ments	Employment		Payroll ($ mil)		Costs ($ mil)		Revenues ($ mil)	
		Total	Constr. workers	Total	Worker payroll	Total	Cost of materials	All sources	Construc-tion
1977	3,283	26,125	19,335	317.0	228.7	582.1	549.9	1,152.8	1,006.6
1982	3,797	35,843	26,402	696.5	492.6	1,312.5	1,209.6	2,610.3	2,422.3
1987	4,636	40,511	28,730	919.5	606.6	1,732.7	1,599.7	3,433.3	3,222.5
1988	4,044[1]	40,445[1]	27,074	947.3[1]	582.4	1,681.2	1,547.2	3,322.5	3,116.1
1989	3,880[1]	38,813[1]	25,514	959.2[1]	559.1	1,631.2	1,496.5	3,215.2	3,013.2
1990	4,013[1]	39,060[1]	24,043	963.8[1]	536.7	1,582.7	1,447.4	3,111.5	2,913.7
1991	4,012[1]	34,995[1]	22,658	878.4[1]	515.3	1,535.6	1,399.9	3,011.1	2,817.5
1992	4,590	32,067	21,352	795.9	494.7	1,490.0	1,354.0	2,913.9	2,724.5
1993	4,583[1]	32,727[1]	20,121	807.5[1]	474.9	1,445.6	1,309.6	2,819.8	2,634.5
1994	4,572	29,205	18,962	751.3	455.9	1,402.6	1,266.7	2,728.8	2,547.5
1995	4,563	27,871	17,869	730.0	437.6	1,360.9	1,225.1	2,640.8	2,463.4
1996	4,554	26,598	16,839	709.2	420.1	1,320.5	1,184.9	2,555.6	2,382.1
1997	4,544	25,383	15,869	689.0	403.3	1,281.2	1,146.1	2,473.1	2,303.4
1998	4,535	24,224	14,954	669.4	387.2	1,243.1	1,108.5	2,393.3	2,227.4

Source: Economic Census of the United States, 1977, 1982, 1987 and 1992. Data for other years are estimates based on the compounded annual growth/decline rates between 1987 and 1992. Footnoted items (1) are from the *County Business Patterns* for the years indicated. Extracted from *Agriculture, Mining, and Construction USA*, Gale, 1998.

SIC 1793 - GLASS AND GLAZING WORK: INDICES OF CHANGE

Year	Estab-lish-ments	Employment		Payroll ($ mil)		Costs ($ mil)		Revenues ($ mil)	
		Total	Constr. workers	Total	Worker payroll	Total	Cost of materials	All sources	Construc-tion
1977	71.5	81.5	90.6	39.8	46.2	39.1	40.6	39.6	36.9
1982	82.7	111.8	123.7	87.5	99.6	88.1	89.3	89.6	88.9
1987	101.0	126.3	134.6	115.5	122.6	116.3	118.1	117.8	118.3
1992	100.0	100.0	100.0	100.0	100.0	100.0	100.0	100.0	100.0

Source: Same as General Statistics but excluding estimates. The values shown reflect change from the base year, 1992. Values above 100 mean greater than 1992, values below 100 mean less than 1992, and a value of 100 in the 1987-91 or 1993-98 period means same as 1992.

SIC 1793 - GLASS AND GLAZING WORK: SELECTED RATIOS

For 1992	Avg. of All Sector	Analyzed Industry	Index
Employees per establishment	8.1	7.0	86
Construction workers per establishment	6.3	4.7	74
Payroll per establishment	205,515	173,409	84
Payroll per employee	25,219	24,821	98
Payroll per construction worker	23,093	23,167	100
Costs per establishment	531,494	324,608	61
Costs per employee	65,220	46,464	71
Costs per construction worker	84,663	69,780	82
Materials as % of costs	52.18	90.88	174
Costs as % of revenues	56.48	51.13	91
Costs as % of construction revenues	57.64	54.69	95
Value added per establishment	409,562	310,225	76
Value added per employee	50,258	44,405	88
Value added per construction worker	65,240	66,689	102
Revenues per establishment	941,057	634,833	67
Revenues per employee	115,478	90,869	79
Revenues per construction worker	149,904	136,469	91
CR as % of total revenues	97.98	93.50	95
Net CR as % of CR	74.06	96.68	131
Investment per establishment	13,794	5,137	37
Investment per employee	1,693	735	43
Investment per construction worker	2,197	1,104	50

Source: Same as General Statistics. The 'Average of Sector' column represents the average of all construction industries. The Index shows the relationship between the Average and the Analyzed Industry. For example, 100 means that they are equal; 500 that the Analyzed Industry is five times the average; 50 means that the Analyzed Industry is half the national average. The abbreviation 'CR' stands for 'construction revenues'; 'na' is used to show that data are 'not available'. Net CR is revenue less work that has been contracted out.

SIC 1794 - EXCAVATION WORK: GENERAL STATISTICS

Year	Estab-lish-ments	Employment		Payroll ($ mil)		Costs ($ mil)		Revenues ($ mil)	
		Total	Constr. workers	Total	Worker payroll	Total	Cost of materials	All sources	Construc-tion
1977	16,521	104,092	91,522	1,207.7	1,020.9	1,376.6	883.8	4,370.2	4,215.7
1982	19,646	135,968	115,059	2,151.9	1,756.7	2,965.4	1,575.4	8,472.6	8,181.3
1987	13,422	95,329	79,198	2,059.8	1,597.5	2,744.7	1,582.8	8,452.4	8,244.4
1988	14,800[1]	99,404[1]	75,520	2,515.8[1]	1,556.0	2,738.6	1,589.6	8,152.1	7,949.0
1989	15,065[1]	98,589[1]	72,012	2,577.1[1]	1,515.6	2,732.5	1,596.4	7,862.5	7,664.3
1990	15,376[1]	101,144[1]	68,667	2,580.0[1]	1,476.3	2,726.5	1,603.2	7,583.2	7,389.7
1991	15,513[1]	90,727[1]	65,478	2,302.5[1]	1,438.0	2,720.4	1,610.1	7,313.8	7,124.9
1992	13,898	77,126	62,437	1,816.8	1,400.6	2,714.4	1,617.0	7,054.0	6,869.7
1993	17,805[1]	87,861[1]	59,537	2,338.7[1]	1,364.3	2,708.4	1,623.9	6,803.4	6,623.6
1994	14,093	70,858	56,772	1,727.8	1,328.9	2,702.4	1,630.8	6,561.8	6,386.3
1995	14,192	67,918	54,135	1,685.0	1,294.4	2,696.4	1,637.8	6,328.7	6,157.5
1996	14,291	65,100	51,621	1,643.2	1,260.8	2,690.5	1,644.8	6,103.8	5,936.9
1997	14,391	62,399	49,223	1,602.5	1,228.0	2,684.5	1,651.8	5,887.0	5,724.2
1998	14,492	59,810	46,937	1,562.8	1,196.2	2,678.6	1,658.9	5,677.9	5,519.1

Source: Economic Census of the United States, 1977, 1982, 1987 and 1992. Data for other years are estimates based on the compounded annual growth/decline rates between 1987 and 1992. Footnoted items (1) are from the *County Business Patterns* for the years indicated. Extracted from *Agriculture, Mining, and Construction USA*, Gale, 1998.

SIC 1794 - EXCAVATION WORK: INDICES OF CHANGE

Year	Estab-lish-ments	Employment		Payroll ($ mil)		Costs ($ mil)		Revenues ($ mil)	
		Total	Constr. workers	Total	Worker payroll	Total	Cost of materials	All sources	Construc-tion
1977	118.9	135.0	146.6	66.5	72.9	50.7	54.7	62.0	61.4
1982	141.4	176.3	184.3	118.4	125.4	109.2	97.4	120.1	119.1
1987	96.6	123.6	126.8	113.4	114.1	101.1	97.9	119.8	120.0
1992	100.0	100.0	100.0	100.0	100.0	100.0	100.0	100.0	100.0

Source: Same as General Statistics but excluding estimates. The values shown reflect change from the base year, 1992. Values above 100 mean greater than 1992, values below 100 mean less than 1992, and a value of 100 in the 1987-91 or 1993-98 period means same as 1992.

SIC 1794 - EXCAVATION WORK: SELECTED RATIOS

For 1992	Avg. of All Sector	Analyzed Industry	Index
Employees per establishment	8.1	5.5	69
Construction workers per establishment	6.3	4.5	71
Payroll per establishment	205,515	130,725	64
Payroll per employee	25,219	23,556	93
Payroll per construction worker	23,093	22,433	97
Costs per establishment	531,494	195,310	37
Costs per employee	65,220	35,195	54
Costs per construction worker	84,663	43,474	51
Materials as % of costs	52.18	59.57	114
Costs as % of revenues	56.48	38.48	68
Costs as % of construction revenues	57.64	39.51	69
Value added per establishment	409,562	312,247	76
Value added per employee	50,258	56,266	112
Value added per construction worker	65,240	69,504	107
Revenues per establishment	941,057	507,556	54
Revenues per employee	115,478	91,461	79
Revenues per construction worker	149,904	112,978	75
CR as % of total revenues	97.98	97.39	99
Net CR as % of CR	74.06	89.22	120
Investment per establishment	13,794	23,846	173
Investment per employee	1,693	4,297	254
Investment per construction worker	2,197	5,308	242

Source: Same as General Statistics. The 'Average of Sector' column represents the average of all construction industries. The Index shows the relationship between the Average and the Analyzed Industry. For example, 100 means that they are equal; 500 that the Analyzed Industry is five times the average; 50 means that the Analyzed Industry is half the national average. The abbreviation 'CR' stands for 'construction revenues'; 'na' is used to show that data are 'not available'. Net CR is revenue less work that has been contracted out.

SIC 1795 - WRECKING AND DEMOLITION WORK: GENERAL STATISTICS

Year	Estab-lish-ments	Employment		Payroll ($ mil)		Costs ($ mil)		Revenues ($ mil)	
		Total	Constr. workers	Total	Worker payroll	Total	Cost of materials	All sources	Construc-tion
1977	978	8,295	6,998	89.0	70.2	47.6	25.9	258.2	240.6
1982	890	8,402	7,201	130.1	107.2	89.2	32.9	403.0	376.9
1987	1,240	14,109	11,686	261.5	195.4	177.0	79.2	958.8	912.5
1988	765[1]	12,043[1]	11,419	291.2[1]	199.1	201.5	93.2	988.0	940.1
1989	747[1]	13,056[1]	11,157	303.3[1]	202.9	229.4	109.5	1,018.0	968.5
1990	832[1]	11,961[1]	10,902	299.6[1]	206.7	261.2	128.8	1,048.9	997.8
1991	857[1]	11,379[1]	10,653	298.1[1]	210.6	297.3	151.5	1,080.7	1,028.0
1992	966	13,112	10,409	296.0	214.6	338.5	178.2	1,113.5	1,059.1
1993	925[1]	9,873[1]	10,171	296.2[1]	218.7	385.4	209.5	1,147.4	1,091.2
1994	874	12,733	9,938	311.1	222.8	438.8	246.4	1,182.2	1,124.2
1995	832	12,548	9,711	318.9	227.0	499.6	289.8	1,218.1	1,158.2
1996	791	12,365	9,489	326.9	231.3	568.7	340.8	1,255.1	1,193.2
1997	753	12,185	9,272	335.2	235.7	647.5	400.7	1,293.2	1,229.4
1998	716	12,008	9,059	343.6	240.1	737.2	471.3	1,332.5	1,266.5

Source: Economic Census of the United States, 1977, 1982, 1987 and 1992. Data for other years are estimates based on the compounded annual growth/decline rates between 1987 and 1992. Footnoted items (1) are from the *County Business Patterns* for the years indicated. Extracted from *Agriculture, Mining, and Construction USA*, Gale, 1998.

SIC 1795 - WRECKING AND DEMOLITION WORK: INDICES OF CHANGE

Year	Estab-lish-ments	Employment		Payroll ($ mil)		Costs ($ mil)		Revenues ($ mil)	
		Total	Constr. workers	Total	Worker payroll	Total	Cost of materials	All sources	Construc-tion
1977	101.2	63.3	67.2	30.1	32.7	14.1	14.5	23.2	22.7
1982	92.1	64.1	69.2	43.9	49.9	26.4	18.5	36.2	35.6
1987	128.4	107.6	112.3	88.3	91.1	52.3	44.5	86.1	86.2
1992	100.0	100.0	100.0	100.0	100.0	100.0	100.0	100.0	100.0

Source: Same as General Statistics but excluding estimates. The values shown reflect change from the base year, 1992. Values above 100 mean greater than 1992, values below 100 mean less than 1992, and a value of 100 in the 1987-91 or 1993-98 period means same as 1992.

SIC 1795 - WRECKING AND DEMOLITION WORK: SELECTED RATIOS

For 1992	Avg. of All Sector	Analyzed Industry	Index
Employees per establishment	8.1	13.6	168
Construction workers per establishment	6.3	10.8	171
Payroll per establishment	205,515	306,447	149
Payroll per employee	25,219	22,577	90
Payroll per construction worker	23,093	20,619	89
Costs per establishment	531,494	350,437	66
Costs per employee	65,220	25,818	40
Costs per construction worker	84,663	32,522	38
Materials as % of costs	52.18	52.63	101
Costs as % of revenues	56.48	30.40	54
Costs as % of construction revenues	57.64	31.96	55
Value added per establishment	409,562	802,304	196
Value added per employee	50,258	59,108	118
Value added per construction worker	65,240	74,457	114
Revenues per establishment	941,057	1,152,742	122
Revenues per employee	115,478	84,926	74
Revenues per construction worker	149,904	106,979	71
CR as % of total revenues	97.98	95.11	97
Net CR as % of CR	74.06	87.62	118
Investment per establishment	13,794	23,944	174
Investment per employee	1,693	1,764	104
Investment per construction worker	2,197	2,222	101

Source: Same as General Statistics. The 'Average of Sector' column represents the average of all construction industries. The Index shows the relationship between the Average and the Analyzed Industry. For example, 100 means that they are equal; 500 that the Analyzed Industry is five times the average; 50 means that the Analyzed Industry is half the national average. The abbreviation 'CR' stands for 'construction revenues'; 'na' is used to show that data are 'not available'. Net CR is revenue less work that has been contracted out.

SIC 1796 - INSTALLING BUILDING EQUIPMENT, N.E.C.: GENERAL STATISTICS

Year	Estab-lish-ments	Employment		Payroll ($ mil)		Costs ($ mil)		Revenues ($ mil)	
		Total	Constr. workers	Total	Worker payroll	Total	Cost of materials	All sources	Construc-tion
1977	2,442	40,474	32,630	752.4	601.6	562.0	469.2	1,947.0	1,899.0
1982	3,754	60,169	49,101	1,449.3	1,144.8	1,303.8	1,038.7	4,255.8	4,189.3
1987	3,777	62,151	50,244	1,857.7	1,447.5	1,779.9	1,363.6	5,502.9	5,359.8
1988	2,976[1]	64,029[1]	52,798	2,157.3[1]	1,502.1	1,866.2	1,425.0	5,732.4	5,589.5
1989	2,852[1]	62,360[1]	55,482	2,067.4[1]	1,558.8	1,956.8	1,489.2	5,971.5	5,829.1
1990	3,040[1]	64,454[1]	58,302	2,216.1[1]	1,617.7	2,051.8	1,556.2	6,220.5	6,078.9
1991	3,108[1]	60,445[1]	61,266	2,137.9[1]	1,678.7	2,151.3	1,626.3	6,479.9	6,339.4
1992	3,889	82,648	64,380	2,324.1	1,742.1	2,255.8	1,699.6	6,750.1	6,611.0
1993	3,548[1]	63,194[1]	67,653	2,438.3[1]	1,807.9	2,365.2	1,776.1	7,031.6	6,894.4
1994	3,935	92,629	71,092	2,542.0	1,876.1	2,480.0	1,856.1	7,324.9	7,189.8
1995	3,958	98,062	74,705	2,658.4	1,946.9	2,600.4	1,939.7	7,630.3	7,497.9
1996	3,981	103,815	78,503	2,780.2	2,020.4	2,726.6	2,027.0	7,948.5	7,819.2
1997	4,004	109,905	82,493	2,907.6	2,096.7	2,858.9	2,118.3	8,280.0	8,154.3
1998	4,028	116,352	86,686	3,040.8	2,175.8	2,997.6	2,213.7	8,625.3	8,503.8

Source: Economic Census of the United States, 1977, 1982, 1987 and 1992. Data for other years are estimates based on the compounded annual growth/decline rates between 1987 and 1992. Footnoted items (1) are from the County Business Patterns for the years indicated. Extracted from Agriculture, Mining, and Construction USA, Gale, 1998.

SIC 1796 - INSTALLING BUILDING EQUIPMENT, N.E.C.: INDICES OF CHANGE

Year	Estab-lish-ments	Employment		Payroll ($ mil)		Costs ($ mil)		Revenues ($ mil)	
		Total	Constr. workers	Total	Worker payroll	Total	Cost of materials	All sources	Construc-tion
1977	62.8	49.0	50.7	32.4	34.5	24.9	27.6	28.8	28.7
1982	96.5	72.8	76.3	62.4	65.7	57.8	61.1	63.0	63.4
1987	97.1	75.2	78.0	79.9	83.1	78.9	80.2	81.5	81.1
1992	100.0	100.0	100.0	100.0	100.0	100.0	100.0	100.0	100.0

Source: Same as General Statistics but excluding estimates. The values shown reflect change from the base year, 1992. Values above 100 mean greater than 1992, values below 100 mean less than 1992, and a value of 100 in the 1987-91 or 1993-98 period means same as 1992.

SIC 1796 - INSTALLING BUILDING EQUIPMENT, N.E.C.: SELECTED RATIOS

For 1992	Avg. of All Sector	Analyzed Industry	Index
Employees per establishment	8.1	21.3	262
Construction workers per establishment	6.3	16.6	263
Payroll per establishment	205,515	597,619	291
Payroll per employee	25,219	28,121	112
Payroll per construction worker	23,093	27,060	117
Costs per establishment	531,494	580,034	109
Costs per employee	65,220	27,294	42
Costs per construction worker	84,663	35,038	41
Materials as % of costs	52.18	75.34	144
Costs as % of revenues	56.48	33.42	59
Costs as % of construction revenues	57.64	34.12	59
Value added per establishment	409,562	1,155,664	282
Value added per employee	50,258	54,380	108
Value added per construction worker	65,240	69,810	107
Revenues per establishment	941,057	1,735,699	184
Revenues per employee	115,478	81,673	71
Revenues per construction worker	149,904	104,848	70
CR as % of total revenues	97.98	97.94	100
Net CR as % of CR	74.06	92.76	125
Investment per establishment	13,794	18,390	133
Investment per employee	1,693	865	51
Investment per construction worker	2,197	1,111	51

Source: Same as General Statistics. The 'Average of Sector' column represents the average of all construction industries. The Index shows the relationship between the Average and the Analyzed Industry. For example, 100 means that they are equal; 500 that the Analyzed Industry is five times the average; 50 means that the Analyzed Industry is half the national average. The abbreviation 'CR' stands for 'construction revenues'; 'na' is used to show that data are 'not available'. Net CR is revenue less work that has been contracted out.

SIC 1799 - SPECIAL TRADE CONTRACTORS, N.E.C.: GENERAL STATISTICS

Year	Estab-lish-ments	Employment		Payroll ($ mil)		Costs ($ mil)		Revenues ($ mil)	
		Total	Constr. workers	Total	Worker payroll	Total	Cost of materials	All sources	Construc-tion
1977	20,626	128,440	107,632	1,383.7	1,085.6	1,915.1	1,530.4	4,607.8	4,407.2
1982	20,446	127,727	102,099	1,833.1	1,331.3	2,671.3	2,042.3	6,365.7	6,076.4
1987	23,198	176,084	141,615	3,089.3	2,268.7	4,672.0	3,439.6	11,294.2	10,814.3
1988	21,876[1]	180,662[1]	144,609	3,724.1[1]	2,418.0	4,893.8	3,587.5	11,817.1	11,332.7
1989	20,868[1]	180,715[1]	147,666	3,945.5[1]	2,577.1	5,126.3	3,741.7	12,364.2	11,876.0
1990	22,471[1]	196,971[1]	150,788	4,263.9[1]	2,746.6	5,369.7	3,902.6	12,936.7	12,445.3
1991	22,634[1]	186,330[1]	153,976	4,151.4[1]	2,927.3	5,624.7	4,070.4	13,535.6	13,041.9
1992	25,270	204,333	157,231	4,435.3	3,119.9	5,891.8	4,245.4	14,162.3	13,667.1
1993	27,296[1]	207,138[1]	160,555	4,911.2[1]	3,325.2	6,171.7	4,427.9	14,818.0	14,322.3
1994	26,150	216,863	163,949	5,125.6	3,543.9	6,464.8	4,618.3	15,504.1	15,008.8
1995	26,601	223,414	167,415	5,510.0	3,777.1	6,771.8	4,816.8	16,221.9	15,728.3
1996	27,060	230,162	170,955	5,923.3	4,025.6	7,093.4	5,023.9	16,973.0	16,482.3
1997	27,527	237,114	174,569	6,367.6	4,290.4	7,430.2	5,239.9	17,758.8	17,272.4
1998	28,002	244,276	178,260	6,845.2	4,572.7	7,783.1	5,465.1	18,581.0	18,100.4

Source: Economic Census of the United States, 1977, 1982, 1987 and 1992. Data for other years are estimates based on the compounded annual growth/decline rates between 1987 and 1992. Footnoted items (1) are from the *County Business Patterns* for the years indicated. Extracted from *Agriculture, Mining, and Construction USA,* Gale, 1998.

SIC 1799 - SPECIAL TRADE CONTRACTORS, N.E.C.: INDICES OF CHANGE

Year	Estab-lish-ments	Employment		Payroll ($ mil)		Costs ($ mil)		Revenues ($ mil)	
		Total	Constr. workers	Total	Worker payroll	Total	Cost of materials	All sources	Construc-tion
1977	81.6	62.9	68.5	31.2	34.8	32.5	36.0	32.5	32.2
1982	80.9	62.5	64.9	41.3	42.7	45.3	48.1	44.9	44.5
1987	91.8	86.2	90.1	69.7	72.7	79.3	81.0	79.7	79.1
1992	100.0	100.0	100.0	100.0	100.0	100.0	100.0	100.0	100.0

Source: Same as General Statistics but excluding estimates. The values shown reflect change from the base year, 1992. Values above 100 mean greater than 1992, values below 100 mean less than 1992, and a value of 100 in the 1987-91 or 1993-98 period means same as 1992.

SIC 1799 - SPECIAL TRADE CONTRACTORS, N.E.C.: SELECTED RATIOS

For 1992	Avg. of All Sector	Analyzed Industry	Index
Employees per establishment	8.1	8.1	100
Construction workers per establishment	6.3	6.2	99
Payroll per establishment	205,515	175,516	85
Payroll per employee	25,219	21,706	86
Payroll per construction worker	23,093	19,843	86
Costs per establishment	531,494	233,156	44
Costs per employee	65,220	28,835	44
Costs per construction worker	84,663	37,473	44
Materials as % of costs	52.18	72.06	138
Costs as % of revenues	56.48	41.60	74
Costs as % of construction revenues	57.64	43.11	75
Value added per establishment	409,562	327,284	80
Value added per employee	50,258	40,475	81
Value added per construction worker	65,240	52,601	81
Revenues per establishment	941,057	560,440	60
Revenues per employee	115,478	69,310	60
Revenues per construction worker	149,904	90,073	60
CR as % of total revenues	97.98	96.50	98
Net CR as % of CR	74.06	90.18	122
Investment per establishment	13,794	11,919	86
Investment per employee	1,693	1,474	87
Investment per construction worker	2,197	1,916	87

Source: Same as General Statistics. The 'Average of Sector' column represents the average of all construction industries. The Index shows the relationship between the Average and the Analyzed Industry. For example, 100 means that they are equal; 500 that the Analyzed Industry is five times the average; 50 means that the Analyzed Industry is half the national average. The abbreviation 'CR' stands for 'construction revenues'; 'na' is used to show that data are 'not available'. Net CR is revenue less work that has been contracted out.

SIC 7353 - HEAVY CONSTRUCTION EQUIPMENT RENTAL: GENERAL STATISTICS

Year	Estab-lish-ments	Employ-ment (000)	Payroll ($ mil.)	Revenues ($ mil.)		Ownership	
				SAS	Census	Sole Prop.	Partner-ships
1987	4,620	38.0	910.4		3,335.3	770	335
1988	4,390	39.8	1,074.6				
1989	3,865	40.0	1,142.8				
1990	3,764	39.6	1,143.2	5,091.0			
1991	3,634	36.1	1,053.1	4,537.0			
1992	3,853	34.7	1,037.0	4,090.0	3,879.4	515	136
1993	3,796	36.8	1,136.8	4,393.0			
1994	3,661[1]	37.3[1]	1,252.0[1]	4,836.0[1]			
1995	3,624[1]	39.7[1]	1,353.9[1]	5,740.0[1]			
1996	3,394[1]	37.0[1]	1,305.0[1]	6,076.0[1]			
1997	3,290[1]	36.8[1]	1,341.4[1]	5,838.6[1]			
1998	3,186[1]	36.6[1]	1,377.9[1]	6,056.7[1]			

Source: Data for 1987 and 1992 are from Census of Service Industries, Bureau of the Census, U.S. Department of Commerce. Data labeled SAS are from the *Service Annual Survey* for 1996, which also presented revisions for ealier years. Data for 1988-1991 and 1993-1995, when shown, are derived from *County Business Patterns* for those years from the Bureau of the Census. Extracted from *Service Industries USA*, 4th edition, Gale, 1998. Note: 1. Projections made by the editor.

SIC 7353 - HEAVY CONSTRUCTION EQUIPMENT RENTAL: INDICES OF CHANGE

Year	Estab-lish-ments	Employ-ment (000)	Payroll ($ mil.)	Revenues ($ mil.)		Ownership	
				SAS	Census	Sole Prop.	Partner-ships
1987	120	110	88		86	150	246
1988	114	115	104				
1989	100	115	110				
1990	98	114	110	124			
1991	94	104	102	111			
1992	100	100	100	100	100	100	100
1993	99	106	110	107			
1994	95[1]	107[1]	121[1]	118[1]			
1995	94[1]	114[1]	131[1]	140[1]			
1996	88[1]	107[1]	126[1]	149[1]			
1997	85[1]	106[1]	129[1]	143[1]			
1998	83[1]	105[1]	133[1]	148[1]			

Source: Same as General Statistics. The values shown reflect change from the base year, 1992, which is always 100. Data points earlier or later than 1992 are less than 1992 if less than 100 and greater than 1992 if greater than 100. Note: 1. Index based on a projected value.

SIC 7353 - HEAVY CONSTRUCTION EQUIPMENT RENTAL: SELECTED RATIOS

For 1992	Average of All Services	Analyzed Industry	Index
Employees per establishment	13	9	67
Revenues per establishment	810,117	1,006,845	124
Payroll per establishment	314,133	269,129	86
Payroll per employee	23,335	29,880	128
Revenue per employee	60,179	111,785	186
Sole proprietors as % of establishments	30.1	13.4	44
Partnerships as % of establishments	5.7	3.5	62

Source: Same as General Statistics. The 'Average of all Services' column represents the average of all service industries of which this SIC is a part. The Index shows the relationship between the Average and the Analyzed Industry. For example, 100 means that they are equal; 500 that the Analyzed Industry is five times the average; 50 means that the Analyzed Industry is half the national average.

FINANCIAL NORMS AND RATIOS

Industry-specific financial norms and ratios are shown in this chapter for twenty-seven industries in the Construction sector. For each industry in the sector, balance sheets are presented for the years 1996 through 1998, with the most recent year shown first. As part of each balance sheet, additional financial averages for net sales, gross profits, net profits after tax, and working capital are shown. The number of establishments used to calculate the averages are shown for each year.

The second table in each display shows D&B Key Business Ratios for the SIC-denominated industry. These data, again, are for the years 1996 through 1998. Ratios measuring solvency (e.g., Quick ratio), efficiency (e.g., Collection period, in days), and profitability (e.g. % return on sales) are shown. A total of 14 ratios are featured. Ratios are shown for the upper quartile, median, and lowest quartile of the D&B sample.

This product includes proprietary data of Dun & Bradstreet Inc.

D&B INDUSTRY NORMS: SIC 1521 - SINGLE-FAMILY HOUSING CONSTRUCTION

	1998 (1341) Estab.		1997 (1932) Estab.		1996 (1963) Estab.	
	$	%	$	%	$	%
Cash	79,187	20.4	70,935	18.9	56,143	19.5
Accounts Receivable	81,904	21.1	81,444	21.7	55,279	19.2
Notes Receivable	4,270	1.1	4,128	1.1	2,591	.9
Inventory	41,922	10.8	44,287	11.8	33,110	11.5
Other Current Assets	56,673	14.6	59,300	15.8	47,218	16.4
Total Current Assets	263,956	68.0	260,094	69.3	194,341	67.5
Fixed Assets	95,102	24.5	83,320	22.2	68,811	23.9
Other Non-current Assets	29,113	7.5	31,902	8.5	24,761	8.6
Total Assets	388,171	100.0	375,316	100.0	287,913	100.0
Accounts Payable	49,298	12.7	53,670	14.3	39,444	13.7
Bank Loans	1,165	.3	751	.2	576	.2
Notes Payable	23,678	6.1	24,771	6.6	18,714	6.5
Other Current Liabilities	79,963	20.6	79,943	21.3	59,310	20.6
Total Current Liabilities	154,104	39.7	159,135	42.4	118,044	41.0
Other Long Term	50,462	13.0	49,542	13.2	42,323	14.7
Deferred Credits	388	.1	1,126	.3	576	.2
Net Worth	183,217	47.2	165,515	44.1	126,970	44.1
Total Liabilities & Net Worth	388,171	100.0	375,318	100.0	287,913	100.0
Net Sales	1,635,344	100.0	1,507,547	100.0	1,081,379	100.0
Gross Profits	389,212	23.8	346,736	23.0	268,182	24.8
Net Profit After Tax	73,590	4.5	67,840	4.5	51,906	4.8
Working Capital	109,852	-	100,961	-	76,297	-

Source: Dun & Bradstreet. Data in this table are copyright (c) 1999 of Dun & Bradstreet. Reprinted by special arrangement with D&B. *Notes:* Values in parentheses above columns indicate the number of establishments in the sample. Data shown are for all companies.

D&B KEY BUSINESS RATIOS: SIC 1521

	1998			1997			1996		
	UQ	MED	LQ	UQ	MED	LQ	UQ	MED	LQ
Solvency									
Quick ratio	2.4	1.1	.4	2.1	1.0	.3	2.2	1.0	.3
Current ratio	3.8	1.7	1.1	3.3	1.7	1.1	3.5	1.7	1.1
Current liabilities/Net worth (%)	19.7	67.9	183.2	25.2	75.6	198.4	23.5	72.2	188.6
Current liabilities/Inventory (%)	72.0	109.5	214.6	65.2	111.8	211.0	64.5	118.0	259.0
Total liabilities/Net worth (%)	32.2	99.8	229.1	39.3	104.4	252.8	38.5	109.7	243.7
Fixed assets/Net worth (%)	14.3	37.1	85.6	13.9	38.1	89.7	14.1	40.3	98.6
Efficiency									
Collection period (days)	9.5	23.7	43.1	9.1	25.6	48.6	9.1	24.5	44.9
Sales to Inventory	59.8	13.6	3.2	78.9	12.5	3.9	71.1	18.1	5.1
Assets/Sales (%)	16.4	28.4	48.6	16.3	28.2	48.2	15.7	27.5	47.7
Sales/Net Working Capital	26.2	11.2	5.7	26.4	11.2	5.6	27.4	11.8	5.7
Accounts payable/Sales (%)	1.7	3.5	6.7	2.0	4.1	7.4	1.8	4.0	6.8
Profitability									
Return - Sales (%)	9.7	4.2	1.2	8.7	3.4	.9	7.8	3.2	1.1
Return - Assets (%)	26.5	11.2	3.1	26.0	8.8	2.0	23.5	8.2	2.2
Return - Net Worth (%)	61.8	29.2	8.9	59.7	22.9	6.7	64.4	22.3	6.7

Source: Dun & Bradstreet. Data in this table are copyright (c) 1999 of Dun & Bradstreet. Reprinted by special arrangement with D&B. *Note:* UQ stands for "Upper Quartile" and represents the top 25 percent of sample; MED stands for "Median"; and LQ stands for "Lower Quartile" and represents the lowest 25 percent.

D&B INDUSTRY NORMS: SIC 1522 - RESIDENTIAL CONSTRUCTION, NEC

	1998 (384) Estab.		1997 (551) Estab.		1996 (466) Estab.	
	$	%	$	%	$	%
Cash	157,437	20.5	155,748	19.2	131,596	19.7
Accounts Receivable	255,739	33.3	249,034	30.7	207,081	31.0
Notes Receivable	9,984	1.3	10,545	1.3	9,352	1.4
Inventory	15,360	2.0	33,259	4.1	24,716	3.7
Other Current Assets	115,966	15.1	124,922	15.4	110,220	16.5
Total Current Assets	554,486	72.2	573,508	70.7	482,965	72.3
Fixed Assets	141,309	18.4	150,880	18.6	127,588	19.1
Other Non-current Assets	72,190	9.4	86,797	10.7	57,448	8.6
Total Assets	767,985	100.0	811,185	100.0	668,001	100.0
Accounts Payable	161,277	21.0	158,992	19.6	125,584	18.8
Bank Loans	2,304	.3	811	.1	-	-
Notes Payable	32,255	4.2	33,259	4.1	36,740	5.5
Other Current Liabilities	119,038	15.5	148,447	18.3	112,224	16.8
Total Current Liabilities	314,874	41.0	341,509	42.1	274,548	41.1
Other Long Term	71,423	9.3	89,230	11.0	67,468	10.1
Deferred Credits	2,304	.3	1,622	.2	668	.1
Net Worth	379,384	49.4	378,823	46.7	325,317	48.7
Total Liabilities & Net Worth	767,985	100.0	811,184	100.0	668,001	100.0
Net Sales	2,260,471	100.0	2,036,299	100.0	1,829,451	100.0
Gross Profits	449,834	19.9	421,514	20.7	375,037	20.5
Net Profit After Tax	131,107	5.8	111,996	5.5	95,131	5.2
Working Capital	239,611	-	231,999	-	208,416	-

Source: Dun & Bradstreet. Data in this table are copyright (c) 1999 of Dun & Bradstreet. Reprinted by special arrangement with D&B. *Notes:* Values in parentheses above columns indicate the number of establishments in the sample. Data shown are for all companies.

D&B KEY BUSINESS RATIOS: SIC 1522

	1998			1997			1996		
	UQ	MED	LQ	UQ	MED	LQ	UQ	MED	LQ
Solvency									
Quick ratio	2.3	1.3	.8	2.0	1.2	.6	2.3	1.2	.7
Current ratio	3.2	1.7	1.2	2.9	1.6	1.2	3.2	1.7	1.2
Current liabilities/Net worth (%)	28.3	86.5	171.9	30.6	78.8	196.6	21.7	76.7	174.7
Current liabilities/Inventory (%)	95.6	236.9	527.8	80.1	139.4	429.4	79.3	158.1	556.5
Total liabilities/Net worth (%)	44.4	106.0	215.7	46.1	101.5	234.9	38.9	95.8	218.8
Fixed assets/Net worth (%)	7.6	21.5	63.6	7.8	21.6	63.2	7.7	20.9	64.2
Efficiency									
Collection period (days)	24.2	47.9	75.6	21.5	42.2	75.6	17.2	40.2	72.7
Sales to Inventory	212.9	64.9	29.3	133.3	27.5	6.8	200.7	94.4	5.0
Assets/Sales (%)	19.4	29.2	60.3	19.7	33.7	61.4	18.0	31.7	55.4
Sales/Net Working Capital	23.4	10.7	4.5	18.9	9.9	4.5	19.3	9.9	4.3
Accounts payable/Sales (%)	3.6	7.1	12.1	3.3	6.3	12.9	2.6	7.0	12.3
Profitability									
Return - Sales (%)	9.7	4.7	1.7	8.7	4.3	1.1	8.7	3.0	1.0
Return - Assets (%)	25.9	11.3	2.7	20.6	7.6	2.6	17.6	7.7	1.8
Return - Net Worth (%)	59.1	27.2	6.6	50.9	20.2	6.3	46.7	19.6	4.7

Source: Dun & Bradstreet. Data in this table are copyright (c) 1999 of Dun & Bradstreet. Reprinted by special arrangement with D&B. *Note:* UQ stands for "Upper Quartile" and represents the top 25 percent of sample; MED stands for "Median"; and LQ stands for "Lower Quartile" and represents the lowest 25 percent.

D&B INDUSTRY NORMS: SIC 1531 - OPERATIVE BUILDERS

	1998 (175) Estab.		1997 (269) Estab.		1996 (283) Estab.	
	$	%	$	%	$	%
Cash	549,889	15.0	227,145	12.1	180,190	13.8
Accounts Receivable	421,582	11.5	180,214	9.6	154,076	11.8
Notes Receivable	51,323	1.4	18,772	1.0	31,337	2.4
Inventory	967,805	26.4	426,131	22.7	257,228	19.7
Other Current Assets	711,190	19.4	443,026	23.6	265,063	20.3
Total Current Assets	2,701,789	73.7	1,295,288	69.0	887,894	68.0
Fixed Assets	590,214	16.1	319,129	17.0	203,694	15.6
Other Non-current Assets	373,925	10.2	262,812	14.0	214,139	16.4
Total Assets	3,665,928	100.0	1,877,229	100.0	1,305,727	100.0
Accounts Payable	344,597	9.4	148,301	7.9	99,235	7.6
Bank Loans	18,330	.5	5,632	.3	-	-
Notes Payable	439,911	12.0	180,214	9.6	112,293	8.6
Other Current Liabilities	813,836	22.2	446,781	23.8	315,986	24.2
Total Current Liabilities	1,616,674	44.1	780,928	41.6	527,514	40.4
Other Long Term	425,248	11.6	274,075	14.6	236,337	18.1
Deferred Credits	3,666	.1	1,877	.1	3,917	.3
Net Worth	1,620,340	44.2	820,349	43.7	537,960	41.2
Total Liabilities & Net Worth	3,665,928	100.0	1,877,229	100.0	1,305,728	100.0
Net Sales	3,793,030	100.0	2,851,740	100.0	2,284,577	100.0
Gross Profits	796,536	21.0	576,051	20.2	486,615	21.3
Net Profit After Tax	182,065	4.8	122,625	4.3	93,668	4.1
Working Capital	1,085,115	-	514,361	-	360,381	-

Source: Dun & Bradstreet. Data in this table are copyright (c) 1999 of Dun & Bradstreet. Reprinted by special arrangement with D&B. *Notes:* Values in parentheses above columns indicate the number of establishments in the sample. Data shown are for all companies.

D&B KEY BUSINESS RATIOS: SIC 1531

	1998			1997			1996		
	UQ	MED	LQ	UQ	MED	LQ	UQ	MED	LQ
Solvency									
Quick ratio	1.3	.4	.2	1.3	.3	.1	1.5	.5	.2
Current ratio	2.6	1.7	1.2	3.1	1.6	1.2	3.5	1.7	1.2
Current liabilities/Net worth (%)	34.8	86.8	217.2	22.9	69.3	204.1	20.7	79.6	200.5
Current liabilities/Inventory (%)	68.9	88.5	133.8	60.8	87.3	126.3	43.4	86.7	114.1
Total liabilities/Net worth (%)	56.8	129.7	226.8	50.4	132.4	255.9	50.1	146.7	283.4
Fixed assets/Net worth (%)	6.9	15.8	52.6	6.5	17.6	55.1	5.7	18.4	65.8
Efficiency									
Collection period (days)	10.2	28.8	79.2	2.9	8.4	41.8	4.8	19.7	46.8
Sales to Inventory	4.0	2.4	1.7	6.2	3.0	1.9	6.4	2.8	1.7
Assets/Sales (%)	44.9	76.3	137.5	38.9	60.2	103.9	45.4	75.6	139.1
Sales/Net Working Capital	9.2	4.1	1.9	14.3	6.6	3.0	12.6	4.6	2.4
Accounts payable/Sales (%)	3.6	6.6	11.7	2.2	4.2	9.7	2.1	4.4	7.6
Profitability									
Return - Sales (%)	7.8	3.4	1.4	8.6	4.4	1.2	10.9	3.0	.1
Return - Assets (%)	11.0	4.6	1.4	12.5	5.9	1.8	11.2	3.2	-.7
Return - Net Worth (%)	29.4	11.6	4.2	37.4	14.4	4.5	33.7	10.7	.4

Source: Dun & Bradstreet. Data in this table are copyright (c) 1999 of Dun & Bradstreet. Reprinted by special arrangement with D&B. *Note:* UQ stands for "Upper Quartile" and represents the top 25 percent of sample; MED stands for "Median"; and LQ stands for "Lower Quartile" and represents the lowest 25 percent.

D&B INDUSTRY NORMS: SIC 1541 - INDUSTRIAL BUILDINGS AND WAREHOUSES

	1998 (928) Estab.		1997 (1291) Estab.		1996 (1209) Estab.	
	$	%	$	%	$	%
Cash	281,505	19.9	225,192	19.1	210,099	18.7
Accounts Receivable	551,693	39.0	464,533	39.4	444,916	39.6
Notes Receivable	11,317	.8	8,253	.7	10,112	.9
Inventory	22,634	1.6	17,685	1.5	20,223	1.8
Other Current Assets	212,190	15.0	165,063	14.0	161,787	14.4
Total Current Assets	1,079,339	76.3	880,726	74.7	847,137	75.4
Fixed Assets	246,140	17.4	218,118	18.5	203,358	18.1
Other Non-current Assets	89,120	6.3	80,173	6.8	73,029	6.5
Total Assets	1,414,599	100.0	1,179,017	100.0	1,123,524	100.0
Accounts Payable	353,649	25.0	288,859	24.5	280,881	25.0
Bank Loans	1,415	.1	-	-	-	-
Notes Payable	29,707	2.1	30,654	2.6	39,323	3.5
Other Current Liabilities	253,213	17.9	202,791	17.2	178,640	15.9
Total Current Liabilities	637,984	45.1	522,304	44.3	498,844	44.4
Other Long Term	103,266	7.3	99,038	8.4	97,747	8.7
Deferred Credits	5,658	.4	2,358	.2	3,371	.3
Net Worth	667,690	47.2	555,317	47.1	523,562	46.6
Total Liabilities & Net Worth	1,414,598	100.0	1,179,017	100.0	1,123,524	100.0
Net Sales	4,325,947	100.0	3,789,567	100.0	3,434,709	100.0
Gross Profits	791,648	18.3	708,649	18.7	656,029	19.1
Net Profit After Tax	160,060	3.7	125,056	3.3	120,215	3.5
Working Capital	441,355	-	358,421	-	348,292	-

Source: Dun & Bradstreet. Data in this table are copyright (c) 1999 of Dun & Bradstreet. Reprinted by special arrangement with D&B. *Notes:* Values in parentheses above columns indicate the number of establishments in the sample. Data shown are for all companies.

D&B KEY BUSINESS RATIOS: SIC 1541

	1998			1997			1996		
	UQ	MED	LQ	UQ	MED	LQ	UQ	MED	LQ
Solvency									
Quick ratio	2.1	1.3	1.0	2.0	1.3	1.0	2.0	1.3	1.0
Current ratio	2.7	1.6	1.3	2.7	1.6	1.3	2.6	1.6	1.3
Current liabilities/Net worth (%)	38.2	105.6	208.7	40.5	100.0	195.6	38.3	99.5	198.1
Current liabilities/Inventory (%)	135.8	274.9	523.3	129.5	220.7	462.8	147.3	299.6	588.8
Total liabilities/Net worth (%)	46.3	125.5	242.6	50.1	118.3	225.3	50.9	123.5	230.8
Fixed assets/Net worth (%)	15.2	28.8	54.1	14.2	30.3	58.1	14.1	30.6	59.5
Efficiency									
Collection period (days)	33.1	49.6	67.4	31.8	49.6	69.4	32.5	50.7	70.1
Sales to Inventory	385.0	118.0	25.2	317.7	110.4	29.5	363.4	133.7	38.7
Assets/Sales (%)	22.9	31.0	44.5	21.9	30.9	43.3	22.5	30.6	43.7
Sales/Net Working Capital	23.0	11.6	5.9	21.7	11.4	6.2	20.4	11.2	6.0
Accounts payable/Sales (%)	3.9	7.4	11.9	3.6	7.2	12.3	4.0	7.2	12.6
Profitability									
Return - Sales (%)	5.6	2.3	.9	5.0	2.2	.6	5.3	2.2	.6
Return - Assets (%)	15.4	6.6	2.5	14.5	6.3	1.8	13.6	5.8	1.9
Return - Net Worth (%)	37.3	17.0	6.5	32.0	14.7	5.5	34.1	14.9	4.7

Source: Dun & Bradstreet. Data in this table are copyright (c) 1999 of Dun & Bradstreet. Reprinted by special arrangement with D&B. *Note:* UQ stands for "Upper Quartile" and represents the top 25 percent of sample; MED stands for "Median"; and LQ stands for "Lower Quartile" and represents the lowest 25 percent.

D&B INDUSTRY NORMS: SIC 1542 - NONRESIDENTIAL CONSTRUCTION, NEC

	1998 (2038) Estab.		1997 (1922) Estab.		1996 (1711) Estab.	
	$	%	$	%	$	%
Cash	264,531	23.0	213,793	21.7	187,025	22.1
Accounts Receivable	442,801	38.5	385,222	39.1	330,043	39.0
Notes Receivable	6,901	.6	7,882	.8	6,770	.8
Inventory	21,853	1.9	17,734	1.8	16,925	2.0
Other Current Assets	178,271	15.5	154,680	15.7	126,093	14.9
Total Current Assets	914,357	79.5	779,311	79.1	666,856	78.8
Fixed Assets	175,970	15.3	151,724	15.4	130,325	15.4
Other Non-current Assets	59,807	5.2	54,187	5.5	49,083	5.8
Total Assets	1,150,134	100.0	985,222	100.0	846,264	100.0
Accounts Payable	323,187	28.1	275,862	28.0	230,184	27.2
Bank Loans	2,300	.2	985	.1	846	.1
Notes Payable	25,303	2.2	23,645	2.4	22,849	2.7
Other Current Liabilities	192,072	16.7	165,517	16.8	140,480	16.6
Total Current Liabilities	542,862	47.2	466,009	47.3	394,359	46.6
Other Long Term	66,708	5.8	64,039	6.5	57,546	6.8
Deferred Credits	1,150	.1	1,970	.2	1,693	.2
Net Worth	539,412	46.9	453,203	46.0	392,667	46.4
Total Liabilities & Net Worth	1,150,132	100.0	985,221	100.0	846,265	100.0
Net Sales	3,789,300	100.0	3,246,982	100.0	2,839,951	100.0
Gross Profits	617,656	16.3	529,258	16.3	477,112	16.8
Net Profit After Tax	128,836	3.4	103,903	3.2	99,398	3.5
Working Capital	371,493	-	313,301	-	272,498	-

Source: Dun & Bradstreet. Data in this table are copyright (c) 1999 of Dun & Bradstreet. Reprinted by special arrangement with D&B. *Notes:* Values in parentheses above columns indicate the number of establishments in the sample. Data shown are for all companies.

D&B KEY BUSINESS RATIOS: SIC 1542

	1998			1997			1996		
	UQ	MED	LQ	UQ	MED	LQ	UQ	MED	LQ
Solvency									
Quick ratio	1.9	1.3	1.0	1.9	1.3	1.0	1.9	1.3	1.0
Current ratio	2.6	1.6	1.2	2.4	1.6	1.3	2.5	1.6	1.3
Current liabilities/Net worth (%)	43.4	104.9	216.5	47.4	100.9	202.0	44.8	103.0	209.9
Current liabilities/Inventory (%)	111.6	245.6	510.5	149.3	306.5	605.4	122.2	269.5	504.4
Total liabilities/Net worth (%)	52.8	120.6	239.5	56.6	116.7	227.5	53.6	123.5	237.6
Fixed assets/Net worth (%)	11.0	23.7	48.9	10.8	23.2	48.9	10.4	24.0	48.6
Efficiency									
Collection period (days)	27.0	46.7	64.6	28.8	47.7	66.4	29.1	45.6	67.2
Sales to Inventory	310.0	111.0	29.8	258.8	92.6	30.6	269.2	85.3	29.7
Assets/Sales (%)	21.2	28.1	39.8	21.3	28.6	39.5	20.2	28.6	39.3
Sales/Net Working Capital	22.6	12.2	6.4	20.7	11.7	6.6	20.8	11.8	6.6
Accounts payable/Sales (%)	4.2	8.1	12.6	4.3	8.1	12.8	4.0	7.8	12.6
Profitability									
Return - Sales (%)	5.5	2.3	.8	5.2	2.2	.8	5.1	2.2	.7
Return - Assets (%)	16.8	7.4	2.5	15.9	6.8	2.3	16.4	6.9	2.2
Return - Net Worth (%)	38.2	17.6	6.7	39.0	17.6	5.9	39.6	17.2	5.8

Source: Dun & Bradstreet. Data in this table are copyright (c) 1999 of Dun & Bradstreet. Reprinted by special arrangement with D&B. *Note:* UQ stands for "Upper Quartile" and represents the top 25 percent of sample; MED stands for "Median"; and LQ stands for "Lower Quartile" and represents the lowest 25 percent.

D&B INDUSTRY NORMS: SIC 1611 - HIGHWAY AND STREET CONSTRUCTION

	1998 (1084) Estab.		1997 (1543) Estab.		1996 (1456) Estab.	
	$	%	$	%	$	%
Cash	290,116	16.7	256,997	15.2	229,381	16.3
Accounts Receivable	470,787	27.1	475,107	28.1	398,251	28.3
Notes Receivable	8,686	.5	8,454	.5	11,258	.8
Inventory	36,482	2.1	35,506	2.1	29,552	2.1
Other Current Assets	173,722	10.0	174,150	10.3	137,910	9.8
Total Current Assets	979,793	56.4	950,214	56.2	806,352	57.3
Fixed Assets	663,618	38.2	639,112	37.8	517,867	36.8
Other Non-current Assets	93,810	5.4	101,446	6.0	83,028	5.9
Total Assets	1,737,221	100.0	1,690,772	100.0	1,407,247	100.0
Accounts Payable	250,160	14.4	258,688	15.3	208,272	14.8
Bank Loans	1,737	.1	1,691	.1	1,407	.1
Notes Payable	67,752	3.9	52,414	3.1	46,439	3.3
Other Current Liabilities	258,846	14.9	253,616	15.0	208,272	14.8
Total Current Liabilities	578,495	33.3	566,409	33.5	464,390	33.0
Other Long Term	269,269	15.5	272,214	16.1	220,938	15.7
Deferred Credits	6,949	.4	6,763	.4	7,036	.5
Net Worth	882,508	50.8	845,386	50.0	714,881	50.8
Total Liabilities & Net Worth	1,737,221	100.0	1,690,772	100.0	1,407,245	100.0
Net Sales	3,992,095	100.0	3,704,290	100.0	3,075,670	100.0
Gross Profits	902,213	22.6	851,987	23.0	735,085	23.9
Net Profit After Tax	163,676	4.1	148,172	4.0	116,875	3.8
Working Capital	401,298	-	383,805	-	341,961	-

Source: Dun & Bradstreet. Data in this table are copyright (c) 1999 of Dun & Bradstreet. Reprinted by special arrangement with D&B. *Notes:* Values in parentheses above columns indicate the number of establishments in the sample. Data shown are for all companies.

D&B KEY BUSINESS RATIOS: SIC 1611

	1998			1997			1996		
	UQ	MED	LQ	UQ	MED	LQ	UQ	MED	LQ
Solvency									
Quick ratio	2.1	1.3	.9	2.0	1.3	.8	2.2	1.3	.9
Current ratio	2.7	1.6	1.2	2.6	1.6	1.2	2.8	1.7	1.2
Current liabilities/Net worth (%)	29.2	63.9	126.9	29.9	62.3	121.1	28.4	60.6	115.8
Current liabilities/Inventory (%)	174.5	362.7	621.5	201.5	374.0	643.6	237.8	421.9	671.8
Total liabilities/Net worth (%)	44.3	97.0	189.2	48.7	100.2	188.3	42.9	96.6	177.4
Fixed assets/Net worth (%)	42.4	74.2	122.6	40.0	73.8	118.7	40.6	70.4	117.4
Efficiency									
Collection period (days)	29.6	45.6	68.6	27.4	46.7	70.5	27.4	46.0	67.2
Sales to Inventory	156.2	74.6	29.0	171.9	72.0	28.8	141.7	61.3	28.8
Assets/Sales (%)	33.9	44.1	60.9	33.2	44.3	61.3	32.2	43.8	58.3
Sales/Net Working Capital	18.6	9.9	5.6	18.2	9.9	5.4	18.1	9.9	5.4
Accounts payable/Sales (%)	3.0	5.6	9.7	3.0	5.9	9.9	2.7	5.6	9.3
Profitability									
Return - Sales (%)	6.9	3.0	1.1	6.8	2.6	.8	6.6	2.8	.8
Return - Assets (%)	13.6	6.5	2.2	13.4	5.7	1.9	13.4	6.4	2.0
Return - Net Worth (%)	29.2	14.0	4.9	27.2	12.9	4.4	26.8	13.6	4.6

Source: Dun & Bradstreet. Data in this table are copyright (c) 1999 of Dun & Bradstreet. Reprinted by special arrangement with D&B. *Note:* UQ stands for "Upper Quartile" and represents the top 25 percent of sample; MED stands for "Median"; and LQ stands for "Lower Quartile" and represents the lowest 25 percent.

D&B INDUSTRY NORMS: SIC 1622 - BRIDGE, TUNNEL, & ELEVATED HIGHWAY CONSTRUCTION

	1998 (178) Estab.		1997 (263) Estab.		1996 (222) Estab.	
	$	%	$	%	$	%
Cash	388,219	21.9	342,154	21.2	304,123	19.1
Accounts Receivable	538,897	30.4	430,920	26.7	480,864	30.2
Notes Receivable	1,773	.1	4,842	.3	9,554	.6
Inventory	24,818	1.4	25,823	1.6	28,661	1.8
Other Current Assets	249,949	14.1	282,438	17.5	251,578	15.8
Total Current Assets	1,203,656	67.9	1,086,177	67.3	1,074,780	67.5
Fixed Assets	473,308	26.7	434,148	26.9	433,096	27.2
Other Non-current Assets	95,725	5.4	93,608	5.8	84,390	5.3
Total Assets	1,772,689	100.0	1,613,933	100.0	1,592,266	100.0
Accounts Payable	280,085	15.8	261,457	16.2	275,462	17.3
Bank Loans	5,318	.3	-	-	-	-
Notes Payable	42,545	2.4	45,190	2.8	57,322	3.6
Other Current Liabilities	296,039	16.7	285,666	17.7	249,986	15.7
Total Current Liabilities	623,987	35.2	592,313	36.7	582,770	36.6
Other Long Term	193,223	10.9	182,374	11.3	178,334	11.2
Deferred Credits	7,091	.4	4,842	.3	9,554	.6
Net Worth	948,389	53.5	834,403	51.7	821,609	51.6
Total Liabilities & Net Worth	1,772,690	100.0	1,613,932	100.0	1,592,267	100.0
Net Sales	3,895,770	100.0	3,405,602	100.0	3,460,761	100.0
Gross Profits	677,864	17.4	643,659	18.9	640,241	18.5
Net Profit After Tax	163,622	4.2	71,518	2.1	76,137	2.2
Working Capital	579,669	-	493,864	-	492,010	-

Source: Dun & Bradstreet. Data in this table are copyright (c) 1999 of Dun & Bradstreet. Reprinted by special arrangement with D&B. *Notes:* Values in parentheses above columns indicate the number of establishments in the sample. Data shown are for all companies.

D&B KEY BUSINESS RATIOS: SIC 1622

	1998			1997			1996		
	UQ	MED	LQ	UQ	MED	LQ	UQ	MED	LQ
Solvency									
Quick ratio	2.4	1.4	1.0	2.1	1.3	.8	2.2	1.3	.9
Current ratio	3.1	1.9	1.4	3.1	1.7	1.3	2.8	1.8	1.3
Current liabilities/Net worth (%)	30.2	63.0	122.6	29.8	72.2	135.0	32.2	76.2	139.6
Current liabilities/Inventory (%)	249.9	439.8	752.1	305.8	481.4	652.3	239.2	442.7	631.2
Total liabilities/Net worth (%)	44.7	88.8	157.6	42.5	100.9	165.4	45.3	97.9	186.3
Fixed assets/Net worth (%)	22.7	48.8	83.9	27.2	48.5	90.3	28.7	50.1	87.5
Efficiency									
Collection period (days)	28.7	50.8	70.9	26.8	46.8	72.4	32.9	51.5	69.7
Sales to Inventory	136.7	72.4	51.0	117.7	58.7	38.4	142.7	75.4	41.8
Assets/Sales (%)	35.7	45.6	63.0	33.8	45.0	61.4	33.9	44.0	55.7
Sales/Net Working Capital	14.4	7.3	3.6	15.3	8.2	4.2	14.3	8.1	4.4
Accounts payable/Sales (%)	3.0	5.8	9.2	3.3	6.2	11.0	4.0	6.8	11.1
Profitability									
Return - Sales (%)	5.5	2.9	1.1	5.8	3.0	.5	4.9	2.5	.4
Return - Assets (%)	10.8	6.2	2.2	12.2	5.6	.8	10.4	5.2	.8
Return - Net Worth (%)	24.6	11.7	4.1	22.2	11.4	1.9	24.9	10.5	1.5

Source: Dun & Bradstreet. Data in this table are copyright (c) 1999 of Dun & Bradstreet. Reprinted by special arrangement with D&B. *Note:* UQ stands for "Upper Quartile" and represents the top 25 percent of sample; MED stands for "Median"; and LQ stands for "Lower Quartile" and represents the lowest 25 percent.

D&B INDUSTRY NORMS: SIC 1623 - WATER, SEWER, AND UTILITY LINES

	1998 (1309) Estab.		1997 (1769) Estab.		1996 (1616) Estab.	
	$	%	$	%	$	%
Cash	218,558	16.0	179,096	15.1	163,884	16.1
Accounts Receivable	408,430	29.9	357,006	30.1	303,338	29.8
Notes Receivable	8,196	.6	8,302	.7	7,125	.7
Inventory	24,588	1.8	20,163	1.7	20,358	2.0
Other Current Assets	140,696	10.3	129,281	10.9	101,791	10.0
Total Current Assets	800,468	58.6	693,848	58.5	596,496	58.6
Fixed Assets	497,219	36.4	423,426	35.7	362,377	35.6
Other Non-current Assets	68,299	5.0	68,792	5.8	59,039	5.8
Total Assets	1,365,986	100.0	1,186,066	100.0	1,017,912	100.0
Accounts Payable	180,310	13.2	160,119	13.5	137,418	13.5
Bank Loans	1,366	.1	1,186	.1	2,036	.2
Notes Payable	56,005	4.1	48,629	4.1	46,824	4.6
Other Current Liabilities	214,460	15.7	190,957	16.1	153,705	15.1
Total Current Liabilities	452,141	33.1	400,891	33.8	339,983	33.4
Other Long Term	195,336	14.3	173,166	14.6	145,561	14.3
Deferred Credits	5,464	.4	4,744	.4	5,090	.5
Net Worth	713,044	52.2	607,267	51.2	527,278	51.8
Total Liabilities & Net Worth	1,365,985	100.0	1,186,068	100.0	1,017,912	100.0
Net Sales	3,022,384	100.0	2,652,992	100.0	2,420,689	100.0
Gross Profits	791,865	26.2	689,778	26.0	641,483	26.5
Net Profit After Tax	160,186	5.3	122,038	4.6	121,034	5.0
Working Capital	348,326	-	292,959	-	256,513	-

Source: Dun & Bradstreet. Data in this table are copyright (c) 1999 of Dun & Bradstreet. Reprinted by special arrangement with D&B. *Notes:* Values in parentheses above columns indicate the number of establishments in the sample. Data shown are for all companies.

D&B KEY BUSINESS RATIOS: SIC 1623

	1998			1997			1996		
	UQ	MED	LQ	UQ	MED	LQ	UQ	MED	LQ
Solvency									
Quick ratio	2.3	1.4	.9	2.3	1.4	.9	2.4	1.4	.9
Current ratio	3.0	1.8	1.2	2.8	1.7	1.3	3.1	1.8	1.2
Current liabilities/Net worth (%)	25.7	58.4	117.7	27.7	62.2	118.1	25.3	60.4	121.7
Current liabilities/Inventory (%)	180.3	387.2	643.8	216.9	394.3	687.6	161.1	359.2	589.4
Total liabilities/Net worth (%)	40.0	88.1	167.6	42.0	91.3	174.6	38.6	88.8	176.9
Fixed assets/Net worth (%)	36.3	67.4	110.9	37.4	67.7	115.9	35.0	66.6	114.8
Efficiency									
Collection period (days)	32.9	50.7	71.2	30.8	52.2	75.2	32.1	50.7	71.9
Sales to Inventory	206.5	74.5	29.3	190.5	83.4	31.7	191.6	79.7	30.1
Assets/Sales (%)	33.2	44.2	60.0	33.2	45.2	61.3	32.5	44.2	60.8
Sales/Net Working Capital	16.6	8.8	5.0	16.2	8.6	4.6	16.0	8.3	4.6
Accounts payable/Sales (%)	2.6	5.2	8.9	2.4	5.3	9.5	2.4	5.3	8.9
Profitability									
Return - Sales (%)	8.8	4.0	1.5	8.1	3.8	1.3	8.5	3.8	1.2
Return - Assets (%)	17.7	8.2	3.1	16.0	8.2	2.8	16.3	7.8	2.5
Return - Net Worth (%)	34.1	17.6	6.6	33.9	17.0	5.9	34.4	16.1	5.2

Source: Dun & Bradstreet. Data in this table are copyright (c) 1999 of Dun & Bradstreet. Reprinted by special arrangement with D&B. *Note:* UQ stands for "Upper Quartile" and represents the top 25 percent of sample; MED stands for "Median"; and LQ stands for "Lower Quartile" and represents the lowest 25 percent.

D&B INDUSTRY NORMS: SIC 1629 - HEAVY CONSTRUCTION, NEC

	1998 (785) Estab.		1997 (1090) Estab.		1996 (986) Estab.	
	$	%	$	%	$	%
Cash	219,921	14.9	178,081	14.8	170,394	14.7
Accounts Receivable	436,891	29.6	351,350	29.2	333,833	28.8
Notes Receivable	10,332	.7	8,423	.7	9,273	.8
Inventory	36,900	2.5	27,675	2.3	31,297	2.7
Other Current Assets	172,690	11.7	129,951	10.8	127,506	11.0
Total Current Assets	876,734	59.4	695,480	57.8	672,303	58.0
Fixed Assets	515,118	34.9	429,561	35.7	405,700	35.0
Other Non-current Assets	84,131	5.7	78,211	6.5	81,140	7.0
Total Assets	1,475,983	100.0	1,203,252	100.0	1,159,143	100.0
Accounts Payable	214,018	14.5	170,862	14.2	168,076	14.5
Bank Loans	1,476	.1	-	-	1,159	.1
Notes Payable	60,515	4.1	44,520	3.7	39,411	3.4
Other Current Liabilities	234,681	15.9	192,520	16.0	191,258	16.5
Total Current Liabilities	510,690	34.6	407,902	33.9	399,904	34.5
Other Long Term	218,445	14.8	175,675	14.6	164,598	14.2
Deferred Credits	7,380	.5	4,813	.4	4,637	.4
Net Worth	739,467	50.1	614,862	51.1	590,003	50.9
Total Liabilities & Net Worth	1,475,982	100.0	1,203,252	100.0	1,159,142	100.0
Net Sales	2,773,382	100.0	2,408,456	100.0	2,529,673	100.0
Gross Profits	732,173	26.4	652,692	27.1	657,715	26.0
Net Profit After Tax	138,669	5.0	110,789	4.6	103,717	4.1
Working Capital	366,044	-	287,578	-	272,398	-

Source: Dun & Bradstreet. Data in this table are copyright (c) 1999 of Dun & Bradstreet. Reprinted by special arrangement with D&B. *Notes:* Values in parentheses above columns indicate the number of establishments in the sample. Data shown are for all companies.

D&B KEY BUSINESS RATIOS: SIC 1629

	1998			1997			1996		
	UQ	MED	LQ	UQ	MED	LQ	UQ	MED	LQ
Solvency									
Quick ratio	2.2	1.3	.8	2.2	1.3	.8	2.2	1.3	.8
Current ratio	3.0	1.7	1.2	2.9	1.7	1.2	2.9	1.7	1.2
Current liabilities/Net worth (%)	26.4	65.1	130.0	25.0	58.8	130.0	25.8	63.3	133.8
Current liabilities/Inventory (%)	195.3	332.6	571.3	148.7	323.2	630.7	142.0	324.6	599.3
Total liabilities/Net worth (%)	40.5	94.4	194.8	38.7	91.3	182.1	40.3	92.8	183.6
Fixed assets/Net worth (%)	28.9	62.4	119.6	30.2	64.0	116.2	32.3	65.3	116.3
Efficiency									
Collection period (days)	32.5	51.1	73.8	31.8	50.4	71.2	29.9	52.8	76.2
Sales to Inventory	151.7	54.5	26.6	144.7	54.4	24.0	126.4	45.5	21.2
Assets/Sales (%)	33.2	47.6	67.8	31.7	45.1	65.6	33.5	47.0	68.0
Sales/Net Working Capital	15.3	8.5	4.6	15.8	8.6	4.8	18.0	9.0	5.0
Accounts payable/Sales (%)	3.0	5.9	10.2	2.6	5.1	9.4	2.6	5.9	10.7
Profitability									
Return - Sales (%)	9.1	3.8	1.2	8.2	3.2	.7	7.8	3.2	.9
Return - Assets (%)	16.1	7.2	2.5	16.7	6.6	1.3	15.0	6.6	1.8
Return - Net Worth (%)	36.0	17.2	5.1	33.9	14.5	3.0	31.8	14.7	4.4

Source: Dun & Bradstreet. Data in this table are copyright (c) 1999 of Dun & Bradstreet. Reprinted by special arrangement with D&B. *Note:* UQ stands for "Upper Quartile" and represents the top 25 percent of sample; MED stands for "Median"; and LQ stands for "Lower Quartile" and represents the lowest 25 percent.

D&B INDUSTRY NORMS: SIC 1711 - PLUMBING, HEATING, AIR-CONDITIONING

	1998 (2216) Estab.		1997 (2060) Estab.		1996 (2035) Estab.	
	$	%	$	%	$	%
Cash	91,143	16.9	83,037	16.8	64,863	16.6
Accounts Receivable	207,634	38.5	190,788	38.6	149,263	38.2
Notes Receivable	2,697	.5	2,471	.5	1,954	.5
Inventory	47,459	8.8	44,484	9.0	36,730	9.4
Other Current Assets	44,763	8.3	41,024	8.3	32,041	8.2
Total Current Assets	393,696	73.0	361,804	73.2	284,851	72.9
Fixed Assets	120,266	22.3	105,280	21.3	85,963	22.0
Other Non-current Assets	25,347	4.7	27,185	5.5	19,928	5.1
Total Assets	539,309	100.0	494,269	100.0	390,742	100.0
Accounts Payable	101,929	18.9	95,888	19.4	75,804	19.4
Bank Loans	1,618	.3	494	.1	-	-
Notes Payable	18,336	3.4	17,794	3.6	15,239	3.9
Other Current Liabilities	88,447	16.4	84,026	17.0	62,128	15.9
Total Current Liabilities	210,330	39.0	198,202	40.1	153,171	39.2
Other Long Term	58,245	10.8	51,898	10.5	45,717	11.7
Deferred Credits	539	.1	989	.2	781	.2
Net Worth	270,193	50.1	243,181	49.2	191,073	48.9
Total Liabilities & Net Worth	539,307	100.0	494,270	100.0	390,742	100.0
Net Sales	1,757,445	100.0	1,746,515	100.0	1,451,974	100.0
Gross Profits	546,565	31.1	541,420	31.0	461,728	31.8
Net Profit After Tax	72,055	4.1	64,621	3.7	55,175	3.8
Working Capital	183,365	-	163,604	-	131,680	-

Source: Dun & Bradstreet. Data in this table are copyright (c) 1999 of Dun & Bradstreet. Reprinted by special arrangement with D&B. *Notes:* Values in parentheses above columns indicate the number of establishments in the sample. Data shown are for all companies.

D&B KEY BUSINESS RATIOS: SIC 1711

	1998			1997			1996		
	UQ	MED	LQ	UQ	MED	LQ	UQ	MED	LQ
Solvency									
Quick ratio	2.5	1.4	1.0	2.3	1.4	.9	2.4	1.5	.9
Current ratio	3.2	1.9	1.3	3.1	1.9	1.3	3.3	1.9	1.3
Current liabilities/Net worth (%)	30.1	70.6	150.0	32.0	73.2	151.8	29.9	69.9	148.4
Current liabilities/Inventory (%)	121.5	253.6	506.6	130.1	254.3	473.1	124.5	249.7	462.8
Total liabilities/Net worth (%)	39.0	90.8	180.5	42.1	93.5	192.9	39.5	90.3	183.9
Fixed assets/Net worth (%)	17.4	34.9	69.1	17.2	34.5	67.2	16.7	34.6	69.2
Efficiency									
Collection period (days)	28.5	47.5	69.0	29.2	46.0	66.4	29.6	46.7	66.8
Sales to Inventory	106.8	42.7	19.3	108.0	40.5	18.6	97.3	39.9	18.7
Assets/Sales (%)	23.2	30.1	39.8	23.2	30.0	39.5	22.8	30.1	39.9
Sales/Net Working Capital	17.3	9.4	5.7	16.6	9.1	5.6	16.5	9.2	5.6
Accounts payable/Sales (%)	3.2	5.4	9.2	3.1	5.4	9.2	3.3	5.3	9.0
Profitability									
Return - Sales (%)	6.5	2.9	.8	6.0	2.5	.8	5.7	2.4	.9
Return - Assets (%)	17.9	7.8	2.3	17.2	7.4	2.3	16.5	7.5	2.5
Return - Net Worth (%)	38.4	17.4	5.7	37.8	16.7	5.1	37.4	16.9	6.0

Source: Dun & Bradstreet. Data in this table are copyright (c) 1999 of Dun & Bradstreet. Reprinted by special arrangement with D&B. *Note:* UQ stands for "Upper Quartile" and represents the top 25 percent of sample; MED stands for "Median"; and LQ stands for "Lower Quartile" and represents the lowest 25 percent.

D&B INDUSTRY NORMS: SIC 1721 - PAINTING AND PAPER HANGING

	1998 (751) Estab.		1997 (1007) Estab.		1996 (1053) Estab.	
	$	%	$	%	$	%
Cash	87,092	18.2	79,197	17.5	64,184	19.6
Accounts Receivable	188,060	39.3	170,161	37.6	117,562	35.9
Notes Receivable	3,350	.7	3,168	.7	2,292	.7
Inventory	14,356	3.0	12,672	2.8	9,824	3.0
Other Current Assets	42,110	8.8	46,613	10.3	30,127	9.2
Total Current Assets	334,968	70.0	311,811	68.9	223,989	68.4
Fixed Assets	114,367	23.9	112,686	24.9	83,832	25.6
Other Non-current Assets	29,190	6.1	28,058	6.2	19,648	6.0
Total Assets	478,525	100.0	452,555	100.0	327,469	100.0
Accounts Payable	53,595	11.2	52,949	11.7	36,677	11.2
Bank Loans	957	.2	453	.1	-	-
Notes Payable	17,705	3.7	19,460	4.3	15,064	4.6
Other Current Liabilities	83,742	17.5	75,124	16.6	51,740	15.8
Total Current Liabilities	155,999	32.6	147,986	32.7	103,481	31.6
Other Long Term	51,202	10.7	47,518	10.5	34,057	10.4
Deferred Credits	1,436	.3	905	.2	655	.2
Net Worth	269,888	56.4	256,147	56.6	189,278	57.8
Total Liabilities & Net Worth	478,525	100.0	452,556	100.0	327,471	100.0
Net Sales	1,465,622	100.0	1,353,816	100.0	1,006,227	100.0
Gross Profits	502,708	34.3	472,482	34.9	378,341	37.6
Net Profit After Tax	80,609	5.5	71,752	5.3	57,355	5.7
Working Capital	178,969	-	163,825	-	120,508	-

Source: Dun & Bradstreet. Data in this table are copyright (c) 1999 of Dun & Bradstreet. Reprinted by special arrangement with D&B. *Notes:* Values in parentheses above columns indicate the number of establishments in the sample. Data shown are for all companies.

D&B KEY BUSINESS RATIOS: SIC 1721

	1998			1997			1996		
	UQ	MED	LQ	UQ	MED	LQ	UQ	MED	LQ
Solvency									
Quick ratio	4.0	1.8	1.1	3.6	1.8	1.0	3.8	1.9	1.2
Current ratio	4.8	2.3	1.4	4.5	2.3	1.4	4.7	2.3	1.5
Current liabilities/Net worth (%)	18.5	48.0	113.5	19.2	50.1	102.2	18.6	45.8	99.4
Current liabilities/Inventory (%)	150.0	312.7	564.7	137.9	289.8	585.3	140.0	311.8	565.2
Total liabilities/Net worth (%)	25.7	66.3	143.8	26.7	65.6	137.7	24.7	63.8	133.6
Fixed assets/Net worth (%)	16.8	36.1	71.0	16.2	34.4	74.2	16.0	36.2	73.2
Efficiency									
Collection period (days)	36.5	56.9	80.7	32.1	55.1	79.9	31.0	51.8	78.1
Sales to Inventory	170.9	67.3	27.3	178.7	83.8	29.6	181.9	78.6	32.6
Assets/Sales (%)	23.7	34.4	48.0	24.3	33.9	49.0	23.7	32.7	47.4
Sales/Net Working Capital	13.8	6.9	4.4	14.1	7.3	4.2	13.8	7.6	4.5
Accounts payable/Sales (%)	1.7	3.3	6.3	1.9	3.5	6.8	1.7	3.4	6.0
Profitability									
Return - Sales (%)	10.5	4.0	1.0	9.5	3.9	1.2	10.0	4.5	1.4
Return - Assets (%)	24.1	8.9	2.1	22.9	9.7	3.1	26.2	10.9	3.7
Return - Net Worth (%)	43.0	18.8	4.7	41.2	18.0	5.5	47.3	21.0	7.3

Source: Dun & Bradstreet. Data in this table are copyright (c) 1999 of Dun & Bradstreet. Reprinted by special arrangement with D&B. *Note:* UQ stands for "Upper Quartile" and represents the top 25 percent of sample; MED stands for "Median"; and LQ stands for "Lower Quartile" and represents the lowest 25 percent.

D&B INDUSTRY NORMS: SIC 1731 - ELECTRICAL WORK

	1998 (1913) Estab.		1997 (1740) Estab.		1996 (2491) Estab.	
	$	%	$	%	$	%
Cash	88,001	16.8	83,297	16.1	68,303	16.7
Accounts Receivable	221,051	42.2	218,848	42.3	169,327	41.4
Notes Receivable	3,143	.6	3,104	.6	2,454	.6
Inventory	33,000	6.3	38,285	7.4	31,902	7.8
Other Current Assets	46,096	8.8	45,529	8.8	35,174	8.6
Total Current Assets	391,291	74.7	389,063	75.2	307,160	75.1
Fixed Assets	108,430	20.7	102,957	19.9	82,618	20.2
Other Non-current Assets	24,096	4.6	25,351	4.9	19,223	4.7
Total Assets	523,817	100.0	517,371	100.0	409,001	100.0
Accounts Payable	86,430	16.5	90,540	17.5	65,849	16.1
Bank Loans	1,048	.2	517	.1	409	.1
Notes Payable	19,905	3.8	19,143	3.7	18,405	4.5
Other Current Liabilities	92,716	17.7	94,679	18.3	69,530	17.0
Total Current Liabilities	200,099	38.2	204,879	39.6	154,193	37.7
Other Long Term	51,858	9.9	51,220	9.9	41,718	10.2
Deferred Credits	1,048	.2	1,552	.3	818	.2
Net Worth	270,813	51.7	259,720	50.2	212,272	51.9
Total Liabilities & Net Worth	523,818	100.0	517,371	100.0	409,001	100.0
Net Sales	1,746,053	100.0	1,592,729	100.0	1,354,369	100.0
Gross Profits	565,721	32.4	504,895	31.7	433,398	32.0
Net Profit After Tax	87,303	5.0	71,673	4.5	66,364	4.9
Working Capital	191,193	-	184,184	-	152,967	-

Source: Dun & Bradstreet. Data in this table are copyright (c) 1999 of Dun & Bradstreet. Reprinted by special arrangement with D&B. *Notes:* Values in parentheses above columns indicate the number of establishments in the sample. Data shown are for all companies.

D&B KEY BUSINESS RATIOS: SIC 1731

	1998			1997			1996		
	UQ	MED	LQ	UQ	MED	LQ	UQ	MED	LQ
Solvency									
Quick ratio	2.9	1.6	1.1	2.7	1.5	1.0	2.9	1.6	1.0
Current ratio	3.7	2.1	1.4	3.3	2.0	1.4	4.0	2.1	1.4
Current liabilities/Net worth (%)	27.7	65.1	143.3	30.6	69.3	152.4	25.1	61.2	142.3
Current liabilities/Inventory (%)	130.2	291.4	548.8	145.5	282.6	529.0	116.0	277.4	528.3
Total liabilities/Net worth (%)	34.6	84.1	177.0	39.5	89.7	198.0	34.0	79.9	175.7
Fixed assets/Net worth (%)	15.8	32.4	63.1	15.5	31.2	62.6	14.3	30.7	60.2
Efficiency									
Collection period (days)	34.0	52.6	73.9	36.5	52.4	73.0	34.7	51.8	72.6
Sales to Inventory	137.3	52.8	22.0	115.7	43.7	18.1	124.4	46.0	18.3
Assets/Sales (%)	24.2	31.5	41.4	23.7	31.3	41.2	23.8	31.1	42.2
Sales/Net Working Capital	14.9	8.3	5.1	14.9	8.4	5.2	14.2	7.9	4.9
Accounts payable/Sales (%)	2.8	4.9	8.1	2.8	5.1	8.5	2.7	4.7	7.9
Profitability									
Return - Sales (%)	8.2	3.5	1.2	7.5	3.2	1.1	7.6	3.3	1.1
Return - Assets (%)	22.9	9.3	3.1	20.0	9.3	3.3	22.3	9.5	2.8
Return - Net Worth (%)	47.7	20.8	7.6	44.5	21.1	7.5	45.0	19.9	6.1

Source: Dun & Bradstreet. Data in this table are copyright (c) 1999 of Dun & Bradstreet. Reprinted by special arrangement with D&B. *Note:* UQ stands for "Upper Quartile" and represents the top 25 percent of sample; MED stands for "Median"; and LQ stands for "Lower Quartile" and represents the lowest 25 percent.

D&B INDUSTRY NORMS: SIC 1741 - MASONRY AND OTHER STONEWORK

	1998 (380) Estab.		1997 (579) Estab.		1996 (552) Estab.	
	$	%	$	%	$	%
Cash	112,289	16.6	116,852	17.5	91,173	19.0
Accounts Receivable	253,664	37.5	261,081	39.1	187,624	39.1
Notes Receivable	5,411	.8	4,674	.7	2,399	.5
Inventory	18,264	2.7	15,358	2.3	11,517	2.4
Other Current Assets	63,585	9.4	68,776	10.3	46,066	9.6
Total Current Assets	453,213	67.0	466,741	69.9	338,779	70.6
Fixed Assets	184,667	27.3	168,935	25.3	115,645	24.1
Other Non-current Assets	38,557	5.7	32,051	4.8	25,432	5.3
Total Assets	676,437	100.0	667,727	100.0	479,856	100.0
Accounts Payable	89,966	13.3	98,824	14.8	69,099	14.4
Bank Loans	2,706	.4	668	.1	960	.2
Notes Payable	29,087	4.3	33,386	5.0	22,073	4.6
Other Current Liabilities	114,318	16.9	118,855	17.8	89,253	18.6
Total Current Liabilities	236,077	34.9	251,733	37.7	181,385	37.8
Other Long Term	84,555	12.5	75,453	11.3	55,663	11.6
Deferred Credits	2,029	.3	2,003	.3	960	.2
Net Worth	353,777	52.3	338,538	50.7	241,847	50.4
Total Liabilities & Net Worth	676,438	100.0	667,727	100.0	479,855	100.0
Net Sales	1,984,544	100.0	2,128,050	100.0	1,606,922	100.0
Gross Profits	575,518	29.0	595,854	28.0	456,366	28.4
Net Profit After Tax	109,150	5.5	121,299	5.7	77,132	4.8
Working Capital	217,136	-	215,008	-	157,392	-

Source: Dun & Bradstreet. Data in this table are copyright (c) 1999 of Dun & Bradstreet. Reprinted by special arrangement with D&B. *Notes:* Values in parentheses above columns indicate the number of establishments in the sample. Data shown are for all companies.

D&B KEY BUSINESS RATIOS: SIC 1741

	1998			1997			1996		
	UQ	MED	LQ	UQ	MED	LQ	UQ	MED	LQ
Solvency									
Quick ratio	3.0	1.6	1.0	2.6	1.5	1.0	3.0	1.6	1.0
Current ratio	3.6	2.0	1.3	3.4	1.8	1.3	3.6	1.9	1.3
Current liabilities/Net worth (%)	24.0	61.3	140.5	26.3	69.5	156.6	26.5	65.6	140.9
Current liabilities/Inventory (%)	145.7	353.5	530.6	163.5	373.5	589.4	159.1	335.0	675.0
Total liabilities/Net worth (%)	37.0	80.4	179.1	39.4	89.5	196.2	33.3	87.8	183.8
Fixed assets/Net worth (%)	21.9	40.5	75.5	20.9	43.2	80.7	16.5	41.3	79.9
Efficiency									
Collection period (days)	36.9	55.9	81.6	36.1	56.6	80.1	34.3	57.3	81.0
Sales to Inventory	306.9	82.4	30.1	234.2	67.6	29.2	250.6	75.0	30.3
Assets/Sales (%)	25.2	33.9	46.0	24.5	32.7	45.1	23.0	32.6	43.8
Sales/Net Working Capital	16.9	9.0	4.9	15.6	9.1	5.2	16.8	8.6	5.2
Accounts payable/Sales (%)	2.5	4.9	8.4	2.5	4.8	8.1	2.3	4.6	7.9
Profitability									
Return - Sales (%)	9.5	3.9	1.3	9.5	4.4	1.2	8.4	3.6	1.2
Return - Assets (%)	24.3	10.5	4.0	25.7	11.7	3.5	23.2	9.3	3.2
Return - Net Worth (%)	49.9	24.4	7.7	52.5	23.2	8.5	50.7	20.5	7.6

Source: Dun & Bradstreet. Data in this table are copyright (c) 1999 of Dun & Bradstreet. Reprinted by special arrangement with D&B. *Note:* UQ stands for "Upper Quartile" and represents the top 25 percent of sample; MED stands for "Median"; and LQ stands for "Lower Quartile" and represents the lowest 25 percent.

D&B INDUSTRY NORMS: SIC 1742 - PLASTERING, DRYWALL, AND INSULATION

	1998 (691) Estab.		1997 (998) Estab.		1996 (946) Estab.	
	$	%	$	%	$	%
Cash	107,797	15.9	102,827	15.5	85,716	16.4
Accounts Receivable	317,289	46.8	306,492	46.2	235,196	45.0
Notes Receivable	4,068	.6	5,307	.8	3,136	.6
Inventory	35,254	5.2	35,824	5.4	29,269	5.6
Other Current Assets	58,305	8.6	65,677	9.9	48,085	9.2
Total Current Assets	522,713	77.1	516,127	77.8	401,402	76.8
Fixed Assets	124,068	18.3	113,442	17.1	94,078	18.0
Other Non-current Assets	31,186	4.6	33,834	5.1	27,178	5.2
Total Assets	677,967	100.0	663,403	100.0	522,658	100.0
Accounts Payable	104,407	15.4	107,471	16.2	85,193	16.3
Bank Loans	678	.1	663	.1	523	.1
Notes Payable	26,441	3.9	28,526	4.3	22,997	4.4
Other Current Liabilities	130,848	19.3	124,720	18.8	95,124	18.2
Total Current Liabilities	262,374	38.7	261,380	39.4	203,837	39.0
Other Long Term	61,017	9.0	59,043	8.9	51,220	9.8
Deferred Credits	2,712	.4	663	.1	2,091	.4
Net Worth	351,865	51.9	342,316	51.6	265,510	50.8
Total Liabilities & Net Worth	677,968	100.0	663,402	100.0	522,658	100.0
Net Sales	2,630,940	100.0	2,342,796	100.0	2,002,285	100.0
Gross Profits	741,925	28.2	627,869	26.8	544,622	27.2
Net Profit After Tax	113,130	4.3	98,397	4.2	84,096	4.2
Working Capital	260,340	-	254,747	-	197,564	-

Source: Dun & Bradstreet. Data in this table are copyright (c) 1999 of Dun & Bradstreet. Reprinted by special arrangement with D&B. *Notes:* Values in parentheses above columns indicate the number of establishments in the sample. Data shown are for all companies.

D&B KEY BUSINESS RATIOS: SIC 1742

	1998			1997			1996		
	UQ	MED	LQ	UQ	MED	LQ	UQ	MED	LQ
Solvency									
Quick ratio	2.9	1.6	1.1	2.7	1.6	1.1	2.7	1.6	1.1
Current ratio	3.4	2.1	1.4	3.3	2.0	1.4	3.5	2.1	1.5
Current liabilities/Net worth (%)	29.4	68.5	151.7	31.8	71.2	144.8	29.1	67.6	145.7
Current liabilities/Inventory (%)	173.4	335.8	598.8	156.6	322.8	529.7	169.7	324.9	562.6
Total liabilities/Net worth (%)	38.5	84.4	181.6	39.6	86.4	170.7	37.7	84.9	176.7
Fixed assets/Net worth (%)	13.0	26.1	55.0	12.4	24.5	49.9	12.6	25.5	53.4
Efficiency									
Collection period (days)	43.4	56.2	73.4	38.0	56.2	77.4	36.5	54.4	74.2
Sales to Inventory	122.2	55.2	27.9	124.1	55.1	26.8	113.2	51.7	26.0
Assets/Sales (%)	23.0	30.3	39.7	22.1	29.5	39.3	20.8	28.5	38.4
Sales/Net Working Capital	14.6	8.1	5.5	15.0	8.4	5.6	13.9	8.1	5.3
Accounts payable/Sales (%)	2.4	4.3	7.2	2.6	4.5	7.2	2.6	4.4	7.0
Profitability									
Return - Sales (%)	7.4	3.2	1.1	7.2	3.5	1.1	7.2	3.1	.9
Return - Assets (%)	23.5	9.6	3.4	23.5	9.5	3.3	21.2	9.0	2.8
Return - Net Worth (%)	46.8	20.5	6.4	46.6	22.4	7.7	44.8	18.8	5.5

Source: Dun & Bradstreet. Data in this table are copyright (c) 1999 of Dun & Bradstreet. Reprinted by special arrangement with D&B. *Note:* UQ stands for "Upper Quartile" and represents the top 25 percent of sample; MED stands for "Median"; and LQ stands for "Lower Quartile" and represents the lowest 25 percent.

D&B INDUSTRY NORMS: SIC 1743 - TERRAZZO, TILE, MARBLE, MOSAIC WORK

	1998 (126) Estab.		1997 (190) Estab.		1996 (192) Estab.	
	$	%	$	%	$	%
Cash	71,322	16.2	60,275	14.8	53,537	17.0
Accounts Receivable	196,355	44.6	160,868	39.5	113,372	36.0
Notes Receivable	881	.2	3,258	.8	3,779	1.2
Inventory	28,617	6.5	35,024	8.6	22,359	7.1
Other Current Assets	30,818	7.0	37,468	9.2	28,973	9.2
Total Current Assets	327,993	74.5	296,893	72.9	222,020	70.5
Fixed Assets	83,209	18.9	88,783	21.8	76,526	24.3
Other Non-current Assets	29,057	6.6	21,585	5.3	16,376	5.2
Total Assets	440,259	100.0	407,261	100.0	314,922	100.0
Accounts Payable	70,881	16.1	63,940	15.7	47,868	15.2
Bank Loans	440	.1	-	-	-	-
Notes Payable	8,805	2.0	16,290	4.0	14,801	4.7
Other Current Liabilities	84,089	19.1	68,420	16.8	47,238	15.0
Total Current Liabilities	164,215	37.3	148,650	36.5	109,907	34.9
Other Long Term	46,667	10.6	43,170	10.6	35,271	11.2
Deferred Credits	440	.1	815	.2	315	.1
Net Worth	228,934	52.0	214,627	52.7	169,427	53.8
Total Liabilities & Net Worth	440,256	100.0	407,262	100.0	314,920	100.0
Net Sales	1,596,409	100.0	1,420,477	100.0	1,204,789	100.0
Gross Profits	488,501	30.6	423,302	29.8	399,990	33.2
Net Profit After Tax	60,664	3.8	62,501	4.4	51,806	4.3
Working Capital	163,775	-	148,243	-	112,112	-

Source: Dun & Bradstreet. Data in this table are copyright (c) 1999 of Dun & Bradstreet. Reprinted by special arrangement with D&B. *Notes:* Values in parentheses above columns indicate the number of establishments in the sample. Data shown are for all companies.

D&B KEY BUSINESS RATIOS: SIC 1743

	1998			1997			1996		
	UQ	MED	LQ	UQ	MED	LQ	UQ	MED	LQ
Solvency									
Quick ratio	2.8	1.6	1.1	3.2	1.6	.9	3.0	1.6	.9
Current ratio	3.9	2.0	1.3	3.8	2.1	1.3	4.0	2.0	1.3
Current liabilities/Net worth (%)	28.2	70.5	149.5	23.4	58.0	151.9	21.0	55.2	122.1
Current liabilities/Inventory (%)	131.2	292.4	517.3	124.6	199.2	384.8	94.6	223.0	434.8
Total liabilities/Net worth (%)	35.4	90.9	165.3	34.6	74.1	187.1	30.3	69.8	160.2
Fixed assets/Net worth (%)	13.5	27.0	55.1	12.9	30.2	67.3	14.0	32.7	68.5
Efficiency									
Collection period (days)	40.7	53.7	71.9	33.8	55.5	69.4	36.9	52.2	73.0
Sales to Inventory	173.7	49.0	22.6	131.6	35.5	13.6	101.1	35.9	20.6
Assets/Sales (%)	23.6	32.2	39.7	21.6	30.4	43.1	23.0	31.7	44.4
Sales/Net Working Capital	15.9	7.4	4.6	15.0	8.6	5.1	15.7	7.6	4.4
Accounts payable/Sales (%)	2.2	4.8	7.9	3.3	4.5	8.1	2.9	5.5	8.8
Profitability									
Return - Sales (%)	6.3	3.2	.7	6.9	3.3	1.4	8.1	3.5	.8
Return - Assets (%)	16.7	9.1	2.4	17.9	8.1	3.1	21.8	9.0	1.8
Return - Net Worth (%)	37.5	14.8	4.2	37.9	16.5	6.3	40.5	18.0	3.3

Source: Dun & Bradstreet. Data in this table are copyright (c) 1999 of Dun & Bradstreet. Reprinted by special arrangement with D&B. *Note:* UQ stands for "Upper Quartile" and represents the top 25 percent of sample; MED stands for "Median"; and LQ stands for "Lower Quartile" and represents the lowest 25 percent.

D&B INDUSTRY NORMS: SIC 1751 - CARPENTRY WORK

	1998 (446) Estab.		1997 (684) Estab.		1996 (654) Estab.	
	$	%	$	%	$	%
Cash	57,771	15.9	51,113	17.3	45,327	20.1
Accounts Receivable	139,523	38.4	103,702	35.1	72,387	32.1
Notes Receivable	2,543	.7	1,773	.6	1,804	.8
Inventory	35,607	9.8	30,136	10.2	22,551	10.0
Other Current Assets	23,254	6.4	23,636	8.0	15,785	7.0
Total Current Assets	258,698	71.2	210,360	71.2	157,854	70.0
Fixed Assets	85,022	23.4	69,726	23.6	55,925	24.8
Other Non-current Assets	19,620	5.4	15,363	5.2	11,726	5.2
Total Assets	363,340	100.0	295,449	100.0	225,505	100.0
Accounts Payable	60,314	16.6	53,476	18.1	37,885	16.8
Bank Loans	727	.2	295	.1	-	-
Notes Payable	14,897	4.1	11,818	4.0	9,697	4.3
Other Current Liabilities	58,861	16.2	51,113	17.3	38,110	16.9
Total Current Liabilities	134,799	37.1	116,702	39.5	85,692	38.0
Other Long Term	40,331	11.1	35,454	12.0	32,247	14.3
Deferred Credits	1,090	.3	295	.1	226	.1
Net Worth	187,120	51.5	142,997	48.4	107,340	47.6
Total Liabilities & Net Worth	363,340	100.0	295,448	100.0	225,505	100.0
Net Sales	1,385,716	100.0	1,272,298	100.0	1,006,383	100.0
Gross Profits	448,972	32.4	399,502	31.4	336,132	33.4
Net Profit After Tax	77,600	5.6	71,249	5.6	60,383	6.0
Working Capital	123,899	-	93,657	-	72,162	-

Source: Dun & Bradstreet. Data in this table are copyright (c) 1999 of Dun & Bradstreet. Reprinted by special arrangement with D&B. *Notes:* Values in parentheses above columns indicate the number of establishments in the sample. Data shown are for all companies.

D&B KEY BUSINESS RATIOS: SIC 1751

	1998			1997			1996		
	UQ	MED	LQ	UQ	MED	LQ	UQ	MED	LQ
Solvency									
Quick ratio	3.1	1.5	.9	2.5	1.4	.9	2.8	1.4	.8
Current ratio	4.1	2.0	1.3	3.4	1.8	1.3	3.8	1.9	1.2
Current liabilities/Net worth (%)	20.3	58.9	147.8	24.8	69.2	153.4	23.7	65.1	155.3
Current liabilities/Inventory (%)	79.9	180.6	386.5	100.4	206.2	344.3	100.7	213.5	358.3
Total liabilities/Net worth (%)	25.8	76.9	195.9	33.5	94.7	195.7	35.6	88.0	200.1
Fixed assets/Net worth (%)	14.1	35.4	78.7	15.8	36.4	80.1	15.4	38.9	84.8
Efficiency									
Collection period (days)	25.2	40.4	58.9	23.5	38.5	60.2	22.6	37.2	57.2
Sales to Inventory	59.2	27.6	15.2	73.2	27.1	14.2	51.7	26.3	13.6
Assets/Sales (%)	18.8	26.2	36.7	17.4	24.6	36.7	16.5	24.8	36.4
Sales/Net Working Capital	21.5	10.9	6.1	22.8	11.6	6.6	18.3	10.4	6.5
Accounts payable/Sales (%)	2.3	4.3	7.9	2.5	5.0	7.9	2.2	4.5	8.2
Profitability									
Return - Sales (%)	10.1	4.6	1.2	9.8	3.8	1.3	10.0	3.6	1.0
Return - Assets (%)	30.8	14.1	3.8	29.4	12.2	3.5	30.8	13.3	3.8
Return - Net Worth (%)	65.5	31.2	9.3	66.9	27.2	8.5	70.2	30.7	9.4

Source: Dun & Bradstreet. Data in this table are copyright (c) 1999 of Dun & Bradstreet. Reprinted by special arrangement with D&B. *Note:* UQ stands for "Upper Quartile" and represents the top 25 percent of sample; MED stands for "Median"; and LQ stands for "Lower Quartile" and represents the lowest 25 percent.

D&B INDUSTRY NORMS: SIC 1752 - FLOOR LAYING AND FLOOR WORK, NEC

	1998 (509) Estab.		1997 (698) Estab.		1996 (670) Estab.	
	$	%	$	%	$	%
Cash	57,208	15.3	53,650	16.1	44,407	15.9
Accounts Receivable	162,277	43.4	139,956	42.0	114,789	41.1
Notes Receivable	2,991	.8	2,333	.7	1,955	.7
Inventory	36,643	9.8	36,655	11.0	31,281	11.2
Other Current Assets	21,313	5.7	19,327	5.8	16,478	5.9
Total Current Assets	280,432	75.0	251,921	75.6	208,910	74.8
Fixed Assets	75,904	20.3	64,313	19.3	56,417	20.2
Other Non-current Assets	17,574	4.7	16,995	5.1	13,965	5.0
Total Assets	373,910	100.0	333,229	100.0	279,292	100.0
Accounts Payable	62,069	16.6	59,315	17.8	49,993	17.9
Bank Loans	1,496	.4	-	-	-	-
Notes Payable	15,704	4.2	13,662	4.1	12,847	4.6
Other Current Liabilities	64,313	17.2	55,649	16.7	43,011	15.4
Total Current Liabilities	143,582	38.4	128,626	38.6	105,851	37.9
Other Long Term	38,139	10.2	33,323	10.0	28,488	10.2
Deferred Credits	1,122	.3	1,000	.3	559	.2
Net Worth	191,068	51.1	170,280	51.1	144,394	51.7
Total Liabilities & Net Worth	373,911	100.0	333,229	100.0	279,292	100.0
Net Sales	1,553,489	100.0	1,412,567	100.0	1,259,350	100.0
Gross Profits	484,689	31.2	432,246	30.6	381,583	30.3
Net Profit After Tax	80,781	5.2	62,153	4.4	60,449	4.8
Working Capital	136,852	-	123,294	-	103,058	-

Source: Dun & Bradstreet. Data in this table are copyright (c) 1999 of Dun & Bradstreet. Reprinted by special arrangement with D&B. *Notes:* Values in parentheses above columns indicate the number of establishments in the sample. Data shown are for all companies.

D&B KEY BUSINESS RATIOS: SIC 1752

	1998			1997			1996		
	UQ	MED	LQ	UQ	MED	LQ	UQ	MED	LQ
Solvency									
Quick ratio	3.0	1.5	1.0	2.8	1.6	1.0	2.8	1.5	1.0
Current ratio	3.8	2.0	1.4	3.6	2.1	1.4	3.9	2.1	1.4
Current liabilities/Net worth (%)	25.0	68.1	150.6	25.0	62.0	156.7	23.3	60.4	143.3
Current liabilities/Inventory (%)	121.5	239.3	445.5	113.3	235.3	466.5	97.6	204.0	403.8
Total liabilities/Net worth (%)	36.8	87.5	179.1	33.6	79.9	185.1	33.5	76.8	170.6
Fixed assets/Net worth (%)	12.8	27.6	62.1	12.1	26.9	58.0	13.3	27.2	62.8
Efficiency									
Collection period (days)	27.0	47.3	67.2	27.2	46.4	65.2	25.9	43.1	63.0
Sales to Inventory	94.6	36.1	19.1	78.3	33.2	16.9	82.3	37.4	15.7
Assets/Sales (%)	19.3	26.3	33.6	17.7	25.5	33.9	17.2	24.6	34.0
Sales/Net Working Capital	18.4	10.1	6.3	19.7	10.1	5.9	20.3	9.9	5.8
Accounts payable/Sales (%)	2.3	4.2	6.9	2.4	4.1	7.0	2.3	4.3	6.8
Profitability									
Return - Sales (%)	7.5	3.1	1.1	7.3	2.9	.8	8.0	3.2	1.0
Return - Assets (%)	25.6	9.8	3.0	23.0	10.0	2.9	25.7	10.3	3.2
Return - Net Worth (%)	55.3	23.6	8.4	54.9	21.6	7.0	54.1	22.0	7.3

Source: Dun & Bradstreet. Data in this table are copyright (c) 1999 of Dun & Bradstreet. Reprinted by special arrangement with D&B. *Note:* UQ stands for "Upper Quartile" and represents the top 25 percent of sample; MED stands for "Median"; and LQ stands for "Lower Quartile" and represents the lowest 25 percent.

D&B INDUSTRY NORMS: SIC 1761 - ROOFING, SIDING, AND SHEET METAL WORK

	1998 (1359) Estab.		1997 (1905) Estab.		1996 (1852) Estab.	
	$	%	$	%	$	%
Cash	105,376	17.8	96,766	17.6	79,701	16.9
Accounts Receivable	217,856	36.8	202,878	36.9	172,135	36.5
Notes Receivable	4,736	.8	3,299	.6	2,358	.5
Inventory	37,296	6.3	36,837	6.7	35,370	7.5
Other Current Assets	58,016	9.8	51,682	9.4	47,632	10.1
Total Current Assets	423,280	71.5	391,462	71.2	337,196	71.5
Fixed Assets	135,568	22.9	125,905	22.9	107,526	22.8
Other Non-current Assets	33,152	5.6	32,438	5.9	26,881	5.7
Total Assets	592,000	100.0	549,805	100.0	471,603	100.0
Accounts Payable	97,088	16.4	92,917	16.9	81,116	17.2
Bank Loans	1,184	.2	550	.1	472	.1
Notes Payable	23,680	4.0	19,793	3.6	19,336	4.1
Other Current Liabilities	94,720	16.0	90,168	16.4	75,928	16.1
Total Current Liabilities	216,672	36.6	203,428	37.0	176,852	37.5
Other Long Term	57,424	9.7	55,530	10.1	49,518	10.5
Deferred Credits	1,184	.2	1,100	.2	943	.2
Net Worth	316,720	53.5	289,747	52.7	244,291	51.8
Total Liabilities & Net Worth	592,000	100.0	549,805	100.0	471,604	100.0
Net Sales	1,893,053	100.0	1,892,258	100.0	1,652,785	100.0
Gross Profits	596,312	31.5	579,031	30.6	510,711	30.9
Net Profit After Tax	87,080	4.6	85,152	4.5	72,723	4.4
Working Capital	206,608	-	188,033	-	160,345	-

Source: Dun & Bradstreet. Data in this table are copyright (c) 1999 of Dun & Bradstreet. Reprinted by special arrangement with D&B. *Notes:* Values in parentheses above columns indicate the number of establishments in the sample. Data shown are for all companies.

D&B KEY BUSINESS RATIOS: SIC 1761

	1998			1997			1996		
	UQ	MED	LQ	UQ	MED	LQ	UQ	MED	LQ
Solvency									
Quick ratio	2.7	1.5	1.0	2.7	1.5	1.0	2.6	1.5	.9
Current ratio	3.6	2.0	1.4	3.4	2.0	1.3	3.5	2.0	1.3
Current liabilities/Net worth (%)	26.1	59.4	127.4	26.4	62.0	136.4	25.5	65.1	135.3
Current liabilities/Inventory (%)	137.5	313.4	560.7	149.1	277.8	523.3	140.7	277.0	496.3
Total liabilities/Net worth (%)	34.6	75.7	162.7	35.7	80.1	172.5	34.9	83.5	178.5
Fixed assets/Net worth (%)	19.5	37.8	70.4	19.0	36.3	67.7	17.6	35.0	67.6
Efficiency									
Collection period (days)	26.6	44.2	67.2	27.7	45.1	66.8	27.5	45.5	65.6
Sales to Inventory	124.6	55.1	25.0	119.1	52.5	24.4	98.6	47.0	22.6
Assets/Sales (%)	22.4	30.5	41.9	22.0	30.1	39.5	21.9	30.2	40.1
Sales/Net Working Capital	16.2	8.8	5.4	17.6	9.3	5.6	16.9	9.3	5.5
Accounts payable/Sales (%)	2.3	4.6	7.9	2.6	4.8	8.2	2.6	4.9	8.2
Profitability									
Return - Sales (%)	7.7	3.3	1.0	7.1	3.0	1.0	6.6	2.9	.8
Return - Assets (%)	21.4	8.9	3.1	20.6	8.7	3.1	20.5	7.8	2.5
Return - Net Worth (%)	42.0	18.4	6.0	40.6	17.6	6.0	43.3	17.2	5.6

Source: Dun & Bradstreet. Data in this table are copyright (c) 1999 of Dun & Bradstreet. Reprinted by special arrangement with D&B. *Note:* UQ stands for "Upper Quartile" and represents the top 25 percent of sample; MED stands for "Median"; and LQ stands for "Lower Quartile" and represents the lowest 25 percent.

D&B INDUSTRY NORMS: SIC 1771 - CONCRETE WORK

	1998 (816) Estab.		1997 (1213) Estab.		1996 (1125) Estab.	
	$	%	$	%	$	%
Cash	111,574	16.0	86,333	15.0	70,870	15.7
Accounts Receivable	249,646	35.8	203,746	35.4	154,830	34.3
Notes Receivable	4,184	.6	3,453	.6	3,611	.8
Inventory	11,157	1.6	10,360	1.8	8,577	1.9
Other Current Assets	50,208	7.2	44,893	7.8	32,952	7.3
Total Current Assets	426,769	61.2	348,785	60.6	270,840	60.0
Fixed Assets	238,489	34.2	196,839	34.2	153,476	34.0
Other Non-current Assets	32,077	4.6	29,929	5.2	27,084	6.0
Total Assets	697,335	100.0	575,553	100.0	451,400	100.0
Accounts Payable	110,179	15.8	96,693	16.8	69,967	15.5
Bank Loans	2,092	.3	-	-	-	-
Notes Payable	25,104	3.6	21,295	3.7	21,216	4.7
Other Current Liabilities	108,087	15.5	90,938	15.8	74,481	16.5
Total Current Liabilities	245,462	35.2	208,926	36.3	165,664	36.7
Other Long Term	104,600	15.0	89,786	15.6	65,904	14.6
Deferred Credits	697	.1	1,151	.2	1,354	.3
Net Worth	346,576	49.7	275,690	47.9	218,478	48.4
Total Liabilities & Net Worth	697,335	100.0	575,553	100.0	451,400	100.0
Net Sales	1,982,613	100.0	1,836,746	100.0	1,537,531	100.0
Gross Profits	592,801	29.9	547,350	29.8	475,097	30.9
Net Profit After Tax	116,974	5.9	91,837	5.0	69,189	4.5
Working Capital	181,308	-	139,860	-	105,176	-

Source: Dun & Bradstreet. Data in this table are copyright (c) 1999 of Dun & Bradstreet. Reprinted by special arrangement with D&B. *Notes:* Values in parentheses above columns indicate the number of establishments in the sample. Data shown are for all companies.

D&B KEY BUSINESS RATIOS: SIC 1771

	1998			1997			1996		
	UQ	MED	LQ	UQ	MED	LQ	UQ	MED	LQ
Solvency									
Quick ratio	2.7	1.5	1.0	2.4	1.4	.9	2.5	1.4	.9
Current ratio	3.1	1.8	1.2	2.8	1.6	1.2	3.1	1.7	1.1
Current liabilities/Net worth (%)	26.8	64.9	143.1	29.3	68.8	146.5	27.0	66.1	152.0
Current liabilities/Inventory (%)	201.1	405.9	672.8	190.5	350.7	601.7	169.0	379.0	626.5
Total liabilities/Net worth (%)	41.7	99.8	190.1	44.5	102.5	207.8	38.2	98.6	209.9
Fixed assets/Net worth (%)	28.9	64.0	115.6	32.2	61.8	116.9	30.1	60.6	114.0
Efficiency									
Collection period (days)	29.9	51.5	74.1	28.1	49.3	73.2	27.0	46.2	70.6
Sales to Inventory	205.2	85.5	34.5	202.1	85.7	41.0	202.9	92.5	37.1
Assets/Sales (%)	25.2	34.4	47.4	24.9	33.6	48.5	23.5	32.8	45.7
Sales/Net Working Capital	19.5	10.1	5.8	20.3	10.6	5.7	21.6	9.9	6.2
Accounts payable/Sales (%)	2.5	4.9	8.6	2.6	5.2	9.1	2.2	4.7	8.5
Profitability									
Return - Sales (%)	10.3	4.6	1.5	8.4	3.5	1.1	7.6	3.3	.9
Return - Assets (%)	23.7	11.0	3.7	21.5	8.7	3.2	19.9	8.9	2.9
Return - Net Worth (%)	47.6	24.6	9.2	45.6	20.6	7.7	44.2	20.1	7.1

Source: Dun & Bradstreet. Data in this table are copyright (c) 1999 of Dun & Bradstreet. Reprinted by special arrangement with D&B. *Note:* UQ stands for "Upper Quartile" and represents the top 25 percent of sample; MED stands for "Median"; and LQ stands for "Lower Quartile" and represents the lowest 25 percent.

D&B INDUSTRY NORMS: SIC 1781 - WATER WELL DRILLING

	1998 (158) Estab.		1997 (208) Estab.		1996 (221) Estab.	
	$	%	$	%	$	%
Cash	83,239	14.4	83,894	13.7	67,191	14.3
Accounts Receivable	150,292	26.0	141,456	23.1	111,828	23.8
Notes Receivable	4,624	.8	6,124	1.0	2,819	.6
Inventory	55,493	9.6	63,073	10.3	45,107	9.6
Other Current Assets	20,232	3.5	39,191	6.4	21,614	4.6
Total Current Assets	313,880	54.3	333,738	54.5	248,559	52.9
Fixed Assets	224,861	38.9	236,985	38.7	190,296	40.5
Other Non-current Assets	39,307	6.8	41,641	6.8	31,011	6.6
Total Assets	578,048	100.0	612,364	100.0	469,866	100.0
Accounts Payable	52,602	9.1	63,073	10.3	45,577	9.7
Bank Loans	3,468	.6	1,225	.2	-	-
Notes Payable	22,544	3.9	34,292	5.6	19,265	4.1
Other Current Liabilities	79,193	13.7	87,568	14.3	62,022	13.2
Total Current Liabilities	157,807	27.3	186,158	30.4	126,864	27.0
Other Long Term	109,251	18.9	98,591	16.1	88,335	18.8
Deferred Credits	1,156	.2	612	.1	1,410	.3
Net Worth	309,834	53.6	327,002	53.4	253,258	53.9
Total Liabilities & Net Worth	578,048	100.0	612,363	100.0	469,867	100.0
Net Sales	1,248,914	100.0	1,050,361	100.0	1,046,282	100.0
Gross Profits	553,269	44.3	474,763	45.2	459,318	43.9
Net Profit After Tax	62,446	5.0	36,763	3.5	47,083	4.5
Working Capital	156,073	-	147,579	-	121,696	-

Source: Dun & Bradstreet. Data in this table are copyright (c) 1999 of Dun & Bradstreet. Reprinted by special arrangement with D&B. *Notes:* Values in parentheses above columns indicate the number of establishments in the sample. Data shown are for all companies.

D&B KEY BUSINESS RATIOS: SIC 1781

	1998			1997			1996		
	UQ	MED	LQ	UQ	MED	LQ	UQ	MED	LQ
Solvency									
Quick ratio	3.7	1.7	.8	2.5	1.2	.7	3.5	1.5	.8
Current ratio	5.3	2.4	1.2	3.9	1.8	1.1	4.7	2.1	1.2
Current liabilities/Net worth (%)	13.6	35.1	88.5	17.4	41.2	92.3	13.2	35.6	76.7
Current liabilities/Inventory (%)	94.9	204.6	379.4	118.2	219.7	464.0	92.3	171.8	367.4
Total liabilities/Net worth (%)	27.1	64.0	123.4	26.4	60.5	123.3	22.3	62.3	133.8
Fixed assets/Net worth (%)	31.3	68.8	110.5	35.0	60.9	117.3	35.4	66.2	117.3
Efficiency									
Collection period (days)	29.5	43.7	72.4	27.4	44.9	64.8	27.4	44.9	68.3
Sales to Inventory	43.5	21.6	11.5	53.1	23.8	12.4	60.4	27.3	11.8
Assets/Sales (%)	37.2	51.1	67.2	35.7	49.4	66.7	37.3	49.7	67.7
Sales/Net Working Capital	11.1	6.2	3.8	12.9	6.1	3.8	12.7	6.1	3.8
Accounts payable/Sales (%)	2.2	4.6	6.9	2.4	4.2	7.3	2.1	3.4	6.2
Profitability									
Return - Sales (%)	7.7	3.6	1.2	7.3	1.9	-.2	7.7	3.4	.9
Return - Assets (%)	13.9	6.7	1.9	11.2	3.5	-.4	15.5	7.6	1.7
Return - Net Worth (%)	34.3	11.1	3.6	21.5	6.4	-.3	25.0	11.7	2.9

Source: Dun & Bradstreet. Data in this table are copyright (c) 1999 of Dun & Bradstreet. Reprinted by special arrangement with D&B. *Note:* UQ stands for "Upper Quartile" and represents the top 25 percent of sample; MED stands for "Median"; and LQ stands for "Lower Quartile" and represents the lowest 25 percent.

D&B INDUSTRY NORMS: SIC 1791 - STRUCTURAL STEEL ERECTION

	1998 (289) Estab.		1997 (395) Estab.		1996 (371) Estab.	
	$	%	$	%	$	%
Cash	140,886	16.1	130,978	16.2	97,319	15.9
Accounts Receivable	356,152	40.7	329,062	40.7	238,706	39.0
Notes Receivable	10,501	1.2	9,702	1.2	4,284	.7
Inventory	21,877	2.5	25,872	3.2	17,750	2.9
Other Current Assets	81,381	9.3	78,425	9.7	56,922	9.3
Total Current Assets	610,797	69.8	574,039	71.0	414,981	67.8
Fixed Assets	223,142	25.5	196,467	24.3	165,870	27.1
Other Non-current Assets	41,128	4.7	38,000	4.7	31,215	5.1
Total Assets	875,067	100.0	808,506	100.0	612,066	100.0
Accounts Payable	119,884	13.7	121,276	15.0	88,138	14.4
Bank Loans	875	.1	809	.1	-	-
Notes Payable	42,878	4.9	34,766	4.3	29,379	4.8
Other Current Liabilities	156,637	17.9	152,808	18.9	110,172	18.0
Total Current Liabilities	320,274	36.6	309,659	38.3	227,689	37.2
Other Long Term	103,258	11.8	86,510	10.7	76,508	12.5
Deferred Credits	875	.1	2,426	.3	2,448	.4
Net Worth	450,660	51.5	409,913	50.7	305,421	49.9
Total Liabilities & Net Worth	875,067	100.0	808,508	100.0	612,066	100.0
Net Sales	2,443,510	100.0	2,504,978	100.0	2,194,240	100.0
Gross Profits	706,174	28.9	701,394	28.0	647,301	29.5
Net Profit After Tax	136,837	5.6	132,764	5.3	133,849	6.1
Working Capital	290,522	-	264,381	-	187,292	-

Source: Dun & Bradstreet. Data in this table are copyright (c) 1999 of Dun & Bradstreet. Reprinted by special arrangement with D&B. *Notes:* Values in parentheses above columns indicate the number of establishments in the sample. Data shown are for all companies.

D&B KEY BUSINESS RATIOS: SIC 1791

	1998			1997			1996		
	UQ	MED	LQ	UQ	MED	LQ	UQ	MED	LQ
Solvency									
Quick ratio	2.9	1.5	1.0	2.7	1.5	1.0	2.7	1.5	1.0
Current ratio	3.6	1.9	1.3	3.3	1.9	1.3	3.3	1.9	1.3
Current liabilities/Net worth (%)	26.0	62.5	144.7	24.6	74.3	152.1	25.8	68.0	154.1
Current liabilities/Inventory (%)	199.3	315.8	548.0	170.7	332.8	540.4	155.9	340.2	510.8
Total liabilities/Net worth (%)	36.3	84.7	187.0	36.4	92.4	190.3	39.6	92.0	190.9
Fixed assets/Net worth (%)	18.5	41.8	79.7	19.2	39.0	78.5	21.2	42.9	87.0
Efficiency									
Collection period (days)	38.7	59.1	84.3	39.3	64.6	84.6	39.4	54.4	80.7
Sales to Inventory	220.1	76.8	22.5	166.6	55.4	22.2	105.8	52.3	22.3
Assets/Sales (%)	29.2	35.7	49.0	26.3	36.5	48.6	25.2	35.4	45.1
Sales/Net Working Capital	13.5	8.5	5.0	17.7	9.3	5.2	15.3	9.2	5.2
Accounts payable/Sales (%)	2.6	4.7	8.3	2.5	5.1	8.6	2.1	4.2	8.1
Profitability									
Return - Sales (%)	8.9	4.6	1.7	7.4	3.5	1.5	9.1	4.0	1.2
Return - Assets (%)	20.4	10.2	3.4	20.5	8.8	3.6	20.9	9.4	3.1
Return - Net Worth (%)	43.9	22.3	7.1	51.2	23.6	9.9	48.7	23.5	8.5

Source: Dun & Bradstreet. Data in this table are copyright (c) 1999 of Dun & Bradstreet. Reprinted by special arrangement with D&B. *Note:* UQ stands for "Upper Quartile" and represents the top 25 percent of sample; MED stands for "Median"; and LQ stands for "Lower Quartile" and represents the lowest 25 percent.

D&B INDUSTRY NORMS: SIC 1793 - GLASS AND GLAZING WORK

	1998 (403) Estab.		1997 (563) Estab.		1996 (540) Estab.	
	$	%	$	%	$	%
Cash	67,695	16.0	53,024	15.4	48,789	16.4
Accounts Receivable	180,238	42.6	142,200	41.3	119,593	40.2
Notes Receivable	1,269	.3	1,722	.5	1,190	.4
Inventory	49,925	11.8	42,694	12.4	40,757	13.7
Other Current Assets	23,693	5.6	17,560	5.1	15,172	5.1
Total Current Assets	322,820	76.3	257,200	74.7	225,501	75.8
Fixed Assets	76,580	18.1	66,796	19.4	58,904	19.8
Other Non-current Assets	23,693	5.6	20,314	5.9	13,090	4.4
Total Assets	423,093	100.0	344,310	100.0	297,495	100.0
Accounts Payable	87,580	20.7	68,862	20.0	58,607	19.7
Bank Loans	846	.2	-	-	-	-
Notes Payable	14,385	3.4	11,018	3.2	12,792	4.3
Other Current Liabilities	59,233	14.0	49,236	14.3	39,864	13.4
Total Current Liabilities	162,044	38.3	129,116	37.5	111,263	37.4
Other Long Term	48,656	11.5	43,727	12.7	35,997	12.1
Deferred Credits	1,269	.3	344	.1	297	.1
Net Worth	211,123	49.9	171,122	49.7	149,937	50.4
Total Liabilities & Net Worth	423,092	100.0	344,309	100.0	297,494	100.0
Net Sales	1,329,550	100.0	1,190,857	100.0	1,037,456	100.0
Gross Profits	468,002	35.2	425,136	35.7	374,522	36.1
Net Profit After Tax	67,807	5.1	59,543	5.0	43,573	4.2
Working Capital	160,775	-	128,084	-	114,238	-

Source: Dun & Bradstreet. Data in this table are copyright (c) 1999 of Dun & Bradstreet. Reprinted by special arrangement with D&B. *Notes:* Values in parentheses above columns indicate the number of establishments in the sample. Data shown are for all companies.

D&B KEY BUSINESS RATIOS: SIC 1793

	1998			1997			1996		
	UQ	MED	LQ	UQ	MED	LQ	UQ	MED	LQ
Solvency									
Quick ratio	2.6	1.5	1.0	2.7	1.5	1.0	2.8	1.6	1.0
Current ratio	3.6	2.1	1.4	3.7	2.1	1.4	3.8	2.1	1.5
Current liabilities/Net worth (%)	28.3	73.5	149.9	28.7	65.1	146.4	26.0	68.8	150.3
Current liabilities/Inventory (%)	108.6	219.5	436.2	113.7	226.8	454.8	99.9	190.6	375.5
Total liabilities/Net worth (%)	35.6	94.4	185.4	39.8	92.1	180.1	34.0	89.7	189.7
Fixed assets/Net worth (%)	12.2	25.2	50.7	14.4	27.8	59.2	13.0	28.9	57.2
Efficiency									
Collection period (days)	28.1	48.6	71.2	31.6	47.5	65.9	30.3	44.7	65.6
Sales to Inventory	72.0	33.2	17.5	62.7	30.3	16.6	52.4	26.3	15.3
Assets/Sales (%)	21.1	29.8	38.9	21.8	29.0	39.9	22.0	28.9	38.7
Sales/Net Working Capital	18.0	8.6	5.3	15.3	8.3	5.4	15.3	8.3	5.2
Accounts payable/Sales (%)	3.2	5.8	9.5	3.2	5.5	9.0	3.1	5.3	9.3
Profitability									
Return - Sales (%)	8.9	3.8	1.3	7.6	3.2	1.3	6.6	2.9	1.0
Return - Assets (%)	27.7	12.1	3.6	23.3	10.0	3.7	20.3	8.2	2.8
Return - Net Worth (%)	58.7	27.8	8.2	49.3	20.4	9.1	43.8	18.8	5.8

Source: Dun & Bradstreet. Data in this table are copyright (c) 1999 of Dun & Bradstreet. Reprinted by special arrangement with D&B. *Note:* UQ stands for "Upper Quartile" and represents the top 25 percent of sample; MED stands for "Median"; and LQ stands for "Lower Quartile" and represents the lowest 25 percent.

D&B INDUSTRY NORMS: SIC 1794 - EXCAVATION WORK

	1998 (1001) Estab.		1997 (1409) Estab.		1996 (1388) Estab.	
	$	%	$	%	$	%
Cash	116,640	12.7	101,399	12.1	78,545	12.6
Accounts Receivable	230,525	25.1	208,665	24.9	145,246	23.3
Notes Receivable	5,511	.6	5,028	.6	3,740	.6
Inventory	13,776	1.5	12,570	1.5	8,727	1.4
Other Current Assets	57,861	6.3	55,309	6.6	40,519	6.5
Total Current Assets	424,313	46.2	382,971	45.7	276,777	44.4
Fixed Assets	456,458	49.7	413,139	49.3	315,426	50.6
Other Non-current Assets	37,656	4.1	41,901	5.0	31,169	5.0
Total Assets	918,427	100.0	838,011	100.0	623,372	100.0
Accounts Payable	94,598	10.3	91,343	10.9	62,337	10.0
Bank Loans	1,837	.2	838	.1	-	-
Notes Payable	41,329	4.5	34,358	4.1	26,182	4.2
Other Current Liabilities	131,335	14.3	134,082	16.0	92,259	14.8
Total Current Liabilities	269,099	29.3	260,621	31.1	180,778	29.0
Other Long Term	195,625	21.3	175,982	21.0	138,389	22.2
Deferred Credits	4,592	.5	3,352	.4	2,493	.4
Net Worth	449,111	48.9	398,055	47.5	301,712	48.4
Total Liabilities & Net Worth	918,427	100.0	838,010	100.0	623,372	100.0
Net Sales	1,727,156	100.0	1,541,250	100.0	1,300,605	100.0
Gross Profits	571,689	33.1	493,200	32.0	433,101	33.3
Net Profit After Tax	107,084	6.2	81,686	5.3	75,435	5.8
Working Capital	155,214	-	122,350	-	95,999	-

Source: Dun & Bradstreet. Data in this table are copyright (c) 1999 of Dun & Bradstreet. Reprinted by special arrangement with D&B. *Notes:* Values in parentheses above columns indicate the number of establishments in the sample. Data shown are for all companies.

D&B KEY BUSINESS RATIOS: SIC 1794

	1998			1997			1996		
	UQ	MED	LQ	UQ	MED	LQ	UQ	MED	LQ
Solvency									
Quick ratio	2.4	1.3	.8	2.2	1.2	.7	2.4	1.2	.7
Current ratio	2.8	1.6	1.0	2.7	1.5	1.0	3.1	1.6	1.0
Current liabilities/Net worth (%)	21.8	54.7	110.9	22.0	56.3	119.9	20.2	49.7	111.9
Current liabilities/Inventory (%)	136.2	364.8	588.9	159.1	321.9	512.6	148.5	365.9	647.6
Total liabilities/Net worth (%)	42.8	95.6	194.3	44.3	106.2	209.7	39.4	94.4	194.4
Fixed assets/Net worth (%)	58.3	99.2	153.4	60.0	101.8	168.7	58.9	99.3	163.8
Efficiency									
Collection period (days)	31.8	51.8	77.4	30.7	52.6	77.0	29.9	47.3	70.5
Sales to Inventory	204.3	77.6	28.0	207.5	74.4	31.0	189.1	99.1	34.0
Assets/Sales (%)	38.3	52.8	73.4	38.6	52.4	72.4	36.1	50.8	71.7
Sales/Net Working Capital	17.9	8.5	4.8	19.1	8.6	4.8	17.6	9.5	5.0
Accounts payable/Sales (%)	2.2	4.8	9.2	2.3	4.9	9.1	1.9	4.6	8.5
Profitability									
Return - Sales (%)	10.0	4.7	1.7	9.2	3.9	1.0	10.5	4.1	1.2
Return - Assets (%)	16.6	8.2	2.9	15.3	7.1	1.6	17.8	7.5	2.0
Return - Net Worth (%)	38.0	18.3	6.6	32.8	15.5	3.9	39.3	17.5	4.8

Source: Dun & Bradstreet. Data in this table are copyright (c) 1999 of Dun & Bradstreet. Reprinted by special arrangement with D&B. *Note:* UQ stands for "Upper Quartile" and represents the top 25 percent of sample; MED stands for "Median"; and LQ stands for "Lower Quartile" and represents the lowest 25 percent.

D&B INDUSTRY NORMS: SIC 1795 - WRECKING AND DEMOLITION WORK

	1998 (110) Estab.		1997 (147) Estab.		1996 (145) Estab.	
	$	%	$	%	$	%
Cash	107,065	11.7	96,797	10.1	78,074	11.0
Accounts Receivable	292,828	32.0	307,643	32.1	200,863	28.3
Notes Receivable	915	.1	-	-	2,839	.4
Inventory	11,896	1.3	16,293	1.7	12,066	1.7
Other Current Assets	74,122	8.1	81,463	8.5	70,267	9.9
Total Current Assets	486,826	53.2	502,196	52.4	364,109	51.3
Fixed Assets	390,743	42.7	397,732	41.5	303,070	42.7
Other Non-current Assets	37,519	4.1	58,462	6.1	42,586	6.0
Total Assets	915,088	100.0	958,390	100.0	709,765	100.0
Accounts Payable	114,386	12.5	115,007	12.0	78,074	11.0
Bank Loans	-	-	-	-	710	.1
Notes Payable	37,519	4.1	51,753	5.4	34,778	4.9
Other Current Liabilities	140,924	15.4	162,926	17.0	112,853	15.9
Total Current Liabilities	292,829	32.0	329,686	34.4	226,415	31.9
Other Long Term	189,423	20.7	177,302	18.5	134,146	18.9
Deferred Credits	915	.1	4,792	.5	7,098	1.0
Net Worth	431,922	47.2	446,610	46.6	342,107	48.2
Total Liabilities & Net Worth	915,089	100.0	958,390	100.0	709,766	100.0
Net Sales	1,696,002	100.0	2,042,520	100.0	1,507,994	100.0
Gross Profits	588,513	34.7	708,754	34.7	544,386	36.1
Net Profit After Tax	111,936	6.6	110,296	5.4	87,464	5.8
Working Capital	193,999	-	172,510	-	137,694	-

Source: Dun & Bradstreet. Data in this table are copyright (c) 1999 of Dun & Bradstreet. Reprinted by special arrangement with D&B. *Notes:* Values in parentheses above columns indicate the number of establishments in the sample. Data shown are for all companies.

D&B KEY BUSINESS RATIOS: SIC 1795

	1998			1997			1996		
	UQ	MED	LQ	UQ	MED	LQ	UQ	MED	LQ
Solvency									
Quick ratio	2.4	1.4	.8	2.1	1.3	.7	2.3	1.3	.8
Current ratio	3.3	1.8	.9	2.7	1.7	1.2	2.9	1.7	1.1
Current liabilities/Net worth (%)	23.5	48.5	126.6	30.6	69.4	130.0	24.3	53.5	140.1
Current liabilities/Inventory (%)	261.8	496.1	643.6	136.8	436.5	688.2	183.1	316.0	583.8
Total liabilities/Net worth (%)	41.0	97.6	239.6	53.5	119.8	219.0	49.2	110.2	208.4
Fixed assets/Net worth (%)	44.5	91.5	148.1	43.0	82.1	149.3	47.4	87.5	153.3
Efficiency									
Collection period (days)	39.5	58.0	78.8	30.0	48.0	68.9	32.5	44.2	77.8
Sales to Inventory	44.8	26.4	17.4	107.4	61.2	19.2	311.2	63.2	31.0
Assets/Sales (%)	33.1	46.6	71.3	32.6	47.2	69.2	31.5	48.7	67.6
Sales/Net Working Capital	12.0	8.9	5.0	19.0	9.1	4.5	20.4	9.3	4.9
Accounts payable/Sales (%)	2.3	5.0	11.0	2.6	4.8	8.5	2.5	4.6	8.4
Profitability									
Return - Sales (%)	12.3	4.8	1.2	10.9	4.2	.8	11.4	3.9	.6
Return - Assets (%)	22.7	7.1	.6	19.3	7.5	1.5	16.5	5.5	.5
Return - Net Worth (%)	43.1	13.7	1.5	40.6	15.5	2.5	40.2	13.5	1.8

Source: Dun & Bradstreet. Data in this table are copyright (c) 1999 of Dun & Bradstreet. Reprinted by special arrangement with D&B. *Note:* UQ stands for "Upper Quartile" and represents the top 25 percent of sample; MED stands for "Median"; and LQ stands for "Lower Quartile" and represents the lowest 25 percent.

D&B INDUSTRY NORMS: SIC 1796 - INSTALLING BUILDING EQUIPMENT, NEC

	1998 (214) Estab.		1997 (318) Estab.		1996 (276) Estab.	
	$	%	$	%	$	%
Cash	118,176	14.8	103,550	13.4	93,200	14.2
Accounts Receivable	328,178	41.1	316,833	41.0	254,002	38.7
Notes Receivable	7,186	.9	7,728	1.0	4,594	.7
Inventory	29,544	3.7	32,456	4.2	30,191	4.6
Other Current Assets	63,879	8.0	74,185	9.6	53,163	8.1
Total Current Assets	546,963	68.5	534,752	69.2	435,150	66.3
Fixed Assets	207,607	26.0	205,555	26.6	190,337	29.0
Other Non-current Assets	43,917	5.5	32,456	4.2	30,848	4.7
Total Assets	798,487	100.0	772,763	100.0	656,335	100.0
Accounts Payable	109,393	13.7	112,051	14.5	88,605	13.5
Bank Loans	3,194	.4	773	.1	-	-
Notes Payable	39,924	5.0	40,956	5.3	24,941	3.8
Other Current Liabilities	136,541	17.1	136,006	17.6	110,264	16.8
Total Current Liabilities	289,052	36.2	289,786	37.5	223,810	34.1
Other Long Term	83,841	10.5	95,050	12.3	74,822	11.4
Deferred Credits	3,992	.5	3,091	.4	2,625	.4
Net Worth	421,601	52.8	384,836	49.8	355,077	54.1
Total Liabilities & Net Worth	798,486	100.0	772,763	100.0	656,334	100.0
Net Sales	2,207,646	100.0	2,487,936	100.0	2,177,508	100.0
Gross Profits	801,375	36.3	796,140	32.0	753,418	34.6
Net Profit After Tax	121,421	5.5	89,566	3.6	121,940	5.6
Working Capital	257,912	-	244,966	-	211,340	-

Source: Dun & Bradstreet. Data in this table are copyright (c) 1999 of Dun & Bradstreet. Reprinted by special arrangement with D&B. *Notes:* Values in parentheses above columns indicate the number of establishments in the sample. Data shown are for all companies.

D&B KEY BUSINESS RATIOS: SIC 1796

	1998			1997			1996		
	UQ	MED	LQ	UQ	MED	LQ	UQ	MED	LQ
Solvency									
Quick ratio	3.9	1.5	1.0	2.7	1.4	.9	3.1	1.6	1.0
Current ratio	4.2	1.8	1.3	3.3	1.8	1.3	3.7	2.0	1.4
Current liabilities/Net worth (%)	19.3	60.1	130.3	26.8	72.3	156.1	19.7	65.2	125.2
Current liabilities/Inventory (%)	172.2	292.6	414.8	146.9	326.8	477.2	143.2	297.8	617.6
Total liabilities/Net worth (%)	26.4	78.2	169.4	35.2	97.0	201.3	29.5	86.3	167.4
Fixed assets/Net worth (%)	15.6	36.3	79.2	20.5	48.2	105.0	20.3	51.1	98.8
Efficiency									
Collection period (days)	39.3	54.8	78.1	33.6	55.1	75.2	35.8	50.4	69.6
Sales to Inventory	112.2	33.8	16.7	101.5	42.8	19.3	144.6	44.1	16.6
Assets/Sales (%)	23.8	35.6	48.8	24.7	33.8	46.4	23.6	33.5	48.0
Sales/Net Working Capital	15.5	8.3	4.6	15.7	10.3	6.0	15.0	8.7	5.1
Accounts payable/Sales (%)	2.2	4.2	7.8	2.3	4.3	8.7	2.0	4.2	7.8
Profitability									
Return - Sales (%)	9.6	3.6	1.1	6.8	2.6	.7	8.7	3.9	1.4
Return - Assets (%)	18.3	7.9	2.3	17.7	7.6	1.6	20.0	10.5	3.8
Return - Net Worth (%)	38.2	15.4	6.0	35.9	17.4	4.3	44.0	18.9	8.0

Source: Dun & Bradstreet. Data in this table are copyright (c) 1999 of Dun & Bradstreet. Reprinted by special arrangement with D&B. *Note:* UQ stands for "Upper Quartile" and represents the top 25 percent of sample; MED stands for "Median"; and LQ stands for "Lower Quartile" and represents the lowest 25 percent.

D&B INDUSTRY NORMS: SIC 1799 - SPECIAL TRADE CONTRACTORS, NEC

	1998 (1579) Estab.		1997 (2221) Estab.		1996 (2097) Estab.	
	$	%	$	%	$	%
Cash	78,980	15.3	69,305	15.3	56,669	15.1
Accounts Receivable	178,091	34.5	158,087	34.9	128,724	34.3
Notes Receivable	3,097	.6	2,718	.6	2,627	.7
Inventory	43,878	8.5	40,314	8.9	34,151	9.1
Other Current Assets	42,329	8.2	38,050	8.4	31,524	8.4
Total Current Assets	346,375	67.1	308,474	68.1	253,695	67.6
Fixed Assets	137,827	26.7	118,678	26.2	100,202	26.7
Other Non-current Assets	32,005	6.2	25,819	5.7	21,392	5.7
Total Assets	516,207	100.0	452,971	100.0	375,289	100.0
Accounts Payable	72,269	14.0	68,399	15.1	54,792	14.6
Bank Loans	1,549	.3	-	-	-	-
Notes Payable	19,100	3.7	20,384	4.5	16,513	4.4
Other Current Liabilities	86,207	16.7	77,458	17.1	63,049	16.8
Total Current Liabilities	179,125	34.7	166,241	36.7	134,354	35.8
Other Long Term	66,591	12.9	58,433	12.9	51,790	13.8
Deferred Credits	1,549	.3	906	.2	1,126	.3
Net Worth	268,944	52.1	227,391	50.2	188,020	50.1
Total Liabilities & Net Worth	516,209	100.0	452,971	100.0	375,290	100.0
Net Sales	1,591,434	100.0	1,437,980	100.0	1,289,817	100.0
Gross Profits	563,368	35.4	498,979	34.7	447,566	34.7
Net Profit After Tax	77,980	4.9	69,023	4.8	59,332	4.6
Working Capital	167,251	-	142,233	-	119,342	-

Source: Dun & Bradstreet. Data in this table are copyright (c) 1999 of Dun & Bradstreet. Reprinted by special arrangement with D&B. *Notes:* Values in parentheses above columns indicate the number of establishments in the sample. Data shown are for all companies.

D&B KEY BUSINESS RATIOS: SIC 1799

	1998			1997			1996		
	UQ	MED	LQ	UQ	MED	LQ	UQ	MED	LQ
Solvency									
Quick ratio	2.9	1.5	.9	2.7	1.4	.8	2.8	1.4	.9
Current ratio	3.9	2.0	1.3	3.7	1.9	1.3	3.7	1.9	1.3
Current liabilities/Net worth (%)	22.0	55.9	129.1	24.4	62.9	145.9	21.9	62.4	138.2
Current liabilities/Inventory (%)	96.6	191.1	402.5	99.6	194.9	405.0	101.7	194.1	436.5
Total liabilities/Net worth (%)	31.8	79.7	174.2	34.9	85.5	194.9	35.8	86.1	194.8
Fixed assets/Net worth (%)	20.5	41.8	84.9	20.3	42.1	87.8	19.8	42.3	87.0
Efficiency									
Collection period (days)	26.7	45.8	69.4	27.0	46.4	71.1	25.9	44.9	69.7
Sales to Inventory	82.0	30.5	14.4	83.7	30.1	13.9	88.2	32.5	13.8
Assets/Sales (%)	22.7	32.9	45.6	22.3	32.3	45.7	22.1	31.6	44.5
Sales/Net Working Capital	16.4	8.5	5.1	17.2	9.2	5.2	16.8	9.1	5.3
Accounts payable/Sales (%)	1.9	3.8	7.4	2.1	4.3	8.2	2.0	4.3	7.9
Profitability									
Return - Sales (%)	8.8	3.6	1.1	8.3	3.2	1.0	8.0	3.0	.9
Return - Assets (%)	22.5	8.8	3.0	22.0	8.8	2.7	21.6	8.8	2.4
Return - Net Worth (%)	49.2	20.4	6.1	49.0	19.6	5.4	47.5	19.1	6.5

Source: Dun & Bradstreet. Data in this table are copyright (c) 1999 of Dun & Bradstreet. Reprinted by special arrangement with D&B. *Note:* UQ stands for "Upper Quartile" and represents the top 25 percent of sample; MED stands for "Median"; and LQ stands for "Lower Quartile" and represents the lowest 25 percent.

D&B INDUSTRY NORMS: SIC 7353 - HEAVY CONSTRUCTION EQUIPMENT RENTAL

	1998 (256) Estab.		1997 (341) Estab.		1996 (338) Estab.	
	$	%	$	%	$	%
Cash	145,366	9.7	130,548	10.1	98,177	10.6
Accounts Receivable	310,215	20.7	231,368	17.9	164,863	17.8
Notes Receivable	10,490	.7	11,633	.9	4,631	.5
Inventory	113,895	7.6	89,186	6.9	60,203	6.5
Other Current Assets	65,939	4.4	59,458	4.6	47,236	5.1
Total Current Assets	645,905	43.1	522,193	40.4	375,110	40.5
Fixed Assets	759,802	50.7	666,959	51.6	475,138	51.3
Other Non-current Assets	92,915	6.2	103,404	8.0	75,948	8.2
Total Assets	1,498,622	100.0	1,292,556	100.0	926,196	100.0
Accounts Payable	109,399	7.3	87,894	6.8	67,612	7.3
Bank Loans	-	-	-	-	926	.1
Notes Payable	109,399	7.3	91,771	7.1	52,793	5.7
Other Current Liabilities	230,788	15.4	191,298	14.8	134,298	14.5
Total Current Liabilities	449,586	30.0	370,963	28.7	255,629	27.6
Other Long Term	337,190	22.5	301,166	23.3	213,951	23.1
Deferred Credits	4,496	.3	3,878	.3	2,779	.3
Net Worth	707,350	47.2	616,549	47.7	453,836	49.0
Total Liabilities & Net Worth	1,498,622	100.0	1,292,556	100.0	926,195	100.0
Net Sales	1,698,462	100.0	1,486,580	100.0	1,224,365	100.0
Gross Profits	847,533	49.9	741,803	49.9	601,163	49.1
Net Profit After Tax	129,083	7.6	104,061	7.0	80,808	6.6
Working Capital	196,320	-	151,229	-	119,479	-

Source: Dun & Bradstreet. Data in this table are copyright (c) 1999 of Dun & Bradstreet. Reprinted by special arrangement with D&B. *Notes:* Values in parentheses above columns indicate the number of establishments in the sample. Data shown are for all companies.

D&B KEY BUSINESS RATIOS: SIC 7353

	1998			1997			1996		
	UQ	MED	LQ	UQ	MED	LQ	UQ	MED	LQ
Solvency									
Quick ratio	2.3	1.0	.5	2.0	1.0	.5	2.3	1.0	.5
Current ratio	2.7	1.4	.9	3.1	1.4	.8	2.8	1.5	.8
Current liabilities/Net worth (%)	22.5	55.9	131.8	20.6	53.3	115.0	20.0	46.8	118.9
Current liabilities/Inventory (%)	90.4	167.4	490.2	81.8	241.3	480.0	85.7	241.2	421.1
Total liabilities/Net worth (%)	42.3	108.0	252.0	36.7	103.3	239.0	31.6	102.9	196.6
Fixed assets/Net worth (%)	50.7	104.8	195.5	51.1	103.2	195.8	47.0	96.6	188.4
Efficiency									
Collection period (days)	31.6	50.4	73.8	32.5	47.1	72.3	29.2	47.5	71.0
Sales to Inventory	60.1	19.4	6.0	56.8	21.6	9.3	64.0	23.4	8.7
Assets/Sales (%)	55.8	80.4	124.1	57.1	79.2	117.1	54.5	76.9	119.7
Sales/Net Working Capital	17.2	7.1	3.7	15.6	6.0	2.9	13.3	6.1	2.6
Accounts payable/Sales (%)	2.0	4.1	9.1	2.6	5.0	9.7	2.5	4.6	7.9
Profitability									
Return - Sales (%)	15.1	5.5	1.1	12.3	5.3	1.5	11.1	4.5	.8
Return - Assets (%)	13.0	6.2	1.2	13.6	6.1	1.7	12.3	5.4	.7
Return - Net Worth (%)	35.1	15.6	4.3	32.2	14.3	4.6	29.4	12.2	1.6

Source: Dun & Bradstreet. Data in this table are copyright (c) 1999 of Dun & Bradstreet. Reprinted by special arrangement with D&B. *Note:* UQ stands for "Upper Quartile" and represents the top 25 percent of sample; MED stands for "Median"; and LQ stands for "Lower Quartile" and represents the lowest 25 percent.

This chapter presents brief profiles of 1,000 companies in the Construction sector. Companies are public, private, and elements of public companies ("public family members").

Each entry features the *D-U-N-S* access number for the company, the company name, its parent (if applicable), address, telephone, sales, employees, the company's primary SIC classification, a brief description of the company's business activity, and the name and title of its chairman, president, or other high-ranking officer. If the company is an exporter, importer, or both, the fact is indicated by the abbreviations EXP, IMP, and IMP EXP shown facing the *D-U-N-S* number.

Rankings of these companies are shown in Chapter 5. Additional financial data—on an aggregated, industry level—are shown in Chapter 3.

This product includes proprietary data of Dun & Bradstreet, Inc.

D-U-N-S 08-034-4989
20TH CENTURY CONSTRUCTION CO
2167 Mentor Ave, Painesville, OH 44077
Phone: (440) 951-5777
Sales: $100,000,000   *Employees:* 5
Company Type: Private   *Employees here:* 5
SIC: 1521
  Contractor of new single-family homes
Brian Pratt, President

D-U-N-S 96-590-5052
A 7 JOINT VENTURE
20 W Howell St, Dorchester, MA
Phone: (617) 265-5200
Sales: $72,275,000   *Employees:* 60
Company Type: Private   *Employees here:* 60
SIC: 1629
  Heavy construction contractor
Alfred P Minervini, President

D-U-N-S 18-652-0383
A & L INDUSTRIAL CONSTRUCTION & MAINTENANCE
1440a E Shipley Ferry Rd, Kingsport, TN 37663
Phone: (423) 239-3826
Sales: $106,800,000   *Employees:* 840
Company Type: Private   *Employees here:* 840
SIC: 1541
  Industrial building construction
Danny J Bateman, President

D-U-N-S 00-791-2025
A C AND S, INC
  (Parent: IREX Corp)
120 N Lime St, Lancaster, PA 17602
Phone: (717) 397-3631
Sales: $99,034,000   *Employees:* 800
Company Type: Public Family Member   *Employees here:* 1
SIC: 1742
  Insulation contractor whol insulation materials & installs fire
   penetration seals
Victor Davidson, President

D-U-N-S 86-939-4627
A V PARTNERSHIP
6 Executive Cir Ste 250, Irvine, CA 92614
Phone: (949) 250-7700
Sales: $100,000,000   *Employees:* 70
Company Type: Private   *Employees here:* 70
SIC: 1521
  Contractor of single-family homes
Ron J Newitt, President

D-U-N-S 36-158-2745
ABLE TELCOM HOLDING CORP
1601 Forum Pl Ste 1110, West Palm Beach, FL 33401
Phone: (561) 688-0400
Sales: $217,481,000   *Employees:* 2,000
Company Type: Public   *Employees here:* 8
SIC: 1623
  Telecommunications installation & service traffic
   management systems & services
Philip M Beshara, President

D-U-N-S 06-452-3459
ABRAMS CONSTRUCTION, INC.
  (Parent: Abrams Industries Inc)
1945 The Exchange Ste 350, Atlanta, GA 30339
Phone: (770) 952-3555
Sales: $146,619,000   *Employees:* 80
Company Type: Public Family Member   *Employees here:* 80
SIC: 1542
  General contractor-nonresidential & industrial buildings
Bobby L Moore Jr, President

D-U-N-S 00-692-4617
ABRAMS INDUSTRIES INC
1945 The Exchange SE, Atlanta, GA 30339
Phone: (770) 953-0304
Sales: $178,591,000   *Employees:* 250
Company Type: Public   *Employees here:* 8
SIC: 1541
  Engages in commercial construction mfg store fixtures &
   displays & develops owns & manages shopping centers &
   office buildings
Jack Breslin, President

D-U-N-S 10-399-4489
ABRAMS INTERNATIONAL INC
111 Congress Ave Ste 2400, Austin, TX 78701
Phone: (512) 322-4000
Sales: $110,000,000   *Employees:* 600
Company Type: Private   *Employees here:* 26
SIC: 1611
  Highway street bridge & dam construction
Sidney E Blandford III, Vice-President

D-U-N-S 00-683-5029
ABSHER CONSTRUCTION CO
8121 Shaw Rd E, Puyallup, WA 98372
Phone: (253) 845-9544
Sales: $70,088,000   *Employees:* 150
Company Type: Private   *Employees here:* 150
SIC: 1542
  General contractor of schools hospitals & other commercial
   buildings
Bryan L Bossier, President

D-U-N-S 18-544-6473
ACTUS CORP/SUNDT, JOINT VENTURE
221 Gateway Rd W Ste 405, Napa, CA 94558
Phone: (707) 252-7511
Sales: $100,000,000   *Employees:* 100
Company Type: Private   *Employees here:* 10
SIC: 1521
  Single-family house construction
Ted C Kennedy, Chairman of the Board

D-U-N-S 08-752-5762
ADC SYSTEMS INTEGRATION, INC.
  (Parent: ADC Telecommunications Inc)
50 Industrial Dr, Chickamauga, GA 30707
Phone: (706) 375-5203
Sales: $130,000,000   *Employees:* 1,000
Company Type: Public Family Member   *Employees here:* 275
SIC: 1731
  Install engineer furnish & telecommunication related
   products
Clark McLellan, Branch Manager

D-U-N-S 08-840-3233
ADCO ELECTRICAL CORP
380 Chelsea Rd, Staten Island, NY 10314
Phone: (718) 494-4400
Sales: $94,928,000   *Employees:* 400
Company Type: Private   *Employees here:* 400
SIC: 1731
  Electrical and communications contractor

D-U-N-S 00-977-0454
ADOLFSON & PETERSON, INC
6701 W 23rd St, Minneapolis, MN 55426
Phone: (612) 544-1561

Sales: $206,000,000   *Employees:* 350
Company Type: Private   *Employees here:* 260
SIC: 1542
   General contractors commercial & industrial buildings &
   apartments
Bob Calderone, Branch Manager

D-U-N-S 00-797-8901
ADVANCE MECHANICAL SYSTEMS INC
2080 S Carboy Rd, Mount Prospect, IL 60056
Phone: (847) 593-2510
Sales: $70,000,000   *Employees:* 225
Company Type: Private   *Employees here:* 225
SIC: 1711
   Plumbing heating air conditioning ventilation refrigeration
   water treatment and pipeline construction
Mary Fortenberry, Branch Manager

D-U-N-S 96-611-4563
AHH HOLDINGS INC
108 Park Place Blvd, Kissimmee, FL 34741
Phone: (407) 846-4130
Sales: $68,366,000   *Employees:* NA
Company Type: Private   *Employees here:* NA
SIC: 1531
   New single-family home sales
Stanley Neff, Branch Manager

D-U-N-S 07-631-9219
AIR SYSTEMS, INC
381 Stockton Ave, San Jose, CA 95126
Phone: (408) 280-1666
Sales: $90,969,000   *Employees:* 120
Company Type: Private   *Employees here:* 120
SIC: 1711
   Mechanical contractor & maintenance
Bruce E McMurray, President

D-U-N-S 13-195-5213
AIRDEX AIR CONDITIONING CORP
   (Parent: Modern Air Conditioning Inc)
9292 49th St, Pinellas Park, FL 33782
Phone: (727) 522-7247
Sales: $150,000,000   *Employees:* 12
Company Type: Public Family Member   *Employees here:* 12
SIC: 1711
   Air conditioning contractor
Garry Brav, President

D-U-N-S 05-128-3901
AIRTRON INC
   (Parent: Group Maintenance America)
7813 N Dixie Dr, Dayton, OH 45414
Phone: (937) 898-0826
Sales: $98,000,000   *Employees:* 600
Company Type: Public Family Member   *Employees here:* 10
SIC: 1711
   Heating & air conditioning contractor
John Losey, President

D-U-N-S 00-581-2276
AJAX PAVING INDUSTRIES INC
   (Parent: HHJ Holdings Ltd)
1 Ajax Dr Ste 200, Madison Heights, MI 48071
Phone: (248) 398-2300
Sales: $100,000,000   *Employees:* 300
Company Type: Private   *Employees here:* 50
SIC: 1611
   Road paving contractor & mfg asphalt paving mixtures
Thomas Amon, President

D-U-N-S 15-093-7027
ALBERICI CORP
2150 Kienlen Ave, St. Louis, MO 63121
Phone: (314) 261-2611
Sales: $531,328,000   *Employees:* 1,500
Company Type: Private   *Employees here:* 40
SIC: 1541
   Holding company general contractor industrial institutional
   commercial & environmental
Brooks T Mancini, President

D-U-N-S 00-945-0362
ALBERT C KOBAYASHI INC
94-535 Ukee St, Waipahu, HI 96797
Phone: (808) 671-6460
Sales: $104,630,000   *Employees:* 175
Company Type: Private   *Employees here:* 169
SIC: 1542
   General contractor of commercial buildings single-family
   residences townhouses and condominiums
Richard Godbout, President

D-U-N-S 01-776-7161
ALBERT M HIGLEY CO
2926 Chester Ave, Cleveland, OH 44114
Phone: (216) 861-2050
Sales: $80,468,000   *Employees:* 180
Company Type: Private   *Employees here:* 180
SIC: 1542
   Commercial & institutional building contractor
Paul Goldman, President

D-U-N-S 00-554-7393
ALDRIDGE ELECTRIC INC (DEL)
28572 N Bradley Rd, Libertyville, IL 60048
Phone: (847) 680-5200
Sales: $80,000,000   *Employees:* 467
Company Type: Private   *Employees here:* 325
SIC: 1731
   Electrical contractor
Mike Morash, President

D-U-N-S 06-739-8685
ALLAN A MYERS INC
   (Parent: America Infrastructure Inc)
1805 Berks Rd, Worcester, PA 19490
Phone: (610) 584-6020
Sales: $118,231,000   *Employees:* 760
Company Type: Private   *Employees here:* 150
SIC: 1629
   Site development contractor & heavy highway & civil
   construction
Dennis Babcock, President

D-U-N-S 01-189-7188
AMBASSADOR CONSTRUCTION CO
317 Madison Ave Fl 12, New York, NY 10017
Phone: (212) 922-1020
Sales: $75,000,000   *Employees:* 46
Company Type: Private   *Employees here:* 46
SIC: 1542
   General contractor of commercial building alterations
J D Baker, President

D-U-N-S 18-797-6139
AMEC HOLDINGS INC
1633 Broadway Fl 24, New York, NY 10019
Phone: (212) 484-0300
Sales: $89,100,000   *Employees:* 700
Company Type: Private   *Employees here:* 100
SIC: 1541
   Holding company
George L Agostini, President

D-U-N-S 04-131-3438
AMELCO CORP
19208 S Vermont Ave, Gardena, CA 90248
Phone: (310) 327-3070
Sales: $107,908,000
Company Type: Private
SIC: 1731
 Electrical mechanical & general industrial contractor
Sue Wingard, Controller

 Employees: 450
 Employees here: 60

D-U-N-S 96-947-4550
AMERALUM INC
 (Parent: BSI Holdings Inc)
1801 Oberlin Rd, Middletown, PA 17057
Phone: (717) 985-9037
Sales: $74,488,000
Company Type: Private
SIC: 1742
 Insulation contractor
F B Mewborn II, Chairman of the Board

 Employees: 730
 Employees here: 7

D-U-N-S 18-062-0254
AMERICAN BRIDGE CO
 (Parent: CEC Investment Corp)
3 Gateway Ctr Ste 1100, Pittsburgh, PA 15222
Phone: (412) 562-4400
Sales: $146,000,000
Company Type: Private
SIC: 1791
 Structural steel erection
Daniel L Baker, President

 Employees: 400
 Employees here: 75

D-U-N-S 96-589-3167
AMERICAN FENCE AND SEC CO INC
2920 N 7th St, Phoenix, AZ 85014
Phone: (602) 734-0500
Sales: $81,082,000
Company Type: Private
SIC: 1799
 Fence contractor and ret fencing materials
Carol Baker, Treasurer

 Employees: 800
 Employees here: 275

D-U-N-S 93-896-3634
AMERICAN RESIDENTIAL SERVICES
5051 Westheimer Rd, Houston, TX 77056
Phone: (713) 599-0100
Sales: $382,518,000
Company Type: Public
SIC: 1711
 Plumbing HVAC & electrical contractor repair and
  maintenance services & retail appliances
Homan Charles I, Chairman of the Board

 Employees: 4,800
 Employees here: 1,336

D-U-N-S 93-261-6949
AMERICAN SPORTS PRODUCTS GROUP
70 W Red Oak Ln, White Plains, NY 10604
Phone: (914) 697-4750
Sales: $130,000,000
Company Type: Private
SIC: 1629
 Contractor of athletic fields & mfg sporting equipment
William A Baker Jr, Partner

 Employees: 300
 Employees here: 2

D-U-N-S 17-368-1735
AMERICON, INC
 (Parent: The Babcock & Wilcox Co)
90 E Tuscarawas Ave, Barberton, OH 44203
Phone: (330) 753-4511
Sales: $87,700,000
Company Type: Public Family Member
SIC: 1711
 Holding company
Glenn S Burns, President

 Employees: 931
 Employees here: 1

D-U-N-S 09-972-4924
AMERILINK CORP
1900 E Dublin Granville R, Columbus, OH 43229
Phone: (614) 895-1313
Sales: $70,000,000
Company Type: Public
SIC: 1623
 Telecommunication design construction installation &
  networking
Danny Bakewell Jr, Partner

 Employees: 588
 Employees here: 78

D-U-N-S 04-316-9309
AMES CONSTRUCTION, INC
14420 County Road 5, Burnsville, MN 55306
Phone: (612) 435-7106
Sales: $271,597,000
Company Type: Private
SIC: 1629
 Heavy construction gold & copper open pit mining and
  highway construction
Robert J Shell, President

 Employees: 750
 Employees here: 150

D-U-N-S 18-476-8547   EXP
AMFELS, INC
Hwy 48, Brownsville, TX 78520
Phone: (956) 831-8220
Sales: $75,500,000
Company Type: Private
SIC: 1629
 Constructs & modifies oil rigs & ships & fabricator of marine
  products including ASME & ASIC products
Brian M Baldwin, Vice-President

 Employees: 660
 Employees here: 655

D-U-N-S 00-377-8412
AMREP CORP
641 Lexington Ave Fl 6, New York, NY 10022
Phone: (212) 705-4700
Sales: $171,368,000
Company Type: Public
SIC: 1521
 Single-family homes & condominium const real estate
  development magazine distributors & subscription
  fulfillment services
Haro M Bedelian, President

 Employees: 1,500
 Employees here: 70

D-U-N-S 05-818-8871
AMREP SOUTHWEST INC
 (Parent: Amrep Corp)
333 Rio Rancho Dr NE, Rio Rancho, NM 87124
Phone: (505) 892-9200
Sales: $104,832,000
Company Type: Public Family Member
SIC: 1521
 Single family new home construction and land development
Panos Papadopoulos, President

 Employees: 193
 Employees here: 112

D-U-N-S 04-741-9031
AMTECH ELEVATOR SERVICES
 (Parent: Amtech Services Inc)
13215 Penn St Ste 600, Whittier, CA 90602
Phone: (562) 698-8177
Sales: $82,068,000
Company Type: Public Family Member
SIC: 1796
 Elevator installation service & repair
Stephen B Ballard, President

 Employees: 604
 Employees here: 16

D-U-N-S 00-283-9751
ANCO INSULATIONS INC
15981 Airline Hwy, Baton Rouge, LA 70817
Phone: (225) 752-2000

Sales: $119,009,000   *Employees:* 1,800
Company Type: Private   *Employees here:* 100
SIC: 1742
 Insulation contractor
Ron Balzer, Vice-President

D-U-N-S 18-584-9387
ANDERSON COLUMBIA CO INC
2 Gordon St, Lake City, FL 32055
Phone: (904) 752-7585
Sales: $100,000,000   *Employees:* 650
Company Type: Private   *Employees here:* 225
SIC: 1611
 Highway/street construction mfg asphalt mixtures/blocks
Stephen M Mockbee, President

D-U-N-S 01-689-6532
ANGELO IAFRATE CONSTRUCTION CO
26400 Sherwood Ave, Warren, MI 48091
Phone: (810) 756-1070
Sales: $150,000,000   *Employees:* 500
Company Type: Private   *Employees here:* 75
SIC: 1611
 Road paving sewer & excavation contractor
Lionel H Barber, Treasurer

D-U-N-S 10-694-3863
ANNING-JOHNSON CO
 (Parent: Anson Industries Inc (del))
1959 Anson Dr, Melrose Park, IL 60160
Phone: (708) 681-1300
Sales: $72,000,000   *Employees:* 400
Company Type: Private   *Employees here:* 150
SIC: 1742
 Acoustical ceiling drywall fireproofing metal floor decks
  metal siding roofing & geotechnical fill contractor
Edwin W Jorden, President

D-U-N-S 04-861-1792
ANTHONY AND SYLVAN POOLS CORP
 (Parent: Essef Corp)
RR 611, Doylestown, PA 18901
Phone: (215) 348-9011
Sales: $140,000,000   *Employees:* 800
Company Type: Public Family Member   *Employees here:* 100
SIC: 1799
 Swimming pool construction
Robert E Barnhill Jr, President

D-U-N-S 01-458-2324
APAC-ALABAMA INC
 (Parent: APAC Holdings Inc)
700 37th St S, Birmingham, AL 35222
Phone: (205) 252-3456
Sales: $114,313,000   *Employees:* 450
Company Type: Public Family Member   *Employees here:* 150
SIC: 1611
 Paving contractor mfg asphalt & whol construction materials
David Pelletier, President

D-U-N-S 04-737-2602
APAC-CAROLINA INC
 (Parent: APAC Holdings Inc)
604 E New Bern Rd, Kinston, NC 28504
Phone: (252) 527-8021
Sales: $236,441,000   *Employees:* 1,000
Company Type: Public Family Member   *Employees here:* 350
SIC: 1611
 Paving contractor asphalt plants and whol construction
  materials
Donald M Barr, President

D-U-N-S 03-919-5045
APAC-FLORIDA INC
 (Parent: APAC Holdings Inc)
1451 Myrtle St, Sarasota, FL 34234
Phone: (941) 355-7178
Sales: $97,820,000   *Employees:* 600
Company Type: Public Family Member   *Employees here:* 275
SIC: 1611
 Highway paving contractor mfg asphalt and whol
  construction materials
Michael D Pattinson, President

D-U-N-S 04-123-7868
APAC-GEORGIA INC
 (Parent: APAC Holdings Inc)
3111 Port Cobb Dr SE, Smyrna, GA 30080
Phone: (404) 351-6301
Sales: $190,766,000   *Employees:* 1,500
Company Type: Public Family Member   *Employees here:* 294
SIC: 1611
 Heavy highway construction including bridges
Georges Ausseil, President

D-U-N-S 19-699-1665
APAC HOLDINGS INC
 (Parent: Ashland Inc)
900 Ashwood Pkwy Ste 700, Atlanta, GA 30338
Phone: (770) 392-5300
Sales: $1,257,143,000   *Employees:* 5,028
Company Type: Public Family Member   *Employees here:* 80
SIC: 1611
 Through subsidiaries pave highways roads airports and
  parking lots operate asphalt plants and whol construction
  materials
Kermit Moser, Vice-President

D-U-N-S 03-942-8339
APAC-MISSISSIPPI INC
 (Parent: APAC Holdings Inc)
900 Ashwood Pkwy, Atlanta, GA 30338
Phone: (770) 392-5300
Sales: $81,492,000   *Employees:* 358
Company Type: Public Family Member   *Employees here:* 6
SIC: 1611
 Paving contractor mfg asphalt and whol sand and gravel
Ben Tucker, Operations-Production-Mfg

D-U-N-S 04-187-4546
APAC-MISSOURI, INC.
 (Parent: APAC Holdings Inc)
1591 E Prathersville Rd, Columbia, MO 65202
Phone: (573) 449-0886
Sales: $115,000,000   *Employees:* 200
Company Type: Public Family Member   *Employees here:* 90
SIC: 1611
 Paving contractor
Donald M Barron, President

D-U-N-S 03-503-7381
APAC-TENNESSEE INC
 (Parent: APAC Holdings Inc)
226 Gill St, Alcoa, TN 37701
Phone: (423) 983-3100
Sales: $196,566,000   *Employees:* 400
Company Type: Public Family Member   *Employees here:* 100
SIC: 1611
 Paving contractor operates asphalt plants & whol
  construction materials
Donald L Duke, President

D-U-N-S 03-993-9236
APAC-TEXAS INC
   (Parent: APAC Holdings Inc)
2121 Irving Blvd, Dallas, TX 75207
Phone: (214) 741-3531
Sales: $69,781,000   *Employees:* 400
Company Type: Public Family Member   *Employees here:* 180
SIC: 1611
   Paving contractor & mfg asphalt
Carl Agsten, General Manager

D-U-N-S 03-523-9920
APAC-VIRGINIA INC
   (Parent: APAC Holdings Inc)
239 Eastwood Dr, Danville, VA 24540
Phone: (804) 792-4211
Sales: $89,646,000   *Employees:* 300
Company Type: Public Family Member   *Employees here:* 100
SIC: 1611
   Paving contractor and whol asphalt sand gravel and maintains
     storage facilities
Michael Barth Jr, President

D-U-N-S 03-585-4939   EXP
API GROUP, INC
2366 Rose Pl, St. Paul, MN 55113
Phone: (651) 636-4320
Sales: $369,295,000   *Employees:* 3,000
Company Type: Private   *Employees here:* 25
SIC: 1742
   Holding company conducting operations through subsidiaries
James H Eacott III, President

D-U-N-S 00-196-2042   EXP
APOGEE ENTERPRISES INC
7900 Xerxes Ave S, Minneapolis, MN 55431
Phone: (612) 835-1874
Sales: $912,831,000   *Employees:* 6,672
Company Type: Public   *Employees here:* 25
SIC: 1791
   Curtainwall window systems & related services contractor
     mfg venetian blinds auto glass repair replacement whol auto
     glass
Stephen Tamanko, President

D-U-N-S 00-955-5442
ARB INC
26000 Commercentre Dr, Lake Forest, CA 92630
Phone: (714) 630-5801
Sales: $205,220,000   *Employees:* 700
Company Type: Private   *Employees here:* 100
SIC: 1542
   Contractor of natural gas petroleum & water pipeline general
     contractor mfg & drives pre-stressed concrete pile
John Westwood, Branch Manager

D-U-N-S 14-499-4779
ARCHER WESTERN CONTRACTORS
   (Parent: The Walsh Group Ltd)
1500 NW 62nd St, Fort Lauderdale, FL 33309
Phone: (954) 938-5339
Sales: $299,527,000   *Employees:* 250
Company Type: Private   *Employees here:* 15
SIC: 1622
   Contractors of commercial buildings highways and bridges
Christophe O Bast, President

D-U-N-S 14-843-5175
ARCTIC SLOPE REGIONAL CONSTRUCTION CO
   (Parent: Arctic Slope Regional Corp)
1230 Agvik St, Barrow, AK 99723
Phone: (907) 852-8633

Sales: $120,400,000   *Employees:* 1,600
Company Type: Private   *Employees here:* 100
SIC: 1623
   Oil & gas pipeline contractors
Kim C Hall, President

D-U-N-S 11-297-5040
ARMADA/HOFFLER CONSTRUCTION CO
1435 Crossways Blvd, Chesapeake, VA 23320
Phone: (757) 366-4000
Sales: $105,954,000   *Employees:* 120
Company Type: Private   *Employees here:* 120
SIC: 1542
   Commercial industrial and institutional contractor
Steven M Lee, President

D-U-N-S 05-772-1219
ARNOLD M DIAMOND INC
333 Glen Head Rd, Glen Head, NY 11545
Phone: (516) 759-0800
Sales: $74,000,000   *Employees:* 40
Company Type: Private   *Employees here:* 10
SIC: 1629
   General contractors of heavy construction & boiler stacks
B E Battaglia, President

D-U-N-S 87-948-6165
ASHTEAD HOLDINGS, INC.
611 Templeton Ave Ste 107, Charlotte, NC 28203
Phone: (704) 348-2676
Sales: $72,600,000   *Employees:* 670
Company Type: Private   *Employees here:* 30
SIC: 7353
   Rents & whol construction equipment
David Bauerly, Chairman of the Board

D-U-N-S 19-323-8870
ASPLUNDH CONSTRUCTION CORP
   (Parent: Asplundh Subsidiary Holdings)
2 Access Rd, Patchogue, NY 11772
Phone: (516) 447-2340
Sales: $67,595,000   *Employees:* 370
Company Type: Private   *Employees here:* 230
SIC: 1731
   Electrical contractor and general construction
Steve Mara, President

D-U-N-S 00-911-3143   EXP
ATKN CO
   (Parent: Guy F Atkinson Company of California)
1005 Oak Hill Rd, Lafayette, CA 94549
Phone: (925) 299-1357
Sales: $370,500,000   *Employees:* 20
Company Type: Private   *Employees here:* 20
SIC: 1629
   Heavy & industrial construction
Frank Van Deventer, President

D-U-N-S 80-659-6441
ATLANTA ARENA CONSTRUCTORS
70 Ellis St NE, Atlanta, GA 30303
Phone: (404) 659-1970
Sales: $75,000,000   *Employees:* 15
Company Type: Private   *Employees here:* 15
SIC: 1542
   Atlanta arena construction
Robert H Baugh, Chairman of the Board

D-U-N-S 10-173-5322
ATLANTIC COAST MECHANICAL INC
   (Parent: HVAC Ltd)
5804 Lease Ln, Raleigh, NC 27613
Phone: (919) 781-6945

Sales: $100,000,000   *Employees:* 150
Company Type: Private   *Employees here:* 65
SIC: 1711
   Mechanical contractor
Larry Persinger, President

D-U-N-S 09-428-0856
ATLANTIC PLANT MAINTENANCE
   (Parent: Viceroy Inc)
3225 Pasadena Blvd, Pasadena, TX 77503
Phone: (713) 740-8000
Sales: $95,159,000   *Employees:* 470
Company Type: Public Family Member   *Employees here:* 22
SIC: 1629
   Power plant construction & pipe fabrication
Sonja Adams, Acting Controller

D-U-N-S 00-692-1365
AUCHTER CO INC
1021 Oak St, Jacksonville, FL 32204
Phone: (904) 355-3536
Sales: $76,000,000   *Employees:* 165
Company Type: Private   *Employees here:* 165
SIC: 1542
   General contractor of commercial & industrial buildings
Frank D King, President

D-U-N-S 00-896-4033
AUSTIN BRIDGE & ROAD, INC
   (Parent: Austin Industries Del Corp)
3535 Travis St Ste 300, Dallas, TX 75204
Phone: (214) 443-5500
Sales: $75,600,000   *Employees:* 600
Company Type: Private   *Employees here:* 40
SIC: 1611
   Highway paving & bridge & highway construction contractor
Benny W Rodriguez, President

D-U-N-S 19-939-6086
AUSTIN COMMERCIAL INC
   (Parent: Austin Industries Del Corp)
3535 Travis St Ste 300, Dallas, TX 75204
Phone: (214) 443-5700
Sales: $400,000,000   *Employees:* 600
Company Type: Private   *Employees here:* 596
SIC: 1542
   General contractor for commercial healthcare and hi-tech
     industries
Ronald E Bayley, President

D-U-N-S 10-583-4857
AUSTIN INDUSTRIAL INC
   (Parent: Austin Industries Del Corp)
8031 Airport Blvd, Houston, TX 77061
Phone: (713) 641-3400
Sales: $99,000,000   *Employees:* 1,050
Company Type: Private   *Employees here:* 75
SIC: 1711
   Industrial & petrochemical maintenance & industrial building
     construction
William S Carter, Chairman of the Board

D-U-N-S 06-895-5640
AUSTIN INDUSTRIES DEL CORP
3535 Travis St Ste 300, Dallas, TX 75204
Phone: (214) 443-5500
Sales: $620,000,000   *Employees:* 5,000
Company Type: Private   *Employees here:* 120
SIC: 1542
   General contractor of commercial industrial road & bridge
     construction
James F Kimsey, President

D-U-N-S 04-526-0007
AVATAR HOLDINGS INC
255 Alhambra Cir Fl 9, Miami, FL 33134
Phone: (305) 442-7000
Sales: $129,084,000   *Employees:* 1,030
Company Type: Public   *Employees here:* 100
SIC: 1521
   Community developer general contractor for single family
     homes water and sewer services
James M Becker, President

D-U-N-S 03-231-1284
B E & K CONSTRUCTION CO
   (Parent: B E & K Inc)
2000 International Park D, Birmingham, AL 35243
Phone: (205) 972-6000
Sales: $632,200,000   *Employees:* 5,000
Company Type: Private   *Employees here:* 250
SIC: 1541
   Contractor of industrial buildings
Thomas B Browne, Chairman of the Board

D-U-N-S 12-282-7819
BABCOCK & WILCOX CONSTRUCTION CO
   (Parent: Americon Inc)
90 E Tuscarawas Ave, Barberton, OH 44203
Phone: (330) 753-4511
Sales: $87,600,000   *Employees:* 930
Company Type: Public Family Member   *Employees here:* 900
SIC: 1711
   Boiler erection & repair
James B Beauchamp, Chief Executive Officer

D-U-N-S 05-910-3481
BAKER CONCRETE CONSTRUCTION
900 N Garver Rd, Monroe, OH 45050
Phone: (513) 539-4000
Sales: $247,000,000   *Employees:* 1,500
Company Type: Private   *Employees here:* 700
SIC: 1771
   Concrete contractor
Leonard Rudofsky, Treasurer

D-U-N-S 78-280-8109
BAKER/MELLON STUART CONSTRUCTION INC
   (Parent: Michael Baker Corp)
Airport Office Park Bldg, Coraopolis, PA 15108
Phone: (412) 269-7111
Sales: $110,000,000   *Employees:* 150
Company Type: Public Family Member   *Employees here:* 50
SIC: 1542
   Contractor of commercial and institutional buildings highway
     street bridge and tunnel construction and construction
     management
Brady Simmerman, Chief Financial Officer

D-U-N-S 84-473-2719
BAKER RESIDENTIAL LP
485 Washington Ave, Pleasantville, NY 10570
Phone: (914) 747-1550
Sales: $75,000,000   *Employees:* 3
Company Type: Private   *Employees here:* 3
SIC: 1531
   Operative builder
William C Hulsey, Chairman of the Board

D-U-N-S 78-305-9074
BALFOUR BEATTY CONSTRUCTION INC
   (Parent: Balfour Beatty Inc)
999 Peachtree St NE, Atlanta, GA 30309
Phone: (404) 875-0356

Sales: $237,110,000   *Employees:* 861
Company Type: Private   *Employees here:* 30
SIC: 1622
   Heavy construction contractor bridges & highways
Harry E Phillips, President

D-U-N-S 02-196-8342
BARCLAY WHITE INC
22 Cassatt Ave, Berwyn, PA 19312
Phone: (610) 296-3700
Sales: $106,492,000   *Employees:* 146
Company Type: Private   *Employees here:* 97
SIC: 1542
   Constuction manager & contractor specializing in commercial
    industrial & institutional construction
Scott Hoisington, President

D-U-N-S 02-482-9988
BARNHILL CONTRACTING CO
2311 N Main St, Tarboro, NC 27886
Phone: (252) 823-1021
Sales: $156,159,000   *Employees:* 920
Company Type: Private   *Employees here:* 120
SIC: 1611
   Highway construction commercial and industrial buildings
    private grading and asphalt laying
Kurt Watzek, President

D-U-N-S 09-926-8468
BARRETT PAVING MATERIALS INC
   (Parent: Colas Inc)
3 Becker Farm Rd, Roseland, NJ
Phone: (973) 533-1001
Sales: $203,178,000   *Employees:* 250
Company Type: Private   *Employees here:* 16
SIC: 1611
   Road paving contractor and manufactures bituminous paving
    materials
David S Weiss, Chief Financial Officer

D-U-N-S 10-869-0918
BARRY BETTE & LED DUKE INC
52 Corporate Cir Ste 1, Albany, NY 12203
Phone: (518) 452-8200
Sales: $300,000,000   *Employees:* 350
Company Type: Private   *Employees here:* 75
SIC: 1542
   Contractors consulting and management services design-build
    services and public works projects (see operations section)
James P Bebout Jr, President

D-U-N-S 08-984-0839
BASIC INDUSTRIES INC
   (Parent: Anco Industries Inc)
16055 Airline Hwy, Baton Rouge, LA 70817
Phone: (225) 752-4333
Sales: $80,000,000   *Employees:* 1,200
Company Type: Private   *Employees here:* 30
SIC: 1742
   Insulation & refractory contractor
R P Bechtel, Chairman of the Board

D-U-N-S 00-332-1833
BATSON-COOK CO
817 4th Ave, West Point, GA 31833
Phone: (706) 643-2500
Sales: $169,938,000   *Employees:* 400
Company Type: Private   *Employees here:* 75
SIC: 1542
   General contractor
M A Hickey, President

D-U-N-S 00-283-7003
BAUGH CONSTRUCTION CO INC
   (Parent: Baugh Enterprises Inc)
900 Poplar Pl S, Seattle, WA 98144
Phone: (206) 726-8000
Sales: $200,000,000   *Employees:* 300
Company Type: Private   *Employees here:* 300
SIC: 1542
   General contractor of commercial & institutional buildings
Michael Decarlo, Manager

D-U-N-S 78-328-5646
BAUGH CONSTRUCTION OREGON INC
   (Parent: Baugh Enterprises Inc)
15500 SW Jay St, Beaverton, OR 97006
Phone: (503) 641-2500
Sales: $225,000,000   *Employees:* 400
Company Type: Private   *Employees here:* 400
SIC: 1542
   Contractor commercial & institutional buildings
John Hainley, Principal

D-U-N-S 10-338-2081
BAUGH ENTERPRISES INC
900 Poplar Pl S, Seattle, WA 98144
Phone: (206) 726-8000
Sales: $221,200,000   *Employees:* 1,000
Company Type: Private   *Employees here:* 70
SIC: 1542
   General contractor of commercial institutional & industrial
    buildings
Lee Smith, Vice-President

D-U-N-S 93-160-5208
BAYLEY CONSTRUCTION, A GEN PARTNR
205 Columbia St, Seattle, WA 98104
Phone: (206) 621-8884
Sales: $170,000,000   *Employees:* 75
Company Type: Private   *Employees here:* 75
SIC: 1542
   Commercial & industrial construction
John T Mitchell, Manager

D-U-N-S 07-488-4115
BAYLOR HEALTH ENTERPRISES INC
   (Parent: Baylor Health Care System)
2625 Elm St Ste 216, Dallas, TX 75226
Phone: (214) 820-2492
Sales: $91,620,000   *Employees:* 300
Company Type: Private   *Employees here:* 100
SIC: 1542
   General contractor of hospitals
M C Wiley, Project Director

D-U-N-S 17-416-1901
BCI CONSTRUCTION, INC
   (Parent: Alternative Living Services)
453 S Webb Rd Ste 500, Wichita, KS 67207
Phone: (316) 681-3744
Sales: $182,875,000   *Employees:* 80
Company Type: Public Family Member   *Employees here:* 30
SIC: 1542
   Nonresidential construction
R M McIlhattan, President

D-U-N-S 00-661-0455
BEACON SKANSKA CONSTRUCTION CO
   (Parent: Sordoni/Skanska Construction Co)
270 Congress St, Boston, MA
Phone: (617) 574-1400

Sales: $150,000,000   *Employees:* 160
Company Type: Private   *Employees here:* 160
SIC: 1542
    Contractor specializing in new construction & remodeling of
    commercial buildings
Sam Halpern, President

D-U-N-S 17-919-1077
BEAZER HOMES ARIZONA INC
    (Parent: Beazer Homes USA Inc)
2005 W 14th St Ste 100, Tempe, AZ 85281
Phone: (602) 967-8655
Sales: $170,499,000   *Employees:* 60
Company Type: Public Family Member   *Employees here:* 60
SIC: 1521
    General contractor single family homes
Joseph A Riedel Jr, Chief Executive Officer

D-U-N-S 17-442-4994
BEAZER HOMES USA INC
5775 Peachtree Dunwoody R, Atlanta, GA 30342
Phone: (404) 250-3420
Sales: $977,409,000   *Employees:* 1,261
Company Type: Public   *Employees here:* 15
SIC: 1521
    General building contractor of single family homes
Dean De Freitas, Manager

D-U-N-S 10-340-1600
BECHTEL CONSTRUCTION CO
    (Parent: Bechtel Construction Operations Inc)
50 Beale St, San Francisco, CA 94105
Phone: (415) 768-1234
Sales: $215,000,000   *Employees:* 175
Company Type: Private   *Employees here:* 5
SIC: 1629
    Heavy construction & construction management
Joseph A Riedel Jr, Chief Executive Officer

D-U-N-S 88-474-1141
BECHTEL CONSTRUCTION OPERATIONS INC
    (Parent: Bechtel Corp)
50 Beale St, San Francisco, CA 94105
Phone: (415) 768-1234
Sales: $595,000,000   *Employees:* 1,275
Company Type: Private   *Employees here:* 25
SIC: 1541
    Industrial construction
Beers C Inc, Partner

D-U-N-S 60-692-6368
BECHTEL/PARSON, BRINKERHOFF
1 South Sta, Boston, MA
Phone: (617) 951-6000
Sales: $250,000,000   *Employees:* 850
Company Type: Private   *Employees here:* 850
SIC: 1622
    Project managers
C R Belger, President

D-U-N-S 09-248-4609
BECON CONSTRUCTION CO
    (Parent: Bechtel Construction Operations Inc)
3000 Post Oak Blvd, Houston, TX 77056
Phone: (713) 235-2000
Sales: $301,000,000   *Employees:* 285
Company Type: Private   *Employees here:* 1
SIC: 1541
    Industrial contractor
C R Belger, President

D-U-N-S 06-450-9458
BEERS CONSTRUCTION CO
    (Parent: Beers Inc)
70 Ellis St NE, Atlanta, GA 30303
Phone: (404) 659-1970
Sales: $1,074,213,000   *Employees:* 1,500
Company Type: Private   *Employees here:* 500
SIC: 1542
    Commercial building construction including office buildings
    tenant construction government public buildings and
    hospitals
Robert Burich, President

D-U-N-S 06-450-9938
BEERS INC
    (Parent: Skanska (USA) Inc)
70 Ellis St NE, Atlanta, GA 30303
Phone: (404) 659-1970
Sales: $1,436,132,000   *Employees:* 2,300
Company Type: Private   *Employees here:* 700
SIC: 1542
    Contractor of new office buildings and hospitals
Thomas F Bell, President

D-U-N-S 88-485-1197
**BELL ATLANTIC COMMUNICATIONS CONSTRUCTION
SERVICES**
    (Parent: Bell Atlantic Corp)
11750 Beltsville Dr, Beltsville, MD 20705
Phone: (301) 586-1100
Sales: $200,000,000   *Employees:* 3,000
Company Type: Public Family Member   *Employees here:* 40
SIC: 1731
    Telephone line construction
Joseph Bell, Chairman of the Board

D-U-N-S 61-298-0789
BELL CORP OF ROCHESTER
1340 Lexington Ave, Rochester, NY 14606
Phone: (716) 458-9090
Sales: $131,900,000   *Employees:* 600
Company Type: Private   *Employees here:* 100
SIC: 1542
    General contractor commercial industrial & governmental
    construction
Joseph M Bell, Chairman of the Board

D-U-N-S 06-988-6331
BELLEVUE HOLDING CO
909 Delaware Ave, Wilmington, DE 19806
Phone: (302) 655-1561
Sales: $70,000,000   *Employees:* 50
Company Type: Private   *Employees here:* 30
SIC: 1542
    Operative builders of commercial buildings
Carolyn M Pavelec, Chief Executive Officer

D-U-N-S 01-752-8402
BELMONT CONSTRUCTORS CO
    (Parent: Stone & Webster Engineering Corp)
2925 Briarpark Dr Ste 260, Houston, TX 77042
Phone: (713) 435-6300
Sales: $80,100,000   *Employees:* 700
Company Type: Public Family Member   *Employees here:* 12
SIC: 1629
    Civil mechanical structural electrical instrumentation pipe
    fabrication & wastewater treatment plants
Steve Watkins, President

D-U-N-S 02-845-8826
BERGELECTRIC CORP
5650 W Centinela Ave, Los Angeles, CA 90045
Phone: (310) 337-1377

Sales: $124,313,000   *Employees:* 900
Company Type: Private   *Employees here:* 360
SIC: 1731
    Electrical contractor
Bruce C Wardell, President

D-U-N-S 01-148-1426
BERKSHIRE POWER CO LLC
200 High St Fl 5, Boston, MA
Phone: (617) 747-9100
Sales: $89,529,000   *Employees:* 60
Company Type: Private   *Employees here:* 30
SIC: 1629
    Power plant construction
John L Brown, Chairman of the Board

D-U-N-S 60-644-7456
BERKSHIRE REALTY CO INC
    (Parent: Berkshire Companies LP)
1000 Parkwood Cir SE, Atlanta, GA 30339
Phone: (770) 955-7527
Sales: $93,002,000   *Employees:* 15
Company Type: Private   *Employees here:* 7
SIC: 1522
    Development and rehabilitation multi-family apartment units
William J Skeffington, Vice-President

D-U-N-S 07-726-2525
BERNARDS BROS INC
610 Ilex St, San Fernando, CA 91340
Phone: (818) 365-9573
Sales: $80,000,000   *Employees:* 80
Company Type: Private   *Employees here:* 80
SIC: 1541
    General contractor industrial and commercial
Robert A Brandt Jr, President

D-U-N-S 05-043-6872
BERRY CONTRACTING, LP
1414 Corn Products Rd, Corpus Christi, TX 78409
Phone: (361) 289-6600
Sales: $225,000,000   *Employees:* 3,200
Company Type: Private   *Employees here:* 1,000
SIC: 1629
    Contractor specializing in industrial fabrication building &
      mining
Joseph D Marsh III, President

D-U-N-S 00-813-3340
BERRY GP, INC
1414 Corn Products Rd, Corpus Christi, TX 78409
Phone: (361) 289-6600
Sales: $135,000,000   *Employees:* 2,733
Company Type: Private   *Employees here:* 400
SIC: 1629
    Petrochemical refinery & chemical plant construction road
      dock facilities & offshore fixed platform construction
Mark Benjamin, Chairman of the Board

D-U-N-S 00-750-4475
BFW CONSTRUCTION CO INC
1111 N General Bruce Dr, Temple, TX 76504
Phone: (254) 778-8941
Sales: $75,000,000   *Employees:* 150
Company Type: Private   *Employees here:* 150
SIC: 1542
    Commercial building contractor
Alvin Benjamin, President

D-U-N-S 04-711-4848
BIG D CONSTRUCTION CORP
4774 S 1300 W, Ogden, UT 84405
Phone: (801) 392-3200

Sales: $176,998,000   *Employees:* 300
Company Type: Private   *Employees here:* 220
SIC: 1541
    New industrial and commercial building construction
T R Benning Jr, Chairman of the Board

D-U-N-S 78-908-2419
BLACK & VEATCH CONSTRUCTION
    (Parent: Black And Veatch Holding Co)
8400 Ward Pkwy, Kansas City, MO 64114
Phone: (913) 458-2000
Sales: $526,942,000   *Employees:* 784
Company Type: Private   *Employees here:* 8
SIC: 1629
    Power plant construction
Lou S Niles, President

D-U-N-S 03-317-6827
BLACK CONSTRUCTION CORP
    (Parent: E E Black Ltd)
P.O. Box 31294, Honolulu, HI 96820
Phone: (808) 836-0454
Sales: $76,500,000   *Employees:* 600
Company Type: Private   *Employees here:* 1
SIC: 1541
    General contractor of new commercial buildings new
      industrial buildings airport runways & highway paving
Kenneth G Benson, Chairman of the Board

D-U-N-S 04-885-1760
BLAKE CONSTRUCTION CO INC
1120 Connecticut Ave NW, Washington, DC 20036
Phone: (202) 828-9000
Sales: $225,000,000   *Employees:* 750
Company Type: Private   *Employees here:* 430
SIC: 1542
    General commercial and custom contractors
Thomas H Bentley III, Chief Executive Officer

D-U-N-S 07-906-6825
BLYTHE CONSTRUCTION INC
    (Parent: Alfred Mcalpine Inc)
2911 N Graham St, Charlotte, NC 28206
Phone: (704) 375-8474
Sales: $134,000,000   *Employees:* 500
Company Type: Private   *Employees here:* 250
SIC: 1611
    General contractor of highways & streets
John R Briscoe, Chief Executive Officer

D-U-N-S 00-604-3665
BMW CONSTRUCTORS INC
1740 W Michigan St, Indianapolis, IN 46222
Phone: (317) 267-0400
Sales: $87,600,000   *Employees:* 765
Company Type: Private   *Employees here:* 200
SIC: 1629
    General industrial contractor
Robert Drinkward, President

D-U-N-S 11-752-7424
BOLDT GROUP INC
2525 N Roemer Rd, Appleton, WI 54911
Phone: (920) 739-7800
Sales: $351,000,000   *Employees:* 2,200
Company Type: Private   *Employees here:* 4
SIC: 1541
    General contractor of industrial commercial and institutional
      buildings construction manager and program manager
Richard L Berger, President

D-U-N-S 15-749-7124
BONITZ OF SOUTH CAROLINA INC
645 Rosewood Dr, Columbia, SC 29201
Phone: (803) 799-0181
Sales: $92,522,000   *Employees:* 850
Company Type: Private   *Employees here:* 26
SIC: 1742
    Holding company (see operations)
Ronald Bergeron, President

D-U-N-S 00-880-1292
BOR-SON CONSTRUCTION, INC
2001 Killebrew Dr Ste 141, Minneapolis, MN 55425
Phone: (612) 854-8444
Sales: $120,000,000   *Employees:* 350
Company Type: Private   *Employees here:* 340
SIC: 1542
    General contractor of commercial buildings
Charles J Berkel, Chairman of the Board

D-U-N-S 15-756-5235
BORAN CRAIG BARBR ENGEL CONSTRUCTION
3606 Enterprise Ave, Naples, FL 34104
Phone: (941) 643-3343
Sales: $145,344,000   *Employees:* 350
Company Type: Private   *Employees here:* 350
SIC: 1522
    Contractor specializing in new construction of multi-family
        residences
Leif A Nesheim, President

D-U-N-S 00-519-8341
BOSTIC BROTHERS CONSTRUCTION INC
410 Cleveland Ave, Burlington, NC 27215
Phone: (336) 228-7876
Sales: $100,000,000   *Employees:* 60
Company Type: Private   *Employees here:* 60
SIC: 1522
    Contractor specializing multi-family home construction and
        apartment operations
Charles J Berkel, Chairman of the Board

D-U-N-S 96-561-6584
BOVIS CONSTRUCTION CORP
    (Parent: Bovis Inc)
200 Park Ave Fl 9, New York, NY 10166
Phone: (212) 592-6700
Sales: $781,402,000   *Employees:* 20
Company Type: Private   *Employees here:* 5
SIC: 1542
    Institutional commercial and industrial building contractor &
        construction management consulting
Lavern Horning, President

D-U-N-S 02-931-6064
BRADDOCK & LOGAN GROUP L.P.
4155 Blackhawk Plaza Cir, Danville, CA 94506
Phone: (925) 736-4000
Sales: $197,800,000   *Employees:* 629
Company Type: Private   *Employees here:* 600
SIC: 1531
    Operative builder
Michael Armitage, Director

D-U-N-S 02-393-5984
BRANCH GROUP INC
442 Rutherford Ave NE, Roanoke, VA 24016
Phone: (540) 982-1678

Sales: $200,000,000   *Employees:* 700
Company Type: Private   *Employees here:* 15
SIC: 1542
    Commercial contractor specializing in office buildings schools
        and institutional buildings and general highway construction
David Marshall, President

D-U-N-S 17-810-9294
BRANCH HIGHWAYS INC
    (Parent: Branch Group Inc)
442 Rutherford Ave NE, Roanoke, VA 24016
Phone: (540) 982-1678
Sales: $95,000,000   *Employees:* 350
Company Type: Private   *Employees here:* 350
SIC: 1611
    Highway construction & grading
Daniel S Berman, President

D-U-N-S 02-397-9508
BRAND SCAFFOLD SERVICE, INC
15450 S Outer 40, Chesterfield, MO 63017
Phone: (314) 519-1000
Sales: $120,100,000   *Employees:* 2,000
Company Type: Private   *Employees here:* 25
SIC: 1799
    Holding company rent sell and erect scaffolding
Adriel Longo, Partner

D-U-N-S 17-788-1687
BRANDENBURG INDUSTRIAL SERVICE CO
2625 S Loomis St, Chicago, IL 60608
Phone: (312) 326-5800
Sales: $75,000,000   *Employees:* 425
Company Type: Private   *Employees here:* 200
SIC: 1622
    Heavy construction & industrial maintenance
Douglas Bernards, President

D-U-N-S 00-507-4302
BRASFIELD & GORRIE, LLC
729 30th St S, Birmingham, AL 35233
Phone: (205) 328-4000
Sales: $550,000,000   *Employees:* 1,600
Company Type: Private   *Employees here:* 125
SIC: 1542
    General contractor
Victor Hallberg, Chairman of the Board

D-U-N-S 00-796-0172
BRICE BUILDING CO INC
2721 2nd Ave N, Birmingham, AL 35203
Phone: (205) 252-9911
Sales: $215,933,000   *Employees:* 730
Company Type: Private   *Employees here:* 275
SIC: 1542
    General contractor
Kenneth J Luhan, President

D-U-N-S 07-844-0773
BRIGHTON HOMES INC
13101 Northwest Fwy, Houston, TX 77040
Phone: (713) 460-0264
Sales: $80,000,000   *Employees:* 92
Company Type: Private   *Employees here:* 92
SIC: 1531
    Operative builder of single-family homes
Ed Martin, President

D-U-N-S 80-541-5783
BRINDERSON
3501 Jamboree Rd Ste 500, Newport Beach, CA 92660
Phone: (949) 737-2600

Sales: $100,000,000
Company Type: Private
SIC: 1629
Employees: 500
Employees here: 500

    Contractor specializing in heavy construction petrochemicals
       and construction management
James A Phillips, President

D-U-N-S 62-522-4902
BROADMOOR
2740 N Arnoult Rd, Metairie, LA 70002
Phone: (504) 885-5400
Sales: $125,000,000
Company Type: Private
SIC: 1541
Employees: 120
Employees here: 120

    Industrial & commercial contractor
Paul Gordon, President

D-U-N-S 17-758-2855
BROWN & ROOT SERVICES CORP
    (Parent: Brown & Root Holdings Inc)
4100 Clinton Dr, Houston, TX 77020
Phone: (713) 676-3011
Sales: $600,000,000
Company Type: Public Family Member
SIC: 1541
Employees: 4,100
Employees here: 200

    Industrial building construction engineering services
Joseph D Bonness III, President

D-U-N-S 02-365-0208
BSI HOLDINGS INC
100 Clock Tower Pl, Carmel, CA 93923
Phone: (831) 622-1840
Sales: $600,000,000
Company Type: Private
SIC: 1742
Employees: 4,000
Employees here: 4

Joseph Bonness III, President

D-U-N-S 18-407-8467   EXP
BTR DUNLOP INC
    (Parent: Btr Dunlop Holdings Del Inc)
1105 N Market St Ste 1300, Wilmington, DE 19801
Phone: (302) 654-7451
Sales: $4,200,000,000
Company Type: Private
SIC: 1611
Employees: 24,000
Employees here: 4

    Holding company
Arturo Diaz Jr, President

D-U-N-S 18-777-1936
BUFFINGTON HOMES INC
    (Parent: The Fortress Group Inc)
8716 N Mopac Expy Ste 100, Austin, TX 78759
Phone: (512) 502-2050
Sales: $100,000,000
Company Type: Public Family Member
SIC: 1521
Employees: 160
Employees here: 128

    Single family home builder
Rick Wylie, President

D-U-N-S 04-222-7413
BUILDER'S MART INC
42251 Sierra Hwy, Lancaster, CA 93535
Phone: (661) 948-2623
Sales: $69,300,000
Company Type: Private
SIC: 1799
Employees: 7
Employees here: 7

    Fence contractor
Dan Beutler, President

D-U-N-S 79-998-0883
BUILDING ONE SERVICES CORP
15500 Wayzata Blvd, Wayzata, MN 55391

Phone: (612) 745-0633
Sales: $297,000,000
Company Type: Public
SIC: 1731
Employees: 4,000
Employees here: 6

    Holding company for electrical contractors & commercial
       cleaning companies
Bob Weik, President

D-U-N-S 04-586-8069
BYERS LOCATE SERVICES, LLC
500 Northridge Rd Ste 300, Atlanta, GA 30350
Phone: (678) 461-3900
Sales: $112,900,000
Company Type: Private
SIC: 1623
Employees: 1,500
Employees here: 25

    Utility locating service
Robert Beylik, President

D-U-N-S 04-404-9088
C A RASMUSSEN INC
2360 Shasta Way, Simi Valley, CA 93065
Phone: (805) 527-9330
Sales: $201,664,000
Company Type: Private
SIC: 1611
Employees: 400
Employees here: 50

    General engineering contractor
George Kougentakis, President

D-U-N-S 04-261-1558
C-B-R DEVELOPMENT CO., INC.
    (Parent: Dennys Inc)
203 E Main St, Spartanburg, SC 29319
Phone: (864) 597-8000
Sales: $176,500,000
Company Type: Public Family Member
SIC: 1542
Employees: 800
Employees here: 800

    General contractors of restaurants
Mike Benteen, President

D-U-N-S 08-529-0336
C C MYERS INC
3286 Fitzgerald Rd, Rancho Cordova, CA 95742
Phone: (916) 635-9370
Sales: $89,431,000
Company Type: Private
SIC: 1622
Employees: 225
Employees here: 43

    Bridge contractors
Jim Dougan, President

D-U-N-S 07-838-0896
C D HENDERSON INC
1985 Forest Ln, Garland, TX 75042
Phone: (972) 272-5466
Sales: $69,000,000
Company Type: Private
SIC: 1542
Employees: 75
Employees here: 75

    Contractor commercial new construction & renovation
Franklin Kohutek, President

D-U-N-S 04-780-9525
C D HENDERSON PROPERTY CO
1985 Forest Ln, Garland, TX 75042
Phone: (972) 272-5466
Sales: $135,000,000
Company Type: Private
SIC: 1542
Employees: 120
Employees here: 120

    Commercial general contractor
William H Munn, President

D-U-N-S 00-578-1356
C D SMITH CONSTRUCTION INC
889 E Johnson St, Fond Du Lac, WI 54935
Phone: (920) 922-0421

Sales: $110,870,000   *Employees:* 380
Company Type: Private   *Employees here:* 380
SIC: 1542
    General contractor commercial institutional & industrial
    buildings
Harry Bielinski, President

D-U-N-S 93-377-6502
C E D CONSTRUCTION PARTNERS
1551 Sandspur Rd, Maitland, FL 32751
Phone: (407) 741-8500
Sales: $111,154,000   *Employees:* 15
Company Type: Private   *Employees here:* 15
SIC: 1522
    General contractors multi-family housing
Michael Bierlein, President

D-U-N-S 83-612-7183
C F JORDAN INC
1940 Northwestern Dr, El Paso, TX 79912
Phone: (915) 877-3333
Sales: $231,083,000   *Employees:* 355
Company Type: Private   *Employees here:* 1
SIC: 1541
    Construction of commercial hospitality educational multi-
    family residential and zoological buildings
Jack Livingood, Chairman of the Board

D-U-N-S 92-958-0561
C F JORDAN RESIDENTIAL LP
1940 Northwestern Dr, El Paso, TX 79912
Phone: (915) 877-3333
Sales: $110,000,000   *Employees:* 50
Company Type: Private   *Employees here:* 6
SIC: 1522
    Multi-family dwelling construction & whol lumber
Harold G Field, President

D-U-N-S 10-723-5665
C P MORGAN CO INC
301 E Carmel Dr Ste E300, Carmel, IN 46032
Phone: (317) 848-4040
Sales: $70,000,000   *Employees:* 100
Company Type: Private   *Employees here:* 100
SIC: 1521
    General contractor single family homes
Ken Burge, Regional Manager

D-U-N-S 00-896-1690
C R MEYER & SONS CO
895 W 20th Ave, Oshkosh, WI 54901
Phone: (920) 235-3350
Sales: $94,484,000   *Employees:* 250
Company Type: Private   *Employees here:* 100
SIC: 1541
    General contractor industrial commercial & health care
    buildings & heavy equipment erection
William H Clark Sr, Purchasing

D-U-N-S 04-076-4144
C RAIMONDO & SONS CONSTRUCTION CO
540 Bergen Blvd, Fort Lee, NJ
Phone: (201) 461-5550
Sales: $115,514,000   *Employees:* 200
Company Type: Private   *Employees here:* 200
SIC: 1542
    General contractor commercial buildings shopping centers &
    industrial buildings
Jim Rein, President

D-U-N-S 00-330-8723
C W MATTHEWS CONTRACTING CO
1600 Kenview Dr NW, Marietta, GA 30060

Phone: (770) 422-7520
Sales: $100,000,000   *Employees:* 540
Company Type: Private   *Employees here:* 100
SIC: 1622
    Highway and bridge contractor
Bill Palmer, President

D-U-N-S 00-681-3109
CACHE VALLEY ELECTRIC CO
919 N 10th W, Logan, UT 84321
Phone: (435) 752-6405
Sales: $69,570,000   *Employees:* 300
Company Type: Private   *Employees here:* 60
SIC: 1731
    Electrical contractor
Joseph Decker, President

D-U-N-S 10-208-7285
CADDELL CONSTRUCTION CO INC
2700 Lagoon Park Dr, Montgomery, AL 36109
Phone: (334) 272-7723
Sales: $143,000,000   *Employees:* 350
Company Type: Private   *Employees here:* 60
SIC: 1542
    Contractor
Robert B Snyder, Chairman of the Board

D-U-N-S 01-835-3420
CADENCE MCSHANE CORP
14860 Montfort Dr Ste 270, Dallas, TX 75240
Phone: (972) 239-2336
Sales: $79,158,000   *Employees:* 70
Company Type: Private   *Employees here:* 70
SIC: 1542
    General contractor
Esteban D Bird, President

D-U-N-S 06-546-9496
CAJUN CONSTRUCTORS, INC.
15635 Airline Hwy, Baton Rouge, LA 70817
Phone: (225) 753-5857
Sales: $112,000,000   *Employees:* 600
Company Type: Private   *Employees here:* 150
SIC: 1623
    Municipal & industrial contractor
Jon R Duncan, President

D-U-N-S 08-219-3079
CAL-AIR INC
12393 Slauson Ave, Whittier, CA 90606
Phone: (562) 698-8301
Sales: $91,000,000   *Employees:* 965
Company Type: Private   *Employees here:* 160
SIC: 1711
    Air conditioning contractor and service
J T Gassman, President

D-U-N-S 09-838-5404   EXP
CAL DIVE INTERNATIONAL INC
400 N Sam Houston Pkwy E, Houston, TX 77060
Phone: (281) 618-0400
Sales: $109,386,000   *Employees:* 432
Company Type: Public   *Employees here:* 75
SIC: 1629
    Marine construction & salvaging
Michael J Blach, President

D-U-N-S 04-448-7569
CALCON CONSTRUCTORS INC
2270 W Bates Ave, Englewood, CO 80110
Phone: (303) 762-1554

Sales: $70,781,000
Company Type: Private
SIC: 1542
   General contractor commercial structures
Ronald Tutor, President

Employees: 95
Employees here: 95

D-U-N-S 06-038-5127
CALIFORNIA PACIFIC HOMES INC
38 Executive Park Ste 200, Irvine, CA 92614
Phone: (949) 759-3167
Sales: $240,000,000
Company Type: Private
SIC: 1531
   Operative builders
Vincent McDonald, President

Employees: 225
Employees here: 25

D-U-N-S 04-750-9526
CALTON HOMES INC
   (Parent: Calton Inc)
500 Craig Rd Ste 2, Englishtown, NJ
Phone: (732) 780-1800
Sales: $122,000,000
Company Type: Public Family Member
SIC: 1531
   Operative builder
Charles Blackman, President

Employees: 101
Employees here: 63

D-U-N-S 01-067-7995
CAPITAL PACIFIC HOLDINGS INC
4100 Macarthur Blvd, Newport Beach, CA 92660
Phone: (949) 622-8400
Sales: $191,098,000
Company Type: Public
SIC: 1531
   Operative builder of single-family homes
Fred A Blair, President

Employees: 217
Employees here: 60

D-U-N-S 00-325-4380
CARL M FREEMAN ASSOCIATES
11325 7th Lcks Rd Ste 238, Potomac, MD 20854
Phone: (301) 983-0400
Sales: $85,000,000
Company Type: Private
SIC: 1531
   Operative builder and property management
Howard M Bender, Chairman of the Board

Employees: 275
Employees here: 20

D-U-N-S 07-592-0348
CASEY INDUSTRIAL INC
4505 Marion St SE, Albany, OR 97321
Phone: (541) 967-8605
Sales: $146,300,000
Company Type: Private
SIC: 1541
   Construction & construction management of industrial plants
John Chadwick, Branch Manager

Employees: 1,153
Employees here: 747

D-U-N-S 01-921-5206
CASHMAN
160 N Washington St, Boston, MA
Phone: (617) 742-4160
Sales: $70,000,000
Company Type: Private
SIC: 1611
   Heavy & highway construction
Thomas Bleigh, President

Employees: 60
Employees here: 60

D-U-N-S 17-959-0773
CASTLE & COOKE INC
10900 Wilshire Blvd, Los Angeles, CA 90024
Phone: (310) 208-3636

Sales: $241,163,000
Company Type: Public
SIC: 1522
   Residential construction nonresidential construction hotel/
    motel operation
Jack G Block, President

Employees: 1,322
Employees here: 7

D-U-N-S 12-272-0998
CATALFUMO CONSTRUCTION AND DEV
4300 Catalfumo Way, Palm Beach Gardens, FL 33410
Phone: (561) 694-3000
Sales: $115,000,000
Company Type: Private
SIC: 1542
   Commercial real estate developer and contractor
Lloyd L Lathrop Jr, President

Employees: 125
Employees here: 125

D-U-N-S 07-607-8435
CATELLUS RESIDENTIAL GROUP
   (Parent: Catellus Development Corp)
5 Park Plz Ste 400, Irvine, CA 92614
Phone: (949) 251-6100
Sales: $105,346,000
Company Type: Public Family Member
SIC: 1531
   Operative builders
Brian A Geary, President

Employees: 150
Employees here: 150

D-U-N-S 03-089-7300
CCBC INC.
1 Graycor Dr, Homewood, IL 60430
Phone: (708) 206-0500
Sales: $200,000,000
Company Type: Private
SIC: 1541
   Holding company
Mike Benteen, President

Employees: 500
Employees here: 1

D-U-N-S 15-181-8457   EXP
CCC GROUP INC
5797 Dietrich Rd, San Antonio, TX 78219
Phone: (210) 661-4251
Sales: $118,175,000
Company Type: Private
SIC: 1541
   Contractor specializing in industrial construction commercial
    construction erection of mining and materials handling
    equipment
L J Blythe, President

Employees: 700
Employees here: 160

D-U-N-S 17-415-2447
CDI CONTRACTORS, LLC
3000 Cantrell Rd, Little Rock, AR 72202
Phone: (501) 666-4300
Sales: $303,908,000
Company Type: Private
SIC: 1542
   General contractors
Thomas Duncan, Branch Manager

Employees: 500
Employees here: 100

D-U-N-S 00-883-1646
CDK CONTRACTING CO
   (Parent: FK Co Inc)
800 S Hutton Rd, Farmington, NM 87401
Phone: (505) 327-5168
Sales: $109,179,000
Company Type: Private
SIC: 1541
   Construction of heavy industrial buildings & power plants
Walter R Boatner, President

Employees: 700
Employees here: 37

D-U-N-S 78-042-5518
CE WARD CONSTRUCTORS, INC
  (Parent: Dunn Industries Inc)
3000 Richmond Ave Ste 200, Houston, TX 77098
Phone: (713) 521-4664
Sales: $80,000,000   *Employees:* 50
Company Type: Private   *Employees here:* 50
SIC: 1542
  Interior construction & renovation contractor
Robert L Mathews, President

D-U-N-S 60-914-3086
CEC INVESTMENT CORP
3 Gateway Ctr Ste 1100, Pittsburgh, PA 15222
Phone: (412) 391-4950
Sales: $145,000,000   *Employees:* 928
Company Type: Private   *Employees here:* 500
SIC: 1791
  Contractors of steel erection & commercial construction
W G Adams, President

D-U-N-S 87-976-8075
CECO CONCRETE CONSTRUCTION LLC
2900 NE Brooktree Ln, Kansas City, MO 64119
Phone: (816) 459-7000
Sales: $105,872,000   *Employees:* 1,200
Company Type: Private   *Employees here:* 22
SIC: 1799
  Concrete form work
Theodore R Bogner, President

D-U-N-S 04-331-3394
CENTEX CONSTRUCTION GROUP INC
  (Parent: Centex Corp)
3710 Rawlins St Ste 1300, Dallas, TX 75219
Phone: (214) 981-5000
Sales: $953,781,000   *Employees:* 1,790
Company Type: Public Family Member   *Employees here:* 35
SIC: 1542
  New construction & renovation of commercial governmental
    medical and light industrial buildings
Michael Collen, Manager

D-U-N-S 05-636-0258
CENTEX CORP
2728 N Harwood St, Dallas, TX 75201
Phone: (214) 981-5000
Sales: $3,975,450,000   *Employees:* 10,259
Company Type: Public   *Employees here:* 400
SIC: 1531
  Operative home builder manufactured homes mortgage
    banking general contractor of office & institutional
    buildings
Kenneth R Field, President

D-U-N-S 05-983-4366
CENTEX FORCUM LANNOM INC
  (Parent: Centex Construction Group Inc)
350 Jere Ford Mem Hwy, Dyersburg, TN 38024
Phone: (901) 285-6503
Sales: $104,638,000   *Employees:* 250
Company Type: Public Family Member   *Employees here:* 240
SIC: 1541
  Contractor of industrial buildings
Oscar C Boldt, Chief Executive Officer

D-U-N-S 86-699-2910
CENTEX LANDIS CONSTRUCTION CO
  (Parent: Centex Construction Co)
241 Industrial Ave, Jefferson, LA 70121
Phone: (504) 833-6070

Sales: $75,000,000   *Employees:* 75
Company Type: Public Family Member   *Employees here:* 75
SIC: 1542
  General commercial contractor
Robert H Boller, President

D-U-N-S 17-501-0040
CENTEX RODGERS CONSTRUCTION CO
  (Parent: Centex Construction Group Inc)
2620 Elm Hill Pike, Nashville, TN 37214
Phone: (615) 889-4400
Sales: $180,000,000   *Employees:* 200
Company Type: Public Family Member   *Employees here:* 60
SIC: 1542
  Nonresidential construction
William E Bolton III, Chairman of the Board

D-U-N-S 00-692-2785
CENTEX ROONEY CONSTRUCTION CO
  (Parent: Centex Construction Group Inc)
6300 NW 5th Way, Fort Lauderdale, FL 33309
Phone: (954) 771-7122
Sales: $350,000,000   *Employees:* 650
Company Type: Public Family Member   *Employees here:* 150
SIC: 1542
  Builds new commercial construction shopping centers
    hospitals post offices hotels condos apt bldgs
Robert Matranga, Chief Executive Officer

D-U-N-S 05-552-7634   EXP
CENTIMARK CORP
12 Grandview Cir, Canonsburg, PA 15317
Phone: (724) 743-7777
Sales: $209,203,000   *Employees:* 1,500
Company Type: Private   *Employees here:* 150
SIC: 1761
  Roofing & flooring contractor
Edward A Bond Sr, Chairman of the Board

D-U-N-S 06-399-2168
CENTURION INDUSTRIES INC
1107 N Taylor Rd, Garrett, IN 46738
Phone: (219) 357-6665
Sales: $78,000,000   *Employees:* 1,000
Company Type: Private   *Employees here:* 80
SIC: 1796
  Millwright mfr sheet metal canopies and commercial roofing
    contractor
George W Rogers, Chairman of the Board

D-U-N-S 08-685-9725
CENTURY CONTRACTORS INC
5100 Smith Farm Rd, Matthews, NC 28104
Phone: (704) 821-8050
Sales: $170,000,000   *Employees:* 900
Company Type: Private   *Employees here:* 50
SIC: 1541
  Industrial building contractor
William Boniface, President

D-U-N-S 62-332-5057
CES/WAY INTERNATIONAL, INC
  (Parent: Sempra Energy Solutions)
2500 City West Blvd, Houston, TX 77042
Phone: (713) 361-7600
Sales: $90,000,000   *Employees:* 175
Company Type: Private   *Employees here:* 120
SIC: 1711
  Mechanical work & installs energy saving devices
Stephen G Bauchman, President

D-U-N-S 00-434-6821
CHAPMAN CORP
331 S Main St, Washington, PA 15301
Phone: (724) 228-1900
Sales: $70,000,000   *Employees:* 300
Company Type: Private   *Employees here:* 300
SIC: 1541
   Industrial building contractors
Wm A Young, President

D-U-N-S 05-765-5102
CHARLES N WHITE CONSTRUCTION CO
115 Issaquena Ave, Clarksdale, MS 38614
Phone: (601) 627-4705
Sales: $142,403,000   *Employees:* 200
Company Type: Private   *Employees here:* 14
SIC: 1542
   Commercial & industrial contractor
Wm A Young, President

D-U-N-S 04-439-9343
CHARLES PANKOW BUILDERS LTD
2476 Lake Ave, Altadena, CA 91001
Phone: (323) 684-2320
Sales: $87,200,000   *Employees:* 132
Company Type: Private   *Employees here:* 52
SIC: 1542
   Commercial building contractor
Donald R Barber, Chairman of the Board

D-U-N-S 04-304-4411
CHARLES R PERRY CONSTRUCTION
2500 NE 18th Ter, Gainesville, FL 32609
Phone: (352) 378-1488
Sales: $75,000,000   *Employees:* 100
Company Type: Private   *Employees here:* 100
SIC: 1542
   Nonresidential construction
Lloyd Thompson, Chairman of the Board

D-U-N-S 18-357-7758
CHARTER BUILDERS, INC.
1501 LBJ Fwy Ste 700, Dallas, TX 75234
Phone: (972) 484-4888
Sales: $100,293,000   *Employees:* 50
Company Type: Private   *Employees here:* 20
SIC: 1542
   Commercial building contractor
Morgan E North, President

D-U-N-S 00-325-2889
CHAS H TOMPKINS CO
   (Parent: J A Jones Construction Co)
1333 H St NW Ste 2, Washington, DC 20005
Phone: (202) 789-0770
Sales: $197,758,000   *Employees:* 149
Company Type: Private   *Employees here:* 100
SIC: 1542
   Commercial building contractor
Anthony J Borrell Jr, Chairman of the Board

D-U-N-S 00-879-6872
CHAS ROBERTS A/C INC
9828 N 19th Ave, Phoenix, AZ 85021
Phone: (602) 943-7291
Sales: $78,522,000   *Employees:* 310
Company Type: Private   *Employees here:* 200
SIC: 1711
   Air conditioning & heating contractor
Wayne Stewart, Chairman of the Board

D-U-N-S 00-516-2300   EXP
CHICAGO BRIDGE & IRON CO ILL
   (Parent: Chicago Bridge & Iron Co Del)
1501 N Division St, Plainfield, IL 60544
Phone: (815) 439-6000
Sales: $97,400,000   *Employees:* 1,080
Company Type: Private   *Employees here:* 4
SIC: 1791
   International holding company supply & construction of plate
     steel structures
Mel Morris, Treasurer

D-U-N-S 07-926-2770
CHIYODA INTERNATIONAL CORP
1100 Olive Way Ste 500, Seattle, WA 98101
Phone: (206) 464-0034
Sales: $70,000,000   *Employees:* 107
Company Type: Private   *Employees here:* 70
SIC: 1541
   New construction and engineering of industrial facilities
Richard L Bostleman, President

D-U-N-S 60-401-5420
CHOATE CONSTRUCTION CO
1640 Powers Ferry Rd SE, Marietta, GA 30067
Phone: (770) 644-2170
Sales: $173,531,000   *Employees:* 360
Company Type: Private   *Employees here:* 66
SIC: 1542
   Commercial building contractor
Bruce D Jaffin, President

D-U-N-S 19-739-7854
CHOICE HOMES-TEXAS, INC
600 Six Flags Dr Ste 642, Arlington, TX 76011
Phone: (817) 652-4900
Sales: $243,847,000   *Employees:* 268
Company Type: Private   *Employees here:* 20
SIC: 1521
   Single-family house construction
John Bouma Sr, Chairman of the Board

D-U-N-S 00-967-3385
CHRISTENSON ELECTRIC INC
111 SW Columbia St, Portland, OR 97201
Phone: (503) 241-4812
Sales: $88,217,000   *Employees:* 600
Company Type: Private   *Employees here:* 40
SIC: 1731
   Electrical contractor
William Moss, Chief Executive Officer

D-U-N-S 00-685-4210
CIANBRO CORP
Hunnewell Sq, Pittsfield, ME
Phone: (207) 487-3311
Sales: $156,281,000   *Employees:* 1,400
Company Type: Private   *Employees here:* 1,250
SIC: 1629
   Heavy construction bridge general commercial & industrial
     construction construction management
Arthur Tye, President

D-U-N-S 02-474-8063
CLANCY & THEYS CONSTRUCTION CO
516 W Cabarrus St, Raleigh, NC 27603
Phone: (919) 834-3601
Sales: $250,000,000   *Employees:* 400
Company Type: Private   *Employees here:* 200
SIC: 1541
   Industrial & commercial contractor
Luther P Cochrane, President

D-U-N-S 07-378-9927
CLARK & SULLIVAN CONSTRUCTORS
   (Parent: C S General Inc)
905 Industrial Way, Sparks, NV 89431
Phone: (775) 355-8500
Sales: $71,376,000   *Employees:* 80
Company Type: Private   *Employees here:* 70
SIC: 1542
   General contractor specializing in commercial & industrial
      buildings
George Chabot, President

D-U-N-S 06-676-7021
CLARK CONSTRUCTION GROUP
   (Parent: Clark Enterprises Inc)
7500 Old Georgetown Rd, Bethesda, MD 20814
Phone: (301) 272-8100
Sales: $1,400,000,000   *Employees:* 3,100
Company Type: Private   *Employees here:* 350
SIC: 1542
   Commercial and industrial building contractor
R M Bowen, President

D-U-N-S 11-904-3008
CLAYCO CONSTRUCTION CO
2199 Innerbelt Business C, St. Louis, MO 63114
Phone: (314) 429-5100
Sales: $155,850,000   *Employees:* 500
Company Type: Private   *Employees here:* 70
SIC: 1541
   General contractor commercial buildings industrial buildings
      & industrial maintenance & repair
David J Bowen, President

D-U-N-S 03-537-8520
CLEVELAND CONSTRUCTION INC
8620 Tyler Blvd, Mentor, OH 44060
Phone: (440) 255-8000
Sales: $103,917,000   *Employees:* 500
Company Type: Private   *Employees here:* 50
SIC: 1542
   General contractor & interior specialty
Matt Bowen, President

D-U-N-S 03-351-6659
CLEVELAND GROUP INC
1281 Fulton Industrial Bl, Atlanta, GA 30336
Phone: (404) 505-4550
Sales: $147,827,000   *Employees:* 255
Company Type: Private   *Employees here:* 25
SIC: 1542
   Construction management electrical and mechanical
      construction and service
Robert L Bowen, President

D-U-N-S 00-283-7144
COCHRAN INC
12500 Aurora Ave N, Seattle, WA 98133
Phone: (206) 367-1900
Sales: $80,974,000   *Employees:* 405
Company Type: Private   *Employees here:* 55
SIC: 1731
   General electrical contractor
Robert J Stamm, Chairman of the Board

D-U-N-S 17-914-3086
CODILLERA CONSTRUCTION CORP
32223 Hwy 6 & 24, Edwards, CO 81632
Phone: (970) 926-3500

Sales: $68,500,000   *Employees:* 500
Company Type: Private   *Employees here:* 500
SIC: 1521
   New construction of residential
Joseph Raphel, Partner

D-U-N-S 60-610-3737
COLAS INC
10 Madison Ave Ste 4, Morristown, NJ
Phone: (973) 290-9082
Sales: $446,745,000   *Employees:* 1,250
Company Type: Private   *Employees here:* 5
SIC: 1611
   Road construction bridge and highway construction & fr
      bituminous road materials
Joe Raphel, General Manager

D-U-N-S 11-532-4766
COLONY HOMES L P
110 Lndnderry Ct Ste 136, Woodstock, GA 30188
Phone: (770) 928-0092
Sales: $125,000,000   *Employees:* 80
Company Type: Private   *Employees here:* 40
SIC: 1521
   General contractor of single-family houses
Timothy A Pixley, President

D-U-N-S 09-713-8846
COLORADO STRUCTURES INC
4720 Forge Rd Ste 106, Colorado Springs, CO 80907
Phone: (719) 522-0500
Sales: $72,870,000   *Employees:* 75
Company Type: Private   *Employees here:* 75
SIC: 1542
   General contractor of commercial buildings & multi-unit
      housing
J C Harrison IV, President

D-U-N-S 80-743-2737
COLSON & COLSON GENERAL CONTRACTORS
2250 McGilchrist St SE, Salem, OR 97302
Phone: (503) 370-7070
Sales: $138,685,000   *Employees:* 75
Company Type: Private   *Employees here:* 75
SIC: 1522
   Residential & commercial buildings contractor
J K Speas, Treasurer

D-U-N-S 05-878-0495
COMERFORDS HEATING & A/C
   (Parent: Service Experts Inc)
7020 Commerce Dr Ste C, Pleasanton, CA 94588
Phone: (925) 463-1253
Sales: $238,692,000   *Employees:* 30
Company Type: Public Family Member   *Employees here:* 30
SIC: 1711
   Heating & air conditioning contractor
Ralph Shivers, President

D-U-N-S 01-584-1703
COMFORT SYSTEMS USA INC
777 Post Oak Blvd Ste 500, Houston, TX 77056
Phone: (713) 830-9600
Sales: $390,122,000   *Employees:* 3,119
Company Type: Public   *Employees here:* 8
SIC: 1711
   Holding company for commercial heating air conditioning
      and ventilation companies
John M Monter, President

D-U-N-S 00-653-2105
COMMERCIAL CONTRACTING CORP
 (*Parent: N A CCC Inc*)
1743 Maplelawn Dr, Troy, MI 48084
Phone: (248) 643-7600
Sales: $110,547,000   *Employees:* 200
Company Type: Private   *Employees here:* 200
SIC: 1796
 Machinery installation contractor
Mark Zilbermann, President

D-U-N-S 02-197-6824
COMMUNICATIONS CONSTRUCTION GROUP
 (*Parent: Dycom Industries Inc*)
235 E Gay St, West Chester, PA 19380
Phone: (610) 696-1800
Sales: $93,000,000   *Employees:* 750
Company Type: Public Family Member   *Employees here:* 55
SIC: 1623
 Cable television contractors
Stephen Branscum, President

D-U-N-S 18-842-9245
COMSTOCK HOLDINGS INC
 (*Parent: Railworks Corp*)
1 N Lexington Ave, White Plains, NY 10601
Phone: (914) 323-3000
Sales: $153,610,000   *Employees:* 1,007
Company Type: Public Family Member   *Employees here:* 57
SIC: 1731
 Electrical contractor
M M Gorrie, Chief Executive Officer

D-U-N-S 79-783-1401
CONCORD DEVELOPMENT CORP ILL
1540 E Dundee Rd Ste 350, Palatine, IL 60074
Phone: (847) 776-0350
Sales: $120,000,000   *Employees:* 140
Company Type: Private   *Employees here:* 50
SIC: 1521
 Single family & multi-family home builder
John R Mills, Branch Manager

D-U-N-S 82-584-2446
CONELLY SWINERTON CONSTRUCTION INC
 (*Parent: Swinerton Inc*)
320 W Alturas St, Tucson, AZ 85705
Phone: (520) 792-2260
Sales: $75,306,000   *Employees:* 50
Company Type: Private   *Employees here:* 44
SIC: 1542
 Contractor of commercial & industrial buildings

D-U-N-S 18-359-0520
CONEX INTERNATIONAL CORP
Hwy 90 W, Beaumont, TX 77713
Phone: (409) 866-9888
Sales: $110,600,000   *Employees:* NA
Company Type: Private   *Employees here:* NA
SIC: 1629
 General contractor
James Rhodes, President

D-U-N-S 18-548-1058
CONLAN CO
1800 Parkway Pl SE, Marietta, GA 30067
Phone: (770) 423-8000
Sales: $81,049,000   *Employees:* 225
Company Type: Private   *Employees here:* 225
SIC: 1542
 General contractors commercial
Darrell D Brechbill, President

D-U-N-S 09-593-3768
CONSULTANT ERECTION CONSTRUCTION INC
145 Divot Ct, Bracey, VA 23919
Phone: (804) 636-2209
Sales: $300,000,000   *Employees:* 8
Company Type: Private   *Employees here:* 8
SIC: 1521
 General contractor of new single-family homes and
  commercial buildings
Fred C Culpepper, Chief Executive Officer

D-U-N-S 62-612-4804
CONTI ENTERPRISES, INC
3001 S Clinton Ave, South Plainfield, NJ
Phone: (908) 755-3185
Sales: $77,123,000   *Employees:* 200
Company Type: Private   *Employees here:* 100
SIC: 1611
 Highway/street construction bridge/tunnel construction &
  water/sewer/utility construction
Brent Zerull, President

D-U-N-S 17-418-7088
CONTINENTAL HOMES INC
 (*Parent: D R Horton Inc*)
7001 N Scottsdale Rd, Scottsdale, AZ 85253
Phone: (602) 483-0006
Sales: $204,500,000   *Employees:* 650
Company Type: Public Family Member   *Employees here:* 200
SIC: 1531
 Operative builder of single family homes
Lou Joseph, President

D-U-N-S 01-788-5732
CORNA/KOKOSING CONSTRUCTION CO
2500 Harrison Rd, Columbus, OH 43204
Phone: (614) 279-8844
Sales: $69,500,000   *Employees:* 321
Company Type: Private   *Employees here:* 321
SIC: 1542
 General contractor commercial & industrial buildings
C M Garver, President

D-U-N-S 08-002-0050
CORRIGAN BROTHERS INC
3545 Gratiot St, St. Louis, MO 63103
Phone: (314) 771-6200
Sales: $75,000,000   *Employees:* 600
Company Type: Private   *Employees here:* 480
SIC: 1711
 Process piping HVAC plumbing & sheet metal contractor
Felix M Drennen III, President

D-U-N-S 00-677-9896
CROWDER CONSTRUCTION CO
1123 E 10th St, Charlotte, NC 28204
Phone: (704) 372-3541
Sales: $104,000,000   *Employees:* 700
Company Type: Private   *Employees here:* 50
SIC: 1629
 Contractor of water & sewer treatment plants and heavy
  industrial construction
Henry Broesche, President

D-U-N-S 00-536-7966
CRUDO BROS., CO. INC.
38415 Schoolcraft Rd, Livonia, MI 48150
Phone: (734) 542-2000
Sales: $77,948,000   *Employees:* 110
Company Type: Private   *Employees here:* 60
SIC: 1541
 Industrial contractor project design & estimating
Douglas M Nelson, Chief Executive Officer

D-U-N-S 02-807-8210
CUPERTINO ELECTRIC INC
(Parent: Synergism Inc)
714 E Evelyn Ave, Sunnyvale, CA 94086
Phone: (408) 991-1000
Sales: $143,570,000   *Employees:* 675
Company Type: Private   *Employees here:* 500
SIC: 1731
    Electrical contractor
Gary L Brinderson, Chairman of the Board

D-U-N-S 08-081-4668
D AND M CONCRETE FLOOR CO
2 Lark St, Fall River, MA
Phone: (508) 675-2423
Sales: $81,977,000   *Employees:* 70
Company Type: Private   *Employees here:* 70
SIC: 1771
    Concrete flooring contractor
William Brisben Jr, President

D-U-N-S 04-329-2481
D L WITHERS CONSTRUCTION LC
3220 E Harbour Dr, Phoenix, AZ 85034
Phone: (602) 438-9500
Sales: $110,073,000   *Employees:* 70
Company Type: Private   *Employees here:* 70
SIC: 1542
    General contractor of commercial industrial and public
      buildings & tenant improvements
Steve E Britt, President

D-U-N-S 09-704-7369
D R HORTON INC
1901 Ascension Blvd, Arlington, TX 76006
Phone: (817) 856-8200
Sales: $2,155,049,000   *Employees:* 2,465
Company Type: Public   *Employees here:* 40
SIC: 1531
    Speculative builder single family homes
John W Broad, Chairman of the Board

D-U-N-S 55-711-4675
D W HUTSON CONSTRUCTION, INC
(Parent: The Fortress Group Inc)
11217 San Jose Blvd, Jacksonville, FL 32223
Phone: (904) 268-2845
Sales: $69,000,000   *Employees:* 41
Company Type: Public Family Member   *Employees here:* 41
SIC: 1521
    Contractor single family homes
John A Stewart, President

D-U-N-S 00-751-2973
DAL-MAC CONSTRUCTION CO
(Parent: Dal-Mac Construction Partners)
111 W Spring Valley Rd, Richardson, TX 75081
Phone: (972) 238-0401
Sales: $165,000,000   *Employees:* 300
Company Type: Private   *Employees here:* 75
SIC: 1542
    General contractor commercial buildings
Jerry Brock, President

D-U-N-S 06-879-7034
DANIEL ENTERPRISES, INC.
1707 E Weber Dr Ste 10, Tempe, AZ 85281
Phone: (602) 967-0000
Sales: $86,148,000   *Employees:* 75
Company Type: Private   *Employees here:* 75
SIC: 1542
    Commercial & industrial building renovation
John R Brooks, President

D-U-N-S 08-477-6343
DANIEL J KEATING CONSTRUCTION CO
1 Bala Ave Ste 400, Bala Cynwyd, PA 19004
Phone: (610) 668-4100
Sales: $250,000,000   *Employees:* 175
Company Type: Private   *Employees here:* 75
SIC: 1542
    General contractor institutional & office buildings
Arthur H Nelson, President

D-U-N-S 79-296-1542
DANIS BUILDING CONSTRUCTION CO
2 River Pl Ste 100, Dayton, OH 45405
Phone: (937) 228-1225
Sales: $124,631,000   *Employees:* 235
Company Type: Private   *Employees here:* 220
SIC: 1542
    General contractor of commercial & industrial buildings
John D Carson, Chairman of the Board

D-U-N-S 36-192-2826
DANIS COMPANIES
2 River Pl Ste 400, Dayton, OH 45405
Phone: (937) 228-1225
Sales: $268,000,000   *Employees:* 745
Company Type: Private   *Employees here:* 17
SIC: 1629
    Waste water & water treatment plant construction
Arthur Nelson, President

D-U-N-S 00-389-7774
DAVID E HARVEY BUILDERS INC
3630 Westchase Dr, Houston, TX 77042
Phone: (713) 783-8710
Sales: $89,064,000   *Employees:* 204
Company Type: Private   *Employees here:* 169
SIC: 1542
    Contractor of commercial buildings
Chester Bross, President

D-U-N-S 00-350-6151
DAVIS ELECTRICAL CONSTRUCTORS
(Parent: Integrated Electrical Services)
429 N Main St, Greenville, SC 29601
Phone: (864) 250-2500
Sales: $100,000,000   *Employees:* 1,000
Company Type: Public Family Member   *Employees here:* 80
SIC: 1731
    Contractor
Byron J Brower, Chairman of the Board

D-U-N-S 18-325-2642
DEGABRIELLE & ASSOC INC
821 Ocean Trl Ste 4, Corolla, NC 27927
Phone: (252) 453-3600
Sales: $88,000,000   *Employees:* 60
Company Type: Private   *Employees here:* 45
SIC: 1521
    General contractor of custom built single family homes
Willie Emberee, Branch Manager

D-U-N-S 01-520-8481
DEMATTEO/FLAT IRON
P.O. Box 285360, Boston, MA
Phone: (617) 561-5042
Sales: $160,000,000   *Employees:* 200
Company Type: Private   *Employees here:* 200
SIC: 1611
    Contruction company
Fletcher Overstreet, Branch Manager

D-U-N-S 07-046-8210
DEVCON CONSTRUCTION INC
555 Los Coches St, Milpitas, CA 95035
Phone: (408) 942-8200
Sales: $602,868,000 *Employees:* 384
Company Type: Private *Employees here:* 100
SIC: 1541
  General contractor industrial & commercial buildings
D J Lesar, Chairman of the Board

D-U-N-S 80-513-4483
DIAMOND HOME SERVICES (DEL)
222 E Church St, Woodstock, IL 60098
Phone: (815) 334-1414
Sales: $161,109,000 *Employees:* 1,200
Company Type: Public *Employees here:* 250
SIC: 1761
  Roofing door & fencing installation contractor and mfr
    fencing
B W Brown, President

D-U-N-S 03-793-7786
DICK CORP
1900 State Rte 51, Clairton, PA 15025
Phone: (412) 384-1000
Sales: $537,513,000 *Employees:* 1,000
Company Type: Private *Employees here:* 1,000
SIC: 1611
  Highway bridge industrial and commercial contractor
Shirley Maus, Treasurer

D-U-N-S 16-086-9780
DILLINGHAM CONSTRUCTION CORP
  (*Parent:* Dillingham Construction Holdings)
5960 Inglewood Dr, Pleasanton, CA 94588
Phone: (925) 463-3300
Sales: $1,022,611,000 *Employees:* 4,000
Company Type: Private *Employees here:* 55
SIC: 1629
  Contractor of heavy commercial & industrial precast &
    stone/rock placement
Sample D Brown, Chairman of the Board

D-U-N-S 15-777-5834
DILLINGHAM CONSTRUCTION PCF LTD
  (*Parent:* Dillingham Construction Corp)
614 Kapahulu Ave, Honolulu, HI 96815
Phone: (808) 735-3211
Sales: $260,400,000 *Employees:* 900
Company Type: Private *Employees here:* 150
SIC: 1542
  General contractor
Richard J Pollak, President

D-U-N-S 00-159-1999
DIMEO CONSTRUCTION CO
75 Chapman St, Providence, RI
Phone: (401) 781-9800
Sales: $105,866,000 *Employees:* 170
Company Type: Private *Employees here:* 70
SIC: 1542
  General contractor-construction mgr of commercial
    institutional & apt bldgs
Bobby C Hewett, Owner

D-U-N-S 87-977-8942
DJB CONSTRUCTION GROUP, INC
  (*Parent:* Beers Construction Co)
3101 Industrial Dr, Raleigh, NC 27609
Phone: (919) 828-6260

Sales: $121,502,000 *Employees:* 228
Company Type: Private *Employees here:* 228
SIC: 1541
  Industrial institutional & commercial construction
Leonard J Brutocao, Chairman of the Board

D-U-N-S 84-207-4510
DOMINION HOMES INC
  (*Parent:* Borror Realty Co)
5501 Frantz Rd, Dublin, OH 43017
Phone: (614) 761-6000
Sales: $207,926,000 *Employees:* 362
Company Type: Public *Employees here:* 300
SIC: 1531
  Operative builder & land developer & whol lumber
Nancy Bryan, Chairman of the Board

D-U-N-S 01-149-2027
DOT BLUE SERVICES INC
  (*Parent:* Northwestern Growth Corp)
500 Fairway Dr Ste 205, Deerfield Beach, FL 33441
Phone: (954) 421-2130
Sales: $200,000,000 *Employees:* 1,375
Company Type: Public Family Member *Employees here:* 40
SIC: 1711
  HVAC contractor
Kay D Wall, Chief Executive Officer

D-U-N-S 05-450-5458
DOUGLAS E BARNHART INC
16981 Via Tazon, San Diego, CA 92127
Phone: (619) 487-1101
Sales: $195,000,000 *Employees:* 250
Company Type: Private *Employees here:* 40
SIC: 1542
  General contractor of commercial buildings
Robert S Shackleford, President

D-U-N-S 00-896-4777
DOVER ELEVATOR CO
  (*Parent:* Dover Elevator International)
6266 Hurt Rd, Horn Lake, MS 38637
Phone: (601) 393-2110
Sales: $4,547,656,000 *Employees:* 2,735
Company Type: Public Family Member *Employees here:* 4
SIC: 1796
  Installation & service of elevators
Michael L Shank, Managing Partner

D-U-N-S 61-780-1915
DPR CONSTRUCTION, INC
555 Twin Dolphin Dr 200, Redwood City, CA 94065
Phone: (650) 592-4800
Sales: $890,588,000 *Employees:* 1,609
Company Type: Private *Employees here:* 465
SIC: 1541
  Technical & commercial building contractors
Robert R Buckley, President

D-U-N-S 00-382-6641
DREES CO
211 Grandview Dr Ste 300, Fort Mitchell, KY 41017
Phone: (606) 578-4200
Sales: $342,773,000 *Employees:* 450
Company Type: Private *Employees here:* 200
SIC: 1521
  General contractor of single family homes & other
    residential buildings and operative builder of single family
    homes
William L Johnsmeyer, President

D-U-N-S 83-546-7143
DUALSTAR TECHNOLOGIES CORP
1130 47th Ave, Long Island City, NY 11101
Phone: (718) 340-6655
Sales: $94,280,000　　　　　　　　　　　*Employees:* 404
Company Type: Public　　　　　　　*Employees here:* 130
SIC: 1711
　　HVAC contractors mechanical contactors installs electrical
　　　systems telephone internet broadcast satellite tv & security
David A Mahas, President

D-U-N-S 02-297-7813
DUININCK BROS INC
408 6th St, Prinsburg, MN 56281
Phone: (320) 978-6011
Sales: $80,000,000　　　　　　　　　　　*Employees:* 50
Company Type: Private　　　　　　　*Employees here:* 25
SIC: 1611
　　General contractor highway construction & bituminous
　　　highway paving
Aldo Falasca, President

D-U-N-S 00-783-6448
DUNN INDUSTRIES, INC.
929 Holmes St, Kansas City, MO 64106
Phone: (816) 474-8600
Sales: $619,000,000　　　　　　　　　*Employees:* 1,000
Company Type: Private　　　　　　*Employees here:* 1,000
SIC: 1542
　　New commercial building contractor
Tom Buffington, President

D-U-N-S 09-569-1085
DUNN INVESTMENT CO
3900 Airport Hwy, Birmingham, AL 35222
Phone: (205) 592-8908
Sales: $226,010,000　　　　　　　　　　*Employees:* 992
Company Type: Private　　　　　　　*Employees here:* 12
SIC: 1542
　　Holding company
Richard B Thompson, President

D-U-N-S 17-572-7478
DUPONT FLOORING SYSTEMS, INC
　　(Parent: Dupont Commercial Flrg Systems)
125 Townpark Dr NW, Kennesaw, GA 30144
Phone: (770) 420-7700
Sales: $450,000,000　　　　　　　　　*Employees:* 2,500
Company Type: Public Family Member　*Employees here:* 100
SIC: 1752
　　Floor covering contractor
Larry Purcell, President

D-U-N-S 04-030-9304
DURA-BUILDERS INC.
5740 Decatur Blvd, Indianapolis, IN 46241
Phone: (317) 821-8100
Sales: $80,000,000　　　　　　　　　　　*Employees:* 50
Company Type: Private　　　　　　　*Employees here:* 50
SIC: 1521
　　New construction of single-family homes
William R Miller, President

D-U-N-S 05-376-3637
DYCOM INDUSTRIES INC
4440 PGA Blvd Ste 600, Palm Beach Gardens, FL 33410
Phone: (561) 627-7171
Sales: $371,363,000　　　　　　　　　*Employees:* 3,834
Company Type: Public　　　　　　　*Employees here:* 24
SIC: 1623
　　Placement and maintenance of telecommunications cable
　　　systems
Joseph Ivey, President

D-U-N-S 92-978-5350
DYN SPECIALTY CONTRACTING INC
　　(Parent: Emcor Group Inc)
1420 Spring Hill Rd, McLean, VA 22102
Phone: (703) 556-8000
Sales: $302,500,000　　　　　　　　*Employees:* 3,200
Company Type: Public Family Member　*Employees here:* 15
SIC: 1711
　　Holding company through subsidiaries operates as a
　　　mechanical & electrical contractor
John Ledecky, Chief Executive Officer

D-U-N-S 08-351-1345
DYNALECTRIC CO
　　(Parent: Dyn Specialty Contracting Inc)
1420 Spring Hill Rd, McLean, VA 22102
Phone: (703) 556-8000
Sales: $237,600,000　　　　　　　　*Employees:* 3,200
Company Type: Public Family Member　*Employees here:* 15
SIC: 1731
　　Electrical contractor
Nick J Bukacek, President

D-U-N-S 09-514-7807
DYNALECTRIC CO OF NEVADA
　　(Parent: Dyn Specialty Contracting Inc)
101 Merritt 7 Ste 7, Norwalk, CT
Phone: (702) 736-8577
Sales: $80,000,000　　　　　　　　　　*Employees:* 100
Company Type: Public Family Member　*Employees here:* 100
SIC: 1731
　　General electrical contractor
Robert Brittan, President

D-U-N-S 19-775-3015
DYNAMIC SYSTEMS, INC
　　(Parent: Faulkner Group Inc)
3901 S Lamar Blvd Ste 300, Austin, TX 78704
Phone: (512) 443-4848
Sales: $150,000,000　　　　　　　　*Employees:* 1,000
Company Type: Private　　　　　　　*Employees here:* 625
SIC: 1711
　　Mechanical contractors
Allan E Bulley Jr, Chairman of the Board

D-U-N-S 95-671-4158
DYNCORP TRI-CITIES SERVICES
　　(Parent: Dyncorp)
2430 Stevens Dr H5-33, Richland, WA 99352
Phone: (509) 376-6068
Sales: $265,900,000　　　　　　　　*Employees:* 1,200
Company Type: Private　　　　　　*Employees here:* 1,200
SIC: 1542
　　Contractor of non-residential buildings
Richard Bunkoff, President

D-U-N-S 00-681-9213
E A HATHAWAY AND CO
　　(Parent: Hathaway Dinwiddie Construction Group)
565 Laurelwood Rd, Santa Clara, CA 95054
Phone: (408) 988-4200
Sales: $80,000,000　　　　　　　　　　*Employees:* 100
Company Type: Private　　　　　　　*Employees here:* 100
SIC: 1542
　　General contractor of commercial buildings
William T Firesheets, President

D-U-N-S 00-961-1484　　　　　　　　　　　　　EXP
E C CO
2121 NW Thurman St, Portland, OR 97210
Phone: (503) 224-3511

Sales: $160,015,000
Employees: 800
Company Type: Private
Employees here: 775
SIC: 1731
   Electrical contractor motor rewinding & repair whol
    electrical apparatus & whol diesel & gas engines
Patrick T Burke, President

D-U-N-S 00-692-6778
E E BLACK LTD
   (Parent: Tutor-Saliba Pacific Inc)
Rogers Blvd, Honolulu, HI 96819
Phone: (808) 836-0454
Sales: $112,000,000
Employees: 800
Company Type: Private
Employees here: 200
SIC: 1629
   Land clearing site work highway and airport runway
    contractor
L C Burlage Sr, Partner

D-U-N-S 01-687-4757
E E REED CONSTRUCTION LC
333 Commerce Green Blvd, Sugar Land, TX 77478
Phone: (281) 933-4000
Sales: $100,000,000
Employees: 125
Company Type: Private
Employees here: 125
SIC: 1542
   General contractor-commercial and industrial buildings
Patricia B Harris, Chairman of the Board

D-U-N-S 00-197-1324
E-J ELECTRIC INSTALLATION CO
4641 Vernon Blvd, Long Island City, NY 11101
Phone: (718) 786-9400
Sales: $80,000,000
Employees: 400
Company Type: Private
Employees here: 400
SIC: 1731
   Electrical work contractors
Michael C Welch, Chairman of the Board

D-U-N-S 03-105-2723
E L HAMM & ASSOCIATES INC
4801 Columbus St, Virginia Beach, VA 23462
Phone: (757) 497-5000
Sales: $87,200,000
Employees: 400
Company Type: Private
Employees here: 53
SIC: 1542
   Management & engineering consultants commercial
    contractors & general warehousing
Thomas R Burns, Chairman of the Board

D-U-N-S 00-831-8503
E L YEAGER CONSTRUCTION CO
   (Parent: Yeager Holdings Inc)
1995 Agua Mansa Rd, Riverside, CA 92509
Phone: (909) 684-5360
Sales: $171,555,000
Employees: 650
Company Type: Private
Employees here: 50
SIC: 1611
   General contractor of highways bridges & dams
Frederick H Burnstead, President

D-U-N-S 09-637-8187
E M J CORP
6148 Lee Hwy Ste 200, Chattanooga, TN 37421
Phone: (423) 855-1550
Sales: $188,921,000
Employees: 200
Company Type: Private
Employees here: 35
SIC: 1542
   Nonresidential construction
Charles D Duff, President

D-U-N-S 10-119-6723
E W HOWELL CO INC
   (Parent: E W Construction Group Inc)
2 Seaview Blvd Fl 3, Port Washington, NY 11050
Phone: (516) 621-1100
Sales: $125,000,000
Employees: 200
Company Type: Private
Employees here: 185
SIC: 1542
   General contractor & construction manager of institutional
    commercial & industrial buildings
John W Burton, Member

D-U-N-S 92-950-8448
EAGLEVENTURES INC
1355b Lynnfield Rd Ste 2, Memphis, TN 38119
Phone: (901) 818-5390
Sales: $270,000,000
Employees: 1,700
Company Type: Private
Employees here: 3
SIC: 1542
   Holding co that through its subs provides non-union gen
    constr mech elect millwright & design service
Harry H Bush, President

D-U-N-S 01-179-5192
EASTERN CONTRACTORS INC
571 Union Ave, Framingham, MA
Phone: (508) 820-4401
Sales: $70,094,000
Employees: 150
Company Type: Private
Employees here: 150
SIC: 1542
   General contractor of municipal buildings & heating
    ventilation & air conditioning work
Harry H Bush, Vice-President

D-U-N-S 15-409-0385
EBY CORP
610 N Main St, Wichita, KS 67203
Phone: (316) 268-3500
Sales: $114,600,000
Employees: 1,000
Company Type: Private
Employees here: 120
SIC: 1629
   Heavy construction contractor
Robert M Bushong, President

D-U-N-S 09-679-0225
ECKER ENTERPRISES INC
5374 N Elston Ave, Chicago, IL 60630
Phone: (773) 685-5500
Sales: $73,673,000
Employees: 400
Company Type: Private
Employees here: 5
SIC: 1742
   Commercial & residential interior & exterior painting &
    decorating drywall plastering acoustical work
Danny L Butler, President

D-U-N-S 00-794-7559
EDWARD KRAEMER & SONS INC
1 Plainview Rd, Plain, WI 53577
Phone: (608) 546-2311
Sales: $140,000,000
Employees: 300
Company Type: Private
Employees here: 150
SIC: 1622
   Bridge construction & produces aggregate
Micheal Samoviski, Chairman

D-U-N-S 01-085-7357
EDWARD ROSE BUILDING CO
30057 Orchard Lake Rd, Farmington Hills, MI 48334
Phone: (248) 539-2255

Sales: $83,400,000   *Employees:* 270
Company Type: Private   *Employees here:* 70
SIC: 1531
    Operative builder & operates apartment buildings
Richard A Byer, President

D-U-N-S 14-850-8351
EGAN COMPANIES
7100 Medicine Lake Rd, Minneapolis, MN 55427
Phone: (612) 544-4131
Sales: $94,723,000   *Employees:* 675
Company Type: Private   *Employees here:* 100
SIC: 1711
    Plumbing & heating contractor mfg sheet metal ventilating
      equipment electrical contracting & piping insulation
Bill Wishlinkski, Vice-President

D-U-N-S 15-374-7514
EICHLEAY HOLDINGS INC
5th & Penn Ave, Pittsburgh, PA 15206
Phone: (412) 361-3000
Sales: $150,000,000   *Employees:* 2,500
Company Type: Private   *Employees here:* 4
SIC: 1541
    Heavy construction contractor & consulting engineers
Joe Bolin, President

D-U-N-S 04-682-2896   EXP
ELGIN NATIONAL INDUSTRIES INC
2001 Bttrfeld Rd Ste 1020, Downers Grove, IL 60515
Phone: (630) 434-7200
Sales: $139,615,000   *Employees:* 672
Company Type: Private   *Employees here:* 12
SIC: 1629
    Engineering services construction of coal and mineral plants
      mfg elec controls mining machinery and equip and mfg
      fasteners
Joseph F Shaughnessy, Chairman of the Board

D-U-N-S 00-408-3234
ELKINS CONSTRUCTORS INC
4501 Beverly Ave, Jacksonville, FL 32210
Phone: (904) 384-6455
Sales: $78,944,000   *Employees:* 150
Company Type: Private   *Employees here:* 150
SIC: 1542
    Contractor specializing in new commercial & health care
      bldgs
Larry Solari, Chief Executive Officer

D-U-N-S 00-893-7641
ELLIOTT-LEWIS CORP
    (Parent: Firstenergy Services Corp)
2701 Grant Ave, Philadelphia, PA 19114
Phone: (215) 698-4400
Sales: $75,000,000   *Employees:* 480
Company Type: Public Family Member   *Employees here:* 276
SIC: 1711
    Contractor specializing in plumbing ventilation heating air
      conditioning refrigeration & building services
John S Thompson, President

D-U-N-S 79-497-1754
ELLIS-DON MICHIGAN INC
    (Parent: Ellis-Don Construction Ltd)
38705 7 Mile Rd Ste 345, Livonia, MI 48152
Phone: (734) 462-1600
Sales: $200,000,000   *Employees:* 40
Company Type: Private   *Employees here:* 40
SIC: 1541
    Contractor specializing in industrial commercial &
      institutional construction
John S Thompson, President

D-U-N-S 06-833-7708
ELMO GREER & SONS INC
Hwy 25 N, London, KY 40741
Phone: (606) 843-6136
Sales: $70,000,000   *Employees:* 200
Company Type: Private   *Employees here:* 160
SIC: 1611
    Highway contractor & mfr asphalt
Bruce W Cash, President

D-U-N-S 09-847-2947
EMBREE CONSTRUCTION GROUP
8050 Airport Rd, Georgetown, TX 78628
Phone: (512) 869-2626
Sales: $99,578,000   *Employees:* 101
Company Type: Private   *Employees here:* 101
SIC: 1542
    General & remodeling contractor of restaurant & store
      buildings
Alan Bird, President

D-U-N-S 01-710-6386   EXP
EMCOR GROUP INC
101 Merritt 7, Norwalk, CT
Phone: (203) 849-7800
Sales: $1,950,868,000   *Employees:* 14,000
Company Type: Public   *Employees here:* 50
SIC: 1731
    Electrical & mechanical contracting & facilities services
George R Edinger, President

D-U-N-S 05-937-1278
ENGELBERTH CONSTRUCTION INC
2000 Mountain View Dr, Colchester, VT
Phone: (802) 655-0100
Sales: $100,767,000   *Employees:* 240
Company Type: Private   *Employees here:* 210
SIC: 1542
    Contractor specializing in new construction of commercial
      industrial & multi-family buildings
John M Ortenzio, President

D-U-N-S 09-347-3452
ENGLE HOMES INC
123 NW 13th St Ste 300, Boca Raton, FL 33432
Phone: (561) 391-4012
Sales: $536,040,000   *Employees:* 744
Company Type: Public   *Employees here:* 40
SIC: 1521
    Single family home construction and real estate developer
John F Dillon, Chairman of the Board

D-U-N-S 09-997-7126
EQUIPMENT SUPPLY CO INC
    (Parent: United Rentals Inc)
1603 Route 130, Burlington, NJ
Phone: (609) 387-4645
Sales: $100,000,000   *Employees:* 250
Company Type: Public Family Member   *Employees here:* 75
SIC: 7353
    Leases aerial work platform equipment
W E Mangum, Chairman of the Board

D-U-N-S 13-958-1219
ESTRIDGE GROUP INC
1041 W Main St, Carmel, IN 46032
Phone: (317) 846-7311
Sales: $85,000,000   *Employees:* 122
Company Type: Private   *Employees here:* 120
SIC: 1521
    General contractor single family homes
Clinton C Myers, President

D-U-N-S 00-693-8807
F A WILHELM CONSTRUCTION CO
3914 Prospect St, Indianapolis, IN 46203
Phone: (317) 359-5411
Sales: $101,700,000
Company Type: Private   *Employees:* 800
                               Employees here: 150
SIC: 1541
   Contractor industrial buildings mechanical contractor and
      commercial buildings
Dan Jordan, Manager

D-U-N-S 87-633-2040
F H PASCHEN, S N NIELSEN, INC.
701 Lee St Ste 550, Des Plaines, IL 60016
Phone: (847) 699-1595
Sales: $93,768,000
Company Type: Private   *Employees:* 150
                               Employees here: 145
SIC: 1542
   General contractor of commercial buildings schools highways
      and bridges
Gordon Campbell, Chief Executive Officer

D-U-N-S 00-678-0316
F N THOMPSON CO
   (Parent: B E & K Inc)
201 Clanton Rd, Charlotte, NC 28217
Phone: (704) 523-0515
Sales: $120,000,000
Company Type: Private   *Employees:* 130
                               Employees here: 45
SIC: 1542
   Commercial and institutional building contractor
Charles D Henderson, President

D-U-N-S 19-502-9830
FACILITY GROUP INC
   (Parent: Facility Holdings Corp)
2233 Lake Park Dr SE, Smyrna, GA 30080
Phone: (770) 437-2700
Sales: $115,831,000
Company Type: Private   *Employees:* 225
                               Employees here: 180
SIC: 1541
   Management company involved in the design and
      construction of food distributing and food processing
      facilities
Michael Sciarrino, Chief Financial Officer

D-U-N-S 14-434-7614
FAIRFIELD DEVELOPMENT INC
5510 Morehouse Dr Ste 200, San Diego, CA 92121
Phone: (619) 457-2123
Sales: $80,000,000
Company Type: Private   *Employees:* 25
                               Employees here: 25
SIC: 1522
   Contractor of multi-family buildings
Charles Floyd, President

D-U-N-S 19-623-1096
FAULKNER GROUP, INC
3901 S Lamar Blvd Ste 370, Austin, TX 78704
Phone: (512) 448-9898
Sales: $300,000,000
Company Type: Private   *Employees:* 2,100
                               Employees here: 15
SIC: 1542
   Contractor specializing in commercial industrial institutional
      and municipal buildings doing both new and renovation
      work
Mildred Frazier, Treasurer

D-U-N-S 01-126-4421
FCI CONSTRUCTORS, INC
507 Fruitvale Ct Ste A, Grand Junction, CO 81504
Phone: (970) 434-9093

Sales: $82,654,000   *Employees:* 150
Company Type: Private   *Employees here:* 75
SIC: 1542
   New construction & renovation of commercial & office
      buildings & industrial buildings
Charles G Erickson III, President

D-U-N-S 18-276-5297
FCL BUILDERS, INC.
1150 Spring Lake Dr, Itasca, IL 60143
Phone: (630) 773-0050
Sales: $108,753,000   *Employees:* 35
Company Type: Private   *Employees here:* 35
SIC: 1541
   Industrial building construction
Janet W Bean, President

D-U-N-S 01-459-8213
FEDERATED HOME & MORTGAGE CO
   (Parent: National Capital Companies Ltd)
1 Country Club Ln, State College, PA 16803
Phone: (814) 238-0535
Sales: $95,000,000   *Employees:* 1,000
Company Type: Private   *Employees here:* 150
SIC: 1522
   Gen contr-apt bldgs & motels operates apt bldgs motels
      restaurants golf club tavern ret gen mdse & provides capital
C F Jordan III, Chairman of the Board

D-U-N-S 18-118-6479
FELIX EQUITIES, INC.
Lincolndale, NY 10540
Phone: (914) 248-8500
Sales: $77,872,000   *Employees:* 350
Company Type: Private   *Employees here:* 20
SIC: 1623
   Gen contractor specializing in sewers pipelines road highways
      and bridge construction foundation work and sewage
      treatment
C F Jordan III, President

D-U-N-S 62-609-2613
FIELDSTONE COMMUNITIES INC
14 Corporate Plaza Dr, Newport Beach, CA 92660
Phone: (949) 640-9090
Sales: $132,000,000   *Employees:* 130
Company Type: Private   *Employees here:* 70
SIC: 1531
   Operative builders
C F Jordan III, Chairman of the Board

D-U-N-S 00-580-3671
FISCHBACH & MOORE ELECTRIC LLC
675 Central Ave, New Providence, NJ
Phone: (908) 508-2600
Sales: $185,600,000   *Employees:* 2,500
Company Type: Private   *Employees here:* 100
SIC: 1731
   General electrical contractor
C F Jordan, Chairman

D-U-N-S 03-780-0398   EXP
FISCHBACH CORP
   (Parent: American International Group)
2775 S Vallejo St, Englewood, CO 80110
Phone: (303) 783-7500
Sales: $400,000,000   *Employees:* 1,000
Company Type: Public Family Member   *Employees here:* 6
SIC: 1731
   Electrical mechanical & general contractor
Clarence Chase, President

D-U-N-S 08-651-5806
FISH CONSTRUCTION CO
11331 Ventura Blvd, Studio City, CA 91604
Phone: (818) 487-1000
Sales: $68,500,000   *Employees:* 500
Company Type: Private   *Employees here:* 12
SIC: 1521
   General contractor of single multi family homes and
      commercial construction
Arthur C Cox Jr, President

D-U-N-S 04-797-5867
FISHEL CO
1810 Arlingate Ln, Columbus, OH 43228
Phone: (614) 274-8100
Sales: $140,872,000   *Employees:* 1,200
Company Type: Private   *Employees here:* 150
SIC: 1623
   Installs telephone & electric utility lines fiberoptic cable cable
      television & gas mains
Andrew Alcorn, Manager

D-U-N-S 07-877-1185
FISHER DEVELOPMENT INC
1485 Bayshore Blvd, San Francisco, CA 94124
Phone: (415) 468-1717
Sales: $310,072,000   *Employees:* 265
Company Type: Private   *Employees here:* 145
SIC: 1542
   General contractors
Henry T Segerstrom, Owner

D-U-N-S 00-842-5084
FISK ELECTRIC CO
   (Parent: Fisk Corp)
111 T C Jester Blvd, Houston, TX 77007
Phone: (713) 868-6111
Sales: $134,102,000   *Employees:* 1,500
Company Type: Private   *Employees here:* 600
SIC: 1731
   General electrical contractor
Richard Taylor, Chief Executive Officer

D-U-N-S 10-275-0130
FK CO, INC
   (Parent: Cornerstone Construction & Metals)
800 S Hutton Rd, Farmington, NM 87401
Phone: (505) 327-5168
Sales: $109,179,000   *Employees:* 700
Company Type: Private   *Employees here:* 35
SIC: 1541
   Industrial facilities & power plant construction company
Gerald D Overaa, President

D-U-N-S 18-228-4216
FLATIRON STRUCTURES CO LLC
10090 I 25 Frontage Rd, Longmont, CO 80504
Phone: (303) 444-1760
Sales: $150,000,000   *Employees:* 320
Company Type: Private   *Employees here:* 60
SIC: 1622
   Bridge construction & heavy concrete work & industrial
      construction
Jerome H Williams, President

D-U-N-S 05-179-0129
FLATLEY CO
50 Braintree Hill Park, Braintree, MA
Phone: (781) 848-2000

Sales: $423,200,000   *Employees:* 4,500
Company Type: Private   *Employees here:* 200
SIC: 1522
   Operates apartments hotels industrial parks office buildings
      shopping crts & nursing homes
Charles P Morgan, President

D-U-N-S 15-113-5134
FLETCHER CONSTRUCTION CO HAWAII LTD
707 Richards St Ste 400, Honolulu, HI 96813
Phone: (808) 533-5000
Sales: $230,000,000   *Employees:* 900
Company Type: Private   *Employees here:* 35
SIC: 1542
   General contractor of commercial buildings apartment
      buildings and condominiums
Charles R Jackson, Chief Executive Officer

D-U-N-S 00-696-9018
FLINT ENGINEERING & CONSTRUCTION CO
   (Parent: Flint Industries Inc)
2440 S Yukon Ave, Tulsa, OK 74107
Phone: (918) 584-0033
Sales: $91,000,000   *Employees:* 1,100
Company Type: Private   *Employees here:* 40
SIC: 1623
   Oil & gas pipeline & plant construction & oil field services
F M Pinkerton, Chief Executive Officer

D-U-N-S 06-455-3092
FLINT INDUSTRIES, INC
   (Parent: Flint Resources Co)
1624 W 21st St, Tulsa, OK 74107
Phone: (918) 587-8451
Sales: $403,000,000   *Employees:* 1,999
Company Type: Private   *Employees here:* 15
SIC: 1542
   Commercial & industrial building contractor pipeline
      construction & oilfield services
Charles Raimondo Sr, President

D-U-N-S 11-191-9205
FLORIDA MIVAN INC
Hollywood Ave, Lake Buena Vista, FL 32830
Phone: (407) 363-4450
Sales: $71,500,000   *Employees:* 330
Company Type: Private   *Employees here:* 300
SIC: 1542
   Commercial construction
Charles J Rallo Jr, Chairman of the Board

D-U-N-S 04-338-3793
FLUOR DANIEL CARIBBEAN INC
   (Parent: Fluor Daniel Inc)
3353 Michelson Dr, Irvine, CA 92698
Phone: (949) 975-2000
Sales: $199,200,000   *Employees:* 1,572
Company Type: Public Family Member   *Employees here:* 1
SIC: 1541
   General contractor-industrial buildings
Ramiro Valdez, President

D-U-N-S 11-510-8599
F.N.F. CONSTRUCTION, INC.
   (Parent: C J Langenfelder & Son Inc)
115 S 48th St, Tempe, AZ 85281
Phone: (602) 784-2910
Sales: $114,222,000   *Employees:* 300
Company Type: Private   *Employees here:* 300
SIC: 1611
   General contractor highway construction & grading &
      excavation contractor & mfg asphalt rubber
Charles D Moody Jr, President

D-U-N-S 06-239-5173
FONTAINE BROS INC
510 Cottage St, Springfield, MA
Phone: (413) 781-2020
Sales: $75,000,000 | *Employees:* 150
Company Type: Private | *Employees here:* 150
SIC: 1542
General building contractor commercial & industrial
Bruce Polishook, Chairman of the Board

D-U-N-S 79-917-1020
FOOTHILLS EASTERN TRANSPORTATION
201 Sandpointe Ave, Santa Ana, CA 92707
Phone: (714) 436-9800
Sales: $83,378,000 | *Employees:* 45
Company Type: Private | *Employees here:* 45
SIC: 1611
Government agency specializing in the construction of
transportation corridors
R E Matthews, Chairman of the Board

D-U-N-S 86-832-1191
FORECAST GROUP, LP
10670 Civic Center Dr, Rancho Cucamonga, CA 91730
Phone: (909) 987-7788
Sales: $198,074,000 | *Employees:* 188
Company Type: Private | *Employees here:* 70
SIC: 1531
Operative builder of single family homes
Robert Chianelli, President

D-U-N-S 09-328-2580
FORTNEY & WEYGANDT, INC.
31269 Bradley Rd, North Olmsted, OH 44070
Phone: (440) 716-4000
Sales: $85,000,000 | *Employees:* 140
Company Type: Private | *Employees here:* 140
SIC: 1542
General contractor commercial institutional & industrial
buildings
James Adamson, President

D-U-N-S 94-578-7588
FORTRESS GROUP INC
1650 Tysons Blvd Ste 600, McLean, VA 22102
Phone: (703) 442-4545
Sales: $445,311,000 | *Employees:* 350
Company Type: Public | *Employees here:* 11
SIC: 1521
Holding company
Greg Bostwick, President

D-U-N-S 17-382-4186
FOSTER WHEELER CONSTRS INC
(*Parent:* Foster Wheeler USA Corp)
Perryville Corporate Park, Clinton, NJ
Phone: (908) 730-4000
Sales: $251,070,000 | *Employees:* 200
Company Type: Public Family Member | *Employees here:* 70
SIC: 1541
Industrial building construction
Robert S Long, President

D-U-N-S 87-737-8414
FOWLER-JONES BEERS CONSTRUCTION
10 W 32nd St, Winston Salem, NC 27105
Phone: (336) 759-7800
Sales: $83,258,000 | *Employees:* 150
Company Type: Private | *Employees here:* 150
SIC: 1542
General contractor specializing in commercial & industrial
construction
James D Laub, President

D-U-N-S 18-481-4879
FRAMATOME USA INC
1911 Fort Myer Dr Ste 705, Arlington, VA 22209
Phone: (703) 527-4747
Sales: $148,500,000 | *Employees:* 2,000
Company Type: Private | *Employees here:* 6
SIC: 1731
Holding company providing management services for
subsidiaries
John Caddell, Chairman of the Board

D-U-N-S 00-697-4232
FRANK A MCBRIDE CO
233 Central Ave, Hawthorne, NJ
Phone: (973) 423-1123
Sales: $82,097,000 | *Employees:* 200
Company Type: Private | *Employees here:* 100
SIC: 1711
Mechanical & sheet metal contractors
James A McShane, Chief Executive Officer

D-U-N-S 04-160-3499
FRANK MESSER & SONS CONSTRUCTION CO
4612 Paddock Rd, Cincinnati, OH 45229
Phone: (513) 242-1541
Sales: $239,611,000 | *Employees:* 400
Company Type: Private | *Employees here:* 280
SIC: 1542
Builder hospitals comm'l/office bldgs schools institutional/
industrial bldgs & warehouses hotels and multi-family
dwellings
L L Grigsby, Chairman of the Board

D-U-N-S 00-978-4638
FREESEN, INC
316 S Pearl Hwy 100, Bluffs, IL 62621
Phone: (217) 754-3304
Sales: $94,538,000 | *Employees:* 250
Company Type: Private | *Employees here:* 250
SIC: 1629
Contractor
Owen Kratz, Chairman of the Board

D-U-N-S 05-388-8038
FREHNER CONSTRUCTION CO INC
4040 Frehner Rd, North Las Vegas, NV 89030
Phone: (702) 649-6250
Sales: $68,823,000 | *Employees:* 250
Company Type: Private | *Employees here:* 250
SIC: 1611
Highway construction contractor
Charles Middleton, Principal

D-U-N-S 60-283-3634   EXP
FRU-CON HOLDING CORP
15933 Clayton Rd, Ballwin, MO 63011
Phone: (314) 391-6700
Sales: $538,157,000 | *Employees:* 2,800
Company Type: Private | *Employees here:* 450
SIC: 1541
General contractor power process industrial environmental
energy commercial & heavy construction
Linda Johnston, Principal

D-U-N-S 12-087-8020
FTR INTERNATIONAL INC
5 Park Plz Ste 1240, Irvine, CA 92614
Phone: (949) 263-8170
Sales: $100,000,000 | *Employees:* 300
Company Type: Private | *Employees here:* 300
SIC: 1542
Global engineering and building contractors
Cal Cox, Chairman of the Board

D-U-N-S 00-480-8028
FULLMAN CO, LLC
5711 SW Hood Ave, Portland, OR 97201
Phone: (503) 224-5200
Sales: $120,000,000   *Employees:* 600
Company Type: Private   *Employees here:* 600
SIC: 1711
    Plumbing/heating/air conditioning contractor
Roy Pool, Branch Manager

D-U-N-S 03-084-7057
FULLMER CONSTRUCTION
1725 S Grove Ave, Ontario, CA 91761
Phone: (909) 947-9467
Sales: $110,000,000   *Employees:* 210
Company Type: Private   *Employees here:* 198
SIC: 1541
    General contractors of new industrial and commercial
        buildings
Donald L Bren, Chairman of the Board

D-U-N-S 07-444-1932
FULTON HOMES CORP
9140 S Kyrene Rd Ste 202, Tempe, AZ 85284
Phone: (602) 753-6789
Sales: $150,000,000   *Employees:* 60
Company Type: Private   *Employees here:* 60
SIC: 1521
    General contractor single family homes
Daniel V Callaghan, President

D-U-N-S 96-508-3199
G B I CONSTRUCTION INC
3120 Medlock Bridge Rd, Norcross, GA 30071
Phone: (770) 448-7008
Sales: $300,000,000   *Employees:* 30
Company Type: Private   *Employees here:* 30
SIC: 1542
    Commercial construction
Michael G Callas, President

D-U-N-S 03-192-6652
G E JOHNSON CONSTRUCTION CO
310 S 14th St, Colorado Springs, CO 80904
Phone: (719) 473-5321
Sales: $152,206,000   *Employees:* 300
Company Type: Private   *Employees here:* 280
SIC: 1542
    General contractor commercial & industrial
Victor Zaccaglin, Chairman of the Board

D-U-N-S 17-514-5788
G J F CONSTRUCTION CORP
1 Wall Street Ct Fl 15, New York, NY 10005
Phone: (212) 635-0760
Sales: $100,365,000   *Employees:* 120
Company Type: Private   *Employees here:* 120
SIC: 1542
    General contractor of commercial & residential building
        alterations and office interiors also new building
        construction
Anthony J Caldarone, President

D-U-N-S 15-275-7639
G L HOMES OF FLORIDA CORP
1401 N University Dr, Pompano Beach, FL 33071
Phone: (954) 753-1730
Sales: $185,000,000   *Employees:* 170
Company Type: Private   *Employees here:* 45
SIC: 1521
    Contractor specializing in new construction of single family
        homes
Bradley A Little, Chief Financial Officer

D-U-N-S 00-482-8893
G W MURPHY CONSTRUCTION CO
    (Parent: Tutor-Saliba Corp)
650 Kakoi St, Honolulu, HI 96819
Phone: (808) 836-0454
Sales: $112,000,000   *Employees:* 250
Company Type: Private   *Employees here:* 250
SIC: 1542
    General contractors of commercial and office buildings
Richard E Gardner, President

D-U-N-S 09-678-8047
GALE INDUSTRIES INC
    (Parent: Masco Corp)
2339 Beville Rd, Daytona Beach, FL 32119
Phone: (904) 304-2222
Sales: $141,700,000   *Employees:* 2,448
Company Type: Public Family Member   *Employees here:* 100
SIC: 1742
    Insulation contractors
George Brestle, President

D-U-N-S 02-743-1444
GALL, LANDAU YOUNG CONSTRUCTION CO
100 116th Ave SE, Bellevue, WA 98004
Phone: (425) 451-8877
Sales: $134,743,000   *Employees:* 200
Company Type: Private   *Employees here:* 200
SIC: 1542
    New construction & remodeling of commercial buildings
William S Orosz Jr, Managing Partner

D-U-N-S 06-989-1919
GAMBONE BROS CONSTRUCTION CO
    (Parent: Gambone Bros Enterprises Inc)
1030 W Germantown Pike, Norristown, PA 19403
Phone: (610) 277-4220
Sales: $85,000,000   *Employees:* 120
Company Type: Private   *Employees here:* 120
SIC: 1521
    General contractor of single family homes & industrial
        buildings
Robert F Campbell Jr, President

D-U-N-S 13-762-9911
GAMMA CONSTRUCTION CO
2808 Joanel St, Houston, TX 77027
Phone: (713) 963-0086
Sales: $80,608,000   *Employees:* 100
Company Type: Private   *Employees here:* 90
SIC: 1542
    General contractor of commercial buildings
Dewain E Campbell, President

D-U-N-S 02-745-2689
GARY MERLINO CONSTRUCTION CO
9125 10th Ave S, Seattle, WA 98108
Phone: (206) 762-9125
Sales: $100,000,000   *Employees:* 325
Company Type: Private   *Employees here:* 15
SIC: 1611
    Highway street water & sewer contractor & mfg ready-mixed
        concrete
Raymond J Camosy, President

D-U-N-S 08-698-4937
GECOS INC
1936 Lee Rd, Winter Park, FL 32789
Phone: (407) 645-5500

Sales: $220,000,000   *Employees:* 1,000
Company Type: Private   *Employees here:* 2
SIC: 1611
    Through subsidiary construction and paving of highways
Steve Campbell, President

D-U-N-S 05-662-6088
GEM INDUSTRIAL INC
    (Parent: Rudolph/Libbe Companies Inc)
6842 Commodore Dr, Walbridge, OH 43465
Phone: (419) 666-6554
Sales: $95,000,000   *Employees:* 1,000
Company Type: Private   *Employees here:* 1,000
SIC: 1711
    Mechanical boiler maintenance & electrical contractors
James P Krapf Sr, President

D-U-N-S 08-373-7403
GENERAL CONSTRUCTION CO
2111 N Northgate Way, Seattle, WA 98133
Phone: (206) 368-6300
Sales: $135,000,000   *Employees:* 500
Company Type: Private   *Employees here:* 466
SIC: 1622
    General contractor heavy civil industrial & marine
    construction
Ralph A Trallo, President

D-U-N-S 93-896-1810
GENERAL PACIFIC CONSTRUCTION
1260 Huntington Dr, South Pasadena, CA 91030
Phone: (323) 257-0883
Sales: $100,000,000   *Employees:* 10
Company Type: Private   *Employees here:* 10
SIC: 1542
    General contractor of commercial & residential structures
Charles R Werkheiser, President

D-U-N-S 00-577-7651
GERALD H PHIPPS INC
1530 W 13th Ave, Denver, CO 80204
Phone: (303) 571-5377
Sales: $146,000,000   *Employees:* 300
Company Type: Private   *Employees here:* 295
SIC: 1542
    Commercial & office building contractor
Albert G Wendt, President

D-U-N-S 15-453-5686
GETSCHOW GROUP INC
229 Van Buren St, Oconto Falls, WI 54154
Phone: (920) 846-8000
Sales: $84,870,000   *Employees:* 650
Company Type: Private   *Employees here:* 120
SIC: 1711
    Mechanical & process piping contractor
Roger Gossett, President

D-U-N-S 05-119-1914
GEUPEL DE MARS INC
    (Parent: Demars Corp)
1919 N Meridian St, Indianapolis, IN 46202
Phone: (317) 924-9192
Sales: $100,000,000   *Employees:* 100
Company Type: Private   *Employees here:* 100
SIC: 1542
    Institutional commercial contractor and industrial contractor
Duwayne Ternes, President

D-U-N-S 04-727-3842
GIANT CONSTRUCTION CO
    (Parent: Giant Food Inc)
6300 Sheriff Rd, Landover, MD 20785

Phone: (301) 386-0439
Sales: $165,400,000   *Employees:* 750
Company Type: Private   *Employees here:* 750
SIC: 1542
    Commercial and industrial building contractor
Robert E Doran III, President

D-U-N-S 09-628-7347
GILBANE BUILDING CO
    (Parent: Gilbane Inc)
7 Jackson Walkway, Providence, RI
Phone: (401) 456-5800
Sales: $910,309,000   *Employees:* 900
Company Type: Private   *Employees here:* 151
SIC: 1541
    Heavy industrial commercial & institutional contracting
    construction management & construction program
    management consultant
James E Bradley, President

D-U-N-S 00-784-5704
GILBERT COMPANIES, INC
    (Parent: Townsend Acquisition Inc)
101 S Main St, Parker City, IN 47368
Phone: (765) 468-3007
Sales: $118,100,000   *Employees:* 1,030
Company Type: Private   *Employees here:* 30
SIC: 1629
    Right of way & brush clearing & transmission & power line
    construction & electrical contractor
Hadi Makarechian, Chairman of the Board

D-U-N-S 05-507-6616
GILBERT SOUTHERN CORP.
    (Parent: Peter Kiewit Sons Inc)
3555 Farnam St, Omaha, NE 68131
Phone: (402) 342-2052
Sales: $84,700,000   *Employees:* 672
Company Type: Private   *Employees here:* 7
SIC: 1611
    Heavy highway & elevated highway construction
Louis Cappelli, President

D-U-N-S 92-630-3249
GLOBAL CONSTRUCTION CO LLC
1 Bala Ave Ste 400, Bala Cynwyd, PA 19004
Phone: (610) 668-4100
Sales: $150,000,000   *Employees:* 80
Company Type: Private   *Employees here:* 3
SIC: 1521
    General contractor of multi dwelling residential buildings
Joseph F Carabetta, Chief Executive Officer

D-U-N-S 03-317-8612
GLOBAL ENERGY EQP GROUP LLC
6120 S Yale Ave Ste 1480, Tulsa, OK 74136
Phone: (918) 488-0828
Sales: $98,300,000   *Employees:* 450
Company Type: Private   *Employees here:* 6
SIC: 1542
    Holding company
Conrad A Solinger, President

D-U-N-S 80-680-8309
GLOBAL INDUSTRIES, LTD
107 Global Cir, Lafayette, LA 70503
Phone: (318) 989-0000
Sales: $379,901,000   *Employees:* 1,563
Company Type: Public   *Employees here:* 60
SIC: 1623
    Pipeline construction services derrick services diving services
    and oil equipment transportation
Osvaldo J Ortiz, President

D-U-N-S 00-637-3443
GOHMANN ASPHALT AND CONSTRUCTION
(Parent: Gohman Construction Inc)
1630 Broadway St, Clarksville, IN 47129
Phone: (812) 282-1349
Sales: $88,000,000   *Employees:* 200
Company Type: Private   *Employees here:* 120
SIC: 1611
   Highway street & bridge construction
Tim Ballard, President

D-U-N-S 02-804-0509
GONSALVES & SANTUCCI INC
5151 Port Chicago Hwy, Concord, CA 94520
Phone: (925) 685-6799
Sales: $122,545,000   *Employees:* 300
Company Type: Private   *Employees here:* 50
SIC: 1541
   General contractor & concrete construction
Carl O Belt Jr, President

D-U-N-S 00-794-3996
GOODFELLOW BROS, INC
1407 Walla Walla Ave, Wenatchee, WA 98801
Phone: (509) 662-7111
Sales: $70,000,000   *Employees:* 300
Company Type: Private   *Employees here:* 30
SIC: 1611
   Construction of highways roads sewers land clearing golf
   course dam irrigation excavating asphalt paving & rock
   crushing
David C Bolander, Chairman of the Board

D-U-N-S 80-252-6780
GOODMAN FAMILY OF BUILDERS
1424 Gables Ct Ste 101, Plano, TX 75075
Phone: (972) 596-0301
Sales: $113,730,000   *Employees:* 156
Company Type: Private   *Employees here:* 130
SIC: 1521
   Single-family house construction
Carl M Freeman, Chairman of the Board

D-U-N-S 18-053-1022
GRACE INDUSTRIES, INC
15145 6th Rd, Whitestone, NY 11357
Phone: (718) 767-9000
Sales: $73,000,000   *Employees:* 100
Company Type: Private   *Employees here:* 100
SIC: 1741
   Concrete block masonry contractor
Peter T Carlino, President

D-U-N-S 04-118-1447
GRAHAM COMPANIES
6843 Main St, Hialeah, FL 33014
Phone: (305) 821-1130
Sales: $156,700,000   *Employees:* 650
Company Type: Private   *Employees here:* 100
SIC: 1531
   Operative builders hotel operation farming land developer
Wayne Carlisle, President

D-U-N-S 14-795-6445
GRANGER MANAGEMENT CORP
415 Boston Tpke, Shrewsbury, MA
Phone: (508) 842-8961
Sales: $99,756,000   *Employees:* 214
Company Type: Private   *Employees here:* 40
SIC: 1542
   General contractor of commercial institutional industrial &
   multi-family buildings
R S Yarborough, Chairman of the Board

D-U-N-S 12-136-0325
GRANGER NORTHERN INC
(Parent: Granger Management Corp)
84 Middle St, Portland, ME
Phone: (207) 774-3500
Sales: $99,756,000   *Employees:* 40
Company Type: Private   *Employees here:* 40
SIC: 1542
   New construction & renovations & repair of commercial &
   industrial buildings
Edward R Carr, President

D-U-N-S 62-282-6360
GRANITE CONSTRUCTION INC
585 W Beach St, Watsonville, CA 95076
Phone: (831) 724-1011
Sales: $1,028,205,000   *Employees:* 1,800
Company Type: Public   *Employees here:* 125
SIC: 1611
   General contractor roads highways bridges dams tunnels
   canals and site preparation
Albert W Turner, General Partner

D-U-N-S 04-957-5371
GRAYCOR INC
(Parent: CCBC Inc)
1 Graycor Dr, Homewood, IL 60430
Phone: (708) 206-0500
Sales: $200,000,000   *Employees:* 500
Company Type: Private   *Employees here:* 1
SIC: 1541
   Holding company
Douglas Carson, President

D-U-N-S 36-289-9130
GREAT LAKES DREDGE & DOCK CORP DEL
(Parent: Blackstone Dredging Partners)
2122 York Rd Fl 2, Oak Brook, IL 60523
Phone: (630) 574-3000
Sales: $258,296,000   *Employees:* 800
Company Type: Private   *Employees here:* 100
SIC: 1629
   Dredging & marine construction river & harbor
   improvements construction of foundations piers & bridges
   & beach renourishment
Charles L Christensen, President

D-U-N-S 10-233-3986
GREEN HOLDINGS INC
2000 S Colorado Blvd Towe, Denver, CA 94111
Phone: (415) 421-0239
Sales: $151,300,000   *Employees:* 1,200
Company Type: Private   *Employees here:* 3
SIC: 1611
   Highway street commercial & mining contractor
Tom Dobson, Chief Executive Officer

D-U-N-S 79-186-0943
GREYSTONE HOMES INC
(Parent: Lennar Corp)
6767 Forest Lawn Dr, Los Angeles, CA 90068
Phone: (323) 436-6300
Sales: $420,000,000   *Employees:* 454
Company Type: Public Family Member   *Employees here:* 33
SIC: 1521
   Single-family house construction
R V Casey, President

D-U-N-S 96-438-1230
GROUP MAINTENANCE AMERICA
8 E Greenway Plz Ste 1500, Houston, TX 77046
Phone: (713) 626-4778

Sales: $437,000,000   *Employees:* 2,800
Company Type: Public   *Employees here:* 11
SIC: 1711
     Plumbing HVAC & electrical contractor
Donald Lamberti, Principal

D-U-N-S 00-438-0705
GRUCON CORP
101 W Pleasant St Ste 201, Milwaukee, WI 53212
Phone: (414) 223-6900
Sales: $88,450,000   *Employees:* 532
Company Type: Private   *Employees here:* 2
SIC: 1711
     Mechanical contractor & construction manager
William Spielvogel, Project Sponsor

D-U-N-S 00-946-7002
GRUPE CO (INC)
3255 W March Ln Fl 4, Stockton, CA 95219
Phone: (209) 473-6000
Sales: $124,800,000   *Employees:* 400
Company Type: Private   *Employees here:* 60
SIC: 1531
     Operative builder property management
Dale Pyatt, Project Sponsor

D-U-N-S 00-890-8519
GUARANTEE ELECTRICAL CO
3405 Bent Ave, St. Louis, MO 63116
Phone: (314) 773-1111
Sales: $80,000,000   *Employees:* 650
Company Type: Private   *Employees here:* 550
SIC: 1731
     Electrical contractor
Jay Cashman, Partner

D-U-N-S 05-170-3098
GUY F ATKINSON CO OF CALIFORNIA
1005 Oak Hill Rd, Lafayette, CA 94549
Phone: (925) 299-1357
Sales: $370,551,000   *Employees:* 20
Company Type: Private   *Employees here:* 20
SIC: 1629
     Heavy industrial and commercial construction
R V Casteel, President

D-U-N-S 95-863-7571
GVL CONTRACTORS LLC
40 Saddle Ridge Rd, Milton, MA
Phone: (617) 989-0805
Sales: $130,000,000   *Employees:* 56
Company Type: Private   *Employees here:* 56
SIC: 1521
     General construction contractor
David H Murdock, Chief Executive Officer

D-U-N-S 03-480-7313
H & M CONSTRUCTION CO., INC
50 Security Dr, Jackson, TN 38305
Phone: (901) 664-6300
Sales: $190,029,000   *Employees:* 250
Company Type: Private   *Employees here:* 100
SIC: 1541
     General contractor of industrial & institutional buildings
Clifford Running, President

D-U-N-S 05-694-8383
H B E CORP
11330 Olive Street Rd, St. Louis, MO 63141
Phone: (314) 567-9000

Sales: $2,455,600,000   *Employees:* 11,000
Company Type: Private   *Employees here:* 550
SIC: 1542
     General contractor hospitals medical office buildings
       healthcare facilities financial facilities and hotels & operates
       hotels
Daniel S Catalfumo, President

D-U-N-S 00-793-6974   EXP
H B ZACHRY CO
     (*Parent:* Zachry Inc)
527 Logwood Ave, San Antonio, TX 78221
Phone: (210) 475-8000
Sales: $665,000,000   *Employees:* 9,000
Company Type: Private   *Employees here:* 300
SIC: 1611
     Highway/bridge/pipeline/dams etc heavy construction
       contractor whol construction machinery/equipment
Catlfumo C Inc, Partner

D-U-N-S 00-388-2685
H J RUSSELL & CO
504 Fair St SW, Atlanta, GA 30313
Phone: (404) 330-1000
Sales: $131,900,000   *Employees:* 600
Company Type: Private   *Employees here:* 211
SIC: 1542
     Construction program management real estate development
       property management and contractor of multi-family
       buildings
Daniel S Catalfumo, President

D-U-N-S 00-693-7122
HAGERMAN CONSTRUCTION CORP
510 W Washington Blvd, Fort Wayne, IN 46802
Phone: (219) 424-1470
Sales: $89,010,000   *Employees:* 160
Company Type: Private   *Employees here:* 30
SIC: 1542
     Commercial institutional & industrial contractor
Raymond Rutter, President

D-U-N-S 62-078-7820
HAKE GROUP INC
1500 Chester Pike, Eddystone, PA 19022
Phone: (610) 876-9291
Sales: $72,000,000   *Employees:* 225
Company Type: Private   *Employees here:* 50
SIC: 1796
     Holding company
John W Vojtech, President

D-U-N-S 96-464-5022
HALLIBURTON DELAWARE, INC
     (*Parent:* Halliburton Co)
500 N Akard St Ste 3600, Dallas, TX 75201
Phone: (214) 978-2600
Sales: $6,592,800,000   *Employees:* 57,300
Company Type: Public Family Member   *Employees here:* 100
SIC: 1629
     Heavy & marine construction contractor & engineering
       services oil field services and specialties
Melvin Gray, Chairman of the Board

D-U-N-S 09-447-1430
HARBERT CORP
1 Riverchase Pkwy S, Birmingham, AL 35244
Phone: (205) 987-5500
Sales: $623,400,000   *Employees:* 2,800
Company Type: Private   *Employees here:* 200
SIC: 1542
     Gas transmission developer and power production
Nita Ing, President

D-U-N-S 00-923-6357
HARBISON-MAHONY-HIGGINS INC
8589 Thys Ct, Sacramento, CA 95828
Phone: (916) 383-4825
Sales: $75,000,000   *Employees:* 100
Company Type: Private   *Employees here:* 100
SIC: 1542
   Nonresidential construction
Ron Schuster, President

D-U-N-S 79-210-2287
HARBOR VIEW HOLDINGS, INC
433 California St Fl 7, San Francisco, CA 94104
Phone: (415) 982-7777
Sales: $130,000,000   *Employees:* 2,500
Company Type: Private   *Employees here:* 20
SIC: 1522
   Hotel contractor & development single-family homes
      contractor commercial property owner & hotel & restaurant
      management
Robins H Jackson, Chairman of the Board

D-U-N-S 00-692-5796
HARDAWAY CO INC
945 Broadway, Columbus, GA 31901
Phone: (706) 322-3274
Sales: $135,000,000   *Employees:* 600
Company Type: Private   *Employees here:* 40
SIC: 1622
   General contractors for road building and heavy construction
      of dams docks power plants marine and bridges
W M Sweetser Jr, President

D-U-N-S 13-105-6467
HARDAWAY GROUP INC
615 Main St, Nashville, TN 37206
Phone: (615) 254-5461
Sales: $115,000,000   *Employees:* 657
Company Type: Private   *Employees here:* 3
SIC: 1542
   General contractor & apartment management
Robert Shiver, President

D-U-N-S 08-696-8344
HARDIN CONSTRUCTION GROUP INC
1380 W Paces Ferry Rd NW, Atlanta, GA 30327
Phone: (404) 264-0404
Sales: $450,000,000   *Employees:* 500
Company Type: Private   *Employees here:* 150
SIC: 1542
   General building contractor and construction management
Leo E Center, Chairman of the Board

D-U-N-S 00-696-0876
HARLAN ELECTRIC CO
   (Parent: MYR Group Inc)
2695 Crooks Rd, Rochester Hills, MI 48309
Phone: (248) 853-4601
Sales: $144,700,000   *Employees:* 1,950
Company Type: Public Family Member   *Employees here:* 250
SIC: 1731
   General electrical contractor
Clyde Jones, President

D-U-N-S 03-615-5612   EXP
HARMON, LTD
   (Parent: Apogee Enterprises Inc)
2001 Killebrew Dr Ste 400, Minneapolis, MN 55425
Phone: (612) 851-9949

Sales: $247,301,000   *Employees:* 1,600
Company Type: Public Family Member   *Employees here:* 150
SIC: 1793
   Curtain wall (glazing) contractor
Michael W Herberholz, President

D-U-N-S 02-086-8758
HARMONY CORP
   (Parent: Turner Industries Ltd)
8687 United Plaza Blvd, Baton Rouge, LA 70809
Phone: (225) 922-5050
Sales: $543,800,000   *Employees:* 4,300
Company Type: Private   *Employees here:* 3,780
SIC: 1541
   Industrial plant repairs & maintenance & industrial
      construction
Robert Van Cleave, President

D-U-N-S 11-824-4722
HARMONY CORP OF TEXAS
   (Parent: Turner Industries Ltd)
3850 Pasadena Blvd, Pasadena, TX 77503
Phone: (713) 477-7440
Sales: $163,000,000   *Employees:* 40
Company Type: Private   *Employees here:* 40
SIC: 1541
   Industrial contractor
David W Quinn, Chief Financial Officer

D-U-N-S 10-866-4368
HARRIS CONTRACTING CO
909 Montreal Cir, St. Paul, MN 55102
Phone: (651) 602-6500
Sales: $70,570,000   *Employees:* 300
Company Type: Private   *Employees here:* 85
SIC: 1711
   Plumbing and mechanical contractor
David R Taylor, President

D-U-N-S 96-259-9221
HATHAWAY DINWIDDIE CONSTRUCTION GROUP
275 Battery St Ste 300, San Francisco, CA 94111
Phone: (415) 986-2718
Sales: $452,000,000   *Employees:* 650
Company Type: Private   *Employees here:* 2
SIC: 1542
   General contractor
Timothy R Eller, Chairman of the Board

D-U-N-S 13-108-4667
HAWKEYE CONSTRUCTION, INC
   (Parent: MYR Group Inc)
1500 NW Graham Ave, Troutdale, OR 97060
Phone: (503) 661-1568
Sales: $431,276,000   *Employees:* 120
Company Type: Public Family Member   *Employees here:* 120
SIC: 1623
   Power line & substations
Barry Wilson, Controller

D-U-N-S 00-287-3693
HAWKINS CONSTRUCTION CO
2512 Deer Park Blvd, Omaha, NE 68105
Phone: (402) 342-1607
Sales: $94,730,000   *Employees:* 250
Company Type: Private   *Employees here:* 250
SIC: 1542
   Commercial buildings & paving & bridge contractor
James Landis, President

D-U-N-S 03-591-0202
HAYDON BUILDING CORP
222 W Southern Ave, Tempe, AZ 85282

Phone: (602) 968-0999
Sales: $70,000,000   *Employees:* 60
Company Type: Private   *Employees here:* 40
SIC: 1541
    Nonresidential /industrial building contruction
Rick Langdon, President

D-U-N-S 04-676-6895   EXP
HAYWARD BAKER INC
    (Parent: Keller Foundations Inc)
1875 Mayfield Rd, Odenton, MD 21113
Phone: (410) 551-8200
Sales: $75,000,000   *Employees:* 175
Company Type: Private   *Employees here:* 20
SIC: 1799
    Ground stabilization contractor
Roland Osgood, Division President

D-U-N-S 78-041-8232
HBG USA INC
1114 Avenue of the Americas, New York, NY 10036
Phone: (212) 626-4400
Sales: $78,100,000   *Employees:* 500
Company Type: Private   *Employees here:* 1
SIC: 1622
    Tunnel construction
Greg Lefera, N/A

D-U-N-S 03-971-5750
HCBECK, LTD
1700 Pacific Ave Ste 3800, Dallas, TX 75201
Phone: (214) 965-1100
Sales: $500,000,000   *Employees:* 200
Company Type: Private   *Employees here:* 70
SIC: 1541
    New construction renovation expansion & tenant work for
    industrial commercial & institutional buildings
Bennie Karnes, President

D-U-N-S 10-716-1366
HENDRICKSON/SCALAMADE
1610 New Hwy, Farmingdale, NY 11735
Phone: (516) 752-2700
Sales: $100,000,000   *Employees:* 400
Company Type: Private   *Employees here:* 400
SIC: 1622
    Heavy construction and highway construction
Timothy R Eller, Chief Executive Officer

D-U-N-S 01-205-9465
HENEGAN CONSTRUCTION CO INC
250 W 30th St, New York, NY 10001
Phone: (212) 947-6441
Sales: $125,000,000   *Employees:* 105
Company Type: Private   *Employees here:* 105
SIC: 1542
    General contractors for commercial alterations &
    construction managers
Philip W Warnick, Manager

D-U-N-S 00-597-5669
HENRY BROS CO
9821 S 78th Ave, Oak Lawn, IL 60457
Phone: (708) 430-5400
Sales: $80,000,000   *Employees:* 50
Company Type: Private   *Employees here:* 50
SIC: 1542
    General contractor of institutional commercial & industrial
    buildings
Joe Arcisz, Manager

D-U-N-S 06-332-2085
HENSEL PHELPS CONSTRUCTION CO
420 6th Ave, Greeley, CO 80631

Phone: (970) 352-6565
Sales: $934,317,000   *Employees:* 1,500
Company Type: Private   *Employees here:* 100
SIC: 1542
    Commercial & industrial contractor
Edward A Whitley, President

D-U-N-S 00-893-7765   EXP
HERMAN GOLDNER CO INC
7777 Brewster Ave, Philadelphia, PA 19153
Phone: (215) 365-5400
Sales: $96,250,000   *Employees:* 350
Company Type: Private   *Employees here:* 335
SIC: 1711
    Mechanical contractor specializing in plumbing heating & air
    conditioning industrial distributor of pipe valves & fittings
Bob L Moss, Chairman of the Board

D-U-N-S 83-967-8356
HIGHLAND FRAMERS OF NORTHERN CALIFORNIA
4920 W Cheyenne Ave Ste B, Las Vegas, NV 89130
Phone: (702) 656-0646
Sales: $70,300,000   *Employees:* 1,200
Company Type: Private   *Employees here:* 40
SIC: 1751
    Carpentry contractor
Paul R Langan, President

D-U-N-S 94-238-5527
HIGHLAND HOMES HOLDINGS INC
12850 Hillcrest Rd, Dallas, TX 75230
Phone: (972) 387-7905
Sales: $323,041,000   *Employees:* 400
Company Type: Private   *Employees here:* 60
SIC: 1521
    Contractor of single family homes
Alfred H Varnum, President

D-U-N-S 00-325-8746
HITT CONTRACTING INC
2704 Dorr Ave, Fairfax, VA 22031
Phone: (703) 846-9000
Sales: $200,000,000   *Employees:* 413
Company Type: Private   *Employees here:* 400
SIC: 1542
    Commercial building contractor renovation & new
    construction
Lester Patzer, President

D-U-N-S 05-441-5021
HOG SLAT INC
206 Fayetteville St, Newton Grove, NC 28366
Phone: (910) 594-0219
Sales: $221,200,000   *Employees:* 1,000
Company Type: Private   *Employees here:* 60
SIC: 1542
    Construct hog breeder facilities & mfg precast concrete floor
    slats & metal equipment for swine confinement
Steven J Yager, President

D-U-N-S 00-332-0850
HOLDER CORP
3333 Cumberland Cir SE, Atlanta, GA 30341
Phone: (770) 988-3000
Sales: $288,127,000   *Employees:* 470
Company Type: Private   *Employees here:* 2
SIC: 1542
    Holding company
Marshall L Gurley, President

D-U-N-S 13-196-1161
HOLIDAY BUILDERS INC
1901 S Harbor City Blvd, Melbourne, FL 32901
Phone: (407) 951-4407

Sales: $74,058,000 *Employees:* 125
Company Type: Private *Employees here:* 10
SIC: 1521
  General contractor of single family homes
Kenneth L Tharp, Chairman of the Board

D-U-N-S 04-320-0344
HOLLADAY CORP
3400 Idaho Ave NW Ste 500, Washington, DC 20016
Phone: (202) 362-2400
Sales: $71,600,000 *Employees:* 750
Company Type: Private *Employees here:* 225
SIC: 1522
  Apartment house building contractor & real estate
    management
Darrell Eggleston, President

D-U-N-S 00-655-6625
HOLLOWAY CONSTRUCTION CO
29250 S Wixom Rd, Wixom, MI 48393
Phone: (248) 349-4943
Sales: $189,200,000 *Employees:* NA
Company Type: Private *Employees here:* NA
SIC: 1611
  Highway street bridge elevated highway & earthmoving
    contractors
Preston M White Jr, President

D-U-N-S 60-523-4293
HOLLY MANAGEMENT LLC
6009 Beltline Rd Ste 100, Dallas, TX 75240
Phone: (972) 701-8485
Sales: $95,000,000 *Employees:* 270
Company Type: Private *Employees here:* 12
SIC: 1521
  Contractor single family home construction real estate
    management & ret mobile homes
James D Armstrong, President

D-U-N-S 80-964-8157
HOLZMANN, PHILIPP USA LTD,
  (Parent: J A Jones Inc)
J A Jones Dr, Charlotte, NC 28287
Phone: (704) 553-3000
Sales: $1,651,004,000 *Employees:* 8,000
Company Type: Private *Employees here:* 8,000
SIC: 1542
  Administrative office
Ray G Anthony, President

D-U-N-S 05-729-8937
HOME PLACE INC
2144 Hilton Dr, Gainesville, GA 30501
Phone: (770) 532-1128
Sales: $72,103,000 *Employees:* 300
Company Type: Private *Employees here:* 50
SIC: 1521
  Operative contractor single family homes
Lynn Leany, President

D-U-N-S 08-446-3850
HOMES BY DAVE BROWN
2164 E Broadway Rd, Tempe, AZ 85282
Phone: (602) 921-1400
Sales: $78,000,000 *Employees:* 100
Company Type: Private *Employees here:* 100
SIC: 1531
  Operative builder
Anthony J Marino, Chief Executive Officer

D-U-N-S 60-654-5119
HOMES HOLDING CORP
  (Parent: Walter Industries Inc)
1500 N Dale Mabry Hwy, Tampa, FL 33607
Phone: (813) 871-4811
Sales: $144,500,000 *Employees:* 1,043
Company Type: Public Family Member *Employees here:* 5
SIC: 1521
  Through its subsidiary operates as a general contractor of
    new single family homes
Raymond Verry, Chief Financial Officer

D-U-N-S 09-873-1318
HORST GROUP INC
320 Granite Run Dr, Lancaster, PA 17601
Phone: (717) 581-9800
Sales: $109,500,000 *Employees:* 500
Company Type: Private *Employees here:* 125
SIC: 1542
  Gen contr-commercial industrial apartment bldg land
    developers property management & operates apartments
Trip Tripathi, President

D-U-N-S 92-976-5030
HORTON D R TEXAS LP
  (Parent: D R Horton Inc)
1901 Ascension Blvd, Arlington, TX 76006
Phone: (817) 856-8200
Sales: $186,916,000 *Employees:* 250
Company Type: Public Family Member *Employees here:* 100
SIC: 1521
  Contractor of single-family homes
Michael D Leach, President

D-U-N-S 78-297-8647
HOSPITALITY WORLDWIDE SERVICES
450 Park Ave Ste 2603, New York, NY 10022
Phone: (212) 223-0699
Sales: $85,442,000 *Employees:* 275
Company Type: Public *Employees here:* 12
SIC: 1522
  Int & ext renov of hotels & purchasing agent of hotel
    furnishings & hotel & restaurant equip & supplies &
    warehousing & transpor
Steve Hadden, N/A

D-U-N-S 07-420-7655
HOUSTON-STAFFORD ELECTRIC
  (Parent: Integrated Electrical Services)
10203 Mula Cir, Stafford, TX 77477
Phone: (281) 498-2212
Sales: $100,000,000 *Employees:* 1,200
Company Type: Public Family Member *Employees here:* 150
SIC: 1731
  Electrical contractor
Jimmy Chancellor, President

D-U-N-S 04-665-0388
HOVNANIAN ENTERPRISES INC
10 Rte 35, Red Bank, NJ
Phone: (732) 747-7800
Sales: $941,947,000 *Employees:* 1,200
Company Type: Public *Employees here:* 100
SIC: 1531
  Operative builder real estate management and mortgage
    banking
Frank Easterling, President

D-U-N-S 61-107-8122
HOVNANIAN PENNSYLVANIA INC
  (Parent: Hovnanian Enterprises Inc)
110 Feldcrest Ave Cn 7825, Edison, NJ
Phone: (732) 225-4001

Sales: $92,900,000   *Employees:* 300
Company Type: Public Family Member   *Employees here:* 110
SIC: 1531
   Operative builder land development mortgage banking real
     estate management
C B Blalock, President

D-U-N-S 05-857-4443
HOWA CONSTRUCTION, INC
663 W 100 S, Salt Lake City, UT 84104
Phone: (801) 328-0678
Sales: $150,000,000   *Employees:* 70
Company Type: Private   *Employees here:* 70
SIC: 1542
   Commercial building contractor
Willard A Freeman, President

D-U-N-S 96-213-4979
HOWARD S WRIGHT CONSTRUCTION CO
425 Pontius Ave N Ste 100, Seattle, WA 98109
Phone: (206) 447-7654
Sales: $210,000,000   *Employees:* 300
Company Type: Private   *Employees here:* 270
SIC: 1542
   Commercial contracting
Charles C Cudd, President

D-U-N-S 02-716-1330
HOWE-BAKER ENGINEERS, INC
   (Parent: Howe-Baker International Inc)
3102 E 5th St, Tyler, TX 75701
Phone: (903) 597-0311
Sales: $91,591,000   *Employees:* 300
Company Type: Private   *Employees here:* 300
SIC: 1629
   Engineering fabrication & construction of processing plants
Michael C Jarrell, President

D-U-N-S 00-692-3197
HUBBARD CONSTRUCTION CO
   (Parent: Hubbard Group Inc)
1936 Lee Rd, Winter Park, FL 32789
Phone: (407) 645-5500
Sales: $240,000,000   *Employees:* 1,259
Company Type: Private   *Employees here:* 534
SIC: 1611
   Construction and paving of highways & asphalt-paving
     manufacturer
Charles J Miller Jr, President

D-U-N-S 00-693-8179
HUBER HUNT & NICHOLS INC
   (Parent: Hunt Corp)
2450 S Tibbs Ave, Indianapolis, IN 46241
Phone: (317) 241-6301
Sales: $900,000,000   *Employees:* 500
Company Type: Private   *Employees here:* 70
SIC: 1542
   General building contractor of commercial office buildings
     stadiums and arenas industrial bldgs & road bldg contractor
Charles N White Sr, Chairman of the Board

D-U-N-S 00-800-1349
HUNT BUILDING CORP
4401 N Mesa St Ste 201, El Paso, TX 79902
Phone: (915) 533-1122
Sales: $160,000,000   *Employees:* 170
Company Type: Private   *Employees here:* 70
SIC: 1522
   General contractor multi family housing
Charles J Pankow Jr, General Partner

D-U-N-S 07-957-1683
HUNT CORP
250 E 96th St Ste 415, Indianapolis, IN 46240
Phone: (317) 575-6301
Sales: $900,000,000   *Employees:* 600
Company Type: Private   *Employees here:* 30
SIC: 1542
   Commercial & industrial contractor
Charles R Perry, President

D-U-N-S 00-582-9601
HUNTER CONTRACTING CO.
701 N Cooper Rd, Gilbert, AZ 85233
Phone: (602) 892-0521
Sales: $67,885,000   *Employees:* 175
Company Type: Private   *Employees here:* 175
SIC: 1611
   Highwaystreet & water treatment plant construction
Michael H Ruehr, President

D-U-N-S 80-977-9259
HYDROCHEM HOLDING, INC
   (Parent: Citicorp Venture Capital Ltd)
5956 Sherry Ln Ste 930, Dallas, TX 75225
Phone: (214) 691-0196
Sales: $78,100,000   *Employees:* 1,300
Company Type: Public Family Member   *Employees here:* 3
SIC: 1799
   Water blasting & chemical cleaning contractor
Colin A Graidage, President

D-U-N-S 10-267-3886   EXP
HYDROCHEM INDUSTRIAL SERVICES
   (Parent: Hydrochem Holding Inc)
900 Georgia Ave, Deer Park, TX 77536
Phone: (713) 393-5702
Sales: $160,604,000   *Employees:* 1,700
Company Type: Public Family Member   *Employees here:* 100
SIC: 1799
   Waterblasting chemical cleaning vacuum services & waste
     minimization
Ward Ritter, President

D-U-N-S 06-540-0434
I A HOLDINGS CORP
   (Parent: Colas Inc)
U.S. Route 202, Concordville, PA 19331
Phone: (610) 459-3136
Sales: $153,404,000   *Employees:* 450
Company Type: Private   *Employees here:* 35
SIC: 1622
   Road and bridge & structure construction also mfg road
     materials water and sewer contracting & long distance
     trucking
Ed Small, President

D-U-N-S 17-670-0805
ICF KAISER ADVANCED TECHNOLOGY
2710 Sunrise Rim Rd, Boise, ID 83705
Phone: (208) 338-8988
Sales: $120,000,000   *Employees:* 150
Company Type: Private   *Employees here:* 25
SIC: 1541
   Commercial & industrial construction
Edward Small, President

D-U-N-S 09-198-9913
ICF KAISER ENGINEERS GROUP
   (Parent: ICF Kaiser International Inc)
9300 Lee Hwy, Fairfax, VA 22031
Phone: (703) 934-3000

Sales: $333,200,000   *Employees:* 2,900
Company Type: Public Family Member   *Employees here:* 650
SIC: 1629
   Heavy construction contractor construction management
     environmental consultant
Charles Roberts Jr, Chief Executive Officer

D-U-N-S 06-114-4291
ICI CONSTRUCTION INC
24707 W Hardy Rd, Spring, TX 77373
Phone: (281) 355-5151
Sales: $72,796,000   *Employees:* 77
Company Type: Private   *Employees here:* 17
SIC: 1542
   General contractor of commercial buildings
Chaz J Glace, Chief Executive Officer

D-U-N-S 03-462-6325
ICOM MECHANICAL INC
477 Burke St, San Jose, CA 95112
Phone: (408) 792-2292
Sales: $99,933,000   *Employees:* 300
Company Type: Private   *Employees here:* 300
SIC: 1711
   Design & installation of HVAC systems
Kevin P Dowd, President

D-U-N-S 62-644-1984
INDUSTRIAL SERVICES TECH
   (Parent: Philip Services Corp)
370 17th St Ste 2300, Denver, CO 80202
Phone: (303) 572-5000
Sales: $95,766,000   *Employees:* 900
Company Type: Private   *Employees here:* 4
SIC: 1541
   Industrial building new construction renovation remodeling
     & repair
Frank Bucci, President

D-U-N-S 01-681-0095
INRECON, L.L.C.
185 Oakland Ave Ste 100, Birmingham, MI 48009
Phone: (248) 594-3188
Sales: $71,853,000   *Employees:* 420
Company Type: Private   *Employees here:* 35
SIC: 1521
   Residential industrial & commercial repair contractor
David Roeder, President

D-U-N-S 15-379-5554
INTECH CONSTRUCTION INC
3001 Market St, Philadelphia, PA 19104
Phone: (215) 243-2000
Sales: $84,019,000   *Employees:* 50
Company Type: Private   *Employees here:* 50
SIC: 1542
   Commercial building construction & management
Joseph P Alteri, President

D-U-N-S 83-983-2631
INTEGRATED ELECTRICAL SERVICES
515 Post Oak Blvd Ste 450, Houston, TX 77027
Phone: (713) 860-1500
Sales: $263,600,000   *Employees:* 3,550
Company Type: Public   *Employees here:* 14
SIC: 1731
   Holding company for electrical contractor
Toomas J Kukk, Chairman of the Board

D-U-N-S 02-935-4755
INTEGRATED ENERGY SERVICES
7 Piedmont Ctr NE Ste 110, Atlanta, GA 30305
Phone: (404) 467-6100

Sales: $160,000,000   *Employees:* 150
Company Type: Private   *Employees here:* 100
SIC: 1711
   Holding company
A W Cherne Jr, President

D-U-N-S 19-604-6809
INTERBETON INC
   (Parent: HBG USA Inc)
1001 Hingham St, Rockland, MA
Phone: (781) 871-6700
Sales: $102,274,000   *Employees:* 500
Company Type: Private   *Employees here:* 5
SIC: 1629
   Heavy civil & marine construction
James A Openshaw Jr, President

D-U-N-S 80-883-5284
INTERNATIONAL ENERGY CORP
250 Hembree Park Dr, Roswell, GA 30076
Phone: (770) 753-0883
Sales: $200,000,000   *Employees:* 115
Company Type: Private   *Employees here:* 115
SIC: 1542
   Builder of power plants
Phillip Cohn, President

D-U-N-S 08-554-8915
INTERNATIONAL MAINTENANCE CORP
8687 United Plaza Blvd, Baton Rouge, LA 70809
Phone: (225) 922-5050
Sales: $430,100,000   *Employees:* 3,400
Company Type: Private   *Employees here:* 530
SIC: 1541
   Industrial maintenance contractor
Ben Shah, Vice-President

D-U-N-S 00-779-7657
INTERSTATE HIGHWAY CONSTRUCTION
7135 S Tucson Way, Englewood, CO 80112
Phone: (303) 790-9100
Sales: $120,000,000   *Employees:* 250
Company Type: Private   *Employees here:* 125
SIC: 1611
   Highway construction resurfacing & airport runway
     contractor
A Suzuki, President

D-U-N-S 04-751-2959   EXP
IREX CORP
120 N Lime St, Lancaster, PA 17602
Phone: (717) 397-3633
Sales: $278,150,000   *Employees:* 1,500
Company Type: Public   *Employees here:* 65
SIC: 1742
   Dist fab of insulation architectural/acoustic & specialty
     products & abatement fire protection & interior finish
     contracting
William M Choate, President

D-U-N-S 02-953-4070
IRISH CONSTRUCTION
   (Parent: Manhattan Capital Corp)
2641 River Ave, Rosemead, CA 91770
Phone: (626) 288-8530
Sales: $75,400,000   *Employees:* 1,000
Company Type: Private   *Employees here:* 600
SIC: 1623
   Cable power & telephone line construction
Dale Lemaster, President

D-U-N-S 00-798-9379
IRVING F JENSEN CO INC
2220 Hawkeye Dr, Sioux City, IA 51105
Phone: (712) 252-1891
Sales: $80,000,000
Company Type: Private
Employees: 100
Employees here: 40
SIC: 1611
General contractor of highways & streets
Andrew B Schmitt, President

D-U-N-S 04-671-6007
ITEQ STORAGE SYSTEMS, INC
(Parent: ITEQ Inc)
4422 Fm 1960 Rd W Ste 350, Houston, TX 77068
Phone: (281) 893-9150
Sales: $90,200,000
Company Type: Private
Employees: 1,000
Employees here: 40
SIC: 1791
Steel tank erection fabricates steel tanks
Lynn D Christensen, President

D-U-N-S 62-080-0540
IVEY MECHANICAL CO
(Parent: Building One Services Corp)
514 N Wells St, Kosciusko, MS 39090
Phone: (601) 289-3646
Sales: $105,000,000
Company Type: Public Family Member
Employees: 750
Employees here: 75
SIC: 1711
Mechanical construction & renovation
Brian Christopher, President

D-U-N-S 07-298-3265
IVORY HOMES
970 Woodoak Ln, Salt Lake City, UT 84117
Phone: (801) 268-0700
Sales: $88,179,000
Company Type: Private
Employees: 80
Employees here: 80
SIC: 1521
Single-family house construction and subdivider and
developer
Robert A Christianson, President

D-U-N-S 00-699-6177
J A JONES INC
J A Jones Dr, Charlotte, NC 28287
Phone: (704) 553-3000
Sales: $1,398,484,000
Company Type: Private
Employees: 6,224
Employees here: 500
SIC: 1542
Commercial institutional industrial plant & process highway
marine & energy construction
Jorge Mas Jr, President

D-U-N-S 03-494-5766
J A TIBERTI CONSTRUCTION CO
1806 Industrial Rd, Las Vegas, NV 89102
Phone: (702) 248-4000
Sales: $121,806,000
Company Type: Private
Employees: 60
Employees here: 60
SIC: 1542
General contractor of industrial & commercial buildings
Alton E Cianchette, Chairman of the Board

D-U-N-S 00-482-1104
J C EVANS CONSTRUCTION CO
13505 Burnet Rd, Austin, TX 78727
Phone: (512) 244-1400

Sales: $90,000,000
Company Type: Private
Employees: 800
Employees here: 700
SIC: 1541
General contractor specializing in commercial & industrial
buildings excavation heavy highway & underground utilities
Charles Kubicki, President

D-U-N-S 79-307-0889
J C HIGGINS CORP
(Parent: Emcor Mechanical/Electrical Services)
70 Hawes Way, Stoughton, MA
Phone: (617) 787-9800
Sales: $122,000,000
Company Type: Public Family Member
Employees: 598
Employees here: 241
SIC: 1711
Plumbing heating ventilation & air conditioning contractor
Jere Meredith, N/A

D-U-N-S 00-800-6561
J D ABRAMS INC
(Parent: Abrams International Inc)
111 Congress Ave Ste 2400, Austin, TX 78701
Phone: (512) 322-4000
Sales: $102,490,000
Company Type: Private
Employees: 572
Employees here: 29
SIC: 1611
Highway street bridge & dam constructor & mfg of pre-
stressed bridge decking of concrete
Walter Canney, Administrator

D-U-N-S 00-890-6844
J E DUNN CONSTRUCTION CO
(Parent: Dunn Industries Inc)
929 Holmes St, Kansas City, MO 64106
Phone: (816) 474-8600
Sales: $417,000,000
Company Type: Private
Employees: 1,000
Employees here: 1,000
SIC: 1542
Commercial building contractor
Frank C Thomas, Principal

D-U-N-S 00-896-0122
J F AHERN CO
855 Morris St, Fond Du Lac, WI 54935
Phone: (920) 921-9020
Sales: $98,451,000
Company Type: Private
Employees: 500
Employees here: 350
SIC: 1711
Mechanical fire protection heating & plumbing contractor
Joseph Nappi, Systems/Data Processing

D-U-N-S 01-950-5429
J F WHITE CONTRACTING CO
1 Gateway Ctr, Newton, MA
Phone: (617) 964-0100
Sales: $147,728,000
Company Type: Private
Employees: 180
Employees here: 50
SIC: 1622
Mass transit bridge tunnel & highway construction
Todd Renfrow, Director

D-U-N-S 01-915-2474
J H BERRA HOLDING CO INC
5091 Baumgartner Rd, St. Louis, MO 63129
Phone: (314) 487-5617
Sales: $90,000,000
Company Type: Private
Employees: 600
Employees here: 3
SIC: 1611
Contractor
B W Wait III, Pe

D-U-N-S 00-610-6520
J H FINDORFF & SON INC
601 W Wilson St, Madison, WI 53703
Phone: (608) 257-5321
Sales: $128,126,000
Company Type: Private   *Employees:* 300
SIC: 1542   *Employees here:* 293
    General contractor & construction manager
David Pickared, Manager

D-U-N-S 00-283-6070
J H KELLY LLC
821 3rd Ave, Longview, WA 98632
Phone: (360) 423-5510
Sales: $127,803,000
Company Type: Private   *Employees:* 800
SIC: 1711   *Employees here:* 500
    Plumbing & mechanical contractor
Frank L Oddo, President

D-U-N-S 02-855-4798
J H MCCORMICK INC
2507 W Empire Ave, Burbank, CA 91504
Phone: (818) 843-2010
Sales: $68,000,000
Company Type: Private   *Employees:* 100
SIC: 1542   *Employees here:* 40
    General contractor of new commercial and industrial
        buildings
Tim Clancy, President

D-U-N-S 11-752-4629
J P CULLEN & SONS INC
330 E Delavan Dr, Janesville, WI 53546
Phone: (608) 754-6601
Sales: $98,425,000
Company Type: Private   *Employees:* 350
SIC: 1542   *Employees here:* 350
    General contractor commercial institutional & industrial
        buildings
Donald Sciaretta, President

D-U-N-S 79-363-0849
J P I NATIONAL CONSTRUCTION
600 Las Colinas Blvd E, Irving, TX 75039
Phone: (972) 556-1700
Sales: $73,163,000
Company Type: Private   *Employees:* 1,182
SIC: 1522   *Employees here:* 65
    General contractor of multi-family dwellings & consulting
        service
James Clark, President

D-U-N-S 60-504-5848
J R AUSTIN CO
12231 Parklawn Dr, Rockville, MD 20852
Phone: (301) 816-1700
Sales: $85,000,000
Company Type: Private   *Employees:* 85
SIC: 1542   *Employees here:* 85
    General contractor of commercial buildings & construction
        management service
Clark Wilson, President

D-U-N-S 14-459-0452
J R ROBERTS ENTERPRISES
7745 Greenback Ln Ste 300, Citrus Heights, CA 95610
Phone: (916) 729-5600
Sales: $250,000,000
Company Type: Private   *Employees:* 230
SIC: 1542   *Employees here:* 80
    General contractor of commercial buildings
Jere L Clark, Executive

D-U-N-S 94-772-7368   EXP
J RAY MCDERMOTT, S.A.
    (Parent: McDermott International Inc)
1450 Poydras St, New Orleans, LA 70112
Phone: (504) 587-5300
Sales: $1,855,486,000
Company Type: Public Family Member   *Employees:* 11,700
SIC: 1629   *Employees here:* 50
    Marine construction services
Robert G Clark, President

D-U-N-S 00-890-7990
J S ALBERICI CONSTRUCTION CO
    (Parent: Alberici Corp)
2150 Kienlen Ave, St. Louis, MO 63121
Phone: (314) 261-2611
Sales: $525,265,000
Company Type: Private   *Employees:* 1,500
SIC: 1541   *Employees here:* 220
    General contractor industrial institutional industrial
        commercial bridge marine & environmental
Thomas J Cleary, Chairman of the Board

D-U-N-S 08-949-1401
JACK B PARSON COMPANIES
    (Parent: Oldcastle Northeast Inc)
2350 S 1900 W, Ogden, UT 84401
Phone: (801) 731-1111
Sales: $145,474,000   *Employees:* 662
Company Type: Private   *Employees here:* 250
SIC: 1611
    Highway & street construction mfg ready mix concrete
James X Clemens, Chairman of the Board

D-U-N-S 07-410-3508   EXP
JACOBS ENGINEERING GROUP INC
1111 S Arroyo Pkwy, Pasadena, CA 91105
Phone: (626) 578-3500
Sales: $2,101,145,000   *Employees:* 23,000
Company Type: Public   *Employees here:* 300
SIC: 1629
    Heavy construction contractor engineering services plant
        maintenance services
Richard G Small, Chief Executive Officer

D-U-N-S 01-209-2540
JAMES G KENNEDY & CO INC
215 E 38th St, New York, NY 10016
Phone: (212) 599-5800
Sales: $75,000,000   *Employees:* 60
Company Type: Private   *Employees here:* 60
SIC: 1542
    General contractor & construction management
James R Cleveland Jr, President

D-U-N-S 00-693-1331
JAMES MCHUGH CONSTRUCTION CO
    (Parent: McHugh Enterprises Inc)
2222 S Indiana Ave, Chicago, IL 60616
Phone: (312) 842-8400
Sales: $113,509,000   *Employees:* 400
Company Type: Private   *Employees here:* 50
SIC: 1542
    Commercial multi-story residential & heavy construction
        contractor
John Grozkowski, Controller

D-U-N-S 86-816-0698
JAY CASHMAN INC
285 Dorchester Ave, Boston, MA
Phone: (617) 268-1300

Sales: $102,400,000   *Employees:* 200
Company Type: Private   *Employees here:* 25
SIC: 1629
   Marine & general construction
Brian Kervick, President

D-U-N-S 00-711-2253
JAYNES CORP
2906 Broadway Blvd NE, Albuquerque, NM 87107
Phone: (505) 345-8591
Sales: $103,534,000   *Employees:* 250
Company Type: Private   *Employees here:* 171
SIC: 1542
   General contractor commercial & industrial buildings
Robert C Overall Sr, President

D-U-N-S 05-934-5124
JE MERIT CONSTRUCTORS, INC
   (Parent: Jacobs Engineering Group Inc)
4848 Loop Central Dr Fl 7, Houston, TX 77081
Phone: (713) 669-8400
Sales: $332,300,000   *Employees:* 7,000
Company Type: Public Family Member   *Employees here:* 70
SIC: 1629
   Heavy construction contractor
John P Case Jr, President

D-U-N-S 15-554-1063
JEFFREY C STONE INC
3333 E Camelback Rd, Phoenix, AZ 85018
Phone: (602) 840-7700
Sales: $116,321,000   *Employees:* 140
Company Type: Private   *Employees here:* 140
SIC: 1542
   General contractor of commercial buildings & hotels
Howard W Hauser, Chief Executive Officer

D-U-N-S 84-787-9251
JERRY PYBUS ELECTRIC
1327 N Tyndall Pkwy, Panama City, FL 32404
Phone: (850) 784-2766
Sales: $300,000,000   *Employees:* 50
Company Type: Private   *Employees here:* 50
SIC: 1731
   Electrical contractor
Fred Hamlin, President

D-U-N-S 00-480-2112
JESCO INC
   (Parent: Eagleventures Inc)
2020 McCullough Blvd, Tupelo, MS 38801
Phone: (601) 842-3240
Sales: $101,700,000   *Employees:* 800
Company Type: Private   *Employees here:* 15
SIC: 1541
   Industrial & commercial building contractor
Jeff Holmes, Branch Manager

D-U-N-S 05-845-6880
JIM WALTER HOMES INC
   (Parent: Homes Holding Corp)
1500 N Dale Mabry Hwy, Tampa, FL 33607
Phone: (813) 871-4611
Sales: $141,200,000   *Employees:* 1,020
Company Type: Public Family Member   *Employees here:* 250
SIC: 1521
   General contractor of single family homes
Gordon W Cochran, President

D-U-N-S 04-830-3440
JMB/URBAN DEVELOPMENT CO.
900 N Michigan Ave, Chicago, IL 60611
Phone: (312) 440-4800

Sales: $379,800,000   *Employees:* 1,218
Company Type: Private   *Employees here:* 150
SIC: 1531
   Operative builder of condominiums & commercial buildings
    & manages commercial & industrial real estate and hotels
Gerald Engle, President

D-U-N-S 09-123-3130
JOE E WOODS INC
63 E Main St Ste 401, Mesa, AZ 85201
Phone: (602) 964-4560
Sales: $124,555,000   *Employees:* 150
Company Type: Private   *Employees here:* 100
SIC: 1522
   General contractor-hotels commercial public & industrial
    buildings
James W Coghlin, President

D-U-N-S 80-738-3716
JOHN CROSLAND CO
   (Parent: Centex Real Estate Corp)
145 Scaleybark Rd, Charlotte, NC 28209
Phone: (704) 523-8111
Sales: $70,600,000   *Employees:* 230
Company Type: Public Family Member   *Employees here:* 145
SIC: 1531
   Speculative builder of single-family homes
James Couchenour, Chief Executive Officer

D-U-N-S 00-695-8193
JOHN E GREEN CO
220 Victor St, Detroit, MI 48203
Phone: (313) 868-2400
Sales: $116,000,000   *Employees:* 350
Company Type: Private   *Employees here:* 225
SIC: 1711
   Mechanical contractor
Michel Roullet, President

D-U-N-S 12-154-3714
JOHN J KIRLIN INC
643 Lofstrand Ln, Rockville, MD 20850
Phone: (301) 424-3410
Sales: $113,200,000   *Employees:* 1,200
Company Type: Private   *Employees here:* 800
SIC: 1711
   Plumbing heating & air conditioning contractor
Angelo Colasanti, Chairman of the Board

D-U-N-S 13-185-4648
JOHN MORIARTY & ASSOCIATES
3 Church St, Winchester, MA
Phone: (781) 729-3900
Sales: $114,937,000   *Employees:* 60
Company Type: Private   *Employees here:* 60
SIC: 1542
   General contractor of new commercial buildings
Thomas D Coleman, Chairman of the Board

D-U-N-S 01-958-5603
JOHN T CALLAHAN & SONS INC
80 1st St, Bridgewater, MA
Phone: (508) 697-9300
Sales: $71,820,000   *Employees:* 100
Company Type: Private   *Employees here:* 90
SIC: 1542
   Contractor commercial buildings & renovations
Thomas M Coleman, Chief Executive Officer

D-U-N-S 07-345-3557
JOHN WLAND HOMES NEIGHBORHOODS
1950 Sullivan Rd, Atlanta, GA 30337
Phone: (770) 996-1400

Sales: $250,637,000   *Employees:* 800
Company Type: Private   *Employees here:* 230
SIC: 1531
   Operative builder
Gregory Bressler, Vice-President

D-U-N-S 02-284-7354
JOHNSON BROS. CORP
23577 Minnesota Highway 2, Litchfield, MN 55355
Phone: (320) 693-2871
Sales: $73,985,000   *Employees:* 600
Company Type: Private   *Employees here:* 60
SIC: 1622
   Bridge tunnel & elevated highway construction industrial
     plant construction & earthwork and underground utilities
Eugene C Gini, President

D-U-N-S 00-484-0864
JONES BROS INC
5760 Old Lebanon Dirt Rd, Mount Juliet, TN 37122
Phone: (615) 754-4710
Sales: $150,000,000   *Employees:* 1,000
Company Type: Private   *Employees here:* 1,000
SIC: 1622
   Bridge asphalt-concrete & grading contractor
Bill Collins, Chief Executive Officer

D-U-N-S 00-678-4565
JONES BROTHERS CONSTRUCTION CORP
10866 Wilshire Blvd, Los Angeles, CA 90024
Phone: (310) 470-1885
Sales: $110,000,000   *Employees:* 119
Company Type: Private   *Employees here:* 4
SIC: 1542
   Contractor of commercial buildings
Raymond M Barry, President

D-U-N-S 02-978-6621
JONES CO CUSTOM HOMES INC
13100 Manchester Rd, St. Louis, MO 63131
Phone: (314) 965-8000
Sales: $131,157,000   *Employees:* 350
Company Type: Private   *Employees here:* 60
SIC: 1521
   Single-family house construction
Harry Collins, Chairman of the Board

D-U-N-S 05-784-7758   EXP
JUPITER INDUSTRIES, INC.
2215 Sanders Rd Ste 385, Northbrook, IL 60062
Phone: (847) 753-8200
Sales: $94,300,000   *Employees:* 1,000
Company Type: Private   *Employees here:* 8
SIC: 1711
   Mechanical contractor mfg fasteners operates real estate
     partnerships oil and gas field services
Thomas Bradbury, Chief Executive Officer

D-U-N-S 08-982-0161
K-FIVE CONSTRUCTION CORP
13769 Main St, Lemont, IL 60439
Phone: (630) 257-5600
Sales: $100,000,000   *Employees:* 80
Company Type: Private   *Employees here:* 80
SIC: 1611
   Highway/street construction local trucking operator
David L Beasley, President

D-U-N-S 82-557-0302
K HOVNANIAN ENTERPRISES, INC
   (Parent: Hovnanian Enterprises Inc)
10 Route 35, Red Bank, NJ
Phone: (732) 747-7800

Sales: $347,900,000   *Employees:* 1,100
Company Type: Public Family Member   *Employees here:* 100
SIC: 1531
   Operative builders
Charles Sanford, Member

D-U-N-S 18-942-6257
KAJIMA U.S.A. INC.
320 Park Ave, New York, NY 10022
Phone: (212) 355-4571
Sales: $950,084,000   *Employees:* 1,440
Company Type: Private   *Employees here:* 9
SIC: 1541
   General contractor of industrial/commercial buildings &
     hotels heavy construction real estate development mgmt
     and consulting
Karla Harding, Director

D-U-N-S 04-434-9389
KALIKOW, H. J. & CO., LLC
101 Park Ave Fl 25, New York, NY 10178
Phone: (212) 808-7000
Sales: $87,200,000   *Employees:* 400
Company Type: Private   *Employees here:* 20
SIC: 1542
   Real estate development and management
E J Olbright, President

D-U-N-S 17-772-3061
KAUFMAN & BROAD HOME CORP
10990 Wilshire Blvd, Los Angeles, CA 90024
Phone: (310) 231-4000
Sales: $2,449,362,000   *Employees:* 3,500
Company Type: Public   *Employees here:* 100
SIC: 1531
   Builds single family homes condominiums apartment
     complexes commercial office buildings mortgage banking
William E Colson, President

D-U-N-S 18-817-6986
KAUFMAN & BROAD OF NORTHERN CALIFORNIA
   (Parent: Kaufman & Broad Home Corp)
3130 Crow Canyon Pl, San Ramon, CA 94583
Phone: (925) 866-9669
Sales: $200,000,000   *Employees:* 92
Company Type: Public Family Member   *Employees here:* 83
SIC: 1531
   Residential contractor
Bruce Lierman, President

D-U-N-S 80-375-0496
KAUFMAN & BROAD OF SAN DIEGO
   (Parent: Kaufman & Broad Home Corp)
12526 High Bluff Dr 400, San Diego, CA 92130
Phone: (619) 259-6000
Sales: $247,565,000   *Employees:* 57
Company Type: Public Family Member   *Employees here:* 57
SIC: 1522
   New construction of single family residential homes
Bill Colgrove, Project Manager

D-U-N-S 06-446-4621
KAUFMAN & BROAD OF SOUTHERN CALIFORNIA
   (Parent: Kaufman & Broad Home Corp)
10990 Wilshire Blvd, Los Angeles, CA 90024
Phone: (310) 231-4000
Sales: $455,083,000   *Employees:* 350
Company Type: Public Family Member   *Employees here:* 90
SIC: 1521
   Single-family house construction residential construction
Daniel Eldridge, President

D-U-N-S 14-812-3169
KCI CONSTRUCTORS, INC.
   (Parent: M W Kellogg Holdings Inc)
601 Jefferson St, Houston, TX 77002
Phone: (713) 753-2000
Sales: $130,000,000
Company Type: Public Family Member
SIC: 1541
   General contractor for industrial buildings
Don L Comerford, President

Employees: NA
Employees here: NA

D-U-N-S 13-195-7722
KEENAN, HOPKINS
3915 Riga Blvd, Tampa, FL 33619
Phone: (813) 628-9330
Sales: $70,528,000
Company Type: Private
SIC: 1542
   Commercial construction
Fred M Ferreira, Chairman of the Board

Employees: 400
Employees here: 200

D-U-N-S 07-684-8985
KEENE CONSTRUCTION CO OF CENTRAL FLORIDA
1400 Hope Rd, Maitland, FL 32751
Phone: (407) 740-6116
Sales: $100,000,000
Company Type: Private
SIC: 1542
   General contractor of commercial buildings
Jack L Lofy, President

Employees: 150
Employees here: 150

D-U-N-S 04-523-5678
KELLER CONSTRUCTION CO LTD
9950 Baldwin Pl, El Monte, CA 91731
Phone: (626) 443-6633
Sales: $100,000,000
Company Type: Private
SIC: 1542
   Commercial building contractor
R R Kipp, President

Employees: 50
Employees here: 43

D-U-N-S 61-675-8074
KELLER FOUNDATIONS, INC
1130 Annapolis Rd Ste 202, Odenton, MD 21113
Phone: (410) 551-8200
Sales: $136,386,000
Company Type: Private
SIC: 1799
   Through subsidiaries is a ground stabilization contractor
Edmund W Wettingel, President

Employees: 300
Employees here: 94

D-U-N-S 01-081-0893
KELLOGG, BROWN & ROOT, INC
   (Parent: Dresser Industries Inc)
601 Jefferson St, Houston, TX 77002
Phone: (713) 676-3011
Sales: $2,300,900,000
Company Type: Public Family Member
SIC: 1629
   Heavy construction engineering services road construction
Thomas C Halperin, Chairman of the Board

Employees: 20,000
Employees here: 5,000

D-U-N-S 00-543-9070
KELSO-BURNETT CO DEL
5200 Newport Dr, Rolling Meadows, IL 60008
Phone: (847) 259-0720
Sales: $73,868,000
Company Type: Private
SIC: 1731
   Electrical contractor
Rick West, President

Employees: 475
Employees here: 290

D-U-N-S 79-932-8471
KENCO COMMUNITIES AT WYCLIFFE
1000 Clint Moore Rd, Boca Raton, FL 33487
Phone: (561) 997-5760
Sales: $80,000,000
Company Type: Private
SIC: 1522
   Contractor specializing in residential construction
Tracy Donovan, President

Employees: 50
Employees here: 30

D-U-N-S 02-583-7287
KENNY CONSTRUCTION CO
   (Parent: Kenny Industries Inc)
250 Northgate Pkwy, Wheeling, IL 60090
Phone: (847) 541-8200
Sales: $200,000,000
Company Type: Private
SIC: 1622
   General contractor & construction manager
Thomas Price, President

Employees: 400
Employees here: 400

D-U-N-S 93-160-4235
KENYON COMPANIES
2602 N 35th Ave, Phoenix, AZ 85009
Phone: (602) 233-1191
Sales: $81,100,000
Company Type: Private
SIC: 1742
   Stucco contractor & mfg insulation chemicals (through
     subsidiaries)
Bernard Yatauro, President

Employees: 1,400
Employees here: 20

D-U-N-S 16-110-0060
KIEWIT, ATKINSON & CASHMAN
451 D St, Boston, MA
Phone: (617) 330-1177
Sales: $301,000,000
Company Type: Private
SIC: 1611
   General contracting
George Tamasi, President

Employees: 60
Employees here: 60

D-U-N-S 05-882-2412
KIEWIT CONSTRUCTION CO
   (Parent: Peter Kiewit Sons Inc)
3555 Farnam St Ste 1000, Omaha, NE 68131
Phone: (402) 342-2052
Sales: $2,325,160,000
Company Type: Private
SIC: 1541
   Industrial commercial subway tunnel highway & residential
     building contractor
George J White Jr, President

Employees: 1,353
Employees here: 11

D-U-N-S 02-492-3799
KIMBALL HILL INC
5999 New Wilke Rd Ste 504, Rolling Meadows, IL 60008
Phone: (847) 255-0500
Sales: $245,787,000
Company Type: Private
SIC: 1521
   Operative builder of single family and multi-residential units
H L Rapaport, Chairman of the Board

Employees: 325
Employees here: 85

D-U-N-S 17-568-4018
KIMMINS CORP
1501 E 2nd Ave, Tampa, FL 33605
Phone: (813) 248-3878

Sales: $113,526,000   *Employees:* 575
Company Type: Public   *Employees here:* 36
SIC: 1799
   Hazardous & non-hazardous waste processing &
   environmental construction
Peter A Pasch, President

D-U-N-S 06-355-2194
KINETICS GROUP, INC
   (Parent: United States Filter Corp)
2805 Mission College Blvd, Santa Clara, CA 95054
Phone: (408) 727-7740
Sales: $388,000,000   *Employees:* 3,460
Company Type: Public Family Member   *Employees here:* 5
SIC: 1711
   Holding company
Greg Benson, President

D-U-N-S 02-235-0136
KINSEL INDUSTRIES INC
8121 Broadway St Ste 300, Houston, TX 77061
Phone: (713) 641-5111
Sales: $75,000,000   *Employees:* 385
Company Type: Private   *Employees here:* 35
SIC: 1623
   General contractor of utility water facilities & sewer
   rehabilitation
Gerald B Alley, President

D-U-N-S 01-515-1186
KINSLEY CONSTRUCTION, INC
2700 Water St, York, PA 17403
Phone: (717) 741-3841
Sales: $143,000,000   *Employees:* 700
Company Type: Private   *Employees here:* 80
SIC: 1541
   Contractor specializing in construction of industrial buildings
   & warehouses commercial buildings & office & shopping
   centers
Robert W Stinson, President

D-U-N-S 00-901-0984
KITCHELL CORP
1707 E Highland Ave, Phoenix, AZ 85016
Phone: (602) 264-4411
Sales: $289,019,000   *Employees:* 700
Company Type: Private   *Employees here:* 30
SIC: 1542
   Holding company active through subsidiaries as general
   contractor commercial public & industrial buildings
B M Shevlin, President

D-U-N-S 01-209-6798
KLEINKNECHT ELECTRIC CO
940 8th Ave, New York, NY 10019
Phone: (212) 989-4500
Sales: $84,228,000   *Employees:* 200
Company Type: Private   *Employees here:* 80
SIC: 1731
   Electrical contractor
Timothy Nightingale, President

D-U-N-S 00-694-2148
KLINGER COMPANIES, INC
2015 7th St, Sioux City, IA 51101
Phone: (712) 277-3900
Sales: $120,700,000   *Employees:* 550
Company Type: Private   *Employees here:* 55
SIC: 1542
   Commercial & industrial contractor
Ronald J Benach, Chairman

D-U-N-S 02-182-8652
KLUKWAN INC
2075 Jordan Ave, Juneau, AK 99801
Phone: (907) 789-7361
Sales: $71,483,000   *Employees:* 300
Company Type: Private   *Employees here:* 30
SIC: 1611
   Highway street & airport construction & logging contractor
O R Hall Jr, Chairman of the Board

D-U-N-S 84-062-2310
KOESTER COMPANIES INC
14649 Highway 41 N, Evansville, IN 47711
Phone: (812) 867-6635
Sales: $82,402,000   *Employees:* 300
Company Type: Private   *Employees here:* 6
SIC: 1629
   Holding company
Daniel V Mey, President

D-U-N-S 10-769-8706
KOKOSING CONSTRUCTION CO
17531 Waterford Rd, Fredericktown, OH 43019
Phone: (740) 694-6315
Sales: $260,000,000   *Employees:* 650
Company Type: Private   *Employees here:* 200
SIC: 1611
   General contractor
Edward D Lothamer Jr, Chairman of the Board

D-U-N-S 02-874-1593
KOLL CO
4343 Von Karman Ave, Newport Beach, CA 92660
Phone: (949) 833-3030
Sales: $406,200,000   *Employees:* 1,828
Company Type: Private   *Employees here:* 300
SIC: 1542
   Construction real estate development property & asset
   management
Brian R Cameron, President

D-U-N-S 08-163-9411
KORTE CONSTRUCTION CO
700 Saint Louis Union Sta, St. Louis, MO 63103
Phone: (314) 231-3700
Sales: $102,270,000   *Employees:* 250
Company Type: Private   *Employees here:* 50
SIC: 1541
   General contractor-industrial & commercial & office
   buildings
Michael Condon, President

D-U-N-S 16-170-6684
KRAEMER BROTHERS, LLC
925 Park Ave, Plain, WI 53577
Phone: (608) 546-2411
Sales: $73,000,000   *Employees:* 125
Company Type: Private   *Employees here:* 125
SIC: 1542
   Nonresidential construction
Donald J O Neill, Chairman of the Board

D-U-N-S 04-546-1498
KRAFT CONSTRUCTION CO
2606 Horseshoe Dr S, Naples, FL 34104
Phone: (941) 643-6000
Sales: $76,067,000   *Employees:* 140
Company Type: Private   *Employees here:* 140
SIC: 1542
   General contractor of commercial buildings
Richard Treml, Vice-President

D-U-N-S 00-696-2104
KRAUS-ANDERSON, INC
525 S 8th St, Minneapolis, MN 55404
Phone: (612) 332-7281
Sales: $465,000,000
Company Type: Private
SIC: 1542
    General contractor of non-residential & residential buildings
      real estate investment mortgage broker & advertising
Richard Treml, President
Employees: 1,000
Employees here: 25

D-U-N-S 08-319-4589
KVAERNER CONSTRUCTION INC
    (Parent: Kvaerner Holdings Inc)
4950 W Kennedy Blvd, Tampa, FL 33609
Phone: (813) 282-7100
Sales: $76,812,000
Company Type: Private
SIC: 1542
    Contractor of commercial & institutional buildings and
      construction project management
Joseph L McCaleb, President
Employees: 175
Employees here: 35

D-U-N-S 79-338-6194
KVAERNER SONGER, INC.
    (Parent: Kvaerner Holdings Inc)
455 Racetrack Rd, Washington, PA 15301
Phone: (724) 223-0800
Sales: $179,000,000
Company Type: Private
SIC: 1711
    Contractor specializing in general plant maintenance
Donald B Smith Jr, President
Employees: 500
Employees here: 60

D-U-N-S 03-568-8795
L & H CO INC DEL
2215 York Rd Ste 304, Hinsdale, IL 60523
Phone: (630) 571-7200
Sales: $67,400,000
Company Type: Private
SIC: 1731
    Electrical highway & pipeline contractor & rebuilds electrical
      motors
John Duplissey, President
Employees: 909
Employees here: 9

D-U-N-S 00-693-1661
L E MYERS CO
    (Parent: MYR Group Inc)
1701 Golf Rd 1012, Rolling Meadows, IL 60008
Phone: (847) 290-1891
Sales: $431,276,000
Company Type: Public Family Member
SIC: 1623
    Construction and maintenance of transmission lines
      distribution systems and substations for electric utilities
Stephen D Conlon, President
Employees: 800
Employees here: 20

D-U-N-S 07-736-3216
L E WENTZ CO
1599 Industrial Rd, San Carlos, CA 94070
Phone: (650) 592-3950
Sales: $110,000,000
Company Type: Private
SIC: 1542
    General contractor commercial & industrial buildings
Gary McElwee, President
Employees: 125
Employees here: 50

D-U-N-S 00-678-1769
L F DRISCOLL CO
9 Presidential Blvd, Bala Cynwyd, PA 19004
Phone: (610) 668-0950

Sales: $250,000,000
Company Type: Private
SIC: 1542
    General contractors of commercial & institutional buildings
      apartment buildings & industrial structures
John H Connell, President
Employees: 250
Employees here: 250

D-U-N-S 00-186-7100
L K COMSTOCK & CO INC
    (Parent: Comstock Holdings Inc)
1 N Lexington Ave, White Plains, NY 10601
Phone: (914) 323-3000
Sales: $153,610,000
Company Type: Public Family Member
SIC: 1731
    Electrical contractor
Ralph Larison, President
Employees: 1,007
Employees here: 57

D-U-N-S 05-835-2022
LAKESIDE INDUSTRIES
6505 226th Pl SE, Issaquah, WA 98027
Phone: (425) 313-2600
Sales: $149,397,000
Company Type: Private
SIC: 1611
    Asphalt paving contractor
Walter P Conrad Jr, President
Employees: 150
Employees here: 150

D-U-N-S 15-036-3661
LANDMARK ORGANIZATION, INC
1250 S Capital of Texas, Austin, TX 78746
Phone: (512) 329-8090
Sales: $73,086,000
Company Type: Private
SIC: 1542
    New commercial construction of medium & large buildings
William Novotny, President
Employees: 50
Employees here: 50

D-U-N-S 06-382-0773
LANDSTAR DEVELOPMENT CORP
550 Biltmore Way Ste 1110, Coral Gables, FL 33134
Phone: (305) 461-2440
Sales: $114,458,000
Company Type: Private
SIC: 1521
    Contractor of new single family homes
Andrew Cummick, Manager
Employees: 150
Employees here: 20

D-U-N-S 10-125-8739
LANE INDUSTRIES INC
965 E Main St, Meriden, CT
Phone: (203) 235-3351
Sales: $284,425,000
Company Type: Private
SIC: 1622
    Highway & bridge airport runway mass transit locks & dams
      and power plant construction & mfg and whol of road build
      material
Stephen W Bisson, President
Employees: 2,175
Employees here: 3

D-U-N-S 09-745-6065
LARWIN CO
16633 Ventura Blvd Ste 13, Encino, CA 91436
Phone: (818) 986-8890
Sales: $80,000,000
Company Type: Private
SIC: 1521
    Single-family house construction
Eric Tessem, President
Employees: 50
Employees here: 20

D-U-N-S 07-125-3470
LATCO INC
Hwy 62 E, Lincoln, AR 72744

Phone: (501) 824-3282
Sales: $70,000,000   Employees: 325
Company Type: Private   Employees here: 100
SIC: 1542
    Poultry house construction
Forrest L Preston, Chairman of the Board

D-U-N-S 00-790-4519
LATHROP CO INC
    (Parent: Turner Construction Co)
460 W Dussel Dr, Maumee, OH 43537
Phone: (419) 893-7000
Sales: $200,000,000   Employees: 200
Company Type: Public Family Member   Employees here: 150
SIC: 1542
    General contractor & construction management
Tommy Blake, President

D-U-N-S 00-781-3587
LAW CO INC
345 Riverview St Ste 300, Wichita, KS 67203
Phone: (316) 268-0200
Sales: $70,000,000   Employees: 200
Company Type: Private   Employees here: 137
SIC: 1542
    Contractor
John S Adams, President

D-U-N-S 02-921-0028
LAWSON ROOFING CO INC
1495 Tennessee St, San Francisco, CA 94107
Phone: (415) 285-1661
Sales: $800,500,000   Employees: 90
Company Type: Private   Employees here: 90
SIC: 1761
    Roofing/siding contractor trade contractor
Ron W Mostyn, President

D-U-N-S 00-696-5917
LAYNE CHRISTENSEN CO
1900 Shawnee Mission Pkwy, Shawnee Mission, KS 66205
Phone: (913) 362-0510
Sales: $294,600,000   Employees: 2,949
Company Type: Public   Employees here: 65
SIC: 1781
    Water well drilling well repair and maintenance
        environmental and exploration drilling
Scott Thompson, President

D-U-N-S 00-780-9676
LAYTON CONSTRUCTION CO
9090 Sandy Pkwy, Sandy, UT 84070
Phone: (801) 568-9090
Sales: $100,000,000   Employees: 300
Company Type: Private   Employees here: 227
SIC: 1542
    Commercial & industrial construction
Thomas N Tidball, President

D-U-N-S 10-733-5184
LCS HOLDINGS, INC.
800 2nd Ave Ste 300, Des Moines, IA 50309
Phone: (515) 245-7600
Sales: $87,200,000   Employees: 400
Company Type: Private   Employees here: 150
SIC: 1542
    Commercial & industrial contractor develops & manages
        retirement homes
Michael L Hauenstein, President

D-U-N-S 03-651-9767
LECHASE CONSTRUCTION SERVICES LLC
    (Parent: Raymond Lechase Inc)
300 Trolley Blvd, Rochester, NY 14606

Phone: (716) 254-3510
Sales: $138,246,000   Employees: 300
Company Type: Private   Employees here: 300
SIC: 1542
    General contractor
H M Juergens, Executive Vice-President

D-U-N-S 08-898-6179
LEE KENNEDY CO INC
1792 Dorchester Ave, Boston, MA
Phone: (617) 825-6930
Sales: $72,134,000   Employees: 75
Company Type: Private   Employees here: 75
SIC: 1542
    Renovation & new construction of office buildings
Kurt G Conti, President

D-U-N-S 09-890-1200
LEHR CONSTRUCTION CORP
902 Broadway Fl 6, New York, NY 10010
Phone: (212) 353-1160
Sales: $200,000,000   Employees: 130
Company Type: Private   Employees here: 130
SIC: 1542
    General contractors of interiors for commercial buildings
Joe McGaugh, President

D-U-N-S 05-537-8061
LENNAR CORP
700 NW 107th Ave Ste 400, Miami, FL 33172
Phone: (305) 559-4000
Sales: $1,303,082,000   Employees: 3,875
Company Type: Public   Employees here: 1,070
SIC: 1531
    Operative builders of single family homes townhouses &
        condominiums & real estate developer
Ed Bryant, Branch Manager

D-U-N-S 03-249-7497
LENNAR HOMES INC
    (Parent: Lennar Corp)
700 NW 107th Ave, Miami, FL 33172
Phone: (305) 559-4000
Sales: $528,266,000   Employees: 300
Company Type: Public Family Member   Employees here: 50
SIC: 1531
    Operative builders specializing in single family homes
        townhouses & condominiums
Richard C Lundquist, President

D-U-N-S 94-951-9342
LENNAR HOMES OF CALIFORNIA
    (Parent: Lennar Corp)
24800 Chrisanta Dr, Mission Viejo, CA 92691
Phone: (949) 598-8500
Sales: $188,000,000   Employees: 90
Company Type: Public Family Member   Employees here: 90
SIC: 1531
    Operative builders and land subdivider
W T Hickcox, President

D-U-N-S 09-678-6447
LEOPARDO COMPANIES, INC.
115 N Brandon Dr, Glendale Heights, IL 60139
Phone: (630) 894-7200
Sales: $120,000,000   Employees: 175
Company Type: Private   Employees here: 175
SIC: 1542
    General contractor of commercial & industrial buildings and
        construction management
Olin Jones, President

D-U-N-S 08-267-1892
LEVITT CORP
(*Parent:* Starrett Corp)
909 3rd Ave, New York, NY 10022
Phone: (212) 751-3100
Sales: $120,378,000
Company Type: Private
SIC: 1531
   Real est dev & bldrs
Jeffrey M Levy, President

        Employees: 493
        Employees here: 25

D-U-N-S 02-142-2662
LEVITT HOMES INC
(*Parent:* Levitt Corp)
7777 Glades Rd Ste 410, Boca Raton, FL 33434
Phone: (561) 482-5100
Sales: $114,442,000
Company Type: Private
SIC: 1522
   General contractor single and multi family houses new
     construction
Naguib Sawiris, President

        Employees: 400
        Employees here: 120

D-U-N-S 06-617-4871
LEWIS HOMES OF CALIFORNIA
1156 N Mountain Ave, Upland, CA 91786
Phone: (909) 985-0971
Sales: $108,900,000
Company Type: Private
SIC: 1531
   Operative builder
Harold T Bieser, Chairman of the Board

        Employees: NA
        Employees here: NA

D-U-N-S 60-420-6664
LEWIS LEASE CRUTCHER
107 Spring St Ste 500, Seattle, WA 98104
Phone: (206) 622-0500
Sales: $107,300,000
Company Type: Private
SIC: 1542
   Commercial construction
Joseph Lizzadro, Chairman of the Board

        Employees: 490
        Employees here: 460

D-U-N-S 06-949-6503
LEXINGTON HOMES, L.L.C.
(*Parent:* Cambridge Properties Partnr)
800 S Milwaukee Ave, Libertyville, IL 60048
Phone: (847) 362-9100
Sales: $99,847,000
Company Type: Private
SIC: 1531
   Operative builder of single and multi-family homes
Dean Haagenson, President

        Employees: 140
        Employees here: 140

D-U-N-S 00-791-5960
LIMBACH CO
(*Parent:* Limbach Co Holding Co)
4 Northshore Ctr, Pittsburgh, PA 15212
Phone: (412) 359-2100
Sales: $220,937,000
Company Type: Private
SIC: 1711
   Heating plumbing & air conditioning contractor
Kendrick G Ellis, President

        Employees: 1,249
        Employees here: 139

D-U-N-S 15-763-4403
LIMBACH HOLDINGS INC
103 Foulk Rd Ste 205-3, Wilmington, DE 19803
Phone: (302) 427-7639

Sales: $329,382,000
Company Type: Private
SIC: 1711
   Mechanical air conditioning & maintenance contractor &
     franchisor
Al E Lucas, Chief Executive Officer

        Employees: 2,510
        Employees here: 1

D-U-N-S 00-894-9836
LINBECK CORP
3810 W Alabama St, Houston, TX 77027
Phone: (713) 621-2350
Sales: $185,000,000
Company Type: Private
SIC: 1542
   General contractor of commercial buildings
Barry D Cooper, Treasurer

        Employees: 760
        Employees here: 75

D-U-N-S 00-806-0170
LINCOLN BUILDERS, INC
1910 Farmerville Hwy, Ruston, LA 71270
Phone: (318) 255-3822
Sales: $78,875,000
Company Type: Private
SIC: 1542
   Commercial & industrial contractors
Paul N Johnson, President

        Employees: 64
        Employees here: 30

D-U-N-S 17-794-3610
LINEAR CONSTRUCTION, INC.
3361 N Palo Verde Ave, Tucson, AZ 85716
Phone: (520) 299-7233
Sales: $200,000,000
Company Type: Private
SIC: 1521
   General contractor for new construction of single & multi-
     family dwellings & commercial building construction &
     remodeling
Ronald T Bellistri, President

        Employees: 6
        Employees here: 6

D-U-N-S 62-210-2226
LOFTIN CONSTRUCTORS, INC.
140 Old Highway 80, Brandon, MS 39042
Phone: (601) 825-4193
Sales: $100,000,000
Company Type: Private
SIC: 1542
   Land work heavy general contractor
Robert Stroup, President

        Employees: 400
        Employees here: 3

D-U-N-S 15-292-2456
LOMBARDY HOLDINGS
8201 Sorensen Ave, Whittier, CA 90607
Phone: (562) 945-1411
Sales: $93,469,000
Company Type: Private
SIC: 1623
   Communications contractor
Eugene R Waken, President

        Employees: 755
        Employees here: 6

D-U-N-S 00-378-6555
LOUIS P CIMINELLI CONSTRUCTION CO
(*Parent:* Louis P Ciminelli Mgt Co)
369 Franklin St, Buffalo, NY 14202
Phone: (716) 855-1200
Sales: $74,000,000
Company Type: Private
SIC: 1542
   General contractor of commercial & industrial buildings
Gary Jennison, Chairman of the Board

        Employees: 25
        Employees here: 25

D-U-N-S 19-066-2122
LP SNYDER LANGSTON
17962 Cowan, Irvine, CA 92614

Phone: (949) 863-9200
Sales: $110,000,000　　　　　　　　　　*Employees:* 100
Company Type: Private　　　　　　　　*Employees here:* 100
SIC: 1542
　　Real estate & construction services
William G Cox, President

D-U-N-S 92-641-4046
LUCENT TECHNOLOGIES SERVICES CO
　　(Parent: Lucent Technologies Inc)
5440 Millstream Rd, McLeansville, NC 27301
Phone: (336) 279-7000
Sales: $70,000,000　　　　　　　　　　*Employees:* 800
Company Type: Public Family Member　　*Employees here:* 200
SIC: 1731
　　Installation of telecommunications equipment engineering
　　　service and temporary help service
Mark S Corna, President

D-U-N-S 00-583-2613
LUNDA CONSTRUCTION CO
620 Gebhardt Rd, Black River Falls, WI 54615
Phone: (715) 284-9491
Sales: $120,000,000　　　　　　　　　　*Employees:* 700
Company Type: Private　　　　　　　　*Employees here:* 150
SIC: 1622
　　Bridge construction
Ronald Cornejo, President

D-U-N-S 04-816-5740
LUNDGREN BROS. CONSTRUCTION
935 Wayzata Blvd E, Wayzata, MN 55391
Phone: (612) 473-1231
Sales: $68,658,000　　　　　　　　　　*Employees:* 200
Company Type: Private　　　　　　　　*Employees here:* 50
SIC: 1521
　　Contractor building new single family construction
Delores Cornell, President

D-U-N-S 00-813-7218
LYDA INC
6228 Bandera Rd, San Antonio, TX 78238
Phone: (210) 684-1770
Sales: $100,000,000　　　　　　　　　　*Employees:* 300
Company Type: Private　　　　　　　　*Employees here:* 150
SIC: 1542
　　Commercial building contractor of new buildings
Wallis H Bryce, President

D-U-N-S 13-073-1797
M A MORTENSON COMPANIES
700 Meadow Ln N, Minneapolis, MN 55422
Phone: (612) 522-2100
Sales: $809,489,000　　　　　　　　　　*Employees:* 1,500
Company Type: Private　　　　　　　　*Employees here:* 300
SIC: 1542
　　Through subsidiaries operates as a general contractor doing
　　　institutional commercial and heavy industrial construction
Edward Elak, N/A

D-U-N-S 08-838-9408
M & H ENTERPRISES INC
1900 Western Ave, Las Vegas, NV 89102
Phone: (702) 385-5257
Sales: $67,749,000　　　　　　　　　　*Employees:* 200
Company Type: Private　　　　　　　　*Employees here:* 200
SIC: 1542
　　General contractor of medical & light commercial buildings
　　　casinos warehouses & industrial buildings
Dennis G Corrigan, President

D-U-N-S 00-791-9442
M B KAHN CONSTRUCTION CO INC
Flintlake & Hwy 555, Columbia, SC 29201

Phone: (803) 736-2950
Sales: $242,000,000　　　　　　　　　　*Employees:* 850
Company Type: Private　　　　　　　　*Employees here:* 65
SIC: 1542
　　General building contractor of new office commercial
　　　institutional & industrial buildings & construction
　　　management
Dan Pool, President

D-U-N-S 06-970-2181
M. D. C. HOLDINGS, INC.
3600 S Yosemite St, Denver, CO 80237
Phone: (303) 773-1100
Sales: $1,263,209,000　　　　　　　　　*Employees:* 1,350
Company Type: Public　　　　　　　　*Employees here:* 100
SIC: 1521
　　General contractor specializing in single-family homes &
　　　mortgage banker
John McCarty, Director

D-U-N-S 07-164-9743
M/I SCHOTTENSTEIN HOMES INC
3 Easton Oval, Columbus, OH 43219
Phone: (614) 418-8000
Sales: $614,004,000　　　　　　　　　　*Employees:* 800
Company Type: Public　　　　　　　　*Employees here:* 250
SIC: 1531
　　Operative builder single family homes
James Clark, Director

D-U-N-S 03-944-1613
M J ANDERSON INC
11382 Prosperity Farms Rd, West Palm Beach, FL 33410
Phone: (561) 627-4744
Sales: $82,039,000　　　　　　　　　　*Employees:* 120
Company Type: Private　　　　　　　　*Employees here:* 120
SIC: 1542
　　Commercial construction and payroll and insurance for the
　　　affiliate companies
Se U Kim, President

D-U-N-S 00-690-6606
M J BROCK & SONS INC
　　(Parent: Ryland Group Inc)
21800 Burbank Blvd, Woodland Hills, CA 91367
Phone: (818) 598-4400
Sales: $74,000,000　　　　　　　　　　*Employees:* 200
Company Type: Public Family Member　　*Employees here:* 30
SIC: 1531
　　Builds single family homes
Michael Saxton, President

D-U-N-S 62-189-6661
M W BUILDERS, INC
　　(Parent: MMC Corp)
11100 Ash St Ste 100, Shawnee Mission, KS 66211
Phone: (913) 469-0101
Sales: $135,000,000　　　　　　　　　　*Employees:* 300
Company Type: Private　　　　　　　　*Employees here:* 220
SIC: 1542
　　Government & commercial general contractor
Cloyce Darnell, Vice-President

D-U-N-S 60-438-1491
M W HOLDINGS INC
2525 E Grand Blvd, Detroit, MI 48211
Phone: (313) 873-2220
Sales: $141,111,000　　　　　　　　　　*Employees:* 400
Company Type: Private　　　　　　　　*Employees here:* 75
SIC: 1791
　　Structural steel erection contractors
James Danella, President

D-U-N-S 02-596-8033
M W KELLOGG CO
  (*Parent:* M W Kellogg - Delaware Inc)
601 Jefferson St, Houston, TX 77002
Phone: (713) 753-2000
Sales: $1,358,000,000
Company Type: Public Family Member   *Employees:* 6,770
                                        Employees here: 3,100
SIC: 1629
  Heavy construction contractor & engineering services
Donald La Belle, Manager

D-U-N-S 78-131-8878
MACOMBER ENTERPRISES, INC
1 Design Center Pl, Boston, MA
Phone: (617) 478-6200
Sales: $80,000,000
Company Type: Private   *Employees:* 120
                          Employees here: 3
SIC: 1542
  Institutional and commercial building contractor
Chet Zurawik, Manager

D-U-N-S 13-105-6707
MAIN STREET OPERATING CO INC
  (*Parent:* Hardaway Group Inc)
615 Main St, Nashville, TN 37206
Phone: (615) 254-5461
Sales: $143,000,000
Company Type: Private   *Employees:* 650
                          Employees here: 2
SIC: 1542
  Commercial industrial & residential building contractor &
    real estate sales & management
John Thompson, Principal

D-U-N-S 01-879-4438
MANAFORT BROTHERS INC
414 New Britain Ave, Plainville, CT
Phone: (860) 229-4853
Sales: $75,000,000
Company Type: Private   *Employees:* 400
                          Employees here: 400
SIC: 1794
  Excavation work concrete & foundations highway & bridge
    rehabilitation & demolition & waste recycling
Bill Johns, Principal

D-U-N-S 05-395-9755
MANHATTAN CONSTRUCTION CO
  (*Parent:* Rooney Brothers Co)
3890 W Northwest Hwy, Dallas, TX 75220
Phone: (214) 357-7400
Sales: $440,000,000
Company Type: Private   *Employees:* 900
                          Employees here: 650
SIC: 1542
  Institutional commercial & industrial building contractor
Alan Hamberlin, President

D-U-N-S 00-978-3127
MARKET & JOHNSON, INC
2350 Galloway St, Eau Claire, WI 54703
Phone: (715) 834-1213
Sales: $83,594,000
Company Type: Private   *Employees:* 300
                          Employees here: 250
SIC: 1542
  General contractor of commercial industrial and institutional
    buildings
Patrick L Murphy, President

D-U-N-S 95-836-3921
MARLEY HOLDINGS L P
9 W 57th St Ste 4200, New York, NY 10019
Phone: (212) 779-1500

Sales: $97,800,000
Company Type: Private   *Employees:* 1,800
                          Employees here: 3
SIC: 1781
  Holding company - water well drilling well & pump repair
    environmental drilling & mineral exploration drilling
    services
Robert Crider, President

D-U-N-S 00-610-2834
MARSHALL ERDMAN & ASSOCIATES
5117 University Ave, Madison, WI 53705
Phone: (608) 238-0211
Sales: $204,253,000
Company Type: Private   *Employees:* 1,112
                          Employees here: 600
SIC: 1542
  Constructs professional buildings & clinics
Rosiland Stock, Branch Manager

D-U-N-S 00-694-4003
MARTIN K EBY CONSTRUCTION CO
  (*Parent:* Eby Corp)
610 N Main St, Wichita, KS 67203
Phone: (316) 268-3500
Sales: $250,000,000
Company Type: Private   *Employees:* 1,499
                          Employees here: 1,133
SIC: 1629
  Heavy construction sewer line bridge & tunnel industrial
    warehouse & commercial building contractor
Stephen W Pavlik, President

D-U-N-S 08-816-5972
MASCARO CONSTRUCTION CO LP
1720 Metropolitan St, Pittsburgh, PA 15233
Phone: (412) 321-4901
Sales: $79,349,000
Company Type: Private   *Employees:* 175
                          Employees here: 175
SIC: 1542
  Commercial buildings contractor
C D Murtagh, Chief Executive Officer

D-U-N-S 00-799-7463
MASS ELECTRIC CONSTRUCTION CO
  (*Parent:* Me Holding Inc)
180 Guest St, Boston, MA
Phone: (617) 254-1015
Sales: $261,584,000
Company Type: Private   *Employees:* 2,050
                          Employees here: 1,000
SIC: 1731
  General electrical contractor
Stephen Bair, General Manager

D-U-N-S 00-692-4385
MASTEC INC
3155 NW 77th Ave, Miami, FL 33122
Phone: (305) 599-1800
Sales: $703,369,000
Company Type: Public   *Employees:* 7,850
                         Employees here: 35
SIC: 1623
  Telecommunications & cable television systems installation
    contractor
Ivan L Crossland, Chief Executive Officer

D-U-N-S 16-165-7119
MATZEL MMFORD ORGANIZATION
100 Village Ct, Hazlet, NJ
Phone: (732) 888-1055
Sales: $120,000,000
Company Type: Private   *Employees:* 100
                          Employees here: 100
SIC: 1521
  Single-family house construction nonresidential construction
Jeff Durbon, President

D-U-N-S 92-641-2453
MBC HOLDINGS, INC
1613d S Defiance St, Archbold, OH 43502
Phone: (419) 445-1015
Sales: $109,184,000   *Employees:* 341
Company Type: Private   *Employees here:* 3
SIC: 1611
　　General highway & bridge contractor & coal mining
John Scheumann, Chairman of the Board

D-U-N-S 62-220-1598
MBK CONSTRUCTION LTD
175 Technology Dr, Irvine, CA 92618
Phone: (949) 789-8300
Sales: $250,000,000   *Employees:* 140
Company Type: Private   *Employees here:* 35
SIC: 1542
　　Commercial building contractor
W B Crouch Jr, President

D-U-N-S 11-897-2512
MCC GROUP, L.L.C.
3001 17th St, Metairie, LA 70002
Phone: (504) 833-8291
Sales: $106,909,000   *Employees:* 250
Company Type: Private   *Employees here:* 40
SIC: 1711
　　Industrial & commercial mechanical contractor
Ross Campesi Jr, President

D-U-N-S 60-654-4336
MCCAR DEVELOPMENT CORP
7000 Central Pkwy NE, Atlanta, GA 30328
Phone: (770) 206-9100
Sales: $70,000,000   *Employees:* 80
Company Type: Private   *Employees here:* 80
SIC: 1521
　　Contractor of new single-family houses
Robert Crown, President

D-U-N-S 08-871-1643
MCCARTHY BUILDING COMPANIES
1341 N Rock Hill Rd, St. Louis, MO 63124
Phone: (314) 968-3300
Sales: $1,127,000,000   *Employees:* 1,500
Company Type: Private   *Employees here:* 120
SIC: 1542
　　General building contractor & construction manager of
　　　institutional commercial & industrial buildings
Licinio Cruz, Chairman of the Board

D-U-N-S 08-486-1954
MCCLURE CO INC
(Parent: PP&L Resources Inc)
4101 N 6th St Unit 4, Harrisburg, PA 17110
Phone: (717) 232-9743
Sales: $70,000,000   *Employees:* 300
Company Type: Public Family Member   *Employees here:* 250
SIC: 1711
　　Contractos specializing in plumbing heating air conditioning
　　　process piping service & maintenance
James O Neill, President

D-U-N-S 05-180-3237
MCCORMICK INC
4000 12th Ave NW, Fargo, ND 58102
Phone: (701) 277-1225
Sales: $80,000,000   *Employees:* 125
Company Type: Private   *Employees here:* 1
SIC: 1611
　　Holding company highway & street construction & power
　　　plant & bridge construction
Fred L Gibbs, Chief Operating Officer

D-U-N-S 04-775-8503   EXP
MCDERMOTT INTERNATIONAL INC
1450 Poydras St, New Orleans, LA 70112
Phone: (504) 587-5400
Sales: $3,674,635,000   *Employees:* 24,700
Company Type: Public   *Employees here:* 400
SIC: 1629
　　Marine construction services mfg power generation systems
　　　& equipment and related services & other activities
Charles H Culp, President

D-U-N-S 07-904-6207
MCGEE BROTHERS CO INC
4608 Carriker Rd, Monroe, NC 28110
Phone: (704) 753-4582
Sales: $74,472,000   *Employees:* 811
Company Type: Private   *Employees here:* 720
SIC: 1741
　　Masonry contractor
O J Knox, President

D-U-N-S 00-679-1313
MCGOUGH CONSTRUCTION CO, INC
2737 Fairview Ave N, St. Paul, MN 55113
Phone: (651) 633-5050
Sales: $168,000,000   *Employees:* 250
Company Type: Private   *Employees here:* 250
SIC: 1542
　　General contractor commercial & industrial construction
Bradley A Cundy, President

D-U-N-S 13-087-2773
MCHUGH ENTERPRISES, INC.
2222 S Indiana Ave, Chicago, IL 60616
Phone: (312) 842-8400
Sales: $87,200,000   *Employees:* 400
Company Type: Private   *Employees here:* 12
SIC: 1542
　　Non-residential multi-story & other residential bldg heavy
　　　construction including bridge tunnel and highway
　　　construction
J B Donaldson Jr, President

D-U-N-S 05-549-6004
MCKINSTRY CO
5005 3rd Ave S, Seattle, WA 98134
Phone: (206) 762-3311
Sales: $70,000,000   *Employees:* 450
Company Type: Private   *Employees here:* 400
SIC: 1711
　　Plumbing ventilation heating & air conditioning fire
　　　protection & industrial piping contractor
James S Ryley, Chief Executive Officer

D-U-N-S 80-592-5500
MCL CONSTRUCTION CORP
1337 W Fullerton Ave, Chicago, IL 60614
Phone: (773) 525-4814
Sales: $85,000,000   *Employees:* 100
Company Type: Private   *Employees here:* 25
SIC: 1521
　　Contractor of condominiums and townhouses
John H Curran, Chairman of the Board

D-U-N-S 19-895-4190
MCSHANE CONSTRUCTION CORP
6400 Shafer Ct Ste 400, Des Plaines, IL 60018
Phone: (847) 292-4300
Sales: $89,988,000   *Employees:* 70
Company Type: Private   *Employees here:* 70
SIC: 1541
　　New construction of industrial office & commercial buildings
Charles P Reid, President

D-U-N-S 80-195-7721
ME HOLDING, INC
(*Parent:* Kiewit Construction Co)
180 Guest St, Boston, MA
Phone: (617) 254-1015
Sales: $261,584,000
Company Type: Private
SIC: 1731
   General electrical contractor
Arlo Dekraai, Sr Manager

    Employees: 1,353
    Employees here: 100

D-U-N-S 87-840-3500
MEADOW VALLEY CORP
4411 S 40th St Ste D-11, Phoenix, AZ 85040
Phone: (602) 437-5400
Sales: $149,979,000
Company Type: Public
SIC: 1611
   Heavy construction contractor
Frederic Mulligan, President

    Employees: 450
    Employees here: 33

D-U-N-S 08-528-3349
MELODY HOMES INC
(*Parent:* Schuler Homes Inc)
11031 Sheridan Blvd, Broomfield, CO 80020
Phone: (303) 466-1831
Sales: $100,000,000
Company Type: Public Family Member
SIC: 1521
   General contractor single-family homes
Joe Becherer, Principal

    Employees: 85
    Employees here: 35

D-U-N-S 18-472-7659
MERCEDES HOMES INC
6767 N Wickham Rd Ste 500, Melbourne, FL 32940
Phone: (407) 259-6972
Sales: $175,831,000
Company Type: Private
SIC: 1521
   General contractor of single family homes
Brad Corbett, Chief Executive Officer

    Employees: 502
    Employees here: 30

D-U-N-S 19-690-5657
MERITAGE CORP
6613 N Scottsdale Rd, Scottsdale, AZ 85250
Phone: (602) 998-8700
Sales: $155,065,000
Company Type: Public
SIC: 1521
   Home builder
Richard W Hubbert, President

    Employees: 190
    Employees here: 4

D-U-N-S 06-126-2622
METRIC CONSTRUCTORS INC
(*Parent:* J A Jones Inc)
J A Jones Dr, Charlotte, NC 28287
Phone: (704) 554-1415
Sales: $380,061,000
Company Type: Private
SIC: 1541
   Industrial institutional & commercial construction
Robert Grimes, President

    Employees: 700
    Employees here: 43

D-U-N-S 04-177-9240
METROPOLITAN MECHANICAL CONTRACTORS
7340 Washington Ave S, Eden Prairie, MN 55344
Phone: (612) 941-7010
Sales: $80,000,000
Company Type: Private
SIC: 1711
   Mechanical heating plumbing air conditioning & fire
     sprinkler contractor
A L Greaves, President

    Employees: 350
    Employees here: 328

D-U-N-S 00-791-6968
MICHAEL BAKER CORP
Airport Office Park 420, Coraopolis, PA 15108
Phone: (412) 269-6300
Sales: $446,432,000
Company Type: Public
SIC: 1611
   Gen contracting-highway eng services facilities mgt services
     oilfield services heavy construction and gen contracting
William E Clark, Chairman of the Board

    Employees: 3,670
    Employees here: 600

D-U-N-S 14-466-2632
MICHAEL/CURRY COMPANIES, INC
5500 Wayzata Blvd Ste 300, Minneapolis, MN 55416
Phone: (612) 546-1400
Sales: $135,000,000
Company Type: Private
SIC: 1542
   Contractor specializing in commercial & industrial
     construction
Subhas Khara, President

    Employees: 400
    Employees here: 4

D-U-N-S 04-252-6087
MICHAEL NICHOLAS INC
565 Randy Rd, Carol Stream, IL 60188
Phone: (630) 682-0900
Sales: $70,000,000
Company Type: Private
SIC: 1751
   Carpentry contractor
Bob Effle, Branch Manager

    Employees: 500
    Employees here: 300

D-U-N-S 00-580-9868
MICHELS PIPELINE CONSTRUCTION
817 W Main St, Brownsville, WI 53006
Phone: (920) 583-3132
Sales: $158,000,000
Company Type: Private
SIC: 1623
   Pipeline & underground utility contractor
Don Nederhood, Chief Executive Officer

    Employees: 500
    Employees here: 250

D-U-N-S 62-697-7425
MICRON CONSTRUCTION INC
(*Parent:* ICF Kaiser Advanced Technology)
2710 Sunrise Rim Rd, Boise, ID 83705
Phone: (208) 338-8988
Sales: $120,000,000
Company Type: Private
SIC: 1541
   General contractor
Angelo Zaffuto, Principal

    Employees: 150
    Employees here: 25

D-U-N-S 06-218-5517
MIDDLESEX CORP
1 Spectacle Pond Rd, Littleton, MA
Phone: (978) 742-4400
Sales: $75,000,000
Company Type: Private
SIC: 1611
   General highway & roadway construction
Bruce Walk, Treasurer

    Employees: 350
    Employees here: 50

D-U-N-S 00-716-8214
MIDWEST MECHANICAL CONTRACTORS INC
(*Parent:* MMC Corp)
4550 W 109th St Ste 100, Shawnee Mission, KS 66211
Phone: (913) 469-2200
Sales: $110,000,000
Company Type: Private
SIC: 1711
   Mechanical contractor
Henry De Mello, President

    Employees: 200
    Employees here: 155

D-U-N-S 13-183-5456
MILBURN INVESTMENTS INC
  (Parent: D R Horton Inc)
4515 Seton Center Pkwy, Austin, TX 78759
Phone: (512) 345-4663
Sales: $725,970,000   *Employees:* 120
Company Type: Public Family Member   *Employees here:* 107
SIC: 1531
  Holding company
Steven Pumper, President

D-U-N-S 00-604-8912
MILESTONE CONTRACTORS, L.P.
5950 S Belmont St, Indianapolis, IN 46217
Phone: (317) 788-1040
Sales: $175,000,000   *Employees:* 250
Company Type: Private   *Employees here:* 35
SIC: 1611
  Road construction sewer & water line constructin bridge
    construction
William W Taylor, Chairman of the Board

D-U-N-S 00-326-1252
MILLER & LONG CO OF MARYLAND
4824 Rugby Ave, Bethesda, MD 20814
Phone: (301) 657-8000
Sales: $73,561,000   *Employees:* 50
Company Type: Private   *Employees here:* 50
SIC: 1771
  Concrete contractor
Kenneth T Sandeno, President

D-U-N-S 00-285-2028
MILLER BUILDING CORP
1410 Commonwealth Dr, Wilmington, NC 28403
Phone: (910) 256-2613
Sales: $152,511,000   *Employees:* 450
Company Type: Private   *Employees here:* 60
SIC: 1541
  Industrial & commercial contractor
Dean F Chase, President

D-U-N-S 00-583-4205
MILLER ELECTRIC CO
2251 Rosselle St, Jacksonville, FL 32204
Phone: (904) 388-8000
Sales: $83,451,000   *Employees:* 691
Company Type: Private   *Employees here:* 350
SIC: 1731
  Electrical contractor
Douglas F Shoffner, President

D-U-N-S 96-577-1140
MIMUN RESOURCES INC
8520 Sweetwater Ln, Houston, TX 77037
Phone: (281) 272-1991
Sales: $300,000,000   *Employees:* 23
Company Type: Private   *Employees here:* 23
SIC: 1623
  Underground utilities contractor
David H Griffin Sr, President

D-U-N-S 07-936-5888
MITCHELL CONSTRUCTION CO
701 North St, Vidalia, GA 30474
Phone: (912) 537-2231
Sales: $100,000,000   *Employees:* 550
Company Type: Private   *Employees here:* 550
SIC: 1542
  General contractor
Robert E Hill, Chairman of the Board

D-U-N-S 62-221-1712
MMC CORP
11100 Ash St Ste 100, Shawnee Mission, KS 66211
Phone: (913) 469-0101
Sales: $269,000,000   *Employees:* 525
Company Type: Private   *Employees here:* 7
SIC: 1711
  Mechanical & general contractors
Donald R Horton, Chairman of the Board

D-U-N-S 04-482-4068
MODERN CONTINENTAL CONSTRUCTION CO
600 Memorial Dr, Cambridge, MA
Phone: (617) 864-6300
Sales: $478,878,000   *Employees:* 2,300
Company Type: Private   *Employees here:* 2,250
SIC: 1622
  General contractor engaged in heavy construction &
    construction of commercial & industrial buildings
M L McAllister, Principal

D-U-N-S 92-717-3658
MODERN-OBAYASHI CORP
148 State St, Boston, MA
Phone: (617) 227-4242
Sales: $75,000,000   *Employees:* 350
Company Type: Private   *Employees here:* 120
SIC: 1622
  Bridge/tunnel construction
Donald R Horton, President

D-U-N-S 05-191-3226
MONSANTO ENVIRO-CHEM SYSTEMS
  (Parent: Monsanto Co)
14522 S Outer 40 Ste 100, Chesterfield, MO 63017
Phone: (314) 275-5700
Sales: $175,000,000   *Employees:* 550
Company Type: Public Family Member   *Employees here:* 380
SIC: 1629
  Heavy construction contractor and engineering services
Thomas D Oxley, President

D-U-N-S 00-511-5654
MONUMENTAL INVESTMENT CORP
2207 Monumental Ave, Baltimore, MD 21227
Phone: (410) 247-2200
Sales: $400,000,000   *Employees:* 1,851
Company Type: Private   *Employees here:* 100
SIC: 1711
  Mechanical construction & construction design &
    engineering services
John Nicholson, Chairman of the Board

D-U-N-S 00-685-3527
MORLEY CONSTRUCTION CO INC
  (Parent: Morley Group Inc)
2901 28th St 100, Santa Monica, CA 90405
Phone: (310) 399-1600
Sales: $90,000,000   *Employees:* 100
Company Type: Private   *Employees here:* 80
SIC: 1771
  General contractor specializing in concrete work earthquake
    retrofit
Douglas L Wilburn, President

D-U-N-S 02-227-8220
MORRISON HOMES, INC
3700 Mansell Rd Ste 300, Alpharetta, GA 30022
Phone: (770) 998-9044

Sales: $301,596,000   *Employees:* 540
Company Type: Private   *Employees here:* 13
SIC: 1521
    Contractor specializing in new construction of single-family
      homes & real estate development
Lawrence D Addario, Chief Operating Officer

D-U-N-S 80-764-4554
MORRISON KNUDSEN CORP
720 Park Blvd, Boise, ID 83712
Phone: (208) 386-5000
Sales: $1,862,174,000   *Employees:* 9,000
Company Type: Public   *Employees here:* 158
SIC: 1622
    General contractor of heavy construction waste remediation
      mining services
Michael D Ambra, President

D-U-N-S 00-969-4779
MORROW-MEADOWS CORP
610 Reyes Dr, Walnut, CA 91789
Phone: (909) 598-7700
Sales: $134,311,000   *Employees:* 820
Company Type: Private   *Employees here:* 520
SIC: 1731
    Electrical contractor
Michael A D Annunzio, President

D-U-N-S 62-365-1965
MORSE DIESEL INTERNATIONAL
    (*Parent:* Amec Holdings Inc)
1633 Broadway Fl 24, New York, NY 10019
Phone: (212) 484-0300
Sales: $76,300,000   *Employees:* 800
Company Type: Private   *Employees here:* 200
SIC: 1522
    Construction managers general contractors construction
      consultants & program managers
H H McJunkin Jr, Chairman of the Board

D-U-N-S 00-481-7490
MOTOR CITY ELECTRIC CO
600 Renaissance Ctr, Detroit, MI 48243
Phone: (313) 567-5300
Sales: $179,000,000   *Employees:* 600
Company Type: Private   *Employees here:* 600
SIC: 1731
    Electrical contractor
Herbert H McJunkin Jr, Principal

D-U-N-S 10-124-1537
MOUNT HOPE ROCK PRODUCTS INC
625 Mount Hope Rd, Wharton, NJ
Phone: (973) 366-7741
Sales: $124,680,000   *Employees:* 200
Company Type: Private   *Employees here:* 184
SIC: 1611
    Highway/street construction asphalt plant
Dale E Lintner Sr, Chairman of the Board

D-U-N-S 12-119-7933
MP WATER RESOURCES GROUP, INC
    (*Parent:* Minnesota Power & Light Co)
30 W Superior St, Duluth, MN 55802
Phone: (218) 722-2641
Sales: $118,992,000   *Employees:* 589
Company Type: Public Family Member   *Employees here:* 1
SIC: 1623
    Water & sewer utility construction
John C Kirby, Chief Executive Officer

D-U-N-S 06-104-4566
MURPHY BROS INC
3150 5th Ave, East Moline, IL 61244
Phone: (309) 752-1227
Sales: $73,628,000   *Employees:* 100
Company Type: Private   *Employees here:* 100
SIC: 1623
    Pipeline contractors
Ernest Dallman, President

D-U-N-S 00-383-3365
MURPHY MECHANICAL CONTRACTORS ENGINEERS
1340 N Price Rd, St. Louis, MO 63132
Phone: (314) 997-6600
Sales: $146,641,000   *Employees:* 700
Company Type: Private   *Employees here:* 500
SIC: 1711
    Mechanical contractor doing process piping plumbing heating
      ventilation refrigeration and air conditioning work
Clarence L Ray, President

D-U-N-S 09-814-6210
MYLER CO INC
970 N Englewood Dr, Crawfordsville, IN 47933
Phone: (765) 362-3353
Sales: $100,000,000   *Employees:* 75
Company Type: Private   *Employees here:* 50
SIC: 1542
    Design & build churches
Daniel P Greguska, President

D-U-N-S 04-534-8588
MYR GROUP INC.
1701 Golf Rd 1012, Rolling Meadows, IL 60008
Phone: (847) 290-1891
Sales: $431,276,000   *Employees:* 4,000
Company Type: Public   *Employees here:* 20
SIC: 1623
    Electric utility line commercial and industrial electrical and
      mechanical construction
Daniel S Falasca, President

D-U-N-S 87-437-6890
MYRICK, BATSON & GUROSKY INC
1 Riverchase Rdg Ste 300, Birmingham, AL 35244
Phone: (205) 444-0776
Sales: $75,000,000   *Employees:* 155
Company Type: Private   *Employees here:* 145
SIC: 1542
    Commercial contractors
Daniel G Schuster, President

D-U-N-S 00-279-5763
N A B CONSTRUCTION CORP
11220 14th Ave, College Point, NY 11356
Phone: (718) 762-0001
Sales: $88,777,000   *Employees:* 400
Company Type: Private   *Employees here:* 400
SIC: 1541
    Industrial building & highway construction
Daniel J Keating III, Chairman of the Board

D-U-N-S 18-377-6814
N A CCC INC
1743 Maplelawn Dr, Troy, MI 48084
Phone: (248) 643-7600
Sales: $74,131,000   *Employees:* 300
Company Type: Private   *Employees here:* 225
SIC: 1796
    Machinery installation contractor
Pierce J Keating, President

D-U-N-S 00-691-5748
NABORS INTERNATIONAL INC
  (*Parent:* Nabors Industries Inc)
515 W Greens Rd Ste 1000, Houston, TX 77067
Phone: (281) 874-0035
Sales: $160,900,000   *Employees:* 1,650
Company Type: Public Family Member   *Employees here:* 4
SIC: 7353
    Oil well drilling
Richard C Russell, President

D-U-N-S 86-809-8054
NASON & CULLEN GROUP INC
500 N Gulph Rd Ste 150, King of Prussia, PA 19406
Phone: (610) 768-9300
Sales: $123,291,000   *Employees:* 195
Company Type: Private   *Employees here:* 5
SIC: 1542
    Holding company which through its subsidiaries commercial
       & industrial builders
Jerry E Kelley, President

D-U-N-S 19-228-0915
NATIONAL BUSINESS GROUP
15319 Chatsworth St, Mission Hills, CA 91345
Phone: (818) 221-6000
Sales: $70,000,000   *Employees:* 455
Company Type: Private   *Employees here:* 40
SIC: 7353
    Rents mfg whls and retails fences and related products
William Darling, President

D-U-N-S 08-153-7599
NATIONAL CAPITAL COMPANIES LTD
1 Country Club Ln, State College, PA 16803
Phone: (814) 238-0534
Sales: $113,800,000   *Employees:* 1,200
Company Type: Private   *Employees here:* 4
SIC: 1522
    Contractor of apt bldgs & motels operates apt bldgs motels
       restaurants golf club tavern ret golf shop & provides capital
James E Megargel Jr, President

D-U-N-S 05-475-7612
NATIONAL CONSTRUCTION ENTERPRISES
1001 W 11th St, Mishawaka, IN 46544
Phone: (219) 259-8581
Sales: $86,900,000   *Employees:* 1,500
Company Type: Private   *Employees here:* 1
SIC: 1742
    Plastering drywall acoustical & lathing contractor
William H Davenport, Chairman of the Board

D-U-N-S 02-131-8381
NATIONAL ENERGY PRODUCTION
  (*Parent:* Enron Corp)
18578 NE 67th Ct, Redmond, WA 98052
Phone: (425) 869-3000
Sales: $200,000,000   *Employees:* 700
Company Type: Public Family Member   *Employees here:* 250
SIC: 1629
    Heavy construction
Tim Davey, President

D-U-N-S 04-578-7087
NATIONAL REFRIGERATION SERVICES
1100 Circle 75 Pkwy SE, Atlanta, GA 30339
Phone: (770) 951-4830
Sales: $108,500,000   *Employees:* 1,150
Company Type: Private   *Employees here:* 3
SIC: 1711
    Refrigerations services
David Christa, President

D-U-N-S 61-208-0937
NATIONSRENT INC
450 E Las Olas Blvd, Fort Lauderdale, FL 33301
Phone: (954) 760-6550
Sales: $200,000,000   *Employees:* 1,000
Company Type: Public   *Employees here:* 100
SIC: 7353
    Equipment rental sales & service
David Harvey Jr, President

D-U-N-S 15-178-3701
NATKIN CONTRACTING LLC
2775 S Vallejo St, Englewood, CO 80110
Phone: (303) 783-7850
Sales: $100,000,000   *Employees:* 200
Company Type: Private   *Employees here:* 55
SIC: 1711
    Mechanical & sheet metal contractor
David Nelson, President

D-U-N-S 04-071-5013
NEENAN CO
2620 E Prospect Rd 100, Fort Collins, CO 80525
Phone: (970) 493-8747
Sales: $88,157,000   *Employees:* 200
Company Type: Private   *Employees here:* 138
SIC: 1542
    Real estate development & commercial construction
Ronnie C Davis, Owner

D-U-N-S 36-151-6271
NEFF CORP
3750 NW 87th Ave Ste 400, Miami, FL 33178
Phone: (305) 513-3350
Sales: $142,019,000   *Employees:* 1,100
Company Type: Public   *Employees here:* 20
SIC: 7353
    Construction and industrial equipment rental whol new &
       used and service and parts
Burton Fisher, President

D-U-N-S 61-783-6002
NEOSHO INC
2953 SW Wanamaker Dr, Topeka, KS 66614
Phone: (785) 273-0200
Sales: $71,913,000   *Employees:* 325
Company Type: Private   *Employees here:* 20
SIC: 1611
    Grading contractor & repair of railroad maintenance
       equipment
Tom C Davis, President

D-U-N-S 01-923-7668
NEW ENGLAND POWER SERVICE CO
  (*Parent:* New England Electric System Vol Assoc)
25 Research Dr, Westborough, MA
Phone: (508) 389-2000
Sales: $206,517,000   *Employees:* 1,305
Company Type: Public Family Member   *Employees here:* 1,305
SIC: 1623
    Electric power line construction administration
Jim Davis, President

D-U-N-S 13-187-7177
NEW FORTIS CORP
  (*Parent:* Hovnanian Enterprises Inc)
151 Jefferson Church Rd, King, NC 27021
Phone: (336) 983-4321
Sales: $133,000,000   *Employees:* 190
Company Type: Public Family Member   *Employees here:* 82
SIC: 1521
    New construction of single-family houses
William M Sumerel, President

D-U-N-S 84-875-5278
NEW URBAN WEST INC
520 Broadway Ste 100, Santa Monica, CA 90401
Phone: (310) 394-3379
Sales: $74,136,000
Company Type: Private   *Employees:* 63
Company Type: Private   *Employees here:* 63
SIC: 1531
  Operative builders
J D Matthews, President

D-U-N-S 11-848-4500
NEWMARK HOME CORP
  (Parent: Newmark Homes Corp)
1200 Soldiers Field Dr, Sugar Land, TX 77479
Phone: (281) 243-0100
Sales: $163,991,000   *Employees:* 200
Company Type: Public   *Employees here:* 60
SIC: 1531
  Speculative & custom builder of single-family homes
Bobby C Kimmel, President

D-U-N-S 00-679-1339
NEWMECH COMPANIES, INC
1633 Eustis St, St. Paul, MN 55108
Phone: (651) 645-0451
Sales: $80,000,000   *Employees:* 300
Company Type: Private   *Employees here:* 292
SIC: 1711
  Mechanical contractor
Charles R Davis, Chief Executive Officer

D-U-N-S 10-719-2858
NEWTRON GROUP, INC
8183 W El Cajon Dr, Baton Rouge, LA 70815
Phone: (225) 927-8921
Sales: $94,601,000   *Employees:* 1,750
Company Type: Private   *Employees here:* 1,342
SIC: 1731
  Electrical & industrial contractors & installation & repair of
  instrumentation
Douglas Lumsden, President

D-U-N-S 94-302-0156
NIELSEN DILLINGHAM BUILDERS
  (Parent: Dillingham Construction Corp)
3127 Jefferson St, San Diego, CA 92110
Phone: (619) 291-6330
Sales: $360,000,000   *Employees:* 700
Company Type: Private   *Employees here:* 300
SIC: 1542
  Nonresidential construction
Ryan Daw, President

D-U-N-S 07-872-5348
NINTEMAN CONSTRUCTION CO
  (Parent: Sundt Construction Inc)
4375 Jutland Dr Ste 200, San Diego, CA 92117
Phone: (619) 490-6800
Sales: $100,000,000   *Employees:* 271
Company Type: Private   *Employees here:* 271
SIC: 1542
  General contractor of commercial buildings
Denise McCullars, Treasurer

D-U-N-S 02-915-8532
N.L. BARNES CONSTRUCTION, INC
449 10th St, San Francisco, CA 94103
Phone: (415) 552-7070
Sales: $135,000,000   *Employees:* 200
Company Type: Private   *Employees here:* 25
SIC: 1542
  Nonresidential construction
John Danis, Chief Executive Officer

D-U-N-S 62-643-5747
NOCUTS, INC
  (Parent: Carolina Telephone & Telg Co)
14111 Capital Blvd, Wake Forest, NC 27587
Phone: (919) 562-4590
Sales: $82,900,000   *Employees:* 1,100
Company Type: Public Family Member   *Employees here:* 884
SIC: 1623
  Underground utilities contractor
Robert R Dawson Jr, Executive

D-U-N-S 03-445-2425
NOR-AM CONSTRUCTION CO
1530 SW Taylor St, Portland, OR 97205
Phone: (503) 228-7177
Sales: $70,000,000   *Employees:* 175
Company Type: Private   *Employees here:* 50
SIC: 1542
  Commercial building construction
Carl W Yost, President

D-U-N-S 00-872-7307
NORTH BROS, INC
  (Parent: Performance Contracting Group)
3250 Woodstock Rd SE, Atlanta, GA 30316
Phone: (404) 627-1381
Sales: $120,000,000   *Employees:* 240
Company Type: Private   *Employees here:* 240
SIC: 1742
  Mfg & contractor of insulation materials
Wilton L Day, President

D-U-N-S 04-230-0384
NORTHERN PIPELINE CONSTRUCTION CO
  (Parent: Southwest Gas Corp)
1 W Deer Valley Rd, Phoenix, AZ 85027
Phone: (602) 582-1235
Sales: $120,000,000   *Employees:* 765
Company Type: Public Family Member   *Employees here:* 25
SIC: 1623
  Gas pipeline construction maintenance & replacement
Richard De Jager, President

D-U-N-S 93-251-5042
NORTHWEST RACING ASSOCIATES LP
2300 Emerald Downs Dr, Auburn, WA 98001
Phone: (253) 288-7000
Sales: $157,000,000   *Employees:* 300
Company Type: Private   *Employees here:* 300
SIC: 1629
  Race track construction & off track betting facility
Alfonso De Luca, President

D-U-N-S 00-421-9882
NORTHWESTERN GROWTH CORP
  (Parent: Northwestern Corp)
125 S Dakota Ave Ste 1100, Sioux Falls, SD 57104
Phone: (605) 367-6960
Sales: $340,400,000   *Employees:* 1,375
Company Type: Public Family Member   *Employees here:* 10
SIC: 1711
  Investment & acquisition company
Richard Gates, Partner

D-U-N-S 07-949-8804
NORWOOD CO
530 Brandywine Pkwy, West Chester, PA 19380
Phone: (610) 431-3500

Sales: $94,226,000   *Employees:* 130
Company Type: Private   *Employees here:* 35
SIC: 1542
    Commercial & industrial building new construction &
       renovation & construction management
Dale DeWitt, President

D-U-N-S 09-384-3118   EXP
NOVA CORP
74 W Sheffield Ave, Englewood, NJ
Phone: (201) 567-4404
Sales: $150,000,000   *Employees:* 60
Company Type: Private   *Employees here:* 60
SIC: 1542
    General contractor/construction manager specializing data
       center & commercial office construction
Richard Smith, President

D-U-N-S 61-281-9599
NSC CORP
49 Danton Dr, Methuen, MA
Phone: (978) 557-7300
Sales: $115,955,000   *Employees:* 850
Company Type: Public   *Employees here:* 20
SIC: 1799
    Specialty contractor
David Tsao, President

D-U-N-S 80-839-4621
NVR, INC
7601 Lewinsville Rd, McLean, VA 22102
Phone: (703) 761-2000
Sales: $1,154,022,000   *Employees:* 2,013
Company Type: Public   *Employees here:* 44
SIC: 1531
    Operative builder of single family houses townhomes
       condominiums and mortgage banking services
Timothy D Word, Managing Partner

D-U-N-S 01-883-8136
O & G INDUSTRIES INC
112 Wall St, Torrington, CT
Phone: (860) 489-9261
Sales: $198,900,000   *Employees:* 649
Company Type: Private   *Employees here:* 100
SIC: 1542
    General contractors commercial & industrial buildings
       highway & sewer contractors & whol construction materials
Daniel B Dearborn, President

D-U-N-S 09-744-5399
O'CONNELL COMPANIES INC
480 Hampden St, Holyoke, MA
Phone: (413) 534-0246
Sales: $91,156,000   *Employees:* 450
Company Type: Private   *Employees here:* 27
SIC: 1541
    General building contractor real estate development
       financing property management
Julius E Ellen, Chief Executive Officer

D-U-N-S 01-087-1333
O'NEIL INDUSTRIES, INC.
2751 N Clybourn Ave, Chicago, IL 60614
Phone: (773) 327-1611
Sales: $244,725,000   *Employees:* 300
Company Type: Private   *Employees here:* 50
SIC: 1542
    General contractor of commercial institutional and industrial
       buildings
Robert G Russo, President

D-U-N-S 78-778-8405
OAKWOOD HOMES LLC
6130 Greenwood Plaza Blvd, Englewood, CO 80111
Phone: (303) 843-6303
Sales: $93,915,000   *Employees:* 120
Company Type: Private   *Employees here:* 100
SIC: 1521
    New construction of single family homes
Neil Deatley, Principal

D-U-N-S 78-297-8548
OBAYASHI U. S. HOLDINGS INC
666 5th Ave Fl 12, New York, NY 10103
Phone: (212) 757-6668
Sales: $250,000,000   *Employees:* 160
Company Type: Private   *Employees here:* 2
SIC: 1542
    Contractor of commercial & industrial buildings & real estate
       investment
A N Deatley, President

D-U-N-S 87-687-9552
OC AMERICA CONSTRUCTION INC
420 E 3rd St Ste 600, Los Angeles, CA 90013
Phone: (213) 687-8700
Sales: $229,356,000   *Employees:* 130
Company Type: Private   *Employees here:* 130
SIC: 1542
    General contractor specializing in commercial and industrial
       building
C D Brown Jr, Chairman of the Board

D-U-N-S 62-076-6626
ODEBRECHT CONTRACTORS OF FLORIDA
    (Parent: Odebrecht of America Inc)
201 Alhambra Cir Ste 1400, Coral Gables, FL 33134
Phone: (305) 445-1165
Sales: $151,155,000   *Employees:* 740
Company Type: Private   *Employees here:* 120
SIC: 1622
    Highway and bridge construction
Joseph Bitzer, Chief Executive Officer

D-U-N-S 02-705-9455
ODEBRECHT OF AMERICA, INC.
1747 Pennsylvania Ave NW, Washington, DC 20006
Phone: (202) 429-6861
Sales: $117,800,000   *Employees:* 750
Company Type: Private   *Employees here:* 2
SIC: 1622

John Amicucci, Shareholder

D-U-N-S 12-227-6124
OGDEN ENERGY GROUP INC
    (Parent: Ogden Corp)
40 Lane Rd, Fairfield, NJ
Phone: (973) 882-9000
Sales: $699,176,000   *Employees:* 355
Company Type: Public Family Member   *Employees here:* 255
SIC: 1629
    Constructs operates and maintains waste-to-energy facilities
       & other environmental services
Bob DeGabrielle, Chief Executive Officer

D-U-N-S 05-609-0319
OKLAND CONSTRUCTION CO
1978 S West Temple, Salt Lake City, UT 84115
Phone: (801) 486-0144

Sales: $220,000,000   *Employees:* 200
Company Type: Private   *Employees here:* 200
SIC: 1542
    New commercial and new industrial building construction
Charles R Martin, President

D-U-N-S 02-733-6650
OLDCASTEL NORTHWEST INC
    (*Parent:* Oldcastle Inc)
18010 Southcenter Pkwy, Tukwila, WA 98188
Phone: (206) 575-3200
Sales: $100,000,000   *Employees:* 250
Company Type: Private   *Employees here:* 20
SIC: 1629
    Heavy construction mfg asphalt whol sand & gravel
David Wakefield, President

D-U-N-S 80-429-6127
OLKER INDUSTRIES, INC
6536 R F D, Long Grove, IL 60047
Phone: (847) 949-1644
Sales: $480,000,000   *Employees:* 10
Company Type: Private   *Employees here:* 10
SIC: 1521
    General contractors
Jerry A Donahue, President

D-U-N-S 00-959-0399
OLTMANS CONSTRUCTION CO
10005 Mission Mill Rd, Whittier, CA 90601
Phone: (562) 948-4242
Sales: $260,099,000   *Employees:* 600
Company Type: Private   *Employees here:* 85
SIC: 1541
    General contractor industrial & commercial buildings
Pablo Del Valle, Managing Partner

D-U-N-S 83-589-6184
ONYX PIPELINE CO LC
802 N Carancahua St, Corpus Christi, TX 78470
Phone: (361) 884-7878
Sales: $101,367,000   *Employees:* 10
Company Type: Private   *Employees here:* 10
SIC: 1623
    Natural gas pipeline
Glenn Pusey, Principal

D-U-N-S 60-224-7645
OPUS U.S. CORP
10350 Bren Rd W, Hopkins, MN 55343
Phone: (612) 656-4444
Sales: $600,000,000   *Employees:* 764
Company Type: Private   *Employees here:* 179
SIC: 1542
    Holding company for the designers builders developers and
      managers of commercial real estate
Ralph Stoy, President

D-U-N-S 18-745-7833
OPUS WEST CORP
    (*Parent:* Opus U.S.Corp)
2415 E Camelback Rd, Phoenix, AZ 85016
Phone: (602) 468-7000
Sales: $220,000,000   *Employees:* 150
Company Type: Private   *Employees here:* 110
SIC: 1542
    General contractor of commercial and industrial buildings
      real estate developer and commercial property operator
Joseph D Chiaie, President

D-U-N-S 07-160-9184
ORLEANS CORP
    (*Parent:* Orleans Homebuilders Inc)
3333 Street Rd Ste 101, Bensalem, PA 19020
Phone: (215) 245-7500
Sales: $100,000,000   *Employees:* 165
Company Type: Public Family Member   *Employees here:* 165
SIC: 1521
    Contractor of single family and multi family homes
Joe Regenhardt, President

D-U-N-S 06-621-0428
OSMAN CONSTRUCTION CORP
70 W Seegers Rd, Arlington Heights, IL 60005
Phone: (847) 593-2700
Sales: $78,415,000   *Employees:* 90
Company Type: Private   *Employees here:* 90
SIC: 1542
    General contractor of new construction of commercial &
      industrial buildings
Larry R Donelson, President

D-U-N-S 04-443-7796
OWL COMPANIES
2465 Campus Dr, Irvine, CA 92612
Phone: (949) 660-4966
Sales: $199,400,000   *Employees:* 1,500
Company Type: Private   *Employees here:* 5
SIC: 1629
    Land preparation construction mgmt services electrical
      services
W A Leone, President

D-U-N-S 94-023-9882
OWNER-BUILDER-ALLIANCE INC
8386 Coconut Blvd, West Palm Beach, FL 33412
Phone: (561) 792-6264
Sales: $100,000,000   *Employees:* 2
Company Type: Private   *Employees here:* 2
SIC: 1521
    Single-family house shell construction
David Greenberg, Treasurer

D-U-N-S 15-687-9231
OXFORD HOLDINGS, INC
3063 NW 23rd Ter, Fort Lauderdale, FL 33311
Phone: (954) 731-2811
Sales: $92,800,000   *Employees:* 425
Company Type: Private   *Employees here:* 25
SIC: 1542
    Through subsidiaries contractor of commercial & office
      buildings new construction
Richard B Demars, Chairman of the Board

D-U-N-S 78-754-6399
P & O INC
8350 E Crescent Pkwy, Englewood, CO 80111
Phone: (303) 773-1700
Sales: $1,930,000,000   *Employees:* 3,800
Company Type: Private   *Employees here:* 30
SIC: 1542
    Institutional commercial and industrial building contractors
      construction management consulting and a cruise ship
      operator
Don Paula, Controller

D-U-N-S 09-633-8223
P J DICK INC
1020 Lebanon Rd, West Mifflin, PA 15122
Phone: (412) 462-9300

Sales: $129,000,000   *Employees:* 200
Company Type: Private   *Employees here:* 195
SIC: 1542
     General contractor and construction management
W G Dement Jr, President

D-U-N-S 79-079-4838
PACIFIC REALTY GROUP, INC.
     (Parent: Pacific USA Holding Corp)
5999 Summerside Dr, Dallas, TX 75252
Phone: (972) 248-5022
Sales: $83,400,000   *Employees:* 270
Company Type: Private   *Employees here:* 70
SIC: 1531
     Residential & commercial development
Raja Jubran, President

D-U-N-S 11-253-1421
PACLANTIC CONSTRUCTION INC
     (Parent: Dillingham Construction Corp)
5960 Inglewood Dr, Pleasanton, CA 94588
Phone: (925) 463-3300
Sales: $190,200,000   *Employees:* 1,500
Company Type: Private   *Employees here:* 1
SIC: 1541
     General contractor of industrial buildings
Dennis J Denier, Chief Executive Officer

D-U-N-S 00-883-0861
PADDOCK POOL CONSTRUCTION CO.
6525 E Thomas Rd, Scottsdale, AZ 85251
Phone: (602) 947-7261
Sales: $72,000,000   *Employees:* 400
Company Type: Private   *Employees here:* 270
SIC: 1799
     Swimming pool contractor ret swimming pool equipment &
       swimming pool maintenance
Patrick Roche, President

D-U-N-S 12-235-5001
PANDA ENERGY INTERNATIONAL
4100 Spring Vly Ste 1001, Dallas, TX 75244
Phone: (972) 980-7159
Sales: $74,502,000   *Employees:* 35
Company Type: Private   *Employees here:* 31
SIC: 1731
     Development construction & operation of cogeneration
       projects & non-utility generators
Dennis J Amoroso, President

D-U-N-S 13-767-8702
PARDEE CONSTRUCTION CO OF NEVADA
     (Parent: Pardee Construction Co)
4835 S Rainbow Blvd, Las Vegas, NV 89103
Phone: (702) 876-2634
Sales: $107,000,000   *Employees:* 100
Company Type: Public Family Member   *Employees here:* 100
SIC: 1521
     Construction of single-family homes
Dennis T Hardy, President

D-U-N-S 08-176-5299
PARKER & LANCASTER CORP
711 Moorefield Park Dr, Richmond, VA 23236
Phone: (804) 323-3100
Sales: $68,604,000   *Employees:* 84
Company Type: Private   *Employees here:* 30
SIC: 1531
     Speculative builder and contract builder of single family
       homes
Leet E Denton, President

D-U-N-S 03-086-6545
PARSONS CORP
100 W Walnut St, Pasadena, CA 91124
Phone: (626) 440-2000
Sales: $1,245,588,000   *Employees:* 10,000
Company Type: Private   *Employees here:* 3,000
SIC: 1629
     Engineering & heavy construction
Colonel R Davis, Principal

D-U-N-S 06-860-7225
PASQUINELLI CONSTRUCTION CO
915 175th St Ste 3, Homewood, IL 60430
Phone: (708) 957-3456
Sales: $100,000,000   *Employees:* 75
Company Type: Private   *Employees here:* 35
SIC: 1531
     Operative builder
Capt Hunter, Branch Manager

D-U-N-S 15-408-2911
PATE & PATE ENTERPRISES INC
300 Valley Wood Dr, The Woodlands, TX 77380
Phone: (281) 353-1444
Sales: $73,818,000   *Employees:* 550
Company Type: Private   *Employees here:* 315
SIC: 1623
     Water sewer & pipeline construction
E D Carlson, Secretary

D-U-N-S 17-435-6386
PAYTON CONSTRUCTION CORP
273 Summer St, Boston, MA
Phone: (617) 423-9035
Sales: $87,324,000   *Employees:* 100
Company Type: Private   *Employees here:* 90
SIC: 1542
     Renovation of commercial & office buildings
Don Drickey, Branch Manager

D-U-N-S 11-883-2153
PCL ENTERPRISES INC
     (Parent: Green Holdings Inc)
2000 Cleo St Ste 400, Denver, CO 80229
Phone: (303) 753-6600
Sales: $714,739,000   *Employees:* 1,200
Company Type: Private   *Employees here:* 81
SIC: 1542
     Governmental commercial & office buildings & highway road
       & bridge construction
Harry Price, Director

D-U-N-S 17-713-9037
PECK/JONES CONSTRUCTION CORP
     (Parent: Jones Brothers Construction Corp)
10866 Wilshire Blvd, Los Angeles, CA 90024
Phone: (310) 470-1885
Sales: $122,000,000   *Employees:* 119
Company Type: Private   *Employees here:* 50
SIC: 1542
     Contractor specializing in commercial and industrial
       buildings
Dan Miller, Branch Manager

D-U-N-S 00-880-2423
PENHALL INTERNATIONAL INC
1801 W Penhall Way, Anaheim, CA 92801
Phone: (714) 778-6677

Sales: $90,000,000
Company Type: Private *Employees:* 700
SIC: 1795 *Employees here:* 7
    Holding company operating through subsidiaries as concrete
      contractor
Stephen Knobbe, Branch Manager

D-U-N-S 12-147-4902
PEPPER COMPANIES INC
643 N Orleans St, Chicago, IL 60610
Phone: (312) 266-4703
Sales: $622,915,000 *Employees:* 900
Company Type: Private *Employees here:* 200
SIC: 1542
    General contractor of commercial & industrial buildings &
      residential homes
William M Derrick, President

D-U-N-S 17-355-2423
PERFORMANCE CONTRACTING GROUP
16047 W 110th St, Shawnee Mission, KS 66219
Phone: (913) 888-8600
Sales: $346,801,000 *Employees:* 5,000
Company Type: Private *Employees here:* 50
SIC: 1742
    Mechanical systems insulation & acoustical contractor
Joe Reghetti, President

D-U-N-S 09-859-9582
PERFORMANCE CONTRACTORS, INC.
9865 Pecue Ln, Baton Rouge, LA 70810
Phone: (225) 751-4156
Sales: $110,000,000 *Employees:* 1,000
Company Type: Private *Employees here:* 1,000
SIC: 1541
    General industrial contractor new construction renovation &
      maintenance
Frank Kocvara, President

D-U-N-S 96-710-7509
PERINI & SLATTERY ASSOC
430 Communipaw Ave Apt 3, Jersey City, NJ
Phone: (201) 915-0006
Sales: $78,000,000 *Employees:* 80
Company Type: Private *Employees here:* 80
SIC: 1542
    Nonresidential construction
Derrick Hodson, President

D-U-N-S 00-695-4432
PERINI CORP
73 Mount Wayte Ave Ste 1, Framingham, MA
Phone: (508) 628-2000
Sales: $1,324,491,000 *Employees:* 2,200
Company Type: Public *Employees here:* 160
SIC: 1542
    Commercial apartment building & heavy const real estate
      development real estate agent-residential/commercial
      property
Patrick O Donnell, President

D-U-N-S 60-693-4008
PERRY HOMES, A JOINT VENTURE
9000 Gulf Fwy Fl 3, Houston, TX 77017
Phone: (713) 947-1750
Sales: $220,000,000 *Employees:* 200
Company Type: Private *Employees here:* 95
SIC: 1531
    Speculative builder of single-family houses
Gary Filizetti, President

D-U-N-S 09-096-3695
PERSEUS FISK, LLC
111 TC Jester, Houston, TX 77007
Phone: (713) 865-9499
Sales: $111,300,000 *Employees:* 1,500
Company Type: Private *Employees here:* 1
SIC: 1731
    Electrical work, nsk
Donald Smith Jr, President

D-U-N-S 15-454-9877
PETER KIEWIT SONS', INC
3555 Farnam St Ste 1000, Omaha, NE 68131
Phone: (402) 342-2052
Sales: $2,096,500,000 *Employees:* 9,393
Company Type: Private *Employees here:* 265
SIC: 1542
    Commercial industrial paving bridge tunnel marine dam &
      land preparation construction & insurance services
Roland Sturm, Managing Member

D-U-N-S 00-185-6145
PETROCELLI ELECTRIC CO INC
1212 43rd Ave, Long Island City, NY 11101
Phone: (718) 937-1200
Sales: $83,382,000 *Employees:* 500
Company Type: Private *Employees here:* 400
SIC: 1731
    Electrical contractor
Richard Crittenden, President

D-U-N-S 10-765-6571
PHILIP ST, INC.
   (Parent: Philip Services Corp)
5200 Cedar Crest St, Houston, TX 77087
Phone: (713) 644-9974
Sales: $146,600,000 *Employees:* 1,278
Company Type: Private *Employees here:* 65
SIC: 1629
    Specialized maintenance & construction services for the
      hydrocarbon processing & production industry
W C Deviney Jr, President

D-U-N-S 00-384-5336
PHILLIPS & JORDAN INC
6621 Wilbanks Rd, Knoxville, TN 37912
Phone: (423) 688-8342
Sales: $90,662,000 *Employees:* 750
Company Type: Private *Employees here:* 150
SIC: 1629
    Heavy construction
Mitchell J Di Carlo, President

D-U-N-S 00-382-1576
PHILLIPS, GETSCHOW CO
   (Parent: Getschow Group Inc)
2860 Greenwald St, Green Bay, WI 54301
Phone: (920) 863-3507
Sales: $84,870,000 *Employees:* 650
Company Type: Private *Employees here:* 100
SIC: 1711
    Mechanical & process piping contracting & custom metal
      fabrication
C S Clegg, Chairman of the Board

D-U-N-S 06-234-5228
PIEDMONT INSULATING CO, INC
663 Arnett Blvd, Danville, VA 24540
Phone: (804) 793-7037

Sales: $200,000,000   *Employees:* 8
Company Type: Private   *Employees here:* 8
SIC: 1742
     Drywall/insulating contractor single-family house
     construction
Wallace Carline, President

D-U-N-S 17-501-7573
PIKE CO INC
1 Circle St, Rochester, NY 14607
Phone: (716) 271-5256
Sales: $100,000,000   *Employees:* 200
Company Type: Private   *Employees here:* 75
SIC: 1542
     Construction managers & general contractor for commercial
     construction
John McFarlane, President

D-U-N-S 00-388-5514
PIKE ELECTRIC INC
100 Pike Way, Mount Airy, NC 27030
Phone: (336) 789-2171
Sales: $277,800,000   *Employees:* 3,700
Company Type: Private   *Employees here:* 300
SIC: 1623
     Electric power line contractor
David E Dick, Chief Executive Officer

D-U-N-S 01-897-0517
PIKE INDUSTRIES, INC
     (Parent: Oldcastle Inc)
3 Eastgate Park Dr, Belmont, NH
Phone: (603) 527-5100
Sales: $145,000,000   *Employees:* 225
Company Type: Private   *Employees here:* 45
SIC: 1611
     Highway construction and street paving contractor
David E Dick, Chief Executive Officer

D-U-N-S 00-577-7677
PINKARD CONSTRUCTION CO
1075 S Yukon St Ste 301, Denver, CO 80226
Phone: (303) 986-4555
Sales: $70,000,000   *Employees:* 50
Company Type: Private   *Employees here:* 48
SIC: 1542
     General contractors of nonresidential buildings & warehouse
     construction
Wayne Williams, Chairman of the Board

D-U-N-S 03-355-1656
PINKERTON & LAWS INC
1810 Water Pl SE Ste 220, Atlanta, GA 30339
Phone: (770) 956-9000
Sales: $95,000,000   *Employees:* 100
Company Type: Private   *Employees here:* 67
SIC: 1542
     General contractor
Ted H Tyson, President

D-U-N-S 00-209-2773
PIZZAGALLI CONSTRUCTION CO
50 Joy Dr, Burlington, VT
Phone: (802) 658-4100
Sales: $250,000,000   *Employees:* 1,000
Company Type: Private   *Employees here:* 100
SIC: 1542
     Commercial & public building sewage & water treatment &
     power plant construction industrial process construction
Ralph Dietze, President

D-U-N-S 04-962-6740
PKF-MARK III, INC
170 Pheasant Run, Newtown, PA 18940
Phone: (215) 968-5031
Sales: $75,000,000   *Employees:* 150
Company Type: Private   *Employees here:* 150
SIC: 1629
     Waste water plant & water treatment plant & highway
     contractor
Harold W Hicks Jr, Branch Manager

D-U-N-S 09-212-5756
PLASTER DEVELOPMENT CO
801 S Rancho Dr Ste E4, Las Vegas, NV 89106
Phone: (702) 385-5031
Sales: $69,000,000   *Employees:* 65
Company Type: Private   *Employees here:* 65
SIC: 1531
     Speculative builder of single-family homes
Sam C Bowen, President

D-U-N-S 92-748-5177
PLATTE RIVER CONSTRUCTORS
2450 S Peoria St Ste 400, Aurora, CO 80014
Phone: (303) 369-7121
Sales: $104,791,000   *Employees:* 51
Company Type: Private   *Employees here:* 51
SIC: 1611
     Highway construction
Donald K Stager, Chairman of the Board

D-U-N-S 79-880-0488
PLEASANT STREET ASSOCIATES
930 Commonwealth Ave, Boston, MA
Phone: (617) 731-5599
Sales: $80,249,000   *Employees:* 125
Company Type: Private   *Employees here:* 75
SIC: 1542
     General contractor of commercial industrial and multi-
     housing buildings
William J Wilson, President

D-U-N-S 01-871-7694
PONTARELLI BUILDERS, INC.
4353 W Lawrence Ave, Chicago, IL 60630
Phone: (773) 794-3100
Sales: $85,000,000   *Employees:* 20
Company Type: Private   *Employees here:* 20
SIC: 1531
     Operative builder of condominiums & real estate manager
William L Higgins III, President

D-U-N-S 00-389-5042
POOLE & KENT CORP
     (Parent: Monumental Investment Corp)
4530 Hollins Ferry Rd, Baltimore, MD 21227
Phone: (410) 247-2200
Sales: $94,300,000   *Employees:* 1,000
Company Type: Private   *Employees here:* 1,000
SIC: 1711
     Mechanical contractors
Don Sundgren, President

D-U-N-S 88-477-9133
POSEIDON OIL PIPELINE CO LLC
600 Travis St Ste 7400, Houston, TX 77002
Phone: (713) 224-7400
Sales: $310,829,000   *Employees:* 60
Company Type: Private   *Employees here:* 60
SIC: 1623
     Construction & transportation of oil through pipeline
William Catlin, President

D-U-N-S 14-621-4242
POTTER CONCRETE CO INC
4820 Gretna St, Dallas, TX 75207
Phone: (214) 630-2191
Sales: $80,000,000
Company Type: Private
SIC: 1771
   Commercial concrete contractor
Thomas Dimeo, Chairman of the Board

Employees: 900
Employees here: 190

D-U-N-S 04-735-8775
POWELL CONSTRUCTION CO
3622 Bristol Hwy, Johnson City, TN 37601
Phone: (423) 282-0111
Sales: $119,032,000
Company Type: Private
SIC: 1542
   Nonresidential construction bituminous coal/lignite surface
     mining & steel erection
Greg Cosko, President

Employees: 500
Employees here: 50

D-U-N-S 10-580-7648
POWER PLANT MAINTENANCE CO
   (Parent: J A Jones Management Services)
S Main St, Society Hill, SC 29593
Phone: (843) 378-4700
Sales: $137,600,000
Company Type: Private
SIC: 1629
   Repair & maint of power plants & industrial plants
Greg Cosko, President

Employees: 1,200
Employees here: 800

D-U-N-S 01-213-7282
POWERSYSTEMS CORP
1246 Concord Rd SE, Smyrna, GA 30080
Phone: (770) 433-8880
Sales: $80,000,000
Company Type: Private
SIC: 1542
   Remodeling contractors and whol construction equipment
Charles Williams, Branch Manager

Employees: 44
Employees here: 44

D-U-N-S 78-296-9992
PRESLEY COMPANIES
19 Corporate Plaza Dr, Newport Beach, CA 92660
Phone: (949) 640-6400
Sales: $329,942,000
Company Type: Public
SIC: 1531
   Operative builder
William T Divane Jr, President

Employees: 376
Employees here: 60

D-U-N-S 92-777-2269
PRIME SERVICE INC
   (Parent: Atlas Copco North America Inc)
16225 Park Ten Pl Ste 200, Houston, TX 77084
Phone: (281) 578-5600
Sales: $326,588,000
Company Type: Private
SIC: 7353
   Heavy construction & industrial equipment rental
Stephen L Kauffman, President

Employees: 2,611
Employees here: 120

D-U-N-S 07-790-4936
PRODUCTION MANAGEMENT COMPANIES
2439 Manhattan Blvd, Harvey, LA 70058
Phone: (504) 366-3594
Sales: $133,300,000
Company Type: Private
SIC: 1629
   Contractors of oil & gas production facilities &
Ed Anderson, President

Employees: 1,162
Employees here: 26

D-U-N-S 07-245-5058
PULICE CONSTRUCTION INC
2033 W Mountain View Rd, Phoenix, AZ 85021
Phone: (602) 944-2241
Sales: $68,189,000
Company Type: Private
SIC: 1611
   General contractor highway construction
Kenneth Baum, President

Employees: 300
Employees here: 300

D-U-N-S 18-620-8351
PULTE CORP
33 Blmfeld Hlls Pkwy 20, Bloomfield Hills, MI 48304
Phone: (248) 644-7300
Sales: $2,866,521,000
Company Type: Public
SIC: 1531
   Operative builder single-family homes townhouses &
     condominiums mortgage banking
Edward J Wolff, President

Employees: 3,778
Employees here: 120

D-U-N-S 04-510-7752
Q I CORP
   (Parent: BSI Holdings Inc)
1121 Alderman Dr, Alpharetta, GA 30005
Phone: (770) 754-4480
Sales: $150,000,000
Company Type: Private
SIC: 1742
   Building insulation contractor
Timothy G Dixon, President

Employees: 1,350
Employees here: 15

D-U-N-S 05-576-5705
QUALITY MECHANICAL CONTRACTORS
3175 Westwood Dr, Las Vegas, NV 89109
Phone: (702) 732-2545
Sales: $82,706,000
Company Type: Private
SIC: 1711
   Mechanical contractor
Mark A Striebel, President

Employees: 420
Employees here: 420

D-U-N-S 04-999-8685
R & D THIEL INC
2340 Newburg Rd, Belvidere, IL 61008
Phone: (815) 544-1699
Sales: $114,179,000
Company Type: Private
SIC: 1751
   Carpentry contractor & mfg wood trusses and wood panels
J D Dennis Jr, President

Employees: 900
Employees here: 600

D-U-N-S 13-132-3123
R J GRIFFIN & CO
800 Mount Vernon Hwy, Atlanta, GA 30327
Phone: (770) 551-8883
Sales: $212,727,000
Company Type: Private
SIC: 1542
   General contractor
Harold Dokmo, Chairman of the Board

Employees: 479
Employees here: 219

D-U-N-S 11-525-4484
R J POMPLUN CO
125 N Market St, Petersburg, VA 23803
Phone: (804) 861-0509
Sales: $110,000,000
Company Type: Private
SIC: 1521
   Single-family house construction nonresidential construction
Edmund S Goulder, President

Employees: 5
Employees here: 5

D-U-N-S 60-737-3412
R M SHOEMAKER HOLDINGS INC
100 Front St Ste 1300, West Conshohocken, PA 19428
Phone: (610) 941-5500
Sales: $234,150,000   *Employees:* 125
Company Type: Private   *Employees here:* 3
SIC: 1541
  Holding company through subsidiaries general contractor of
    industrial & commercial buildings
C R Dobson, Chairman of the Board

D-U-N-S 08-955-1790
R P INDUSTRIES INC
105 Reynolds Rd, Franklin, TN 37064
Phone: (615) 595-2400
Sales: $71,500,000   *Employees:* 75
Company Type: Private   *Employees here:* 75
SIC: 1542
  Contractor of commercial & industrial buildings
Douglas G Borror, President

D-U-N-S 36-136-7147
R SANDERS & ASSOC CUSTOM BUILDERS
  (Parent: Highland Homes Holdings Inc)
12850 Hillcrest Rd, Dallas, TX 75230
Phone: (972) 387-7905
Sales: $103,623,000   *Employees:* 89
Company Type: Private   *Employees here:* 75
SIC: 1521
  New construction of single family homes
Don A Galloway, President

D-U-N-S 08-157-3172
R W GRANGER & SONS INC
  (Parent: Granger Management Corp)
415 Boston Tpke Ste 307, Shrewsbury, MA
Phone: (508) 842-8961
Sales: $85,000,000   *Employees:* 134
Company Type: Private   *Employees here:* 134
SIC: 1542
  General contractor of commercial institutional industrial &
    multi-family buildings
Donald R Krueger, President

D-U-N-S 01-025-4816
RADNOR HOMES, INC
  (Parent: Pulte Home Corp)
5544 Franklin Pike, Nashville, TN 37220
Phone: (615) 377-9260
Sales: $75,000,000   *Employees:* 74
Company Type: Public Family Member   *Employees here:* 70
SIC: 1521
  Single & multi-family construction & land development
Greg Phillips, Treasurer

D-U-N-S 09-174-0084
RAFN CO
1721 132nd Ave NE, Bellevue, WA 98005
Phone: (425) 702-6600
Sales: $80,000,000   *Employees:* 180
Company Type: Private   *Employees here:* 180
SIC: 1542
  General contractor commercial buildings & multi-family
    dwellings
Terrance K Donley, Chairman of the Board

D-U-N-S 09-897-5501
RAGNAR BENSON, INC.
  (Parent: The Austin Co)
250 S Northwest Hwy, Park Ridge, IL 60068
Phone: (847) 698-4900

Sales: $104,837,000   *Employees:* 150
Company Type: Private   *Employees here:* 70
SIC: 1541
  Contractor of industrial commercial institutional &
    government buildings
Donna R Arbogast, Owner

D-U-N-S 80-972-7084
RAILROAD TRACK CONSTRUCTION CO
  (Parent: Florida East Coast Railway Co)
1 Malaga St, St. Augustine, FL 32084
Phone: (904) 826-2202
Sales: $250,520,000   *Employees:* 20
Company Type: Public Family Member   *Employees here:* 20
SIC: 1629
  Railroad track construction
James A Donohoe III, President

D-U-N-S 02-496-7189
RAILWORKS CORP
1104 Kenilworth Dr, Baltimore, MD 21204
Phone: (410) 467-9505
Sales: $248,000,000   *Employees:* 1,900
Company Type: Public   *Employees here:* 20
SIC: 1731
  Holding company
Roy F Greenwald, President

D-U-N-S 06-598-3553
RAMEX CONSTRUCTION CO, INC
1209 Genoa Red Bluff Rd, Pasadena, TX 77504
Phone: (281) 487-9000
Sales: $67,513,000   *Employees:* 310
Company Type: Private   *Employees here:* 35
SIC: 1623
  Underground utility contractor bridges & commercial
    building construction & street & highway paving
Steve Kasper, Secretary

D-U-N-S 05-513-8853
RANDALL ABB CORP
  (Parent: Abb Lummus Global Inc)
10255 Richmond Ave, Houston, TX 77042
Phone: (713) 735-6800
Sales: $89,617,000   *Employees:* 370
Company Type: Private   *Employees here:* 110
SIC: 1629
  Installation & mfg of natural gas processing equipment
William R Dooley, Chairman of the Board

D-U-N-S 03-744-5905
R.A.S. BUILDERS, INC
180 E Hampden Ave Ste 201, Englewood, CO 80110
Phone: (303) 762-0505
Sales: $195,941,000   *Employees:* 150
Company Type: Private   *Employees here:* 45
SIC: 1542
  Commercial interior finishing contractor
Donald B Murphy, President

D-U-N-S 00-317-0628
REA CONSTRUCTION CO
  (Parent: J A Jones Inc)
6135 Pk Drv Suth Ste 400, Charlotte, NC 28210
Phone: (704) 553-6500
Sales: $170,223,000   *Employees:* 900
Company Type: Private   *Employees here:* 250
SIC: 1611
  Constructs concrete and asphalt highways and asphalt paving
R B Cavalline, President

D-U-N-S 18-895-6726
REALEN HOMES CONSTRUCTION CO
    (*Parent:* Realen Homes Inc)
725 Talamore Dr, Ambler, PA 19002
Phone: (215) 628-3300
Sales: $102,000,000   *Employees:* 125
Company Type: Private   *Employees here:* 100
SIC: 1531
    Operative builder of single-family houses
Thomas E Doster III, Chairman of the Board

D-U-N-S 03-446-6789
RED SIMPSON INC
4615 Parliament Dr, Alexandria, LA 71303
Phone: (318) 487-1074
Sales: $133,900,000   *Employees:* 1,780
Company Type: Private   *Employees here:* 500
SIC: 1623
    Power line contractor
Patrick L Johnson, President

D-U-N-S 05-849-8650
REF-CHEM CORP
1128 S Grandview Ave, Odessa, TX 79761
Phone: (915) 332-8531
Sales: $73,725,000   *Employees:* 1,015
Company Type: Private   *Employees here:* 400
SIC: 1629
    Industrial plant construction specializing in refineries
      petrochemical & chemical plants
Craig Rowe, Managing Member

D-U-N-S 08-315-0672
REGIS HOMES CORP
18802 Bardeen Ave, Irvine, CA 92612
Phone: (949) 756-5959
Sales: $156,700,000   *Employees:* 500
Company Type: Private   *Employees here:* 500
SIC: 1531
    Operative builder & real estate property manager
Joel Spizey, President

D-U-N-S 00-982-3915
RENTENBACH ENG CO
2400 Sutherland Ave, Knoxville, TN 37919
Phone: (423) 546-2440
Sales: $95,762,000   *Employees:* 200
Company Type: Private   *Employees here:* 34
SIC: 1541
    Nonresidential construction industrial building construction
Joel Spivey, President

D-U-N-S 85-899-5517
RESCO HOLDINGS INC
    (*Parent:* Wheelabrator Technologies Inc)
Liberty Ln, Hampton, NH
Phone: (603) 929-3000
Sales: $229,700,000   *Employees:* 2,000
Company Type: Public Family Member   *Employees here:* NA
SIC: 1629
    Holding company
Douglas E Barnhart, Chief Executive Officer

D-U-N-S 79-607-7360
RICHMOND AMERICAN HOMES, INC.
    (*Parent:* M D C Holdings Inc)
3010 E Camelback Rd, Phoenix, AZ 85016
Phone: (602) 956-4100
Sales: $155,056,000   *Employees:* 90
Company Type: Public Family Member   *Employees here:* 90
SIC: 1521
    General residential construction
Doyle Wilson, President

D-U-N-S 14-837-9076
RICHMOND AMERICAN HOMES OF CALIFORNIA
    (*Parent:* M D C Holdings Inc)
2280 Diamond Blvd Ste 500, Concord, CA 94520
Phone: (925) 687-1812
Sales: $182,445,000   *Employees:* 300
Company Type: Public Family Member   *Employees here:* 22
SIC: 1521
    General contractor of single family homes
Jenny Neff-Ross, Secretary

D-U-N-S 62-191-9513
RICHMOND AMERICAN HOMES OF COLORADO
    (*Parent:* M D C Holdings Inc)
4600 S Ulster St Ste 400, Denver, CO 80237
Phone: (303) 773-1100
Sales: $360,000,000   *Employees:* 300
Company Type: Public Family Member   *Employees here:* 150
SIC: 1531
    Operative builder
Nigel P Davis, President

D-U-N-S 02-241-8776
RICHMOND AMERICAN HOMES OF MARYLAND
    (*Parent:* M D C Holdings Inc)
3701 Pender Dr Ste 200, Fairfax, VA 22030
Phone: (703) 352-0800
Sales: $76,365,000   *Employees:* 93
Company Type: Public Family Member   *Employees here:* 92
SIC: 1521
    Contractor specializing in construction of single family homes
      & townhouses
Gerald F Dowling, President

D-U-N-S 14-820-1676
RICHMOND AMERICAN HOMES OF VIRGINIA
    (*Parent:* M D C Holdings Inc)
3701 Pender Dr Ste 200, Fairfax, VA 22030
Phone: (703) 352-0800
Sales: $111,129,000   *Employees:* 190
Company Type: Public Family Member   *Employees here:* 190
SIC: 1521
    Contractor of single family homes & townhouses
Samuel J Bue, President

D-U-N-S 05-087-2167
RITCHIE CORP
    (*Parent:* Ritchie Companies Inc)
2020 Amidon St, Wichita, KS 67203
Phone: (316) 838-9301
Sales: $113,740,000   *Employees:* 330
Company Type: Private   *Employees here:* 50
SIC: 1611
    Paving contractors manufactures concrete mixes operates
      ready mid concrete plant wholesales hand tool sand &
      gravel
Michael Ford, Branch Manager

D-U-N-S 11-747-9402
RIVER CITY CONSTRUCTION L.L.C.
1050 W Washington St, East Peoria, IL 61611
Phone: (309) 694-3120
Sales: $120,895,000   *Employees:* 250
Company Type: Private   *Employees here:* 235
SIC: 1542
    Commercial & industrial contractor
Peter C Nosler, Chief Executive Officer

D-U-N-S 79-869-6928
ROBINS AND MORTON GROUP
400 Shades Creek Pkwy, Birmingham, AL 35209
Phone: (205) 870-1000

Sales: $210,000,000   *Employees:* 250
Company Type: Private   *Employees here:* 50
SIC: 1542
    General contractor
Thomas Hyde, Chief Financial Officer

D-U-N-S 02-131-8571
ROBISON CONSTRUCTION INC
1216 140th Avenue Ct E, Sumner, WA 98390
Phone: (253) 863-5200
Sales: $75,246,000   *Employees:* 280
Company Type: Private   *Employees here:* 280
SIC: 1623
    Underground utilities highway & industrial construction
R F Burner, Branch Manager

D-U-N-S 05-815-1689
ROCHE CONSTRUCTORS INC
361 71st Ave, Greeley, CO 80634
Phone: (970) 356-3611
Sales: $75,672,000   *Employees:* 100
Company Type: Private   *Employees here:* 35
SIC: 1542
    General contractor specializing in commercial & industrial
    buildings
James T Driver, President

D-U-N-S 88-448-7042
ROCKY MOUNTAIN REMEDIATION SERVICES LLC
1819 Denver West Dr, Golden, CO 80401
Phone: (303) 215-1103
Sales: $99,974,000   *Employees:* 700
Company Type: Private   *Employees here:* 700
SIC: 1799
    Environmental services contractor
Earl W Pitchford, President

D-U-N-S 00-978-0180
ROEL CONSTRUCTION CO, INC
3366 Kurtz St, San Diego, CA 92110
Phone: (619) 297-4156
Sales: $128,336,000   *Employees:* 260
Company Type: Private   *Employees here:* 260
SIC: 1542
    General contractor new commercial buildings
Howard S Mura, N/A

D-U-N-S 05-013-4089
ROGERS-O'BRIEN CONSTRUCTION CO
11145 Morrison Ln, Dallas, TX 75229
Phone: (972) 243-1335
Sales: $107,862,000   *Employees:* 188
Company Type: Private   *Employees here:* 120
SIC: 1541
    New construction & renovation industrial building contractor
J S Jeffress, Branch Manager

D-U-N-S 10-712-5957
ROONEY BROTHERS CO
111 W 5th St Ste 1000, Tulsa, OK 74103
Phone: (918) 583-6900
Sales: $384,800,000   *Employees:* 1,732
Company Type: Private   *Employees here:* 1
SIC: 1542
    Institutional commercial & industrial building contractor
    whol building materials mfg electronic assemblies
Gregory Cuneo, President

D-U-N-S 80-482-8556
ROSEMONT EXPOSITION SERVICES INC
9301 Bryn Mawr Ave, Des Plaines, IL 60018
Phone: (847) 696-2208

Sales: $114,400,000   *Employees:* 900
Company Type: Private   *Employees here:* 900
SIC: 1541
    Exhibit construction for trade shows
Ben H Hall Jr, President

D-U-N-S 00-796-8621
ROSENDIN ELECTRIC INC
985 Timothy Dr, San Jose, CA 95133
Phone: (408) 286-2800
Sales: $166,700,000   *Employees:* 1,200
Company Type: Private   *Employees here:* 1,000
SIC: 1731
    Electrical contractor
William M Ducci, Chairman of the Board

D-U-N-S 00-987-2888
ROTH BROS INC
(Parent: Firstenergy Corp)
3847 Crum Rd, Youngstown, OH 44515
Phone: (330) 793-5571
Sales: $75,000,000   *Employees:* 500
Company Type: Public Family Member   *Employees here:* 300
SIC: 1711
    Heating air conditioning roofing & sheet metal contractor
Peter Edwards, Chairman of the Board

D-U-N-S 06-817-0844
ROTTLUND CO INC
2681 Long Lake Rd 301, St. Paul, MN 55113
Phone: (651) 638-0500
Sales: $160,830,000   *Employees:* 248
Company Type: Public   *Employees here:* 56
SIC: 1531
    Operative builder of townhomes & single family homes
Francis Dugan, Chief Executive Officer

D-U-N-S 02-291-2059
ROXCO LTD
(Parent: Loftin Constructors Inc)
140 Old Highway 80, Brandon, MS 39042
Phone: (601) 825-4193
Sales: $100,000,000   *Employees:* 450
Company Type: Private   *Employees here:* 400
SIC: 1542
    Commercial multi-residental & industrial contractors
Francis Dugan, Chief Executive Officer

D-U-N-S 00-785-0530
ROY ANDERSON CORP
11400 Reichold Rd, Gulfport, MS 39503
Phone: (228) 896-4000
Sales: $201,348,000   *Employees:* 300
Company Type: Private   *Employees here:* 265
SIC: 1542
    Nonresidential & industrial building construction
L C Marcon, President

D-U-N-S 18-856-7259
ROYAL IMPERIAL GROUP INC
900 W Jackson Blvd Ste 7e, Chicago, IL 60607
Phone: (312) 738-1717
Sales: $176,500,000   *Employees:* 800
Company Type: Private   *Employees here:* 20
SIC: 1542
    Development of commercial and multi-residential buildings
    and management service for retirement centers
Harlton G Dunbar, Chairman of the Board

D-U-N-S 11-824-8285
ROYCE HOMES, INC
14614 Falling Creek Dr, Houston, TX 77068
Phone: (281) 440-5091

.*Sales:* $100,000,000   *Employees:* 412
Company Type: Private   *Employees here:* 180
SIC: 1521
  General contractor of single-family homes
Dennis E King, President

D-U-N-S 78-949-6015
RR WESTMINSTER HOLDING DE CORP
  (Parent: Clarendon Nat Insur Md Corp)
1177 Avenue of the Americas, New York, NY 10036
Phone: (212) 790-9700
Sales: $109,384,000   *Employees:* 300
Company Type: Private   *Employees here:* 1
SIC: 1542
  General contractor commercial & industrial construction &
    operator of hotels
Terrence P Dunn, President

D-U-N-S 00-284-5360
RUDOLPH & SLETTEN INC
989 E Hillsdale Blvd, Foster City, CA 94404
Phone: (650) 572-1919
Sales: $487,000,000   *Employees:* 900
Company Type: Private   *Employees here:* 100
SIC: 1541
  Industrial & commercial & institutional building contractor
James S French, President

D-U-N-S 15-133-8688
RUDOLPH/LIBBE COMPANIES INC
6494 Latcha Rd, Walbridge, OH 43465
Phone: (419) 241-5000
Sales: $266,321,000   *Employees:* 1,000
Company Type: Private   *Employees here:* 200
SIC: 1541
  Industrial & commercial contractor
Keith McLoughlin, Chairman of the Board

D-U-N-S 00-419-3405
RUHLIN CO
6931 Ridge Rd, Sharon Center, OH 44274
Phone: (330) 239-2800
Sales: $70,000,000   *Employees:* 150
Company Type: Private   *Employees here:* 150
SIC: 1611
  Highway & bridge construction & commercial construction
Francis J Van Antwerp Jr, President

D-U-N-S 00-431-0892
RUSCILLI CONSTRUCTION CO INC
2041 Arlingate Ln, Columbus, OH 43228
Phone: (614) 876-9484
Sales: $180,000,000   *Employees:* 110
Company Type: Private   *Employees here:* 90
SIC: 1541
  Construction management & general contractor
David Rowe, Chief Executive Officer

D-U-N-S 15-530-3365
RUST CONSTRUCTORS INC
  (Parent: Raytheon Engineers Constrs International)
1200 Corp Dr Ste 450, Birmingham, AL 35242
Phone: (205) 995-6600
Sales: $821,600,000   *Employees:* 6,500
Company Type: Public Family Member   *Employees here:* 50
SIC: 1541
  General contractor
D T Dankert, President

D-U-N-S 02-281-9288
RYAN COMPANIES U.S., INC
  (Parent: Ryan Properties Inc)
900 2nd Ave S Ste 700, Minneapolis, MN 55402

Phone: (612) 336-1200
Sales: $189,273,000   *Employees:* 450
Company Type: Private   *Employees here:* 1
SIC: 1542
  General contractor building new commercial office and
    industrial buildings
Bill Dutra, Chief Executive Officer

D-U-N-S 13-151-1644
RYAN INC EASTERN
786 S Military Trl, Deerfield Beach, FL 33442
Phone: (954) 427-5599
Sales: $75,000,000   *Employees:* 300
Company Type: Private   *Employees here:* 30
SIC: 1794
  Excavating & grading contractor golf course construction and
    underground utilities contractor
Joe Pigford, President

D-U-N-S 06-816-3195
RYAN PROPERTIES, INC.
900 2nd Ave S Ste 700, Minneapolis, MN 55402
Phone: (612) 336-1200
Sales: $198,821,000   *Employees:* 450
Company Type: Private   *Employees here:* 325
SIC: 1542
  General contractor of commercial retail office medical &
    industrial buildings
Thomas R Pledger, Chairman of the Board

D-U-N-S 02-258-5913
RYLAND GROUP INC
11000 Broken Land Pkwy, Columbia, MD 21044
Phone: (410) 715-7000
Sales: $1,649,806,000   *Employees:* 2,270
Company Type: Public   *Employees here:* 350
SIC: 1531
  Operative builders of single family homes & mortgage-
    banking
Jeffrey M Levy, President

D-U-N-S 02-150-1325
S & B ENGINEERS AND CONSTRUCTORS
7809 Park Place Blvd, Houston, TX 77087
Phone: (713) 645-4141
Sales: $382,479,000   *Employees:* 2,000
Company Type: Private   *Employees here:* 1,100
SIC: 1629
  Heavy construction contractor of industrial plants and design
    & engineering service
James Kleinkauf, President

D-U-N-S 92-708-7163
S B C C, INC
511 Division St, Campbell, CA 95008
Phone: (408) 379-5500
Sales: $135,000,000   *Employees:* 130
Company Type: Private   *Employees here:* 130
SIC: 1542
  Nonresidential construction
Jeffrey M Levy, President

D-U-N-S 00-278-3918
S E JOHNSON COMPANIES INC
1345 Ford St, Maumee, OH 43537
Phone: (419) 893-8731
Sales: $270,975,000   *Employees:* 1,516
Company Type: Private   *Employees here:* 654
SIC: 1611
  Road & bridge contractor mfg asphalt & limestone quarry
Joe Seal, Branch Manager

D-U-N-S 03-902-4971
S H FLEMING & CO INC
8707 W Chester Pike, Upper Darby, PA 19082
Phone: (610) 449-6612
Sales: $120,000,000   *Employees:* 20
Company Type: Private   *Employees here:* 4
SIC: 1721
    Painting contractor
Tim Homer, Manager

D-U-N-S 02-915-4101
S J AMOROSO CONSTRUCTION CO
348 Hatch Dr, Foster City, CA 94404
Phone: (650) 349-6691
Sales: $226,622,000   *Employees:* 300
Company Type: Private   *Employees here:* 35
SIC: 1542
    General contractor commercial buildings
Ken Hart, Senior Vice-President

D-U-N-S 15-060-5418
S M & P UTILITY RESOURCES INC
    (Parent: I W C Resources Corp)
11455 N Meridian St, Carmel, IN 46032
Phone: (317) 581-7800
Sales: $82,900,000   *Employees:* 1,100
Company Type: Public Family Member   *Employees here:* 25
SIC: 1623
    Cable locator contractor
Jeff Levy, President

D-U-N-S 02-481-9682
S T WOOTEN CORP
3801 Black Creek Rd SE, Wilson, NC 27893
Phone: (252) 291-5165
Sales: $90,000,000   *Employees:* 500
Company Type: Private   *Employees here:* 50
SIC: 1611
    Highway & street construction
Hal Turner, President

D-U-N-S 93-788-8956
SAFE SITES OF COLORADO, LLC
    (Parent: CBS Corp)
Hwy 93 & Cactus Ave, Golden, CO 80403
Phone: (303) 966-3143
Sales: $156,420,000   *Employees:* 637
Company Type: Public Family Member   *Employees here:* 637
SIC: 1799
    Stabilize and repackage special nuclear materials
Ramon Bonin, Chairman of the Board

D-U-N-S 09-776-1795
SALMON & ALDER ASSOCIATES
623 N 1250 W, Centerville, UT 84014
Phone: (801) 295-0184
Sales: $237,709,000   *Employees:* 70
Company Type: Private   *Employees here:* 70
SIC: 1711
    Heating air conditioning & electrical contractor
John M Hess, President

D-U-N-S 11-329-9648
SAN JOSE CONSTRUCTION CO, INC
1210 Coleman Ave, Santa Clara, CA 95050
Phone: (408) 986-8711
Sales: $84,067,000   *Employees:* 130
Company Type: Private   *Employees here:* 115
SIC: 1542
    General contractor-commercial buildings
William W Fleeman, President

D-U-N-S 02-871-7015
SAN LUIS TANK PIPING CONSTRUCTION CO
    (Parent: Matrix Service Co)
825 26th St, Paso Robles, CA 93446
Phone: (805) 238-0888
Sales: $214,877,000   *Employees:* 90
Company Type: Public Family Member   *Employees here:* 90
SIC: 1791
    Structural steel erection
Randy J Rehmann, President

D-U-N-S 00-893-8961
SARGENT ELECTRIC CO
2801 Liberty Ave, Pittsburgh, PA 15222
Phone: (412) 391-0588
Sales: $69,887,000   *Employees:* 600
Company Type: Private   *Employees here:* 400
SIC: 1731
    Contractor
W R Dengler, President

D-U-N-S 07-722-8849
SASCO ELECTRIC
12900 Alondra Blvd, Artesia, CA 90703
Phone: (562) 926-0900
Sales: $297,079,000   *Employees:* 4,000
Company Type: Private   *Employees here:* 1,100
SIC: 1731
    Electrical contractor
Noble Larsen, President

D-U-N-S 00-379-1852
SCHIAVONE CONSTRUCTION CO
1600 Paterson Plank Rd, Secaucus, NJ
Phone: (201) 867-5070
Sales: $88,321,000   *Employees:* 300
Company Type: Private   *Employees here:* 300
SIC: 1629
    Subway elevated highway bridge and tunnel contractor
Bob Webb, Branch Manager

D-U-N-S 08-372-2850
SCHUFF STEEL CO
420 S 19th Ave, Phoenix, AZ 85009
Phone: (602) 252-7787
Sales: $138,218,000   *Employees:* 781
Company Type: Public   *Employees here:* 382
SIC: 1791
    Structural steel erection contractor & steel fabrication
Robert Frix, Vice-President

D-U-N-S 02-897-3472
SCL CONSTRUCTION
7401t Spring V, Springfield, VA 22150
Phone: (703) 913-7885
Sales: $150,000,000   *Employees:* 21
Company Type: Private   *Employees here:* 21
SIC: 1521
    General contractor
Jim Bricker, President

D-U-N-S 10-291-3811
SCOTT COMPANIES INC
1717 Doolittle Dr, San Leandro, CA 94577
Phone: (510) 895-2333
Sales: $94,300,000   *Employees:* 1,000
Company Type: Private   *Employees here:* 400
SIC: 1711
    Mechanical contractor
Denise Schneider, President

D-U-N-S 17-679-1002
SECURITY TECHNOLOGIES GROUP
(Parent: Security Tech Holding Corp)
150 S Pine Island Rd, Fort Lauderdale, FL 33324
Phone: (954) 424-5999
Sales: $75,000,000
Company Type: Private   *Employees:* 700
   Employees here: 4
SIC: 1731
   Installation & monitoring of access control systems burglar
     alarms fire alarms & closed circuit tv & guard protective
     services
Ronald W Hathaway, Chairman of the Board

D-U-N-S 00-282-4159
SELLEN CONSTRUCTION CO INC
228 9th Ave N, Seattle, WA 98109
Phone: (206) 682-7770
Sales: $184,846,000   *Employees:* 500
Company Type: Private   *Employees here:* 500
SIC: 1542
   General contractor of commercial & institutional buildings
Robert N Reeves Jr, President

D-U-N-S 96-020-5870
SERVICE EXPERTS INC
6 Cadillac Dr Ste 400, Brentwood, TN 37027
Phone: (615) 371-9990
Sales: $238,692,000   *Employees:* 3,500
Company Type: Public   *Employees here:* 50
SIC: 1711
   Provides residential HVAC services and replacement
     equipment
Nafa Khalaf, President

D-U-N-S 05-147-6992
SHAPELL INDUSTRIES INC
8383 Wilshire Blvd, Beverly Hills, CA 90211
Phone: (323) 655-7330
Sales: $408,000,000   *Employees:* 300
Company Type: Private   *Employees here:* 50
SIC: 1531
   Operative builders mortgage financing and escrow service
William K Deshler, Chairman of the Board

D-U-N-S 04-145-6567
SHASTA INDUSTRIES INC
2950 N 7th St, Phoenix, AZ 85014
Phone: (602) 258-8981
Sales: $69,000,000   *Employees:* 500
Company Type: Private   *Employees here:* 250
SIC: 1799
   Swming pool & gunite contractor whol swming pool chmcls
     swming pool mntnnce & mfg pvc valves & pool cleaning sys
Dalton W Ceos, N/A

D-U-N-S 04-705-6460
SHAWMUT WOODWORKING & SUPPLY
560 Harrison Ave, Boston, MA
Phone: (617) 338-6200
Sales: $126,698,000   *Employees:* 179
Company Type: Private   *Employees here:* 179
SIC: 1542
   General contractor of commercial buildings restaurants
     institutions & hospital projects
Ronald Tutor, President

D-U-N-S 94-506-3865
SHEA HOMES LP
655 Brea Canyon Rd, Walnut, CA 91789
Phone: (909) 594-9500

Sales: $1,200,000,000   *Employees:* 588
Company Type: Private   *Employees here:* 575
SIC: 1521
   General contractors-single family houses
Terry E Mbr, President

D-U-N-S 94-435-6336
SHEA-TRAYLOR-HEALY JOINT VENTURE
164 Meadow St, Framingham, MA
Phone: (508) 788-0300
Sales: $71,000,000   *Employees:* 200
Company Type: Private   *Employees here:* 200
SIC: 1531
   Operative builders
Allen D Larson, President

D-U-N-S 00-781-8933
SHEEHAN PIPE LINE CONSTRUCTION CO
1924 S Utica Ave Ste 1100, Tulsa, OK 74104
Phone: (918) 747-3471
Sales: $71,128,000   *Employees:* 67
Company Type: Private   *Employees here:* 50
SIC: 1623
   Gas & pipeline contractor
William Oftedal, President

D-U-N-S 08-990-2563
SHELCO INC
6805 Monroe Rd, Charlotte, NC 28212
Phone: (704) 367-5600
Sales: $280,000,000   *Employees:* 240
Company Type: Private   *Employees here:* 135
SIC: 1541
   Industrial & commercial building construction
Robert J Bauer, Chairman of the Board

D-U-N-S 00-430-0158
SHELLY & SANDS INC
3570 S River Rd, Zanesville, OH 43701
Phone: (740) 453-0721
Sales: $100,000,000   *Employees:* 600
Company Type: Private   *Employees here:* 12
SIC: 1611
   Road & asphalt paving contractor
E K Halvorson, President

D-U-N-S 05-962-7224
SHIEL-SEXTON CO INC
8035 Castleton Rd, Indianapolis, IN 46250
Phone: (317) 842-4941
Sales: $116,449,000   *Employees:* 150
Company Type: Private   *Employees here:* 150
SIC: 1542
   Commercial and industrial building contractor
Butch Dahlke, Branch Manager

D-U-N-S 05-540-7076
SHIMIZU AMERICA CORP
800 Wilshire Blvd Ste 800, Los Angeles, CA 90017
Phone: (213) 362-7510
Sales: $142,000,000   *Employees:* 138
Company Type: Private   *Employees here:* 38
SIC: 1542
   General contractor
James F Sattler, Chief Executive Officer

D-U-N-S 12-254-7532
SHOOK NATIONAL CORP
4977 Northcutt Pl, Dayton, OH 45414
Phone: (937) 276-6666

Sales: $112,000,000   *Employees:* 266
Company Type: Private   *Employees here:* 13
SIC: 1629
   Water & sewage treatment plant contractor & general
     contractor commercial buildings
Gene F Guidi, Chairman of the Board

D-U-N-S 87-927-6376
SILVERADO CONSTRUCTORS
22 Executive Cir 200, Irvine, CA 92614
Phone: (949) 752-0990
Sales: $260,000,000   *Employees:* 760
Company Type: Private   *Employees here:* 760
SIC: 1611
   Highway/street construction
Eugene R Berwald, President

D-U-N-S 11-503-8192
SITHE ENERGIES USA INC
   (Parent: Sithe Energies Inc)
450 Lexington Ave Fl 37, New York, NY 10017
Phone: (212) 450-9000
Sales: $335,844,000   *Employees:* 240
Company Type: Private   *Employees here:* 4
SIC: 1629
   Operator owner & developer of energy plants
Robin J Snell, President

D-U-N-S 09-239-9013
SKANSKA (U.S.A.), INC.
60 Arch St, Greenwich, CT
Phone: (203) 629-8840
Sales: $2,060,690,000   *Employees:* 3,700
Company Type: Private   *Employees here:* 7
SIC: 1542
   Holding company
Eric Sambol, President

D-U-N-S 62-111-6326
SLATTERY ASSOCIATES INC (DEL)
   (Parent: Skanska (USA) Inc)
1616 Whitestone Expy, Whitestone, NY 11357
Phone: (718) 767-2600
Sales: $237,865,000   *Employees:* 350
Company Type: Private   *Employees here:* 4
SIC: 1623
   Sewer highway bridge tunnel subway pile driving &
     mechanical contracting
Erdmen T Mackenzie, President

D-U-N-S 11-529-5636
SLAYDEN CONSTRUCTION INC
500 Willamette Ave, Stayton, OR 97383
Phone: (503) 769-1969
Sales: $90,000,000   *Employees:* 163
Company Type: Private   *Employees here:* 163
SIC: 1542
   General contractor commercial buildings highway & street
     work sewer & water main work waste treatment plant
     construction
E K Simonds, Chairman of the Board

D-U-N-S 36-293-9332
SLETTEN CONSTRUCTION OF NEVADA
   (Parent: Sletten Inc)
5825 Polaris Ave, Las Vegas, NV 89118
Phone: (702) 739-8770
Sales: $70,828,000   *Employees:* 200
Company Type: Private   *Employees here:* 200
SIC: 1542
   General contractor commercial institutional & industrial
     buildings
Phillip Schiavone, President

D-U-N-S 12-206-5287
SLETTEN INC
1000 25th St N Ste 4, Great Falls, MT 59401
Phone: (406) 761-7920
Sales: $134,713,000   *Employees:* 200
Company Type: Private   *Employees here:* 3
SIC: 1542
   New construction of commercial institutional & industrial
     buildings
Robert J Corrigan, Treasurer

D-U-N-S 00-791-9871
SLOAN CONSTRUCTION CO
   (Parent: Colas Inc)
1600 W Washington St, Greenville, SC 29601
Phone: (864) 271-9090
Sales: $130,000,000   *Employees:* 400
Company Type: Private   *Employees here:* 25
SIC: 1611
   Highway paving resurfacing & maintenance & airport runway
     construction
Howard L Rowland, President

D-U-N-S 01-221-6888
SOBRATO CONSTRUCTION INC
10600 N De Anza Blvd, Cupertino, CA 95014
Phone: (408) 446-0799
Sales: $450,000,000   *Employees:* 15
Company Type: Private   *Employees here:* 15
SIC: 1542
   Nonresidential construction
J R Mann Jr, President

D-U-N-S 06-211-5472
SOFEC INC
   (Parent: Fmc Corp)
6677 Gessner Dr, Houston, TX 77040
Phone: (713) 510-6600
Sales: $80,000,000   *Employees:* 120
Company Type: Public Family Member   *Employees here:* 120
SIC: 1629
   Construction of marine terminals & other specialized
     equipment
James H Eacott III, President

D-U-N-S 02-051-8445
SOLTEK OF SAN DIEGO
2424 Congress St Ste A, San Diego, CA 92110
Phone: (619) 296-6247
Sales: $111,949,000   *Employees:* 150
Company Type: Private   *Employees here:* 150
SIC: 1542
   General contractor
Bryan E Kornblau, Chairman of the Board

D-U-N-S 78-733-5827
SORDONI/SKANSKA CONSTRUCTION CO
   (Parent: Skanska (USA) Inc)
400 Interpace Pkwy Bldg C, Parsippany, NJ
Phone: (973) 334-5300
Sales: $1,100,000,000   *Employees:* 850
Company Type: Private   *Employees here:* 50
SIC: 1541
   Contractor of industrial buildings warehouses & corporate
     buildings
Alfred D Spotts, President

D-U-N-S 03-494-4686
SOUTHERN NEVADA PAVING INC
3555 Polaris Ave, Las Vegas, NV 89103
Phone: (702) 876-5226

Sales: $89,575,000
Company Type: Private
SIC: 1611
Employees: 400
Employees here: 23
Grading and paving contractor
Fred J Schuber Jr, President

D-U-N-S 04-116-2926
SOUTHLAND INDUSTRIES
1661 E 32nd St, Long Beach, CA 90807
Phone: (562) 424-8638
Sales: $176,884,000
Company Type: Private
SIC: 1711
Employees: 521
Employees here: 200
Air conditioning contractor
Jack Hatcher, Chairman of the Board

D-U-N-S 11-269-7560
SOUTHWEST RECREATIONAL INDS
(Parent: American Sports Products Group)
701 Leander Dr, Leander, TX 78641
Phone: (512) 259-0080
Sales: $85,927,000
Company Type: Private
SIC: 1629
Employees: 800
Employees here: 52
Constructor of athletic fields specializing in running tracks
and football fields
Robert M Earl, President

D-U-N-S 60-915-9785
SOVEREIGN HOMES CORP
8440 Walnut Hill Ln Lb2, Dallas, TX 75231
Phone: (214) 361-9292
Sales: $167,500,000
Company Type: Private
SIC: 1521
Employees: 175
Employees here: 162
Single-family home builder
Laird E Smith, President

D-U-N-S 82-540-9501
SPAW GLASS HOLDING CORP
13603 Westland East Blvd, Houston, TX 77041
Phone: (281) 970-5300
Sales: $152,699,000
Company Type: Private
SIC: 1542
Employees: 170
Employees here: 1
Holding company
Robert East, Chief Executive Officer

D-U-N-S 11-330-8837
SPIE GROUP INC
1415 S Roselle Rd, Palatine, IL 60067
Phone: (847) 925-3330
Sales: $77,200,000
Company Type: Private
SIC: 1731
Employees: 1,040
Employees here: 1,040
Electrical contractor
Ramesh K Motwane, President

D-U-N-S 01-808-4590
STAHL CONSTRUCTION CO
5900 Rowland Rd, Hopkins, MN 55343
Phone: (612) 931-9300
Sales: $100,000,000
Company Type: Private
SIC: 1542
Employees: 55
Employees here: 52
Contractor specializing in public & commercial buildings and
construction management services
Harry L Sloan, President

D-U-N-S 05-129-3207
STAKER PAVING AND CONSTRUCTION CO
(Parent: Oldcastle Inc)
1000 W Center St, North Salt Lake, UT 84054

Phone: (801) 298-7500
Sales: $79,068,000
Company Type: Private
SIC: 1611
Employees: 230
Employees here: 135
Contractor in highway or street paving resurfacing and
airport runways blacktopping and mfg asphalt paving
mixtures
Joseph Stern, President

D-U-N-S 00-838-8373
STANDARD PACIFIC CORP
1565 Macarthur Blvd, Costa Mesa, CA 92626
Phone: (714) 668-4300
Sales: $584,571,000
Company Type: Public
SIC: 1531
Employees: 430
Employees here: 100
Operative builder
Joe Stewart, President

D-U-N-S 04-810-5746
STARSTONE CONSTRUCTION CO
900 State Rte 51, Clairton, PA 15025
Phone: (412) 384-1270
Sales: $87,200,000
Company Type: Private
SIC: 1542
Employees: 400
Employees here: 400
Commercial and industrial building contractior
Paul S Ebensteiner, President

D-U-N-S 02-467-5258
STEBBINS ENTERPRISES INC
1359 Hooksett Rd, Hooksett, NH
Phone: (603) 623-8811
Sales: $80,000,000
Company Type: Private
SIC: 1542
Employees: 200
Employees here: 115
Holding company through its subsidiaries operates as a
contractor specializing in new construction commercial
buildings
Martin K Eby Jr, Chairman of the Board

D-U-N-S 14-455-1249
STELLAR GROUP INC
2900 Hartley Rd, Jacksonville, FL 32257
Phone: (904) 260-2900
Sales: $202,595,000
Company Type: Private
SIC: 1541
Employees: 350
Employees here: 120
General contractor of refrigerated warehouses & other
industrial bldgs
Donald W Schmid, President

D-U-N-S 05-039-2307
STEVENS PAINTON CORP
7850 Freeway Cir Ste 100, Cleveland, OH 44130
Phone: (440) 234-7888
Sales: $91,396,000
Company Type: Private
SIC: 1541
Employees: 500
Employees here: 10
Heavy industrial building construction contractor
Paul Roebuck, President

D-U-N-S 87-746-5666
STEWART-LEDLOW INC
154 Commissioner Dr, Meridianville, AL 35759
Phone: (256) 828-1779
Sales: $200,000,000
Company Type: Private
SIC: 1742
Employees: 35
Employees here: 35
Drywall contractor
Donald A Goldstein, Chairman of the Board

D-U-N-S 05-376-5699
STILES CORP
6400 N Andrews Ave, Fort Lauderdale, FL 33309
Phone: (954) 776-9300
Sales: $150,458,000   *Employees:* 250
Company Type: Private   *Employees here:* 75
SIC: 1541
   General contractor industrial & commercial buildings new
   construction
Amy Eckman, President

D-U-N-S 05-668-8781
STRUCTURE-TONE, INC
15 E 26th St Fl 8, New York, NY 10010
Phone: (212) 481-6100
Sales: $154,200,000   *Employees:* 700
Company Type: Private   *Employees here:* 535
SIC: 1542
   General contractor & construction management
Edwin S Bell Jr, President

D-U-N-S 00-477-6787
STURGEON ELECTRIC CO
   (Parent: Harlan Electric Co)
12150 E 112th Ave, Henderson, CO 80640
Phone: (303) 286-8000
Sales: $74,200,000   *Employees:* 1,000
Company Type: Public Family Member   *Employees here:* 125
SIC: 1731
   General electrical contractor & electric power line
   construction
Kenna Prophet, President

D-U-N-S 10-790-4625
SUFFOLK CONSTRUCTION CO
65 Allerton St, Boston, MA
Phone: (617) 445-3500
Sales: $378,009,000   *Employees:* 400
Company Type: Private   *Employees here:* 125
SIC: 1542
   General contractor of commercial & institutional buildings
J D Harris, President

D-U-N-S 01-713-3732
SUMMIT COMPANIES OF JACKSONVILLE
6877 Phillips Industrial, Jacksonville, FL 32256
Phone: (904) 268-5500
Sales: $167,754,000   *Employees:* 100
Company Type: Private   *Employees here:* 4
SIC: 1542
   Holding company
William Alexander, President

D-U-N-S 60-331-9088
SUMMIT CONTRACTORS INC
   (Parent: Summit Cmpnies of Jacksonville)
6877 Phillips Industrial, Jacksonville, FL 32256
Phone: (904) 268-5500
Sales: $167,753,000   *Employees:* 100
Company Type: Private   *Employees here:* 45
SIC: 1542
   Commercial and multi family residential construction
Penn Cassels Jr, President

D-U-N-S 10-177-6490
SUNBELT RENTALS INC
   (Parent: Ashtead Holdings Inc)
611 Templeton Ave Ste 107, Charlotte, NC 28203
Phone: (704) 348-2676

Sales: $72,600,000   *Employees:* 670
Company Type: Private   *Employees here:* 30
SIC: 7353
   Rents construction equipment
Dennis Nelson, President

D-U-N-S 79-887-1364
SUNCO BUILDING CORP
4500 PGA Blvd Ste 400, Palm Beach Gardens, FL 33418
Phone: (561) 627-2112
Sales: $82,500,000   *Employees:* 600
Company Type: Private   *Employees here:* 35
SIC: 1521
   General contractor of new single-family houses
David R Kraemer, President

D-U-N-S 04-555-2585
SUNDANCE HOMES, INC.
201 N Wells St Ste 1800, Chicago, IL 60606
Phone: (312) 338-3300
Sales: $131,556,000   *Employees:* 140
Company Type: Public   *Employees here:* 40
SIC: 1531
   Operative builders
Sheldon Rose, President

D-U-N-S 78-729-4933
SUPERFOS CONSTRUCTION (U.S.)
2999 Ross Clark Cir, Dothan, AL 36301
Phone: (334) 794-2198
Sales: $100,000,000   *Employees:* 2,500
Company Type: Private   *Employees here:* 1
SIC: 1611
   Holding company
Steven M Edwards, President

D-U-N-S 00-484-4981
SUPERIOR CONSTRUCTION CO INC
2045 E Dunes Hwy, Gary, IN 46402
Phone: (219) 886-3728
Sales: $78,673,000   *Employees:* 400
Company Type: Private   *Employees here:* 300
SIC: 1622
   Bridge highway and industrial building construction
Gary A Edwards, President

D-U-N-S 00-946-0791
SWINERTON & WALBERG CO
   (Parent: Swinerton Inc)
580 California St, San Francisco, CA 94104
Phone: (415) 421-2980
Sales: $558,772,000   *Employees:* 729
Company Type: Private   *Employees here:* 250
SIC: 1542
   General contractor
Edward A Lieske, President

D-U-N-S 84-975-4288
SWINERTON INC
580 California St, San Francisco, CA 94104
Phone: (415) 421-2980
Sales: $500,589,000   *Employees:* 1,100
Company Type: Private   *Employees here:* 250
SIC: 1542
   General contractor
Larry Bashore, President

D-U-N-S 92-831-3055
SYCAMORE CONSTRUCTION LTD
8041 Hosbrook Rd Ste 230, Cincinnati, OH 45236
Phone: (513) 489-2460

Sales: $200,000,000
Company Type: Private
SIC: 1522
  General contractor of apartment buildings
Robert Egizii, Chief Executive Officer

Employees: 80
Employees here: 15

D-U-N-S 13-161-9637
SYNERGISM INC
722 E Evelyn Ave, Sunnyvale, CA 94086
Phone: (408) 739-5000
Sales: $157,484,000
Company Type: Private
SIC: 1731
  Electrical contractor
Chris Condy, President

Employees: 800
Employees here: 3

D-U-N-S 15-178-4485
T I C HOLDINGS INC
2211 Elk River Rd, Steamboat Springs, CO 80487
Phone: (970) 879-2561
Sales: $420,506,000
Company Type: Private
SIC: 1541
  Industrial construction
Gerald L Egan, Chairman of the Board

Employees: 3,000
Employees here: 120

D-U-N-S 18-519-1905
T J LAMBRECHT CONSTRUCTION
Joliet, IL 60432
Phone: (815) 726-7722
Sales: $70,797,000
Company Type: Private
SIC: 1794
  Earth excavation road building underground sewer & water
    contractor
Gerald L Egan, Chairman of the Board

Employees: 500
Employees here: 500

D-U-N-S 00-694-8202
T L JAMES & CO INC
106 W Mississippi Ave, Ruston, LA 71270
Phone: (318) 255-7912
Sales: $252,095,000
Company Type: Private
SIC: 1611
  Road bridge dredging & heavy construction & forestry
Raymond C Beil, President

Employees: 1,377
Employees here: 150

D-U-N-S 13-134-9888
TAISEI AMERICA CORP
301 E Ocean Blvd, Long Beach, CA 90802
Phone: (562) 432-5020
Sales: $103,000,000
Company Type: Private
SIC: 1541
  Contractor of industrial and commercial buildings land
    subdivider and developer
Bill Eichelberger, President

Employees: 82
Employees here: 35

D-U-N-S 02-622-0772
TARGET GENERAL INC
3036 E Greenway Rd, Phoenix, AZ 85032
Phone: (602) 494-0800
Sales: $145,000,000
Company Type: Private
SIC: 1542
  General contractor commercial institutional & industrial
    buildings
George F Eichleay, President

Employees: 80
Employees here: 80

D-U-N-S 07-487-6079
TAYLOR BALL, INC.
5000 Westown Pkwy Ste 250, West Des Moines, IA 50266
Phone: (515) 244-4500

Sales: $235,367,000
Company Type: Private
SIC: 1542
  Commercial contractor
Thomas D Eilerson, President

Employees: 400
Employees here: 8

D-U-N-S 00-736-8780
TDINDUSTRIES, INC.
13850 Diplomat Dr, Dallas, TX 75234
Phone: (972) 888-9500
Sales: $125,000,000
Company Type: Private
SIC: 1711
  Mechanical contractor repair air conditioning equipment &
    new home contractor

Employees: 918
Employees here: 650

D-U-N-S 00-691-1135
TEICHERT INC
3500 American River Dr, Sacramento, CA 95864
Phone: (916) 484-3011
Sales: $347,824,000
Company Type: Private
SIC: 1611
  Heavy construction whol grading & paving materials & mfg
    redi-mix
Larry A McKinney, President

Employees: 1,200
Employees here: 100

D-U-N-S 08-647-9037
TELLEPSEN CORP
777 Benmar Dr Ste 400, Houston, TX 77060
Phone: (281) 447-8100
Sales: $115,000,000
Company Type: Private
SIC: 1542
  General contractor of commercial & light industrial projects
John S Elder, President

Employees: 300
Employees here: 300

D-U-N-S 06-459-8725
TEMPCO DISASTER SERVICES, INC
1505 Gardena Ave, Glendale, CA 91204
Phone: (818) 507-6900
Sales: $71,500,000
Company Type: Private
SIC: 1542
  Contractor for insurance repairs
James E Pfleeger, President

Employees: 330
Employees here: 41

D-U-N-S 06-859-6782
TENNIS CORP OF AMERICA
3611 W Kinzie St, Chicago, IL 60624
Phone: (773) 463-1234
Sales: $200,000,000
Company Type: Private
SIC: 1799
  Builds owns operates & manages tennis & fitness centers real
    estate investment franchising & ret tennis equip
Jaime Jurado, President

Employees: 1,800
Employees here: 130

D-U-N-S 05-563-6856
THERMA CORP
1601 Las Plumas Ave, San Jose, CA 95133
Phone: (408) 433-5577
Sales: $200,000,000
Company Type: Private
SIC: 1711
  Plumbing heating & air conditioning contractor
James W Lacy, President

Employees: 1,200
Employees here: 1,200

D-U-N-S 00-894-8473
THOS S BYRNE INC
900 Summit Ave, Fort Worth, TX 76102
Phone: (817) 335-3394

Sales: $115,000,000   *Employees:* 150
Company Type: Private   *Employees here:* 10
SIC: 1542
    General contractor for commercial building construction
Thomas C Fitzpatrick, Sr Chairman of the Board

D-U-N-S 00-794-1958
TIDEWATER CONSTRUCTION CORP
   (*Parent:* Tidewater Skanska Group Inc)
809 S Military Hwy, Virginia Beach, VA 23464
Phone: (757) 420-4140
Sales: $150,000,000   *Employees:* 1,000
Company Type: Private   *Employees here:* 75
SIC: 1541
    Heavy marine and industrial construction
Fred C Schulte, Chairman of the Board

D-U-N-S 02-354-8787
TILCON CONNECTICUT, INC.
   (*Parent:* Tilcon Inc)
909 Foxon Rd, North Branford, CT
Phone: (203) 484-2881
Sales: $75,600,000   *Employees:* 198
Company Type: Private   *Employees here:* 100
SIC: 1611
    Highway & street paving contractor whol sand gravel &
     crushed stone
Robert Knuth, President

D-U-N-S 02-366-5045
TILCON INC
   (*Parent:* Oldcastle Inc)
Black Rock Ave, New Britain, CT
Phone: (860) 223-3651
Sales: $100,800,000   *Employees:* 1,561
Company Type: Private   *Employees here:* 300
SIC: 1611
    Highway & street paving contractor & whol sand gravel &
     crushed stone
Jeff Smith, Chairman of the Board

D-U-N-S 02-046-4892
TIMEC ACQUISITION CORP
155 Corporate Pl, Vallejo, CA 94590
Phone: (707) 642-2222
Sales: $114,600,000   *Employees:* 1,000
Company Type: Private   *Employees here:* 1
SIC: 1629
    Contractor specializing in maintenance and refurbishing of
     refineries and petrochemical plants
B L Allred, President

D-U-N-S 78-568-3343
TOLL HOLDINGS, INC
   (*Parent:* Toll Brothers Inc)
3103 Philmont Ave, Huntingdon Valley, PA 19006
Phone: (215) 938-8000
Sales: $125,200,000   *Employees:* 905
Company Type: Public Family Member   *Employees here:* 905
SIC: 1521
    Builder of single family homes townhouses & condominiums
Robert E Huddleston, President

D-U-N-S 01-184-7571
TORCON INC
214 E Grove St, Westfield, NJ
Phone: (908) 232-8900
Sales: $400,000,000   *Employees:* 200
Company Type: Private   *Employees here:* 50
SIC: 1542
    Construction management project consultant of commercial
     institutional & industrial buildings
H C Elliott III, President

D-U-N-S 15-982-3368
TOWNSEND ACQUISITION INC
700 S Council St, Muncie, IN 47305
Phone: (765) 284-4461
Sales: $118,100,000   *Employees:* 1,030
Company Type: Private   *Employees here:* 2
SIC: 1629
    Right of way & brush clearing transmission line construction
     & electrical contractor
William R Sautter, President

D-U-N-S 18-303-5393
TRANSEASTERN PROPERTIES INC
3300 N University Dr, Pompano Beach, FL 33065
Phone: (954) 346-9700
Sales: $92,772,000   *Employees:* 100
Company Type: Private   *Employees here:* 100
SIC: 1521
    Construction of residential & commercial buildings
Geoffrey M Smith, President

D-U-N-S 00-693-7023
TRAYLOR BROS INC
835 N Congress Ave, Evansville, IN 47715
Phone: (812) 477-1542
Sales: $185,713,000   *Employees:* 1,000
Company Type: Private   *Employees here:* 75
SIC: 1622
    Tunnel & bridge construction
Donald Smith, Chairman of the Board

D-U-N-S 04-114-0195
TRI-CITY ELECTRICAL CONTRACTORS
   (*Parent:* Building One Services Corp)
430 West Dr, Altamonte Springs, FL 32714
Phone: (407) 788-3500
Sales: $103,955,000   *Employees:* 1,250
Company Type: Public Family Member   *Employees here:* 750
SIC: 1731
    Electrical contractor
Richard Ellsworth, President

D-U-N-S 00-893-9043
TRUMBULL CORP
1020 Lebanon Rd, West Mifflin, PA 15122
Phone: (412) 462-9300
Sales: $78,250,000   *Employees:* 700
Company Type: Private   *Employees here:* 400
SIC: 1611
    Heavy highway construction excavating contractor & mfg
     asphalt road materials
Russell L Broad, President

D-U-N-S 61-508-3169
TULLY CONSTRUCTION CO INC
12750 Northern Blvd, Flushing, NY 11368
Phone: (718) 446-7000
Sales: $150,000,000   *Employees:* 250
Company Type: Private   *Employees here:* 250
SIC: 1611
    Heavy construction of streets roads & bridges
Rex Greer, President

D-U-N-S 10-327-3827
TURNER CORP
375 Hudson St Rm 700, New York, NY 10014
Phone: (212) 229-6000
Sales: $3,170,744,000   *Employees:* 3,000
Company Type: Public   *Employees here:* 100
SIC: 1542
    General building contractor construction management
     consulting services & real estate investment
Mike King, President

D-U-N-S 00-977-2062
TURNER INDUSTRIES LTD
8687 United Plaza Blvd, Baton Rouge, LA 70809
Phone: (225) 922-5050
Sales: $550,000,000   *Employees:* 7,000
Company Type: Private   *Employees here:* 1,300
SIC: 1541
    Industrial construction & maintenance & equipment rental &
      pipe fabrication
Philip Annis, Chief Executive Officer

D-U-N-S 08-593-5690
TUTOR-SALIBA CORP
15901 Olden St, Sylmar, CA 91342
Phone: (818) 362-8391
Sales: $433,640,000   *Employees:* 1,200
Company Type: Private   *Employees here:* 60
SIC: 1542
    General building contractor of new commercial buildings
      roads bridges and subways rigging contractor and real estate
      dev
Jeffrey M Levy, Chairman of the Board

D-U-N-S 60-991-4064
U. S. GENERATING CO LLC
7500 Old Georgetown Rd, Bethesda, MD 20814
Phone: (301) 718-6800
Sales: $79,151,000   *Employees:* 1,541
Company Type: Private   *Employees here:* 100
SIC: 1629
    Development construction & management of electric
      generation facilities
Jeffrey M Levy, President

D-U-N-S 87-907-4474
UNITED HOMES INC
    (*Parent:* United Development Mgt Co)
2100 Golf Rd Ste 110, Rolling Meadows, IL 60008
Phone: (847) 427-4500
Sales: $108,501,000   *Employees:* 55
Company Type: Private   *Employees here:* 3
SIC: 1521
    Holding company
Jeff Beamen, Manager

D-U-N-S 00-958-6041
UNITED RENTALS NORTH AMERICA
    (*Parent:* United Rentals Inc)
1581 Cummins Dr Ste 155, Modesto, CA 95358
Phone: (209) 544-9000
Sales: $273,200,000   *Employees:* 2,800
Company Type: Public Family Member   *Employees here:* 80
SIC: 7353
    Equipment rental company with an extensive line of
      construction industrial commercial & residential equipment
Robert Caya, President

D-U-N-S 05-362-7352
U.S. CONTRACTORS INC
622 Commerce St, Clute, TX 77531
Phone: (409) 265-7451
Sales: $165,666,000   *Employees:* 1,800
Company Type: Private   *Employees here:* 1,800
SIC: 1629
    General contractor of petrochemical plants
Jeffrey M Levy, President

D-U-N-S 00-890-7313
U.S. ENGINEERING CO
3433 Roanoke Rd, Kansas City, MO 64111
Phone: (816) 753-6969

Sales: $109,597,000   *Employees:* 525
Company Type: Private   *Employees here:* 200
SIC: 1711
    Mechanical plumbing heating & air conditioning contractor
Randall P Birdwell, Chief Executive Officer

D-U-N-S 05-157-1438
U.S. HOME CORP
10707 Clay Rd, Houston, TX 77041
Phone: (713) 877-2311
Sales: $1,497,649,000   *Employees:* 1,954
Company Type: Public   *Employees here:* 81
SIC: 1531
    Operative home builder
Kevin J Spellman, President

D-U-N-S 08-956-0403
UNIVERSAL CONSTRUCTORS INC
2548 Morrison St, McMinnville, TN 37110
Phone: (931) 668-2876
Sales: $123,260,000   *Employees:* 55
Company Type: Private   *Employees here:* 40
SIC: 1522
    General contractor of residential buildings
Arthur Andersen Jr, President

D-U-N-S 04-660-2728
**UNIVERSITY MECHANICAL & ENGINEERING
CONTRACTORS**
    (*Parent:* Emcor Mechanical/Electrical Services)
4464 Alvarado Canyon Rd, San Diego, CA 92120
Phone: (619) 283-3181
Sales: $86,000,000   *Employees:* 750
Company Type: Public Family Member   *Employees here:* 250
SIC: 1711
    Mechanical contractors
Meredith L Reiter, President

D-U-N-S 60-384-6437
UST LEASING CORP
    (*Parent:* U.S.Trust)
40 Glen Ave, Newton, MA
Phone: (617) 965-0366
Sales: $285,213,000   *Employees:* 25
Company Type: Public Family Member   *Employees here:* 25
SIC: 7353
    Equipment leasing
Domingo Sadurni, Partner

D-U-N-S 13-147-2680
UTILX CORP
22404 66th Ave S, Kent, WA 98032
Phone: (253) 395-0200
Sales: $82,464,000   *Employees:* 515
Company Type: Public   *Employees here:* 90
SIC: 1623
    Underground utilities contractor
Shaker Anthony I, President

D-U-N-S 18-792-7397
VALENZUELA ENGINEERING INC
3130 Skyway Dr Ste 702, Santa Maria, CA 93455
Phone: (805) 349-2811
Sales: $68,036,000   *Employees:* 300
Company Type: Private   *Employees here:* 290
SIC: 1542
    Public building construction
Mike R Brister, President

D-U-N-S 00-794-4184
VECELLIO & GROGAN, INC.
2251 Robert C Byrd Dr, Beckley, WV 25801
Phone: (304) 252-6575

Sales: $200,000,000   *Employees:* 1,200
Company Type: Private   *Employees here:* 350
SIC: 1611
   Highway & bridge construction golf course construction &
      site development
Otto A Engelberth, Chairman of the Board

D-U-N-S 04-758-6581
VENTURE CONSTRUCTION CO
5660 Peachtree Industrial, Norcross, GA 30071
Phone: (770) 441-2404
Sales: $150,709,000   *Employees:* 300
Company Type: Private   *Employees here:* 40
SIC: 1542
   Commercial construction
Steve Hill, President

D-U-N-S 14-773-4172
VHC, INC
3090 Holmgren Way, Green Bay, WI 54304
Phone: (920) 336-7278
Sales: $100,000,000   *Employees:* 1,100
Company Type: Private   *Employees here:* 4
SIC: 1731
   Electrical contractor general contractor commercial industrial
      & homes processing pipe contractor & owns commercial
      buildings
David Shapiro, Chief Financial Officer

D-U-N-S 62-690-0898
VICEROY, INC.
(Parent: General Electric Co)
3225 Pasadena Blvd, Pasadena, TX 77503
Phone: (281) 740-8000
Sales: $97,868,000   *Employees:* 549
Company Type: Public Family Member   *Employees here:* 76
SIC: 1629
   Power plant construction pipe fabrication & installs power
      generation systems
A D Dalton Jr, President

D-U-N-S 17-562-4253
VRATSINAS CONSTRUCTION CO
216 Louisiana St, Little Rock, AR 72201
Phone: (501) 376-0017
Sales: $131,781,000   *Employees:* 154
Company Type: Private   *Employees here:* 150
SIC: 1542
   Contractor-commercial buildings
Thomas E White, Chairman of the Board

D-U-N-S 00-693-2032
W E O'NEIL CONSTRUCTION CO
(Parent: O'Neil Industries Inc)
2751 N Clybourn Ave, Chicago, IL 60614
Phone: (773) 327-1611
Sales: $153,690,000   *Employees:* 200
Company Type: Private   *Employees here:* 80
SIC: 1542
   General contractor of commercial industrial and institutional
      buildings
Pat Rucker, President

D-U-N-S 06-467-6240
W G MILLS INC
3301 Whitfield Ave, Sarasota, FL 34243
Phone: (941) 758-6441
Sales: $72,625,000   *Employees:* 125
Company Type: Private   *Employees here:* 40
SIC: 1542
   General contractor of commercial & institutional bldgs
Jack F Beck, Chairman of the Board

D-U-N-S 00-403-2132
W G YATES & SONS CONSTRUCTION CO
104 Gully Ave, Philadelphia, MS 39350
Phone: (601) 656-5411
Sales: $319,849,000   *Employees:* 2,000
Company Type: Private   *Employees here:* 1,000
SIC: 1542
   Commercial and industrial contractor
Richard A Sperber, President

D-U-N-S 14-750-5523
W M GRACE COMPANIES INC
7575 N 16th St Ste 1, Phoenix, AZ 85020
Phone: (602) 956-8254
Sales: $176,500,000   *Employees:* 800
Company Type: Private   *Employees here:* 40
SIC: 1542
   General contractor convention center and hotel operator
James R Bullock Jr, President

D-U-N-S 00-581-0890
W M JORDAN CO INC
11010 Jefferson Ave, Newport News, VA 23601
Phone: (757) 596-6341
Sales: $150,000,000   *Employees:* 200
Company Type: Private   *Employees here:* 200
SIC: 1542
   Commercial & industrial contractor
R K Ray, Secretary

D-U-N-S 00-326-3555
W M SCHLOSSER CO INC
2400 51st Pl, Hyattsville, MD 20781
Phone: (301) 773-1300
Sales: $75,000,000   *Employees:* 250
Company Type: Private   *Employees here:* 50
SIC: 1542
   New commercial building contractors
Mario Reiriz, President

D-U-N-S 00-793-0936
W S BELLOWS CONSTRUCTION CORP
1906 Afton St, Houston, TX 77055
Phone: (713) 680-2132
Sales: $130,000,000   *Employees:* 300
Company Type: Private   *Employees here:* 300
SIC: 1542
   General contractor commercial and institutional construction
Larry Talbert, President

D-U-N-S 03-237-6709
W W GAY MECHANICAL CONTRACTORS
526 Stockton St, Jacksonville, FL 32204
Phone: (904) 388-2696
Sales: $67,500,000   *Employees:* 717
Company Type: Private   *Employees here:* 500
SIC: 1711
   Mechanical contractors including fire sprinkler installation
Robert Epifano, President

D-U-N-S 16-109-4818
W W INVESTMENT CO
1637 N Warson Rd, St. Louis, MO 63132
Phone: (314) 427-6733
Sales: $106,458,000   *Employees:* 1,236
Company Type: Private   *Employees here:* 40
SIC: 1799
   Waterproofing roofing masonry and concrete restoration
      contractor
James H Pugh Jr, President

D-U-N-S 00-653-7161
WALBRIDGE ALDINGER CO
613 Abbott St, Detroit, MI 48226
Phone: (313) 963-8000
Sales: $630,000,000
Company Type: Private
SIC: 1541
    General contractor & construction manager industrial &
    commercial buildings
Lowell Cave, President

Employees: 600
Employees here: 100

D-U-N-S 13-746-1604
WALDINGER CORP
2601 Bell Ave, Des Moines, IA 50321
Phone: (515) 284-1911
Sales: $82,986,000
Company Type: Private
SIC: 1711
    Mechanical & sheet metal contractor
Patrick J Trompeter, President

Employees: 600
Employees here: 220

D-U-N-S 04-854-4209
WALKER ENGINEERING INC
    (*Parent:* Building One Services Corp)
10999 Petal St, Dallas, TX 75238
Phone: (214) 349-5900
Sales: $96,000,000
Company Type: Public Family Member
SIC: 1731
    Electrical contracting
David P Bleile, President

Employees: 850
Employees here: 550

D-U-N-S 01-930-5200
WALSH BROTHERS INC
150 Hampshire St, Cambridge, MA
Phone: (617) 876-0375
Sales: $88,981,000
Company Type: Private
SIC: 1542
    General contractor of new construction of commercial
    buildings hospital school and institutional buildings
Peter J Corogin, President

Employees: 140
Employees here: 112

D-U-N-S 05-361-1034
WALSH CONSTRUCTION CO
3015 SW 1st Ave, Portland, OR 97201
Phone: (503) 222-4375
Sales: $120,000,000
Company Type: Private
SIC: 1522
    Contractor of residential & commercial buildings
Steven F McDonald, President

Employees: 350
Employees here: 220

D-U-N-S 12-147-6675
WALSH GROUP LTD
929 W Adams St, Chicago, IL 60607
Phone: (312) 563-5400
Sales: $959,103,000
Company Type: Private
SIC: 1542
    General contractor of commercial & office buildings new
    construction highway construction and factory construction
Ernest F Bock, President

Employees: 1,439
Employees here: 700

D-U-N-S 17-543-6658
WALTER & SCI CONSTRUCTION USA
441 SW 41st St, Renton, WA 98055
Phone: (425) 251-5332
Sales: $219,225,000
Company Type: Private
SIC: 1622
    Tunnel highway & bridge construction
Erwin Geis, Chief Executive Officer

Employees: 207
Employees here: 150

D-U-N-S 14-799-0758
WALTON CONSTRUCTION CO INC
3252 Roanoke Rd, Kansas City, MO 64111
Phone: (816) 753-2121
Sales: $308,000,000
Company Type: Private
SIC: 1542
    Commercial & industrial building contractor
Edward Storey, Chief Executive Officer

Employees: 300
Employees here: 100

D-U-N-S 03-714-1256
WARDE ELECTRIC CONTRACTING
100 Wells Ave, Congers, NY 10920
Phone: (914) 268-0453
Sales: $100,000,000
Company Type: Private
SIC: 1731
    Electrical contractor
Roger B Coe, President

Employees: 100
Employees here: 100

D-U-N-S 04-132-6406
WARMINGTON HOMES
3090 Pullman St, Costa Mesa, CA 92626
Phone: (714) 557-5511
Sales: $170,000,000
Company Type: Private
SIC: 1531
    Operative builders
James H Estes, President

Employees: 246
Employees here: 75

D-U-N-S 07-826-2268
WASHINGTON COSCAN INC
    (*Parent:* Brookfield Homes Ltd)
8521 Leesburg Pike, Vienna, VA 22182
Phone: (703) 356-9090
Sales: $74,673,000
Company Type: Private
SIC: 1521
    Contractor of single family homes and real estate
    development
Paul Estridge Jr, President

Employees: 90
Employees here: 30

D-U-N-S 02-268-6208
WASHINGTON HOMES INC
1802 Brightseat Rd Fl 6, Landover, MD 20785
Phone: (301) 772-8900
Sales: $240,703,000
Company Type: Public
SIC: 1531
    Operative builder-single family homes townhomes
    condominiums
Randy Etter, President

Employees: 377
Employees here: 45

D-U-N-S 16-140-9818
WASTE MANAGEMENT INDUS SERVICES
    (*Parent:* Rust International Inc)
1980 Highway 146 N, La Porte, TX 77571
Phone: (713) 307-2100
Sales: $150,000,000
Company Type: Public Family Member
SIC: 1799
    Industrial cleaning
Evans Lloyd I, President

Employees: 2,500
Employees here: 300

D-U-N-S 00-320-3254
WATSON ELECTRICAL CONSTRUCTION CO
    (*Parent:* Building One Services Corp)
490 Ward Blvd, Wilson, NC 27893
Phone: (252) 237-7511

Sales: $110,000,000   *Employees:* 1,200
Company Type: Public Family Member   *Employees here:* 225
SIC: 1731
    Electrical contractor
David Heneberry, Chairman of the Board

D-U-N-S 04-292-0728   EXP
WEATHERFORD U.S., INC
    (Parent: Weatherford International)
515 Post Oak Blvd, Houston, TX 77027
Phone: (713) 693-4000
Sales: $147,300,000   *Employees:* 1,511
Company Type: Public Family Member   *Employees here:* 150
SIC: 7353
    Oil field services
David M Parker, Chairman of the Board

D-U-N-S 00-690-2431
WEBB DEL CORP
6001 N 24th St, Phoenix, AZ 85016
Phone: (602) 808-8000
Sales: $1,177,767,000   *Employees:* 3,200
Company Type: Public   *Employees here:* 300
SIC: 1521
    Operative builder and real estate development
Ronald E Pierson, President

D-U-N-S 08-356-2694
WEEKLEY HOMES, LP
1300 Post Oak Blvd, Houston, TX 77056
Phone: (713) 963-0500
Sales: $503,000,000   *Employees:* 790
Company Type: Private   *Employees here:* 112
SIC: 1531
    Builder of single-family homes
Konrad E Poth, President

D-U-N-S 04-466-5230
WEEKS MARINE INC
216 North Ave E, Cranford, NJ
Phone: (908) 272-4010
Sales: $164,537,000   *Employees:* 500
Company Type: Private   *Employees here:* 45
SIC: 1629
    Dredging & marine contractors
Richard J Seikaly, President

D-U-N-S 02-300-8949
WEIS BUILDERS, INC
8009 34th Ave S Ste 1300, Minneapolis, MN 55425
Phone: (612) 858-9999
Sales: $100,000,000   *Employees:* 100
Company Type: Private   *Employees here:* 60
SIC: 1542
    General contractor building commercial apartment &
      industrial buildings
F D Reardon, President

D-U-N-S 00-694-1454
WEITZ CO INC
400 Locust St Ste 300, Des Moines, IA 50309
Phone: (515) 698-4260
Sales: $500,000,000   *Employees:* 660
Company Type: Private   *Employees here:* 17
SIC: 1542
    Commercial construction & renovation
Sid Baron, President

D-U-N-S 09-665-6251
WELBRO CONSTRUCTORS INC
800 Trafalgar Ct Ste 200, Maitland, FL 32751
Phone: (407) 475-0800

Sales: $90,000,000   *Employees:* 300
Company Type: Private   *Employees here:* 1
SIC: 1522
    General contractor of hotels & condominiums and
      specialized public buildings
Dick Scales, N/A

D-U-N-S 04-438-9377
WELCON MANAGEMENT CO
490 Ward Blvd, Wilson, NC 27893
Phone: (252) 237-7511
Sales: $115,000,000   *Employees:* 1,203
Company Type: Private   *Employees here:* 3
SIC: 1731
    Electrical contractor
Salvatore Fichera, President

D-U-N-S 06-151-5573
WELDED CONSTRUCTION CO
26933 Eckel Rd, Perrysburg, OH 43551
Phone: (419) 874-3548
Sales: $116,436,000   *Employees:* 700
Company Type: Private   *Employees here:* 10
SIC: 1623
    Oil & gas pipeline contractor
Jaime F Olivencia, Partner

D-U-N-S 05-857-5051
WELSBACH ELECTRIC CORP (DEL)
    (Parent: Emcor Mechanical/Electrical Services)
11101 14th Ave, College Point, NY 11356
Phone: (718) 670-7900
Sales: $80,000,000   *Employees:* 350
Company Type: Public Family Member   *Employees here:* 350
SIC: 1731
    Electrical contractor
James M Wilhelm, President

D-U-N-S 00-980-8627
WESTCOTT CONSTRUCTION CORP
135 E Washington St, North Attleboro, MA
Phone: (508) 695-3561
Sales: $68,314,000   *Employees:* 100
Company Type: Private   *Employees here:* 100
SIC: 1542
    General construction
James Gray, President

D-U-N-S 16-109-1111
WESTERN GROUP INC
    (Parent: W W Investment Co)
1637 N Warson Rd, St. Louis, MO 63132
Phone: (314) 427-6733
Sales: $106,458,000   *Employees:* 1,236
Company Type: Private   *Employees here:* 40
SIC: 1799
    Waterproofing roofing masonry and concrete restoration
      contractor
Richard Maloni, President

D-U-N-S 05-502-9375
WESTERN NATIONAL PROPERTIES
8 Executive Cir, Irvine, CA 92614
Phone: (949) 862-6200
Sales: $95,000,000   *Employees:* 1,000
Company Type: Private   *Employees here:* 130
SIC: 1522
    Apartment building developers
Frank Paschen Jr, Chairman of the Board

D-U-N-S 13-085-8319
WESTERN STATES FIRE PROTECTION
   (Parent: API Group Inc)
7026 S Tucson Way, Englewood, CO 80112
Phone: (303) 792-0022
Sales: $132,338,000   *Employees:* 700
Company Type: Private   *Employees here:* 100
SIC: 1711
   Fire sprinkler system installation
Jimmy U Crane, Chairman of the Board

D-U-N-S 00-260-9535
WESTERN SUMMIT CONSTRUCTORS
   (Parent: T I C Holdings Inc)
5470 N Valley Hwy, Denver, CO 80216
Phone: (303) 298-9500
Sales: $87,065,000   *Employees:* 500
Company Type: Private   *Employees here:* 75
SIC: 1629
   Waste water & sewage treatment plant construction
Ted C Kennedy, Chairman of the Board

D-U-N-S 00-890-9129
WESTERN WATERPROOFING CO
   (Parent: Western Group Inc)
1637 N Warson Rd, St. Louis, MO 63132
Phone: (314) 427-6733
Sales: $81,523,000   *Employees:* 854
Company Type: Private   *Employees here:* 7
SIC: 1799
   Waterproofing roofing masonry and concrete restoration
   contractor
Ken Kefalas, President

D-U-N-S 80-937-8425
WESTMINSTER HOMES, INC.
   (Parent: Washington Homes Inc)
2706 N Church St, Greensboro, NC 27405
Phone: (336) 375-6200
Sales: $71,584,000   *Employees:* 85
Company Type: Public Family Member   *Employees here:* 35
SIC: 1542
   General contractor
David J Farr, President

D-U-N-S 02-359-7826
WESTRA CONSTRUCTION INC
W 7185 Hwy 49, Waupun, WI 53963
Phone: (920) 324-3545
Sales: $96,557,000   *Employees:* 275
Company Type: Private   *Employees here:* 200
SIC: 1542
   General contractor-commercial industrial & institutional
   buildings
Robert L Moultrie, Chairman of the Board

D-U-N-S 00-692-0755
WHITE CONSTRUCTION CO
U.S. Hwy 19, Chiefland, FL 32626
Phone: (352) 493-1444
Sales: $72,309,000   *Employees:* 600
Company Type: Private   *Employees here:* 15
SIC: 1611
   Road construction / dairy farm / asphalt plant
Kenneth R Karr, President

D-U-N-S 07-792-8521
WHITE-SPUNNER CONSTRUCTION
2654 Cameron St, Mobile, AL 36607
Phone: (334) 471-5189

Sales: $70,000,000   *Employees:* 35
Company Type: Private   *Employees here:* 35
SIC: 1542
   General contractor
Roland Fagen, Chief Executive Officer

D-U-N-S 00-695-0604
WHITING-TURNER CONTG CO INC
300 E Joppa Rd Ste 8, Baltimore, MD 21286
Phone: (410) 821-1100
Sales: $1,036,957,000   *Employees:* 1,839
Company Type: Private   *Employees here:* 987
SIC: 1542
   Heavy construction and construction management
Maynard Fahs Jr, President

D-U-N-S 05-115-3724
WHITTAKER CONSTRUCTION INC
   (Parent: The Fortress Group Inc)
355 Mid Rivers Mall Dr, St. Peters, MO 63376
Phone: (314) 970-1511
Sales: $85,000,000   *Employees:* 375
Company Type: Public Family Member   *Employees here:* 366
SIC: 1521
   General contractor of single-family homes
Christophe Hashioka, President

D-U-N-S 55-648-8831
WILDER CONSTRUCTION CO
1525 Marine View Dr, Everett, WA 98201
Phone: (425) 551-3100
Sales: $142,689,000   *Employees:* 250
Company Type: Private   *Employees here:* 200
SIC: 1611
   Highway construction asphalt paving underground utilities
   contractor & environmental remediation work
Joseph Falco, Treasurer

D-U-N-S 18-668-6002
WILLBROS USA, INC
2431 E 61st St Ste 700, Tulsa, OK 74136
Phone: (918) 748-7000
Sales: $106,421,000   *Employees:* 700
Company Type: Private   *Employees here:* 115
SIC: 1623
   Oil & gas pipeline construction contractor & consulting
   engineer
Michael Falconite, President

D-U-N-S 95-802-1990
WILLIAMS GROUP INTERNATIONAL
2076 W Park Pl, Stone Mountain, GA 30087
Phone: (770) 879-4000
Sales: $214,057,000   *Employees:* 1,500
Company Type: Private   *Employees here:* 200
SIC: 1799
   Specialized industrial services
Michael W Fann, President

D-U-N-S 02-147-5181
WILLIAMS INDUSTRIES INC
11000 Brittmoore Park Dr, Houston, TX 77041
Phone: (713) 849-1400
Sales: $97,000,000   *Employees:* 200
Company Type: Private   *Employees here:* 200
SIC: 1542
   General commercial contractor
Kenneth Stonecipher, President

D-U-N-S 05-140-3194
WILLIARD INC
   (Parent: EFG Holdings Inc)
375 Highland Ave, Jenkintown, PA 19046

Phone: (215) 885-5000
Sales: $118,666,000   *Employees:* 500
Company Type: Private   *Employees here:* 475
SIC: 1711
   Mechanical contractor
Abraham S Fassberg, President

D-U-N-S 04-931-7449
WILSON ELECTRIC CO, INC.
   (Parent: Building One Services Corp)
15475 N Greenway Hayden L, Scottsdale, AZ 85260
Phone: (602) 991-0100
Sales: $71,009,000   *Employees:* 750
Company Type: Public Family Member   *Employees here:* 510
SIC: 1731
   Electrical contractor computer syst svs fiber optic
      telecommunication & data cabling
Jack W Sanford, Chairman of the Board

D-U-N-S 09-656-9983
WINCHESTER HOMES INC
   (Parent: Weyerhaeuser Real Estate Co)
6305 Ivy Ln Ste 800, Greenbelt, MD 20770
Phone: (301) 474-4411
Sales: $155,969,000   *Employees:* 220
Company Type: Public Family Member   *Employees here:* 16
SIC: 1531
   Operative builder of single family houses
Steven Nelson, Chief Executive Officer

D-U-N-S 09-176-3417
WINTER CONSTRUCTION CO INC
   (Parent: Winter Group of Companies Inc)
1900 Emery St NW Ste 30, Atlanta, GA 30318
Phone: (404) 588-3300
Sales: $200,000,000   *Employees:* 360
Company Type: Private   *Employees here:* 341
SIC: 1542
   Commercial institutional and industrial building construction
Royce W Faulkner, Chairman

D-U-N-S 08-623-5538
WINTER PARK CONSTRUCTION CO
221 Circle Dr, Maitland, FL 32751
Phone: (407) 644-8923
Sales: $100,000,000   *Employees:* 83
Company Type: Private   *Employees here:* 83
SIC: 1522
   Commercial construction
David A Phillips, President

D-U-N-S 00-286-6366
WOHLSEN CONSTRUCTION CO
548 Steel Way, Lancaster, PA 17601
Phone: (717) 299-2500
Sales: $135,000,000   *Employees:* 375
Company Type: Private   *Employees here:* 120
SIC: 1542
   General contractor of institutional commercial & industrial
      buildings & construction management services
John Nelson, General Manager

D-U-N-S 00-289-8088
WOLVERINE BUILDING INC
4045 Barden St SE, Grand Rapids, MI 49512
Phone: (616) 949-3360
Sales: $71,500,000   *Employees:* 100
Company Type: Private   *Employees here:* 100
SIC: 1541
   Contractor of industrial commercial and institutional
      buildings
Ed Forsman, President

D-U-N-S 08-969-2149
WOODROW TAYLOR HOMES INC
24461 Ridge Route Dr, Laguna Hills, CA 92653
Phone: (949) 581-2626
Sales: $147,294,000   *Employees:* 183
Company Type: Private   *Employees here:* 183
SIC: 1521
   General contractor of single family homes and real estate
      developer
Greg Cosko, President

D-U-N-S 03-024-1269
WORTH CONSTRUCTION INC
24 Taylor Ave, Bethel, CT
Phone: (203) 797-8788
Sales: $127,959,000   *Employees:* 125
Company Type: Private   *Employees here:* 125
SIC: 1542
   Contractor of commercial buildings such as convention
      centers office buildings hospitals schools & industrial
      buildings
David Hathcock, President

D-U-N-S 60-582-9316
WORTHINGTON COMMUNITIES INC
17380 Winkler Rd, Fort Myers, FL 33908
Phone: (941) 482-8828
Sales: $74,489,000   *Employees:* 85
Company Type: Private   *Employees here:* 85
SIC: 1521
   Contractor specializing in new construction of single and
      multi-family homes
Frances E Mason, President

D-U-N-S 83-937-5425
YEAGER HOLDINGS, INC
1995 Agua Mansa Rd, Riverside, CA 92509
Phone: (909) 684-5360
Sales: $171,555,000   *Employees:* 500
Company Type: Private   *Employees here:* 80
SIC: 1611
   General contractor
Felix Petrillo, President

D-U-N-S 00-699-5682
YONKERS CONTRACTING CO INC
969 Midland Ave, Yonkers, NY 10704
Phone: (914) 965-1500
Sales: $270,641,000   *Employees:* 2,500
Company Type: Private   *Employees here:* 2,000
SIC: 1611
   General contractor highways bridges whol construction
      materials construction of comm & inst bldgs & electrical
      contractor
Felix Petrillo, President

D-U-N-S 08-077-4656
YORK CONSTRUCTION CO INC
   (Parent: Beers Construction Co)
1164 Woodruff Rd, Greenville, SC 29607
Phone: (864) 297-9700
Sales: $67,704,000   *Employees:* 125
Company Type: Private   *Employees here:* 125
SIC: 1541
   Contractor specializing in industrial & commercial buildings
John B Meek, President

D-U-N-S 00-116-8020
YORK RESEARCH CORP
280 Park Ave Rm 2700 W, New York, NY 10017
Phone: (212) 557-6200

Sales: $502,980,000
Company Type: Public
SIC: 1629
   Develops owns & operates co-generation & renewable
     energy projects and brokers wholesale energy transactions
Richard L Scott, President

Employees: 44
Employees here: 25

   D-U-N-S 02-155-8440   EXP
ZACHRY INC
527 Logwood Ave, San Antonio, TX 78221
Phone: (210) 475-8000
Sales: $800,000,000
Company Type: Private
SIC: 1611
   Highway/bridge/pipeline/dams etc heavy construction
     contractor mfg portland cement sand/gravel quarry
Whitworth Ferguson Jr, President

Employees: 10,000
Employees here: 400

   D-U-N-S 04-373-7824
ZAMIAS CONSTRUCTION CO INC
300 Market St Ste 102, Johnstown, PA 15901
Phone: (814) 535-5549
Sales: $150,000,000
Company Type: Private
SIC: 1542
   General contractor
J R Sutton, President

Employees: 20
Employees here: 20

   D-U-N-S 17-677-0030
ZARING NATIONAL CORP
11300 Cornell Park Dr, Cincinnati, OH 45242
Phone: (513) 489-8849
Sales: $223,957,000
Company Type: Public
SIC: 1521
   Holding company for general contractor of single family
     homes land development retail manufactured housing
     mortgage brokers
Keith Ferrell, Treasurer

Employees: 428
Employees here: 17

   D-U-N-S 17-506-9095
ZURN CONSTRUCTORS, INC
   (*Parent:* Zurn Industries Inc)
1 Zurn Pl, Erie, PA 16505
Phone: (814) 452-2111
Sales: $85,200,000
Company Type: Public Family Member
SIC: 1629
   Waste water and sewage treatment plant construction mfg
     pre stressed concrete beams and fire sprinkler system
     installation
Philip Fester, President

Employees: 744
Employees here: 3

CHAPTER 5 - PART I

RANKINGS AND COMPANIES

The companies presented in Chapter 4 - Company Directory are arranged in this chapter in rank order: by sales and by number of employees. Each company's name, rank, location, type, sales, employment figure, and primary SIC are shown. Only companies with reported sales data are included in the "rankings by sales" table; similarly, only companies that report employment data are ranked in the "rankings by employment" table.

Company type is either Public, Private, or Public Family Member. The last category is used to label corporate entities that belong to a group of companies, the relationship being that of a subsidiary or element of a parent. The parents of Public Family Member companies can be found in the company's directory entry presented in Chapter 4.

This product includes proprietary data of Dun & Bradstreet, Inc.

D&B COMPANY RANKINGS BY SALES

Company	Rank	Location	Type	Sales ($ mil.)	Employ-ment	Primary SIC
Halliburton Delaware, Inc	1	Dallas, TX	Public Family Member	6,592.8	57,300	1629
Dover Elevator Co	2	Horn Lake, MS	Public Family Member	4,547.7	2,735	1796
BTR Dunlop Inc	3	Wilmington, DE	Private	4,200.0	24,000	1611
Centex Corp	4	Dallas, TX	Public	3,975.4	10,259	1531
McDermott International Inc	5	New Orleans, LA	Public	3,674.6	24,700	1629
Turner Corp	6	New York, NY	Public	3,170.7	3,000	1542
Pulte Corp	7	Bloomfield Hills, MI	Public	2,866.5	3,778	1531
H B E Corp	8	St. Louis, MO	Private	2,455.6	11,000	1542
Kaufman & Broad Home Corp	9	Los Angeles, CA	Public	2,449.4	3,500	1531
Kiewit Construction Co	10	Omaha, NE	Private	2,325.2	1,353	1541
Kellogg, Brown & Root, Inc	11	Houston, TX	Public Family Member	2,300.9	20,000	1629
D R Horton Inc	12	Arlington, TX	Public	2,155.0	2,465	1531
Jacobs Engineering Group Inc	13	Pasadena, CA	Public	2,101.1	23,000	1629
Peter Kiewit Sons', Inc	14	Omaha, NE	Private	2,096.5	9,393	1542
Skanska (U.S.A.), Inc.	15	Greenwich, CT	Private	2,060.7	3,700	1542
Emcor Group Inc	16	Norwalk, CT	Public	1,950.9	14,000	1731
P & O Inc	17	Englewood, CO	Private	1,930.0	3,800	1542
Morrison Knudsen Corp	18	Boise, ID	Public	1,862.2	9,000	1622
J Ray McDermott, S.A.	19	New Orleans, LA	Public Family Member	1,855.5	11,700	1629
Holzmann, Philipp USA Ltd	20	Charlotte, NC	Private	1,651.0	8,000	1542
Ryland Group Inc	21	Columbia, MD	Public	1,649.8	2,270	1531
U.S. Home Corp	22	Houston, TX	Public	1,497.6	1,954	1531
Beers Inc	23	Atlanta, GA	Private	1,436.1	2,300	1542
Clark Construction Group	24	Bethesda, MD	Private	1,400.0	3,100	1542
J A Jones Inc	25	Charlotte, NC	Private	1,398.5	6,224	1542
M W Kellogg Co	26	Houston, TX	Public Family Member	1,358.0	6,770	1629
Perini Corp	27	Framingham, MA	Public	1,324.5	2,200	1542
Lennar Corp	28	Miami, FL	Public	1,303.1	3,875	1531
M. D. C. Holdings, Inc.	29	Denver, CO	Public	1,263.2	1,350	1521
Apac Holdings Inc	30	Atlanta, GA	Public Family Member	1,257.1	5,028	1611
Parsons Corp	31	Pasadena, CA	Private	1,245.6	10,000	1629
Shea Homes LP	32	Walnut, CA	Private	1,200.0	588	1521
Webb Del Corp	33	Phoenix, AZ	Public	1,177.8	3,200	1521
NVR, Inc	34	McLean, VA	Public	1,154.0	2,013	1531
McCarthy Building Companies	35	St. Louis, MO	Private	1,127.0	1,500	1542
Sordoni/Skanska Construction Co	36	Parsippany, NJ	Private	1,100.0	850	1541
Beers Construction Co	37	Atlanta, GA	Private	1,074.2	1,500	1542
Whiting-Turner Contg Co Inc	38	Baltimore, MD	Private	1,037.0	1,839	1542
Granite Construction Inc	39	Watsonville, CA	Public	1,028.2	1,800	1611
Dillingham Construction Corp	40	Pleasanton, CA	Private	1,022.6	4,000	1629
Beazer Homes USA Inc	41	Atlanta, GA	Public	977.4	1,261	1521
Walsh Group Ltd	42	Chicago, IL	Private	959.1	1,439	1542
Centex Construction Group Inc	43	Dallas, TX	Public Family Member	953.8	1,790	1542
Kajima U.S.A. Inc.	44	New York, NY	Private	950.1	1,440	1541
Hovnanian Enterprises Inc	45	Red Bank, NJ	Public	941.9	1,200	1531
Hensel Phelps Construction Co	46	Greeley, CO	Private	934.3	1,500	1542
Apogee Enterprises Inc	47	Minneapolis, MN	Public	912.8	6,672	1791
Gilbane Building Co	48	Providence, RI	Private	910.3	900	1541
Huber Hunt & Nichols Inc	49	Indianapolis, IN	Private	900.0	500	1542
Hunt Corp	50	Indianapolis, IN	Private	900.0	600	1542
DPR Construction, Inc	51	Redwood City, CA	Private	890.6	1,609	1541
Rust Constructors Inc	52	Birmingham, AL	Public Family Member	821.6	6,500	1541
M A Mortenson Companies	53	Minneapolis, MN	Private	809.5	1,500	1542
Lawson Roofing Co Inc	54	San Francisco, CA	Private	800.5	90	1761
Zachry Inc	55	San Antonio, TX	Private	800.0	10,000	1611
Bovis Construction Corp	56	New York, NY	Private	781.4	20	1542
Milburn Investments Inc	57	Austin, TX	Public Family Member	726.0	120	1531
PCL Enterprises Inc	58	Denver, CO	Private	714.7	1,200	1542
Mastec Inc	59	Miami, FL	Public	703.4	7,850	1623
Ogden Energy Group Inc	60	Fairfield, NJ	Public Family Member	699.2	355	1629
H B Zachry Co	61	San Antonio, TX	Private	665.0	9,000	1611
B E & K Construction Co	62	Birmingham, AL	Private	632.2	5,000	1541
Walbridge Aldinger Co	63	Detroit, MI	Private	630.0	600	1541
Harbert Corp	64	Birmingham, AL	Private	623.4	2,800	1542
Pepper Companies Inc	65	Chicago, IL	Private	622.9	900	1542
Austin Industries Del Corp	66	Dallas, TX	Private	620.0	5,000	1542
Dunn Industries, Inc.	67	Kansas City, MO	Private	619.0	1,000	1542
M/I Schottenstein Homes Inc	68	Columbus, OH	Public	614.0	800	1531
Devcon Construction Inc	69	Milpitas, CA	Private	602.9	384	1541
Brown & Root Services Corp	70	Houston, TX	Public Family Member	600.0	4,100	1541

D&B COMPANY RANKINGS BY SALES

Company	Rank	Location	Type	Sales ($ mil.)	Employ-ment	Primary SIC
BSI Holdings Inc	71	Carmel, CA	Private	600.0	4,000	1742
Opus U.S. Corp	72	Hopkins, MN	Private	600.0	764	1542
Bechtel Construction Operations Inc	73	San Francisco, CA	Private	595.0	1,275	1541
Standard Pacific Corp	74	Costa Mesa, CA	Public	584.6	430	1531
Swinerton & Walberg Co	75	San Francisco, CA	Private	558.8	729	1542
Brasfield & Gorrie, LLC	76	Birmingham, AL	Private	550.0	1,600	1542
Turner Industries Ltd	77	Baton Rouge, LA	Private	550.0	7,000	1541
Harmony Corp	78	Baton Rouge, LA	Private	543.8	4,300	1541
Fru-Con Holding Corp	79	Ballwin, MO	Private	538.2	2,800	1541
Dick Corp	80	Clairton, PA	Private	537.5	1,000	1611
Engle Homes Inc	81	Boca Raton, FL	Public	536.0	744	1521
Alberici Corp	82	St. Louis, MO	Private	531.3	1,500	1541
Lennar Homes Inc	83	Miami, FL	Public Family Member	528.3	300	1531
Black & Veatch Construction	84	Kansas City, MO	Private	526.9	784	1629
J S Alberici Construction Co	85	St. Louis, MO	Private	525.3	1,500	1541
Weekley Homes, Lp	86	Houston, TX	Private	503.0	790	1531
York Research Corp	87	New York, NY	Public	503.0	44	1629
Swinerton Inc	88	San Francisco, CA	Private	500.6	1,100	1542
Hcbeck, Ltd	89	Dallas, TX	Private	500.0	200	1541
Weitz Co Inc	90	Des Moines, IA	Private	500.0	660	1542
Rudolph & Sletten Inc	91	Foster City, CA	Private	487.0	900	1541
Olker Industries, Inc	92	Long Grove, IL	Private	480.0	10	1521
Modern Continental Construction Co	93	Cambridge, MA	Private	478.9	2,300	1622
Kraus-Anderson, Inc	94	Minneapolis, MN	Private	465.0	1,000	1542
Kaufman & Broad of S California	95	Los Angeles, CA	Public Family Member	455.1	350	1521
Hathaway Dinwiddie Constr Grp	96	San Francisco, CA	Private	452.0	650	1542
Dupont Flooring Systems, Inc	97	Kennesaw, GA	Public Family Member	450.0	2,500	1752
Hardin Construction Group Inc	98	Atlanta, GA	Private	450.0	500	1542
Sobrato Construction Inc	99	Cupertino, CA	Private	450.0	15	1542
Colas Inc	100	Morristown, NJ	Private	446.7	1,250	1611
Michael Baker Corp	101	Coraopolis, PA	Public	446.4	3,670	1611
Fortress Group Inc	102	McLean, VA	Public	445.3	350	1521
Manhattan Construction Co	103	Dallas, TX	Private	440.0	900	1542
Group Maintenance America	104	Houston, TX	Public	437.0	2,800	1711
Tutor-Saliba Corp	105	Sylmar, CA	Private	433.6	1,200	1542
Hawkeye Construction, Inc	106	Troutdale, OR	Public Family Member	431.3	120	1623
L E Myers Co	107	Rolling Meadows, IL	Public Family Member	431.3	800	1623
MYR Group Inc.	108	Rolling Meadows, IL	Public	431.3	4,000	1623
International Maintenance Corp	109	Baton Rouge, LA	Private	430.1	3,400	1541
Flatley Co	110	Braintree, MA	Private	423.2	4,500	1522
T I C Holdings Inc	111	Steamboat Springs, CO	Private	420.5	3,000	1541
Greystone Homes Inc	112	Los Angeles, CA	Public Family Member	420.0	454	1521
J E Dunn Construction Co	113	Kansas City, MO	Private	417.0	1,000	1542
Shapell Industries Inc	114	Beverly Hills, CA	Private	408.0	300	1531
Koll Co	115	Newport Beach, CA	Private	406.2	1,828	1542
Flint Industries, Inc	116	Tulsa, OK	Private	403.0	1,999	1542
Austin Commercial Inc	117	Dallas, TX	Private	400.0	600	1542
Fischbach Corp	118	Englewood, CO	Public Family Member	400.0	1,000	1731
Monumental Investment Corp	119	Baltimore, MD	Private	400.0	1,851	1711
Torcon Inc	120	Westfield, NJ	Private	400.0	200	1542
Comfort Systems USA Inc	121	Houston, TX	Public	390.1	3,119	1711
Kinetics Group, Inc	122	Santa Clara, CA	Public Family Member	388.0	3,460	1711
Rooney Brothers Co	123	Tulsa, OK	Private	384.8	1,732	1542
American Residential Services	124	Houston, TX	Public	382.5	4,800	1711
S & B Engineers and Constructors	125	Houston, TX	Private	382.5	2,000	1629
Metric Constructors Inc	126	Charlotte, NC	Private	380.1	700	1541
Global Industries, Ltd	127	Lafayette, LA	Public	379.9	1,563	1623
JMB/Urban Development Co.	128	Chicago, IL	Private	379.8	1,218	1531
Suffolk Construction Co	129	Boston, MA	Private	378.0	400	1542
Dycom Industries Inc	130	Palm Beach Gardens, FL	Public	371.4	3,834	1623
Guy F Atkinson Co of California	131	Lafayette, CA	Private	370.6	20	1629
Atkn Co	132	Lafayette, CA	Private	370.5	20	1629
Api Group, Inc	133	St. Paul, MN	Private	369.3	3,000	1742
Nielsen Dillingham Builders	134	San Diego, CA	Private	360.0	700	1542
Richmond Am Homes of Colorado	135	Denver, CO	Public Family Member	360.0	300	1531
Boldt Group Inc	136	Appleton, WI	Private	351.0	2,200	1541
Centex Rooney Construction Co	137	Fort Lauderdale, FL	Public Family Member	350.0	650	1542
K Hovnanian Enterprises, Inc	138	Red Bank, NJ	Public Family Member	347.9	1,100	1531
Teichert Inc	139	Sacramento, CA	Private	347.8	1,200	1611
Performance Contracting Group	140	Shawnee Mission, KS	Private	346.8	5,000	1742

D&B COMPANY RANKINGS BY SALES

Company	Rank	Location	Type	Sales ($ mil.)	Employ-ment	Primary SIC
Drees Co	141	Fort Mitchell, KY	Private	342.8	450	1521
Northwestern Growth Corp	142	Sioux Falls, SD	Public Family Member	340.4	1,375	1711
Sithe Energies USA Inc	143	New York, NY	Private	335.8	240	1629
ICF Kaiser Engineers Group	144	Fairfax, VA	Public Family Member	333.2	2,900	1629
JE Merit Constructors, Inc	145	Houston, TX	Public Family Member	332.3	7,000	1629
Presley Companies	146	Newport Beach, CA	Public	329.9	376	1531
Limbach Holdings Inc	147	Wilmington, DE	Private	329.4	2,510	1711
Prime Service Inc	148	Houston, TX	Private	326.6	2,611	7353
Highland Homes Holdings Inc	149	Dallas, TX	Private	323.0	400	1521
W G Yates & Sons Construction Co	150	Philadelphia, MS	Private	319.8	2,000	1542
Poseidon Oil Pipeline Co LLC	151	Houston, TX	Private	310.8	60	1623
Fisher Development Inc	152	San Francisco, CA	Private	310.1	265	1542
Walton Construction Co Inc	153	Kansas City, MO	Private	308.0	300	1542
CDI Contractors, LLC	154	Little Rock, AR	Private	303.9	500	1542
Dyn Specialty Contracting Inc	155	McLean, VA	Public Family Member	302.5	3,200	1711
Morrison Homes, Inc	156	Alpharetta, GA	Private	301.6	540	1521
Becon Construction Co	157	Houston, TX	Private	301.0	285	1541
Kiewit, Atkinson & Cashman	158	Boston, MA	Private	301.0	60	1611
Barry Bette & Led Duke Inc	159	Albany, NY	Private	300.0	350	1542
Consultant Erection Construction Inc	160	Bracey, VA	Private	300.0	8	1521
Faulkner Group, Inc	161	Austin, TX	Private	300.0	2,100	1542
G B I Construction Inc	162	Norcross, GA	Private	300.0	30	1542
Jerry Pybus Electric	163	Panama City, FL	Private	300.0	50	1731
Mimun Resources Inc	164	Houston, TX	Private	300.0	23	1623
Archer Western Contractors	165	Fort Lauderdale, FL	Private	299.5	250	1622
Sasco Electric	166	Artesia, CA	Private	297.1	4,000	1731
Building One Services Corp	167	Wayzata, MN	Public	297.0	4,000	1731
Layne Christensen Co	168	Shawnee Mission, KS	Public	294.6	2,949	1781
Kitchell Corp	169	Phoenix, AZ	Private	289.0	700	1542
Holder Corp	170	Atlanta, GA	Private	288.1	470	1542
UST Leasing Corp	171	Newton, MA	Public Family Member	285.2	25	7353
Lane Industries Inc	172	Meriden, CT	Private	284.4	2,175	1622
Shelco Inc	173	Charlotte, NC	Private	280.0	240	1541
Irex Corp	174	Lancaster, PA	Public	278.1	1,500	1742
Pike Electric Inc	175	Mount Airy, NC	Private	277.8	3,700	1623
United Rentals North America	176	Modesto, CA	Public Family Member	273.2	2,800	7353
Ames Construction, Inc	177	Burnsville, MN	Private	271.6	750	1629
S E Johnson Companies Inc	178	Maumee, OH	Private	271.0	1,516	1611
Yonkers Contracting Co Inc	179	Yonkers, NY	Private	270.6	2,500	1611
Eagleventures Inc	180	Memphis, TN	Private	270.0	1,700	1542
MMC Corp	181	Shawnee Mission, KS	Private	269.0	525	1711
Danis Companies	182	Dayton, OH	Private	268.0	745	1629
Rudolph/Libbe Companies Inc	183	Walbridge, OH	Private	266.3	1,000	1541
Dyncorp Tri-Cities Services	184	Richland, WA	Private	265.9	1,200	1542
Integrated Electrical Services	185	Houston, TX	Public	263.6	3,550	1731
Mass Electric Construction Co	186	Boston, MA	Private	261.6	2,050	1731
ME Holding, Inc	187	Boston, MA	Private	261.6	1,353	1731
Dillingham Construction PCF Ltd	188	Honolulu, HI	Private	260.4	900	1542
Oltmans Construction Co	189	Whittier, CA	Private	260.1	600	1541
Kokosing Construction Co	190	Fredericktown, OH	Private	260.0	650	1611
Silverado Constructors	191	Irvine, CA	Private	260.0	760	1611
Gr Lakes Dredge & Dock Corp Del	192	Oak Brook, IL	Private	258.3	800	1629
T L James & Co Inc	193	Ruston, LA	Private	252.1	1,377	1611
Foster Wheeler Constrs Inc	194	Clinton, NJ	Public Family Member	251.1	200	1541
John Wland Homes Neighborhoods	195	Atlanta, GA	Private	250.6	800	1531
Railroad Track Construction Co	196	St. Augustine, FL	Public Family Member	250.5	20	1629
Bechtel/Parson, Brinkerhoff	197	Boston, MA	Private	250.0	850	1622
Clancy & Theys Construction Co	198	Raleigh, NC	Private	250.0	400	1541
Daniel J Keating Construction Co	199	Bala Cynwyd, PA	Private	250.0	175	1542
J R Roberts Enterprises	200	Citrus Heights, CA	Private	250.0	230	1542
L F Driscoll Co	201	Bala Cynwyd, PA	Private	250.0	250	1542
Martin K Eby Construction Co	202	Wichita, KS	Private	250.0	1,499	1629
MBK Construction Ltd	203	Irvine, CA	Private	250.0	140	1542
Obayashi U. S. Holdings Inc	204	New York, NY	Private	250.0	160	1542
Pizzagalli Construction Co	205	Burlington, VT	Private	250.0	1,000	1542
Railworks Corp	206	Baltimore, MD	Public	248.0	1,900	1731
Kaufman & Broad of San Diego	207	San Diego, CA	Public Family Member	247.6	57	1522
Harmon, Ltd	208	Minneapolis, MN	Public Family Member	247.3	1,600	1793
Baker Concrete Construction	209	Monroe, OH	Private	247.0	1,500	1771
Kimball Hill Inc	210	Rolling Meadows, IL	Private	245.8	325	1521

D&B COMPANY RANKINGS BY SALES

Company	Rank	Location	Type	Sales ($ mil.)	Employ-ment	Primary SIC
O'Neil Industries, Inc.	211	Chicago, IL	Private	244.7	300	1542
Choice Homes-Texas, Inc	212	Arlington, TX	Private	243.8	268	1521
M B Kahn Construction Co Inc	213	Columbia, SC	Private	242.0	850	1542
Castle & Cooke Inc	214	Los Angeles, CA	Public	241.2	1,322	1522
Washington Homes Inc	215	Landover, MD	Public	240.7	377	1531
California Pacific Homes Inc	216	Irvine, CA	Private	240.0	225	1531
Hubbard Construction Co	217	Winter Park, FL	Private	240.0	1,259	1611
Frank Messer & Sons Constr Co	218	Cincinnati, OH	Private	239.6	400	1542
Comerfords Heating & A/C	219	Pleasanton, CA	Public Family Member	238.7	30	1711
Service Experts Inc	220	Brentwood, TN	Public	238.7	3,500	1711
Slattery Associates Inc (Del)	221	Whitestone, NY	Private	237.9	350	1623
Salmon & Alder Associates	222	Centerville, UT	Private	237.7	70	1711
Dynalectric Co	223	McLean, VA	Public Family Member	237.6	3,200	1731
Balfour Beatty Construction Inc	224	Atlanta, GA	Private	237.1	861	1622
Apac-Carolina Inc	225	Kinston, NC	Public Family Member	236.4	1,000	1611
Taylor Ball, Inc.	226	West Des Moines, IA	Private	235.4	400	1542
R M Shoemaker Holdings Inc	227	West Conshohocken, PA	Private	234.1	125	1541
C F Jordan Inc	228	El Paso, TX	Private	231.1	355	1541
Fletcher Construction Co Hawaii Ltd	229	Honolulu, HI	Private	230.0	900	1542
Resco Holdings Inc	230	Hampton, NH	Public Family Member	229.7	2,000	1629
OC America Construction Inc	231	Los Angeles, CA	Private	229.4	130	1542
S J Amoroso Construction Co	232	Foster City, CA	Private	226.6	300	1542
Dunn Investment Co	233	Birmingham, AL	Private	226.0	992	1542
Baugh Construction Oregon Inc	234	Beaverton, OR	Private	225.0	400	1542
Berry Contracting, LP	235	Corpus Christi, TX	Private	225.0	3,200	1629
Blake Construction Co Inc	236	Washington, DC	Private	225.0	750	1542
Zaring National Corp	237	Cincinnati, OH	Public	224.0	428	1521
Baugh Enterprises Inc	238	Seattle, WA	Private	221.2	1,000	1542
Hog Slat Inc	239	Newton Grove, NC	Private	221.2	1,000	1542
Limbach Co	240	Pittsburgh, PA	Private	220.9	1,249	1711
Gecos Inc	241	Winter Park, FL	Private	220.0	1,000	1611
Okland Construction Co	242	Salt Lake City, UT	Private	220.0	200	1542
Opus West Corp	243	Phoenix, AZ	Private	220.0	150	1542
Perry Homes, a Joint Venture	244	Houston, TX	Private	220.0	200	1531
Walter & Sci Construction USA	245	Renton, WA	Private	219.2	207	1622
Able Telcom Holding Corp	246	West Palm Beach, FL	Public	217.5	2,000	1623
Brice Building Co Inc	247	Birmingham, AL	Private	215.9	730	1542
Bechtel Construction Co	248	San Francisco, CA	Private	215.0	175	1629
San Luis Tank Piping Constr Co	249	Paso Robles, CA	Public Family Member	214.9	90	1791
Williams Group International	250	Stone Mountain, GA	Private	214.1	1,500	1799
R J Griffin & Co	251	Atlanta, GA	Private	212.7	479	1542
Howard S Wright Construction Co	252	Seattle, WA	Private	210.0	300	1542
Robins and Morton Group	253	Birmingham, AL	Private	210.0	250	1542
Centimark Corp	254	Canonsburg, PA	Private	209.2	1,500	1761
Dominion Homes Inc	255	Dublin, OH	Public	207.9	362	1531
New England Power Service Co	256	Westborough, MA	Public Family Member	206.5	1,305	1623
Adolfson & Peterson, Inc	257	Minneapolis, MN	Private	206.0	350	1542
Arb Inc	258	Lake Forest, CA	Private	205.2	700	1542
Continental Homes Inc	259	Scottsdale, AZ	Public Family Member	204.5	650	1531
Marshall Erdman & Associates	260	Madison, WI	Private	204.3	1,112	1542
Barrett Paving Materials Inc	261	Roseland, NJ	Private	203.2	250	1611
Stellar Group Inc	262	Jacksonville, FL	Private	202.6	350	1541
C A Rasmussen Inc	263	Simi Valley, CA	Private	201.7	400	1611
Roy Anderson Corp	264	Gulfport, MS	Private	201.3	300	1542
Baugh Construction Co Inc	265	Seattle, WA	Private	200.0	300	1542
Bell Atlantic Comm Constr Serv	266	Beltsville, MD	Public Family Member	200.0	3,000	1731
Branch Group Inc	267	Roanoke, VA	Private	200.0	700	1542
CCBC Inc.	268	Homewood, IL	Private	200.0	500	1541
Dot Blue Services Inc	269	Deerfield Beach, FL	Public Family Member	200.0	1,375	1711
Ellis-Don Michigan Inc	270	Livonia, MI	Private	200.0	40	1541
Graycor Inc	271	Homewood, IL	Private	200.0	500	1541
Hitt Contracting Inc	272	Fairfax, VA	Private	200.0	413	1542
International Energy Corp	273	Roswell, GA	Private	200.0	115	1542
Kaufman & Broad of N California	274	San Ramon, CA	Public Family Member	200.0	92	1531
Kenny Construction Co	275	Wheeling, IL	Private	200.0	400	1622
Lathrop Co Inc	276	Maumee, OH	Public Family Member	200.0	200	1542
Lehr Construction Corp	277	New York, NY	Private	200.0	130	1542
Linear Construction, Inc.	278	Tucson, AZ	Private	200.0	6	1521
National Energy Production	279	Redmond, WA	Public Family Member	200.0	700	1629
Nationsrent Inc	280	Fort Lauderdale, FL	Public	200.0	1,000	7353

D&B COMPANY RANKINGS BY SALES

Company	Rank	Location	Type	Sales ($ mil.)	Employ- ment	Primary SIC
Piedmont Insulating Co, Inc	281	Danville, VA	Private	200.0	8	1742
Stewart-Ledlow Inc	282	Meridianville, AL	Private	200.0	35	1742
Sycamore Construction Ltd	283	Cincinnati, OH	Private	200.0	80	1522
Tennis Corp of America	284	Chicago, IL	Private	200.0	1,800	1799
Therma Corp	285	San Jose, CA	Private	200.0	1,200	1711
Vecellio & Grogan, Inc.	286	Beckley, WV	Private	200.0	1,200	1611
Winter Construction Co Inc	287	Atlanta, GA	Private	200.0	360	1542
Owl Companies	288	Irvine, CA	Private	199.4	1,500	1629
Fluor Daniel Caribbean Inc	289	Irvine, CA	Public Family Member	199.2	1,572	1541
O & G Industries Inc	290	Torrington, CT	Private	198.9	649	1542
Ryan Properties, Inc.	291	Minneapolis, MN	Private	198.8	450	1542
Forecast Group, LP	292	Rancho Cucamonga, CA	Private	198.1	188	1531
Braddock & Logan Group L.P.	293	Danville, CA	Private	197.8	629	1531
Chas H Tompkins Co	294	Washington, DC	Private	197.8	149	1542
Apac-Tennessee Inc	295	Alcoa, TN	Public Family Member	196.6	400	1611
R.A.S. Builders, Inc	296	Englewood, CO	Private	195.9	150	1542
Douglas E Barnhart Inc	297	San Diego, CA	Private	195.0	250	1542
Capital Pacific Holdings Inc	298	Newport Beach, CA	Public	191.1	217	1531
Apac-Georgia Inc	299	Smyrna, GA	Public Family Member	190.8	1,500	1611
Paclantic Construction Inc	300	Pleasanton, CA	Private	190.2	1,500	1541
H & M Construction Co., Inc	301	Jackson, TN	Private	190.0	250	1541
Ryan Companies U.S., Inc	302	Minneapolis, MN	Private	189.3	450	1542
Holloway Construction Co	303	Wixom, MI	Private	189.2	NA	1611
E M J Corp	304	Chattanooga, TN	Private	188.9	200	1542
Lennar Homes of California	305	Mission Viejo, CA	Public Family Member	188.0	90	1531
Horton D R Texas LP	306	Arlington, TX	Public Family Member	186.9	250	1521
Traylor Bros Inc	307	Evansville, IN	Private	185.7	1,000	1622
Fischbach & Moore Electric LLC	308	New Providence, NJ	Private	185.6	2,500	1731
G L Homes of Florida Corp	309	Pompano Beach, FL	Private	185.0	170	1521
Linbeck Corp	310	Houston, TX	Private	185.0	760	1542
Sellen Construction Co Inc	311	Seattle, WA	Private	184.8	500	1542
BCI Construction, Inc	312	Wichita, KS	Public Family Member	182.9	80	1542
Richmond Am Homes of California	313	Concord, CA	Public Family Member	182.4	300	1521
Centex Rodgers Construction Co	314	Nashville, TN	Public Family Member	180.0	200	1542
Ruscilli Construction Co Inc	315	Columbus, OH	Private	180.0	110	1541
Kvaerner Songer, Inc.	316	Washington, PA	Private	179.0	500	1711
Motor City Electric Co	317	Detroit, MI	Private	179.0	600	1731
Abrams Industries Inc	318	Atlanta, GA	Public	178.6	250	1541
Big D Construction Corp	319	Ogden, UT	Private	177.0	300	1541
Southland Industries	320	Long Beach, CA	Private	176.9	521	1711
C-B-R Development Co., Inc.	321	Spartanburg, SC	Public Family Member	176.5	800	1542
Royal Imperial Group Inc	322	Chicago, IL	Private	176.5	800	1542
W M Grace Companies Inc	323	Phoenix, AZ	Private	176.5	800	1542
Mercedes Homes Inc	324	Melbourne, FL	Private	175.8	502	1521
Milestone Contractors, L.P.	325	Indianapolis, IN	Private	175.0	250	1611
Monsanto Enviro-Chem Systems	326	Chesterfield, MO	Public Family Member	175.0	550	1629
Choate Construction Co	327	Marietta, GA	Private	173.5	360	1542
E L Yeager Construction Co	328	Riverside, CA	Private	171.6	650	1611
Yeager Holdings, Inc	329	Riverside, CA	Private	171.6	500	1611
Amrep Corp	330	New York, NY	Public	171.4	1,500	1521
Beazer Homes Arizona Inc	331	Tempe, AZ	Public Family Member	170.5	60	1521
Rea Construction Co	332	Charlotte, NC	Private	170.2	900	1611
Bayley Construction, a Gen Partnr	333	Seattle, WA	Private	170.0	75	1542
Century Contractors Inc	334	Matthews, NC	Private	170.0	900	1541
Warmington Homes	335	Costa Mesa, CA	Private	170.0	246	1531
Batson-Cook Co	336	West Point, GA	Private	169.9	400	1542
McGough Construction Co, Inc	337	St. Paul, MN	Private	168.0	250	1542
Summit Companies of Jacksonville	338	Jacksonville, FL	Private	167.8	100	1542
Summit Contractors Inc	339	Jacksonville, FL	Private	167.8	100	1542
Sovereign Homes Corp	340	Dallas, TX	Private	167.5	175	1521
Rosendin Electric Inc	341	San Jose, CA	Private	166.7	1,200	1731
U.S. Contractors Inc	342	Clute, TX	Private	165.7	1,800	1629
Giant Construction Co	343	Landover, MD	Private	165.4	750	1542
Dal-Mac Construction Co	344	Richardson, TX	Private	165.0	300	1542
Weeks Marine Inc	345	Cranford, NJ	Private	164.5	500	1629
Newmark Home Corp	346	Sugar Land, TX	Public	164.0	200	1531
Harmony Corp of Texas	347	Pasadena, TX	Private	163.0	40	1541
Diamond Home Services (Del)	348	Woodstock, IL	Public	161.1	1,200	1761
Nabors International Inc	349	Houston, TX	Public Family Member	160.9	1,650	7353
Rottlund Co Inc	350	St. Paul, MN	Public	160.8	248	1531

D&B COMPANY RANKINGS BY SALES

Company	Rank	Location	Type	Sales ($ mil.)	Employ-ment	Primary SIC
Hydrochem Industrial Services	351	Deer Park, TX	Public Family Member	160.6	1,700	1799
E C Co	352	Portland, OR	Private	160.0	800	1731
Dematteo/Flat Iron	353	Boston, MA	Private	160.0	200	1611
Hunt Building Corp	354	El Paso, TX	Private	160.0	170	1522
Integrated Energy Services	355	Atlanta, GA	Private	160.0	150	1711
Michels Pipeline Construction	356	Brownsville, WI	Private	158.0	500	1623
Synergism Inc	357	Sunnyvale, CA	Private	157.5	800	1731
Northwest Racing Associates Lp	358	Auburn, WA	Private	157.0	300	1629
Graham Companies	359	Hialeah, FL	Private	156.7	650	1531
Regis Homes Corp	360	Irvine, CA	Private	156.7	500	1531
Safe Sites of Colorado, LLC	361	Golden, CO	Public Family Member	156.4	637	1799
Cianbro Corp	362	Pittsfield, ME	Private	156.3	1,400	1629
Barnhill Contracting Co	363	Tarboro, NC	Private	156.2	920	1611
Winchester Homes Inc	364	Greenbelt, MD	Public Family Member	156.0	220	1531
Clayco Construction Co	365	St. Louis, MO	Private	155.9	500	1541
Meritage Corp	366	Scottsdale, AZ	Public	155.1	190	1521
Richmond American Homes, Inc.	367	Phoenix, AZ	Public Family Member	155.1	90	1521
Structure-Tone, Inc	368	New York, NY	Private	154.2	700	1542
W E O'Neil Construction Co	369	Chicago, IL	Private	153.7	200	1542
Comstock Holdings Inc	370	White Plains, NY	Public Family Member	153.6	1,007	1731
L K Comstock & Co Inc	371	White Plains, NY	Public Family Member	153.6	1,007	1731
I A Holdings Corp	372	Concordville, PA	Private	153.4	450	1622
Spaw Glass Holding Corp	373	Houston, TX	Private	152.7	170	1542
Miller Building Corp	374	Wilmington, NC	Private	152.5	450	1541
G E Johnson Construction Co	375	Colorado Springs, CO	Private	152.2	300	1542
Green Holdings Inc	376	Denver, CA	Private	151.3	1,200	1611
Odebrecht Contractors of Florida	377	Coral Gables, FL	Private	151.2	740	1622
Venture Construction Co	378	Norcross, GA	Private	150.7	300	1542
Stiles Corp	379	Fort Lauderdale, FL	Private	150.5	250	1541
Airdex Air Conditioning Corp	380	Pinellas Park, FL	Public Family Member	150.0	12	1711
Angelo Iafrate Construction Co	381	Warren, MI	Private	150.0	500	1611
Beacon Skanska Construction Co	382	Boston, MA	Private	150.0	160	1542
Dynamic Systems, Inc	383	Austin, TX	Private	150.0	1,000	1711
Eichleay Holdings Inc	384	Pittsburgh, PA	Private	150.0	2,500	1541
Flatiron Structures Co LLC	385	Longmont, CO	Private	150.0	320	1622
Fulton Homes Corp	386	Tempe, AZ	Private	150.0	60	1521
Global Construction Co LLC	387	Bala Cynwyd, PA	Private	150.0	80	1521
Howa Construction, Inc	388	Salt Lake City, UT	Private	150.0	70	1542
Jones Bros Inc	389	Mount Juliet, TN	Private	150.0	1,000	1622
Nova Corp	390	Englewood, NJ	Private	150.0	60	1542
Q I Corp	391	Alpharetta, GA	Private	150.0	1,350	1742
SCL Construction	392	Springfield, VA	Private	150.0	21	1521
Tidewater Construction Corp	393	Virginia Beach, VA	Private	150.0	1,000	1541
Tully Construction Co Inc	394	Flushing, NY	Private	150.0	250	1611
W M Jordan Co Inc	395	Newport News, VA	Private	150.0	200	1542
Waste Management Indus Services	396	La Porte, TX	Public Family Member	150.0	2,500	1799
Zamias Construction Co Inc	397	Johnstown, PA	Private	150.0	20	1542
Meadow Valley Corp	398	Phoenix, AZ	Public	150.0	450	1611
Lakeside Industries	399	Issaquah, WA	Private	149.4	150	1611
Framatome USA Inc	400	Arlington, VA	Private	148.5	2,000	1731
Cleveland Group Inc	401	Atlanta, GA	Private	147.8	255	1542
J F White Contracting Co	402	Newton, MA	Private	147.7	180	1622
Weatherford U.S., Inc	403	Houston, TX	Public Family Member	147.3	1,511	7353
Woodrow Taylor Homes Inc	404	Laguna Hills, CA	Private	147.3	183	1521
Murphy Mech Contractors Engineers	405	St. Louis, MO	Private	146.6	700	1711
Abrams Construction, Inc.	406	Atlanta, GA	Public Family Member	146.6	80	1542
Philip St, Inc.	407	Houston, TX	Private	146.6	1,278	1629
Casey Industrial Inc	408	Albany, OR	Private	146.3	1,153	1541
American Bridge Co	409	Pittsburgh, PA	Private	146.0	400	1791
Gerald H Phipps Inc	410	Denver, CO	Private	146.0	300	1542
Jack B Parson Companies	411	Ogden, UT	Private	145.5	662	1611
Boran Craig Barbr Engel Constr	412	Naples, FL	Private	145.3	350	1522
CEC Investment Corp	413	Pittsburgh, PA	Private	145.0	928	1791
Pike Industries, Inc	414	Belmont, NH	Private	145.0	225	1611
Target General Inc	415	Phoenix, AZ	Private	145.0	80	1542
Harlan Electric Co	416	Rochester Hills, MI	Public Family Member	144.7	1,950	1731
Homes Holding Corp	417	Tampa, FL	Public Family Member	144.5	1,043	1521
Cupertino Electric Inc	418	Sunnyvale, CA	Private	143.6	675	1731
Caddell Construction Co Inc	419	Montgomery, AL	Private	143.0	350	1542
Kinsley Construction, Inc	420	York, PA	Private	143.0	700	1541

D&B COMPANY RANKINGS BY SALES

Company	Rank	Location	Type	Sales ($ mil.)	Employ-ment	Primary SIC
Main Street Operating Co Inc	421	Nashville, TN	Private	143.0	650	1542
Wilder Construction Co	422	Everett, WA	Private	142.7	250	1611
Charles N White Construction Co	423	Clarksdale, MS	Private	142.4	200	1542
Neff Corp	424	Miami, FL	Public	142.0	1,100	7353
Shimizu America Corp	425	Los Angeles, CA	Private	142.0	138	1542
Gale Industries Inc	426	Daytona Beach, FL	Public Family Member	141.7	2,448	1742
Jim Walter Homes Inc	427	Tampa, FL	Public Family Member	141.2	1,020	1521
M W Holdings Inc	428	Detroit, MI	Private	141.1	400	1791
Fishel Co	429	Columbus, OH	Private	140.9	1,200	1623
Anthony and Sylvan Pools Corp	430	Doylestown, PA	Public Family Member	140.0	800	1799
Edward Kraemer & Sons Inc	431	Plain, WI	Private	140.0	300	1622
Elgin National Industries Inc	432	Downers Grove, IL	Private	139.6	672	1629
Colson & Colson Gen Contractors	433	Salem, OR	Private	138.7	75	1522
Lechase Construction Services LLC	434	Rochester, NY	Private	138.2	300	1542
Schuff Steel Co	435	Phoenix, AZ	Public	138.2	781	1791
Power Plant Maintenance Co	436	Society Hill, SC	Private	137.6	1,200	1629
Keller Foundations, Inc	437	Odenton, MD	Private	136.4	300	1799
Berry GP, Inc	438	Corpus Christi, TX	Private	135.0	2,733	1629
C D Henderson Property Co	439	Garland, TX	Private	135.0	120	1542
General Construction Co	440	Seattle, WA	Private	135.0	500	1622
Hardaway Co Inc	441	Columbus, GA	Private	135.0	600	1622
M W Builders, Inc	442	Shawnee Mission, KS	Private	135.0	300	1542
Michael/Curry Companies, Inc	443	Minneapolis, MN	Private	135.0	400	1542
N.L. Barnes Construction, Inc	444	San Francisco, CA	Private	135.0	200	1542
S B C C, Inc	445	Campbell, CA	Private	135.0	130	1542
Wohlsen Construction Co	446	Lancaster, PA	Private	135.0	375	1542
Gall, Landau Young Construction Co	447	Bellevue, WA	Private	134.7	200	1542
Sletten Inc	448	Great Falls, MT	Private	134.7	200	1542
Morrow-Meadows Corp	449	Walnut, CA	Private	134.3	820	1731
Fisk Electric Co	450	Houston, TX	Private	134.1	1,500	1731
Blythe Construction Inc	451	Charlotte, NC	Private	134.0	500	1611
Red Simpson Inc	452	Alexandria, LA	Private	133.9	1,780	1623
Production Management Companies	453	Harvey, LA	Private	133.3	1,162	1629
New Fortis Corp	454	King, NC	Public Family Member	133.0	190	1521
Western States Fire Protection	455	Englewood, CO	Private	132.3	700	1711
Fieldstone Communities Inc	456	Newport Beach, CA	Private	132.0	130	1531
Bell Corp of Rochester	457	Rochester, NY	Private	131.9	600	1542
H J Russell & Co	458	Atlanta, GA	Private	131.9	600	1542
Vratsinas Construction Co	459	Little Rock, AR	Private	131.8	154	1542
Sundance Homes, Inc.	460	Chicago, IL	Public	131.6	140	1531
Jones Co Custom Homes Inc	461	St. Louis, MO	Private	131.2	350	1521
Adc Systems Integration, Inc.	462	Chickamauga, GA	Public Family Member	130.0	1,000	1731
American Sports Products Group	463	White Plains, NY	Private	130.0	300	1629
GVL Contractors LLC	464	Milton, MA	Private	130.0	56	1521
Harbor View Holdings, Inc	465	San Francisco, CA	Private	130.0	2,500	1522
KCI Constructors, Inc.	466	Houston, TX	Public Family Member	130.0	NA	1541
Sloan Construction Co	467	Greenville, SC	Private	130.0	400	1611
W S Bellows Construction Corp	468	Houston, TX	Private	130.0	300	1542
Avatar Holdings Inc	469	Miami, FL	Public	129.1	1,030	1521
P J Dick Inc	470	West Mifflin, PA	Private	129.0	200	1542
Roel Construction Co, Inc	471	San Diego, CA	Private	128.3	260	1542
J H Findorff & Son Inc	472	Madison, WI	Private	128.1	300	1542
Worth Construction Inc	473	Bethel, CT	Private	128.0	125	1542
J H Kelly LLC	474	Longview, WA	Private	127.8	800	1711
Shawmut Woodworking & Supply	475	Boston, MA	Private	126.7	179	1542
Toll Holdings, Inc	476	Huntingdon Valley, PA	Public Family Member	125.2	905	1521
Broadmoor	477	Metairie, LA	Private	125.0	120	1541
Colony Homes L P	478	Woodstock, GA	Private	125.0	80	1521
E W Howell Co Inc	479	Port Washington, NY	Private	125.0	200	1542
Henegan Construction Co Inc	480	New York, NY	Private	125.0	105	1542
Tdindustries, Inc.	481	Dallas, TX	Private	125.0	918	1711
Grupe Co (Inc)	482	Stockton, CA	Private	124.8	400	1531
Mount Hope Rock Products Inc	483	Wharton, NJ	Private	124.7	200	1611
Danis Building Construction Co	484	Dayton, OH	Private	124.6	235	1542
Joe E Woods Inc	485	Mesa, AZ	Private	124.6	150	1522
Bergelectric Corp	486	Los Angeles, CA	Private	124.3	900	1731
Nason & Cullen Group Inc	487	King of Prussia, PA	Private	123.3	195	1542
Universal Constructors Inc	488	McMinnville, TN	Private	123.3	55	1522
Gonsalves & Santucci Inc	489	Concord, CA	Private	122.5	300	1541
Calton Homes Inc	490	Englishtown, NJ	Public Family Member	122.0	101	1531

D&B COMPANY RANKINGS BY SALES

Company	Rank	Location	Type	Sales ($ mil.)	Employ-ment	Primary SIC
J C Higgins Corp	491	Stoughton, MA	Public Family Member	122.0	598	1711
Peck/Jones Construction Corp	492	Los Angeles, CA	Private	122.0	119	1542
J A Tiberti Construction Co	493	Las Vegas, NV	Private	121.8	60	1542
DJB Construction Group, Inc	494	Raleigh, NC	Private	121.5	228	1541
River City Construction L.L.C.	495	East Peoria, IL	Private	120.9	250	1542
Klinger Companies, Inc	496	Sioux City, IA	Private	120.7	550	1542
Arctic Slope Region Construction Co	497	Barrow, AK	Private	120.4	1,600	1623
Levitt Corp	498	New York, NY	Private	120.4	493	1531
Brand Scaffold Service, Inc	499	Chesterfield, MO	Private	120.1	2,000	1799
Bor-Son Construction, Inc	500	Minneapolis, MN	Private	120.0	350	1542
Concord Development Corp Ill	501	Palatine, IL	Private	120.0	140	1521
F N Thompson Co	502	Charlotte, NC	Private	120.0	130	1542
Fullman Co, LLC	503	Portland, OR	Private	120.0	600	1711
ICF Kaiser Advanced Technology	504	Boise, ID	Private	120.0	150	1541
Interstate Highway Construction	505	Englewood, CO	Private	120.0	250	1611
Leopardo Companies, Inc.	506	Glendale Heights, IL	Private	120.0	175	1542
Lunda Construction Co	507	Black River Falls, WI	Private	120.0	700	1622
Matzel Mmford Organization	508	Hazlet, NJ	Private	120.0	100	1521
Micron Construction Inc	509	Boise, ID	Private	120.0	150	1541
North Bros, Inc	510	Atlanta, GA	Private	120.0	240	1742
Northern Pipeline Construction Co	511	Phoenix, AZ	Public Family Member	120.0	765	1623
S H Fleming & Co Inc	512	Upper Darby, PA	Private	120.0	20	1721
Walsh Construction Co	513	Portland, OR	Private	120.0	350	1522
Powell Construction Co	514	Johnson City, TN	Private	119.0	500	1542
Anco Insulations Inc	515	Baton Rouge, LA	Private	119.0	1,800	1742
MP Water Resources Group, Inc	516	Duluth, MN	Public Family Member	119.0	589	1623
Williard Inc	517	Jenkintown, PA	Private	118.7	500	1711
Allan A Myers Inc	518	Worcester, PA	Private	118.2	760	1629
CCC Group Inc	519	San Antonio, TX	Private	118.2	700	1541
Gilbert Companies, Inc	520	Parker City, IN	Private	118.1	1,030	1629
Townsend Acquisition Inc	521	Muncie, IN	Private	118.1	1,030	1629
Odebrecht of America, Inc.	522	Washington, DC	Private	117.8	750	1622
Shiel-Sexton Co Inc	523	Indianapolis, IN	Private	116.4	150	1542
Welded Construction Co	524	Perrysburg, OH	Private	116.4	700	1623
Jeffrey C Stone Inc	525	Phoenix, AZ	Private	116.3	140	1542
John E Green Co	526	Detroit, MI	Private	116.0	350	1711
NSC Corp	527	Methuen, MA	Public	116.0	850	1799
Facility Group Inc	528	Smyrna, GA	Private	115.8	225	1541
C Raimondo & Sons Constr Co	529	Fort Lee, NJ	Private	115.5	200	1542
Apac-Missouri, Inc.	530	Columbia, MO	Public Family Member	115.0	200	1611
Catalfumo Construction and Dev	531	Palm Beach Gardens, FL	Private	115.0	125	1542
Hardaway Group Inc	532	Nashville, TN	Private	115.0	657	1542
Tellepsen Corp	533	Houston, TX	Private	115.0	300	1542
Thos S Byrne Inc	534	Fort Worth, TX	Private	115.0	150	1542
Welcon Management Co	535	Wilson, NC	Private	115.0	1,203	1731
John Moriarty & Associates	536	Winchester, MA	Private	114.9	60	1542
Eby Corp	537	Wichita, KS	Private	114.6	1,000	1629
Timec Acquisition Corp	538	Vallejo, CA	Private	114.6	1,000	1629
Landstar Development Corp	539	Coral Gables, FL	Private	114.5	150	1521
Levitt Homes Inc	540	Boca Raton, FL	Private	114.4	400	1522
Rosemont Exposition Services Inc	541	Des Plaines, IL	Private	114.4	900	1541
Apac-Alabama Inc	542	Birmingham, AL	Public Family Member	114.3	450	1611
F.N.F. Construction, Inc.	543	Tempe, AZ	Private	114.2	300	1611
R & D Thiel Inc	544	Belvidere, IL	Private	114.2	900	1751
National Capital Companies Ltd	545	State College, PA	Private	113.8	1,200	1522
Ritchie Corp	546	Wichita, KS	Private	113.7	330	1611
Goodman Family of Builders	547	Plano, TX	Private	113.7	156	1521
Kimmins Corp	548	Tampa, FL	Public	113.5	575	1799
James McHugh Construction Co	549	Chicago, IL	Private	113.5	400	1542
John J Kirlin Inc	550	Rockville, MD	Private	113.2	1,200	1711
Byers Locate Services, LLC	551	Atlanta, GA	Private	112.9	1,500	1623
Cajun Constructors, Inc.	552	Baton Rouge, LA	Private	112.0	600	1623
E E Black Ltd	553	Honolulu, HI	Private	112.0	800	1629
G W Murphy Construction Co	554	Honolulu, HI	Private	112.0	250	1542
Shook National Corp	555	Dayton, OH	Private	112.0	266	1629
Soltek of San Diego	556	San Diego, CA	Private	111.9	150	1542
Perseus Fisk, LLC	557	Houston, TX	Private	111.3	1,500	1731
C E D Construction Partners	558	Maitland, FL	Private	111.2	15	1522
Richmond Am Homes of Virginia	559	Fairfax, VA	Public Family Member	111.1	190	1521
C D Smith Construction Inc	560	Fond Du Lac, WI	Private	110.9	380	1542

D&B COMPANY RANKINGS BY SALES

Company	Rank	Location	Type	Sales ($ mil.)	Employ-ment	Primary SIC
Conex International Corp	561	Beaumont, TX	Private	110.6	NA	1629
Commercial Contracting Corp	562	Troy, MI	Private	110.5	200	1796
D L Withers Construction LC	563	Phoenix, AZ	Private	110.1	70	1542
Abrams International Inc	564	Austin, TX	Private	110.0	600	1611
Baker/Mellon Stuart Constr Inc	565	Coraopolis, PA	Public Family Member	110.0	150	1542
C F Jordan Residential LP	566	El Paso, TX	Private	110.0	50	1522
Fullmer Construction	567	Ontario, CA	Private	110.0	210	1541
Jones Brothers Construction Corp	568	Los Angeles, CA	Private	110.0	119	1542
L E Wentz Co	569	San Carlos, CA	Private	110.0	125	1542
LP Snyder Langston	570	Irvine, CA	Private	110.0	100	1542
Midwest Mechanical Contractors Inc	571	Shawnee Mission, KS	Private	110.0	200	1711
Performance Contractors, Inc.	572	Baton Rouge, LA	Private	110.0	1,000	1541
R J Pomplun Co	573	Petersburg, VA	Private	110.0	5	1521
Watson Electrical Construction Co	574	Wilson, NC	Public Family Member	110.0	1,200	1731
U.S. Engineering Co	575	Kansas City, MO	Private	109.6	525	1711
Horst Group Inc	576	Lancaster, PA	Private	109.5	500	1542
Cal Dive International Inc	577	Houston, TX	Public	109.4	432	1629
RR Westminster Holding DE Corp	578	New York, NY	Private	109.4	300	1542
MBC Holdings, Inc	579	Archbold, OH	Private	109.2	341	1611
CDK Contracting Co	580	Farmington, NM	Private	109.2	700	1541
FK Co, Inc	581	Farmington, NM	Private	109.2	700	1541
Lewis Homes of California	582	Upland, CA	Private	108.9	NA	1531
FCL Builders, Inc.	583	Itasca, IL	Private	108.8	35	1541
United Homes Inc	584	Rolling Meadows, IL	Private	108.5	55	1521
National Refrigeration Services	585	Atlanta, GA	Private	108.5	1,150	1711
Amelco Corp	586	Gardena, CA	Private	107.9	450	1731
Rogers-O'Brien Construction Co	587	Dallas, TX	Private	107.9	188	1541
Lewis Lease Crutcher	588	Seattle, WA	Private	107.3	490	1542
Pardee Construction Co of Nevada	589	Las Vegas, NV	Public Family Member	107.0	100	1521
MCC Group, L.L.C.	590	Metairie, LA	Private	106.9	250	1711
A & L Industrial Constr & Maint	591	Kingsport, TN	Private	106.8	840	1541
Barclay White Inc	592	Berwyn, PA	Private	106.5	146	1542
W W Investment Co	593	St. Louis, MO	Private	106.5	1,236	1799
Western Group Inc	594	St. Louis, MO	Private	106.5	1,236	1799
Willbros USA, Inc	595	Tulsa, OK	Private	106.4	700	1623
Armada/Hoffler Construction Co	596	Chesapeake, VA	Private	106.0	120	1542
Ceco Concrete Construction LLC	597	Kansas City, MO	Private	105.9	1,200	1799
Dimeo Construction Co	598	Providence, RI	Private	105.9	170	1542
Catellus Residential Group	599	Irvine, CA	Public Family Member	105.3	150	1531
Ivey Mechanical Co	600	Kosciusko, MS	Public Family Member	105.0	750	1711
Ragnar Benson, Inc.	601	Park Ridge, IL	Private	104.8	150	1541
Amrep Southwest Inc	602	Rio Rancho, NM	Public Family Member	104.8	193	1521
Platte River Constructors	603	Aurora, CO	Private	104.8	51	1611
Centex Forcum Lannom Inc	604	Dyersburg, TN	Public Family Member	104.6	250	1541
Albert C Kobayashi Inc	605	Waipahu, HI	Private	104.6	175	1542
Crowder Construction Co	606	Charlotte, NC	Private	104.0	700	1629
Tri-City Electrical Contractors	607	Altamonte Springs, FL	Public Family Member	104.0	1,250	1731
Cleveland Construction Inc	608	Mentor, OH	Private	103.9	500	1542
R Sanders & Assoc Custom Builders	609	Dallas, TX	Private	103.6	89	1521
Jaynes Corp	610	Albuquerque, NM	Private	103.5	250	1542
Taisei America Corp	611	Long Beach, CA	Private	103.0	82	1541
J D Abrams Inc	612	Austin, TX	Private	102.5	572	1611
Jay Cashman Inc	613	Boston, MA	Private	102.4	200	1629
Interbeton Inc	614	Rockland, MA	Private	102.3	500	1629
Korte Construction Co	615	St. Louis, MO	Private	102.3	250	1541
Realen Homes Construction Co	616	Ambler, PA	Private	102.0	125	1531
F A Wilhelm Construction Co	617	Indianapolis, IN	Private	101.7	800	1541
Jesco Inc	618	Tupelo, MS	Private	101.7	800	1541
Onyx Pipeline Co LC	619	Corpus Christi, TX	Private	101.4	10	1623
Tilcon Inc	620	New Britain, CT	Private	100.8	1,561	1611
Engelberth Construction Inc	621	Colchester, VT	Private	100.8	240	1542
G J F Construction Corp	622	New York, NY	Private	100.4	120	1542
Charter Builders, Inc.	623	Dallas, TX	Private	100.3	50	1542
20th Century Construction Co	624	Painesville, OH	Private	100.0	5	1521
A V Partnership	625	Irvine, CA	Private	100.0	70	1521
Actus Corp/Sundt, Joint Venture	626	Napa, CA	Private	100.0	100	1521
Ajax Paving Industries Inc	627	Madison Heights, MI	Private	100.0	300	1611
Anderson Columbia Co Inc	628	Lake City, FL	Private	100.0	650	1611
Atlantic Coast Mechanical Inc	629	Raleigh, NC	Private	100.0	150	1711
Bostic Brothers Construction Inc	630	Burlington, NC	Private	100.0	60	1522

D&B COMPANY RANKINGS BY SALES

Company	Rank	Location	Type	Sales ($ mil.)	Employ-ment	Primary SIC
Brinderson	631	Newport Beach, CA	Private	100.0	500	1629
Buffington Homes Inc	632	Austin, TX	Public Family Member	100.0	160	1521
C W Matthews Contracting Co	633	Marietta, GA	Private	100.0	540	1622
Davis Electrical Constructors	634	Greenville, SC	Public Family Member	100.0	1,000	1731
E E Reed Construction LC	635	Sugar Land, TX	Private	100.0	125	1542
Equipment Supply Co Inc	636	Burlington, NJ	Public Family Member	100.0	250	7353
FTR International Inc	637	Irvine, CA	Private	100.0	300	1542
Gary Merlino Construction Co	638	Seattle, WA	Private	100.0	325	1611
General Pacific Construction	639	South Pasadena, CA	Private	100.0	10	1542
Geupel De Mars Inc	640	Indianapolis, IN	Private	100.0	100	1542
Hendrickson/Scalamade	641	Farmingdale, NY	Private	100.0	400	1622
Houston-Stafford Electric	642	Stafford, TX	Public Family Member	100.0	1,200	1731
K-Five Construction Corp	643	Lemont, IL	Private	100.0	80	1611
Keene Constr Co of Central Florida	644	Maitland, FL	Private	100.0	150	1542
Keller Construction Co Ltd	645	El Monte, CA	Private	100.0	50	1542
Layton Construction Co	646	Sandy, UT	Private	100.0	300	1542
Loftin Constructors, Inc.	647	Brandon, MS	Private	100.0	400	1542
Lyda Inc	648	San Antonio, TX	Private	100.0	300	1542
Melody Homes Inc	649	Broomfield, CO	Public Family Member	100.0	85	1521
Mitchell Construction Co	650	Vidalia, GA	Private	100.0	550	1542
Myler Co Inc	651	Crawfordsville, IN	Private	100.0	75	1542
Natkin Contracting LLC	652	Englewood, CO	Private	100.0	200	1711
Ninteman Construction Co	653	San Diego, CA	Private	100.0	271	1542
Oldcastle Northwest Inc	654	Tukwila, WA	Private	100.0	250	1629
Orleans Corp	655	Bensalem, PA	Public Family Member	100.0	165	1521
Owner-Builder-Alliance Inc	656	West Palm Beach, FL	Private	100.0	2	1521
Pasquinelli Construction Co	657	Homewood, IL	Private	100.0	75	1531
Pike Co Inc	658	Rochester, NY	Private	100.0	200	1542
Roxco Ltd	659	Brandon, MS	Private	100.0	450	1542
Royce Homes, Inc	660	Houston, TX	Private	100.0	412	1521
Shelly & Sands Inc	661	Zanesville, OH	Private	100.0	600	1611
Stahl Construction Co	662	Hopkins, MN	Private	100.0	55	1542
Superfos Construction (U.S.)	663	Dothan, AL	Private	100.0	2,500	1611
VHC, Inc	664	Green Bay, WI	Private	100.0	1,100	1731
Warde Electric Contracting	665	Congers, NY	Private	100.0	100	1731
Weis Builders, Inc	666	Minneapolis, MN	Private	100.0	100	1542
Winter Park Construction Co	667	Maitland, FL	Private	100.0	83	1522
Rocky Mountain Remed Serv LLC	668	Golden, CO	Private	100.0	700	1799
Icom Mechanical Inc	669	San Jose, CA	Private	99.9	300	1711
Lexington Homes, L.L.C.	670	Libertyville, IL	Private	99.8	140	1531
Granger Management Corp	671	Shrewsbury, MA	Private	99.8	214	1542
Granger Northern Inc	672	Portland, ME	Private	99.8	40	1542
Embree Construction Group	673	Georgetown, TX	Private	99.6	101	1542
A C and S, Inc	674	Lancaster, PA	Public Family Member	99.0	800	1742
Austin Industrial Inc	675	Houston, TX	Private	99.0	1,050	1711
J F Ahern Co	676	Fond Du Lac, WI	Private	98.5	500	1711
J P Cullen & Sons Inc	677	Janesville, WI	Private	98.4	350	1542
Global Energy Eqp Group LLC	678	Tulsa, OK	Private	98.3	450	1542
Airtron Inc	679	Dayton, OH	Public Family Member	98.0	600	1711
Viceroy, Inc.	680	Pasadena, TX	Public Family Member	97.9	549	1629
Apac-Florida Inc	681	Sarasota, FL	Public Family Member	97.8	600	1611
Marley Holdings L P	682	New York, NY	Private	97.8	1,800	1781
Chicago Bridge & Iron Co Ill	683	Plainfield, IL	Private	97.4	1,080	1791
Williams Industries Inc	684	Houston, TX	Private	97.0	200	1542
Westra Construction Inc	685	Waupun, WI	Private	96.6	275	1542
Herman Goldner Co Inc	686	Philadelphia, PA	Private	96.3	350	1711
Walker Engineering Inc	687	Dallas, TX	Public Family Member	96.0	850	1731
Industrial Services Tech	688	Denver, CO	Private	95.8	900	1541
Rentenbach Eng Co	689	Knoxville, TN	Private	95.8	200	1541
Atlantic Plant Maintenance	690	Pasadena, TX	Public Family Member	95.2	470	1629
Branch Highways Inc	691	Roanoke, VA	Private	95.0	350	1611
Federated Home & Mortgage Co	692	State College, PA	Private	95.0	1,000	1522
Gem Industrial Inc	693	Walbridge, OH	Private	95.0	1,000	1711
Holly Management LLC	694	Dallas, TX	Private	95.0	270	1521
Pinkerton & Laws Inc	695	Atlanta, GA	Private	95.0	100	1542
Western National Properties	696	Irvine, CA	Private	95.0	1,000	1522
Adco Electrical Corp	697	Staten Island, NY	Private	94.9	400	1731
Hawkins Construction Co	698	Omaha, NE	Private	94.7	250	1542
Egan Companies	699	Minneapolis, MN	Private	94.7	675	1711
Newtron Group, Inc	700	Baton Rouge, LA	Private	94.6	1,750	1731

D&B COMPANY RANKINGS BY SALES

Company	Rank	Location	Type	Sales ($ mil.)	Employ- ment	Primary SIC
Freesen, Inc	701	Bluffs, IL	Private	94.5	250	1629
C R Meyer & Sons Co	702	Oshkosh, WI	Private	94.5	250	1541
Jupiter Industries, Inc.	703	Northbrook, IL	Private	94.3	1,000	1711
Poole & Kent Corp	704	Baltimore, MD	Private	94.3	1,000	1711
Scott Companies Inc	705	San Leandro, CA	Private	94.3	1,000	1711
Dualstar Technologies Corp	706	Long Island City, NY	Public	94.3	404	1711
Norwood Co	707	West Chester, PA	Private	94.2	130	1542
Oakwood Homes LLC	708	Englewood, CO	Private	93.9	120	1521
F H Paschen, S N Nielsen, Inc.	709	Des Plaines, IL	Private	93.8	150	1542
Lombardy Holdings	710	Whittier, CA	Private	93.5	755	1623
Berkshire Realty Co Inc	711	Atlanta, GA	Private	93.0	15	1522
Communications Construction Group	712	West Chester, PA	Public Family Member	93.0	750	1623
Hovnanian Pennsylvania Inc	713	Edison, NJ	Public Family Member	92.9	300	1531
Oxford Holdings, Inc	714	Fort Lauderdale, FL	Private	92.8	425	1542
Transeastern Properties Inc	715	Pompano Beach, FL	Private	92.8	100	1521
Bonitz of South Carolina Inc	716	Columbia, SC	Private	92.5	850	1742
Baylor Health Enterprises Inc	717	Dallas, TX	Private	91.6	300	1542
Howe-Baker Engineers, Inc	718	Tyler, TX	Private	91.6	300	1629
Stevens Painton Corp	719	Cleveland, OH	Private	91.4	500	1541
O'Connell Companies Inc	720	Holyoke, MA	Private	91.2	450	1541
Cal-Air Inc	721	Whittier, CA	Private	91.0	965	1711
Flint Engineering & Construction Co	722	Tulsa, OK	Private	91.0	1,100	1623
Air Systems, Inc	723	San Jose, CA	Private	91.0	120	1711
Phillips & Jordan Inc	724	Knoxville, TN	Private	90.7	750	1629
Iteq Storage Systems, Inc	725	Houston, TX	Private	90.2	1,000	1791
Ces/Way International, Inc	726	Houston, TX	Private	90.0	175	1711
J C Evans Construction Co	727	Austin, TX	Private	90.0	800	1541
J H Berra Holding Co Inc	728	St. Louis, MO	Private	90.0	600	1611
Morley Construction Co Inc	729	Santa Monica, CA	Private	90.0	100	1771
Penhall International Inc	730	Anaheim, CA	Private	90.0	700	1795
S T Wooten Corp	731	Wilson, NC	Private	90.0	500	1611
Slayden Construction Inc	732	Stayton, OR	Private	90.0	163	1542
Welbro Constructors Inc	733	Maitland, FL	Private	90.0	300	1522
McShane Construction Corp	734	Des Plaines, IL	Private	90.0	70	1541
Apac-Virginia Inc	735	Danville, VA	Public Family Member	89.6	300	1611
Randall Abb Corp	736	Houston, TX	Private	89.6	370	1629
Southern Nevada Paving Inc	737	Las Vegas, NV	Private	89.6	400	1611
Berkshire Power Co LLC	738	Boston, MA	Private	89.5	60	1629
C C Myers Inc	739	Rancho Cordova, CA	Private	89.4	225	1622
Amec Holdings Inc	740	New York, NY	Private	89.1	700	1541
David E Harvey Builders Inc	741	Houston, TX	Private	89.1	204	1542
Hagerman Construction Corp	742	Fort Wayne, IN	Private	89.0	160	1542
Walsh Brothers Inc	743	Cambridge, MA	Private	89.0	140	1542
N A B Construction Corp	744	College Point, NY	Private	88.8	400	1541
Grucon Corp	745	Milwaukee, WI	Private	88.4	532	1711
Schiavone Construction Co	746	Secaucus, NJ	Private	88.3	300	1629
Christenson Electric Inc	747	Portland, OR	Private	88.2	600	1731
Ivory Homes	748	Salt Lake City, UT	Private	88.2	80	1521
Neenan Co	749	Fort Collins, CO	Private	88.2	200	1542
Degabrielle & Assoc Inc	750	Corolla, NC	Private	88.0	60	1521
Gohmann Asphalt and Construction	751	Clarksville, IN	Private	88.0	200	1611
Americon, Inc	752	Barberton, OH	Public Family Member	87.7	931	1711
Babcock & Wilcox Construction Co	753	Barberton, OH	Public Family Member	87.6	930	1711
BMW Constructors Inc	754	Indianapolis, IN	Private	87.6	765	1629
Payton Construction Corp	755	Boston, MA	Private	87.3	100	1542
Charles Pankow Builders Ltd	756	Altadena, CA	Private	87.2	132	1542
E L Hamm & Associates Inc	757	Virginia Beach, VA	Private	87.2	400	1542
Kalikow, H. J. & Co., LLC	758	New York, NY	Private	87.2	400	1542
LCS Holdings, Inc.	759	Des Moines, IA	Private	87.2	400	1542
McHugh Enterprises, Inc.	760	Chicago, IL	Private	87.2	400	1542
Starstone Construction Co	761	Clairton, PA	Private	87.2	400	1542
Western Summit Constructors	762	Denver, CO	Private	87.1	500	1629
National Construction Enterprises	763	Mishawaka, IN	Private	86.9	1,500	1742
Daniel Enterprises, Inc.	764	Tempe, AZ	Private	86.1	75	1542
Univ Mech & Engineer Contractors	765	San Diego, CA	Public Family Member	86.0	750	1711
Southwest Recreational Inds	766	Leander, TX	Private	85.9	800	1629
Hospitality Worldwide Services	767	New York, NY	Public	85.4	275	1522
Zurn Constructors, Inc	768	Erie, PA	Public Family Member	85.2	744	1629
Carl M Freeman Associates	769	Potomac, MD	Private	85.0	275	1531
Estridge Group Inc	770	Carmel, IN	Private	85.0	122	1521

D&B COMPANY RANKINGS BY SALES

Company	Rank	Location	Type	Sales ($ mil.)	Employ- ment	Primary SIC
Fortney & Weygandt, Inc.	771	North Olmsted, OH	Private	85.0	140	1542
Gambone Bros Construction Co	772	Norristown, PA	Private	85.0	120	1521
J R Austin Co	773	Rockville, MD	Private	85.0	85	1542
MCL Construction Corp	774	Chicago, IL	Private	85.0	100	1521
Pontarelli Builders, Inc.	775	Chicago, IL	Private	85.0	20	1531
R W Granger & Sons Inc	776	Shrewsbury, MA	Private	85.0	134	1542
Whittaker Construction Inc	777	St. Peters, MO	Public Family Member	85.0	375	1521
Getschow Group Inc	778	Oconto Falls, WI	Private	84.9	650	1711
Phillips, Getschow Co	779	Green Bay, WI	Private	84.9	650	1711
Gilbert Southern Corp.	780	Omaha, NE	Private	84.7	672	1611
Kleinknecht Electric Co	781	New York, NY	Private	84.2	200	1731
San Jose Construction Co, Inc	782	Santa Clara, CA	Private	84.1	130	1542
Intech Construction Inc	783	Philadelphia, PA	Private	84.0	50	1542
Market & Johnson, Inc	784	Eau Claire, WI	Private	83.6	300	1542
Miller Electric Co	785	Jacksonville, FL	Private	83.5	691	1731
Edward Rose Building Co	786	Farmington Hills, MI	Private	83.4	270	1531
Pacific Realty Group, Inc.	787	Dallas, TX	Private	83.4	270	1531
Petrocelli Electric Co Inc	788	Long Island City, NY	Private	83.4	500	1731
Foothills Eastern Transportation	789	Santa Ana, CA	Private	83.4	45	1611
Fowler-Jones Beers Construction	790	Winston Salem, NC	Private	83.3	150	1542
Waldinger Corp	791	Des Moines, IA	Private	83.0	600	1711
Nocuts, Inc	792	Wake Forest, NC	Public Family Member	82.9	1,100	1623
S M & P Utility Resources Inc	793	Carmel, IN	Public Family Member	82.9	1,100	1623
Quality Mechanical Contractors	794	Las Vegas, NV	Private	82.7	420	1711
FCI Constructors, Inc	795	Grand Junction, CO	Private	82.7	150	1542
Sunco Building Corp	796	Palm Beach Gardens, FL	Private	82.5	600	1521
Utilx Corp	797	Kent, WA	Public	82.5	515	1623
Koester Companies Inc	798	Evansville, IN	Private	82.4	300	1629
Frank A McBride Co	799	Hawthorne, NJ	Private	82.1	200	1711
Amtech Elevator Services	800	Whittier, CA	Public Family Member	82.1	604	1796
M J Anderson Inc	801	West Palm Beach, FL	Private	82.0	120	1542
D and M Concrete Floor Co	802	Fall River, MA	Private	82.0	70	1771
Western Waterproofing Co	803	St. Louis, MO	Private	81.5	854	1799
Apac-Mississippi Inc	804	Atlanta, GA	Public Family Member	81.5	358	1611
Kenyon Companies	805	Phoenix, AZ	Private	81.1	1,400	1742
American Fence and Sec Co Inc	806	Phoenix, AZ	Private	81.1	800	1799
Conlan Co	807	Marietta, GA	Private	81.0	225	1542
Cochran Inc	808	Seattle, WA	Private	81.0	405	1731
Gamma Construction Co	809	Houston, TX	Private	80.6	100	1542
Albert M Higley Co	810	Cleveland, OH	Private	80.5	180	1542
Pleasant Street Associates	811	Boston, MA	Private	80.2	125	1542
Belmont Constructors Co	812	Houston, TX	Public Family Member	80.1	700	1629
Aldridge Electric Inc (Del)	813	Libertyville, IL	Private	80.0	467	1731
Basic Industries Inc	814	Baton Rouge, LA	Private	80.0	1,200	1742
Bernards Bros Inc	815	San Fernando, CA	Private	80.0	80	1541
Brighton Homes Inc	816	Houston, TX	Private	80.0	92	1531
CE Ward Constructors, Inc	817	Houston, TX	Private	80.0	50	1542
Duininck Bros Inc	818	Prinsburg, MN	Private	80.0	50	1611
Dura-Builders Inc.	819	Indianapolis, IN	Private	80.0	50	1521
Dynalectric Co of Nevada	820	Norwalk, CT	Public Family Member	80.0	100	1731
E A Hathaway and Co	821	Santa Clara, CA	Private	80.0	100	1542
E-J Electric Installation Co	822	Long Island City, NY	Private	80.0	400	1731
Fairfield Development Inc	823	San Diego, CA	Private	80.0	25	1522
Guarantee Electrical Co	824	St. Louis, MO	Private	80.0	650	1731
Henry Bros Co	825	Oak Lawn, IL	Private	80.0	50	1542
Irving F Jensen Co Inc	826	Sioux City, IA	Private	80.0	100	1611
Kenco Communities at Wycliffe	827	Boca Raton, FL	Private	80.0	50	1522
Larwin Co	828	Encino, CA	Private	80.0	50	1521
Macomber Enterprises, Inc	829	Boston, MA	Private	80.0	120	1542
McCormick Inc	830	Fargo, ND	Private	80.0	125	1611
Metropolitan Mechanical Contractors	831	Eden Prairie, MN	Private	80.0	350	1711
Newmech Companies, Inc	832	St. Paul, MN	Private	80.0	300	1711
Potter Concrete Co Inc	833	Dallas, TX	Private	80.0	900	1771
Powersystems Corp	834	Smyrna, GA	Private	80.0	44	1542
Rafn Co	835	Bellevue, WA	Private	80.0	180	1542
Sofec Inc	836	Houston, TX	Public Family Member	80.0	120	1629
Stebbins Enterprises Inc	837	Hooksett, NH	Private	80.0	200	1542
Welsbach Electric Corp (Del)	838	College Point, NY	Public Family Member	80.0	350	1731
Mascaro Construction Co Lp	839	Pittsburgh, PA	Private	79.3	175	1542
Cadence McShane Corp	840	Dallas, TX	Private	79.2	70	1542

D&B COMPANY RANKINGS BY SALES

Company	Rank	Location	Type	Sales ($ mil.)	Employment	Primary SIC
U. S. Generating Co LLC	841	Bethesda, MD	Private	79.2	1,541	1629
Staker Paving and Construction Co	842	North Salt Lake, UT	Private	79.1	230	1611
Elkins Constructors Inc	843	Jacksonville, FL	Private	78.9	150	1542
Lincoln Builders, Inc	844	Ruston, LA	Private	78.9	64	1542
Superior Construction Co Inc	845	Gary, IN	Private	78.7	400	1622
Chas Roberts A/C Inc	846	Phoenix, AZ	Private	78.5	310	1711
Osman Construction Corp	847	Arlington Heights, IL	Private	78.4	90	1542
Trumbull Corp	848	West Mifflin, PA	Private	78.3	700	1611
HBG USA Inc	849	New York, NY	Private	78.1	500	1622
Hydrochem Holding, Inc	850	Dallas, TX	Public Family Member	78.1	1,300	1799
Centurion Industries Inc	851	Garrett, IN	Private	78.0	1,000	1796
Homes by Dave Brown	852	Tempe, AZ	Private	78.0	100	1531
Perini & Slattery Assoc	853	Jersey City, NJ	Private	78.0	80	1542
Crudo Bros., Co. Inc.	854	Livonia, MI	Private	77.9	110	1541
Felix Equities, Inc.	855	Lincolndale, NY	Private	77.9	350	1623
Spie Group Inc	856	Palatine, IL	Private	77.2	1,040	1731
Conti Enterprises, Inc	857	South Plainfield, NJ	Private	77.1	200	1611
Kvaerner Construction Inc	858	Tampa, FL	Private	76.8	175	1542
Black Construction Corp	859	Honolulu, HI	Private	76.5	600	1541
Richmond Am Homes of Maryland	860	Fairfax, VA	Public Family Member	76.4	93	1521
Morse Diesel International	861	New York, NY	Private	76.3	800	1522
Kraft Construction Co	862	Naples, FL	Private	76.1	140	1542
Auchter Co Inc	863	Jacksonville, FL	Private	76.0	165	1542
Roche Constructors Inc	864	Greeley, CO	Private	75.7	100	1542
Austin Bridge & Road, Inc	865	Dallas, TX	Private	75.6	600	1611
Tilcon Connecticut, Inc.	866	North Branford, CT	Private	75.6	198	1611
Amfels, Inc	867	Brownsville, TX	Private	75.5	660	1629
Irish Construction	868	Rosemead, CA	Private	75.4	1,000	1623
Conelly Swinerton Construction Inc	869	Tucson, AZ	Private	75.3	50	1542
Robison Construction Inc	870	Sumner, WA	Private	75.2	280	1623
Ambassador Construction Co	871	New York, NY	Private	75.0	46	1542
Atlanta Arena Constructors	872	Atlanta, GA	Private	75.0	15	1542
Baker Residential LP	873	Pleasantville, NY	Private	75.0	3	1531
BFW Construction Co Inc	874	Temple, TX	Private	75.0	150	1542
Brandenburg Industrial Service Co	875	Chicago, IL	Private	75.0	425	1622
Centex Landis Construction Co	876	Jefferson, LA	Public Family Member	75.0	75	1542
Charles R Perry Construction	877	Gainesville, FL	Private	75.0	100	1542
Corrigan Brothers Inc	878	St. Louis, MO	Private	75.0	600	1711
Elliott-Lewis Corp	879	Philadelphia, PA	Public Family Member	75.0	480	1711
Fontaine Bros Inc	880	Springfield, MA	Private	75.0	150	1542
Harbison-Mahony-Higgins Inc	881	Sacramento, CA	Private	75.0	100	1542
Hayward Baker Inc	882	Odenton, MD	Private	75.0	175	1799
James G Kennedy & Co Inc	883	New York, NY	Private	75.0	60	1542
Kinsel Industries Inc	884	Houston, TX	Private	75.0	385	1623
Manafort Brothers Inc	885	Plainville, CT	Private	75.0	400	1794
Middlesex Corp	886	Littleton, MA	Private	75.0	350	1611
Modern-Obayashi Corp	887	Boston, MA	Private	75.0	350	1622
Myrick, Batson & Gurosky Inc	888	Birmingham, AL	Private	75.0	155	1542
PKF-Mark III, Inc	889	Newtown, PA	Private	75.0	150	1629
Radnor Homes, Inc	890	Nashville, TN	Public Family Member	75.0	74	1521
Roth Bros Inc	891	Youngstown, OH	Public Family Member	75.0	500	1711
Ryan Inc Eastern	892	Deerfield Beach, FL	Private	75.0	300	1794
Security Technologies Group	893	Fort Lauderdale, FL	Private	75.0	700	1731
W M Schlosser Co Inc	894	Hyattsville, MD	Private	75.0	250	1542
Washington Coscan Inc	895	Vienna, VA	Private	74.7	90	1521
Panda Energy International	896	Dallas, TX	Private	74.5	35	1731
Worthington Communities Inc	897	Fort Myers, FL	Private	74.5	85	1521
Ameralum Inc	898	Middletown, PA	Private	74.5	730	1742
McGee Brothers Co Inc	899	Monroe, NC	Private	74.5	811	1741
Sturgeon Electric Co	900	Henderson, CO	Public Family Member	74.2	1,000	1731
New Urban West Inc	901	Santa Monica, CA	Private	74.1	63	1531
N A CCC Inc	902	Troy, MI	Private	74.1	300	1796
Holiday Builders Inc	903	Melbourne, FL	Private	74.1	125	1521
Arnold M Diamond Inc	904	Glen Head, NY	Private	74.0	40	1629
Louis P Ciminelli Construction Co	905	Buffalo, NY	Private	74.0	25	1542
M J Brock & Sons Inc	906	Woodland Hills, CA	Public Family Member	74.0	200	1531
Johnson Bros. Corp	907	Litchfield, MN	Private	74.0	600	1622
Kelso-Burnett Co Del	908	Rolling Meadows, IL	Private	73.9	475	1731
Pate & Pate Enterprises Inc	909	The Woodlands, TX	Private	73.8	550	1623
Ref-Chem Corp	910	Odessa, TX	Private	73.7	1,015	1629

D&B COMPANY RANKINGS BY SALES

Company	Rank	Location	Type	Sales ($ mil.)	Employ- ment	Primary SIC
Ecker Enterprises Inc	911	Chicago, IL	Private	73.7	400	1742
Murphy Bros Inc	912	East Moline, IL	Private	73.6	100	1623
Miller & Long Co of Maryland	913	Bethesda, MD	Private	73.6	50	1771
J P I National Construction	914	Irving, TX	Private	73.2	1,182	1522
Landmark Organization, Inc	915	Austin, TX	Private	73.1	50	1542
Grace Industries, Inc	916	Whitestone, NY	Private	73.0	100	1741
Kraemer Brothers, LLC	917	Plain, WI	Private	73.0	125	1542
Colorado Structures Inc	918	Colorado Springs, CO	Private	72.9	75	1542
ICI Construction Inc	919	Spring, TX	Private	72.8	77	1542
W G Mills Inc	920	Sarasota, FL	Private	72.6	125	1542
Ashtead Holdings, Inc.	921	Charlotte, NC	Private	72.6	670	7353
Sunbelt Rentals Inc	922	Charlotte, NC	Private	72.6	670	7353
White Construction Co	923	Chiefland, FL	Private	72.3	600	1611
A 7 Joint Venture	924	Dorchester, MA	Private	72.3	60	1629
Lee Kennedy Co Inc	925	Boston, MA	Private	72.1	75	1542
Home Place Inc	926	Gainesville, GA	Private	72.1	300	1521
Anning-Johnson Co	927	Melrose Park, IL	Private	72.0	400	1742
Hake Group Inc	928	Eddystone, PA	Private	72.0	225	1796
Paddock Pool Construction Co.	929	Scottsdale, AZ	Private	72.0	400	1799
Neosho Inc	930	Topeka, KS	Private	71.9	325	1611
Inrecon, L.L.C.	931	Birmingham, MI	Private	71.9	420	1521
John T Callahan & Sons Inc	932	Bridgewater, MA	Private	71.8	100	1542
Holladay Corp	933	Washington, DC	Private	71.6	750	1522
Westminster Homes, Inc.	934	Greensboro, NC	Public Family Member	71.6	85	1542
Florida Mivan Inc	935	Lake Buena Vista, FL	Private	71.5	330	1542
R P Industries Inc	936	Franklin, TN	Private	71.5	75	1542
Tempco Disaster Services, Inc	937	Glendale, CA	Private	71.5	330	1542
Wolverine Building Inc	938	Grand Rapids, MI	Private	71.5	100	1541
Klukwan Inc	939	Juneau, AK	Private	71.5	300	1611
Clark & Sullivan Constructors	940	Sparks, NV	Private	71.4	80	1542
Sheehan Pipe Line Construction Co	941	Tulsa, OK	Private	71.1	67	1623
Wilson Electric Co, Inc.	942	Scottsdale, AZ	Public Family Member	71.0	750	1731
Shea-Traylor-Healy Joint Venture	943	Framingham, MA	Private	71.0	200	1531
Sletten Construction of Nevada	944	Las Vegas, NV	Private	70.8	200	1542
T J Lambrecht Construction	945	Joliet, IL	Private	70.8	500	1794
Calcon Constructors Inc	946	Englewood, CO	Private	70.8	95	1542
John Crosland Co	947	Charlotte, NC	Public Family Member	70.6	230	1531
Harris Contracting Co	948	St. Paul, MN	Private	70.6	300	1711
Keenan, Hopkins	949	Tampa, FL	Private	70.5	400	1542
Highland Framers of N Calif	950	Las Vegas, NV	Private	70.3	1,200	1751
Eastern Contractors Inc	951	Framingham, MA	Private	70.1	150	1542
Absher Construction Co	952	Puyallup, WA	Private	70.1	150	1542
Advance Mechanical Systems Inc	953	Mount Prospect, IL	Private	70.0	225	1711
Amerilink Corp	954	Columbus, OH	Public	70.0	588	1623
Bellevue Holding Co	955	Wilmington, DE	Private	70.0	50	1542
C P Morgan Co Inc	956	Carmel, IN	Private	70.0	100	1521
Cashman	957	Boston, MA	Private	70.0	60	1611
Chapman Corp	958	Washington, PA	Private	70.0	300	1541
Chiyoda International Corp	959	Seattle, WA	Private	70.0	107	1541
Elmo Greer & Sons Inc	960	London, KY	Private	70.0	200	1611
Goodfellow Bros, Inc	961	Wenatchee, WA	Private	70.0	300	1611
Haydon Building Corp	962	Tempe, AZ	Private	70.0	60	1541
Latco Inc	963	Lincoln, AR	Private	70.0	325	1542
Law Co Inc	964	Wichita, KS	Private	70.0	200	1542
Lucent Technologies Services Co	965	McLeansville, NC	Public Family Member	70.0	800	1731
McCar Development Corp	966	Atlanta, GA	Private	70.0	80	1521
McClure Co Inc	967	Harrisburg, PA	Public Family Member	70.0	300	1711
McKinstry Co	968	Seattle, WA	Private	70.0	450	1711
Michael Nicholas Inc	969	Carol Stream, IL	Private	70.0	500	1751
National Business Group	970	Mission Hills, CA	Private	70.0	455	7353
Nor-Am Construction Co	971	Portland, OR	Private	70.0	175	1542
Pinkard Construction Co	972	Denver, CO	Private	70.0	50	1542
Ruhlin Co	973	Sharon Center, OH	Private	70.0	150	1611
White-Spunner Construction	974	Mobile, AL	Private	70.0	35	1542
Sargent Electric Co	975	Pittsburgh, PA	Private	69.9	600	1731
Apac-Texas Inc	976	Dallas, TX	Public Family Member	69.8	400	1611
Cache Valley Electric Co	977	Logan, UT	Private	69.6	300	1731
Corna/Kokosing Construction Co	978	Columbus, OH	Private	69.5	321	1542
Builder's Mart Inc	979	Lancaster, CA	Private	69.3	7	1799
C D Henderson Inc	980	Garland, TX	Private	69.0	75	1542

D&B COMPANY RANKINGS BY SALES

Company	Rank	Location	Type	Sales ($ mil.)	Employ- ment	Primary SIC
D W Hutson Construction, Inc	981	Jacksonville, FL	Public Family Member	69.0	41	1521
Plaster Development Co	982	Las Vegas, NV	Private	69.0	65	1531
Shasta Industries Inc	983	Phoenix, AZ	Private	69.0	500	1799
Frehner Construction Co Inc	984	North Las Vegas, NV	Private	68.8	250	1611
Lundgren Bros. Construction	985	Wayzata, MN	Private	68.7	200	1521
Parker & Lancaster Corp	986	Richmond, VA	Private	68.6	84	1531
Codillera Construction Corp	987	Edwards, CO	Private	68.5	500	1521
Fish Construction Co	988	Studio City, CA	Private	68.5	500	1521
Ahh Holdings Inc	989	Kissimmee, FL	Private	68.4	NA	1531
Westcott Construction Corp	990	North Attleboro, MA	Private	68.3	100	1542
Pulice Construction Inc	991	Phoenix, AZ	Private	68.2	300	1611
Valenzuela Engineering Inc	992	Santa Maria, CA	Private	68.0	300	1542
J H McCormick Inc	993	Burbank, CA	Private	68.0	100	1542
Hunter Contracting Co.	994	Gilbert, AZ	Private	67.9	175	1611
M & H Enterprises Inc	995	Las Vegas, NV	Private	67.7	200	1542
York Construction Co Inc	996	Greenville, SC	Private	67.7	125	1541
Asplundh Construction Corp	997	Patchogue, NY	Private	67.6	370	1731
Ramex Construction Co, Inc	998	Pasadena, TX	Private	67.5	310	1623
W W Gay Mechanical Contractors	999	Jacksonville, FL	Private	67.5	717	1711
L & H Co Inc Del	1000	Hinsdale, IL	Private	67.4	909	1731

D&B COMPANY RANKINGS BY EMPLOYMENT

Company	Rank	Location	Type	Sales ($ mil.)	Employ-ment	Primary SIC
Halliburton Delaware, Inc	1	Dallas, TX	Public Family Member	6,592.8	57,300	1629
McDermott International Inc	2	New Orleans, LA	Public	3,674.6	24,700	1629
BTR Dunlop Inc	3	Wilmington, DE	Private	4,200.0	24,000	1611
Jacobs Engineering Group Inc	4	Pasadena, CA	Public	2,101.1	23,000	1629
Kellogg, Brown & Root, Inc	5	Houston, TX	Public Family Member	2,300.9	20,000	1629
Emcor Group Inc	6	Norwalk, CT	Public	1,950.9	14,000	1731
J Ray McDermott, S.A.	7	New Orleans, LA	Public Family Member	1,855.5	11,700	1629
H B E Corp	8	St. Louis, MO	Private	2,455.6	11,000	1542
Centex Corp	9	Dallas, TX	Public	3,975.4	10,259·	1531
Parsons Corp	10	Pasadena, CA	Private	1,245.6	10,000	1629
Zachry Inc	11	San Antonio, TX	Private	800.0	10,000	1611
Peter Kiewit Sons', Inc	12	Omaha, NE	Private	2,096.5	9,393	1542
H B Zachry Co	13	San Antonio, TX	Private	665.0	9,000	1611
Morrison Knudsen Corp	14	Boise, ID	Public	1,862.2	9,000	1622
Holzmann, Philipp USA Ltd	15	Charlotte, NC	Private	1,651.0	8,000	1542
Mastec Inc	16	Miami, FL	Public	703.4	7,850	1623
JE Merit Constructors, Inc	17	Houston, TX	Public Family Member	332.3	7,000	1629
Turner Industries Ltd	18	Baton Rouge, LA	Private	550.0	7,000	1541
M W Kellogg Co	19	Houston, TX	Public Family Member	1,358.0	6,770	1629
Apogee Enterprises Inc	20	Minneapolis, MN	Public	912.8	6,672	1791
Rust Constructors Inc	21	Birmingham, AL	Public Family Member	821.6	6,500	1541
J A Jones Inc	22	Charlotte, NC	Private	1,398.5	6,224	1542
Apac Holdings Inc	23	Atlanta, GA	Public Family Member	1,257.1	5,028	1611
Austin Industries Del Corp	24	Dallas, TX	Private	620.0	5,000	1542
B E & K Construction Co	25	Birmingham, AL	Private	632.2	5,000	1541
Performance Contracting Group	26	Shawnee Mission, KS	Private	346.8	5,000	1742
American Residential Services	27	Houston, TX	Public	382.5	4,800	1711
Flatley Co	28	Braintree, MA	Private	423.2	4,500	1522
Harmony Corp	29	Baton Rouge, LA	Private	543.8	4,300	1541
Brown & Root Services Corp	30	Houston, TX	Public Family Member	600.0	4,100	1541
BSI Holdings Inc	31	Carmel, CA	Private	600.0	4,000	1742
Building One Services Corp	32	Wayzata, MN	Public	297.0	4,000	1731
Dillingham Construction Corp	33	Pleasanton, CA	Private	1,022.6	4,000	1629
MYR Group Inc.	34	Rolling Meadows, IL	Public	431.3	4,000	1623
Sasco Electric	35	Artesia, CA	Private	297.1	4,000	1731
Lennar Corp	36	Miami, FL	Public	1,303.1	3,875	1531
Dycom Industries Inc	37	Palm Beach Gardens, FL	Public	371.4	3,834	1623
P & O Inc	38	Englewood, CO	Private	1,930.0	3,800	1542
Pulte Corp	39	Bloomfield Hills, MI	Public	2,866.5	3,778	1531
Pike Electric Inc	40	Mount Airy, NC	Private	277.8	3,700	1623
Skanska (U.S.A.), Inc.	41	Greenwich, CT	Private	2,060.7	3,700	1542
Michael Baker Corp	42	Coraopolis, PA	Public	446.4	3,670	1611
Integrated Electrical Services	43	Houston, TX	Public	263.6	3,550	1731
Kaufman & Broad Home Corp	44	Los Angeles, CA	Public	2,449.4	3,500	1531
Service Experts Inc	45	Brentwood, TN	Public	238.7	3,500	1711
Kinetics Group, Inc	46	Santa Clara, CA	Public Family Member	388.0	3,460	1711
International Maintenance Corp	47	Baton Rouge, LA	Private	430.1	3,400	1541
Berry Contracting, LP	48	Corpus Christi, TX	Private	225.0	3,200	1629
Dyn Specialty Contracting Inc	49	McLean, VA	Public Family Member	302.5	3,200	1711
Dynalectric Co	50	McLean, VA	Public Family Member	237.6	3,200	1731
Webb Del Corp	51	Phoenix, AZ	Public	1,177.8	3,200	1521
Comfort Systems USA Inc	52	Houston, TX	Public	390.1	3,119	1711
Clark Construction Group	53	Bethesda, MD	Private	1,400.0	3,100	1542
Api Group, Inc	54	St. Paul, MN	Private	369.3	3,000	1742
Bell Atlantic Comm Constr Serv	55	Beltsville, MD	Public Family Member	200.0	3,000	1731
T I C Holdings Inc	56	Steamboat Springs, CO	Private	420.5	3,000	1541
Turner Corp	57	New York, NY	Public	3,170.7	3,000	1542
Layne Christensen Co	58	Shawnee Mission, KS	Public	294.6	2,949	1781
ICF Kaiser Engineers Group	59	Fairfax, VA	Public Family Member	333.2	2,900	1629
Fru-Con Holding Corp	60	Ballwin, MO	Private	538.2	2,800	1541
Group Maintenance America	61	Houston, TX	Public	437.0	2,800	1711
Harbert Corp	62	Birmingham, AL	Private	623.4	2,800	1542
United Rentals North America	63	Modesto, CA	Public Family Member	273.2	2,800	7353
Dover Elevator Co	64	Horn Lake, MS	Public Family Member	4,547.7	2,735	1796
Berry GP, Inc	65	Corpus Christi, TX	Private	135.0	2,733	1629
Prime Service Inc	66	Houston, TX	Private	326.6	2,611	7353
Limbach Holdings Inc	67	Wilmington, DE	Private	329.4	2,510	1711
Dupont Flooring Systems, Inc	68	Kennesaw, GA	Public Family Member	450.0	2,500	1752
Eichleay Holdings Inc	69	Pittsburgh, PA	Private	150.0	2,500	1541
Fischbach & Moore Electric LLC	70	New Providence, NJ	Private	185.6	2,500	1731

D&B COMPANY RANKINGS BY EMPLOYMENT

Company	Rank	Location	Type	Sales ($ mil.)	Employ-ment	Primary SIC
Harbor View Holdings, Inc	71	San Francisco, CA	Private	130.0	2,500	1522
Superfos Construction (U.S.)	72	Dothan, AL	Private	100.0	2,500	1611
Waste Management Indus Services	73	La Porte, TX	Public Family Member	150.0	2,500	1799
Yonkers Contracting Co Inc	74	Yonkers, NY	Private	270.6	2,500	1611
D R Horton Inc	75	Arlington, TX	Public	2,155.0	2,465	1531
Gale Industries Inc	76	Daytona Beach, FL	Public Family Member	141.7	2,448	1742
Beers Inc	77	Atlanta, GA	Private	1,436.1	2,300	1542
Modern Continental Construction Co	78	Cambridge, MA	Private	478.9	2,300	1622
Ryland Group Inc	79	Columbia, MD	Public	1,649.8	2,270	1531
Boldt Group Inc	80	Appleton, WI	Private	351.0	2,200	1541
Perini Corp	81	Framingham, MA	Public	1,324.5	2,200	1542
Lane Industries Inc	82	Meriden, CT	Private	284.4	2,175	1622
Faulkner Group, Inc	83	Austin, TX	Private	300.0	2,100	1542
Mass Electric Construction Co	84	Boston, MA	Private	261.6	2,050	1731
NVR, Inc	85	McLean, VA	Public	1,154.0	2,013	1531
Able Telcom Holding Corp	86	West Palm Beach, FL	Public	217.5	2,000	1623
Brand Scaffold Service, Inc	87	Chesterfield, MO	Private	120.1	2,000	1799
Framatome USA Inc	88	Arlington, VA	Private	148.5	2,000	1731
Resco Holdings Inc	89	Hampton, NH	Public Family Member	229.7	2,000	1629
S & B Engineers and Constructors	90	Houston, TX	Private	382.5	2,000	1629
W G Yates & Sons Construction Co	91	Philadelphia, MS	Private	319.8	2,000	1542
Flint Industries, Inc	92	Tulsa, OK	Private	403.0	1,999	1542
U.S. Home Corp	93	Houston, TX	Public	1,497.6	1,954	1531
Harlan Electric Co	94	Rochester Hills, MI	Public Family Member	144.7	1,950	1731
Railworks Corp	95	Baltimore, MD	Public	248.0	1,900	1731
Monumental Investment Corp	96	Baltimore, MD	Private	400.0	1,851	1711
Whiting-Turner Contg Co Inc	97	Baltimore, MD	Private	1,037.0	1,839	1542
Koll Co	98	Newport Beach, CA	Private	406.2	1,828	1542
Anco Insulations Inc	99	Baton Rouge, LA	Private	119.0	1,800	1742
Granite Construction Inc	100	Watsonville, CA	Public	1,028.2	1,800	1611
Marley Holdings L P	101	New York, NY	Private	97.8	1,800	1781
Tennis Corp of America	102	Chicago, IL	Private	200.0	1,800	1799
U.S. Contractors Inc	103	Clute, TX	Private	165.7	1,800	1629
Centex Construction Group Inc	104	Dallas, TX	Public Family Member	953.8	1,790	1542
Red Simpson Inc	105	Alexandria, LA	Private	133.9	1,780	1623
Newtron Group, Inc	106	Baton Rouge, LA	Private	94.6	1,750	1731
Rooney Brothers Co	107	Tulsa, OK	Private	384.8	1,732	1542
Eagleventures Inc	108	Memphis, TN	Private	270.0	1,700	1542
Hydrochem Industrial Services	109	Deer Park, TX	Public Family Member	160.6	1,700	1799
Nabors International Inc	110	Houston, TX	Public Family Member	160.9	1,650	7353
DPR Construction, Inc	111	Redwood City, CA	Private	890.6	1,609	1541
Arctic Slope Region Construction Co	112	Barrow, AK	Private	120.4	1,600	1623
Brasfield & Gorrie, LLC	113	Birmingham, AL	Private	550.0	1,600	1542
Harmon, Ltd	114	Minneapolis, MN	Public Family Member	247.3	1,600	1793
Fluor Daniel Caribbean Inc	115	Irvine, CA	Public Family Member	199.2	1,572	1541
Global Industries, Ltd	116	Lafayette, LA	Public	379.9	1,563	1623
Tilcon Inc	117	New Britain, CT	Private	100.8	1,561	1611
U. S. Generating Co LLC	118	Bethesda, MD	Private	79.2	1,541	1629
S E Johnson Companies Inc	119	Maumee, OH	Private	271.0	1,516	1611
Weatherford U.S., Inc	120	Houston, TX	Public Family Member	147.3	1,511	7353
Alberici Corp	121	St. Louis, MO	Private	531.3	1,500	1541
Amrep Corp	122	New York, NY	Public	171.4	1,500	1521
Apac-Georgia Inc	123	Smyrna, GA	Public Family Member	190.8	1,500	1611
Baker Concrete Construction	124	Monroe, OH	Private	247.0	1,500	1771
Beers Construction Co	125	Atlanta, GA	Private	1,074.2	1,500	1542
Byers Locate Services, LLC	126	Atlanta, GA	Private	112.9	1,500	1623
Centimark Corp	127	Canonsburg, PA	Private	209.2	1,500	1761
Fisk Electric Co	128	Houston, TX	Private	134.1	1,500	1731
Hensel Phelps Construction Co	129	Greeley, CO	Private	934.3	1,500	1542
Irex Corp	130	Lancaster, PA	Public	278.1	1,500	1742
J S Alberici Construction Co	131	St. Louis, MO	Private	525.3	1,500	1541
M A Mortenson Companies	132	Minneapolis, MN	Private	809.5	1,500	1542
McCarthy Building Companies	133	St. Louis, MO	Private	1,127.0	1,500	1542
National Construction Enterprises	134	Mishawaka, IN	Private	86.9	1,500	1742
Owl Companies	135	Irvine, CA	Private	199.4	1,500	1629
Paclantic Construction Inc	136	Pleasanton, CA	Private	190.2	1,500	1541
Perseus Fisk, LLC	137	Houston, TX	Private	111.3	1,500	1731
Williams Group International	138	Stone Mountain, GA	Private	214.1	1,500	1799
Martin K Eby Construction Co	139	Wichita, KS	Private	250.0	1,499	1629
Kajima U.S.A. Inc.	140	New York, NY	Private	950.1	1,440	1541

D&B COMPANY RANKINGS BY EMPLOYMENT

Company	Rank	Location	Type	Sales ($ mil.)	Employ-ment	Primary SIC
Walsh Group Ltd	141	Chicago, IL	Private	959.1	1,439	1542
Cianbro Corp	142	Pittsfield, ME	Private	156.3	1,400	1629
Kenyon Companies	143	Phoenix, AZ	Private	81.1	1,400	1742
T L James & Co Inc	144	Ruston, LA	Private	252.1	1,377	1611
Dot Blue Services Inc	145	Deerfield Beach, FL	Public Family Member	200.0	1,375	1711
Northwestern Growth Corp	146	Sioux Falls, SD	Public Family Member	340.4	1,375	1711
Kiewit Construction Co	147	Omaha, NE	Private	2,325.2	1,353	1541
ME Holding, Inc	148	Boston, MA	Private	261.6	1,353	1731
M. D. C. Holdings, Inc.	149	Denver, CO	Public	1,263.2	1,350	1521
Q I Corp	150	Alpharetta, GA	Private	150.0	1,350	1742
Castle & Cooke Inc	151	Los Angeles, CA	Public	241.2	1,322	1522
New England Power Service Co	152	Westborough, MA	Public Family Member	206.5	1,305	1623
Hydrochem Holding, Inc	153	Dallas, TX	Public Family Member	78.1	1,300	1799
Philip St, Inc.	154	Houston, TX	Private	146.6	1,278	1629
Bechtel Construction Operations Inc	155	San Francisco, CA	Private	595.0	1,275	1541
Beazer Homes USA Inc	156	Atlanta, GA	Public	977.4	1,261	1521
Hubbard Construction Co	157	Winter Park, FL	Private	240.0	1,259	1611
Colas Inc	158	Morristown, NJ	Private	446.7	1,250	1611
Tri-City Electrical Contractors	159	Altamonte Springs, FL	Public Family Member	104.0	1,250	1731
Limbach Co	160	Pittsburgh, PA	Private	220.9	1,249	1711
W W Investment Co	161	St. Louis, MO	Private	106.5	1,236	1799
Western Group Inc	162	St. Louis, MO	Private	106.5	1,236	1799
JMB/Urban Development Co.	163	Chicago, IL	Private	379.8	1,218	1531
Welcon Management Co	164	Wilson, NC	Private	115.0	1,203	1731
Basic Industries Inc	165	Baton Rouge, LA	Private	80.0	1,200	1742
Ceco Concrete Construction LLC	166	Kansas City, MO	Private	105.9	1,200	1799
Diamond Home Services (Del)	167	Woodstock, IL	Public	161.1	1,200	1761
Dyncorp Tri-Cities Services	168	Richland, WA	Private	265.9	1,200	1542
Fishel Co	169	Columbus, OH	Private	140.9	1,200	1623
Green Holdings Inc	170	Denver, CA	Private	151.3	1,200	1611
Highland Framers of N Calif	171	Las Vegas, NV	Private	70.3	1,200	1751
Houston-Stafford Electric	172	Stafford, TX	Public Family Member	100.0	1,200	1731
Hovnanian Enterprises Inc	173	Red Bank, NJ	Public	941.9	1,200	1531
John J Kirlin Inc	174	Rockville, MD	Private	113.2	1,200	1711
National Capital Companies Ltd	175	State College, PA	Private	113.8	1,200	1522
PCL Enterprises Inc	176	Denver, CO	Private	714.7	1,200	1542
Power Plant Maintenance Co	177	Society Hill, SC	Private	137.6	1,200	1629
Rosendin Electric Inc	178	San Jose, CA	Private	166.7	1,200	1731
Teichert Inc	179	Sacramento, CA	Private	347.8	1,200	1611
Therma Corp	180	San Jose, CA	Private	200.0	1,200	1711
Tutor-Saliba Corp	181	Sylmar, CA	Private	433.6	1,200	1542
Vecellio & Grogan, Inc.	182	Beckley, WV	Private	200.0	1,200	1611
Watson Electrical Construction Co	183	Wilson, NC	Public Family Member	110.0	1,200	1731
J P I National Construction	184	Irving, TX	Private	73.2	1,182	1522
Production Management Companies	185	Harvey, LA	Private	133.3	1,162	1629
Casey Industrial Inc	186	Albany, OR	Private	146.3	1,153	1541
National Refrigeration Services	187	Atlanta, GA	Private	108.5	1,150	1711
Marshall Erdman & Associates	188	Madison, WI	Private	204.3	1,112	1542
Flint Engineering & Construction Co	189	Tulsa, OK	Private	91.0	1,100	1623
K Hovnanian Enterprises, Inc	190	Red Bank, NJ	Public Family Member	347.9	1,100	1531
Neff Corp	191	Miami, FL	Public	142.0	1,100	7353
Nocuts, Inc	192	Wake Forest, NC	Public Family Member	82.9	1,100	1623
S M & P Utility Resources Inc	193	Carmel, IN	Public Family Member	82.9	1,100	1623
Swinerton Inc	194	San Francisco, CA	Private	500.6	1,100	1542
VHC, Inc	195	Green Bay, WI	Private	100.0	1,100	1731
Chicago Bridge & Iron Co Ill	196	Plainfield, IL	Private	97.4	1,080	1791
Austin Industrial Inc	197	Houston, TX	Private	99.0	1,050	1711
Homes Holding Corp	198	Tampa, FL	Public Family Member	144.5	1,043	1521
Spie Group Inc	199	Palatine, IL	Private	77.2	1,040	1731
Avatar Holdings Inc	200	Miami, FL	Public	129.1	1,030	1521
Gilbert Companies, Inc	201	Parker City, IN	Private	118.1	1,030	1629
Townsend Acquisition Inc	202	Muncie, IN	Private	118.1	1,030	1629
Jim Walter Homes Inc	203	Tampa, FL	Public Family Member	141.2	1,020	1521
Ref-Chem Corp	204	Odessa, TX	Private	73.7	1,015	1629
Comstock Holdings Inc	205	White Plains, NY	Public Family Member	153.6	1,007	1731
L K Comstock & Co Inc	206	White Plains, NY	Public Family Member	153.6	1,007	1731
Adc Systems Integration, Inc.	207	Chickamauga, GA	Public Family Member	130.0	1,000	1731
Apac-Carolina Inc	208	Kinston, NC	Public Family Member	236.4	1,000	1611
Baugh Enterprises Inc	209	Seattle, WA	Private	221.2	1,000	1542
Centurion Industries Inc	210	Garrett, IN	Private	78.0	1,000	1796

D&B COMPANY RANKINGS BY EMPLOYMENT

Company	Rank	Location	Type	Sales ($ mil.)	Employ- ment	Primary SIC
Davis Electrical Constructors	211	Greenville, SC	Public Family Member	100.0	1,000	1731
Dick Corp	212	Clairton, PA	Private	537.5	1,000	1611
Dunn Industries, Inc.	213	Kansas City, MO	Private	619.0	1,000	1542
Dynamic Systems, Inc	214	Austin, TX	Private	150.0	1,000	1711
Eby Corp	215	Wichita, KS	Private	114.6	1,000	1629
Federated Home & Mortgage Co	216	State College, PA	Private	95.0	1,000	1522
Fischbach Corp	217	Englewood, CO	Public Family Member	400.0	1,000	1731
Gecos Inc	218	Winter Park, FL	Private	220.0	1,000	1611
Gem Industrial Inc	219	Walbridge, OH	Private	95.0	1,000	1711
Hog Slat Inc	220	Newton Grove, NC	Private	221.2	1,000	1542
Irish Construction	221	Rosemead, CA	Private	75.4	1,000	1623
Iteq Storage Systems, Inc	222	Houston, TX	Private	90.2	1,000	1791
J E Dunn Construction Co	223	Kansas City, MO	Private	417.0	1,000	1542
Jones Bros Inc	224	Mount Juliet, TN	Private	150.0	1,000	1622
Jupiter Industries, Inc.	225	Northbrook, IL	Private	94.3	1,000	1711
Kraus-Anderson, Inc	226	Minneapolis, MN	Private	465.0	1,000	1542
Nationsrent Inc	227	Fort Lauderdale, FL	Public	200.0	1,000	7353
Performance Contractors, Inc.	228	Baton Rouge, LA	Private	110.0	1,000	1541
Pizzagalli Construction Co	229	Burlington, VT	Private	250.0	1,000	1542
Poole & Kent Corp	230	Baltimore, MD	Private	94.3	1,000	1711
Rudolph/Libbe Companies Inc	231	Walbridge, OH	Private	266.3	1,000	1541
Scott Companies Inc	232	San Leandro, CA	Private	94.3	1,000	1711
Sturgeon Electric Co	233	Henderson, CO	Public Family Member	74.2	1,000	1731
Tidewater Construction Corp	234	Virginia Beach, VA	Private	150.0	1,000	1541
Timec Acquisition Corp	235	Vallejo, CA	Private	114.6	1,000	1629
Traylor Bros Inc	236	Evansville, IN	Private	185.7	1,000	1622
Western National Properties	237	Irvine, CA	Private	95.0	1,000	1522
Dunn Investment Co	238	Birmingham, AL	Private	226.0	992	1542
Cal-Air Inc	239	Whittier, CA	Private	91.0	965	1711
Americon, Inc	240	Barberton, OH	Public Family Member	87.7	931	1711
Babcock & Wilcox Construction Co	241	Barberton, OH	Public Family Member	87.6	930	1711
CEC Investment Corp	242	Pittsburgh, PA	Private	145.0	928	1791
Barnhill Contracting Co	243	Tarboro, NC	Private	156.2	920	1611
Tdindustries, Inc.	244	Dallas, TX	Private	125.0	918	1711
L & H Co Inc Del	245	Hinsdale, IL	Private	67.4	909	1731
Toll Holdings, Inc	246	Huntingdon Valley, PA	Public Family Member	125.2	905	1521
Bergelectric Corp	247	Los Angeles, CA	Private	124.3	900	1731
Century Contractors Inc	248	Matthews, NC	Private	170.0	900	1541
Dillingham Construction PCF Ltd	249	Honolulu, HI	Private	260.4	900	1542
Fletcher Construction Co Hawaii Ltd	250	Honolulu, HI	Private	230.0	900	1542
Gilbane Building Co	251	Providence, RI	Private	910.3	900	1541
Industrial Services Tech	252	Denver, CO	Private	95.8	900	1541
Manhattan Construction Co	253	Dallas, TX	Private	440.0	900	1542
Pepper Companies Inc	254	Chicago, IL	Private	622.9	900	1542
Potter Concrete Co Inc	255	Dallas, TX	Private	80.0	900	1771
R & D Thiel Inc	256	Belvidere, IL	Private	114.2	900	1751
Rea Construction Co	257	Charlotte, NC	Private	170.2	900	1611
Rosemont Exposition Services Inc	258	Des Plaines, IL	Private	114.4	900	1541
Rudolph & Sletten Inc	259	Foster City, CA	Private	487.0	900	1541
Balfour Beatty Construction Inc	260	Atlanta, GA	Private	237.1	861	1622
Western Waterproofing Co	261	St. Louis, MO	Private	81.5	854	1799
Bechtel/Parson, Brinkerhoff	262	Boston, MA	Private	250.0	850	1622
Bonitz of South Carolina Inc	263	Columbia, SC	Private	92.5	850	1742
M B Kahn Construction Co Inc	264	Columbia, SC	Private	242.0	850	1542
NSC Corp	265	Methuen, MA	Public	116.0	850	1799
Sordoni/Skanska Construction Co	266	Parsippany, NJ	Private	1,100.0	850	1541
Walker Engineering Inc	267	Dallas, TX	Public Family Member	96.0	850	1731
A & L Industrial Constr & Maint	268	Kingsport, TN	Private	106.8	840	1541
Morrow-Meadows Corp	269	Walnut, CA	Private	134.3	820	1731
McGee Brothers Co Inc	270	Monroe, NC	Private	74.5	811	1741
A C and S, Inc	271	Lancaster, PA	Public Family Member	99.0	800	1742
American Fence and Sec Co Inc	272	Phoenix, AZ	Private	81.1	800	1799
Anthony and Sylvan Pools Corp	273	Doylestown, PA	Public Family Member	140.0	800	1799
C-B-R Development Co., Inc.	274	Spartanburg, SC	Public Family Member	176.5	800	1542
E C Co	275	Portland, OR	Private	160.0	800	1731
E E Black Ltd	276	Honolulu, HI	Private	112.0	800	1629
F A Wilhelm Construction Co	277	Indianapolis, IN	Private	101.7	800	1541
Gr Lakes Dredge & Dock Corp Del	278	Oak Brook, IL	Private	258.3	800	1629
J C Evans Construction Co	279	Austin, TX	Private	90.0	800	1541
J H Kelly LLC	280	Longview, WA	Private	127.8	800	1711

D&B COMPANY RANKINGS BY EMPLOYMENT

Company	Rank	Location	Type	Sales ($ mil.)	Employ-ment	Primary SIC
Jesco Inc	281	Tupelo, MS	Private	101.7	800	1541
John Wland Homes Neighborhoods	282	Atlanta, GA	Private	250.6	800	1531
L E Myers Co	283	Rolling Meadows, IL	Public Family Member	431.3	800	1623
Lucent Technologies Services Co	284	McLeansville, NC	Public Family Member	70.0	800	1731
M/I Schottenstein Homes Inc	285	Columbus, OH	Public	614.0	800	1531
Morse Diesel International	286	New York, NY	Private	76.3	800	1522
Royal Imperial Group Inc	287	Chicago, IL	Private	176.5	800	1542
Southwest Recreational Inds	288	Leander, TX	Private	85.9	800	1629
Synergism Inc	289	Sunnyvale, CA	Private	157.5	800	1731
W M Grace Companies Inc	290	Phoenix, AZ	Private	176.5	800	1542
Weekley Homes, Lp	291	Houston, TX	Private	503.0	790	1531
Black & Veatch Construction	292	Kansas City, MO	Private	526.9	784	1629
Schuff Steel Co	293	Phoenix, AZ	Public	138.2	781	1791
BMW Constructors Inc	294	Indianapolis, IN	Private	87.6	765	1629
Northern Pipeline Construction Co	295	Phoenix, AZ	Public Family Member	120.0	765	1623
Opus U.S. Corp	296	Hopkins, MN	Private	600.0	764	1542
Allan A Myers Inc	297	Worcester, PA	Private	118.2	760	1629
Linbeck Corp	298	Houston, TX	Private	185.0	760	1542
Silverado Constructors	299	Irvine, CA	Private	260.0	760	1611
Lombardy Holdings	300	Whittier, CA	Private	93.5	755	1623
Ames Construction, Inc	301	Burnsville, MN	Private	271.6	750	1629
Blake Construction Co Inc	302	Washington, DC	Private	225.0	750	1542
Communications Construction Group	303	West Chester, PA	Public Family Member	93.0	750	1623
Giant Construction Co	304	Landover, MD	Private	165.4	750	1542
Holladay Corp	305	Washington, DC	Private	71.6	750	1522
Ivey Mechanical Co	306	Kosciusko, MS	Public Family Member	105.0	750	1711
Odebrecht of America, Inc.	307	Washington, DC	Private	117.8	750	1622
Phillips & Jordan Inc	308	Knoxville, TN	Private	90.7	750	1629
Univ Mech & Engineer Contractors	309	San Diego, CA	Public Family Member	86.0	750	1711
Wilson Electric Co, Inc.	310	Scottsdale, AZ	Public Family Member	71.0	750	1731
Danis Companies	311	Dayton, OH	Private	268.0	745	1629
Engle Homes Inc	312	Boca Raton, FL	Public	536.0	744	1521
Zurn Constructors, Inc	313	Erie, PA	Public Family Member	85.2	744	1629
Odebrecht Contractors of Florida	314	Coral Gables, FL	Private	151.2	740	1622
Ameralum Inc	315	Middletown, PA	Private	74.5	730	1742
Brice Building Co Inc	316	Birmingham, AL	Private	215.9	730	1542
Swinerton & Walberg Co	317	San Francisco, CA	Private	558.8	729	1542
W W Gay Mechanical Contractors	318	Jacksonville, FL	Private	67.5	717	1711
Amec Holdings Inc	319	New York, NY	Private	89.1	700	1541
Arb Inc	320	Lake Forest, CA	Private	205.2	700	1542
Belmont Constructors Co	321	Houston, TX	Public Family Member	80.1	700	1629
Branch Group Inc	322	Roanoke, VA	Private	200.0	700	1542
CCC Group Inc	323	San Antonio, TX	Private	118.2	700	1541
CDK Contracting Co	324	Farmington, NM	Private	109.2	700	1541
Crowder Construction Co	325	Charlotte, NC	Private	104.0	700	1629
FK Co, Inc	326	Farmington, NM	Private	109.2	700	1541
Kinsley Construction, Inc	327	York, PA	Private	143.0	700	1541
Kitchell Corp	328	Phoenix, AZ	Private	289.0	700	1542
Lunda Construction Co	329	Black River Falls, WI	Private	120.0	700	1622
Metric Constructors Inc	330	Charlotte, NC	Private	380.1	700	1541
Murphy Mech Contractors Engineers	331	St. Louis, MO	Private	146.6	700	1711
National Energy Production	332	Redmond, WA	Public Family Member	200.0	700	1629
Nielsen Dillingham Builders	333	San Diego, CA	Private	360.0	700	1542
Penhall International Inc	334	Anaheim, CA	Private	90.0	700	1795
Rocky Mountain Remed Serv LLC	335	Golden, CO	Private	100.0	700	1799
Security Technologies Group	336	Fort Lauderdale, FL	Private	75.0	700	1731
Structure-Tone, Inc	337	New York, NY	Private	154.2	700	1542
Trumbull Corp	338	West Mifflin, PA	Private	78.3	700	1611
Welded Construction Co	339	Perrysburg, OH	Private	116.4	700	1623
Western States Fire Protection	340	Englewood, CO	Private	132.3	700	1711
Willbros USA, Inc	341	Tulsa, OK	Private	106.4	700	1623
Miller Electric Co	342	Jacksonville, FL	Private	83.5	691	1731
Cupertino Electric Inc	343	Sunnyvale, CA	Private	143.6	675	1731
Egan Companies	344	Minneapolis, MN	Private	94.7	675	1711
Elgin National Industries Inc	345	Downers Grove, IL	Private	139.6	672	1629
Gilbert Southern Corp.	346	Omaha, NE	Private	84.7	672	1611
Ashtead Holdings, Inc.	347	Charlotte, NC	Private	72.6	670	7353
Sunbelt Rentals Inc	348	Charlotte, NC	Private	72.6	670	7353
Jack B Parson Companies	349	Ogden, UT	Private	145.5	662	1611
Amfels, Inc	350	Brownsville, TX	Private	75.5	660	1629

D&B COMPANY RANKINGS BY EMPLOYMENT

Company	Rank	Location	Type	Sales ($ mil.)	Employ-ment	Primary SIC
Weitz Co Inc	351	Des Moines, IA	Private	500.0	660	1542
Hardaway Group Inc	352	Nashville, TN	Private	115.0	657	1542
Anderson Columbia Co Inc	353	Lake City, FL	Private	100.0	650	1611
Centex Rooney Construction Co	354	Fort Lauderdale, FL	Public Family Member	350.0	650	1542
Continental Homes Inc	355	Scottsdale, AZ	Public Family Member	204.5	650	1531
E L Yeager Construction Co	356	Riverside, CA	Private	171.6	650	1611
Getschow Group Inc	357	Oconto Falls, WI	Private	84.9	650	1711
Graham Companies	358	Hialeah, FL	Private	156.7	650	1531
Guarantee Electrical Co	359	St. Louis, MO	Private	80.0	650	1731
Hathaway Dinwiddie Constr Grp	360	San Francisco, CA	Private	452.0	650	1542
Kokosing Construction Co	361	Fredericktown, OH	Private	260.0	650	1611
Main Street Operating Co Inc	362	Nashville, TN	Private	143.0	650	1542
Phillips, Getschow Co	363	Green Bay, WI	Private	84.9	650	1711
O & G Industries Inc	364	Torrington, CT	Private	198.9	649	1542
Safe Sites of Colorado, LLC	365	Golden, CO	Public Family Member	156.4	637	1799
Braddock & Logan Group L.P.	366	Danville, CA	Private	197.8	629	1531
Amtech Elevator Services	367	Whittier, CA	Public Family Member	82.1	604	1796
Abrams International Inc	368	Austin, TX	Private	110.0	600	1611
Airtron Inc	369	Dayton, OH	Public Family Member	98.0	600	1711
Apac-Florida Inc	370	Sarasota, FL	Public Family Member	97.8	600	1611
Austin Bridge & Road, Inc	371	Dallas, TX	Private	75.6	600	1611
Austin Commercial Inc	372	Dallas, TX	Private	400.0	600	1542
Bell Corp of Rochester	373	Rochester, NY	Private	131.9	600	1542
Black Construction Corp	374	Honolulu, HI	Private	76.5	600	1541
Cajun Constructors, Inc.	375	Baton Rouge, LA	Private	112.0	600	1623
Christenson Electric Inc	376	Portland, OR	Private	88.2	600	1731
Corrigan Brothers Inc	377	St. Louis, MO	Private	75.0	600	1711
Fullman Co, LLC	378	Portland, OR	Private	120.0	600	1711
H J Russell & Co	379	Atlanta, GA	Private	131.9	600	1542
Hardaway Co Inc	380	Columbus, GA	Private	135.0	600	1622
Hunt Corp	381	Indianapolis, IN	Private	900.0	600	1542
J H Berra Holding Co Inc	382	St. Louis, MO	Private	90.0	600	1611
Johnson Bros. Corp	383	Litchfield, MN	Private	74.0	600	1622
Motor City Electric Co	384	Detroit, MI	Private	179.0	600	1731
Oltmans Construction Co	385	Whittier, CA	Private	260.1	600	1541
Sargent Electric Co	386	Pittsburgh, PA	Private	69.9	600	1731
Shelly & Sands Inc	387	Zanesville, OH	Private	100.0	600	1611
Sunco Building Corp	388	Palm Beach Gardens, FL	Private	82.5	600	1521
Walbridge Aldinger Co	389	Detroit, MI	Private	630.0	600	1541
Waldinger Corp	390	Des Moines, IA	Private	83.0	600	1711
White Construction Co	391	Chiefland, FL	Private	72.3	600	1611
J C Higgins Corp	392	Stoughton, MA	Public Family Member	122.0	598	1711
MP Water Resources Group, Inc	393	Duluth, MN	Public Family Member	119.0	589	1623
Amerilink Corp	394	Columbus, OH	Public	70.0	588	1623
Shea Homes LP	395	Walnut, CA	Private	1,200.0	588	1521
Kimmins Corp	396	Tampa, FL	Public	113.5	575	1799
J D Abrams Inc	397	Austin, TX	Private	102.5	572	1611
Klinger Companies, Inc	398	Sioux City, IA	Private	120.7	550	1542
Mitchell Construction Co	399	Vidalia, GA	Private	100.0	550	1542
Monsanto Enviro-Chem Systems	400	Chesterfield, MO	Public Family Member	175.0	550	1629
Pate & Pate Enterprises Inc	401	The Woodlands, TX	Private	73.8	550	1623
Viceroy, Inc.	402	Pasadena, TX	Public Family Member	97.9	549	1629
C W Matthews Contracting Co	403	Marietta, GA	Private	100.0	540	1622
Morrison Homes, Inc	404	Alpharetta, GA	Private	301.6	540	1521
Grucon Corp	405	Milwaukee, WI	Private	88.4	532	1711
MMC Corp	406	Shawnee Mission, KS	Private	269.0	525	1711
U.S. Engineering Co	407	Kansas City, MO	Private	109.6	525	1711
Southland Industries	408	Long Beach, CA	Private	176.9	521	1711
Utilx Corp	409	Kent, WA	Public	82.5	515	1623
Mercedes Homes Inc	410	Melbourne, FL	Private	175.8	502	1521
Angelo Iafrate Construction Co	411	Warren, MI	Private	150.0	500	1611
Blythe Construction Inc	412	Charlotte, NC	Private	134.0	500	1611
Brinderson	413	Newport Beach, CA	Private	100.0	500	1629
CCBC Inc.	414	Homewood, IL	Private	200.0	500	1541
CDI Contractors, LLC	415	Little Rock, AR	Private	303.9	500	1542
Clayco Construction Co	416	St. Louis, MO	Private	155.9	500	1541
Cleveland Construction Inc	417	Mentor, OH	Private	103.9	500	1542
Codillera Construction Corp	418	Edwards, CO	Private	68.5	500	1521
Fish Construction Co	419	Studio City, CA	Private	68.5	500	1521
General Construction Co	420	Seattle, WA	Private	135.0	500	1622

D&B COMPANY RANKINGS BY EMPLOYMENT

Company	Rank	Location	Type	Sales ($ mil.)	Employ-ment	Primary SIC
Graycor Inc	421	Homewood, IL	Private	200.0	500	1541
Hardin Construction Group Inc	422	Atlanta, GA	Private	450.0	500	1542
HBG USA Inc	423	New York, NY	Private	78.1	500	1622
Horst Group Inc	424	Lancaster, PA	Private	109.5	500	1542
Huber Hunt & Nichols Inc	425	Indianapolis, IN	Private	900.0	500	1542
Interbeton Inc	426	Rockland, MA	Private	102.3	500	1629
J F Ahern Co	427	Fond Du Lac, WI	Private	98.5	500	1711
Kvaerner Songer, Inc.	428	Washington, PA	Private	179.0	500	1711
Michael Nicholas Inc	429	Carol Stream, IL	Private	70.0	500	1751
Michels Pipeline Construction	430	Brownsville, WI	Private	158.0	500	1623
Petrocelli Electric Co Inc	431	Long Island City, NY	Private	83.4	500	1731
Powell Construction Co	432	Johnson City, TN	Private	119.0	500	1542
Regis Homes Corp	433	Irvine, CA	Private	156.7	500	1531
Roth Bros Inc	434	Youngstown, OH	Public Family Member	75.0	500	1711
S T Wooten Corp	435	Wilson, NC	Private	90.0	500	1611
Sellen Construction Co Inc	436	Seattle, WA	Private	184.8	500	1542
Shasta Industries Inc	437	Phoenix, AZ	Private	69.0	500	1799
Stevens Painton Corp	438	Cleveland, OH	Private	91.4	500	1541
T J Lambrecht Construction	439	Joliet, IL	Private	70.8	500	1794
Weeks Marine Inc	440	Cranford, NJ	Private	164.5	500	1629
Western Summit Constructors	441	Denver, CO	Private	87.1	500	1629
Williard Inc	442	Jenkintown, PA	Private	118.7	500	1711
Yeager Holdings, Inc	443	Riverside, CA	Private	171.6	500	1611
Levitt Corp	444	New York, NY	Private	120.4	493	1531
Lewis Lease Crutcher	445	Seattle, WA	Private	107.3	490	1542
Elliott-Lewis Corp	446	Philadelphia, PA	Public Family Member	75.0	480	1711
R J Griffin & Co	447	Atlanta, GA	Private	212.7	479	1542
Kelso-Burnett Co Del	448	Rolling Meadows, IL	Private	73.9	475	1731
Atlantic Plant Maintenance	449	Pasadena, TX	Public Family Member	95.2	470	1629
Holder Corp	450	Atlanta, GA	Private	288.1	470	1542
Aldridge Electric Inc (Del)	451	Libertyville, IL	Private	80.0	467	1731
National Business Group	452	Mission Hills, CA	Private	70.0	455	7353
Greystone Homes Inc	453	Los Angeles, CA	Public Family Member	420.0	454	1521
Amelco Corp	454	Gardena, CA	Private	107.9	450	1731
Apac-Alabama Inc	455	Birmingham, AL	Public Family Member	114.3	450	1611
Drees Co	456	Fort Mitchell, KY	Private	342.8	450	1521
Global Energy Eqp Group LLC	457	Tulsa, OK	Private	98.3	450	1542
I A Holdings Corp	458	Concordville, PA	Private	153.4	450	1622
McKinstry Co	459	Seattle, WA	Private	70.0	450	1711
Meadow Valley Corp	460	Phoenix, AZ	Public	150.0	450	1611
Miller Building Corp	461	Wilmington, NC	Private	152.5	450	1541
O'Connell Companies Inc	462	Holyoke, MA	Private	91.2	450	1541
Roxco Ltd	463	Brandon, MS	Private	100.0	450	1542
Ryan Companies U.S., Inc	464	Minneapolis, MN	Private	189.3	450	1542
Ryan Properties, Inc.	465	Minneapolis, MN	Private	198.8	450	1542
Cal Dive International Inc	466	Houston, TX	Public	109.4	432	1629
Standard Pacific Corp	467	Costa Mesa, CA	Public	584.6	430	1531
Zaring National Corp	468	Cincinnati, OH	Public	224.0	428	1521
Brandenburg Industrial Service Co	469	Chicago, IL	Private	75.0	425	1622
Oxford Holdings, Inc	470	Fort Lauderdale, FL	Private	92.8	425	1542
Inrecon, L.L.C.	471	Birmingham, MI	Private	71.9	420	1521
Quality Mechanical Contractors	472	Las Vegas, NV	Private	82.7	420	1711
Hitt Contracting Inc	473	Fairfax, VA	Private	200.0	413	1542
Royce Homes, Inc	474	Houston, TX	Private	100.0	412	1521
Cochran Inc	475	Seattle, WA	Private	81.0	405	1731
Dualstar Technologies Corp	476	Long Island City, NY	Public	94.3	404	1711
Adco Electrical Corp	477	Staten Island, NY	Private	94.9	400	1731
American Bridge Co	478	Pittsburgh, PA	Private	146.0	400	1791
Anning-Johnson Co	479	Melrose Park, IL	Private	72.0	400	1742
Apac-Tennessee Inc	480	Alcoa, TN	Public Family Member	196.6	400	1611
Apac-Texas Inc	481	Dallas, TX	Public Family Member	69.8	400	1611
Batson-Cook Co	482	West Point, GA	Private	169.9	400	1542
Baugh Construction Oregon Inc	483	Beaverton, OR	Private	225.0	400	1542
C A Rasmussen Inc	484	Simi Valley, CA	Private	201.7	400	1611
Clancy & Theys Construction Co	485	Raleigh, NC	Private	250.0	400	1541
E L Hamm & Associates Inc	486	Virginia Beach, VA	Private	87.2	400	1542
E-J Electric Installation Co	487	Long Island City, NY	Private	80.0	400	1731
Ecker Enterprises Inc	488	Chicago, IL	Private	73.7	400	1742
Frank Messer & Sons Constr Co	489	Cincinnati, OH	Private	239.6	400	1542
Grupe Co (Inc)	490	Stockton, CA	Private	124.8	400	1531

D&B COMPANY RANKINGS BY EMPLOYMENT

Company	Rank	Location	Type	Sales ($ mil.)	Employment	Primary SIC
Hendrickson/Scalamade	491	Farmingdale, NY	Private	100.0	400	1622
Highland Homes Holdings Inc	492	Dallas, TX	Private	323.0	400	1521
James McHugh Construction Co	493	Chicago, IL	Private	113.5	400	1542
Kalikow, H. J. & Co., LLC	494	New York, NY	Private	87.2	400	1542
Keenan, Hopkins	495	Tampa, FL	Private	70.5	400	1542
Kenny Construction Co	496	Wheeling, IL	Private	200.0	400	1622
LCS Holdings, Inc.	497	Des Moines, IA	Private	87.2	400	1542
Levitt Homes Inc	498	Boca Raton, FL	Private	114.4	400	1522
Loftin Constructors, Inc.	499	Brandon, MS	Private	100.0	400	1542
M W Holdings Inc	500	Detroit, MI	Private	141.1	400	1791
Manafort Brothers Inc	501	Plainville, CT	Private	75.0	400	1794
McHugh Enterprises, Inc.	502	Chicago, IL	Private	87.2	400	1542
Michael/Curry Companies, Inc	503	Minneapolis, MN	Private	135.0	400	1542
N A B Construction Corp	504	College Point, NY	Private	88.8	400	1541
Paddock Pool Construction Co.	505	Scottsdale, AZ	Private	72.0	400	1799
Sloan Construction Co	506	Greenville, SC	Private	130.0	400	1611
Southern Nevada Paving Inc	507	Las Vegas, NV	Private	89.6	400	1611
Starstone Construction Co	508	Clairton, PA	Private	87.2	400	1542
Suffolk Construction Co	509	Boston, MA	Private	378.0	400	1542
Superior Construction Co Inc	510	Gary, IN	Private	78.7	400	1622
Taylor Ball, Inc.	511	West Des Moines, IA	Private	235.4	400	1542
Kinsel Industries Inc	512	Houston, TX	Private	75.0	385	1623
Devcon Construction Inc	513	Milpitas, CA	Private	602.9	384	1541
C D Smith Construction Inc	514	Fond Du Lac, WI	Private	110.9	380	1542
Washington Homes Inc	515	Landover, MD	Public	240.7	377	1531
Presley Companies	516	Newport Beach, CA	Public	329.9	376	1531
Whittaker Construction Inc	517	St. Peters, MO	Public Family Member	85.0	375	1521
Wohlsen Construction Co	518	Lancaster, PA	Private	135.0	375	1542
Asplundh Construction Corp	519	Patchogue, NY	Private	67.6	370	1731
Randall Abb Corp	520	Houston, TX	Private	89.6	370	1629
Dominion Homes Inc	521	Dublin, OH	Public	207.9	362	1531
Choate Construction Co	522	Marietta, GA	Private	173.5	360	1542
Winter Construction Co Inc	523	Atlanta, GA	Private	200.0	360	1542
Apac-Mississippi Inc	524	Atlanta, GA	Public Family Member	81.5	358	1611
C F Jordan Inc	525	El Paso, TX	Private	231.1	355	1541
Ogden Energy Group Inc	526	Fairfield, NJ	Public Family Member	699.2	355	1629
Adolfson & Peterson, Inc	527	Minneapolis, MN	Private	206.0	350	1542
Barry Bette & Led Duke Inc	528	Albany, NY	Private	300.0	350	1542
Bor-Son Construction, Inc	529	Minneapolis, MN	Private	120.0	350	1542
Boran Craig Barbr Engel Constr	530	Naples, FL	Private	145.3	350	1522
Branch Highways Inc	531	Roanoke, VA	Private	95.0	350	1611
Caddell Construction Co Inc	532	Montgomery, AL	Private	143.0	350	1542
Felix Equities, Inc.	533	Lincolndale, NY	Private	77.9	350	1623
Fortress Group Inc	534	McLean, VA	Public	445.3	350	1521
Herman Goldner Co Inc	535	Philadelphia, PA	Private	96.3	350	1711
J P Cullen & Sons Inc	536	Janesville, WI	Private	98.4	350	1542
John E Green Co	537	Detroit, MI	Private	116.0	350	1711
Jones Co Custom Homes Inc	538	St. Louis, MO	Private	131.2	350	1521
Kaufman & Broad of S California	539	Los Angeles, CA	Public Family Member	455.1	350	1521
Metropolitan Mechanical Contractors	540	Eden Prairie, MN	Private	80.0	350	1711
Middlesex Corp	541	Littleton, MA	Private	75.0	350	1611
Modern-Obayashi Corp	542	Boston, MA	Private	75.0	350	1622
Slattery Associates Inc (Del)	543	Whitestone, NY	Private	237.9	350	1623
Stellar Group Inc	544	Jacksonville, FL	Private	202.6	350	1541
Walsh Construction Co	545	Portland, OR	Private	120.0	350	1522
Welsbach Electric Corp (Del)	546	College Point, NY	Public Family Member	80.0	350	1731
MBC Holdings, Inc	547	Archbold, OH	Private	109.2	341	1611
Florida Mivan Inc	548	Lake Buena Vista, FL	Private	71.5	330	1542
Ritchie Corp	549	Wichita, KS	Private	113.7	330	1611
Tempco Disaster Services, Inc	550	Glendale, CA	Private	71.5	330	1542
Gary Merlino Construction Co	551	Seattle, WA	Private	100.0	325	1611
Kimball Hill Inc	552	Rolling Meadows, IL	Private	245.8	325	1521
Latco Inc	553	Lincoln, AR	Private	70.0	325	1542
Neosho Inc	554	Topeka, KS	Private	71.9	325	1611
Corna/Kokosing Construction Co	555	Columbus, OH	Private	69.5	321	1542
Flatiron Structures Co LLC	556	Longmont, CO	Private	150.0	320	1622
Chas Roberts A/C Inc	557	Phoenix, AZ	Private	78.5	310	1711
Ramex Construction Co, Inc	558	Pasadena, TX	Private	67.5	310	1623
Ajax Paving Industries Inc	559	Madison Heights, MI	Private	100.0	300	1611
American Sports Products Group	560	White Plains, NY	Private	130.0	300	1629

D&B COMPANY RANKINGS BY EMPLOYMENT

Company	Rank	Location	Type	Sales ($ mil.)	Employ-ment	Primary SIC
Apac-Virginia Inc	561	Danville, VA	Public Family Member	89.6	300	1611
Baugh Construction Co Inc	562	Seattle, WA	Private	200.0	300	1542
Baylor Health Enterprises Inc	563	Dallas, TX	Private	91.6	300	1542
Big D Construction Corp	564	Ogden, UT	Private	177.0	300	1541
Cache Valley Electric Co	565	Logan, UT	Private	69.6	300	1731
Chapman Corp	566	Washington, PA	Private	70.0	300	1541
Dal-Mac Construction Co	567	Richardson, TX	Private	165.0	300	1542
Edward Kraemer & Sons Inc	568	Plain, WI	Private	140.0	300	1622
F.N.F. Construction, Inc.	569	Tempe, AZ	Private	114.2	300	1611
FTR International Inc	570	Irvine, CA	Private	100.0	300	1542
G E Johnson Construction Co	571	Colorado Springs, CO	Private	152.2	300	1542
Gerald H Phipps Inc	572	Denver, CO	Private	146.0	300	1542
Gonsalves & Santucci Inc	573	Concord, CA	Private	122.5	300	1541
Goodfellow Bros, Inc.	574	Wenatchee, WA	Private	70.0	300	1611
Harris Contracting Co	575	St. Paul, MN	Private	70.6	300	1711
Home Place Inc	576	Gainesville, GA	Private	72.1	300	1521
Hovnanian Pennsylvania Inc	577	Edison, NJ	Public Family Member	92.9	300	1531
Howard S Wright Construction Co	578	Seattle, WA	Private	210.0	300	1542
Howe-Baker Engineers, Inc	579	Tyler, TX	Private	91.6	300	1629
Icom Mechanical Inc	580	San Jose, CA	Private	99.9	300	1711
J H Findorff & Son Inc	581	Madison, WI	Private	128.1	300	1542
Keller Foundations, Inc	582	Odenton, MD	Private	136.4	300	1799
Klukwan Inc	583	Juneau, AK	Private	71.5	300	1611
Koester Companies Inc	584	Evansville, IN	Private	82.4	300	1629
Layton Construction Co	585	Sandy, UT	Private	100.0	300	1542
Lechase Construction Services LLC	586	Rochester, NY	Private	138.2	300	1542
Lennar Homes Inc	587	Miami, FL	Public Family Member	528.3	300	1531
Lyda Inc	588	San Antonio, TX	Private	100.0	300	1542
M W Builders, Inc	589	Shawnee Mission, KS	Private	135.0	300	1542
Market & Johnson, Inc	590	Eau Claire, WI	Private	83.6	300	1542
McClure Co Inc	591	Harrisburg, PA	Public Family Member	70.0	300	1711
N A CCC Inc	592	Troy, MI	Private	74.1	300	1796
Newmech Companies, Inc	593	St. Paul, MN	Private	80.0	300	1711
Northwest Racing Associates Lp	594	Auburn, WA	Private	157.0	300	1629
O'Neil Industries, Inc.	595	Chicago, IL	Private	244.7	300	1542
Pulice Construction Inc	596	Phoenix, AZ	Private	68.2	300	1611
Richmond Am Homes of California	597	Concord, CA	Public Family Member	182.4	300	1521
Richmond Am Homes of Colorado	598	Denver, CO	Public Family Member	360.0	300	1531
Roy Anderson Corp	599	Gulfport, MS	Private	201.3	300	1542
RR Westminster Holding DE Corp	600	New York, NY	Private	109.4	300	1542
Ryan Inc Eastern	601	Deerfield Beach, FL	Private	75.0	300	1794
S J Amoroso Construction Co	602	Foster City, CA	Private	226.6	300	1542
Schiavone Construction Co	603	Secaucus, NJ	Private	88.3	300	1629
Shapell Industries Inc	604	Beverly Hills, CA	Private	408.0	300	1531
Tellepsen Corp	605	Houston, TX	Private	115.0	300	1542
Valenzuela Engineering Inc	606	Santa Maria, CA	Private	68.0	300	1542
Venture Construction Co	607	Norcross, GA	Private	150.7	300	1542
W S Bellows Construction Corp	608	Houston, TX	Private	130.0	300	1542
Walton Construction Co Inc	609	Kansas City, MO	Private	308.0	300	1542
Welbro Constructors Inc	610	Maitland, FL	Private	90.0	300	1522
Becon Construction Co	611	Houston, TX	Private	301.0	285	1541
Robison Construction Inc	612	Sumner, WA	Private	75.2	280	1623
Carl M Freeman Associates	613	Potomac, MD	Private	85.0	275	1531
Hospitality Worldwide Services	614	New York, NY	Public	85.4	275	1522
Westra Construction Inc	615	Waupun, WI	Private	96.6	275	1542
Ninteman Construction Co	616	San Diego, CA	Private	100.0	271	1542
Edward Rose Building Co	617	Farmington Hills, MI	Private	83.4	270	1531
Holly Management LLC	618	Dallas, TX	Private	95.0	270	1521
Pacific Realty Group, Inc.	619	Dallas, TX	Private	83.4	270	1531
Choice Homes-Texas, Inc	620	Arlington, TX	Private	243.8	268	1521
Shook National Corp	621	Dayton, OH	Private	112.0	266	1629
Fisher Development Inc	622	San Francisco, CA	Private	310.1	265	1542
Roel Construction Co, Inc	623	San Diego, CA	Private	128.3	260	1542
Cleveland Group Inc	624	Atlanta, GA	Private	147.8	255	1542
Abrams Industries Inc	625	Atlanta, GA	Public	178.6	250	1541
Archer Western Contractors	626	Fort Lauderdale, FL	Private	299.5	250	1622
Barrett Paving Materials Inc	627	Roseland, NJ	Private	203.2	250	1611
C R Meyer & Sons Co	628	Oshkosh, WI	Private	94.5	250	1541
Centex Forum Lannom Inc	629	Dyersburg, TN	Public Family Member	104.6	250	1541
Douglas E Barnhart Inc	630	San Diego, CA	Private	195.0	250	1542

D&B COMPANY RANKINGS BY EMPLOYMENT

Company	Rank	Location	Type	Sales ($ mil.)	Employ- ment	Primary SIC
Equipment Supply Co Inc	631	Burlington, NJ	Public Family Member	100.0	250	7353
Freesen, Inc	632	Bluffs, IL	Private	94.5	250	1629
Frehner Construction Co Inc	633	North Las Vegas, NV	Private	68.8	250	1611
G W Murphy Construction Co	634	Honolulu, HI	Private	112.0	250	1542
H & M Construction Co., Inc	635	Jackson, TN	Private	190.0	250	1541
Hawkins Construction Co	636	Omaha, NE	Private	94.7	250	1542
Horton D R Texas LP	637	Arlington, TX	Public Family Member	186.9	250	1521
Interstate Highway Construction	638	Englewood, CO	Private	120.0	250	1611
Jaynes Corp	639	Albuquerque, NM	Private	103.5	250	1542
Korte Construction Co	640	St. Louis, MO	Private	102.3	250	1541
L F Driscoll Co	641	Bala Cynwyd, PA	Private	250.0	250	1542
MCC Group, L.L.C.	642	Metairie, LA	Private	106.9	250	1711
McGough Construction Co, Inc	643	St. Paul, MN	Private	168.0	250	1542
Milestone Contractors, L.P.	644	Indianapolis, IN	Private	175.0	250	1611
Oldcastle Northwest Inc	645	Tukwila, WA	Private	100.0	250	1629
River City Construction L.L.C.	646	East Peoria, IL	Private	120.9	250	1542
Robins and Morton Group	647	Birmingham, AL	Private	210.0	250	1542
Stiles Corp	648	Fort Lauderdale, FL	Private	150.5	250	1541
Tully Construction Co Inc	649	Flushing, NY	Private	150.0	250	1611
W M Schlosser Co Inc	650	Hyattsville, MD	Private	75.0	250	1542
Wilder Construction Co	651	Everett, WA	Private	142.7	250	1611
Rottlund Co Inc	652	St. Paul, MN	Public	160.8	248	1531
Warmington Homes	653	Costa Mesa, CA	Private	170.0	246	1531
Engelberth Construction Inc	654	Colchester, VT	Private	100.8	240	1542
North Bros, Inc	655	Atlanta, GA	Private	120.0	240	1742
Shelco Inc	656	Charlotte, NC	Private	280.0	240	1541
Sithe Energies USA Inc	657	New York, NY	Private	335.8	240	1629
Danis Building Construction Co	658	Dayton, OH	Private	124.6	235	1542
J R Roberts Enterprises	659	Citrus Heights, CA	Private	250.0	230	1542
John Crosland Co	660	Charlotte, NC	Public Family Member	70.6	230	1531
Staker Paving and Construction Co	661	North Salt Lake, UT	Private	79.1	230	1611
DJB Construction Group, Inc	662	Raleigh, NC	Private	121.5	228	1541
Advance Mechanical Systems Inc	663	Mount Prospect, IL	Private	70.0	225	1711
C C Myers Inc	664	Rancho Cordova, CA	Private	89.4	225	1622
California Pacific Homes Inc	665	Irvine, CA	Private	240.0	225	1531
Conlan Co	666	Marietta, GA	Private	81.0	225	1542
Facility Group Inc	667	Smyrna, GA	Private	115.8	225	1541
Hake Group Inc	668	Eddystone, PA	Private	72.0	225	1796
Pike Industries, Inc	669	Belmont, NH	Private	145.0	225	1611
Winchester Homes Inc	670	Greenbelt, MD	Public Family Member	156.0	220	1531
Capital Pacific Holdings Inc	671	Newport Beach, CA	Public	191.1	217	1531
Granger Management Corp	672	Shrewsbury, MA	Private	99.8	214	1542
Fullmer Construction	673	Ontario, CA	Private	110.0	210	1541
Walter & Sci Construction USA	674	Renton, WA	Private	219.2	207	1622
David E Harvey Builders Inc	675	Houston, TX	Private	89.1	204	1542
Apac-Missouri, Inc.	676	Columbia, MO	Public Family Member	115.0	200	1611
C Raimondo & Sons Constr Co	677	Fort Lee, NJ	Private	115.5	200	1542
Centex Rodgers Construction Co	678	Nashville, TN	Public Family Member	180.0	200	1542
Charles N White Construction Co	679	Clarksdale, MS	Private	142.4	200	1542
Commercial Contracting Corp	680	Troy, MI	Private	110.5	200	1796
Conti Enterprises, Inc	681	South Plainfield, NJ	Private	77.1	200	1611
Dematteo/Flat Iron	682	Boston, MA	Private	160.0	200	1611
E M J Corp	683	Chattanooga, TN	Private	188.9	200	1542
E W Howell Co Inc	684	Port Washington, NY	Private	125.0	200	1542
Elmo Greer & Sons Inc	685	London, KY	Private	70.0	200	1611
Foster Wheeler Constrs Inc	686	Clinton, NJ	Public Family Member	251.1	200	1541
Frank A McBride Co	687	Hawthorne, NJ	Private	82.1	200	1711
Gall, Landau Young Construction Co	688	Bellevue, WA	Private	134.7	200	1542
Gohmann Asphalt and Construction	689	Clarksville, IN	Private	88.0	200	1611
Hcbeck, Ltd	690	Dallas, TX	Private	500.0	200	1541
Jay Cashman Inc	691	Boston, MA	Private	102.4	200	1629
Kleinknecht Electric Co	692	New York, NY	Private	84.2	200	1731
Lathrop Co Inc	693	Maumee, OH	Public Family Member	200.0	200	1542
Law Co Inc	694	Wichita, KS	Private	70.0	200	1542
Lundgren Bros. Construction	695	Wayzata, MN	Private	68.7	200	1521
M & H Enterprises Inc	696	Las Vegas, NV	Private	67.7	200	1542
M J Brock & Sons Inc	697	Woodland Hills, CA	Public Family Member	74.0	200	1531
Midwest Mechanical Contractors Inc	698	Shawnee Mission, KS	Private	110.0	200	1711
Mount Hope Rock Products Inc	699	Wharton, NJ	Private	124.7	200	1611
N.L. Barnes Construction, Inc	700	San Francisco, CA	Private	135.0	200	1542

D&B COMPANY RANKINGS BY EMPLOYMENT

Company	Rank	Location	Type	Sales ($ mil.)	Employ- ment	Primary SIC
Natkin Contracting LLC	701	Englewood, CO	Private	100.0	200	1711
Neenan Co	702	Fort Collins, CO	Private	88.2	200	1542
Newmark Home Corp	703	Sugar Land, TX	Public	164.0	200	1531
Okland Construction Co	704	Salt Lake City, UT	Private	220.0	200	1542
P J Dick Inc	705	West Mifflin, PA	Private	129.0	200	1542
Perry Homes, a Joint Venture	706	Houston, TX	Private	220.0	200	1531
Pike Co Inc	707	Rochester, NY	Private	100.0	200	1542
Rentenbach Eng Co	708	Knoxville, TN	Private	95.8	200	1541
Shea-Traylor-Healy Joint Venture	709	Framingham, MA	Private	71.0	200	1531
Sletten Construction of Nevada	710	Las Vegas, NV	Private	70.8	200	1542
Sletten Inc	711	Great Falls, MT	Private	134.7	200	1542
Stebbins Enterprises Inc	712	Hooksett, NH	Private	80.0	200	1542
Torcon Inc	713	Westfield, NJ	Private	400.0	200	1542
W E O'Neil Construction Co	714	Chicago, IL	Private	153.7	200	1542
W M Jordan Co Inc	715	Newport News, VA	Private	150.0	200	1542
Williams Industries Inc	716	Houston, TX	Private	97.0	200	1542
Tilcon Connecticut, Inc.	717	North Branford, CT	Private	75.6	198	1611
Nason & Cullen Group Inc	718	King of Prussia, PA	Private	123.3	195	1542
Amrep Southwest Inc	719	Rio Rancho, NM	Public Family Member	104.8	193	1521
Meritage Corp	720	Scottsdale, AZ	Public	155.1	190	1521
New Fortis Corp	721	King, NC	Public Family Member	133.0	190	1521
Richmond Am Homes of Virginia	722	Fairfax, VA	Public Family Member	111.1	190	1521
Forecast Group, LP	723	Rancho Cucamonga, CA	Private	198.1	188	1531
Rogers-O'Brien Construction Co	724	Dallas, TX	Private	107.9	188	1541
Woodrow Taylor Homes Inc	725	Laguna Hills, CA	Private	147.3	183	1521
Albert M Higley Co	726	Cleveland, OH	Private	80.5	180	1542
J F White Contracting Co	727	Newton, MA	Private	147.7	180	1622
Rafn Co	728	Bellevue, WA	Private	80.0	180	1542
Shawmut Woodworking & Supply	729	Boston, MA	Private	126.7	179	1542
Albert C Kobayashi Inc	730	Waipahu, HI	Private	104.6	175	1542
Bechtel Construction Co	731	San Francisco, CA	Private	215.0	175	1629
Ces/Way International, Inc	732	Houston, TX	Private	90.0	175	1711
Daniel J Keating Construction Co	733	Bala Cynwyd, PA	Private	250.0	175	1542
Hayward Baker Inc	734	Odenton, MD	Private	75.0	175	1799
Hunter Contracting Co.	735	Gilbert, AZ	Private	67.9	175	1611
Kvaerner Construction Inc	736	Tampa, FL	Private	76.8	175	1542
Leopardo Companies, Inc.	737	Glendale Heights, IL	Private	120.0	175	1542
Mascaro Construction Co Lp	738	Pittsburgh, PA	Private	79.3	175	1542
Nor-Am Construction Co	739	Portland, OR	Private	70.0	175	1542
Sovereign Homes Corp	740	Dallas, TX	Private	167.5	175	1521
Dimeo Construction Co	741	Providence, RI	Private	105.9	170	1542
G L Homes of Florida Corp	742	Pompano Beach, FL	Private	185.0	170	1521
Hunt Building Corp	743	El Paso, TX	Private	160.0	170	1522
Spaw Glass Holding Corp	744	Houston, TX	Private	152.7	170	1542
Auchter Co Inc	745	Jacksonville, FL	Private	76.0	165	1542
Orleans Corp	746	Bensalem, PA	Public Family Member	100.0	165	1521
Slayden Construction Inc	747	Stayton, OR	Private	90.0	163	1542
Beacon Skanska Construction Co	748	Boston, MA	Private	150.0	160	1542
Buffington Homes Inc	749	Austin, TX	Public Family Member	100.0	160	1521
Hagerman Construction Corp	750	Fort Wayne, IN	Private	89.0	160	1542
Obayashi U. S. Holdings Inc	751	New York, NY	Private	250.0	160	1542
Goodman Family of Builders	752	Plano, TX	Private	113.7	156	1521
Myrick, Batson & Gurosky Inc	753	Birmingham, AL	Private	75.0	155	1542
Vratsinas Construction Co	754	Little Rock, AR	Private	131.8	154	1542
Absher Construction Co	755	Puyallup, WA	Private	70.1	150	1542
Atlantic Coast Mechanical Inc	756	Raleigh, NC	Private	100.0	150	1711
Baker/Mellon Stuart Constr Inc	757	Coraopolis, PA	Public Family Member	110.0	150	1542
BFW Construction Co Inc	758	Temple, TX	Private	75.0	150	1542
Catellus Residential Group	759	Irvine, CA	Public Family Member	105.3	150	1531
Eastern Contractors Inc	760	Framingham, MA	Private	70.1	150	1542
Elkins Constructors Inc	761	Jacksonville, FL	Private	78.9	150	1542
F H Paschen, S N Nielsen, Inc.	762	Des Plaines, IL	Private	93.8	150	1542
FCI Constructors, Inc	763	Grand Junction, CO	Private	82.7	150	1542
Fontaine Bros Inc	764	Springfield, MA	Private	75.0	150	1542
Fowler-Jones Beers Construction	765	Winston Salem, NC	Private	83.3	150	1542
ICF Kaiser Advanced Technology	766	Boise, ID	Private	120.0	150	1541
Integrated Energy Services	767	Atlanta, GA	Private	160.0	150	1711
Joe E Woods Inc	768	Mesa, AZ	Private	124.6	150	1522
Keene Constr Co of Central Florida	769	Maitland, FL	Private	100.0	150	1542
Lakeside Industries	770	Issaquah, WA	Private	149.4	150	1611

D&B COMPANY RANKINGS BY EMPLOYMENT

Company	Rank	Location	Type	Sales ($ mil.)	Employ-ment	Primary SIC
Landstar Development Corp	771	Coral Gables, FL	Private	114.5	150	1521
Micron Construction Inc	772	Boise, ID	Private	120.0	150	1541
Opus West Corp	773	Phoenix, AZ	Private	220.0	150	1542
PKF-Mark III, Inc	774	Newtown, PA	Private	75.0	150	1629
R.A.S. Builders, Inc	775	Englewood, CO	Private	195.9	150	1542
Ragnar Benson, Inc.	776	Park Ridge, IL	Private	104.8	150	1541
Ruhlin Co	777	Sharon Center, OH	Private	70.0	150	1611
Shiel-Sexton Co Inc	778	Indianapolis, IN	Private	116.4	150	1542
Soltek of San Diego	779	San Diego, CA	Private	111.9	150	1542
Thos S Byrne Inc	780	Fort Worth, TX	Private	115.0	150	1542
Chas H Tompkins Co	781	Washington, DC	Private	197.8	149	1542
Barclay White Inc	782	Berwyn, PA	Private	106.5	146	1542
Concord Development Corp Ill	783	Palatine, IL	Private	120.0	140	1521
Fortney & Weygandt, Inc.	784	North Olmsted, OH	Private	85.0	140	1542
Jeffrey C Stone Inc	785	Phoenix, AZ	Private	116.3	140	1542
Kraft Construction Co	786	Naples, FL	Private	76.1	140	1542
Lexington Homes, L.L.C.	787	Libertyville, IL	Private	99.8	140	1531
MBK Construction Ltd	788	Irvine, CA	Private	250.0	140	1542
Sundance Homes, Inc.	789	Chicago, IL	Public	131.6	140	1531
Walsh Brothers Inc	790	Cambridge, MA	Private	89.0	140	1542
Shimizu America Corp	791	Los Angeles, CA	Private	142.0	138	1542
R W Granger & Sons Inc	792	Shrewsbury, MA	Private	85.0	134	1542
Charles Pankow Builders Ltd	793	Altadena, CA	Private	87.2	132	1542
F N Thompson Co	794	Charlotte, NC	Private	120.0	130	1542
Fieldstone Communities Inc	795	Newport Beach, CA	Private	132.0	130	1531
Lehr Construction Corp	796	New York, NY	Private	200.0	130	1542
Norwood Co	797	West Chester, PA	Private	94.2	130	1542
OC America Construction Inc	798	Los Angeles, CA	Private	229.4	130	1542
S B C C, Inc	799	Campbell, CA	Private	135.0	130	1542
San Jose Construction Co, Inc	800	Santa Clara, CA	Private	84.1	130	1542
Catalfumo Construction and Dev	801	Palm Beach Gardens, FL	Private	115.0	125	1542
E E Reed Construction LC	802	Sugar Land, TX	Private	100.0	125	1542
Holiday Builders Inc	803	Melbourne, FL	Private	74.1	125	1521
Kraemer Brothers, LLC	804	Plain, WI	Private	73.0	125	1542
L E Wentz Co	805	San Carlos, CA	Private	110.0	125	1542
McCormick Inc	806	Fargo, ND	Private	80.0	125	1611
Pleasant Street Associates	807	Boston, MA	Private	80.2	125	1542
R M Shoemaker Holdings Inc	808	West Conshohocken, PA	Private	234.1	125	1541
Realen Homes Construction Co	809	Ambler, PA	Private	102.0	125	1531
W G Mills Inc	810	Sarasota, FL	Private	72.6	125	1542
Worth Construction Inc	811	Bethel, CT	Private	128.0	125	1542
York Construction Co Inc	812	Greenville, SC	Private	67.7	125	1541
Estridge Group Inc	813	Carmel, IN	Private	85.0	122	1521
Air Systems, Inc	814	San Jose, CA	Private	91.0	120	1711
Armada/Hoffler Construction Co	815	Chesapeake, VA	Private	106.0	120	1542
Broadmoor	816	Metairie, LA	Private	125.0	120	1541
C D Henderson Property Co	817	Garland, TX	Private	135.0	120	1542
G J F Construction Corp	818	New York, NY	Private	100.4	120	1542
Gambone Bros Construction Co	819	Norristown, PA	Private	85.0	120	1521
Hawkeye Construction, Inc	820	Troutdale, OR	Public Family Member	431.3	120	1623
M J Anderson Inc	821	West Palm Beach, FL	Private	82.0	120	1542
Macomber Enterprises, Inc	822	Boston, MA	Private	80.0	120	1542
Milburn Investments Inc	823	Austin, TX	Public Family Member	726.0	120	1531
Oakwood Homes LLC	824	Englewood, CO	Private	93.9	120	1521
Sofec Inc	825	Houston, TX	Public Family Member	80.0	120	1629
Jones Brothers Construction Corp	826	Los Angeles, CA	Private	110.0	119	1542
Peck/Jones Construction Corp	827	Los Angeles, CA	Private	122.0	119	1542
International Energy Corp	828	Roswell, GA	Private	200.0	115	1542
Crudo Bros., Co. Inc.	829	Livonia, MI	Private	77.9	110	1541
Ruscilli Construction Co Inc	830	Columbus, OH	Private	180.0	110	1541
Chiyoda International Corp	831	Seattle, WA	Private	70.0	107	1541
Henegan Construction Co Inc	832	New York, NY	Private	125.0	105	1542
Calton Homes Inc	833	Englishtown, NJ	Public Family Member	122.0	101	1531
Embree Construction Group	834	Georgetown, TX	Private	99.6	101	1542
Actus Corp/Sundt, Joint Venture	835	Napa, CA	Private	100.0	100	1521
C P Morgan Co Inc	836	Carmel, IN	Private	70.0	100	1521
Charles R Perry Construction	837	Gainesville, FL	Private	75.0	100	1542
Dynalectric Co of Nevada	838	Norwalk, CT	Public Family Member	80.0	100	1731
E A Hathaway and Co	839	Santa Clara, CA	Private	80.0	100	1542
Gamma Construction Co	840	Houston, TX	Private	80.6	100	1542

D&B COMPANY RANKINGS BY EMPLOYMENT

Company	Rank	Location	Type	Sales ($ mil.)	Employ-ment	Primary SIC
Geupel De Mars Inc	841	Indianapolis, IN	Private	100.0	100	1542
Grace Industries, Inc	842	Whitestone, NY	Private	73.0	100	1741
Harbison-Mahony-Higgins Inc	843	Sacramento, CA	Private	75.0	100	1542
Homes by Dave Brown	844	Tempe, AZ	Private	78.0	100	1531
Irving F Jensen Co Inc	845	Sioux City, IA	Private	80.0	100	1611
J H McCormick Inc	846	Burbank, CA	Private	68.0	100	1542
John T Callahan & Sons Inc	847	Bridgewater, MA	Private	71.8	100	1542
LP Snyder Langston	848	Irvine, CA	Private	110.0	100	1542
Matzel Mmford Organization	849	Hazlet, NJ	Private	120.0	100	1521
MCL Construction Corp	850	Chicago, IL	Private	85.0	100	1521
Morley Construction Co Inc	851	Santa Monica, CA	Private	90.0	100	1771
Murphy Bros Inc	852	East Moline, IL	Private	73.6	100	1623
Pardee Construction Co of Nevada	853	Las Vegas, NV	Public Family Member	107.0	100	1521
Payton Construction Corp	854	Boston, MA	Private	87.3	100	1542
Pinkerton & Laws Inc	855	Atlanta, GA	Private	95.0	100	1542
Roche Constructors Inc	856	Greeley, CO	Private	75.7	100	1542
Summit Companies of Jacksonville	857	Jacksonville, FL	Private	167.8	100	1542
Summit Contractors Inc	858	Jacksonville, FL	Private	167.8	100	1542
Transeastern Properties Inc	859	Pompano Beach, FL	Private	92.8	100	1521
Warde Electric Contracting	860	Congers, NY	Private	100.0	100	1731
Weis Builders, Inc	861	Minneapolis, MN	Private	100.0	100	1542
Westcott Construction Corp	862	North Attleboro, MA	Private	68.3	100	1542
Wolverine Building Inc	863	Grand Rapids, MI	Private	71.5	100	1541
Calcon Constructors Inc	864	Englewood, CO	Private	70.8	95	1542
Richmond Am Homes of Maryland	865	Fairfax, VA	Public Family Member	76.4	93	1521
Brighton Homes Inc	866	Houston, TX	Private	80.0	92	1531
Kaufman & Broad of N California	867	San Ramon, CA	Public Family Member	200.0	92	1531
Lawson Roofing Co Inc	868	San Francisco, CA	Private	800.5	90	1761
Lennar Homes of California	869	Mission Viejo, CA	Public Family Member	188.0	90	1531
Osman Construction Corp	870	Arlington Heights, IL	Private	78.4	90	1542
Richmond American Homes, Inc.	871	Phoenix, AZ	Public Family Member	155.1	90	1521
San Luis Tank Piping Constr Co	872	Paso Robles, CA	Public Family Member	214.9	90	1791
Washington Coscan Inc	873	Vienna, VA	Private	74.7	90	1521
R Sanders & Assoc Custom Builders	874	Dallas, TX	Private	103.6	89	1521
J R Austin Co	875	Rockville, MD	Private	85.0	85	1542
Melody Homes Inc	876	Broomfield, CO	Public Family Member	100.0	85	1521
Westminster Homes, Inc.	877	Greensboro, NC	Public Family Member	71.6	85	1542
Worthington Communities Inc	878	Fort Myers, FL	Private	74.5	85	1521
Parker & Lancaster Corp	879	Richmond, VA	Private	68.6	84	1531
Winter Park Construction Co	880	Maitland, FL	Private	100.0	83	1522
Taisei America Corp	881	Long Beach, CA	Private	103.0	82	1541
Abrams Construction, Inc.	882	Atlanta, GA	Public Family Member	146.6	80	1542
BCI Construction, Inc	883	Wichita, KS	Public Family Member	182.9	80	1542
Bernards Bros Inc	884	San Fernando, CA	Private	80.0	80	1541
Clark & Sullivan Constructors	885	Sparks, NV	Private	71.4	80	1542
Colony Homes L P	886	Woodstock, GA	Private	125.0	80	1521
Global Construction Co LLC	887	Bala Cynwyd, PA	Private	150.0	80	1521
Ivory Homes	888	Salt Lake City, UT	Private	88.2	80	1521
K-Five Construction Corp	889	Lemont, IL	Private	100.0	80	1611
McCar Development Corp	890	Atlanta, GA	Private	70.0	80	1521
Perini & Slattery Assoc	891	Jersey City, NJ	Private	78.0	80	1542
Sycamore Construction Ltd	892	Cincinnati, OH	Private	200.0	80	1522
Target General Inc	893	Phoenix, AZ	Private	145.0	80	1542
ICI Construction Inc	894	Spring, TX	Private	72.8	77	1542
Bayley Construction, a Gen Partnr	895	Seattle, WA	Private	170.0	75	1542
C D Henderson Inc	896	Garland, TX	Private	69.0	75	1542
Centex Landis Construction Co	897	Jefferson, LA	Public Family Member	75.0	75	1542
Colorado Structures Inc	898	Colorado Springs, CO	Private	72.9	75	1542
Colson & Colson Gen Contractors	899	Salem, OR	Private	138.7	75	1522
Daniel Enterprises, Inc.	900	Tempe, AZ	Private	86.1	75	1542
Lee Kennedy Co Inc	901	Boston, MA	Private	72.1	75	1542
Myler Co Inc	902	Crawfordsville, IN	Private	100.0	75	1542
Pasquinelli Construction Co	903	Homewood, IL	Private	100.0	75	1531
R P Industries Inc	904	Franklin, TN	Private	71.5	75	1542
Radnor Homes, Inc	905	Nashville, TN	Public Family Member	75.0	74	1521
A V Partnership	906	Irvine, CA	Private	100.0	70	1521
Cadence McShane Corp	907	Dallas, TX	Private	79.2	70	1542
D and M Concrete Floor Co	908	Fall River, MA	Private	82.0	70	1771
D L Withers Construction LC	909	Phoenix, AZ	Private	110.1	70	1542
Howa Construction, Inc	910	Salt Lake City, UT	Private	150.0	70	1542

D&B COMPANY RANKINGS BY EMPLOYMENT

Company	Rank	Location	Type	Sales ($ mil.)	Employment	Primary SIC
McShane Construction Corp	911	Des Plaines, IL	Private	90.0	70	1541
Salmon & Alder Associates	912	Centerville, UT	Private	237.7	70	1711
Sheehan Pipe Line Construction Co	913	Tulsa, OK	Private	71.1	67	1623
Plaster Development Co	914	Las Vegas, NV	Private	69.0	65	1531
Lincoln Builders, Inc	915	Ruston, LA	Private	78.9	64	1542
New Urban West Inc	916	Santa Monica, CA	Private	74.1	63	1531
A 7 Joint Venture	917	Dorchester, MA	Private	72.3	60	1629
Beazer Homes Arizona Inc	918	Tempe, AZ	Public Family Member	170.5	60	1521
Berkshire Power Co LLC	919	Boston, MA	Private	89.5	60	1629
Bostic Brothers Construction Inc	920	Burlington, NC	Private	100.0	60	1522
Cashman	921	Boston, MA	Private	70.0	60	1611
Degabrielle & Assoc Inc	922	Corolla, NC	Private	88.0	60	1521
Fulton Homes Corp	923	Tempe, AZ	Private	150.0	60	1521
Haydon Building Corp	924	Tempe, AZ	Private	70.0	60	1541
J A Tiberti Construction Co	925	Las Vegas, NV	Private	121.8	60	1542
James G Kennedy & Co Inc	926	New York, NY	Private	75.0	60	1542
John Moriarty & Associates	927	Winchester, MA	Private	114.9	60	1542
Kiewit, Atkinson & Cashman	928	Boston, MA	Private	301.0	60	1611
Nova Corp	929	Englewood, NJ	Private	150.0	60	1542
Poseidon Oil Pipeline Co LLC	930	Houston, TX	Private	310.8	60	1623
Kaufman & Broad of San Diego	931	San Diego, CA	Public Family Member	247.6	57	1522
GVL Contractors LLC	932	Milton, MA	Private	130.0	56	1521
Stahl Construction Co	933	Hopkins, MN	Private	100.0	55	1542
United Homes Inc	934	Rolling Meadows, IL	Private	108.5	55	1521
Universal Constructors Inc	935	McMinnville, TN	Private	123.3	55	1522
Platte River Constructors	936	Aurora, CO	Private	104.8	51	1611
Bellevue Holding Co	937	Wilmington, DE	Private	70.0	50	1542
C F Jordan Residential LP	938	El Paso, TX	Private	110.0	50	1522
CE Ward Constructors, Inc	939	Houston, TX	Private	80.0	50	1542
Charter Builders, Inc.	940	Dallas, TX	Private	100.3	50	1542
Conelly Swinerton Construction Inc	941	Tucson, AZ	Private	75.3	50	1542
Duininck Bros Inc	942	Prinsburg, MN	Private	80.0	50	1611
Dura-Builders Inc.	943	Indianapolis, IN	Private	80.0	50	1521
Henry Bros Co	944	Oak Lawn, IL	Private	80.0	50	1542
Intech Construction Inc	945	Philadelphia, PA	Private	84.0	50	1542
Jerry Pybus Electric	946	Panama City, FL	Private	300.0	50	1731
Keller Construction Co Ltd	947	El Monte, CA	Private	100.0	50	1542
Kenco Communities at Wycliffe	948	Boca Raton, FL	Private	80.0	50	1522
Landmark Organization, Inc	949	Austin, TX	Private	73.1	50	1542
Larwin Co	950	Encino, CA	Private	80.0	50	1521
Miller & Long Co of Maryland	951	Bethesda, MD	Private	73.6	50	1771
Pinkard Construction Co	952	Denver, CO	Private	70.0	50	1542
Ambassador Construction Co	953	New York, NY	Private	75.0	46	1542
Foothills Eastern Transportation	954	Santa Ana, CA	Private	83.4	45	1611
Powersystems Corp	955	Smyrna, GA	Private	80.0	44	1542
York Research Corp	956	New York, NY	Public	503.0	44	1629
D W Hutson Construction, Inc	957	Jacksonville, FL	Public Family Member	69.0	41	1521
Arnold M Diamond Inc	958	Glen Head, NY	Private	74.0	40	1629
Ellis-Don Michigan Inc	959	Livonia, MI	Private	200.0	40	1541
Granger Northern Inc	960	Portland, ME	Private	99.8	40	1542
Harmony Corp of Texas	961	Pasadena, TX	Private	163.0	40	1541
FCL Builders, Inc.	962	Itasca, IL	Private	108.8	35	1541
Panda Energy International	963	Dallas, TX	Private	74.5	35	1731
Stewart-Ledlow Inc	964	Meridianville, AL	Private	200.0	35	1742
White-Spunner Construction	965	Mobile, AL	Private	70.0	35	1542
Comerfords Heating & A/C	966	Pleasanton, CA	Public Family Member	238.7	30	1711
G B I Construction Inc	967	Norcross, GA	Private	300.0	30	1542
Fairfield Development Inc	968	San Diego, CA	Private	80.0	25	1522
Louis P Ciminelli Construction Co	969	Buffalo, NY	Private	74.0	25	1542
UST Leasing Corp	970	Newton, MA	Public Family Member	285.2	25	7353
Mimun Resources Inc	971	Houston, TX	Private	300.0	23	1623
SCL Construction	972	Springfield, VA	Private	150.0	21	1521
Atkn Co	973	Lafayette, CA	Private	370.5	20	1629
Bovis Construction Corp	974	New York, NY	Private	781.4	20	1542
Guy F Atkinson Co of California	975	Lafayette, CA	Private	370.6	20	1629
Pontarelli Builders, Inc.	976	Chicago, IL	Private	85.0	20	1531
Railroad Track Construction Co	977	St. Augustine, FL	Public Family Member	250.5	20	1629
S H Fleming & Co Inc	978	Upper Darby, PA	Private	120.0	20	1721
Zamias Construction Co Inc	979	Johnstown, PA	Private	150.0	20	1542
Atlanta Arena Constructors	980	Atlanta, GA	Private	75.0	15	1542

D&B COMPANY RANKINGS BY EMPLOYMENT

Company	Rank	Location	Type	Sales ($ mil.)	Employ-ment	Primary SIC
Berkshire Realty Co Inc	981	Atlanta, GA	Private	93.0	15	1522
C E D Construction Partners	982	Maitland, FL	Private	111.2	15	1522
Sobrato Construction Inc	983	Cupertino, CA	Private	450.0	15	1542
Airdex Air Conditioning Corp	984	Pinellas Park, FL	Public Family Member	150.0	12	1711
General Pacific Construction	985	South Pasadena, CA	Private	100.0	10	1542
Olker Industries, Inc	986	Long Grove, IL	Private	480.0	10	1521
Onyx Pipeline Co LC	987	Corpus Christi, TX	Private	101.4	10	1623
Consultant Erection Construction Inc	988	Bracey, VA	Private	300.0	8	1521
Piedmont Insulating Co, Inc	989	Danville, VA	Private	200.0	8	1742
Builder's Mart Inc	990	Lancaster, CA	Private	69.3	7	1799
Linear Construction, Inc.	991	Tucson, AZ	Private	200.0	6	1521
20th Century Constrruction Co	992	Painesville, OH	Private	100.0	5	1521
R J Pomplun Co	993	Petersburg, VA	Private	110.0	5	1521
Baker Residential LP	994	Pleasantville, NY	Private	75.0	3	1531
Owner-Builder-Alliance Inc	995	West Palm Beach, FL	Private	100.0	2	1521

MERGERS & ACQUISITIONS

The following essay presents a look at merger and acquisition activity in the Construction sector. A general overview of M&A activity is followed by a listing of actual merger and acquisition events. Purchasing companies are listed in alphabetical order, with a paragraph set aside for each acquisition.

This essay discusses recent merger and acquisition activity in the industry and its effect on the industry. The essay is followed by a list of significant acquisitions and mergers.

During the late 1990s it was speculated that the U.S. was undergoing the biggest merger boom in its history—and the construction industry was not unaffected. Construction has seen its fair share of mergers and acquisitions in recent years, although this industry didn't see nearly the number of consolidations that occurred in the telecommunications and banking industries, for example. Construction transactions have occurred on both a national and an international level, and some of the acquisitions included companies in industries that are related to construction but aren't construction companies themselves, such as manufacturers of building products and supplies.

According to Hugh L. Rice and Andrew W. Arnold, merger and acquisition specialists at FMI, a management consulting firm for clients in construction and related fields, acquisitions in the construction industry are a fairly recent phenomenon. Historically, construction firms that wanted to expand into another market simply opened a new office in that market. It wasn't until 1975 that interest dawned in construction company acquisitions, and the interest never really waned. The nation as a whole saw a major merger boom during the mid-1980s, and the construction industry continued to take part in the merger mania of the mid- to late-1990s.

As in other industries, buyers and sellers of construction companies are motivated by growth, expansion, diversification, development, customer demand, asset accumulation, competitive consolidation, credit needs, risk, declining markets, and a good offer. Growth is the main reason construction companies acquire other companies; in general, buyers of construction companies are interested in expanding their business by moving into geographical areas in which the market is growing. Many construction companies seek geographic diversity in order to reduce the risk of an economic downturn in one area destroying the entire business. Diversification of operations is another key reason construction companies purchase other firms. Survival is key to any business and having interest in more than one segment of an industry is a wise strategy in ensuring that survival. Establishing a start-up

company remains a way to enter a new market, but a faster and often less expensive way is to buy an already-established operation.

Growth is a clear incentive for larger companies to buy smaller firms, but why do these smaller companies want to be bought? According to industry experts, such as the ones at FMI, the construction industry is highly risky by nature: large amounts of money can be lost in short periods of time. Increasingly, owners of smaller construction companies are deciding to reduce their risk by selling their company, or some segment of it, to a larger firm. Another prevalent force causing construction companies to sell out is the undercapitalization of the industry—a situation that some analysts predict will continue into the twenty-first century. Due to credit constraints and lack of capital, it is expected that many construction firms will need to seek financial partners. As a result, mergers and acquisitions in the industry will continue.

One of the corporations leading the industry in acquisitions by swallowing up smaller entities across the United States is Group Maintenance America Corp. (GroupMAC). Headquartered in Houston, Texas, the corporation was founded in 1996 to merge heating, ventilation, and air-conditioning (HV-AC) companies, plumbing companies, and electrical services companies to create a national service company. Within three years, GroupMAC had operations in 106 locations, served residential and commercial customers in 28 states, and had annual revenues of approximately $1.4 billion.

In June 1999 alone, GroupMAC completed the acquisition of five platform companies and one satellite company with annual revenues of $117 million. Those companies included Cardinal Contracting Corp. of Indianapolis, Indiana; Klassic Air Conditioning, Inc., of Houston, Texas; L.T. Mechanical, Inc., of Charlotte, North Carolina; Tower Electric Co. of Fairfax, Virginia; and Vermont Mechanical, Inc., of South Burlington, Vermont.

Another top acquisition-minded construction company is Integrated Electrical Services, Inc. (IES), which in June, 1999, acquired seven companies with combined annual revenues of approximately $135 million. IES, however, sought diversification through acquisitions that extended beyond the bounds of the industry into areas that are growing faster than construction. According to IES, the firms acquired in June, 1999, "strengthened the corporation's capabilities in the information technology (which includes data and telecommunications), power line, commercial, and industrial markets." The completion of these transactions, along with the nine acquisitions completed the preceding month, brought Integrated Electrical Services' total annual revenue to approximately $1.1 billion.

Acquisitions also stretched across international waters during the late 1990s. Masco Corp., a Taylor, Michigan-based maker of kitchen cabinets and bathroom fixtures, announced in May, 1999, that it would buy Avocet Hardware PLC of the United Kingdom for an undisclosed sum and Gummers of Birmingham, England, for $150 million in cash.

U.S. construction firms were also bought out by overseas firms. In June, 1999, Wienerberger Baustoffindustrie AG of Austria signed a definitive agreement to acquire General Shale LLC of Johnson City, Tennessee, from the Etex/Marley Group for $260 million. Pioneer International Ltd., an Australian building products giant, acquired 14 small integrated aggregates and concrete operations in the United States between July, 1997, and July, 1999. Ireland's CRH PLC purchased Thompson-McCully Companies, a Michigan asphalt company, for $422 million, and Sordoni Skanska of Sweden purchased Alex J. Etkin Inc., a Detroit-area company, in July, 1999.

Mergers & Acquisitions

Ace Hardware Corp. and **Builder Marts of America** (BMA) announced in June 1999 a strategic merger that created the largest wholesale buying and distribution group in the lumber, building materials and millwork industry. [*PRNewswire*, 6/30/99.]

Acme Brick Co., a subsidiary of **Justin Industries**, agreed to purchase **Eureka Brick & Tile** of Clarksville, Arkansas, for an undisclosed sum. [*Fort Worth Star-Telegram*, 6/25/99.]

—purchased **Texas Clay Industries**, a brick manufacturer, in January 1999.

ACR Group Inc. acquired **Beaumont A/C Supply Inc.**, a Beaumont, Texas-based wholesale distributor of air-conditioning equipment and supplies. [*Business Wire*, 1/27/99.]

Affordable Homes of America, Inc., acquired **Big Mountain Construction Company, Inc.** in July 1999. [*PRNewswire*, 7/7/99.]

—acquired **Realty Center, Inc.** in June 1999. [*PRNewswire*, 7/6/99.]

American Homestar Corp. signed definitive agreements in May 1998 to acquire **R-Anell Custom Homes, Inc.**, and its related manufacturing operations, **Gold Medal Homes, Inc.**, and **Gold Medal Homes of North Carolina, Inc.**, estimated at $50 million. [*Business Wire*, 5/29/98.]

Andersen Corp. agreed in March 1999 to purchase **Morgan Products** for approximately $41 million in a deal that merges the largest wood window and patio door manufacturer in the U.S. with one of the industry's biggest millwork wholesalers. [*National Home Center News*, 3/22/99, p. 1.]

—acquired **Rima Building Center** on April 13, 1999, for an undisclosed amount. [*National Home Center News*, 5/3/99, p. 5.]

—acquired **Tri-City Lumber** of Kalispell, Montana, on March 22, 1999, for an undisclosed amount. [*National Home Center News*, 5/3/99, p. 5.]

Atrium Companies, a Dallas-based vinyl window manufacturer and fabricator, purchased **Champagne Industries Inc.** of Denver for an undisclosed amount in June 1999. [*Plastics News*, 6/7/99, p. 27.]

—agreed to purchase **Heat Inc.**, owner of **Best Built Inc.**, a manufacturer of vinyl windows and doors, for approximately $85 million in April 1999. [*New York Times*, 4/22/99, p. C4.]

Bechtel National, Inc., announced in April 1999 it had reached an agreement with **CBS Corp.** to acquire two industrial divisions, formerly parts of **Westinghouse Electric Corp.**, that provide supplies and technical services to the U.S. Navy's Nuclear

Propulsion Program. [Company press release, 4/29/99.]

Bracknell Corp. acquired **Preferred Electric, Inc.**, a Chicago-based electrical services business, and its affiliates in June 1999 for approximately $10 million. [*Canada NewsWire*, 6/30/99.]

BSL Holdings, Inc., a building products distribution company, agreed in April 1999 to pay $30 million and assume $5 million in debt in exchange for **Holmes Lumber**. [*National Home Center News*, 4/19/99, p. 5.]

—agreed to acquire **Paty Lumber Co.** in June 1999. [*PRNewswire*, 6/29/99.]

—acquired **Kellogg Lumber Co.** of Denver, Colorado, in July 1999 in an undisclosed transaction. [*PRNewswire*, 7/14/99.]

—is the parent of **Builders' Supply & Lumber Co.**, which acquired **Durham Manufacturing Company, Inc.**, of Gallatin, Tennessee, in an undisclosed transaction in June 1999. [*PRNewswire*, 6/30/99.]

Cal Dive International, Inc., and **Aker Marine Contractors, Inc.**, announced that Cal Dive acquired Hvide Marine's majority equity interest in a $39 million Dove anchor handling and sub-sea construction vessel in June 1999. [*PR Newswire*, 6/21/99.]

Cameron Ashley Building Products, Inc., announced in June 1998 it had signed a letter of intent to acquire the assets of **Gerard Demers Inc.**, a distributor of building material products, for undisclosed terms. [*Business Wire*, 6/3/98.]

—acquired **Ozark Construction Supply Co.** of Columbia, Missouri, a specialty products company that primarily distributes vinyl siding, windows, and doors, for an undisclosed sum in June 1998. [*Business Wire*, 7/24/98.]

—acquired **Lafayette WoodWorks, Inc.**, of Lafayette, Louisiana, a millworks specialty company, for an undisclosed sum in June 1998. [*Business Wire*, 7/24/98.]

Cannon Valley Woodwork of Cannon Falls, Minnesota, a designer of unfinished kitchen and bathroom

cabinets, acquired Iowa-based **Brammer Co.**, a prefinished kitchen cabinet producer, in May 1999. [*National Home Center News*, 5/3/99, p. 15.]

Carmeuse/Lafarge North American Lime Joint Venture announced in June 1998 it would acquire stock in **Global Stone Ingersoll Ltd.** and **Global Stone Detroit Lime Co.** for $62 million from **Oglebay Norton Co.** of Cleveland, Ohio. [*Industrial Specialties News*, 6/28/99, p. 4.]

Celotex, a Tampa-based building materials supplier, acquired **Capaul**, a Wisconsin ceiling and wall supplier, in May 1999. [*National Home Center News*, 5/3/99, p. 15.]

Centex Homes, the home-building subsidiary of Dallas-based **Centex Corp.**, acquired the home-building operating assets of Chicago-based **Sundance Homes, Inc.**, for approximately $50 million in July 1999. [*PRNewswire*, 7/12/99.]

Champion Enterprises, Inc. acquired **Care Free Homes, Inc.**, a manufactured home retail organization headquartered in Salt Lake City, for an undisclosed sum in June 1999. [Company press release, 6/11/99.]

Clark Steel Framing Systems of Cincinnati acquired **Delta Metal Products, Inc.**, of Dallas, a steel framing producer for the residential and commercial construction markets, in an undisclosed deal in April 1999. [*American Metal Market*, 4/12/99, p. 6.]

Crossmann Communities, Inc. acquired **Homes by Huff & Co., Inc.**, of Raleigh-Durham, North Carolina, in June 1999. [*PRNewswire*, 6/21/99.]

Dayton Superior Corp. acquired the assets of **Cempro, Inc.**, a manufacturer of blended cementitious chemical products used in the construction market, for an undisclosed sum in January 1999. [*Business Wire*, 1/11/99.]

D.R. Horton, Inc., a housing contractor, acquired **Century Title Agency, Inc.**, in July 1999. [*PRNewswire*, 7/7/99.]

Elo Electric Co., a lighting designer and installation firm, merged with its sister company, **ProNet Communications, Inc.**, a telecommunications and computer installation firm, to form **Dynalink Corp.** in June 1999. [*Crain's Cleveland Business*, 7/5/99.]

Florida Rock Industries, Inc., announced in July 1999 it had sold in a cash transaction the highway and heavy construction assets and operations of its subsidiary, **Harper Bros., Inc.**, located in Fort Myers, Florida, to **Harper Bros. Construction, Inc.**, a subsidiary of **Superfos Construction, Inc.** [*Business Wire*, 7/2/99.]

General Roofing Services, Inc., a leading national provider of commercial roofing services, acquired **B&R Roofing Co.** and **Northwest Roofing Co.**, both located in Fresno, California, for undisclosed sums in July 1999. [*PRNewswire*, 7/14/99.]

—acquired **Top Concepts**, with locations in Houston, Dallas, and Austin, Texas, for an undisclosed sum in July 1999. [*PRNewswire*, 7/14/99.]

Gibraltar acquired **K&W Metal Fabricators**, doing business as **Weather Guard Building Products**, a Denver-based manufacturer and distributor of a full line of metal building products for industrial, commercial, and residential applications, in June 1999 for an undisclosed amount. [*PRNewswire*, 7/1/99.]

Ginsite Materials, Inc., of Fort Lauderdale, Florida, agreed to merge with **Envirocon**, a Denver-based construction industry supplier, in June 1999. [*Business Wire*, 6/30/99.]

Group Maintenance America Corp. acquired **Airtron, Inc.**, one of the country's largest privately-owned residential and light commercial HVAC contractors, in February 1997. [*Contracting Business*, 6/1/97, p. 18.]

—merged with **United Service Alliance** in June 1997. [*Contracting Business*, 6/1/97, p 18.]

—acquired five platform companies in June 1999: **Cardinal Contracting Corp.** of Indianapolis, Indiana; **Klassic Air Conditioning, Inc.**, of Houston, Texas; **L.T. Mechanical, Inc.**, of Charlotte, North Carolina; **Tower Electric Co.** of Fairfax, Virginia; and **Vermont Mechanical, Inc.**, of South Burlington, Vermont.

—acquired **Trinity Contractors, Inc.**, in November 1998. [Company press release, 11/13/98.]

—purchased **Dynalink Corp.** in July 1999. [*Crain's Cleveland Business*, 7/5/99.]

Hanson Building Materials America, Inc., a subsidiary of **Hanson PLC**, acquired **Tidewater Sand & Gravel, Inc.**, and **Moe Sand Co.**, the largest marine-dredged aggregates producer in the San Francisco Bay area, for $44.0 million in cash in July 1999. [*PRNewswire*, 7/7/99.]

—signed an agreement to acquire the **North American Brick Group** for Can$390 million in April 1999. [*Industrial Specialties News*, 4/26/99.]

Home Depot purchased **Georgia Lighting**, an Atlanta-based specialty lighting designer, for an undisclosed sum in July 1999. [*Wall Street Journal*, 7/6/99, p. A6.]

ICF Kaiser International, Inc., finalized the sale of its Consulting Group to the Group's management and **CM Equity Partners, L.P.**, for $64 million in cash plus $6.6 million in interest-bearing notes, in June 1999. [*PRNewswire*, 6/30/99.]

Insituform Technologies, Inc., a worldwide provider of trenchless technologies for the improvement of sewer, gas, and industrial pipes, acquired its Insituform Process licensee in the Netherlands for approximately $11.8 million in July 1999. [*Business Wire*, 6/1/99.]

Integrated Electrical Services, Inc., acquired **Bartley & DeVary Electric, Inc.**, of Milton, Delaware, in June 1999 for an undisclosed sum. [Company press release, 6/18/99.]

—acquired **California Communications, Inc.**, an information technology firm in Ontario, California, in June 1999 for an undisclosed sum. [Company press release, 6/18/99.]

—acquired **Canova Electrical Contracting, Inc.**, a firm in East McKeesport, Pennsylvania, in June 1999 for an undisclosed sum. [Company press release, 6/18/99.]

—acquired **Carroll Systems, Inc.**, an information technology firm in Austin, Texas, in June 1999 for an undisclosed sum. [Company press release, 6/18/99.]

—acquired **Delco Electric, Inc.**, of Oklahoma City in June 1999 for an undisclosed sum. [Company press release, 6/18/99.]

—acquired **DKD Electric Co.** of Albuquerque in June 1999 for an undisclosed sum. [Company press release, 6/18/99.]

—acquired **E.P. Breaux Electrical Inc.**, located in New Iberia, Louisiana, in June 1999 for an undisclosed sum. [Company press release, 6/18/99.]

—acquired **Federal Communications Group**, an information technology firm in New Iberia, Louisiana, in June 1999 for an undisclosed sum. [Company press release, 6/18/99.]

—acquired **ICG Electric, Inc.**, a power line firm in Colorado Springs, in June 1999 for an undisclosed sum. [Company press release, 6/18/99.]

—acquired **Murray Electrical Contractors, Inc.**, an industrial firm in Rosenburg, Oregon, in June 1999 for an undisclosed sum. [Company press release, 6/18/99.]

—acquired **New Tech Electric, Inc.**, a firm in Hillsboro, Oregon, in June 1999 for an undisclosed sum. [Company press release, 6/18/99.]

—acquired Nashville-based **Pan American Electric, Inc.**, in June 1999 for an undisclosed sum. [Company press release, 6/18/99.]

—acquired **Putzel Electrical Contractors**, located in Macon, Georgia, in June 1999 for an undisclosed sum. [Company press release, 6/18/99.]

—acquired **Tech Electric Company, Inc.**, a firm in Raleigh, North Carolina, in June 1999 for an undisclosed sum. [Company press release, 6/18/99.]

—acquired **Tesla Power & Automation, Inc.**, a Houston-based industrial prefabrication firm, in June 1999 for an undisclosed sum. [Company press release, 6/18/99.]

—acquired **Valentine Electrical, Inc.**, of Ashland, Virginia, in June 1999 for an undisclosed sum. [Company press release, 6/18/99.]

Integrated Homes, Inc., entered into a letter of intent to acquire San Jose-based **Digital Interiors, Inc.**, a pioneer in the home networking industry and residential systems integrator, for approximately $24.8 million in June 1999. [*PRNewswire*, 6/18/99.]

Jacobs Engineering Group Inc. and **Sverdrup Corp.** announced in January 1999 the completion of their merger, creating a global firm in engineering, architecture, construction, maintenance, operations, consulting, and technology. [*Business Wire*, 1/13/99.]

Jeld-Wen announced its plan to acquire **Rugby Building Products**, an Alpharetta, Georgia, millwork wholesaler, from its parent company, **Rugby Group (UK)**, in May 1999. [*National Home Center News*, 5/3/99, p. 5.]

Juno Lighting, Inc. approved a merger with **Fremont Investors** in June 1999. [*PRNewswire*, 6/29/99.]

Justin Industries, Inc., of Fort Worth, Texas, entered into an agreement to acquire **Eureka Brick & Tile** of Clarksville, Arkansas, in June 1999. [*Industrial Specialties News*, 6/28/99, p. 4.]

Lanoga Corp. of Redmond, Washington, acquired the largest independent home center retailer in the Denver market, **Home Lumber & Supply** of Littleton, Colorado, for an undisclosed amount in April 1999. [*National Home Center News*, 4/5/99, p. 1.]

L.B. Foster Co. agreed to purchase **CXT Inc.**, a Spokane-based manufacturer of engineered prestressed and precast concrete products primarily used in the railroad and transit industries, for an undisclosed amount in April 1999. [*American Metal Market*, 4/20/99, p. 4.]

Lennox International Inc., an international manufacturer of heating, air-conditioning, and refrigeration equipment, agreed to buy the heating and air-conditioning division of **The Ducane Co.** for an undisclosed sum in June 1999. [*State* (Columbia, SC), 6/3/99.]

LG&E Energy purchased **CRC Holdings Corp.**, the parent company of Houston-based **CRC-Evans Pipeline International**, a gas-pipeline construction supplier, for $83.5 million in July 1999.

Masco Corp., a Michigan-based maker of kitchen cabinets and bathroom fixtures, announced in May 1999 that it would buy **Avocet Hardware PLC** of the United Kingdom for an undisclosed sum. [*New York Times, 5/1/99, p. B3.*]

—acquired the **Cary Group**, a fiberglass insulation installation operation, for an undisclosed sum in April 1999. [*New York Times, 4/14/99, p. C4.*]

—purchased **Faucet Queens Inc.** of Vernon, Illinois; **GMU Group** of Azumaya, Spain; and **Gummers** of Birmingham, England, for a total of $150 million in cash in April 1999. [*Crain's Detroit Business, 4/5/99, p. 3.*]

Michael Baker Corp., an engineering, construction management and operations, and technical services firm, announced its exploration into the acquisition of **Steen Production Service, Inc.**, of Lafayette, Louisiana, in June 1999. [*Business Wire, 6/29/99.*]

—acquired **GeoResearch, Inc.**, and created **Baker GeoResearch, Inc.**, in September 1998 for an undisclosed sum. [*Business Wire, 9/30/98.*]

Morrison Knudsen Corp., a construction and engineering company, acquired the government services operations of **Westhinghouse Electric Co.** from **CBS Corp.** on March 22, 1999. [*Associated Press Newswires, 7/10/99.*]

New Holland N.V. acquired **Case Corp.**, maker of farm and construction equipment and machinery, in June 1999 for an undisclosed amount. [*Business Wire, 6/99.*]

Nortek Inc. purchased **Peachtree, Thermal-Gard** and **Caradon Windows & Doors**. [*Corporate Money, 4/14/99, p. 7.*]

Numex Corp. announced its negotiations to acquire **Modular Structures International, Inc.**, a California-based manufacturer of prefab modular office units and school classrooms. [*Business Wire, 2/28/99.*]

Oldcastle Materials Group, a subsidiary of **CRH PLC**, an international building materials company, purchased **Thompson-McCully Companies**, an integrated aggregates, asphalt, and paving contractor based in Michigan, for more than $340 million in July 1999. [*PRNewswire, 7/8/99.*]

—acquired **Millington Quarry**, an aggregate and asphalt producer based in Millington, New Jersey. [*PRNewswire, 7/5/99.*]

—acquired **Dell Contractors, Inc.**, an integrated aggregates, asphalt, and paving contractor located in northern New Jersey, in July 1999. [*PRNewswire, 7/5/99.*]

Pelican Companies Inc., a retailer of building materials, acquired **Triangle Building Supply**, a North Carolina lumberyard, for an undisclosed amount in March 1999. [*National Home Center News, 4/19/99, p. 56.*]

Pioneer International Ltd., an Australian building products giant, acquired 14 small integrated aggregate and concrete operations in the United States between July 1997 and July 1999, all ranging between $33.18 million and $39.81 million. [*Asia Pulse, 5/11/99.*]

Quanta Services Inc., a Houston-based electrical contractor, acquired **H.L. Chapman Pipeline Construction**, Inc., in April 1999. [*Dow Jones Business News, 5/3/99.*]

Reliant Building Products, a leading vinyl and aluminum window manufacturer controlled by **Keystone Inc.** and its affiliates, acquired **Care-Free Window Group**, a vinyl window company, in January 1998. [*Business Wire, 1/29/98.*]

Seigle's Building Centers Inc., a supplier of doors, moldings, and hardware based in Elgin, Illinois, acquired its West Chicago competitor, **DuPage Millwork Inc.**, for about $2 million in April 1999. [*Crain's Chicago Business, 4/26/99, p. 32.*]

Sordoni Skanska Construction Co. of Parsippany, New Jersey, acquired **Alex J. Etkin Inc.** of Farmington Hills, Michigan, for $13 million. [*Detroit Free Press, 7/9/99.*]

Southwest Recreational Industries, Inc. bought **Martin Surfacing**, a subsidiary of **Desseaux Corporation of North America** and a manufacturer of running tracks and gym flooring systems, in June 1999 in an undisclosed transaction. [*PRNewswire, 6/23/99.*]

Stonegate Resources LLC acquired **Bagnal Builders Supply Co.** of Columbia, South Carolina, in June 1999. [*PRNewswire, 6/28/99.*]

—acquired **MBS Holdings**, a leading Dallas-based building materials supplier, in June 1999. [*PRNewswire, 6/24/99.*]

TRC Companies, an engineering and construction company, acquired **A&H Engineers**, a New York-based transportation, consulting, and engineering firm, for an undisclosed amount in June 1999. [*Dow Jones Business News, 6/1/99.*]

Trinity Contractors, Inc., a subsidiary of **Group Maintenance America Corp.**, acquired **Electrical Associates of Dallas, Inc.**, in June 1999 for an undisclosed sum. [Company press release, 6/16/99.]

Turner Corp., one of the largest construction firms in the United States, announced on July 16, 1999, that it was evaluating an offer by an unidentified investment group to buy the company. [*New York Times, 7/17/99.*]

URS Corp., an engineering and construction management firm based in San Francisco, acquired the **Dames & Moore Group**, a Los Angeles-based engineering firm, for approximately $300 million in June 1999. [*Business Wire, 6/24/99.*]

U.S. Industries, Inc. announced in February 1999 it had reached an agreement with **Huffy Corporation, Inc.** to acquire the assets of **True Temper Hardware Co.** for $100 million. [*Business Wire, 2/12/99.*]

—acquired **Zurn Industries, Inc.**, a manufacturer of HVAC and plumbing equipment, in a $765 million transaction in February 1998. [*Business Wire, 2/17/98.*]

U.S. Silica Co., a producer of sand, acquired **George F. Pettinos, Inc.**, a Pennsylvania-based producer of silica sand for the construction industry, a coater of silica sand, and a reseller of a variety of other products for the foundry industry, in July 1998 for an undisclosed amount. [*Business Wire, 7/27/98.*]

Walter Industries, Inc., announced that its homebuilding and financing subsidiary, **Jim Walter Homes, Inc.** acquired **Crestline Homes, Inc.**, a North Carolina-based builder of modular homes, in an undisclosed transaction in March 1999. [Company press release, 3/12/99.]

Weitzer Homebuilders Inc. announced in February 1999 its intention to acquire all of the homebuilding operations of **Century Partners Group, Ltd.** [*Business Wire, 2/17/99.*]

Wienerberger Baustoffindustrie AG of Austria signed a definitive agreement in June 1999 to acquire **General Shale LLC** of Johnson City, Tennessee, from the **Etex/Marley Group** for $260 million. [*Industrial Specialties News, 6/28/99, p. 4.*]

Further Reading

Aley, James, and Matt Siegel. "First: The Fallout from Merger Mania." *Fortune,* 2 March 1998, p. 26.

"Australia's Pioneer Buys U.S. Concrete Business, Seeks More." *Asia Pulse,* 11 May 1999.

"GroupMAC Press Release." 16 June 1999. Available from http://www.groupmac.com

"Integrated Electrical Services Becomes Billion-Dollar Company, Completes Seven Acquisitions with Combined Revenues of $135 Million." *PRNewswire,* 18 June 1999.

"Ireland's CRH Buys Michigan Asphalt Company." *Dow Jones Business News,* 8 July 1999.

Levin, Dorin. *Detroit Free Press,* 7 July 1999.

"Masco Corp. Will Buy Avocet Hardware PLC for Undisclosed Amount of Cash." *New York Times,* 1 May 1999, p. B3.

Rice, Hugh L., and Andrew W. Arnold. "Why Would Anyone Want to Buy a Construction Company?"

Available from http://www.fminet.com/ARTICLES/-gc/buyconst.shtml

"Wienerberger Enters U.S. Market, Buys General Shale." *Industrial Specialties News,* 28 June 1999, p. 4.

—K. Burton

ASSOCIATIONS

This chapter presents a selection of business and professional associations active in the Construction sector. The information shown is adapted from Gale's *Encyclopedia of Associations* series and provides detailed and comprehensive information on nonprofit membership organizations.

Entries are arranged in alphabetical order. Categories included are name, address, contact person, telephone, toll-free number, fax number, E-mail address and web site URL (when provided). A text block shows founding date, staff, number of members, budget, and a general description of activities.

ABG DIVISION UNITED STEEL WORKERS
3362 Hollenberg Dr.
Bridgeton, MO 63044
John Murphy, Dir.
PH: (314)739-6142
FX: (314)739-1216
Founded: 1982. **Members:** 45,000. AFL-CIO; Canadian Labour Congress.

AIR BALANCE CONSULTANTS
4207 Maycrest Ave.
Los Angeles, CA 90032-1237
Hall Evans, Coord.
Founded: 1967. **Members:** 35. Professional engineers engaged in air balancing (the balancing of air conditioning systems).

AIR-CONDITIONING AND REFRIGERATION INSTITUTE
4301 N. Fairfax Dr., Ste. 425
Arlington, VA 22203
Clifford H. Rees, Jr., Pres.
PH: (703)524-8800
FX: (703)528-3816
E-mail: ari@ari.org
URL: http://www.ari.org
Founded: 1953. **Staff:** 45. **Members:** 207. **Budget:** $9,000,000. Manufacturers of air conditioning, refrigeration, and heating products and components. Develops and establishes equipment and application standards and certifies performance of certain industry products; provides credit and statistical services to members. Provides representation and technical assistance to government entities in federal, state, and local legislative matters; provides public relations, consumer education, and promotional programs for the industry.

AIR CONDITIONING CONTRACTORS OF AMERICA
1712 New Hampshire Ave., NW
Washington, DC 20009
Roger Jask, CEO/Exec.VP
PH: (202)483-9370
FX: (202)588-1217
E-mail: comm@acca.org
URL: http://www.acca.org
Founded: 1969. **Staff:** 24. **Members:** 3,800. **Budget:** $4,000,000. Contractors involved in installation and service of heating, air conditioning, and refrigeration systems. Associate members are utilities, manufacturers, wholesalers, and other market-oriented businesses. Monitors utility competition and operating practices of HVAC manufacturers and wholesalers. Provides consulting services, technical training, and instructor certification program; offers management seminars. Operates annual educational institute.

AIR DIFFUSION COUNCIL
104 S. Michigan Ave., Ste. 1500
Chicago, IL 60603-5908
Jack Lagershausen, Exec.Dir.
Founded: 1960. **Members:** 50. Manufacturers and suppliers of flexible air duct. Administers industry-wide testing and rating standards for members' products. Participates in activities related to air duct standardization.

AIR DISTRIBUTION INSTITUTE
4415 W. Harrison St., Ste. 322
Hillside, IL 60162
Patricia H. Keating, Gen.Mgr.
PH: (708)449-2933
FX: (708)449-0837
Founded: 1947. **Staff:** 2. **Members:** 26. Manufacturers of prefabricated pipes, ducts, and fittings used in the residential air distribution industry. Promotes the industry and works to improve its products. Conducts sales surveys and compiles statistics.

AIR MOVEMENT AND CONTROL ASSOCIATION
30 W. University Dr.
Arlington Heights, IL 60004-1893
Peter N. Hanly, Exec.VP & CEO

PH: (847)394-0150
FX: (847)253-0088
E-mail: amca@amca.org
URL: http://www.AMCA.org
Founded: 1955. **Staff:** 23. **Members:** 255. **Budget:** $2,500,000. Manufacturers of air moving and control equipment and related air systems equipment. Conducts research on improvement of methods of testing; develops standard codes for fans, louvers, dampers, shutters, and similar equipment. Operates testing laboratory and performance certification programs for fans and other devices.

AMERICAN ARCHITECTURAL MANUFACTURERS ASSOCIATION
1827 Walden Office Sq., Ste. 104
Schaumburg, IL 60173-4268
Steve Sullivan, Exec. VP
PH: (847)303-5664
FX: (847)303-5774
E-mail: webmaster@aamanet.org
URL: http://www.aamanet.org
Founded: 1962. **Staff:** 10. **Members:** 280. **Budget:** $2,500,000. Manufacturers of architectural products including: prime and combination storm windows; sliding glass and combination storm doors; window and curtain-walls; store fronts and entrances; siding; soffits, fascia, gutters, downspouts, skylights, space enclosures, and mobile home components. Conducts research. Presents film programs to architectural and builder organizations and governmental agencies. Has appointed technical committees and task groups. Compiles statistics.

AMERICAN ASSOCIATION OF AUTOMATIC DOOR MANUFACTURERS
1300 Sumner Ave.
Cleveland, OH 44115-2851
John H. Addington, Exec.Dir.
PH: (216)241-7333
FX: (216)241-0105
E-mail: aaadm@taol.com
URL: http://www.taol.com/aaadm
Founded: 1994. **Staff:** 3. **Members:** 7. Manufacturers of automatically operated pedestrian doors. (Automatic folding, sliding and swinging doors used in grocery stores and other businesses.) Works to promote the industry and provide a forum for members to communicate. Offers certification program for inspectors.

AMERICAN CONCRETE INSTITUTE
PO Box 9094
Farmington Hills, MI 48333-9094
James G. Toscas, Exec.VP
PH: (248)848-3700
FX: (248)848-3701
E-mail: techinq@aci-ini.org
URL: http://www.aci-int.org
Founded: 1905. **Staff:** 70. **Members:** 17,500. **Budget:** $7,600,000. Technical society of engineers, architects, contractors, educators, and others interested in improving techniques of design construction and maintenance of concrete products and structures. Operates speakers' bureau; offers specialized education seminars. Maintains 112 technical committees.

AMERICAN COUNCIL FOR CONSTRUCTION EDUCATION
1300 Hudson Ln., Ste. 3
Monroe, LA 71201-6054
Daniel E. Dupree, Exec.VP
PH: (318)323-2816
FX: (318)323-2413
E-mail: acce@iamerica.net
URL: http://www.calpoly.edu/~cm/acce
Founded: 1974. **Staff:** 2. **Members:** 150. **Budget:** $200,000. Construction-oriented associations, corporations, and individuals united to: promote and improve construction education at the postsecondary level; engage in accrediting construction education programs offered by colleges and universities nationwide; maintain

procedures consistent with the accrediting policies of the Commission on Recognition of Postsecondary Accreditation and report the results of its activities and list the colleges and universities with accredited programs of study in construction; review at regular intervals the criteria, standards, and procedures that the council has adopted to evaluate programs in construction education. Provides visiting teams for campus program evaluations; compiles statistics.

AMERICAN FENCE ASSOCIATION
5300 Memorial Dr., Ste. 116
Stone Mountain, GA 30083
Terry Dempsey, Jr., CAE, Exec.VP
PH: (404)299-5413
TF: (800)822-4342
FX: (404)299-8927
E-mail: afa@mindspring.com
URL: http://www.americanfenceassoc.org
Founded: 1962. **Staff:** 6. **Members:** 1,340. **Budget:** $1,500,000. Fence contractors, manufacturers, and wholesalers; associate members are general contractors, architects, and insurance companies. Promotes the fence industry in 17 countries. Sponsors field training school and certification program.

AMERICAN FIBERBOARD ASSOCIATION
1210 W. Northwest Hwy.
Palatine, IL 60067-1897
Curtis Peterson, Exec.VP
PH: (847)934-8394
FX: (847)934-8803
E-mail: afa@entranceramp.com
Founded: 1991. **Staff:** 4. **Members:** 6. Fiberboard manufacturing companies. Provides research and fiberboard certification to members.

AMERICAN HARDBOARD ASSOCIATION
1210 W. Northwest Hwy.
Palatine, IL 60067
C. Curtis Peterson, Exec.VP
PH: (847)934-8800
FX: (847)934-8803
E-mail: ccpeters@starnetusa.com
Founded: 1974. **Staff:** 4. **Members:** 6. **Budget:** $1,000,000. Manufacturers representing major U.S. producers of hardboard.

AMERICAN INSTITUTE OF CONSTRUCTORS
1300 N. 17th St., Ste. 830
Arlington, VA 22209
Richard W. Singer, Contact
PH: (703)812-2021
FX: (703)812-8234
URL: http://www.aicnet.org
Founded: 1971. **Staff:** 2. **Members:** 1,600. **Budget:** $200,000. Professionals engaged in construction practice, education, and research. Serves as the certifying body for the professional constructor. Objectives are to promote the study and to advance the practice of construction. Facilitates the exchange of information and ideas relating to construction. Conducts educational programs.

AMERICAN INSTITUTE OF INSPECTORS
1117 47th St.
Sacramento, CA 95819
Brent Foster, Chmn.
PH: (800)877-4770
FX: (916)348-0607
E-mail: notesfield@aol.com
URL: http://www.inspection.org
Founded: 1989. **Members:** 280. Certified home inspectors. Works to set standards for impartial evaluations of residential properties. Certifies members in four areas: residential homes, mobile homes, mechanics, and earthquake hazard reduction. Maintains speakers' bureau.

AMERICAN INSTITUTE OF STEEL CONSTRUCTION
1 E. Wacker Dr., Ste. 3100
Chicago, IL 60601-2001
Lou Gurthet, Pres.
PH: (312)670-2400
FX: (312)670-5403
URL: http://www.aisc.org
Founded: 1921. **Staff:** 40. **Members:** 3,000. **Budget:** $6,500,000. Fabricators who erect structural steel for buildings and bridges. Sponsors research cooperatively with other industry groups and independently at engineering colleges. Program includes studies on welded and bolted connections, composite design, allowable stress and load factor design in steel, buckling problems, and techniques of painting structural steel. Collects and releases market data and statistics; develops specifications and standard practice codes. Conducts technical lecture program. Assembles photographic exhibits of steel structures.

AMERICAN SOCIETY OF HOME INSPECTORS
PO Box 95588
Palatine, IL 60095
Robert J. Paterkiewicz, CAE, Contact
TF: (800)743-2744
FX: (847)290-1920
E-mail: hq@ashi.com
URL: http://www.ashi.com
Founded: 1976. **Staff:** 10. **Members:** 6,000. **Budget:** $2,000,000. Professional home inspectors whose goals are to: establish home inspector qualifications; set standards of practice for home inspections; adhere to a code of ethics; keep the concept of "objective third party" intact; inform members of the most advanced methods and techniques. Conducts seminars through regional chapters.

AMERICAN SOCIETY OF PROFESSIONAL ESTIMATORS
11141 Georgia Ave., Ste. 412
Wheaton, MD 20902
Beverly S. Perrell, Dir. of Administration
PH: (301)929-8848
FX: (301)929-0231
E-mail: aspesbo@aol.com
URL: http://www.aspenational.com
Founded: 1957. **Staff:** 2. **Members:** 2,500. **Budget:** $250,000. Construction cost estimators. Develops professional and ethical standards in construction estimating. Offers continuing education to established professionals; provides certification for estimators.

AMERICAN SUPPLY ASSOCIATION
222 Merchandise Mart, Ste. 1360
Chicago, IL 60654
Inge Calderon, Exec.VP
PH: (312)464-0090
FX: (312)464-0091
E-mail: asaemail@interserv.com
URL: http://www.asa.net/tech
Founded: 1970. **Staff:** 22. **Members:** 1,050. **Budget:** $8,000,000. National association of wholesale, distributors, and manufacturers of plumbing and heating, cooling, pipes, valves, and fittings. Compiles statistics on operating costs and makes occasional studies of compensation, fringe benefits, wages, and salaries. Conducts research studies and forecasting surveys. Offers group insurance. Maintains management institutes, home study courses under the ASA Education Foundation and Endowment program, provides technology and produces a CD-ROM catalogue of manufacturers.

ARCHITECTURAL WOODWORK INSTITUTE
1952 Isaac Newton Sq.
Reston, VA 20190
Judith B. Durham, Exec.VP
PH: (703)733-0600
FX: (703)733-0584
E-mail: jdurham@awinet.org
URL: http://www.awinet.org
Founded: 1953. **Staff:** 6. **Members:** 850. **Budget:** $1,200,000. Manufacturers of architectural woodwork products (casework,

fixtures, and panelings) and associated suppliers of equipment and materials. Works to: raise industry standards; research new and improved materials and methods; publish technical data helpful in the design and use of architectural woodwork. Conducts seminars and training course.

ASPHALT EMULSION MANUFACTURERS ASSOCIATION

3 Church Cir., Ste. 250
Annapolis, MD 21401
Michael R. Krissoff, Exec.Dir.
PH: (410)267-0023
E-mail: 74603.3345@compuserve.com
URL: http://www.aema.org
Founded: 1973. **Staff:** 2. **Members:** 150. **Budget:** $250,000. Seeks to foster: advancement and improvement of the asphalt emulsion industry; expanded and more efficient use of emulsion as a result of an improved state of the art; provision of information to users through guide specifications and answers to specific questions.

ASPHALT INSTITUTE

Research Park Dr.
PO Box 14052
Lexington, KY 40512-4052
Edward L. Miller, Pres.
PH: (606)288-4960
FX: (606)288-4999
URL: http://www.asphaltinstitute.org
Founded: 1919. **Staff:** 42. **Members:** 48. **Budget:** $3,000,000. Refiners of asphalt products from crude petroleum and related asphalt businesses. Conducts extensive program of education, research, and engineering service related to asphalt products. Sponsors workshops and seminars. Compiles statistics; maintains library.

ASPHALT ROOFING MANUFACTURERS ASSOCIATION

4041 Powder Mill Rd., Ste. 404
Beltsville, MD 20705-3106
Richard D. Snyder, Exec.VP
PH: (301)348-2002
FX: (301)348-2020
Founded: 1915. **Staff:** 8. **Members:** 52. **Budget:** $950,000. Manufacturers of asphalt shingles, rollgoods, built-up roofing systems (BUR) and modified bitumen roofing systems. Compiles statistics.

ASSOCIATED AIR BALANCE COUNCIL

1518 K St. NW
Washington, DC 20005
Kenneth M. Sufka, Exec.Dir.
PH: (202)737-0202
FX: (202)638-4833
E-mail: aabchq@aol.com
URL: http://www.aabchq.com
Founded: 1965. **Staff:** 5. **Members:** 146. Certified test and balance engineers. Works to upgrade air testing and balancing within the building industry through exchange of technical information and professional standards. Offers recommendations to the manufacturing segment concerning air handling equipment and to the professional sector regarding design of air handling systems. Holds Apprenticeship Training Program for Balancing Technicians; conducts testing and balancing seminars for engineers.

ASSOCIATED CONSTRUCTION DISTRIBUTORS INTERNATIONAL

4595 Towne Lake Pkwy., Bldg. 300, Ste. 230
Woodstock, GA 30189
Tom Goetz, VP
PH: (770)516-1636
FX: (770)516-1303
Founded: 1974. **Staff:** 3. **Members:** 36. **Budget:** $300,000. Independent construction material and equipment distributors specializing in concrete and masonry supplies and equipment. Promotes improved communication and greater professionalism among members. Maintains library; conducts annual financial statistical survey of member firms; sponsors occasional technical seminars.

ASSOCIATED SCHOOLS OF CONSTRUCTION

Auburn University
119 Dudley Hall
Auburn, AL 36849-5315
F. Eugene Rebholz, Asst.Sec.-Treas.
PH: (334)844-5383
FX: (334)844-5386
E-mail: molhend@mail.auburn.edu
Founded: 1965. **Members:** 91. Colleges and universities offering a program leading to an undergraduate or advanced degree with major emphasis on construction. Aims to establish objectives for the development of construction education and to assist institutions of higher education in establishing construction education and management programs. Has undertaken an intensive study of the curricula of member institutions, with resulting recommendations. Compiles statistics.

ASSOCIATION OF ASPHALT PAVING TECHNOLOGISTS

400 Selby Ave., Ste. I
St. Paul, MN 55102
Eugene L. Skok, Sec.-Treas.
PH: (651)293-9188
FX: (651)293-9193
E-mail: aaptbev@aol.com
Founded: 1924. **Staff:** 2. **Members:** 825. **Budget:** $135,000. Engineers and chemists engaged in asphalt paving or related fields such as materials and construction equipment.

ASSOCIATION OF MAJOR CITY BUILDING OFFICIALS

505 Huntmar Park Dr., Ste. 210
Herndon, VA 20170
Jill Moreschi, Sec.
PH: (703)481-2020
TF: (800)DOC-CODE
FX: (703)481-3596
Founded: 1974. **Members:** 36. National forum of city and county building officials united to discuss mutual interests and problems. Focuses on issues of public safety in the buildings, administrative techniques, and building codes. Encourages the development of comprehensive training and educational programs for building code enforcement personnel. Provides scientific and technical resources for the improvement of building codes and for innovative building technology and products to reduce the cost of construction and maintain safety levels.

ASSOCIATION OF MEZZANINE MANUFACTURERS

8720 Red Oak Blvd., Ste. 201
Charlotte, NC 28217
John Nofsinger, Mng.Dir.
PH: (704)522-7826
FX: (704)522-7826
URL: http://www.mhia.org/
Founded: 1989. **Staff:** 2. **Members:** 13. **Budget:** $50,000. Mezzanine manufacturers. Promotes mezzanine industry and strives to create recognition for the industry in the marketplace. Develops design and manufacturer standards and regulations to benefit the consumer. Strives to improve related tools and equipment to increase productivity and profitability within the industry. Conducts educational and research programs; compiles statistics.

ASSOCIATION OF REFRIGERANT AND DESUPERHEATING MANUFACTURING

Addison Products Company
PO Box 607776
ECU Division
Orlando, FL 32860-7776
Rodney E. Weaver, Pres.
PH: (407)292-4400
FX: (407)290-1329
E-mail: admin@addison-hvac.com
URL: http://www.addison-hvac.com
Founded: 1987. **Members:** 15. Manufacturers of desuperheaters and heat recovery systems. Seeks to improve waste heat recovery

systems. Conducts research; advocates certification of all heat recovery systems.

ASSOCIATION OF THE WALL AND CEILING INDUSTRIES -INTERNATIONAL

803 West Broad St., Ste. 600
Falls Church, VA 22046-3108
Steven A. Etkin, Exec.VP
PH: (703)534-8300
FX: (703)534-8307
E-mail: info@awci.org
URL: http://www.AWCI.ORG
Founded: 1976. **Staff:** 12. **Members:** 1,000. **Budget:** $1,800,000.
Acoustical tile, drywall, demountable partitions, lathing and plaster-
ing, fireproofing, light-gauge steel framing, stucco and exterior
insulation finish systems.

BRICK INDUSTRY ASSOCIATION

11490 Commerce Park Dr.
Reston, VA 20191
Nelson J. Cooney, Pres.
PH: (703)620-0010
FX: (703)620-3928
E-mail: brickinfo@bia.org
URL: http://www.bia.org
Founded: 1934. **Staff:** 13. **Members:** 50. **Budget:** $1,500,000.
Manufacturers of clay brick.

BRIDGE GRID FLOORING MANUFACTURERS ASSOCIATION

231 S. Church St.
Mount Pleasant, PA 15666
Daniel H. Copeland, Exec.Dir.
PH: (412)547-2660
FX: (412)547-2660
E-mail: bgfma@aol.com
Founded: 1985. **Staff:** 1. **Members:** 5. Manufacturers of bridge
grid decks; associate members are suppliers of steel used in the con-
struction of bridge grid decks. Seeks to increase the use of steel
bridge grid decks by promoting their use among consultants, state
bridge engineers, bridge owners, and other specifying agencies.
Conducts research, in conjunction with universities, on engineering
characteristics of steel grid decks. Maintains speakers' bureau.

BUILDING AND CONSTRUCTION TRADES DEPARTMENT -AFL-CIO

1155 15th St. NW, 4th Fl.
Washington, DC 20005
Robert A. Georgine, Contact
PH: (202)347-1461
FX: (202)628-0724
URL: http://www.buildingtrades.org/
Members: 4,500,000. Federation of labor unions in the construction
industry including asbestos workers, bricklayers, masons, plasterers,
carpenters, electrical workers, elevator constructors, operating engineers, granite cutters, hod carriers, common laborers, iron workers,
carpet, tile and stone workers, painters, decorators, paper hangers,
plumbers, steam fitters, roofers, boilermakers, lathers, sheet metal
workers, and other related trades. Maintains liaison with Center to
Protect Workers Rights, which provides independent research and
support.

BUILDING OFFICIALS AND CODE ADMINISTRATORS INTERNATIONAL

4051 W. Flossmoor Rd.
Country Club Hills, IL 60478-5795
Paul K. Heilstedt, P.E., CEO
FX: (708)799-4981
E-mail: member@bocai.org
URL: http://www.bocai.org
Founded: 1915. **Staff:** 100. **Members:** 14,500. **Budget:**
$10,000,000. Governmental officials and agencies and other inter-
ests concerned with administering or formulating building, fire, me-
chanical, plumbing, zoning, housing regulations. Promulgates the

BOCA National Codes and the ICC International Codes suitable for
adoption by reference by governmental entities. Provides services
for maintaining the codes up-to-date. Supplies information on quality and acceptability of building materials and systems and on new
construction techniques and materials. Maintains services for all
members in connection with codes and their administration; provides consulting, training and education, plan review, and other advisory services; conducts correspondence courses; prepares in-serv-
ice training programs and assists local organizations in such activities. Maintains placement services.

CELLULOSE INSULATION MANUFACTURERS ASSOCIATION

136 S. Keowee St.
Dayton, OH 45402
Daniel Lea, Exec. Officer
PH: (513)222-2462
TF: (888)881-2462
FX: (513)222-5794
E-mail: cima@dayton.net
URL: http://www.cellulose.org
Founded: 1982. **Staff:** 2. **Members:** 38. **Budget:** $400,000. Manu-
facturers of cellulose insulation. Promotes quality control; represents
the interests of the industry. Supports research into the characteris-
tics and performance of cellulose insulation.

CENTRAL WHOLESALERS ASSOCIATION

PO Box 310
Caledonia, OH 43314-0310
Dan L. Schlosser, Exec.VP
PH: (419)845-2023
FX: (419)845-2026
Founded: 1974. **Staff:** 1. **Members:** 111. Wholesale distributors of
plumbing, heating, and cooling supplies. Provides a forum for the
exchange of ideas and information pertaining to the industry. Con-
ducts surveys; sponsors seminars and educational programs. Com-
piles statistics; reports on wages and business conditions.

CERAMIC TILE DISTRIBUTORS ASSOCIATION

800 Roosevelt Rd.
Bldg. C, Ste. 20
Glen Ellyn, IL 60137
Rick Church, Exec. Dir.
PH: (630)545-9415
TF: (800)938-CTDA
FX: (630)790-3095
URL: http://www.ctdahome.org
Founded: 1978. **Staff:** 3. **Members:** 500. Wholesale distributors
and manufacturers of ceramic tile and related products. Promotes the
increase of sales volumes in the ceramic tile industry through educa-
tional programs and networking. Promotes independent ceramic tile
distributors and represents their interests. Provides technical infor-
mation; compiles statistics. Sponsors competitions. Maintains insurance program for members and speakers' bureau.

CHAIN LINK FENCE MANUFACTURERS INSTITUTE

9891 Broken Land Pkwy., No. 300
Columbia, MD 21046
Mark Levin, CAE, Exec.VP
PH: (301)596-2583
FX: (301)596-2594
Founded: 1960. **Staff:** 2. **Members:** 52. Firms engaged in the manufacture of chain link fencing. Provides a forum in which members
can meet to be educated and exchange ideas on operations and management; promotes use of chain link fence. Collects statistics; works
with consumers and governments to develop standards and specifications with the goal of upgrading the quality of the product. Maintains speakers' bureau.

COMMERCIAL REFRIGERATOR MANUFACTURERS ASSOCIATION

1200 19th St., Ste. 300
Washington, DC 20036
Sharon Butalla, Exec.Dir.

PH: (202)857-1145
FX: (202)223-4579
Founded: 1933. **Staff:** 2. **Members:** 45. **Budget:** $140,000. Manufacturers of refrigerated display cases and cabinets, food service refrigerators, and sectional cooling rooms. Seeks to provide a voice for manufacturers and suppliers to address industry developments and problems with companies who share common interests. Maintains a continuing presence within Congress and government agencies to monitor and respond to policies and regulations affecting the industry and represent the collective interests of members. Acts as clearinghouse on information including foreign sales opportunities, technological developments, domestic markets, and other data of importance to the refrigeration industry. Provides technical information concerning regulations to governmental agencies. Conducts research to eliminate waste and increase efficiency of the production, distribution, and marketing of merchandise, products, or equipment related to the industry. Has developed a health and sanitation standard for retail food store refrigerators. Compiles statistics.

COMPOSITES FABRICATORS ASSOCIATION
1655 Ft. Myer Dr., Ste. 510
Arlington, VA 22209
Missy Henriksen, Exec.Dir.
PH: (703)525-0511
FX: (703)525-0743
E-mail: cfa-info@cfa-hq.org
URL: http://www.cfa-hq.org
Founded: 1979. **Staff:** 8. **Members:** 800. Companies engaged in the hand layup or sprayup of fiberglass in open molds or engaged in filament winding or resin transfer molding. Products requiring this process include boats, swimming pools, and bathroom fixtures. Conducts educational and research programs; compiles statistics. Sponsors product specialty seminars.

CONCRETE REINFORCING STEEL INSTITUTE
933 Plum Grove Rd.
Schaumburg, IL 60173
Charles E. Slater, Pres.
PH: (847)517-1200
FX: (847)517-1206
URL: http://www.crsi.org
Founded: 1924. **Staff:** 19. **Members:** 180. Producers, fabricators, and distributors of reinforcing steel bars used in reinforced concrete construction. Conducts research; provides technical information on reinforced concrete design and construction practices.

CONSTRUCTION INDUSTRY EMPLOYERS ASSOCIATION
PO Box 4189
Buffalo, NY 14217
James C. Logan, Exec.VP
PH: (716)875-4744
FX: (716)875-4412
Founded: 1867. **Staff:** 4. **Members:** 100. Construction firms. Represents member firms in labor negotiations and assists with labor relations. Conducts educational programs.

CONSTRUCTION OWNERS ASSOCIATION OF AMERICA
1200 Peachtree Center Harris Tower
233 Peachtree St., NE
Atlanta, GA 30303
PH: (800)994-2622
TF: (800)255-8325
FX: (404)577-3551
URL: http://www.coaa.org
Founded: 1994. **Staff:** 2. **Members:** 200. Public and private owners of construction projects. Promotes and fosters the interests of construction owners. Works to standardize construction contract forms and documentation. Provides educational programs.

CONSTRUCTION SPECIFICATIONS INSTITUTE
601 Madison St.
Alexandria, VA 22314-1791
Gregory Balestrero, Exec.Dir.

PH: (703)684-0300
TF: (800)689-2900
FX: (703)684-0465
E-mail: csimail@csinet.org
URL: http://www.csinet.org
Founded: 1948. **Staff:** 57. **Members:** 17,700. **Budget:** $10,500,000. Individuals concerned with the specifications and documents used for construction projects. Membership includes architects, professional engineers, specifiers, contractors, product manufacturers, teachers and research workers in architectural and engineering fields, and building maintenance engineers. Dedicated to advancing construction technology through communication, service, education, and research. Certifies construction specifiers and others involved in construction and allied industries. Maintains 20 committees including Certification, Credentials, Specifications Competition, and Technical Documents. Sponsors competitions; maintains speakers' bureau; offers seminars.

COOLING TOWER INSTITUTE
PO Box 73383
Houston, TX 77273
Virginia A. Manser, Admin.
PH: (281)583-4087
FX: (281)537-1721
E-mail: vmanser@cti.org
URL: http://www.cti.org
Founded: 1950. **Staff:** 3. **Members:** 400. **Budget:** $800,000. Seeks to improve technology, design, and performance of water conservation apparatus. Has developed standard specifications for cooling towers; provides inspection services. Conducts research through technical subcommittees. Sponsors projects; maintains speakers' bureau.

EIFS INDUSTRY MEMBERS ASSOCIATION
3000 Corporate Center Dr. Ste 270
Morrow, GA 30260
Steve Klamke, Exec.Dir.
PH: (770)968-7945
TF: (800)294-3462
FX: (770)968-5818
URL: http://www.eifsfacts.com
Founded: 1981. **Staff:** 4. **Members:** 325. **Budget:** $2,000,000. Those in the exterior insulation and finish systems industry. Dedicated to improving the exterior insulation industry and widening the use of its products through collective action. Conducts educational and research programs.

ENERGY EFFICIENT BUILDING ASSOCIATION
500 Energy Efficient Bldg.
Silver Spring, MD 20910
James S. Golden, Exec.Dir.
PH: (612)851-9940
FX: (612)851-9507
E-mail: eebanews@aol.com
URL: http://www.eeba.org
Founded: 1982. **Staff:** 3. **Members:** 400. **Budget:** $250,000. Architects, builders and building material suppliers, contractors, scientists, homeowners, and other individuals and businesses with an interest in energy efficient construction. Fosters the development, dissemination, and acceptance of information relevant to the design, construction, and operation of energy and resource efficient buildings which provide quality living environments. Serves as a forum for the exchange of information and ideas among members.

ENVIRONMENTAL INFORMATION ASSOCIATION
4915 Auburn Ave., Ste. 303
Bethesda, MD 20814
PH: (301)961-4999
TF: (888)343-4342
FX: (301)961-3094
Founded: 1983. **Staff:** 5. **Members:** 1,000. Individuals and corporations concerned about environmental management and control. Collects and disseminates information concerning environmental risks in buildings to interested professionals, building owners, and

the public. Serves as a clearinghouse of information on effective environmental management. Promotes high standards of professionalism among members. Maintains EIA Asbestos Abatement Worker and Training Program and offers operations and maintenance programs for management. Provides consulting and referral service to members on health issues. Maintains speakers' bureau; compiles statistics.

EVAPORATIVE COOLING INSTITUTE
PO Box 3ECI
Las Cruces, NM 88003-8001
Robert Foster, Treas.
PH: (505)646-4104
FX: (505)646-2960
Founded: 1989. **Members:** 60. Manufacturers of evaporative apparatus; designers, specifiers, and users of heating, ventilating, and air conditioning systems; sales representatives; representatives of educational and governmental agencies; interested individuals. Seeks to advance the art and science of evaporative air cooling and air conditioning by: promoting the technology and industry; collecting and publishing information on applying, installing, operating, and maintaining evaporative systems; disseminating information on codes, standards, and certification programs; identifying and encouraging research; maintaining contact with related trade associations, professional societies, government agencies, and customers.

EXPANDED SHALE CLAY AND SLATE INSTITUTE
2225 E. Murray Holladay Rd., Ste. 102
Salt Lake City, UT 84117
John P. Ries, Exec.Dir.
PH: (801)272-7070
FX: (801)272-3377
Founded: 1952. **Staff:** 2. **Members:** 21. Manufacturers of rotary kiln produced shale, clay, and slate lightweight aggregate. Promotes the extensive use of rotary kiln produced lightweight aggregate in the concrete masonry, ready-mix, and precast markets. Disseminates educational materials to the building industry based on research and development. Works with other technical organizations to maintain product quality, life-safety, and professional integrity throughout the construction industry and related building code bodies.

FACING TILE INSTITUTE
Box 8880
Canton, OH 44711
Paul Tauer, Dir. of Sales
PH: (330)488-1211
FX: (330)488-0333
Founded: 1934. **Members:** 3. Manufacturers of glazed brick and/or structural glazed tile. Promotes the use of glazed and unglazed facing tile for interior and exterior use in all phases of construction. Presently inactive.

FOUNDATION OF THE WALL AND CEILING INDUSTRY
803 W. Broad St., Ste. 600
Falls Church, VA 22046
Steven A. Etkin, Exec.VP
PH: (703)543-8300
FX: (703)534-8307
E-mail: info@awci.org
URL: http://www.awci.org
Founded: 1978. **Staff:** 1. **Budget:** $50,000. National and local contractors, manufacturers of construction products, architects, specifiers, and distributors/suppliers of wall and ceiling products. Seeks to support and expand the wall and ceiling industry's educational and research activities. Operates information clearinghouse.

GLAZING INDUSTRY CODE COMMITTEE
2945 SW Wanamaker St., Ste. A
Topeka, KS 66614
William J. Birch, Admin.
PH: (785)271-0208
FX: (785)271-0166
E-mail: gicc@glasswebsite.com
URL: http://www.glasswebsite.com

Founded: 1983. **Members:** 19. **Budget:** $95,000. Trade association for the glazing industry. Represents members' interests before the model building codes.

HEARTH EDUCATION FOUNDATION
2700 Fairview Ave. N.
St. Paul, MN 55115-1306
Tracy Wurzel, Exec.Dir.
Founded: 1981. **Staff:** 2. Seeks to serve the public interest in advancing the safe and efficient use of hearth appliances including wood stoves, fireplaces, pallet and gas appliances. Provides certification exams to wood stove, fireplace, pellet and gas appliance installers and inspectors.

HEAT EXCHANGE INSTITUTE
1300 Summer Ave.
Cleveland, OH 44115-2851
John H. Addington, Sec.-Treas.
PH: (216)241-7333
FX: (216)241-0105
E-mail: hei@taol.com
URL: http://www.taol.com/hei
Founded: 1933. **Staff:** 3. **Members:** 17. Manufacturers of steam condensers, closed feedwater heaters, steam jet ejectors, liquid ring vacuum pumps, power plant heat exchangers, and deaerators.

HOME VENTILATING INSTITUTE DIVISION OF THE AIR MOVEMENT CONTROL ASSOCIATION
30 W. University Dr.
Arlington Heights, IL 60004
Dale Rammien, Exec.Dir.
PH: (847)394-0150
FX: (847)253-0088
E-mail: amca@amca.org
Founded: 1955. **Staff:** 2. **Members:** 34. A voluntary organization for manufacturer self-regulation. Conducts a program for certified performance ratings for powered and static residential ventilating equipment. Ratings are specified to meet air change standards for the whole house. Participates in the development of standards and codes. Partakes in ventilation research projects.

HYDRONICS INSTITUTE DIVISION OF GAMA
PO Box 218
35 Russo Pl.
Berkeley Heights, NJ 07922
PH: (908)464-8200
FX: (908)464-7818
Founded: 1970. **Staff:** 6. **Members:** 55. Manufacturers of hydronic (hot water and steam) heating and cooling equipment. Sponsors educational programs in selected cities. Compiles statistics.

INDUSTRIAL HEATING EQUIPMENT ASSOCIATION
1901 N. Fort Myer Dr.
Arlington, VA 22209
James J. Houston, CAE, Exec.VP
PH: (703)525-2513
FX: (703)525-2513
E-mail: ihea@ihea.org
URL: http://www.ihea.org
Founded: 1929. **Staff:** 2. **Members:** 50. **Budget:** $200,000. Manufacturers of industrial furnaces, ovens, combustion equipment, atmosphere generators, induction and dielectric heating equipment, industrial heaters, process controls, fuel saving and heating devices, and heat recovery equipment.

INSULATED STEEL DOOR INSTITUTE
30200 Detroit Rd.
Cleveland, OH 44145-1967
J. J. Wherry, Mng.Dir.
PH: (440)899-0010
FX: (440)892-1404
URL: http://www.isdi.org
Founded: 1975. **Staff:** 5. **Members:** 8. Manufacturers of insulated

steel door systems for residential applications, united for development of performance specifications and standards.

INTERNATIONAL ASSOCIATION OF COLD STORAGE
  CONTRACTORS
7315 Wisconsin Ave., No. 1200N
Bethesda, MD 20814
J. William Hudson, Exec.Dir.
PH: (301)652-5674
FX: (301)652-7269
E-mail: email@iarw.org
Founded: 1981. **Members:** 75. **Budget:** $75,000. Seeks to ensure high standards and professionalism in the cold storage insulation industry which involves insulating, designing, and building coolers, freight cars, industrial freezers, and other types of industrial refrigeration. Objectives are: to improve business operations; to carry out insurance survey work; to act as a clearinghouse for technical information. Compiles industry statistics.

INTERNATIONAL ASSOCIATION OF HEAT AND FROST
  INSULATORS AND ASBESTOS WORKERS
1776 Massachusetts Ave. NW, Ste. 301
Washington, DC 20036-1989
William G. Bernard, Gen.Pres.
PH: (202)785-2388
FX: (202)429-0568
Founded: 1910. **Staff:** 23. **Members:** 18,000. AFL-CIO.

INTERNATIONAL ASSOCIATION OF MACHINISTS AND
  AEROSPACE WORKERS, WOODWORKERS DISTRICT
  LODGE 1
25 Cornell Ave.
Gladstone, OR 97027
Chuck Macrae, Pres./DBR
PH: (503)656-1475
FX: (503)657-2254
Founded: 1937. **Staff:** 13. **Members:** 8,000. AFL-CIO. Union which represents woodworkers in the logging, sawmill, plywood, particleboard, hardboard, and tree nursery industries.

INTERNATIONAL ASSOCIATION OF PLUMBING AND
  MECHANICAL OFFICIALS
20001 Walnut Dr. S
Walnut, CA 91789-2825
Donald Laughlin, Chief Admin. Officer
PH: (909)595-8449
FX: (909)594-3690
E-mail: iapmo@earthlink.net
URL: http://www.iapmo.org
Founded: 1926. **Staff:** 21. **Members:** 4,500. **Budget:** $4,000,000. Government agencies, administrative officials, sales representatives, manufacturers, associations, and members of associations related to the plumbing field. Sponsors and writes Uniform Plumbing Codes; also sponsors Uniform Mechanical Code. Sponsors speakers' bureau.

INTERNATIONAL BROTHERHOOD OF PAINTERS AND
  ALLIED TRADES
United Unions Bldg.
1750 New York Ave. NW
Washington, DC 20006
A. L. Monroe, Gen.Pres.
PH: (202)637-0720
FX: (202)637-0771
Founded: 1887. **Members:** 162,295. AFL-CIO.

INTERNATIONAL CAST POLYMER ASSOCIATION
8201 Greensboro Dr., Ste. 300
McAllen, VA 22102-3810
Tim Rugh, Exec. VP
PH: (703)610-9034
FX: (703)610-9005
E-mail: icpa@icpa-hq.com
URL: http://www.icpa-hq.com

Founded: 1974. **Staff:** 6. **Members:** 330. **Budget:** $900,000. Firms and corporations that make cast polymer products (such as cast marble vanity tops and solid surface countertops); firms and corporations that supply raw materials and production equipment to manufacturers of cast polymer products. Promotes the merits of certified cast polymer products to their markets; works to expand these markets for the benefit of manufacturers, suppliers, and sellers of these products; firms that fabricate/install cast polymer products. Develops and promotes industry-wide standards of product quality and acceptability for the protection of purchasers of cast polymer products. Represents the cast polymer industry before government, code bodies, and regulatory agencies of all types. Defends the industry against unwarranted regulations and seeks to guarantee its source and supply of raw materials; helps members improve their skills as businessmen; educates the public on how the industry sells its products. Works to develop reliable industry-wide market data to guide members in planning operations; strives to advance the interests of the industry and of members within the boundaries set by law. Participates in standards, product testing and certification programs, technical exchange, marketing and business educational activities, production data, and informal exchanges. Conducts research programs; compiles statistics.

INTERNATIONAL CODE COUNCIL
5203 Leesburg Pike, Ste. 708
Falls Church, VA 22041
Richard P. Kuchnicki, CEO
PH: (703)931-4533
FX: (703)379-1546
E-mail: staff@intlcode.org
URL: http://www.intlcode.org
Founded: 1972. **Staff:** 4. Three model code organizations with a membership of about 12000 cities, states, counties, and towns. Represents building officials at all levels of government. Develops, recommends, and promotes new product acceptance, uniform regulations, and adoption of model codes. Maintains Board for the Coordination of the Model Codes and National Evaluation Service. Administers nationally recognized Certified Building Official Program.

INTERNATIONAL COMPRESSOR REMANUFACTURERS
  ASSOCIATION
PO Box 33092
Kansas City, MO 64114
Olive L. Snider, Exec.Sec.
PH: (816)333-7205
FX: (913)764-7422
Founded: 1965. **Staff:** 2. **Members:** 60. **Budget:** $30,000. Persons, firms, and corporations engaged in the business of remanufacturing and rebuilding refrigeration and air conditioning compressors. Seeks to foster trade, commerce, and interest of those engaged in the rebuilding, exchanging, and repairing of refrigeration and allied equipment. Promotes uniformity and certainty in the trade customs of those with an interest in the industry. Collects and disseminates information of value to members and the public; arbitrates differences among members.

INTERNATIONAL CONFERENCE OF BUILDING
  OFFICIALS
5360 Workman Mill Rd.
Whittier, CA 90601-2298
Jon Traw, Pres.
PH: (562)699-0541
TF: (800)284-4406
FX: (562)695-4694
URL: http://www.icbo.org
Founded: 1922. **Staff:** 135. **Members:** 16,000. **Budget:** $15,000,000. Representatives of local, regional, and state governments. Seeks to publish, maintain, and promote the Uniform Building Code and related documents; investigate and research principles underlying safety to life and property in the construction, use, and location of buildings and related structures; develop and promulgate uniformity in regulations pertaining to building construction; educate the building official; formulate guidelines for the administration of building inspection departments. Conducts training programs,

courses, and certification programs for code enforcement inspectors. Maintains speakers' bureau.

INTERNATIONAL DISTRICT ENERGY ASSOCIATION
1200 19th St. NW, Ste. 300
Washington, DC 20036-2401
John L. Fiegel, Exec.Dir.
PH: (202)429-5111
FX: (202)429-5113
E-mail: idea@dc.sba.com
Founded: 1909. **Staff:** 6. **Members:** 770. **Budget:** $800,000. Suppliers of space heating by means of steam and hot water, and air conditioning by means of steam and chilled water, via piping systems from a central station to groups of buildings.

INTERNATIONAL DOOR ASSOCIATION
PO Box 117
28 Lowry Dr.
West Milton, OH 45383
Christopher S. Long, Exec.VP
PH: (937)698-4186
Founded: 1973. **Members:** 750. Individuals and companies who manufacture, sell, or install overhead garage doors and openers. Objective is to promote the industry and increase training and educational opportunities. Has written a code of business practices; compiles statistics. Conducts seminars.

INTERNATIONAL GROUND SOURCE HEAT PUMP
  ASSOCIATION
Oklahoma State University
490 Cordell S.
Stillwater, OK 74078
James Bose, Exec.Dir.
PH: (405)744-5175
TF: (800)626-4747
FX: (405)744-5283
E-mail: jbose@master.ceat.okstate.edu
Founded: 1987. **Staff:** 11. **Members:** 2,000. **Budget:** $500,000. Manufacturers, distributors, and contractors in the ground source heat pump systems and products industry. Seeks to educate the public about ground source heat pump systems and promote their use as economical energy saving systems. (The system consists of a water source heat pump connected to a plastic pipe buried in the ground in which the earth supplies energy for space heating, domestic water heating, and a place to waste excess heat during cooling cycles.) Sponsors teleconferences and exhibits at trade shows.

INTERNATIONAL INSTITUTE OF AMMONIA
  REFRIGERATION
1200 19th St. NW, No. 300
Washington, DC 20036-2401
M. Kent Anderson, Pres.
PH: (202)857-1110
FX: (202)223-4579
Founded: 1971. **Staff:** 6. **Members:** 1,200. **Budget:** $550,000. Ammonia equipment manufacturers, consultants, contractors, wholesalers, and anhydrous ammonia users from 20 countries. Works to provide education, information, and standards for the proper and safe use of ammonia as a refrigerant.

INTERNATIONAL MASONRY INSTITUTE
  APPRENTICESHIP AND TRAINING
Annapolis 42 E. St.
Annapolis, MD 21401
Joan Bassett Baggett-Calambokidis, Pres.
PH: (410)280-1305
FX: (301)261-2855
Founded: 1970. Nonmembership organization serving as a joint labor-management trust between the International Union of Bricklayers and Allied Craftsmen (IUBAC) and contractors who employ the Union's members. Provides training, apprenticeship, and technical assistance.

INTERNATIONAL MOBILE AIR CONDITIONING
  ASSOCIATION
PO Box 9000
Fort Worth, TX 76147-2000
Frank Allison, Exec.Dir.
PH: (817)338-1100
FX: (817)338-1451
E-mail: imac@iamerica.net
Founded: 1958. **Staff:** 5. **Members:** 500. **Budget:** $225,000. Manufacturers of complete air-conditioning systems and other installed accessories for automobiles, trucks, recreational vehicles, farm and off-highway vehicles, marine and aircraft; manufacturers of component parts; distributors of units; membership figure represents participants from 39 countries.

INTERNATIONAL SLURRY SURFACING ASSOCIATION
1200 19th St. NW, Ste. 300
Washington, DC 20036-2401
John L. Fiegel, Exec.Dir.
PH: (202)857-1160
FX: (202)223-4579
E-mail: brianbrown@dc.sba.com
URL: http://www.history.rochester.edu/issa
Founded: 1962. **Staff:** 2. **Members:** 225. **Budget:** $210,000. Dedicated to the interests, education, and success of slurry surfacing professionals and corporations around the world. Promotes ethics and quality and provides members with information, technical assistance, and ongoing opportunities for networking and professional development.

INTERNATIONAL UNION OF BRICKLAYERS AND
  ALLIED CRAFTSMEN
815 15th St. NW
Washington, DC 20005
John T. Joyce, Pres.
PH: (202)783-3788
FX: (202)393-0219
Founded: 1865. **Members:** 106,000. AFL-CIO.

INTERNATIONAL UNION OF OPERATING ENGINEERS
1125 17th St. NW
Washington, DC 20036
Frank Hanley, Pres.
PH: (202)429-9100
FX: (202)429-0316
E-mail: webmaster@iuoe.org
URL: http://www.iuoe.org
Founded: 1896. **Members:** 370,000. AFL-CIO.

ITALIAN TRADE COMMISSION
499 Park Ave.
New York, NY 10022
Massimo Mamberti, Trade Commiss., Exec.Dir.
PH: (212)980-1500
FX: (212)758-1050
E-mail: newyork@italtrade.com
URL: http://www.italtrade.com
Founded: 1980. **Staff:** 4. Promotes the Italian tile industry. Informs retailers, distributors, architects, builders, and other consumers of the availability of Italian ceramic tile in the U.S. Disseminates educational materials. Compiles statistics; conducts research programs.

LABORERS' INTERNATIONAL UNION OF NORTH
  AMERICA
905 16th St. NW
Washington, DC 20006
Arthur A. Coia, Gen.Pres.
PH: (202)737-8320
FX: (202)737-2754
URL: http://www.liuna.org
Founded: 1903. **Members:** 750,000. AFL-CIO.

MAPLE FLOORING MANUFACTURERS ASSOCIATION
60 Revere Dr., Ste. 500
Northbrook, IL 60062
Kevin R. Hacke, Exec.Dir.
PH: (847)480-9138
FX: (847)480-9282
E-mail: mfma@maplefloor.org
URL: http://www.maplefloor.org
Founded: 1897. **Staff:** 2. **Members:** 150. **Budget:** $350,000. Manufacturers and installers of Northern Maple hardwood flooring. Establishes uniform grades and standards for MFMA hard maple.

MASONRY SOCIETY
3970 Broadway, Ste. 201-D
Boulder, CO 80304-1135
William D. Palmer, Exec.Dir.
PH: (303)939-9700
FX: (303)541-9215
E-mail: masonry@compuserve.com
Founded: 1977. **Staff:** 2. **Members:** 1,000. **Budget:** $500,000. Architects, engineers, manufacturers, mason contractors, craftsmen, students, educators, and other individuals interested in the use of masonry. Seeks to unite the specialized disciplines involved in the design, manufacture, and construction of masonry structures for the exchange of technical and practical information. Provides a forum for design professionals (architects and engineers) to become involved with the masonry industry. Advocates the establishment of a national building standard for masonry. Sponsors educational programs and publishes technical documents on all aspects of masonry. Maintains speakers' bureau.

MATERIALS AND METHODS STANDARDS ASSOCIATION
PO Box 350
Grand Haven, MI 49417-0350
Harvey J. Powell, Pres.
PH: (616)842-7844
FX: (616)842-1547
Founded: 1962. **Members:** 43. Corporations, firms, and individuals engaged in the manufacture and sale of products in the ceramic tile and dimensional stone industries. Establishes standards of quality and performance of materials and methods for installation and use. Participates in the writing of industry standards with the Tile Council of America, American National Standards Institute, and Marble Institute of America.

METAL BUILDING MANUFACTURERS ASSOCIATION
1300 Summer Ave.
Cleveland, OH 44115-2851
Charles M. Stockinger, Gen.Mgr.
PH: (216)241-7333
FX: (216)241-0105
E-mail: mbma@mbma.com
URL: http://www.mbma.com
Founded: 1956. **Staff:** 4. **Members:** 80. Manufacturers of metal building systems. Conducts research programs and compiles statistics. Associate members - suppliers.

METAL CONSTRUCTION ASSOCIATION
104 S. Michigan Ave., Ste. 1500
Chicago, IL 60603
David W. Barrack, Exec.Dir.
PH: (312)201-0193
FX: (312)201-0214
E-mail: 74733.1624@compuserve.com
Founded: 1983. **Staff:** 5. **Members:** 100. Individuals engaged in the manufacture, design, engineering, sale, or installation of metal used in construction; others interested in the metal construction industry. Promotes the use of metal in all construction applications. Represents all sectors of the metal construction industry; fosters improved communication within the industry; serves as liaison between members and other industry organizations. Collects and disseminates information. Maintains Merit Award Program to acknowledge outstanding buildings, products, and systems in the industry. Plans programs in institutional advertising, voluntary standards, and

statistics; proposed educational programs include structure erection, estimating, and bookkeeping. Compiles statistics.

METAL FRAMING MANUFACTURERS ASSOCIATION
401 N. Michigan Ave.
Chicago, IL 60611-4267
Jack M. Springer, Exec.Dir.
PH: (312)644-6610
FX: (312)321-5144
Founded: 1981. **Staff:** 2. **Members:** 7. **Budget:** $12,000. Manufacturers of ferrous and nonferrous metal framing systems. Promotes the use of metal framing (continuous slot metal channel) systems; develops industry standards; collects industry statistics.

MOBILE AIR CONDITIONING SOCIETY WORLDWIDE
PO Box 100
East Greenville, PA 18041
Simon Oulouhojian, COO, Pres.
PH: (215)679-2220
FX: (215)541-4635
Founded: 1981. **Staff:** 12. **Members:** 1,600. Distributors, service specialists, installers, manufacturers, and suppliers of automotive and truck air conditioners and parts. Works to disseminate information and develop specialized education.

NATIONAL ACADEMY OF CODE ADMINISTRATION
803 County Admin. Bldg.
138 E. Court St.
Cincinnati, OH 45202
Ralph W. Liebing, Exec.Dir.
Founded: 1970. **Members:** 900. Operates in the areas of education, certification, and training of code enforcement and administration personnel. Has established a voluntary national professional certification examination for building officials/code administrators. Program includes training workshops and self-study courses in the areas of code administration, law, management, and technology. Seeks to raise the professional level of the building official. Maintains speakers' bureau. Conducts law and management seminars for code administrators.

NATIONAL AIR FILTRATION ASSOCIATION
1518 K St NW, Ste. 503
Washington, DC 20005
Kenneth M. Sufka, Exec.Dir.
PH: (202)628-5328
TF: (800)941-6274
FX: (202)638-4833
E-mail: nafahq@aol.com
Founded: 1980. **Members:** 200. Companies which sell or service air filtration media to commercial and industrial users; manufacturers of air filtration media. Promotes the sale and use of air filtration media. Offers technical education to members; conducts regional workshops.

NATIONAL ASPHALT PAVEMENT ASSOCIATION
NAPA Bldg.
5100 Forbes Blvd.
Lanham, MD 20706-4413
Mike Acott, Pres.
PH: (301)731-4748
TF: (888)468-6499
FX: (301)731-4621
E-mail: napa@hotmix.org
URL: http://www.hotmix.org
Founded: 1955. **Staff:** 20. **Members:** 750. **Budget:** $1,500,000. Manufacturers and producers of scientifically proportioned hot mix asphalt for use in all paving, including highways, airfields, and environmental usages. Membership includes hot mix producers, paving contractors, equipment manufacturers, engineering consultants, and others. Supports research and publishes in formation on: producing, stockpiling, and feeding of the aggregate to the manufacturing facility; drying; methods of screening, storing, and proportioning in the manufacturing facility; production of the hot mix asphalt; transporting mix to paver; laydown procedure and rolling; general workman-

ship; and related construction practices and materials. Is committed to product quality, environmental control, safety and health, and energy conservation. Conducts training programs on a variety of technical and managerial topics for industry personnel. Maintains speakers' bureau and Hot Mix Asphalt Hall of Fame.

NATIONAL ASSOCIATION OF BRICK DISTRIBUTORS
11490 Commerce Park Dr., Ste. 300
Reston, VA 20191
Jennifer Chomicki, Dir. of Comm.
PH: (703)620-0010
FX: (703)620-3928
Founded: 1956. **Staff:** 2. **Members:** 400. **Budget:** $500,000. Distributors and manufacturers of structural clay products and their suppliers. Promotes the sale and use of all types of clay products.

NATIONAL ASSOCIATION OF FLOOR COVERING DISTRIBUTORS
401 N. Michigan
Chicago, IL 60611
Mariann B. Gregory, Exec.Dir.
PH: (312)321-6836
FX: (312)245-1085
E-mail: mgregory@sba.com
URL: http://www.nafcd.com
Founded: 1971. **Staff:** 2. **Members:** 285. **Budget:** $500,000. Floor covering distributors and firms selling to them. Objectives are to promote, protect, and advance the best interests of wholesale floor covering distribution; to foster sound business principles in all phases of floor covering wholesaling; to increase the use of wholesale floor covering products by the retailer; to improve understanding between manufacturers and wholesalers of floor covering products, and increase distribution of floor covering and related products through wholesale distribution channels; to improve the conditions under which the industry must operate; to collect and disseminate pertinent industry data; to assist its members through education, research, and training. Conducts surveys; compiles statistics.

NATIONAL ASSOCIATION OF INDEPENDENT RESURFACERS
5806 W. 127th St.
Alsip, IL 60658
Nancy Surprenant, Exec.Sec.
PH: (708)371-8237
Founded: 1973. **Members:** 100. Individuals and firms in the business of resanding and refinishing bowling lanes. Purposes are: to cooperate with proprietors; to improve safety standards, finishes, and equipment, thus reducing fire hazards; to convince the insurance industry that insuring resurfacers is a good investment; to enhance the status of the resurfacing industry and give resurfacers a representative voice in the bowling industry; to keep abreast of federal, state, and local legislation affecting resurfacers; to exchange ideas for resurfacers' mutual benefit. Conducts resurfacers training school and sales training seminar.

NATIONAL ASSOCIATION OF STORE FIXTURE MANUFACTURERS
3595 Sheridan St., No. 200
Hollywood, FL 33021
Klein Merriman, Exec.Dir.
PH: (954)893-7300
FX: (954)893-7500
E-mail: nasfm@nasfm.org
URL: http://www.nasfm.org
Founded: 1956. **Staff:** 8. **Members:** 600. **Budget:** $1,000,000. Represents the interests of manufacturers of store fixtures and displays. Provides networking opportunities for members. Conducts educational programs.

NATIONAL ASSOCIATION OF THE REMODELING INDUSTRY
4900 Seminary Rd., Ste. 320
Alexandria, VA 22311
William C. Carmichael, Exec.VP

PH: (703)575-1100
FX: (703)575-1121
E-mail: info@nari.org
URL: http://www.nari.org
Founded: 1982. **Staff:** 15. **Members:** 5,500. Remodeling contractors, manufacturers of building products, lending institutions, and wholesalers and distributors. Promotes the common business interests of those engaged in the home improvement and remodeling industries. Encourages ethical conduct, good business practices, and professionalism in the home improvement and remodeling industry. Conducts seminars, workshops, and promotional programs. Monitors legislation and regulations affecting the industry. Compiles statistics.

NATIONAL CONFERENCE OF STATES ON BUILDING CODES AND STANDARDS
505 Huntmar Park Dr., Ste. 210
Herndon, VA 20170
Robert C. Wible, Exec.Dir.
PH: (703)467-2045
TF: (800)DOC-CODE
FX: (703)481-3596
E-mail: jweisel@ncbcs.org
URL: http://www.ncsbcs.org
Founded: 1967. **Staff:** 55. **Members:** 280. **Budget:** $4,500,000. States (including District of Columbia, Puerto Rico, and the Virgin Islands), building code officials, building-related manufacturers, associations, educators, and consumer groups seeking a cooperative solution to the multiple problems in the entire building regulatory system. Seeks to: provide a forum for discussion of problems related to the administration of building programs by state regulatory officers; provide a mechanism for developing solutions to problems identified by the conference; assist in the development of programs leading to the adoption and administration of uniform comprehensive building codes and standards where such uniformity is deemed necessary for interstate purposes; encourage acceptance of modular and industrialized building and pre-assembled building components; develop an effective voice for state officials before the American National Standards Institute and the committees of nationally recognized standards-generating organizations; develop standards and code practices that will encourage the introduction and uniform recognition of innovations in building materials; establish standards for building accessibility by disabled individuals; support the evolution of comprehensive training and educational programs at recognized educational institutions for personnel connected with the enforcement of building regulations; foster cooperation among government officials concerned with building regulations, and between these officials and the design, manufacturing, business, and consumer interests affected by their activities. Co-sponsors International Building Safety Week every April. Compiles statistics.

NATIONAL COUNCIL OF ACOUSTICAL CONSULTANTS
66 Morris Ave., Ste. 1A
Springfield, NJ 07081-1409
Peter Allen, Exec.Sec.
PH: (973)564-5859
FX: (973)564-7480
Founded: 1962. **Members:** 130. Firms of acoustical consultants. Dedicated to management and related concerns of professional acoustical consulting firms and to safeguarding the interests of the individuals they serve. Sponsors educational programs; maintains speakers' bureau.

NATIONAL COUNCIL OF THE HOUSING INDUSTRY
1201 15th St. NW
Washington, DC 20005
James R. Birdsong, Staff VP
PH: (202)822-0520
TF: (800)368-5242
FX: (202)822-0374
URL: http://www.nahb.com
Founded: 1964. **Staff:** 4. **Members:** 88. **Budget:** $600,000. Manufacturers of goods and services for the American housing industry.

Provides support for the effort of the industry to fill the housing needs of American families.

NATIONAL ENVIRONMENTAL BALANCING BUREAU
8575 Grovement Circle
Gaithersburg, MD 20877-4121
Michael P. Dolim, Exec.VP
PH: (301)977-3698
FX: (301)977-9589
E-mail: mrnebb@aol.com
Founded: 1971. **Staff:** 4. **Members:** 553. **Budget:** $600,000. Qualified heating, ventilation, and air-conditioning contractors specializing in the fields of air and hydronic systems balancing, sound vibration measuring, testing of heating and cooling systems, building systems commissioning, and testing of cleanrooms. Seeks to establish and maintain industry standards, procedures, and specifications for testing, adjusting, and balancing work; certify those firms that meet the qualification requirements; establish educational programs to provide competent management and supervision of testing and balancing (TAB) work. Establishes professional qualifications for TAB supervisors. Maintains chapters in Australia and Canada.

NATIONAL FENESTRATION RATING COUNCIL
1300 Spring St., Ste. 500
Silver Spring, MD 20910
James Krahn, Chair
PH: (301)589-6372
FX: (301)588-0854
E-mail: nfrcusa@aol.com
URL: http://www.nfrc.org
Founded: 1990. **Staff:** 4. **Members:** 140. **Budget:** $1,000,000. Individuals, organizations, and corporations interested in production, regulation, promotion, and development of technology related to fenestration products. Develops national voluntary energy performance rating system for fenestration products; coordinates certification and labeling activities to ensure uniform rating application. Promotes consumer awareness of fenestration ratings in an effort to encourage informed purchase of windows, doors, and skylights. Conducts efficiency testing. Maintains speakers' bureau; conducts educational and research programs.

NATIONAL HOUSING ENDOWMENT
1201 15th St. NW
Washington, DC 20005-2800
Bruce S. Silver, Exec. Dir.
PH: (202)822-0274
TF: (800)368-5242
FX: (202)861-2177
Founded: 1987. **Staff:** 2. **Budget:** $200,000. Created by the National Association of Home Builders of the U.S. Provides funds for research on the housing industry and education and training programs for skilled workers and management personnel in the field. Offers scholarships and university campus programs to assure that the housing industry retains the quality personnel necessary for growth and stability. Supports activities that promote a quality home and living environment for all Americans and contribute to the development and advancement of community life.

NATIONAL INSTITUTE OF BUILDING SCIENCES
1090 Vermont Ave. NW, Ste. 700
Washington, DC 20005-4905
David A. Harris, Pres.
PH: (202)289-7800
FX: (202)289-1092
E-mail: nibs@nibs.org
URL: http://www.nibs.org
Founded: 1976. **Staff:** 25. **Members:** 800. Individuals and organizations, including architects, engineers, builders, contractors, realtors, universities, and all levels of government interested in the building industry. Created by Congress to promote a favorable and coherent building regulatory environment and encourage new technology in the building industry.

NATIONAL KEROSENE HEATER ASSOCIATION
1816 Old Natchez Trace
Franklin, TN 37069
J. Thomas Smith, Gen. Counsel
PH: (615)790-0770
FX: (615)790-6700
E-mail: nkha@nashville.com
Founded: 1981. **Staff:** 3. **Members:** 10. **Budget:** $540,000. Manufacturers, importers, distributors, and retailers of kerosene heaters in the U.S.; associate members include those active in selling, manufacturing, or dealing in machinery, supplies, or services used by the kerosene heater industry. Objectives are: to promote the kerosene heater as a cost efficient, supplemental heating system that reduces heating expenses while conserving energy; to encourage maximum safety and efficiency in kerosene heaters marketed in the U.S.; to educate the public and regulatory bodies about the safe operation and benefits of these heaters; to support member companies and their customers. Has established minimum product safety standards for members; campaigns for comprehensive product safety standards and legislation. Operates task forces.

NATIONAL OAK FLOORING MANUFACTURERS ASSOCIATION
PO Box 3009
Memphis, TN 38173-0009
Stan Elberg, Exec.VP
PH: (901)526-5016
FX: (901)526-7022
E-mail: info@nofma.org
URL: http://www.nofma.org
Founded: 1909. **Staff:** 7. **Members:** 25. Manufacturers of hardwood flooring. Promotes standardization; conducts grade labeling and inspection service; maintains research program in grading, handling, and installation; compiles statistics.

NATIONAL PATIO ENCLOSURE ASSOCIATION
12625 Frederick St. 1-5, 315
Moreno Valley, CA 92553
Tom Brandon, Exec.Dir.
PH: (909)485-8881
FX: (909)924-3078
Founded: 1954. **Members:** 80. Promotes the general welfare of manufacturers and retailers of patio enclosures and related products such as patio covers.

NATIONAL REFRIGERATION CONTRACTORS ASSOCIATION
1900 Arch St.
Philadelphia, PA 19103-1498
Elizabeth B. Franks, Exec.Dir.
PH: (215)564-3484
FX: (215)963-9785
E-mail: assnhqt@netaxs.com
Founded: 1948. **Staff:** 2. **Members:** 80. **Budget:** $50,000. Distributors, contractors, and manufacturers of commercial refrigeration equipment.

NATIONAL ROOFING FOUNDATION
O'Hare International Center
10255 W. Higgins, Ste. 600
Rosemont, IL 60018-5607
Christopher Seidel, Exec.Dir.
PH: (847)299-9070
FX: (847)299-1183
E-mail: nrca@roofonline.org
URL: http://www.nrea.net
Founded: 1970. **Staff:** 1. **Budget:** $1,000,000. Sponsors programs and projects that support the highest-quality programs for roofing contractors, ensure timely and forward-thinking industry responses to major economic and technological issues, and enhance the long-term viability and attractiveness of the roofing industry. Administers a scholarship program.

NATIONAL SASH AND DOOR JOBBERS ASSOCIATION
10225 Robert Trent Jones Pkwy.
New Port Richey, FL 34655-4649
Robert T. O'Keefe, Pres. & CEO
PH: (727)372-3665
TF: (800)786-SASH
FX: (727)372-2879
E-mail: info@nsdja.com
URL: http://www.nsdja.com
Founded: 1964. **Staff:** 7. **Members:** 1,050. **Budget:** $1,600,000.
Wholesale distributors of windows, door, millwork, and related products. Conducts research and statistical studies. Offers millwork home study course and audiovisual program dealing with product knowledge; furnishes group insurance. Compiles statistics.

NATIONAL SLAG ASSOCIATION
110 W Lancaster Ave., Ste. 2
Wayne, PA 19087
Robert Y. Twitmyer, Pres.
PH: (610)971-4840
FX: (610)971-4841
E-mail: useslag@aol.com
URL: http://www.nationalslagassoc.org
Founded: 1918. **Staff:** 2. **Members:** 78. Membership is comprised of Organizations actively engaged in iron and steel slag processing, refining, and/or the marketing of these slags. Organizations that are actively involved in activities directly connected with the iron and steel slag industry such as users, manufacturer's of equipment, suppliers, and service firms. Seeks to communicate and exchange pertinent slag industry information to the membership. Supports/promotes iron and steel slag interests at all levels, provides initiative and leadership, fosters humanistic and user-friendly levels of communications, and nurtures a positive relationship with all governmental and environmental agencies and the steel slag industry.

NATIONAL STANDARD PLUMBING CODE COMMITTEE
180 S. Washington St.
PO Box 6808
Falls Church, VA 22040
Bob Shepherd, Tech.Dir.
PH: (703)237-8100
TF: (800)533-7694
FX: (703)237-7442
E-mail: naphcc@naphcc.org
Founded: 1970. **Staff:** 2. **Members:** 12. Sponsored by National Association of Plumbing-Heating-Cooling Contractors. Has developed and updates a model plumbing code. NAPHCC serves as a secretariat and publisher of the code.

NATIONAL TILE ROOFING MANUFACTURERS ASSOCIATION
PO Box 40337
Eugene, OR 97404-0049
Richard K. Olson, Pres.
PH: (541)689-0366
FX: (541)689-5530
URL: http://www.ntrma.org
Founded: 1975. **Staff:** 1. **Members:** 41. **Budget:** $350,000. Manufacturers and suppliers of clay and concrete roofing tiles; cement companies; mineral pigment producers; and others furnishing equipment and materials for manufacturing roof tiles. Promotes the use of "firesafe" roof construction, especially clay and concrete tile roofs; educates the architectural, design, and construction industries regarding the advantages of tile roofs; presents to the home-owning public the advantages and economies of tile roofs. Conducts international programs for architects, builders, building inspectors, and roofing contractors; provides sound/slide presentations, speakers, mailers, and specifications relating to tile roof construction. roof construction.

NATIONAL WOOD FLOORING ASSOCIATION
16388 Westwoods Business Pk.
Ellisville, MO 63021
Edward S. Korczak, CAE, Exec.Dir.

TF: (800)422-4556
FX: (314)391-6137
E-mail: natlwood@aol.com
URL: http://www.woodfloors.org
Founded: 1985. **Staff:** 10. **Members:** 1,800. **Budget:** $1,500,000. Individuals, firms, and corporations engaged in the manufacture, distribution, installation, or sale of wood flooring and allied products. Purposes are to: unite all segments of the wood flooring industry; coordinate marketing and advertising programs of members; educate professionals and consumers about the benefits of wood flooring; increase the market share of the wood flooring industry. Works to develop product standards and a code of professional ethics within the industry. Sponsors training seminars for management and sales personnel; conducts promotional programs on the care and maintenance of wood floors. Disseminates information on new products and services; maintains speakers' bureau; compiles statistics. Maintains hall of fame on wood floor products and installation. Is developing a certification program for sanders, finishers, and installers of hardwood floors.

NORTH AMERICAN BUILDING MATERIAL DISTRIBUTION ASSOCIATION
401 N. Michigan Ave.
Chicago, IL 60611
Kevin Gammonley, V. Pres.
PH: (312)321-6845
TF: (888)747-7862
FX: (312)644-0310
E-mail: nbmda@sba.com
URL: http://www.nbmda.org
Founded: 1952. **Staff:** 5. **Members:** 400. **Budget:** $1,200,000. Building material distributors and manufacturers operating in more than 1500 locations. Represents industry when appropriate. Distributes member and industry information; provides networking opportunities to distributors and manufacturers in the building material industry. Maintains education foundation; provides charitable programs.

NORTH AMERICAN INSULATION MANUFACTURERS ASSOCIATION
44 Canal Center Plz., Ste. 310
Alexandria, VA 22314
Kenneth D. Mentzer, Exec.VP
PH: (703)684-0084
FX: (703)684-0427
E-mail: insulation@naima.org
URL: http://www.naima.org
Founded: 1933. **Staff:** 9. **Members:** 16. **Budget:** $4,000,000. Manufacturers of fiber glass, rock wool, and slag wool insulation products. Promotes energy efficiency and environmental preservation through the use of fiber glass, rock wool, and slag wool insulation products. Encourages safe production and use of insulation products.

NORTHAMERICAN HEATING, REFRIGERATION, AND AIRCONDITIONING WHOLESALERS ASSOCIATION
PO Box 16790
1389 Dublin Rd.
Columbus, OH 43216
James D. Wilder, Exec.VP
PH: (614)488-1835
FX: (614)488-0482
E-mail: nhrawmail@nhraw.org
URL: http://www.nhraw.org
Founded: 1947. **Staff:** 10. **Members:** 1,100. Wholesalers of heating, air conditioning, sheet metal, duct work, refrigerants, and their components.

OPERATIVE PLASTERERS AND CEMENT MASONS INTERNATIONAL ASSOCIATION OF U.S. AND CANADA
14405 Laurel Place, Ste. 300
Laurel, MD 20707
John J. Dougherty, Gen.Pres.

PH: (301)470-4200
FX: (301)470-2502
E-mail: opcmiaintl@opcnia.org
URL: http://www.opcmia.org
Founded: 1864. **Staff:** 15. **Members:** 50,000. AFL-CIO.

PACKAGED ICE ASSOCIATION
PO Box 1199
Tampa, FL 33601-1199
Jane McEwen, Exec.Dir.
E-mail: mborden@mercury.interpath.net
URL: http://www.packagedice.com
Founded: 1917. **Staff:** 5. **Members:** 160. Manufacturers and distributors of packaged ice; associate members are manufacturers of ice making equipment and supplies. Major activities are in public relations, technology, sanitation, government relations, and merchandising. Sponsors hall of fame.

PLUMBING AND DRAINAGE INSTITUTE
45 Bristol Dr., Ste. 101
South Easton, MA 02375-1916
William C. Whitehead, Exec.Sec.
PH: (508)230-3516
TF: (800)589-8956
FX: (508)230-3529
E-mail: info@pdionline.org
URL: http://www.pdionline.org
Founded: 1928. **Staff:** 1. **Members:** 14. Manufacturers of engineered plumbing and drainage products. Distributes publications to architects, engineers, contractors, and other plumbing industry representatives. Works on codes and standards for plumbing drainage products.

PLUMBING MANUFACTURERS INSTITUTE
1340 Remington Rd.
Ste. A
Schaumburg, IL 60173
Barbara C. Higgens, Exec.Dir.
PH: (847)884-9764
FX: (847)884-9775
URL: http://www.pmihome.org
Founded: 1956. **Staff:** 4. **Members:** 50. Manufacturers of plumbing products.

POLYISOCYANURATE INSULATION MANUFACTURERS ASSOCIATION
1001 Pennsylvania Ave. NW
Washington, DC 20004
Jared O. Blum, Pres.
PH: (202)624-2709
FX: (202)628-3856
E-mail: pima@pima.org
URL: http://www.pima.org
Founded: 1986. **Staff:** 3. **Members:** 22. **Budget:** $1,000,000. Companies and individuals involved in the manufacture of polyisocyanurate roofing and wall insulations; associate members are suppliers to the industry. Promotes the industry and represents its legislative and regulatory interests at the state and federal levels; develops product application standards. Addresses issues such as toxicity, building codes, fire performance, energy conservation, environmental effects of insulation, and the import industry. Conducts research; sponsors educational programs; compiles statistics.

PORCELAIN ENAMEL INSTITUTE
4004 Hillsboro Pike, Ste. 224B
Nashville, TN 37215
Tom Sanford, Exec.VP
PH: (615)385-0758
FX: (615)385-5463
E-mail: penamel@aol.com
URL: http://www.porcelainenamel.com
Founded: 1931. **Staff:** 4. **Members:** 100. Trade association of the porcelain enamel industry. Manufacturers of major appliances, sanitaryware, architectural porcelain enamel, signs, and other porcelain enamel products; suppliers to the industry such as producers of steel, aluminum, and porcelain enamel frit; chemical companies. Conducts market development and promotion programs, develops test methods for evaluation of porcelain enamel properties, and maintains weather resistance testing sites jointly with the National Bureau of Standards. Serves as information clearinghouse.

POST-TENSIONING INSTITUTE
1717 W. Northern Ave., Ste. 114
Phoenix, AZ 85021
Gerard McGuire, Exec.Dir.
PH: (602)870-7540
FX: (602)870-7541
Founded: 1976. **Staff:** 3. **Members:** 800. **Budget:** $450,000. Post-tensioning material fabricators, manufacturers of prestressing steel and P/T accessories and supplies, concrete construction organizations, professional engineers, architects, and contractors. Seeks to advance the use of post-tensioning materials through research, technical development, and marketing efforts. Compiles information of benefit to users of post-tensioning materials. Cooperates in the adoption and maintenance of standard specifications for the design, fabrication, and installation of post-tensioning materials. Conducts research programs.

REFRIGERATION SERVICE ENGINEERS SOCIETY
1666 Rand Rd.
Des Plaines, IL 60016-3552
Joe Ziemba, Exec.VP
PH: (847)297-6464
FX: (847)297-5038
E-mail: rses@starnetinc.com
URL: http://www.rses.org
Founded: 1933. **Staff:** 38. **Members:** 30,000. **Budget:** $5,000,000. Persons engaged in refrigeration, air-conditioning and heating installation, service, sales, and maintenance. Conducts training courses and certification testing. Maintains a hall of fame and a speakers' bureau.

REINFORCED CONCRETE RESEARCH COUNCIL
Texas A&M University
Dept. of Civil Engineering
College Station, TX 77843-3136
Joseph M. Bracci, Sec.
PH: (409)845-3750
FX: (409)845-6554
E-mail: j-bracci@tamu.edu
Founded: 1948. **Members:** 40. Persons engaged or interested in reinforced concrete research. Sponsors research on structural concrete.

RESILIENT FLOOR COVERING INSTITUTE
966 Hungerford Dr., Ste. 12-B
Rockville, MD 20850
Douglas W. Wiegand, Mng.Dir.
PH: (301)340-8580
FX: (301)340-7283
Founded: 1929. **Staff:** 2. **Members:** 25. **Budget:** $700,000. Manufacturers of vinyl composition tile, solid vinyl tile, or sheet vinyl and rubber tile.

RUBBER PAVEMENTS ASSOCIATION
312 Massachusetts Ave. NE
Washington, DC 20002-5702
Gordon McDougall, Exec.Dir.
Founded: 1985. **Staff:** 3. **Members:** 24. **Budget:** $300,000. Suppliers and processors of asphalt rubber products. To promote the efficient use of ground scrap tire rubber in asphalt products. Conducts national and international seminars; presents technical papers and films. Maintains bibliography; operates speakers' bureau. Bestows awards for individual contributions to the industry and for outstanding performance.

SAFETY GLAZING CERTIFICATION COUNCIL
PO Box 9
Henderson Harbor, NY 13651
John G. Kent, Admin.
PH: (315)938-7444
FX: (315)938-7453
E-mail: jgkent@gisco.net
URL: http://www.sgcc.org
Founded: 1971. **Staff:** 3. **Members:** 122. Manufacturers of safety glazing products, building code administrators, and others responsible for the safety of the public. Maintains certification and testing program for safety glazing material used in buildings. Certification activities include: accrediting laboratories to conduct safety glazing testing; initial and periodic testing by an accredited laboratory, and complaint testing in the event of a substantiated complaint; formal appeals procedure.

SCAFFOLD INDUSTRY ASSOCIATION
20335 Ventura Blvd., No. 310
Woodland Hills, CA 91364
Gary Larson, Exec.VP
PH: (818)610-0320
FX: (818)610-0323
Founded: 1972. **Staff:** 8. **Members:** 1,000. **Budget:** $1,500,000. Firms or individuals that manufacture, sell, or contract for the erection and/or rental of scaffolding, aerial platforms, and shoring or for any device used in the support of workers, material, or equipment. Activities include meetings, educational seminars, research, accident prevention insurance programs for members. Provides safety training aids such as videos, slides, warning signs and a scaffolder training program.

SCAFFOLDING, SHORING AND FORMING INSTITUTE
1300 Sumner Ave.
Cleveland, OH 44115-2851
John H. Addington, Mng.Dir.
PH: (216)241-7333
FX: (216)241-0105
E-mail: sssi@taol.com
URL: http://www.taol.com/ssfi
Founded: 1960. **Staff:** 3. **Members:** 16. Manufacturers of scaffolding, shoring, and forming. Establishes recommended criteria and inspection guidelines for the proper and safe use of scaffolding, shoring, and forming in concrete construction.

SHEET METAL AND AIR CONDITIONING CONTRACTORS' NATIONAL ASSOCIATION
4201 Lafayette Center Dr.
Chantilly, VA 20151-1209
John W. Sroka, Exec.VP
PH: (703)803-2980
FX: (703)803-3732
E-mail: info@smacna.org
URL: http://www.smacna.org
Founded: 1943. **Staff:** 35. **Members:** 1,956. **Budget:** $7,900,000. Ventilating, air handling, warm air heating, architectural and industrial sheet metal, kitchen equipment, testing and balancing, siding, and decking and specialty fabrication contractors. Prepares standards and codes; sponsors research and educational programs on sheet metal duct construction and fire damper (single and multi-blade) construction. Engages in legislative and labor activities; conducts business management and contractor education programs.

SOUTHERN BUILDING CODE CONGRESS, INTERNATIONAL
900 Montclair Rd.
Birmingham, AL 35213
William J. Tangye, CEO
PH: (205)591-1853
FX: (205)592-7001
URL: http://www.sbcci.org
Founded: 1940. **Staff:** 75. **Members:** 13,500. **Budget:** $10,000,000. Active members are state, county, municipal, or other government subdivisions (2400); associate members are trade associations, architects, engineers, contractors, and related groups or persons (5100). Seeks to develop, maintain, and promote the adoption of the Standard Building, Gas, Plumbing, Mechanical, Fire Prevention, and Housing Codes. Encourages uniformity in building regulations through the Standard Codes and their application and enforcement. Provides technical and educational services to members and others; participates in the development of nationally recognized consensus standards. Provides research on new materials and methods of construction; conducts seminars on code enforcement, inspection, and special topics.

SPRI
200 Reservoir St., No. 309A
Needham, MA 02494
Linda King, Mng.Dir.
PH: (781)444-0242
FX: (781)444-6111
E-mail: lkspri@aol.com
URL: http://www.spri.org
Founded: 1982. **Staff:** 2. **Members:** 45. **Budget:** $350,000. Manufacturers and marketers of all components used in flexible membrane roofing systems, representing thermoplastic thermoset, and modified bitumen products. Works to guide materials growth in the roofing industry; increase credibility of flexible membrane roofing systems and technology in the marketplace; aid in the development of standards by organizations and code-establishing agencies; and establish relations with consulting engineers, the National Bureau of Standards, and ASTM. Monitors related legislative activities. Conducts educational and research programs; compiles statistics; maintains speakers' bureau.

STEAMFITTING INDUSTRY PROMOTION FUND
44 W. 28th St.
New York, NY 10001
Raymond W. Hopkins, Administrator
PH: (212)481-1493
FX: (212)447-6439
E-mail: nymca@aol.com

STEEL DECK INSTITUTE
PO Box 25
Fox River Grove, IL 60021-0025
Steven A. Roehrig, Mng.Dir.
PH: (847)462-1930
FX: (847)462-1940
E-mail: steve@sdi.org
URL: http://www.sdi.org
Founded: 1936. **Staff:** 2. **Members:** 23. **Budget:** $200,000. Manufacturers of steel decks (12); associate members (11) are manufacturers of allied products. Formulates and publishes design specifications; conducts and sponsors research and test programs; compiles statistics.

STEEL DOOR INSTITUTE
30200 Detroit Rd.
Cleveland, OH 44145
J. J. Wherry, Mng.Dir.
PH: (440)899-0010
FX: (440)892-1404
URL: http://www.steeldoor.org
Founded: 1954. **Staff:** 5. **Members:** 11. Manufacturers of standard, all-metal doors and frames used in commercial applications.

STEEL JOIST INSTITUTE
3127 10th Ave. Ext. N
Myrtle Beach, SC 29577-6760
R. Donald Murphy, Mgr.Dir.
Founded: 1928. **Staff:** 2. **Members:** 15. Manufacturers engaged in the production of open web, longspan, and deep longspan steel joists; K-, LH-, and DLH-series; and joist girders. Formulates standards for design, manufacture, and use; assists in the development of building code regulations. Conducts seminars.

STEEL WINDOW INSTITUTE
1300 Sumner Ave.
Cleveland, OH 44115-2851
John H. Addington, Exec.Sec.
PH: (216)241-7333
FX: (216)241-0105
E-mail: swi@taol.com
URL: http://www.taol.com/swi
Founded: 1920. **Staff:** 3. **Members:** 8. Manufacturers of solid section steel windows.

STUCCO MANUFACTURERS ASSOCIATION
2402 Vista Nobleza
Newport Beach, CA 92660-3545
Robert F. Welch, Exec.Sec.
PH: (408)649-3466
FX: (408)647-1552
Founded: 1957. **Staff:** 1. **Members:** 30. **Budget:** $28,000. Manufacturers of stucco products.

SUBMERSIBLE WASTEWATER PUMP ASSOCIATION
1806 Johns Dr.
Glenview, IL 60025
Charles Stolberg, Exec.Dir.
PH: (847)729-7972
FX: (708)729-3670
Founded: 1976. **Staff:** 5. **Members:** 30. Manufacturers of submersible wastewater pumps and systems for municipal and industrial applications and manufacturers of component parts and accessory items for those pumps and systems. Promotes the submersible wastewater pump as a superior product and as a method for handling waste in any application.

**SUMP AND SEWAGE PUMP MANUFACTURERS
   ASSOCIATION**
PO Box 647
Northbrook, IL 60065-0647
Pamela W. Franzen, Mng.Dir.
PH: (847)559-9233
FX: (847)559-9235
E-mail: 103061.1063@compuserve.com
Founded: 1956. **Staff:** 3. **Members:** 32. Manufacturers of residential sump pumps (cellar drainers) and sewage pumps. Seeks to: develop and promulgate quality standards; implement a certification and labeling program for all products conforming to these standards; investigate market size and activity; promote improved provisions in building codes on the use of sump and sewage pumps.

**SUPPLIERS OF ADVANCED COMPOSITE MATERIALS
   ASSOCIATION**
1600 Wilson Blvd., Ste. 901
Arlington, VA 22209
William H. Werst, Jr., Exec.Dir.
PH: (703)841-1556
FX: (703)841-1559
E-mail: sacma@ibm.net
Founded: 1984. **Staff:** 5. **Members:** 10. **Budget:** $400,000. Associate members are engaged in the construction of fiber-reinforced advanced composite finished products; manufacturers of machinery and equipment; suppliers of ancillary materials used to test advanced composite products. Affiliate members are related industries and organizations engaged in research involving development of advanced composite materials. Regular members produce carbon/graphite materials, resins, and pre-impregnated materials for use in producing advanced composite structural shapes. Represents the industry before public, governmental, and quasi-governmental bodies; collects and publishes industry, statistics; encourages the use of advanced composite materials in specific markets through promotional and market development programs; addresses environmental, health, and safety problems; develops recommended test methods. Holds semi-annual industry related conferences.

TILE COUNCIL OF AMERICA
100 Clemson Research Blvd.
Anderson, SC 29625
Robert E. Daniels, Exec.Dir.
PH: (864)646-8453
FX: (864)646-2821
E-mail: literature@carol.net
URL: http://www.tileusa.com
Founded: 1945. **Staff:** 6. **Members:** 84. **Budget:** $1,000,000. Manufacturers of domestic ceramic tile for floors, walls, and related products. Promotes increase in the marketability of ceramic tile. Conducts testing program on tile and tile installation materials. Supervises international licensing program with 16 licensees. Compiles statistics.

TRUSS PLATE INSTITUTE
583 D'Onofrio Dr., Ste. 200
Madison, WI 53719
Charles B. Goehring, Mng.Dir.
PH: (608)833-5900
FX: (608)833-4360
Founded: 1961. **Staff:** 3. **Members:** 400. Firms manufacturing metal connector plates for wood trusses; firms producing trusses; suppliers of materials for trusses. Develops consensus design criteria in accordance with ANSI's accredited procedures for the Development and Coordination of American National Standards. Disseminates information to the public, including design specifications, truss bracing recommendations, and a quality control manual; conducts statistical survey and research programs.

**TUBULAR EXCHANGER MANUFACTURERS
   ASSOCIATION**
25 N. Broadway
Tarrytown, NY 10591
Richard C. Byrne, Sec.
PH: (914)332-0040
FX: (914)332-1541
E-mail: tema@tema.org
URL: http://www.tema.org
Founded: 1939. **Staff:** 2. **Members:** 20. Manufacturers of heat exchangers and allied equipment.

**UNITED ASSOCIATION OF JOURNEYMEN AND
   APPRENTICES OF THE PLUMBING AND PIPE FITTING
   INDUSTRY OF THE U.S. AND CANADA**
PO Box 37800
Washington, DC 20013
Martin Maddaloni, Gen.Pres.
PH: (202)628-5823
FX: (202)628-5024
Founded: 1889. **Members:** 325,000. AFL-CIO.

**UNITED BROTHERHOOD OF CARPENTERS AND
   JOINERS OF AMERICA**
101 Constitution Ave. NW
Washington, DC 20001
Douglas J. McCarron, Gen.Pres.
PH: (202)546-6206
FX: (202)546-5724
Founded: 1881. **Members:** 500,000. AFL-CIO.

**UNITED UNION OF ROOFERS, WATERPROOFERS AND
   ALLIED WORKERS**
1660 L St. NW, Ste. 800
Washington, DC 20036
Earl Kruse, Pres.
PH: (202)463-7663
FX: (202)463-6906
Members: 25,000. AFL-CIO.

USED OIL MANAGEMENT ASSOCIATION
2550 M St. NW
Washington, DC 20037-1350
Mary Beth Bosco, Contact

PH: (202)457-6420
FX: (202)457-6315
URL: http://www.uoma.com
Founded: 1981. **Members:** 5. Manufacturers and distributors of appliances used to convert waste oil into heat. Serves as a forum for manufacturers to exchange information necessary to improve the quality and safety of their products. Promotes interests of the industry by providing information to public officials which will enable them to properly consider the passage of new legislation and to reexamine existing laws which the association feels unnecessarily restrict the use of waste oil burning appliances.

VINYL SIDING INSTITUTE
1801 K St. NW, Ste. 600K
Washington, DC 20006-1301
Jery Y. Huntley, Exec.Dir.
URL: http://www.vinylsiding.org
Founded: 1976. **Staff:** 4. **Members:** 66. A division of the Society of the Plastics Industry. Vinyl siding manufacturers and suppliers. Compiles statistics.

VINYL WINDOW AND DOOR INSTITUTE
1801 K St. NW, Ste. 600K
Washington, DC 20006-1301
Juliette Lang Cahn, Exec.Dir.
Founded: 1981. **Staff:** 5. **Members:** 58. A division of The Society of the Plastics Industry. Companies that extrude plastic lineals; machinery, resin, materials, and hardware suppliers; fabricators of vinyl windows. Promotes the vinyl window and door industry through the development of technical and marketing programs. Develops standards for vinyl windows and doors promulgated by the ASTM. Has developed a certification program to serve as a third party quality control system for window manufacturers. Has also established public relations program geared to product enhancement and the promotion of an increased market for vinyl windows and doors. Compiles statistics for use in the decision-making process of the window and door industry. Conducts studies on weathering, impact, and color.

WHOLESALE DISTRIBUTORS ASSOCIATION
10935 Estate Ln.
Ste. 400
Dallas, TX 75238
Sandi Erstamer, Exec.Dir.
PH: (214)349-7100
FX: (214)349-7946
Founded: 1929. **Staff:** 3. **Members:** 140. Wholesalers representing the plumbing, heating, piping, and cooling industries. Provides a forum for the exchange of information and ideas among members. Represents members in Washington, DC on legislative and regulatory issues. Maintains Wholesale Distributors Association Educational Foundation, which provides scholarships to students pursuing careers in the industry. Conducts seminars and research programs; compiles statistics.

WINDOW AND DOOR MANUFACTURERS ASSOCIATION
1400 E. Touhy Ave., No. 470
Des Plaines, IL 60018
Alan J. Campbell, Pres.
PH: (847)299-5200
TF: (800)223-2301
FX: (847)299-1286
URL: http://www.nwwda.org
Founded: 1927. **Staff:** 6. **Members:** 140. Manufacturers of woodwork products such as doors, windows, frames, and related products. Fosters, promotes, and protects members' interests; encourages product use. Establishes quality and performance standards; conducts research in all areas of door and window manufacture. Issues seals of approval for wood preservative treatment, hardwood doors, and window unit manufacture.

WIRE REINFORCEMENT INSTITUTE
PO Box 450
301 E. Sandusky St.
Findlay, OH 45839-0450
Roy H. Reiterman, Tech. Dir.
PH: (419)425-9473
FX: (419)425-5741
E-mail: wwri@bright.net
URL: http://www.bright.net/~rreiter
Founded: 1930. **Staff:** 2. **Members:** 45. **Budget:** $500,000. Manufacturers of steel welded wire reinforcement (WWR) and wire products for the reinforcement of concrete and other construction materials. Works to disseminate technical information and extend the use of welded wire reinforcement through scientific and market research, consumer education, engineering, product development, and general construction technology. Provides technical service to users and specifiers of welded wire reinforcement such as architects, consulting engineers, contractors, and governmental department engineers. Conducts research programs on properties and performance of welded wire fabric.

WOOD MOULDING AND MILLWORK PRODUCERS ASSOCIATION
507 1st St.
Woodland, CA 95695-4025
Bob Weiglein, Exec.VP
PH: (530)661-9591
TF: (800)550-7889
FX: (530)661-9586
E-mail: bob@wmmpa.com
URL: http://www.wmmpa.com
Founded: 1963. **Staff:** 3. **Members:** 120. **Budget:** $590,000. Manufacturers of wood mouldings and millwork. Provides promotion, standardization, and marketing information services.

WOOD TRUSS COUNCIL OF AMERICA
One WTCA Center Dr., Ste. 14
6425 Normandy Ln.
Madison, WI 53719-1133
Kirk Grundahl, P.E., Exec.Dir.
PH: (608)274-4849
FX: (608)274-3329
E-mail: wtca@woodtruss.com
URL: http://www.woodtruss.com
Founded: 1983. **Staff:** 6. **Members:** 750. Manufacturers and suppliers of structural wood components. Promotes the interests of members, manufacturers, and suppliers of related products. Encourages the use of structural wood components; supports research and development; provides educational services.

CONSULTANTS

Consultants and consulting organizations active in the Construction sector are featured in this chapter. Entries are adapted from Gale's *Consultants and Consulting Organizations Directory* (*CCOD*). Each entry represents an expertise which may be of interest to business organizations, government agencies, non-profit institutions, and individuals requiring technical and other support. The listees shown are located in the United States and Canada.

In Canada, the use of the term "consultant" is restricted. The use of the word, in this chapter, does not necessarily imply that the firm has been granted the "consultant" designation in Canada.

Entries are arranged in alphabetical order. Categories include contact information (address, phone, fax, web site, E-mail); names and titles of executive officers; and a descriptive block that begins with founding year and staff.

3D/INTERNATIONAL
1900 W. Loop S., Ste. 600
Houston, TX 77027
J.V. Neuhaus, III, Chairman/CEO
PH: (713)871-7000
FX: (713)871-7171
URL: http://www.3di.com/
Founded: 1955. **Staff:** 325. Services include architecture, civil engineering, construction management, cost estimating, economics and finance, electrical engineering, hazardous materials management, hydraulics and hydrology, indoor pollution studies, industrial hygiene, interior architecture, land planning, landscape architecture, mechanical engineering, planning and urban design, project management, space planning, transportation engineering, and wastewater engineering. Experienced in office buildings, hotels and condominiums, shopping and convention centers, banking and financial institutions, resorts, airports, healthcare, educational, exhibition, manufacturing, correctional and defense facilities, transitways and new towns.

ABAX INC.
51-09 2nd St.
Long Island City, NY 11101
PH: (718)784-2229
TF: (800)427-5567
FX: (718)784-2296
Founded: 1980. **Staff:** 35. Consults in the field of specialty construction and environmental services, including medical waste incineration, emission monitoring, asbestos, and lead paint abatement.

ABC—ADVANCED BUSINESS CONCEPTS
130 Fairlane Dr.
Industry, PA 15052
PH: (412)643-5253
FX: (412)643-6497
Firm offers special knowledge in construction materials and equipment.

ABIDE INTERNATIONAL INC.
401 Park Place, Ste. 203
Kirkland, WA 98033
Charles R. Hinson, President
PH: (425)827-7944
FX: (425)827-8564
Founded: 1985. **Staff:** 35. Consulting firm provides construction management services.

ABRAMS & TANAKA ASSOCIATES, INC.
3214 Nebraska Ave.
Santa Monica, CA 90404
William W. Parmenter, President
PH: (310)453-8861
FX: (310)828-5357
E-mail: abrtan@ata.cnchost.com
Founded: 1977. **Staff:** 8. Provides food facilities consultation and planning. Services include preliminary design, design development, equipment planning, preparation of construction documents, and construction administration. Industries served: food service for hotels, restaurants, in-plant employee feeding, healthcare, clubs, airports, theme parks, and government agencies.

ACAESA CO.
1248 Bedford Hwy.
Bedford, NS, Canada B4A 1C6
Johan D. Koppernaes, Chairman/CEO
PH: (902)835-8348
FX: (902)835-0134
Founded: 1992. **Staff:** 60. Offers conceptual designs, feasibility studies, business plans, preparation of construction plans, specifications and contract documents, construction management, construction inspection, and start-up and commissioning of: fish processing plants and fishing vessels, dairies and food processing plants, cold storages and ice making plants, environmental plants—air, water and sewage, mineral resource exploration and evaluation, solid and liquid waste pollution prevention plants, transportation systems shipping, railways, trucking and air, and harbors, wharves, schools, hospitals, and town halls. Industries served: fishing vessel owners, fish plant owners, beverage companies, cheese companies, dairies, railroad companies, ship owners, aquaculture companies, mining and construction, federal, provincial and municipal governments, and governmental infrastructure corporations.

ACRES INTERNATIONAL LTD.
480 University Ave.
Toronto, ON, Canada M5G 1V2
O.T. Sigvaldason, President
PH: (416)595-2000
FX: (416)595-2004
E-mail: toronto@acres.com
URL: http://www.acres.com
Founded: 1924. **Staff:** 600. Large Canadian consulting engineering firm offering project and construction management services to a wide variety of industries in the power, transportation and mining/heavy industrial sectors. Facilities include fully equipped laboratories for physical modeling to scale, soil and rock mechanical investigations, hydraulic and aerodynamic model testing, chemical analysis and biological testing, as well as modern computer facilities. Serves private industries as well as government agencies.

W. R. ADAMS CO., INC.
500 E. 2nd St.
PO Box 1953
Rome, GA 30162-1953
Walter R. Adams, Chairman & CEO
PH: (706)295-2703
FX: (706)234-4065
E-mail: info@wradams.com
URL: http://www.wradams.com
Founded: 1986. Offers operations-based planning services with a team expertise unmatched in the industry. Offers architectural, design, planning, programming, and operational expertise in providing services that include: service-specific planning; facility assessment; CON application assistance; operational & space programming; master facility planning basic cost estimating; site planning/ land use studies.

ADI GROUP INC.
1133 Regent St., Ste. 300
Fredericton, NB, Canada E3B 3Z2
Hollis B. Cole, President/CEO
PH: (506)452-9000
FX: (506)459-3954
E-mail: adigroup@adi.ca
URL: http://www.adi.ca
Founded: 1945. **Staff:** 230. Provides consulting services in most engineering disciplines, architecture, environmental science, geomatics, and business planning, as well as design-build services for a wide variety of environmental, transportation, and building projects. Geographic Areas Served: North America, the Caribbean, Mexico, South America, Europe, India and Southeast Asia. ADI also has licensing agreements with companies in India, Mexico Turkey, United Kingdom and Israel.

ADVANCE STRUCTURES
1990 N. California Blvd., Ste. 26
PO Box 5636
Walnut Creek, CA 94596
Gerald Wiggen, Owner
PH: (510)938-6380
FX: (510)938-6380
Founded: 1964. **Staff:** 3. Consulting firm is active in the manufacturing and distribution of housing, primarily steel-framed homes.

AEP ASSOCIATES, INC.
485 Notch Rd.
Little Falls, NJ 07424-1955
Stanley John Lacz, President

PH: (201)256-7575
FX: (201)890-7848
Founded: 1965. **Staff:** 4. Provides comprehensive professional services in the following areas: architectural-building, programming, cost analysis, construction documents, construction inspection, and interior design; landscape architecture; engineering-site plans, energy studies, storm drainage, foundations, structures, plumbing, water supply, heating, air conditioning, electrical lighting, and land subdivisions; planning-master plan studies, zoning ordinance, variances, application to government agencies; governmental approvals-stream encroachment, wet lands, planning boards, and boards of adjustment; expert witness-site visit, reports, and testimony. Clients have included leading corporations; municipal, county, state, and federal governmental agencies; various developers; organizations and individuals for mercantile, educational, and medical projects; and homeowners.

AGR INTERNATIONAL INC.
500 Sun Valley Dr.
Roswell, GA 30076
James Dodd, President
PH: (770)594-0963
FX: (770)594-7304
Founded: 1990. **Staff:** 8. Engineering firm specializes in providing construction management services.

AGRA MONENCO INC.
2010 Winston Park Dr., Ste. 100
Oakville, ON, Canada L6H 6A3
Bob Van Adel, President
PH: (905)829-5400
FX: (905)829-5625
URL: http://www.agra.com
Founded: 1907. **Staff:** 1320. International corporation specialized in engineering, construction, project development, management information systems and the environment for power, process and infrastructure industries. Services include: economic, financial and technical feasibility studies; exploration and site selection; project planning and financing; conceptual and detailed design; process design; estimating; project management; procurement and logistics support; specifications and equipment selection; construction management; commissioning and operations assistance; maintenance and rehabilitation; management consulting; resource planning and development; socioeconomic impact assessments; system planning, development and implementation; computer software development and hardware selection; training and transfer of technology; and research. Industries served: utilities, private power, financing institutions, governments, and private companies.

AIG CONSULTANTS, INC.
72 Wall St., 9th Fl.
New York, NY 10270
PH: (212)770-3630
FX: (212)785-8287
Founded: 1979. **Staff:** 200. Consulting company with extensive experience in containing and solving a wide range of industrial and commercial problems related to risk management, loss control, and quality improvement. Provides clients with analyses of current or potential risks, recommendations for corrective actions and follow-up assessment to contain risk and ensure profitability. Areas of expertise include environmental services (property transfer assessments, hospital medical waste plans, compliance audits, environmental risk assessments, hazardous materials/waste management); healthcare services (quality improvement, accreditation, peer review, risk management consulting); industrial hygiene (asbestos abatement); and property conservation (casualty, fleet, ergonomics, products liability, construction). Industries served: all manufacturing and service industries, as well as government agencies.

AINLEY GRAHAM AND ASSOCIATES LTD.
2724 Fenton Rd.
Gloucester, ON, Canada K1T 3T7
T.W. Hardy, President

PH: (613)822-1052
FX: (613)822-1573
E-mail: mailbox@ainleygraham.com
Founded: 1962. **Staff:** 25. Offers consulting, planning and engineering services from concept through construction and final commissioning, for municipal, provincial/state, and federal governments, and the private sector in environmental, water supply, sewage collection municipal, transportation, and structural sectors.

AIR LAND SURVEYS, INC.
7990 M-15
Clarkston, MI 48348
Gary R. Stonerock, President
PH: (248)625-4890
FX: (248)625-4893
E-mail: airlands@aol.com
Founded: 1969. **Staff:** 23. Services include aerial photography, digital mapping, land surveying, digital ortho photo, construction layout, architectural surveys, and G.P.S. (Global Positions by Satellites) surveys. Industries served: local, state and federal governments, engineers, surveyors, land planners, developers and airport planners. Geographic areas served: Great Lakes region.

ALAIMO GROUP CONSULTANTS
200 High St.
Mount Holly, NJ 08060
Richard A. Alaimo, President
PH: (609)267-8310
FX: (609)267-7452
Founded: 1967. **Staff:** 105. Offers civil, sanitary, mechanical, electrical, and structural engineering consulting services. Also active in the following: highway design; environmental planning; landfill design; resource recovery; waste systems; site, urban, and regional planning; surveying; construction management; and construction field services. Serves private industries as well as government agencies.

ALBECON
1531 S. Edgewood, Ste. P
Baltimore, MD 21227
Lloyd Bernstein, President/CEO
PH: (410)368-9098
FX: (410)368-9097
E-mail: lloyd@albecon.com
URL: http://www.albecon.com
Founded: 1994. A full-service general contractor offering A/E/C project management services to business-commercial building owners, design groups, and facilities managers. Experience in cost estimating and consulting, project management, and property management and support services. Specializes in health care facilities and med-tech fit-outs. As cost consultants, prepares estimates and budget projections. As construction managers, reviews site development plans and A/E specifications to identify specific design, material and phasing options. As general contractors, builds and renovate health care, commercial, industrial, retail, office and multi-family buildings. As property managers, oversees operations of hospital-owned office and research facilities.

ALLEN ENGINEERING CORP.
819 S. Fifth St.
PO Box 819
Paragould, AR 72450
PH: (501)236-7751
TF: (800)643-0095
FX: (501)236-3934
URL: http://www.alleneng.com
Firm offers expertise in construction materials, engineering, and training.

ALLGEIER, MARTIN & ASSOCIATES, INC.
Box 2627
Joplin, MO 64803
Vernon R. Lawson, Chairman

PH: (417)624-5703
FX: (417)624-7558
Founded: 1954. **Staff:** 103. Offers complete engineering consulting services, from planning through construction inspection and start-up. Professional staff has expertise in civil, electrical, structural, mechanical, sanitary, and geological engineering; and surveying and mapping. Clients include utilities; municipal, county, state, and federal governments; industrial firms; institutions; developers; builders; and other professionals.

ALPHA CORP.
45665 Willow Pond Plaza
Sterling, VA 20164
Edwin D. Heine, Chairman
PH: (703)709-2206
FX: (703)709-0643
E-mail: mail@alphacorporation.com
Founded: 1979. **Staff:** 85. Provides a full range of engineering design, estimating, management, scheduling, and claims analysis services. Specialties include: civil and structural design; rehabilitation and underpinning of bridges and buildings; support of excavation (slurry walls, cofferdams, tiebacks); marine and underground construction; construction management; and review, analysis, and evaluation of construction disputes, including expert testimony and litigation/negotiation support. Particular industries served include: construction, data processing, energy, insurance, iron and steel, manufacturing, marine, mining, transportation, and government agencies. agencies. Geographic areas served: U.S.

AMERICAN MINE SERVICES, INC.
12570 E. 39th Ave.
Denver, CO 80239
Jim Lamb, Vice President
PH: (303)371-4000
FX: (303)371-4004
E-mail: amsdenver@aol.com
Founded: 1976. **Staff:** 9. Offers underground construction, exploration drilling, engineering and consulting services to the mining industry, as well as government agencies.

AMERICAN VECTOR CORP.
834 S. Vine St.
Hinsdale, IL 60521
Robert L. Hinkle, President
PH: (630)655-3959
FX: (630)655-3959
Founded: 1985. **Staff:** 4. Provides consultation in construction planning, estimating, scheduling, and management. Also offers expertise in changes and extras to construction contracts.

AMMANN & WHITNEY
96 Morton St.
New York, NY 10014
Nick Ivonoff, President, CEO
PH: (212)524-7200
FX: (212)524-7215
E-mail: AWMKTG-2@aol.com
Founded: 1946. **Staff:** 165. Engineering firm involved in the transportation and facilities/buildings fields. Provides feasibility studies, inspection and new/rehabilitation design of structures, as well as construction management services.

AMON CONSULTING
PO Box 1131
Mount Juliet, TN 37121
Paul G. Amon, President
PH: (615)758-4349
FX: (615)754-0480
E-mail: michele@amonconsulting.com
URL: http://www.amonconsulting.com
A multi-service consulting project management and engineering services firm. Handles everything from preconstruction cost analysis to construction management. Services include cost estimating, project planning, scheduling, cost engineering, value engineering, and plant and equipment assessments.

AMTECH ROOFING CONSULTANTS
14107 Haymeadow Dr.
Dallas, TX 75240
Robert F. Alford, President
PH: (972)980-3733
TF: (800)828-2465
FX: (972)980-3736
Founded: 1981. **Staff:** 21. Provides assistance on roof problems and/or projects. Services concentrate on providing design review, existing roof system evaluation, developing plans and specifications, quality control monitor, testing of roof systems and presenting seminars on roof maintenance. Industries served: commercial and industrial. Geographic areas served: no limitations.

ANDERSON ENGINEERING
1901 E. Lincoln Ave.
Sunnyside, WA 98944-0089
Vernon L. Anderson, P.E., Principal
PH: (509)837-4454
FX: (509)839-7143
E-mail: andeng@televar.com
Founded: 1971. **Staff:** 4. Offers engineering services in the design, construction, operation, and maintenance of food processing and storage facilities, commercial and industrial structures, materials handling systems, water and waste handling and treatment systems, and real estate subdivisions. Also offers construction materials testing and inspection.

AQUATECH CONSULTANCY, INC.
135 Paul Dr. #200
San Rafael, CA 94903
Manfred "Fred" Honeck, PE, Principal
PH: (415)472-3538
FX: (415)507-0555
E-mail: info@noleak.com
URL: http://www.noleak.com
Founded: 1997. Waterproofing; window/wall performance testing (ASTM-AAMA); EIFS systems; sealants; epoxy; polyester, polyurethane & elastometric coatings; industrial floorings; construction defect investigation. Multi-discipline experts on staff; full E&O liability insurance; more than 10 years with trial and litigation support.

AQUATIC CONSULTING SERVICES
3833 Lamont St., 4C
San Diego, CA 92109
Alison Osinski, Ph.D., Principal
PH: (619)270-6024
FX: (619)270-3459
E-mail: alisonh2o@aol.com
URL: http://www.poolspaworld.com/experts/aquaticconsultingservices
Provides consultation, investigation, research, and expert testimony on swimming pool construction defects cases, and all water-related personal injury cases, including drowning and near drowning, spinal injury, slip-and fall, boating and PWC accidents, waterslide and diving injuries, occurring at commercial and residential swimming pools, waterparks or open water facilities. Specializes in aquatic risk management, swimming pool design, maintenance, management and operation, water quality, boating safety, supervision issues, barrier effectiveness, staff qualification and training, code compliance, signage and warnings.

AQUATIC DESIGN & CONSTRUCTION LTD.
3450 Meridian Rd.
Okemos, MI 48864
PH: (517)347-5537
FX: (517)347-4999
E-mail: shrimpone@aol.com
Offers services in aquatic design, project planning, engineering, GPS surveying, GIS mapping, feasibility studies, construction management, and CAD design. Specializes in shrimp farming. Fluent in Spanish.

ARCADIS GERAGHTY & MILLER
1099 18th St., Ste. 2100
Denver, CO 80202-1921
John V. Boyette, President
PH: (303)294-1200
FX: (303)294-1221
URL: http://www.gmgw.com
Founded: 1957. **Staff:** 1300. ARCADIS Geraghty & Miller provides a full spectrum of consulting and engineering services in the fields of environment and infrastructure for the private and public sectors.

THE ARCHITECTS COLLABORATIVE INC.
124 Mount Auburn St., Ste. 200N
Cambridge, MA 02138
John F. Hayes, President
PH: (617)576-5706
FX: (617)547-1431
Founded: 1945. **Staff:** 66. Offers consulting services in architectural design, urban design, campus planning, urban and regional planning, landscape architecture, interior architecture, graphic design, equipment planning, programming, space analysis, computer-aided drafting capability (CAD), feasibility studies, cost analysis and control, building and materials research, construction documents, and construction administration. Worldwide clients are in business, industry, government, education, medicine, and the arts.

ARCHITECTURAL RESEARCH CONSULTING
415 Washington
Denver, CO 80203
David Ballast, Contact
PH: (303)733-7725
FX: (303)733-8988
Founded: 1981. **Staff:** 1. Offers applied research and information services to architects, interior designers and others in the building industry. Activities involve assisting in a wide range of information needs in such areas as building product and building system evaluation, codes and regulations, office systems, building type studies, programming needs, among others. Services are offered on a fee basis.

ARCHITECTURAL TESTING INC.
130 Derry Ct.
York, PA 17402-9405
Henry Taylor, President/Founder
PH: (717)764-7700
FX: (717)764-4129
URL: http://www.testati.com
Firm specializes in building envelope testing and related work.

ARMENCO URBAN DEVELOPMENT CO., LLC
128 Harbor Island Cir. S
Memphis, TN 38103
Edmund H. Armentrout, President
PH: (901)526-5458
FX: (901)526-5458
E-mail: edarmen@aol.com
Provides consulting services in development, retail analysis, financial feasibility studies, housing, public-private partnerships, office development and major public facilities such as convention centers, sports facilities and museums.

ARMS CONSULTING
1501 Quail St., Ste. 100
Newport Beach, CA 92660
TF: (800)266-2767
E-mail: info@armscnsltng.com
URL: http://www.armsconsltng.com
Founded: 1986. Provides services in the areas of communications consulting, project management, construction management, and furniture procurement. Offers information on spatial uses, building codes, ADA compliance, and city ordinances. Also offers budget projections.

ARNOLD & ASSOCIATES INC.
14275 Midway Rd., Ste. 170
Addison, TX 75001
Nancy Arnold, President
PH: (972)991-1144
TF: (800)535-6329
FX: (972)991-7302
E-mail: earnold267@aol.com
Founded: 1990. **Staff:** 9. Roofing consultant provides expertise in waterproofing and restoration to the construction industry worldwide.

ASAI ARCHITECTURE-PLANNING—INTERIOR DESIGN
1200 Grand Blvd.
Kansas City, MO 64106
Stephen N. Abend, Contact
PH: (816)221-5011
FX: (816)221-5014
E-mail: asai@asaiarchitecture.com
Founded: 1968. **Staff:** 30. Provides programming, planning and urban design, architecture, engineering, interior design, space planning, graphics, landscape architecture, energy engineering, construction documents, feasibility studies, zoning and codes analysis, development analysis, computer aided design, computer based specifications, cost estimating, construction management, and value engineering. Projects include the design of criminal justice, educational, library, recreational, governmental/public, and healthcare facilities; and multi-family housing. Also experienced in historic preservation and restoration. Industries served: criminal justice, public administration, corporate administration, education (elementary, secondary, higher), and recreation.

ASSOCIATED CONSTRUCTION TECHNOLOGIES, INC.
919 Conestoga Rd., Ste. 104, Bldg. 2
Rosemont, PA 19010
Patricia J. Sheridan, President
PH: (610)526-9022
FX: (610)526-9027
E-mail: info@act-inc-pa.com
URL: http://www.act-inc-pa.com
Founded: 1984. **Staff:** 8. Provides scheduling evaluation, performance oversight, dispute resolution, design errors and omissions reviews, termination assistance, cost overrun audits, damages valuation, and changed conditions investigations. Specialists include engineers, architects, and those expert in construction scheduling, cost estimating, highway, roofing, water intrusion, scheduling, OSHA and safety regulation.

ASSOCIATED ENGINEERING
12 W. 32nd St.
New York, NY 10001
H.C. Fisher, Contact
PH: (212)564-5666
FX: (212)967-5365
Founded: 1978. **Staff:** 36. Offers complete scope of engineering services and counsel on matters involving power plants, chemical, industrial and pharmaceutical process plants, and general building structures. Activities also include dock facilities, water works, materials handling, substitute energy, and general work efforts as well as construction management services.

ASSOCIATED WALL & CEILING SERVICES INC.
PO Box 1573
Roswell, GA 30077-1573
Urban G. Rump, President
PH: (770)442-1991
FX: (770)442-0635
Founded: 1990. **Staff:** 2. Consulting and business appraisal firm working exclusively with the interior and exterior finishes industry. Specializes in firms engaged in drywall, lath and plaster, acoustical ceilings and exterior finish systems. Services offered include operations consulting, troubleshooting, expert witness testimony and contract arbitration, and business appraisals in situations such as estate

valuations, buy/sell agreements, financing, eminent domain, and ESOP valuations.

AUERBACH & ASSOCIATES, INC.
27 W. 20th St., Ste. 1204
New York, NY 10011
Steve Friedlander, Contact
PH: (212)645-3956
FX: (212)645-4094
E-mail: auerbachny@aol.com
Founded: 1971. Offers architectural design services, specializing in performing arts, conference, and convention facilities. Conducts feasibility studies; plans facility design and documentation; creates lighting, sound, and stage rigging systems; and oversees construction.

AUSTIN, TSUTSUMI & ASSOCIATES, INC.
501 Sumner St., Ste. 521
Honolulu, HI 96817
Ted S. Kawahigashi, President
PH: (808)533-3646
FX: (808)526-1267
E-mail: ata@lava.net
Founded: 1934. **Staff:** 47. A firm of professional engineers and surveyors specializing in all phases of civil, hydraulic, structural, traffic, and sanitary engineering. Offers master planning, preparation of feasibility reports and contract documents, and consultation during construction. Projects have included airport pavements and facilities; drainage systems; highways and freeways; civilian and military housing; irrigation projects; sewerage systems, sewage treatment plants; city street improvements; structural design for bridges, offices, industrial buildings and school structures; industrial and residential subdivisions; tunnels, water supply and distribution systems; water treatment plants; dams, traffic studies, construction surveillance, field surveys and miscellaneous civil engineering work. Serves private industries as well as government agencies.

AUTOMATIC CONTROLS & EQUIPMENT, LTD.
403 E. Main St.
Morgantown, PA 19543-0768
Joseph G. Stein, President
PH: (610)286-7766
FX: (610)286-7304
URL: http://www.automatic.controls.com
Founded: 1983. **Staff:** 4. Specialists in the design, installation and repair of coil conversion equipment for the steel industry. Offers expertise in integrating the design, construction, installation and repair of electrical, mechanical, pneumatic, and hydraulic equipment. Provides complete set up of plant operations. Particular specialty area is stainless steel and aluminum coil polishing and buffing. Conducts used machinery inspections and negotiations for new and used equipment.

AVACON CORP.
1300 S. Valley Vista Dr.
Diamond Bar, CA 91765
Joseph J. Garcia, President
PH: (909)861-3844
FX: (909)860-3170
E-mail: avacorp@aol.com
Founded: 1977. **Staff:** 22. Offers civil, structural, environmental, transportation engineering, surveying and construction management, building evaluation and information systems solutions. Provides quality control for public, private and military works. Services include conceptual studies, EIS/EIR site assessments and development, designs/plans, specifications, construction estimates and bid documents, contract administration, and field engineering. Industries served: military, public works, private developers, and private business. Geographic areas served: western U.S.

AWA INC.
93 Penwood Dr.
Murray Hill, NJ 07974
A. William Allen, President

PH: (908)464-8537
FX: (908)464-8537
Founded: 1990. **Staff:** 2. Offers consultation on all phases of project development and management from conception through startup, both domestic and worldwide. Areas of service include market research, process and economic feasibility, cost estimates, environmental considerations, site selection, planning and staffing, contractor selection, project control, procurement, contracts, labor relations, training and startup. Industries served: manufacturers of titanium metal, magnesium metal, chlorine, titanium dioxide pigments, nonferrous die castings, refractories, petroleum and petrochemical products, gasoline from methanol, power generation from coal, sulfuric acid and other chemicals.

C. AYERS LTD.
5225 Jeffs-Doty Rd.
Ottawa Lake, MI 49267
PH: (734)854-6494
FX: (734)854-7359
Construction firm offers counseling and training.

AZTEC ENGINEERING
7575 Northway Dr.
Hanover Park, IL 60103
Javier Lopez, President
PH: (630)830-1671
Founded: 1986. **Staff:** 4. Provides electrical engineering consultation (including power distribution, indoor-outdoor lighting design in commercial, industrial, institutional buildings, roadway lighting design, estimation, cost and supervision). Particular expertise in complete hi-mast lighting design including pole foundation. Primarily serves the construction industry and government as an industry as well as the home furnishings and products industry.

BACKSTAGE THEATRE PRODUCTION AND CONSULTATION
5299 Sixth Ave.
Delta, BC, Canada V4M 1L6
Gregg Burhoe, Contact
PH: (604)943-5149
FX: (604)943-5189
Provides comprehensive production support for the performing arts, including theater design, construction, and conversion; lighting renovation; project management; and equipment rental.

MICHAEL BAKER CORP.
PO Box 12259
Pittsburgh, PA 15231
Charles I. Homan, C.E.O. & President
PH: (412)269-6300
TF: (800)642-2537
FX: (412)269-2534
E-mail: corpcom@mbakercorp.com
URL: http://www.mbakercorp.com
Founded: 1940. **Staff:** 3700. Offers consulting, design engineering, and program management services for highway and transportation; environmental management; industrial facilities and structures; aerial photography, mapping, and surveying; data conversion; Geographic Information Services and energy-related engineering operations and maintenance services. Serves private industries as well as government agencies. Geographic areas served: Worldwide.

BALL CONSTRUCTION MANAGEMENT
25477 via Alcira
Valencia, CA 91355
Chris Ball, Principal Consultant
PH: (800)919-7899
FX: (805)254-0576
E-mail: cheis@ballem.com
Offers construction litigation support, field investigations and documentation, document organization and analysis, schedule analysis, cost estimating, code review, technical analysis and reports, settlement conference support, and trial exhibits.

BALPORT CO., INC.
656 Guy Lombardo Ave.
Freeport, NY 11520
Anthony Tarantino, President
PH: (516)623-0675
FX: (516)623-1260
Founded: 1988. **Staff:** 2. Over 40 years experience in every phase of elevator industry, including labor-relations. Services include accident investigation, expert witness, equipment advisory, surveys, Americans with Disabilities Act (handicapped) lifts, and construction and service contract review. Industries served: elevator industry, architects, engineers, general contractors, building owners, construction managers, and municipalities.

ROBERT B. BALTER CO.
18 Music Fair Rd.
Owings Mills, MD 21117
David A. Easterbrooks, Director of Marketing
PH: (410)363-1555
FX: (410)363-8073
Founded: 1963. **Staff:** 90. Offers geotechnical, environmental, and construction engineering consultation and design to firms and individuals engaged in the planning and erection of architectural and civil engineering structures. Services provided range from development of foundation criteria and design, complete surface and subsurface exploratory work, including drilling, rock coring and geophysical investigations, through laboratory testing and analyses, and the inspection and supervision of construction. Environmental services include Phase I and Phase II assessments through Phase III remediation design.

BALTES/VALENTINO ASSOCIATES, LTD.
7250 N. 16th St., Ste. 102
Phoenix, AZ 85020
Robert T. Baltes, Chairman/CEO
PH: (602)371-1333
FX: (602)371-0675
E-mail: tav@buaeng.com
Founded: 1972. **Staff:** 30. Performs surveys, energy studies, and mechanical, plumbing, and electrical designs for all building types, including clean rooms and computer facilities. Industries served: commercial, resort, industrial, institutional, military, and government.

BARBA-ARKHON INTERNATIONAL INC.
Laurel Corporate Center
10000 Midlantic Dr., Ste. 300 E
Mount Laurel, NJ 08054
Evans M. Barba, CEO & Chairman of the Board
PH: (609)235-5000
TF: (800)966-2272
FX: (609)235-3005
E-mail: info@barba-arkhon.com
URL: http://www.barba-arkhon.com
Founded: 1983. **Staff:** 30. Provides program management and claims services for all types of construction, supply and service contracts, including infrastructure, government and commercial buildings, power projects, ship repair and overhaul, and aerospace projects. Specifically, these services include: development of contracts and procedures, troubleshooting ongoing projects, CPM schedule preparation and updating, change order management, training, assessment of construction quality, A/E and contractor performance evaluations, claims analysis, damage calculations, dispute resolution, and expert witness testimony. Clients include national and European law firms, Fortune 500 companies, federal agencies, state and county governments, municipalities, developers, sureties and insurance companies, government defense contractors, design and engineering firms, general and trade contractors, and banks.

BARNHART, JOHNSON, FRANCIS AND WILD, INC.
31 Ensign Dr.
Avon, CT 06001
Charles V. Francis, President

PH: (860)678-0064
FX: (860)677-4809
E-mail: bjfw@bjfw.com
Founded: 1975. **Staff:** 20. Provides multi-disciplined total project professional engineering services, including consultation, investigation, evaluation, management, planning, design supervision of construction, in connection with public or privately owned structures, buildings, equipment and processes. Disciplines include mechanical, electrical, structural, and civil Engineering, and asbestos and lead-based paint abatement design.

BARRIENTOS & ASSOCIATES INC.
7601 Ganser Way
Madison, WI 53719-2074
Julian Barrientos, P.E., Contact
PH: (608)833-8560
FX: (608)833-8921
Founded: 1964. **Staff:** 35. Consulting engineering and architecture firm offering services for infrastructure projects in transportation, criminal justice, higher education, utilities, water resources, parks and recreation, convention centers, bridges and highways.

PEDRO L. BARRINGTON
1030 Society Hill
Cherry Hill, NJ 08003
Pedro L. Barrington, Principal
PH: (609)489-1778
FX: (609)489-1786
A business development and marketing professional, specializing in the development and implementation of business plans dealing with products and services. Experience in architectural design, construction supervision, and retail banking and ATM operations.

BARTON MALOW CO.
27777 Franklin Rd., Ste. 800
Southfield, MI 48034
Ben Maibach, Jr., Chairman
PH: (248)351-4500
FX: (248)351-5795
E-mail: info@bmco.com
URL: http://www.bmco.com
Founded: 1924. Pre-design services include pre-design implementation schedules; conceptual estimates; facilities assessment; program budget development; team coordination; cash flow/financial decision support; program scope refinement; agency coordination and review; master plan implementation schedule; construction phasing/logistics studies; project scope definition; staff support/management procedures; C.O.N. assistance (healthcare) design phase services include master construction schedules; generating contractor participation; cost models; drawing review; schematic estimates; equal employment opportunity; design development estimates; bid packaging strategy; construction document estimates; project-specific bid documents; guaranteed maximum price; value analysis; constructability review; coordination of contract documents; long-lead equipment purchasing; pre-qualification of contractors; bid—process management: subcontractor personnel review; bid analysis/scope review—bid receipt; and pre-bid conference. Construction phase services include establishing on-site organization; review contractor applications for payment; control / coordination of trade contractors; assistance in obtaining necessary permits; determining contractor resources; establishing labor policies; controlling and monitoring schedules; inspecting work of contractors; conducting progress meetings; implementing total quality management; installing project management software; cost control—status of allowances; field information requests status of changes ; change order management; billing summary; safety program ; shop drawings and samples processing ; material handling; material installation ; maintaining records; project filing system; monthly progress report; schedule updates; processing bulletins and field orders; contractor evaluation; reviewing impact of changes; and progress photos.

BATHEJA AND ASSOCIATES

4822 Dodge
Omaha, NE 68132
Shan L. Batheja, President
PH: (402)551-8353
FX: (402)551-3906
E-mail: bateja@radiks.net
Founded: 1979. **Staff:** 20. Multidisciplined firm offers services in architecture, civil and structural engineering, surveying, and construction management. Serves private industries as well as government agencies.

BDM ENVIRONMENTAL

4221 Forbes Blvd., Ste. 240
Lanham, MD 20706
Carol Wilson Hodges, Vice President
PH: (301)459-9677
FX: (301)459-3064
E-mail: chodges@atsbdm.com
URL: http://www.bdm.com
Acts as an expert witness on environmental matters. Specializes in environmental insurance claims; hydrology/hydrogeology/ environmental engineering; site characterization/remediation/air dispersion/ groundwater/fate and transport modeling; release timing/ forensic investigations for soil and groundwater contamination; contaminant fingerprinting; CERCLA potentially responsible party negotiations; cost allocation/recovery; agency negotiations; hazardous waste management/minimization; innovative technology assessment; pollution prevention; industrial process re-engineering; engineering services; construction management; petroleum technologies; landfill management; information technologies; environmental compliance assessments; and environmental management systems.

BE & K, INC.

2000 International Park Dr.
Birmingham, AL 35243
Ted C. Kennedy, CEO
PH: (205)969-3600
FX: (205)972-6651
URL: http://www.bek.com
Founded: 1982. **Staff:** 291. A high technology engineering/ construction/consulting firm specializing in services to the process industries of industrial power generation, pulp and paper, oil and gas, refining, and chemicals.

DON L. BECK ASSOCIATES INC.

10050 N. Foothill Blvd.
Cupertino, CA 95014-5601
Don L. Beck, CEO and CFO
PH: (408)973-8688
FX: (408)973-8714
Founded: 1981. **Staff:** 9. A management consulting firm specializing in building facilities planning and management worldwide.

BECKER-JOHNSON, INC.

2601 Platte Place
Colorado Springs, CO 80909
Johnny B. Johnson, President
PH: (719)473-5653
FX: (719)634-5983
Founded: 1955. **Staff:** 14. Offers design and inspection for water supply distribution and treatment, wastewater distribution and treatment, industrial wastes, flood control facilities, and town and community planning. Also offers counsel in urban renewal, hydrology, construction layout, and environmental engineering. Clients in local government, private owners, and industry.

BECKWITH CONSULTING GROUP

PO Box 162
Medina, WA 98039
Tom Beckwith, Contact
PH: (206)453-6026
FX: (206)453-1871
Founded: 1983. **Staff:** 4. Firm provides urban planning, design and

development services to government and private industry. These include economic base studies, market and economic feasibility studies, site planning and physical development concepts, urban design and architectural design developments, architectural programs and building space plans, financial lenders packages and life-cycle analysis, project development and construction administration. Group also experienced with comprehensive plans and redevelopment programs, urban design guidelines and zoning ordinances, environmental impact statements and plans, capital improvement programs and fiscal management systems.

BRIAN A. BEECHER AND ASSOCIATES

350 Kresge Ln., Ste. B.
Sparks, NV 89431
Brian A. Beecher, Owner
PH: (702)356-7870
Founded: 1965. **Staff:** 2. Building design consultants with additional expertise in mine plant and facility design, structural and miscellaneous steel detailing, and construction estimating.

ROBERT BEIN, WILLIAM FROST AND ASSOCIATES

14725 Alton Pky.
Irvine, CA 92618
Robert W. Bein, Contact
PH: (714)472-3505
FX: (714)472-8373
URL: http://www.cbf.com
Founded: 1944. **Staff:** 300. Professional consultants providing planning, engineering, surveying, environmental and related services, including civil, mechanical and electrical design, structural and traffic engineering, and energy consulting and energy management services to the building design and construction industry. Serves private industry and government agencies in the western U.S., in Mexico, and Asia.

HOWARD K. BELL, CONSULTING ENGINEERS, INC.

PO Box 546
Lexington, KY 40585-0546
Theo Greene, Jr., President
PH: (606)278-5412
FX: (606)278-2911
E-mail: hkbell@lex.infi.net
Founded: 1914. **Staff:** 66. Multi-discipline firm providing water and wastewater engineering. Professional services include wastewater collection and treatment, wastewater operations assistance, sewer rehabilitation surveys and design, infiltration/inflow analysis evaluations, 201 facilities planning, storm drainage improvements, watershed evaluation studies, water storage and distribution, sludge stabilization/de-watering, KPDES permit assistance, asbestos abatement services, environmental site assessments, solid/hazardous waste, groundwater monitoring, underground storage tanks (UST), industrial waste, permitting and closure plans, environmental audits, lagoon/landfill design, mapping, master planning, dams, and related projects.

THE BENHAM COMPANIES

9400 N. Broadway
Oklahoma City, OK 73156
Donald L. Wickens, President/CEO
PH: (405)478-5353
FX: (405)478-5660
E-mail: lroach@benham.com
URL: http://www.benham.com
Founded: 1909. **Staff:** 900. Offers clients throughout the U.S. and abroad expertise involving some 25 professional disciplines in planning, design, architecture, engineering, and construction. Specific areas of activity include: design and planning; architecture; graphics and drafting; modeling; environmental; the various engineering disciplines such as civil, structural, mechanical, controls, electrical, power, and energy; and other specialized disciplines. Industries served: chemical, defense, food and beverage, municipal, power medical, corrections, retail, and recreation.

MICHAEL BENZA & ASSOCIATES, INC.
6860 W. Snowville Rd.
Brecksville, OH 44141
Michael Benza, Contact
PH: (440)526-4206
FX: (440)546-2691
Founded: 1972. **Staff:** 35. Civil, structural, architectural, sanitary and municipal consultants whose areas of expertise include sewage treatment and collection; water supply treatment and distribution; commercial, industrial, and municipal structures; foundations, land utilization and planning for industrial, commercial and residential projects; roads, bridges, airports, city planning; and construction and design survey service. Industries served: utilities (gas and electric), steel, automobile, construction, developers, and government agencies.

BERMELLO, AJAMIL & PARTNERS, INC.
2601 S. Bayshore Dr.
Miami, FL 33133
Willy Bermello, Principal
PH: (786)859-2050
FX: (786)859-7835
E-mail: info@bamiami.com
URL: http://www.bamiami.com
Founded: 1939. Architecture services in the areas of facilities survey and building certification; ADA surveys; zoning analysis; site planning; and architectural design. Planning, Urban Design & Landscape Architecture services include environmental planning; master planning; comprehensive planning; neighborhood planning; rezoning; development of regional impacts (DRI); major use permits; feasibility analysis; highest and best use studies; redevelopment plans; design of outdoor spaces; landscape architecture; and park design. Construction services include; project management; cost estimating; plans processing and permitting; construction administration; construction engineering & inspection (CE&I); and post-evaluation analysis.

BETHESDA ENGINEERS AND SURVEYORS
PO Box 30808
Bethesda, MD 20824
Ken West, President
PH: (301)654-7907
FX: (301)654-7908
Founded: 1990. **Staff:** 7. Offers civil engineering and land surveying consulting services in land development and storm-water management systems, water, sewer, utility, road and street design, hydrologic and floodplain studies, construction inspection, construction management, topographic and boundary surveys. Services include design, investigations, feasibility studies, permits processing and construction surveying. Geographic areas served: metropolitan Washington DC, Maryland, and northern Virginia.

BICYCLE ACCIDENT INVESTIGATION
PO Box 230
San Jose, CA 95103-0230
Alexander LaRiviere, Principal
PH: (408)294-2412
TF: (888)231-7574
FX: (408)294-8649
E-mail: bikexpert@aol.com
URL: http://www.bikexport.com
Founded: 1982. Offers expert testimony and consulting in regard to the design, construction, and repairing of bicycles, and as well as the operation of all foreign and domestic bicycles and the cause of bicycle failure. Also specializes in the mechanical aspects of bicycle accidents involving roadways, vehicles, railroad crossings, rider error or mechanical failure. Explains the chain of events that show the order in which certain evidence is created, and evaluates the types of damage done.

CLEM B. BINNINGS, II
1104 2nd St.
New Orleans, LA 70130
Clem B. Binnings, II, Contact
PH: (504)891-0963
Civil engineering consultant specializing in foundations, construction claims, construction accident investigations, and expert testimony.

ROBERT R. BISACCIA INC.
171 Madison Ave., Ste. 1501
New York, NY 10016
Robert Bisaccia, President
PH: (212)686-6277
FX: (212)545-0924
Founded: 1967. **Staff:** 7. Firm provides construction and construction management services to clients in the metropolitan New York area.

WALTER P. BISHOP CONSULTING ENGINEER PC
740 Broadway, 9th Fl.
New York, NY 10003-9518
Walter Bishop, Contact
PH: (212)420-8282
FX: (212)505-6201
Consulting engineering firm assists with construction.

BLACK & VEATCH
PO Box 8405
Kansas City, MO 64114
P.J. Adam, CEO & Chairman of the Board
PH: (913)458-2000
FX: (913)458-2934
E-mail: info@bv.com
URL: http://www.bv.com
Founded: 1915. **Staff:** 8000. A global engineering and construction firm serving utilities, industry and governmental agencies worldwide. Provides engineering, procurement and construction services to the electric power industry. Capabilities include fossil-fueled plants, simple and combined cycleplants, and cogeneration. Also provides engineering services in the infrastructure field, including water and wastewater, solid and hazardous waste management, hydraulic structures, and transportation. In the process field, Black & Veatch provides engineering, procurement, and construction in gas processing, sulfur recovery, and liquefaction of natural gas.

BLYMYER ENGINEERS, INC.
1829 Clement Ave.
Alameda, CA 94501
H.S. Lewis, President
PH: (510)521-3773
TF: (800)753-3773
FX: (510)865-2594
E-mail: blymyer.com
Founded: 1961. **Staff:** 35. Offers design engineering and construction management consulting for transportation facilities and major material handling equipment. Also advises on terminal/depot spill prevention counter measures and industrial equipment design and installation. Environmental Division consists of three departments: Underground Storage Tank Services, Environmental Planning and Assessment, and Geotechnical and Remediation Services. Services include environmental audit and site assessment services, soil and groundwater sampling, remediation design, and storm water compliance services. Serves private industries as well as government agencies.

OSCAR J. BOLDT CONSTRUCTION CO.
2525 N. Roemer Rd.
Appleton, WI 54912
Warren F. Parsons, President
PH: (920)739-6321
TF: (800)992-6538
FX: (920)739-4409
URL: http://www.boldt.com
Founded: 1889. **Staff:** 2000. Construction consultants with expertise in the following areas: site investigation, construction troubleshooting, construction contract methods, conceptual estimating, project accounting methods, contractor/A/E selection services, value en-

gineering, concrete placement techniques, project management, construction purchasing techniques, budget control, program management, scheduling, and solving construction and machinery installation problems. Serves government also.

MARC BOOGAY CONSULTING ENGINEER
2141 El Camino Real
Oceanside, CA 92054
PH: (760)721-1959
FX: (760)721-0911
E-mail: boogay@sdnc.quik.com
Staff: 3. Phase I and Phase II environmental site assessments. Design of remediations for contaminated soil or groundwater. Monitoring of progress in site remediation. Asbestos surveys in buildings. Design of asbestos abatements and asbestos operation-management plans. Building engineering inspection. Seismic, probable maximum loss reports. Forensic investigations, expert witness testimony, litigation support.

BOOKER ASSOCIATES, INC.
1139 Olive St.
St. Louis, MO 63101
Robert C. Flory, CEO
PH: (314)421-1476
FX: (314)421-1741
Founded: 1949. **Staff:** 240. An engineering, architectural, planning, landscape architecture, and construction management firm providing professional services to federal, state and local governments, general commercial and institutional clients, and various industrial clients including chemical, automotive, and general light and heavy industries. Specializing in transportation design including bridge, road and airport, and blast resistant facility design.

BOVIS CONSTRUCTION CORP.
33 New Montgomery St., Ste. 1400
San Francisco, CA 94105
James D'Agostino, COO
PH: (415)512-0586
FX: (415)512-0589
URL: http://www.bovis.com
Founded: 1979. International construction management firm.

BOYKEN INTERNATIONAL, INC.
8800 Roswell Rd., Ste. 270
Atlanta, GA 30350
Donald R. Boyken, CCC, Chairman & CEO
PH: (770)992-3210
TF: (800)842-5489
FX: (770)992-1489
E-mail: dboyken@boyken.com
URL: http://www.boyken.com
Founded: 1980. **Staff:** 35. Professional construction consulting firm offering program management services, cost and schedule controls, expert witness testimony, litigation support services, property evaluation inspections, owner's representative services and value engineering.

T.J. BOYLE & ASSOCIATES—LANDSCAPE ARCHITECTS & SITE PLANNING CONSULTANTS
301 College St.
Burlington, VT 05401
Terrence J. Boyle, Contact
PH: (802)658-3555
FX: (802)863-1562
E-mail: tjboyle@sprynet.com
URL: http://www.home.sprynet.com/spynet/tyboyle
Founded: 1967. **Staff:** 4. Landscape architects and planning consultants providing services in the areas of land planning, site planning, park and recreation planning, power transmission routing, urban design and streetscapes. Also offers site design and engineering, cost opinions, bid documents and construction administration. Industries served: private sector, transmission lines services, and local and state government agencies.

A. DAVID BRAYTON, CONSTRUCTION SAFETY CONSULTANTS
2328 Mapleview Ave.
Portage, MI 49024-6774
A. David Brayton, Principal
PH: (616)323-8311
FX: (616)323-8156
E-mail: davebray@net-link.net
Specializes in construction safety matters including, injuries and reconstructions; warning labels, behavior and OSHA.

BREEN ENGINEERING
1615 W. Abram St., Ste. 200
Arlington, TX 76013-1787
James E. Breen, President
PH: (817)275-4711
FX: (817)275-4711
Founded: 1978. **Staff:** 3. Building construction consultants offering complete inspection services of residential and commercial structures (includes structural, equipment and systems). Clients include real estate brokers, investors (real estate), and builders/developers.

JAMES R. BRENZEL, CPA
1155 Crane St., Ste. 5
Menlo Park, CA 94025
James R. Brenzel, CPA
PH: (415)325-3667
FX: (415)325-3667
Certified public accountant specializing in income taxation; litigation support; forensic accounting; business valuation; professional practice valuation; economic and financial analysis; contract disputes; construction contractor-developer-investor disputes; partnership and stockholder disputes; orderly liquidations, split-ups and dissolution; damage quantification and lost profits; rental real estate accounting; management and analysis; accounting and taxation for mining and oil and gas; accounting taxation for trusts and estates.

BRIGGS ASSOCIATES, A TUNDRA CORP. CO.
400 Hingham St.
Rockland, MA 02370
Charles H. Gross, Senior Vice President
PH: (617)871-6040
FX: (617)871-7982
Founded: 1983. **Staff:** 220. Consulting engineers serving the construction industry. Consulting engineering services include land use planning and permitting, municipal planning and zoning, site/civil development engineering, groundwater modeling and hydrogeology, geotechnical engineering, and roofing failure analysis. Also offers the following environmental services: asbestos abatement, planning and consulting; environmental permitting/impact statements; site certifications; solid hazardous waste investigations and management; water supply and wastewater management; indoor air quality surveys; and technical assistance audits. A variety of building construction quality assurance/quality control services are available. Serves private industries as well as government agencies.

BROWN AND CALDWELL
PO Box 8045
Walnut Creek, CA 94596
Craig Goehring, CEO/Chairman
PH: (925)937-9010
TF: (800)727-2224
FX: (925)937-9026
URL: http://www.brownandcaldwell.com
Founded: 1947. **Staff:** 800. Consulting engineers and scientists active in planning, design, and construction management for water, wastewater, hazardous waste projects, solid waste management, storm water management, and energy. Extensive experience in environmental engineering and services for competitive performance. Industries served: aerospace, agriculture and forestry, banking and finance, chemical, construction, energy industries, food processing, government agencies, healthcare, manufacturing, mining, petroleum, pharmaceuticals, utilities, and others.

E.R. BROWNELL & ASSOCIATES, INC.
3152 Coral Way
Miami, FL 33145
Angel Lopez, President
PH: (305)446-3511
FX: (305)444-2034
Founded: 1953. **Staff:** 43. Civil engineering firm specializes in transportation, land development and land surveying: construction stakeout, property and topographical surveys; water, sewer, road, and pavement design; structural engineering: bridges and buildings; and utility engineering: telephone conduit and cable design projects; construction engineering and inspection of roadway projects. Serves the following industries: banking and finance, construction, legal profession, real estate and government.

BROWNLEE CONSTRUCTION CONSULTANTS
1500 Riverfront Dr., Ste. 106
Little Rock, AR 72203
Porter Brownlee, Contact
PH: (501)666-9401
FX: (501)666-9402
E-mail: spb3@aol.com
Founded: 1982. **Staff:** 3. Offers construction consulting that includes market study, investment analysis, budgeting, construction costs projections, financial design, contract administration, scheduling, construction cost control, and contract draw certification; some construction-related litigation support may also be provided. Serves private industry as well as government agencies.

BRW, INC.
700 3rd St., S.
Minneapolis, MN 55415
Doug Differt, Vice President
PH: (612)370-0700
TF: (800)966-2794
FX: (612)370-1378
URL: http://www.brw.inc.com
Founded: 1956. **Staff:** 600. Multidisciplinary consulting firm provides professional services-concept through construction-in transportation, civil and structural engineering, planning, and urban design.

BRYANT ASSOCIATES, INC.
160 North Washington Ste. 700
Boston, MA 02114-2127
John J. Phillips, P.E., Vice President
PH: (617)248-0300
FX: (617)248-0212
E-mail: bama@bryant-engrs.com
URL: http://www.bryant-engrs.com
Founded: 1976. **Staff:** 84. Offers civil and structural engineering, landscape architecture, and surveying services in the field of transportation and environmental and site development. Transportation projects include highways, expressways, bridges, railroads, mass transit facilities, street improvements, ports, and airports. Environmental projects include sanitary and storm sewers, water collection systems, grading, drainage, and erosion control. Serves private industries as well as government agencies.

BUCHART-HORN, INC.
445 W. Philadelphia
York, PA 17405-7055
George D. Barnes, President
PH: (717)852-1400
TF: (800)274-2224
FX: (717)852-1401
Founded: 1946. **Staff:** 321. Offers complete architectural/ engineering services: transportation, environmental, rate analysis/ valuation, operations management, training, surveys, construction management, recreation, analytical testing, and aerial mapping. Serves private industry as well as government agencies.

BUCHER, WILLIS & RATLIFF CORP.
7920 Ward Pky.
Kansas City, MO 64114-2021
James Ray Flemons, Contact
PH: (816)363-2696
TF: (800)748-8276
FX: (816)363-0027
E-mail: bwr@bwrcorp.com
URL: http://www.bwrcorp.com
Founded: 1957. **Staff:** 230. Professional consulting engineers, planners and architects offering engineering services in studying the feasibility, planning, design, plan preparation, specification writing and inspection of construction for bridges, highways, streets, dams, airports, industrial and domestic water and waste treatment facilities, environmental compliance, water and sewerage systems and cross country utilities. Firm also offers planning services in comprehensive planning, recreational planning, urban renewal planning, airport planning, transportation planning, off-street parking and zoning for statewide, regional and local governmental agencies, as well as architectural services in the design of governmental centers, group housing, schools, swimming pools and commercial and industrial buildings. Also offers services of aerial photography, complete technical photography, surveying and photogrammetry to support the above described professional services.

BUERKI BRENNAN ASSOCIATES
10134 N. Port Washington Rd.
Mequon, WI 53092
Robert E. Brennan, Contact
PH: (414)241-4446
Founded: 1967. **Staff:** 3. Offers consulting assistance to architects, engineers, and owners of performing arts facilities; emphasis on new construction and renovation. Serves private industries as well as government agencies.

BUILDING INFORMATION SYSTEMS, INC.
12268 SW 50th St.
Cooper City, FL 33330
Ralph M. Hippard, President
PH: (954)252-9933
FX: (954)252-9977
E-mail: buildingfl@aol.com
URL: http://members.aol.com/BUILDINGFL/SYSTEMS.html
Founded: 1997. **Staff:** 2. Management and leadership systems for residential and light commercial builders.

BURGESS AND NIPLE, LTD.
5085 Reed Rd.
Columbus, OH 43220-2581
Owen B. March, Executive Director
PH: (614)459-2050
TF: (800)282-1961
FX: (614)451-1385
E-mail: info@burnip.com
URL: http://www.burgessniple.com
Founded: 1912. **Staff:** 616. Consulting engineers and architects providing services to municipal, county, state and federal governments; individuals; and utilities, corporations, and industries. Services include: architecture, bridge design and inspection, computer services, construction services, flood control, hydroelectric power development, laboratory analyses, land development, landscape architecture, mechanical and electrical design, mining and reclamation, process engineering, sludge management, solid and hazardous waste management, storm drainage, structures, transportation, urban and regional planning, utility services, value engineering, water facilities, water resources, and wastewater facilities.

H.H. BURKITT PROJECT MANAGEMENT, INC.
1730 Bldg.
Portland, OR 97221-2547
H.H. Burkitt, President/CEO
PH: (503)297-4520
FX: (503)297-4519

Founded: 1976. **Staff:** 137. Offers a full range of professional engineering and project management services.

BURNHAM CONSULTANTS, LTD.

Burnham Ctr. Bldg., 111 W. Washington St., Ste. 1601
Chicago, IL 60602
TF: (800)407-7990
FX: (312)220-0194
E-mail: 102164.2461@compuserve.com
Processes and manages municipal approvals to expedite construction projects in Chicago and surrounding suburbs. Processing services include site permits, certificates of occupancy, contractor licensing, public way leasing, zoning variances, and building historical data.

BURNS & MCDONNELL

9400 Ward Pky.
Kansas City, MO 64114
Dave G. Ruf, Jr., Chairman and CEO
PH: (816)333-9400
FX: (816)333-3690
E-mail: busder@burnsmcd.com
URL: http://www.burnsmcd.com
Founded: 1898. **Staff:** 1262. Engineers and architects offering the following types of services: reports and studies, engineering and architectural design, professional construction management, general consultations. Typical projects include: industrial/commercial facilities; airports and aerospace facilities; water supply and wastewater systems; electric power generation, transmission and distribution; air pollution control systems and testing; civil works including bridges and roads; hazardous waste management; and process engineering for food, chemicals, and petroleum; environmental audits and assessments; biological surveys; permitting; waste handling and incineration; solid waste management and remedial investigations; design and construction oversight.

BURNS AND ROE ENTERPRISES

700 and 800 Kindermack Rd.
Oradell, NJ 07649
K. Keith Roe, President
PH: (201)265-2000
FX: (201)986-4459
Founded: 1974. **Staff:** 1800. BRISC functions equally well as consulting engineer and a full service contractor. Services include planning, project financing, technical and economic studies, cost estimating, site selection, engineering, design, scale modeling, procurement, scheduling, logistic support, construction management, quality assurance, start-up and test, and operating maintenance and operation. Industries served: defense and aerospace, chemical, construction, energy industries, transportation, government agencies, communications, manufacturing, and pharmaceutical.

BUTLAK ENGINEERING

6304 Inwood St.
Cheverly, MD 20785
Paul E. Butlak, Contact
PH: (240)822-5274
FX: (240)773-7047
Founded: 1985. A consulting engineering enterprise serving the needs of contractors, engineers, architects, and owners. The services available are categorized as follows: scheduling services, estimating services, claim analysis services, litigation support, lender support, educational services, and construction management.

TED BUTTERISS MANAGEMENT & TECHNOLOGY

451 Pebble Beach Pl.
Fullerton, CA 92835
PH: (714)441-2280
FX: (714)441-2281
E-mail: Global_Tradelinks@compuserve.com
URL: http://www.consultapc.org/Butter2.htm
Offers services in business management, project management, engineering management, and plant construction and startup management. Business management services include performing energy audits, reviewing work processes, and auditing management practices.

Project management services include feasibility services, preparing requests for proposal, and project management training. Engineering management services include specification production and control, quality control management, and determining design document requirements.

CALDWELL CONSULTING ASSOCIATES

PO Box 29143
Richmond, VA 23242-0143
Cary Cohen, President
PH: (804)740-2469
FX: (804)740-0335
E-mail: info@caldwell.com
Founded: 1977. **Staff:** 7. Offers training services to industry and government with specialization in government procurement, electric utility, engineering and construction. Develops procedures and policies for purchasing and contract administration. Involved in claims preparation and/or defense for construction and government projects.

CAMP AND ASSOCIATES, INC.

5833 Stewart Pky.
Douglasville, GA 30135
William W. Camp, President
PH: (770)949-0723
FX: (770)942-0112
Founded: 1979. **Staff:** 20. Offers complete range of architectural and engineering services for industrial, military and governmental clients. Services include study, design, construction management for office, warehouse, manufacturing; process systems, utilities systems; water, wastewater, solid waste disposal; and hazardous and toxics evaluation and system design. Staff includes registered professionals in architecture and civil, structural, mechanical, electrical, environmental, chemical, and sanitary engineering.

CAMPBELL & JOHNSON, ENGINEERS

113 W. 7th St.
Concordia, KS 66901-2801
Eric W. Johnson, President
PH: (913)243-1755
FX: (913)243-1757
Founded: 1969. **Staff:** 8. Offers consulting civil engineering services to private firms and small municipalities and counties in Kansas. Activities include bridge design, building design, land surveying, and construction management. Also provide extensive architectural services.

THE CAMPBELL GROUP

607 W. Chicago Blvd.
Tecumseh, MI 49286
PH: (517)426-6458
E-mail: info@campgroup.com
URL: http://www.campgroup.com
An association of building industry and communications specialists assisting the industry in improving systems and procedures, improving quality and customer satisfaction, improving employee understanding and performance, and improving business results.

LOUIS H. CAMPBELL—ARCHITECTURAL CONSULTANT FOR PERFORMANCE SPACES

1012 Burning Tree Pky.
Denton, TX 76201
Louis H. Campbell, President
PH: (940)383-2110
FX: (940)383-2110
Founded: 1983. **Staff:** 2. Develops architectural program for public performance spaces working with either architect or client-owner for the development, specification, on-site inspection during construction and installation, and systems orientation to client/owner representatives upon acceptance of facility. Experience in new or renovated facilities. International as well as domestic project history. Industries served: architecture, arts, construction, systems design engineering, and government agencies.

CANAC INTERNATIONAL INC.
1100 University, 5th Fl.
Montreal, PQ, Canada H3B 3A5
A.R. Pozniak, President
PH: (514)399-3593
FX: (514)399-3967
Founded: 1971. **Staff:** 50. Provides comprehensive management (administration, planning, information systems, costing, project control), engineering, procurement, training and other consulting services in relation with the design, construction, operations, direct management and maintenance of new or existing railways, intermodal transportation networks and telecommunications. Included is direct or consultative management of any aspect of existing railway operations or design and construction of new rail lines and railway facilities.

CANARAIL CONSULTANTS INC.
1140 Maisonneuve Blvd. W, Ste. 1050
Montreal, PQ, Canada H3A 1M8
Hovig Bedikian, President
PH: (514)985-0930
FX: (514)985-0929
E-mail: inbox@canarail.com
URL: http://www.canarail.com
Founded: 1990. **Staff:** 75. Railway consulting capabilities include feasibility studies, project management services, procurement and tendering services, civil engineering, preliminary and detailed design, railway rehabilitation, construction supervision, technical assistance, institutional reforms, privatization, training and transfer of technology, economic and transport studies, railway operations, maintenance planning and procedures for motive power, rolling stock, and railway marketing studies and assistance in railway costing, management information systems, electrification, signaling and telecommunications.

CANNON
2170 Whitehaven Rd.
Grand Island, NY 14072
John D. Cannon, Chairman
PH: (716)773-6800
FX: (716)773-5909
Founded: 1945. **Staff:** 300. A full-service architectural/engineering/planning organization with specialized experience in project research, planning, and design. Projects range in scale from a single structure to joint development complexes and in variety from corporate headquarters to multi-industry complexes, secondary schools to university campuses, health clinics to hospitals and medical centers, and research and production facilities. Industries served: healthcare, education, corporate/commercial, government, and industry.

CANNON GROUP / ROOF & BUILDING CONSULTANTS
12 E. Stow Rd., Ste. 210
Marlton, NJ 08053-3163
Herbert Cannon, Principal
PH: (609)983-9595
TF: (800)233-6986
FX: (609)983-2662
URL: http://www.cannon-roof.com/
Founded: 1982. **Staff:** 10. A consulting and design firm composed of registered architects and roofing consultants specializing in the investigation and remediation of failed roofing, waterproofing and moisture control systems. Investigates and prepares reports in legal cases. Services include investigation and analysis, litigation and mediation, design and construction, construction inspections, maintenance programs, roof asset management, project profiles.

CAPITAL PROJECT MANAGEMENT, INC.
531 Plymouth Rd., Ste. 508
Plymouth Meeting, PA 19462-1642
Michael F. D'Onofrio, Principal
PH: (610)260-0500
FX: (610)260-0400
E-mail: cpmi@cpmiteam.com
URL: http://www.cpmiteam.com

an engineering consulting firm specializing in contract dispute analysis and resolution; project management oversight; project controls; and surety evaluations. Experienced in analyzing and resolving construction and manufacturing contract disputes. Evaluates technical, schedule and cost issues; develops dispute resolution strategies; assists in settlement negotiations; and provides expert witness testimony.

CAPLAN ENGINEERING CO.—ELECTRICAL CONSULTANTS
7531 Roslyn St.
Pittsburgh, PA 15218
PH: (412)271-4700
FX: (412)271-8120
Founded: 1959. **Staff:** 8. Offers electrical design consulting to commercial, industrial, educational, and institutional facilities. Scope of design services include lighting, power, security, fire alarm, computer, life-safety, electric heat and special systems. Also offers utility rate and cost analysis, power factor study, and site observation. Serves private industries as well as government agencies.

CARTER & BURGESS, INC.
PO Box 985006
Fort Worth, TX 76107
Wilton N. Hammond, Chairman
PH: (817)735-6000
FX: (817)735-5646
URL: http://www.c-.com
Founded: 1939. **Staff:** 700. Full-service engineering, architectural, planning, and environmental firm. It is organized into ten integrated, client-centered business divisions, including: Transportation, Facilities, Warehouse/Distribution, Federal Programs, Land Development, Planning/Landscape Architecture, Public Works, Survey, Environmental/Geographic Information Systems, and Acoustical/Theatrical. Services include mechanical, electrical, plumbing (MEP), fire protection design, structural engineering, 3-D modeling, Graphic Information Systems and Remote Sensing, environmental studies, environmental engineering, architecture, lighting design, noise/vibration control, and construction services.

CARTER CONTRACTING & DEVELOPING INC.
810 Oak Shadow Ct.
Mansfield, TX 76063
Ted Carter, Contact
PH: (817)473-7377
FX: (817)473-7922
Construction firm specializes in hotel renovation.

CARUOLO ASSOCIATES, INC.
The Commons at Valley Forge East, Ste. 85
PO Box 1150
Valley Forge, PA 19482-1150
John Caruolo, P.E., President
PH: (610)983-3694
FX: (610)983-9202
Founded: 1986. **Staff:** 3. Full-service transportation consulting firm specializing in transportation planning, traffic engineering, and construction management for highways, bus and rail systems. Also experienced in roadway design, traffic studies, operations planning, costing, environmental studies, and service analysis.

W. MARTIN "RED" CASS & ASSOCIATES
PO Box 1466
Citrus Heights, CA 95611
W. Martin Cass, Contact
PH: (916)989-9161
Founded: 1970. **Staff:** 2. Administrator of Shoring Safety Training School in Sacramento, California. Operates only facility currently training personnel working in the underground construction industry. Also serves as expert witness in construction accidents. Serves agricultural, forestry, construction, insurance, legal, manufacturing, transportation and utilities industries, as well as government agencies. Jean L. Wood woman-owned firm.

CCL CONSTRUCTION CONSULTANTS
7219 Metcalf Ave., Ste. 202
Overland Park, KS 66204-1974
Harry Callahan, Chairman of Board
PH: (913)491-8626
TF: (800)533-8626
FX: (913)491-9469
E-mail: cclcc@ix.netcom.com
URL: http://www.cclcon.com
Founded: 1986. **Staff:** 30. Construction consultant firm providing services to attorneys, contractors, and building owners worldwide.

C.C.R.M., INC.
923 Old Manoa Rd.
Havertown, PA 19083
Walter Lee Sheppard, Jr., President
PH: (610)449-2167
Founded: 1976. **Staff:** 1. Consultants in corrosion and chemically resistant masonry ("acid-resistant" brickwork, monolithic surfacing materials, tank and other vessel linings, polymer concretes and cements) and construction, inspection, trouble shooting and repair of these materials, plus design, selection, and specification preparation for them. Handles forensic work in these subjects. Serves private industries as well as government agencies worldwide.

CDI—ENGINEERING
12727 Featherwood Dr., Ste. 200
Houston, TX 77034
James E. Musick, Vice President.
PH: (713)484-7622
TF: (800)324-7882
FX: (713)484-9956
Founded: 1952. **Staff:** 1500. Full service engineering, procurement and construction management company offering full discipline service to heavy industry, refining, chemical, petrochemical, steel, aluminum, government agencies, and electronics manufacturing. Also supplies technical manpower to these industries. Engineering disciplines include process, mechanical, instrumentation, piping, structural, civil, environmental, and electrical. Also offers architectural services.

CEM SERVICES, INC.
7609 Epsilon Dr.
Gaithersburg, MD 20885
S.P. Verma, President
PH: (301)869-6820
FX: (301)869-7435
Founded: 1984. **Staff:** 10. Construction management and design engineers offering civil, structural, architectural and geotechnical project development.

CENTENNIAL ENGINEERING, INC.
PO Drawer 1307
Arvada, CO 80001-1307
Larry R. Thomas, President
PH: (303)420-0221
FX: (303)940-4335
URL: http://www.mkcentennial.com
Founded: 1974. **Staff:** 450. Consulting engineering firm providing transportation planning and traffic engineering; roadway, street, light rail transit and railroad design; bridge design and structural analysis; hydrologic studies and hydraulics; flood plain analysis; surveying and construction management services to private businesses, and local, state, regional and federal government agencies.

CENTRAL ENGINEERS & ARCHITECTS
910 Grove St.
Beaver Dam, WI 53916
Dan J. Prunuske, Contact
PH: (414)887-3127
FX: (414)887-7996
Founded: 1951. **Staff:** 10. Provides a complete range of consulting services including architectural, municipal and environmental engineering, planning, and surveying. These services extend from project conception and design, through construction, to completion. Specific activities include: feasibility studies, reports, planning, cost estimates, engineering design, surveys, detailed plans and specifications, project implementation and management, construction supervision, and assistance in preparation of funding and grant applications. Industries served: municipal government, industrial and commercial firms, and state government.

CENTURY CONSTRUCTORS & ENGINEERS
375 Chipeta Way
Salt Lake City, UT 84108
George B. Martin, Senior Vice President
PH: (801)582-2002
FX: (801)582-1440
Founded: 1894. **Staff:** 300. Engineering and construction company offering a wide range of services including the following: feasibility studies, process studies, process engineering, engineering and design, purchasing, expediting, inspection, schedule/cost control, operator training services, construction, construction management, project management, environmental impact assessment, estimating, and start-up services. Industries served: chemicals, petrochemical, refining, minerals processing, pharmaceutical, general industrial, and pipeline.

CENTURY ENGINEERING, INC.
32 West Rd.
Towson, MD 21204
James T. Johnson, Sr., President
PH: (410)823-8070
FX: (410)823-2184
Founded: 1974. **Staff:** 180. Offers engineering expertise in the following areas: highways, bridges, mechanical, electrical, civil, structural, and marine. Also offers construction management, inspection, geotechnical, and hydrological services. Serves private industries as well as government agencies.

CENTURY WEST ENGINEERING CORP.
825 NE Multnomah, Ste. 425
Portland, OR 97232
J. Ned Dempsey, President
PH: (503)231-6078
FX: (503)231-6482
URL: http://www.centurywest.com
Founded: 1969. **Staff:** 85. General engineering consultants offering services in aviation, structural agricultural, civil, environmental, geotechnical, hydrologic and sanitary engineering, as well as industrial/hazardous waste management services. Also offers landscape architecture, planning, surveying, drafting, laboratory and field testing services, and construction management and inspection. Serves private industries as well as government agencies.

CGA MANAGEMENT SERVICES, INC.
1492 Lake Murray Blvd.
Columbia, SC 29212
Nelson W. Meek, Contact
PH: (803)781-9140
FX: (803)781-1692
Founded: 1989. **Staff:** 12. Provides pre-architectural site and facility planning, project management and construction management services, transition and activation services, primarily for criminal justice system and facilities. Industries served: primarily corrections; local, state, and federal jail and prison facilities.

CH2M HILL
6060 S. Willow Dr.
Englewood, CO 80111
James W. Poirot, Chairman of the Board
PH: (303)771-0900
FX: (303)770-2616
URL: http://www.ch2m.com/
Founded: 1946. **Staff:** 7000. International consulting firm of engineers, planners, economists and scientists in many technical fields. Services include general civil engineering; structural engineering; municipal and industrial wastewater, solid waste and water resources

management; construction management; toxic and hazardous waste management; irrigation; transportation; and environmental studies. Serves private industries as well as government agencies.

HOMER L. CHASTAIN & ASSOCIATES, LLP
5 N. Country Club Rd.
Decatur, IL 62521
P.A. Hazenfield, Contact
PH: (217)422-8544
FX: (217)422-0398
E-mail: hlc@hlcllp.com
URL: http://www.pagedepot.com/hlcllp/transportation.htm
Founded: 1954. **Staff:** 50. Provides civil, structural, industrial design, urban planning, and construction engineering. Range of activity includes streets, highways, freeways, bridges, buildings, water supply, sewage, waste planning, dams, and drainage. Also offers environmental impact studies, material controls, municipal engineering, feasibility studies and valuations, precise surveys and topographic mapping, geodetic triangulation and leveling, and electronic computer services. Planning includes grant applications, TIF districts, zoning and ordinance writing and creating master plans.

CHCG ARCHITECTS INC.
135 W. Green St., Ste. 200
Pasadena, CA 91105
Armando Gonzalez, Contact
PH: (818)568-1428
FX: (818)568-8026
E-mail: chcg28@aol.com
Founded: 1964. **Staff:** 30. In addition to architectural services, the firm offers consulting in space planning, interior design, and allied construction management. Specializes in health, education, government and industrial projects; work includes various types of buildings and complexes, such as civic, educational, recreational, medical, commercial and industrial architecture, as well as master planning. Certified minority owned business.

CHESAPEAKE SYSTEMS CONSULTANTS, INC.
909 N. Cobb Pky., NE, Ste. 104
Marietta, GA 30062
Robert C. Waner, President
PH: (770)419-9988
FX: (770)419-0437
Firm provides failure investigations, power system analysis, power quality surveys and analysis, feasibility studies, site measurements, electrical system design, substation design and construction, and surge protection.

CHICAGO ROOFING CONTRACTORS ASSOCIATION
4415 W. Harrison St., Ste. 242-C
Hillside, IL 60162
PH: (708)449-3340
FX: (708)449-0837
E-mail: crcainfo@crca.org
URL: http://www.crca.org/index.html
Seeks to remain in close contact, through public relations activities, with architects, engineers, contractors and other segments of the construction industry, including property owners and the general public, so that communications efforts are coordinated and channeled to the best interests of members, their employees, the industry and public welfare.

MAX A. CHOW & ASSOCIATES
PO Box 9023054
San Juan, PR 00902
Max A. Chow, Contact
PH: (787)721-7963
FX: (787)721-7963
E-mail: chow@kirbe.com
Founded: 1979. **Staff:** 3. Provides the following consulting services: urban planning and design, architectural design, construction supervision, municipal development, and recreational planning and design. Specialty in tropical architecture.

CHRISTENSEN & RHOADS—ARCHITECTURE PLANNING INTERIORS
310 N. Irwin St., Ste. 17
Hanford, CA 93230
Donald J. Christensen, Contact
PH: (209)584-3371
FX: (209)584-5423
Founded: 1972. **Staff:** 4. Architect and planning consultant with experience in the environmental design fields including planning, landscape architecture, construction, and architectural practice. Projects have encompassed the broad range of building types, including residential, commercial, industrial, educational, health, public buildings, recreational structures and grounds, urban design plans, and comprehensive plans for cities. Three special interests in practice are energy-conserving design, recreational and sports facility design, and historic preservation and adaptive re-use. Serves private industries as well as government agencies.

THE CITY GROUP
281 Delsea Dr.
Sewell, NJ 08080
R.P. Pacitti, President
PH: (609)256-1921
FX: (609)256-1922
Founded: 1989. **Staff:** 5. Building design and construction consultants with major focus areas including construction management, project management, contract administration services, construction claims consulting, expert review and witness, constructability reviews, and construction feasibility studies. Also conducts ARPA resource and labor productivity reviews and value engineering reviews for the industrial manufacturing, process-chemical and petrochemical, environmental (hazardous waste, air pollution control, and wastewater treatment), cogeneration and general utility, and pharmaceutical facility construction industries, as well as government agencies worldwide.

CIVIC ASSOCIATES, INC., CONSULTING AND FORENSIC ENGINEERS
3500 Rainbow Blvd.
Kansas City, KS 66103
Frank W. Sharp, Jr., P.E., Senior Engineer
PH: (913)677-5230
FX: (913)831-9789
Founded: 1975. **Staff:** 10. Firm engaged in a diversity of design and/or construction-related activities including: construction inspections; construction management and estimates; civil, structural, mechanical, electrical, and industrial engineering; water, wastewater, and pollution control engineering; forensic engineering services and related expert testimony; and safety and risk analysis.

CLARK PATTERSON & ASSOCIATES
186 N. Water St.
Rochester, NY 14604-1122
Phillip J. Clark, President
PH: (716)454-4570
FX: (716)232-5836
Founded: 1975. **Staff:** 100. Multi-disciplined engineering firm providing planning, design, and construction management services. Meeting the engineering needs of commercial, industrial, and municipal clients, the firm offers civil, mechanical, electrical, structural, and land survey and development services.

CLARK REPORTS
925 Sherwood Dr.
PO Box 185
Lake Bluff, IL 60044
TF: (800)222-0255
E-mail: info@clarkreports.com
URL: http://www.clarkreports.com
Founded: 1962. Provides advanced notification of projects in the planning and pre-planning stages throughout North America.

CLEANING CONSULTANT SERVICES, INC.
PO Box 1273
Seattle, WA 98111
William R. Griffin, President
PH: (206)682-9748
FX: (206)622-6876
URL: http://www.cleaningconsultants.com
Founded: 1976. **Staff:** 14. Management consultants to cleaning and maintenance contractors, property managers, hospitals, schools, hotels, building owners, facility directors, and small business owners in the cleaning industry. Services are designed to increase efficiency and profit through training and the use of time-saving techniques on the job; increase the useful life of building surfaces and equipment; encourage self development of cleaning and maintenance professionals; and make the world a clean and safe place to live. Specific consulting services relate to: cleaning contract specifications development and negotiation, claim and dispute resolution, expert court testimony, independent certified cleaning and maintenance inspections, training program and materials development, building start-up and long-range maintenance planning, architect and engineering services regarding cleaning, and building maintenance. Serves all industries in need of cleaning and maintenance services.

J.P. CLEMENT & ASSOCIATES
1528 Northview Dr.
Thousand Oaks, CA 91362
John P. Clement, Director
PH: (805)494-9325
E-mail: jpclement@juno.com
Specializes in traffic engineering consulting. Experience in site planning, traffic control devices (warning, construction, regulatory, and construction signs, delineation, signals as contributing factors to traffic collisions), highway design, speed humps, geometric features, construction zones, roadside obstacles, design, construction, and maintenance, and operation.

CLEMONS, RUTHERFORD & ASSOCIATES, INC.
2027 Thomasville Rd.
Tallahassee, FL 32312
William D. Rutherford, President
PH: (850)385-6153
FX: (850)386-8420
E-mail: cra@clemons-rutherford.com
Founded: 1960. **Staff:** 31. Architectural consultants specializing in medical, educational, computer facilities, correctional and religious facilities. Industries served: healthcare, educational, corrections, advanced technological, and government agencies.

NED CLYDE CONSTRUCTION, INC.
159 Mason Cir.
Concord, CA 94520
Ned Clyde, Principal
PH: (925)689-5411
FX: (925)246-8164
Founded: 1981. **Staff:** 15. Construction services include underpinning and releveling buildings; the design and installation of drainage systems, erosion control measures, and retaining walls; and the design and repair of earth slides. Provides contract claims merit analysis and claims quantum valuation. Offers expert testimony in litigation cases.

CMD ASSOCIATES, INC.
1800 Westlake Ave. N, Ste. 203
Seattle, WA 98109
Robert G. Thomas, Jr., Principal
PH: (206)285-6811
FX: (206)285-0752
E-mail: rthomas@eifs.com
URL: http://www.eifs.com
Founded: 1988. Exterior Insulation and Finish Systems (EIFS) consultants. EIFS is a type of cladding for exterior building walls that provides insulation, weatherproofing and aesthetics in an integrated, composite system.

CODE SOURCE PC
2939 Wilson, Ste. 100
Grandville, MI 49418
Robert Bush, President
TF: (800)200-2633
E-mail: codeman@codesourcepc.com
URL: http://www.codesourcepc.com
Founded: 1993. **Staff:** 300. Full service building code consulting for architects, municipalities, and businesses.

COFFEY-LEE ASSOCIATES, INC.
2425 E. Commercial Blvd., Ste 403
Fort Lauderdale, FL 33308
James P. Lee, Contact
PH: (954)772-0770
FX: (954)772-1036
Founded: 1972. **Staff:** 5. Offers counsel to shelter industry and investors on building projects for planning, zoning, community relations, labor, design review, material specifications, contracts, management, scheduling, and quality control. Clients in construction, investment, building material organizations. Principally active with large scale organizations in the United States.

EDWIN COGERT & ASSOCIATES
16161 Ventura Blvd., #665
Encino, CA 91436
Ed Cogert, Contact
PH: (818)990-1721
FX: (818)906-9926
Founded: 1974. **Staff:** 3. Construction and management consultants. Work with architects, designers and developers and provide conceptual estimate of costs, obtain bids, and build projects. Also offers expert witness and construction litigation consulting services which include investigating and reporting on construction defects and forensic construction, giving testimony in court, and pricing out cost to correct defects, and construction arbitrators. Industries served: architects, designers, decorators, developers, and legal community.

COLBERT, MATZ, ROSENFELT, INC.
2835 Smith Ave. Ste. G
Baltimore, MD 21209
Robert S. Rosenfelt, Vice President
PH: (410)653-3838
FX: (410)653-7953
Founded: 1994. **Staff:** 17. Engineering consulting firm offers planning and zoning for commercial site development projects; planning and zoning for residential land development projects; land surveying services for all types of projects—boundary surveys, certifications, construction stake out services and as-built surveys; and construction and land development construction management services including contracting and coordinating environmental and geotechnical services. Industries served: commercial and residential land development, construction, home building, banks, title companies, and private homeowners. Geographic areas served: Baltimore County, Baltimore City, Anne Arundel County, Howard County, Carroll County, and Harford County—all in Maryland.

COMMAND DATA
2204 Lakeshore Dr., Ste. 206
Birmingham, AL 35209
TF: (800)624-1872
FX: (205)870-1405
Firm offers consulting and expertise in construction materials and equipment.

COMMERCIAL COST CONTROL, INC.
1086 Longwood Dr.
Woodstock, GA 30189
Calvin Boydstun, Partner
PH: (770)924-7811
FX: (770)924-8011
URL: http://www.commercialcostcontrol.com
A construction audit firm dedicated to providing value to clients by

reducing or recovering capital and expense cost items while maintaining sensitivity to the partnership between clients and their vendors. Construction audit services, "cost plus" project audit, "lump sum" project audit, lease audit services, subtenant portfolio audits, utility audit and consultation, bill verification, rate audits, deregulation opportunity assessments, and accounts payable audit services.

COMMERCIAL DEVELOPERS INC.
615 Griswold, Ste. 1220
Detroit, MI 48226-3222
George D. Cutler, President
PH: (313)961-7980
FX: (313)961-7980

COMMUNITY PLANNING, INC.
745 Fort St., Ste. 400
Honolulu, HI 96813-3804
Bernard P. Kea, President
PH: (808)531-4252
FX: (808)526-2476
Founded: 1957. **Staff:** 14. Offers counsel to developers on land and community planning, subdivision layouts and housing developments. Also prepares engineering construction plans and cost estimates; prepares final survey subdivision plans and descriptions; provides land surveys including property stakeout, topographic and construction control surveys; and construction management.

COMPREHENSIVE SERVICES CORP.
10650 Irma Dr., Unit 14
Denver, CO 80233-3626
Dick Memmer, President
PH: (303)457-9033
FX: (303)450-7303

CONCRETE PLANTS INC.
821 W. Benfield Rd., Ste. 7
Severna Park, MD 21146
PH: (410)987-4542
FX: (410)987-3640
Firm provides services in appraisals, construction consulting, designing, and engineering.

CONCRETE SCIENCE
5468 Briar Ridge Dr.
Castro Valley, CA 94552-1709
Ashok Kakade, Consultant
PH: (510)581-2342
FX: (510)581-4178
E-mail: amkakade@concretescience.com
URL: http://www.concretescience.com
Specializes in concrete, masonry and stucco. Consulting in construction practices. Offers failure investigation and repair recommendations.

CONNERLY & ASSOCIATES
Sacramento, CA 95818
Ward Connerly, President
PH: (916)456-4784
FX: (916)456-7672
Founded: 1973. **Staff:** 14. Offers land-use consulting and assistance on building and construction projects throughout California.

CONSTRUCTION CONSULTING SERVICES
53 Cambridge Dr. W.
Copiague, NY 11726-3231
William J. Graf, Founder
PH: (516)842-8497
E-mail: wjgraf@sprynet.com
URL: http://home.sprynet.com/sprynet/wjgraf
Founded: 1990. Construction consulting services. Prepares due diligence reports on real estate properties and engineering; and evaluations of the architectural, structural, mechanical, electrical, plumbing, vertical transportation, and life safety systems of commercial and industrial buildings.

CONSTRUCTION DYNAMICS
1711 E. Gableview St.
Palmdale, CA 93550
Paul C. Womack, Contact
PH: (661)947-9415
FX: (661)947-1803
E-mail: womack@rglobal.net
Founded: 1978. Offers construction management consulting and owner's representative services, including project scheduling, estimating, administration, coordination, and troubleshooting.

CONSTRUCTION ECONOMISTS OF AMERICA, INC.
PO Box 1053
Lewiston, NY 14092
Norman H. Matthews, President
PH: (716)754-7841
FX: (716)754-8524
Founded: 1979. **Staff:** 6. Services include quantity surveying, cost engineering, and mortgage monitoring. Specializes in tender preparations, scrutinizing of extras to contract, and claims preparation and defense. Also provides construction litigation support services, construction cost monitoring, life cycle costing, and valuations for expropriation and taxation. Industries served: commercial, institutional, industrial and environmental construction including airports, hydroelectric plants, refineries, pulp and paper, and steelmaking.

CONSTRUCTION EXPERTS, INC.
PO Box 231832
Encinitas, CA 92023-1832
Robert R. George, President
PH: (760)809-0663
E-mail: info@constructionguy.com
URL: http://www.constructionguy.com
Founded: 1994. Provides consultation, assistance and guidance to construction companies in the process of developing in-house construction training programs for both craft and supervisory workers.

CONSTRUCTION INTERFACE SERVICES, INC.
2 N. Front St.
Wilmington, NC 28401
TF: (888)899-6312
FX: (910)762-4703
URL: http://www.constructor.com
Provides project management consulting services and seminars to services to contractors, attorneys, sureties, lending institutions, owners, and design professionals.

CONSTRUCTION INVESTIGATION CONSULTANTS
2931 NE 39th Ct.
Lighthouse Point, FL 33064
Stanley F. Boor, President and Senior Consultant
PH: (954)783-4771
FX: (954)783-5044
Construction technology specialists, providing legal assistance, evaluation and analysis in reviewing construction documents, drawings and records; reviewing legal documents, depositions and interrogatories; assistance in discovery and production; preparation of questions for interrogatories and depositions; assistance in developing case strategy; participation in negotiations/settlements agreements; preparation of trial exhibits; and expert witness testimony. Specializes in the review and analysis of construction practices and procedures versus applicable building codes and industry standards.

CONSTRUCTION MANAGEMENT CONSOLIDATED INC.
24420 Zermatt
Valencia, CA 91355
PH: (805)254-7370
FX: (805)254-7370
Construction management consultants.

CONSTRUCTION MANAGEMENT RESOURCES (CMR)
448 S. "E" St.
Santa Rosa, CA 95404
Kenji P. Hoshino, Principal

PH: (707)575-4652
FX: (707)575-4710
Offers construction forensic engineering services, including contract claims merit analysis; claims quantum valuation; expert testimony in CPM-scheduling; loss of productivity analysis; litigation document management; construction management software; construction litigation support and consulting; graphic exhibit production; and electronic/computer data audit and production support during discovery.

CONSTRUCTION PERFORMANCE SPECIALISTS, INC.
PO Box 7996
Tyler, TX 75711
Donald F. McDonald, Jr., President
PH: (903)581-0200
FX: (903)581-0393
E-mail: 74003.1406@compuserve.com
Founded: 1987. **Staff:** 5. Construction litigation support consultants to attorneys and contractors. Services include: documentation review and providing of expert testimony regarding construction delay and impact claims. Experts in the use of CPM scheduling and analysis, pricing of impacts, and productivity measurement and analysis. Serves construction industries and contracts, as well as government agencies worldwide.

CONSTRUCTION SERVICE INDUSTRIES
PO Box 566
Mentor, OH 44061
PH: (440)428-7572
E-mail: csiincor@aol.com
URL: http://members.aol.com/csiincor
Provides project scheduling, estimating and general construction consulting services to contractors, architects and owners. These services assist those involved in the construction process to plan, organize and control their projects. Offers the following project scheduling and estimating services: Critical Path Method (CPM) scheduling; pure logic and flow chart scheduling; Project progress updating; resource and man-hour analysis; delay cost analysis; Cost control systems; change order and extra work cost.

CONSTRUCTION TESTING, INC.
925 N. Jerome St.
Allentown, PA 18103
PH: (610)433-6871
FX: (610)433-7594
E-mail: mike@constest.com
URL: http://www.constest.com
Founded: 1991. Specializing in testing and inspection of concrete, soil structural steel, aggregates, concrete masonry units & mortar, structural clay brick, bituminous concrete, and high strength non-shrink grout.

CONSUL-TECH ENGINEERING INC.
3141 Commerce Pky.
Miramar, FL 33025
Andy Garganta, Principal
PH: (954)438-4300
TF: (888)438-4308
FX: (954)438-1433
E-mail: corp@consul-t.com
URL: http://www.consul-t.com
Founded: 1982. **Staff:** 135. Consulting engineering firm specializes in civil engineering, environmental and wetland permitting, land planning, land surveying, transportation engineering, construction management, and forensic engineering.

THE CONSULTANTS GROUP
Columbia, SC
PH: (803)732-6100
FX: (803)732-6100
E-mail: Mamacher@worldnet.att.net
URL: http://www.stuccosystems.com
Offers buyers involved in the construction of their new home or office the service of on site consulting (Third party monitoring). Provides project management. Creates report furnished with the text and

photographic documentation of construction process to illustrate client's buildings compliance or non-compliance with building codes.

CONSULTANTS RESOURCE GROUP, INC.
7520 W. Waters Ave., Ste. 16
Tampa, FL 33615
Edward H. Hicks, President
PH: (813)888-6341
FX: (813)888-7389
URL: http://mobilehomepark.com
Founded: 1980. Serves the manufactured housing land development industry and offers expertise in area market surveys, competitive analysis, manufacturer liaison, project feasibility, loan packaging, business plans, marketing plans, sales training, zoning and land use approvals. Firm also offers mortgage brokerage services for conventional development loans, permanent loan income property financing and FHA 207(m) land lease community approvals. Personnel placement and recruitment also available for M/H industry.

CONTINENTAL PLACER INC.
216 Computer Dr., W.
Albany, NY 12205
John Helhert, President
PH: (518)458-9203
FX: (518)458-9206
E-mail: cpigold@aol.com
Founded: 1988. **Staff:** 25. Firm provides expertise in geology, mining, mine planning, environmental permitting, groundwater supply, remediation, computer modeling, and environmental site assessments.

COOLEX TECHNOLOGIES INTERNATIONAL INC.
PO Box 395
Greenbelt, MD 20768-0395
Oyedemi C. Oluokun, President/CEO
PH: (301)982-9224
FX: (301)982-9727
Founded: 1986. **Staff:** 12. Provides consulting engineering services in traffic engineering, transportation engineering, environmental studies, architectural services, and traffic impact analysis. Also performs construction management services including construction inspection and training of construction inspectors. Works for industrialists, individuals, institutions, local, state and federal government agencies. Geographic areas served: U.S.

R. G. COPPINGER & ASSOCIATES
1429 New Cir. Rd. NE
Lexington, KY 40509-1019
R.G. Coppinger, Owner
PH: (606)269-5534
FX: (606)266-1533
Founded: 1970. **Staff:** 11. Construction management consulting firm.

CORPORATE FACILITY SERVICES
9 Daffodil Ln.
San Carlos, CA 94070-1552
David Bourland, Principal
PH: (650)610-9111
FX: (650)610-9119
URL: http://www.corpfacserv.com
Founded: 1993. An outsource facilities department providing project management services for construction, furniture and relocation projects in Silicon Valley and the San Francisco Bay Area. The principal services provided include planning and budgeting; assessing current and future facility requirements; exploring and analyzing logical approaches; articulating objectives on behalf of management; directing the conceptual design process developing budget estimates documenting plans for evaluation by management.

CORROSION AND MATERIALS TECHNOLOGY, INC.
23 Manchester Dr.
Westfield, NJ 07090-2255
W.J. Neill, Jr., President

PH: (908)233-3509
FX: (908)233-8966
Founded: 1986. **Staff:** 1. Corrosion and materials engineering consultant to the petroleum refining and chemical industries, as well as others. Certified by NACE International as a Corrosion Specialist. Past Chairman of American Petroleum Institute (API), Manufacturing, Contractors, and Designers Subcommittee on Corrosion and Materials. Assists with the selection of materials of construction and corrosion allowances for maintenance and new construction, development of appropriate follow-up on nondestructive examination (ultrasonic thickness, ultrasonic flaw detection, wet fluorescent magnetic particle, radiography) of pressure vessels, heat exchangers, piping, de-aerators, and tanks. Works with world-class metallurgical laboratory on failure analysis and rapid development of cost effective solutions. Extensive working knowledge of ASME Boiler and Pressure Vessel Code (material requirements, Code Stamp Quality Control Manual, Code Stamp Applications and Renewals, Welding Procedure Specifications, Tests, and Welder Performance Tests). Extensive working knowledge of the National Board Inspection Code including "R" stamp applications and renewals. Extensive working knowledge of API 510, pressure vessel inspection code, API 570, piping inspection code, and API 653, tank inspection, repair, alteration, and reconstruction. Follow-up of jurisdictional requirements on boilers and pressure vessels; market exploration studies; market development studies; investigating committee review of plant problems; and expert witness services. Industries served: petroleum refining and marketing, petrochemical, alloy steels and others.

CORSER & ASSOCIATES, INC.
34184-B Pacific Coast Hwy., Ste. 223
Dana Point, CA 92629-2889
Samuel Corser Gale, President
PH: (714)493-3823
FX: (714)493-4489
E-mail: CORSER@atsroof-rite-way.com
URL: http://www.roof-rite-way.com
Provides forensic roofing/waterproofing expert witness services, including discovery of commercial/industrial/residential building construction defects.

CORTEZ, INC.
700 Roper Pky.
PO Box 25
Ocoee, FL 34761
Paul Robertson, Contact
PH: (407)656-4397
TF: (800)477-1589
FX: (407)656-4557
Founded: 1973. **Staff:** 9. Serves beverage processing concerns in the areas of construction management; custom design, fabrication, and installation; packaging support; and single source turnkey projects.

COSMOPOLITAN CHAMBER OF COMMERCE
1326 S. Michigan Ave.
Chicago, IL 60605
Consuelo M. Pope, President/CEO
PH: (312)786-0212
TF: (877)786-0212
FX: (312)786-9079
E-mail: cchamber@aol.com
URL: http://www.cchamber.org
Founded: 1933. **Staff:** 6. Consulting, education and training in Electronic Commerce. Consults to major corporations, general contractors, government entities, municipal agencies, and participants in the construction industry on the use of minority businesses.

**COST, PLANNING, AND MANAGEMENT
   INTERNATIONAL, INC.**
100 E. Grand, Ste. 280
Des Moines, IA 50309
Richard Janssen, President & Treasurer

PH: (515)244-1166
TF: (800)247-CPMI
FX: (515)244-5040
E-mail: pamadeo@cpmi.com
Founded: 1970. **Staff:** 50. Offers construction management services, owner's representation, development, facility programming and planning, cost management, schedule management, and construction claims management. Serves public and quasi-public clients as well as government agencies.

COX ASSOCIATES
2901 Curry Ford Rd.
Orlando, FL 32806-5824
Bud Reeger, President
PH: (407)896-4341
FX: (407)896-2238
E-mail: coxassoc96@aol.com
Founded: 1957. **Staff:** 15. Architectural consultants provide roofing services to contractors and government agencies in the U.S.

CRD CAMPBELL, INC.
One Campbell Plaza
59th & Arsenal
St. Louis, MO 63139-1764
Kenneth E. Chandler, PE, Chairman and CEO
PH: (314)781-2004
FX: (314)781-0037
Founded: 1992. **Staff:** 50. A professional services organization of engineers, architects, planners, and construction managers that specializes in air and surface transportation, which include roads, highways, bridges, railroads, parking structures and airport facilities. Airfield facilities include terminals, runways, taxiways, aprons, aircraft hangars and maintenance facilities. Firm also officers quality control/quality assurance inspection, materials testing, and construction management services, as well as program management and design services for infrastructure, industrial, healthcare, and municipal building projects.

CREAK MOSKAL & ASSOCIATES INC.
104 Parkview Dr.
Louisville, KY 40245
Ronald E. Creak, President
PH: (502)241-2774
FX: (502)243-0907
Founded: 1991. **Staff:** 3. Firm provides consulting services in the field of vertical transportation. Offers litigation support services, including expert witness testimony to attorneys involved in litigation arising from personal injury accidents which occur on vertical transportation equipment. Consulting services also provided to architects, general contractors, developers, and building owners for preparation of specifications, maintenance audits, construction management, final inspection, and traffic analysis.

CREATIVE RESOURCE MANAGEMENT
835 18th Ave.
Salt Lake City, UT 84103
Frieda A. McCoy, Contact
PH: (801)328-8986
FX: (801)575-8314
Founded: 1982. **Staff:** 4. Provides consulting assistance in all phases of program management from planning and design, through implementation and operations. These services encompass: project management, scheduling, contracts management, information management, configuration management, planning and organizational management, and quality assurance documentation control. Industries served: construction, utilities, nuclear and energy industries; and financial institutions.

CRITERIUM-HARE ENGINEERS
8637 Cherry Ln., Ste. B
Laurel, MD 20707
Victor Hare, President

PH: (301)953-1711
FX: (301)490-5993
E-mail: vhare@criterium-hare.com
URL: http://criterium-hare.com
Founded: 1983. **Staff:** 3. Engineering consulting firm offering services in the following areas: general civil engineering, structural repair designs, construction inspection, supervision, inspection reports, underwater inspections, commercial buildings, and condominiums; structural consulting, swimming pools, tennis courts and recreational areas. Also provides expert court testimony.

CRSS INC.
1177 W. Loop S, Ste. 900
Houston, TX 77027
William Utt, President
PH: (713)552-2000
FX: (713)552-2416
Founded: 1946. **Staff:** 2200. Large engineering/architecture design company active in the independent power/cogeneration industry. Serves private industries as well as government agencies.

CS2 DESIGN GROUP, LLC
837 Oakton St.
Elk Grove Village, IL 60007
PH: (847)981-1880
FX: (847)981-1885
E-mail: info@cs2designgroup.com
URL: http://www.cs2designgroup.com
A consulting engineering company licensed to practice mechanical and electrical systems design for buildings. Scope of services include construction documents for bidding, field construction administration, health/life/safety reports, permit acquisitions, and building system studies and reports.

CTL ENGINEERING, INC.
2860 Fisher Rd.
Columbus, OH 43204
C.K. Satyapriya, P.E., President
PH: (614)276-8123
TF: (800)229-8123
FX: (614)276-6377
E-mail: ctl@ctleng.com
URL: http://www.ctleng.com
Founded: 1927. **Staff:** 200. Offers consulting engineering, independent laboratory testing and independent inspection services. Areas of expertise involve energy, chemical, pulp and paper, transportation and construction. Clients include manufacturers, architects, government agencies, contractors, insurance companies, attorneys, engineering firms, developers, and private individuals.

LEO A. DALY
8600 Indian Hills Dr.
Omaha, NE 68114
S.L. Condit, Senior Vice President
PH: (402)391-8111
FX: (402)391-8564
URL: http://www.leoadaly.com
Founded: 1915. **Staff:** 750. Full architectural, engineering, planning, interiors and construction services including program/project management for institutional, commercial and governmental clients. Project types include hotels, office buildings, educational facilities, laboratories, high-tech industrial facilities, government and military buildings, recreational facilities, healthcare facilities, air transportation terminals and support facilities, retail and distribution facilities, land use and specific site master plans, financial and banking facilities, and religious structures. Also offers expertise in water supply, treatment and distribution, waste water treatment; environmental engineering; infrastructure engineering; power generation and distribution.

DANIEL, MANN, JOHNSON, & MENDENHALL
3250 Wilshire Blvd.
Los Angeles, CA 90010
Raymond W. Holdsworth, President/CEO

PH: (213)381-3663
FX: (213)383-3656
URL: http://www.jmjm.com
Founded: 1946. **Staff:** 1500. Large, international architectural and engineering consulting firm. Provides professional consulting services to both public and private clients. Since its founding, DMJM has successfully executed a broad variety of assignments exceeding $30 billion in construction costs. Much of this work has been directed toward meeting the many requirements of commercial, industrial, institutional, and governmental clients within the United States and overseas. Many of these projects have received international recognition for their innovative, functional, and aesthetically pleasing solutions to complex, one-of-a-kind problems. Specific areas of activity include architecture, planning (urban, regional), transportation, public works, industrial and defense, energy, and management services.

DARCON INC.
300 Scarlet Blvd.
PO Box 1579
Oldsmar, FL 34677
James Crane, President
PH: (813)855-8993
FX: (813)855-7860
Engineering and construction consulting firm.

DASILVA & ASSOCIATES
37 W. 28th St. 5th Fl.
New York, NY 10001
Peter N. DaSilva, President
PH: (212)889-1840
FX: (212)696-1986
E-mail: dsaarch@aol.com
Founded: 1977. **Staff:** 16. An architectural and planning firm, specializing in health facility consultation. Services range from program needs, costs and scheduling analysis; through long-range plans, programming, design and construction administration; to interior design, medical equipment selection and specification. Activities include consultation on reuse, retrofit and reconfiguration of existing plants. Serves private industries as well as government agencies

STEPHEN M. DAVIS, ARCHITECTS-PLANNERS
8055 SW 92nd St.
Miami, FL 33156
Stephen M. Davis, Contact
PH: (305)279-9300
FX: (305)279-9480
Founded: 1963. **Staff:** 3. Architectural consultants offering services in site planning, industrial plant layout, energy management, and construction management.

WILLIAM R. DAWSON
1502C Walnut St.
Berkeley, CA 94709
PH: (510)549-3241
FX: (510)549-1066
Specializes in structural engineer building and bridge structures, including structural design and review, structural specifications, construction administration, inspection, errors and omissions, industry standards, and failure analysis.

DB FLETT & ASSOCIATES
1655 N. Main St., Ste. 310
Walnut Creek, CA 94596
Douglas Flett, Principal
PH: (510)935-7710
FX: (510)935-7763
Civil engineering services in land development, drainage and flood control, surveying, construction, and errors and omissions. Investigates design and construction deficiencies. Offers litigation support and expert testimony in professional negligence; dispute resolution and claims; and boundary and easements cases.

DE LEUW, CATHER & CO.
1133 15th St. NW, Ste. 800
Washington, DC 20005-2701
R.S. O'Neil, President
PH: (202)775-3300
FX: (202)775-3422
Founded: 1919. **Staff:** 1100. Provides services in the planning, design and construction management of highways, public transportation facilities, railroads, ports and harbors, bridges, tunnels and transit maintenance facilities. Also offers a complete range of engineering management services in planning, developing and implementing operations and maintenance management systems and training programs. Industries served: public and private sectors: highways, railroads, public transportation, and infrastructure.

DEL VALLE CONSULTING
11768 Tammy Way
Grass Valley, CA 95949
John D. Payne, President
PH: (916)272-2500
FX: (916)272-8647
E-mail: jdpayne@oro.net
Specializes in concrete design and construction. Provides post-tension investigations, construction cost estimates, and building topographic plans and surface models.

DELTEX CORP.
PO Box 1769
Stockton, CA 95201
Herman Miller, President
PH: (209)948-3111
FX: (209)933-0307
E-mail: mill@gotnet.net
Founded: 1970. **Staff:** 1. Provides construction project management contract, resident engineering, and construction inspection services. Industries served: government agencies, public works, including wastewater, treatment plants and power plants.

DESCO DEVELOPMENT
3675 Mount Diablo Blvd., Ste. 270
Lafayette, CA 94549
Louis L. Rozenfeld, Contact
PH: (510)283-8470
FX: (510)283-9671
E-mail: focus@value.net
Founded: 1975. **Staff:** 17. Construction management consultants.

DEVELOPERS LAND CONSTRUCTION COORDINATION
3220 Corporate Ct., Ste. A
Ellicott City, MD 21042
John Stevens, Secretary/Treasurer
PH: (410)480-9810
FX: (410)480-9813
Founded: 1991. Firm is committed to managing the construction activities that produce the necessary public facilities in proposed communities. Services can include: on-site supervision; review of all construction drawings for cost effectiveness, construction ease and compliance to existing codes, specifications and techniques; creation of construction budgets; collection of subcontractor bids, negotiation of prices, and establishment of contracts to obtain maximum value; coordination of all contracts, scheduling of all subcontractors to realize timely completion and potential savings; communication with engineers and government agencies to streamline and consolidate the completion of infrastructure; and quality control. Also provides dedication services and bond reduction programs. Industries served: development community and homebuilding industry.

DEVELOPMENT CONSULTANTS GROUP, INC.
3305 Breckinridge Blvd., Ste. 102
Duluth, GA 30096
J. Dennis Billew, President

PH: (770)279-1710
FX: (770)921-9426
E-mail: ps@dcginc.net
URL: http://www.dcginc.net
Founded: 1985. **Staff:** 25. A full service consulting firm offering land planning and engineering expertise from project conception to completion. Services include pre-purchase site research and feasibility studies; rezoning applications and presentations; zoning variance assistance; land planning; boundary and topographic surveying; civil engineering design; pre-construction assistance; construction monitoring; construction staking; record drawing; and plats. Capabilities include planning and engineering of roadways and streets, water and sewer systems, site grading, erosion control facilities, and storm water management systems for low, medium, and high density residential projects, office and commercial parks, individual commercial and office sites, and public sector projects. Special areas of expertise include river corridor reviews, floodplain management, wetlands delineation and engineering services, urban drainage/storm water management consulting, lake and dam analysis and design, and erosion control facilities design. Serves private industries as well as government agencies.

DEWBERRY DESIGN GROUP INC.
119 N. Robinson, Ste. 700
Oklahoma City, OK 73102
Ken Wilkinson, COO
PH: (405)239-4700
FX: (405)239-4750
Founded: 1942. **Staff:** 200. Offers architectural, engineering, planning, interior design and landscape architectural consulting services. Also provides related construction management services, graphic and signage design as well as energy conservation planning.

DHILLON ENGINEERING, INC.
11400 Cronridge Dr., Ste. D
Owings Mills, MD 21117
Gurmeet S. Dhillon, President
PH: (410)356-1095
FX: (410)363-4675
Founded: 1985. **Staff:** 20. Offers services in civil, structural, electrical, and mechanical engineering for design of roads, bridges, drainage and marine structures, and water supply and sewage systems. Designs commercial and residential buildings and investigates and renovates existing ones. Prepares preliminary reports, construction documents, cost estimate and specifications, and provides construction management.

VINOD H. DHOLAKIA—ARCHITECT
89-06 120th St.
Richmond Hill, NY 11418-3211
Vinod H. Dholakia, President
PH: (718)847-6208
Founded: 1986. **Staff:** 3. Architect and interior designer of residential, commercial (stores, offices and restaurants) and industrial buildings and spaces including: zoning analysis and code compliance, space planning, lighting design, graphic design and furniture and furnishings selections. Active in new and renovation/conversion projects costing from $5,000 to $50,000,000. Industries served: home owners, businesses, real estate investors and developers, retail corporations, and government agencies. Architect work limited to the states of New York and New Jersey. All other work anywhere in the United States and Canada.

D'HUY ENGINEERING, INC.
453 Main St.
Bethlehem, PA 18018
Gerard D'Huy, President
PH: (610)865-3000
FX: (610)861-0181
E-mail: dei@early.com
Founded: 1976. **Staff:** 15. Structural design, project management and forensic engineering firm. A specialty is the analysis of structural failures. Firm performs structural design and analysis; building evaluation and retrofit design; furnace, preheater and process struc-

ture design; project management; facilities engineering; forensic engineering and failure analysis; facade investigation and repair.

JOHN DICKERMAN AND ASSOCIATES
9030 Bronson Dr.
Potomac, MD 20854
John M. Dickerman, Contact
PH: (301)983-2547
Founded: 1964. **Staff:** 3. Specializes in construction, real estate and housing; marketing of manufactured building materials and products; financing of homes, apartments, and related community elements. Involved in Federal government programs in housing and urban affairs. The firm has done numerous corporate acquisition and investment analyses, management studies, and executive search assignments in the field of building and manufacturing.

DIGITAL ENGINEERING CORP.
9841 Broken Land Pky. Ste. 106
Columbia, MD 21046
Jack Hedjazi, President
PH: (410)290-5244
FX: (410)290-5246
E-mail: info@digitalcorp.com
URL: http://www.digitalcorp.com
Founded: 1986. **Staff:** 12. Services include civil engineering, GPS Survey, land planning, environmental issues, and construction management. Additional services include: digital mapping expertise, GIS and computer hardware, as well as software assistance. Industries served: utilities, local, state and federal government.

DKI GROUP ENGINEERS, INC. (WORLD H.Q.)
One Van Patten Dr.
Clifton Park, NY 12065
D.K. Gupta, P.E., President
PH: (518)877-8000
FX: (518)877-8001
E-mail: dkil23@aol.com
URL: http://www.dkiUSA.com
Founded: 1978. Consulting engineers specializing in environmental, energy, transportation, planning, construction management, hazardous and toxic wastes management, and energy management. Also offers expertise in areas of railroads/mass transit, airports, bridges, highways, signals/communications, and railroads/transits/airports, and tunnels. Serves federal, state, and municipal governments and the private sector worldwide.

DL ENGINEERING
8180 Lakeview Ctr.
Odessa, TX 79765
Don Lawrence, Contact
PH: (915)563-0033
TF: (800)725-7250
FX: (915)563-0088
E-mail: dleng@aol.com
Staff: 6. Firm's basic industrial plant professional engineering services include process, civil/structural, electrical, control systems, instrumentation, and project management. Has experience in plant design, construction, start-up, and operations of large and small industrial projects from grass roots to completed plants. Employs the latest state-of-the-art computer-aided engineering, design, drafting, and office automation systems. Industries served: petrochemical, refining, power generation, power distribution (electrical), and commercial building in the Southwest.

DLR GROUP
400 Essex Ct.
Omaha, NE 68114
Bryce Pearsall, Contact
PH: (402)393-4100
FX: (402)393-8747
Founded: 1966. Provides professional architectural and building engineering consulting services to private industry, federal, state and local governmental agencies, schools, municipalities and developers.

F.W. DODGE MARKET ANALYSIS GROUP
24 Hartwell Ave.
Lexington, MA 02173
TF: (800)591-4462
FX: (617)860-6884
E-mail: info@mcgraw-hill.com
URL: http://www.mag.fwdodge.com
Serves the information needs of the construction, financial, and real estate industries by providing historical and forecast information, market demand indicators, and custom market studies, tailored and customized to meet specific market needs.

DONNELL CONSULTANTS INC., THEATRE CONSTRUCTION PROJECT AND COST MANAGEMENT
One North Dale Mabry, Ste. 1040
Tampa, FL 33609
Athol Joffe, Contact
PH: (813)875-8074
FX: (813)878-2963
E-mail: dci1040@aol.com
Founded: 1986. **Staff:** 14. Advises on comprehensive capital costs for performing arts centers. Conducts feasibility studies; program analysis and budgeting; cost control; project and design team management.

DORGAN ASSOCIATES, INC.
7601 Ganser Way
Madison, WI 53719-1227
Charles E. Dorgan, Secretary/Treasurer
PH: (608)827-6880
FX: (608)827-6886
E-mail: dai@dorganai.com
Founded: 1984. **Staff:** 7. Engineering design, applied and developmental research services to local, national and international clients. Development and application of emerging technologies including thermal energy storage, cold air distribution, building commissioning process, and dual path air-conditioning systems. The firm recently completed the second phase of research to link and quantify the productivity benefits of maintaining good indoor air quality in commercial and institutional buildings. Provides research and testing of HVAC equipment and systems, and expert witness and accident investigation of HVAC systems, gas combustion equipment, and controls.

CHARLES E. & JOAN MARIE DORGAN ENGINEERING & EDUCATION CONSULTANTS
305 Valley View St.
Verona, WI 53593-1535
PH: (608)845-7483
FX: (608)845-5599
E-mail: cedorgan@atsfacstaff.wisc.edu
Engineering consultants specializing in HVAC and R in schools, offices, industrial facilities, supermarkets, and residential homes. Concerned with patents, product liability, design, installation, fire, VAV, controls, thermal storage, roofs, envelopes and tax issues. Also involved in indoor air quality: design and installation in schools, government, office, jails, and residential buildings; and product liability of agricultural machinery, controls, gas and electric appliances, printing and other presses, construction.

DOW GEOLOGICAL SERVICES, INC.
5735 SW Urish Rd.
Topeka, KS 66610
Verne E. Dow, President
PH: (913)478-4952
FX: (913)478-4070
Founded: 1983. **Staff:** 2. Consultant in oil and gas exploration, development and evaluation; construction materials; exploration, development, and evaluation; and environmental geology as related to hydrogeology and groundwater pollution (hydrocarbon pollution and remedial solutions). Industries served: oil and gas, construction aggregates, and government agencies.

DOWL ENGINEERS
4040 B St.
Anchorage, AK 99503
Melvin R. Nichols, Contact
PH: (907)562-2000
FX: (907)563-3953
Founded: 1962. **Staff:** 50. Provides services in the areas of: planning, landscape architecture, surveying and mapping, geology and geotechnical engineering, civil design, environmental services, construction administration, materials testing, and computer science. Clients include architects and construction contractors; private developers; military and other government agencies; and commercial concerns in Alaska and Pacific Northwest.

DRAPER & ASSOCIATES
6520 Powers Ferry Rd., Ste. 225
Atlanta, GA 30339
PH: (404)256-3601
FX: (404)256-3922
URL: http://www.draperandassociates.com
Provides construction project management services. The firm has managed projects ranging from single facility renovations to billion-dollar multi-project environments.

DRAWINGBOARD INFORMATION SYSTEMS INC.
16730 Northview Cres.
Surrey, BC, Canada V4P 2W1
PH: (604)241-9816
FX: (604)241-9817
E-mail: info@dwg.com
URL: http://www.dwg.com/
Provides links to associations, consultants, building products, office equipment, and information resources of interest to the design and construction industries.

DRENSE, INC.
10101 Southwest Fwy., Ste. 650
Houston, TX 77074
PH: (713)771-8877
URL: http://www.compassnet.com/drenond
Provides management and consulting services in all phases of environmental projects including initial site assessments, construction, remediation, and site closure.

DURRANT GROUP INC.
942 Cycare Plaza
Dubuque, IA 52004-0509
Gordon E. Mills, AIA, Vice President & Secy/Treas.
PH: (319)583-9131
FX: (319)557-9078
E-mail: cmarsden@durrant.com
URL: http://www.durrant.com
Founded: 1933. **Staff:** 250. Offers architectural, engineering and construction management services. Expertise includes space planning, programming and master planning, architecture, energy management, power distribution, systems/energy evaluation, cost and schedule management, and project management and financing. Serves private industry as well as government agencies.

E-B-L ENGINEERS, INC.
The Professional Engineering Center
8005 Harford Rd.
Baltimore, MD 21234
Moritz Bukowitz, Chairman of the Board
PH: (410)668-8000
FX: (410)668-8001
E-mail: ebl@eblengineers.com
URL: http://www.eblengineers.com
Founded: 1972. **Staff:** 42. Offers mechanical, electrical, and fire protection engineering consulting services for commercial, governmental agencies, industrial and institutional buildings. These services include surveys and reports, feasibility studies and preparation of plans and specifications for new construction and renovation pro-

jects, including code compliance consultation and fire/life safety analysis. Geographic areas served: primarily Mid-Atlantic region.

EAGLE ENTERPRISES
26200 W. 108th St.
Olathe, KS 66061
Charles L. Huston, President
PH: (913)829-5099
FX: (913)829-5099
E-mail: hustoncl@aol.com
Involved in the evaluation of construction and engineering project management, licensing, procurement, and testing management. Provides damage calculations of management deficiencies including schedule impact.

EAPC ARCHITECTS ENGINEERS
3100 DeMers Ave.
Grand Forks, ND 58201
Ray Engen, President
PH: (701)775-5507
TF: (888)303-3272
FX: (701)772-3605
E-mail: eapc@corpcomm.net
Founded: 1967. **Staff:** 59. Active in land use planning, architecture, civil engineering, structural engineering, mechanical engineering, electrical engineering, industrial engineering, forensic engineering, and construction management, including design/build. Serves clients in the following industries: construction, energy, healthcare, education and food processing.

EARTH ARCHITECTURE CENTER INTERNATIONAL
5928 Guadalupe Trail, NW
Albuquerque, NM 87107
Paul G. McHenry, Jr., AIA, Managing Director
PH: (505)345-2613
FX: (505)345-2613
E-mail: mchenry@unm.edu
Staff: 3. Offers customized research on earth building architecture (abode, dammed earth) and related topics using in-house database of 1300 annotated references and file of more than 10,000 photos. Currently assembling roster of organizations associated with earth building worldwide.

EARTH TECHNOLOGY CORP. (USA)
100 W. Broadway, Ste. 5000
Long Beach, CA 90802
Diane Creel, President/CEO
PH: (562)495-4449
TF: (800)688-9828
FX: (562)495-2825
Founded: 1970. **Staff:** 2000. International provider of total water management, engineering and construction, transportation, and environmental services and remediation for government and industry. Provides contract operations and design/build/finance/operate services for public and private water supply and wastewater treatment systems, as well as traditional engineering, design, and planning services for water/wastewater management. Also provides environmental, engineering, and construction services for transportation systems. Provides a full range of engineering, design/build, and construction management services for the rehabilitation, relocation, and new construction of various facility types including manufacturing operations, universities, hospitals, and municipal and federal facilities. Services include chemical/process engineering, and architecture and interior design. The firm's environmental services and remediation division offers the full spectrum of environmental and remediation services, from site assessment/investigation to remedial design and cleanup. Its services include remediation design and construction, facility decontamination and demolition, strategic environmental management, brownfield redevelopment, air quality consulting and engineering, and resource management and planning.

EARTHQUAKE AND STRUCTURES, INC.

6355 Telegraph Ave., Ste. 101
Oakland, CA 94609
B.K. Paul, Principal
PH: (510)601-1065
FX: (510)601-1808
Provides structural engineering consulting. Offers structural analysis and design of residential, commercial, industrial, institutional, recreational and community facilities; independent design review, report and expert witness testimony; failure investigations, analysis and modification design; foundation, retaining wall and drainage failure analysis and design; structural assessment and upgrading of existing structures including masonry buildings; seismic retrofit and bracing of masonry, concrete, steel and wood structures; and civil engineering, construction management and feasibility studies.

EAST HILL GROUP

67 Spring Ln.
Englewood, NJ 07631
Rolf Hoexter, Contact
PH: (201)567-2720
FX: (201)567-6968
E-mail: 74024.3124@compuserve.com
Founded: 1985. **Staff:** 2. Organization of engineering and organizational development consultants who focus on increasing profitability by improving customer satisfaction and increasing product/service quality. Areas of expertise include the following: manufacturing methods and cost reduction; manufacturing control systems; product design; business systems for such operations as cost collection, order entry, and others; machinery selection and installation; quality control systems; plant layout; construction management; microcomputer applications; and management and supervisory training and development. Industries served: for engineering and methods improvement consulting: graphic arts machinery and equipment, precision machinery building, aerospace component and parts manufacturing, facilities planning and construction; for total quality management consulting: most manufacturing and service industries.

EBC INDUSTRIES, INC.

1830 E. Joppa Rd.
Baltimore, MD 21234-2735
Altan Kemahli, President
PH: (410)882-9444
FX: (410)882-9554
Founded: 1973. **Staff:** 6. Offers architectural, structural design, and construction management consulting.

ECOLOGY AND ENVIRONMENT, INC.

Buffalo Corporate Center
368 Pleasant View Dr.
Lancaster, NY 14086-1397
Gerhard J. Neumaier, President
PH: (716)684-8060
FX: (716)684-0844
E-mail: nrs02@ene.com
Founded: 1970. **Staff:** 800. A firm of international specialists on environmental issues with over 75 individual disciplines represented on its full-time professional staff. The company provides hazardous, solid, medical, and nuclear waste remedial investigations, feasibility studies, and mitigative action management; environmental engineering design, planning and construction management; compliance audits; environmental impact assessments; hazardous materials management and emergency spill response; hazards and risk analysis; air and water quality analyses and pollution control engineering; hydrogeological studies; occupational health and industrial hygiene studies; socioeconomic studies; archaeological and cultural resources analyses; and related environmental work. Macroenvironmental emphasis is on global warming, ozone depletion, acid precipitation, and deforestation. The firm's certified Analytical Services Center provides complete chemical analytical laboratory services and is equipped to perform sampling and field monitoring programs in air, water, soil, groundwater and noise pollution abatement. Serves private industries as well as government agencies.

EDGE GROUP, CONSULTANTS, PLANNERS & ARCHITECTS

444 Bunker Rd.
West Palm Beach, FL 33405
Donald R. Edge, President
PH: (561)585-9307
FX: (561)585-9628
Founded: 1960. **Staff:** 4. Offers consulting and planning services for the design, construction, and correction of buildings. Specializes in healthcare facilities; planning, programming and design of healthcare facilities of any type, and safety correction and remodeling of healthcare facilities. Industries served: government agencies, hospitals, psychiatric hospitals, medical offices, clinics, nursing homes, and long-term care facilities.

EI ASSOCIATES

115 Evergreen Pl.
East Orange, NJ 07018
Peter A. Cipriano, President
PH: (201)672-5100
FX: (201)672-1784
E-mail: eia@superlink.net
Founded: 1944. **Staff:** 210. Offers architectural, engineering, and construction services to all industries, government agencies, and educational institutions.

ELECTRACK—A DIVISION OF HEERY INTERNATIONAL, INC.

Metro-plex II
8201 Corporate Dr., Ste. 800
Landover, MD 20785
Don McAlpine, Vice President
PH: (301)306-0118
FX: (301)577-9472
Founded: 1972. **Staff:** 165. Firm offers complete design and construction services to transportation authorities. Provides expertise in the planning, design, and construction of light rail, monorail, trolley bus, and mainline rail systems, including high-speed rail. Focuses on the design and construction management of electrification systems, including traction power, operational simulations, catenary, third rail, and people mover systems.

EME, INC.

903 Commerce Dr.
Oak Brook, IL 60521
Ken Yoshitani, President
PH: (630)990-0470
FX: (630)990-0474
Founded: 1979. **Staff:** 22. Provides engineering/design/construction support services for facility engineering projects. Emphasis is on energy conservation and management. Industries served: industrials, institutions (educational, hospitals), commercial, and government in metropolitan Chicago area.

ENERGY ENVIRONMENTAL RESEARCH CORP.

18 Mason St.
Irvine, CA 92618
Dr. Thomas Tyson, Chairman/President
PH: (714)859-8851
TF: (800)500-4337
FX: (714)859-3194
Founded: 1977. **Staff:** 120. Specializes in application of high-technology solutions to practical problems in the area of energy and environmental engineering. Provides research and development, systems design and evaluation, regulatory support and development, product development, and engineering construction services to public and private sectors. Historically, EER has specialized in development of combustion control systems to minimize air pollutant emissions from fossil fuel-fired boilers. That continues as a large business area for EER through programs such as the Clean Coal Technology Program, which is sponsored by federal and state governments, as well as private industry. Firm is also considered a leader in the incineration/thermal treatment of both municipal and hazardous waste. Included in its skills are combustion process specification en-

gineering analysis, process evaluations system specification and analysis, process evaluation system specification, and permit assistance. Industries served: chemical, petrochemical, air pollution control, electric power, government, and natural gas.

ENERGY RELATED PROJECTS, INC.
3647 Pallos Verdas Dr.
Dallas, TX 75229
Jaime Urrea, President
PH: (214)353-9761
FX: (214)353-9765
E-mail: erp@metronet.com
URL: http://www.metronet.com/~erp/
Founded: 1993. **Staff:** 4. Firm assists in the optimization of heating, ventilation, and air conditioning (HVAC) systems. Serves hospitals, retail and industrial businesses, office buildings, and hotels worldwide. Specializes in turnkey chiller replacements that offer the best possible return on investment.

ENGINEERING & CONSTRUCTION SERVICES INC.
3275 Progress Dr., Ste. 2A
Orlando, FL 32826
M.J. Parker, President
PH: (407)438-1987
TF: (800)642-7722
FX: (407)823-8299
Founded: 1990. **Staff:** 23. Firm offers engineering and construction management services. Industries served: government, transportation, and insurance.

ENGINEERING DESIGN CORP.
5150 SW Griffith Dr.
Beaverton, OR 97005
Shantu Shah, Pres.
PH: (503)644-0883
TF: (800)EDI-SHAH
FX: (503)626-2622
Founded: 1985. Provides engineering design services, specializing in UPS (uninterruptible power systems) for commercial and industrial facilities. Also offers equipment and materials selection, construction management and documents, testing and power-up, and safety and operations training.

ENGINEERING MANAGEMENT CONSULTANTS
PO Box 1087
El Granada, CA 94018-1087
G.M. Quraishi, President
PH: (415)726-2088
FX: (415)726-0230
Founded: 1975. **Staff:** 20. A team of architects, engineers, consultants and constructors who have worked on major United States and international projects. Experienced in electrical design and construction of generation, transmission and distribution systems for industrial, commercial and institutional facilities including nuclear/fossil power plants. Expert in PERT/CPM planning and scheduling, responsible for developing and implementing quality assurance, control and inspection programs for major projects. Active in design of defense projects, hospitals, schools, computer facilities, high rises, cogeneration and sewage plant projects, energy conservation and power systems studies. Related experience in program/project management, engineering/construction management, and procurement.

ENGINEERS INTERNATIONAL, INC.
98 E. Naperville Rd., Ste. 201
Westmont, IL 60559
Madan M. Singh, President
PH: (630)963-3444
FX: (630)963-3433
Founded: 1975. **Staff:** 35. Provides engineering and research services to industry and government, in the fields of civil/military construction, and in minerals, energy, mining, environmental and materials testing fields.

ENSIGN ENGINEERING
3272 Tierney Pl.
Bronx, NY 10465
Regina Gallagher Marengo, President
PH: (718)792-2271
FX: (718)792-2271
E-mail: eepc@ensignengineering.com
URL: http://www.ensignengineering.com
Founded: 1993.

ENTECH, ENGINEERS, INC.
1356 E. Edinger Ave.
Santa Ana, CA 92705
Jay Sehgal, President
PH: (714)836-1013
FX: (714)836-0687
Founded: 1979. **Staff:** 31. A firm of multidisciplined consulting engineers. Expertise includes preparation of feasibility studies, planning and funding documents and plans, specifications and construction cost estimates for federal, state and local government projects and commercial, industrial, hospital/medical and recreational facilities. In-house capabilities include civil, environmental structural, sanitary, mechanical and electrical engineering.

ENVIRONMENTAL & ENGINEERING SERVICES, INC.
687 NW 5th St.
Corvallis, OR 97330
Fred Shaub, Principal
PH: (541)754-1062
FX: (541)753-3948
E-mail: eesi@peak.org
URL: http://www.peak.org/~eesi
Founded: 1979. Provides mechanical and electrical engineering services, with a special emphasis in renovation and energy upgrades. Offers a wide range of HVAC, electrical, and controls engineering services including feasibility assessments, master planning, budgeting, cost analysis, design, computer-aided drafting, energy use modeling, facility management, and construction management.

ENVIRONMENTAL ENGINEERING CORP.
6 S. Orange Ave.
PO Box 343
South Orange, NJ 07079
Pradeep Lamba, Contact
PH: (973)762-8969
FX: (973)762-3771
Founded: 1969. **Staff:** 4. Firm provides comprehensive environmental consulting services, including design of pollution control systems, environmental compliance and permitting, site assessments and investigations, remediation services, storage tank management, hazardous analysis and risk assessment, construction management, and others. Serves chemical and allied industries, municipalities, environmental attorneys, and environmental contractors in the U.S., primarily the Northeast.

ENVIRONMENTAL HYDROGEOENGINEERING, INC.
2 Foxboro Ln.
Manalapan, NJ 07726-3221
Philip A. Haderer, President
PH: (732)780-0596
FX: (732)780-6221
E-mail: ehe07726@aol.com
URL: http://members.aol.com/ehe07726/ehe.html
Consulting environmental engineers and hydrogeologists. Services include Phase I & II Environmental Site Assessments; environmental auditing; UST management; asbestos & lead studies; indoor air quality; environmental permits; ISRA compliance; preliminary assessments; site investigations; groundwater modeling; feasibility studies; treatability studies; preliminary design; final design; cost estimating; construction management; and expert witnesses.

ENVIRONMENTAL RESOURCES MANAGEMENT

855 Springdale Dr.
Exton, PA 19341
Paul H. Woodruff, Founder
PH: (610)524-3500
TF: (800)544-3117
FX: (610)524-7335
E-mail: mkt_info@erm.com
URL: http://www.erm.com
Founded: 1977. **Staff:** 2400. A global environmental, health and safety consulting organization with more than 120 locations in 34 countries. One of the world's largest providers of environmental consulting and engineering services to industry offering site assessment and remediation, hazardous and solid waste management, air and water pollution control, human health and ecological risk assessment, process safety, management consulting, information management, analytical services and turnkey construction to address all environmental challenges.

ERDENBERGER, INC.

PO Box 501239
Atlanta, GA 31150
Peter Erdenberger, Contact
PH: (770)552-0368
FX: (770)552-0208
Founded: 1988. **Staff:** 5. Provides consulting services to international clients, small to medium American firms, legal, financial firms, and state or local agencies providing initial services to clients for the establishment of a new facility. The firm offers expertise to senior management issues ranging from feasibility studies to operations start-up. Specific areas of consultation are as follows: feasibility studies, preliminary engineering, site selection, engineering and construction liaison, equipment startup, and environmental issues. Also active in preparation of new facility infrastructures for transportation, personnel selection and training, quality control, production, plant engineering, sales and marketing, customer service, cost accounting, and overall management. Industries served: manufacturing and services industries, and government agencies.

ERDMAN ANTHONY CONSULTING ENGINEERS

3 Crossgate Dr., Ste. 100
Mechanicsburg, PA 17055-2459
Russell J. Bullock, President
PH: (717)766-1741
FX: (717)766-5516
E-mail: penn@erdmananthony.com
URL: http://www.erdmananthony.com
Founded: 1954. **Staff:** 240. Provides skilled and comprehensive engineering, surveying, and associated services for public agencies and private industry. Includes transportation, environmental, structures, mechanical/electrical, survey and mapping, landscape architecture, and construction inspection in the northeastern United States.

ERLIN, HIME ASSOCIATES—DIVISION OF WISS, JANNEY, ELSTNER ASSOCIATES, INC.

330 Pfingston Rd.
Northbrook, IL 60062
J.D. Connolly, Contact
PH: (847)272-7730
FX: (847)291-5189
E-mail: jdc@wje.com
Founded: 1971. **Staff:** 25. Offers consulting on the failure of materials of construction, primarily through petrographic studies and chemical analyses. Also specialized chemical and instrumental analyses. Serves private industries as well as government agencies.

ERTECH APPLIED ROOFING TECHNOLOGY

1919 San Juan Rd.
Aromas, CA 95004
Richard Tippett, Principal
TF: (800)272-7474
FX: (831)726-1938
E-mail: rtippett@aol.com
URL: http://ertechinc.com

Founded: 1979. **Staff:** 2. A waterproofing consultant specializing in failures, investigation, redesign and construction management from roof to subgrade.

ESA MANAGEMENT & ENGINEERING CONSULTANTS

9422-6 Compass Point Dr. S.
San Diego, CA 92126
Edward D. Richardson, President
PH: (619)578-3695
FX: (619)542-0634
Founded: 1985. **Staff:** 1. Offers problem-solving technical, engineering, and management services to a broad range of clients, which includes government, private, and public sector clients. Among the services provided by ESA are the following: vendor/supplier surveys, operation concepts studies, competitive product evaluations, forms control, productivity/work measurements, space planning, materials management studies, manufacturing engineering studies, construction project coordination, fleet vehicle appraisals, transit (DOT) bus line inspections, facility studies, maintenance reviews, and work place methods layouts. Industries served: transit, private and industrial/manufacturing, and government.

ETC LABORATORIES

22560 Glenn Dr., Ste. 118
Sterling, VA 20164
Joseph D. Shuffleton, President
PH: (703)450-6220
FX: (703)444-2285
URL: http://www.etc-web.com
Founded: 1982. Pavement construction, inspection and evaluation services in asphalt rehabilitation and reconstruction; maintenance programs/inspection guidelines; subsurface drainage systems; surface drainage features (concrete curbs and gutter assemblies, drainage construction).

ETES CORP.

PO Box 8259
Chicago, IL 60680
Rod J. Oancea, President
PH: (312)332-1067
FX: (219)923-4812
E-mail: rjo@etes.com
Founded: 1974. **Staff:** 15. Offers services in engineering, construction management, security, data processing and office automation, energy conservation and management, and microsystems integration and related software to commercial and industrial clients.

EVANS AMERICAN CORP.

15710 John F. Kennedy Blvd.
Houston, TX 77032-2346
Nelson R. Bean, President
PH: (281)590-6000
FX: (281)590-8300
Founded: 1986. **Staff:** 26. Construction management consultants.

EVANS KUHN & ASSOCIATES INC.

727 E. Bethany Home Rd., Ste. D-225
Phoenix, AZ 85014
George L. Evans, President
PH: (602)241-0782
FX: (602)248-9158
Founded: 1977. **Staff:** 31. Civil engineering consultants specializing in highway design, water and sewer collection and distribution design, site selection and analysis, surface hydrology, surveying construction administration services and value engineering. Staff specialists in airport design, surface hydrology, land surveying and civil engineering. Practice includes investigations, consultation, and preparation of designs and construction documents. Serves private industries and government agencies in Arizona.

EVEREST ENGINEERING

915 W. Liberty Dr.
Wheaton, IL 60187-4846
Jagan N. Gosain, President

PH: (630)462-9797
FX: (630)462-9941
Founded: 1983. **Staff:** 20. Firm provides geotechnical and construction engineering services in Illinois and Wisconsin.

EXICO INC.
Federated Investors Tower
1001 Liberty Ave., Ste. 603
Pittsburgh, PA 15222
Eustace O. Uku, President
PH: (412)261-3073
TF: (800)TLE-XICO
FX: (412)261-0626
E-mail: exicoine@aol.com
Founded: 1980. **Staff:** 15. Offers general management services, financing, marketing, franchising, environmental consulting, construction management and international business. Industries served: architect/engineering, construction, banks and financial companies, manufacturing, medical, dental, retail and wholesaling.

EXPLOSION INVESTIGATORS
13100 SE Spring Mountain Rd.
Portland, OR 97236-6702
William E. Gale, Jr., Principal
PH: (503)698-2700
TF: (800)229-7773
FX: (503)698-1511
E-mail: sales@FireExperts.com
URL: http://www.fireexperts.com
Loss prevention engineering specialists in industrial and commercial fire/explosion investigations; and facility/building design and construction issues.

FAAS METALLURGY AND WELDING
22907 Felbar Ave.
Torrance, CA 90505
B.P. Faas, Contact
PH: (310)530-5664
FX: (310)530-5664
E-mail: BPFAAS@aol.com
Founded: 1977. **Staff:** 2. Welding, metallurgical, and quality control consultant who provides specifications and procedures for construction, fabrication, repair, manufacturing and joining metal products. Services also include failure analysis, inspection and product liability investigations, and testimony. Includes monitoring of industrial codes and specifications, and fabrication procedures. Industries served: attorneys; manufacturers; heavy industry, particularly construction; petroleum and chemical; buildings; pipeline; and power plants.

ROBERT FAASS, CONSULTING ENGINEER
6812 96th Pl.
Seabrook, MD 20706
Robert Faass, P.E.
PH: (301)731-5772
E-mail: faass@erols.com
Founded: 1987. **Staff:** 2. Evaluates mechanical, electrical, environmental control, and illumination systems of buildings; and provides power quality and energy management services. Develops guide specifications for mechanical and electrical construction. Provides forensic engineering services. Industries served: technology users, historic preservation, and computer media storage.

F.A.B.E. ASSOCIATES CONSTRUCTION CONSULTANTS
68 Fletcher St.
Winchester, MA 01890
F.A. Bares, President
PH: (781)729-3656
FX: (781)729-8531
E-mail: bares@fabe.ultranet.com
URL: http://www.wozbol.std.com/~fbares
Founded: 1988. **Staff:** 3. Testifies in courts, at depositions and pretrial hearings on heavy construction, building, environmental and remediation construction, including personal injuries, accidents, stabi-

lity and collapses of excavations and trenches, soil movements, septic problems, water infiltration and water damages, bridge failures, foundations, vibration damages, tunneling, soil improvement, jet-grouting, slurry trenches, code violations, and applications.

EDWARD W. FACE CO. INC.
427 W. 35th St.
Norfolk, VA 23508-3201
Bradbury R. Face, President
PH: (757)624-2121
FX: (757)624-2128
URL: http://www.faceco.com
Founded: 1980. **Staff:** 20. Offers building expertise especially in concrete construction.

H. FAIR ASSOCIATES, INC.
500 Main St.
Armonk, NY 10504
Harlan W. Fair, President
PH: (914)273-3457
FX: (914)273-3247
Founded: 1976. Construction management organization offering a wide range of engineering services. Particular expertise in project planning and construction claims. Also offers expert testimony.

FAISANT ASSOCIATES, INC.
810 Light St., Ste. 201
Baltimore, MD 21230
PH: (410)783-1696
FX: (410)783-1753
E-mail: faisant@erols.com
Founded: 1950. **Staff:** 7. Provides structural engineering services in all type of building design; foundation design; structural investigations and reports; and structural product development. Serves private industries and government agencies in Maryland and surrounding states.

FALKIN ASSOCIATES INC.
10303 Meridian Ave. N.
Seattle, WA 98133-9483
Harlan Falkin, President
PH: (206)527-3417
FX: (206)524-3873
E-mail: Falkinassociates@worldnet.att.net
Founded: 1976. **Staff:** 10. Construction management consultants.

FANNING FANNING & ASSOCIATES INC.
2555 74th St.
Lubbock, TX 79423
Norris Fanning, President
PH: (806)745-2533
FX: (806)745-3596
E-mail: fanning@onramp.net
URL: http://rampages.onramp.net/~fanning
Founded: 1956. Firm specializes in engineering services for Mechanical, Electrical, Plumbing design and plant layout, HVAC, energy conservation and management, utilities, district heating & cooling plants and communications for institutional, commercial and industrial buildings. Design services for drawings, specifications and bid documents, master planning, engineering reports, estimates, analysis, feasibility studies, and construction phase services.

FARD ENGINEERS, INC.
1291 Oakland Blvd.
Walnut Creek, CA 94596
Sean Fard, Contact
PH: (510)932-5505
FX: (510)932-0555
E-mail: mailbox@fard.com
URL: http://www.fard.com
Founded: 1991. **Staff:** 17. Designs mechanical and electrical systems for all types of buildings. Serves the construction industry in California, Oregon, Arizona, Washington, and Nevada.

M. RUSSEL FELDMAN & ASSOCIATES
85 Langley Rd.
Newton, MA 02159
M. Russel Feldman, Contact
PH: (617)964-3915
Founded: 1979. **Staff:** 6. Offers real estate, planning and design services to clients in the private and public sectors. To private sector clients, offers comprehensive development services, physical and facilities planning studies, and construction management; financial services including market surveys, operating projections, estimates of hard and soft project costs, feasibility analyses, project packaging, financing proposals, and negotiations with public agencies, lenders and investors. Also consults to local and state governments at the program/policy design level and on individual projects.

WAYNE E. FERRELL, JR.
PO Box 24448
Jackson, MS 39225-4448
Wayne E. Ferrell, Jr., Contact
PH: (601)969-4700
FX: (601)969-4715
E-mail: airlaw@mslawyer.com
Staff: 3. Specializes in aviation accidents, airports, aircraft finance, aviation litigation, and aircraft maintenance and operations.

FEWELL GEOTECHNICAL ENGINEERING, LTD.
96-1416 Waihona Pl.
Pearl City, HI 96782-1973
Richard B. Fewell, President
PH: (808)455-6569
FX: (808)456-7062
E-mail: fge@alcha.net
Founded: 1976. **Staff:** 28. Consultants in geotechnical engineering. Services include investigations, reports and construction quality control; test borings, laboratory testing, and analysis for both building and heavy construction. Serves private industries as well as government agencies.

FINKBEINER, PETTIS & STROUT, INC.
4405 Talmadge Rd.
Toledo, OH 43623-0807
Gary W. Johnson, Contact
PH: (419)473-1121
FX: (419)473-2108
URL: http://www.fpsengineering.com
Founded: 1900. **Staff:** 215. Consulting engineers in the fields of waterworks systems, water treatment plants, sewer systems, sewage treatment plants, highway and bridges, drainage and paving. Also feasibility studies, design, plans and specifications, supervision of construction and appraisals, comprehensive planning, flood plain management and hydrology. Does projects in public works and industrial categories. Serves private industries as well as government agencies.

EWELL W. FINLEY & PARTNERS, INC.
34-18 Northern Blvd.
Long Island City, NY 11101
Ananda De Silva, Contact
PH: (718)482-7000
FX: (718)937-5938
E-mail: ewfpc@email.msn.com
Founded: 1966. **Staff:** 72. EWF, one of the oldest 100 percent minority-owned consulting engineering firms in the United States, offers diversified services under a single management. Specific services include master planning, feasibility studies, concepts, design, working drawings, specifications, contract documents, project cost analysis, reports, surveys, operation and maintenance manuals, and construction review. Projects range from new construction and the renovation of existing facilities to historic preservation. Major disciplines of engineering and design are: civil engineering, structural engineering, environmental engineering, value engineering, transportation engineering, geotechnical engineering, surveying, and construction review. For clients in government and private industry, EWF has completed assignments that include: airports, bridges and

tunnels, commercial buildings, correctional facilities, educational, cultural, and religious institutions, government buildings, highways, hospitals and medical facilities, industrial parks, office buildings, parking facilities, parks and recreational complexes, people-mover facilities, railroads, rapid transit systems, light rail systems, rehabilitation and historic preservation, residential buildings, sewage collection and treatment plants, shopping centers, storm water management and flood control, and water supply and distribution systems.

FISHBECK, THOMPSON, CARR & HUBER, INC.
6090 E. Fulton
Ada, MI 49301-0211
James E. Smalligan, P.E., Vice President
PH: (616)676-3824
FX: (616)676-8173
URL: http://www.headquarters.com/ftch
Founded: 1956. **Staff:** 200. A professional environmental, architectural/engineering, and civil engineering consulting firm. Works with clients from the industrial, governmental, institutional, and private sectors. Projects range from small feasibility, planning, and regulatory studies to very large design and construction projects.

GERALD R.A. FISHE
PO Box 478
Fort Lauderdale, FL 33302-0478
Gerald R.A. Fishe, Contact
PH: (954)581-4998
FX: (954)581-4998
Founded: 1966. **Staff:** 1. Consulting forensic engineer. Registered in fields of mechanical, electrical and civil engineering in Florida, Georgia, Alabama, Missouri, Illinois and Iowa. Consulting forensic services rendered include roofing, building construction, coatings, slip or trip and fall events, automobile accident events, building element failures, construction site injuries, electrical injuries, initial ignition determination fire cause, machinery caused injuries and component failures, and bulkhead failures. Industries served: any that have events or problems listed above that require investigation, legal profession and insurance industry, as well as government agencies. Geographic areas served: United States and Bahamas; available anywhere clients need services.

FISHER ASSOCIATES
PO Box 51968
Durham, NC 27717
C. Page Fisher, Contact
PH: (919)493-1815
FX: (919)493-3625
Founded: 1955. **Staff:** 1. Consulting engineer specializing in geotechnical services and construction litigation matters.

F.J.M. ENGINEERS, INC.
10455 Jefferson Hwy.
Baton Rouge, LA 70809
Oren C. Furnish, President
PH: (504)292-5030
FX: (504)293-6007
E-mail: fjmeng@aol.com
Founded: 1977. **Staff:** 40. Firm serves as project engineers and construction managers to the following industries: bauxite/alumina, mining; specialty chemicals, cement, petrochemicals; agriculture, petroleum, material handling, and power generation. Provide feasibility studies, project management, design construction management and contract personnel.

FLANAGAN & ASSOCIATES, INC.
2394 Mariner Sq. Dr.
Alameda, CA 94501
Michael J. Flanagan, Ph.D., President
PH: (510)521-6002
FX: (510)521-8264
E-mail: flanagan@ricochet.net
Designs, implements, and supervises the construction of instrumentation, SCADA and distributed digital control systems for the water and wastewater industry. Provides expert witness and claims analy-

sis services, including discovery, report preparation, interrogatories, depositions, and jury trial preparation.

FLEMING CORP.
400 Olive St.
St. Louis, MO 63102
Charles E. Fleming, President
PH: (314)241-9550
FX: (314)241-9556
Founded: 1968. **Staff:** 101. Offers architecture, engineering, planning, and construction management consulting services for firms in the governmental, commercial, and private sectors.

FLUOR DANIEL WILLIAMS BROTHERS
4500 S. 129th E. Ave.
Tulsa, OK 74134
PH: (918)610-9500
FX: (918)610-9510
Founded: 1964. **Staff:** 300. Consulting engineering firm with specific expertise in the fields of oil and gas exploration, drilling and production, pipelining and gathering systems for onshore and offshore operations, and process plant facilities for the refining and petrochemical industries. These technical skills are supported by capabilities in feasibility studies, project planning and management, environmental studies and evaluations, procurement, expediting, shop inspection, right-of-ways acquisitions, construction management, field inspection, and facility operations and maintenance. Provides geological and reservoir engineering services for the disciplines of petroleum engineering, reservoir analysis/appraisal, structural, and field analysis. Processing services range from economic feasibility studies to process simulation, design, detailed engineering, procurement, inspection and expediting, construction management, field operation, and laboratory analyses. Also offers marine services for the development, design, engineering, project management and construction management of offshore and related facilities for the oil and gas industry. Over the years, specialized knowledge been acquired in remote locations where logistic planning and support services are as important as technical developments. Particular experience has been gained in harsh climates-arctic, desert and jungle-as well as in crossing several of the major mountain ranges of the world.

FMI CORP.
5151 Glenwood Ave.
Raleigh, NC 27622
Robert Andrews, Chairman and CEO
PH: (919)787-8400
TF: (800)669-1364
FX: (919)785-9320
URL: http://www.fminet.com
Founded: 1952. **Staff:** 130. Provides management consulting and educational services for the construction industry. Services include strategic planning, business evaluations and plans, benchmarking, total quality management, project partnering, mergers and acquisitions, stock valuations, target marketing, construction market forecasting, educational products and public programs, and group programs and travel. Clients include contractors, manufacturers and distributors of building materials products, construction materials producers, surety companies, trade associations and other providers of services to the construction industry. Serves private industries as well as government agencies.

FOGEL & ASSOCIATES, INC.
1170 Broadway, Ste. 510
New York, NY 10001
Irving M. Fogel, P.E., President
PH: (212)686-6500
FX: (212)684-1487
E-mail: fogeleng@worldnet.att.net
URL: http://www.fogeleng.com
Founded: 1969. **Staff:** 2. Services offered include construction project management, construction loan management, construction claims, expert testimony, and surety consulting. Clients include

banks, contractors, owners, surety companies, lenders, and government agencies worldwide.

THOMAS FOK AND ASSOCIATES LTD.
3896 Mahoning Ave.
Youngstown, OH 44515
Thomas D.Y. Fok, Chairman
PH: (330)799-1501
FX: (330)799-2519
Founded: 1976. **Staff:** 32. Services include the planning and design of bridges, highways, airports, parks, wastewater collection treatment and disposal, water supply distribution systems; traffic control and parking facilities; building foundation and structural framing; field surveying; and project inspection and construction management. Serves cities and municipalities, county, and state governmental departments as well as developers, contractors and private citizens.

FOOD PLANT ENGINEERING, INC.
1710 S. 24th Ave.
Yakima, WA 98902
Barry Hulet, President
PH: (509)248-5530
FX: (509)453-3008
E-mail: bhulet@corp.foodplant.com
URL: http://www.foodplant.com
Founded: 1976. **Staff:** 30. Consulting architects and engineers specializing in systems design and feasibility studies for food processing plants and materials handling systems. Offers operations improvement programs and construction project management services. Works primarily with food processing businesses. Geographic areas served: U.S. and international.

FOODPRO INTERNATIONAL, INC.
PO Box 53110
San Jose, CA 95153
M. William Washburn, President
PH: (408)227-2332
FX: (408)227-4908
E-mail: foodpro@best.com
URL: http://www.foodpro.net
Founded: 1974. **Staff:** 65. Offers a complete range of consulting engineering services from studies (planning, feasibility, site selection, etc.) through construction and equipment installation management including all the engineering disciplines (industrial, refrigeration, electrical, etc.) necessary for complete plans and specifications.

FORENSIC BUILDING INVESTIGATORS
8414 Bieriot Ave., Ste. 100
Los Angeles, CA 90045-3027
James M. Collins, Principal
PH: (310)645-0707
FX: (310)337-9107
Specializes in construction defects. Provides forensic investigation and analysis and repair of buildings.

FORENSIS GROUP, INC.
711 E. Walnut St., Ste. 409
Pasadena, CA 91101
Mercy Steenwyk, Director
PH: (626)795-5000
TF: (800)555-5422
FX: (626)795-1950
E-mail: forensis@earthlink.net
URL: http://www.forensisgroup.com
Full spectrum of consulting and expert testimony in forensic technical engineering; failure analysis; safety; architecture; construction (defects and cost estimates); earthquake; accident reconstruction; environmental; fires and explosions; product liability; economics; appraisal; slip and fall. Experts average 35 years of professional experience.

FOSDICK & HILMER, INC.
36 E. Fourth St., Ste. 320
Cincinnati, OH 45202
James W. Pretz, Chairman
PH: (513)241-5640
FX: (513)241-3659
Founded: 1905. **Staff:** 39. Offers technical and management services on construction, energy, and environmental matters. Emphasis is on energy supply and delivery; M/E systems for commercial, institutional and industrial facilities; power plant design and construction; air and water pollution control; and construction project issues. Services include planning and analytical studies, management audits, engineering, project management and support; and plant operation troubleshooting. Specific expertise includes power plant construction/modification; instrumentation and controls; building/facilities M/E systems. Serves private industry and government agencies in the continental U.S.

FOSROC INC.
150 Carley Ct.
Georgetown, KY 40324
PH: (502)863-6800
FX: (502)863-4010
Firm offers extensive knowledge in construction design.

FOWLIE & ASSOCIATES
630 Skyline Rd.
Ventura, CA 93003
Elmore I. Fowlie, President
PH: (805)644-0201
FX: (805)644-0201
Founded: 1977. **Staff:** 4. Offers environmentally conscious architectural services, including interior design, urban planning, building program development, and site analysis. Industries served: educational, industrial, residential, commercial, and municipal facilities in southern California.

P.L. FRANK, INC.
5850 Ellsworth Ave., Ste. 301
Pittsburgh, PA 15232
Philip L. Frank, Principal
PH: (412)361-7707
FX: (412)362-3062
E-mail: plfinc@aol.com
Provides expert mechanical engineering testimony in the areas of HVAC, plumbing, infectious disease control, energy conservation, retro fit, and new construction.

SCOTT B. FRANKLIN & ASSOCIATES
68 S. Main St.
PO Box 270754
West Hartford, CT 06107
Marshall Franklin, President
PH: (860)561-4832
FX: (860)521-5560
Founded: 1986. **Staff:** 7. Provides construction services to clients in the U.S.

FRAZIER-SIMPLEX, INC.
PO Box 493
Washington, PA 15301
J.E. Frazier, II, Chairman of the Board
PH: (412)225-1100
FX: (412)225-3114
E-mail: info@frazier-simplex.com
URL: http://www.frazier-simplex.com
Founded: 1918. **Staff:** 25. Engineering consultancy specializing in services to the glass and steel industries (suspended refractories), and to the construction industry.

SAMUEL K. FRESHMAN
6151 W. Century Blvd., Ste. 300
Los Angeles, CA 90045

PH: (310)410-2300
FX: (310)410-2919
E-mail: standard@deltanet.com
Attorney acting as an expert witness in legal malpractice, real estate brokerage malpractice, leases, syndication, construction property management, due diligence, conflict of interest, title insurance, escrow, and development. Acts as an arbitrator and mediator.

FROMHERZ ENGINEERS INC.
2740 Indiana Ave
Kenner, LA 70062
Jay Shah, President
PH: (504)466-5060
FX: (504)466-0064
E-mail: feimink@aol.com
Founded: 1989. **Staff:** 14. Multidisciplined engineering firm offers expertise in the following: architectural, civil, structural, mechanical, electrical, construction, and environmental services. Also provides inspection services. Industries served: chemical, petrochemical, transportation, and energy. Geographic areas served: Gulf-South U.S., Central America, East Africa, and India.

**FRU-CON CONSTRUCTION CORP., FRU-CON
   ENGINEERING INC.**
15933 Clayton Rd.
Ballwin, MO 63022-0100
Bruce A. Frost, President/CEO
PH: (314)391-6700
FX: (314)391-4513
Founded: 1872. **Staff:** 2000. Firm provides construction, engineering, project development, and technical services to the industrial manufacturing, process, energy, heavy civil, environmental, commercial, healthcare, and educational markets. Serves public and private clients both domestically and internationally.

FULGENZI ENGINEERING
2722 W. 10th
Amarillo, TX 79102
George Maddox, P.E., Ph.D., Contact
PH: (806)373-3084
FX: (806)373-3085
E-mail: johnkayf@ar.net
Founded: 1962. **Staff:** 6. Offers services in the areas of structural, environmental, geohydraulic and hydraulic engineering; geology, general construction, and project design and management, including plant layout and design. Also offers expertise in plastic and corrosion related to industrial waste. Industries served: copper refinery, petrochemical, and cement industries in Texas, New Mexico, Colorado, Oklahoma, and Arizona.

G & T ASSOCIATES INC.
11925 Pearl Rd., Ste. 401
Strongsville, OH 44136-3340
Chandu Patel, Contact
PH: (440)572-0555
FX: (440)572-0320
E-mail: gtassocoh@aol.com
Founded: 1986. **Staff:** 24. Offers assistance in the field of civil and structural engineering. Specializes in preparation of design and construction documents, construction management, and construction inspection. Primarily serves the construction, food and beverage, iron and steel, lumber, pulp, and paper, pharmaceutical, government, and transportation industries. Also offers environmental engineering services and general contracting services.

GA DEVELOPMENT GROUP, INC.
PO Box 817
Washington Crossing, PA 18977
Joseph E. Gaudet, President
PH: (215)493-5191
FX: (215)493-9163
Firm provides construction and environmental engineering consulting.

GAI CONSULTANTS, INC.
570 Beatty Rd.
Monroeville, PA 15146
A.M. DiGioia, Jr., President
PH: (412)856-6400
FX: (412)856-4970
Founded: 1958. **Staff:** 438. Provides planning, study, and design services in civil, environmental, geotechnical, and structural engineering, transmission lines, environmental sciences, energy, mining, water resources, industrial/hazardous waste management, transportation, archaeology and cultural resources, site development, and construction monitoring. Industries served: chemicals, metals, mining, energy, utilities, iron and steel, transportation, construction, agriculture and forestry, manufacturing, real estate, hazardous/solid waste management, and government agencies.

GALYARDT ASSOCIATES, INC.
1506 Mt. View Rd., Ste. 102
PO Box 7197
Rapid City, SD 57709-7197
Gary E. Galyardt, President
PH: (605)343-5282
FX: (605)343-2378
E-mail: galyrdt@aol.com
Founded: 1968. **Staff:** 7. Offers consultation, special studies and reports, site development, the design of facilities and inspection during construction. Projects include public, commercial and industrial buildings, libraries, water works, sewers, highways, bridges, streets, drainage and general municipal engineering.

ROBERT J. GANLEY—CONSULTING ENGINEERS
152 Delaware Ave.
Delmar, NY 12054
Robert J. Ganley, Contact
PH: (518)439-0836
FX: (518)439-0836
Founded: 1959. **Staff:** 3. Provides design, specifications and supervision of construction for water supply, sewerage, sewage treatment and drainage projects both municipal and private clients (industrial buildings and facilities).

GARING, TAYLOR & ASSOCIATES, INC.
141 S. Elm St.
Arroyo Grande, CA 93420
R. James Garing, President
PH: (805)489-1321
FX: (805)489-6723
E-mail: garing@aol.com
Provides forensic civil engineering analysis including structures, drainage systems, and construction litigation. Performs investigative analysis of land development, conditions of approval, local government approvals; as well as highway geometry and traffic analysis; application and suitability of materials, and installation methods.

GAUDET ASSOCIATES, INC.
The Piers at Penn's Landing, Pier 5
Philadelphia, PA 19106
Joseph E. Gaudet, President
PH: (215)351-4045
Founded: 1970. **Staff:** 50. A firm of consulting engineers active in construction management, project management, real estate development, facilities engineering and design.

GBL INTERNATIONAL INC.
93 Kerrs Corner Rd.
Blairstown, NJ 07825
Thomas Lang, President
PH: (908)362-6773
FX: (908)362-6773
E-mail: tlang@cpatch.com
URL: http://www.gbl.idsite.com/
Services the real estate development, building, civil and heavy highway construction industries in all market segments in Central and Eastern Europe and the former Soviet Union. Active in other tech-

nology and infrastructure projects in Poland, Ukraine, Russia, the Baltics, and Central Asia, including developing joint ventures in all types of aggregate based construction materials for the building and road construction industries, systems integration and nuclear engineering. Areas of experience are accounting, construction, finance, government affairs, import-export, law, manufacturing, marketing, nuclear safety, real estate, transportation.

GE CO.
GE Business Information Center
320 Great Oaks Office Park
Albany, NY 12203-5965
PH: (212)869-5555
TF: (800)626-2004
FX: (212)334-2463
E-mail: cgal@mindspring.com
URL: http://www.ge.com
Firm offers special knowledge in the following areas: construction materials, equipment, financial services, plastics, power systems, industrial controls, motors, transportation leasing, aircraft engines, and factory automation.

GEMINI GEOTECHNICAL ASSOCIATES, INC.
1 Cate St.
Portsmouth, NH 03801
PH: (603)427-0141
E-mail: crb@geminigeo.com
URL: http://www.geminigeo.com
Founded: 1989. Geotechnical and environmental engineers and consultants. Geotechnical engineering services include geotechnical design of shallow and deep building foundations; geotechnical engineering for cellular and communication towers; forensic investigations of settlement, subsidence, and drainage damage; design of earth dams and embankments; soil and rock slope stability analysis; design and engineering for sheetpiling, anchors, and bracing for deep excavations; design of rock blasting programs and preblast surveys; design development and implementation of instrumentation programs; foundation installation inspections and construction support services; engineering geology and geologic mapping. The environmental services includes Phase 1 Environmental Site Assessments; Phase II Comprehensive Site Investigations; human health risk assessments; brownfields studies; remedial action plans; soil and groundwater remediation systems; and underground storage tank design and closure.

R.J. GENEREUX & ASSOCIATES, LTD.
2060 Broad St.
Regina, SK, Canada S4P 1Y3
PH: (306)525-6121
FX: (306)522-9744
Founded: 1965. **Staff:** 17. Consultants providing transportation engineering, traffic engineering, road and street planning and design, airports, transit engineering, drainage, municipal engineering, site engineering, heavy construction engineering, contract administration, and project management.

GEOLEX, INC.
PO Box 374
Aptos, CA 95001
William B. Wigginton, Principal
PH: (831)662-0609
FX: (831)662-0609
E-mail: wwigginton@aol.com
Founded: 1992. **Staff:** 1. Firm specializes in landslide identification and repair, foundation failure, construction failure analysis, groundwater resources and studies, soil testing, roadway construction and failure investigations, and insurance causation studies.

GEORGE, MILES AND BUHR, LLP
206 Downtown Plaza
Salisbury, MD 21801
James R. Thomas, Jr., PE, Managing Partner

PH: (410)742-3115
TF: (800)789-4GMB
FX: (410)548-5790
E-mail: gmb@gmbnet.com
URL: http://www.gmbnet.com
Founded: 1960. **Staff:** 61. Multi-disciplined architectural/ engineering firm with special emphasis on comprehensive civil-sanitary engineering services, new construction, maintenance and repair of existing structures, structural design, feasibility studies, evaluation reports, facilities plans, design and preparation of contract documents, and construction management. Serves private industries and government agencies.

GEOSYNTEC CONSULTANTS
621 NW 53rd St., Ste. 650
Boca Raton, FL 33487
Rudolph Bonaparte, Ph.D., P.E., President/CEO
PH: (561)995-0900
FX: (561)995-0925
E-mail: annep@geosyntec.com
URL: http://www.geosyntec.com
Founded: 1983. **Staff:** 280. Firm offers expertise in geotechnical engineering, geoenvironmental engineering, hydrogeology, and hydrology and related engineering and scientific disciplines. Also provides construction services and quality assurance experience for environment and geotechnical projects. Laboratory facilities are on—site for materials testing.

GEOTEC ASSOCIATES
302 Beverly Rd.
Newark, DE 19711
Robert Nicholls, President
PH: (302)368-0427
FX: (302)368-0427
Founded: 1960. **Staff:** 3. Provides geotechnical and construction materials testing, analysis, and design for highways, bridges, buildings, and process industries. Also offers settlement, shear failure, and seepage analyses and design. Conducts forensic testing for construction materials failure analyses, expert testimony; evaluations of concrete product manufacturing operations, and composite construction products market research and development. Industries served: manufacturing and process industries; federal, state, and local governments.

GEOTEST ENGINEERING, INC.
5600 Bintliff Dr.
Houston, TX 77036
V.N. Vijayvergiya, President
PH: (713)266-0588
FX: (713)266-2977
E-mail: geosta14@aol.com
Founded: 1979. **Staff:** 41. Geotechnical engineering consultants offering the following services: soil borings in a variety of soil conditions in shallow waters, marshy areas and in deep waters offshore; laboratory and field test data on soils and rocks; inspection of footings, mats and excavations for proper bearing capacity; supervision of braced excavation, de-watering and tiebacks; and other foundation and construction problems. Serves private industries as well as government agencies.

GHT LTD.
1010 N. Glebe Rd., Ste. 200
Arlington, VA 22201-4749
James E. Cummings, Principal
PH: (703)243-1200
FX: (703)276-1376
E-mail: ght@ghtltd.com
URL: http://www.ghtltd.com
Founded: 1965. Design services in mechanical engineering: (heating, ventilating, and air-conditioning (HVAC) systems; energy conservation technology; systems analysis; building management and automation systems.); electrical engineering: (lighting, power supply and distribution, standby and uninterruptible power supply (ups); energy analysis.); plumbing engineering: (sanitary, storm drainage, and

disposal; water supply, gas, compressed air, clinical and laboratory services.) Telecommunications and security engineering services include voice, data, security design: (application of structured cabling design standards; building and campus telecommunications planning and evaluation; grounding and RFI shielding design.) Life safety engineering services include safety criteria analysis; fire alarm, fire suppression and smoke evacuation systems; emergency systems. Utilities planning services include utilities assessment; redesign for existing facilities, master planning and design for future facilities. Engineering studies/energy modeling services include engineering studies provide estimates of life expectancy and replacement or upgrade costs for mechanical and electrical equipment and systems. Construction phase services include site visits to ensure correct contractor implementation of plans and specifications. Coordination between designers, contractors, owners, architects and property managers through personal contact, field reports and punch lists.

GIBSON TOURNEY KIM, INC.
519 Tennessee Ave., Ste. 300
Fort Wayne, IN 46805
Dick L. Gibson, President
PH: (219)424-4950
FX: (219)422-8464
Founded: 1946. **Staff:** 9. Architectural and structural consultants working with commercial, institutional and religious buildings, as well as government agencies. Provides construction supervision (financial, insurance, developer), and space planning and interior design (offices, shops, restaurants).

GIFFELS ASSOCIATES LTD.
30 International Blvd.
Rexdale, ON, Canada M9W 5P3
J. Shufelt, Contact
PH: (416)675-5950
FX: (416)675-4620
E-mail: geninfok@giffels.com
URL: http://www.giffels.com
Founded: 1949. **Staff:** 250. Offers multidiscipline architectural and engineering design services related to planning, design, construction, and project management of major capital projects for industry, institutions and government. Projects include buildings, industrial plant facilities, highways, roads, bridges, and transit systems. Also provides expertise in CADD computer systems and applications, generates software under contract or via license, and offers technical training in these areas. Industries served: architecture, construction services, engineering, plant layout/interior design/space planning, traffic and parking, transportation—highway, computer technology, industrial process engineering, environmental engineering, and government agencies.

GILSON, MCKELLAR, MCWHORTER & ASSOCIATES
949 E. 12400 S
Draper, UT 84020
Larry R. Gilson, Contact
PH: (801)571-9414
FX: (801)571-9449
Founded: 1950. **Staff:** 24. Offers complete engineering services including feasibility reports, design and supervision of construction on municipal and industrial water supply and distribution; design and supervision of construction of office buildings, vehicle maintenance buildings, fire stations, warehouses; building repair, modification and expansion; sewage and industrial wastes collection and treatment; irrigation dams, reservoirs, canals and pressure piping, flood control including dams, reservoirs, storm sewers; basin water quality studies and environmental evaluations.

GLEASON, FLOYD & ASSOCIATES
1 Georgia Center, Ste. 610
Atlanta, GA 30308
Roger William (Bill) Mott, VP
PH: (404)872-5400
FX: (404)888-0806
E-mail: gfaa@mindspring.com
Founded: 1977. **Staff:** 12. Consultants serving the construction and

related industries in such areas as claim analysis, management systems, planning and scheduling, estimating, feasibility studies, productivity assessment, cost and schedule controls, quality control, audit services, value engineering, construction administration, training seminars, and construction claims. Also serves as expert witness in relevant cases. Serves private industries as well as government agencies.

JAY O. GLERUM & ASSOCIATES, INC.
18434 47th Pl. NE
Seattle, WA 98155
PH: (206)362-9293
FX: (206)363-0219
Founded: 1987. Advises on theater and performing arts production technology. Specializes in stage machinery systems design, inspection, and accident investigation.

GLOBAL UNIVERSAL INC.
11701 South Fwy.
Burleson, TX 76028
Ronald Welborn, President
PH: (817)293-9334
FX: (817)293-9336

GME CONSULTANTS, INC.
14000 21st Ave. N.
Minneapolis, MN 55447
William Kwasny, Principal
PH: (612)559-1859
FX: (612)559-0720
Forensic engineering services are geotechnical and environmental. Performs building condition surveys; vibration monitoring; roofing surveys and design; slope movement/failure evaluation; distressed structures analysis ; floor slab moisture investigations; the effects of new construction on existing structures; and non-destructive testing.

SAMUEL J. GORDON, PH.D.
1555 Los Olivos Rd.
Santa Rosa, CA 95404-2010
, Principal
PH: (707)539-6012
FX: (707)539-0827
E-mail: samjgordon@aol.com
A mechanical/manufacturing engineer and environmental assessor specializing in discovery support, analysis and testimony regarding mechanical, electromechanical, hydraulic, pneumatic and steam operated manufacturing, construction, and agricultural and marine machinery.

LEON GOTTLIEB & ASSOCIATES
4601 Sendero Pl.
Tarzana, CA 91356-4821
Leon Gottlieb, President
PH: (818)757-1131
FX: (818)757-1131
E-mail: LGottlieb@aol.com
URL: http://lawinfo.com/biz/gottlieb
Founded: 1969. Consultant and expert testimony on franchising, fast food, restaurants, management, operations of all types, hotels, retail, service industries, advertising, promotion, sales, multi-level marketing, convenience stores, food courts, shopping malls, food manufacturing, distribution, brokerage, licensing agreements, training manuals, security, safety, injury, construction, equipment, site selection, turn-around problems, and profit and loss damage assessment. Expert witness/arbitration experience.

GOVE ASSOCIATES, INC.
1601 Portage St.
Kalamazoo, MI 49001
M.E. Schuur, Executive Vice President
PH: (616)385-0011
TF: (800)632-5753
FX: (616)382-6972
Founded: 1946. **Staff:** 75. Architects and engineers providing con-

sulting services in the areas of land surveying, civil engineering, community planning, construction services, environmental services, GIS mapping, and architecture. Industries served: municipalities.

GOYLE ENGINEERING, INC.
115 Rauch Dr.
Marietta, OH 45750
R.K. Goyle, President
PH: (614)374-5607
FX: (614)374-3825
E-mail: goyle@sbrynet.com
Founded: 1983. **Staff:** 4. Soils and materials engineering consultant provides the following: independent testing lab, construction materials testing and inspection, geotechnical studies, and construction inspection. Serves private industries as well as government agencies.

GRAEF, ANHALT, SCHLOEMER & ASSOCIATES, INC.
125 South 84th St.
Milwaukee, WI 53214
Richard M. Bub, P.E., President
PH: (414)259-1500
FX: (414)259-0037
Founded: 1961. **Staff:** 250. Consulting services to industries, architects, developers, government, and municipalities including site investigation, environmental audits, surveying, cost analysis, investigations, reports, design, construction documents, and inspections; for buildings, water supply, solid waste, sewage treatment facilities, drainage, site development, streets, bridges, and parking facilities; and foundations, geotechnical, and structural engineering for all types of buildings and structures.

JOHN GRAHAM ASSOCIATES
900 Fourth Ave., Ste. 700
Seattle, WA 98164
Roderick R. Kirkwood, Contact
PH: (206)461-6000
FX: (206)461-6049
Founded: 1900. **Staff:** 50. Full service architectural and engineering consultants. Services include: architectural and interior design; landscape architecture; mechanical, electrical, structural, and civil engineering; urban design and planning; space analysis and programming; construction administration; and graphic design. Serves private industries as well as government agencies.

GRAHAM LANDSCAPE ARCHITECTURE
229 Prince George St.
Annapolis, MD 21401
J. Patrick Graham, Contact
PH: (410)269-5886
FX: (410)268-4032
E-mail: grahamla@bayserve.net
Founded: 1984. **Staff:** 7. Provides support to architects and owners/ developers in the complete range of landscape design services from programming and site analysis through schematic design and design development, including construction documents and construction observation or specialized construction management. A landscape maintenance manual is prepared specifically for each project. Areas of expertise include Health Care gardens, interior landscape, rooftop gardens, and historic preservation. Industries served: institutional, office and commercial, residential, and government projects.

GRECON, INC.
2251 Drusilla Ln., Ste. A
Baton Rouge, LA 70809
Stephen Spohrer, P.E.
PH: (504)927-6362
FX: (504)927-6366
E-mail: grecon@tlxnet.net
Founded: 1982. Construction engineers and consultants.

GREELEY AND HANSEN
100 S. Wacker Dr., Ste. 1400
Chicago, IL 60606
Thomas J. Sullivan, Managing Partner

PH: (312)558-9000
TF: (800)837-9779
FX: (312)558-1006
E-mail: info@greeley-hansen.com
URL: http://www.greely-hansen.com
Founded: 1914. **Staff:** 290. Offers sanitary and environmental engineering studies, designs, and construction services for water supply, purification, transmission, storage and distribution; sanitary sewerage; primary, secondary and advanced treatment of domestic and industrial wastewater; storm water, flood control; collection, transfer and disposal of solid wastes; valuations, rate studies and financial feasibility studies. Industries served: municipalities and other governmental authorities, as well as the private sector.

GREENMAN-PEDERSEN, INC.
325 W. Main St.
Babylon, NY 11702
Michael Buoncore, Secretary/Treasurer
PH: (516)587-5060
TF: (800)347-9221
FX: (516)587-5029
E-mail: gpi@gpinet.com
Founded: 1966. **Staff:** 320. Consulting engineering firm that provides planning, design, construction, inspection, aerial photographic and photogrammetric mapping services to a number of county government offices, municipal and regional authorities, state agencies, Department of Defense agencies, school districts, industrial concerns, private individuals and other professional firms. Some major areas of service and expertise are highway and traffic engineering, coastal and marine engineering, environmental science and engineering, architecture, interior design, landscape architecture, and water resources management. The firm is also involved in assisting municipalities and school districts in securing federal funding, and is thoroughly acquainted with the many sources for development funds and guides clients through the intricate procedures involved in receiving project approvals.

DAVID GREIG & ASSOCIATES
650—1380 Burrard St.
Vancouver, BC, Canada V6Z 2B7
G. David Greig, President
PH: (604)683-5333
FX: (604)683-5330
E-mail: dgreig@dgadesign.com
Founded: 1980. **Staff:** 10. Food service facility planners and management consultants who conduct conceptual/programming/research and preparation/evaluation of request for proposal documents for food service operator on behalf of facility owner. Also performs existing facility evaluation and food service facility design. Will provide guidance through specifications, bid process, and construction supervision. Industries served: food service including hospitality, institutional, healthcare, recreation facilities, and government agencies. Services include Interior Design and Computer Graphics Design.

GREINER ENGINEERING, INC.
909 E. Las Colinas Blvd., Ste. 1900
Irving, TX 75039-3907
Arnold Davidson, Treasurer
PH: (214)869-1001
FX: (214)869-3111
Founded: 1908. **Staff:** 1500. A technical services organization offering engineering, architectural, and planning counsel to public and private agencies such as state and federal highway departments, airport authorities, developers, and local public works clients and school districts. Serves 34 state highway departments and eight of America's ten largest airports.

GRIFFIN STRUCTURAL GROUP
3085 Humphrey Rd.
Loomis, CA 95650
Robert D. Griffin, Principal
PH: (916)652-7160
FX: (916)652-7198

An expert witness in construction deficiencies and plan checking, construction administration, building design and review, project management, and construction defects and failure analysis. Reviews construction documents. Inspects existing structures for professional registration. Performs seismic analysis and investigation. Designs major seismic bracing systems, including rigid frames, concrete shear walls, and diagonal braces.

EVERETT GRIFFITH JR. & ASSOCIATES, INC.
408 N. 3rd St.
Lufkin, TX 75901
Wayne Stolz, President
PH: (409)634-5528
FX: (409)634-7989
Founded: 1955. **Staff:** 19. Offers consulting services in civil, mechanical, electrical, structural, and industrial engineering for municipal works, government agencies, state agencies, hospital, heavy industry and light industry.

CLAYFORD T. GRIMM P.E., INC.
1904 Wooten Dr.
Austin, TX 78757
Clayford T. Grimm, President
PH: (512)452-2354
FX: (512)452-6315
E-mail: ctgpeinc@xmail.utexas.net
URL: http://www.abuildnet.com/users2/000441.shtml
Founded: 1971. Consulting architectural engineer on design, construction, maintenance, restoration, and demolition of brick, stone, terra cotta, and concrete masonry structures. Particular emphasis on functional performance and failure investigation.

GSE ASSOCIATES, INC.
991 Grand Caillou Rd.
Houma, LA 70363
Arthur A. DeFraites, Jr., President
PH: (504)876-6380
FX: (504)876-0621
E-mail: houma@gulf-south.com
URL: http://www.gulf-south.com
Founded: 1972. **Staff:** 41. Multi-disciplinary firm offering consulting, civil, structural, sanitary, environmental, mechanical, electrical, landscape architecture and surveying services for municipal, industrial, commercial, and private clientele. Consulting services include investigations and studies; design and preparation of plans, specifications, and contract documents; construction administration and project representation of: roads, streets, highways, bridges; storm water management, water treatment, storage, distribution; fire protection systems; wastewater collection, treatment; solid waste projects, electrical transmission, substation, distribution, controls; and mechanical HVAC system.

GUSTAFSON, POULSEN & ASSOCIATES, INC.
7901 Stoneridge Dr., Ste. 528
Pleasanton, CA 94588-3657
Lawrence Gustafson, Contact
PH: (510)463-8843
FX: (510)463-8872
Founded: 1977. **Staff:** 15. Construction management consultants offer CPM scheduling and related services, construction management, construction claims analysis, and construction estimating. Industries served: construction (commercial development, institutional, industrial, residential, heavy engineering, and maritime), along with construction claim resolution, construction loan monitoring, corporate reorganization scheduling, software implementation scheduling, and manufacturing scheduling; and legal profession.

HAAN CONSTRUCTION CONSULTANTS
718 Shelbourne Dr.
Marlton, NJ 08053
PH: (609)985-9600
FX: (609)985-9614
Offers a combination of project management and claims analysis services to the construction industry. Clients include attorneys, own-

ers, developers, contractors, government agencies, architects, engineers, construction managers, insurers and sureties.

THE HAIST CORP.
925 Village Center, Ste. One
Lafayette, CA 94549
Whitney S. Haist, Principal
PH: (925)283-2070
FX: (925)284-1843
E-mail: haist@jps.net
URL: http://www.jps.net/haist/haistcor.htm
Consulting services in practices and standards, uniform building codes, and failure analysis. Offers cost of repair estimating and destructive testing.

HALDEMAN POWELL & PARTNERS
15303 Dallas Pky., Ste. 300, LB30
Dallas, TX 75248
Edward B. Haldeman, Jr., President
PH: (972)701-9000
FX: (972)991-3008
E-mail: aoffice@haldeman-powell.com
URL: http://www.haldeman-powell.com
Founded: 1975. **Staff:** 40. Offers basic architectural services, zoning assistance services, master planning, construction administration, relocation coordination, interior design, corporate and tenant space planning, computer-aided drafting and design, model building, renderings, and facilities programming. Services include the following building types: office buildings; hotels; retail centers; industrial facilities; recreational, educational, aviation, high-rise housing, institutional, and computer facilities.

HAMMOND, COLLIER & WADE—LIVINGSTONE
ASSOCIATES, INC.
4010 Stone Way N., Ste. 300
Seattle, WA 98103-8090
Bruce Livingstone, President
PH: (206)632-2664
TF: (800)562-7707
FX: (206)632-0947
URL: http://www.hcwl.com
Founded: 1943. **Staff:** 51. Offers civil and municipal engineering, land surveying services, and materials testing laboratory. Representative project areas include water and sewer utility design and hydraulic engineering; flood control, drainage, and hydrology; subdivision engineering, grading, roads and parking; urban, environmental and site planning; G.I.S. and facilities mapping, legal, topographic and boundary surveys, hydrographic, creek restoration, and hazardous waste site surveying.

HAN-PADRON ASSOCIATES, LLP
11 Penn Plaza
New York, NY 10001
Dennis V. Padron, Contact
PH: (212)736-5466
FX: (212)629-4406
E-mail: hpany@han-padron.com
URL: http://www.han-padron.com
Founded: 1979. **Staff:** 120. Consulting services include planning, design and construction supervision for marine terminals, ports and harbors, coastal structures, single point moorings, pipelines, conveyors, offshore structures, tank farms, bulk storage facilities and marinas for the energy, mining, and marine transportation industries and for various federal, state and local government agencies.

HANLEY-MCCARTNEY INC.
11726 San Vicente Blvd., Ste. 400
Los Angeles, CA 90049-5044
Reid McCartney, Contact
PH: (310)207-4633
FX: (310)207-3876
Founded: 1987. **Staff:** 2. Consulting firm offering construction and construction management services to architects, clients in business and industry, and the general public.

WILLIAM H. HARELSON
325 Mt. Sherman Dr.
Leadville, CO 80461
W.H. Harelson, Contact
PH: (719)486-0507
Founded: 1983. **Staff:** 2. Offers services in mining and tunneling engineering. Also provides services as expert witness in construction management and inspection, and in computer software. Serves private industries as well as government agencies.

HARZA ENGINEERING CO.
Sears Tower
233 S. Wacker Dr.
Chicago, IL 60606-6392
J.E. Lindell, Vice President
PH: (312)831-3000
FX: (312)831-3999
E-mail: info@harza.com
URL: http://www.harza.com
Founded: 1920. **Staff:** 800. An international consulting firm that provides quality engineering, environmental, and architectural services to private enterprises and government agencies in the development of water, energy, and land resources. Specializes in the planning, design, permitting, and construction management of dams and reservoirs; pumped storage projects; hydroelectric facilities; water supply systems; fish hatchery and passage facilities; private power development; electrical power transmission and distribution systems; navigation locks; waterfront facilities; parks and recreational facilities; educational facilities; pharmaceutical facilities; roads, highways, and bridges; tunnels and underground structures; water; and wastewater treatment facilities. Other services include: agriculture and irrigation development; dam inspection and rehabilitation; equipment acquisition management; technology transfer and training; environmental studies and mitigation; flood control; and water quality monitoring.

HATCH ASSOCIATES
2800 Speakman Dr.
Mississauga, ON, Canada L5K 2R7
R.R. Nolan, President/CEO
PH: (905)855-7600
FX: (905)855-8270
E-mail: tomreid@hatch.ca
URL: http://www.hatch.ca
Founded: 1955. **Staff:** 2300. Offers comprehensive engineering (ISO 9001-94 registered), procurement, project and construction management services in the following fields: iron and steel, nonferrous metals and minerals, information technology, energy, petrochemical, pulp and paper, rapid transit and tunneling, pharmaceuticals and industrial/manufacturing. Specific services include feasibility studies, assistance with project financing, technology transfer, process development, systems development, environmental assessment studies and pollution control. Industries served: chemical, energy, iron and steel, pulp and paper, manufacturing, mining, transportation, base metals and minerals, transit and tunneling, utilities, and government agencies.

HAWK ENGINEERING
PO Box 427
Binghamton, NY 13902
William C. Drachler, President
PH: (607)648-4168
TF: (800)945-4295
FX: (607)648-4777
E-mail: hawkeng@stnx.lrun.com
URL: http://hawkeng.com
Founded: 1955. **Staff:** 34. Consulting engineers whose services include civil engineering and planning, construction coordination, environmental engineering and planning, survey mapping and GIS, landscape architecture, and related endeavors. Serves private industries as well as government agencies.

HAYES LARGE ARCHITECTS
Logan Blvd. and 5th Ave.
Altoona, PA 16603
J. Richard Fruth, Contact
PH: (814)946-0451
FX: (814)946-9054
E-mail: altoona@Mayeslarge.com
Founded: 1922. **Staff:** 120. Offers architecture, structural engineering, landscape architecture, energy conservation, interior design, planning and programming, food service design, laboratory equipment development, cost estimating, value engineering and construction administration. Clients include public and private schools, colleges and universities, corporate, continuing care, hospital, retirement communities, commercial and industrial, government and religious.

HCMA CONSULTING GROUP
7150 SW Fir Loop, Ste. 100
Tigard, OR 97223
Robert Hafner, President
PH: (503)620-4329
TF: (800)587-4329
FX: (503)620-9360
E-mail: admin@hcma.com
URL: http://www.hcma.com
Founded: 1962. **Staff:** 20. Engineering consulting firm offering Structural, Mechanical, Civil and Electrical Engineering and Construction Management Services for industrial, commercial and government clients. HCMA specializes in the forest products industry and offers those clients a complete one-stop consulting service starting in the forest with resource/process/market analysis and feasibility studies-to the existing mill with training productivity, profitability, improvement services, operations management and research, economic studies, computer services and business appraisals.

HDO ARCHITECTS
2960 Camino Diablo, Ste. 110
Walnut Creek, CA 94596
Randall Harris, Principal
PH: (925)934-4206
FX: (925)934-8618
Consultation services in wood frame construction and reconstruction.

THE HELFENBEIN CO.
4070 Fragile Sail Way
Ellicott City, MD 21042
Christian Helfenbein, Contact
PH: (410)461-1111
FX: (410)461-1296
Founded: 1976. Architectural design firm specializing in commercial design/build services. Maintains computer-aided design capabilities. Also custom cabinetry design and fabrication.

HELLMUTH, OBATA & KASSABAUM, INC.
One Metropolitan Square
St. Louis, MO 63102
Gyo Obata, Co-Chairman
PH: (314)421-2000
TF: (800)788-5518
FX: (314)621-0944
E-mail: debbie.dempsey@hok.com
URL: http://www.hok.com
Founded: 1955. **Staff:** 2000. Offers complete architectural and engineering consulting services including site selection, facility programming, architectural software systems, master planning, design, bidding and contract documents, construction administration and supervision, landscape architecture, interior design, graphic design, lighting design, architectural renderings, models, sports facilities planning and design, store planning, and facility management. Engineering services include mechanical/electrical and civil.

HELP/SIMINS FALOTICO GROUP INC.
100 St. Mary's Ave.
Staten Island, NY 10305
Thomas Masucci, President
PH: (718)448-3400
TF: (800)435-7099
FX: (718)448-3499
E-mail: helpco@help-co-inc.com
URL: http://www.helpco-inc.com
Founded: 1980. **Staff:** 17. Provides complete integration of services in architecture, engineering, environmental, and construction management, computer-aided-design, industrial hygiene, energy management, and training and certification. Includes design, inspections, analysis, project management, and quality control for existing or new facilities including industrial, residential, government, commercial, utilities, and medical.

VERNON G. HENRY & ASSOCIATES INC.
515 Post Oak Blvd., Ste. 205
Houston, TX 77027
Vernon G. Henry, President
PH: (713)627-7666
E-mail: henryinc@flash.net
Founded: 1967. **Staff:** 15. Services range from development of comprehensive plans for cities, large scale new communities and public parks to detailed subdivision platting and landscape plans for office parks, shopping centers and other commercial projects. Involves coordination with architectural, engineering, environmental and market analysis firms. Also offers counsel in traffic analysis, development feasibility and site selection. Regularly provides expert witness court testimony in litigation involving zoning, deed restrictions and eminent domain proceedings. Additional capabilities include evaluation of existing vegetation, irrigation systems design, outdoor lighting design, design of decks, shade structures, pools, fountains and water features, as well as construction management.

HIGH-POINT RENDEL
225 Broadway, Ste. 2200
San Diego, CA 92101
Gene Bennett, President and CEO
PH: (619)230-0336
TF: (800)229-9050
FX: (619)230-0613
Founded: 1980. **Staff:** 150. A worldwide financial, contractual, and management consultancy, offering construction claim evaluations, management analysis of construction firms and projects, owner representation services, property and casualty services, surety and defective construction investigations, fidelity claim services, and bank problem loan and customer evaluation services. Other services include construction management, hazardous waste evaluation, forensic engineering and project feasibility and constructability. Industries served: real estate development, construction, engineering, architecture, financiers, litigation, insurance, owner, public agencies, and government agencies.

HIGHLIGHTS CORP.
825 Hammonds Ferry Rd., Ste. B
Linthicum Heights, MD 21090
Joseph C. Huang, CEO
PH: (410)636-9930
FX: (410)636-9940
Founded: 1969. **Staff:** 46. Offers architectural and engineering design consulting specializing in construction services: general contracting, construction management, construction inspection, and construction estimating. Serves private industries as well as government agencies.

HILL INTERNATIONAL, INC.
1 Levitt Pky.
Willingboro, NJ 08046
Irvin E. Richter, Chairman/CEO

PH: (609)871-5800
FX: (609)871-5714
E-mail: sturichter@hillintl.com
URL: http://www.hillintl.com
Founded: 1976. **Staff:** 200. Provides comprehensive engineering, construction and management consulting services to contractors, public/private owners, architect/engineers, lenders, sureties, and their counsel. Services include staff training, organizational studies including evaluation of contract delivery systems and project administration practices, development of project controls, project management and oversight support, troubled project turnaround, project staff augmentation, cost tracking and control, cost estimating, CPM scheduling, delay/acceleration and disruption/inefficiency analyses, damages evaluation, claim analysis and negotiation, defective design and construction forensics, neutral dispute evaluation and mediation, technical evaluation of performance disputes, alternative dispute resolution and litigation support and expert witness services.

RICHARD HILL, P.C.
2 W. 32nd St.
New York, NY 10001
Richard Hill, President
PH: (212)594-7070
FX: (212)736-7667
Founded: 1957. **Staff:** 3. Design of heating, ventilating, air conditioning, plumbing, fire protection and electrical systems for new construction and tenant change in existing buildings. Feasibility and existing installation evaluation reports. Code compliance studies. Industries served: real estate, government, architects, and designers in New York, New Jersey, and Connecticut.

THE HILLIER GROUP
500 Alexander Park, CN23
Princeton, NJ 08543-0023
J. Robert Hillier, CEO
PH: (609)452-8888
TF: (800)HIL-LIER
FX: (609)452-8332
E-mail: nstern@hillier.com
URL: http://www.hillier.com
Founded: 1966. **Staff:** 420. Provides services in architecture, planning, interior design, engineering, construction management, strategic facilities planning, real estate evaluation, and graphic design. Industries served: public and private sector.

HISTORIC EXTERIOR PAINT COLORS CONSULTING
3661 Waldenwood Dr.
Ann Arbor, MI 48105
Robert Schweitzer, Consultant
PH: (734)668-0298
E-mail: robs@umich.edu
URL: http://www.arts-crafts.com/market/robs
Provides exterior paint color consulting — historic, contemporary, new construction, commercial, residential museums.

HKA ELEVATOR CONSULTING
27401 Los Altos, Ste. 480
Mission Viejo, CA 92691
Daryl Anderson, President
PH: (949)348-9711
FX: (949)348-9751
E-mail: hka@hkaconsulting.com
URL: http://www.hkaconsulting.com
Founded: 1963. **Staff:** 6. A consulting firm specializing in the business of vertical and horizontal transportation. Assists clients in the development of people and material transportation systems for market segments such as airports, commercial offices, retail malls, hospitals, hotels, residential, parking facilities, museums, libraries, schools, correctional facilities, and public transit facilities. Its client base consists of architects, developers, building owners and managers, contractors and public agencies such as federal, state, country and city entities. Additionally, the firm's expertise allows for expert witness services to be offered to attorneys and insurance companies. Elevator consulting services for projects in which the property and

vertical transportation systems are already installed include the following services: due diligence, performance analysis, maintenance contract, modernization, bid review, A.D.A. compliance, capital expenditure/5 year plan, expert witness, and insurance claims. Elevator consulting services for new construction projects in which the vertical transportation systems have yet to be designed or installed require the following phases of services: schematic design, design development, construction doc., bidding, and construction administration.

HLW INTERNATIONAL LLP
115 5th Ave.
New York, NY 10003
Leevi Kiil, Contact
PH: (212)353-4600
FX: (212)353-4666
Founded: 1885. **Staff:** 211. A full service architecture/engineering/planning/interior design firm, offering complete professional design services including architecture; mechanical, electrical, plumbing, and structural engineering; master planning; site planning; landscape architecture; interior design; facilities management; construction management, communications, and graphics. The firm's areas of specialization include the design of research and development facilities, academic facilities, communications buildings, advertising agencies, broadcasting facilities, financial institutions, and automated offices, as well as flexible corporate facilities for the 1990s. Industries served: pharmaceutical, electronics, chemical, consumer products, consumer services, communications, banking, advertising, media, healthcare, and government agencies.

HOLDREN CONSTRUCTION MANAGEMENT
9280 Metcalf Ave., Ste. 292G
Overland Park, KS 66212-1478
Stephen L. Holdren, President
PH: (913)492-2328
FX: (913)492-2328
E-mail: sholdren@sprynet.com
Founded: 1984. **Staff:** 3. Provides consulting and analysis to the construction industry. This includes project management, CPM scheduling, proposals for government contracts, construction cost estimates, construction claims analysis, litigation support, and expert testimony. Specialized expertise in contractor document review, expert testimony related to schedule delays and impact analysis, and loss of efficiency claims. Clients include: contractors, consulting engineers, law firms, government agencies, and surety companies.

H.H. HOLMES TESTING LABORATORIES, INC.
170 Shepard Ave.
Wheeling, IL 60090
Scott R. Nelson, President
PH: (847)541-4040
E-mail: scott@hhholmestesting.com
URL: http://www.hhholmestesting.com
Founded: 1936. Lab services: encompass the full range of construction materials testing. Primary fields of testing are in soils, concrete, aggregate, asphalt, masonry, steel and research. The lab is equipped to handle testing requirements. Field services: field staff consult in a broad range of construction testing services. Drill services: performs concrete inspections, soil bearing inspections, nuclear density testing of soils and asphalt, core drilling of concrete and asphalt, masonry inspections and steel testing.

HOLZMACHER, MCLENDON & MURRELL
575 Broad Hollow Rd.
Melville, NY 11747
Gary J. Miller, Contact
PH: (516)756-8000
FX: (516)694-4122
URL: http://www.ham.com
Founded: 1933. **Staff:** 120. Offers environmental engineering expertise in water resource management, wastewater management, solid waste management and resource recovery, hazardous materials/air pollution control, infrastructure/site engineering, construction management, environmental science, community planning and de-

velopment, architecture and structural engineering, surveying and mapping and analytical laboratory services for government and industry.

HOME BUILDERS NETWORK
205 E. Ridgeville Blvd., Ste. C
Mount Airy, MD 21771
Al Trellis, Founder
TF: (800)206-0974
E-mail: consult@hbnnet.com
URL: http://www.hbnnet.com
Founded: 1991. Helps builders increase their competitiveness through information, education, and consulting. Also works with industry manufacturers to help them better serve their builder customers. Works directly with builders in the areas of marketing, product design, land acquisition, and management. Also works with architects to facilitate the creation of housing product lines for builders.

THE HOMESTAR GROUP
4646 N. Hermitage
Chicago, IL 60640
Ronald L. Gan, President
PH: (773)878-7078
FX: (773)878-7255
E-mail: homestar1@aol.com
URL: http://members.aol.com/consulths
A full service construction consulting firm specializing in analyzing and reorganizing construction projects that are not progressing as planned. Provides project analysis, financial analysis, project recovery services, and litigation support.

HORNER & SHIFRIN, INC.
5200 Oakland Ave.
St. Louis, MO 63110
Leonard C. Kirberg, President
PH: (314)531-4321
FX: (314)531-6966
E-mail: hs@hornershifrin.com
URL: http://www.hornershifrin.com
Founded: 1933. **Staff:** 80. Offers engineering and architectural design and construction management services, including financial feasibility studies; field surveying; design; preparation of plans and specifications; and construction management for civil, architectural, structural, mechanical, and electrical projects. Typical projects include airports, highways, bridges, commercial and industrial buildings, sewerage and water treatment and distribution systems, flood control, storm drainage systems, docks, and industrial sites and parks. Serves clients in all industries located in the Midwest.

GEORGE THOMAS HOWARD ASSOCIATES, INC.
7046 Hollywood Blvd., 7th Fl.
Hollywood, CA 90028-6063
George Thomas Howard, Chairman/CEO
PH: (213)462-2343
FX: (213)461-3553
Founded: 1970. **Staff:** 12. The firm is principally involved in the design of public assembly facilities including theatres, auditoriums, lecture halls, legislative chambers, meeting rooms, convention halls, theme parks, etc. and all associated special facilities and systems for both new construction and renovation/retrofit. Services include acoustics, audio systems; projection; architectural display and theatrical lighting; seating and sightlines; theatrical rigging; theatrical draperies; stage floors; stage lifts; and video monitoring systems. In addition the firm consults on the design of new and the remodeling of existing motion picture and television studio facilities and the design of museum, hotel and casino security systems. Serves private sector as well as government agencies worldwide.

C.W. HOWE ASSOCIATES
1424 4th St., Ste. 501
Santa Monica, CA 90401
Carl Howe, Principal

PH: (310)395-9688
FX: (310)395-0698
E-mail: carl@cwhowe.com
URL: http://www.cwhowe.com
Founded: 1983. **Staff:** 4. Provides structural analysis and design of single and multi family residential, hillside construction, commercial, government and aerospace facilities, amusement park rides, seismic retrofitting. Offers construction defect analysis and claims resolution, building code review, real estate prepurchase reports, insurance claims forensic engineering, failure analysis, and expert witness testimony.

HOYER-SCHLESINGER-TURNER, INC.
300 W. Adams St.
Chicago, IL 60606
Amos Turner, President
PH: (312)263-0556
FX: (312)263-0820
Founded: 1963. **Staff:** 15. Provides consulting engineering, design, purchasing of equipment and construction management in the following disciplines: civil, architectural, structural, mechanical, electrical and instrumentation. Serves the chemical, petrochemical, food, pharmaceutical, minerals, steel, and plating industries, as well as government agencies.

HUITT-ZOLLARS INC.
500 W 7th St., Ste. 300
Fort Worth, TX 76102
Robert L. Zollars, President
PH: (817)335-3000
FX: (817)335-1025
Founded: 1975. **Staff:** 310. Provides professional consulting services to public and private clients in the areas of civil, structural, transportation, architecture, MEP, HVAC, environmental engineering, land surveying, and construction administration. Projects undertaken have included general public works, mixed-use planned developments, commercial/industrial parks, renovation of existing structures, environmental assessments, medical facilities, environmental engineering, traffic engineering, transportation planning, feasibility studies, construction administration and inspection. Serves private industries as well as government agencies.

I & F EQUIPMENT INC.
6069 Oakbrook Pky.
Norcross, GA 30093
Larry Z. Isaacson, ASA, Senior member
PH: (770)840-7060
TF: (800)427-2819
FX: (770)840-7069
E-mail: sales@ifequip.com
URL: http://www.ifequip.com
Founded: 1998. Specializes in appraisals of firms that manufacture concrete products.

ICF KAISER INTERNATIONAL, INC.
9300 Lee Hwy.
Fairfax, VA 22031-1207
James O. Edwards, Chairman of the Board & CEO
PH: (703)934-3600
TF: (800)423-4860
FX: (703)934-3740
URL: http://www.icfkaiser.com
Founded: 1969. **Staff:** 5000. Firm is one of the United States' largest engineering, construction, and consulting services companies. It provides fully integrated capabilities to clients in four related market areas: environment, infrastructure, industry, and energy. Recognized for its economic and financial analyses, strategic and management advice, organizational development and implementation skills, and design and execution of cutting-edge information technologies. Specific areas of expertise include the environment, energy, housing and community development, economic strategy, transportation, and education and training. ICF Kaiser is also recognized as a global provider of conceptual and detailed engineering, program and project management, and construction management and construction servi-

ces for the environmental, industrial, infrastructure, and refining and petrochemical sectors.

IDCON INC.
7200 Falls of Neuse Rd.
Raleigh, NC 27615-5311
Christer Idhammar, CEO & Pres
PH: (919)847-8764
TF: (800)849-2041
FX: (919)847-8647
E-mail: info@idcon.com
URL: http://www.idcon.com
Founded: 1985. **Staff:** 12. Offers maintenance management services to manufacturing industry in North America and worldwide.

ILF CONSULTANTS INC.
3911 Old Lee Hwy., Ste. 42E
Fairfax, VA 22030
PH: (703)383-1280
FX: (703)383-1281
E-mail: johnijenkins@ibm.net
Engineers and architects specializing in tunnel construction.

IMAGE BUILDERS CONSORTIUM, INC.
521 W. Briardale Ave.
Orange, CA 92865
PH: (714)998-8811
FX: (714)998-5858
E-mail: image@connectnet.com
Founded: 1990. **Staff:** 50. Provider guarantees higher efficiency, better service, and lower costs. Use of a custom-tailored provider program from the occupied building specialists will reduce burden and increase profitability. Total facilities service from design build to maintenance and repair is available.

INBERG-MILLER ENGINEERS
124 E. Main
Riverton, WY 82501
J. Roger Miller, CEO
PH: (307)856-8136
FX: (307)856-3851
E-mail: imeriv@wyoming.com
Founded: 1971. **Staff:** 31. Consulting civil, geotechnical, and environmental engineering firm specializing in site and utilities engineering and surveying, construction materials and water testing. Serves private industries as well as government agencies.

INCINERATOR CONSULTANTS INC.
11204 Longwood Grove Dr.
Reston, VA 20194-1302
Calvin R. Brunner, President
PH: (703)437-1790
FX: (703)437-9048
E-mail: cbrunner@clark.net
URL: http://www.clark.net/pub/cbrunner
Founded: 1986. **Staff:** 1. An engineering firm specializing in incinerator systems technology. This includes all types of systems: for hospital waste disposal, hazardous waste disposal, treatment plant sludges, refuse or trash burning, general industrial waste disposal, VOCs and institutional waste stream disposal, and contaminated sites. Tasks include evaluation, planning, incinerator design seminars, applications seminars, conceptual design, bid package preparation, permitting, equipment procurement, construction administration, construction management, operator training, operations assistance, design manuals, trouble-shooting, inspections, and expert testimony. Industries served: any industry which generates waste; also institutions (universities, hospitals, etc.), and local, state, and federal governments.

INDUCTIVE ENGINEERING
602 State St.
Cedar Falls, IA 50613
Dale M. Gumz, Owner
PH: (319)266-0476

Founded: 1970. An engineering consultant for agriculture, construction, consumer products, and specialty machines. Forensic and safety services include accident reconstruction, design analysis, human factors, manufacturing processes, mechanical and electrical, occupational safety, product liability, product and machine design. Acts as an expert witness.

INNOVATIVE CONSULTANTS, INC.
3740 Campus Dr., Ste. 200
Newport Beach, CA 92660
Robert C. Thomas, President
PH: (714)756-8750
FX: (714)261-8419
Founded: 1972. **Staff:** 9. Provides project management, construction management, engineering, and process development for industry on water pollution control, water reuse, and resource recovery. Services include permit negotiation and processing, waste sampling and evaluation for compliance, monitoring and reporting; as well as studies, evaluations and process development in associated areas of water and resource recovery.

INSTITUTE FOR PRODUCTS, ENGINEERING & CONSTRUCTION
1121 Prospect St.
Westfield, NJ 07090-4240
Edna Zdenek, Contact
PH: (908)233-2973
TF: (888)212-1155
FX: (908)654-5937
E-mail: ipec@forensicengineers.com
URL: http://www.forensicengineers.com
Founded: 1971. **Staff:** 3. Provides studies, reports, and extensive litigation support. Expertise in construction, construction documentation, product liability, engineering, architecture, fire protection systems, codes and standards, Americans with Disabilities Act compliance, welding, automobiles, off-road vehicles and heavy equipment. All staff members hold appropriate licenses and degrees in one or more of the following: architecture, metallurgy, mechanical engineering, electrical engineering, structural engineering, chemical engineering, and engineering management. Staff is experienced with litigation, including testimony at trial, alternative dispute resolution and administrative hearings. Specialized expertise includes correctional facilities, gambling casinos, carnival and amusement parks, commercial and industrial buildings. Industries served: government agencies, educational and institutional facilities.

INTERFACE CONSULTING INTERNATIONAL
One Riverway, Ste. 2350
Houston, TX 77056
Frank Adams, President
PH: (713)626-2525
TF: (800)496-1089
FX: (713)626-2555
E-mail: interface@interface-consulting.com
URL: http://www.interface.consulting.com
Founded: 1986. An international consultant in claims management and dispute resolution, Interface combines innovative technology with hands-on experience to provide cost-effective, results-oriented solutions to construction conflicts. Interface consultants work to resolve a variety of construction problems including delays, disruptions, productivity and damages. Interface serves construction owners, contractors and their attorneys with disputes in the petrochemical, marine, wastewater, utilities, environmental, roads & bridges and commercial industries.

INTERTECH ASSOCIATES, INC.
77-55 Schanck Rd., Ste. B-9
Freehold, NJ 07728
Perry L. Schwartz, P.E.P.P.N.C.E.
PH: (732)431-4236
FX: (732)780-1597
E-mail: ia@intertechassociates.com
URL: http://www.intertechassociates.com
Founded: 1974. A consulting engineering organization specializing

in telecommunications and electronics systems for commercial, government education facilities. Works with developers, owners, and tenants on the design, evaluation, and implementation of intelligent building systems, such as voice, data, access control, video, security, alarms, radio, and other associated systems.

INTERTRADE PACKAGE MACHINERY
751 S. Center St.
Adrian, MI 49221
John Brannen, Contact
PH: (517)265-6608
FX: (517)265-2131
Provides manufacturers a wide range of expertise, including plant engineering, construction management, contract installation and maintenance, packaging consultation and maintenance, and assorted processing and refrigeration equipment.

IRZ CONSULTING
505 E. Main
Hermiston, OR 97838
PH: (541)567-0252
FX: (541)567-4239
E-mail: irz@eoni.com
URL: http://www.irz.com/IRZ
Founded: 1984. A full-service irrigation engineering and consulting firm. Specializes in large scale irrigation development, design, and construction management.

ISES CORP.
2165 W. Park Ct., Ste. N
Stone Mountain, GA 30087
PH: (770)879-7376
TF: (800)881-ISES
FX: (770)879-7825
E-mail: rickh@isescorp.com
URL: http://www.isescorp.com
Founded: 1980. Seeks to provide clients with operations/ management tool that identifies and quantifies areas requiring the necessary actions and costs to renovate, retrofit, restore, and modernize existing buildings to an improved condition. Specializes in facility condition analysis; elevator engineering; security analysis; utility system and infrastructure analysis; operations and maintenance analysis; facilities financing; and facility condition analysis.

IVEY CONSTRUCTION SERVICES
5225 Bothe Ave.
San Diego, CA 92122
William Ivey, Mechanical Engineer
PH: (619)587-1146
FX: (619)587-0060
Founded: 1994. HVAC, plumbing and piping experts. Provides construction consulting and technical services to the construction industry and legal community. Services include construction management, cost analysis, claim preparation, delay impact analysis, forensic investigation and expert witness testimony.

JACKSON AND TULL CHARTERED ENGINEERS
2705 Bladensburg Rd. NE
Washington, DC 20018
Knox W. Tull, Jr., President
PH: (202)333-9100
FX: (202)526-2876
Founded: 1974. **Staff:** 342. Offers civil and structural design engineering services, including storm water management; water supply and treatment; highway, bridge, and railroad design, mass transportation, dam inspection, and construction inspection and management. Also provides expertise in aerospace engineering.

C. E. JACKSON, JR.
PO Box 1226
McComb, MS 39649-1226
C. E. Jackson, Jr., Principal Executive
PH: (601)684-1107
E-mail: c.e.jackson@ieee.org
URL: http://www.telapex.com/~cejjrpe/resour01.htm
Construction consulting services in construction safety, civil engineering, construction management, electrical safety, construction engineering, OSHA regulations, arbitration/mediation, public safety, demolition, steel erection, trenching/excavation, highway work-zone safety, and construction equipment safety.

JACOBS ENGINEERING GROUP INC.
251 S. Lake Ave.
Pasadena, CA 91101
Joseph J. Jacobs, Chairman
PH: (626)449-2171
FX: (626)578-6916
Founded: 1947. A design/construction firm which offers a wide range of services to industry. The federal government and aerospace, high-tech facilities, petroleum and petrochemical, pharmaceutical, food, nonferrous metals, pulp and paper, fertilizer and chemical industries are primary clients. Services, in addition to engineering, design and construction, include feasibility, market and economic analyses, process design, complete environmental engineering services, architectural design, and plant maintenance services.

J.A.M.S/ENDISPUTE
1920 Main St., Ste. 300
Irvine, CA 92614-7279
John J. (Jack) Unroe, President & CEO
PH: (714)244-1818
TF: (800)352-5267
FX: (714)224-1818
URL: http://www.jams-endispute.com
Founded: 1994. **Staff:** 200. Provider of dispute resolution services including, but not limited to, employment, environmental, construction and insurance claims settlement. Also assists companies in designing dispute resolution programs for employee population.

JAVASSOCIATES, LLC
12-147 Blvd. Dr.
Danbury, CT 06810
John A. Vossler, PE, President
PH: (203)748-5489
TF: (800)782-JAVA
FX: (203)748-5489
E-mail: jvossler@javassociates.com
URL: http://www.javassociates.com
Founded: 1988. **Staff:** 2. Provides consulting and scheduling services for the planning, development and construction management of small to large building programs. Specialization in the development and construction of high tech manufacturing buildings and support facilities for industrial waste treatment, chemical distribution and bulk chemical storage. Expertise includes a knowledge and understanding of regulatory agencies, building codes, and environmental and land use considerations for successful project development. Industries served: high-tech industrial, environmental, university and governmental.

J.C. ESTIMATING, INC./JCE CO.
39-B N. Lawn Ave.
Elmsford, NY 10523-2623
Carole Shillito, President
PH: (914)592-6080
FX: (914)592-6247
E-mail: JCECO@worldnet.att.net
Founded: 1980. **Staff:** 25. A construction consulting firm providing a broad scope of services, from bid estimates for contractors and budget estimates for owners and users, to change order estimates for multi-billion dollar projects, as well as on-site supervision and management. Services cover the full range of project, planning and implementation; from the conceptual design to completion and any resultant claims and scheduling. The firm will also provide services on a temporary or on-call basis, an alternative to maintaining a full-time staff.

JDE CONSTRUCTION MANAGEMENT LTD.
Canada Trust Tower
10104—103 Ave., Ste. 1103
Edmonton, AB, Canada T5J 0H8
PH: (403)429-4849
TF: (800)667-4849
FX: (403)429-4843
E-mail: jde@jdecm.com
URL: http://www.jdecm.com
Construction consultants. Specializes in providing solutions that encourage the prevention, mitigation, and equitable settlement of construction disputes.

JENKINS CONSTRUCTION INC.
3011 W. Grand Blvd.
305 Fisher Bldg.
Detroit, MI 48202
James B. Jenkins, President
PH: (313)871-6040
FX: (313)871-6044
Founded: 1989. **Staff:** 30. Provides construction management and general contracting services to clients throughout the Metro Detroit area.

JOFFKO INTERNATIONAL ASSOCIATES
8038 El Rio St.
Houston, TX 77054-4184
Achilles Kozakis, Contact
PH: (713)644-3888
FX: (713)644-3015
Founded: 1974. **Staff:** 19. Consultants in the design and building profession who provide complete architectural, planning, engineering, contracting, maintenance, procurement and construction management services. Global operations include the Middle East, North and West Africa, and the Far East as well as ongoing projects in the United States.

JOHNSON ENGINEERING CONSULTANTS
368 Huron St.
Stratford, ON, Canada N5A 5T5
David G. Johnson, P. Eng.
PH: (519)271-9923
FX: (519)271-5353
E-mail: bjohnson@golden.net
URL: http://www.golden.net/~bjohnson/
Founded: 1963. Consulting engineering firm offering a range of civil engineering services from conceptual design through field design, drafting, and overall project management. Services include subdivision studies and design, municipal drains, structural design and analysis of any structure constructed out of steel, concrete, masonry, or wood (including manure tanks and bridges), formwork and falsework design, building design for commercial, industrial, residential, municipal, and agricultural (barns, shops, etc.), Ontario Building Code and Ontario Fire Code review, mechanical and electrical building services design, site plan agreements, lot grading plans, site investigation, construction layout, supervision, construction management including cost estimates, technical specifications, and contract documents, computerized and hand drafting, environmental studies, and storm water management.

JORDAN, KAISER AND SESSIONS
279 Lower Woodville Rd.
Natchez, MS 39120
PH: (601)442-3628
FX: (601)442-5511
E-mail: jkscs@bkbank.com
Founded: 1955. **Staff:** 36. Offers general civil engineering counsel including studies, reports, evaluations; surveying; design and supervision of construction of utilities systems, airfields, roads and streets and drainage systems.

JOSEPHSON-WERDOWATZ & ASSOCIATES, INC.
6370 Lusk Blvd., Ste. F200
San Diego, CA 92121-2753
Carl H. Josephson, President
PH: (619)558-2181
TF: (800)558-2181
FX: (619)558-2188
E-mail: cjosephson@jwa-se.com
Founded: 1988. **Staff:** 20. Provides construction defect investigations and evaluations; and structural design and analysis; building code review and analysis; computer presentations and animations; and alternative dispute resolution.

J.R.L. EXECUTIVE RECRUITERS
2700 Rockcreek Pky., Ste. 303
Kansas City, MO 64117
Larry E. Eason, President
PH: (816)471-4022
FX: (816)471-8634
Founded: 1987. **Staff:** 10. Executive recruiting segment of affiliation provides professional search specialists in the following areas: engineering/technical, data processing, warehousing/manufacturing, and computerized search for permanent and temporary personnel. The Engineering and Technical Services segment (Division of J.R.L. Executive Recruiters), offers construction management, contract engineering and technical services. Provides supervision of municipal, commercial, and industrial/manufacturing developments. Industries served: consulting, manufacturing, chemical, rubber/plastics, agricultural/foods processing, automotive, petrochemical, petroleum, pharmaceutical, paper, brewing/bottling, material handling, electronics, computer, explosives, heavy equipment, printing, environment, nuclear power, power utilities, packaging, industrial, and government agencies.

KAISER-TAULBEE ASSOCIATES, INC.
PO Box 480
Lexington, KY 40585-0480
Robert L. Kaiser, President
PH: (606)253-2459
FX: (606)259-1864
E-mail: wthomas@mis.net
Founded: 1981. **Staff:** 12. Engineering consultants providing mechanical, electrical engineering design, energy management, and construction supervision services. These services offered for developers of office buildings, retail shopping centers, apartment complexes, condos, schools, hospitals, manufacturing facilities, churches, restaurants, and newspaper facilities.

KALIN ASSOCIATES, INC
154 Wells Ave.
Newton Center, MA 02459
Mark J. Kalin, President
PH: (617)964-5477
FX: (617)964-5788
URL: http://www.spec-net.com/kalin.html
Independent specifications firm specializing in preparation of technical specifications and bidding documents for construction projects, and preparation of guide specifications for building product manufacturers. Related services include development of master specifications for agencies and design firms; computer automation of technical documents; specification coordination for large projects.

KARL KARDEL CONSULTANCY
479 Mountain Ave.
Piedmont, CA 94611
Karl Kardel, Principal
PH: (510)261-4149
FX: (510)547-1756
Founded: 1959. **Staff:** 12. Provides consultation in water invasion in above and below grade leaks. Offers problem resolution in finishes and coatings and forensic analysis in building failures. Specializes in historic conservation, architectural finishes, and water invasion. Gives analysis for managed case cost controls.

DREW A. KARTIGANER, ARCHITECT
555 Blooming Grove Tpke., Rte. 94
New Windsor, NY 12553
Drew A. Kartiganer, Contact
PH: (914)562-4499
FX: (914)562-8828
Founded: 1987. **Staff:** 3. Offers architectural design in residential and commercial areas, along with interior design expertise in the corporate and retail fields. Also designs master plan development for subdivisions, commercial and residential user. Offers expertise in historic renovations, housing and site plan analysis for commercial and residential use. Industries served: commercial, residential, and interior designers in the mid-Hudson region.

KASPER GROUP, INC.
968 Fairfield Ave.
Bridgeport, CT 06605
Joseph T. Kasper, President
PH: (203)579-1902
FX: (203)696-2323
URL: http://www.kaspergroup.com
Founded: 1963. **Staff:** 50. Offers consulting services in architecture, engineering (civil, structural, environmental, transportation, mechanical, electrical); planning (construction site and community); construction management; and surveying (land, hydrographic and aerial).

KAZEL MOUNTAIN MINES CORP.
PO Box 1428
Fairplay, CO 80440
William G. Kazel, President
PH: (719)836-3100
Founded: 1972. **Staff:** 5. Offers services in mine contracting, evaluation and equipment sales. Serves private industries as well as government agencies.

KBA ENGINEERING
25 S. Washington Ave.
Jermyn, PA 18433
Al Brocavich, President
PH: (717)876-5744
FX: (717)876-4299
E-mail: kba@icontech.com
Founded: 1982. **Staff:** 14. Offers the following consulting services: civil and structural engineering design; solid waste management studies for municipalities; plant and environmental engineering for industry; pavement management for municipalities; construction management; and materials testing.

KCI TECHNOLOGIES, INC.
10 N. Park Dr.
Hunt Valley, MD 21030-1888
PH: (410)316-7800
TF: (800)572-7496
FX: (410)316-7817
URL: http://www.kci.com
Founded: 1988. **Staff:** 450. Offers complete engineering and planning services-consultation, investigations, feasibility studies, reports, planning design, plans, specifications and construction services. Areas of work: commercial, industrial, institutional and public facilities; highways, airports, water, waste water, solid waste and environmental systems, and telecommunication tower construction. New design or renovation design for heating, air conditioning, plumbing, lighting, power, energy, telecommunications, refrigeration, controls, central plants, urban development, town planning, transportation and environmental systems, storm sewers, flood control installations, railroads and bridges, airports and mass transit. Industries served: public, developers, telecommunications, chemical, manufacturing, and government agencies.

KEESEN WATER MANAGEMENT, INC.
420 S. Marion Pky., Ste. 1502
Denver, CO 80209
Mary Stuart, President

PH: (303)695-7711
TF: (800)878-7781
FX: (303)695-1413
E-mail: khauna@aol.com
Founded: 1982. **Staff:** 3. Irrigation system design and consulting firm offers evaluations, operation management and construction services. Leads educational seminars and prepares informational reports. Special skills include: computer (CAD) irrigation design, experience in specifying and operating computerized central/satellite control systems, water audits and evaluation of irrigation systems, and a familiarity with many types of soil moisture systems. Industries served: developers, land planners, government agencies, grounds maintenance personnel, grounds managers, homeowner's associations, and any other entity requiring knowledge of irrigation systems or related fields. Also serves government agencies.

KELLAM AND ASSOCIATES, INC.
131 Dillmont Dr., Ste. 200
Columbus, OH 43235
Richard L. Myers, President
PH: (614)888-5131
FX: (614)888-2755
Founded: 1953. **Staff:** 25. Offers services in architecture, structural, electrical, mechanical, plumbing engineering, and construction management.

KELLEY MARINA DEVELOPMENT CO.
Tucker's Wharf
PO Box 212
Marblehead, MA 01945
William H. Kelley, President
PH: (617)639-4454
FX: (617)639-4640
E-mail: kmr@shore.net
Founded: 1986. **Staff:** 2. Consults on all phases of waterfront development, operations and management. Services include, but are not limited to: initial concept and planning, site layout and configuration, financial planning and implementation, equipment evaluation and selection, construction bidding and supervision, marina marketing, and marina management. Also experienced in golf course management and safety programs. Industries served: marina, golf, banking, and government agencies. Geographic areas served: East Coast.

KENNEDY/JENKS CONSULTANTS
622 Folsom St.
San Francisco, CA 94107
David D. Kennedy, President
PH: (415)243-2150
FX: (415)896-0999
URL: http://www.kennedyjenks.com
Founded: 1919. **Staff:** 330. The firm provides environmental consulting engineering services including feasibility studies, planning and preliminary design, final design, management of construction, operational assistance, and plant monitoring. Fields of activity include water supply, treatment and distribution, wastewater collection, treatment and disposal, wastewater reclamation and reuse, hazardous and toxic waste remedial work, industrial waste treatment, environmental impact assessments, and energy conservation systems. Serves private industries as well as government agencies.

KENNEDY SAFETY SERVICES, INC.
137 Ruhle Rd.
Ballston Spa, NY 12020
George S. Kennedy, Principal
PH: (518)885-2560
FX: (518)884-8756
E-mail: kssinc@worldnet.att.net
An accident and safety specialist in litigation consulting, safety training and education issues, safety management, personal injury investigation, accident investigation and reconstruction, OSHA compliance and regulations, product safety, construction, and occupational safety and health issues. Concentrates on the following areas: trenching, excavation, confined space entry, stairways, scaffolds, ladders, slips, falls, fall protection, electrical hazards, materials

handling, loading docks, forklifts, tools, equipment, machine guarding, lockout/tagout, personal protective equipment, hazardous materials, and hazard communication.

KFA SERVICES
6710 128th St., SW
Edmonds, WA 98026
Michael S. Katz, Contact
PH: (206)745-6860
FX: (206)745-6860
Founded: 1983. Offers consulting services in financial, accounting, and economic analysis including business valuations, financial projections and feasibility analysis, cost accounting, economic loss determination, mergers and acquisitions, and business policy and planning assistance. Also provides litigation support and construction claims analysis. Serves private industries as well as government agencies.

KGA, INC.
PO Box 635
Laguna Beach, CA 92651
Kurt Grosz, President
PH: (949)499-7474
FX: (949)499-8560
E-mail: socal@kgainc.com
URL: http://www.kgainc.com
Construction and engineering professionals who specialize in construction claims consultation and litigation support. Acts as mediators for construction related disputes. Specializes in analysis of contracts, drawings and specifications, building codes, construction defects, OSHA, change orders, construction sequencing, cost of repair, and scheduling.

KHANNA CONSULTING ENGINEERS, INC.
1091 Industrial Rd., Ste. 260
San Carlos, CA 94070
Mohan D.S. Khanna, President
PH: (650)598-0300
Founded: 1984. **Staff:** 4. Engineering consultant specializing in commercial and residential construction and development. Also offers structural engineering services including expertise in transportation, bridges, rails, highways, right-of-way engineering, as well as preliminary studies. Industrial experience includes: plant layout, piping, pipe hangers, foundations, steel frames, concrete frames, vibratory machine foundations, lateral analysis, and computer applications. Additional experience in waste water plants, water transportation, culverts, and other related items.

KINSEY ASSOCIATES
486 Rte. 24, Bldg. 2
Hackettstown, NJ 07840
L. John Belle, II, President
PH: (908)850-6488
FX: (908)850-6379
E-mail: kinsey@sprynet.com
Founded: 1962. **Staff:** 5. Park and recreation consultants offering a wide range of services including master plans, feasibility studies, recreation studies, and site planning and design of tennis courts, swimming pools; shelters, park sites, golf courses, ice arenas, ski areas, and camps. Serves private industries as well as government agencies.

KINTECH SERVICES, INC.
2900 Vernon Pl.
Cincinnati, OH 45219
A.P. Hallam, President
PH: (513)281-2900
FX: (513)281-1123
Founded: 1929. **Staff:** 110. Provides engineering, design, procurement, and construction management services for industrial plants. Serves all industries with emphasis on the process industries, chemical, pharmaceutical, and food.

GEORGE B. KIRK
PO Box 129
Mi Wuk Village, CA 95346
George B. Kirk, Contact
PH: (209)586-1603
FX: (209)586-1603
Founded: 1979. **Staff:** 1. Provides consulting services including technical appraisals for new ventures, and technical support for attorneys in litigation concerning building materials. Industries served: gypsum manufacturers and government agencies.

DONALD L. KISELEWSKI, INC.
4705 Holly Dr.
Palm Beach Gardens, FL 33418-4505
PH: (561)622-8538
FX: (561)694-8104
E-mail: DLRK@aol.com
An expert witness for construction defects and personal injury matters involving buildings, including modular construction, certified plans examination, conventional building construction, inspection, failure investigation, code compliance, restoration, evaluation, material analysis, and litigation.

KJWW ENGINEERING CONSULTANTS
623—26th Ave.
Rock Island, IL 61201
Vernon M. Wegerer, President
PH: (309)788-0673
FX: (309)786-5967
URL: http://www.kjww.com
Founded: 1961. **Staff:** 135. Designs mechanical, electrical, and structural systems for buildings. Specialties include the following: heating, ventilating, air conditioning, plumbing, process piping, fire protection, electrical distribution, asbestos removal, cogeneration, telecommunications, data systems and lighting. Also provides project and long-range planning, life cycle analysis, energy conservation, studies, cost estimates, construction observation, and systems commissioning. Industries served: healthcare, manufacturing, research, government, food processing, and education.

KLEINFELDT CONSULTANTS LTD.
2400 Meadowpine Blvd., Ste. 100
Mississauga, ON, Canada L5N 6S2
PH: (905)542-1600
FX: (905)542-9210
URL: http://www.kcl.ca/
Founded: 1961. Provides consulting engineering services to building owners, property managers and land developers. Assignments in building science, municipal engineering, land development services, structural engineering, mechanical/electrical engineering, forensic services, project management, environmental engineering. Offers a design, management and construction inspection team.

KLOCKNER STADLER HURTER LTD.
1400 Fort St., Ste. 900
Montreal, PQ, Canada H3H 2T1
Peter Schmid, President
PH: (514)932-4611
FX: (514)932-9700
E-mail: promo@ksh.ca
Founded: 1979. **Staff:** 400. Engineers and contractors to the forestry, pulp and paper industry. Assumes full turn-key responsibility. Services offered include: studies, basic and detailed engineering, project management and PM services, procurement, expediting, inspection and shipping of equipment, construction and construction management, financing, and operation management. Has designed, supplied and constructed pulp and paper mills, wood processing plants and forestry projects in many parts of the world. Pulp and paper industry projects have been designed to process soft and hardwoods, as well as non-wood fibers such as bagasse, bamboo, kenaf, sisal, reeds and straw.

KMK CONSULTANTS LTD.
220 Advance Blvd.
Brampton, ON, Canada L6T 4J5
T.H. Montgomery, Director
PH: (905)459-4780
FX: (905)459-7869
E-mail: kmk@kmk.on.ca
Founded: 1959. **Staff:** 55. Consulting engineers, planners, and landscape architects specializing in municipal engineering and planning projects. Services include design, project initiation and management, construction administration, and commissioning. Experienced with land development, subdivision engineering, landscape planning. Industries served: federal and provincial government ministries and departments; government agencies, regional and local municipalities; private industry and land development companies and institutions in Ontario, Canada.

JAX KNEPPERS ASSOCIATES, INC.
2950 Buskirk Ave., Ste. 180
Walnut Creek, CA 94596
PH: (510)933-3914
TF: (800)833-4371
FX: (510)933-9370
E-mail: jaxkneppers@earthlink.net
URL: http://www.jaxkneppers.com
Specializes in construction defect claims; standard of care analysis for architects, engineers and contractors; cost analysis and estimates; insurance losses, delay impact analysis; schedule analysis; project management; value engineering; construction document preparation; reconstruction cost estimates; and building damage assessment. Provides trial exhibits and graphics.

CALVIN KERN KOBSA & THE ADAM KERN GROUP
111 W. Monument St.
Baltimore, MD 21201
Calvin K. Kobsa, President
PH: (410)837-2277
FX: (410)837-7213
Founded: 1962. **Staff:** 3. Consulting services include architectural design, feasibility studies, cost estimates, inspection, and construction troubleshooting. Industries served: all private, institutional and public organizations.

KOHN ENGINEERING
4220 Mountain Rd.
Macungie, PA 18062
Don Kohn, Principal
PH: (610)967-4766
FX: (610)967-6468
E-mail: kohneng@voicenet.com
URL: http://www.voicenet.com/~kohneng
Founded: 1995. Specializes in program assessment: identifies cost effectiveness; assures compliance; determines ability to prevent or respond to fire emergency. Nuclear compliance: performs audits; provides technical and licensing; fire protection; functional inspections; surveillance reduction evaluations. Code compliance: interprets codes; reviews compliance; evaluates cost effective alternatives; negotiates code requirements design: evaluates cost effective alternatives; prepares specifications; creates drawings; reviews documents. Program development: creates integrated fire protection program; outlines objectives; defines organizational relationships; specifies design requirements; identifies operating requirements; creates procedures, fire response, maintenance. Litigation support: technical support; investigations; expert witnesses. Project management: program; design; construction; startup inspections: Facility. Equipment property insurance: negotiates insurance recommendations; evaluates cost-effective alternatives; reviews compliance; develops action plans to implement requirements. Vendor assistance: technical support; code interpretation; compliance support; product testing support. Training: code requirements; insurance requirements; hazard identification; and fire protection features.

KORA MANAGEMENT SERVICES
289 Cedar St.
Sudbury, ON, Canada P3B 1M8
Mitchell R. Speigel, President
PH: (705)675-7454
FX: (705)675-6302
E-mail: mrspeigel@compuserve.com
URL: http://www.korams.com
Founded: 1995. Specializes in construction, real estate development and management advice, and dispute resolution services. Experienced in property management, administration, and on-site construction. Offers services in five languages throughout North and South America.

JOHN P. KOSS ASSOCIATES, INC.
19640 Cypress Cir.
Miami, FL 33018-6258
John Peter Koss, President
PH: (305)829-3631
FX: (305)829-2484
E-mail: oleboss@aol.com
Founded: 1989. Provides engineering expertise for beverage industry in the following areas: management, construction management, facilities planning and engineering, warehousing, and distribution.

R. KRAFT INC.
129 Shorecliff Dr.
Rochester, NY 14612-3925
Ralph Kraft, President
PH: (716)621-6946
TF: (800)447-4754
FX: (716)621-2778
E-mail: clnrmsrvs@aol.com
URL: http://www.cleanroomservices.com
Founded: 1977. **Staff:** 6. Provides consulting for cleanroom design and construction of new cleanrooms, consulting of existing cleanrooms for more efficient operations and production yields, third party audits, certification services, QA programs for proper cleanroom construction methodology, training seminars for cleanroom constructors, operators, maintenance and support personnel, airflow visualization studies, witness plate sampling, fabric and product evaluation studies for cleanroom compatibility. Industries served: microelectronics, medical device/packaging, optical, pharmaceuticals, biotechnology, film manufacturing, injection molding, food processing and other environments requiring ultra-clean manufacturing facilities, as well as government agencies.

FRANCIS KRAHE & ASSOC. INC.
580 Broadway St., Ste. 100
Laguna Beach, CA 92651-1874
Francis J. Krahe, II, President
PH: (714)376-0744
FX: (714)376-0747
E-mail: fdkrachc@fkaild.com
URL: http://www.fkaild.com
Founded: 1983. **Staff:** 10. Firm offers architectural lighting design, providing both architectural and engineering services. Experienced with custom fixture design, construction management, and cost and energy management.

KRAUSER, WELSH, & CIRZ, INC.
161 Madison Ave.
Morristown, NJ 07962-2135
Barry J. Krauser, Contact
PH: (201)538-3188
FX: (201)538-8741
Founded: 1965. **Staff:** 31. The firm's professional real estate appraisal and consulting assignments and capabilities encompass: commercial/industrial valuations, lease and acquisition decisions, land-use analysis, construction management, market and feasibility studies, joint venture/limited partnership, financial analysis and tax consulting. Also offers expert testimony for property owners and by special assignment of the court or reviewing agency.

KRUMBEIN ENGINEERING, LTD.
361 SE 2nd
Pendleton, OR 97801
David H. Krumbein, President
PH: (541)276-3244
Founded: 1975. **Staff:** 1. Civil engineering consultant specializing in property and construction surveys.

KSS ENTERPRISES
PO Box 1824
Kihei, HI 96753
Karen S. Seddon, Owner
PH: (808)874-3450
FX: (808)874-3450
E-mail: kseddon@mavi.net
Founded: 1993. **Staff:** 1. Provides construction management and construction company organization.

**LA TRAY ENGINEERING CONSTRUCTION &
   CONSULTING**
7 Fabian Ct.
Novato, CA 94947
Patrick R. La Tray, Principal
PH: (415)898-2295
Offers services that include concrete failure analysis, coefficient of friction analysis, soil movement, drainage degradation/failures, concrete and masonry waterproofing failures analysis, structure inspection, structural failure analysis, and construction arbitration in litigation.

LABELLA ASSOCIATES, P.C.
300 State St., Ste. 201
Rochester, NY 14614
Salvatore A. LaBella, Contact
PH: (716)454-6110
FX: (716)454-3066
E-mail: labella@frontiernet.net
Founded: 1978. **Staff:** 70. Areas of specialization include: civil engineering, encompassing highway and street design; traffic planning, analysis, and design; structural design, inspections and load ratings for bridges and buildings; general municipal engineering for water distribution, sewers, drainage control; construction services; site development; and land survey. Environmental engineering services include hazardous material management, regulatory compliance and permit applications, training, solid waste management, landfills, recycling, composting, wastewater and water treatment, environmental site investigations, underground storage tank management, asbestos management and an in-house laboratory. Also offers architectural services with expertise in building design, mechanical/ electrical engineering and programming for renovations and additions, roofs, libraries, public facilities, educational and religious facilities, and industrial and commercial buildings.

LAC COMMUNICATIONS, INC.
Altavista 21-Q-46
Ponce, PR 00731
Luis A. Capestany, President
PH: (787)844-1448
FX: (787)843-0030
Founded: 1986. **Staff:** 16. Engineering firm with planning, design and construction capabilities in the communications field including CATV, telephone, microwave, earth station, and tower systems. Can perform both aerial and underground work. Industries served: telecommunications, government agencies, and general construction.

LANGFORD MANAGEMENT ASSOCIATES, INC.
The Graham Bldg., Ste. 1200
15th & Ranstead Sts.
Philadelphia, PA 19102
PH: (215)561-1960
FX: (215)561-1977
E-mail: langfordma@aol.com
Construction, engineer and environmental consultants. Provides a staff of engineers and construction experts to examine, confirm and

develop case evidence for insurance claims, personal injury, product liability, business interruption, construction litigation, and environmental litigation.

RONALD LASLEY & ASSOCIATES
PO Box 758
Palisade, CO 81526
Ronald Lasley, Contact
PH: (970)464-5156
FX: (970)464-5156
Founded: 1981. **Staff:** 1. Construction claims consultants provide services to the construction industry in regard to contract disputes. The firm's clients include attorneys, contractors, subcontractors, manufacturers, owners, government, sureties and design firms. The firm performs factual research, critical path schedule analysis and damages calculation on construction projects which are in dispute. Computers are used extensively during research and preparation of reports. Expert testimony is provided as well.

HOWARD LAST, P.E.
91 Arleigh Rd.
Great Neck, NY 11021
Howard Last, P.E.
PH: (516)466-8552
FX: (516)466-8552
Founded: 1985. **Staff:** 3. Specialist in the design of instrumentation and control systems for water and wastewater treatment facilities for municipalities and industrial firms. Offers assistance during construction and start-up of control systems. Assists with the preparation of field wiring and piping diagrams. Provides training of operating personnel. Existing instrumentation systems evaluated for upgrade and modernization. Is also an expert witness.

LAW COMPANIES GROUP, INC.
112 Townpark Dr.
Kennesaw, GA 30144
R.K. Sehgal, Chairman and CEO
PH: (770)421-3400
FX: (770)421-3486
Founded: 1946. Law Companies Group, Inc. is a corporation which is wholly owned by its employees. Firm is organized to provide the benefits of a worldwide organization focused on quality services delivered at a local level. Law consists of three groups whose staff number over 4,000 in over 100 worldwide locations. The three separate groups serve the engineering, environmental, and international markets.

LAW COMPANIES GROUP, INC.
3 Ravinia Dr., Ste. 1830
Atlanta, GA 30346
Andrew Young, Chairman and CEO
PH: (770)396-8000
FX: (770)390-3289
Founded: 1947. **Staff:** 1500. Law Companies International Group provides consulting services for all types of construction projects primarily through its subsidiary Sir Alexander Gibb & Partners Limited and related Gibb companies. Gibb offers a full range of consulting services. These include project management, feasibility and pre-investment studies; site investigation surveys and models; project planning and detailed design; tender documentation and evaluation; contract administration and measurement; supervision of construction; procurement; technical assistance and training; and operations and maintenance. Industries served: public entities, industrial companies, property owners and developers. Geographic areas served: international.

**LAW/CRANDALL, INC.—SUBSIDIARY OF LAW
   COMPANIES GROUP, INC.**
200 Citadel Dr.
Los Angeles, CA 90040-1554
LeRoy Crandall, Chairman
PH: (213)889-5300
FX: (213)721-6700
Founded: 1954. **Staff:** 465. Firm offers a full range of consulting

services including site evaluation, comprehensive investigation and reports, geologic-seismic evaluation, engineering and environmental geology, materials engineering, and geotechnical inspection and testing services. Serves the industrial, commercial, and institutional markets in both public and private sectors worldwide.

LAWGIBB GROUP

112 Townpark Dr.
Kennesaw, GA 30144
Bruce C. Coles, Chairman and CEO
PH: (770)360-0600
FX: (770)360-0580
URL: http://www.lawgibb.com
Founded: 1946. **Staff:** 4300. Leading engineering, environmental and design consulting services company. Serves the industrial, commercial, and government market sectors throughout the world.

LAWLER, MATUSKY AND SKELLY ENGINEERS

1 Blue Hill Plz.
Pearl River, NY 10965
Peter M. McGroddy, COO
PH: (914)735-8300
FX: (914)735-7466
E-mail: lms@eng.com
URL: http://www.lmseng.com
Founded: 1965. **Staff:** 130. Offers environmental engineering and science consulting services that include planning, engineering studies, environmental assessment, permit negotiations, site engineering, process design, pilot plant operations, construction design and specifications, consultation during construction, bench scale testing, waste management and groundwater resource planning (contamination and hazardous materials assessment, preliminary site assessment, field sampling and monitoring for wastes, soils, groundwater and surface water, remediation design, QA/QC compliance procedures), feasibility and treatability studies, modeling, biological and water quality sampling and analysis, and expert witness testimony. Industries served: utilities, chemical, pharmaceutical, banking, electronics, construction, food, automation, telecommunications, computers, aerospace, cosmetics, petroleum, metals, paper, real estate, textile, insurance, dairy, and government agencies.

LEA INTERNATIONAL, LTD.

802-595 St.
Vancouver, BC, Canada V6C 2T5
N.E. Weeks, President
PH: (604)609-2272
FX: (604)609-7008
E-mail: leainternational@lea.com
URL: http://www.lea.ca
Founded: 1962. **Staff:** 150. A company of professional engineers, planners and economists specializing in consulting for all aspects of transportation, including planning and feasibility, project management and construction supervision, design, maintenance, training and technical assistance for highways, bridges, airport facilities, marine works, rail, transit and traffic, together with transportation planning, multi-modal transport planning, pavement management and computer applications covering all aspects of the movement of people, goods, and related services, both domestic and overseas.

A.C. LEADBETTER & SON, INC.

110 Arco Dr.
Toledo, OH 43607
PH: (419)537-9081
FX: (419)536-9134
Founded: 1946. Provides engineering consulting and design and construction services to the glass industry.

RICHARD A. LEBOEUF CONSULTANTS INC.

98 Freemans Bridge Rd.
Scotia, NY 12302
Richard A. LeBoeuf, President
PH: (518)399-4635
TF: (800)892-3025
FX: (518)382-5889

Founded: 1983. **Staff:** 10. Construction and roofing consultants.

ANDREW J. LECHNER, P.E.

2828 Burnaby Park Loop SE
Olympia, WA 98501-3884
Andrew J. Lechner, P.E.
PH: (360)705-3997
FX: (360)705-6519
Founded: 1986. **Staff:** 1. Metal industries consultants specialize in facility planning, project management and project engineering and construction management. Services available predominantly for nonferrous, aluminum sheet, plate, rod, bar, foil wire and extrusions. Also offers review of existing facilities to improve production, reduce costs, and improve quality. Industries served: basic and secondary metal producers.

DAVID H. LEE & ASSOCIATES, INC.

23011 Moulton Pky., Ste. D-11
Laguna Hills, CA 92653
PH: (714)461-5690
FX: (714)461-7901
E-mail: dhlee@pacbell.net
URL: http://www.dhla.com
A geotechnical engineering consulting firm specializing in new construction, investigations, arbitration, expert witness testimony, forensic studies of residential, commercial and industrial structures for insurance companies, earth movement (settlement, soil creep, landslides and expansive soils), foundation distress, slope stability, retaining walls, pipelines, design and construction deficiencies. Geotechnical monitoring includes slope inclinometers, settlement sensors, pneumatic transducers, tilt meters, piezometers, and manometer surveys.

LEE RESOURCES, INC.

880 S. Pleasantburg Dr., Ste. 1-F
Greenville, SC 29607-2413
Bill Lee, President
PH: (864)232-5264
TF: (800)277-7888
E-mail: info@leeresources.com
URL: http://www.leeresources.com
Founded: 1987. **Staff:** 18. Consulting service assists clients in the lumber and building supply industry to improve organizational productivity. Specializes in site selection; site planning; facility design and specification; equipment requirements and procurement; personnel needs and job descriptions; inventory assortment; proforma P&L budgets; initial capitalization requirements;

LEHR ASSOCIATES, CONSULTING ENGINEERS

130 W. 30th St.
New York, NY 10001-4092
Louis G. Piccirillo, Contact
PH: (212)947-8050
FX: (212)967-2059
E-mail: la@lehrassoc.com
Founded: 1969. **Staff:** 54. A full service consulting engineering firm providing mechanical, electrical, sanitary, and fire/life safety systems design for office buildings and renovations, medical and healthcare facilities, computer facilities, financial institutions, government agencies, retail and commercial buildings, educational facilities, residential housing, and hotels and major resorts. Also provides specialized services in: energy management, facilities management, including initial start-up of operations and maintenance, central utilities, site utilities and thorough construction phase project management. Industries served: commercial buildings, hotels, hospitals, schools, office buildings, shopping centers, and residential structures.

LEMNA TECHNOLOGIES

1408 Northland Dr., Ste. 310
St. Paul, MN 55120
Viet Ngo, President/CEO

PH: (651)688-0836
FX: (651)688-8813
E-mail: techsales@lemna.com
URL: http://www.lemna.com
Founded: 1983. Provides engineering, design and troubleshooting for wastewater treatment plants for industries and municipalities. Services include engineering assessment, chemical treatment, system design, manuals, start-up and personnel training, design/construction/management of patented Lemna treatment systems. Serves private industries as well as government agencies. with a total employment of more than 300 professionals. They use local and international subcontractors for construction and procurement of materials.

LUIS LEMUS CONSULTING ENGINEERS, INC.
5455 Dashwood, Ste. 100
Bellaire, TX 77401
Luis Lemus, Jr., President
PH: (713)661-9880
FX: (713)668-9813
Founded: 1978. **Staff:** 5. Consultants in the preparation of complete design and construction documents in structural and civil engineering (e.g., roadways, bridges, commercial and residential buildings, water and sanitary sewer drainage projects). Serves private industries as well as government agencies.

LENDERS' ARCHITECTURAL, LTD.
137 N. Wabash, Ste. 504
Chicago, IL 60602
Roy L. Stanger, AIA, President
PH: (312)346-2929
FX: (312)346-4788
Founded: 1989. **Staff:** 7. Construction risk management and remediation/repair consultants to the real estate development industry. For existing buildings, the firm identifies needed repairs and estimates cost of accomplishing them; prepares a maintenance plan and estimates its long-term cost. For construction and mortgage purposes, reviews budgeted costs for project and comments on their adequacy; reviews project documentation and comments on completeness and conformity to codes; conducts monthly reviews of the progress of the work, and comments on the appropriateness of the payout requests as related to the work in place, the quality of the work, and whether construction is keeping pace with the schedule; comments on conformance of the work to contract drawings and codes. For existing office buildings, shopping centers, and industrial buildings, the firm inventories space to determine net rentable area, net usable area, and construction area. Industries served: real estate development, banks, condominiums and cooperatives, building owners, and government agencies.

B.H. LEVELTON AND ASSOCIATES
No. 1, 12791 Clarke Pl.
Richmond, BC, Canada V6V 2H9
P.T. Seabrook, President
PH: (604)278-1411
FX: (604)278-1042
E-mail: levelton@unixg.ubc.ca
Founded: 1966. **Staff:** 85. Offers technical counsel in the following areas: construction materials design and testing, metallurgy, failure analysis, non-destructive testing, corrosion, cathodic protection, environmental engineering and testing, chemical and mechanical process engineering, geotechnical engineering, and feasibility studies. Serves private industries including pulp and paper, wood products, construction, and mining, as well as government agencies.

W.M. LEWIS & ASSOCIATES, INC.
Bank One Plaza, Ste. 300
PO Box 1383
Portsmouth, OH 45662
William M. Lewis, Jr., President
PH: (740)354-3238
FX: (740)353-2198
Founded: 1958. **Staff:** 19. Serves privately- and municipally-owned electric utilities and electric cooperatives in the planning, design and supervision of construction of hydroelectric generation, transmission, distribution and substations. Also performs cost-of-service and rates analyses.

L.F. RESEARCH
5611 County Ct.
Roscoe, IL 61073
Derek N. Walton, Owner, President
PH: (815)633-4504
FX: (815)633-4504
E-mail: lfresearch@aol.com
URL: http://members.aol.com/lfresearch
Founded: 1992. **Staff:** 9. Services include electromagnetic compatibility design, reviews of electrical schematics, PWB layouts, and mechanical construction. Tests for conducted and radiated emissions, conducted immunity, and radiated immunity.

LG & E POWER ENGINEERS AND CONSTRUCTORS, INC.
3200 Park Center Dr.
Costa Mesa, CA 92626
Donald Yamano, President
PH: (714)955-4000
FX: (714)955-4017
Founded: 1969. **Staff:** 60. Provides environmental, design, engineering, procurement, construction and startup services to the steam and power generation, industrial process, and petrochemical industries; as well as government agencies and utilities. Expertise includes cogeneration, power production, gas compression, and gas treatment facilities worldwide.

LIEBMANN ASSOCIATES, INC.—CONSTRUCTION CONSULTANTS
210 Interstate N. Pky., Ste. 700
Atlanta, GA 30339
Seymour W. Liebmann, President
PH: (770)952-8798
FX: (404)237-4516
Founded: 1979. **Staff:** 4. Offers general construction consulting services to the construction industry, law firms, government agencies, insurance companies, and financial and real estate firms. Specific services include expert witness testimony in construction matters and claims litigation and arbitration, cost analysis and evaluations, forensic services, and inspections and evaluations of physical facilities.

T.Y. LIN INTERNATIONAL
825 Battery St.
San Francisco, CA 94111
William Kallas, President
PH: (415)291-3700
FX: (415)433-0807
E-mail: postmaster@tylin.com
URL: http://www.tylin.com
Founded: 1954. **Staff:** 655. Offers a full range of structural and civil engineering services for complex infrastructure projects, including concept studies, preliminary design, plans and details for complete construction documents, preparation of specifications, checking of shop drawings, jobsite inspection and supervision, and value engineering. Also specializes in seismic analysis and retrofit design, transportation planning and traffic engineering. Projects have included bridges, highways, mass transit systems, convention centers, maritime structures, medical facilities, industrial complexes, office buildings, and parking structures. Serves private industries as well as government agencies.

WILL LINDSAY AND ASSOCIATES
1885 W. Commonwealth, Unit N
Fullerton, CA 92833
Will H. Lindsay, Jr., P.E.
PH: (714)525-4959
FX: (714)525-5150
Founded: 1958. **Staff:** 2. Offers consulting and construction services on systems for the manufacture or process of materials and finishes, while eliminating problems of pollution control of air, water,

noise, solid waste or toxic materials. This includes representation as an expert to the various boards and agencies cognizant with the control of these requirements. Also serves government agencies.

LINGNELL CONSULTING SERVICES
1270 Shores Ct.
Rockwall, TX 75087
A. William Lingnell, P.E., CC, APC
PH: (972)771-1600
FX: (214)771-1600
Specializes in technical management, building walls, windows, and glass; design, engineering, quality improvement programs, product development, and expert witness services.

COLIN C. LIVINGSTON, REAL ESTATE ANALYST/ CONSULTANT
Piedmont, CA 94611
PH: (510)654-7580
FX: (510)654-4340
Consulting in construction lending; commercial and residential real estate lending; banking; and mortgage banking; provides feasibility studies and market analysis for real estate development.

LOCKWOOD, ANDREWS & NEWNAM, INC.
1500 CityWest Blvd.
Houston, TX 77042
J. Anthony Boyd, Vice President
PH: (713)266-6900
FX: (713)266-2089
E-mail: mkth@lan-inc.com
URL: http://www.lan-inc.com
Founded: 1935. **Staff:** 230. Consulting engineering and architectural design, construction management and program management services. Specific services include preliminary studies, development and analysis of options, site selection, master planning, facility layout, special studies, energy and water conservation, traffic and transportation, preliminary design, detailed design, alternative design evaluation and construction services. Industry served: Aerospace, Research & Development, Educational, Industrial, Federal Agencies, Energy Systems/Cogeneration, Commercial Facilities, Health Care, Water/ Wastewater, Transit/Transportation. National.

LOCKWOOD GREENE ENGINEERS, INC.
PO Box 491
Spartanburg, SC 29304
Donald R. Luger, CEO
PH: (864)578-2000
FX: (864)599-4117
E-mail: Lockwood@lg.com
URL: http://www.lg.com
Founded: 1832. **Staff:** 3500. Planning, engineering, architecture and construction management of industrial, institutional, and commercial facilities. Industries served: general manufacturing, aerospace/defense, foods and beverages, printing and publishing, pharmaceutical, microelectronics, chemicals, research and development, textiles, steel, transportation, and government agencies.

LARRY B. LOETHEN
PO Box 3722
Quincy, IL 62305-3722
Larry B. Loethen, Sr., Contact
PH: (217)223-4777
FX: (217)223-8763
Founded: 1969. **Staff:** 3. Offers expertise in marketing and sales of flooring products, including carpet, tile, vinyl, wood, and others. Industries served: flooring and floor products, government, and general business in midwestern U.S.

LOSS ANALYSIS ENGINEERING, INC.
1420 N. Sam Houston Pky. E., Ste. 110
Houston, TX 77032
Richard T. Frantz, President
PH: (800)452-0870
FX: (281)442-5600

An independent investigative engineering company specializing in accident/failure analysis, forensic engineering, fire and explosion cause analysis for the insurance and legal communities. Capabilities encompass electrical, mechanical, chemical, construction, civil, structural, environmental, marine, electronics, energy, and vehicle accident reconstructions. Investigations provide evidence collection, objective analysis and practical interpretation of the data and a clear presentation of facts and conclusions that enables client to make decisions regarding insurance coverage, subrogation, litigation and repairs.

AUGUST C. LOZANO, P.E., INC.
500 Grand Ave.
Englewood, NJ 07631
August C. Lozano, President
PH: (201)871-7068
FX: (201)871-0206
E-mail: anglozano@aol.com
Founded: 1987. **Staff:** 5. The company specializes in structural and civil engineering design; preparation and processing of construction claims; construction management engineering reports; management, planning and inspection; construction methods and procedures; new work, rebuilding and alterations; and forensic engineering. Industries served: municipalities, attorneys, homeowners, and owners of commercial buildings.

LUDELL MANUFACTURING CO.
5200 W. State St.
Milwaukee, WI 53208
TF: (800)558-0800
FX: (414)476-9864
Firm offers extensive knowledge in engineering.

RAYMOND J. LYNCH, P.E., CONSULTING ENGINEERS
250 Rockland Ave.
River Vale, NJ 07675
Raymond J. Lynch, P.E., President
PH: (201)666-6178
FX: (201)666-6178
Founded: 1980. **Staff:** 4. Consulting engineers active in construction, energy conservation, design of plants and offices, plumbing-HVAC, and fire protection services. Industries served: hospital services, pharmaceutical, industrial/commercial buildings, and government agencies. Geographic areas served: Northeast Coast—North Carolina to Massachusetts.

THE LZA GROUP, INC.
641 Ave. of the Americas
New York, NY 10011
Charles H. Thornton, Chairman of the Board
PH: (212)741-1300
FX: (212)989-2040
E-mail: jzuliani@lzagroup.com
URL: http://www.LZAGroup.com
Founded: 1956. **Staff:** 360. Total engineering and architectural services for industrial-type facilities, warehouse/distribution facilities, special structures, parking garages, aviation and transportation facilities, laboratories, and suburban offices. Firm's capabilities include architecture, structural engineering, mechanical engineering (HVAC and plumbing), fire protection, electrical engineering (power distribution, lighting, communication systems, fire alarms, security systems), construction services, site utilities (power generation, water supply, sewage disposal, boilers), civil engineering (roads/rail, pavements, retaining walls, site drainage, piers/bulkheads), industrial engineering, cost estimating, and scheduling. Industries served: transportation, food, pharmaceutical, retail, aviation, real estate development, manufacturing, utilities, including government agencies.

HUNTLY G. MACDONALD
1021 Kingston Ln.
Alameda, CA 94501
PH: (510)521-4863
FX: (510)522-4344
Provides construction equipment and mining equipment appraisals.

A consultant in personal injury litigation regarding construction and mining equipment. Offers on-site studies and investigation. Provides document reviews, expert opinion memorandums, and report briefs.

IAN MACKINLAY ARCHITECTURE, INC.
26 O'Farrell S t., 2nd Fl.
San Francisco, CA 94108
PH: (415)243-4191
FX: (415)243-9769
E-mail: ima.arch@ix.netcom.com
Founded: 1990. **Staff:** 9. Architecture consultant providing expert analysis and testimony regarding architectural design and construction defects; building code compliance; roofing and waterproofing systems; and problems related to building in the snow and cold. Provides litigation strategy and organization, as well as product research and documentation.

MACLAUGHLAN CORNELIUS AND FILONI INC.
200 The Bank Tower
Pittsburgh, PA 15222
Albert L. Filoni, Contact
PH: (412)281-6568
FX: (412)288-2439
E-mail: mcf@usaor.net
Supervises architectural design, construction, and renovation of performing arts facilities. Conducts feasibility studies and master planning; provides all documentation; designs sets; and serves in advisory capacity for various projects.

HENRY J. MAGAZINER
2 Franklin Town Blvd. (2404)
Philadelphia, PA 19103-1237
Henry J. Magaziner, F.A.I.A.
PH: (215)575-9360
FX: (215)545-8397
Founded: 1948. **Staff:** 2. Arbitration of construction cases; expert witnessing in connection with accidents involving building deficiencies, ADA accessibility, inspection of buildings to determine their suitability for new uses, regulation compliance, and safety inspections. Critical inspection of museum buildings. National Register and Historic Landmark studies.

MAGUIRE GROUP, INC.
One Ct. St.
New Britain, CT 06051
Richard J. Repeta, President/CEO
PH: (203)224-9141
FX: (203)224-9147
Founded: 1938. **Staff:** 320. Offers comprehensive architectural, engineering, and planning consulting services to a full range of public and private sector clients. Specific areas of expertise include water and wastewater engineering, transportation engineering and infrastructure construction, environmental planning, design of port/ marine facilities, building systems design, design of waste-to-energy facilities, materials recycling centers and sanitary landfills, and construction administration and inspection services.

MAHALI-SHAFER THEATRE SERVICE
5293 SW Kenny Rd.
Lake Oswego, OR 97035
Kermit Shafer, Contact
PH: (503)228-1720
FX: (503)598-7603
Firm consults on theatre, lighting and scene design, and commercial lighting. Offers design, construction specifications, restoration, space conversion, and project supervision.

MAHARISHI GLOBAL CONSTRUCTION
500 N. 3rd St., Ste. 110
Fairfield, IA 52556
PH: (515)472-9605
FX: (515)472-9083
E-mail: reception@MGC-Vastu.com
URL: http://www.mgc-vastu.com

Consulting services to designers and builders of homes and institutional and commercial buildings, pre-designed homes and office buildings providing drawings and specifications .

NATHAN D. MAIER ENGINEERS INC.
8080 Park Ln. N. Park 2, Ste. 600
Dallas, TX 75231
Jean B. Maier, President
PH: (214)739-4741
FX: (214)739-5961
E-mail: ndmce@ndmce.com
URL: http://ndmce.com
Founded: 1984. **Staff:** 55. A civil engineering consulting firm with expertise in land development services, hydrology and hydraulics, environmental engineering, structural, transportation, traffic, surveying, municipal services and land planning. Industries served: municipalities, private land developers, financial institutions, and federal agencies.

JAMES J. MALLETT
416 N. Baylen St.
Pensacola, FL 32501
PH: (850)438-7794
FX: (850)438-7839
E-mail: malletteng@mallett-eng.com
A civil/structural construction consulting engineer specializing in documents, reports, investigations, and limited litigation.

MANAGEMENT COUNSELING CORP.
5059 Newport Ave., Ste. 206
San Diego, CA 92107
Mark A. Johnson, CEO, Chairman
PH: (619)225-9436
FX: (619)225-8496
Founded: 1962. **Staff:** 8. Consultants offering construction management and construction support services from project concept through warranty. Services include: critical path scheduling, cost estimating, constructibility analysis, contract administration, construction coordination, and claims analysis and prevention. Industries served: construction.

MANDEVILLE BERGE BOX-ARCHITECTS, ENGINEERS, PLANNERS, INTERIORS
500 Union St., Ste. 740
Seattle, WA 98101
Duane H. Box, AIA, Managing Partner
PH: (206)682-0120
FX: (206)682-0122
E-mail: mbbarch@juno.com
Founded: 1957. **Staff:** 10. Provides professional architectural/ engineering/planning services to a broad clientele. Services are in three general categories: (1) comprehensive architectural services with full control and coordination of engineering functions; (2) long range land use planning; (3) construction management. Clients include commercial and religious institutions, municipalities, governmental agencies, industries, banking, military, healthcare, multi-family residential, libraries, and recreation in western United States and Pacific islands.

MANUFACTURERS' SURVEY ASSOCIATES
30 Technology Pky. S., Ste. 100
Norcross, GA 30092
TF: (800)999-5502
FX: (770)417-4344
E-mail: info@msaonl.com
URL: http://www.msaonl.com
A provider of information for the construction industry. Offers information on commercial construction, architects and specifiers and CAD and technical information for manufacturer's building products.

MARATHON ENGINEERS/ARCHITECTS/PLANNERS, LLC
2323 E. Capitol Dr.
Appleton, WI 54913-8028
Chris J. Cox, Executive Vice President
PH: (920)954-2000
FX: (920)954-2020
URL: http://www.marathon-eap.com
Founded: 1966. **Staff:** 140. Provides engineering/architectural/ planning services to industrial, commercial, and institutional clients with a strong focus on research, engineering, pilot plant laboratory and office complexes. Specializes in providing consulting engineering to the pulp and paper, chemical and food processing industries. Disciplines include the following: architectural design, interior design, structural engineering, process engineering, civil engineering, plumbing and piping engineering, electrical engineering, instrumentation, heating, ventilation and air conditioning engineering, energy conservation audits, retrofit of existing mechanical systems, cost estimating, and construction observation. Marathon has served clients throughout the United States, Canada and on a smaller scale the foreign markets.

MARATHON SYSTEM SERVICES, INC.
3400 Industrial Ln., Unit 1
Broomfield, CO 80020-1650
Gary Glasscock, President
PH: (303)469-3700
FX: (303)469-3737
URL: http://www.marasyssys.com
Founded: 1979. **Staff:** 30. Data processing consultants specializing in service to the construction industry. Consults on obtaining and using automated management information in construction companies.

MARITECH ENGINEERING, INC.
1519 Alameda Dr.
Austin, TX 78704-3101
C. Michael Donoghue, President
PH: (512)326-3232
Founded: 1987. **Staff:** 2. Specialists in the structural design of conventional building and waterfront structures, fixed and floating breakwaters. Performs wind and wave studies and offers construction administration services.

THE MARK GROUP, INC.
3480 Buskirk Ave., Ste. 120
Pleasant Hill, CA 94523
David K. Rogers, Principal
PH: (510)946-1055
FX: (510)946-9813
Specializes in geotechnical failure analysis, construction quality assurance, cost recovery and technical documentation, soil and groundwater cleanup, management, environmental compliance audits, underground tank removal, air toxic monitoring, risk assessment, and worker exposure.

MARKETS BY DESIGN
97 Buttermill Ave.
Concord, ON, Canada L4K 3X2
TF: (888)617-7111
FX: (905)669-4385
URL: http://www.markets-by-design.com
Provides services in design, signage and construction to the retail industry. Experience in feasibility studies; conceptual development of building and marketing parameters; site planning and civic coordination; base building design signage, communication and fixture design; full coordination of construction, construction documents, and contract administration; and post construction services.

MARMAC, ENGINEERING & DESIGN
15621 Red Hill Ave., Ste. 200
Tustin, CA 92780
Arthur W. Akers, President
PH: (714)258-8500
FX: (714)258-5000

Founded: 1970. **Staff:** 70. A multidisciplined consulting engineering company active with oil, gas, refinery, and power industries. Significant experience in the following areas: pipelines, power plants and cogeneration, environmental reports, hazardous waste clean up, fine chemical process, refinery process and optimization, design of oil and gas production facilities, related land services, and design of oil, gas and product storage facilities.

S.J. MARSDEN & CO., INC.
Rte. 3, Box 93
Rogersville, MO 65742-9214
Stephen J. Marsden, President
PH: (417)753-4000
TF: (800)753-9199
FX: (417)753-2000
E-mail: herbal@dialnet.net
URL: http://www.herbaladvantage.com
Founded: 1980. **Staff:** 4. Provides counsel, development and management services for domestic and international projects. Specializes in agricultural project design, feasibility studies, and construction supervision for greenhouse projects and related support systems for vegetable, flower, or grass fodder production in soil or hydroponics. Related services include construction supervision, management supervision, project start-up, vegetable packing systems, flower grading systems, selective personnel recruiting, product procurement, systems evaluation, site analysis surveys, and soil testing.

MARSTON & MARSTON, INC.
13515 Barrett Parkway Dr., Ste. 260
Ballwin, MO 63021
Donald D. Marston, Chairman
PH: (314)984-8800
FX: (314)984-8770
E-mail: mining@marston.com
Founded: 1977. **Staff:** 40. Engineering services to the mining industry include surface and underground mine design and planning, mining project feasibility studies, mine management, geologic services, cost estimating, reserve evaluation, due diligence reports, and operations audits. Industries served: coal, base and precious metals, industrial minerals, rare earths, and strategic metals companies, electric power utilities, financial institutions, and government agencies.

MARTIN & HUANG INTERNATIONAL INC.
48 S. Chester Ave.
Pasadena, CA 91106
King M. Huang, President
PH: (626)585-9680
FX: (626)585-9685
E-mail: mhi999@aol.com
Founded: 1976. **Staff:** 16. Consulting structural engineering service in United States, Far East, Asia and Middle East. Project assignments have encompassed all types of building structures. Expertise includes: high rise public and commercial buildings, convention halls, sports facilities, hospitals and hotel apartments. Also experienced in most forms of transportation facilities including airports, ports, harbors, bridges, heavy and light rail projects. Provides construction management and construction phase consultations as well. Serves government agencies also.

R.R. MARTIN CONSULTANTS
185 E. Lake Samm Pky. SE
Redmond, WA 98053
Rodney R. Martin, Contact
PH: (206)868-6781
FX: (206)868-2908
Founded: 1982. **Staff:** 2. Offers construction management consulting services for owners, contractors, subcontractors, material suppliers, sureties, lending institutions and the legal profession. Services include: preliminary assessment of construction issues, review and analysis of documentation for claims, scheduling and scheduling analysis, cost/time, impact analysis, financial analysis, claim preparation and presentation, claim negotiation support, computer support services, arbitration/litigation support, and expert witness testimony. Serves private industries as well as government agencies.

STEPHEN P. MASLAN & CO.
8011 Paseo, Ste. 201
Kansas City, MO 64131
Stephen P. Maslan, Contact
PH: (816)444-6260
FX: (816)444-8789
E-mail: maslaneng@osns.com
URL: http://www.osns.com/maslan
Founded: 1982. **Staff:** 6. Licensed construction management engineer prepares plans and specifications for buildings and structures including manufacturing plants, warehouses, schools and housing projects. Supervises construction and construction management. Investigates building failures and makes interior designs and layout.

MASONRY & CONCRETE CONSULTANTS, INC.
5211 Berry Creek
Houston, TX 77017
Turner Smith, President
PH: (713)944-1148
FX: (713)944-1723
Specializes in general construction, including masonry and stone, jobsite workmanship, contract claims, and basic building failures.

MATERIAL HANDLING SYSTEMS
2200 Litton Ln.
Hebron, KY 41048
Paula Holmes, Contact
PH: (606)334-2400
FX: (606)334-2845
Provides services in the areas of construction management, conveyor systems design, materials handling equipment, automated storage/retrieval systems, and software development.

MAY & HOLBROOK ARCHITECTS
901 N. Calvert St.
Baltimore, MD 21202
Patricia Holbrook, Partner
PH: (410)752-1554
FX: (410)727-4819
Founded: 1972. **Staff:** 8. Full architectural services include programming, planning, space plans, interior design, construction documents, construction administration, value engineering, construction management, project management, and facilities management for all building types. Industries served: public and private client-agents and owners.

MCCORMACK INTERNATIONAL CONSULTANTS
PO Box 164
New Ipswich, NH 03071
Dr. James J. McCormack, CMC, DBA, Ph.D., Contact
PH: (603)878-3282
FX: (603)878-3282
E-mail: drmcc@mccintlconslt.mv.com
URL: http://globallook.mcni.com/mccormac.html
Founded: 1982. **Staff:** 5. Organizational analysis/restructuring, maintenance/materials management, exports, technology transfer, construction management-fossil/nuclear, feasibility-cost/benefit studies, project evaluation/turnaround, post-reengineering appraisal, train trainers, productivity (work sampling), studies in addition to: International—restructure privatized companies, technology transfer, small/medium enterprise development/turnaround, product distribution analysis, facility and contiguous infrastructure appraisal, train trainers.

G.E. MCCOY & ASSOCIATES CONSULTING
835 18th Ave.
Salt Lake City, UT 84103
Gerald E. McCoy, President
PH: (801)328-8986
FX: (801)575-8314
Founded: 1984. **Staff:** 2. Provides consulting assistance specifically related to construction and contracts management. Services encompass on-site project management, leasehold improvements, management of tenant buildout and reviewing and negotiating contracts for

clients involving architecture engineering and construction. Prepares and negotiates contracts, claims and changes for clients as well as acts as clients' representative at contractor/owner meetings. Industries served: large corporations, developers, contractors, construction, and energy industries.

PATRICK J. MCENTEGART
24-16 Steinway St., Ste. 636
Long Island City, NY 11103
Patrick J. McEntegart, Contact
PH: (718)634-0460
FX: (718)278-1769
Founded: 1987. **Staff:** 8. Firm provides cost engineering, construction management, feasibility studies, and budgeting services. Serves the construction, agriculture, and manufacturing industries worldwide.

MCFARLAND-JOHNSON, INC.
PO Box 1980
Binghamton, NY 13902
James C. Kerins, Jr., Vice President
PH: (607)723-9421
FX: (607)723-4979
E-mail: mcfarland@mjinc.com
Founded: 1946. **Staff:** 90. Consulting engineers offering engineering services in industrial and municipal buildings, urban renewal, mechanical, electrical, and environmental systems, planning, design and inspection of railroads, highways, bridges, airports, sewage treatment and collection systems, water treatment and distribution systems, and parking facilities. Also provides mortgage loan inspection services. Industries served: manufacturing, assembly plants, communications, transportation, financial institutions, industrial development agencies, government agencies, and energy retrofit controls.

MCKAY/MOORE PARTNERSHIP
Seattle, WA 98117-4142
Patricia Moore, Founder
PH: (206)781-0676
FX: (206)781-0676
E-mail: mckaymoore@strabo.com
URL: http://www.strabo.com/mckaymoore
Founded: 1995. Provides cost estimating services to owners and design professionals involved in construction projects. Other services include value engineering cost support, expert witness, and cost estimate review/quality control. Certified as a Women's Business Enterprise for the state of Washington and as a Disadvantaged Business Enterprise.

DAVY MCKEE CORP.
300 S. Riverside Plaza, 18th Fl.
Chicago, IL 60606
D.T. Wetzel, Contact
TF: (800)592-6618
Founded: 1906. **Staff:** 10000. Engineering and construction firm serving the process industries, food, pharmaceuticals, biotechnology, chemicals, petroleum, iron and steel, petrochemical, polymers, nonferrous metals, fertilizers, and plastics. Also serves the power industry.

PATRICK J. MCMACKIN—MANAGEMENT CONSULTING SERVICES
204 W. Neversink Rd.
Reading, PA 19606
Patrick J. McMackin, Contact
PH: (610)370-2001
FX: (610)370-2001
Founded: 1989. **Staff:** 1. Active in the field of project and construction management program development, offering system implementation, training, project application and implementation. Industries served: utilities, government, and manufacturing.

JOHN MCNAIR AND ASSOCIATES
LB&B Bldg.
Waynesboro, VA 22980
John W. McNair, Jr., P.E.
PH: (540)942-1161
FX: (540)942-1163
E-mail: jma@brucheum.com
Founded: 1958. **Staff:** 5. Full service engineering firm concentrating activities in the fields of civil, structural, electrical/mechanical and environmental engineering and construction management. Serves private industries as well as government agencies.

MCNEELY ENGINEERING CONSULTANTS LTD.
260 Terence Matthews Crescent
Kanata, ON, Canada K2M 2C7
P.A. McNeely, President
PH: (613)591-7500
FX: (613)591-8864
E-mail: mcneely@compmore.net
Founded: 1975. **Staff:** 100. Offers feasibility studies, detailed design and construction supervision for transportation, municipal, structural, agricultural and water resources projects. Typical projects include roads, bridges, airports, transit systems, water supply systems, sewerage and sewage treatment plants, waste management systems, environmental assessments, pollution control studies, storm water management systems, erosion control, flood prevention, agricultural drainage, office buildings, reservoirs, and storage tanks. Serves private industries as well as government agencies.

MDA ENGINEERING, INC.
795 Fletcher Ln.
Hayward, CA 94544
Joseph McQuillan, Principal
PH: (510)889-8144
FX: (510)889-8281
E-mail: mda@mdaengineering.com
URL: http://www.mdaengineering.com
Founded: 1987. Provides mechanical engineering consulting services, and to assist in building construction projects. Offers a spectrum of mechanical engineering, consulting services. Experience in computer-aided design/engineering and energy analysis/simulation.

MDC SYSTEMS
55 West Ave.
Wayne, PA 19087
John B. Stetson, Division President
PH: (610)975-6600
FX: (610)975-6600
E-mail: info@mdcsystems.com
URL: http://www.mdcsystems.com
Founded: 1967. **Staff:** 175. Project management consultants providing construction related services such as construction/project management, construction inspection, project management oversight (PMO), CPM scheduling, cost estimating, and design and construction claims analysis and litigation support. Industries served: aviation planning and engineering, transportation educational, hospital/healthcare, general building, ports/waterfront/marine structures, wastewater, correctional, and government agencies.

R. S. MEANS CO., INC.
100 Construction Plaza
Kingston, MA 02364
Perry B. Sells, Contact
PH: (617)585-7880
TF: (800)448-8182
FX: (617)585-7466
URL: http://www.rmeans.com
Founded: 1942. **Staff:** 70. Provides construction cost information and consulting services. Industries served: building construction, engineering, architecture, education, and government agencies.

MEAT INDUSTRIES CONSULTANTS, LTD.
222 Park Dr.
Eastchester, NY 10709
Gary Hyman, President
PH: (914)337-8625
FX: (914)723-0215
Founded: 1967. **Staff:** 5. Processing and Warehousing Specialists. Emphasis is on reducing labor costs and increasing productivity, design of a new addition or new facilities providing turnkey professional services, architectural/engineering services, procurement. Industries served: meat, poultry, fish, and bakery.

MECKLER ENGINEERS GROUP
17525 Ventura Blvd., Ste. 307
Encino, CA 91316-3817
Milton Meckler, President/CEO
PH: (818)995-7672
FX: (818)995-8161
Founded: 1980. **Staff:** 8. An industrial, manufacturing, process environmental and mechanical engineering consulting firm for construction projects and industry; HVAC and plumbing systems; engineering and energy studies, utilities planning, life safety, support systems and specifications, computer simulation, forensic evaluation, surveys, economics, remediation, and construction management. Areas of expertise include energy analysis, indoor air quality, fire and smoke modeling; desiccant system design and analysis; accident reconstruction, product liability, failure analysis, air and water pollution, and waste management. Industries served: heating, ventilating, refrigeration and air conditioning; gas and electric utilities; government agencies; educational, institutional and healthcare.

MERIDIAN CONSTRUCTION MANAGEMENT
4303 S. Napa St.
Spokane, WA 99203
Mark D'Agostino, Contact
PH: (509)443-0252
FX: (509)443-1875
E-mail: mdagos@aol.com
Founded: 1998. **Staff:** 1. Represents owners, developers, contractors, and architects by employing principles of trust and leadership that delivers results to ensure commercial projects are completed within budget and on schedule. Meridian's contractor experience enables it to effectively assess issues and offer solutions on your project. Industries served: construction, development, retail, real estate.

MERIDIAN CONSULTING GROUP, INC.
650 E. Algonquin Rd., Ste. 207
Schaumburg, IL 60173
William G. Sarver, Chairman
PH: (847)303-5533
FX: (847)303-5547
E-mail: RCCogburn@aol.com
URL: http://meridian-consulting.com
Founded: 1986. Specializes in contract surety claims, construction management, scheduling and cost control, estimating, construction claims, litigation support, specification writing, and property and casualty claims, and E&O claims.

DWIGHT W. MICHENER
4980 Old State Rte. 73
Waynesville, OH 45068
Dwight W. Michener, Contact
PH: (513)897-7236
Founded: 1970. **Staff:** 2. Agricultural consultant specializing in irrigation and drainage engineering, including tile drains, surface drains, small dams, surface and sprinkler irrigation, land leveling, channels, and rock dams. Also offers income tax preparation. Serves private industries as well as government agencies. Active internationally with experience in Ethiopia, Turkey, Pakistan, Iraq, and Syria.

MIDGLEY-CLAUER ASSOCIATES, INC.
4438 Leffingwell Rd.
Canfield, OH 44406
Wesley R. Midgley, President
PH: (216)533-7460
FX: (216)533-7460
Founded: 1978. **Staff:** 2. Offers services in structural analysis and design, specializing in cold-formed steel applications. Serves the storage rack industry and the cold-formed steel framing industry. Analyses and designs storage rack buildings, cold-formed steel bearing walls for one, two, and three story buildings as well as curtain walls. Also investigates structural accidents.

MIDWEST EQUIPMENT CO.
PO Box 10353
Green Bay, WI 54307
Joseph R. Senecal, President
PH: (920)494-6475
FX: (920)494-4212
Firm offers expertise in construction materials and equipment, as well as appraisals, in all concrete equipment, Red-mix, block, pipe, sand, gravel, and heavy construction equipment.

MIRALLES ASSOCIATES, INC.
729 W. Woodbury Rd.
Altadena, CA 91001
Adolfo E. Miralles, President
PH: (626)791-7691
FX: (626)791-0901
E-mail: miralles@ix.netcom.com
Founded: 1972. **Staff:** 16. A full service architectural firm specializing in master planning, space planning, architectural and interpretive design, and construction management. Expertise includes accurate cost estimating and timely completion of projects. Serves private industries as well as government agencies in the southwestern U.S.

MODULAR CONSULTANTS INC.
3109 Crabtree Ln.
Elkhart, IN 46514
Steven A. Sabo, President
PH: (219)264-5761
FX: (219)264-5761
E-mail: sasabo5313@aol.com
Founded: 1995. **Staff:** 2. Offers services in the design and construction of factory built buildings, business planning for factory built buildings, site set up design and review of factories, and plant layout and design of factories. Expert witness on modular, mobile, and R.V. buildings.

MOFFAT KINOSHITA ASSOCIATES INC.
124 Merton St.
Toronto, ON, Canada M4S 2Z2
Don Moffat, Contact
PH: (416)488-5811
FX: (416)488-5829
Founded: 1965. **Staff:** 31. Consulting architects and planners offering services in space programming, master planning, site planning, building design and construction administration. Experienced with cultural facilities, parks and recreation facilities, housing, educational facilities, and renovations of all kinds. Serves private industries as well as government agencies.

MOISTURE CONTROL TECHNOLOGIES
842 W. Lodi Ave.
Lodi, CA 95240
Don Bush, Sr., FRCI, RRC, President
PH: (209)333-4390
TF: (800)886-6210
FX: (209)333-4393
Founded: 1981. **Staff:** 6. Consulting firm with principal interests in the quality of survey and analysis design, application and maintenance of roofing, waterproofing and moistureproofing systems. Also offers services in construction management and as expert witness.

Industries served: architecture, engineering, construction, developers, building owners (low and high rise), and government agencies.

MARIANO D. MOLINA—MECHANICAL & ELECTRICAL CONSULTING ENGINEERS
65 Bleecker St.
New York, NY 10012
Mariano D. Molina, President
PH: (212)677-0777
FX: (212)677-9156
E-mail: mom2nyo@aol.com
Founded: 1978. **Staff:** 65. Engineering consultants offer complete design and construction supervision. Offers expertise on mechanical, electrical, plumbing, fire protection, security, communications, lighting, vertical and horizontal transportation systems and energy conservation measures. Industries served: architects, government agencies, major corporations, developers, transit authorities, healthcare, educational, industrial, and correction facilities.

MONEX RESOURCES INC.
45 NE Loop 410, Ste. 700
San Antonio, TX 78216
PH: (210)349-4069
FX: (210)349-8512
E-mail: bmti@boralmti.com
URL: http://www.boralmti.com
Construction materials firm offers extensive knowledge in engineering.

MOON CONSULTING
677 Greenbrier Dr.
Heyburn, ID 83336
Eugene Durell Moon, Principal
PH: (208)678-0637
Offers services in geological exploration and mine evaluation. Specializes in mine, legal property, construction and civil engineering surveys and design, and nuclear plant operation. Familiar with all aspects of shielding, radioactivity, quality assurance, power and safety on nuclear plants.

MORRISON-KNUDSEN ENGINEERS, INC.
1 Market Steuart, Ste. 400
San Francisco, CA 94105
James Ellis, President
PH: (415)442-7300
FX: (415)442-7405
Founded: 1945. **Staff:** 450. Consulting engineers, domestic and worldwide whose services range from conceptual development, financial planning, and field investigations to engineering, project management, and quality control, including: program management for private sector clients and government agencies; construction management from construction planning through start-up; procurement and complete logistics support, including materials control, expediting and shipping, warehousing and source inspection; comprehensive project control systems for small to mega projects, including planning and scheduling, estimating, cost engineering, materials, and document control; and operations and maintenance including repair, alterations, communications, transportation services, purchasing and contracting in all major public utilities, transportation and military facilities. Specific market segments cover electric utilities; transportation; water resources; oil and gas; hazardous waste design; minerals such as base metals, industrial metals, precious metals, and strategic minerals; and public works.

MOTION INDUSTRIES INC.
1605 Alton Rd.
Birmingham, AL 35210
PH: (205)956-1122
FX: (205)951-1170
URL: http://www.motion-industries.com
Firm provides extensive knowledge in construction materials and equipment, designing, engineering, and training.

MS CONSULTANTS, INC.
333 E. Federal St.
Youngstown, OH 44503
Thomas F. Mosure, President
PH: (330)744-5321
FX: (330)744-5256
URL: http://www.msconsultants.com
Founded: 1960. **Staff:** 174. Full-service engineering/architectural firm offering services in civil (highway, structures, traffic, airports, environmental, geotechnical, hydrologic/hydraulic) engineering; surveying; mechanical engineering; electrical engineering; construction engineering; planning and environmental science; and architecture. Client population is 70 percent public sector and 30 percent private sector.

MUESER RUTLEDGE CONSULTING ENGINEERS
708 Third Ave.
New York, NY 10017
Joel Moskowitz, Partner
PH: (212)490-7110
FX: (212)490-6654
E-mail: mail@mrce.com
URL: http://www.mrce.com
Founded: 1910. **Staff:** 100. Geotechnical and structural foundation engineering services provided for: Foundation design: building foundations; transportation structures; special structures & excavation support; temporary structures; claim support; underpinning. Geotechnical services: investigations, analyses and recommendations; field observation and testing; groundwater control and waste containment; ground improvement. Instrumentation: marine and water-related structures; waterfront development studies; piers, wharves and bulkheads; outfalls and intakes; cellular cofferdams; dams & dikes; wastewater treatment plants.

MULTICOMM SCIENCES INTERNATIONAL, INC.
266 W. Main St.
Denville, NJ 07834
Victor J. Nexon, President
PH: (201)627-7400
FX: (201)625-1002
Founded: 1952. Consulting engineers specializing in telecommunications for terrestrial and satellite systems. Services include studies, specifications, construction supervision and evaluation, computerized frequency data, planning, selection and protection. Serves private, common carrier and government facilities, domestic and international.

MURPHY & DITTENHAFER INC.
800 N. Charles St.
Baltimore, MD 21201
Michael V. Murphy, AIA, Contact
PH: (410)625-4823
FX: (410)625-4674
E-mail: mvm@murphdittarch.com
Founded: 1985. **Staff:** 25. Provides full range of architectural interior design, and planning consultation including master plans and strategic plans in addition to preliminary design, construction documentation, and construction administration. Firm serves a wide range of clients, private and public, with specialties in affordable housing, higher and secondary education, religious institutions, museums, historic districts, libraries, social service agencies, urban renewal and planning authorities. Full CADD utilization.

NANNIS & ASSOCIATES, INC.
5266 Old Norcross Rd.
Norcross, GA 30071
Walid A. Nannis, President
PH: (770)300-9955
FX: (770)300-0770
E-mail: nannis@dscga.com
Founded: 1931. **Staff:** 8. Consultants in the design analysis and the rendering of plans and specifications for all types of structures including shoring and bracing systems, foundations, educational, civic,

and industrial complexes, multi-rise buildings, and parking garages. Analysis in all types of construction materials.

NBBJ
111 S. Jackson St.
Seattle, WA 98104
Friedrich Bohm, Chairman
PH: (206)223-5555
FX: (206)621-2300
E-mail: nbbjinfo@nbbj.com
URL: http://www.nbbj.com
Founded: 1943. **Staff:** 750. NBBJ is the second largest architectural firm in the United States-fifth largest in the world-and employs over 600 people in six U.S. cities including: Seattle, Columbus, San Francisco, Los Angeles, New York, and Research Triangle Park, as well as Tokyo. The firm's services include: Programming, Architecture, Planning and Design, Facilities Management, Economics and Financial Feasibility, Land Use Planning, Graphic Design and Signage. The firm's markets are diverse and include: Airport/Transportation, Commercial Mixed-use, Corporate Design/Interiors, Criminal Justice, Graphic Design, Health Care, Higher Education, Hospitality/Resort/Recreation, Performing Arts, Planning, Research/Advanced Technology, Retail, Senior Housing/Assisted Living, and Sports & Entertainment.

NEBRASKA TESTING GROUP, MAXIM TECHNOLOGIES, INC.
5058 South 111th St.
Omaha, NE 68137
Al Rahman, Manager, Omaha Operations
PH: (402)331-4453
FX: (402)331-5961
Founded: 1955. **Staff:** 50. A commercial and independent testing, engineering and consulting laboratory providing service to government, business, industry and individuals in the fields of soil and material engineering, construction testing, industrial hygiene, chemical, bacteriological and environmental sciences, non-destructive testing and related services. Industries served: engineering, environmental, construction services, and government agencies.

WALDEMAR S. NELSON AND CO., INC.
1200 St. Charles Ave.
New Orleans, LA 70130
Waldemar S. Nelson, Chairman
PH: (504)523-5281
FX: (504)523-4587
E-mail: jim.cospolich@wsnelson.com
URL: http://www.wsnelson.com
Founded: 1945. **Staff:** 310. Offers complete engineering, project management, and construction management services including preparation of economic and feasibility studies, planning, permitting, conceptual and preliminary engineering, detailed design and specifications, construction management, start-up assistance, and support throughout the life of the facility. Industries served: energy, oil and gas production, industrial, institutional, military, local, city, state, and federal government.

NELSON CONSULTING
3303 Lee Pky., Ste. 410
Dallas, TX 75219-5109
Erik L. Nelson, Ph.D., President
PH: (214)528-8765
FX: (214)528-9098
E-mail: Enelson528@aol.com
Forensic and consulting architectural engineering services includes damage assessments and construction cost estimating, building investigations, condition surveys, foundation distress, laser elevation surveys and 3-D CAD rendering, reports and studies, expert witness and litigation support. Forensic and investigative experience includes cause, evaluation, damage assessment and remedial repair for foundation and superstructure damage sustained due to various causes, such as expansive soils, tornadoes, water leaks, fire, explosions and roof collapses.

NESTOR ASSOCIATES, INC.
Atrium Executive Center
80 Orville Dr.
Bohemia, NY 11716
Stephen J. Marmaroff, President
PH: (516)665-6070
FX: (516)567-0611
Founded: 1983. **Staff:** 3. A consulting firm offering a wide range of technical and management services to business and industry, with particular emphasis on (1) electrical energy supply and power plant construction, operation, maintenance and management analysis, (2) air and water pollution control, and (3) project management and forensic services for surety companies. Services include planning, analytical studies and audits, engineering, construction support, operational troubleshooting, electrical generation, project implementation, litigation support, and rate case testimony. Serves private industry as well as government agencies.

THE NETTLESHIP GROUP
2665 Main St., Ste. 220
Santa Monica, CA 90405
Patricia S. Nettleship, CEO
PH: (310)392-8585
FX: (310)392-8580
E-mail: tng@nettleship.com
URL: http://www.nettleship.com
Founded: 1978. **Staff:** 80. Multidisciplined consulting firm composed of skilled professionals engaged in project management information systems and administration of design and construction services for large complex capital programs. Firm's computer specialists are expert in specifying, installing, maintaining, and implementing fully integrated local and wide area networked computer systems. Industries served: public agencies, airports, light rail, subway systems, highways, wastewater, correctional facilities, and large architectural/engineering firms working on major infrastructure projects.

NEUNDORFER ENGINEERED SYSTEMS
4590 Hamann Pky.
Willoughby, OH 44094
PH: (440)942-8990
FX: (440)942-6824
E-mail: sales@neundorfer.com
URL: http://www.neundorfer.com
Firm offers extensive knowledge in construction materials and inspection.

W.F. NEWELL & ASSOCIATES, INC.
255 Rolling Hills Rd.
Mooresville, NC 28115
William F. Newell, Jr., President
PH: (704)664-0832
FX: (704)664-3142
E-mail: wfnewell@pobox.com
Specializes in welding and welding engineering for machining, material technologies, piping, pressure vessels, power generation (nuclear, fossil, hydro), industrial, manufacturing, heavy and highway construction, and auto racing.

NEWMAN PARTNERSHIP INC, THE
2800 Centenary Blvd.
Shreveport, LA 71104-3355
Michael T. Newman, Partner
PH: (318)424-8414
FX: (318)424-3167
E-mail: newman@prysm.net
URL: http://www.newmaninc.com
Founded: 1973. Environmental services include: Asbestos Containing Material (ACM) surveys, evaluations, sampling and analysis, management plans, operation and maintenance programs, abatement project design, abatement contract administration, project air monitoring, and claim documentation, Phase I Site Assessments per ASTM guidelines, historical research, on-site investigations, optional sampling, hazards evaluation, asbestos, lead (paint, soil, water), PCB's, other issues; Phase II and Phase III assessments, un-

derground storage tanks, indoor air sampling, volatile organic chemicals, personnel questionnaires, building evaluations; lead in paint and water sampling; pre-purchase inspections that include building code compliance, fire code, A.D.A., construction and maintenance reviews, building systems review, HVAC, electrical, and structural; repair, upgrade, renovation cost estimates; and review of current regulations regarding asbestos for schools and public buildings.

NICHOLS REAL ESTATE & GENERAL CONTRACTING
1633 Clear View Dr.
Beverly Hills, CA 90210
Barbara Nichols, President
PH: (310)273-6369
Specializes in real estate standards of care, disclosure requirements, custom and practice, agency relationships, damage valuation, construction and materials. Provides litigation consultation and document review, data analysis and research, evidence development and evaluation, deposition preparation and expert witness testimony.

NIELSEN-WURSTER GROUP INC.
345 Wall St.
Princeton, NJ 08540
Kris R. Nielsen, President
PH: (609)497-7300
FX: (609)497-3412
E-mail: njnwg@aol.com
URL: http://www.nielsen-wurster.com
Founded: 1976. **Staff:** 40. Offers engineering management consulting services in the following areas: construction disputes and forensic engineering specializing in claim analysis, litigation support, and expert testimony; power (nuclear, fossil and hydro)-providing prudency, management and construction audits; technical services-scheduling and estimating; and construction management-full on-site and technical services for full project management. Industries served: construction, industrial, forest/products, pharmaceutical, government, utilities, banking, lending, insurance, and other Fortune 500 companies.

NIRO INC.
9165 Rumsey Rd.
Columbia, MD 21045
Heather Szymanski, Marketing
PH: (410)997-8700
FX: (410)997-5021
E-mail: hvs@niroinc.com
URL: http://www.niroinc.com
Offers physical plant engineering; construction management; custom design, fabrication, and installation services; and equipment appraisal.

NOFSINGER INC.—A BURNS & MCDONNELL CO.
9400 Ward Pky.
Kansas City, MO 64114
Donald F. Greenwood, President
PH: (816)361-7999
FX: (816)333-3690
E-mail: rnofsin@burnsmcd.com
URL: http://www.burnsmcd.com
Founded: 1950. **Staff:** 90. Provides engineering and consulting services for the process industries. Activities include chemical, mechanical, instrument, electrical and civil engineering for the food, petroleum, chemical, and petrochemical industries, including consulting, process and economic feasibility studies, process engineering and detailed design engineering. Works with various government agencies. The company also provides construction design build capabilities and start-up services.

NOLAN-SCOTT INC.
403 Allegheny Ave.
Towson, MD 21204
John E. Nolan, CEO
PH: (410)296-7262
FX: (410)583-5832
Founded: 1974. **Staff:** 21. Firm offers design, engineering, and con-

struction services, specializing in integrating design, cost control and schedule.

NOLTE ASSOCIATES, INC.
1750 Creekside Oaks Dr., Ste. 200
Sacramento, CA 95833
George S. Nolte, Jr., President
PH: (916)641-1500
FX: (916)641-9222
E-mail: info@nolte.com
URL: http://www.nolte.com
Founded: 1949. **Staff:** 250. Consultants to both public and private enterprises throughout the western United States and Central America in their respective roles in the community development process. Provides engineering, planning, and other professional services related to the planning, design, and implementation of land use and infrastructure changes to support the expanding economies and improve the quality of local communities. Specific services include: land use, transportation and storm, sanitary and water system master planning; landscape architecture; civil and structural engineering for site development, highways, roadways, and transit; design of water supply treatment and distribution facilities; domestic and industrial wastewater collection and treatment facilities; flood control and drainage facilities; surveying, and mapping; construction/program management and inspection; assessment proceedings; environmental analysis and EIR/EIS document preparation; and federal, state, and local agency permit and entitlement processing.

NORMANDALE ASSOCIATES INC.
4045 Plateau Rd.
Reno, NV 89509
James N. Verhey, CMC, President
PH: (702)747-0606
TF: (800)397-0607
FX: (702)747-4886
Founded: 1978. **Staff:** 5. Facility development and project management firm offering the following services for expansions, consolidations and relocation planning: strategic real estate site selection studies; property documentation and valuation; buyer/ tenant representation; furniture and equipment inventories, procurement, installation coordination; move/relocation management; excess property disposition. Serves private corporations, health systems, hospitals and clinics, as well as government agencies.

GLORIA NOVAK, LIBRARY BUILDING CONSULTANT
18430 Round Mountain Ranch Rd.
Nevada City, CA 95959
Gloria Novak, Contact
PH: (530)478-9608
FX: (530)478-9608
Founded: 1974. **Staff:** 1. Offers library building consulting for academic, school, public, institutional, and special libraries for new buildings, additions to existing buildings, remodeling and renovation, and conversion of non-library buildings to library use. Specific services include, but are not limited to, feasibility studies, building programs, site and architect selection, and critical evaluation of building design, drawings and specifications; interior design-layout, selection and specification of furniture and equipment; specialized planning for non-print media, computer services, handicapped access, conservation of energy, book storage facilities, safety and security, space utilization studies, and library lighting. Serves libraries and government agencies worldwide.

O'BRIEN KREITZBERG
50 Fremont St., 24th Fl.
San Francisco, CA 94105
Alan Krusi, CEG,RG, President
PH: (415)777-0188
FX: (415)777-3023
E-mail: info@okpcm.com
URL: http://www.okpcm.com
Founded: 1972. **Staff:** 800. Founded in 1972 and headquartered in San Francisco, California, O'Brien Kreitzberg (OK) is the nation's oldest and largest firm specializing in program and construction

management. With more than 20 offices around the world, the firm is able to provide comprehensive and proactive services in any location. OK has managed a wide range of projects, from the planning and design stages through construction and occupancy, for owners in the public and private sectors. OK's Program and construction management services include schedule and cost control, estimating, value engineering, constructability reviews, contract administration, inspection/quality control and quality assurance. The firm also provides claims avoidance/dispute resolution, insurance consulting and risk assessment services.

OCCIDENTAL EXPRESS
297 Kansas St.
San Francisco, CA 94103
Henry Karnilowicz, Principal
PH: (415)621-7533
FX: (415)621-7583
E-mail: occexp@aol.com
Founded: 1975. **Staff:** 5. Residential and commercial construction, including second story and room additions, alteration and renovation, kitchens and bathrooms, seismic retrofitting, tenant improvement, compliance with ADA requirements, fire, water and smoke damage repair, and insurance claims assistance and services.

OGILVIE CONSULTANTS LTD.
23 Croydon Rd.
Toronto, ON, Canada M6C 1S6
Alan F. Ogilvie, President, P.E.
PH: (416)781-7820
FX: (416)789-3530
E-mail: ogilvie@inforamp.net
Founded: 1972. **Staff:** 4. Mechanical engineers offering consulting and building services to clients in manufacturing, industrial, institutional, and commercial industries and municipal governments in Canada.

WILSON OKAMOTO AND ASSOCIATES, INC.
1907 S. Beretania St., Ste 400
Honolulu, HI 96811
Gary T. Okamoto, President
PH: (808)946-2277
FX: (808)946-2253
E-mail: woa@aloha.net
Founded: 1947. **Staff:** 55. Offers complete technical consulting services ranging from land use planning, master planning, feasibility reports, environmental, and economic studies to the preparation of detailed civil, structural, and architectural designs, working drawings, specifications and cost estimates, and construction management. Serves private industries as well as government agencies.

OLVER INC.
1116 S. Main St.
Blacksburg, VA 24060
John W. Olver, CEO
PH: (540)552-5548
FX: (540)552-5577
E-mail: olver@olver.com
URL: http://www.olver.com
Founded: 1973. **Staff:** 72. Provides consultation in the fields of civil, sanitary, mechanical, electrical, structural, chemical and environmental engineering. Services include preliminary evaluations, environmental design, construction management, municipal and industrial clients. Industrial clients include manufacturing, printing, poultry, textiles, pharmaceutical, chemical, and paper.

OLYMPIC ASSOCIATES CO.
701 Dexter Ave. N., Ste. 301
Seattle, WA 98109
Peter E. Jobs, President
PH: (206)285-4300
FX: (206)285-4371
E-mail: info@oac_intl.com
Founded: 1955. **Staff:** 20. Offers the following services: architectural; civil, structural, mechanical, and electrical engineering; plan-

ning; and construction management including scheduling, estimating, value engineering, claims analysis and constructability studies. Serves private industries as well as government agencies.

OMEGA ENGINEERING CONSULTANTS, INC.
10456 W. Atlantic Blvd.
Coral Springs, FL 33071
Andrew M. Knysh, President
PH: (954)344-6303
TF: (800)286-6342
FX: (954)344-0191
E-mail: webmaster@omega-engineering.com
URL: http://www.omega-engineering.com
A consulting firm providing inspection, analysis, advice, support and expert testimony. Staff includes professional engineers, electrical, mechanical, plumbing and roofing experts. Services include due diligence condition surveys, damage assessment failure analysis, contract review, project and accident reconstruction, field-testing of materials, cost estimation and turnover surveys.

ONSITE SYCOM ENERGY CORP.
701 Palomar Airport Rd., Ste. 200
Carlsbad, CA 92009
Richard T. Sperberg, CEO
PH: (760)931-2400
FX: (760)931-2405
URL: http://onsitesycom.com
Founded: 1982. **Staff:** 160. Firm offers a full range of professional consulting services for energy efficiency services, including lighting retrofits, and energy management systems, equipment upgrades, HVAC modifications, high efficiency motors, industrial process improvements and cogeneration/small power systems. Additionally offers a full range of professional consulting within various target markets such as utilities, product suppliers and government in the area of market assessments, business strategy, public policy analysis, and environmental impact/feasibility studies.

ORTH-RODGERS AND ASSOCIATES, INC.
230 S. Broad St., 16th Fl.
Philadelphia, PA 19102
H. Richard Orth, Contact
PH: (215)735-1932
FX: (215)735-5954
E-mail: oraphila@ix.netcom.com
URL: http://www.pw1.netcom.com/~oraphila/index.htm
Founded: 1977. **Staff:** 64. Provides professional engineering services to the public sector (municipalities, counties and state Departments of Public Works and Transportation), to private sector land developers, to site planners, and to industrial/commercial organizations. Traffic engineering projects include: highway access and intersection design, site engineering, parking demand/feasibility studies, facilities studies, signalization and signing, construction inspection, traffic impact studies, traffic counts, speed delay analysis, preparation of traffic control and monitoring plans.

OWNER SERVICES GROUP, INC.
200 W. 22nd St., Ste. 209
Lombard, IL 60148-4883
Ian Parr, Contact
PH: (630)916-7500
TF: (800)443-8607
FX: (630)916-7502
E-mail: tstat@ccsos.com
URL: http://www.ccsos.com
Founded: 1992. **Staff:** 12. Construction Management, Owner Representation, Project Management, Cost Management, Facility Management, Dispute Resolution.

PACE ENGINEERING, INC.
9310 Topanga Canyon Blvd., Ste. 220A
Chatsworth, CA 91311
Charles G. Novak, Principal

PH: (818)407-9407
FX: (818)407-9400
E-mail: paceeng@iswest.net
Founded: 1967. Specializes in fire and arson investigations, litigation support, accident reconstruction, mechanical and electrical failures, civil engineering, building restoration plans, slip and fall analysis, soils and geological investigations, brake failures, building codes, code compliance, construction defects, consulting engineering, cost estimating, design defects, electrical codes, fire protection, equipment failures, forensic engineering, land development, land surveying, plumbing and fire sprinkler failures, product liability, safety engineering, seismic analysis, soft tissue, soil and foundation, soil movement, structural failures, tire/brake failure, and water intrusion.

ROBERT PACIFICO ASSOCIATES
111 Van Buren St.
Woodstock, IL 60098
Robert Pacifico, Contact
PH: (815)338-8808
FX: (815)338-8818
E-mail: pacifico@stans.com
Founded: 1986. **Staff:** 5. Specialists in food facility planning and laundry facility planning. Services include the following: feasibility studies; management advisory services; predesign programming; construction document services; bid negotiation and construction management; systems analysis; and menu, labor/staffing, and operations analysis. Industries served: institutional, correctional, educational, business and industry, hospitality, healthcare in both commercial and noncommercial sectors.

JOHN PAOLUCCIO CONSULTING ENGINEERS, INC.
5038 Salida Blvd.
Salida, CA 95368
John A. Paoluccio, President
PH: (209)545-1662
FX: (209)545-3533
E-mail: jpce@sonnet.com
URL: http://www.jpce.com
Founded: 1972. Engineering consultants specializing in the design of mechanical and HVAC systems, energy conservation analysis and design, fire protection systems and agricultural mechanical projects. Also offers construction management and expert witness services. Clients include laboratory research facilities, industrial and food processing plants, military and government facilities, schools, churches, hospitals, and commercial projects in California.

PARADIGM CONSULTANTS, INC.
2501 Central Pky., Ste. A3
Houston, TX 77092
Thomas B. Lansley, Contact
PH: (713)686-6771
FX: (713)686-6795
E-mail: info@thelabtexas.com
URL: http://www.thelabtexas.com
Founded: 1995. **Staff:** 40. Provides environmental, geotechnical, and construction materials engineering and testing services. Tests, inspects, evaluates, and monitors materials and processes used in construction. Experienced in environmental engineering and soil and water contamination problems.

PARSONS BRINCKERHOFF
One Penn Plaza
New York, NY 10119
Thomas J. O'Neill, President and Chief Executive Officer
PH: (212)465-5000
FX: (212)465-5096
E-mail: pbinfo@pbworld.com
URL: http://www.pbworld.com
Founded: 1885. **Staff:** 7700. An international engineering firm, with more than 200 (corporate and project) offices worldwide, specializing in planning, engineering, construction management and operations and maintenance services.

PARSONS CORP.
100 W. Walnut St.
Pasadena, CA 91124
James F. McNulty, President and CEO
PH: (818)440-2000
FX: (818)440-2630
URL: http://www.parsons.com
Founded: 1944. **Staff:** 9000. Offers worldwide engineering consulting and construction management services for: petroleum refining; chemical and gas processing plants; airports and terminals; port and harbor facilities; rapid transit systems; water and sewerage systems; conventional and nuclear power generation; solid waste handling and treatment; environmental protection systems; and defense and aerospace facilities. The Parsons Corporation comprises The Ralph M. Parsons Company; De Leuw, Cather and Company; Barton-Aschman Associates, Inc.; Harland Bartholomew and Associates, Inc.; Parsons Main, Inc.; Parsons Constructors Inc.; Parsons Construction Services, Inc.; Parsons Municipal Services, Inc.; The Ralph M. Parsons Company, Ltd.; Saudi Arabian Parsons Limited; Parsons Engineering Science, Inc. and Parsons S.I.P. Inc.

PARSONS MAIN, INC.
101 Huntington Ave Prudential Center
Boston, MA 02199
James T. Callahan, President
PH: (617)262-3200
FX: (617)859-2575
Founded: 1893. **Staff:** 1300. Provides complete planning and feasibility studies; economic and financial analyses; design engineering; architectural services; preparation of specifications; bid evaluation and procurement assistance; construction management; design-build projects; plant start-up and commissioning; operator training and management consulting services in the fields of electric power and energy technology; hydroelectric and thermal power generating plants; electric power transmission and distribution systems; water supply, irrigation and flood control; industrial facilities and manufacturing plants; printing and publishing plants; pulp and paper facilities; land, air and water pollution control and remediation projects; hazardous and toxic waste materials management; and licensing and environmental assistance. Industries served: power, printing and publishing, pulp and paper, manufacturing/process, environmental engineering, and government agencies.

PARSONS POWER GROUP INC.
2675 Morgantown Rd.
Reading, PA 19607
Harry W. Sauer, VP, G-UB-MK
PH: (610)855-2000
FX: (610)855-2001
Founded: 1906. **Staff:** 1100. An engineering consultancy serving utility, industrial, and governmental clients throughout the world. Services include planning, design, quality assurance, and project and construction management. Work ranges from design of new facilities to specialized assistance for increased efficiency and availability of operating plants. Typical projects include nuclear and fossil-fueled power generating plants, electrical transmission and distribution systems, design of new plants, modernization and automation of existing industrial and government facilities, development of advanced energy systems, and environmental control systems.

PARSONS TRANSPORTATION GROUP
1133 15th St., NW
Washington, DC 20005
Andrew Bonds, Jr., Senior Vice President
PH: (202)775-3300
FX: (202)775-3422
Firm offers expertise in planning, design, and construction management to rail and bus industries. Has extensive knowledge in corridor studies, alternative analyses, maintenance facilities, terminals, intermodal facilities, guideway, structures, and systems.

PARSONSON & ASSOCIATES, INC.
105 Mark Trail
Atlanta, GA 30328
Peter S. Parsonson, Ph.D., President
PH: (404)894-2244
FX: (404)894-1742
E-mail: peter.parsonson@ce.gatech.edu
URL: http://www.ce.gatech.edu/ttarsons/
Specializes in traffic accident investigation and reconstruction; traffic safety engineering; highway design, construction, and maintenance; signs, signals, and markings; and engineering interpretation of contracts, and standards. Experienced in cases involving human factors, pedestrians, trucks, motorcycles, intersections, shoulders, drop-offs, driveways, skidding, hydroplaning, contractors, duty to warn of hazards.

JOHN W. PARTLOW
3231 Vineyard Ave. #2
Pleasanton, CA 94566
PH: (925)846-7530
FX: (925)846-6910
A claim litigation consultant specializing in bad faith analysis, complex litigation, large commercial losses, bond, construction defect litigation, environmental pollution, property and casualty losses, coverage analysis, and industry practices and standards.

THE PAVLIK DESIGN TEAM
1301 E. Broward Blvd.
Fort Lauderdale, FL 33301
Ronald J. Pavlik, CEO/President
PH: (954)523-3300
FX: (954)524-8370
E-mail: rjpavlik1@aol.com
URL: http://www.members.aol.com/rjpavlik1/pavlik.html
Founded: 1969. **Staff:** 88. Provides interior and architectural services, including master planning; design; lighting; signage; graphics; conceptual feasibility studies; construction documentation, specifications, management; cost analysis; database management; 3-D studio animation; customer software libraries. Specializes in retail stores. Industries served: retail, hospitality, and general commercial.

PEABODY'S MACHINE DIVISION OF TESTING
5301 Lord's Mine Trail
Placerville, CA 95667
Geoffrey Peabody, President
PH: (530)622-9399
Founded: 1977. **Staff:** 6. Manufacturing process consultant for industries incorporating welding and welding inspection. Services include procedure development, certification, code analysis and compliance, welding instruction, failure analysis, personnel evaluation, construction management, and acceptance criteria development.

PEARMAN CONSTRUCTION
2001 Hoover Ave.
5105309455
5105309444
Oakland, CA 94602
Donald V. Pearman, President
PH: (510)530-9444
FX: (510)530-9455
Offers expert witness investigation and testimony in construction. Specializes in structural pest damage, foundation defects, deck failure, and water infiltration. Provides whole-house defect analysis; photo and video documentation, and reporting.

J.N. PEASE ASSOCIATES
2925 E. Independence Blvd.
Charlotte, NC 28218
PH: (704)376-6423
FX: (704)332-6177
E-mail: info@inpease.com
Founded: 1938. **Staff:** 55. Provides services in the areas of architecture, building engineering, civil/environmental engineering, planning, and interior design.

PECK & ASSOCIATES CONSTRUCTION, INC.
2430 S. Atlantic Ave., Ste. F
Daytona Beach, FL 32118
Edwin Peck, Jr., President, Chief Executive
PH: (904)255-7336
FX: (904)238-3663
E-mail: susan@peckcompanies.com
URL: http://www.peckcompanies.com
Founded: 1974. A representative for Florida's pre-engineered metal buildings. Deals with estimating, purchasing, expediting, detailing and value engineering.

PENNONI ASSOCIATES INC.
1600 Callowhill St.
Philadelphia, PA 19130
Eric Flicker, Vice President
PH: (215)561-0460
FX: (215)496-0063
Founded: 1966. **Staff:** 420. Consulting professionals providing services in civil, sanitary, environmental, structural, mechanical, electrical, industrial, transportation, and municipal engineering, solid and hazardous waste management, planning, landscape architecture, surveying, building systems design, and geographic information systems (GIS) to local, county, state and federal governmental bodies and private industry and land development clients.

PERFORMANCE ASSOCIATES INTERNATIONAL, INC.
760 E. Pusch View Ln.
Tucson, AZ 85737
S.R. Brown, Contact
PH: (520)544-2220
FX: (520)544-2255
E-mail: performance@perfnet.com
URL: http://www.perfnet.com
Founded: 1983. **Staff:** 45. Write custom plant operating manuals and multimedia systems, conduct operator training, and implement operations and maintenance improvement programs.

W. CHARLES PERRY & ASSOCIATES
231 W. 41st Ave.
San Mateo, CA 94403-4303
W. Charles Perry, Principal
PH: (650)638-9241
FX: (650)638-9242
URL: http://www.wcharlesperry.com
Specializes in failure analysis and accident reconstruction involving industrial accidents, automobile accidents, personal injuries, building fires, industrial fires and industrial explosions. Provides design evaluations of products and buildings at the system and component level. Provides risk analysis of product designs, instructions and human behavior. Provides safety evaluation of construction sites and industrial facilities.

PERRY-CARRINGTON ENGINEERING CORP.
214 W. Second St.
Marshfield, WI 54449-2719
David L. LaFontaine, P.E., President
PH: (715)384-2133
FX: (715)384-9787
Founded: 1949. **Staff:** 15. Consulting engineers and land surveyors serving local government and private industry. Recent experience with design of water pollution control systems as well as other kinds of water systems management and distribution. Also active in civil engineering, municipal projects, transportation (bridges, highways, airports), and construction management and inspection.

PFEIFFER ENGINEERING CO.
2701 Lindsay Ave.
Louisville, KY 40206-2222
John C. Pfeiffer, President
PH: (502)897-1630
FX: (502)895-3894
URL: http://www.pfeiffereng.com
Founded: 1981. **Staff:** 19. Offers industrial control systems design,

construction supervision, and start-up assistance. Also furnishes engineering services and hardware/software design. Industries served include: chemical, food processing, packaging, tobacco, explosives, automotive, and metal forming. Serves private industries as well as government agencies.

PHILIP ENVIRONMENTAL SERVICES CORP.
210 W. Sand Bank Rd.
Columbia, IL 62236
Jenny Penland, President
PH: (618)281-7173
FX: (618)281-5120
URL: http://www.philipinc.com
Founded: 1975. **Staff:** 646. Environmental and industrial services firm specializing in consulting, remediation, demolition/ decommissioning, and waste management. Specific services include: strategic resource management (SRM); industrial redevelopment; ecological and wetland services; PCB line and concrete cleaning; remedial investigations and feasibility studies; environmental pre-acquisition and compliance audits; remedial design; groundwater, soil, surface water, and air sampling; contamination assessment; risk assessments; RCRA closure projects; hazardous waste investigations; emergency response; and analytical services. Additional expertise in asbestos consulting and abatement, geotechnical engineering, soils and materials testing, and construction for private and public sector clients. Industries served: chemical, manufacturing, transportation, petroleum, electronics, food and beverage, pulp and paper, and utilities.

LESTER P. PICARD—PROJECT ENGINEERING
139 Wilson Ave.
Houma, LA 70364
Lester P. Picard, Contact
PH: (504)868-3845
FX: (504)522-0554
E-mail: lppicard@neworleans.walkhaydel.com
Founded: 1988. **Staff:** 1. Project management consultant provides project engineering services to chemical processing industry. Offers complete project management or related services including estimating, scheduling, cost control, progress reporting, and start-up assistance. Turnaround scheduling and control also available. Experience in maintenance and construction. Industries served: chemical processing, metals, oil refining, and material handling.

MALCOLM PIRNIE, INC.
104 Corporate Park Dr.
White Plains, NY 10602-0751
Paul L. Busch, CEO, Chairman, President
PH: (914)694-2100
TF: (800)759-5020
FX: (914)694-9286
URL: http://www.pirnie.com
Founded: 1895. **Staff:** 1100. Independent environmental engineering sciences and consulting firm. Provides professional engineering and management services to public and private clients worldwide. Specializes in drinking water, wastewater, hazardous and solid wastes, air quality and environmental remediation. Activities include engineering, planning, science and management consulting relative to water supply, distribution, treatment and storage; water reclamation/reuse; water resource development, control and modeling; wastewater collection and treatment; drainage; storm water management and flood control; hazardous waste management and control; solid waste management and resource recovery; construction services; operation and maintenance; utility financing and management programs; environmental impact assessments; odor control; and atmospheric sciences. Industries Served: Municipalities, government, industry and federal agencies.

PJ MATERIALS CONSULTANTS
11 Wagoners Trl.
Guelph, ON, Canada N1G 3M9
Paul Jeffs, Founder

PH: (519)767-0702
FX: (519)821-2870
E-mail: pjmc@mgl.ca
URL: http://www.mgl.ca/~pjmc
Founded: 1989. Firm provides technical advice in the design, specification, construction, restoration and protection of concrete and masonry structures.

PLAIN AND SIMPLE SEMINARS
20 Teaberry Ln.
Attleboro, MA 02703
David A. Purdy, Contact
PH: (508)226-3318
Independent consultant teaches training seminars for managers, superintendents, supervisors, foremen, and tradesmen in construction work. Topics include: listening, teambuilding, motivation, scheduling, planning, communications, safety, materials, methods, project management, and others.

PLANNING MASTERS
3343 William Dr.
Newbury Park, CA 91320
Chase Lichtenstein, President
PH: (805)499-7526
FX: (805)499-8356
E-mail: chasewl@aol.com
Founded: 1985. **Staff:** 1. Management consulting firm provides project management training and implementation services to organizations that require expeditious implementation of new or revised programs. Specializes in the management of limited resources. Additionally consults on construction management and maintenance management. Industries served: manufacturing, chemical, pharmaceutical, and construction.

PLANT PROFILES INC.
1015 E. Felicidad Dr.
Fallbrook, CA 92028-2717
Chuck Gubser, Consultant
PH: (760)723-5710
FX: (760)728-3820
E-mail: chuck@tfb.com
Plant Profiles is a consulting group offering the design engineering, procurement services, and project management of custom designed concrete batching, aggregate processing, material storage and bulk material handling systems for the concrete, construction materials, and mining industries.

PLATINUM ENERGY SERVICES, INC.
100 Executive Way, Ste. 203
Ponte Vedra Beach, FL 32082
John Paparelli, President
PH: (904)273-0039
FX: (904)273-8437
E-mail: Platcon@aol.com
Founded: 1995. **Staff:** 30. Steam and electric generating plant due diligence review, pre-investment studies, plant condition assessments, planning and scheduling, preparation of capital and O&M cost estimates, preparation of EPC bidding documents, review of proposals and negotiation contracts, monitoring of engineering and construction progress, review of power purchase agreements, spare parts inventory control, procurement of equipment and materials, preparation of lead time reports, evaluation of change orders, and expediting and reporting services.

PMSI ARCHITECTS, ENGINEERS AND CONSTRUCTION MANAGERS
7 S. Dewey St.
Eau Claire, WI 54701
Premal J. Sheth, President
PH: (715)834-6661
FX: (715)834-3559
E-mail: pmsiaecm@discover-net.net
Founded: 1977. **Staff:** 25. Architectural/engineering design and construction management services. Serves private industries as well as government agencies.

JERRY L. POLLAK, ARCHITECT
14209 Chandler Blvd.
Sherman Oaks, CA 91401
Jerry L. Pollak, Contact
PH: (818)909-3757
FX: (818)997-7999
Founded: 1970. **Staff:** 1. Offers counsel in architecture, construction, safety issues and urban design. Provides expert witness and consulting to attorneys on issues relating to expertise including construction, malpractice, safety, codes, and construction methodology. Serves private industries as well as government agencies.

POOLE FIRE PROTECTION ENGINEERING, INC.
1317 S. Fountain Dr.
Olathe, KS 66061
John "Jack" W. Poole,, III, President
PH: (913)829-8650
TF: (800)285-3473
FX: (913)829-8690
E-mail: pfpe@tfs.net
Founded: 1991. **Staff:** 7. Provide state-of-the-art, cost effective fire protection engineering and code consulting services. Offer a practical approach to conventional fire protection and life safety concerns, as well as those unique to specialized industries. Services include the following principal categories: building construction and code analysis, regulatory compliance, risk management/loss control, computer fire and egress modeling applications, construction management, suppression and detection design principles and system maintenance, and legal testimony/deposition review. Industries served: architects and engineers, insurance industry, government services, manufacturing, and legal industry.

J.W. POST & ASSOCIATES, INC.
19834 Sundance Dr.
Humble, TX 77346
Jeffrey W. Post, President
PH: (281)852-3745
FX: (281)852-7689
Founded: 1982. **Staff:** 1. Expertise in welding engineering, including materials selection, preparation or review of welding procedures or welder performance qualifications, design and implementation of repair procedures and techniques including heat straightening or heat cambering, inspection and non-destructive testing techniques, provided to owners or contractors primarily engaged in steel construction.

GERALD POTAPA & ASSOCIATES
32500 Concord, Ste. 301
Madison Heights, MI 48071
Gerald Potapa, President
PH: (313)585-6763
FX: (313)585-6767
Founded: 1976. **Staff:** 9. Provides mechanical and electrical engineering services related to the construction industry-commercial, institutional and industrial.

POWER ENGINEERS INC.
PO Box 1066
Hailey, ID 83333
Pete VanDerMeulen, Contact
PH: (208)788-3456
FX: (208)788-2082
URL: http://www.powereng.com
Founded: 1976. **Staff:** 400. A consulting engineering firm that offers multidiscipline engineering and support needs for utilities and industrial process facilities. Services include electrical power line and substation design, electrical instrumentation and control engineering, civil/structural, mechanical, communications, systems, architectural, conservation and energy analysis, and geotechnical engineering. Support services include system studies, SCADA, land and environmental (including geographic information systems), and sur-

veying. Additionally, offers complete construction management, inspection, and procurement services. Industries served: electric utilities, industrial process and food facilities, government agencies and institutions, oil and gas, mining, telecommunication firms, and pulp and paper.

PREZANT ASSOCIATES, INC.
330 6th Ave. N., Ste. 200
Seattle, WA 98109
Brad Prezant, CEO
PH: (206)281-8858
FX: (206)281-8922
URL: http://www.prezant.com
Founded: 1987. Industrial hygiene consulting, laboratory and health/safety training organization. Firm is divided into three departments: consulting, training and laboratory. Provides risk management consultation services to property owners and managers, construction firms, industrial and manufacturing facilities, school districts and universities, municipalities and utilities and regulatory agencies. Specializes in analyzing asbestos, metals, and volatile organic compounds. Conducts hazardous materials surveys and designed demolition/renovation materials removal plans and specifications.

PROFESSIONAL CONSTRUCTION CONSULTANTS, INC.
1116 Wyoming Ave.
El Paso, TX 79902
Ricardo A. Baca, President
PH: (915)533-1176
FX: (915)533-1249
Founded: 1976. **Staff:** 4. Provides consulting services related to the cost of construction. Services include, but are not limited to, cost comparisons of structural systems and wall systems, recommendations for substitutions of materials, recommendations for possible alternates, and value engineering on architectural and structural systems. Extensive experience in working with contractors supports capability to point out possible conflicts (architect/engineer vs. contractor), to suggest optional ways of construction, and to point out possible mistakes or conflicting data during the design stage and assist the architect/engineer in the correction of them. Serves private industries as well as government agencies.

PROFESSIONAL ENGINEERING INSPECTIONS, INC.
PO Box 271492
Houston, TX 77277
Don Robinson, President
PH: (713)664-1264
FX: (713)664-9134
E-mail: office@profengineering.com
URL: http://www.profengineering.com
Specializes in residential inspections, commercial inspections and consulting, structural inspection-mechanical and electrical, pools and spas- foundation, roof- energy loss, quality of construction- condition of property, and capital reserve studies- special inspections.

PROFIT ASSOCIATES, INC.
PO Box 38026
Charleston, SC 29414
Bob Rogers, Managing Director
PH: (803)763-5718
FX: (803)763-5719
E-mail: bobrog@awod.com
URL: http://www.awod.com/gallery/business/proasc
A team of management and turnaround specialists providing consulting services. Focuses on the problems of small to medium-sized businesses in the manufacturing, distribution, construction, software, health care, and transportation industries. Specializes in employee productivity and incentives, management re-engineering, profit and expense controls, production planning, strategic business planning, marketing and public relations, or ISO 9000 support.

PROJECT MANAGEMENT SERVICES, INC.
PO Box 4113
Rockville, MD 20849
Douglas N. Mitten, Contact
PH: (301)340-0527
FX: (301)424-3660
E-mail: pmsimail@aol.com
URL: http://www.libra.wcupa.edu/Valu/Link/pmsindex.html
Founded: 1987. **Staff:** 12. Independent construction cost estimating, scheduling and value engineering services. Provides risk analyses, cost analyses, range estimating, surety value analysis(sm) facility security (CPTED) studies, and asbestos cost estimating. Provides master, preconstruction, and construction scheduling. Value engineering workshops and program studies are by certified value specialists. Claims review and expert witness services provided as well. Develops software in related fields.

J.P. PROSSER & ASSOCIATES, INC.
65 Broad St.
Boston, MA 02109
John P. Prosser, President
PH: (617)357-8110
FX: (617)357-7410
Founded: 1982. **Staff:** 3. Offers general consulting in real estate development, construction and property management, including workouts of distressed property. Additional areas of expertise in code compliance, energy management and construction inspection/certification. Serves private industries as well as government agencies.

NATHAN PUTCHAT ASSOCIATES
PO Box 965
Hobe Sound, FL 33475
Nathan Putchat, Contact
PH: (561)546-2972
FX: (561)546-9654
Founded: 1940. **Staff:** 4. Engineers and planners involved in the following areas: building construction, heavy construction, construction cost analysis and project management, claims preparation and documentation, construction trade practices, building construction failures, marine casualty investigation, fire and arson investigation, automotive and heavy equipment accident reconstruction, oceanographic and estuarine ecological and marine problems, and water, wastewater and solid wastes.

QORE
11420 Johns Creek Pky.
Duluth, GA 30097
Dave Albin, President
PH: (770)476-3555
FX: (770)476-0213
E-mail: duluth@qore.net
URL: http://www.qore.net
Founded: 1969. **Staff:** 465. Geotechnical engineering consultants offering the following services: construction materials testing, geology and hydrogeology, environmental assessments, nondestructive testing, and evaluation. Serves private industries as well as government agencies.

RAILWAY SYSTEMS DESIGN INC.
464 S. Old Middletown Rd.
Media, PA 19063
Ashok K. Kheny, President
PH: (610)565-9300
FX: (610)565-9309
E-mail: gsmedmlb@interamp.com
Firm offers special knowledge in design engineering and construction management of signal and communication systems, traction electrification systems, catenary systems, and transit and railroad operations.

RATHS, RATHS & JOHNSON, INC.
835 Midway Dr.
Willowbrook, IL 60521
Otto C. Guedelhoefer, Senior Principal
PH: (630)325-6160
TF: (800)826-6822
FX: (630)325-2866
E-mail: info@rrj.com
URL: http://www.rrj.com
Founded: 1966. **Staff:** 30. Forensic engineering services include, failure analysis, structural problem analysis, construction and problem resolution. Provides performance evaluation, structural repair design, material evaluation and testing, full scale testing, mock-up testing, models for courtroom exhibits, presentation graphics, condition assessment, and repair of distressed or aged structures.

OFFICE OF RICHARD W. RAUSEO
1184 Edinburgh Rd.
San Dimas, CA 91773
PH: (818)859-2400
FX: (818)859-2402
E-mail: rauseo@ibm.net
Concerned with construction defects, building code compliance with emphasis on the building shell, construction accident reconstruction, and safety analysis.

RAYMAR ENGINEERING
3000 Citrus Cir., Ste. 204
Walnut Creek, CA 94598
Martin Fohrman, Principal
PH: (510)944-5266
FX: (510)944-9963
Provides civil engineering services. Specializes in structures, land development drainage/flood control, surveying, and construction errors and omissions. Investigates design and construction deficiencies. Provides litigation support.

A.G. RAYMOND & CO.
3101 E. Essex Cir.
Raleigh, NC 27608
Arthur G. Raymond, Jr., President
PH: (919)782-7077
FX: (919)782-7263
E-mail: agrco@mindspring.com
Founded: 1981. **Staff:** 7. Management and technical consultants to the forest and wood products industry. Services include: feasibility analysis, materials utilization, plant location, long-range planning, facilities design and planning, equipment specification, methods improvement, and production control systems. Also provides services in construction management, facilities engineering (structural, electrical, and mechanical design), and computer applications through associated firms for complete turnkey projects.

RAYTHEON ENGINEERS AND CONSTRUCTORS, INC.
PO Box 101
Birmingham, AL 35201
Rodney C. Gilbert, Chairman/CEO
PH: (205)995-7878
TF: (800)247-3122
FX: (205)995-7777
Founded: 1905. **Staff:** 7000. Leading company providing environmental engineering, consulting, infrastructure and construction services to governmental and industrial clients. Industries served: pulp and paper, metals, aerospace, food and beverage, chemicals, energy, government, electronics, and general manufacturing.

RAYTHEON ENGINEERS & CONSTRUCTORS INTERNATIONAL INC.
141 Spring St.
Lexington, MA 02173
Charles Q. Miller, Chairman/CEO
PH: (617)862-6600
FX: (617)860-2845
Founded: 1993. **Staff:** 16000. Offers consulting services in engineering, design, construction, and maintenance of utility and industrial power plants petroleum and mining facilities, chemical, pharmaceutical and biotechnology, foods, metals, and general manufacturing plants, high-technology research laboratories, government facilities, and infrastructure facilities in transportation, highways, and water resources. Also provides special consulting on site planning, environmental assessments and testing, process technologies, control systems integration, environmental engineering, generation planning and licensing, and quality programs.

THE RBA GROUP
One Evergreen Place
Morristown, NJ 07960
William Garro, President
PH: (973)898-0300
FX: (973)984-5421
Founded: 1968. **Staff:** 300. Offers large-scale development planning, transportation planning and engineering, and architectural design, as well as a diverse portfolio of expertise which includes: roadway planning and engineering; structural engineering; architectural rehabilitation; urban design, land development and site engineering; environmental permitting; surveying; and construction services. Also works in bicycle/pedestrian planning, traffic calming strategies, downtown revitalization development, golf course design support, and cultural resource management.

RESIDENTIAL CONSTRUCTION SERVICES
404 Allen Rd.
Oconomowoc, WI 53066
PH: (414)567-5833
FX: (414)567-2617
E-mail: Rstolz5833@aol.com
URL: http://members.aol.com/RStolz5833/rcs/index.htm
Provides residential design and drafting of single and multifamily dwellings from conception through final plans, including floor plans, detailing, specifications, cross sections, foundations, electrical, cabinets, and structural.

RESIDENTIAL DESIGN CONSULTANTS
363 W. Stuart Ave.
Fresno, CA 93704
Louis A. Hall, CKD, CBD, CID
PH: (559)435-1740
FX: (559)435-1740
E-mail: louhall@thesocket.com
URL: http://www.kitchenbathdesigner.com
Founded: 1984. **Staff:** 1. Offers residential design and construction consulting with emphasis on kitchen and bath design and remodeling. Provides seminars and training programs to residential remodeling and interior design related industries in the U.S. Relating to sales training, relationship building, creating and creativity and credibility strategies, vocational sales teaming.

RESOURCE MANAGEMENT INTERNATIONAL, INC.
3100 Zinfandel Dr., Ste. 600
Rancho Cordova, CA 95670-6026
Ronald O. Nichols, Senior Managing Director
PH: (916)852-1300
FX: (916)852-1073
E-mail: laura_wendel@rmiinc.com
URL: http://www.rmiinc.com
Founded: 1979. **Staff:** 275. Consulting firm specializing in the fields of electric power, natural gas, water resources and telecommunications. Capabilities include strategic planning and marketing, competitive assessments, organizational development and restructuring, training, customer service programs, new product and service development, engineering studies, geographic information system design and implementation, system planning and design, generation and transmission siting/routing, operations and maintenance, construction management, economic analyses, competitive analyses, competitive market pricing, tariff design, fuel supply planning, financing strategies, resource planning, load forecasting, regulatory compliance programs and environmental assessments, contract development and negotiation, dispute resolution and arbitration and

comprehensive project management. RMI serves both providers and users of energy, water, and telecommunication services and products, including public and private utility companies, independent service providers and distributors, business and industry, governments, institutions, multilateral development banks and bilateral agencies, regulatory commissions, and the legal and financial communities.

REVAY AND ASSOCIATES LTD.
4333 Rue Ste. Catherine Ouest
Montreal, PQ, Canada H3Z 1P9
PH: (514)932-2188
FX: (514)939-0776
E-mail: revay@dsuper.net
URL: http://www.revay.com
Founded: 1970. Firm specializes in management consulting services. Prepares and conduct in-depth surveys and studies for government and the construction industry.

RICHEY RESOURCES CO.
1700 W. Loop S, Ste. 800
Houston, TX 77027-3007
Thomas Richey, Owner
PH: (713)622-0877
TF: (800)346-3354
FX: (713)622-0876
E-mail: 110034.2263@compuserve.com
Founded: 1957. **Staff:** 1. Advises U.S. businesses on marketing, management, sales, and training.

RICHMOND STERLING, INC.
235 Peachtree St. NE, Ste. 888
Atlanta, GA 30303
PH: (404)525-9606
FX: (404)525-4416
E-mail: pnm@richmondsterling.com
URL: http://www.richmondsterling.com
An independent construction consulting firm that provides project management, owner's representative services and independent cost management to users of the construction industry. Provides a complete management and control system; supervises the overall budget and schedule; solicits and evaluates bids, recommends a contractor, and awards the contract; directs the contractor in the performance of the contract; operates as the in-house manager of design and construction processes; ensures the owner's directives are accurately given to the design; professionals and contractor, then correctly executed; enables the owner to properly manage the project's development within schedule and budget constraints; monitors and controls the project budgets independently of design and construction teams; monitors contractor pricing and valuations of the work in progress; controls and mitigate extra costs; monitors the cash flow through all phases of construction.

RIDER HUNT ACKROYD, LLC
999 3rd Ave., Ste. 830
Seattle, WA 98104
Peter D. Ackroyd, President
PH: (206)223-2055
FX: (206)223-2056
E-mail: rhasea@aol.com
Founded: 1981. **Staff:** 10. Firm provides construction management and cost estimation services. Advises on cost containment.

RIDGE & ASSOCIATES, INC.
PO Box 1091
Findlay, OH 45839
Larry J. Hoover, President
PH: (419)423-3641
FX: (419)423-0136
E-mail: lasereng@bright.net
URL: http://www.rareyroth.com/ridge
Founded: 1976. **Staff:** 11. Engineering consultancy offers services in the areas of petroleum storage, handling, and dispensing facilities. Typical facilities are terminals, tank farms, bulk plants, pipeline

pumping stations, and aviation fuel facilities. Also offers investigative engineering services, contract drafting, computer-assisted drafting and multi-discipline engineering services to general industry. Also supplies machine design services through an affiliated company, Omega Mechanical Design, Inc. Industries served are primarily petroleum, manufacturing and transportation, as well as government agencies and insurance companies.

P. PAUL RIDILLA
71 Triplet Lake Dr., N.
Casselberry, FL 32707
P. Paul Ridilla, President
PH: (407)699-8515
FX: (407)695-7225
Founded: 1972. **Staff:** 2. Provides management consulting and training for construction and service industries. Specializes in construction foreman training, construction superintendent training, and construction estimator training. Also provides counseling for construction employees.

ROARING BROOK CONSULTANTS, INC.
15 Sewall Rd.
South Berwick, ME 03908
Keith T. Kallberg, General Manager
PH: (207)384-2643
FX: (207)384-5383
E-mail: keith@rbc.mv.com
URL: http://www.aecnet.com/rbc/home.htm
Specializes in civil engineering, structural engineering, land surveying, forensic engineering, Phase I environmental site assessments, condition inspections, repair designs, repair estimates, code compliance evaluation, site development, construction management, construction schedule and claims analysis. Provides property inspection reports with detail and explanation. Offers construction management for new construction and repair projects.

ROBINSON & WOOD, INC.
227 N. 1st St.
San Jose, CA 95113
Archie S. Robinson, Principal
PH: (408)298-7120
FX: (408)298-0477
E-mail: rw@r-winc.com
Specializes in insurance defense in automobile, trucking, fire, casualty, product liability, construction, landslide and subsidence, insurance coverage, bad faith, government discrimination, legal and medical malpractice, environmental law, intellectual property cases.

JOHN R. ROGERS ASSOCIATES, INC.
10332 Richview Dr.
St. Louis, MO 63127
John R. Rogers, P.E., President
PH: (314)965-6635
FX: (314)965-6635
E-mail: jtaurus@juno.com
Founded: 1984. **Staff:** 4. Engineering consultants providing feasibility studies, cost estimates, designs, plans, and specifications for projects requiring industrial and electrical engineering services. The work ranges from automation, communications and economics, to operations planning, noise, and vibration abatement and training. Firm provides engineering services to industrial and commercial firms, to institutions, to government agencies, and to owners, architects, contractors, and other engineering firms. Forensic investigations and opinions are provided, when required.

ROMERO MANAGEMENT ASSOCIATES
1805 W. Ave. K Ste. 202
Lancaster, CA 93534
Teresa Romero, Principal
PH: (805)940-0540
FX: (805)940-0546
E-mail: rma@as.net
URL: http://web.as.net/~rma
Founded: 1991. Provides consulting services for school districts in

the area of energy management. Offers complete review of design including value engineering, constructability, and bid documents.

ROSSER INTERNATIONAL, INC.
524 W. Peachtree St. NW
Atlanta, GA 30308
Paul C. Rosser, Chairman Emeritus
PH: (404)876-3800
TF: (800)523-6478
FX: (404)888-6861
Founded: 1947. **Staff:** 200. Provides architectural, engineering, and program management services involving facilities design for sports arenas and stadiums, criminal justice, aviation, military, healthcare, offices, computers, broadcast, and laboratories. Offers comprehensive package from concept through construction quality documents. Industries served: all in public and private sector in the U.S. and worldwide.

ROTHBERG TAMBURINI WINSOR
1600 Stout St., Ste. 1800
Denver, CO 80202-3126
Michael Rothberg, President
PH: (303)825-5999
FX: (303)825-0642
E-mail: rtw@rtweng.com
URL: http://www.rtweng.com/rtw
Founded: 1984. **Staff:** 40. Provides site development and master plans; utility system analysis and design; water quality analysis; water/wastewater facility and process design; electrical, control, and SCADA systems; facility upgrades, expansions, and retrofits; construction management; value engineering; expert testimony; process control operations training and troubleshooting; and facility startups. Industries served: all government and private sector in the United States.

ROUX ASSOCIATES, INC.
1377 Motor Pky., Ste. 403
Hauppauge, NY 11788-5258
Paul H. Roux, President
PH: (516)232-2600
TF: (800)322-ROUX
FX: (516)232-9898
Founded: 1981. **Staff:** 130. An environmental consulting firm specializing in investigating and solving a broad range of ground-water and soil contamination problems for industrial clients nationwide. Other activities include environmental property transfer assessment, underground storage tank management, and remediation design and construction management. Industries served include: aerospace, agriculture, apparel and textiles, banking and finance, chemicals, electronics, energy, lumber, pulp, and paper, mining, petroleum, pharmaceutical and utilities.

ROY ASSOCIATES, INC.
594 Marrett Rd.
Lexington, MA 02173-7605
Swapan Roy, Contact
PH: (617)863-0101
FX: (617)863-1151
E-mail: rai@sprynet.com
Founded: 1985. **Staff:** 4. Structural and civil engineering firm also specializes in minor architectural renovation work. Industries served: federal agencies, state agencies, architects, and industrial facilities.

RUMMEL, KLEPPER & KAHL, LLP
81 Mosher St.
Baltimore, MD 21217
William K. Hellmann, Contact
PH: (410)728-2900
TF: (800)787-3755
FX: (410)728-2992
URL: http://www.rkkengineers.com
Founded: 1923. **Staff:** 350. Engineering services for studies, planning, design and construction inspection of highways; bridges;

dams; water and gas supply, water and wastewater treatment, industrial wastewater treatment, and solid waste collection and disposal facilities; rapid transit facilities; railroads; ports; natural gas/pipeline facilities; industrial and commercial developments; and park and recreational facilities. Also, geotechnical engineering for heavy construction and structures; construction monitoring services to lending institutions; and engineering for private waterfront development. Industries served: private industries and developers as well as government agencies.

RUSSELL PROGRAM MANAGEMENT, INC.
504 Fair St. SW
Atlanta, GA 30313
Herman J. Russell, Chairman/CEO
PH: (404)330-0858
FX: (404)330-0922
Founded: 1984. **Staff:** 56. A consulting firm of architects, engineers, and contractors providing project coordination and management information services to organizations involved in capital improvement programs. Industries served: transportation, correctional, educational, healthcare, environmental, industrial/commercial, and civic centers. Geographic areas served: southeastern United States.

SAARMAN CONSTRUCTION, LTD.
683 McAllister St.
San Francisco, CA 94102
Paul Saarman, Principal
PH: (415)749-2700
FX: (415)749-2709
Firm specializes in residential and commercial insurance restoration, and cost of repairs in fire, water, and smoke damage. Provides expert witness testimony. Evaluates construction defects.

DAVID SABSAY
667 Montgomery Rd.
Sebastopol, CA 95472
David Sabsay, Contact
PH: (707)823-6936
FX: (707)823-3726
E-mail: dsabsay@sonic.net
Library consultant whose services include building programs; site and architect selection; construction budgeting and financing; critical evaluation of building design, drawings and specifications; and interior design. Also involved in media and computer services. Serves private industries as well as government agencies.

SAGE CONSTRUCTION CONSULTING
1623 Blake St., Ste. 400
Denver, CO 80202-1337
Richard E. Tasker, President
PH: (303)571-0237
TF: (800)288-2663
FX: (303)893-2849
E-mail: sageco@aol.com
URL: http://www.sageconsult.com
Founded: 1985. **Staff:** 14. Offers forensic expertise in the field of construction. Industries served: insurance, bonding, legal, and general public in the United States.

SAI CONSTRUCTION AND LAND SURVEYORS INC.
23 Narragansett Ave.
Jamestown, RI 02835
Barbara A. Szepatowski, President
PH: (401)423-0430
TF: (800)498-0653
FX: (401)423-0037
Founded: 1989. **Staff:** 24. Firm offers expertise in land surveying, civil and environmental engineering, wetlands biology, land use planning, technical writing, drafting, environmental permitting, and field technology. Has support staff familiar with all phases of local, state, and federal regulations. Experience ranges from metes and bound surveys of single lots and multi-lot land development projects, to hazardous waste surveying, to construction layout. Serves

private, industrial, and public sector clients in Rhode Island, Connecticut, and Massachusetts.

SAJAN INC.
2150 N. 107th St., Ste. 520
Seattle, WA 98133
Suresh L. Malik, President
PH: (206)363-6762
FX: (206)363-6769
Founded: 1980. **Staff:** 25. Consulting engineers experienced in highways, structural, bridges, storm drainage, sanitary sewers, water supply, surveying, and construction management. Industries served: marine and transportation.

SALES & MARKETING EXCELLENCE
8230 Elizabeth Ln.
La Plata, MD 20646
PH: (301)932-1744
FX: (301)934-0533
E-mail: dgehris@bellatlantic.net
Firm offers training in construction materials and equipment.

JEFFREY PETER SALVIN
19320 SW 129th Ave.
Miami, FL 33177
Jeffrey P. Salvin, Contact
PH: (305)251-8770
FX: (305)251-8770
E-mail: pejeff@aol.com
Founded: 1978. **Staff:** 3. Specializes in construction claims including change order analysis, delay, acceleration, loss of productivity, impact, weather delay, and other construction-related litigation analyses. Extensive experience in serving legal profession.

CHARLES J. SAMO
19701 Constellation Ln.
Huntington Beach, CA 92646
PH: (714)964-1687
TF: (800)201-8555
FX: (714)964-8060
Specializes in construction safety, compliance, accident reconstruction, slip and fall, damage to underground utilities, natural gas and oil pipeline accidents, overhead and underground high voltage lines, gas safety and electrical safety, pipeline safety, and traffic safety. Prepares computer graphics and exhibits.

**STEVE SAMUELS, ARCHITECTURAL WOODWORK
  CONSULTANT**
202 Cleveland Dr.
Croton on Hudson, NY 10520
Steve Samuels, Contact
PH: (914)271-9364
FX: (914)271-6488
E-mail: samuels@interactive.net
Founded: 1988. **Staff:** 2. Provides architectural woodwork expertise, specializing in cost effective programming, designing, engineering, estimation, specification, and evaluation of architectural woodwork. Also offers project management, quality control, document preparation, site evaluation, needs analysis, and code compliance review. Serves government agencies in the U.S., primarily Greater-New York area.

SANDWELL INTERNATIONAL INC.
Park Place
Vancouver, BC, Canada V6C 2X8
Alan Pyatt, Chairman/President/CEO
PH: (604)684-0055
FX: (604)684-7533
E-mail: info@Sandwell.com
URL: http://www.sandwell.com
Founded: 1949. **Staff:** 800. An engineering contractor operating worldwide in the pulp and paper, bulk handling, marine and energy sectors.

SAUNDERS CONSTRUCTION, INC.
PO Box 3908
6950 S Jordan Rd.
Englewood, CO 80155
PH: (303)699-9000
FX: (303)680-7448
URL: http://www.saundersci.com
Founded: 1972. **Staff:** 185. A general construction contractor. Project team of professional estimators and engineers. The company has a wide range of expertise including medical, industrial and manufacturing, retail, office, education, recreation, automotive, and church projects, along with campus settings and municipal facilities. Contract structures include design-build, lump-sum and GMP formats.

J.D. SCHAEFER & ASSOCIATES
35 W. Seaview Ave.
San Rafael, CA 94901-2353
J.D. Schaefer, Owner
PH: (415)485-0354
TF: (888)875-1955
FX: (415)485-0354
E-mail: jdrower@linex.com
Founded: 1989. **Staff:** 2. Assists with claims preparation and analysis. Services in investigation, discovery, interrogatories, depositions, construction management, contract administration (scheduling, inspections, industry standards, and specifications), and crisis management.

SCHARF-GODFREY INC.
24-E Montgomery Village Ave.
Gaithersburg, MD 20879
Robin Godfrey, President
PH: (301)990-0101
FX: (301)990-1777
E-mail: info@scharf-godrey.com
Founded: 1920. **Staff:** 15. Provides construction costing for projects involving airports, office buildings, military and housing projects, hospitals, educational facilities, laboratories, bridges, highways, rail/transit facilities, corrections facilities, and water/ wastewater treatment plants. Also skilled in arbitration, bid evaluation, change order evaluation, contract administration and negotiations, cost surveys, expert testimony, life cycle costing, project management, quantity surveys, scheduling/CPM, and value engineering to architects, engineers, facility owners, government agencies, and developers worldwide. Certified woman-owned enterprise (WBE).

CHARLES S. SCHECK ASSOCIATES
9306 N. Lotus Ave.
Skokie, IL 60077
Charles S. Scheck, President
PH: (847)966-7869
Founded: 1981. **Staff:** 2. Planning consultants specializing in urban development, zoning administration, residential rehabilitation, capital improvement programming, policy, and development. Industries served: real estate development; state, county and municipal governments.

F.J. SCHROEDER & ASSOCIATES
1926 Westholme Ave.
Los Angeles, CA 90025
Frederick J. Schroeder, Contact
PH: (310)470-2655
FX: (310)470-6378
E-mail: fjsacons@aol.com
URL: http://www.mcninet.com/GlobalLook/Fjschroe.html
Founded: 1985. **Staff:** 2. Provides consulting services in the following areas to professional engineering firms, public agencies, and other clients involved in public infrastructure design, construction, operation and maintenance: strategic management, project planning and management, primary and secondary research, marketing auditing, planning and program implementation, new business planning, interim management, and other management services. Industries served: professional engineering firms, government agencies and

others involved in planning, design construction, operation and maintenance of public works infrastructure.

THOMAS G. SCHULTZ, PH.D.
17540 Hoot Owl Way
Morgan Hill, CA 95037-6524
PH: (408)779-0611
FX: (408)776-0390
Provides highway and traffic engineering analysis, including geometric features, roadside obstacles, signing, signals, warnings and delineation as contributing factors to the occurrence of an automobile accident. Analyzes the planning, design, construction, maintenance and operation of highways to include accident experience of road sections or intersections and comparison to system standards. Determines the relationship of specific design or operational features to accident patterns or to the occurrence of a specific accident.

SCINETEX CORP.
1655 N. Ft. Myer Dr., Ste. 400
Arlington, VA 22209
PH: (703)276-3377
FX: (703)276-0996
Civil engineering firm provides complete construction management services to industrial clients.

SE TECHNOLOGIES INC.
98 Vanadium Rd.
Bridgeville, PA 15017
Paul L. Spence, Vice President of Environmental Services
PH: (412)221-1100
FX: (412)257-6103
E-mail: se@vanadium.com
Founded: 1977. **Staff:** 430. Offers counsel and services in the areas of civil and environmental engineering, solid waste management, geology and hydrogeology, environmental science, construction management, and industrial safety and hygiene.

DON SEARLES, DREDGING SPECIALISTS
43 Dewitt Ave.
Mattoon, IL 61938
Don Searles, Dir. of Operations
PH: (217)234-3344
FX: (217)234-3347
E-mail: dredesp@advant.com
URL: http://www.dredgingspeciliasts.com
Provides consulting, claims investigations and litigation assistance in the dredging, including hydraulic and mechanical methods; dredging of rivers harbors, lakes, sludge, sand and gravel; the design, construction, operation and repair of rotary-basket and bucket-wheel cutterhead dredges; pre-dredging site investigations; dredge material analysis and production estimates; and spoil-area design. Also provides assistance in sludge engineering, including design, construction, operation and repair of sludge dredges; the design and construction of pumping systems; sludge de-watering by belt-press and plate and frame filter press. Also involved in fluid power hydraulic systems, including the design, construction, operation and repair.

SEAWORTHY SYSTEMS, INC.
22 Main St.
Centerbrook, CT 06409
David A. O'Neil, President
PH: (860)767-9061
FX: (860)767-1263
E-mail: mtoyen@seaworthysys.com
URL: http://www.seaworthysys.com
Founded: 1973. **Staff:** 50. Active in ship design and construction management, ship owner technical representation and liaison, propulsion plant improvement, alternative fuel conversions, economic analysis and trade-off studies, marine and industrial test programs, laboratory services, expert witness and other litigation support services, marine industry forecasting services, and software development. Industries served: maritime and industrial firms, as well as government agencies.

SECOR INTERNATIONAL INC.
12034—134th Ct. NE
Redmond, WA 98052-2442
PH: (425)372-1600
URL: http://www.secor.com
Founded: 1989. **Staff:** 700. Services include environmental restoration, environmental permitting and compliance, construction and remediation, risk assessment, land and resource management, environmental process engineering, water and wastewater treatment and supply, air quality management, environmental management information systems, waste management, industrial hygiene, and geochemistry services.

SELLMEYER ENGINEERING
PO Box 356
McKinney, TX 75069
J.S. Sellmeyer, President
PH: (972)542-2056
FX: (972)542-2056
E-mail: selmeyer@flash.net
Founded: 1980. **Staff:** 3. Broadcast and communications engineering consultants offering the following services: FCC applications, transmitter plant design, construction supervision, broadcast studio facilities planning and construction, AM directional antenna design, and adjustment and measurements.

SELTEC/BMG CONTROLS INC.
1279 Quarry Ln.
Pleasanton, CA 94566
PH: (510)426-7800
FX: (510)484-4676
Firm offers counseling in construction materials and design.

SEVENTH GENERATION STRATEGIES, INC.
Sustainable Technology Center
650 Mullis St., Ste. 201
Friday Harbor, WA 98250
James G. Sackett, President and Founder
PH: (360)378-8588
FX: (360)378-6477
E-mail: info@sevengensys.com
URL: http://www.sevengensys.com
A multi-disciplinary firm offering performance and economic solutions to building owners, designers and developers. Provides whole system design and technologies to meet power, heating, cooling, sewage, water and other project requirements on an integrated basis.

SHAH ASSOCIATES
2635 Pettit
Bellmore, NY 11710
Natvar M. Shah, President
PH: (516)826-3001
FX: (516)826-3008
Founded: 1890. **Staff:** 60. Performs consulting engineering services in the areas of environmental, surveying, community planning, site planning/development sanitary design, mechanical and electrical, structural design, civil design, construction management, and utility services. Industries served: state, federal and municipal, architecture, developers, telecommunications, utility, and commercial builders/owners. Geographic areas served: New York, New Jersey, and Connecticut, Northeast and Midwest.

SHAH ASSOCIATES PC
1188 Meadowbrook Rd.
Merrick, NY 11566
Natvar M. Shah, President
PH: (516)292-0314
FX: (516)481-0615
Founded: 1977. **Staff:** 110. A consulting engineering firm which specializes in the design, estimating, survey, and construction inspection of highways, bridges, tunnels, subway systems, commercial and industrial buildings, sewer systems, waterfront structures, and many other civil engineering-related projects. Serves various state

transportation departments, other private consultants and clients, and city and local authorities.

DAN SHANAHAN
PO Box 3
Georgetown, TX 78627
PH: (512)930-4966
FX: (888)991-1111
E-mail: omabarb@rytebyte.com
Consulting engineer offers the design and construction of residential and commercial complexes, apartment buildings, shopping centers, gymnasiums, assembly halls, marinas, sea walls, roads, utilities, treatment facilities, large effluent disposal areas, and solid waste disposal sites. Specializes in civil, environmental, structural engineering, and investigative engineering.

L.W. SHEBSES & ASSOCIATES
PO Box 250095
West Bloomfield, MI 48325-0095
Leonard Shebses, Contact
PH: (248)851-5340
FX: (248)851-5042
Founded: 1975. **Staff:** 5. Shopping center consultant specializing in marketing, property management, rezoning coordination, land acquisition, site development, lease negotiations, systems organization, and construction management. Has innovated numerous property control and personnel accountability systems. Industries served: shopping center owners, government agencies, and retailers.

SHELADIA ASSOCIATES INC.
15825 Shady Grove Rd., Ste. 100
Rockville, MD 20850
Pravin N. Sheladia, Chairman
PH: (301)590-3939
FX: (301)948-7174
E-mail: sheladia@mindspring.com
Founded: 1974. **Staff:** 120. Provides study, analysis, planning, design and construction management services in engineering/architectural disciplines. Specific expertise in highways, bridges, mass transits, sanitary, environmental, hazardous waste management, water resources, hydrology, hydraulics, land, surveying, civil, electrical, mechanical and architectural projects. Services also include program planning, program management, monitoring and evaluation, MIS and systems analysis. Industries served: municipal agencies, transportation, housing, commercial, and industrial.

SHERLOCK HOMES
Atlanta, GA
Robert D. Seely, Contact
PH: (404)876-3845
Founded: 1989. **Staff:** 1. Provides structural and mechanical evaluation of residential and small commercial buildings. Industries served: real estate. Geographic areas served: metropolitan Atlanta and surrounding counties.

SHILSTONE & ASSOCIATES, INC.
9400 NCX Tower
Dallas, TX 75231-5033
James M. Shilstone, President
PH: (214)361-9681
TF: (800)782-8649
FX: (214)361-7925
E-mail: jay.shilstone@shilstone.com
URL: http://www.shilstone.com
Founded: 1977. **Staff:** 3. Construction industry consultants offering technical support for planning and construction of concrete structures for both structural and architectural concrete using precast and cast-in-place methods. Provides process technology to owners, architects, engineers, contractors and suppliers in the construction industry worldwide. Also offers special consultation and testimony in legal matters.

SHOOSHANIAN ENGINEERING ASSOCIATES INC.
330 Congress St.
Boston, MA 02210
Edward Shooshanian, Chairman
PH: (617)426-0110
FX: (617)426-7358
Founded: 1961. **Staff:** 75. Engineering firm specializing in design and construction services for a variety of industries.

SHORELINE CONTRACTORS INC.
Lloyd Palmaymesa, President
PH: (619)283-2024
E-mail: Info@shoreline-contractors.com
URL: http://www.shoreline-contractors.com
Founded: 1977. General building contractors involved from the initial concept, through design, contracting and completion of a project.

SIDAWI & ASSOCIATES CONSULTING ENGINEERS
3184-K Airway Ave.
Costa Mesa, CA 92626
Zac Sidawi, Pres.
PH: (714)966-1416
FX: (714)966-1502
E-mail: zsidawl@earthlink.net
Founded: 1979. **Staff:** 5. Specializes in water and wastewater systems engineering. Includes civil/sanitary and electrical engineers with extensive experience in preparation of documents for potable and reclaimed water and wastewater systems facilities; as well as feasibility studies and master plans; hydraulic networks analyses; quantity and construction cost estimates; construction phase services; and facilities start-up. Industries served: municipalities, water districts, land developers, and other engineering companies in California, Arizona, and Nevada.

SIDHU ASSOCIATES, INC.
2033 York Rd.
Timonium, MD 21093
Devindar S. Sidhu, President
PH: (410)561-5130
FX: (410)561-0954
Founded: 1977. **Staff:** 34. Mechanical/electrical design and construction management firm experienced in HVAC, plumbing, fire protection, power distribution, lighting, energy conservation, EMCS, communication systems, and CCTV for commercial, industrial, and institutional buildings. Also experienced with recreational facilities and highways, wastewater treatment plants, hazardous waste management and other environmental services, high voltage power transmission and distribution lines, radar and communication systems, and construction management for buildings and transit facilities. Serves private industry as well as government agencies.

LAWRENCE SIEGEL
Box 869
Columbia, MD 21044
Lawrence Siegel, Consultant
PH: (410)997-9210
FX: (410)997-0927
E-mail: lscourt@compuserve.com
URL: http://ourworld.compuserve.com/homepages/lscourt
Founded: 1975. Serving government agencies and architects with needs assessment, security analysis and design, facility planning, master planning, feasibility and pre-design, facility programming.

SIERRA DELTA CORP.
3281 S. Highland Dr.
Las Vegas, NV 89109-1044
Robert I. Eidemiller, President, Chief Executive Officer
PH: (702)734-7144
FX: (702)734-2542

JOSEPH C. SILVERN & ASSOCIATES
324 Greenwood St.
Evanston, IL 60201
Joseph C. Silvern, Contact

PH: (847)866-8888
FX: (847)866-8889
Founded: 1955. **Staff:** 1. Specialist in cost analysis of electrical portion of construction projects: budgets, contractor estimates, owner evaluation, claims by contractor or owner representative against claims, and product pricing.

SIMONS-CONKEY INC.
800 Marquette Ave., Ste. 1200
Minneapolis, MN 55402
William O. Vaughn, President
PH: (612)332-8326
FX: (612)332-2423
Founded: 1956. **Staff:** 90. Provides consulting engineering services primarily to the manufacturing and process industries with emphasis on beverages and food. A list of services include: feasibility studies, engineering design (process, electrical, mechanical, structural, civil), site layout, plant layout, cost estimates, construction review, start-up assistance, energy management, and project management. Serves private industries as well as government agencies.

SIMONS, LI & ASSOCIATES, INC.
3150 Bristol St., Ste. 500
Costa Mesa, CA 92626
Ruh-Ming Li, President
PH: (714)513-1280
FX: (714)513-1278
Founded: 1980. **Staff:** 40. A civil engineering consulting firm, with services offered in water resources engineering, environmental analysis and engineering, erosion and sedimentation, construction management, land development and planning, drainage and flood control, transportation, and computer services. Serves government, business, and industry, both nationally and internationally.

SIMPSONS COMMERCIAL INTERIORS—A DIVISION OF HUDSON'S BAY CO.
11 Allstate Pky., Main Fl.
Markham, ON, Canada L3R 9T8
James G. Hatch, Contact
PH: (905)479-7007
FX: (905)479-6919
Founded: 1929. **Staff:** 65. Offers professional services, including design and planning, procurement, and installation for all commercial interior environments. Fields of activity include: interior design (consulting and planning); interior construction and renovation; business interiors (commercial and private offices); commercial floor-coverings; commercial and institutional food services; hotel, motel and hospitality environments; institutional environments; and national accounts. Serves private industries as well as government agencies.

SINAK CORP.
861 Sixth Ave., Ste. 411
San Diego, CA 92101
Stan Kuerbis, President
PH: (619)231-1771
FX: (619)231-9364
E-mail: sinakcorp@aol.com
URL: http://www.sinakcorp.com
Founded: 1979. Firm offers expertise in construction materials and equipment.

SITE-BLAUVELT ENGINEERS, INC.
200 E. Park Dr., Ste. 100
Mount Laurel, NJ 08054-1299
R. W. Price, P.E., Vice President
PH: (609)273-1224
TF: (800)966-SITE
FX: (609)273-9244
Founded: 1961. **Staff:** 260. A consulting organization specializing in the fields of highway/bridge design, geotechnical engineering, civil engineering, surveying, structural engineering, construction inspection and testing, and consulting on distressed facilities. Projects include apartment complexes, office buildings, shopping centers, ho-

tels, highways, bridges, manufacturing facilities, and government and public facilities. Also maintain drill rigs, ASHTO certified soils and concrete testing labs, and a soils analysis laboratory, field test equipment and CADD systems. Industries served: transportation, public utilities, petroleum and chemical producers, commercial, healthcare, educational, and local, state and federal government agencies.

GARY A. SMITH, CPA
1984 Tice Valley Blvd.
Walnut Creek, CA 94595
PH: (510)933-6920
FX: (510)947-2996
Provides forensic accounting and financial analysis. Handles construction claims, damages and lost profits, securities and investments, fraud investigations, real estate, bankruptcy, accountant's liability, and business valuation.

SMITH-EMERY CO.
Los Angeles, CA
PH: (213)749-3411
E-mail: mktla@smithemery.com
URL: http://www.smithemery.com
Construction testing and inspection services. Acts as a single source of testing and inspection for all construction related services in the commercial building market, from the soil to the roof. Offers inspection, testing and failure analysis services including post tensioning, curtain wall testing, masonry inspection and tests, flatness testing & flat jack testing, batch plant inspection, seismic evaluation, non-destructive examinations, laboratory mock-ups, concrete placement, construction materials testing, concrete compression tests, roofing inspections and tests, wood structure inspection, reinforcing steel placement, gypsum inspection, and metallurgical lab testing.

FREDERICK A. SMITH ENGINEERS
33 Lockwood Dr.
Charleston, SC 29401
Cameron E. Smith, Contact
PH: (803)722-0827
FX: (803)897-2815
Founded: 1965. **Staff:** 4. Offers counsel on project development, site surveys, construction plans and specification, and construction supervision. Specialized services offered in the area of acoustics (sound level measurements and attenuation), and the design of specialized communications systems, and airport lighting and landing systems. Serves private industries as well as government agencies.

RAYMOND M. SMITH
1010 El Camino Real, Ste. 300
Menlo Park, CA 94025-4345
PH: (415)321-1252
FX: (415)321-2268
A litigation consultant offering expert testimony and arbitration regarding: architectural and construction disputes, code violations, construction defects and failures, and architectural malpractice. Provides investigative analysis, construction inspection and accident investigation.

S.N.A.P. PRODUCTION SERVICES
18653 Ventura Blvd., Ste. 295
Tarzana, CA 91356
Barry M. Seybert, Contact
PH: (818)340-0283
FX: (818)340-0577
Founded: 1979. **Staff:** 6. Specialists in studio design for television production offer particular expertise in video and multi-image productions. Serves commercial, industrial, and educational facilities primarily; some experience with government agencies.

SNC-LAVALIN INTERNATIONAL INC.
2 Place Felix Martin
Montreal, PQ, Canada H2Z 1Z3
Michael Novak, President

PH: (514)393-1000
FX: (514)866-0419
E-mail: user-id@snc-lavalin.com
Founded: 1936. **Staff:** 6200. Consulting services include studies, project management, engineering, procurement, construction and construction management, planning and research, scientific applications and transfer of technology. Also provides complementary services such as market, economic and financial feasibility studies, aerial photography, hydrogeological and geotechnical studies, environmental studies, computer services, purchasing, plant commissioning, and technical assistance and training. Offers the above-mentioned services in virtually all fields of engineering and applied sciences. Industries served: agriculture and forestry, automotive, chemical, construction, data processing and computers, energy industries, government as an industry, healthcare, iron and steel, lumber, pulp and paper, manufacturing, petroleum, mining, transportation, and utilities.

SOIL ENGINEERING CONSTRUCTION
927 Arguello St.
Redwood City, CA 94063
George Drew, Principal
PH: (415)367-9595
FX: (415)367-8139
Geotechnical, soils, foundation consultants and constructors .Provides forensic investigations and expert witness testimony. Specializes in foundations, retaining walls, landslides, settlement, failure analysis, site remediation plans and hazardous waste disposal analysis, drainage system and erosion control (evaluations redesign and pricing).

SOJ, LTD.-ARCHITECTS AND PLANNERS
5820 York Rd.
Baltimore, MD 21212
Harry C. Hess, III, President
PH: (410)433-4600
FX: (410)323-4127
Founded: 1962. **Staff:** 7. Consultants in architecture, interior design, planning and construction management. Industries served: school systems, criminal justice, healthcare, commercial (banks, shopping centers, etc.), light industrial, and housing.

SOLUTIONS FOR ENVIRONMENTAL HARMONY
5 Abode Rd.
New Lebanon, NY 12125
David Iman Adler, Landscape Architect
PH: (518)794-9796
FX: (518)794-8060
E-mail: dodler@taconic.net
URL: http://www.taconic.net/adler/index.html
A full service landscape architecture firm. Specializes in landscape architectural design, garden design, environmental impact statements, environmental site planning, environmental assessment, ecological restoration, wetlands design and mitigation, pond design, wildlife habitat restoration, community built projects, playground design and construction.

SPA & ASSOCIATES, INC.
451 Sunrise Hwy.
Lynbrook, NY 11563
Salvatore P. Accomando, President
PH: (516)593-1688
FX: (516)593-2080
Founded: 1980. **Staff:** 4. Provides mechanical and electrical design consulting for commercial and industrial clients. Also designs energy conservation programs and audits construction management services. Serves private industries as well as government agencies.

ARTHUR L. SPAET & ASSOCIATES
58 W. 40th St.
New York, NY 10018
Roy Sokoloski, President
PH: (212)302-2180
FX: (212)391-2148

Founded: 1963. **Staff:** 20. Architectural and engineering design firm provides consulting expertise in construction contract documents, construction administration and facilities management. Preservation department specializing in exterior and interior building rehabilitation, including landmark properties restoration. Comprehensive services including architectural, mechanical, plumbing, electrical, fire and life safety design. Industries served: academic, industrial, financial, government, healthcare, housing, corporate, and retail. Geographic areas served: New York, New Jersey, and Connecticut.

SPEXWEST
PO Box 3861
Laguna Hills, CA 92654-3861
PH: (714)832-2222
TF: (888)SPE-XWES
FX: (714)832-2222
URL: http://www.deltanet.com/spexwest
A multi-faceted and multi-disciplined company engaged in construction specifications consulting, construction administration, and litigation support.

SSFM ENGINEERS, INC.
501 Sumner St., Ste. 502
Honolulu, HI 96817
Michael P. Matsumoto, President/CEO
PH: (808)531-1308
FX: (808)521-7348
E-mail: projects@ssfm.com
URL: http://www.ssfm.com
Founded: 1959. **Staff:** 47. Offers project management, structural engineering, civil engineering, and other services.

ROBERT M. STAFFORD INC.
10815 Statesville Rd.
Charlotte, NC 28269-7647
Stuart W. Sutton, President
PH: (704)875-0207
TF: (800)545-6159
FX: (704)875-0408
E-mail: charlotteoffice@robertmstaffordinc.com
URL: http://www.robertmstaffordinc.com
Founded: 1964. **Staff:** 26. Engineering firm provides roofing, waterproofing, and construction design services to commercial industries and contractors in the U.S. and Canada.

STANDARD AND POOR'S DRI UTILITY COST INFORMATION SERVICE
1200 G St. NW, 10th Fl.
Washington, DC 20005
Alton Adams, Contact
PH: (202)383-2000
TF: (800)933-3374
FX: (202)383-2005
E-mail: dri.mcgraw-hill.com
URL: http://www.dri.mcgraw-hill.com
Founded: 1978. **Staff:** 400. The DRI/McGraw-Hill Utility Cost Information Service maintains computer-based models of electric and gas utility construction costs, operation and maintenance costs, and nuclear plant decommissioning costs. Analysis and forecasts of inflation induced increases in these expenses are provided for both company planning purposes and for special applications, such as rate proceedings. Industries served: electric and gas utilities, state and local governments (public utility commissions) and agencies of the federal government—federal power authorities and the Department of Energy.

STANDARD TESTING AND ENGINEERING CO.
3400 N. Lincoln Blvd.
Oklahoma City, OK 73105
Thomas J. Kelly, President
PH: (405)528-0541
TF: (800)725-0541
FX: (405)528-0559

Founded: 1951. **Staff:** 120. Civil and environmental engineers offering services in construction management, structural engineering, soil/site analysis, testing, environmental audit, and clean-up consulting. Industries served: construction, energy, architecture design, steel fabrication, environmental, and industrial hygiene, as well as government agencies.

THE STANLEY GROUP
Stanley Bldg., 225 Iowa Ave.
Muscatine, IA 52761
Greg G. Thomopulos, President
PH: (319)264-6600
FX: (319)264-6658
E-mail: info@stanleygroup.com
URL: http://www.stanleygroup.com
Founded: 1913. **Staff:** 487. International consultants in the fields of engineering, architecture, planning, management, economics, and environmental sciences. Specific areas of activity include air, water, and noise pollution; electric power generation, transmission, and distribution; energy use and conservation; value engineering; industrial development; construction management; natural resources management; transportation; urban and regional development; and surveying. Design Build Service Representative projects include power plants, power systems, utilities, buildings, industrial plants, water supply, pollution control, highways and streets, bridges, ports and harbors, airports, environmental studies, comprehensive planning, land development, and infrastructure. Services provided are studies, reports, design, construction management, and consultation. Industries served: food and beverage processors; steel mills; industrial complexes; automotive manufacturers; manufacturing plants; chemical process industries; distribution, warehouses, operations; as well as government agencies.

STANLEY TECHNOLOGY GROUP, INC.
10160 112th St.
Edmonton, AB, Canada T5K 2L6
R.P. Triffo, President & CEO
PH: (403)917-7000
FX: (403)917-7330
Founded: 1954. **Staff:** 1200. Provides environmental scientific, engineering, construction and project management services in the following areas: project management; conceptual design, feasibility studies and project development; environmental studies, permitting and design; multidiscipline design engineering services; structural and architectural design for buildings; site planning and development; water effluent treatment processes and design; instrumentation and control for proprietary processes; design of utilities, services, and offsite facilities; railway, road planning and transportation; containment and waste management; computer aided design and drafting; procurement and subcontracting services; construction management and inspection; site surveying; commissioning; and system trouble shooting, monitoring and optimization. Firm is able to provide an all inclusive service package, or if required, on a discipline basis either as a prime consultant or in support of a project manager. Market sectors served industrial, municipal, and commercial-institutional worldwide.

STOTTLER STAGG & ASSOCIATES—ARCHITECTS, ENGINEERS, PLANNERS, INC.
8680 N. Atlantic Ave.
Cape Canaveral, FL 32920
Richard H. Stottler, Jr., President
PH: (407)783-1320
FX: (407)783-7065
Founded: 1959. **Staff:** 140. Professional consulting services to all sizes of governmental and private clients in the U.S., primarily in the southwest, but also Europe. Offers complete in-house capabilities in the fields of architecture, engineering, planning, surveying, environmental, and construction management. Provides extensive computer capability and automated drafting systems.

STRUCTURAL SURVEYS, INC.
61 Highbrook Ave.
Pelham, NY 10803
Karl Tannert, President
PH: (914)738-6323
FX: (914)738-8868
Founded: 1985. **Staff:** 6. Provides architects, engineers, general contractors, and owners with advanced skills for evaluating the soundness of existing structures. Also provides new engineering products and technologies such as corraudit surveys, cathodic protection systems, waterproofing and crack repair treatments all geared to the complete restoration and preservation of structures.

STUEVEN ENGINEERING CONSULTANTS
425 W. 5th, Ste. 103
Escondido, CA 92025
PH: (760)735-8577
FX: (760)735-8578
E-mail: hjs@stueven-engineering.com
URL: http://www.stueven-engineering.com
A mechanical consulting engineering firm dedicated to professional engineering, planning, design and construction administration services for heating, ventilation and air conditioning systems, plumbing and process systems.

STV GROUP
205 W. Welsh Dr.
Douglassville, PA 19518
D.M. Servedio, President & Chief Executive Officer
PH: (610)385-8200
FX: (610)385-8501
E-mail: info@stvinc.com
URL: http://www.stvinc.com
Founded: 1968. **Staff:** 1000. An international engineering, architectural, planning, environmental, and construction management firm serving the following industries: aerospace, chemical, electronics, energy, food and beverage, government agencies, healthcare, iron and steel, manufacturing, mining, petroleum, pharmaceutical, plastics, pulp and paper, rubber, transportation and infrastructure, and advanced technology. The firm is actively engaged in architecture; civil, chemical, defense, electrical, environmental, industrial, mechanical, process, structural, and sanitary engineering; materials handling; pollution control; resource recovery, and transportation. Also infrastructure, technical manuals, site development, and surveying.

SVERDRUP CORP.
13723 Riverport Dr.
Maryland Heights, MO 63043
R.E. Beumer, Chairman/CEO
PH: (314)436-7600
TF: (800)325-7910
FX: (314)770-5105
E-mail: info@sverdrup.com
URL: http://www.sverdrup.com
Founded: 1928. **Staff:** 5000. A professional services firm with broad capabilities in providing total project management for capital facilities and technical systems, or for any combination of engineering, architecture, planning, construction and facility operations. Markets served are advanced technology, architecture, aviation, justice, environmental, food and beverage, pharmaceutical, public works and transportation. The company's flexible approach to project management includes design/build, construction management, program management and traditional design/bid/build. It also provides contractual services for the operation of aerospace and industrial research, development and test centers. In addition to engineers, architects and planners, the staff includes interior designers, scientists, economists and specialists in construction, project management, finance and computer science. Serves private industries as well as government agencies. Sverdrup is a Jacobs Engineering Group Inc. company.

SWANSON ASSOCIATES
No. 7 Sage Ct.
Austin, TX 78737
George P. Swanson, President
PH: (512)288-9097
FX: (512)288-9096
E-mail: info@geoswan.com
URL: http://www.geoswan.com
Founded: 1987. Environmentally-conscience construction firm services include non-toxic, "breathing" construction consulting; natural low impact energy and site utility development consulting; CADD custom and stock natural building design plans; site supervision, construction management and general contracting.

SYLVA ENGINEERING CORP.
1303-B Sherwood Forest
Houston, TX 77043
Cesar E. Sylva, President
PH: (713)973-7239
FX: (713)973-7359
E-mail: sec@sylvaeng.com
URL: http://www.sylvaeng.com
Founded: 1985. **Staff:** 29. Offers general consulting, civil and municipal engineering services with specialties in traffic and transportation, coastal and marine, and environmental concerns. Industries served include construction, marine, transportation, utilities as well as government agencies.

TANKTITE INC.
1950 Greenwood Lake Tpke.
PO Box 6000
Hewitt, NJ 07421
TF: (800)828-TANK
FX: (973)728-8854
URL: http://www.tanktite.com
Provides a range of site investigation and facility assessment, environmental engineering and design, project management and construction supervision services associated with site remediation. Services include assessment of environmental liabilities, real estate transaction audits, subsurface investigations, geo-environmental engineering, site cleanup, facilities decommissioning and waste management.

JOE B. TAYLOR, ARCHITECT-CONSULTANT, NCARB
PO Box 7334
Little Rock, AR 72217
Joe B. Taylor, Owner
PH: (501)847-1900
FX: (501)847-2900
Founded: 1976. **Staff:** 1. Consultant and expert witness for plaintiffs and defendants in construction litigation dealing with building problems including: severe weather and structural damage, defective construction including roofs, foundations, structural failure, code violations and total projects, and personal injury litigation. Services also include interpretation of contract documents (plans specifications, construction contracts), Investigations and detailed reports. Industries served: municipal governments, schools, churches, commercial and residential projects.

TECHNA-FLO INC.
PO Box 3479
Englewood, CO 80155
J.W. Haskins, Contact
PH: (303)699-9844
FX: (303)693-8449
Founded: 1975. Firm offers extensive knowledge in construction materials, design, and engineering of bulk material systems.

TECHNICAL INSPECTIONS ASSOCIATES
25 Shawnee
Lake Forest, IL 60045-2831
Felix J. (Gene) Lyczko, MSME

PH: (847)295-2156
FX: (847)295-7242
E-mail: flyzcko@ameritech.net
Founded: 1978. Provides general expert witness and inspection services, including construction management; structural inspections; heating, ventilating and air conditioning inspections; roofing systems; chemistry; welding; boilers; subsurface inspections; electrical inspection; engines and vehicles; fires and explosions; heavy equipment; machine design; metallurgy; and safety. Industries served: legal profession, insurance industry, and government agencies worldwide.

TEMPEST CO.
13326 A St.
Omaha, NE 68144-3641
PH: (402)334-3332
TF: (888)334-3332
FX: (402)334-9033
E-mail: inquire@tempestcompany.com
URL: http://www.tempestcompany.com
A construction consulting firm specializing in management consulting, marketing and proposal preparation, strategic bidding, and estimating and bidding practices.

TENG & ASSOCIATES, INC.
205 N. Michigan Ave., 36th Fl.
Chicago, IL 60601-5914
Ivan J. Dvorak, P.E., CEO and President
PH: (312)616-0000
FX: (312)616-6069
E-mail: design@teng.com
URL: http://www.teng.com
Founded: 1959. **Staff:** 257. Offers a full range of design services including architectural design, urban design, planning, landscape architecture, interior design, civil, structural, mechanical, plumbing, electrical, and environmental engineering.

TETRA DESIGN, INC.
1055 Wilshire Blvd., Ste. 1885
Los Angeles, CA 90017
Robert H. Uyeda, President
PH: (213)250-7440
FX: (213)481-0947
E-mail: tetdesign@aol.com
Founded: 1975. **Staff:** 10. Architecture, space planning and interior design consultants specializing in new construction and renovation of office buildings, maintenance structures for vehicle maintenance and container terminals, shopping centers, and low/moderate income housing. Industries served: ports facilities, governmental facilities, housing, commercial, industrial, and renovation/retrofit.

MORTON G. THALHIMER, INC.
PO Box 702
Richmond, VA 23218
PH: (804)648-5881
FX: (804)697-3479
Advises clients on industrial and commercial locations, real estate investments, office feasibility, and construction management.

THORBURN ASSOCIATES
PO Box 20399
Castro Valley, CA 94546-8399
Lisa Thorburn, CSI
PH: (510)886-7826
FX: (510)886-7828
E-mail: ta@ta-inc.com
URL: http://www.ta-inc.com
Founded: 1992. **Staff:** 10. Acoustical Consulting and Audiovisual System Design services include sound isolation; room acoustics; mechanical noise and vibration control; environmental noise studies; video, audio, control, and projection system designs; project management; acoustical/certification testing and measurement for all types of projects and facilities.

TIPPETT & GEE, INC.
502 N. Willis
Abilene, TX 79603
Louis S. Gee, CEO
PH: (915)673-8291
FX: (915)672-5251
E-mail: jsanders@tsppetgee.com
URL: http://www.tippettgee.com
Founded: 1954. **Staff:** 41. Offers engineering design, consulting, architecture, and construction management services to the electrical power industry and commercial buildings. Primary activity is in the power plant design field, steam and gas turbines. Design experience in plants fired by gas, oil, coal and lignite. Performs engineering design on associated projects such as transmission lines and substations. Also prepares studies and reports on electric utility related items.

TISDEL ASSOCIATES
113 Main St.
Canton, NY 13617
Ronald E. Berry, Contact
PH: (315)386-8542
FX: (315)386-2974
Founded: 1969. **Staff:** 15. Civil and sanitary consulting engineers active in study, design and construction services, water pollution control, solid waste disposal, industrial plant design, water treatment and distribution, airport, and bridge construction. Industries served: paper, aluminum, meat processing, glass, office products, electronics, cogeneration, facilities, and government agencies.

TOCCI BUILDING CORP.
130 New Boston St.
Woburn, MA 01801
John L. Tocci, President
PH: (617)935-5500
FX: (617)935-1888
URL: http://www.tocci.com
Founded: 1922. **Staff:** 45. Provides cost analysis and construction management services; conceptual design cost estimating; cost modeling; value optimization; and project scheduling. Serves retail, healthcare, institutional, R&D, and technology industries in New England.

RICHARD TOLER, SECURITY CONSULTANT
PO Box 35456
Richmond, VA 23235
Richard A. Toler, President
PH: (804)320-0337
FX: (804)320-1660
Founded: 1982. **Staff:** 3. Offers services in electronic protection, surveillance, and countermeasures. Also involved in loss prevention, training, and security engineering. Serves commercial and industrial industry, security directors, and residential homeowners.

R. L. TOWNSEND & ASSOCIATES, INC.
10,000 N. Central Expy., Ste. 1006
Dallas, TX 75231
Rich Townsend, Principal
PH: (972)208-1222
FX: (972)208-4643
E-mail: info@rltownsend.com
URL: http://www.rltownsend.com
Founded: 1984. Firm provides construction contract cost control advisory and audit services to "owner" organizations. Clients include organizations contracting with design firms, construction management firms and construction contractors to build new facilities and/or renovate existing facilities. Construction projects include manufacturing plants, petrochemical plants, office buildings, retail developments, hotel/resort buildings, gas and oil pipelines, local government buildings, banks, airport terminals, airport infrastructure, college and university buildings, hospitals and medical centers. Construction cost control and audit services: construction contract compliance audit services; construction contract control advisory services; construction cost monitoring services; comprehensive advisory/audit services; construction cost control and audit training.

TRAFFIC & CIVIL ENGINEERING CONSULTING SERVICES
PO Box 961
Los Gatos, CA 95031
James C. Jeffrey, Principal
PH: (408)377-6222
FX: (408)377-6240
Specializes in site planning, land use, environmental and their administrative review; and roadway and parking design, construction and maintenance of traffic control devices and systems, including compliance with standards of practice. Analyzes need for roadway accident mitigation measures related to street design/construction, access and land use.

TRANSCON CONSULTING, LTD.
1913 Huguenot Rd., Ste. 201
Richmond, VA 23235
Richard L. Ott, President
PH: (804)897-1382
FX: (804)897-1383
E-mail: milestone@transcon.net
URL: http://www.transcon.net
Founded: 1993. Provides management and services to the transportation and commercial construction industry. These services include preparation of construction schedules; preparation of delay impact analyses to prove/disprove claims preparation, review and analysis of claims between parties on construction projects; assistance in all aspects of construction administration management; expert witness testimony in legal actions; technical and educational services to the construction industry.

TRANSMETRICS, INC.
660 S. Figueroa St., Ste. 2000
Los Angeles, CA 90017
Jack Ybarra, President
PH: (213)688-1400
FX: (213)688-1571
E-mail: transla@ida.net
Firm provides special knowledge in civil engineering, planning, and construction management. Also assists in the design of highways, railways, and airports, including light rail, heavy rail, commuter, inter-city, and high-speed rail.

TRANSVIRON, INC.
1624 York Rd.
Lutherville, MD 21093
Charles S. Bao, President
PH: (410)321-6961
FX: (410)494-9321
Founded: 1961. **Staff:** 11. A multidisciplined consulting engineering firm which provides civil and environmental engineering services to public agencies and private firms. Recent experience in wastewater collection and treatment, water supply and distribution, storm water management, highways and bridges, hazardous waste management, water and wastewater treatment plant operations and construction management.

TRAUTMAN ASSOCIATES, ARCHITECTS/ENGINEERS
470 Franklin St.
Buffalo, NY 14202
Paul M. Markwart, President
PH: (716)883-4400
FX: (716)883-4268
E-mail: mailbox@trautmanassoc.com
Founded: 1956. **Staff:** 45. Provides architectural and engineering services for schools, commercial, municipal, and industrial clients. Specializes in new buildings, building additions and renovations, and adaptive reuse. Has expertise in mechanical, civil, electrical, and structural engineering.

TRENDS MANAGEMENT CONSULTING, INC.
301 S. Church St., Ste. 256
PO Box 1153
Rocky Mount, NC 27802
Lillian Thompson, Contact
PH: (919)446-0060
FX: (919)446-1756
E-mail: lthompson1@sprintmail.com
Founded: 1991. **Staff:** 1. Design and management consulting firm, specializing in aligning the work space and core work flow to strategic initiatives. Solves the elimination of non-value added activity that impacts productivity and the bottom line. Helps manage transition by facilitating project, design, or improvement teams, through planning development, and implementation processes, to achieve desired results. Offers services in four areas: planning, consulting, facilitating, and coordinating of work. Industries served: for-profit, non-profit, and government entities experiencing transition.

TRI-TECH PLANNING CONSULTANTS, INC.
11 Farmingdale Rd.
West Babylon, NY 11704
Richard M. Geller, President
PH: (516)587-4300
FX: (516)587-0158
Founded: 1967. **Staff:** 40. Construction management consultants specializing in scheduling and construction claims litigation services. Particular expertise in cost control systems, payment requisitions, change orders and management reporting which are all computerized and integrated with project scheduling systems.

TRS CONSULTANTS, INC.
5000 Executive Pky., Ste. 390
San Ramon, CA 94583-4210
PH: (510)275-9870
FX: (510)275-9930
Provides engineering and construction management services to transportation, transit, environmental, and facilities projects.

DAVID G. TUNNICLIFF CONSULTING ENGINEER
9624 Larimore Ave.
Omaha, NE 68134-3038
David G. Tunnicliff, Contact
PH: (402)572-9431
Founded: 1979. **Staff:** 2. Offers engineering and research on mineral aggregates and bituminous materials, mixtures, pavements, and construction, including mixture design, structural design, pavement evaluation, and construction site safety. Serves private industries as well as government agencies.

TURNAROUND & CRISIS MANAGEMENT, INC.
2 Mid America Plz., Ste. 714
Oakbrook Terrace, IL 60181
PH: (630)990-9000
FX: (630)990-9693
E-mail: info@turnrnd.com
URL: http://www.turnrnd.com
Turnaround management firm. Dedicated to providing turnaround consulting, crisis and interim management, and corporate renewal and asset recovery services to financially distressed and underperforming companies in the manufacturing, wholesale distribution, service and construction-related industries.

UCIC CONSULTANTS
151 Kalmus Dr., Ste. C-250
Costa Mesa, CA 92626
Hugh E. Cronin, President
PH: (714)979-7997
FX: (714)979-2742
E-mail: ucic@pacbell.net
Founded: 1976. **Staff:** 33. Firm was founded to provide engineering, auditing, and management services to the construction industry. Services include estimating, scheduling, quality assurance, claims, quality control, auditing, and cost control. Industries served: construction, including government agencies.

U.S. ENCON INC.
4728 Ponte Vedra Dr.
Marietta, GA 30067
Peter Sullivan, R.A., R.E.M., C.E.A., R.E.P.A.
PH: (770)951-9177
FX: (770)951-8178
Staff: 12. Construction and environmental management firm offers expertise in lender/owner representation, quality control, litigation support, Phases I, II & III Environmental Assessments, construction loan management, and Americans with Disabilities Act (ADA) audits. Serves lending industry, hospitality (hotels/motels), and commercial real estate developers (HUD) in the U.S. and the Caribbean.

UPP GEOTECHNOLOGY, INC.
1330 S. Bascom Ave., Ste. B
San Jose, CA 95128
R. Rexford Upp, Principal
PH: (408)275-1336
FX: (408)287-3079
Specializes in earth movement, including landslides, soil creep, expansive soil and erosion. Provides faults and earthquake hazard evaluation. Inspects grading and drainage. Interprets aerial photos. Investigates distressed foundations and structures, including hillside single family homes, multi-family residential complexes, and commercial and industrial developments.

URBITRAN ASSOCIATES, INC.
71 West 23rd St., 11th Fl.
New York, NY 10010
Fruma Narov, PE, Secretary
PH: (212)366-6200
FX: (212)366-6214
E-mail: urbitran@ix.netcom.com
Founded: 1973. **Staff:** 182. Consulting engineers and planners specializing in transportation, traffic and parking, and related civil/ environmental engineering topics. Also offers construction management services. Serves government and public agencies, as well as private developers. Serves tri-state area, with projects throughout the U.S., as well as Europe and Asia.

URS GREINER, INC.
100 California St., Ste. 500
San Francisco, CA 94111-4529
Irwin L. Rosenstein, President
PH: (415)774-2700
TF: (800)327-8877
FX: (415)398-1904
Founded: 1929. **Staff:** 3046. Provides planning, architectural/ engineering design, and program and construction management services for today's complex surface and air transportation, facilities, telecommunications, hazardous waste, environmental, and water resources projects. Industries served: Federal, state, and local governmental agencies as well as public sector clients (petroleum, manufacturing, and industrial companies and commercial developers).

USAQUATICS, INC.
2355 Polaris Ln., No. 110
Plymouth, MN 55447
PH: (612)745-9016
FX: (612)745-9243
URL: http://www.usaquaticsinc.com
Specializes in consultation, design, and project construction management for renovations, expansion or new construction of multi-use swimming pools, aquatic facilities and aquatic parks.

USKH INC.
2515 A St.
Anchorage, AK 99503
Leo VonScheben, Contact
PH: (907)276-4245
FX: (907)258-4653
E-mail: leo@uskh.com
URL: http://www.uskh.com
Founded: 1972. **Staff:** 85. Provides services in architecture, civil,

mechanical and structural engineering. Also offers assistance with planning, survey, landscape architecture, interior design, and construction administration.

VANBOERUM & FRANK ASSOCIATES, INC.

330 S. 300 E., Ste. 200
Salt Lake City, UT 84111
Joseph V. Simmons, PE
PH: (801)530-3148
FX: (801)530-3150
E-mail: lsimons@vbvta.com
URL: http://www.vbta.com
Founded: 1972. **Staff:** 45. Offers complete mechanical, civil & geotechnical engineering consulting services which include the following: Heating, Ventilation, Air Conditioning, Energy Conservation, Refrigeration, Air Quality, Plumbing, Fire Protection, Boiler/Chiller Plants, Ammonia Plants, Cogeneration, Civil Engineering, Geotechnical/Environmental. VBFA has designed hospital and laboratory facilities, recreational facilities, arenas, prison and jail facilities, university and school facilities, hotel and condominiums, office buildings, museums, libraries, and convention centers.

C. VARGAS & ASSOCIATES, LTD.—CONSULTING ENGINEERS

8596 Arlington Expy.
Jacksonville, FL 32211
Clark Vargas, P.E., President
PH: (904)725-7131
FX: (904)725-4749
E-mail: vargas2000@aol.com
Founded: 1978. **Staff:** 18. Offers mechanical, electrical, and civil engineering services, specifically in the areas of water and wastewater, paving and drainage, and subdivision development. Serves municipalities, industrial and commercial clients, and land developers.

VAUGHN WOODWORK CONSULTANTS

269 Linsey
North Attleboro, MA 02760-4729
Norman L. "Woody" Vaughn, Jr., Contact
PH: (508)695-8193
FX: (508)695-8179
E-mail: Wood.Expert@woody-vaughn.com
URL: http://www.woody-vaughn.com
Founded: 1992. Firm offers architectural woodwork and management advisory services for woodworking, construction, and design industries. Expert witness.

VECTOR ENGINEERING, INC.

12438 Loma Rica Dr., Ste. C
Grass Valley, CA 95945
Mark E. Smith, Principal
PH: (530)272-2448
FX: (530)272-8533
E-mail: vector@rectoreng.com
URL: http://www.vectoreng.com
Founded: 1986. **Staff:** 70. Specializes in geomembrane liners, clay liners, landfill caps, closures, leachate collection, construction quality, construction claims, geotechnical engineering, earthworks, operations, and slope stability.

VEENSTRA & KIMM, INC., ENGINEERS & PLANNERS

3000 Westown Pky.
West Des Moines, IA 50266-1320
H.R. Veenstra, Jr., President
PH: (515)225-8000
TF: (800)241-8000
FX: (515)225-7848
Founded: 1961. **Staff:** 55. The practice includes a wide range of consulting services involving sewer systems and wastewater treatment plants; water supply, distribution, storage and treatment; streets and highways; airports; bridges; land surveys and site planning; swimming pools; solid waste disposal systems; and expert testimony on engineering matters in litigations. Complete services are offered

to cities, counties, industries, regional areas and state and federal agencies covering all aspects of comprehensive planning and related fields. The type of services provided varies with the client and the project. It may include preliminary cost estimates, preliminary studies and reports, rate and feasibility studies, preparation of plans and specifications, assistance in awarding construction contracts and monitoring of construction.

ANIL VERMA ASSOCIATES, INC.

911 Wilshire Blvd., Ste. 1700
Los Angeles, CA 90017
Anil Verma, President
PH: (213)624-6908
FX: (213)624-1188
E-mail: anilverma@aol.com
Founded: 1985. **Staff:** 23. Firm offers special knowledge in architecture, engineering, construction management, project management, planning, landscape architecture, GIS, mapping, and computer drafting services.

VHS ASSOCIATES, INC.

22 Commercial Blvd.
Novato, CA 94949
Charles C. Swensen, Jr., Principal
PH: (415)884-2988
FX: (415)884-2065
E-mail: cswensenjr@vhsinc.com
Founded: 1974. **Staff:** 10. Offers consultation in the evaluation of construction and property loss problems, building condition surveys, and forensic investigation to establish cause and determine extent of damage. Reviews design to identify and evaluate questions of code compliance and faulty construction. Other services include civil and geophysical engineering, planning, estimating, scheduling, and performance evaluation.

VILICAN-LEMAN & ASSOCIATES, INC.

28316 Franklin Rd.
Southfield, MI 48034-5503
Claude Coates, President
PH: (248)356-8181
FX: (248)356-0902
Founded: 1955. **Staff:** 11. Provides planning and design services to communities (cities, townships, counties and regional agencies) and to private developers. Planning activities for municipalities include the full range of master plan development, environmental and site analysis studies, zoning ordinance preparation and administration, and consultation on special problems. The firm offers a wide range of services to private developers including site planning, landscape architectural services, including preparation of detailed construction drawings and specifications, and contract administration of design projects.

VISIONS, INC.

101 Essex Ct.
Omaha, NE 68114-3778
James J. Riskowski, Principal, President
PH: (402)393-6124
FX: (402)393-8747
E-mail: info@visions-edtech.com
URL: http://www.visions-edtech.com
Firm plans and develops educational technology systems. Experienced in educational facility planning; architecture; engineering; voice, video and data system design; space programming; cost control and innovative funding; building codes; construction administration; and CAD.

VOELKER, CASTILLA & KOPCZYNSKI, INC.

4106 Office Pky.
Dallas, TX 75204
Richard J. Voelker, Chairman of the Board
PH: (214)823-1202
FX: (214)821-1454
Founded: 1991. **Staff:** 16. Corporate facilities engineering firm specializes in construction management, software and relocation con-

sulting services. Also offers expertise in institutional property services including consulting, leasing and property management. Industries served: electronics, energy, and education.

DAVID VOLKERT & ASSOCIATES, INC.
3809 Moffett Rd.
Mobile, AL 36670
David G. Volkert, Chairman
PH: (334)342-1070
FX: (334)342-7962
E-mail: volkert@volkert.com
URL: http://www.volkert.com
Founded: 1925. **Staff:** 450. A multi-disciplinary design firm of engineers, architects and planners offering complete civil, structural, electrical, and sanitary, engineering consulting and design services, as well as architectural, environmental, bridge inspection, land planning, surveying, construction inspection, construction management and right-of-way acquisition services, to public and private clients. Major projects include bridges, highways, tunnels; rapid transit, recreational, educational, wastewater treatment, and material handling facilities; seaports, airports, utilities, and subdivision development. and South America.

J.P. VRANESH
1662 Glen Oak Ct.
Lafayette, CA 94549
J.P. Vranesh, Contact
PH: (925)939-1679
FX: (925)935-0145
Founded: 1990. **Staff:** 3. Management and hands-on capabilities and understanding in the engineering, procurement and construction business, their organization, and industries served, and the knowledge and experience relevant to the areas of involvement. All areas of procurement from bidding, specification, purchasing/contracting, expediting, inspection, traffic and logistics, receiving, protection, inventory control, warehousing and issuance. Also human resources of same. Industries served: all engineering, procurement, and construction; and suppliers to heavy construction.

VS ENGINEERING INC.
4275 N. High School Rd.
Indianapolis, IN 46254
Bhagwan C. Patel, President
PH: (317)293-3542
FX: (317)293-4737
Founded: 1980. **Staff:** 15. Multidisciplined engineering firm offers expertise in the following areas: planning, design and land surveying, and construction management of highways and bridges; environmental, wastewater, water, flood control, utility, and sitework. Also specializes in structural engineering projects for government and private industries. Geographic areas served: Midwest area, including Indiana, Ohio, Illinois, Wisconsin and Michigan.

MARK L. WADDELL
14506 Boydton Plank Rd.
Dinwiddie, VA 23841
Mark L. Waddell, CC, APC
PH: (804)469-4303
Consulting services in industrial construction management; acts as project coordinator, evaluation, owner representation, and contract administration.

WAGNER-HOHNS-INGLIS, INC.
100 High St.
Mount Holly, NJ 08060
Gordon H. Curtis, President
PH: (609)261-0100
FX: (609)261-8584
E-mail: whi-corp@whi-inc.com
URL: http://www.whi-inc.com
Founded: 1964. **Staff:** 35. Consultants to the construction industry. Organized in four major construction service areas: Claims and Litigation, Critical Path Method (CPM) Construction Scheduling, Project Management and a spectrum of Special Management Services

geared to provide solutions to construction management and claims problems. The firm has assisted law firms, building owners/ developers, contractors, insurance and surety companies, architect/ engineers, governmental agencies (whether town, city, county, state or federal) to resolve some of the nation's most complex construction disputes. Firm will discuss and accept construction consulting assignments anywhere in the world.

J.S. WAGNER ROOFING SPECIALIST
4909 46th Ave.
Hyattsville, MD 20781
Chuck Wagner, President
PH: (301)927-9030
FX: (301)927-3505
Founded: 1914. Firm offers roofing expertise on removal, re-roofing, and roof repair of shingle, slate, tile, copper, tin, slate, and ornamental metal roofs.

WALDRON ENTERPRISES
371 Kings Hwy. W
Haddonfield, NJ 08033
A. James Waldron, Contact
PH: (609)428-3742
FX: (609)428-3742
Founded: 1961. **Staff:** 14. Offers the following consulting services: establishing and analyzing project schedules via network planning techniques of CPM, PERT; establishing cost control procedures; monitoring and updating schedules; preparation of claims and litigation analyses; testimony as an expert witness in claims and litigation. Clients include the construction, manufacturing, power generating industries, and government agencies.

WALK, HAYDEL & ASSOCIATES, INC.
600 Carondelet St.
New Orleans, LA 70130
F.H. Walk, Co-chairman
PH: (504)586-8111
FX: (504)522-0554
Founded: 1959. **Staff:** 600. Offers consulting project management, engineering, architectural, construction management, and environmental consulting services to commercial, industrial and governmental clients. Complete multidiscipline engineering services include site selection, feasibility studies, environmental impact assessments and permitting, facility conceptual and detail design, procurement, and construction management services.

WALLACE ENGINEERING
201 W. 5th, Ste. 200
Tulsa, OK 74103
Thomas W. Wallace, President/Principal
PH: (918)584-5858
FX: (918)584-8689
E-mail: email@wallacesc.com
URL: http://www.wallacesc.com
Forensic structural and civil engineering firm. Investigations in compliance with building codes and standards, building, roof, foundation, retaining wall or bridge collapses, structural failure of masonry, steel, joists, wood, concrete designs. Analyzes structural design and specifications of buildings, bridges and highways, roof drainage and ponding, wind/seismic/snow loads, materials, underwater bridge investigations, floor vibration. Performs civil site feasibility studies and underwater scour and silting studies and mapping.

WALLIS & ASSOCIATES, CONSULTING ENGINEERS, INC.
8031 Broadway
San Antonio, TX 78209-2674
William E. Wallis, President
PH: (210)824-7471
FX: (210)824-7473
Founded: 1958. **Staff:** 4. Provides technical expertise to engineering, construction and energy related sectors; assists with the preparation of bidding and construction documents, and the administration of construction activities. Industries served: manufacturing, educa-

tion, construction, energy production, and governmental agencies in Texas.

FREDERICK WARD ASSOCIATES, INC.
7900 Sudley Rd., Ste. 711
Manassas, VA 20109
David R. Hall, Managing Principal
PH: (703)361-7718
FX: (703)361-0117
E-mail: drhall@fwava.com
URL: http://www.mnsinc.com/fwava
Forensic civil/structural engineering firm. Specializes in construction disputes; accident investigation, analysis; accident location surveys; GPS surveys; civil design (site, highways, bridges); building collapses; marine construction; underwater evidence recovery; underwater mapping; code analysis; land planning/design; and geotechnical investigation.

WARD ASSOCIATES P.C. ARCHITECTS, LANDSCAPE ARCHITECTS, ENGINEERS
1500 Lakeland Ave.
Bohemia, NY 11716
Anthony D. Carlisto, Vice President
PH: (516)563-4800
FX: (516)563-4807
E-mail: wardpc@earthlink.net
URL: http://www.waropc.com
Founded: 1971. **Staff:** 20. Park, recreation and sports consultants, architecture, landscape architecture, and engineering firm offering the following services: schematic studies, construction plans and specifications, inspections, cost analyses, and construction management for institutional, municipal and commercial projects.

FREDERICK A. WEBSTER
PO Box 4043
Menlo Park, CA 94025
PH: (415)321-6939
FX: (415)473-0989
Specializes in structural damage and distress, foundation damage, and construction-related errors and damage. Provides statistically-based investigations and structural design and analysis.

WEDGCO ENGINEERING
15020 Shady Grove Rd., Ste. 450
Rockville, MD 20850-3364
W.E.D. Geoghegan, President
PH: (301)340-0006
FX: (301)340-0097
E-mail: wedgco@aol.com
URL: http://www.wedgcoengineering.com
Founded: 1963. **Staff:** 26. Develops designs and specifications for heating, ventilating and air conditioning systems, refrigeration systems, thermal storage systems, energy management systems, ground source heat pump systems, plumbing systems, electrical power distribution systems, and lighting systems. Industries served: architectural designers, developers, contractors, building owners; institutional and governmental agencies, as well as the building industry.

PHIL WEINERT ENGINEERING
6755 Earl Dr., Ste. 105
Colorado Springs, CO 80918
PH: (719)548-5019
FX: (719)548-5034
E-mail: pweinert@msn.com
Concerned with construction claims, construction problem resolution, dam construction, mediation, facility management, and contract construction management. Performs system analysis, environmental studies, structural analysis.

WESTERN TECHNOLOGIES INC.
3737 E. Broadway Rd.
Phoenix, AZ 85040
Randolph Marwig, P.E., Managing Director
PH: (602)437-3737
TF: (800)580-3737
FX: (602)470-1341
E-mail: wt-phx@primenet.com
Founded: 1955. **Staff:** 275. Offers services in quality management of construction materials and geotechnical and environmental engineering. Services include construction administration, quality management of materials, materials research, geotechnical services, environmental engineering, materials engineering and testing, and non-destructive examinations. Industries served: architects, engineers, developers, mechanical contractors, steel fabricators, public works, and government agencies in Arizona, Nevada, southern California, New Mexico, and Mexico.

ROY F. WESTON, INC.
1 Weston Way
West Chester, PA 19380-1499
Roy F. Weston, Chairman Emeritus
PH: (610)701-3000
FX: (610)701-3186
E-mail: webmaster@rfweston.com
URL: http://www.rfweston.com
Founded: 1957. **Staff:** 2300. WESTON is a leading infrastructure redevelopment services firm for Fortune 500 and government decision-makers worldwide. With more than 40 years of experience, the company creates lasting economic value for its clients, especially by bringing facilities, land or other resources compromised by the effects of past development back to productive use. WESTON's infrastructure redevelopment services include consulting, construction remediation and redevelopment, and knowledge systems and solutions. The company is based in West Chester, PA, and has 60 offices throughout the United States.

WEXCO INTERNATIONAL CORP.
3226 Thatcher Ave.
Marina del Rey, CA 90292-5556
Stephen C. Wexler, Ph.D., Principal
PH: (310)306-3877
FX: (310)306-3877
Firm involved in construction consulting, engineering, and safety and management. Specializes in construction defects and damages, costs to repair, policy coverage, construction claims, delay impact analysis, CPM scheduling, contract disputes, damage calculations, safety engineering, building codes, and safety regulation compliance.

JAMES WILLIAM WHITE
1309 State St.
La Crosse, WI 54601
James William White, Contact
PH: (608)784-8043
E-mail: jw5535@aol.com
Founded: 1980. Provides consulting services regarding library buildings. Services include feasibility studies; building programs; site and architect selection; construction budgeting and financing; critical evaluation of building design, drawings and specifications; and interior design. Serves private industries as well as government agencies. Geographic areas served: Midwest.

WHITMAN, REQUARDT AND ASSOCIATES LLP
2315 Saint Paul St.
Baltimore, MD 21218
C. Richard Lortz, Contact
PH: (410)235-3450
FX: (410)243-5716
E-mail: baltimore@wrallp.com
URL: http://www.wrallp.com
Founded: 1915. **Staff:** 300. Provides consulting engineering services in the civil, sanitary, highway, land, planning, structural, soils, marine, mechanical, electrical and solid waste management fields as well as supporting architectural design services. These services usually include reports, studies, designs, plans and specifications, and observation of construction. Serves private industries as well as government agencies.

WIER & ASSOCIATES INC.
4300 Beltway Pl., Ste. 130
Arlington, TX 76018
John P. Wier, President
PH: (817)467-7700
TF: (800)499-7070
FX: (817)467-7713
E-mail: JohnW@WierAssociates.com
URL: http://www.wier-assoc.com
Founded: 1978. **Staff:** 40. General civil engineering, land surveying, and land planning specialists providing services to private sector businesses, developers, industry, and municipal and state governments, specializing in the north central Texas area around the Dallas-Fort Worth metroplex. Offers services predominantly in the areas of feasibility studies, planning, design, and construction administration of projects concerning streets, storm drainage, water distribution, and sanitary sewer collection.

VICTOR WILBURN ARCHITECTS
2 Wisconsin Cir., Ste. 700
Chevy Chase, MD 20815
Victor H. Wilburn, Contact
PH: (240)244-0617
FX: (240)537-1143
Founded: 1963. **Staff:** 7. Architectural consulting firm providing the following professional services: feasibility studies, conceptual design studies, analysis of requirements, space management planning, and site planning. Also prepares construction drawings, specifications, and contract documents. Expertise extends to areas of construction supervision, construction management, community planning, and other related specialties as required. Serves private industries as well as government agencies.

WILEY & WILSON—ARCHITECTS, ENGINEERS, PLANNERS
2310 Langhorne Rd.
Lynchburg, VA 24505
H.L. Lytton, Contact
PH: (804)947-1901
FX: (804)947-1647
Founded: 1901. **Staff:** 120. Offers comprehensive design and report services in the fields of civil, mechanical, electrical and structural engineering, as well as architectural planning and design, and urban, regional and comprehensive planning. Special strengths lie in the areas of water and waste treatment, heating, ventilating and air conditioning; plumbing, fire prevention systems; power plants, structures, highways, streets, subways, electric distribution systems; commercial, institutional and industrial architecture, building renovations; plant and process design and layout, fuel conversion process, noise control; construction administration and management; environmental impact analysis, water quality management and computer modeling. Industries served: apparel and textiles, chemical, communications (electronic), data processing and computer, education, electronics, food and beverage, government agencies, manufacturing, pharmaceutical, printing, publishing, transportation, and utilities.

VERLE A. WILLIAMS & ASSOCIATES, INC.
Williams Engineering Center
San Diego, CA 92121
Ron Rybak, Vice President
PH: (619)458-9121
FX: (619)458-1929
E-mail: vwilli3853@aol.com
URL: http://www.vawa.com
Founded: 1981. **Staff:** 22. Engineers offering the following services: full mechanical, electrical, and energy systems design services for clients concerned with effective operation and energy consumption; energy conservation studies; studies and design for alternate energy projects, such as cogeneration, incineration and Thermal Energy Storage (TES) systems; energy management system feasibility studies, operation evaluations, contract design; lighting system feasibility studies and design; construction observation and coordination services; operator training; industrial plant energy analyses; energy utilization training programs; energy awareness program development and management; building systems operation tracking and maintenance enhancement; automatic control system design; and Irrigation System Conservation and Automatic Central Control System Management and Operation. Clients include: healthcare and educational institutions, commercial, airport, industrial and military organizations, and other consultants.

WILLIAMS-RUSSELL AND JOHNSON, INC.
771 Spring St. NW
Atlanta, GA 30308-1038
Pelham C. Williams, President/CEO
PH: (404)853-6800
FX: (404)853-6932
Founded: 1976. **Staff:** 160. Provides consultant engineering, architecture, and planning services to public, private military, governmental, and institutional clients from project inception through completion. Principal areas of expertise include civil and environmental engineering, electrical engineering, mechanical engineering, structural engineering, and construction/program management services. Serves private industries as well as government agencies.

WILSON AND CO. ENGINEERS AND ARCHITECTS
4775 Indian School Rd. NE
Albuquerque, NM 87110
Herbert H. Bassett, Contact
PH: (505)254-4000
FX: (505)254-4055
URL: http://www.wilsonco.com
Founded: 1932. **Staff:** 250. Provides consulting engineering, architectural and planning services for municipal, state and federal government; for commercial businesses and industry; and for institutions such as schools and hospitals. Typical projects include city, regional, and industrial planning; design of streets, highways, railroads and bridges, water treatment, wastewater treatment facilities, photogrammetry; design and improvement of airports; design of programs for management of industrial waste; and construction related services.

WINTON ENGINEERING, INC.
340 16th St., Ste. 200
San Diego, CA 92101-7606
Guy W. Winton, III, President
PH: (619)696-8955
FX: (619)696-8959
E-mail: guyiii@home.com
Founded: 1961. **Staff:** 10. Civil engineering design services include subdivisions and grading, storm drains, hydrology and hydraulics, sedimentation studies, septic systems, sewer and water systems, pumping stations, water wells and tanks, and road and highway design. Also offers land surveying and residential/commercial/industrial planning. Provides forensic engineering in the areas of flooding, construction, defects, standard of care, and motor vehicle accident reconstruction. Industries served: owners, developers, government agencies, and legal profession.

WISS, JANNEY, ELSTNER ASSOCIATES, INC.
330 Pfingsten Rd.
Northbrook, IL 60062-2095
Jerry G. Stockbridge, President
PH: (847)272-7400
FX: (847)291-9599
Founded: 1956. **Staff:** 235. Provides a wide range of consulting services in all areas of construction technology. Specialties include structural evaluations, failure investigations, condition surveys, construction problem solving, facade and roof evaluations, construction materials evaluation, testing and instrumentation, repair and rehabilitation, and historic preservation. Has served more than 10,000 clients, from individuals to large corporations and governmental agencies.

WLW & ASSOCIATES, INC.
729 Rte. 83, Ste. 323
Bensenville, IL 60106
Alex L. Wlodzimierski, President
PH: (630)766-6606
FX: (630)766-6607
Founded: 1968. **Staff:** 8. Consultants in structural, mechanical, electrical engineering, and architectural additions/remodeling/designing. Services include estimating, cost control, and budget studies.

WOLFORD ENGINEERING SERVICES
2255 Ewing Chapel Rd.
Dacula, GA 30019
Farley E. Wolford, Contact
PH: (770)962-9403
FX: (770)962-9403
Founded: 1982. **Staff:** 2. Civil engineer and land surveyor offers site planning and engineering. Services include: boundary, topographic and construction surveys and hydrologic studies. Provides water, sewer and transportation engineering services to business and industry, including real estate development, construction, governments and private entities.

WOODWARD-CLYDE
4582 S. Ulster St., Ste. 600
Denver, CO 80237
Jean-Yves Perez, President/CEO
PH: (303)740-2600
TF: (800)776-3296
FX: (303)740-2650
E-mail: info@wcc.com
URL: http://www.wcc.com
Founded: 1950. **Staff:** 2600. Offers consulting services in all types of engineering, including civil, geotechnical, and environmental sciences, and design and construction phase services. Services include complete programs in all areas of solid and hazardous waste management. Also provides special technical and laboratory services, and computerized database information management. Industries served: oil and gas, chemical, pulp and paper, and mining.

YAGER EQUIPMENT SALES
603 Sunrise Dr.
Waxahachie, TX 75165
PH: (972)938-9772
FX: (972)937-9772
Firm provides special knowledge in appraisals, construction materials, design, engineering, inspection, permitting, testing, and training.

YARMUS J ENGINEERING PC
230 N. Main St.
New City, NY 10956-5302
Dr. James Yarmus, Principal
PH: (914)634-3580
E-mail: yarmus@compuserve.com
URL: http://www.ourworld.compuserve.com/homepages/yarmus
Founded: 1977. Firm specializes in engineering and construction-related consulting.

YBI
880 W. 1st St., Ste. 203
Los Angeles, CA 90012
Yale Barkan, Principal
PH: (213)620-0272
FX: (213)617-0558
Forensic liability investigations in construction defects and product and appliance defects, including electrical shock/electrocution, industrial explosions, building and safety code violations, and electrical fire cause and origin. Provides failure analysis on computers, transformers, DC and AC motors, industrial process control systems, controllers, toasters, toaster ovens, microwave ovens, hair dryers, relays, and analog and digital circuits.

YOUNGLOVE CONSTRUCTION CO.
2015 E. 7th
PO Box 8800
Sioux City, IA 51102
Michael A. Gunsch, Exec. VP
PH: (712)277-3906
FX: (712)277-5300
E-mail: mgunsch@younglove-const.com
URL: http://www.youngloveconst.com
Provides architectural engineering services to manufacturing industry, including facilities planning and construction management.

BRUCE G. ZIMMERMAN
18671 Paseo Cortez
Irvine, CA 92612
Bruce G. Zimmerman, Contact
PH: (714)854-5145
FX: (714)509-7419
URL: http://www.dealmaker.com
Founded: 1979. **Staff:** 2. Serves as expert witness and consultant regarding shopping center real estate, land and building development, construction, zoning, leasing/sales, tenant relocation, broker standards, operating covenants, entitlements, due diligence, project finance, management, and valuation. Also specializes in joint venture formation, management, and dissolution, economic loss evaluation, and structured settlements. Member of California Bar Association (inactive), general contractor, and real estate broker. Industries served: shopping center real estate, land development, retail, banking and finance, and legal profession.

ZS ENGINEERING
99 Tulip Ave., No. 102
Floral Park, NY 11001-1959
Zygmunt Staszewski, Principal
PH: (516)328-3200
FX: (516)328-6195
Founded: 1989. Offers engineering consulting services to building owners and contractors.

TRADE INFORMATION SOURCES

Adapted from Gale's *Encyclopedia of Business Information Sources* (*EBIS*), the entries featured in this chapter show trade journals and other published sources, including web sites and databases. Entries list the title of the work, the name of the author (where available), name and address of the publisher, frequency or year of publication, prices or fees, and Internet address (in many cases).

ABC TODAY\ASSOCIATED BUILDERS AND
  CONTRACTORS NATIONAL MEMBERSHIP DIRECTORY
Associated Builders and Contractors
1300 N. 17th St.
Alexandria, VA 22209
PH: (703)812-2000
Annual. $150.00. List of approximately 19,000 member construction contractors and suppliers.

ABERDEEN'S CONCRETE CONSTRUCTION
Aberdeen Group
426 S. Westgate St.
Addison, IL 60101
PH: (800)837-0870
FX: (630)543-3112
E-mail: aberdeen@wocnet.com
Monthly. $27.00 per year. Covers methods of building with precast, prestressed, and other forms of concrete. Emphasis is on technology and new products or construction procedures.

ABERDEEN'S CONCRETE JOURNAL: THE CONCRETE
  PRODUCER'S FAVORITE MAGAZINE
Aberdeen Group
426 S. Westgate St.
Addison, IL 60101
PH: (800)837-0870
FX: (630)543-3112
E-mail: aberdeen@wocnet.com
Monthly. $33.00 per year. Covers the production and marketing of various concrete products, including precast and prestressed concrete.

ABERDEEN'S CONCRETE REPAIR DIGEST: THE
  MAGAZINE FOR THE CONCRETE REPAIR SPECIALIST
Aberdeen Group
426 S. Westgate St.
Addison, IL 60101
PH: (800)837-0870
FX: (630)543-3112
E-mail: aberdeen@wocnet.com
Bimonthly. $21.00 per year. Edited for specialists in the repair, maintenance, and restoration of concrete construction. Covers technology, marketing, and management.

ABERDEEN'S CONCRETE SOURCEBOOK
Aberdeen Group
426 S. Westgate St.
Addison, IL 60101
PH: (800)837-0870
FX: (630)543-3112
E-mail: aberdeen@wocnet.com
Annual. $30.00. Provides information on manufacturers of equipment, products, and materials for the concrete construction industry. Includes indexes by company, product, and trade name.

ABERDEEN'S CONSTRUCTION MARKETING TODAY
Aberdeen Group
426 S. Westgate St.
Addison, IL 60101
PH: (800)837-0870
FX: (630)543-3112
E-mail: aberdeen@wocnet.com
Monthly. $39.00 per year. Edited for sellers of construction products and services. Covers advertising, marketing, sales promotion, construction trade shows, and industry trends.

ABERDEEN'S MAGAZINE OF MASONRY
  CONSTRUCTION
Aberdeen Group
426 S. Westgate St.
Addison, IL 60101
PH: (800)837-0870
FX: (630)543-3112
E-mail: aberdeen@wocnet.com
Monthly. $27.00 per year. Covers the business, production, and marketing aspects of various kind of masonry construction: brick, concrete block, glass block, etc.

ACI MANUAL OF CONCRETE PRACTICE
American Concrete Institute
Redford Sta.
PO Box 19150
Detroit, MI 48219
PH: (313)532-2600
FX: (313)533-4747
Free to members; non-members, $592.50 per set.

AMERICAN CEMENT DIRECTORY
Bradley Pulverizer Co.
123 S. Third St.
Allentown, PA 18105
PH: (800)355-1186
FX: (610)770-9400
Annual. $67.00. About 200 cement manufacturing plants in the United States, Canada, Mexico, Central and South America.

AMERICAN HOUSING SURVEY FOR THE UNITED
  STATES
Available from U.S. Government Printing Office
Washington, DC 20402
PH: (202)512-1800
FX: (202)512-2250
E-mail: gpoaccess@gpo.gov
URL: http://www.access.gpo.gov
Biennial. $39.00. Issued by the U.S. Census Bureau. Covers both owner-occupied and renter-occupied housing. Includes data on such factors as condition of building, type of mortgage, utility costs, and housing occupied by minorities. (Current Housing Reports, H150.)

AMERICAN LAND PLANNING LAW
Clark Boardman Callaghan
155 Pfingsten Rd.
Deerfield, IL 60015
PH: (800)328-4880
FX: (847)948-8955
URL: http://www.westgroup.com
Norman Williams, Jr. $750.00 Eight volumes. Periodic supplementation.

AMERICAN SOCIETY OF CIVIL ENGINEERS\OFFICIAL
  REGISTER
American Society of Civil Engineers
345 E. 47th St.
New York, NY 10017-2398
PH: (800)548-2723
FX: (212)980-4681
E-mail: tpowell@asce.org
URL: http://www.pubs.asce.org
Annual. Free.

AMERICAN SOCIETY OF CIVIL
  ENGINEERS\PROCEEDINGS
American Society of Civil Engineers
345 E. 47th St.
New York, NY 10017-2398
PH: (800)548-2723
FX: (212)980-4681
E-mail: tpowell@asce.org
URL: http://www.pubs.asce.org
Monthly. $2,289.00 per year. Consists of the Journals of the various Divisions of the Society.

AMERICAN SOCIETY OF CIVIL
  ENGINEERS\TRANSACTIONS
American Society of Civil Engineers
345 E. 47th St.
New York, NY 10017-2398

PH: (800)548-2723
FX: (212)980-4681
E-mail: tpowell@asce.org
URL: http://www.pubs.asce.org
Annual. $140.00.

ASCE NEWS
American Society of Civil Engineers
345 E. 47th St.
New York, NY 10017-2398
PH: (800)548-2723
FX: (212)705-7712
E-mail: tpowell@asce.org
URL: http://www.pubs.asce.org
Monthly. $36.00 per year. Newsletter.

BASIC CONSTRUCTION MATERIALS
Prentice-Hall
One Lake St.
Upper Saddle River, NJ 07458
PH: (800)223-1360
FX: (800)445-6991
URL: http://www.prenhall.com
Charles Herubin and Theodore Marotta. 1996. $58.00. Fifth edition.

BLUE BOOK OF BUILDING AND CONSTRUCTION
PO Box 500
Jefferson Valley, NY 10535
PH: (800)431-2584
FX: (914)245-5781
Annual. Controlled circulation. 11 regional editions. Lists architects, contractors, subcontractors, manufacturers and suppliers of constructions materials and equipment.

BUILDER: OFFICIAL PUBLICATION OF THE NATIONAL ASSOCIATION OF HOME BUILDERS
Hanley-Wood, Inc.
One Thomas Circle, Ste. 600
Washington, DC 20005
PH: (202)452-0800
FX: (202)785-1974
E-mail: johnbutter@builderonline.com
URL: http://www.builderonline.com
National Association of Home Builders of the United States. Monthly. $29.95 per year. Covers the home building and remodeling industry in general, including design, construction, and marketing.

BUILDING CONSTRUCTION COST DATA
R.S. Means Co., Inc.
PO Box 800
Kingston, MA 02364-0800
PH: (800)448-8182
FX: (617)585-7466
URL: http://www.rsmeans.com
Annual. $86.95. Lists over 20,000 entries for estimating.

BUILDING CONSTRUCTION HANDBOOK
Butterworth-Heinemann
225 Wildwood Ave.
Woburn, MA 01081
PH: (800)366-2665
FX: (617)933-6333
Ray Chudley. 1995. $28.95. Second edition.

BUILDING DESIGN AND CONSTRUCTION
Cahners Publishing Inc.
PO Box 5080
Des Plaines, IL 60017-5080
PH: (800)662-7776
FX: (847)635-9950
E-mail: marketaccess@cahners.com
URL: http://www.cahners.com
Monthly. $99.90 per year. For non-residential building owners, contractors, engineers and architects.

BUILDING MATERIAL RETAILER
National and Building Material Dealers Association
40 Ivy St. SE
Washington, DC 20003
PH: (800)328-9125
Monthly. $25.00 per year. Includes special feature issues on hand and power tools, lumber, roofing, kitchens, flooring, windows and doors, and insulation.

BUILDING OFFICIALS AND CODE ADMINISTRATORS INTERNATIONAL\MEMBERSHIP DIRECTORY
Building Officials and Code Administrators International
4051 W. Flossmoor Rd.
Country Club Hills, IL 60478
PH: (708)799-2300
FX: (708)799-4981
E-mail: boca@bocai.org
Annual. $16.00. Approximately 14,000 construction code officials, architects, engineers, trade associations, and manufacturers.

BUILDING SUPPLY BUSINESS
Cahners Publishing Co.
PO Box 5080
Des Plaines, IL 60017-5080
PH: (800)662-7776
FX: (847)390-2690
E-mail: marketaccess@cahners.com
URL: http://www.cahners.com
Monthly. $70.00 per year. For retailers of lumber and building materials.

BUILDING SUPPLY HOME CENTERS RETAIL GIANTS REPORT
Cahners Publishing Co.
PO Box 5080
Des Plaines, IL 60017-5080
PH: (800)662-7776
FX: (847)390-2690
E-mail: marketaccess@cahners.com
URL: http://www.cahners.com
Annual. $30.00. Lists major retailers of a wide variety of building and home improvement materials, products, fixtures, accessories, equipment, and tools.

BUILDINGS: THE FACILITIES CONSTRUCTION AND MANAGEMENT JOURNAL
Stamats Communications, Inc.
PO Box 1888
Cedar Rapids, IA 52406-1888
PH: (800)553-8878
FX: (319)364-4278
URL: http://www.buildings.com
Monthly. $70.00 per year. Serves professional building ownership/management organizations.

THE CARPENTER
United Brotherhood of Carpenters and Joiners of America
101 Constitution Ave. NW
Washington, DC 20001
PH: (202)546-6206
FX: (202)547-8979
Bimonthly. $10.00 per year.

CARPENTERS AND BUILDERS LIBRARY
Macmillan Publishing Co., Inc.
200 Old Tappan Rd.
Old Tappan, NJ 07675
PH: (800)223-2336
FX: (800)445-6991
John E. Ball. 1991. Four volumes. $21.95 per volume. Sixth revised edition.

CARPENTRY FOR RESIDENTIAL CONSTRUCTION
Craftsman Book Co.
PO Box 6500
Carlsbad, CA 92008
PH: (800)829-8123
FX: (619)438-0398
Byron Maguire. 1987. $19.75.

CEE NEWS
Intertech Publishing Corp.
PO Box 12901
Overland Park, KS 66282-2901
PH: (800)621-9907
FX: (800)633-6219
Monthly. Free to qualified personnel.

CEMENT AND CONCRETE RESEARCH
Elsevier Science
655 Ave. of the Americas
New York, NY 10010
PH: (888)437-4636
FX: (212)633-3680
E-mail: usinfo-f@elsevier.com
URL: http://www.elsevier.com
Monthly. $1280.00 per year. Text in English, French, German and Russian.

CEMENT AND CONCRETE TERMINOLOGY
American Concrete Institute
Redford Sta.
PO Box 19150
Detroit, MI 48219
PH: (313)532-2600
FX: (313)533-4747
1990. $54.50.

CEMENT DATA BOOK: INTERNATIONAL PROCESS ENGINEERING IN THE CEMENT INDUSTRY
French and European Publications, Inc.
Rockefeller Center Promenade
610 Fifth Ave.
New York, NY 10020-2479
PH: (212)581-8810
FX: (212)265-1094
Walter H. Duda. 1985. $950.00. Third edition. Three volumes. Vol.1, $375.00; vol.2, $325.00; vol.3, $250.00. Text in English and German.

CEMENT, QUARRY AND MINERAL AGGREGATES NEWSLETTER
National Safety Council, Periodicals Dept.
1121 Spring Lake Dr.
Itasca, IL 60143
PH: (800)621-7619
FX: (630)775-2068
Bimonthly. Members, $15.00 per year; non-members, $19.00 per year.

CENSUS OF CONSTRUCTION INDUSTRIES: ROOFING SIDING AND SHEET METAL WORK SPECIAL TRADE CONTRACTORS
U.S. Bureau of the Census
Washington, DC 20233-0800
PH: (301)457-4100
FX: (301)457-3842
URL: http://www.census.gov
Quinquennial.

CENSUS OF CONSTRUCTION: SUBJECT BIBLIOGRAPHY NO. 157
Available from U.S. Government Printing Office
Washington, DC 20402
PH: (202)512-1800
FX: (202)512-2250

Annual. Free. Lists government publications.

CERAMIC TILE
Available from FIND/SVP, Inc.
625 Ave. of the Americas
New York, NY 10011-2002
PH: (800)346-3787
FX: (212)807-2716
E-mail: catalog@findsvp.com
URL: http://www.findsvp.com
1997. $995.00. Market research report published by specialists in business information. Presents market data relative to demographics, sales growth, shipments, exports, imports, price trends, and end-use. Includes company profiles.

CFMA BUILDING PROFITS
Construction Financial Management Association
707 State Rd., Ste. 223
Princeton, NJ 08540-1413
PH: (609)683-5000
FX: (609)683-4821
Bimonthly. Controlled circulation. Covers the financial side of the construction industry.

CIVIL ENGINEERING DATABASE
American Society of Civil Engineers
345 E. 47th St.
New York, NY 10017-2398
PH: (800)548-2723
FX: (212)980-4681
Provides abstracts of the U.S. and international literature of civil engineering, 1975 to date. Inquire as to online cost and availability.

CIVIL ENGINEERING: ENGINEERED DESIGN AND CONSTRUCTION
American Society of Civil Engineers
345 E. 47th St.
New York, NY 10017-2398
PH: (800)548-2723
FX: (212)980-4681
E-mail: tpowell@asce.org
URL: http://www.pubs.asce.org
Monthly. $98.00 per year.

CIVIL ENGINEERING PRACTICE: ENGINEERING SUCCESS BY ANALYSIS OF FAILURE
McGraw-Hill
1221 Avenue of the Americas
New York, NY 10020
PH: (800)722-4726
FX: (800)262-4729
David D. Piesold. 1991. $52.00.

COMPLETE BUILDING EQUIPMENT MAINTENANCE DESK BOOK
Prentice Hall
One Lake St.
Upper Saddle River, NJ 07458
PH: (800)223-1360
FX: (800)445-6991
URL: http://www.prenhall.com
Sheldon J. Fuchs, editor. 1993. Second edition. Price on application.

CONCRETE
Advanstar Communications, Inc.
7500 Old Oak Blvd.
Cleveland, OH 44130
PH: (800)346-0085
FX: (216)891-2726
URL: http://www.advanstar.com
The Concrete Society. Bimonthly. $75.00 per year. Information for ready mix, precast, prestressed, masonry and pipe producers.

CONCRETE ABSTRACTS
American Concrete Institute
Redford Sta.
PO Box 19150
Detroit, MI 48219
PH: (313)532-2600
FX: (313)538-0655
Bimonthly. Members, $166.00; non-members, $194.00 per year.

CONCRETE CONSTRUCTION BUYERS' GUIDE ISSUE
Aberdeen Group
426 S. Westgate St.
Addison, IL 60101
PH: (800)837-0870
FX: (630)543-3112
E-mail: aberdeen@wocnet.com
Annual. $3.00. Lists sources of products and services related to building with concrete.

CONCRETE INTERNATIONAL
American Concrete Institute
Redford Sta.
PO Box 19150
Detroit, MI 48219
PH: (313)532-2600
FX: (313)538-0655
Monthly. $109.00 per year. Covers practical technology, industry news, and business management relating to the concrete construction industry.

CONCRETE JOURNAL BUYERS' GUIDE ISSUE
Aberdeen Group
426 S. Westgate St.
Addison, IL 60101
PH: (800)837-0870
FX: (630)543-3112
E-mail: aberdeen@wocnet.com
Annual. $3.00. Lists manufacturers or suppliers of concrete-related products and services.

CONCRETE PRODUCTS
Intertec Publishing Corp.
29 N. Wacker Dr.
Chicago, IL 60606
PH: (800)621-9907
FX: (800)633-6219
Monthly. $36.00 per year.

CONCRETE REPAIR DIGEST BUYERS' GUIDE ISSUE
Aberdeen Group
426 S. Westgate St.
Addison, IL 60101
PH: (800)837-0870
FX: (630)543-3112
E-mail: aberdeen@wocnet.com
Annual. $3.00. Lists sources of products and services for concrete repair and maintenance specialists.

CONSTRUCTION ARBITRATION HANDBOOK
Shepard's
555 Middle Creek Parkway
Colorado Springs, CO 80921
PH: (800)743-7393
FX: (800)525-0053
James Acret. 1985. $110.00. Explains the arbitration of disputes involving builders.

CONSTRUCTION CONTRACTING
John Wiley and Sons, Inc.
605 Third Ave.
New York, NY 10158-0012
PH: (800)225-5945
FX: (212)850-6088
Richard H. Clough and Glenn A. Sears. 1994. $67.95. Sixth edition.

CONSTRUCTION COST INDEXES
R.S. Means Co., Inc.
PO Box 800
Kingston, MA 02364-0800
PH: (800)448-8182
FX: (617)585-7466
Quarterly. $210.00 per year.

CONSTRUCTION EQUIPMENT BUYER'S GUIDE
Cahners Publishing Co.
PO Box 5080
Des Plaines, IL 60017-5080
PH: (800)662-7776
FX: (847)390-2690
E-mail: marketaccess@cahners.com
URL: http://www.cahners.com
Annual. $49.95. Included in subscription to *Construction Equipment.*

CONSTRUCTION EQUIPMENT DISTRIBUTION
Associated Equipment Distributors
615 W. 22nd St.
Oak Brook, IL 60521
PH: (800)338-0650
FX: (708)574-0132
Monthly. Members, $20.00 per year; non-members, $40.00 per year.

CONSTRUCTION EQUIPMENT OPERATION AND MAINTENANCE
Construction Publications Inc.
PO Box 1689
Cedar Rapids, IA 52406
PH: (319)366-1597
FX: (319)362-8808
Clark K. Parks, editor. Bimonthly. $12.00 per year. Information for users of construction equipment and industry news.

CONSTRUCTION INDUSTRY ANNUAL FINANCIAL SURVEY
Construction Financial Management Association
707 State Rd., Ste. 223
Princeton, NJ 08540
PH: (609)683-5000
FX: (609)683-4821
Annual. $149.00. Contains key financial ratios for various kinds and sizes of construction contractors.

CONSTRUCTION LABOR REPORT
Bureau of National Affairs, Inc.
1250 23rd St. NW
Washington, DC 20037
PH: (800)372-1033
FX: (202)822-8092
URL: http://www.bna.com.
Weekly. $893.00 per year. Two volumes. Looseleaf.

CONSTRUCTION LAW ADVISER: MONTHLY PRACTICAL ADVICE FOR LAWYERS AND CONSTRUCTION PROFESSIONALS
Clark Boardman Callaghan
155 Pfingsten Rd.
Deerfield, IL 60015
PH: (800)328-4880
FX: (847)948-8955
URL: http://www.westgroup.com
Monthly. $295.00 per year. Newsletter.

CONSTRUCTION MATERIALS: TYPES, USES, AND APPLICATIONS
John Wiley & Sons, Inc.
605 Third Ave.
New York, NY 10158-0012
PH: (800)225-5945
FX: (212)850-6088

Caleb Hornbostel. 1991. $150.00. Second edition.

CONSTRUCTION REVIEW
Available from U.S. Government Printing Office
Washington, DC 20402
PH: (202)512-1800
FX: (202)512-2250
Industry and Trade Administration, U.S. Dept. of Commerce. Quarterly. $18.00 per year. Provides virtually all of the government's current statistics pertaining to construction.

CONSTRUCTION SPECIFIER: FOR COMMERCIAL AND INDUSTRIAL CONSTRUCTION
Construction Specifications Institute
601 Madison St.
Alexandria, VA 22314
PH: (800)689-2900
FX: (703)684-0465
URL: http://www.csinet.org
Monthly. Free to members; non-members, $36.00 per year; universities, $30.00 per year. Technical aspects of the construction industry.

CONSTRUCTION SPECIFIER\MEMBER DIRECTORY
Construction Specifications Institute
601 Madison St.
Alexandria, VA 22314
PH: (800)689-2900
FX: (703)684-0465
URL: http://www.csinet.org
Annual. $30.00. Roster of construction specifiers by the institute, and 17,200 members.

CONSTRUCTOR: THE MANAGEMENT MAGAZINE OF THE CONSTRUCTION INDUSTRY
Associated General Contractors of America
AGC Information, Inc.
1957 E St. NW
Washington, DC 20006
PH: (202)393-2040
FX: (202)628-7369
URL: http://www.agc.org
Monthly. Members, $15.00 per year; non-members, $100.00 per year.

COST OF DOING BUSINESS AND FINANCIAL POSITION SURVEY OF THE RETAIL LUMBER AND BUILDING MATERIAL DEALERS OF THE NORTHEASTERN STATES
Northeastern Retail Lumber Association
585 N. Greenbush Rd.
Rensselaer, NY 12144-9453
PH: (800)292-6752
Annual. Free to members; non-members, $300.00. Includes sales figures, profit margins, pricing methods, rates of return, and other financial data for retailers of lumber and building supplies in the Northeast.

DESIGN OF CONCRETE STRUCTURES
McGraw-Hill, Inc.
1221 Ave. of the Americas
New York, NY 10020-1095
PH: (800)722-4726
FX: (212)512-2821
Arthur H. Nilson. 1997. 12th edition. Price on application.

DESIGN COST & DATA: THE COST ESTIMATING MAGAZINE FOR ARCHITECTS, BUILDERS AND SPECIFIERS
L. M. Rector Corp.
8602 North 40th St.
Tampa, FL 33604
PH: (813)989-9300
FX: (813)980-3982
Bimonthly. $64.80 per year. Provides a preliminary cost estimating

system for architects, contractors, builders, and developers, utilizing historical data. Includes case studies of actual costs.

DICTIONARY OF ARCHITECTURE, BUILDING, CONSTRUCTION AND MATERIALS
French and European Publishers, Inc.
Rockefeller Center Promenade
610 Fifth Ave.
New York, NY 10020-2479
PH: (212)581-8810
FX: (212)265-1094
H. Bucksch. 1983. Second edition. Two volumes. $295.00 per volume.

DICTIONARY OF ARCHITECTURE AND CONSTRUCTION
McGraw-Hill, Inc.
1221 Ave. of the Americas
New York, NY 10020-1095
PH: (800)722-4726
FX: (212)512-2821
Cyril M. Harris. 1993. $65.00. Second edition.

DICTIONARY OF BUILDING
G P Courseware
8908 S. Yale Ave., Ste. 250
Tulsa, OK 74137-3543
PH: (918)655-2152
FX: (918)494-4957
Randall McMullan. 1991. $59.50.

DIRECTORY OF BUILDING PRODUCTS HARDLINES DISTRIBUTORS
Chain Store Guide Information Services
3922 Coconut Palm Dr.
Tampa, FL 33619
PH: (800)927-9292
FX: (813)664-6882
E-mail: valkelly@sprynet.com
URL: http://www/d-net.com/csgis
Biennial. $260.00. Includes hardware, housewares, and building supply distributors.

DIRECTORY OF HOME CENTER OPERATORS AND HARDWARE CHAINS
Chain Store Guide Information Services
3922 Coconut Palm Dr.
Tampa, FL 33619
PH: (800)927-9292
FX: (813)664-6882
E-mail: valkelly@sprynet.com
URL: http://www.d-net.com/csgis
Annual. $290.00. Nearly 5,800 home center operators, paint and home decorating chains, and lumber and building materials companies.

DODGE REPORTS
F. W. Dodge Group
McGraw-Hill Information Systems Co.
1221 Ave. of the Americas
New York, NY 10020
PH: (212)512-2000
Daily. Price on application. Individual reports on new construction jobs.

DODGE/SCAN
F. W. Dodge Group
McGraw-Hill Information Systems Co.
1221 Ave. of the Americas
New York, NY 10020
PH: (212)512-2000
Price on application. Provides plans and specifications of new construction jobs.

DOOR HARDWARE
Available from FIND/SVP, Inc.
625 Ave. of the Americas
New York, NY 10011-2002
PH: (800)346-3787
FX: (212)807-2716
E-mail: catalog@findsvp.com
URL: http://www.findsvp.com
1997. $995.00. Market research report published by specialists in business information. Covers locks, closers, doorknobs, security devices, and other door hardware. Presents market data relative to demographics, sales growth, shipments, exports, imports, price trends, and end-use. Includes company profiles.

DOORS
Available from FIND/SVP, Inc.
625 Ave. of the Americas
New York, NY 10011-2002
PH: (800)346-3787
FX: (212)807-2716
E-mail: catalog@findsvp.com
URL: http://www.findsvp.com
1997. $995.00. Market research report published by specialists in business information. Covers residential doors, including garage doors. Presents market data relative to demographics, sales growth, shipments, exports, imports, price trends, and end-use. Includes company profiles.

THE ECOLOGY OF LAND USE: A BIBLIOGRAPHIC GUIDE
Sage Publications, Inc.
PO Box 5084
Thousand Oaks, CA 91359-9924
PH: (805)499-0721
FX: (805)499-0871
E-mail: libraries@sagepub.com
URL: http://www.sagepub.com
Graham Trelstad. 1994. $10.00.

ELECTRICAL CONSTRUCTION AND MAINTENANCE
Intertec Publishing Corp.
PO Box 12901
Overland Park, KS 66282-2901
PH: (800)621-9907
FX: (800)633-6219
Monthly. Free to qualified personnel; others, $45.00 per year.

ELECTRICAL CONSTRUCTION MATERIALS DIRECTORY
Underwriters Laboratories, Inc.
333 Pfingsten Rd.
Northbrook, IL 60062-2096
PH: (708)272-8800
FX: (708)272-8129
E-mail: directories@ul.com
Annual. $22.00. Lists construction materials manufacturers authorized to use UL label.

ELECTRICAL CONTRACTOR MAGAZINE
National Electrical Contractors Association
Three Bethesda Metro Center, Ste. 1100
Bethesda, MD 20814
PH: (301)657-3110
FX: (301)961-6495
Monthly.

ENCYCLOPEDIA OF ARCHITECTURE: DESIGN, ENGINEERING AND CONSTRUCTION
John Wiley and Sons, Inc.
605 Third Ave.
New York, NY 10158-0012
PH: (800)526-5368
FX: (212)850-6088

Joseph A. Wilkes and R. T. Packard, editors. 1988-89. $1,225.00. Six volumes. $275.00 per volume.

ENR DIRECTORY OF CONTRACTORS
McGraw-Hill, Inc.
1221 Avenue of the Americas
New York, NY 10020-1095
PH: (800)722-4726
FX: (212)512-2821
Biennial. $97.00. Four regional editions. About 3,900 general and specialty contractors and approximately 4,000 construction managers; about 200 contractors receive in-depth profiles. The top 400 construction contractors and international contractors are also listed.

ENR (ENGINEERING NEWS-RECORD)
McGraw-Hill, Inc.
1221 Ave. of the Americas
New York, NY 10020-1095
PH: (800)722-4726
FX: (212)512-2821
Weekly. $69.00 per year.

ENR TOP 400 CONSTRUCTION CONTRACTORS
McGraw-Hill, Inc.
1221 Ave of the Americas
New York, NY 10020
PH: (800)722-4726
FX: (212)512-2821
Annual. $10.00. Lists 400 United States contractors receiving largest dollar volume of contracts in preceding calendar year.

ENR TOP INTERNATIONAL CONTRACTORS
McGraw-Hill, Inc.
1221 Ave of the Americas
New York, NY 10020
PH: (800)722-4726
FX: (212)512-2821
Annual. $10.00. Lists over 200 contractors (including United States firms) competing outside their own national borders who received largest dollar volume of foreign contracts in preceding calendar year.

EQUIPMENT TODAY
Johnson Hill Press, Inc.
PO Box 803
Fort Atkinson, WI 53538-0803
PH: (800)547-7377
FX: (414)563-1699
Monthly. $60.00 per year.

EXPENDITURES FOR RESIDENTIAL UPKEEP AND IMPROVEMENT
Available from U.S. Government Printing Office
Washington, DC 20402
PH: (202)512-1800
FX: (202)512-2250
Quarterly. $8.00 per year. Bureau of the Census Construction Report, C50. Provides estimates of spending for housing maintenance, repairs, additions, alterations, and major replacements.

FLUID ABSTRACTS: CIVIL ENGINEERING
Elsevier Science
655 Ave. of the Americas
New York, NY 10010
PH: (888)437-4636
FX: (212)633-3680
E-mail: usinfo-f@elsevier.com
URL: http://www.elsevier.com
Monthly. $1,002.00 per year. Annual cumulation. Includes the literature of coastal structures. Published in England by Elsevier Science Publishing Ltd.

FOREST PRODUCTS JOURNAL
Forest Products Research Society
2801 Marshall Ct.
Madison, WI 53705
PH: (608)231-1361
FX: (608)231-2152
10 times a year. $135.00 per year.

**FORMS AND AGREEMENTS FOR ARCHITECTS,
ENGINEERS AND CONTRACTORS**
Clark Boardman Callaghan
155 Pfingsten Rd.
Deerfield, IL 60015
PH: (800)328-4880
FX: (847)948-8955
URL: http://www.westgroup.com
Albert Dib. Four looseleaf volumes. $495.00. Periodic supplementation. Covers evaluation of construction documents and alternative clauses. Includes pleadings for litigation and resolving of claims.

**FUNDAMENTALS OF CONSTRUCTION ESTIMATING AND
COST ACCOUNTING, WITH COMPUTER
APPLICATIONS**
Prentice Hall
One Lake St.
Upper Saddle River, NJ 07458
PH: (800)223-1360
FX: (800)445-6991
URL: http://www.prenhall.com
Keith Collier. 1987. $66.00. Second edition.

GOVERNMENT CONTRACTOR
Federal Publications, Inc.
1120 20th St. NW, Ste. 500 S
Washington, DC 20036-3483
PH: (800)922-4330
FX: (202)659-2233
E-mail: bbolger@fedpub.com
URL: http://www.fedpub.com
Weekly. $1,032.00 per year.

GOVERNMENT CONTRACTS REPORTS
Commerce Clearing House, Inc.
4025 W. Peterson Ave.
Chicago, IL 60646-6085
PH: (800)248-3248
FX: (800)224-8299
$2,120.00 per year. 10 looseleaf volumes. Weekly updates. Laws and regulations affecting government contracts.

**HARDWARE AGE HOME IMPROVEMENT MARKET:
WHO MAKES IT BUYER'S GUIDE**
Chilton Co.
201 King of Prussia Rd.
Radnor, PA 19089-0230
PH: (800)695-1214
FX: (610)964-4284
E-mail: homeimpvmt@aol.com
URL: http://www.chilton.com
Annual. $25.00. Lists about 4,100 manufacturers of a wide variety of hardware and other products, including automotive, electrical, lawn and garden, plumbing, building, home improvement, housewares, paint, hand tools, and power tools. Includes company name, product, and brand name indexes. Included in subscription to *Hardware Age*.

**HARDWARE AGE HOME IMPROVEMENT MARKET:
"WHO'S WHO" VERIFIED DIRECTORY OF HOME
IMPROVEMENT**
Chilton Co.
201 King of Prussia Rd.
Radnor, PA 19089-0230

PH: (800)695-1214
FX: (610)964-4284
URL: http://www.chilton.com
Biennial. $195.00. Lists about 2,500 wholesalers, specialty distributors, and manufacturers' representatives. Covers a wide variety of hardware items and other products.

THE HOME DO-IT-YOURSELF MARKET
Available from FIND/SVP, Inc.
625 Ave. of the Americas
New York, NY 10011-2002
PH: (800)346-3787
FX: (212)807-2716
E-mail: catalog@findsvp.com
URL: http://www.findsvp.com
1997. $2,500.00. Market research report published by Packaged Facts. Covers the market for lumber, finishing materials, tools, hardware, etc.

**HOUSING AFFAIRS LETTER: WEEKLY WASHINGTON
REPORT ON HOUSING**
C D Publications
8204 Fenton St.
Silver Springs, MD 20910-2889
PH: (301)588-6380
FX: (301)588-6385
Community Services Development, Inc. Weekly. $399.00 per year.

**HOUSING FINANCIAL MARKETS AND THE WIDER
ECONOMY**
John Wiley and Sons, Inc.
605 Third Ave.
New York, NY 10158-0012
PH: (800)225-5945
FX: (212)850-6088
David Miles. 1995. $80.00.

HOUSING MARKET REPORT
C D Publications
8204 Fenton St.
Silver Springs, MD 20910-2889
PH: (301)588-6380
FX: (301)588-6385
Community Development Services, Inc. Semimonthly. $337.00 per year. Real estate outlook for U.S. housing markets.

HOUSING STARTS
Available from U.S. Government Printing Office
Washington, DC 20402
PH: (202)512-1800
FX: (202)512-2250
U.S. Bureau of the Census. Monthly. $21.00 per year. Construction Reports: C-20.

HOUSING STATISTICS OF THE UNITED STATES
Bernan Press
4611-F Assembly Dr.
Lanham, MD 20706-4391
PH: (800)274-4447
FX: (800)865-3450
E-mail: info@bernan.com
URL: http://www.bernan.com
Patrick A. Simmons, editor. 1997. $59.00.

**ILLUSTRATED DICTIONARY OF BUILDING MATERIALS
AND TECHNIQUES: AN INVALUABLE SOURCEBOOK
TO THE TOOLS, TERMS, MATERIALS, AND
TECHNIQUES USED BY BUILDING**
John Wiley and Sons, Inc.
605 Third Ave.
New York, NY 10158-0012
PH: (800)225-5945
FX: (212)850-6088
Paul Bianchina. 1993. $47.95. Contains 4,000 definitions of building

and building materials terms, with 500 illustrations. Includes materials grades, measurements, and specifications.

INSTITUTE ON PLANNING, ZONING AND EMINENT DOMAIN, SOUTHWESTERN LEGAL FOUNDATION: PROCEEDINGS, 1971-1994

Fred B. Rothman and Co.
10368 W. Centennial Rd.
Littleton, CO 80127
PH: (800)457-1986
FX: (303)978-1457
1994. $1,824.00. 24 volumes.

INTERNATIONAL CONFERENCE OF BUILDING OFFICIALS\MEMBERSHIP ROSTER

International Conference of Building Officials
5360 Workman Mill Rd.
Whittier, CA 90601-2298
PH: (800)336-1963
FX: (310)692-3853
Annual. $20.50.

INTERNATIONAL CONFERENCE OF BUILDING OFFICIALS\UNIFORM BUILDING CODE

International Conference of Building Officials
5360 Workman Mill Rd.
Whittier, CA 90601-2298
PH: (800)336-1963
FX: (310)699-8031
Triennial. Two volumes. Members, $107.15; non-members, $139.90.

JOURNAL OF HOUSING AND COMMUNITY DEVELOPMENT

National Association of Housing and Redevelopment Officials
630 Eye St. NW
Washington, DC 20001-3736
PH: (202)289-3500
FX: (202)429-8181
Bimonthly. $24.00 per year.

JOURNAL OF HOUSING ECONOMICS

Academic Press, Inc., Journals Div.
525 B St., Ste. 1900
San Diego, CA 92101-4495
PH: (800)321-5068
FX: (800)235-0256
E-mail: apsubs@acad.com
URL: http://www.apnet.com
Quarterly. $150.00 per year.

KITCHEN CABINETS AND OTHER CABINETWORK

Available from FIND/SVP, Inc.
625 Ave. of the Americas
New York, NY 10011-2002
PH: (800)346-3787
FX: (212)807-2716
E-mail: catalog@findsvp.com
URL: http://www.findsvp.com
1997. $995.00. Market research report published by specialists in business information. Covers both custom and stock cabinets. Presents market data relative to demographics, sales growth, shipments, exports, imports, price trends, and end-use. Includes company profiles.

LAND USE DIGEST

Urban Land Institute
625 Indian Ave. NW, Ste. 400
Washington, DC 20004-2930
PH: (800)321-5011
FX: (212)624-7140
E-mail: bookstore@uli.org
URL: http://www.uli.org
Monthly.

LAND USE AND ENVIRONMENT LAW REVIEW

Clark Boardman Callaghan
155 Pfingsten Rd.
Deerfield, IL 60015
PH: (800)328-4880
FX: (847)948-8955
URL: http://www.westgroup.com
Annual. $130.00.

LAND USE LAW REPORT

Business Publishers, Inc.
951 Pershing Dr.
Silver Spring, MD 20910-4464
PH: (800)274-0122
FX: (301)585-9075
E-mail: bpinews@bpinews.com
URL: http://www.bpinews.com
Biweekly. $273.00 per year. Provides current reports on planning issues affecting urban, suburban, agricultural and natural resources land jurisdictions.

LAND USE LAW AND ZONING DIGEST

American Planning Association
122 S. Michigan Ave., Ste. 1600
Chicago, IL 60603-6107
PH: (312)431-9100
FX: (312)431-9985
Monthly. $250.00 per year. Covers judicial decisions and state laws affecting zoning and land use. Edited for city planners and lawyers. Supplement available *Zoning News*.

MAGAZINE OF MASONRY CONSTRUCTION BUYERS' GUIDE ISSUE

Aberdeen Group
426 S. Westgate St.
Addison, IL 60101
PH: (800)837-0870
FX: (630)543-3112
E-mail: aberdeen@wocnet.com
Annual. $3.00. Lists manufacturers or suppliers of products and services related to masonry construction.

MATERIALS HANDBOOK

McGraw-Hill
1221 Ave. of the Americas
New York, NY 10020
PH: (800)722-4726
FX: (212)512-2821
George S. Brady and others. 1996. $89.95. 14th edition.

MEANS LABOR RATES FOR THE CONSTRUCTION INDUSTRY

R.S. Means Co., Inc.
PO Box 800
Kingston, MA 02364-0800
PH: (800)448-8182
FX: (617)585-7466
Annual. $174.95.

MODERN CARPENTRY: BUILDING CONSTRUCTION DETAILS IN EASY-TO-UNDERSTAND FORM

Goodheart-Willcox Co., Inc.
18604 W. Creek Dr.
Tinley Park, IL 60477-6243
PH: (800)323-0440
FX: (708)687-5068
Willis H. Wagner and Howard S. Smith. 1996. $45.28.

NAHRO DIRECTORY OF LOCAL AGENCIES AND RESOURCE GUIDE

National Association of Housing and Redevelopment Officials
630 Eye St. NW
Washington, DC 20001-3736

PH: (202)289-3500
FX: (202)289-8181
Triennial. Members, $80.00; non-members, $100.00.

NATIONAL HOME CENTER NEWS: THE NEWSPAPER FOR RETAILERS SERVING HOMEOWNERS AND CONTRACTORS
Lebhar-Friedman, Inc.
425 Park Ave.
New York, NY 10022
PH: (212)756-5000
FX: (212)756-5139
Biweekly. $79.00 per year. Includes special feature issues on hardware and tools, building materials, millwork, electrical supplies, lighting, and kitchens.

NEW ONE-FAMILY HOUSES SOLD
Available from U.S. Government Printing Office
Washington, DC 20402
PH: (202)512-1800
FX: (202)512-2250
Monthly. $20.00 per year. Bureau of the Census Construction Report, C25. Provides data on new, privately-owned, one-family homes sold during the month and for sale at the end of the month.

NEW USES FOR OBSOLETE BUILDINGS
Urban Land Institute
1025 Thomas Jefferson St. NW, Ste. 500 W.
Washington, DC 20007
PH: (800)321-5011
FX: (202)624-7152
E-mail: bookstore@uli.org
URL: http://www.uli.org
1996. $64.95. Covers various aspects of redevelopment: zoning, building codes, environment, economics, financing, and marketing. Includes eight case studies and 75 descriptions of completed "adaptive use projects."

NORTH AMERICAN BUILDING MATERIAL DISTRIBUTION ASSOCIATION\MEMBERSHIP AND PRODUCT DIRECTORY
National American Building Material Distribution Association
401 N. Michigan Ave.
Chicago, IL 60611-4274
PH: (312)321-6845
FX: (312)644-0310
E-mail: nbmda@sba.com
Annual. $795.00. About 200 wholesale distributors of building products who are members, and 150 manufacturers in that field who are associate members andover 600 of their locations.

NORTH AMERICAN WHOLESALE LUMBER ASSOCIATION\DISTRIBUTION DIRECTORY
North American Wholesale Lumber Association
3601 West Algonquin Rd., No. 400
Rolling Meadows, IL 60008-3108
PH: (800)527-8258
FX: (708)870-0201
E-mail: nawla@aol.com
Annual. $50.00. Over 550 wholesalers and manufacturers of lumber and related forest products.

NTIS ALERTS: BUILDING INDUSTRY TECHNOLOGY
National Technical Information Service
U.S. Department of Commerce, Technology Administration
5285 Port Royal Rd.
Springfield, VA 22161
PH: (800)553-6847
FX: (703)321-8547
Semimonthly. $160.00 per year. Provides descriptions of government-sponsored research reports and software, with ordering information. Covers architecture, construction management, building materials, maintenance, furnishings, and related subjects.

PROFESSIONAL BUILDER
Cahners Publishing Co.
PO Box 5080
Des Plaines, IL 60017-5080
PH: (800)662-7776
FX: (847)635-9950
E-mail: marketaccess@cahners.com
URL: http://www.cahners.com
14 times a year. $89.00 per year. Provides price and market forecasts on industrial products, components and materials. Office products, business systems and transportation.

PROSALES: FOR DEALERS AND DISTRIBUTORS SERVING THE PROFESSIONAL CONTRACTOR
Hanley-Wood, Inc.
One Thomas Circle, Ste. 600
Washington, DC 20005
PH: (202)452-0800
FX: (202)785-1974
Nine times a year. $36.00 per year. Includes special feature issues on selling, credit, financing, and the marketing of power tools.

RECOGNIZED COMPONENT DIRECTORY
Underwriters Laboratories, Inc.
333 Pfingsten Rd.
Northbrook, IL 60062-2096
PH: (708)272-8800
FX: (708)272-8129
E-mail: directories@ul.com
Annual. $60.00. Supplement issued each year at $35.00. Lists electrical component manufacturers authorized to use UL label.

REINFORCED CONCRETE FUNDAMENTALS
John Wiley and Sons, Inc.
605 Third Ave.
New York, NY 10158-0012
PH: (800)526-5368
FX: (212)850-6088
Phil M. Ferguson and others. 1988. $86.95. Fifth edition.

REMODELING: EXCELLENCE IN PROFESSIONAL REMODELING
Hanley-Wood, Inc.
One Thomas Circle, Ste. 600
Washington, DC 20005
PH: (202)452-0800
FX: (202)785-1974
E-mail: editor@builderonline.com
URL: http://www.remodeling.hw.net
Monthly. $44.95 per year. Covers new products, construction, management, and marketing for remodelers.

REMODELING PRODUCT GUIDE
Hanley-Wood, Inc.
One Thomas Circle, Ste. 600
Washington, DC 20005
PH: (202)452-0800
FX: (202)785-1974
E-mail: cweber@hanley-wood.com
Annual. $10.00. A directory of products and services for the home remodeling industry.

ROOF FRAMING
Craftsman Book Co.
PO Box 6500
Carlsbad, CA 92008
PH: (800)829-8123
FX: (619)438-0398
Marshall Gross. 1989. $22.00. Revised edition. (Home Craftsman Books).

RSI (ROOFING, SIDING, INSULATION)
Advanstar Communications, Inc.
7500 Old Oak Blvd.
Cleveland, OH 44130
PH: (800)346-0085
FX: (216)891-2726
URL: http://www.advanstar.com
Monthly. $36.00 per year.

THE SOURCE: WOODWORKING INDUSTRY DIRECTORY
Cahners Publishing Co.
PO Box 5080
Des Plaines, IL 60017-5080
PH: (800)662-7776
FX: (847)390-2618
E-mail: marketaccess@cahners.com
URL: http://www.cahners.com
Annual. $25.00. A product-classified listing of more than 1,800 suppliers to the furniture and cabinet industries.

STANDARD HANDBOOK FOR CIVIL ENGINEERS
McGraw-Hill
1221 Ave. of the Americas
New York, NY 10020
PH: (800)722-4726
FX: (212)512-2821
Frederick S. Merritt and others. 1995. $120.00. Fourth edition.

STANDARD HANDBOOK OF STRUCTURAL DETAILS FOR BUILDING CONSTRUCTION
McGraw-Hill
1221 Ave. of the Americas
New York, NY 10020
PH: (800)722-4726
FX: (212)512-2821
Morton Newman. 1993. $99.95. Second edition.

THE SUBCONTRACTOR
American Subcontractors Association
1004 Duke St.
Alexandria, VA 22314-3588
PH: (703)684-3450
Monthly. $40.00 per year.

TILE AND DECORATIVE SURFACES
Tile and Decorative Surfaces Co.
6300 Variel Ave., Ste. 1
Woodland Hills, CA 91367-2513
PH: (800)401-9215
FX: (818)704-6500
E-mail: trademags@earthlink.net
URL: http://www.infotile.com
Monthly. $50.00 per year.

TILE AND DECORATIVE SURFACES: DIRECTORY AND PURCHASING GUIDE ISSUE
Tile and Decorative Surfaces Co.
6300 Variel Ave., Ste. 1
Woodland Hills, CA 91367-2513
PH: (800)401-9215
FX: (818)704-6500
E-mail: trademags@earthlink.net
URL: http://www.infotile.com
Annual. $20.00. List of over 2,000 manufacturers and distributors of the products and tile setting materials.

TILE DESIGN AND INSTALLATION
Business News Publishing Co.
755 W. Big Beaver, 10th Fl.
Troy, MI 48084
PH: (800)837-7370
URL: http://www.bnp.com
Quarterly. $55.00 per year.

U.S. FLOOR COVERINGS INDUSTRY
Available from FIND/SVP, Inc.
625 Ave. of the Americas
New York, NY 10011-2002
PH: (800)346-3787
FX: (212)807-2716
E-mail: catalog@findsvp.com
URL: http://www.findsvp.com
1997. $995.00. Market research report published by specialists in business information. Covers carpets, hardwood flooring, and tile. Presents market data relative to demographics, sales growth, shipments, exports, imports, price trends, and end-use. Includes company profiles.

U.S. GLASS, METAL, AND GLAZING
Key Communications, Inc.
PO Box 569
Garrisonville, VA 22463
PH: (540)720-5584
FX: (540)720-5687
E-mail: usglass@aol.com
URL: http://www.usglass.com
Monthly. $35.00 per year. Edited for glass fabricators, glaziers, distributors, and retailers. Special feature issues are devoted to architectural glass, mirror glass, windows, storefronts, hardware, machinery, sealants, and adhesives. Regular topics include automobile glass and fenestration (window design and placement).

U.S. HOUSING MARKETS
Lomas Mortgage USA
33300 Five Mile Rd., Ste. 202
Livonia, MI 48154
PH: (800)755-6269
FX: (313)397-2020
Quarterly. $180.00 per year. Includes eight interim reports. Provides data on residential building permits, apartment building completions, rental vacancy rates, sales of existing homes, average home prices, housing affordability, etc. All major U.S. cities and areas are covered.

UNITED STATES CENSUS OF CONSTRUCTION INDUSTRIES
U.S. Bureau of the Census
Washington, DC 20233-0800
PH: (202)512-1800
FX: (202)512-2250
URL: http://www.census.gov
Quinquennial. Results presented in reports, tape, and CD-ROM files.

VALUE OF NEW CONSTRUCTION PUT IN PLACE
Available from U.S. Government Printing Office
Washington, DC 20402
PH: (202)512-1800
FX: (202)512-2250
U.S. Bureau of the Census. Monthly. $27.00 per year.

VINYL SHEET AND FLOOR TILE
Available from FIND/SVP, Inc.
625 Ave. of the Americas
New York, NY 10011-2002
PH: (800)346-3787
FX: (212)807-2716
E-mail: catalog@findsvp.com
URL: http://www.findsvp.com
1997. $995.00. Market research report published by specialists in business information. Presents vinyl flooring market data relative to demographics, sales growth, shipments, exports, imports, price trends, and end-use. Includes company profiles.

WINDOWS
Available from FIND/SVP, Inc.
625 Ave. of the Americas
New York, NY 10011-2002

PH: (800)346-3787
FX: (212)807-2716
E-mail: catalog@findsvp.com
URL: http://www.findsvp.com
1997. $995.00. Market research report published by specialists in business information. Covers metal, wood, and vinyl windows. Presents market data relative to demographics, sales growth, shipments, exports, imports, price trends, and end-use. Includes company profiles.

WOOD DIGEST
Johnson Hill Press, Inc.
PO Box 803
Fort Atkinson, WI 53538-0803
PH: (800)547-7377
FX: (414)536-1701
Monthly. $50.00 per year.

***WOOD AND WOOD PRODUCTS: FURNITURE, CABINETS,
    WOODWORKING AND ALLIED PRODUCTS
    MANAGEMENT AND OPERATIONS***
Vance Publishing Corp.
PO Box 1414
Lincolnshire, IL 60069-1414
PH: (800)621-2845
FX: (708)634-4379
Monthly. $45.00 per year.

WOODTURNER'S BIBLE
TAB Books, Inc.
11 W. 19th St.
New York, NY 10011-4285
PH: (212)337-4097
FX: (212)337-6056
Percy Blandford. 1990. $26.95. Third edition.

***WOODWORKING FACTBOOK: BASIC INFORMATION ON
    WOOD FOR WOOD CARVERS, HOME WOODSHOP
    CRAFTSMEN, TRADESMEN AND INSTRUCTORS***
Robert Speller and Sons Publishers, Inc.
Madison Square Sta.
PO Box 411
New York, NY 10159
PH: (212)473-0333
Donald G. Coleman. $22.50.

Information presented in this chapter is adapted from Gale's *Trade Shows Worldwide* (*TSW*). Entries present information needed for all those planning to visit or to participate in trade shows for the Construction sector. *TSW* entries include U.S. and Canadian shows and exhibitions.

Entries are arranged in alphabetical order by the name of the event and include the exhibition management company with full contact information, frequency of the event, audience, and principal exhibits.

A/E/C SYSTEMS AND CFC FALL
415 Eagleview Blvd., Ste. 106
Exton, PA 19341-1153
PH: (610)458-7070
TF: (800)451-1196
FX: (610)458-7171
URL: http://www.aecsystems.com
Frequency: Annual. **Audience:** Construction professionals, including architects, engineers, facility managers, surveyors, managers, subcontractors, and home builders. **Principal Exhibits:** Computer hardware and software for the construction industry, including scheduling, estimating, design, office, and project management systems, and information on management consultant services. **Held in conjunction with:** A/E/C Systems Show; Build USA Fall; Construction Maryland; JointCost Management Societies Symposium.

A/E/C SYSTEMS\INTERNATIONAL COMPUTER AND MANAGEMENT SHOW FOR THE DESIGN AND CONSTRUCTION INDUSTRIES
415 Eagleview Blvd., Ste. 106
Exton, PA 19341-1153
PH: (610)458-7070
TF: (800)451-1196
FX: (610)458-7171
URL: http://www.aecsystems.com
Frequency: Annual. **Audience:** Design and construction professionals. **Principal Exhibits:** Architects, designers, civil Eng., Surveyors, power and process Eng., GIS, contractors, facilities managers/ owners, mechanical, manufacturing engineers. **Incorporating:** Autodesk Expo; Bentley MicroStation Mall; Build USA; Construction LosAngeles; E/NET.

AGC CONSTRUCTOR EXHIBITION
1957 E. St., NW
Washington, DC 20006-5107
PH: (202)393-2040
FX: (202)628-7369
Frequency: Annual. **Audience:** Contractors, subcontractors, and trade professionals. **Principal Exhibits:** Heavy and light construction equipment, trucks, building materials, and management services.

AMERICA EAST CONVENTION AND EXPOSITION
585 N. Greenbush Rd.
Rensselaer, NY 12144-9453
PH: (518)286-1010
TF: (800)292-6752
FX: (518)286-1755
E-mail: clnrla@aol.com
URL: http://www.nrla.org/
Frequency: Annual. **Audience:** Building material retailers, architects and contractors. **Principal Exhibits:** Building material products, services and technologies.

AMERICAN INSTITUTE OF BUILDING DESIGN ANNUAL CONVENTION
991 Post Rd. East
Westport, CT 06880
PH: (203)227-3640
TF: (800)366-2423
FX: (203)227-8624
Frequency: Annual. **Audience:** Building designers, drafting professionals, architects, and builders. **Principal Exhibits:** Building products, including: roofing, windows, doors, floor covering, fire places, spas/jacuzzis, lumber, intercom systems, alarm systems, and appliances; computer-aid design technology, computer hardware/ software, and plan publishers.

AMERICAN SOCIETY OF PLUMBING ENGINEERS MEETING
3617 Thousand Oaks Blvd., No. 210
Westlake Village, CA 91362-3649

PH: (805)495-7120
FX: (805)495-4861
E-mail: aspehq@aol.com
Frequency: Biennial. **Principal Exhibits:** Exhibits for the plumbing engineering industry.

AMERICAN SUPPLY ASSOCIATION CONFERENCE
222 Merchandise Mart, Ste. 1360
Chicago, IL 60654-1202
PH: (312)464-0090
FX: (312)464-0091
E-mail: asaemail@interserv.com
URL: http://www.asanet.com
Frequency: Biennial. **Principal Exhibits:** Equipment, supplies, and services for wholesalers, distributors, and manufacturers of plumbing and heating pipes, valves, and fittings.

ATLANTIC BUILDING MATERIALS SHOW
95 Foundry St., Ste. 203
Moncton, NB, Canada E1C 5H7
PH: (506)858-0700
FX: (506)859-0064
E-mail: absda@nbnet.nb.ca
Frequency: Annual. **Audience:** Dealers, manufacturers, distributors, builders, architects, and government officials. **Principal Exhibits:** Building materials and hardware.

BATIMAT NORTH AMERICA, THE INTERNATIONAL CONSTRUCTION INDUSTRY EXPOSITION
1 Penn Plaza
New York, NY 10119-0002
PH: (212)714-1300
TF: (800)829-3976
FX: (212)643-4803
Frequency: Annual. **Principal Exhibits:** Building industry equipment, supplies, and services. **Held in conjunction with:** InterPlan.

BAUTECH/STROYTECH\INTERNATIONAL TRADE FAIR FOR THE BUILDING ENGINEERING AND CITY RE-DEVELOPMENT
PO Box 2460
Germantown, MD 20875-2460
PH: (301)515-0012
FX: (301)515-0016
E-mail: glahe@glahe.com
Frequency: Biennial. **Principal Exhibits:** Building, road construction, construction and city re-development projects.

BRICK SHOW
11490 Commerce Park Dr.
Reston, VA 22091
PH: (703)620-0010
FX: (703)620-3928
URL: http://www.bia.org
Frequency: Annual. **Audience:** Brick distributors, manufacturers, and industry suppliers. **Principal Exhibits:** Displays related to the brick industry.

BUFFALO CONSTRUCTION EXPO
431 Ohio Pike, Ste. 104 S.
Cincinnati, OH 45255
PH: (704)331-9095
FX: (704)344-0504
Principal Exhibits: Equipment, supplies, and services for the construction industry.

BUILD EXPO
383 Main Ave.
PO Box 6059
Norwalk, CT 06851
PH: (203)840-5358
FX: (203)840-4804
E-mail: inquiry@nepcon.reedexpo.com

Frequency: Annual. **Principal Exhibits:** Equipment, supplies, and services for building.

THE BUILDERS' SHOW
1201 15th St. NW
Washington, DC 20005-2800
PH: (202)861-2109
TF: (800)368-5242
FX: (202)861-2104
URL: http://www.nahb.com/expos
Frequency: Annual. **Audience:** Trade. **Principal Exhibits:** Building products, equipment, and services.

BUILDERS TRADE SHOW
1738 Elton Rd., Ste. 200
Silver Spring, MD 20903-1725
PH: (301)925-9486
FX: (301)925-9411
Frequency: Annual. **Principal Exhibits:** Construction equipment, supplies, and services.

BUILDEX/BC CONSTRUCTION SHOW
1755 W. Broadway, Ste. 206
Vancouver, BC, Canada V6J 4S5
PH: (604)739-2112
FX: (604)739-2124
Frequency: Annual. **Audience:** Building and hardware retailers, architects, and allied building industry trade. **Principal Exhibits:** Building construction and hardware equipment, supplies, and services.

BUILDING COMPONENT & MANUFACTURING CONFERENCE
5937 Meadowood Dr., Ste. 14
Madison, WI 53711-4125
PH: (608)274-4849
FX: (608)274-3329
E-mail: wtca@woodtruss.com
URL: http://www.woodtruss.com
Frequency: Annual. **Principal Exhibits:** Structural wood components and related articles.

THE BUILDING INDUSTRY SHOW
1330 S. Valley Vista Dr.
Diamond Bar, CA 91765
PH: (909)396-9993
FX: (909)396-9846
E-mail: biasocal@ix.netcom.com
Frequency: Annual. **Audience:** Builders, contractors, and related building industry professionals. **Principal Exhibits:** Products and services for the building industry.

BUILDING MATERIALS EXPO
1727 Dillingham Blvd.
Honolulu, HI 96819
PH: (808)847-4666
FX: (808)842-0129
E-mail: bia@pixi.com
Frequency: Annual. **Audience:** Architects, builders, developers, designers, specifiers, engineers, realtors, subcontractors, and other principals from the building industry. **Principal Exhibits:** Materials and services used in the building trade.

BUILDING PRODUCTS SHOWCASE
PO Box 1699
Olympia, WA 98507-1699
PH: (360)943-3054
FX: (360)943-1219
Frequency: Annual. **Audience:** Building material and home center retail dealers and nonmember trade professionals. **Principal Exhibits:** Building materials and services.

BUILDING AND REPAIR
PO Box 2460
Germantown, MD 20875-2460
PH: (301)515-0012
FX: (301)515-0016
E-mail: glahe@glahe.com
Principal Exhibits: Building and repair equipment, supplies, and services.

BUILDINGS SHOW
The Merchandise Mart, Ste. 470
200 World Trade Center
Chicago, IL 60654
PH: (312)527-7979
FX: (312)527-7888
Frequency: Annual. **Audience:** Trade professionals. **Principal Exhibits:** Building products and commercial furnishings and finishes.

CALGARY HOME AND GARDEN SHOW
999 8th St. SW, Ste. 300
Calgary, AB, Canada T2R 1N7
PH: (403)209-3555
TF: (888)799-2545
FX: (403)244-5517
URL: http://www.southex.com
Frequency: Annual. **Audience:** General public. **Principal Exhibits:** Interior and exterior home products; home and garden supplies.

CALGARY HOME & INTERIOR DESIGN SHOW
999 8th St. SW, Ste. 300
Calgary, AB, Canada T2R 1N7
PH: (403)209-3555
TF: (888)799-2545
FX: (403)244-5517
URL: http://www.southex.com
Frequency: Annual. **Audience:** General public. **Principal Exhibits:** Products and services for the home, including electrical, plumbing, heating, and air conditioning equipment; building products, paints, roofing, and insulation; hardware, tools, and appliances; floor coverings; landscaping equipment and supplies; interior decorations; furnishings; antiques; and home entertainment equipment.

CAM EXPO WEST
1625 S. Woodward
PO Box 3204
Bloomfield Hills, MI 48302
PH: (248)972-1000
FX: (248)972-1001
Frequency: Annual. **Audience:** Construction professionals. **Principal Exhibits:** Construction equipment, products, and services.

CENTRAL PENNSYLVANIA INDUSTRIAL AND CONSTRUCTION SHOW
164 Lake Front Dr.
Cockeysville, MD 21030-2215
PH: (410)252-1167
TF: (800)638-6396
FX: (410)560-0477
E-mail: info@isoa.com
URL: http://www.isoa.com
Frequency: Annual. **Principal Exhibits:** Industrial and construction equipment, supplies, and services.

CHARLOTTE CONSTRUCTION EXPO
800 Briar Creek Rd., Ste. DD-507
Charlotte, NC 28205
PH: (704)344-8136
FX: (704)342-0760
E-mail: expo_group@pol.com
Frequency: Annual. **Principal Exhibits:** Construction equipment, supplies, and services.

CHICAGO BUILDINGS & REAL ESTATE SHOW
383 Main Ave.
PO Box 6059
Norwalk, CT 06851
PH: (203)840-5358
FX: (203)840-4804
E-mail: inquiry@nepcon.reedexpo.com
Frequency: Annual. **Audience:** Property managers, owners, managers, architects, engineers and designers. **Principal Exhibits:** Products and services needed to build, operate and maintain, renovate and restore buildings.

CINCINNATI CONSTRUCTION EXPO
431 Ohio Pike, Ste. 104 S.
Cincinnati, OH 45255
PH: (704)331-9095
FX: (704)344-0504
Frequency: Annual. **Audience:** Business professionals. **Principal Exhibits:** Building products and services for architects, contractors, and builders.

CIPHEX TORONTO
295 The West Mall, Ste. 330
Toronto, ON, Canada M9C 4Z4
PH: (416)695-0447
TF: (800)NEX-CIPH
FX: (416)695-0450
E-mail: ciph@ican.net
URL: http://www.ciph.com
Frequency: Biennial. **Audience:** Trade only. **Principal Exhibits:** Plumbing, heating, refrigeration, ventilation and air-conditioning trades equipment, supplies, and services.

CIPHEX/WEST
295 The West Mall, Ste. 330
Toronto, ON, Canada M9C 4Z4
PH: (416)695-0447
TF: (800)NEX-CIPH
FX: (416)695-0450
E-mail: ciph@ican.net
URL: http://www.ciph.com
Frequency: Biennial. **Audience:** Trade professionals. **Principal Exhibits:** Plumbing, heating, refrigeration, ventilating and air-conditioning trades equipment, supplies, and services.

CONEX\CONNECTICUT CONSTRUCTION EXPOSITION
94 Murphy Rd.
Hartford, CT 06114
PH: (860)247-8363
TF: (800)753-9776
FX: (860)947-6900
URL: http://www.keypro.com
Frequency: Annual. **Audience:** Construction and related trades, including subcontractors, public works and municipal officials. **Principal Exhibits:** Construction equipment, supplies, and services.

CONEXPO-CON/AGG
111 E. Wisconsin Ave., Ste. 1000
Milwaukee, WI 53202-4879
PH: (414)272-0943
TF: (800)867-6060
FX: (414)272-2672
E-mail: conexpo@cimanet.com
URL: http://www.conexpoconagg.com
Frequency: Triennial. **Audience:** Construction and related equipment contractors, manufacturers, distributors, engineers, and government officials. **Principal Exhibits:** Construction industry equipment, supplies, and services.

CONSTRUCO\INTERNATIONAL EXHIBITION OF THE CONSTRUCTION INDUSTRY
Av. Fundidora 501, Local 22
Col. Obrera
64010 Monterrey, Nuevo Leon, Mexico

PH: 8 369 6660
Principal Exhibits: Construction equipment, supplies, and services.

CONSTRUCTION FINANCIAL MANAGEMENT ASSOCIATION ANNUAL CONFERENCE AND EXHIBITION
Princeton Gateway Corporate Campus
707 State Rd., Ste. 223
Princeton, NJ 08540-1413
PH: (609)683-5000
FX: (609)683-4821
E-mail: conferences@cfma.org
URL: http://www.cfma.org
Frequency: Annual. **Audience:** Contractors, subcontractors, architects, real estate developers, and engineers. **Principal Exhibits:** Equipment, supplies, and services for the construction industry.

CONSTRUCTION MATERIALS RECYCLING SEMINAR
6300 South Syracuse Way, Ste. 650
Englewood, CO 80111
PH: (303)220-0600
FX: (303)770-0253
URL: http://www.intertec.com
Audience: Recyclers, crushed stone producers, construction and demolition contractors, concrete producers, sand/gravel/asphalt producers, gypsum manufacturers, etc. **Principal Exhibits:** Construction and demolition manufacturing supplies.

CONSTRUCTION SPECIFICATIONS INSTITUTE ANNUAL CONVENTION EXHIBIT
601 Madison St.
Alexandria, VA 22314-1791
PH: (703)684-0300
TF: (800)689-2900
FX: (703)684-0465
E-mail: csimail@csinet.org
URL: http://www.csinet.org
Frequency: Annual. **Audience:** Architects, Contractors, designers, owners, facility managers, engineers. **Principal Exhibits:** Products and services used in non-residential construction.

CONSTRUCTO EXPO
441 Boul. LeBeau
St. Laurent, PQ, Canada H4N 1S2
PH: (514)745-5720
FX: (514)339-2267
Frequency: Annual. **Audience:** Construction professionals, architects, engineers, designers, building owners, developers, municipal representatives. **Principal Exhibits:** Construction products, tools and equipment, and related services.

CUSTOM BUILDER CONFERENCE AND EXPO
13760 Noel Rd., Ste. 500
Dallas, TX 75240
PH: (972)239-3060
TF: (800)527-0207
FX: (972)419-7855
Frequency: Annual. **Principal Exhibits:** Construction equipment, supplies, and services.

DESIGN & CONSTRUCTION EXPO
1625 S. Woodward
PO Box 3204
Bloomfield Hills, MI 48302
PH: (248)972-1000
FX: (248)972-1001
Frequency: Annual. **Audience:** Trade professionals. **Principal Exhibits:** Construction industry equipment, supplies, and services.

DOOR AND HARDWARE INSTITUTE ANNUAL CONVENTION AND EXPOSITION
14170 Newbrook Dr.
Chantilly, VA 22021-2223

PH: (703)222-2010
FX: (703)222-2410
URL: http://www.dhi.org
Frequency: Annual. **Audience:** Industry distributors, sales representatives, and manufacturers; engineers; and facility administrators. **Principal Exhibits:** Doors, hardware, and specialty building products.

EASTERN CONVENTION & EXPO
604 E. Baltimore Pke.
Media, PA 19063
PH: (610)565-6144
TF: (800)296-EAST
FX: (610)565-0968
E-mail: office@ebmda.org
URL: http://www.ebmda.org
Frequency: Annual. **Audience:** Representatives from independent retail home centers and lumberyards; building material dealers. **Principal Exhibits:** Building industry equipment, supplies, and services.

EDMONTON HOME AND GARDEN SHOW
999 8th St. SW, Ste. 300
Calgary, AB, Canada T2R 1N7
PH: (403)209-3555
TF: (888)799-2545
FX: (403)244-5517
URL: http://www.southex.com
Frequency: Annual. **Audience:** General public. **Principal Exhibits:** Kitchen cabinets, furniture, fireplaces, interior design, renovation products, new construction.

**EM\ENVIRONMENTAL MANAGEMENT CONFERENCE
AND EXPOSITION**
USEPA
Federal Center
61 Forsythe St. SW
Atlanta, GA 30303
PH: (404)562-9900
Frequency: Annual. **Audience:** Building owners and facility managers, contractors, consultants, regulators, architects, engineers, and government agencies. **Principal Exhibits:** Equipment, supplies, and services for quantifying, managing or remediating environmental hazards in buildings, and facilities.

FORT WORTH CONSTRUCTION EXPO
431 Ohio Pike, Ste. 104 S.
Cincinnati, OH 45255
PH: (704)331-9095
FX: (704)344-0504
Principal Exhibits: Construction equipment, supplies, and services.

**GULF INTERNATIONAL EXHIBITION\INTERNATIONAL
TRADE FAIR FOR BUILDING, CONSTRUCTION, PUBLIC
WORKS, ELECTRONIC ENGINEERING, AND
CONSUMER GOODS**
PO Box 2460
Germantown, MD 20875-2460
PH: (301)515-0012
FX: (301)515-0016
E-mail: glahe@glahe.com
Frequency: Biennial. **Principal Exhibits:** Building, construction, public works, electrical equipment, electronic engineering, communication, office systems, education, production technology, material transport and consumer goods.

THE HOME AUTOMATION SHOW & CONFERENCE
383 Main Ave.
PO Box 6059
Norwalk, CT 06851
PH: (203)840-5358
FX: (203)840-4804
E-mail: inquiry@nepcon.reedexpo.com
Frequency: Annual. **Audience:** Dealers, installers, distributors,

contractors, service providers and utility engineers. **Principal Exhibits:** Home automation, equipment and services.

HOME AND GARDEN EXPO SHOW AND SALE
1801 MacKay
Regina, SK, Canada S4N 6E7
PH: (306)757-0322
FX: (306)569-9144
Frequency: Annual. **Principal Exhibits:** Home building and remodeling equipment, supplies, and services.

HOME AND GARDEN TRADE SHOW/LETHBRIDGE
3401 S. Parkside Dr. S.
Lethbridge, AB, Canada T1J 4R3
PH: (403)328-4491
FX: (403)320-8139
E-mail: lethexhb@telusplanet.net
URL: http://www.telusplanet.net/public/lethexhb
Frequency: Annual. **Audience:** General public, including home and apartment owners and equipment suppliers. **Principal Exhibits:** Home building materials, cabinets, interior furnishings and fixtures, and landscaping supplies.

HOME IDEAS & LIFESTYLES SHOW
7895 49th Ave., Ste. 10
Red Deer, AB, Canada T4P 2B4
PH: (403)346-5321
FX: (403)342-1301
E-mail: cahba@rttinc.com
URL: http://www.albertaweb.com/cahba
Frequency: Annual. **Audience:** Central Alberta. **Principal Exhibits:** Shelter construction and related products.

**ICCON\INTERNATIONAL COMMERCIAL
CONSTRUCTION EXPOSITION**
1201 15th St. NW
Washington, DC 20005-2800
PH: (202)861-2109
TF: (800)368-5242
FX: (202)861-2104
URL: http://www.nahb.com/expos
Audience: Trade. **Principal Exhibits:** Equipment, supplies, and services for the construction industries. **Held in conjunction with:** International Builders' Show.

**ICUEE\INTERNATIONAL CONSTRUCTION AND UTILITY
EQUIPMENT EXPOSITION**
10 S. Riverside Plaza, Ste. 1220
Chicago, IL 60606-3710
PH: (312)321-1470
FX: (312)321-1480
Frequency: Biennial. **Audience:** Professionals in the utility, construction, outside plant/telco and electric power industries. **Principal Exhibits:** Utility and construction equipment, supplies, and services.

**ILLINOIS ASSOCIATION OF PLUMBING, HEATING, AND
COOLING CONTRACTORS CONVENTION AND EXPO**
821 S. Grand Ave., W.
Springfield, IL 62704
PH: (217)522-7219
FX: (217)522-4315
Frequency: Annual. **Audience:** Architects, engineers, plumbing inspectors, and plumbers. **Principal Exhibits:** Plumbing, heating, and air conditioning products.

INDIANAPOLIS CONSTRUCTION EXPO
431 Ohio Pike, Ste. 104 S.
Cincinnati, OH 45255
PH: (704)331-9095
FX: (704)344-0504
Principal Exhibits: Equipment, supplies, and services for the construction industry.

INTERNATIONAL ASSOCIATION OF PLUMBING AND
MECHANICAL OFFICIALS CONFERENCE
20001 Walnut Dr. S
Walnut, CA 91789-2825
PH: (909)595-8449
FX: (909)594-3690
E-mail: iapmo@earthlink.net
URL: http://www.iapmo.org
Frequency: Annual. **Audience:** Plumbing industry. **Principal Exhibits:** Plumbing equipment, supplies, and services.

INTERNATIONAL CEMENT SEMINAR
6300 South Syracuse Way, Ste. 650
Englewood, CO 80111
PH: (303)220-0600
FX: (303)770-0253
URL: http://www.intertec.com
Audience: Executive and senior management level cement plant operators. **Principal Exhibits:** Products and services for the cement production industry.

INTERNATIONAL ROAD FEDERATION MEETING
2600 Virginia Ave., NW Ste. 208
Washington, DC 20037
PH: (202)338-4641
FX: (202)338-8104
Audience: Road associations, private sector firms, and public sector firms. **Principal Exhibits:** Road and highway transportation improvement equipment, supplies, and services.

IOWA LUMBER CONVENTION
1405 Lilac Dr. N., Ste. 130
Golden Valley, MN 55422
PH: (612)544-6822
FX: (612)544-0820
URL: http://www.NLASSN.org
Frequency: Annual. **Audience:** Retail lumber and building material dealers. **Principal Exhibits:** Products and services ultimately sold or used by retail lumber and building material dealers.

KENTUCKY ASSOCIATION OF PLUMBING, HEATING,
AND COOLING CONTRACTORS CONVENTION
1501 Durrett Ln.
Louisville, KY 40213
PH: (502)451-5577
FX: (502)451-5551
Frequency: Annual. **Audience:** Plumbing contractors and heating and cooling contractors. **Principal Exhibits:** Plumbing, heating, and air conditioning equipment, supplies, and services.

LITS\LONDON INDUSTRIAL TECHNOLOGY SHOW
383 Main Ave.
PO Box 6059
Norwalk, CT 06851
PH: (203)840-5358
FX: (203)840-4804
E-mail: inquiry@nepcon.reedexpo.com
Frequency: Biennial. **Audience:** Engineers, maintenance and plant managers. **Principal Exhibits:** Materials handling, welding, fabricating equipment, supplies,, and services.

MASCON MASSACHUSETTS CONSTRUCTION EXPO
2302 Horse Pen Rd.
Herndon, VA 22071-3499
PH: (703)713-1900
FX: (703)713-1910
URL: http://www.ncma.org
Frequency: Biennial. **Audience:** Construction industry and related professionals, including architects, engineers, contractors, and construction firm owners and managers. **Principal Exhibits:** Construction equipment, supplies, and services.

MASON CONTRACTORS ASSOCIATION OF AMERICA
CONVENTION
1550 Spring Rd., Ste. 320
Oakbrook, IL 60521
PH: (708)782-6767
FX: (708)620-6767
Frequency: Annual. **Audience:** Mason contractors and related industry officials. **Principal Exhibits:** Masonry equipment, supplies, and services.

MASONRY EXPO
2302 Horse Pen Rd.
Herndon, VA 22071-3499
PH: (703)713-1900
FX: (703)713-1910
URL: http://www.ncma.org
Frequency: Annual. **Audience:** Manufacturers of concrete block, concrete pavers, mason contractors, brick manufacturers and distributors, architects, contractors, and builders. **Principal Exhibits:** Masonry equipment, supplies, and services.

MASSACHUSETTS ASSOCIATION OF PLUMBING/
HEATING/COOLING CONTRACTORS CONVENTION
AND TRADESHOW
178 Forbes Rd., Ste. 218
Braintree, MA 02184
PH: (617)843-3800
TF: (800)542-7422
FX: (781)843-1178
E-mail: phcc@shore.net
Frequency: Biennial. **Audience:** Trade professionals and the general public. **Principal Exhibits:** Plumbing, heating and cooling equipment, supplies, and services.

MECANEX
8175 Boul. St. Laurent
Montreal, PQ, Canada H2P 2M1
PH: (514)382-2668
FX: (514)382-1566
Frequency: Annual. **Audience:** Mechanical contracting industry professional. **Principal Exhibits:** New products, services and technologies in plumbing, heating, air-conditioning, fire-protection, ventilation and refrigeration. Also tools, equipment, and services for contractors.

METALCON INTERNATIONAL TRADE SHOW
10 Midland Ave.
Newton, MA 02158
PH: (617)965-0055
TF: (800)526-5455
FX: (617)965-5152
Frequency: Annual. **Audience:** Architects, engineers, contractors, building owners, and developers. **Principal Exhibits:** Building systems components supplies, accessories and services for the metal construction industry.

MIACON\MIAMI INTERNATIONAL CONSTRUCTION
SHOW/EXPO
3400 Coral Way, 3rd Fl.
Miami, FL 33145
PH: (305)441-2865
FX: (305)529-9217
E-mail: miacon@wwen.com
URL: http://www.miacon.com
Frequency: Annual. **Audience:** Qualified buyers from Latin America, the Caribbean, Brazil and southeastern U.S. **Principal Exhibits:** Equipment, machinery, supplies, and services for the construction, and mining industries. **Held in conjunction with:** Miamin, The Miami International Mining Show.

MID-AMERICA HARDWARE & BUILDING MATERIALS
EXPOSITION
6321 Blue Ridge Blvd.
Kansas City, MO 64133-4809

PH: (816)931-2102
Frequency: Annual. **Audience:** Home center operators, retail lumber and building materials dealers, and hardware dealers. **Principal Exhibits:** Building materials and hardware products.

MIDWEST CONTRACTORS EXPO
320 Laura St.
Wichita, KS 67211
PH: (316)262-8860
FX: (316)262-2782
Frequency: Annual. **Principal Exhibits:** Plumbing, heating and cooling equipment, supplies, and services.

MISSISSIPPI BUILDING PRODUCTS TRADE SHOW
PO Box 474
Carthage, MS 39051-0474
PH: (601)267-5522
FX: (601)267-5522
Frequency: Annual. **Audience:** Building material retailers. **Principal Exhibits:** Building materials and related equipment, supplies, and services.

MOS-CON
5995 Bent Pine Dr., No. 3311
Orlando, FL 32822
PH: (407)851-7222
FX: (407)851-0950
E-mail: expocorp@compuserve.com
Frequency: Annual. **Audience:** Buyers, government leaders, industry and finance. **Principal Exhibits:** Construction, quarry, aggregate, publics works, waste management equipment, products services and publications.

NATIONAL ASSOCIATION OF DEMOLITION CONTRACTORS ANNUAL CONVENTION
16 N. Franklin St.
Doylestown, PA 18901
PH: (215)348-4949
TF: (800)541-2412
FX: (215)348-8422
Frequency: Annual. **Audience:** Demolition contractors and equipment manufacturers. **Principal Exhibits:** Demolition equipment, supplies, and services.

NATIONAL BUILDING PRODUCTS EXPOSITION & CONFERENCE
383 Main Ave.
PO Box 6059
Norwalk, CT 06851
PH: (203)840-5358
FX: (203)840-4804
E-mail: inquiry@nepcon.reedexpo.com
Frequency: Annual. **Audience:** Building products retailers and manufacturers; contractors; architects. **Principal Exhibits:** Building products and related equipment, supplies, and services. **Held in conjunction with:** National Hardware Show.

NATIONAL FRAME BUILDERS CONFERENCE AND RURAL BUILDER SHOW
4840 W. 15th St., Ste. 1000
Lawrence, KS 66049-3876
PH: (913)843-2444
TF: (800)557-6957
FX: (913)843-7555
E-mail: nfba@postframe.org
Frequency: Annual. **Audience:** Rural contractors. **Principal Exhibits:** Products and services related to post-frame construction.

NATIONAL HARDWARE SHOW
383 Main Ave.
PO Box 6059
Norwalk, CT 06851

PH: (203)840-5358
FX: (203)840-4804
E-mail: inquiry@nepcon.reedexpo.com
Frequency: Annual. **Audience:** Wholesalers, mass merchandisers, and hardware, home center, and lawn and garden retailers and dealers. **Principal Exhibits:** Hardware; lawn and garden equipment; outdoor living, home improvement, and building products, automotive aftermarket products, and retail information technology. **Held in conjunction with:** National Building Products Exposition and Conference.

NATIONAL PAVEMENT MAINTENANCE EXPOSITION AND CONFERENCE
426 S. Westgate
Addison, IL 60101
PH: (630)543-0870
TF: (800)837-0870
FX: (630)543-3112
Frequency: Annual. **Audience:** Pavement contractors, distributors, and dealers of pavement maintenance products and equipment, and property owners and managers. **Principal Exhibits:** Pavement maintenance equipment, supplies, and services.

NATIONAL PLUMBING-HEATING-COOLING PIPING PRODUCERS EXPOSITION
180 S. Washington St.
PO Box 6808
Falls Church, VA 22046
PH: (703)237-8100
TF: (800)533-7694
FX: (703)237-7442
Frequency: Annual. **Principal Exhibits:** Equipment, supplies, and services for plumbing, heating, and cooling.

NEBRASKA BUILDING PRODUCTS EXPO
6321 Blue Ridge Blvd.
Kansas City, MO 64133-4809
PH: (816)931-2102
Principal Exhibits: Building products exhibition.

NEW ENGLAND HOME SHOW
383 Main Ave.
PO Box 6059
Norwalk, CT 06851
PH: (203)840-5358
FX: (203)840-4804
E-mail: inquiry@nepcon.reedexpo.com
Frequency: Annual. **Audience:** Home owners, prospective home owners, condominium owners, apartment dwellers, and general public. **Principal Exhibits:** Homebuilding and improvement equipment, supplies, and services, including bathroom and kitchen supplies, building materials, appliances, doors and windows, swimming pools, hot tubs, and spas.

NEX\NORTH AMERICAN EXPOSITION
295 The West Mall, Ste. 330
Toronto, ON, Canada M9C 4Z4
PH: (416)695-0447
TF: (800)NEX-CIPH
FX: (416)695-0450
E-mail: ciph@ican.net
URL: http://www.ciph.com
Frequency: Biennial. **Audience:** Contractors, distributors, specifiers, architects, engineers, interior designers. **Principal Exhibits:** Plumbing, heating, and cooling contractors, wholesalers, distributors, manufacturers, representatives.

NORTH AMERICAN BUILDING MATERIAL DISTRIBUTION ASSOCIATION CONVENTION
401 N. Michigan Ave.
Chicago, IL 60611

PH: (312)321-6845
TF: (888)747-7862
FX: (312)644-0310
E-mail: nbmda@sba.com
URL: http://www.nbmda.org
Frequency: Annual. **Audience:** wholesale distributors of building materials and specialty products. **Principal Exhibits:** Building materials and specialty products marketed through wholesale distributors, and distribution support services.

NORTHWESTERN BUILDING PRODUCTS EXPO
1405 Lilac Dr. N., Ste. 130
Golden Valley, MN 55422
PH: (612)544-6822
FX: (612)544-0820
URL: http://www.NLASSN.org
Frequency: Annual. **Audience:** Retail lumber and building material dealers. **Principal Exhibits:** Any product or service that is ultimately sold or used by retail lumber and building material dealers.

THE OHIO PLUMBING HEATING COOLING EXPO
18961 Rivers Edge Dr.
Chagrin Falls, OH 44023
PH: (216)543-4011
FX: (216)543-1699
E-mail: OHIOPHCC@aol.com
Frequency: Annual. **Principal Exhibits:** Products, tools, and services used by plumbing and heating contractors.

PHILCONTRUCT\INTERNATIONAL TRADE FAIR FOR CONSTRUCTION AND BUILDING MATERIALS
20 Harrison Ave.
Waldwick, NJ 07463-1709
PH: (201)652-7070
FX: (201)652-3898
E-mail: 74161.1167@compuserve.com
URL: http://www.kallman.com
Principal Exhibits: Equipment, supplies, and services for the construction industry.

POWER SHOW OHIO
6124 Avery Rd.
PO Box 68
Dublin, OH 43017
PH: (614)889-1309
FX: (614)889-0463
Frequency: Annual. **Audience:** Trade professionals and general public. **Principal Exhibits:** Construction equipment, agricultural equipment, and outdoor power equipment.

PROMIT INTERNATIONAL EXPO
Gardens Plaza Bldg.
3300 PGA Blvd., Ste. 520
Palm Beach Gardens, FL 33410
PH: (407)624-1139
FX: (407)625-4042
E-mail: npbc@disasters-hazardmit.org
URL: http://www.disasters-hazardmit.org
Principal Exhibits: Equipment, supplies, and services for the protection of buildings against natural and human-made disasters such as hurricanes, earthquakes, floods, fires, explosions, slides, terrorism, and environmental problems.

RAPID EXCAVATION & TUNNELING CONFERENCE
PO Box 625002
Littleton, CO 80162
PH: (303)973-9550
TF: (800)763-3132
FX: (303)979-3461
E-mail: smenet@aol.com
URL: http://www.smenet.org
Principal Exhibits: Excavation equipment.

REHVAC\THE INTERNATIONAL HEATING, VENTILATING AND AIR-CONDITIONING EXPOSITION
383 Main Ave.
PO Box 6059
Norwalk, CT 06851
PH: (203)840-5358
FX: (203)840-4804
E-mail: inquiry@nepcon.reedexpo.com
Frequency: Annual. **Audience:** Trade professionals. **Principal Exhibits:** Air-conditioning, refrigeration systems and parts, environmental protection systems.

RES-COM\THE PRESIDENTIAL & COMMERCIAL CONSTRUCTION EXPO/BUFFALO
3494 Delaware Ave.
Buffalo, NY 14217
PH: (716)871-1125
TF: (800)222-4465
FX: (716)871-9638
E-mail: ppminc@buffnet.net
Frequency: Annual. **Audience:** Construction buyers, specifiers, and architects. **Principal Exhibits:** Construction and building products and related equipment, supplies, and services.

RESTOREX/REFURBEX\PRODUCTS AND SERVICES FOR BUILDING RESTORATION AND REFURBISHMENT
PO Box 4105
Macon, GA 31208
Frequency: Biennial. **Audience:** Architects, builders, planners, designers, restorers, hotel owners, and home owners. **Principal Exhibits:** Windows, doors, stained glass, paints, wallpapers, structural cleaning equipment, bricks, timber, and related equipment and services.

RETAIL OPERATIONS AND CONSTRUCTION EXPO
1600 Golf Rd., Ste. 550
Rolling Meadows, IL 60005
PH: (847)290-0770
TF: (800)638-6296
FX: (847)290-0771
Frequency: Annual. **Audience:** Trade only; retailers, store designers, operations and construction professionals, brand marketers, visual merchandisers. **Principal Exhibits:** Overhead lighting, wall coverings, construction material, data processing equipment, and security systems. **Held in conjunction with:** GlobalShop; The Store Fixturing Show; The Visual Merchandising Show.

RICHMOND INDUSTRIAL AND CONSTRUCTION SHOW
164 Lake Front Dr.
Cockeysville, MD 21030-2215
PH: (410)252-1167
TF: (800)638-6396
FX: (410)560-0477
E-mail: info@isoa.com
URL: http://www.isoa.com
Frequency: Annual. **Audience:** Trade professionals. **Principal Exhibits:** Industrial equipment, supplies, and services.

SAE EARTHMOVING INDUSTRY CONFERENCE AND EXPOSITION
400 Commonwealth Dr.
Warrendale, PA 15096-0001
PH: (412)776-4841
FX: (412)776-0210
E-mail: meetings@sae.org
URL: http://www.sae.org
Frequency: Annual. **Principal Exhibits:** Earthmoving equipment and related propulsion systems, design, manufacturing, and maintenance.

**SHEET METAL AND AIR-CONDITIONING
  CONTRACTORS NATIONAL ASSOCIATION
  CONVENTION/EXHIBITION FORUM**
4201 Lafayette Center Dr.
PO Box 221230
Chantilly, VA 22022-1230
PH: (703)803-2980
FX: (703)803-3732
E-mail: info@smacna.org
URL: http://www.smacna.org
Frequency: Annual. **Audience:** Owners of sheet metal and air-conditioning contracting firms. **Principal Exhibits:** Limited to table tops only.

SHOWCASE
607 4th St. SE
Medicine Hat, AB, Canada T1A 0L1
PH: (403)527-5214
FX: (403)527-5182
Frequency: Annual. **Principal Exhibits:** Home handyman, food fair, auto village, images and lifestyles.

**SOUTHEAST ROOFING AND SHEET METAL
  SPECTACULAR TRADE EXPOSITION**
Drawer 4850
Winter Park, FL 32793
PH: (407)671-3772
FX: (407)679-0010
Frequency: Annual. **Audience:** Roofing, sheet metal, and air conditioning contractors, architects, specifiers, and building officials. **Principal Exhibits:** Roofing and sheet metal supplies and products.

**STONEXPO/MARBLE INSTITUTE OF AMERICA
  CONVENTION**
30 Eden Alley, Ste. 301
Columbus, OH 43215
PH: (614)459-0840
FX: (614)459-3904
E-mail: psabel@aol.com
URL: http://marble-institute.com
Frequency: Annual. **Audience:** Trade only. **Principal Exhibits:** Marble, stone, and related equipment, supplies, and services.

SURFACES
383 Main Ave.
PO Box 6059
Norwalk, CT 06851
PH: (203)840-5358
FX: (203)840-4804
E-mail: inquiry@nepcon.reedexpo.com
Frequency: Annual. **Principal Exhibits:** Equipment, supplies, and services for building.

**TEXAS SOCIETY OF ARCHITECTS PRODUCTS
  EXHIBITION**
816 Congress Ave., Ste. 970
Austin, TX 78701-2443
PH: (512)478-7386
TF: (800)478-7386
FX: (512)478-0528
Frequency: Annual. **Audience:** Association members and persons affiliated with the building industry. **Principal Exhibits:** Designing and building materials and related services.

TIANJIN CONSTRUCTION
PO Box 2460
Germantown, MD 20875-2460
PH: (301)515-0012
FX: (301)515-0016
E-mail: glahe@glahe.com
Frequency: Biennial. **Principal Exhibits:** Construction equipment, supplies, and services.

WORCESTER HOME SHOW/FALL
PO Box 785
Westborough, MA 01581-0785
PH: (508)836-2222
FX: (508)836-0231
Frequency: Annual. **Audience:** Trade professionals and general public. **Principal Exhibits:** Goods and services for in and outside the home.

WORCESTER HOME SHOW/SPRING
PO Box 785
Westborough, MA 01581-0785
PH: (508)836-2222
FX: (508)836-0231
Frequency: Annual. **Audience:** Trade professionals and general public. **Principal Exhibits:** Goods and services for in and outside the home.

**WORLD CONGRESS OF THE WORLD FEDERATION OF
  BUILDING SERVICE CONTRACTORS**
10201 Lee Hwy., Ste. 225
Fairfax, VA 22030
PH: (703)359-7090
TF: (800)368-3414
FX: (703)352-0493
Frequency: Biennial. **Principal Exhibits:** Building service contracting equipment, supplies, and services.

**WORLD ORGANIZATION OF BUILDING OFFICIALS
  CONGRESS**
Site 18, Box 31, SS1
Calgary, AB, Canada T2M 4N3
PH: (403)239-2889
FX: (403)547-4546
Frequency: Triennial. **Principal Exhibits:** Exhibits relating to the dissemination of technical information on buildings; promotion of the standardization of construction materials, building equipment, and appliances; unification of legislation on buildings, with particular emphasis on codes, procedures, and directives aimed at ensuring safety; and the development of methods of preventing fires and other hazards in buildings.

PART II
AGRICULTURE

FOREWORD

THE CHANGING STRUCTURE OF U.S. AGRICULTURE

C. Phillip Baumel

History of U.S. Agriculture

For nearly a century following the 1607 settlement in Jamestown, Virginia, agriculture remained concentrated along the Atlantic coast. Agricultural production was labor-based, with the huge demand for labor being supplied by large families, indentured prisoners from England and, later, by slaves from Africa.

Agricultural technology remained labor-based for the next two centuries as agriculture spread into the Ohio Valley and the Deep South. This westward movement was spurred by federal land acts designed to facilitate the settlement process and to raise revenue for the government. The early acts in 1784 and 1785 allowed land to be sold in minimum lots of 640 acres and maximum lots of one-half of a township. Later acts reduced the maximum size, first to 320 acres and eventually to 160 acres. Some very large farms were created out of these sales. Slave labor permitted the development of large plantations in the Deep South and large cattle ranches were formed in the Southwest, an area of low rainfall. However, the majority of the farms consisted of 80 to 360 acres. One reason for the small-sized farms was the lack of capital to buy more land. More important, the labor-based technology severely limited the number of acres that could be farmed. Given the technology of the time and the abolition of slavery, most large farms and plantations were eventually sold to small farmers.

As the westward migration proceeded, public and private investments were made in roads, bridges, railroads, markets, processing facilities, warehouses and, later, in water resources. These investments allowed farmers to begin shifting from subsistence farming to commercial farming, i.e., selling some of their output into commercial markets. By 1933, most farmers had shifted to commercial farming. Between 1933 and 1970, farmers began buying an increasing share of their production inputs from commercial markets. This substitution of tractors and equipment, fertilizers, seed, energy and purchased feeds for farm-produced inputs and family labor enabled farmers to operate more land with less labor. Today, it is commonplace for individual Midwestern grain farmers to operate 2,000 to 4,000 acres. The number of acres operated—but not necessarily owned—by individual farmers, continues to increase unabated.

The Four Agricultural Revolutions

American agriculture has undergone four major technological revolutions. The first was the Mechanical Revolution, which started in the mid-19th century. The mechanical planter, threshing machine and cotton gin were all developed at this time. By 1857, John Deere was producing 10,000 cheap, efficient plows per year. Machines became larger and more efficient but remained horse-drawn. Relatively efficient gasoline-powered tractors were available by 1920 and farmers rapidly adopted this innovation. Tractors were an efficient substitute for farm labor and freed up millions of acres of land that had been used to produce feed for farm horses. The major results of the Mechanical Revolution were the substitution of machinery for human and animal power and a major reduction in the number of farms and people employed in agriculture.

The second revolution, the Biological-Chemical Revolution, built upon and extended the Mechanical Revolution. This revolution occurred between 1930 and 1980 and brought forth discoveries and refinements in plant genetics, hybridization of field crops, synthetic fertilizers and herbicides and insecticides. The Biological-Chemical Revolution dramatically increased productivity and the use of purchased inputs, and accelerated the transformation of farming to a business endeavor. It also set the stage for specialized crop farms and eliminated the need for livestock waste as the source of plant food.

The advent of gene splicing and insertion unleashed the magic of DNA recombinant research. These discoveries initiated the third revolution—the Biogenetic Revolution—which promises new species, new products and plants that are resistant to disease, drought and insects. Crop varieties developed for specific end-user needs are now reaching grocery store shelves. "Designer" commodities are expected to replace many undifferentiated, generic, bulk commodities that have been the standard agricultural output for centuries.

The fourth revolution emerged in the early 1980s. Made possible by new electronic technologies, the Managerial Revolution addresses the need to coordinate and manage the food system through electronic communication and data management systems. The integration of satellite and computer technologies, telephone, fax, and digital cameras enables the coordination of the production chain from inputs to retail distribution. Previous agricultural revolutions resulted in higher levels of specialization and structural change in the supply, production and processing sectors. The emerging system integrates and coordinates these sectors using information and management technologies and allows finely tuned micro-management at the primary agricultural production level.

The four agricultural revolutions have profoundly impacted the structure of U.S. agriculture. These impacts include the development of unique plant and animal genetics and the industrialization and globalization of agriculture. U.S. agriculture has been globalized by changing world trade policies and accelerated economic growth in densely-populated foreign nations. Rising incomes in these areas have created a demand for better diets, thus increasing the demand for U.S. farm products.

Agricultural Exports

During most of the past 150 years U.S. agriculture has had a large surplus production capacity, producing more than what is needed for domestic consumption. This excess production capacity has allowed the United States to be a major force in world export markets. During the past 25 years, U.S. agriculture has been heavily dependent on export demand. Preliminary estimates place the 1998-99 value of U.S. agricultural exports at $49 billion. Table 1 shows the approximate percentages of U.S. output that are exported, while Table 2 shows the dominance of U.S. agriculture in world production and exports of corn, soybeans, cotton and wheat.

Table 1: U.S. agricultural exports as a percentage of total production

Commodity	Percent
Corn	25
Grain sorghum	40
Soybeans	45
Wheat	45
Rice	40
Cotton	42
Broilers	15
Beef	8
Pork	6

Table 2: Typical U.S. percentage shares of world production and exports of selected agricultural products[1]

Commodity	% of world production	% of world exports
Corn	40	60
Soybeans	45	60
Soybean meal	33	15
Cotton	20	25
Wheat	12	24
Rice	2	12

Although the United States ships agricultural products to a wide range of countries, its largest market for meat and grain is Asia. Latin America is a rapidly developing market for these products. Major competitors of the U.S. in meat, grain and oilseed exports include Canada, the European Union (EU), Argentina, Brazil, and Australia. Modestly reduced subsidies in EU agriculture and strong growth in U.S. exports of grains, oilseeds and meats to Mexico, encouraged by the North American Free Trade Agreement (NAFTA), has improved the position of U.S. agricultural exports in world markets. NAFTA, in turn, has increased the competition in U.S. markets from Mexican fruits and vegetables and from Canadian wheat.

For a number of years trade sanctions have been applied to certain countries hostile to the United States. In 1999, such sanctions were eased for Iran, Morocco and the Sudan. However, easing sanctions is not expected to bring a large surge in U.S. agricultural exports since other countries already supply those markets and will compete aggressively. Sanctions remain against several other countries, including North Korea and Cuba.

Industrialization of Agriculture

The pressures to reduce costs and gain a larger share of the global food and fiber markets have led to a frantic effort in agricultural industries to adopt new technologies and to consolidate firms and farms into larger, lower-cost, integrated, industrial-like production systems. Industrial agriculture utilizes large-scale, specialized production units, intensive and standardized production practices, the separation of labor and management from ownership, the extensive use of computerized management and the intensive substitution of capital for labor.

Poultry and Livestock

Egg production is an early example of industrialized agriculture. Historically, eggs were produced on small family farms in the Corn Belt. Eggs were assembled at cooperatives or creameries and shipped to population centers.

New confinement production technologies, introduced in the 1950s and 1960s, have reduced production costs, greatly diminished labor requirements and increased the productivity of hens and the quality of the eggs. These technologies include housing large numbers of layers in one building. The buildings are environmentally friendly, with automated feed and watering systems that serve several buildings. The egg gathering, cleaning and packaging systems are also automated. Several connected buildings can house and feed millions of birds with minimal labor and maximum feed and production efficiency.

Initially, industrialized egg production units were built near large consuming areas, shifting almost all egg production from Iowa, at one time the largest egg producing state in the country, to modern production units located close to urban areas in California. Unlike the family-farm egg production units, the large California units were investor-owned, managed by professional managers and staffed by non-family workers. However, as the California units depreciated and local envi-

ronmental restrictions increased building costs, egg production began to shift back to the Midwest.

Broilers quickly followed the egg model. Today, most broilers are produced in confinement in large, company-owned units or in family-farm units that work under contract with large, integrated broiler-producing firms like Tyson Foods.

Beef cattle feeding was the next product to follow the egg model. Cattle feeding also shifted from Iowa in the early 1970s, the largest cattle feeding state in the country, and from other Corn Belt states to large, specialized, investor-owned cattle feedlots located in the High Plains, from central Nebraska down to the Texas Panhandle.

Industrialization of the pork industry is now underway. Large-scale swine production units dot the landscape across all of Iowa and North Carolina and, to a lesser extent, Missouri, Illinois, Nebraska, Oklahoma, Utah and other states.

The dairy industry is in the early stages of moving toward industrialization. Historically, dairy production was centered in Wisconsin, Minnesota, northeast Iowa, northern Illinois and the northeastern United States. Later, large-scale industrialized dairy units were built in the West, and California soon became the leading milk producing state. However, urban sprawl and environmental concerns have encouraged some milk producers to move from California into Texas, New Mexico and Idaho.

Today, nearly all poultry, a high percentage of beef and increasing amounts of dairy and swine are grown in the industrial production model. Indeed, the largest producers or contractors for livestock production are large, industrialized food firms. Table 3 identifies some of the major producers of each type of livestock.

Table 3: Major U.S. livestock producers by class of livestock

Broilers	Swine	Cattle
Tyson Foods	Murphy Family	Cactus Feeders
Gold Kist	Smithfield	Wayne/Conti
Perdue Farms	Wayne/Conti	Con Agra
Con Agra Poultry	Seaboard	Cargill
Pilgrims Pride	Prestige Farms	National Farms
Wayne/Conti	Tyson Foods	J.R. Simplot Co.
Seaboard Corp.	Cargill	Cattlco

(As of September, 1999, Murphy Family Farms was being bought by Smithfield Foods.)

To illustrate the dominance of these firms, the largest 50 pork producers will market about 50 percent of the 1999 pork production[2], and the six largest broiler producers sold about 50 percent of the broilers. However, family farms are adopting the technologies used by corporate livestock producers in an effort to survive and thrive in the era of industrialized agriculture.

Crop Production

The grain industry is slowly moving toward industrialized production. Grain production is still dominated by family farms and family-owned farm corporations. However, the number of acres operated by individual commercial farmers continues to rise. Corn Belt grain production operations of 2,000 to 4,000 acres operated by one farmer plus some part-time help are now common. These large, minimum-labor farm operations are made possible by large-size machinery, new production technologies such as no-till agriculture, custom herbicide and pesticide applications and cost-reducing biotechnology.

For example, genetically modified "Roundup Ready" soybeans can withstand the "Roundup" herbicide, which kills all plants except those that have the "Roundup Ready" gene. This development eliminates the need for cultivating soybeans and for repeated applications of less effective herbicides. Another example, Bt corn is toxic to the European corn borer, thus eliminating the need for some pesticide applications. And no-till agriculture, i.e., no ground preparation prior to or after planting, allows residue from last year's production to remain on the soil surface. Weeds and insects are controlled by biotechnology and chemical applications. All of these new technologies reduce costs and labor requirements, increase yields and increase the potential number of acres one person can farm, which facilitates the trend toward larger farms.

Biotechnology also is enabling farmers to produce "differentiated quality" products. Examples of differentiated grain qualities include:

- high oil corn to increase the energy content of feed
- high sucrose soybeans for human food
- reduced saturated fat in soy oil for human consumption
- high oleic fatty acid in corn and soybeans to increase oil stability
- high saturated fat in soybeans to reduce trans-fatty acids in shortenings

Many other genetic modifications of corn, soybeans and other grain products are under development in university, government and private biotechnology laboratories.

Most differentiated quality grains in commercial use are produced under contract with seed companies or end-user firms. By 1997, contractual arrangements for production and/or marketing of agricultural commodities were widespread. Nearly one-third of all U.S. crops and livestock, in dollar value, were grown or sold under production or marketing contracts. Production contracts specify sources and types of inputs and management practices to be used in production, while marketing contracts specify market outlets, price, quality premiums or discounts and other related details that are established before the production process is completed. Two-thirds of the farms using contractual arrangements were small family farms, with annual gross sales under $250,000. However, farms with more than $250,000 in sales accounted for more than three-fourths of the total value of products sold under contract[3].

Agricultural Input Industries

Major consolidations have occurred among and between local retail farm supply firms and manufacturers of these products. The most dramatic consolidations have taken place in the seed and chemical businesses. The major agricultural chemical companies—Dow,

Dupont, Monsanto and Novartis—have purchased almost all the major producers of seed for the grain and cotton sectors. These acquisitions facilitate and complement the agricultural chemical companies' entrance into the life sciences and enable them to bundle the sale of seeds, chemicals and financing. These acquisitions also gained them access to herbicide- and insect-resistant crop varieties which substitute for some farm chemicals. It also ensures that the research of the acquired companies complements the goals of the chemical companies. Some major acquisitions by these four chemical companies include:

- Dow: Mycogen, Illinois Foundation Seeds
- Dupont: Pioneer HiBred International, Protein Technology International
- Monsanto: Asgrow, DeKalb, Holdens, Cargill International Seeds, Delta and Pineland, Calgene
- Novartis: Northrup King

Historically, there have been numerous manufacturers of farm machinery. Famous brand names include John Deere, International Harvester, Case, Allis Chalmers, Stieger, Oliver, Ford, Massey-Ferguson and New Holland. However, the declining number of farms, the increasing size of tractors, combines and planters and the advent of no-till agriculture have reduced the number of units sold. To adjust, the industry has consolidated to maintain economies of size, research and development budgets and to increase worldwide market share. Today's major farm machinery manufacturers include John Deere, New Holland, AGCO and Komotsu.

The animal health industry, makers of biological pharmaceuticals and feed additives, has also consolidated. Today it is a global industry dominated by Merial, Pfizer, Bayer and Akzo Nobel.

Marketing Industries

Similar consolidations have taken place in the marketing industries. Historically, farmers sold to cooperatives and other local buyers. Today, many of these local organizations have been consolidated into large, multiple-location firms—with as many as 25 locations—that buy commodities from farmers up to 30 miles away. These consolidations were encouraged by economies of size in distribution and transportation, obsolete facilities and increased farmer mobility

brought about by farmer purchases of semi-tractor-trailer trucks.

Consolidation is also occurring in the meat-packing and grain merchandising, exporting and processing sectors. The most dramatic consolidation of grain facilities occurred in 1999 when Cargill purchased most of Continental Grain's grain-handling facilities. Farmland Industries and Harvest States, two of the largest U.S. farmer-owned cooperatives, have announced merger plans. Growmark, a large Illinois-based cooperative, and Countrymark, a large Ohio- and Indiana-based cooperative, have formed joint ventures with Archer Daniels Midland Company (ADM). ADM also has an alliance with Novartis, a major seed producer. ConAgra has joint ventures with ADM, Farmland Industries and Harvest States. Most of these same companies, particularly Cargill, ConAgra, Farmland Industries and ADM, are also major grain and/or meat processors. These latter industries are highly concentrated, as shown in Table 4:

Table 4: Top four concentration ratios in selected agricultural industries

Industry	Percent of total[4]
Grain storage	24
Grain export facilities	59
Beef packers	79
Pork packers	57
Flour milling	62
Wet corn milling	74
Soybean crushing	80
Ethanol production	67

Transportation

Agriculture requires substantial transportation services. About 60 percent of the tons shipped by barge on the Mississippi River system are grains. About 17 percent of the total carloads hauled by railroads are agricultural and forest products. Like other input industries, there have been major consolidations within the barge and railroad industries. Five barge companies operate about 55 percent of all dry cargo barges on the Mississippi River system. There are about 350 railroad firms in the United States, yet the six U.S. Class I railroads originate about 99 percent of all U.S. grain car loadings.

There is substantially more competition in the trucking sector. Of particular significance is the rapid growth of farmer-owned semi trucks, which enable farmers to bypass the nearby railroad to access a competing railroad or to haul directly to processor and feeder markets.

Future Changes and Outlook

Recent changes in U.S. agriculture have been driven by two main forces. The first is survival; the second will be discussed in the next section. Agricultural firms have long known that the survivors in the global food system will be the low-cost producers, processors and distributors of consistently high-quality foods to consumers. The low commodity prices in the late 1990s have accelerated this cost-reducing trend, and agricultural input and marketing firms will continue to consolidate into fewer but larger firms.

Low commodity prices have also increased the number of farmers exiting agriculture during the late 1990s. The number of U.S. farms reached its peak in 1935 at 6.8 million and had declined to an estimated 2.1 million farms by 1997. The 1997 average size of a U.S. farm was 436 acres, almost triple the 150 acres per farm in 1935. Nearly three-fourths of these farms are non-commercial, i.e., farms with gross annual sales of less than $50,000. These small farm operators rely on off-farm employment and/or investments for most of their income and they account for only 10 percent of gross farm product sales. They contribute significantly to rural social structures and are economically important to rural businesses, but they are only small contributors to the nation's food and natural fiber supplies.

Commercial farms comprise 27 percent of all farms but account for 90 percent of gross sales. Within this group, the largest four percent of all farms account for 50 percent of gross sales. The top one percent of all farms produce slightly more than 25 percent of the total gross sales. Extremely large farms are concentrated more in fruit and vegetable, dairy, livestock and poultry production than in major field crops[5]. Some observers suggest that the number of commercial

farms in the U.S. might eventually decline to as few as 20,000 to 30,000 in the next 15 to 25 years. At the same time, the number of non-commercial farms is likely to increase.

Supply Chains

The second driver of future consolidations is the emergence of innovative ways to deliver new and consistently high-quality foods to consumers[6]. Figure 1, on the next page, illustrates the decision-making process in traditional agriculture, in which each entity operates independently and attempts to maximize its own profits.

Figure 2 illustrates the decision-making process in supply chain agriculture—sometimes called alliances. Supply chains or alliances are groups of input suppliers and/or farmers and/or marketing firms joined together in some form of business structure to produce a consistently high-quality product at the lowest possible price. The shaded area in Figure 2 illustrates coordination among all stages of input supply, production and processing. All the participants in the shaded area are committed to the production and delivery of a consistent size, type and quality product at a specified time and place. The purpose is to maximize joint profits and to distribute them according to the contribution and economic power of each participant. The coordination and commitment mechanism is typically a contract, or it could be ownership, joint ventures, franchises, new-generation closed cooperatives (which are similar to limited partnerships) or other forms of coordination or cooperation. Supply chains will tend to adopt the latest technologies, including precision farming and use of the Internet and emerging biotechnologies in order to compete in price, quality and consistency.

Supply chains or alliances can range from several farmers coordinating among themselves to all the participants in the production-marketing chain. There is a wide range in the type and size of supply chains or alliances. The key to success is a coordinated, *interdependent* effort in contrast to the fiercely *independent* actions of farmers in traditional agriculture.

In traditional agriculture, risk management decisions (price, production and financial) are made by individual producers using private- and public-sector supplied tools. Under the emerging structure, risk management

Figure 1: Traditional agriculture

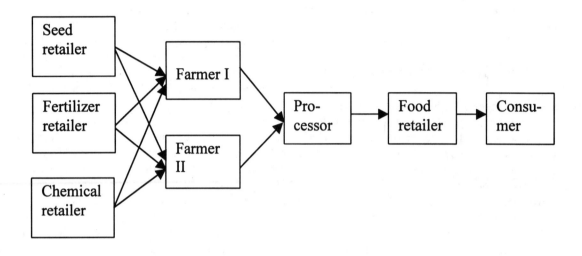

Figure 2: Supply chain agriculture

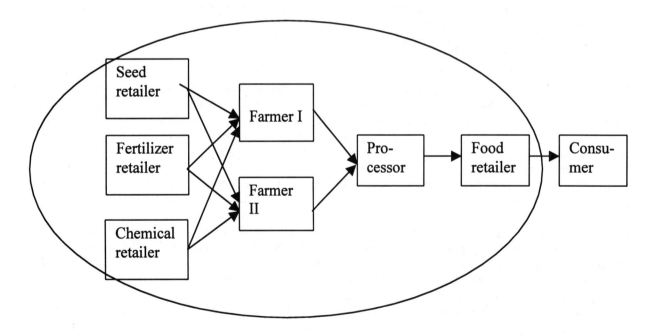

will be wrapped into the total system, with some of the individual areas of risk being offset elsewhere in the system. For example, in late 1998 and early 1999 hog prices were at record lows in real terms and producers faced extreme losses; meanwhile, retail pork prices were relatively high. This meant that fully integrated hog farms—those involved from breeding stock to retail—experienced substantial profits as losses in production were more than offset by profits in processing and wholesaling. Hence, price risk in the emerging structure appears likely to be much lower than under the traditional system.

While many in the agricultural sector are excited about the emerging structure, others express great concern about the potential economic disadvantage of farmers in a structure dominated by a few global companies. In this latter view, the farmer changes from an independent and innovative entrepreneur to a person with people-management skills exercising a very narrow range of management initiatives. Results from the "broiler model" raise concerns that most of the "added value" may be retained by global firms rather than being passed back to farmers and rural communities.

Precision Farming

Precision agriculture uses the latest developments in information technologies to increase productivity while decreasing the cost of production and minimizing environmental impacts. Producers know that yields are higher in some parts of a field than in others. This field variability can be caused by non-uniform soil properties such as nutrient availability, soil moisture, landscape, pests, soil compaction and drainage. With precision agriculture, producers vary inputs across the field using computerized machinery that is precisely controlled by satellites, local sensors and computer software. More inputs are applied in nutrient-deficient or pest-infested areas of the field and less are applied elsewhere. This increases yields and minimizes inputs, thus reducing costs and environmental damage. Precision agriculture can also identify the fields that are best suited for specific types of new, biotechnology-generated products.

Emerging Technologies

The first generation of agricultural biotechnology products included insect- and herbicide-resistant seeds.

These cost-reducing/yield-increasing technologies have been widely adopted by agriculture. Approximately 50 percent of the 1999 U.S. acreage of corn, soybeans and cotton were planted with transgenic herbicide- or insect-resistant seeds. First-generation, quality-differentiated products have been less widely adopted by farmers. One reason for the limited of success of the latter products is that, in many cases, the additional cost of the seed, identity preservation and lower yields are greater than the additional value of the products. Moreover, the modifications that were designed to improve animal feed rations compete with traditional feed ingredients that also are produced by agriculture. Substitution of these modified grains for traditional feed ingredients has essentially become a zero sum game for agriculture. This suggests that future biotechnology developments must meet at least the following conditions:

1. The value of the modification must be increased through:

- stacking two or more high-value modifications into the same seed

- developing plants that produce products that are highly valued for human consumption. These most highly valued modifications are likely to be used as nutraceuticals, i.e., food ingredients that provide health benefits beyond traditional foods, such as foods that contain anti-cancer ingredients. A second class of high-value plant modifications is pharmaceuticals that contain naturally-produced compounds that substitute for chemical or synthetic drug compounds.

2. Developing high-yielding varieties of modified crops so that the value of the modified seeds is not offset by the cost of reduced yields.

The rapid adoption of the Internet as a method of communication has created an array of new agricultural marketing and coordination activities. The Internet allows the use of e-mail for offering and accepting contracts for the production and sale of specific types of modified grains, fibers and animal products. New businesses use the Internet to offer the sale and delivery of agricultural inputs to the farm. These e-businesses bypass traditional local input suppliers, including farmer-owned cooperatives, by offering the same quality inputs at reduced prices. Typically, input e-businesses target farmers who operate large numbers of acres and buy large quantities of inputs. This type of buying helps large-scale farmers become the low-cost, surviving producers. The Internet also is a mechanism that can be efficiently used to coordinate large, complex supply chains at a low cost.

Major Issues Surrounding These Changes

Cost-cutting

The need to remain the low-cost producer to meet domestic and global competition will continue. The rapid consolidation of firms for efficiency and coordination is raising concerns about market power, monopoly pricing, the declining number of farmers and the demise of many rural towns.

Genetically Modified Foods

The second driver of consolidation—the development of genetically modified foods and fibers—is beginning to meet stiff public resistance. European consumers have raised serious concerns about the human and environmental safety of genetically modified plants. This concern has led the European Union to slow the approval of genetically modified crops. Several European food store chains have announced that they will no longer accept foods containing genetically modified materials. These bans on the use of genetically modified foods in some export markets have raised great concern in agricultural circles. The big questions are:

- Will the genetically modified foods be proven as safe as claimed by the large U.S. life science companies?
- Will the higher qualities and lower costs of the genetically modified foods overcome the fears expressed by environmentalists and many consumers?
- Will a sector of the consuming public continue to prefer non-genetically modified foods?
- Will the growing market for organic foods continue?

Regardless of the outcomes, these concerns have sometimes resulted in premium prices for conventional grains over genetically modified grains. One possible response to this controversy is for U.S. agriculture to develop a segregated marketing system to provide non-genetically modified foods to those markets that are willing to pay for them.

Environmental Concerns

The shift to herbicides and insecticides, synthetic and chemical fertilizers, genetically modified crops and the industrialization of animal agriculture has raised numerous questions and concerns about their impacts on the environment. Industrialized animal agriculture has created concerns about the concentration of large numbers of animals in small areas, in which 12 to 18 months of animal waste is collected in earthen and concrete pits and in aboveground concrete and steel containers. The environmental concerns include high levels of odor, potential leakage of the animal wastes into groundwater and spillage into rivers and streams. Environmental concerns from extensive use of agricultural chemicals include nitrogen, phosphate, herbicide and pesticide pollution of groundwater and streams. Nitrogen fertilizer runoff into the Mississippi River has been blamed as a contributor to hypoxia—oxygen deficient areas in the Gulf of Mexico. The loss of oxygen has resulted in the loss of aquatic animal life in a large area south of the mouth of the Mississippi River.

While these issues have been vigorously discussed, the content of the discussion has focused more on what could happen than what is likely to happen. There has been little discussion of the tradeoffs from these developments. For example, the concentration of livestock production into small areas means there are large areas that are no longer involved in animal production and therefore have no more pollution from animal wastes. Moreover, the animal waste management practices of industrialized agriculture tend to be more environmentally friendly than the methods used by traditional animal production.

The use of no-till cropping and chemicals increases the concentration of some chemicals in the soil. However, these technologies also greatly reduce soil erosion. There has been little research and public discussion of such tradeoffs as these and the net environmental effects of these new production methods. These tradeoffs need to be quantified and incorporated into public environmental debates.

Public Policies

A major public policy dating back to at least the 1930s has been price supports and subsidies to maintain a large number of family farms, the vitality of rural communities and to provide a stable, reliable, low-cost food supply. Today, the two types of subsidies that are used to achieve these goals are direct payments to farmers and indirect subsidies. Direct payment subsidies have a maximum payment limit per person so that extremely large subsidies are not paid to large, efficient farms. The limits vary somewhat depending on the type of payment but typically range from $50,000 to $75,000 per person. Payments are collected in cases in which gross farm income is severely depressed. The payments help cover essential costs but still leave typical producers with large, negative net incomes.

The logic behind the subsidies is that agriculture is heavily dependent on biological processes and is subject to much greater risks than many industries. Moreover, the economic health of the agricultural sector is critically important to the nation since it is the source of food production. In 1999, the incomes of several key sectors of Midwestern agriculture were severely depressed. The severe pressures reflect global changes in farm policies and sharply reduced export demand because of the Asian financial crisis.

Indirect subsidies are those which indirectly affect farmers through reduced production costs or enhanced prices for agricultural products. In many cases, these subsidies benefit rural consumers and other rural businesses, as well as farmers. These subsidies are not size-specific, but affect all sizes of farms equally. A partial list of such subsidies includes:

• Market information
• Rural roads
• Vehicle license fees
• Waterway operation and maintenance and construction costs
• Rural electricity
• Irrigation water supplies in arid and semi-arid areas
• Flood control
• Ethanol fuels
• Corn sweeteners, through sugar import quotas
• Interest rates on government loans
• Soil conservation practices
• Crop insurance

• Research and extension
• Grading and inspection of farm products
• Domestic demand enhancements
• Market development and promotion work

The number of farms has declined rapidly since 1935; thus it is uncertain whether these subsidies have achieved their goals of maintaining a large number of family farms and the vitality of rural communities. The most that can be said is that these subsidies may have had a modest impact on the structure of U.S. agriculture.

Conclusions

The structure of U.S. agriculture has been changing since the mid-1800s and is now entering a period of unprecedented change. The driving forces of these changes are technology—especially biotechnology and computerized management and control—industrialization, supply chains and globalization. The key questions now facing agriculture and society in general are:

• Where are these changes taking agriculture?
• What are the gains and losses from this changing structure?
• Who gains and loses from these changes?
• What can be done to manage these changes?

Agricultural economist Michael Boehlje suggests three alternatives to manage these changes:[7]

• Let the market shape the direction of these changes.
• Restrict or prohibit change.
• Attempt to shape the direction and magnitude of these changes.

A thorough discussion and understanding of all the issues and consequences is needed before society decides which course of action to pursue.

Notes

1. World Agricultural Outlook Board, USDA. *World Agricultural Supply and Demand Estimates.* Washington, D.C. July 12, 1999, WASDE 352.

2. Freese, Betsy. "Pork Powerhouses, 1998." *Successful Farming* Vol. 96, No. 10, 1998.

3. Banker, David, and Janet Perry. "More farmers contracting to manage risk." *Agricultural Outlook.* Economic Research Service, USDA. Washington, D.C. January/February 1999, pp. 6-7.

4. Heffernan, William. "Consolidation in the Food and Agriculture System." Unpublished report to the National Farmers Union. February 5, 1999.

5. Economic Research Service, USDA. "Structural and Financial Characteristics of U.S. Farms, 1994: The 19th Annual Family Farm Report to the Congress." Washington, D.C.

6. Drabenstrott, Mark. "Consolidation in U.S. agriculture leading to new rural landscape and public policy considerations." *Feedstuffs* Vol. 71, No. 20, May 17, 1999.

7. Boehlje, Michael, Purdue University. "Positioning your business for the 21st Century." *Agriculture in the 21st Century—Surviving and Thriving.* College of Agriculture and Home Economics Experiment Station, University Extension, Iowa State University, Ames, IA, March 8, 1999.

—C. Phillip Baumel

C. Phillip Baumel is a Charles F. Curtiss Distinguished Professor in Agriculture and a Professor of Economics at Iowa State University, Ames, Iowa. Professor Baumel is a Fellow in the American Agricultural Economics Association and the author of over 300 referred and non-referred articles. He has served as a consultant to local, regional and international firms, to state and federal governments and to private agencies.

CHAPTER 1 - PART II

INDUSTRY OVERVIEW

This chapter presents a comprehensive overview of the Agriculture industry. Major topics covered include an Industry Snapshot, Organization and Structure, Background and Development, Pioneers in the Industry, Current Conditions and Future Projections, Industry Leaders, Work Force, and North America and the World. A suggested list for further reading, including web sites to visit, completes the chapter. Additional company information is presented in Chapter 6 - Mergers & Acquisitions.

Industry Snapshot

Agriculture, lumber, and fishing have one thing in common—the harvesting of a plant or animal for human consumption. Experts project that the world's population had approached six billion by the late 1990s. Growing at a rate of 86 million per year, the number of people inhabiting the Earth is expected to reach about 10 billion by the mid-21st century.

As the number of consumers of food and paper products grows, so does the pressure on the Earth's resources. In response, each sector of the agriculture industry has implemented strategies to help ensure that these increased needs will be met in future generations. Biotechnology has exploded onto the agricultural scene, producing crops with greater yields and enhanced nutrition. Regulations in commercial fishing have attempted to abate the depletion of fish stocks in the world's waters. And reforestation is now a chief component in the logging industry.

The agriculture industry encompasses these 51 SICs (Standard Industrial Classification codes):

Cash Grains
0111: Wheat; **0112: Rice**; **0115 Corn**; **0116: Soybeans**; and **0119: Cash Grains, Not Elsewhere Classified**.

Fields Crops, Except Cash Grains
0131: Cotton; **0132: Tobacco**; **0133: Sugarcane and Sugar Beets**; **0134: Irish Potatoes**; and **0139: Field Crops Except Cash Grains, Not Elsewhere Classified**.

Vegetables and Melons
0161: Vegetables and Melons.

Fruits and Tree Nuts
0171: Berry Crops; **0172: Grapes**; **0173: Tree Nuts**; **0174: Citrus Fruits**; **0175: Deciduous Tree Fruits**; and **0179: Fruits and Tree Nuts, Not Elsewhere Classified**.

Horticultural Specialties
0181: Ornamental Floriculture and Nursery Products and **0182: Food Crops Grown Under Cover**.

General Farms, Primarily Crop
0191: General Farms, Primarily Crop, such as those farms that derive more than half of their sales from crops.

Livestock, Except Dairy and Poultry
0211: Beef Cattle Feedlots; **0212: Beef Cattle, Except Feedlots**; **0213: Hogs**; and **0214: Sheep and Goats**.

Dairy Farms
0241: Dairy Farms.

Poultry and Eggs
0251: Broiler, Fryer, and Roaster Chickens; **0252: Chicken Eggs**; **0253: Turkey and Turkey Eggs**; **0254: Poultry Hatcheries**; and **0259: Poultry and Eggs, Not Elsewhere Classified**, including duck, geese, pigeon, and quail farms.

Animal Specialties
0271: Fur-Bearing Animals and Rabbits; **0272: Horses and Other Equines**; **0273: Animal Aquaculture**; and **0279: Animal Specialties, Not Elsewhere Classified**, including apiaries, aviaries, kennels, and alligator, earthworm, and silkworm farms.

Soil Preparation Services
0711: Soil Preparation Services.

Crop Services
0721: Crop Planting, Cultivating, and Protecting; **0722: Crop Harvesting, Primarily by Machine**; **0723: Crop Preparation Services for Market, Except Cotton Ginning**; and **0724: Cotton Ginning**.

Animal Services, Except Veterinary
0751: Livestock Services, Except Veterinary, such as artificial insemination services, custom slaughtering, livestock breeding services, and sheep shearing; and **0752: Animal Specialty Services, Except Veterinary**, such as horse training.

Farm Labor and Management Services
0761: Farm Labor Contractors and Crew Leaders and **0762: Farm Management Services**.

0811: Timber Tracts.

Forest Nurseries and Gathering of Forest Products

0831: Forest Nurseries and Gathering of Forest Products.

Fishing, Hunting, and Trapping

0912: Finfish; 0913: Shellfish; 0919: Miscellaneous Marine Products; 0921: Fish Hatcheries and Preserves; and 0971: Hunting and Trapping and Game Propagation.

Logging

2411: Logging.

Organization and Structure

Farming

The agribusiness industry is focused on the raising of plants or animals for distribution to processing companies, which further develop the raw goods for public consumption. After this stage, the processed products are sold to producers of food, beverages, clothing, or other materials. For example, farmers sell corn to processors for transformation into corn syrup, which is then sold to soft drink manufacturers.

When crops or livestock are ready for market, the farmer transports them directly to food processors, storage centers, or wholesale markets or auctions. Their primary means of transportation are trucks, railroads, and river or ocean vessels.

By far, family-owned farms represent the largest group of the U.S. farming sector, with corporate-owned farms making up only a small percentage of farms. Overall, the number of farms across the country is on the decline, as consolidation of land emerges as a means of increasing productivity. Innovations in mechanization, seed technology, and other labor-saving technologies have steadily reduced the number of necessary farm laborers.

The farming cooperative has gained popularity as a defense against the economic pressures facing farmers. These cooperatives are associations of independent farmers that assist in the marketing and distribution of goods and share profits among members.

Grains are grown on about half of the world's total cropland. The largest U.S. grain crop is corn, which is used as livestock feed or is made into cornstarch, corn syrup, ethanol fuel, or dextrose for a variety of consumer and industrial products. Soybeans are the second-largest U.S. crop and are used in oil, whole soybean, and protein products. Wheat ranks third and is used primarily for flour. Other notable grain crops are barley, millet, rice, oats, rye, sorghum, and such feed crops as alfalfa, clover, and varieties of grass.

Cotton is the world's most important non-food crop. Like most other crops, the harvesting of cotton is highly mechanized. However, handpicking is often the preferred method of harvesting, since ripening stages and the quality and coloration of the lint varies between plants and cannot be distinguished by a mechanical harvester.

Tobacco is another important specialty crop. It is used for smoking, chewing, and snuffing. After harvest, the tobacco leaves are cured by air, fire, flue, or the sun. They are then graded, or packaged together with similarly sized leaves, and shipped for processing.

Livestock farming entails the breeding and raising of animals for the purpose of food, toil, or pleasure. Cattle represents the world's largest livestock group. They are used as draft animals, milk producers, and a source of meat. Sheep and goats are raised for wool, meat, and milk. The pig—one of the first domesticated animals—is raised primarily for meat. Horses are raised for use as draft animals and mounts for ranches; as pets, for pleasure riding; and as investments, for racing and show.

Poultry farming entails the raising of chickens, turkeys, ducks, geese, guinea fowl, and squabs for meat or egg production. The U.S. chicken farming industry is a model in efficiency for rearing animals of uniform quality at low cost through continued research in nutrition, breeding, and disease control. The farming of other poultry has not approached the popularity of chickens in the U.S., but is nonetheless practiced in nearly every country throughout the world.

Dairy farming has become increasingly automated, thereby enabling the management of large numbers of animals. By the mid-1990s farms of 5,000 milking cows had become fairly typical. Milking machines are utilized to extract milk, usually twice each day. The perishable nature of milk demands that it be cooled to and maintained at 50 degrees Fahrenheit or lower within two hours. It is then held in cooling tanks or cans, which are picked up by tankers that deliver the milk to plants for processing.

Fishing

Fishing industry techniques vary depending on the species sought. In general, there are four main methods: entrapping nets, lines, traps, and encircling nets, which include the purse seine, haul seine, and trawl seine. Some ships are equipped with freezers or canners that process the fish shortly after catch, but most transport the fish to onshore processors.

The most popular types of fish for human consumption are cod, flatfish, haddock, herring, salmon, and tuna. These and other marine fish represent about 80 percent of the world's catch. Freshwater fish, such as bass, carp, catfish, and perch, constitute about 10 percent. Shellfish are classified into two general categories: crustaceans, including crabs, crayfish, lobster, and shrimp; and mollusks, like clams, oysters, mussels, scallops, and snails.

Since ancient times fishing has been an important industry for virtually all countries. In recent years, however, this industry has become threatened by over-exploitation, which has depleted the stocks of the world's species. A number of causes are behind this decline, including technological advances in fishing techniques, increased sizes of fishing fleets, and the impact of pollution.

Because of these threats to the industry, as well as ongoing territorial disputes, governments have entered into numerous domestic and international agreements over fishing rights. Among recent regulations are the 1983 Law of the Sea, which grants countries a 200-mile ocean territory in which to regulate fishing activities, and the passage of a 1996 bill calling for the U.S. National Marine Fisheries Service to eliminate overfishing and to establish other conservation efforts for the industry.

Logging

Logging entails selecting harvestable trees; chopping them down; bucking, or sawing them to desired lengths; and skidding, or transporting, them to a sawmill. Before logging can begin, paths must be cleared into the timber tract. After completion of a logging project, reclamation must be done to comply with environmental regulations and with the logic of conservation for the propagation of the resource for future use. Reforestation is typically accomplished by purchasing seedlings from tree nurseries on a contract basis.

Paper and forest product manufacturers usually own large tracts of land to meet their supply requirements. When timber can be purchased at a low price, however, these companies may opt to acquire their supplies on the open market from private- or government-owned land or timber harvesting companies.

Background and Development

Reduced to their most simplistic levels, fishing and hunting have served to meet the basic requirements for sustaining carnivorous life. These endeavors, therefore, predate the human species, as they were practiced by prehistoric animals, just as they are by their contemporary counterparts.

As industries, however, fishing and hunting arose relatively recently. Fur trading developed into a lucrative and booming industry among Europeans by the 1700s. Hunters and trappers engaged in the capture of such North American animals as the beaver, otter, lynx, and other forest-dwellers even before the establishment of the United States of America. These hunters and trappers took more prey than nature could replenish, however. By 1700 the beaver was virtually non-existent east of the Appalachian Mountains. The population of wild turkeys and bison were also drastically reduced by that time.

In more recent years the fur industry has come to rely upon fur farms, where animals are bred and killed for their hides. Hunting remains largely a sustainable activity in non-industrial regions, where it is a means of satisfying food and clothing requirements. In other regions, hunting is a recreational pursuit wherein the attainment of food or hide is, at the most, of secondary concern, behind the capture of a trophy or simply the "thrill of the hunt" itself.

Fishing, on the other hand, has evolved into an important commercial enterprise throughout the world. Thousands of years ago, artificial breeding of fish was developed in China. This practice emerged in Europe in the 1300s. By the 1780s trout hatcheries were maintained in Germany and Norway. Americans operated five commercial hatcheries by 1870. Offshore, humans increasingly took to boats, eventually amassing fleets of fishing vessels. As they ventured farther into the ocean, conflicts between competing fishers arose, sometimes with violent results. These disputes led to the establishment of national boundaries of fishing waters and numerous agreements over fishing rights.

Like fishing and hunting, forestry and logging are extensions of prehistoric consumption of natural resources. Wood was gathered from trees for myriad uses, including fire, tools, and the construction of shelter. Forests were regarded as self-perpetuating, limitless resources. Yet as societies developed more uses for wood and populations continued to grow, forests began to diminish. As early as 5,000 years ago China suffered a shortage of wood. The same problem arose in ancient Greece and Rome, and by the Middle Ages some European countries had adopted regulations restricting deforestation. The New World provided Europe with sorely needed lumber as early as 1621, just one year after the *Mayflower* landed. In 1623 America's first sawmill began operation and by mid-century an industry based on producing ship masts and timbers was well developed. The advent of railroads not only transported lumber and people throughout the U.S., it also required enormous amounts of wood for railroad ties.

Only in the 19th century was a determined effort to protect and replenish the forest undertaken. Forest management in Europe involved the control of harvesting, prevention of soil erosion, and the limitation of timber production. Arbor Day, devoted to the planting of trees, was first proclaimed in 1872 in Nebraska. After World War II, the U.S. federal government, along with private lumber and paper industries, reached a consensus that proper management of forests was the only way to ensure their existence into future generations.

The propagation of forests, however, had long been at odds with an industry that took center stage—agriculture. To farmers, the forest was a waste of valuable land. As a result, for most of the history of this industry, little regard was paid to deforestation in the name of agriculture.

Unlike the other sectors of the industry, crop and livestock agriculture developed as the systematic modification of a natural resource for later use or consumption. Like other animals, humans had long been gatherers of plants, but only with the development of agriculture did they invest in raising such plants instead of relying on nature alone to provide them.

Historians widely date the emergence of agriculture at about 10,000 years ago. This Neolithic Revolution occurred at the end of the last Ice Age, when hunter-gatherers settled in villages in the Middle East. As reported in a November 1998 issue of *Science* magazine, however, recent archaeological evidence suggests that agricultural settlements arose much earlier than that, as early as 13,000 years ago in the Near East. Regardless of the exact time period, though, agriculture and animal domestication have existed for a long time and have played a crucial role in the development of modern industries.

Pepper, avocado, and amaranth were domesticated in the Americas by 7000 BC, followed by corn at around 3500 BC. Pigs are believed to have been the first domesticated animals, arising in Jarmo (Iraq) by 6750 BC. Domesticated cattle dates to 6000 BC in Greece. China provides evidence of the cultivation of millet by 5000 BC, of rice in the following millennium, of wheat by 1300 BC, and of barley and soybeans by 1100 BC.

By the Roman epoch agriculture was a well-developed industry, producing most of the crops associated with the contemporary Mediterranean region, including a variety of grains and legumes, as well as olives, fruit trees, turnips, and radishes. Textbooks on farming techniques were produced by this time period, and an array of effective farming implements had been developed.

An agricultural recession struck Europe in the late 13th century and lasted through the 14th century. Bad weather destroyed crops, resulting in years of famine.

Plagues, particularly the Black Death, followed, wiping out about one-third of Europe's population. The Hundred Years' War and other military strikes further reduced the number of laborers available to work the arable land, which, as a result, sat idle.

The development of the Norfolk four-course system signaled an important change in European agriculture. It was characterized by the elimination of a fallow year for the land and put an emphasis on fodder crops. In this system, wheat was grown in the first year, turnips in the second, and barley in the third. In the fourth year clover and ryegrass were grown and grazed upon by farm animals, which further fertilized the soil with their nutrient-rich droppings. The four-course system was adopted throughout much of Europe by the end of the 19th century.

During this time, improvements in farming tools and machinery were developed at a rapid pace. They included the Rotherham plow, the horse-drawn hoe, and the seed drill. Farming textbooks and societies increased in number, representing the rising importance of commercial agriculture in national economies. An agricultural school was founded in 1727 in Germany, where the first agricultural high school was later established in 1806.

The first steam-powered plows were invented in the 1830s, but not until three decades later did they evolve into practical instruments. Their widespread adoption was followed rapidly by the mechanization of other farm implements, such as hay rakes, hay loaders, potato spinners, threshing drums, and milking machines. Off the farm, steam power facilitated the transport of goods, particularly by railroad.

The internal combustion engine, introduced in the late 19th century, soon became the primary source of power for farming. By 1907 about 600 tractors were in use; that number skyrocketed to 3.4 million by 1950. Like the railroad, the introduction and proliferation of the automobile, truck, and airplane had a great impact on agriculture, as farmers could more readily transport goods to market and supplies to the farm. After World War II self-propelled machines were invented for a variety of agricultural tasks, including spraying, harvesting, and baling.

During the 1800s experiments with the hybridization of plants led to improved varieties of crops, not to mention the establishment of the scientific field of genetics. Gregor Mendel published the first scientific research on the topic, but some farmers were already conducting practical experiments with their own crops. New varieties of hybrid potatoes, corn, wheat, and rice were continually developed throughout the mid-1900s, by which time businesses, government agencies, and agricultural societies had become involved in the field as well. These innovations, along with the increased use of fertilizers and irrigation, led to the so-called Green Revolution of the 1950s and 1960s.

As the field of genetics developed so did its application to agriculture. Researchers began isolating genes that would produce a desired trait in a plant, such as making it less susceptible to damage by insects or fertilizers, capable of greater yields, or more nutritious. The Flavr Savr tomato, introduced by Calgene in May 1994, was one of the first genetically engineered seeds that was commercially available; it was a failure, however, due to its high cost. In 1996 Monsanto unveiled a soybean that was resistant to that company's highly effective Roundup herbicide, and it was soon widely accepted by farmers. Increasingly, chemical companies have begun working with seed manufacturers to develop new breeds of plants and, in so doing, have established a new industry—life sciences.

Pioneers in the Industry

John Deere

Born in 1804, this native of Vermont became a blacksmith apprentice at age 17. Four years later he established his own shop and worked there until 1837, when he headed west. He settled in Grand Detour, Illinois, and again founded a blacksmith enterprise. Over time, Deere observed that he was making the same sorts of repairs to the wooden and cast iron plows that were used at the time. Deducing that they were ill-suited to the heavy prairie soil, he joined with Major Leonard Andrus to devise improved plows. In 1838 the partners settled on a design incorporating a steel cutter and a wrought iron moldboard, and that year they sold three different models.

In 1839 Deere and Andrus designed 10 improved models, followed by 40 new versions in 1840. By

1846 the partners were selling one thousand plows annually. Realizing that Grand Detour was not well situated for receiving supplies and for marketing the plows, Deere sold his interest in the partnership to Andrus in 1847 and moved to Moline, Illinois. Once there, he began importing English steel and soon developed the nation's first cast steel plow. By 1855 he was manufacturing 10,000 plows per year.

In 1868 he incorporated his business as Deere & Company, of which he remained president until his death in 1886. His company remains in existence and is one of the most well-known names in agricultural machinery and products. It also manufactures tools for other industries, including construction and grounds care.

Gregor Mendel

Gregor Mendel is credited as being the father of genetics, a field that is the basis for an agricultural revolution. As with many great thinkers, the full import of his work was realized only after this death.

Born in 1822 in Austria, Mendel became an Augustinian monk at age 21. He studied science on his own and later at the University of Vienna. He then became a teacher, although he had failed the examination for teaching certification.

Meanwhile, in 1856, he began working and experimenting in the small monastery garden. There, Mendel observed that certain traits of garden peas were passed to descendants in predictable patterns. He theorized that each parent plant contributes half of a pair of heredity units, now called genes, that account for a certain characteristic of the hybrid progeny. These experiments and accompanying calculations led to his formulation of the principles of segregation and of independent assortment.

Mendel reported his findings to the Natural Science Society in 1865 and published them the following year. They were universally ignored, but Mendel continued his work as a researcher and teacher until his death in 1884. In 1900, while pouring through the available research in this area of study, three scientists independently discovered Mendel's data and theories, which were later confirmed experimentally. Posthumously, then, Mendel has contributed enormously to the scientific fields of genetics, biology, botany, and anthropology, as well as to their practical applications in such industries as agriculture and animal husbandry.

Louis Pasteur

Louis Pasteur was a brilliant and revolutionary scientist who had a great impact in science, industry, and medicine. Among other achievements, he is known as the founder of microbiology.

Born in 1822 in Dole, France, Pasteur earned successive degrees in science, eventually becoming a doctor of philosophy at age 25. His initial research in fermentation encouraged a brewer to approach him with the problem of undesirable substances that appeared during the fermentation of alcohol from grain and sugar. Pasteur theorized that these substances were the products of microorganisms, later called germs, that were always in existence in air. This led him to postulate that food decomposes when it comes into contact with these minute organisms, a theory that was controversial because it was in contrast with the widely accepted theory of the spontaneous generation of bacterial life.

Pasteur then proved that heating substances, a process later known as pasteurization, killed these unwanted organisms, thereby enabling the products' uncontaminated manufacture, preservation, and transportation. The beverage industries that immediately benefited from these discoveries were milk, alcohol, and vinegar.

Perhaps his most famous work, however, was on vaccines. Using his self-acquired knowledge of microbiology, Pasteur invented a vaccine against anthrax, a disease that struck sheep, and against chicken cholera, which affected fowl. Most importantly, he developed a vaccine against rabies. After applying this treatment to animals, he first saved the life of a child who had been bitten by a rabid dog in 1885.

Despite becoming partially paralyzed in 1868, Pasteur continued his research and his responsibilities as head of the Pasteur Institute, dedicated to further research on treatments for rabies, until his death in 1895.

Eli Whitney

Well known as the inventor of the cotton gin (short for "engine"), Eli Whitney is often overlooked as the inventor of the concept of mass-production. Still, his cotton-associated fame is not undeserved, as he revolutionized America's cotton and textile industries with his small box.

Whitney was born in 1765 in Massachusetts and graduated from Yale in 1792. He moved to Georgia to take a teaching position but upon arrival learned that it had already been filled. Stranded and unemployed, he befriended the manager of a large plantation. There, Whitney observed that the South had the resources to meet the great demand for cotton but was hampered by the tedious process of handpicking the product. Within days he had invented a simple yet efficient machine that separated cotton by spinning it around a drum and extracting the unwanted seeds and hulls with metal hooks. In March 1794 he received a patent for his invention but he never benefited financially from it: the simplicity of its design inspired farmers to pirate, rather than purchase, the cotton gin.

Undeterred, Whitney turned to the manufacture of muskets for the government. At that time, each component was formed individually and, as a result, would fit only for that musket for which it had been designed. Whitney revolutionized industry by mass producing parts to precise, uniform specifications, thereby enabling the interchangeability of components. With this concept, a broken part didn't spell the uselessness of the entire musket—that part could simply be replaced by another. He demonstrated the genius of mass production before an assembly that included Thomas Jefferson. Whitney died in 1825.

Current Conditions and Future Projections

The worldwide agriculture industry was well entrenched in a serious depression in 1999, with farm prices in 1998 the lowest of the decade. A May 1999 issue of *U.S. News & World Report* relates alarming figures.

The U.S. hog market was the bleakest of the agricultural sectors, with pork prices in December 1998 at only nine cents per pound—lower than prices during the Great Depression. By the time that farmers realized the state of the market, however, they were already raising the next generation of hogs, thereby worsening their prospects.

This agricultural crisis is reminiscent of that of the 1980s. But unlike that crunch, farmers in the 1990s are finding that alternative agricultural avenues do not offer any relief. Grain prices, even for the usually low-risk corn and soybeans, were depressed as well, with soybean futures reaching a 12-year low of $4.50 per bushel in March 1999. Even dairy farming declined, dropping 37 percent in February. As a result, the U.S. Congress set aside $6 billion in emergency aid in the autumn of 1998 and another $566 million in May 1999.

Ironically, this dire situation arose from an agricultural high in the mid-1990s. Commodity prices reached record levels in 1995 and the trade environment was encouraging. In response, Congress passed the Freedom to Farm bill, which paid farmers to sign up for a program of decreased government subsidies.

With this windfall and an over-confidence in the market, farmers upped production, planting greater amounts of higher-yield seed varieties and increasing their livestock numbers. This led to a glut of corn, soybeans, and wheat, which spelled trouble for farmers when the Asian economic crisis hit.

Another industry sector that is in the midst of a crisis is commercial fishing, which is suffering from the over-exploitation of global fish stocks. The National Academy of Sciences reported in a December 1998 issue of *Business Week* that 30 percent of stocks—including orange roughy, shark, swordfish, and tuna—are on the decline and another 44 percent are borderline. In response, the Food & Agriculture Organization, a unit of the United Nations, agreed to implement a reduction of the fishing fleets of member countries, which total 3.5 million fishing boats worldwide.

Industry Leaders

Archer Daniels Midland Co.

John W. Daniels began crushing flaxseed for the production of linseed oil in 1878. In 1903 George P. Archer joined Daniels Linseed Co. and the firm was renamed Archer Daniels. It acquired the Midland Linseed Products Co. in 1923, forming Archer Daniels Midland Co. (ADM).

During the 1930s the company's research department delved into the alteration of the chemical structure of linseed oil, resulting in the successful extraction of lecithin from soybean oil. This discovery was responsible for a 10-fold reduction in the cost of lecithin, an ingredient in heavy demand for candy and other food products. In 1938 ADM's assets reached $22.5 million. By 1949, with sales of $277 million, the company was the nation's leading processor of linseed oil and soybeans and the fourth-largest flour miller.

In 1967 ADM acquired the Fleischmann Malting Co., a provider of malting products for the food and beverage industries. Four years later ADM purchased Corn Sweeteners Inc., a producer of high-fructose syrups, glutens, oil, and caramel color. Such acquisitions continued throughout the 1970s and into the 1980s. Among its notable purchases was the Columbian Peanut Co., which made ADM the leading U.S. peanut sheller.

Price fixing allegations against ADM surfaced in 1995. In October 1996 the company pled guilty to the price fixing of lysine and citric acid and it agreed to pay $100 million in fines—the largest penalty ever imposed in a criminal antitrust suit. ADM also agreed to pay an additional $90 million to settle related civil suits.

By the late 1990s, Archer Daniels Midland was one of the world's leading processors of corn, wheat, and oilseed. For fiscal 1998, the company's oilseed products generated revenues of $10.1 billion, accounting for 63 percent of ADM's total revenues. Corn products brought in $2.2 billion, or 13 percent. Wheat and other milled products accounted for $1.5 billion, followed by the $1.2 billion derived from other products.

Cargill Inc.

The largest private company in the U.S., Cargill is the leading exporter of grain and the largest salt company, and its Excel Corporation controls 20 percent of the nation's cattle production. Cargill operates in such diverse businesses as fertilizer, grain, hybrid seeds, steelmaking, financial services, and food processing.

William Wallace Cargill formed a partnership with his brother Sam in 1867 for the operation of a grain flat house in Iowa. The young company soon began acquiring flat houses to take advantage of the agricultural explosion that accompanied the railroad expansion following the Civil War. During the remainder of the century, it also ventured into the operation of grain elevators and warehouses, and then into shipbuilding and lumber. By 1890 the company operated 71 grain flat houses, 28 coal sheds, and two flour mills.

Cargill expanded internationally by opening a Canadian unit in 1928, and it soon established sales offices overseas. In 1936 its diverse array of company operations were united as Cargill, Inc. The firm reorganized in 1943 into four market divisions: seed, grain, warehouses, and shipbuilding. It expanded into the salt industry by initiating salt barging in 1954. Cargill then diversified into the broiler chicken industry in 1966 by purchasing the Paramount Poultry brand; into flour milling by acquiring Burrus Mills in 1972; and into the steel-making industry by acquiring North Star Steel Co. in 1974. Further acquisitions took Cargill into the beef processing and malting businesses in 1979. The 1997 acquisition of the North American salt production, processing, and marketing assets of Akzo Nobel ranked Cargill behind only Morton Salt in U.S. salt production.

By 1998 Cargill's agriculture sector produced a variety of feed, seed, and fertilizer. Its food processing unit included corn and wheat wet milling for the production of corn syrups, glucose, dry sweeteners, citric acid, sodium citrate, corn starch, and flour. This sector also processed cocoa, oranges, peanuts, soybeans, oils, beef, pork, poultry, and eggs. In addition, Cargill's industrial operations included steel, recycling, and fertilizers.

Dean Foods Co.

His experience in brokering evaporated milk enabled Sam Dean to establish the Dean Evaporated Milk Co. in 1925. One decade later the company expanded into fresh milk, and in 1943 its research and development laboratory produced a powdered, non-dairy coffee creamer. Four years later Dean diversified into ice cream, and then into pickles with its 1961 purchase of Green Bay Food Company.

A difficult dairy market in the 1970s spurred Dean to expand through the purchase of small, but healthy, companies to add to its product line-up. The industry underwent a turnaround, however, in the mid-1980s as a growing public awareness of the health benefits of calcium drove dairy sales. By 1984 dairy products accounted for nearly 70 percent of Dean's sales, which approached $1 billion.

Dean entered the frozen and canned vegetables industry through its 1986 merger with Larsen Company, and by the following year it ranked third in the nation in that market. After several other acquisitions to build this line, including the 1993 purchase of the Birds Eye brand, Dean Foods exited vegetables by selling those operations to Agrilink Foods in September 1998.

In 1998 Dean Foods remained the leading dairy processor and distributor in the U.S., with net income of $106 million on sales of $2.7 billion. Its Dairy Products business, consisting of fluid milk and cultured products, ice creams, and extended shelf life products, accounted for $1.6 billion in revenues. The Pickle Products group, which generated $349 million in sales, encompassed pickles, peppers, relishes, olives, sauces, and syrups. The Specialty Products group produced $335 million in sales of non-dairy creamers and other powdered products, dips and dressings, and aseptic shelf stable puddings and cheese sauces.

IBP, Inc.

The world's leading processor of beef had its start in 1961 as Iowa Beef Packers, Inc. By 1964 the company had become one of the most efficient in the industry, requiring only 32 minutes to process a steer from plant door to freezer. Three years later it revolutionized the industry by introducing the boxed beef concept—packaging smaller parts of the animal in boxes rather than the standard shipment of whole carcasses to customers.

In 1970, after the settlement of a long and violent union strike, the company changed its name to Iowa Beef Processors. During the 1970s the firm was embroiled in a number of scandals, including charges of bribing supermarket buyers and union officials and of maintaining ties with the Mafia. By 1974, however, the company had become the world's largest beef processor.

Occidental Petroleum Corp. purchased the firm in 1981. The following year Iowa Beef Processors expanded into pork processing and changed its name to IBP,

Inc. to reflect its diminished emphasis on beef. By 1990 the company was the nation's leading supplier of fresh pork.

For fiscal 1998, IBP sold 14.3 billion pounds of fresh meat for a total of $11 billion. Its Foodbrands America unit recorded revenues of $1.05 billion. Transcontinental Cold Storage posted revenues of $25 million. IBP Leather, one of the world's largest suppliers of cow hides for the leather industry, posted sales of $601 million.

Monsanto Co.

In 1901 John Francis Queeny founded Monsanto Chemical Works for the production of saccharin. The company soon expanded into caffeine, vanillin, and aspirin. Monsanto went public in 1927 and two years later it doubled in size and diversified into rubber chemicals by acquiring Rubber Services Laboratories Co. and Nitro Co. During the 1930s the newly renamed Monsanto Chemical Co. ventured into the soap and detergents industry and then into plastics and resins.

In a foreshadowing of its success in the agricultural industry, Monsanto began marketing Randox, a herbicide capable of killing weeds before they broke ground, in 1956. Eight years later the company dropped the word "Chemical" from its name to reflect its diverse operations.

The company made significant strides in the agriculture sector during the 1980s. In 1982 it was the first to modify a plant cell genetically, and the next year it acquired Jacob Hartz Seed Co. In 1988 Monsanto acquired Greensweep, maker of lawn and garden products.

In 1995 the U.S. Environmental Protection Agency approved the raising of plants that had been bioengineered to produce their own pesticide. That year Monsanto purchased a 49.9 percent stake in Calgene Inc. It acquired the remaining stake in 1997. It acquired both Asgrow Agronomics and Monsoy, the second-largest soybean seed marketers in the U.S. and the world, respectively, in 1996.

In 1997 Monsanto purchased a stake in DEKALB Genetics Corp., the second-largest seed company in the U.S. It also completely exited the chemicals business by spinning off its chemicals operations as Solutia Inc. The next year it acquired the remainder of DEKALB Genetics, along with Plant Breeding International Cambridge Ltd. and the international seed business of Cargill Inc.

Monsanto's Agricultural Products sector generated 1998 revenues in excess of $4 billion. Its Nutrition & Consumer Products unit recorded sales of $1.5 billion, while its Pharmaceuticals operations accounted for $2.9 billion in revenues.

Pioneer Hi-Bred International, Inc.

Pioneer Hi-Bred is the nation's largest developer and producer of seed, particularly hybrid varieties. In addition to corn, which comprised about 75 percent of the company's 1998 sales, it also offers soybean, alfalfa, canola, wheat, sorghum, and sunflower hybrids.

In 1926 Henry Agard Wallace, along with his brother Jim and several other partners, established the Hi-Bred Corn Co. in Iowa to develop and market hybrid seed corn. Its products were sold via mail order by advertising in the Wallace family farming newspaper. Growing sales prompted the company to purchase 80 additional acres and to create a Parent Seed Department in 1929. Four years later Henry resigned to become the U.S. Secretary of Agriculture; he became Vice President of the U.S. under Franklin D. Roosevelt in 1941.

Hi-Bred was afforded the opportunity to provide a practical demonstration of the advantages of hybrid corn when a severe drought struck in 1934. That year the company changed its name to Pioneer Hi-Bred to distinguish itself from the increasing number of hybrid seed companies. By 1972 Pioneer and its primary rival, DeKalb AgResearch Inc., each held 22 percent of the nation's hybrid seed corn market. Pioneer went public the following year. In 1979 it increased its share of the seed corn market to 34 percent as DeKalb's hold fell to 14 percent.

In 1989 Pioneer added the word "International" to its name to reflect its global reach, as it operated in 32 countries. Four years later the company entered into a joint venture with Kraft Food Ingredients to produce specialty oils from sunflower and other oilseed crops. Two years later it entered into a joint venture with Mycogen Corp. to develop genetically engineered crops that are resistant to insects. In 1998 DuPont Co. acquired a 20 percent stake in Pioneer by entering into a joint venture, Optimum Quality Grains, to research and develop new methods and uses for grain. In March 1999 DuPont agreed to buy the remaining 80 percent of Pioneer for $7.7 billion. Pioneer's 1998 revenues were $1.8 billion, with net income of $270 million.

Tyson Foods, Inc.

In 1935 John Tyson founded a small business for buying chickens and transporting them for sale outside of Arkansas. He soon began incubating chicks for sale to local growers and then established a company feed mill. Tyson's Feed & Hatchery continued its vertical integration by acquiring a broiler farm in 1943, and in 1958 the company completed the construction of its first processing plant. By the end of the decade it was processing 96,000 broilers each week.

The company went public as Tyson's Foods in 1963. That year it also made its first acquisition, Garrett Poultry Co. By mid-decade the industry's production of broilers soared, forcing prices down and smaller companies out of business. Tyson took advantage of this environment by purchasing struggling competitors and by 1969 Tyson supplied two percent of the nation's chickens.

The 1970s brought increased consumer awareness of the nutritional benefits of poultry, and Tyson's broiler production hit 72 million in 1970. The next year the company changed its name to Tyson Foods, Inc. It diversified into hog farming and by the end of the decade it was the nation's leading supplier of live swine. To shield itself from the cyclicity of the commodities market Tyson acted to expand its involvement in value-added products; it acquired such companies as Krispy Kitchens, Ocoma Foods, and the Wilson Food Corp.

Tyson leapt over ConAgra, Inc., in 1986 to become the nation's largest poultry producer. These two companies engaged in a two-year battle to acquire Holly Farms Corp., the nation's leading chicken producer. In 1989 Tyson succeeded, paying $1.3 billion for Holly Farms. With that purchase, Tyson's revenues doubled to $2.5 billion and its operations expanded into beef processing for the first time. It acquired McCarty Farms in 1995 and Hudson Foods in 1998.

In 1998 Tyson was the world's largest poultry company and the nation's seventh-largest hog producer. Its sales that year reached $7.41 billion, with net income of $25.1 million.

Weyerhaeuser Co.

Weyerhaeuser is the largest producer of softwood lumber in North America and the world's largest pulp producer. It was founded by Frederick Weyerhaeuser, who purchased a lumberyard in 1858. In 1900 he entered into a partnership to purchase a 900,000-acre tract of timber in Washington. This business, Weyerhaeuser Timber Co., opened the nation's first tree farm in 1941.

A depressed timber market spurred the company to diversify into wood products, including wood pulp, containerboard, and particleboard; the firm dropped the word "Timber" from its moniker to reflect this expanded focus. Weyerhaeuser went public in 1963, providing it with the capital to expand overseas by opening an office in Tokyo.

The destruction of thousands of acres of timber due to the 1980 eruption of Mt. Saint Helens, combined with the cyclical nature of the industry, prompted the firm to strengthen its core businesses and drop less successful operations. During the 1990s Weyerhaeuser purchased 200,000 acres of timberland in Georgia and 193,000 acres in New Zealand.

The company's Timberlands unit, incorporating Weyerhaeuser's working forests (5.3 million acres in the U.S. alone), seed orchards, nurseries, and greenhouses, generated $636 million in revenues in 1998. The Pulp, Paper, and Packaging sector, comprised of bleached paperboard, containerboard packaging and recycling, fine paper, newsprint, and pulp, accounted for $4.3 billion in sales. Wood Products, which generated $4.5 billion in sales, encompassed architectural doors, building materials distribution, panels business, Northwest hardwoods, and softwood lumber. Weyerhaeuser Real Estate Company, a homebuilding enterprise, had revenues of $1.2 billion in 1998.

Work Force

Farmers and Farm Managers

The duties of the farmer depend on the type of farm operated. Because those tasks require specialized management techniques and skills, the typical farmer is involved in only a handful of different markets.

Crop farmers are engaged in the planning, planting, cultivation, harvest, and marketing of grain, vegetables, fruits, and fiber plants. Livestock and dairy farmers raise, breed, and market animals or animal products. Horticultural specialty farmers tend to such greenhouse plants as flowers, shrubs, sod, and fruits and vegetables. Aquaculture farmers raise fish and shellfish in vessels for sale as food or for recreational fishing.

The *Agriculture Fact Book 1998,* published by the U.S. Department of Agriculture, noted that employment on U.S. farms in 1997 was 2.9 million, down from 9.9 million in 1950. This decline is attributed to increased mechanization and labor-saving technology, a trend toward fewer and larger farms, and relatively low wages. Yet this employment decline is believed to have stabilized, as efficiencies gained from technology and major consolidation of farms has leveled off.

According to the *Fact Book,* 69 percent of farm laborers in 1997 were family workers, with the remaining 31 percent being hired workers. The hourly rate for such hired help varied from $5.69 in Wyoming to $10.13 in Hawaii, with a national average of $7.36. The necessity for hiring workers depends greatly on the type of farm. For highly mechanized farms, including grain, livestock, and poultry, labor accounted for less than five percent of total farm expenses in 1992. Horticultural specialty farms, however, called for the greatest proportion of labor expenses (45 percent), followed by fruit and tree nut farms (40 percent) and vegetable and melon farms (37 percent).

Working conditions for farmers are typically strenuous, requiring long days of physical work. For crop farmers, the majority of fieldwork is concentrated during planting and harvesting seasons. Much of the planning, marketing, and machinery repair takes place during the off-season, at which time many farmers are employed in a second occupation as well. In 1996 about 39 percent of small farm operators engaged in non-farm work to a great extent, according to the *Agriculture Fact Book*. That year, the average household income for operators of small farms, which comprised about three-quarters of all U.S. farms, was $50,360, about 84 percent of which was derived from off-farm pursuits.

While most farmers and farm managers gain experience in agriculture as workers on their family's farms, many others combine formal education with several years of practical work experience. Fields of study include agronomy, dairy science, agriculture business and economics, crop and fruit science, horticulture, and animal science. As science and technology become more important in the agricultural industry, such college or university educations become increasingly vital. Indeed, even operators who have been raised on farms are finding it necessary to enroll in the occasional class to keep abreast of changes in the industry.

For the industry overall, the *1998-99 Occupational Outlook Handbook* predicts that the employment of U.S. farmers will remain constant or even decline slightly through the year 2006. The aforementioned technological advances and consolidation of farms is expected to result in an industry that supports new workers only to replace farmers who are retiring or otherwise departing from the industry. The only farming sector expected to undergo the opposite trend is aquaculture. This area is expected to experience steady growth through 2006 in response to declining worldwide fish stocks in natural waters.

Loggers

The modern logging and timber cutting process, while becoming increasingly mechanized, still entails strenuous physical activity on the part of the worker. The typical logger is part of a small crew, numbering four to eight laborers, that works outdoors regardless of weather conditions. Job hazards include falling trees and tree limbs, dangerous equipment, and high-decibel noise levels from machinery, as well as precarious terrain and poisonous flora and fauna.

Various specialties comprise the logging occupation. The faller cuts down trees with axes or chain saws. The bucker uses a chain saw to trim excess foliage from the felled tree and hew it to a manageable length.

The choke setter attaches steel cables or chains to the logs, which are then skidded, or dragged, by tractor operators to a loading area. There, the grapple loader lifts them into trucks.

According to the *Occupational Outlook Handbook*, 33,000 log handling equipment operators were employed in the U.S. in 1996. Logging tractor operators held 21,000 jobs, fallers and buckers held 17,000, and miscellaneous loggers held 11,000. Employment in the industry is expected to decline slightly through 2006 in response to increased mechanical innovations and the reduced availability of harvestable timber.

About one-third of loggers are self-employed, working in turn for self-employed logging contractors. Earnings vary widely based on geographic region, with Alaska and the northwest U.S. providing greater salaries than in the South, due to cost of living differences.

Although most training is acquired through on-the-job experience, formal training is available from such trade organizations as the Northeastern Loggers Association and the American Pulpwood Association. In addition, state forestry and logging associations offer specialized training for fallers, the most skilled of the logging occupations.

Fishers

Commercial fishing requires a boat with a crew that includes a captain, a first mate, a boatswain, and several deckhands. The captain oversees the vessel and the entire fishing operation, from the selection of the fishing site and duration of the trip to the sale of the catch. The first mate is the second-in-command and fills in when the captain is off duty. The boatswain supervises the deckhands, which are charged with most of the physical labor required, including sailing and fishing tasks.

Most training for commercial fishers is acquired on the job, although some colleges and vocational schools offer courses in fishing technology, seamanship, navigation, and vessel repair and maintenance. Licensing is required for captains and mates of vessels greater than 200 gross tons. Additionally, certain fish-processing crew members are required to obtain merchant mariner's documents from the U.S. Coast Guard.

The *1998-99 Occupational Outlook Handbook* estimates that about 45,000 fishers were employed in the U.S. in 1996. It predicted that this number would decline through 2006 due to reduced fish populations in the world's waters. This decline is also attributable to improvements in fishing technology and the disenchantment of fishers over the occupation's lack of steady income, which varies widely according to market conditions.

North America and the World

In 1997 the U.S. agriculture industry exported $57.1 billion in products while importing $35.2 billion, creating a trade surplus of $21.9 billion. This balance was significantly lower than the 1996 peak of $28.1 billion and is attributable to a continued decline in farm prices and to the Asian financial crisis.

Asia was, by far, the largest importer of U.S. agricultural products, accounting for a $19 billion trade surplus for the U.S. Europe accounted for a $4 billion surplus, followed by Africa with $1.4 billion, Mexico with $1.1 billion, and Canada with $171 million. With South America, the U.S. had the largest trade deficit— $2.8 billion. Australia and Oceania accounted for a $1.2 billion trade deficit, followed by Central America with a $1.1 billion deficit.

David Marchick, Deputy Assistant Secretary for Trade Policy and Programs, believes that agricultural trade plays a key role in the U.S. economy. His address to the Global Agricultural Attache Conference, as reported in the September 1998 *U.S. Department of State Dispatch,* stresses that "the future of U.S. agriculture lies in trade."

Unfortunately, a number of trade barriers exist for U.S. farmers. Not only do they face substantial tariffs, they are also discouraged from exporting by significant non-tariff barriers. Among these are "unjustified sanitary and phytosanitary restrictions to our agricultural exports, technical barriers such as labeling requirements, and slow approvals for genetically modified products." The World Trade Organization is charged with addressing these and other barriers to global agricultural trade. It is slowly making strides to improve the condition of fair trade between member countries.

Research and Technology

Biotechnology

The use of hybrid crops, fertilizers, and irrigation in the 1950s and 1960s sparked the so-called Green Revolution. Since then, the use of genetically modified seeds, fertilizers, and pesticides has exploded, changing not only the foods that we eat, but also the very business of agriculture.

A new industry, life science, is the convergence of agriculture, genetics, and food sciences. Life science tackles three main goals:

The first is to increase crop yields. This can be accomplished in a number of ways, one of which is to make the crops more resistant to herbicides. Monsanto developed the first commercial success in this area. That company's Roundup herbicide was so powerful that it killed not only weeds but also the crops that it was designed to protect, so in 1996 the company introduced a soybean containing a gene that was able to withstand the effects of Roundup. This gene was later inserted into corn and cotton, providing those crops with the same resistance.

Another tactic for increasing crop production is to engineer a plant in a way that increases the number of bushels yielded per acre. Increasing yield per acre is a pressing need in the agriculture industry, since the world's population is rising while the amount of arable land is shrinking. Yield can be increased by engineering a plant to emit its own pesticide. By the late 1990s research was being conducted on cotton, potato, and corn varieties that fended off worms and other pests without the use of external pesticides.

Life science's second mission is to develop plants with enhanced nutrition. Soybeans and corn have been modified to produce oil that contains less saturated fat than the natural varieties. Livestock feed has also been introduced to enable the animal to fatten up quicker through the absorption of enhanced protein.

The third arm of life science is rooted in medicine and pharmaceuticals. Geneticists have begun research into plants that can help ward off diseases. For example, they are working on ways to increase a tomato's content of lycopene, a chemical believed to have cancer-prevention properties.

Biotechnology and life science are not without their critics, however. These critics ask that oft-posed question regarding breakthroughs in scientific frontiers—it can be done, but should it be done? Several compelling arguments have been put forth to limit genetic modification in agriculture.

Critics charge that the world's food supply could be at risk if the majority of crops have similar or identical genetic structure, since this lack of diversity could make them all vulnerable to sudden shifts in climate or to the development of new strains of insects or diseases. The use of plants that emit pesticides could result in the evolution of insects that are tougher and less resistant to those pesticides. And genes inserted into crops could do damage to non-agricultural vegetation if they should escape off the farm, producing weeds that are resistant to herbicides or trees that are sterile.

By and large, farmers are conservative in regard to biotechnology, but many have slowly embraced it. However, they are greatly concerned about the relationship with seed companies that has emerged as an offshoot of biotechnology. In this relationship, which has been dubbed "bioserfdom," farmers have essentially become contract laborers of the large chemical and seed companies.

Genetically engineered seeds are licensed by the seed companies to farmers, who must sign contracts that restrict their use, prevent the farmers from planting their own seeds, and prohibit the practice of saving unplanted seeds for the next season. Monsanto, one of the industry's giants, has even resorted to suing farmers in breach of those contracts for up to $1 million and threatening them with criminal charges.

In March 1999 the U.S. Department of Agriculture established a panel to address this and other issues related to life science. This advisory panel will consist of 25 research and social scientists, farmers, and consumers, all of whom were to be appointed in late 1999.

Further Reading

"Agriculture." *Britannica CD 98 Multimedia Edition, 1994-1998.* Encyclopedia Britannica, Inc.

Archer Daniels Midland Co. Form 10-K. 24 September 1998. Available from http://www.admworld.com/financial/filings.htm

Baker, Beth. "A New Advisory Panel Will Help USDA Tackle the Thorny Issues Raised by Agricultural Biotechnology." *BioScience,* June 1999.

"Big Harvests, Bigger Blues." *Business Week,* 15 March 1999.

Cohen, Warren. "The Seeds of Discontent." *U.S. News & World Report,* 24 May 1999.

"Commercial Fishing." *Britannica CD 98 Multimedia Edition, 1994-1998.* Encyclopedia Britannica, Inc.

Dean Foods Co. 1998 Annual Report. Available from http://www.deanfoods.com

"Fields of Genes." *Business Week,* 12 April 1999.

Harlan, Jack R. *The Living Fields: Our Agricultural Heritage.* Cambridge: Cambridge University Press, 1995.

"Hook, Line, and Extinction." *Business Week,* 14 December 1998.

Hunt, Kimberly N., and AnnaMarie L. Sheldon, eds. *Notable Corporate Chronologies,* 2nd ed. Detroit: Gale Research, 1999.

IBP, Inc., 1998 Annual Report. Available from http://www.ibpinc.com

"Livestock." *Britannica CD 98 Multimedia Edition, 1994-1998.* Encyclopedia Britannica, Inc.

MacCleery, Douglas W. *America's Forests: A History of Resiliency and Recovery.* Durham: Forest History Society, 1994.

Monsanto Co. 1998 Annual Report. Available from http://www.monsanto.com/monsanto/investor/report/ 98

Pringle, Heather. "The Slow Birth of Agriculture." *Science,* 20 November 1998.

U.S. Bureau of Labor Statistics. *1998-99 Occupational Outlook Handbook.*

U.S. Department of Agriculture. *Agriculture Fact Book 98.* Available from http://www.usda.gov/news/ pubs/fbook98

U.S. Department of State. "The Importance of Agriculture to the United States." *U.S. Department of State Dispatch,* September 1998.

"United States Foreign Trade Highlights." Office of Trade & Economic Analysis, International Trade Administration. Available from http://www.ita.doc.gov/ industry/otea/usfth/aggregate

Wells, Susan, and Gordon Shepherd. "Threats and Conflicts." *UNESCO Courier,* July-August 1998.

Weyerhaeuser Co. 1998 Annual Report. Available from http://www.weyerhaeuser.com/annualreport/ wyar98

White, William C., and Donald N. Collins. *Opportunities in Agriculture Careers.* Lincolnwood: VGM Career Horizons, 1988.

Wille, Christopher M. *Opportunities in Forestry Careers.* Lincolnwood: VGM Career Horizons, 1992.

—Deborah J. Untener

INDUSTRY STATISTICS & PERFORMANCE INDICATORS

This chapter presents statistical information on the Agriculture industry. This view of the industry is through the lens of federal statistics. All the data shown are drawn from government sources, including the 100 percent surveys of the Economic Census and the partial surveys of services and other industries conducted annually by the U.S. Department of Commerce. Tables include general statistics, indices of change, and selected ratios.

SIC 07— - AGRICULTURAL SERVICES, FORESTRY, AND FISHING: GENERAL STATISTICS

Year	Establishments				Mid-March Employ-ment	Payroll	
	Total	With less than 10 employees	With 10-49 employees	With 50 or more employees		Total[1] ($ 000)	1st Quarter annualized[2] ($ 000)
1987	75,687	65,433	9,409	845	437,869	6,467,849	5,289,084
1988	73,764	62,927	9,865	972	461,768	7,161,195	5,848,288
1989	79,461	67,763	10,662	1,036	489,293	7,801,338	6,315,436
1990	84,811	71,994	11,728	1,089	531,010	8,650,036	7,083,308
1991	91,286	78,056	12,122	1,108	543,652	9,086,006	7,483,488
1992	97,245	82,724	13,314	1,207	593,518	10,040,725	8,294,820
1993	100,347	85,496	13,683	1,168	588,362	10,251,640	7,961,028
1994	104,390	90,173	13,058	1,159	586,069	11,204,284	8,617,936
1995	108,353	92,897	14,165	1,291	630,157	12,099,036	9,727,444
1996	113,547[3]				659,338[3]	12,611,692[3]	9,958,062[3]
1997	118,130[3]				683,332[3]	13,295,148[3]	10,469,842[3]
1998	122,713[3]				707,326[3]	13,978,604[3]	10,981,621[3]

Source: County Business Patterns, U.S. Department of Commerce, Bureau of the Census, Washington, DC 20233-0800. Extracted from *Agriculture, Mining, and Construction USA*, Gale, 1998. Notes: 1. Actual total payroll for the year. 2. 1st quarter payroll, multiplied by 4. 3. Trend projections.

SIC 07— - AGRICULTURAL SERVICES, FORESTRY, AND FISHING: INDICES OF CHANGE

Year	Establishments				Mid-March Employ-ment	Payroll	
	Total	With less than 10 employees	With 10-49 employees	With 50 or more employees		Total[1] ($ 000)	1st Quarter annualized[2] ($ 000)
1987	77.8	79.1	70.7	70.0	73.8	64.4	63.8
1988	75.9	76.1	74.1	80.5	77.8	71.3	70.5
1989	81.7	81.9	80.1	85.8	82.4	77.7	76.1
1990	87.2	87.0	88.1	90.2	89.5	86.1	85.4
1991	93.9	94.4	91.0	91.8	91.6	90.5	90.2
1992	100.0	100.0	100.0	100.0	100.0	100.0	100.0
1993	103.2	103.4	102.8	96.8	99.1	102.1	96.0
1994	107.3	109.0	98.1	96.0	98.7	111.6	103.9
1995	111.4	112.3	106.4	107.0	106.2	120.5	117.3
1996	116.8[3]				111.1[3]	125.6[3]	120.1[3]
1997	121.5[3]				115.1[3]	132.4[3]	126.2[3]
1998	126.2[3]				119.2[3]	139.2[3]	132.4[3]

Source: Same as General Statistics. The values shown reflect change from the base year, 1992. Values above 100 mean greater than 1992, values below 100 mean less than 1992, and a value of 100 in the 1987-91 or 1993-98 period means same as 1992. Notes: 1. Actual total payroll for the year. 2. 1st quarter payroll, multiplied by 4. 3. Trend projections.

SIC 0700 - AGRICULTURAL SERVICES: GENERAL STATISTICS

| Year | Establishments | | | | Mid-March Employ-ment | Payroll | |
	Total	With less than 10 employees	With 10-49 employees	With 50 or more employees		Total[1] ($ 000)	1st Quarter annualized[2] ($ 000)
1987	71,992	62,364	8,872	756	409,364	5,956,665	4,811,528
1988	70,291	60,126	9,293	872	432,453	6,589,097	5,311,964
1989	76,005	64,963	10,112	930	460,060	7,214,260	5,763,588
1990	81,328	69,196	11,154	978	500,048	7,985,961	6,482,660
1991	87,513	74,972	11,561	980	510,142	8,343,346	6,778,668
1992	93,251	79,443	12,727	1,081	559,574	9,250,618	7,504,384
1993	95,956	81,791	13,112	1,053	555,686	9,501,264	7,292,316
1994	99,784	86,222	12,513	1,049	551,507	10,346,530	7,860,016
1995	103,543	88,751	13,607	1,185	595,842	11,204,230	8,870,056
1996	108,821[3]				623,357[3]	11,663,600[3]	9,075,808[3]
1997	113,258[3]				646,531[3]	12,298,757[3]	9,542,948[3]
1998	117,696[3]				669,706[3]	12,933,913[3]	10,010,087[3]

Source: County Business Patterns, U.S. Department of Commerce, Bureau of the Census, Washington, DC 20233-0800. Extracted from *Agriculture, Mining, and Construction USA*, Gale, 1998. Notes: 1. Actual total payroll for the year. 2. 1st quarter payroll, multiplied by 4. 3. Trend projections.

SIC 0700 - AGRICULTURAL SERVICES: INDICES OF CHANGE

| Year | Establishments | | | | Mid-March Employ-ment | Payroll | |
	Total	With less than 10 employees	With 10-49 employees	With 50 or more employees		Total[1] ($ 000)	1st Quarter annualized[2] ($ 000)
1987	77.2	78.5	69.7	69.9	73.2	64.4	64.1
1988	75.4	75.7	73.0	80.7	77.3	71.2	70.8
1989	81.5	81.8	79.5	86.0	82.2	78.0	76.8
1990	87.2	87.1	87.6	90.5	89.4	86.3	86.4
1991	93.8	94.4	90.8	90.7	91.2	90.2	90.3
1992	100.0	100.0	100.0	100.0	100.0	100.0	100.0
1993	102.9	103.0	103.0	97.4	99.3	102.7	97.2
1994	107.0	108.5	98.3	97.0	98.6	111.8	104.7
1995	111.0	111.7	106.9	109.6	106.5	121.1	118.2
1996	116.7[3]				111.4[3]	126.1[3]	120.9[3]
1997	121.5[3]				115.5[3]	133.0[3]	127.2[3]
1998	126.2[3]				119.7[3]	139.8[3]	133.4[3]

Source: Same as General Statistics. The values shown reflect change from the base year, 1992. Values above 100 mean greater than 1992, values below 100 mean less than 1992, and a value of 100 in the 1987-91 or 1993-98 period means same as 1992. Notes: 1. Actual total payroll for the year. 2. 1st quarter payroll, multiplied by 4. 3. Trend projections.

SIC 0711 - SOIL PREPARATION SERVICES: GENERAL STATISTICS

| Year | Establishments | | | | Mid-March Employ-ment | Payroll | |
	Total	With less than 10 employees	With 10-49 employees	With 50 or more employees		Total[1] ($ 000)	1st Quarter annualized[2] ($ 000)
1987	581	477	88	16	4,498	73,757	62,192
1988	528	425	91	12	5,036	78,561	72,548
1989	498	397	91	10	4,190	78,888	72,648
1990	523	428	88	7	3,658	77,881	65,444
1991	543	451	82	10	3,800	73,920	64,236
1992	606	506	90	10	4,047	79,009	69,632
1993	643	539	92	12	4,416	88,353	72,956
1994	630	534	88	8	4,339	120,070	83,548
1995	626	525	90	11	4,842	105,231	94,760
1996	637[3]				4,230[3]	106,865[3]	85,937[3]
1997	649[3]				4,207[3]	110,866[3]	88,417[3]
1998	661[3]				4,183[3]	114,866[3]	90,898[3]

Source: County Business Patterns, U.S. Department of Commerce, Bureau of the Census, Washington, DC 20233-0800. Extracted from *Agriculture, Mining, and Construction USA*, Gale, 1998. Notes: 1. Actual total payroll for the year. 2. 1st quarter payroll, multiplied by 4. 3. Trend projections.

SIC 0711 - SOIL PREPARATION SERVICES: INDICES OF CHANGE

| Year | Establishments | | | | Mid-March Employ-ment | Payroll | |
	Total	With less than 10 employees	With 10-49 employees	With 50 or more employees		Total[1] ($ 000)	1st Quarter annualized[2] ($ 000)
1987	95.9	94.3	97.8	160.0	111.1	93.4	89.3
1988	87.1	84.0	101.1	120.0	124.4	99.4	104.2
1989	82.2	78.5	101.1	100.0	103.5	99.8	104.3
1990	86.3	84.6	97.8	70.0	90.4	98.6	94.0
1991	89.6	89.1	91.1	100.0	93.9	93.6	92.3
1992	100.0	100.0	100.0	100.0	100.0	100.0	100.0
1993	106.1	106.5	102.2	120.0	109.1	111.8	104.8
1994	104.0	105.5	97.8	80.0	107.2	152.0	120.0
1995	103.3	103.8	100.0	110.0	119.6	133.2	136.1
1996	105.2[3]				104.5[3]	135.3[3]	123.4[3]
1997	107.1[3]				103.9[3]	140.3[3]	127.0[3]
1998	109.0[3]				103.4[3]	145.4[3]	130.5[3]

Source: Same as General Statistics. The values shown reflect change from the base year, 1992. Values above 100 mean greater than 1992, values below 100 mean less than 1992, and a value of 100 in the 1987-91 or 1993-98 period means same as 1992. Notes: 1. Actual total payroll for the year. 2. 1st quarter payroll, multiplied by 4. 3. Trend projections.

SIC 0720 - CROP SERVICES: GENERAL STATISTICS

| Year | Establishments | | | | Mid-March Employment | Payroll | |
	Total	With less than 10 employees	With 10-49 employees	With 50 or more employees		Total[1] ($ 000)	1st Quarter annualized[2] ($ 000)
1987	3,309	2,645	520	144	33,271	503,248	422,928
1988	3,135	2,456	520	159	37,167	564,106	494,520
1989	3,092	2,381	550	161	37,536	597,270	515,240
1990	3,265	2,514	595	156	36,603	640,402	546,444
1991	3,447	2,687	600	160	38,133	662,542	555,844
1992	3,760	2,883	691	186	42,704	751,205	640,052
1993	3,936	3,089	670	177	43,292	781,842	658,504
1994	4,019	3,174	643	202	47,223	902,226	731,292
1995	4,058	3,188	682	188	45,579	921,866	791,504
1996	4,120[3]				47,641[3]	956,940[3]	796,186[3]
1997	4,225[3]				49,092[3]	1,007,061[3]	835,470[3]
1998	4,331[3]				50,542[3]	1,057,183[3]	874,755[3]

Source: County Business Patterns, U.S. Department of Commerce, Bureau of the Census, Washington, DC 20233-0800. Extracted from *Agriculture, Mining, and Construction USA*, Gale, 1998. Notes: 1. Actual total payroll for the year. 2. 1st quarter payroll, multiplied by 4. 3. Trend projections.

SIC 0720 - CROP SERVICES: INDICES OF CHANGE

| Year | Establishments | | | | Mid-March Employment | Payroll | |
	Total	With less than 10 employees	With 10-49 employees	With 50 or more employees		Total[1] ($ 000)	1st Quarter annualized[2] ($ 000)
1987	88.0	91.7	75.3	77.4	77.9	67.0	66.1
1988	83.4	85.2	75.3	85.5	87.0	75.1	77.3
1989	82.2	82.6	79.6	86.6	87.9	79.5	80.5
1990	86.8	87.2	86.1	83.9	85.7	85.2	85.4
1991	91.7	93.2	86.8	86.0	89.3	88.2	86.8
1992	100.0	100.0	100.0	100.0	100.0	100.0	100.0
1993	104.7	107.1	97.0	95.2	101.4	104.1	102.9
1994	106.9	110.1	93.1	108.6	110.6	120.1	114.3
1995	107.9	110.6	98.7	101.1	106.7	122.7	123.7
1996	109.6[3]				111.6[3]	127.4[3]	124.4[3]
1997	112.4[3]				115.0[3]	134.1[3]	130.5[3]
1998	115.2[3]				118.4[3]	140.7[3]	136.7[3]

Source: Same as General Statistics. The values shown reflect change from the base year, 1992. Values above 100 mean greater than 1992, values below 100 mean less than 1992, and a value of 100 in the 1987-91 or 1993-98 period means same as 1992. Notes: 1. Actual total payroll for the year. 2. 1st quarter payroll, multiplied by 4. 3. Trend projections.

SIC 0740 - VETERINARY SERVICES: GENERAL STATISTICS

| Year | Establishments | | | | Mid-March Employ-ment | Payroll | |
	Total	With less than 10 employees	With 10-49 employees	With 50 or more employees		Total[1] ($ 000)	1st Quarter annualized[2] ($ 000)
1987	16,748	13,822	2,897	29	98,553	1,390,710	1,260,524
1988	16,687	13,508	3,146	33	104,471	1,512,528	1,321,484
1989	17,667	14,147	3,484	36	112,136	1,684,660	1,462,824
1990	18,214	14,387	3,789	38	120,886	1,884,418	1,637,556
1991	19,282	15,092	4,140	50	129,160	2,085,613	1,810,188
1992	20,136	15,499	4,572	65	139,139	2,320,296	2,018,584
1993	20,631	15,713	4,854	64	145,711	2,474,470	2,111,248
1994	21,543	16,272	5,212	59	153,309	2,680,994	2,294,600
1995	22,033	16,261	5,695	77	164,314	2,961,468	2,575,792
1996	22,805[3]				170,723[3]	3,079,997[3]	2,635,737[3]
1997	23,520[3]				178,900[3]	3,272,847[3]	2,795,045[3]
1998	24,235[3]				187,077[3]	3,465,696[3]	2,954,353[3]

Source: County Business Patterns, U.S. Department of Commerce, Bureau of the Census, Washington, DC 20233-0800. Extracted from *Agriculture, Mining, and Construction USA*, Gale, 1998. Notes: 1. Actual total payroll for the year. 2. 1st quarter payroll, multiplied by 4. 3. Trend projections.

SIC 0740 - VETERINARY SERVICES: INDICES OF CHANGE

| Year | Establishments | | | | Mid-March Employ-ment | Payroll | |
	Total	With less than 10 employees	With 10-49 employees	With 50 or more employees		Total[1] ($ 000)	1st Quarter annualized[2] ($ 000)
1987	83.2	89.2	63.4	44.6	70.8	59.9	62.4
1988	82.9	87.2	68.8	50.8	75.1	65.2	65.5
1989	87.7	91.3	76.2	55.4	80.6	72.6	72.5
1990	90.5	92.8	82.9	58.5	86.9	81.2	81.1
1991	95.8	97.4	90.6	76.9	92.8	89.9	89.7
1992	100.0	100.0	100.0	100.0	100.0	100.0	100.0
1993	102.5	101.4	106.2	98.5	104.7	106.6	104.6
1994	107.0	105.0	114.0	90.8	110.2	115.5	113.7
1995	109.4	104.9	124.6	118.5	118.1	127.6	127.6
1996	113.3[3]				122.7[3]	132.7[3]	130.6[3]
1997	116.8[3]				128.6[3]	141.1[3]	138.5[3]
1998	120.4[3]				134.5[3]	149.4[3]	146.4[3]

Source: Same as General Statistics. The values shown reflect change from the base year, 1992. Values above 100 mean greater than 1992, values below 100 mean less than 1992, and a value of 100 in the 1987-91 or 1993-98 period means same as 1992. Notes: 1. Actual total payroll for the year. 2. 1st quarter payroll, multiplied by 4. 3. Trend projections.

SIC 0750 - ANIMAL SERVICES, EXCEPT VETERINARY: GENERAL STATISTICS

| Year | Establishments | | | | Mid-March Employ-ment | Payroll | |
	Total	With less than 10 employees	With 10-49 employees	With 50 or more employees		Total[1] ($ 000)	1st Quarter annualized[2] ($ 000)
1987	6,886	6,223	611	52	31,510	368,905	350,848
1988	6,470	5,806	613	51	31,354	380,385	352,180
1989	6,564	5,888	628	48	31,153	384,003	359,288
1990	7,352	6,643	665	44	33,659	428,595	392,820
1991	7,931	7,208	668	55	35,831	463,112	432,488
1992	8,786	8,016	717	53	38,117	504,901	464,240
1993	9,074	8,293	727	54	39,527	532,764	474,028
1994	9,375	8,623	699	53	39,241	553,690	493,480
1995	9,700	8,916	736	48	40,488	572,623	521,808
1996	10,135[3]				41,866[3]	599,300[3]	536,915[3]
1997	10,554[3]				43,071[3]	625,452[3]	558,410[3]
1998	10,972[3]				44,275[3]	651,604[3]	579,905[3]

Source: County Business Patterns, U.S. Department of Commerce, Bureau of the Census, Washington, DC 20233-0800. Extracted from *Agriculture, Mining, and Construction USA*, Gale, 1998. Notes: 1. Actual total payroll for the year. 2. 1st quarter payroll, multiplied by 4. 3. Trend projections.

SIC 0750 - ANIMAL SERVICES, EXCEPT VETERINARY: INDICES OF CHANGE

| Year | Establishments | | | | Mid-March Employ-ment | Payroll | |
	Total	With less than 10 employees	With 10-49 employees	With 50 or more employees		Total[1] ($ 000)	1st Quarter annualized[2] ($ 000)
1987	78.4	77.6	85.2	98.1	82.7	73.1	75.6
1988	73.6	72.4	85.5	96.2	82.3	75.3	75.9
1989	74.7	73.5	87.6	90.6	81.7	76.1	77.4
1990	83.7	82.9	92.7	83.0	88.3	84.9	84.6
1991	90.3	89.9	93.2	103.8	94.0	91.7	93.2
1992	100.0	100.0	100.0	100.0	100.0	100.0	100.0
1993	103.3	103.5	101.4	101.9	103.7	105.5	102.1
1994	106.7	107.6	97.5	100.0	102.9	109.7	106.3
1995	110.4	111.2	102.6	90.6	106.2	113.4	112.4
1996	115.4[3]				109.8[3]	118.7[3]	115.7[3]
1997	120.1[3]				113.0[3]	123.9[3]	120.3[3]
1998	124.9[3]				116.2[3]	129.1[3]	124.9[3]

Source: Same as General Statistics. The values shown reflect change from the base year, 1992. Values above 100 mean greater than 1992, values below 100 mean less than 1992, and a value of 100 in the 1987-91 or 1993-98 period means same as 1992. Notes: 1. Actual total payroll for the year. 2. 1st quarter payroll, multiplied by 4. 3. Trend projections.

SIC 0760 - FARM LABOR AND MANAGEMENT SERVICES: GENERAL STATISTICS

| Year | Establishments | | | | Mid-March Employ-ment | Payroll | |
	Total	With less than 10 employees	With 10-49 employees	With 50 or more employees		Total[1] ($ 000)	1st Quarter annualized[2] ($ 000)
1987	807	622	135	50	11,593	128,184	129,676
1988	679	524	114	41	9,973	112,229	107,508
1989	670	506	128	36	9,007	112,452	105,112
1990	775	596	134	45	10,763	135,753	123,872
1991	771	595	134	42	9,817	132,188	125,208
1992	849	650	140	59	12,337	161,164	150,864
1993	925	738	135	52	11,797	161,553	148,648
1994	945	767	132	46	10,181	170,921	149,888
1995	949	769	140	40	10,452	176,526	166,080
1996	958[3]				10,733[3]	180,866[3]	162,525[3]
1997	984[3]				10,734[3]	188,085[3]	167,934[3]
1998	1,010[3]				10,735[3]	195,303[3]	173,343[3]

Source: County Business Patterns, U.S. Department of Commerce, Bureau of the Census, Washington, DC 20233-0800. Extracted from *Agriculture, Mining, and Construction USA*, Gale, 1998. Notes: 1. Actual total payroll for the year. 2. 1st quarter payroll, multiplied by 4. 3. Trend projections.

SIC 0760 - FARM LABOR AND MANAGEMENT SERVICES: INDICES OF CHANGE

| Year | Establishments | | | | Mid-March Employ-ment | Payroll | |
	Total	With less than 10 employees	With 10-49 employees	With 50 or more employees		Total[1] ($ 000)	1st Quarter annualized[2] ($ 000)
1987	95.1	95.7	96.4	84.7	94.0	79.5	86.0
1988	80.0	80.6	81.4	69.5	80.8	69.6	71.3
1989	78.9	77.8	91.4	61.0	73.0	69.8	69.7
1990	91.3	91.7	95.7	76.3	87.2	84.2	82.1
1991	90.8	91.5	95.7	71.2	79.6	82.0	83.0
1992	100.0	100.0	100.0	100.0	100.0	100.0	100.0
1993	109.0	113.5	96.4	88.1	95.6	100.2	98.5
1994	111.3	118.0	94.3	78.0	82.5	106.1	99.4
1995	111.8	118.3	100.0	67.8	84.7	109.5	110.1
1996	112.8[3]				87.0[3]	112.2[3]	107.7[3]
1997	115.9[3]				87.0[3]	116.7[3]	111.3[3]
1998	119.0[3]				87.0[3]	121.2[3]	114.9[3]

Source: Same as General Statistics. The values shown reflect change from the base year, 1992. Values above 100 mean greater than 1992, values below 100 mean less than 1992, and a value of 100 in the 1987-91 or 1993-98 period means same as 1992. Notes: 1. Actual total payroll for the year. 2. 1st quarter payroll, multiplied by 4. 3. Trend projections.

SIC 0761 - FARM LABOR CONTRACTORS: GENERAL STATISTICS

| Year | Establishments | | | | Mid-March Employ-ment | Payroll | |
	Total	With less than 10 employees	With 10-49 employees	With 50 or more employees		Total[1] ($ 000)	1st Quarter annualized[2] ($ 000)
1987	108	64	25	19	4,548	45,581	46,660
1988	91	52	26	13	3,996	35,859	34,380
1989	111	71	30	10	2,834	34,860	29,764
1990	195	139	38	18	4,054	49,200	37,220
1991	202	139	45	18	4,318	47,729	42,120
1992	240	171	43	26	5,603	58,530	52,024
1993	358	272	57	29	5,984	71,720	59,912
1994	384	297	58	29	5,696	74,901	63,484
1995	365	275	68	22	6,091	79,752	67,524
1996	421[3]				6,195[3]	81,084[3]	65,859[3]
1997	458[3]				6,462[3]	86,062[3]	69,206[3]
1998	496[3]				6,729[3]	91,039[3]	72,554[3]

Source: County Business Patterns, U.S. Department of Commerce, Bureau of the Census, Washington, DC 20233-0800. Extracted from *Agriculture, Mining, and Construction USA*, Gale, 1998. Notes: 1. Actual total payroll for the year. 2. 1st quarter payroll, multiplied by 4. 3. Trend projections.

SIC 0761 - FARM LABOR CONTRACTORS: INDICES OF CHANGE

| Year | Establishments | | | | Mid-March Employ-ment | Payroll | |
	Total	With less than 10 employees	With 10-49 employees	With 50 or more employees		Total[1] ($ 000)	1st Quarter annualized[2] ($ 000)
1987	45.0	37.4	58.1	73.1	81.2	77.9	89.7
1988	37.9	30.4	60.5	50.0	71.3	61.3	66.1
1989	46.3	41.5	69.8	38.5	50.6	59.6	57.2
1990	81.3	81.3	88.4	69.2	72.4	84.1	71.5
1991	84.2	81.3	104.7	69.2	77.1	81.5	81.0
1992	100.0	100.0	100.0	100.0	100.0	100.0	100.0
1993	149.2	159.1	132.6	111.5	106.8	122.5	115.2
1994	160.0	173.7	134.9	111.5	101.7	128.0	122.0
1995	152.1	160.8	158.1	84.6	108.7	136.3	129.8
1996	175.3[3]				110.6[3]	138.5[3]	126.6[3]
1997	191.0[3]				115.3[3]	147.0[3]	133.0[3]
1998	206.7[3]				120.1[3]	155.5[3]	139.5[3]

Source: Same as General Statistics. The values shown reflect change from the base year, 1992. Values above 100 mean greater than 1992, values below 100 mean less than 1992, and a value of 100 in the 1987-91 or 1993-98 period means same as 1992. Notes: 1. Actual total payroll for the year. 2. 1st quarter payroll, multiplied by 4. 3. Trend projections.

SIC 0762 - FARM MANAGEMENT SERVICES: GENERAL STATISTICS

Year	Establishments				Mid-March Employ-ment	Payroll	
	Total	With less than 10 employees	With 10-49 employees	With 50 or more employees		Total[1] ($ 000)	1st Quarter annualized[2] ($ 000)
1987	506	413	79	14	4,059	65,969	63,648
1988	397	321	59	17	3,973	59,881	58,660
1989	379	308	58	13	3,032	60,104	57,736
1990	405	325	66	14	3,549	67,052	63,956
1991	430	351	68	11	3,447	68,135	65,912
1992	494	392	80	22	5,097	85,354	83,400
1993	505	412	74	19	4,915	82,650	80,356
1994	489	401	72	16	4,287	93,502	84,428
1995	497	411	69	17	4,101	93,654	95,288
1996	486[3]				4,539[3]	96,369[3]	93,082[3]
1997	491[3]				4,633[3]	100,490[3]	97,041[3]
1998	496[3]				4,727[3]	104,612[3]	101,000[3]

Source: County Business Patterns, U.S. Department of Commerce, Bureau of the Census, Washington, DC 20233-0800. Extracted from *Agriculture, Mining, and Construction USA*, Gale, 1998. Notes: 1. Actual total payroll for the year. 2. 1st quarter payroll, multiplied by 4. 3. Trend projections.

SIC 0762 - FARM MANAGEMENT SERVICES: INDICES OF CHANGE

Year	Establishments				Mid-March Employ-ment	Payroll	
	Total	With less than 10 employees	With 10-49 employees	With 50 or more employees		Total[1] ($ 000)	1st Quarter annualized[2] ($ 000)
1987	102.4	105.4	98.8	63.6	79.6	77.3	76.3
1988	80.4	81.9	73.8	77.3	77.9	70.2	70.3
1989	76.7	78.6	72.5	59.1	59.5	70.4	69.2
1990	82.0	82.9	82.5	63.6	69.6	78.6	76.7
1991	87.0	89.5	85.0	50.0	67.6	79.8	79.0
1992	100.0	100.0	100.0	100.0	100.0	100.0	100.0
1993	102.2	105.1	92.5	86.4	96.4	96.8	96.4
1994	99.0	102.3	90.0	72.7	84.1	109.5	101.2
1995	100.6	104.8	86.3	77.3	80.5	109.7	114.3
1996	98.4[3]				89.1[3]	112.9[3]	111.6[3]
1997	99.4[3]				90.9[3]	117.7[3]	116.4[3]
1998	100.3[3]				92.7[3]	122.6[3]	121.1[3]

Source: Same as General Statistics. The values shown reflect change from the base year, 1992. Values above 100 mean greater than 1992, values below 100 mean less than 1992, and a value of 100 in the 1987-91 or 1993-98 period means same as 1992. Notes: 1. Actual total payroll for the year. 2. 1st quarter payroll, multiplied by 4. 3. Trend projections.

SIC 0780 - LANDSCAPE AND HORTICULTURAL SERVICES: GENERAL STATISTICS

| Year | Establishments | | | | Mid-March Employment | Payroll | |
	Total	With less than 10 employees	With 10-49 employees	With 50 or more employees		Total[1] ($ 000)	1st Quarter annualized[2] ($ 000)
1987	40,543	35,730	4,366	447	216,965	3,322,988	2,444,552
1988	39,414	34,323	4,539	552	230,059	3,727,525	2,787,576
1989	43,772	38,246	4,917	609	248,953	4,095,032	3,038,948
1990	46,903	40,754	5,497	652	274,112	4,485,151	3,436,308
1991	51,415	45,260	5,530	625	273,048	4,573,704	3,492,580
1992	55,268	48,490	6,106	672	304,212	5,082,821	3,871,300
1993	59,475	52,238	6,547	690	306,090	5,393,224	3,773,208
1994	62,228	55,866	5,683	679	294,854	5,866,475	4,075,992
1995	64,834	57,838	6,180	816	326,366	6,383,492	4,659,544
1996	68,643[3]				341,956[3]	6,598,932[3]	4,750,485[3]
1997	72,062[3]				355,522[3]	6,965,277[3]	5,000,443[3]
1998	75,482[3]				369,088[3]	7,331,622[3]	5,250,401[3]

Source: County Business Patterns, U.S. Department of Commerce, Bureau of the Census, Washington, DC 20233-0800. Extracted from *Agriculture, Mining, and Construction USA*, Gale, 1998. Notes: 1. Actual total payroll for the year. 2. 1st quarter payroll, multiplied by 4. 3. Trend projections.

SIC 0780 - LANDSCAPE AND HORTICULTURAL SERVICES: INDICES OF CHANGE

| Year | Establishments | | | | Mid-March Employment | Payroll | |
	Total	With less than 10 employees	With 10-49 employees	With 50 or more employees		Total[1] ($ 000)	1st Quarter annualized[2] ($ 000)
1987	73.4	73.7	71.5	66.5	71.3	65.4	63.1
1988	71.3	70.8	74.3	82.1	75.6	73.3	72.0
1989	79.2	78.9	80.5	90.6	81.8	80.6	78.5
1990	84.9	84.0	90.0	97.0	90.1	88.2	88.8
1991	93.0	93.3	90.6	93.0	89.8	90.0	90.2
1992	100.0	100.0	100.0	100.0	100.0	100.0	100.0
1993	107.6	107.7	107.2	102.7	100.6	106.1	97.5
1994	112.6	115.2	93.1	101.0	96.9	115.4	105.3
1995	117.3	119.3	101.2	121.4	107.3	125.6	120.4
1996	124.2[3]				112.4[3]	129.8[3]	122.7[3]
1997	130.4[3]				116.9[3]	137.0[3]	129.2[3]
1998	136.6[3]				121.3[3]	144.2[3]	135.6[3]

Source: Same as General Statistics. The values shown reflect change from the base year, 1992. Values above 100 mean greater than 1992, values below 100 mean less than 1992, and a value of 100 in the 1987-91 or 1993-98 period means same as 1992. Notes: 1. Actual total payroll for the year. 2. 1st quarter payroll, multiplied by 4. 3. Trend projections.

SIC 0800 - FORESTRY: GENERAL STATISTICS

| Year | Establishments | | | | Mid-March Employ-ment | Payroll | |
	Total	With less than 10 employees	With 10-49 employees	With 50 or more employees		Total[1] ($ 000)	1st Quarter annualized[2] ($ 000)
1987	1,796	1,405	332	59	17,692	264,425	262,040
1988	1,699	1,310	326	63	17,875	273,171	260,356
1989	1,687	1,299	321	67	17,125	254,370	237,152
1990	1,798	1,391	340	67	17,981	287,955	266,024
1991	1,995	1,587	340	68	18,525	300,701	282,708
1992	2,138	1,723	348	67	18,588	340,130	318,896
1993	2,251	1,848	343	60	17,716	348,400	293,172
1994	2,382	1,970	354	58	19,462	417,686	376,612
1995	2,512	2,101	347	64	20,488	459,495	438,028
1996	2,522[3]				19,808[3]	442,828[3]	398,981[3]
1997	2,618[3]				20,089[3]	465,504[3]	417,535[3]
1998	2,713[3]				20,370[3]	488,180[3]	436,090[3]

Source: County Business Patterns, U.S. Department of Commerce, Bureau of the Census, Washington, DC 20233-0800. Extracted from *Agriculture, Mining, and Construction USA*, Gale, 1998. Notes: 1. Actual total payroll for the year. 2. 1st quarter payroll, multiplied by 4. 3. Trend projections.

SIC 0800 - FORESTRY: INDICES OF CHANGE

| Year | Establishments | | | | Mid-March Employ-ment | Payroll | |
	Total	With less than 10 employees	With 10-49 employees	With 50 or more employees		Total[1] ($ 000)	1st Quarter annualized[2] ($ 000)
1987	84.0	81.5	95.4	88.1	95.2	77.7	82.2
1988	79.5	76.0	93.7	94.0	96.2	80.3	81.6
1989	78.9	75.4	92.2	100.0	92.1	74.8	74.4
1990	84.1	80.7	97.7	100.0	96.7	84.7	83.4
1991	93.3	92.1	97.7	101.5	99.7	88.4	88.7
1992	100.0	100.0	100.0	100.0	100.0	100.0	100.0
1993	105.3	107.3	98.6	89.6	95.3	102.4	91.9
1994	111.4	114.3	101.7	86.6	104.7	122.8	118.1
1995	117.5	121.9	99.7	95.5	110.2	135.1	137.4
1996	118.0[3]				106.6[3]	130.2[3]	125.1[3]
1997	122.4[3]				108.1[3]	136.9[3]	130.9[3]
1998	126.9[3]				109.6[3]	143.5[3]	136.7[3]

Source: Same as General Statistics. The values shown reflect change from the base year, 1992. Values above 100 mean greater than 1992, values below 100 mean less than 1992, and a value of 100 in the 1987-91 or 1993-98 period means same as 1992. Notes: 1. Actual total payroll for the year. 2. 1st quarter payroll, multiplied by 4. 3. Trend projections.

SIC 0900 - FISHING, HUNTING, AND TRAPPING: GENERAL STATISTICS

Year	Establishments				Mid-March Employ-ment	Payroll	
	Total	With less than 10 employees	With 10-49 employees	With 50 or more employees		Total[1] ($ 000)	1st Quarter annualized[2] ($ 000)
1987	1,826	1,623	187	16	8,420	176,340	138,832
1988	1,679	1,447	208	24	9,067	216,523	188,788
1989	1,682	1,454	203	25	9,426	253,623	220,580
1990	1,609	1,368	207	34	10,555	299,401	249,876
1991	1,714	1,465	200	49	12,764	368,454	341,288
1992	1,798	1,534	221	43	12,553	349,665	364,832
1993	2,087	1,836	208	43	12,704	319,285	299,608
1994	2,168	1,957	172	39	12,951	344,577	296,688
1995	2,236	2,022	183	31	11,871	348,527	330,456
1996	2,151[3]				13,972[3]	409,234[3]	390,112[3]
1997	2,204[3]				14,537[3]	432,138[3]	414,579[3]
1998	2,257[3]				15,102[3]	455,041[3]	439,046[3]

Source: County Business Patterns, U.S. Department of Commerce, Bureau of the Census, Washington, DC 20233-0800. Extracted from *Agriculture, Mining, and Construction USA*, Gale, 1998. Notes: 1. Actual total payroll for the year. 2. 1st quarter payroll, multiplied by 4. 3. Trend projections.

SIC 0900 - FISHING, HUNTING, AND TRAPPING: INDICES OF CHANGE

Year	Establishments				Mid-March Employ-ment	Payroll	
	Total	With less than 10 employees	With 10-49 employees	With 50 or more employees		Total[1] ($ 000)	1st Quarter annualized[2] ($ 000)
1987	101.6	105.8	84.6	37.2	67.1	50.4	38.1
1988	93.4	94.3	94.1	55.8	72.2	61.9	51.7
1989	93.5	94.8	91.9	58.1	75.1	72.5	60.5
1990	89.5	89.2	93.7	79.1	84.1	85.6	68.5
1991	95.3	95.5	90.5	114.0	101.7	105.4	93.5
1992	100.0	100.0	100.0	100.0	100.0	100.0	100.0
1993	116.1	119.7	94.1	100.0	101.2	91.3	82.1
1994	120.6	127.6	77.8	90.7	103.2	98.5	81.3
1995	124.4	131.8	82.8	72.1	94.6	99.7	90.6
1996	119.7[3]				111.3[3]	117.0[3]	106.9[3]
1997	122.6[3]				115.8[3]	123.6[3]	113.6[3]
1998	125.5[3]				120.3[3]	130.1[3]	120.3[3]

Source: Same as General Statistics. The values shown reflect change from the base year, 1992. Values above 100 mean greater than 1992, values below 100 mean less than 1992, and a value of 100 in the 1987-91 or 1993-98 period means same as 1992. Notes: 1. Actual total payroll for the year. 2. 1st quarter payroll, multiplied by 4. 3. Trend projections.

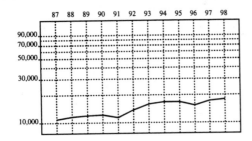

87 88 89 90 91 92 93 94 95 96 97 98

Revenues ($ millions)

SIC 2411 LOGGING: GENERAL STATISTICS

Year	Estab-lish-ments	Employment			Compensation		Production ($ mil.)		
		Total (000)	Production		Payroll ($ mil.)	Wages ($/hr)	Cost of Materials	Value of Shipments	Capital Inves.
			Workers (000)	Hours (mil.)					
1987	11,936	85.8	72.2	131.3	1,515.5	9.14	6,801.5	10,938.2	349.3
1988		86.9	73.0	136.5	1,591.4	9.09	7,350.6	11,663.8	221.5
1989	11,915	81.7	68.0	132.4	1,595.6	9.50	7,576.3	12,017.4	353.9
1990		83.4	68.9	134.4	1,647.3	9.55	7,930.4	12,229.0	405.9
1991		78.1	65.4	126.0	1,560.6	9.80	7,280.2	11,434.3	292.9
1992	13,010	83.6	69.4	131.2	1,693.1	9.96	8,763.3	13,844.5	375.5
1993		86.2	71.6	138.9	1,774.9	9.86	10,121.3	15,976.4	366.0
1994		87.2	71.7	142.4	1,820.2	9.96	10,856.7	16,817.7	469.0
1995		86.8	71.0	140.7	1,890.8	10.41	10,707.4	16,775.5	592.4
1996		83.0	68.3	134.1	1,856.0	10.76	9,660.5	15,411.1	539.4
1997		85.6[1]	69.7[1]	140.5[1]	1,951.2[1]	10.69[1]	10,840.2[1]	17,293.0[1]	510.4[1]
1998		86.0[1]	69.8[1]	141.8[1]	2,000.7[1]	10.84[1]	11,255.6[1]	17,955.8[1]	528.5[1]
1999		86.3[1]	69.8[1]	143.0[1]	2,050.1[1]	11.00[1]	11,671.1[1]	18,618.6[1]	546.7[1]
2000		86.7[1]	69.9[1]	144.2[1]	2,099.5[1]	11.16[1]	12,086.6[1]	19,281.5[1]	564.9[1]

Source: 1987 and 1992 Economic Census; *Annual Survey of Manufactures*, 88-91, 93-96. Establishment counts for non-Census years are from *County Business Patterns*. Extracted from *Manufacturing USA*, 6th Edition, Gale, 1998. Note: 1. Projections by the editors.

SIC 2411 LOGGING: INDICES OF CHANGE

Year	Estab-lish-ments	Employment			Compensation		Production ($ mil.)		
		Total (000)	Production		Payroll ($ mil.)	Wages ($/hr)	Cost of Materials	Value of Shipments	Capital Inves.
			Workers (000)	Hours (mil.)					
1987	92	103	104	100	90	92	78	79	93
1988		104	105	104	94	91	84	84	59
1989	92	98	98	101	94	95	86	87	94
1990		100	99	102	97	96	90	88	108
1991		93	94	96	92	98	83	83	78
1992	100	100	100	100	100	100	100	100	100
1993		103	103	106	105	99	115	115	97
1994		104	103	109	108	100	124	121	125
1995		104	102	107	112	105	122	121	158
1996		99	98	102	110	108	110	111	144
1997		102[1]	100[1]	107[1]	115[1]	107[1]	124[1]	125[1]	136[1]
1998		103[1]	101[1]	108[1]	118[1]	109[1]	128[1]	130[1]	141[1]
1999		103[1]	101[1]	109[1]	121[1]	110[1]	133[1]	134[1]	146[1]
2000		104[1]	101[1]	110[1]	124[1]	112[1]	138[1]	139[1]	150[1]

Source: Same as General Statistics. Values reflect change from the base year, 1992. Values above 100 mean greater than 1992, values below 100 mean less than 1992, and a value of 100 in the 1982-91 or 1993-2000 period means same as 1992. Note: 1. Projections by the editors.

SIC 2411 LOGGING: SELECTED RATIOS

For 1996	Average of All Manufacturing	Analyzed Industry	Index
Employees per Establishment	46	6	14
Payroll per Establishment	1,332,320	130,138	10
Payroll per Employee	29,181	20,252	69
Production Workers per Establishment	31	5	17
Wages per Establishment	734,496	100,442	14
Wages per Production Worker	23,390	18,829	81
Hours per Production Worker	2,025	1,890	93
Wages per Hour	11.55	9.96	86
Value Added per Establishment	3,842,210	393,490	10
Value Added per Employee	84,153	61,236	73
Value Added per Production Worker	122,353	73,765	60
Cost per Establishment	4,239,462	673,582	16
Cost per Employee	92,853	104,824	113
Cost per Production Worker	135,003	126,272	94
Shipments per Establishment	8,100,800	1,064,143	13
Shipments per Employee	177,425	165,604	93
Shipments per Production Worker	257,966	199,488	77
Investment per Establishment	278,244	28,862	10
Investment per Employee	6,094	4,492	74
Investment per Production Worker	8,861	5,411	61

Source: Same as General Statistics. The 'Average of All Manufacturing' column represents the average of all manufacturing industries reported for the most recent complete year available. The Index shows the relationship between the Average and the Analyzed Industry. For example, 100 means that they are equal; 500 that the Analyzed Industry is five times the average; 50 means that the Analyzed Industry is half the national average. The abbreviation 'na' is used to show that data are 'not available'.

CHAPTER 3 - PART II

FINANCIAL NORMS AND RATIOS

Industry-specific financial norms and ratios are shown in this chapter for thirty-two industries in the Agriculture sector. For each industry in the sector, balance sheets are presented for the years 1996 through 1998, with the most recent year shown first. As part of each balance sheet, additional financial averages for net sales, gross profits, net profits after tax, and working capital are shown. The number of establishments used to calculate the averages are shown for each year.

The second table in each display shows D&B Key Business Ratios for the SIC-denominated industry. These data, again, are for the years 1996 through 1998. Ratios measuring solvency (e.g., Quick ratio), efficiency (e.g., Collection period, in days), and profitability (e.g. % return on sales) are shown. A total of 14 ratios are featured. Ratios are shown for the upper quartile, median, and lowest quartile of the D&B sample.

This product includes proprietary data of Dun & Bradstreet Inc.

D&B INDUSTRY NORMS: SIC 0111 - WHEAT

	1998 (22) Estab.		1997 (23) Estab.		1996 (38) Estab.	
	$	%	$	%	$	%
Cash	45,149	3.7	26,840	6.1	89,575	11.3
Accounts Receivable	69,554	5.7	22,000	5.0	47,562	6.0
Notes Receivable	28,066	2.3	2,200	.5	-	-
Inventory	213,543	17.5	77,879	17.7	28,537	3.6
Other Current Assets	59,792	4.9	34,759	7.9	51,526	6.5
Total Current Assets	416,104	34.1	163,678	37.2	217,200	27.4
Fixed Assets	640,629	52.5	219,117	49.8	331,349	41.8
Other Non-current Assets	163,513	13.4	57,199	13.0	244,152	30.8
Total Assets	1,220,246	100.0	439,994	100.0	792,701	100.0
Accounts Payable	43,929	3.6	13,640	3.1	12,683	1.6
Bank Loans	-	-	-	-	-	-
Notes Payable	107,382	8.8	55,439	12.6	43,599	5.5
Other Current Liabilities	156,191	12.8	66,879	15.2	98,295	12.4
Total Current Liabilities	307,502	25.2	135,958	30.9	154,577	19.5
Other Long Term	219,644	18.0	84,039	19.1	163,296	20.6
Deferred Credits	-	-	-	-	-	-
Net Worth	693,100	56.8	219,997	50.0	474,828	59.9
Total Liabilities & Net Worth	1,220,246	100.0	439,994	100.0	792,701	100.0
Net Sales	657,485	100.0	1,222,281	100.0	607,683	100.0
Gross Profits	200,533	30.5	710,145	58.1	207,828	34.2
Net Profit After Tax	76,926	11.7	61,114	5.0	17,623	2.9
Working Capital	108,602	-	27,719	-	62,623	-

Source: Dun & Bradstreet. Data in this table are copyright (c) 1999 of Dun & Bradstreet. Reprinted by special arrangement with D&B. *Notes:* Values in parentheses above columns indicate the number of establishments in the sample. Data shown are for all companies.

D&B KEY BUSINESS RATIOS: SIC 0111

	1998			1997			1996		
	UQ	MED	LQ	UQ	MED	LQ	UQ	MED	LQ
Solvency									
Quick ratio	.6	.4	.1	.7	.3	.1	1.7	.5	.3
Current ratio	2.4	1.5	.7	2.5	1.4	.7	2.4	1.3	.5
Current liabilities/Net worth (%)	24.8	33.8	47.0	15.4	27.8	95.4	9.1	21.4	32.9
Current liabilities/Inventory (%)	73.9	96.0	179.1	46.4	95.2	255.3	241.7	265.0	326.8
Total liabilities/Net worth (%)	38.4	55.9	100.0	15.4	84.8	134.2	21.2	40.0	124.7
Fixed assets/Net worth (%)	65.3	98.5	156.9	52.5	86.2	135.8	38.1	78.7	131.5
Efficiency									
Collection period (days)	7.8	18.5	30.6	19.2	50.6	82.5	4.8	12.4	103.3
Sales to Inventory	5.7	2.8	1.9	3.7	3.6	2.6	10.0	8.9	7.8
Assets/Sales (%)	81.1	145.4	188.8	24.6	88.3	143.3	34.8	75.9	471.5
Sales/Net Working Capital	9.5	4.1	1.7	14.5	7.3	7.1	5.6	5.5	1.6
Accounts payable/Sales (%)	1.2	4.1	7.8	6.9	13.7	15.9	3.1	3.1	3.1
Profitability									
Return - Sales (%)	24.3	9.0	3.1	6.2	3.0	-6.7	4.7	3.8	2.0
Return - Assets (%)	11.5	6.6	3.4	4.6	2.1	-7.6	6.7	.7	-2.5
Return - Net Worth (%)	21.8	16.2	6.3	14.7	8.6	-7.7	12.9	8.9	4.8

Source: Dun & Bradstreet. Data in this table are copyright (c) 1999 of Dun & Bradstreet. Reprinted by special arrangement with D&B. *Note:* UQ stands for "Upper Quartile" and represents the top 25 percent of sample; MED stands for "Median"; and LQ stands for "Lower Quartile" and represents the lowest 25 percent.

D&B INDUSTRY NORMS: SIC 0115 - CORN

	1998 (38) Estab.		1997 (34) Estab.		1996 (38) Estab.	
	$	%	$	%	$	%
Cash	93,369	6.4	155,821	7.5	58,751	6.6
Accounts Receivable	75,862	5.2	101,803	4.9	110,381	12.4
Notes Receivable	-	-	51,940	2.5	1,780	.2
Inventory	294,695	20.2	322,030	15.5	143,317	16.1
Other Current Assets	107,958	7.4	60,251	2.9	68,543	7.7
Total Current Assets	571,884	39.2	691,845	33.3	382,772	43.0
Fixed Assets	675,465	46.3	1,103,214	53.1	393,454	44.2
Other Non-current Assets	211,539	14.5	282,556	13.6	113,942	12.8
Total Assets	1,458,888	100.0	2,077,615	100.0	890,168	100.0
Accounts Payable	59,814	4.1	78,949	3.8	80,115	9.0
Bank Loans	5,836	.4	16,621	.8	-	-
Notes Payable	62,732	4.3	172,442	8.3	73,884	8.3
Other Current Liabilities	196,950	13.5	274,245	13.2	81,895	9.2
Total Current Liabilities	325,332	22.3	542,257	26.1	235,894	26.5
Other Long Term	233,422	16.0	386,437	18.6	145,097	16.3
Deferred Credits	-	-	-	-	-	-
Net Worth	900,133	61.7	1,148,922	55.3	509,176	57.2
Total Liabilities & Net Worth	1,458,887	100.0	2,077,616	100.0	890,167	100.0
Net Sales	1,083,581	100.0	1,611,681	100.0	1,398,440	100.0
Gross Profits	586,217	54.1	886,425	55.0	872,627	62.4
Net Profit After Tax	137,615	12.7	99,924	6.2	123,063	8.8
Working Capital	246,552	-	149,588	-	146,877	-

Source: Dun & Bradstreet. Data in this table are copyright (c) 1999 of Dun & Bradstreet. Reprinted by special arrangement with D&B. *Notes:* Values in parentheses above columns indicate the number of establishments in the sample. Data shown are for all companies.

D&B KEY BUSINESS RATIOS: SIC 0115

	1998			1997			1996		
	UQ	MED	LQ	UQ	MED	LQ	UQ	MED	LQ
Solvency									
Quick ratio	1.6	.3	.1	1.3	.6	.2	.8	.5	.3
Current ratio	4.9	2.2	.9	4.0	1.4	.8	4.5	1.3	.9
Current liabilities/Net worth (%)	11.4	26.0	48.6	8.0	18.8	63.8	12.4	22.9	70.2
Current liabilities/Inventory (%)	32.9	89.0	169.0	42.7	94.9	306.3	76.4	137.0	177.0
Total liabilities/Net worth (%)	21.5	39.9	90.0	15.7	57.2	119.4	25.6	63.5	129.1
Fixed assets/Net worth (%)	56.0	77.3	106.9	64.9	79.4	103.7	33.6	58.6	125.6
Efficiency									
Collection period (days)	9.5	30.0	41.9	6.7	8.0	42.0	24.5	29.2	65.3
Sales to Inventory	13.0	2.0	1.6	7.2	3.2	2.0	4.1	3.1	1.5
Assets/Sales (%)	68.6	117.4	180.5	118.4	203.5	230.3	99.2	130.7	188.8
Sales/Net Working Capital	4.3	3.3	1.5	5.3	3.3	1.6	6.7	5.0	4.1
Accounts payable/Sales (%)	1.1	20.2	22.6	.9	2.2	4.8	2.7	3.8	7.1
Profitability									
Return - Sales (%)	16.4	10.5	3.7	6.6	3.7	-.6	12.0	9.1	6.5
Return - Assets (%)	9.4	6.9	2.5	2.6	1.7	-.3	6.4	3.9	2.6
Return - Net Worth (%)	10.9	8.6	2.9	8.2	2.5	.1	14.4	8.3	5.1

Source: Dun & Bradstreet. Data in this table are copyright (c) 1999 of Dun & Bradstreet. Reprinted by special arrangement with D&B. *Note:* UQ stands for "Upper Quartile" and represents the top 25 percent of sample; MED stands for "Median"; and LQ stands for "Lower Quartile" and represents the lowest 25 percent.

D&B INDUSTRY NORMS: SIC 0134 - IRISH POTATOES

	1998 (34) Estab.		1997 (34) Estab.		1996 (26) Estab.	
	$	%	$	%	$	%
Cash	317,656	9.9	206,160	4.3	99,550	3.7
Accounts Receivable	218,188	6.8	393,142	8.2	215,243	8.0
Notes Receivable	6,417	.2	19,178	.4	21,524	.8
Inventory	381,829	11.9	685,602	14.3	473,536	17.6
Other Current Assets	48,130	1.5	139,038	2.9	59,192	2.2
Total Current Assets	972,220	30.3	1,443,120	30.1	869,045	32.3
Fixed Assets	1,835,348	57.2	2,819,117	58.8	1,469,036	54.6
Other Non-current Assets	401,081	12.5	532,180	11.1	352,461	13.1
Total Assets	3,208,649	100.0	4,794,417	100.0	2,690,542	100.0
Accounts Payable	227,814	7.1	282,871	5.9	118,384	4.4
Bank Loans	-	-	28,767	.6	-	-
Notes Payable	189,310	5.9	431,498	9.0	34,977	1.3
Other Current Liabilities	372,203	11.6	599,302	12.5	425,106	15.8
Total Current Liabilities	789,327	24.6	1,342,438	28.0	578,467	21.5
Other Long Term	683,442	21.3	920,528	19.2	707,613	26.3
Deferred Credits	-	-	4,794	.1	2,691	.1
Net Worth	1,735,880	54.1	2,526,658	52.7	1,401,773	52.1
Total Liabilities & Net Worth	3,208,649	100.0	4,794,418	100.0	2,690,544	100.0
Net Sales	3,619,957	100.0	3,605,188	100.0	4,105,963	100.0
Gross Profits	1,259,745	34.8	1,384,392	38.4	1,753,246	42.7
Net Profit After Tax	130,318	3.6	205,496	5.7	160,133	3.9
Working Capital	182,893	-	100,683	-	290,578	-

Source: Dun & Bradstreet. Data in this table are copyright (c) 1999 of Dun & Bradstreet. Reprinted by special arrangement with D&B. *Notes:* Values in parentheses above columns indicate the number of establishments in the sample. Data shown are for all companies.

D&B KEY BUSINESS RATIOS: SIC 0134

	1998			1997			1996		
	UQ	MED	LQ	UQ	MED	LQ	UQ	MED	LQ
Solvency									
Quick ratio	.4	.2	.1	.6	.3	.2	.8	.6	.4
Current ratio	1.3	.9	.5	2.8	1.1	.7	2.2	1.6	1.1
Current liabilities/Net worth (%)	1.5	12.2	39.2	19.9	42.5	100.6	14.4	26.1	51.4
Current liabilities/Inventory (%)	37.2	69.3	86.2	41.0	117.0	223.0	62.8	95.1	220.1
Total liabilities/Net worth (%)	5.0	26.2	74.1	45.6	99.1	158.0	33.7	81.0	127.0
Fixed assets/Net worth (%)	40.7	58.5	77.9	85.1	128.5	166.3	71.6	92.6	122.2
Efficiency									
Collection period (days)	15.3	17.2	21.9	20.5	36.9	54.7	18.3	29.2	52.8
Sales to Inventory	6.8	4.6	3.4	8.4	5.3	1.8	10.7	4.9	2.2
Assets/Sales (%)	40.3	60.2	67.8	84.9	121.9	180.2	58.2	77.6	148.5
Sales/Net Working Capital	3.1	3.0	1.9	42.1	6.2	1.9	12.4	6.2	2.3
Accounts payable/Sales (%)	.5	2.3	6.4	1.4	3.0	8.6	.9	3.5	6.5
Profitability									
Return - Sales (%)	6.5	4.7	-.3	6.8	5.3	.8	6.6	3.6	-.8
Return - Assets (%)	5.8	3.5	-.5	4.4	2.7	.6	7.4	6.0	-1.4
Return - Net Worth (%)	12.4	3.5	-7.3	11.0	6.6	.6	15.5	10.6	-6.2

Source: Dun & Bradstreet. Data in this table are copyright (c) 1999 of Dun & Bradstreet. Reprinted by special arrangement with D&B. *Note:* UQ stands for "Upper Quartile" and represents the top 25 percent of sample; MED stands for "Median"; and LQ stands for "Lower Quartile" and represents the lowest 25 percent.

D&B INDUSTRY NORMS: SIC 0139 - FIELD CROPS, EXCEPT CASH GRAINS, NEC

	1998 (25) Estab.		1997 (42) Estab.		1996 (40) Estab.	
	$	%	$	%	$	%
Cash	102,385	9.3	60,034	5.2	65,663	8.8
Accounts Receivable	105,688	9.6	152,393	13.2	79,094	10.6
Notes Receivable	-	-	27,708	2.4	2,985	.4
Inventory	127,706	11.6	128,149	11.1	88,048	11.8
Other Current Assets	68,257	6.2	65,806	5.7	63,425	8.5
Total Current Assets	404,036	36.7	434,090	37.6	299,215	40.1
Fixed Assets	588,988	53.5	568,012	49.2	362,639	48.6
Other Non-current Assets	107,889	9.8	152,393	13.2	84,317	11.3
Total Assets	1,100,913	100.0	1,154,495	100.0	746,171	100.0
Accounts Payable	37,431	3.4	55,416	4.8	30,593	4.1
Bank Loans	-	-	-	-	-	-
Notes Payable	80,367	7.3	79,660	6.9	55,217	7.4
Other Current Liabilities	129,908	11.8	126,994	11.0	62,678	8.4
Total Current Liabilities	247,706	22.5	262,070	22.7	148,488	19.9
Other Long Term	116,697	10.6	187,028	16.2	117,895	15.8
Deferred Credits	-	-	3,463	.3	-	-
Net Worth	736,511	66.9	701,933	60.8	479,788	64.3
Total Liabilities & Net Worth	1,100,914	100.0	1,154,494	100.0	746,171	100.0
Net Sales	1,402,875	100.0	1,000,000	100.0	927,623	100.0
Gross Profits	467,157	33.3	373,000	37.3	233,761	25.2
Net Profit After Tax	166,942	11.9	67,000	6.7	129,867	14.0
Working Capital	156,330	-	172,020	-	150,727	-

Source: Dun & Bradstreet. Data in this table are copyright (c) 1999 of Dun & Bradstreet. Reprinted by special arrangement with D&B. *Notes:* Values in parentheses above columns indicate the number of establishments in the sample. Data shown are for all companies.

D&B KEY BUSINESS RATIOS: SIC 0139

	1998			1997			1996		
	UQ	MED	LQ	UQ	MED	LQ	UQ	MED	LQ
Solvency									
Quick ratio	1.9	.9	.2	1.5	.7	.2	2.0	.8	.3
Current ratio	7.9	1.4	1.2	4.7	2.0	.8	5.2	2.1	1.1
Current liabilities/Net worth (%)	10.3	39.3	61.0	7.3	33.2	50.7	11.5	25.5	41.5
Current liabilities/Inventory (%)	56.6	123.0	221.9	58.4	102.7	153.6	44.6	84.5	197.4
Total liabilities/Net worth (%)	14.9	40.4	90.6	31.9	50.3	125.6	18.9	52.3	112.7
Fixed assets/Net worth (%)	51.1	78.1	109.6	38.8	82.7	119.2	71.7	86.5	99.5
Efficiency									
Collection period (days)	18.5	23.0	49.3	20.7	31.0	40.0	10.3	15.3	116.5
Sales to Inventory	11.4	6.3	3.9	18.4	8.5	4.0	23.7	8.4	3.1
Assets/Sales (%)	57.7	83.7	117.3	48.3	76.2	156.5	30.9	52.7	168.0
Sales/Net Working Capital	10.7	5.4	2.0	8.3	5.4	3.8	50.8	13.9	6.4
Accounts payable/Sales (%)	.7	2.9	6.6	1.0	4.3	6.7	.7	1.3	5.7
Profitability									
Return - Sales (%)	20.5	6.7	3.3	16.6	6.5	.8	35.8	13.4	1.4
Return - Assets (%)	15.6	6.3	2.1	20.2	6.6	2.0	27.3	4.7	2.8
Return - Net Worth (%)	17.1	9.5	3.5	34.4	10.2	3.7	30.9	10.0	5.1

Source: Dun & Bradstreet. Data in this table are copyright (c) 1999 of Dun & Bradstreet. Reprinted by special arrangement with D&B. *Note:* UQ stands for "Upper Quartile" and represents the top 25 percent of sample; MED stands for "Median"; and LQ stands for "Lower Quartile" and represents the lowest 25 percent.

D&B INDUSTRY NORMS: SIC 0161 - VEGETABLES AND MELONS

	1998 (87) Estab.		1997 (117) Estab.		1996 (119) Estab.	
	$	%	$	%	$	%
Cash	171,883	6.9	187,338	9.5	203,026	11.2
Accounts Receivable	378,640	15.2	341,153	17.3	246,532	13.6
Notes Receivable	17,437	.7	17,748	.9	19,940	1.1
Inventory	137,008	5.5	167,618	8.5	130,517	7.2
Other Current Assets	194,302	7.8	167,618	8.5	164,959	9.1
Total Current Assets	899,270	36.1	881,475	44.7	764,974	42.2
Fixed Assets	1,332,712	53.5	842,036	42.7	861,049	47.5
Other Non-current Assets	259,069	10.4	248,470	12.6	186,712	10.3
Total Assets	2,491,051	100.0	1,971,981	100.0	1,812,735	100.0
Accounts Payable	246,614	9.9	149,871	7.6	112,390	6.2
Bank Loans	17,437	.7	1,972	.1	-	-
Notes Payable	117,079	4.7	84,795	4.3	112,390	6.2
Other Current Liabilities	361,202	14.5	352,985	17.9	244,719	13.5
Total Current Liabilities	742,332	29.8	589,623	29.9	469,499	25.9
Other Long Term	361,202	14.5	374,677	19.0	331,730	18.3
Deferred Credits	4,982	.2	3,944	.2	3,625	.2
Net Worth	1,382,533	55.5	1,003,739	50.9	1,007,880	55.6
Total Liabilities & Net Worth	2,491,049	100.0	1,971,983	100.0	1,812,734	100.0
Net Sales	4,567,921	100.0	4,844,547	100.0	3,315,059	100.0
Gross Profits	1,694,699	37.1	1,584,167	32.7	1,067,449	32.2
Net Profit After Tax	114,198	2.5	96,891	2.0	76,246	2.3
Working Capital	156,936	-	291,853	-	295,476	-

Source: Dun & Bradstreet. Data in this table are copyright (c) 1999 of Dun & Bradstreet. Reprinted by special arrangement with D&B. *Notes:* Values in parentheses above columns indicate the number of establishments in the sample. Data shown are for all companies.

D&B KEY BUSINESS RATIOS: SIC 0161

	1998			1997			1996		
	UQ	MED	LQ	UQ	MED	LQ	UQ	MED	LQ
Solvency									
Quick ratio	1.4	.6	.4	2.0	.9	.5	2.1	1.0	.4
Current ratio	2.2	1.2	.7	3.3	1.6	1.0	3.3	1.8	1.0
Current liabilities/Net worth (%)	18.3	39.6	110.7	15.2	41.9	97.6	11.9	39.9	83.8
Current liabilities/Inventory (%)	164.9	362.5	591.4	101.5	194.6	388.7	92.1	219.9	408.1
Total liabilities/Net worth (%)	26.4	74.0	156.8	33.4	83.8	178.4	27.3	62.7	164.0
Fixed assets/Net worth (%)	63.4	96.6	131.1	39.2	86.6	130.2	45.1	73.6	139.9
Efficiency									
Collection period (days)	9.9	31.4	42.0	20.4	32.5	49.6	9.7	24.3	51.6
Sales to Inventory	165.5	42.2	23.9	41.2	22.3	6.8	53.1	31.7	8.5
Assets/Sales (%)	30.2	50.1	63.0	28.8	49.2	103.3	31.5	45.3	87.3
Sales/Net Working Capital	42.8	21.2	8.8	36.4	11.1	5.6	30.0	9.1	4.5
Accounts payable/Sales (%)	1.4	3.8	7.8	1.8	5.1	7.3	1.1	2.5	7.0
Profitability									
Return - Sales (%)	4.7	2.8	-.9	8.8	2.6	-.6	8.0	3.2	-.4
Return - Assets (%)	11.4	5.5	-2.3	11.9	5.0	.1	12.9	6.6	-1.5
Return - Net Worth (%)	20.9	14.1	-5.3	33.0	12.6	.9	26.6	10.2	-.8

Source: Dun & Bradstreet. Data in this table are copyright (c) 1999 of Dun & Bradstreet. Reprinted by special arrangement with D&B. *Note:* UQ stands for "Upper Quartile" and represents the top 25 percent of sample; MED stands for "Median"; and LQ stands for "Lower Quartile" and represents the lowest 25 percent.

D&B INDUSTRY NORMS: SIC 0172 - GRAPES

	1998 (24) Estab.		1997 (36) Estab.		1996 (27) Estab.	
	$	%	$	%	$	%
Cash	216,982	4.2	218,681	5.8	212,509	5.6
Accounts Receivable	588,951	11.4	373,266	9.9	368,097	9.7
Notes Receivable	-	-	7,541	.2	-	-
Inventory	1,048,746	20.3	795,547	21.1	804,500	21.2
Other Current Assets	428,797	8.3	135,733	3.6	447,788	11.8
Total Current Assets	2,283,476	44.2	1,530,768	40.6	1,832,894	48.3
Fixed Assets	2,619,281	50.7	2,028,456	53.8	1,832,893	48.3
Other Non-current Assets	263,478	5.1	211,140	5.6	129,024	3.4
Total Assets	5,166,235	100.0	3,770,364	100.0	3,794,811	100.0
Accounts Payable	408,132	7.9	256,385	6.8	223,894	5.9
Bank Loans	10,332	.2	-	-	-	-
Notes Payable	242,813	4.7	67,867	1.8	151,792	4.0
Other Current Liabilities	459,795	8.9	388,347	10.3	417,429	11.0
Total Current Liabilities	1,121,072	21.7	712,599	18.9	793,115	20.9
Other Long Term	1,425,881	27.6	1,334,709	35.4	1,005,625	26.5
Deferred Credits	-	-	45,244	1.2	56,922	1.5
Net Worth	2,619,281	50.7	1,677,812	44.5	1,939,148	51.1
Total Liabilities & Net Worth	5,166,234	100.0	3,770,364	100.0	3,794,810	100.0
Net Sales	6,458,748	100.0	2,582,422	100.0	4,838,876	100.0
Gross Profits	3,093,740	47.9	1,053,628	40.8	1,916,195	39.6
Net Profit After Tax	600,664	9.3	165,275	6.4	130,650	2.7
Working Capital	1,162,402	-	818,169	-	1,039,778	-

Source: Dun & Bradstreet. Data in this table are copyright (c) 1999 of Dun & Bradstreet. Reprinted by special arrangement with D&B. *Notes:* Values in parentheses above columns indicate the number of establishments in the sample. Data shown are for all companies.

D&B KEY BUSINESS RATIOS: SIC 0172

	1998			1997			1996		
	UQ	MED	LQ	UQ	MED	LQ	UQ	MED	LQ
Solvency									
Quick ratio	1.5	.8	.3	1.1	.6	.3	2.1	.7	.3
Current ratio	3.5	2.4	1.5	2.5	1.7	1.1	4.3	2.7	1.7
Current liabilities/Net worth (%)	16.3	33.5	85.8	6.0	11.9	36.4	12.9	33.7	72.4
Current liabilities/Inventory (%)	43.5	91.4	165.7	56.3	89.3	112.5	26.0	72.7	278.3
Total liabilities/Net worth (%)	40.2	85.8	159.2	22.7	63.5	115.3	22.1	69.9	166.0
Fixed assets/Net worth (%)	80.8	113.8	138.2	52.1	67.5	107.0	41.0	87.4	120.2
Efficiency									
Collection period (days)	26.7	35.0	56.2	18.6	21.9	28.5	17.2	30.0	63.3
Sales to Inventory	11.4	4.0	1.7	4.2	3.0	2.8	6.5	3.8	2.6
Assets/Sales (%)	50.1	74.9	209.8	47.8	85.2	103.1	60.5	83.2	107.0
Sales/Net Working Capital	10.5	3.4	2.1	4.4	3.1	2.0	13.3	7.3	2.8
Accounts payable/Sales (%)	4.7	7.6	9.9	4.2	7.8	9.9	3.3	6.3	11.2
Profitability									
Return - Sales (%)	8.9	5.8	3.2	4.6	4.2	1.0	5.0	3.1	1.7
Return - Assets (%)	7.7	4.1	2.7	3.7	2.8	2.0	9.3	3.3	1.7
Return - Net Worth (%)	29.2	9.6	5.0	8.1	5.9	5.2	21.2	8.6	3.6

Source: Dun & Bradstreet. Data in this table are copyright (c) 1999 of Dun & Bradstreet. Reprinted by special arrangement with D&B. *Note:* UQ stands for "Upper Quartile" and represents the top 25 percent of sample; MED stands for "Median"; and LQ stands for "Lower Quartile" and represents the lowest 25 percent.

D&B INDUSTRY NORMS: SIC 0174 - CITRUS FRUITS

	1998 (24) Estab.		1997 (35) Estab.		1996 (33) Estab.	
	$	%	$	%	$	%
Cash	456,152	5.3	642,420	7.9	484,056	6.5
Accounts Receivable	843,451	9.8	780,662	9.6	744,701	10.0
Notes Receivable	206,559	2.4	24,396	.3	14,894	.2
Inventory	499,185	5.8	471,650	5.8	588,314	7.9
Other Current Assets	1,024,190	11.9	699,343	8.6	186,175	2.5
Total Current Assets	3,029,537	35.2	2,618,471	32.2	2,018,140	27.1
Fixed Assets	3,838,561	44.6	3,773,199	46.4	3,514,991	47.2
Other Non-current Assets	1,738,541	20.2	1,740,225	21.4	1,913,883	25.7
Total Assets	8,606,639	100.0	8,131,895	100.0	7,447,014	100.0
Accounts Payable	395,905	4.6	341,540	4.2	305,328	4.1
Bank Loans	-	-	-	-	-	-
Notes Payable	275,412	3.2	333,408	4.1	163,834	2.2
Other Current Liabilities	929,517	10.8	593,628	7.3	871,301	11.7
Total Current Liabilities	1,600,834	18.6	1,268,576	15.6	1,340,463	18.0
Other Long Term	1,463,129	17.0	1,642,643	20.2	1,757,495	23.6
Deferred Credits	94,673	1.1	113,847	1.4	67,023	.9
Net Worth	5,448,003	63.3	5,106,829	62.8	4,282,033	57.5
Total Liabilities & Net Worth	8,606,639	100.0	8,131,895	100.0	7,447,014	100.0
Net Sales	9,315,926	100.0	11,853,130	100.0	12,048,488	100.0
Gross Profits	3,251,258	34.9	3,781,148	31.9	3,409,722	28.3
Net Profit After Tax	959,540	10.3	794,160	6.7	903,637	7.5
Working Capital	1,428,702	-	1,349,895	-	677,678	-

Source: Dun & Bradstreet. Data in this table are copyright (c) 1999 of Dun & Bradstreet. Reprinted by special arrangement with D&B. *Notes:* Values in parentheses above columns indicate the number of establishments in the sample. Data shown are for all companies.

D&B KEY BUSINESS RATIOS: SIC 0174

	1998			1997			1996		
	UQ	MED	LQ	UQ	MED	LQ	UQ	MED	LQ
Solvency									
Quick ratio	1.8	1.0	.5	2.5	1.1	.6	1.5	.6	.4
Current ratio	4.3	2.1	1.2	4.9	2.1	1.5	2.7	1.7	.8
Current liabilities/Net worth (%)	8.6	27.2	38.1	4.5	13.2	40.4	3.8	6.3	16.2
Current liabilities/Inventory (%)	54.2	208.6	648.2	37.7	73.3	142.0	41.9	90.5	147.1
Total liabilities/Net worth (%)	30.0	38.8	126.1	18.9	34.8	97.5	6.3	27.5	62.1
Fixed assets/Net worth (%)	33.2	52.9	120.4	44.5	63.1	104.8	43.1	59.7	84.1
Efficiency									
Collection period (days)	17.2	27.4	57.3	17.6	33.5	83.9	19.7	31.4	51.1
Sales to Inventory	104.1	51.9	4.6	79.3	31.0	3.8	17.8	6.4	3.1
Assets/Sales (%)	53.0	87.5	184.0	88.2	137.1	323.0	71.9	96.8	133.2
Sales/Net Working Capital	22.8	3.1	2.5	6.3	3.3	1.8	5.8	3.8	2.8
Accounts payable/Sales (%)	1.5	2.6	3.8	1.1	2.6	4.6	1.0	2.2	4.2
Profitability									
Return - Sales (%)	14.7	5.4	1.0	12.9	9.7	.9	6.3	3.5	2.1
Return - Assets (%)	12.2	3.2	1.1	8.7	2.9	.9	3.9	2.2	1.8
Return - Net Worth (%)	17.5	4.4	3.3	14.3	5.9	2.2	8.2	6.5	4.1

Source: Dun & Bradstreet. Data in this table are copyright (c) 1999 of Dun & Bradstreet. Reprinted by special arrangement with D&B. *Note:* UQ stands for "Upper Quartile" and represents the top 25 percent of sample; MED stands for "Median"; and LQ stands for "Lower Quartile" and represents the lowest 25 percent.

D&B INDUSTRY NORMS: SIC 0175 - DECIDUOUS TREE FRUITS

	1998 (66) Estab.		1997 (73) Estab.		1996 (57) Estab.	
	$	%	$	%	$	%
Cash	128,677	8.9	153,929	8.9	122,645	6.6
Accounts Receivable	151,810	10.5	164,306	9.5	180,251	9.7
Notes Receivable	2,892	.2	10,377	.6	24,157	1.3
Inventory	115,665	8.0	140,092	8.1	150,519	8.1
Other Current Assets	67,953	4.7	86,477	5.0	100,346	5.4
Total Current Assets	466,997	32.3	555,181	32.1	577,918	31.1
Fixed Assets	809,656	56.0	989,295	57.2	970,011	52.2
Other Non-current Assets	169,160	11.7	185,060	10.7	310,329	16.7
Total Assets	1,445,813	100.0	1,729,536	100.0	1,858,258	100.0
Accounts Payable	83,857	5.8	88,206	5.1	115,212	6.2
Bank Loans	-	-	12,107	.7	-	-
Notes Payable	66,507	4.6	108,961	6.3	150,519	8.1
Other Current Liabilities	164,823	11.4	183,331	10.6	174,676	9.4
Total Current Liabilities	315,187	21.8	392,605	22.7	440,407	23.7
Other Long Term	394,707	27.3	503,295	29.1	481,289	25.9
Deferred Credits	1,446	.1	5,189	.3	9,291	.5
Net Worth	734,474	50.8	828,448	47.9	927,271	49.9
Total Liabilities & Net Worth	1,445,814	100.0	1,729,537	100.0	1,858,258	100.0
Net Sales	2,000,438	100.0	2,000,000	100.0	1,687,700	100.0
Gross Profits	1,096,240	54.8	1,082,000	54.1	914,733	54.2
Net Profit After Tax	-2,000	-	78,000	3.9	-5,063	-
Working Capital	151,811	-	162,576	-	137,512	-

Source: Dun & Bradstreet. Data in this table are copyright (c) 1999 of Dun & Bradstreet. Reprinted by special arrangement with D&B. *Notes:* Values in parentheses above columns indicate the number of establishments in the sample. Data shown are for all companies.

D&B KEY BUSINESS RATIOS: SIC 0175

	1998			1997			1996		
	UQ	MED	LQ	UQ	MED	LQ	UQ	MED	LQ
Solvency									
Quick ratio	3.0	.9	.4	2.0	1.0	.4	2.0	.7	.2
Current ratio	5.0	1.2	.7	4.1	1.5	1.0	3.1	1.6	.8
Current liabilities/Net worth (%)	8.3	25.3	85.7	8.8	22.7	80.8	14.5	34.3	91.9
Current liabilities/Inventory (%)	57.9	163.9	276.9	89.7	146.9	279.6	87.2	149.8	208.2
Total liabilities/Net worth (%)	24.8	83.7	177.9	27.6	84.3	141.3	23.7	86.3	206.1
Fixed assets/Net worth (%)	45.6	102.0	158.6	73.4	96.9	161.4	43.7	94.5	198.0
Efficiency									
Collection period (days)	18.6	38.4	94.2	9.1	34.3	56.9	12.8	24.5	59.2
Sales to Inventory	26.8	6.9	3.4	36.2	14.1	4.9	13.7	10.4	3.6
Assets/Sales (%)	61.8	105.1	165.5	59.7	80.8	139.6	55.1	87.1	144.0
Sales/Net Working Capital	26.6	4.3	2.0	19.1	6.0	3.3	13.0	6.3	3.0
Accounts payable/Sales (%)	1.6	5.1	9.8	1.2	3.7	5.9	2.4	5.6	8.7
Profitability									
Return - Sales (%)	7.7	1.4	-.4	10.9	4.7	.8	5.5	2.2	-2.3
Return - Assets (%)	7.3	2.3	-.8	7.5	2.6	.8	7.0	2.0	-5.4
Return - Net Worth (%)	15.4	5.5	-1.7	16.6	4.7	1.5	19.8	3.2	-27.8

Source: Dun & Bradstreet. Data in this table are copyright (c) 1999 of Dun & Bradstreet. Reprinted by special arrangement with D&B. *Note:* UQ stands for "Upper Quartile" and represents the top 25 percent of sample; MED stands for "Median"; and LQ stands for "Lower Quartile" and represents the lowest 25 percent.

D&B INDUSTRY NORMS: SIC 0181 - ORNAMENTAL NURSERY PRODUCTS

	1998 (204) Estab.		1997 (283) Estab.		1996 (285) Estab.	
	$	%	$	%	$	%
Cash	124,581	10.6	105,589	10.1	104,338	11.1
Accounts Receivable	132,808	11.3	135,907	13.0	133,477	14.2
Notes Receivable	5,876	.5	3,136	.3	2,820	.3
Inventory	280,896	23.9	219,542	21.0	188,936	20.1
Other Current Assets	48,187	4.1	55,408	5.3	43,239	4.6
Total Current Assets	592,348	50.4	519,582	49.7	472,810	50.3
Fixed Assets	485,397	41.3	446,402	42.7	391,031	41.6
Other Non-current Assets	97,549	8.3	79,453	7.6	76,138	8.1
Total Assets	1,175,294	100.0	1,045,437	100.0	939,979	100.0
Accounts Payable	91,673	7.8	84,681	8.1	67,678	7.2
Bank Loans	5,876	.5	3,136	.3	2,820	.3
Notes Payable	58,765	5.0	44,954	4.3	48,879	5.2
Other Current Liabilities	159,840	13.6	148,452	14.2	140,057	14.9
Total Current Liabilities	316,154	26.9	281,223	26.9	259,434	27.6
Other Long Term	206,852	17.6	221,633	21.2	173,896	18.5
Deferred Credits	1,175	.1	5,227	.5	3,760	.4
Net Worth	651,113	55.4	537,356	51.4	502,889	53.5
Total Liabilities & Net Worth	1,175,294	100.0	1,045,439	100.0	939,979	100.0
Net Sales	2,297,720	100.0	2,118,557	100.0	1,571,786	100.0
Gross Profits	1,084,524	47.2	900,387	42.5	696,301	44.3
Net Profit After Tax	135,565	5.9	82,624	3.9	61,300	3.9
Working Capital	276,195	-	238,360	-	213,375	-

Source: Dun & Bradstreet. Data in this table are copyright (c) 1999 of Dun & Bradstreet. Reprinted by special arrangement with D&B. *Notes:* Values in parentheses above columns indicate the number of establishments in the sample. Data shown are for all companies.

D&B KEY BUSINESS RATIOS: SIC 0181

	1998			1997			1996		
	UQ	MED	LQ	UQ	MED	LQ	UQ	MED	LQ
Solvency									
Quick ratio	1.7	.7	.3	2.3	.8	.4	1.9	.9	.4
Current ratio	3.6	2.0	1.1	4.3	2.2	1.2	4.4	2.1	1.2
Current liabilities/Net worth (%)	12.8	39.1	79.0	13.2	37.2	95.3	12.3	39.3	91.3
Current liabilities/Inventory (%)	38.8	81.9	153.7	45.6	89.4	219.9	56.3	100.8	240.5
Total liabilities/Net worth (%)	25.5	66.4	165.7	30.7	70.4	185.5	26.4	71.1	164.5
Fixed assets/Net worth (%)	39.3	69.3	124.9	42.8	74.5	125.0	37.3	70.4	121.8
Efficiency									
Collection period (days)	12.8	24.8	39.4	14.8	28.5	43.6	17.1	34.0	56.4
Sales to Inventory	11.3	6.5	2.4	25.6	7.9	3.4	18.4	7.7	2.5
Assets/Sales (%)	36.0	57.7	88.0	32.9	52.4	85.6	35.7	60.4	90.9
Sales/Net Working Capital	11.0	6.7	2.5	12.0	6.7	3.1	11.3	6.3	2.9
Accounts payable/Sales (%)	1.9	3.9	7.3	1.6	4.2	7.7	2.0	4.1	7.0
Profitability									
Return - Sales (%)	9.0	3.4	.7	8.5	2.7	.7	8.6	2.5	.3
Return - Assets (%)	10.7	5.4	1.2	12.2	5.0	1.4	13.3	4.2	.2
Return - Net Worth (%)	23.9	10.8	3.3	20.8	9.9	3.7	24.4	9.1	.7

Source: Dun & Bradstreet. Data in this table are copyright (c) 1999 of Dun & Bradstreet. Reprinted by special arrangement with D&B. *Note:* UQ stands for "Upper Quartile" and represents the top 25 percent of sample; MED stands for "Median"; and LQ stands for "Lower Quartile" and represents the lowest 25 percent.

D&B INDUSTRY NORMS: SIC 0182 - FOOD CROPS GROWN UNDER COVER

	1998 (13) Estab.		1997 (23) Estab.		1996 (18) Estab.	
	$	%	$	%	$	%
Cash	100,315	7.1	110,115	10.1	111,283	12.4
Accounts Receivable	313,660	22.2	175,530	16.1	198,335	22.1
Notes Receivable	29,671	2.1	27,256	2.5	1,795	.2
Inventory	144,114	10.2	109,025	10.0	91,539	10.2
Other Current Assets	36,735	2.6	51,242	4.7	33,205	3.7
Total Current Assets	624,495	44.2	473,168	43.4	436,157	48.6
Fixed Assets	693,726	49.1	510,237	46.8	426,286	47.5
Other Non-current Assets	94,663	6.7	106,845	9.8	35,000	3.9
Total Assets	1,412,884	100.0	1,090,250	100.0	897,443	100.0
Accounts Payable	178,023	12.6	143,913	13.2	124,745	13.9
Bank Loans	1,413	.1	-	-	5,385	.6
Notes Payable	15,542	1.1	9,812	.9	56,539	6.3
Other Current Liabilities	166,720	11.8	103,574	9.5	86,155	9.6
Total Current Liabilities	361,698	25.6	257,299	23.6	272,824	30.4
Other Long Term	309,422	21.9	267,111	24.5	135,514	15.1
Deferred Credits	-	-	-	-	-	-
Net Worth	741,764	52.5	565,840	51.9	489,108	54.5
Total Liabilities & Net Worth	1,412,884	100.0	1,090,250	100.0	897,446	100.0
Net Sales	2,098,797	100.0	2,232,826	100.0	2,220,148	100.0
Gross Profits	973,842	46.4	683,245	30.6	834,776	37.6
Net Profit After Tax	125,928	6.0	-	-	15,541	.7
Working Capital	262,797	-	215,870	-	163,335	-

Source: Dun & Bradstreet. Data in this table are copyright (c) 1999 of Dun & Bradstreet. Reprinted by special arrangement with D&B. *Notes:* Values in parentheses above columns indicate the number of establishments in the sample. Data shown are for all companies.

D&B KEY BUSINESS RATIOS: SIC 0182

	1998			1997			1996		
	UQ	MED	LQ	UQ	MED	LQ	UQ	MED	LQ
Solvency									
Quick ratio	1.6	1.4	.8	2.2	1.0	.4	2.0	1.1	.8
Current ratio	2.5	1.9	1.6	3.2	2.1	1.0	2.6	1.7	1.2
Current liabilities/Net worth (%)	18.6	30.2	107.0	17.0	29.2	67.9	22.0	59.5	92.1
Current liabilities/Inventory (%)	119.8	142.6	176.8	140.6	196.2	297.3	148.3	202.1	303.1
Total liabilities/Net worth (%)	50.3	102.0	159.6	30.9	53.7	119.0	36.4	66.9	140.8
Fixed assets/Net worth (%)	67.3	101.5	139.6	48.6	70.8	117.4	50.7	69.9	128.3
Efficiency									
Collection period (days)	21.2	29.6	54.4	24.9	28.8	44.0	24.4	27.0	33.1
Sales to Inventory	24.3	11.5	9.3	43.1	20.2	10.0	48.5	34.7	13.1
Assets/Sales (%)	23.0	72.6	97.7	32.2	47.2	70.9	23.1	34.3	62.7
Sales/Net Working Capital	13.1	5.5	4.7	11.3	6.9	5.0	17.7	7.7	7.1
Accounts payable/Sales (%)	2.9	6.0	6.9	2.8	5.8	6.5	1.9	5.5	6.9
Profitability									
Return - Sales (%)	11.0	7.9	4.1	6.0	1.7	-.1	5.2	2.9	1.5
Return - Assets (%)	15.6	8.6	6.9	8.3	2.6	-.5	7.9	5.7	3.4
Return - Net Worth (%)	21.3	18.3	13.0	18.5	10.3	2.4	19.3	8.9	4.0

Source: Dun & Bradstreet. Data in this table are copyright (c) 1999 of Dun & Bradstreet. Reprinted by special arrangement with D&B. *Note:* UQ stands for "Upper Quartile" and represents the top 25 percent of sample; MED stands for "Median"; and LQ stands for "Lower Quartile" and represents the lowest 25 percent.

D&B INDUSTRY NORMS: SIC 0191 - GENERAL FARMS, PRIMARILY CROP

	1998 (91) Estab.		1997 (111) Estab.		1996 (128) Estab.	
	$	%	$	%	$	%
Cash	78,705	6.3	105,109	8.8	105,447	9.6
Accounts Receivable	96,195	7.7	109,887	9.2	86,774	7.9
Notes Receivable	17,490	1.4	14,333	1.2	8,787	.8
Inventory	112,436	9.0	107,498	9.0	86,774	7.9
Other Current Assets	61,215	4.9	76,443	6.4	82,381	7.5
Total Current Assets	366,041	29.3	413,270	34.6	370,163	33.7
Fixed Assets	748,322	59.9	597,212	50.0	501,973	45.7
Other Non-current Assets	134,923	10.8	183,941	15.4	226,272	20.6
Total Assets	1,249,286	100.0	1,194,423	100.0	1,098,408	100.0
Accounts Payable	51,221	4.1	34,638	2.9	38,444	3.5
Bank Loans	12,493	1.0	9,555	.8	-	-
Notes Payable	83,702	6.7	53,749	4.5	53,822	4.9
Other Current Liabilities	144,917	11.6	206,635	17.3	114,235	10.4
Total Current Liabilities	292,333	23.4	304,577	25.5	206,501	18.8
Other Long Term	217,376	17.4	193,497	16.2	213,091	19.4
Deferred Credits	3,748	.3	5,972	.5	3,295	.3
Net Worth	735,829	58.9	690,376	57.8	675,522	61.5
Total Liabilities & Net Worth	1,249,286	100.0	1,194,422	100.0	1,098,409	100.0
Net Sales	1,531,764	100.0	1,456,497	100.0	933,783	100.0
Gross Profits	669,381	43.7	575,316	39.5	330,559	35.4
Net Profit After Tax	110,287	7.2	88,846	6.1	81,239	8.7
Working Capital	73,708	-	108,692	-	163,663	-

Source: Dun & Bradstreet. Data in this table are copyright (c) 1999 of Dun & Bradstreet. Reprinted by special arrangement with D&B. *Notes:* Values in parentheses above columns indicate the number of establishments in the sample. Data shown are for all companies.

D&B KEY BUSINESS RATIOS: SIC 0191

	1998			1997			1996		
	UQ	MED	LQ	UQ	MED	LQ	UQ	MED	LQ
Solvency									
Quick ratio	.9	.4	.2	1.6	.6	.3	2.3	.8	.3
Current ratio	2.1	1.4	.6	2.3	1.4	.9	4.9	2.0	1.1
Current liabilities/Net worth (%)	12.5	41.9	73.4	9.3	34.6	68.9	8.2	18.1	60.2
Current liabilities/Inventory (%)	65.7	84.8	134.4	91.6	132.9	223.1	61.7	108.3	175.2
Total liabilities/Net worth (%)	31.6	72.7	131.1	24.6	60.7	122.6	20.0	51.7	101.6
Fixed assets/Net worth (%)	72.0	97.0	147.4	55.9	91.6	124.0	43.0	71.8	122.7
Efficiency									
Collection period (days)	6.2	22.5	35.3	12.8	25.6	58.8	16.0	39.5	75.5
Sales to Inventory	11.8	5.3	2.9	8.7	5.2	3.2	9.3	5.6	4.0
Assets/Sales (%)	60.7	81.8	157.1	57.1	99.0	149.6	53.8	81.8	147.0
Sales/Net Working Capital	18.8	5.7	3.4	23.8	12.3	5.6	11.4	5.8	2.1
Accounts payable/Sales (%)	1.7	4.3	6.3	2.4	4.1	5.7	1.9	3.3	6.2
Profitability									
Return - Sales (%)	15.0	5.7	1.4	8.3	2.5	.3	18.1	3.7	1.1
Return - Assets (%)	10.9	6.0	1.8	6.9	5.0	.7	8.9	4.8	1.3
Return - Net Worth (%)	19.2	11.4	3.9	11.5	8.1	1.4	14.8	6.6	2.6

Source: Dun & Bradstreet. Data in this table are copyright (c) 1999 of Dun & Bradstreet. Reprinted by special arrangement with D&B. *Note:* UQ stands for "Upper Quartile" and represents the top 25 percent of sample; MED stands for "Median"; and LQ stands for "Lower Quartile" and represents the lowest 25 percent.

D&B INDUSTRY NORMS: SIC 0211 - BEEF CATTLE FEEDLOTS

	1998 (64) Estab.		1997 (115) Estab.		1996 (113) Estab.	
	$	%	$	%	$	%
Cash	221,544	4.6	228,187	5.6	255,552	6.1
Accounts Receivable	1,011,396	21.0	961,644	23.6	1,064,100	25.4
Notes Receivable	250,441	5.2	134,467	3.3	100,545	2.4
Inventory	1,281,101	26.6	986,092	24.2	858,821	20.5
Other Current Assets	235,992	4.9	273,009	6.7	414,748	9.9
Total Current Assets	3,000,474	62.3	2,583,399	63.4	2,693,766	64.3
Fixed Assets	1,319,631	27.4	1,083,886	26.6	1,005,449	24.0
Other Non-current Assets	496,066	10.3	407,476	10.0	490,156	11.7
Total Assets	4,816,171	100.0	4,074,761	100.0	4,189,371	100.0
Accounts Payable	481,617	10.0	411,551	10.1	427,316	10.2
Bank Loans	9,632	.2	-	-	-	-
Notes Payable	1,093,271	22.7	566,392	13.9	569,754	13.6
Other Current Liabilities	438,271	9.1	851,625	20.9	833,685	19.9
Total Current Liabilities	2,022,791	42.0	1,829,568	44.9	1,830,755	43.7
Other Long Term	385,294	8.0	464,523	11.4	456,641	10.9
Deferred Credits	19,265	.4	-	-	16,757	.4
Net Worth	2,388,820	49.6	1,780,671	43.7	1,885,217	45.0
Total Liabilities & Net Worth	4,816,170	100.0	4,074,762	100.0	4,189,370	100.0
Net Sales	11,630,972	100.0	10,487,249	100.0	15,333,376	100.0
Gross Profits	2,256,409	19.4	2,118,424	20.2	2,928,675	19.1
Net Profit After Tax	441,977	3.8	304,130	2.9	429,335	2.8
Working Capital	977,683	-	753,830	-	863,011	-

Source: Dun & Bradstreet. Data in this table are copyright (c) 1999 of Dun & Bradstreet. Reprinted by special arrangement with D&B. *Notes:* Values in parentheses above columns indicate the number of establishments in the sample. Data shown are for all companies.

D&B KEY BUSINESS RATIOS: SIC 0211

	1998			1997			1996		
	UQ	MED	LQ	UQ	MED	LQ	UQ	MED	LQ
Solvency									
Quick ratio	1.0	.5	.3	1.0	.6	.4	1.0	.7	.4
Current ratio	1.8	1.4	1.1	2.1	1.4	1.0	2.2	1.4	1.1
Current liabilities/Net worth (%)	25.4	97.6	270.6	40.9	115.1	238.1	46.9	95.9	187.8
Current liabilities/Inventory (%)	92.4	131.3	233.2	92.5	142.1	268.6	103.3	235.7	469.6
Total liabilities/Net worth (%)	34.5	117.6	290.2	63.8	137.3	315.6	48.5	129.8	234.6
Fixed assets/Net worth (%)	32.4	68.9	93.6	32.7	61.7	116.4	29.2	51.2	92.9
Efficiency									
Collection period (days)	22.9	41.8	68.0	29.6	47.5	78.1	28.7	40.7	57.9
Sales to Inventory	15.2	8.6	3.3	32.2	11.3	4.1	17.3	12.9	6.1
Assets/Sales (%)	37.1	59.8	78.3	32.6	52.9	69.2	35.4	48.4	77.5
Sales/Net Working Capital	15.5	9.4	4.0	12.2	7.8	3.4	13.1	8.4	5.5
Accounts payable/Sales (%)	2.8	4.2	7.5	1.7	4.4	7.1	3.0	5.3	7.7
Profitability									
Return - Sales (%)	6.0	3.0	1.1	6.8	3.1	1.5	7.0	2.9	1.6
Return - Assets (%)	10.7	4.5	3.0	13.2	6.2	2.7	12.2	7.1	3.8
Return - Net Worth (%)	29.0	14.7	4.8	32.0	21.7	8.6	30.4	19.1	8.1

Source: Dun & Bradstreet. Data in this table are copyright (c) 1999 of Dun & Bradstreet. Reprinted by special arrangement with D&B. *Note:* UQ stands for "Upper Quartile" and represents the top 25 percent of sample; MED stands for "Median"; and LQ stands for "Lower Quartile" and represents the lowest 25 percent.

D&B INDUSTRY NORMS: SIC 0212 - BEEF CATTLE, EXCEPT FEEDLOTS

	1998 (39) Estab.		1997 (49) Estab.		1996 (66) Estab.	
	$	%	$	%	$	%
Cash	128,195	7.0	169,602	6.5	133,351	8.8
Accounts Receivable	104,388	5.7	206,132	7.9	109,106	7.2
Notes Receivable	53,110	2.9	117,417	4.5	39,399	2.6
Inventory	146,509	8.0	401,826	15.4	154,566	10.2
Other Current Assets	173,980	9.5	169,602	6.5	77,283	5.1
Total Current Assets	606,182	33.1	1,064,579	40.8	513,705	33.9
Fixed Assets	1,021,901	55.8	1,155,903	44.3	572,804	37.8
Other Non-current Assets	203,281	11.1	388,780	14.9	428,845	28.3
Total Assets	1,831,364	100.0	2,609,262	100.0	1,515,354	100.0
Accounts Payable	42,121	2.3	70,450	2.7	54,553	3.6
Bank Loans	20,145	1.1	-	-	-	-
Notes Payable	87,905	4.8	153,946	5.9	68,191	4.5
Other Current Liabilities	144,678	7.9	401,826	15.4	254,580	16.8
Total Current Liabilities	294,849	16.1	626,222	24.0	377,324	24.9
Other Long Term	194,125	10.6	454,012	17.4	190,935	12.6
Deferred Credits	-	-	7,828	.3	7,577	.5
Net Worth	1,342,390	73.3	1,521,200	58.3	939,520	62.0
Total Liabilities & Net Worth	1,831,364	100.0	2,609,262	100.0	1,515,356	100.0
Net Sales	1,776,229	100.0	3,629,300	100.0	1,343,672	100.0
Gross Profits	504,449	28.4	1,477,125	40.7	525,376	39.1
Net Profit After Tax	131,441	7.4	50,810	1.4	-13,437	-
Working Capital	311,331	-	438,356	-	136,382	-

Source: Dun & Bradstreet. Data in this table are copyright (c) 1999 of Dun & Bradstreet. Reprinted by special arrangement with D&B. *Notes:* Values in parentheses above columns indicate the number of establishments in the sample. Data shown are for all companies.

D&B KEY BUSINESS RATIOS: SIC 0212

	1998			1997			1996		
	UQ	MED	LQ	UQ	MED	LQ	UQ	MED	LQ
Solvency									
Quick ratio	4.0	.3	.2	2.1	.4	.2	2.3	.5	.2
Current ratio	11.1	2.0	.8	3.9	2.2	.9	5.9	1.6	.8
Current liabilities/Net worth (%)	2.1	16.0	43.5	7.7	24.1	76.6	3.1	12.0	59.3
Current liabilities/Inventory (%)	53.1	116.5	244.5	90.9	154.4	190.5	36.1	130.9	358.9
Total liabilities/Net worth (%)	4.8	35.4	77.7	12.8	53.7	122.3	7.9	18.1	77.3
Fixed assets/Net worth (%)	49.1	76.3	103.5	40.2	86.7	117.6	29.3	58.9	107.9
Efficiency									
Collection period (days)	3.3	20.5	33.5	5.9	21.9	44.8	7.6	18.6	43.4
Sales to Inventory	14.0	6.1	3.5	29.4	3.7	2.7	16.7	5.2	4.1
Assets/Sales (%)	67.7	98.0	248.7	63.4	108.0	396.2	42.7	252.6	415.9
Sales/Net Working Capital	14.1	3.9	1.2	5.3	3.6	2.5	3.4	1.6	1.0
Accounts payable/Sales (%)	1.4	2.7	6.1	1.4	3.6	6.2	2.2	5.8	7.3
Profitability									
Return - Sales (%)	14.7	6.3	-.4	5.4	2.0	-7.3	13.0	1.8	-3.6
Return - Assets (%)	12.2	3.4	-.2	8.2	1.3	-.8	6.2	1.2	-2.8
Return - Net Worth (%)	15.6	4.0	-.1	9.3	3.8	-1.2	10.1	3.4	-2.5

Source: Dun & Bradstreet. Data in this table are copyright (c) 1999 of Dun & Bradstreet. Reprinted by special arrangement with D&B. *Note:* UQ stands for "Upper Quartile" and represents the top 25 percent of sample; MED stands for "Median"; and LQ stands for "Lower Quartile" and represents the lowest 25 percent.

D&B INDUSTRY NORMS: SIC 0213 - HOGS

	1998 (39) Estab.		1997 (36) Estab.		1996 (34) Estab.	
	$	%	$	%	$	%
Cash	34,871	1.8	146,434	4.1	136,994	5.6
Accounts Receivable	65,868	3.4	189,292	5.3	124,763	5.1
Notes Receivable	13,561	.7	121,433	3.4	90,514	3.7
Inventory	536,632	27.7	946,461	26.5	592,010	24.2
Other Current Assets	116,238	6.0	310,725	8.7	119,870	4.9
Total Current Assets	767,170	39.6	1,714,345	48.0	1,064,151	43.5
Fixed Assets	951,214	49.1	1,550,053	43.4	1,108,185	45.3
Other Non-current Assets	218,915	11.3	307,153	8.6	273,988	11.2
Total Assets	1,937,299	100.0	3,571,551	100.0	2,446,324	100.0
Accounts Payable	65,868	3.4	110,718	3.1	100,299	4.1
Bank Loans	-	-	-	-	-	-
Notes Payable	187,918	9.7	535,733	15.0	276,435	11.3
Other Current Liabilities	201,479	10.4	357,155	10.0	401,197	16.4
Total Current Liabilities	455,265	23.5	1,003,606	28.1	777,931	31.8
Other Long Term	536,632	27.7	535,733	15.0	447,677	18.3
Deferred Credits	-	-	-	-	-	-
Net Worth	945,402	48.8	2,032,212	56.9	1,220,716	49.9
Total Liabilities & Net Worth	1,937,299	100.0	3,571,551	100.0	2,446,324	100.0
Net Sales	3,244,086	100.0	3,968,345	100.0	2,589,506	100.0
Gross Profits	1,057,572	32.6	1,380,984	34.8	893,380	34.5
Net Profit After Tax	233,574	7.2	202,386	5.1	157,960	6.1
Working Capital	311,905	-	710,738	-	286,220	-

Source: Dun & Bradstreet. Data in this table are copyright (c) 1999 of Dun & Bradstreet. Reprinted by special arrangement with D&B. *Notes:* Values in parentheses above columns indicate the number of establishments in the sample. Data shown are for all companies.

D&B KEY BUSINESS RATIOS: SIC 0213

	1998			1997			1996		
	UQ	MED	LQ	UQ	MED	LQ	UQ	MED	LQ
Solvency									
Quick ratio	.4	.3	.1	1.0	.3	.2	.7	.3	.1
Current ratio	2.4	1.5	1.1	4.8	1.8	1.1	1.8	1.2	.9
Current liabilities/Net worth (%)	24.3	54.8	71.7	13.8	36.6	83.7	31.6	54.9	69.2
Current liabilities/Inventory (%)	41.3	72.7	89.3	44.1	76.3	127.9	42.7	98.1	116.0
Total liabilities/Net worth (%)	74.3	102.0	169.5	22.8	86.8	151.5	36.7	71.3	103.5
Fixed assets/Net worth (%)	69.9	105.3	141.9	55.6	98.8	133.6	59.2	96.6	112.9
Efficiency									
Collection period (days)	10.2	15.3	23.0	8.3	12.1	18.4	12.1	12.1	12.7
Sales to Inventory	3.9	3.1	2.5	4.5	2.9	2.1	3.9	3.3	2.8
Assets/Sales (%)	54.8	75.3	257.6	61.7	67.9	80.9	86.5	116.1	230.2
Sales/Net Working Capital	9.1	4.6	1.5	44.0	9.5	3.6	39.6	12.8	9.6
Accounts payable/Sales (%)	1.1	2.8	7.5	1.5	4.3	8.1	3.6	4.6	5.1
Profitability									
Return - Sales (%)	9.0	3.6	-2.3	9.8	3.3	2.1	9.1	5.6	3.2
Return - Assets (%)	11.7	5.4	-1.3	8.2	4.9	2.9	7.2	4.8	2.8
Return - Net Worth (%)	14.4	9.1	-10.3	17.7	12.8	7.1	12.2	9.0	5.8

Source: Dun & Bradstreet. Data in this table are copyright (c) 1999 of Dun & Bradstreet. Reprinted by special arrangement with D&B. *Note:* UQ stands for "Upper Quartile" and represents the top 25 percent of sample; MED stands for "Median"; and LQ stands for "Lower Quartile" and represents the lowest 25 percent.

D&B INDUSTRY NORMS: SIC 0241 - DAIRY FARMS

	1998 (59) Estab.		1997 (76) Estab.		1996 (71) Estab.	
	$	%	$	%	$	%
Cash	165,559	5.8	141,504	6.0	113,492	8.4
Accounts Receivable	151,287	5.3	96,694	4.1	66,204	4.9
Notes Receivable	14,272	.5	4,717	.2	2,702	.2
Inventory	236,921	8.3	202,822	8.6	128,354	9.5
Other Current Assets	199,813	7.0	134,429	5.7	63,502	4.7
Total Current Assets	767,852	26.9	580,166	24.6	374,254	27.7
Fixed Assets	1,575,665	55.2	1,327,780	56.3	706,624	52.3
Other Non-current Assets	510,949	17.9	450,455	19.1	270,219	20.0
Total Assets	2,854,466	100.0	2,358,401	100.0	1,351,097	100.0
Accounts Payable	88,488	3.1	110,845	4.7	31,075	2.3
Bank Loans	2,854	.1	-	-	-	-
Notes Payable	111,324	3.9	115,562	4.9	67,555	5.0
Other Current Liabilities	319,700	11.2	297,159	12.6	245,900	18.2
Total Current Liabilities	522,366	18.3	523,566	22.2	344,530	25.5
Other Long Term	919,138	32.2	719,312	30.5	374,254	27.7
Deferred Credits	-	-	7,075	.3	4,053	.3
Net Worth	1,412,961	49.5	1,108,448	47.0	628,260	46.5
Total Liabilities & Net Worth	2,854,465	100.0	2,358,401	100.0	1,351,097	100.0
Net Sales	2,664,848	100.0	1,213,874	100.0	1,204,589	100.0
Gross Profits	1,364,402	51.2	608,151	50.1	470,994	39.1
Net Profit After Tax	7,995	.3	33,988	2.8	14,455	1.2
Working Capital	245,484	-	56,602	-	29,724	-

Source: Dun & Bradstreet. Data in this table are copyright (c) 1999 of Dun & Bradstreet. Reprinted by special arrangement with D&B. *Notes:* Values in parentheses above columns indicate the number of establishments in the sample. Data shown are for all companies.

D&B KEY BUSINESS RATIOS: SIC 0241

	1998			1997			1996		
	UQ	MED	LQ	UQ	MED	LQ	UQ	MED	LQ
Solvency									
Quick ratio	1.1	.4	.1	1.4	.3	.1	.8	.3	.2
Current ratio	4.2	1.9	.9	2.9	1.2	.7	4.0	1.1	.6
Current liabilities/Net worth (%)	8.4	30.2	71.8	10.4	42.4	70.3	7.3	17.1	97.7
Current liabilities/Inventory (%)	74.5	118.3	253.3	78.0	161.4	242.5	100.0	177.9	289.2
Total liabilities/Net worth (%)	47.3	73.0	200.5	43.4	107.4	179.1	23.9	72.5	173.6
Fixed assets/Net worth (%)	73.0	98.0	172.7	80.3	100.9	172.0	66.7	96.2	165.1
Efficiency									
Collection period (days)	22.6	34.0	40.2	17.4	27.0	39.1	25.2	31.8	46.4
Sales to Inventory	30.7	11.0	4.3	20.4	12.0	7.5	32.9	22.1	13.9
Assets/Sales (%)	61.5	105.0	185.5	62.8	95.2	198.9	52.3	80.5	126.0
Sales/Net Working Capital	8.4	6.7	3.7	13.1	9.9	2.9	7.7	5.6	1.8
Accounts payable/Sales (%)	.6	3.2	8.7	3.9	5.2	14.0	2.1	3.4	8.9
Profitability									
Return - Sales (%)	6.3	2.2	-1.2	7.4	5.1	1.6	3.6	.2	-4.4
Return - Assets (%)	10.5	1.3	-.6	9.2	3.0	1.2	1.5	.1	-2.1
Return - Net Worth (%)	18.1	5.0	-.6	25.8	4.5	2.4	3.5	.8	-12.3

Source: Dun & Bradstreet. Data in this table are copyright (c) 1999 of Dun & Bradstreet. Reprinted by special arrangement with D&B. *Note:* UQ stands for "Upper Quartile" and represents the top 25 percent of sample; MED stands for "Median"; and LQ stands for "Lower Quartile" and represents the lowest 25 percent.

D&B INDUSTRY NORMS: SIC 0252 - CHICKEN EGGS

	1998 (27) Estab.		1997 (31) Estab.		1996 (28) Estab.	
	$	%	$	%	$	%
Cash	202,851	6.3	243,100	7.3	116,361	5.1
Accounts Receivable	499,078	15.5	512,842	15.4	228,158	10.0
Notes Receivable	25,759	.8	29,971	.9	2,282	.1
Inventory	621,433	19.3	692,670	20.8	431,218	18.9
Other Current Assets	183,532	5.7	193,148	5.8	93,545	4.1
Total Current Assets	1,532,653	47.6	1,671,731	50.2	871,564	38.2
Fixed Assets	1,429,617	44.4	1,405,320	42.2	1,010,739	44.3
Other Non-current Assets	257,589	8.0	253,091	7.6	399,276	17.5
Total Assets	3,219,859	100.0	3,330,142	100.0	2,281,579	100.0
Accounts Payable	186,752	5.8	189,818	5.7	132,332	5.8
Bank Loans	74,057	2.3	-	-	-	-
Notes Payable	154,553	4.8	99,904	3.0	177,963	7.8
Other Current Liabilities	476,539	14.8	356,325	10.7	200,779	8.8
Total Current Liabilities	891,901	27.7	646,047	19.4	511,074	22.4
Other Long Term	595,674	18.5	715,981	21.5	622,871	27.3
Deferred Credits	35,418	1.1	9,990	.3	-	-
Net Worth	1,696,866	52.7	1,958,124	58.8	1,147,634	50.3
Total Liabilities & Net Worth	3,219,859	100.0	3,330,142	100.0	2,281,579	100.0
Net Sales	10,226,912	100.0	5,747,596	100.0	6,550,240	100.0
Gross Profits	2,239,694	21.9	1,655,308	28.8	1,349,349	20.6
Net Profit After Tax	674,976	6.6	275,885	4.8	85,153	1.3
Working Capital	640,752	-	1,025,684	-	360,489	-

Source: Dun & Bradstreet. Data in this table are copyright (c) 1999 of Dun & Bradstreet. Reprinted by special arrangement with D&B. *Notes:* Values in parentheses above columns indicate the number of establishments in the sample. Data shown are for all companies.

D&B KEY BUSINESS RATIOS: SIC 0252

	1998			1997			1996		
	UQ	MED	LQ	UQ	MED	LQ	UQ	MED	LQ
Solvency									
Quick ratio	1.6	.8	.4	4.5	1.4	.5	.9	.5	.3
Current ratio	3.4	2.4	1.0	4.6	3.1	1.9	2.6	1.8	1.0
Current liabilities/Net worth (%)	17.0	32.6	62.8	16.3	27.6	48.7	13.3	33.8	115.2
Current liabilities/Inventory (%)	49.7	121.4	183.2	51.8	95.9	163.9	73.5	96.7	168.2
Total liabilities/Net worth (%)	33.4	59.2	139.3	30.5	53.3	181.2	35.9	84.0	214.6
Fixed assets/Net worth (%)	48.5	88.7	113.3	43.4	68.0	114.1	49.9	90.9	146.6
Efficiency									
Collection period (days)	20.8	31.8	51.5	15.5	24.5	39.3	16.3	34.7	49.1
Sales to Inventory	13.9	8.6	3.9	17.8	9.1	4.4	10.9	7.3	5.6
Assets/Sales (%)	42.9	53.4	96.4	40.7	47.8	80.0	45.2	62.4	100.2
Sales/Net Working Capital	17.5	4.2	2.9	6.9	5.1	3.0	10.0	5.8	3.5
Accounts payable/Sales (%)	1.7	3.9	4.8	1.1	2.3	4.2	2.7	4.9	8.1
Profitability									
Return - Sales (%)	12.6	4.0	1.2	7.7	5.7	3.6	3.4	1.2	-1.2
Return - Assets (%)	11.1	7.5	2.8	17.3	13.0	4.2	7.8	1.1	-3.4
Return - Net Worth (%)	20.0	16.1	8.7	32.7	21.6	11.4	12.8	1.7	-17.1

Source: Dun & Bradstreet. Data in this table are copyright (c) 1999 of Dun & Bradstreet. Reprinted by special arrangement with D&B. *Note:* UQ stands for "Upper Quartile" and represents the top 25 percent of sample; MED stands for "Median"; and LQ stands for "Lower Quartile" and represents the lowest 25 percent.

D&B INDUSTRY NORMS: SIC 0711 - SOIL PREPARATION SERVICES

	1998 (43) Estab.		1997 (50) Estab.		1996 (56) Estab.	
	$	%	$	%	$	%
Cash	74,655	17.1	52,098	9.8	48,811	14.6
Accounts Receivable	114,820	26.3	155,762	29.3	95,950	28.7
Notes Receivable	4,366	1.0	5,316	1.0	4,680	1.4
Inventory	27,504	6.3	29,770	5.6	20,059	6.0
Other Current Assets	25,322	5.8	31,897	6.0	14,041	4.2
Total Current Assets	246,667	56.5	274,843	51.7	183,541	54.9
Fixed Assets	157,605	36.1	218,493	41.1	123,698	37.0
Other Non-current Assets	32,307	7.4	38,276	7.2	27,080	8.1
Total Assets	436,579	100.0	531,612	100.0	334,319	100.0
Accounts Payable	29,251	6.7	57,946	10.9	41,790	12.5
Bank Loans	-	-	-	-	-	-
Notes Payable	11,788	2.7	26,581	5.0	18,722	5.6
Other Current Liabilities	56,319	12.9	53,693	10.1	46,136	13.8
Total Current Liabilities	97,358	22.3	138,220	26.0	106,648	31.9
Other Long Term	92,991	21.3	116,423	21.9	46,805	14.0
Deferred Credits	2,183	.5	532	.1	3,009	.9
Net Worth	244,048	55.9	276,438	52.0	177,858	53.2
Total Liabilities & Net Worth	436,580	100.0	531,613	100.0	334,320	100.0
Net Sales	1,231,989	100.0	1,317,356	100.0	966,906	100.0
Gross Profits	648,026	52.6	516,404	39.2	389,663	40.3
Net Profit After Tax	89,935	7.3	55,329	4.2	59,948	6.2
Working Capital	149,310	-	136,624	-	76,894	-

Source: Dun & Bradstreet. Data in this table are copyright (c) 1999 of Dun & Bradstreet. Reprinted by special arrangement with D&B. *Notes:* Values in parentheses above columns indicate the number of establishments in the sample. Data shown are for all companies.

D&B KEY BUSINESS RATIOS: SIC 0711

	1998			1997			1996		
	UQ	MED	LQ	UQ	MED	LQ	UQ	MED	LQ
Solvency									
Quick ratio	4.3	2.0	1.2	2.3	1.3	.7	3.9	1.2	.7
Current ratio	5.0	2.6	1.8	3.6	1.8	1.1	4.6	1.6	.9
Current liabilities/Net worth (%)	15.0	33.7	73.3	8.6	16.0	38.5	15.4	48.1	104.1
Current liabilities/Inventory (%)	85.3	109.4	242.1	10.6	59.3	132.6	46.4	138.4	210.2
Total liabilities/Net worth (%)	25.4	86.4	182.2	28.1	52.8	91.0	34.7	74.8	155.5
Fixed assets/Net worth (%)	33.1	60.1	116.6	28.9	51.8	86.3	30.4	59.2	107.2
Efficiency									
Collection period (days)	22.2	66.6	98.9	21.7	55.3	87.2	26.1	79.6	90.4
Sales to Inventory	50.2	15.1	6.1	27.5	12.9	8.9	61.8	31.0	12.2
Assets/Sales (%)	31.6	42.6	54.2	29.0	51.0	87.8	29.6	45.4	63.6
Sales/Net Working Capital	8.7	5.1	3.7	11.9	5.7	3.0	21.6	10.1	4.6
Accounts payable/Sales (%)	1.5	3.7	5.0	1.9	5.3	7.7	2.8	4.3	9.7
Profitability									
Return - Sales (%)	12.8	8.5	2.5	6.4	2.5	.9	10.8	3.1	.8
Return - Assets (%)	27.5	21.3	6.0	10.6	4.3	2.0	13.1	7.0	1.3
Return - Net Worth (%)	51.7	29.5	14.7	15.4	9.1	4.4	26.0	13.5	2.6

Source: Dun & Bradstreet. Data in this table are copyright (c) 1999 of Dun & Bradstreet. Reprinted by special arrangement with D&B. *Note:* UQ stands for "Upper Quartile" and represents the top 25 percent of sample; MED stands for "Median"; and LQ stands for "Lower Quartile" and represents the lowest 25 percent.

D&B INDUSTRY NORMS: SIC 0721 - CROP PLANTING AND PROTECTING

	1998 (55) Estab.		1997 (73) Estab.		1996 (86) Estab.	
	$	%	$	%	$	%
Cash	88,073	11.7	89,031	10.4	72,544	14.1
Accounts Receivable	112,914	15.0	182,341	21.3	85,920	16.7
Notes Receivable	21,830	2.9	14,553	1.7	5,659	1.1
Inventory	39,143	5.2	66,773	7.8	37,558	7.3
Other Current Assets	24,088	3.2	41,091	4.8	30,355	5.9
Total Current Assets	286,048	38.0	393,789	46.0	232,036	45.1
Fixed Assets	382,401	50.8	380,092	44.4	240,783	46.8
Other Non-current Assets	84,309	11.2	82,182	9.6	41,674	8.1
Total Assets	752,758	100.0	856,063	100.0	514,493	100.0
Accounts Payable	75,276	10.0	73,621	8.6	31,384	6.1
Bank Loans	2,258	.3	4,280	.5	-	-
Notes Payable	63,232	8.4	79,614	9.3	44,246	8.6
Other Current Liabilities	91,084	12.1	97,591	11.4	68,942	13.4
Total Current Liabilities	231,850	30.8	255,106	29.8	144,572	28.1
Other Long Term	135,496	18.0	163,508	19.1	107,529	20.9
Deferred Credits	-	-	1,712	.2	6,174	1.2
Net Worth	385,412	51.2	435,736	50.9	256,218	49.8
Total Liabilities & Net Worth	752,758	100.0	856,062	100.0	514,493	100.0
Net Sales	1,194,273	100.0	1,370,692	100.0	1,215,559	100.0
Gross Profits	520,703	43.6	588,027	42.9	566,450	46.6
Net Profit After Tax	45,382	3.8	71,276	5.2	65,640	5.4
Working Capital	54,199	-	138,682	-	87,464	-

Source: Dun & Bradstreet. Data in this table are copyright (c) 1999 of Dun & Bradstreet. Reprinted by special arrangement with D&B. *Notes:* Values in parentheses above columns indicate the number of establishments in the sample. Data shown are for all companies.

D&B KEY BUSINESS RATIOS: SIC 0721

	1998			1997			1996		
	UQ	MED	LQ	UQ	MED	LQ	UQ	MED	LQ
Solvency									
Quick ratio	2.1	.8	.4	2.2	1.0	.5	3.1	1.2	.4
Current ratio	2.5	1.4	.7	3.3	1.5	1.0	5.1	1.6	.8
Current liabilities/Net worth (%)	12.8	55.4	103.7	23.1	54.2	101.8	14.8	29.1	99.1
Current liabilities/Inventory (%)	148.8	260.5	541.9	128.6	195.3	313.1	96.0	215.2	368.1
Total liabilities/Net worth (%)	35.9	105.7	171.3	47.5	102.4	153.6	19.1	85.5	152.0
Fixed assets/Net worth (%)	53.3	92.4	149.0	53.9	86.7	144.6	40.9	92.6	177.0
Efficiency									
Collection period (days)	19.4	33.2	55.5	23.8	41.3	65.9	17.2	34.0	58.0
Sales to Inventory	104.8	32.7	15.2	133.1	32.0	15.0	77.1	26.7	17.6
Assets/Sales (%)	35.9	52.8	81.4	37.7	55.9	78.3	34.7	43.2	61.0
Sales/Net Working Capital	29.6	9.6	4.8	26.8	7.8	3.4	17.9	7.4	4.3
Accounts payable/Sales (%)	1.4	6.1	10.1	2.2	5.2	8.0	2.4	4.3	7.1
Profitability									
Return - Sales (%)	6.4	1.6	-.1	8.9	3.4	.8	7.4	4.0	2.0
Return - Assets (%)	13.4	2.5	.2	14.6	6.8	1.7	11.3	8.9	2.9
Return - Net Worth (%)	23.6	7.5	-.1	38.8	11.9	4.0	23.5	11.8	6.1

Source: Dun & Bradstreet. Data in this table are copyright (c) 1999 of Dun & Bradstreet. Reprinted by special arrangement with D&B. *Note:* UQ stands for "Upper Quartile" and represents the top 25 percent of sample; MED stands for "Median"; and LQ stands for "Lower Quartile" and represents the lowest 25 percent.

D&B INDUSTRY NORMS: SIC 0722 - CROP HARVESTING

	1998 (20) Estab.		1997 (17) Estab.		1996 (19) Estab.	
	$	%	$	%	$	%
Cash	130,722	11.6	266,496	20.1	213,014	13.7
Accounts Receivable	152,133	13.5	192,249	14.5	185,027	11.9
Notes Receivable	33,807	3.0	55,686	4.2	13,994	.9
Inventory	107,057	9.5	55,686	4.2	85,517	5.5
Other Current Assets	67,615	6.0	70,270	5.3	116,614	7.5
Total Current Assets	491,334	43.6	640,387	48.3	614,166	39.5
Fixed Assets	498,096	44.2	452,116	34.1	679,469	43.7
Other Non-current Assets	137,483	12.2	233,350	17.6	261,215	16.8
Total Assets	1,126,913	100.0	1,325,853	100.0	1,554,850	100.0
Accounts Payable	63,107	5.6	140,540	10.6	230,118	14.8
Bank Loans	-	-	-	-	-	-
Notes Payable	28,173	2.5	30,495	2.3	99,510	6.4
Other Current Liabilities	120,580	10.7	192,249	14.5	216,124	13.9
Total Current Liabilities	211,860	18.8	363,284	27.4	545,752	35.1
Other Long Term	126,214	11.2	294,339	22.2	233,227	15.0
Deferred Credits	3,381	.3	-	-	-	-
Net Worth	785,458	69.7	668,229	50.4	775,870	49.9
Total Liabilities & Net Worth	1,126,913	100.0	1,325,852	100.0	1,554,849	100.0
Net Sales	3,383,074	100.0	2,059,939	100.0	15,594,000	100.0
Gross Profits	1,288,951	38.1	537,644	26.1	3,477,462	22.3
Net Profit After Tax	182,686	5.4	140,076	6.8	810,888	5.2
Working Capital	279,474	-	277,104	-	68,413	-

Source: Dun & Bradstreet. Data in this table are copyright (c) 1999 of Dun & Bradstreet. Reprinted by special arrangement with D&B. *Notes:* Values in parentheses above columns indicate the number of establishments in the sample. Data shown are for all companies.

D&B KEY BUSINESS RATIOS: SIC 0722

	1998			1997			1996		
	UQ	MED	LQ	UQ	MED	LQ	UQ	MED	LQ
Solvency									
Quick ratio	3.5	.8	.5	2.9	1.1	.7	1.6	.7	.3
Current ratio	5.6	2.1	1.7	3.9	1.7	1.4	2.3	1.1	.6
Current liabilities/Net worth (%)	5.4	18.0	55.0	14.4	24.7	72.9	17.8	51.7	168.4
Current liabilities/Inventory (%)	64.7	144.2	220.4	88.2	101.9	142.2	132.3	137.9	143.5
Total liabilities/Net worth (%)	8.0	36.1	100.7	34.4	73.4	204.2	38.0	92.0	172.7
Fixed assets/Net worth (%)	38.8	61.2	100.4	40.8	67.2	84.0	51.3	92.1	137.9
Efficiency									
Collection period (days)	3.3	19.4	39.8	4.9	17.6	48.9	55.3	62.4	92.9
Sales to Inventory	14.1	9.6	7.9	28.0	8.7	5.7	98.4	98.4	98.4
Assets/Sales (%)	34.8	45.0	56.0	30.8	34.4	50.6	27.1	42.5	55.1
Sales/Net Working Capital	13.4	5.6	4.7	13.4	10.8	6.1	19.1	10.5	9.6
Accounts payable/Sales (%)	.8	2.0	5.5	.5	4.0	4.4	1.3	5.3	12.6
Profitability									
Return - Sales (%)	4.9	3.1	.7	7.4	2.8	.2	4.0	2.4	1.6
Return - Assets (%)	11.0	3.5	1.2	8.8	3.7	-1.6	12.0	6.3	4.6
Return - Net Worth (%)	20.8	7.2	1.8	13.9	4.4	-4.6	60.3	28.3	13.0

Source: Dun & Bradstreet. Data in this table are copyright (c) 1999 of Dun & Bradstreet. Reprinted by special arrangement with D&B. *Note:* UQ stands for "Upper Quartile" and represents the top 25 percent of sample; MED stands for "Median"; and LQ stands for "Lower Quartile" and represents the lowest 25 percent.

D&B INDUSTRY NORMS: SIC 0723 - CROP PREPARATION SERVICES FOR MARKET

	1998 (171) Estab.		1997 (235) Estab.		1996 (224) Estab.	
	$	%	$	%	$	%
Cash	421,115	14.2	308,658	13.9	320,451	15.1
Accounts Receivable	604,982	20.4	479,641	21.6	464,760	21.9
Notes Receivable	35,587	1.2	15,544	.7	19,100	.9
Inventory	397,390	13.4	308,658	13.9	286,496	13.5
Other Current Assets	154,211	5.2	131,013	5.9	118,843	5.6
Total Current Assets	1,613,285	54.4	1,243,514	56.0	1,209,650	57.0
Fixed Assets	1,112,100	37.5	812,725	36.6	734,279	34.6
Other Non-current Assets	240,214	8.1	164,321	7.4	178,264	8.4
Total Assets	2,965,599	100.0	2,220,560	100.0	2,122,193	100.0
Accounts Payable	364,769	12.3	306,437	13.8	320,451	15.1
Bank Loans	2,966	.1	4,441	.2	2,122	.1
Notes Payable	145,314	4.9	108,807	4.9	112,476	5.3
Other Current Liabilities	575,326	19.4	353,069	15.9	343,795	16.2
Total Current Liabilities	1,088,375	36.7	772,754	34.8	778,844	36.7
Other Long Term	477,462	16.1	364,172	16.4	322,573	15.2
Deferred Credits	17,794	.6	19,985	.9	12,733	.6
Net Worth	1,381,970	46.6	1,063,648	47.9	1,008,042	47.5
Total Liabilities & Net Worth	2,965,601	100.0	2,220,559	100.0	2,122,192	100.0
Net Sales	5,461,961	100.0	4,928,859	100.0	4,584,705	100.0
Gross Profits	1,518,425	27.8	1,532,875	31.1	1,251,624	27.3
Net Profit After Tax	245,788	4.5	231,656	4.7	197,142	4.3
Working Capital	524,911	-	470,758	-	430,805	-

Source: Dun & Bradstreet. Data in this table are copyright (c) 1999 of Dun & Bradstreet. Reprinted by special arrangement with D&B. _Notes:_ Values in parentheses above columns indicate the number of establishments in the sample. Data shown are for all companies.

D&B KEY BUSINESS RATIOS: SIC 0723

	1998			1997			1996		
	UQ	MED	LQ	UQ	MED	LQ	UQ	MED	LQ
Solvency									
Quick ratio	1.6	1.0	.5	1.9	1.0	.6	1.6	1.0	.6
Current ratio	2.3	1.4	1.1	2.9	1.4	1.1	2.6	1.4	1.0
Current liabilities/Net worth (%)	30.7	80.0	152.8	23.7	62.3	149.1	27.6	76.3	163.7
Current liabilities/Inventory (%)	99.2	217.9	405.9	94.2	194.3	399.6	103.4	211.0	385.1
Total liabilities/Net worth (%)	49.6	100.8	239.1	40.0	106.6	237.6	42.9	118.0	242.2
Fixed assets/Net worth (%)	46.6	73.9	129.6	44.2	81.4	127.5	38.9	74.4	118.4
Efficiency									
Collection period (days)	16.0	30.9	53.0	15.3	36.1	61.9	16.4	34.7	62.1
Sales to Inventory	47.5	24.7	10.2	39.6	17.4	8.1	37.5	17.2	9.0
Assets/Sales (%)	31.6	60.1	101.0	31.3	54.8	94.9	30.8	51.8	98.4
Sales/Net Working Capital	16.6	9.2	4.8	21.2	8.8	4.7	22.1	8.5	4.5
Accounts payable/Sales (%)	1.9	4.6	8.8	2.0	4.9	13.3	2.0	4.6	9.9
Profitability									
Return - Sales (%)	8.2	2.4	-	7.2	3.4	.9	6.4	2.9	.9
Return - Assets (%)	14.2	3.7	-.1	15.4	4.7	1.5	13.0	5.3	1.8
Return - Net Worth (%)	29.9	8.8	.2	29.4	11.4	4.2	34.0	11.3	4.3

Source: Dun & Bradstreet. Data in this table are copyright (c) 1999 of Dun & Bradstreet. Reprinted by special arrangement with D&B. _Note:_ UQ stands for "Upper Quartile" and represents the top 25 percent of sample; MED stands for "Median"; and LQ stands for "Lower Quartile" and represents the lowest 25 percent.

D&B INDUSTRY NORMS: SIC 0724 - COTTON GINNING

	1998 (72) Estab.		1997 (109) Estab.		1996 (118) Estab.	
	$	%	$	%	$	%
Cash	302,421	15.1	331,358	17.6	255,740	16.3
Accounts Receivable	214,298	10.7	222,161	11.8	194,550	12.4
Notes Receivable	8,011	.4	15,062	.8	10,983	.7
Inventory	130,181	6.5	126,142	6.7	101,982	6.5
Other Current Assets	84,117	4.2	64,012	3.4	39,224	2.5
Total Current Assets	739,028	36.9	758,735	40.3	602,479	38.4
Fixed Assets	941,310	47.0	918,766	48.8	792,322	50.5
Other Non-current Assets	322,449	16.1	205,216	10.9	174,154	11.1
Total Assets	2,002,787	100.0	1,882,717	100.0	1,568,955	100.0
Accounts Payable	166,231	8.3	171,327	9.1	105,120	6.7
Bank Loans	-	-	1,883	.1	-	-
Notes Payable	108,150	5.4	88,488	4.7	94,137	6.0
Other Current Liabilities	282,393	14.1	252,284	13.4	196,119	12.5
Total Current Liabilities	556,774	27.8	513,982	27.3	395,376	25.2
Other Long Term	326,454	16.3	306,883	16.3	258,877	16.5
Deferred Credits	-	-			1,569	.1
Net Worth	1,119,558	55.9	1,061,852	56.4	913,131	58.2
Total Liabilities & Net Worth	2,002,786	100.0	1,882,717	100.0	1,568,953	100.0
Net Sales	2,513,762	100.0	2,184,477	100.0	2,011,519	100.0
Gross Profits	766,697	30.5	644,421	29.5	613,513	30.5
Net Profit After Tax	160,881	6.4	218,448	10.0	179,025	8.9
Working Capital	182,253	-	244,753	-	207,102	-

Source: Dun & Bradstreet. Data in this table are copyright (c) 1999 of Dun & Bradstreet. Reprinted by special arrangement with D&B. *Notes:* Values in parentheses above columns indicate the number of establishments in the sample. Data shown are for all companies.

D&B KEY BUSINESS RATIOS: SIC 0724

	1998			1997			1996		
	UQ	MED	LQ	UQ	MED	LQ	UQ	MED	LQ
Solvency									
Quick ratio	1.7	1.0	.4	2.1	1.1	.6	2.4	1.0	.6
Current ratio	2.6	1.3	.8	3.1	1.5	.9	3.2	1.5	1.0
Current liabilities/Net worth (%)	15.4	33.5	70.9	13.7	34.0	84.5	15.4	32.0	75.6
Current liabilities/Inventory (%)	98.8	246.7	467.0	87.9	196.8	516.0	82.9	195.6	416.2
Total liabilities/Net worth (%)	27.1	58.9	98.8	26.2	64.2	129.3	24.8	62.3	139.4
Fixed assets/Net worth (%)	45.7	79.0	124.1	50.2	80.8	117.0	51.1	76.3	129.2
Efficiency									
Collection period (days)	4.4	21.5	45.6	14.8	29.6	51.5	10.6	20.1	37.2
Sales to Inventory	52.3	19.9	7.7	56.6	21.3	10.4	57.2	23.4	7.4
Assets/Sales (%)	58.3	87.7	113.1	47.1	79.0	139.9	45.4	90.1	142.2
Sales/Net Working Capital	20.7	6.8	3.0	15.8	6.3	3.6	13.0	7.2	3.3
Accounts payable/Sales (%)	1.3	4.7	11.1	.9	4.4	10.2	.8	2.3	7.0
Profitability									
Return - Sales (%)	18.3	6.1	1.2	19.5	6.1	1.5	18.0	6.3	1.5
Return - Assets (%)	23.1	5.3	1.7	21.1	9.2	2.6	20.3	8.1	1.9
Return - Net Worth (%)	38.8	10.9	3.2	37.4	19.3	4.4	37.2	13.0	3.4

Source: Dun & Bradstreet. Data in this table are copyright (c) 1999 of Dun & Bradstreet. Reprinted by special arrangement with D&B. *Note:* UQ stands for "Upper Quartile" and represents the top 25 percent of sample; MED stands for "Median"; and LQ stands for "Lower Quartile" and represents the lowest 25 percent.

D&B INDUSTRY NORMS: SIC 0742 - VETERINARY SERVICES, SPECIALTIES

	1998 (42) Estab.		1997 (79) Estab.		1996 (98) Estab.	
	$	%	$	%	$	%
Cash	42,730	20.0	38,458	19.0	30,424	24.7
Accounts Receivable	12,178	5.7	17,812	8.8	10,593	8.6
Notes Receivable	2,350	1.1	1,012	.5	985	.8
Inventory	26,920	12.6	21,658	10.7	11,948	9.7
Other Current Assets	9,401	4.4	8,299	4.1	4,681	3.8
Total Current Assets	93,579	43.8	87,239	43.1	58,631	47.6
Fixed Assets	74,137	34.7	85,821	42.4	47,915	38.9
Other Non-current Assets	45,935	21.5	29,349	14.5	16,629	13.5
Total Assets	213,651	100.0	202,409	100.0	123,175	100.0
Accounts Payable	15,383	7.2	16,800	8.3	11,455	9.3
Bank Loans	-	-	-	-	-	-
Notes Payable	427	.2	7,287	3.6	3,203	2.6
Other Current Liabilities	27,134	12.7	32,790	16.2	20,201	16.4
Total Current Liabilities	42,944	20.1	56,877	28.1	34,859	28.3
Other Long Term	31,407	14.7	44,327	21.9	28,330	23.0
Deferred Credits	-	-	-202	-	-	-
Net Worth	139,300	65.2	101,406	50.1	59,987	48.7
Total Liabilities & Net Worth	213,651	100.0	202,408	100.0	123,176	100.0
Net Sales	966,463	100.0	837,901	100.0	613,771	100.0
Gross Profits	738,378	76.4	532,067	63.5	433,936	70.7
Net Profit After Tax	49,290	5.1	46,922	5.6	58,308	9.5
Working Capital	50,635	-	30,361	-	23,773	-

Source: Dun & Bradstreet. Data in this table are copyright (c) 1999 of Dun & Bradstreet. Reprinted by special arrangement with D&B. *Notes:* Values in parentheses above columns indicate the number of establishments in the sample. Data shown are for all companies.

D&B KEY BUSINESS RATIOS: SIC 0742

	1998			1997			1996		
	UQ	MED	LQ	UQ	MED	LQ	UQ	MED	LQ
Solvency									
Quick ratio	3.7	1.5	.7	2.6	1.1	.6	3.5	1.1	.5
Current ratio	4.9	3.6	1.5	4.5	2.1	1.0	5.6	1.9	1.0
Current liabilities/Net worth (%)	9.1	15.6	46.1	12.0	41.8	93.6	7.4	30.4	101.2
Current liabilities/Inventory (%)	45.1	87.4	273.4	58.1	139.0	304.8	88.2	162.8	302.4
Total liabilities/Net worth (%)	14.3	41.0	89.9	25.4	76.8	185.0	12.8	43.2	125.2
Fixed assets/Net worth (%)	21.7	52.8	84.7	41.0	62.7	136.6	28.2	63.6	100.5
Efficiency									
Collection period (days)	2.6	6.0	13.9	6.9	24.1	46.0	4.8	7.5	16.8
Sales to Inventory	48.5	34.2	23.3	57.8	33.9	20.3	50.3	26.9	18.6
Assets/Sales (%)	14.3	18.8	25.1	9.3	18.5	36.8	13.5	20.7	34.9
Sales/Net Working Capital	29.4	18.0	9.7	44.1	17.5	8.0	35.9	20.1	9.3
Accounts payable/Sales (%)	1.5	2.1	4.1	1.1	2.8	4.7	1.5	2.8	4.7
Profitability									
Return - Sales (%)	10.7	1.8	.6	14.7	4.4	1.9	14.7	6.6	2.5
Return - Assets (%)	31.0	7.8	3.0	59.0	14.6	2.2	47.9	22.3	4.1
Return - Net Worth (%)	38.8	13.7	5.6	102.2	19.9	3.9	140.9	44.1	16.0

Source: Dun & Bradstreet. Data in this table are copyright (c) 1999 of Dun & Bradstreet. Reprinted by special arrangement with D&B. *Note:* UQ stands for "Upper Quartile" and represents the top 25 percent of sample; MED stands for "Median"; and LQ stands for "Lower Quartile" and represents the lowest 25 percent.

D&B INDUSTRY NORMS: SIC 0751 - LIVESTOCK SERVICES, EXCEPT VETERINARY

	1998 (21) Estab.		1997 (26) Estab.		1996 (22) Estab.	
	$	%	$	%	$	%
Cash	360,889	12.4	544,280	19.5	327,200	13.1
Accounts Receivable	477,305	16.4	463,336	16.6	457,080	18.3
Notes Receivable	20,373	.7	-	-	-	-
Inventory	279,398	9.6	273,536	9.8	207,310	8.3
Other Current Assets	276,488	9.5	97,691	3.5	154,858	6.2
Total Current Assets	1,414,453	48.6	1,378,843	49.4	1,146,448	45.9
Fixed Assets	1,140,875	39.2	1,088,560	39.0	986,594	39.5
Other Non-current Assets	355,068	12.2	323,777	11.6	364,665	14.6
Total Assets	2,910,396	100.0	2,791,180	100.0	2,497,707	100.0
Accounts Payable	130,968	4.5	150,724	5.4	194,821	7.8
Bank Loans	-	-	-	-	-	-
Notes Payable	90,222	3.1	86,527	3.1	107,401	4.3
Other Current Liabilities	360,889	12.4	326,568	11.7	247,273	9.9
Total Current Liabilities	582,079	20.0	563,819	20.2	549,495	22.0
Other Long Term	334,696	11.5	418,677	15.0	387,145	15.5
Deferred Credits	-	-	2,791	.1	-	-
Net Worth	1,993,621	68.5	1,805,893	64.7	1,561,067	62.5
Total Liabilities & Net Worth	2,910,396	100.0	2,791,180	100.0	2,497,707	100.0
Net Sales	3,636,221	100.0	8,944,979	100.0	6,248,462	100.0
Gross Profits	1,836,292	50.5	4,418,820	49.4	3,742,829	59.9
Net Profit After Tax	76,361	2.1	125,230	1.4	199,951	3.2
Working Capital	832,373	-	815,025	-	596,952	-

Source: Dun & Bradstreet. Data in this table are copyright (c) 1999 of Dun & Bradstreet. Reprinted by special arrangement with D&B. *Notes:* Values in parentheses above columns indicate the number of establishments in the sample. Data shown are for all companies.

D&B KEY BUSINESS RATIOS: SIC 0751

	1998			1997			1996		
	UQ	MED	LQ	UQ	MED	LQ	UQ	MED	LQ
Solvency									
Quick ratio	2.8	1.1	.9	4.0	2.1	1.0	5.6	1.7	1.0
Current ratio	5.2	2.6	1.6	4.9	3.3	2.2	7.1	2.6	1.7
Current liabilities/Net worth (%)	13.1	17.3	41.6	13.4	18.8	28.2	9.6	19.3	36.9
Current liabilities/Inventory (%)	114.0	158.2	229.8	104.8	133.0	201.6	69.6	136.1	207.7
Total liabilities/Net worth (%)	13.1	25.3	65.4	18.9	25.9	56.4	17.0	37.5	74.1
Fixed assets/Net worth (%)	27.9	46.7	80.9	23.4	48.7	80.5	34.2	62.7	92.4
Efficiency									
Collection period (days)	17.2	30.7	58.0	13.7	24.7	58.1	23.9	35.0	56.8
Sales to Inventory	59.0	29.3	9.9	38.6	16.0	11.7	54.2	16.9	11.6
Assets/Sales (%)	33.2	60.7	85.8	20.6	59.5	67.8	32.1	58.2	72.9
Sales/Net Working Capital	18.4	10.1	2.2	14.6	6.3	3.6	12.5	7.1	3.7
Accounts payable/Sales (%)	1.3	2.5	4.9	1.8	3.6	4.3	1.9	3.7	4.8
Profitability									
Return - Sales (%)	9.7	5.7	-.6	4.4	2.8	-2.4	4.7	3.4	1.6
Return - Assets (%)	38.6	5.3	-.8	7.8	4.8	-5.2	14.1	7.0	1.8
Return - Net Worth (%)	41.8	6.2	-.9	9.5	5.9	-7.5	16.7	8.2	1.9

Source: Dun & Bradstreet. Data in this table are copyright (c) 1999 of Dun & Bradstreet. Reprinted by special arrangement with D&B. *Note:* UQ stands for "Upper Quartile" and represents the top 25 percent of sample; MED stands for "Median"; and LQ stands for "Lower Quartile" and represents the lowest 25 percent.

D&B INDUSTRY NORMS: SIC 0752 - ANIMAL SPECIALTY SERVICES, EXCEPT VETERINARY

	1998 (42) Estab.		1997 (48) Estab.		1996 (60) Estab.	
	$	%	$	%	$	%
Cash	93,614	12.8	108,937	16.3	62,514	14.5
Accounts Receivable	44,613	6.1	52,130	7.8	32,335	7.5
Notes Receivable	2,925	.4	668	.1	431	.1
Inventory	78,255	10.7	64,159	9.6	18,970	4.4
Other Current Assets	91,420	12.5	68,838	10.3	22,850	5.3
Total Current Assets	310,827	42.5	294,732	44.1	137,100	31.8
Fixed Assets	370,068	50.6	328,817	49.2	244,881	56.8
Other Non-current Assets	50,464	6.9	44,778	6.7	49,149	11.4
Total Assets	731,359	100.0	668,327	100.0	431,130	100.0
Accounts Payable	56,315	7.7	37,426	5.6	19,401	4.5
Bank Loans	-	-	-	-	-	-
Notes Payable	21,941	3.0	13,367	2.0	22,419	5.2
Other Current Liabilities	47,538	6.5	76,189	11.4	29,317	6.8
Total Current Liabilities	125,794	17.2	126,982	19.0	71,137	16.5
Other Long Term	82,644	11.3	65,496	9.8	83,208	19.3
Deferred Credits	-	-	1,337	.2	-	-
Net Worth	522,922	71.5	474,512	71.0	276,785	64.2
Total Liabilities & Net Worth	731,360	100.0	668,327	100.0	431,130	100.0
Net Sales	916,723	100.0	670,396	100.0	730,687	100.0
Gross Profits	469,362	51.2	442,461	66.0	500,521	68.5
Net Profit After Tax	93,506	10.2	70,392	10.5	86,952	11.9
Working Capital	185,034	-	167,750	-	65,963	-

Source: Dun & Bradstreet. Data in this table are copyright (c) 1999 of Dun & Bradstreet. Reprinted by special arrangement with D&B. *Notes:* Values in parentheses above columns indicate the number of establishments in the sample. Data shown are for all companies.

D&B KEY BUSINESS RATIOS: SIC 0752

	1998			1997			1996		
	UQ	MED	LQ	UQ	MED	LQ	UQ	MED	LQ
Solvency									
Quick ratio	4.8	1.3	.6	3.4	1.5	.5	3.6	1.2	.6
Current ratio	8.5	3.0	1.6	9.3	2.3	1.4	8.5	2.5	1.0
Current liabilities/Net worth (%)	4.4	11.5	50.8	4.4	10.8	47.2	2.6	14.4	34.0
Current liabilities/Inventory (%)	46.8	84.3	192.9	80.8	166.1	225.5	29.6	140.9	352.0
Total liabilities/Net worth (%)	8.4	32.0	103.4	6.3	21.2	67.2	4.0	29.0	139.8
Fixed assets/Net worth (%)	46.9	75.9	104.3	44.9	74.9	103.5	42.0	80.2	176.5
Efficiency									
Collection period (days)	4.8	16.6	34.5	7.3	10.6	55.1	2.2	9.5	56.9
Sales to Inventory	40.1	19.5	7.3	56.7	22.1	10.0	57.8	41.5	18.5
Assets/Sales (%)	48.7	101.2	195.0	31.0	94.4	190.1	51.5	122.4	185.1
Sales/Net Working Capital	12.9	8.2	2.3	10.8	4.5	1.6	13.4	4.2	2.4
Accounts payable/Sales (%)	1.7	2.9	5.6	3.6	4.5	6.5	1.2	3.2	5.1
Profitability									
Return - Sales (%)	13.6	8.1	5.2	21.8	12.1	5.0	19.4	8.2	3.1
Return - Assets (%)	13.3	8.9	3.9	26.7	18.4	5.5	18.8	6.1	.8
Return - Net Worth (%)	28.5	15.6	6.2	38.7	23.0	7.6	25.1	9.4	.9

Source: Dun & Bradstreet. Data in this table are copyright (c) 1999 of Dun & Bradstreet. Reprinted by special arrangement with D&B. *Note:* UQ stands for "Upper Quartile" and represents the top 25 percent of sample; MED stands for "Median"; and LQ stands for "Lower Quartile" and represents the lowest 25 percent.

D&B INDUSTRY NORMS: SIC 0762 - FARM MANAGEMENT SERVICES

	1998 (23) Estab.		1997 (32) Estab.		1996 (28) Estab.	
	$	%	$	%	$	%
Cash	87,072	11.0	165,890	15.5	75,639	9.5
Accounts Receivable	151,980	19.2	195,857	18.3	141,724	17.8
Notes Receivable	3,958	.5	4,281	.4	6,370	.8
Inventory	16,623	2.1	41,740	3.9	46,976	5.9
Other Current Assets	79,948	10.1	77,059	7.2	50,161	6.3
Total Current Assets	339,581	42.9	484,827	45.3	320,870	40.3
Fixed Assets	364,119	46.0	410,979	38.4	378,195	47.5
Other Non-current Assets	87,863	11.1	174,452	16.3	97,136	12.2
Total Assets	791,563	100.0	1,070,258	100.0	796,201	100.0
Accounts Payable	31,663	4.0	82,410	7.7	38,218	4.8
Bank Loans	-	-	-	-	15,924	2.0
Notes Payable	39,578	5.0	96,323	9.0	46,180	5.8
Other Current Liabilities	40,370	5.1	116,658	10.9	105,895	13.3
Total Current Liabilities	111,611	14.1	295,391	27.6	206,217	25.9
Other Long Term	135,357	17.1	232,246	21.7	188,699	23.7
Deferred Credits	1,583	.2	6,422	.6	-	-
Net Worth	543,012	68.6	536,199	50.1	401,285	50.4
Total Liabilities & Net Worth	791,563	100.0	1,070,258	100.0	796,201	100.0
Net Sales	3,256,216	100.0	4,524,099	100.0	4,688,914	100.0
Gross Profits	914,997	28.1	1,447,712	32.0	1,486,386	31.7
Net Profit After Tax	221,423	6.8	312,163	6.9	234,446	5.0
Working Capital	227,971	-	189,435	-	114,653	-

Source: Dun & Bradstreet. Data in this table are copyright (c) 1999 of Dun & Bradstreet. Reprinted by special arrangement with D&B. *Notes:* Values in parentheses above columns indicate the number of establishments in the sample. Data shown are for all companies.

D&B KEY BUSINESS RATIOS: SIC 0762

	1998			1997			1996		
	UQ	MED	LQ	UQ	MED	LQ	UQ	MED	LQ
Solvency									
Quick ratio	9.3	2.2	.9	2.4	1.3	.9	1.8	1.2	.6
Current ratio	13.1	3.9	2.1	3.5	1.9	1.3	2.4	1.8	1.2
Current liabilities/Net worth (%)	5.8	10.1	35.9	11.1	40.7	138.2	14.2	45.2	112.6
Current liabilities/Inventory (%)	137.4	189.2	472.9	168.0	375.8	510.8	94.9	237.5	447.4
Total liabilities/Net worth (%)	23.2	52.9	75.9	38.4	140.9	179.9	32.3	89.0	144.6
Fixed assets/Net worth (%)	32.1	65.8	111.0	29.5	67.4	148.7	39.4	91.2	154.1
Efficiency									
Collection period (days)	13.2	25.9	61.2	20.4	32.9	84.0	23.0	48.6	107.3
Sales to Inventory	88.6	55.4	32.0	88.4	77.1	17.5	67.3	27.3	21.8
Assets/Sales (%)	30.1	53.4	67.6	25.2	42.6	82.7	17.7	33.6	62.6
Sales/Net Working Capital	9.9	4.7	4.0	21.6	4.6	3.6	34.1	5.9	4.1
Accounts payable/Sales (%)	1.9	2.8	2.9	2.7	3.8	6.5	5.3	7.3	11.2
Profitability									
Return - Sales (%)	14.2	3.7	2.2	12.8	5.4	2.4	10.2	4.4	.8
Return - Assets (%)	6.9	4.4	3.6	15.0	9.6	2.6	28.5	5.0	1.0
Return - Net Worth (%)	11.9	6.4	5.1	48.1	14.5	8.7	76.1	12.7	5.5

Source: Dun & Bradstreet. Data in this table are copyright (c) 1999 of Dun & Bradstreet. Reprinted by special arrangement with D&B. *Note:* UQ stands for "Upper Quartile" and represents the top 25 percent of sample; MED stands for "Median"; and LQ stands for "Lower Quartile" and represents the lowest 25 percent.

D&B INDUSTRY NORMS: SIC 0781 - LANDSCAPE COUNSELING AND PLANNING

	1998 (192) Estab.		1997 (248) Estab.		1996 (234) Estab.	
	$	%	$	%	$	%
Cash	58,634	17.4	41,273	11.8	37,349	14.6
Accounts Receivable	105,473	31.3	99,334	28.4	71,629	28.0
Notes Receivable	674	.2	1,749	.5	1,023	.4
Inventory	17,860	5.3	22,385	6.4	17,396	6.8
Other Current Assets	19,882	5.9	21,336	6.1	13,047	5.1
Total Current Assets	202,523	60.1	186,077	53.2	140,444	54.9
Fixed Assets	118,615	35.2	141,306	40.4	101,559	39.7
Other Non-current Assets	15,838	4.7	22,385	6.4	13,814	5.4
Total Assets	336,976	100.0	349,768	100.0	255,817	100.0
Accounts Payable	38,415	11.4	41,972	12.0	31,977	12.5
Bank Loans	1,011	.3	700	.2	256	.1
Notes Payable	18,871	5.6	19,937	5.7	15,349	6.0
Other Current Liabilities	57,286	17.0	65,756	18.8	49,884	19.5
Total Current Liabilities	115,583	34.3	128,365	36.7	97,466	38.1
Other Long Term	54,927	16.3	72,752	20.8	48,605	19.0
Deferred Credits	337	.1	350	.1	767	.3
Net Worth	166,129	49.3	148,302	42.4	108,978	42.6
Total Liabilities & Net Worth	336,976	100.0	349,769	100.0	255,816	100.0
Net Sales	1,217,930	100.0	1,284,843	100.0	905,164	100.0
Gross Profits	535,889	44.0	551,198	42.9	383,790	42.4
Net Profit After Tax	85,255	7.0	60,388	4.7	44,353	4.9
Working Capital	86,940	-	57,712	-	42,978	-

Source: Dun & Bradstreet. Data in this table are copyright (c) 1999 of Dun & Bradstreet. Reprinted by special arrangement with D&B. *Notes:* Values in parentheses above columns indicate the number of establishments in the sample. Data shown are for all companies.

D&B KEY BUSINESS RATIOS: SIC 0781

	1998			1997			1996		
	UQ	MED	LQ	UQ	MED	LQ	UQ	MED	LQ
Solvency									
Quick ratio	2.7	1.4	.9	2.3	1.2	.6	1.9	1.1	.7
Current ratio	3.7	1.8	1.2	2.8	1.5	.9	2.5	1.5	1.0
Current liabilities/Net worth (%)	23.8	59.4	149.4	25.4	63.5	138.1	29.5	75.6	148.5
Current liabilities/Inventory (%)	120.4	291.6	552.0	119.1	299.8	619.1	118.8	235.0	508.6
Total liabilities/Net worth (%)	32.9	99.0	225.4	54.5	116.0	214.4	53.3	120.7	219.4
Fixed assets/Net worth (%)	37.7	65.8	159.2	38.6	74.3	143.6	42.8	81.0	145.7
Efficiency									
Collection period (days)	23.7	43.8	72.3	20.4	38.9	64.4	22.1	43.1	67.5
Sales to Inventory	117.7	35.7	15.6	70.1	37.1	18.1	64.2	26.3	12.0
Assets/Sales (%)	21.9	34.6	46.7	23.7	34.0	45.5	22.2	31.5	43.0
Sales/Net Working Capital	21.6	11.2	5.8	22.8	10.5	6.0	26.3	12.9	6.9
Accounts payable/Sales (%)	1.8	3.9	7.4	1.5	4.0	7.9	2.1	4.0	7.0
Profitability									
Return - Sales (%)	10.6	4.4	1.2	7.5	3.2	1.2	8.2	3.1	.9
Return - Assets (%)	24.4	11.0	2.7	20.1	7.5	3.1	25.2	8.5	2.6
Return - Net Worth (%)	56.7	23.3	6.7	39.3	19.7	8.5	52.4	20.2	7.4

Source: Dun & Bradstreet. Data in this table are copyright (c) 1999 of Dun & Bradstreet. Reprinted by special arrangement with D&B. *Note:* UQ stands for "Upper Quartile" and represents the top 25 percent of sample; MED stands for "Median"; and LQ stands for "Lower Quartile" and represents the lowest 25 percent.

D&B INDUSTRY NORMS: SIC 0782 - LAWN AND GARDEN SERVICES

	1998 (700) Estab.		1997 (971) Estab.		1996 (1009) Estab.	
	$	%	$	%	$	%
Cash	59,595	15.0	51,435	13.5	36,378	13.7
Accounts Receivable	106,078	26.7	102,489	26.9	69,039	26.0
Notes Receivable	3,178	.8	2,286	.6	2,390	.9
Inventory	25,030	6.3	23,241	6.1	17,260	6.5
Other Current Assets	14,700	3.7	20,193	5.3	14,870	5.6
Total Current Assets	208,581	52.5	199,644	52.4	139,937	52.7
Fixed Assets	164,481	41.4	160,401	42.1	110,462	41.6
Other Non-current Assets	24,235	6.1	20,955	5.5	15,135	5.7
Total Assets	397,297	100.0	381,000	100.0	265,534	100.0
Accounts Payable	42,113	10.6	41,910	11.0	28,943	10.9
Bank Loans	397	.1	381	.1	266	.1
Notes Payable	18,673	4.7	19,431	5.1	15,666	5.9
Other Current Liabilities	65,951	16.6	68,961	18.1	43,813	16.5
Total Current Liabilities	127,134	32.0	130,683	34.3	88,688	33.4
Other Long Term	80,254	20.2	80,391	21.1	53,903	20.3
Deferred Credits	795	.2	1,143	.3	531	.2
Net Worth	189,113	47.6	168,783	44.3	122,411	46.1
Total Liabilities & Net Worth	397,296	100.0	381,000	100.0	265,533	100.0
Net Sales	1,314,360	100.0	1,157,302	100.0	916,076	100.0
Gross Profits	527,058	40.1	486,067	42.0	400,325	43.7
Net Profit After Tax	70,975	5.4	57,865	5.0	42,139	4.6
Working Capital	81,446	-	68,961	-	51,248	-

Source: Dun & Bradstreet. Data in this table are copyright (c) 1999 of Dun & Bradstreet. Reprinted by special arrangement with D&B. *Notes:* Values in parentheses above columns indicate the number of establishments in the sample. Data shown are for all companies.

D&B KEY BUSINESS RATIOS: SIC 0782

	1998			1997			1996		
	UQ	MED	LQ	UQ	MED	LQ	UQ	MED	LQ
Solvency									
Quick ratio	2.6	1.3	.8	2.3	1.2	.7	2.4	1.2	.7
Current ratio	3.2	1.7	1.1	3.0	1.6	1.0	3.3	1.6	1.1
Current liabilities/Net worth (%)	23.9	57.7	126.2	26.9	62.6	152.0	23.1	59.0	129.0
Current liabilities/Inventory (%)	109.0	220.6	480.9	124.9	268.7	500.8	107.9	216.3	467.9
Total liabilities/Net worth (%)	46.3	97.6	189.0	50.0	108.4	222.7	41.4	92.3	201.4
Fixed assets/Net worth (%)	43.9	81.8	137.5	48.2	88.2	151.2	42.2	79.9	142.5
Efficiency									
Collection period (days)	21.5	35.8	59.1	18.3	36.1	58.4	21.0	36.5	59.7
Sales to Inventory	85.9	35.1	15.7	114.5	45.0	14.9	99.4	37.6	13.7
Assets/Sales (%)	25.1	34.7	48.1	21.2	31.5	46.3	23.9	33.3	46.9
Sales/Net Working Capital	21.9	11.3	6.0	25.5	12.7	6.6	25.8	11.5	6.1
Accounts payable/Sales (%)	1.8	3.9	6.7	1.5	3.3	6.1	1.5	3.5	6.9
Profitability									
Return - Sales (%)	9.4	3.9	1.2	7.8	3.4	1.0	7.7	2.9	.7
Return - Assets (%)	21.5	9.9	3.4	22.3	9.3	2.5	17.8	8.0	1.9
Return - Net Worth (%)	48.2	20.7	8.5	53.5	21.6	7.1	45.3	19.0	4.4

Source: Dun & Bradstreet. Data in this table are copyright (c) 1999 of Dun & Bradstreet. Reprinted by special arrangement with D&B. *Note:* UQ stands for "Upper Quartile" and represents the top 25 percent of sample; MED stands for "Median"; and LQ stands for "Lower Quartile" and represents the lowest 25 percent.

D&B INDUSTRY NORMS: SIC 0783 - ORNAMENTAL SHRUB AND TREE SERVICES

	1998 (78) Estab.		1997 (106) Estab.		1996 (117) Estab.	
	$	%	$	%	$	%
Cash	42,840	14.4	62,197	15.8	36,562	13.7
Accounts Receivable	58,608	19.7	80,306	20.4	49,106	18.4
Notes Receivable	1,488	.5	1,181	.3	1,601	.6
Inventory	7,438	2.5	11,022	2.8	9,341	3.5
Other Current Assets	14,875	5.0	20,470	5.2	12,010	4.5
Total Current Assets	125,249	42.1	175,176	44.5	108,620	40.7
Fixed Assets	157,677	53.0	186,592	47.4	139,311	52.2
Other Non-current Assets	14,578	4.9	31,886	8.1	18,948	7.1
Total Assets	297,504	100.0	393,654	100.0	266,879	100.0
Accounts Payable	19,933	6.7	30,705	7.8	16,546	6.2
Bank Loans	298	.1	1,575	.4	-	-
Notes Payable	18,148	6.1	24,013	6.1	18,415	6.9
Other Current Liabilities	52,063	17.5	65,740	16.7	49,373	18.5
Total Current Liabilities	90,442	30.4	122,033	31.0	84,334	31.6
Other Long Term	69,021	23.2	92,903	23.6	69,922	26.2
Deferred Credits	298	.1	1,181	.3	267	.1
Net Worth	137,744	46.3	177,538	45.1	112,356	42.1
Total Liabilities & Net Worth	297,505	100.0	393,655	100.0	266,879	100.0
Net Sales	1,051,907	100.0	1,097,429	100.0	851,395	100.0
Gross Profits	510,175	48.5	591,514	53.9	425,698	50.0
Net Profit After Tax	48,388	4.6	74,625	6.8	57,043	6.7
Working Capital	34,808	-	53,143	-	24,286	-

Source: Dun & Bradstreet. Data in this table are copyright (c) 1999 of Dun & Bradstreet. Reprinted by special arrangement with D&B. *Notes:* Values in parentheses above columns indicate the number of establishments in the sample. Data shown are for all companies.

D&B KEY BUSINESS RATIOS: SIC 0783

	1998			1997			1996		
	UQ	MED	LQ	UQ	MED	LQ	UQ	MED	LQ
Solvency									
Quick ratio	2.1	1.1	.6	2.4	1.2	.8	2.2	1.1	.6
Current ratio	3.0	1.4	.8	3.8	1.4	1.0	2.8	1.3	.7
Current liabilities/Net worth (%)	19.8	44.3	114.8	20.8	55.1	122.3	17.8	52.7	124.6
Current liabilities/Inventory (%)	191.4	336.0	577.0	166.0	300.0	581.2	93.8	257.1	409.6
Total liabilities/Net worth (%)	21.9	99.3	165.9	39.8	100.3	203.5	45.5	109.9	276.4
Fixed assets/Net worth (%)	55.3	99.5	175.6	52.7	99.9	190.8	59.5	109.1	264.1
Efficiency									
Collection period (days)	17.9	28.7	44.5	20.1	31.0	46.0	20.1	28.1	50.4
Sales to Inventory	197.4	113.1	32.3	133.4	68.2	31.4	87.6	43.7	15.8
Assets/Sales (%)	25.5	33.9	49.7	28.0	38.1	49.5	24.9	35.6	55.5
Sales/Net Working Capital	15.0	9.4	6.0	20.0	10.4	6.2	18.7	9.4	5.2
Accounts payable/Sales (%)	.9	1.9	3.7	1.1	1.6	4.6	1.4	2.7	5.1
Profitability									
Return - Sales (%)	7.2	3.5	.7	11.4	4.0	.9	9.3	4.6	2.3
Return - Assets (%)	22.1	8.8	2.1	26.1	8.4	1.8	21.5	12.7	3.8
Return - Net Worth (%)	44.7	22.0	5.4	69.0	29.0	4.1	47.9	28.7	7.5

Source: Dun & Bradstreet. Data in this table are copyright (c) 1999 of Dun & Bradstreet. Reprinted by special arrangement with D&B. *Note:* UQ stands for "Upper Quartile" and represents the top 25 percent of sample; MED stands for "Median"; and LQ stands for "Lower Quartile" and represents the lowest 25 percent.

D&B INDUSTRY NORMS: SIC 0811 - TIMBER TRACTS

	1998 (32) Estab.		1997 (29) Estab.		1996 (44) Estab.	
	$	%	$	%	$	%
Cash	288,728	7.5	690,408	7.2	68,864	6.3
Accounts Receivable	454,265	11.8	872,599	9.1	103,843	9.5
Notes Receivable	3,850	.1	28,767	.3	24,048	2.2
Inventory	639,051	16.6	1,505,473	15.7	171,614	15.7
Other Current Assets	323,375	8.4	1,045,201	10.9	60,119	5.5
Total Current Assets	1,709,269	44.4	4,142,448	43.2	428,488	39.2
Fixed Assets	1,466,738	38.1	3,758,887	39.2	473,304	43.3
Other Non-current Assets	673,699	17.5	1,687,663	17.6	191,289	17.5
Total Assets	3,849,706	100.0	9,588,998	100.0	1,093,081	100.0
Accounts Payable	300,277	7.8	220,547	2.3	42,630	3.9
Bank Loans	-	-	326,026	3.4	5,465	.5
Notes Payable	146,289	3.8	364,382	3.8	85,260	7.8
Other Current Liabilities	388,820	10.1	699,997	7.3	97,284	8.9
Total Current Liabilities	835,386	21.7	1,610,952	16.8	230,639	21.1
Other Long Term	800,739	20.8	1,371,227	14.3	186,917	17.1
Deferred Credits	3,850	.1	38,356	.4	3,279	.3
Net Worth	2,209,732	57.4	6,568,463	68.5	672,245	61.5
Total Liabilities & Net Worth	3,849,707	100.0	9,588,998	100.0	1,093,080	100.0
Net Sales	2,867,635	100.0	5,222,330	100.0	3,182,421	100.0
Gross Profits	1,075,363	37.5	2,402,272	46.0	1,365,259	42.9
Net Profit After Tax	65,956	2.3	443,898	8.5	302,330	9.5
Working Capital	873,884	-	2,531,496	-	197,848	-

Source: Dun & Bradstreet. Data in this table are copyright (c) 1999 of Dun & Bradstreet. Reprinted by special arrangement with D&B. *Notes:* Values in parentheses above columns indicate the number of establishments in the sample. Data shown are for all companies.

D&B KEY BUSINESS RATIOS: SIC 0811

	1998			1997			1996		
	UQ	MED	LQ	UQ	MED	LQ	UQ	MED	LQ
Solvency									
Quick ratio	1.8	1.3	.4	3.8	1.4	.5	3.0	1.1	.3
Current ratio	5.8	2.2	1.3	10.0	4.2	1.6	5.6	2.6	.9
Current liabilities/Net worth (%)	6.0	23.6	64.6	5.5	12.6	68.2	4.7	13.4	55.6
Current liabilities/Inventory (%)	48.5	93.2	220.5	46.4	94.6	151.5	70.3	149.8	257.7
Total liabilities/Net worth (%)	15.8	63.9	245.7	11.4	20.4	149.0	15.5	27.5	94.0
Fixed assets/Net worth (%)	20.3	61.0	125.2	21.7	62.3	110.7	55.0	96.2	158.2
Efficiency									
Collection period (days)	15.7	36.1	106.2	13.9	30.3	68.3	20.8	48.6	140.2
Sales to Inventory	14.7	5.4	3.3	36.1	15.2	4.2	8.2	3.3	.8
Assets/Sales (%)	38.5	107.3	253.0	118.7	191.4	313.5	85.2	258.8	427.0
Sales/Net Working Capital	9.2	5.1	1.0	5.6	1.6	1.2	7.1	1.7	.4
Accounts payable/Sales (%)	2.7	5.7	10.2	2.5	3.7	5.6	1.5	3.9	11.4
Profitability									
Return - Sales (%)	14.5	6.6	2.0	26.4	13.2	6.2	17.1	12.3	6.4
Return - Assets (%)	14.0	7.9	.8	13.2	9.1	4.1	10.6	5.2	2.8
Return - Net Worth (%)	28.7	11.6	1.1	18.4	15.3	6.3	21.2	6.7	3.6

Source: Dun & Bradstreet. Data in this table are copyright (c) 1999 of Dun & Bradstreet. Reprinted by special arrangement with D&B. *Note:* UQ stands for "Upper Quartile" and represents the top 25 percent of sample; MED stands for "Median"; and LQ stands for "Lower Quartile" and represents the lowest 25 percent.

D&B INDUSTRY NORMS: SIC 0851 - FORESTRY SERVICES

	1998 (29) Estab.		1997 (53) Estab.		1996 (43) Estab.	
	$	%	$	%	$	%
Cash	95,213	18.1	112,316	17.8	144,349	18.3
Accounts Receivable	92,057	17.5	108,530	17.2	133,306	16.9
Notes Receivable	13,151	2.5	5,679	.9	789	.1
Inventory	12,099	2.3	35,966	5.7	61,526	7.8
Other Current Assets	48,396	9.2	74,457	11.8	71,780	9.1
Total Current Assets	260,916	49.6	336,948	53.4	411,750	52.2
Fixed Assets	202,000	38.4	225,263	35.7	271,345	34.4
Other Non-current Assets	63,125	12.0	68,778	10.9	105,698	13.4
Total Assets	526,041	100.0	630,989	100.0	788,793	100.0
Accounts Payable	45,240	8.6	44,169	7.0	51,272	6.5
Bank Loans	-	-	-	-	3,944	.5
Notes Payable	32,089	6.1	30,918	4.9	38,651	4.9
Other Current Liabilities	75,224	14.3	116,102	18.4	173,535	22.0
Total Current Liabilities	152,553	29.0	191,189	30.3	267,402	33.9
Other Long Term	88,901	16.9	108,530	17.2	124,629	15.8
Deferred Credits	-	-	8,834	1.4	1,578	.2
Net Worth	284,588	54.1	322,435	51.1	395,186	50.1
Total Liabilities & Net Worth	526,042	100.0	630,988	100.0	788,795	100.0
Net Sales	1,508,054	100.0	2,476,565	100.0	1,694,143	100.0
Gross Profits	450,908	29.9	733,063	29.6	367,629	21.7
Net Profit After Tax	40,717	2.7	104,016	4.2	89,790	5.3
Working Capital	108,364	-	145,759	-	144,349	-

Source: Dun & Bradstreet. Data in this table are copyright (c) 1999 of Dun & Bradstreet. Reprinted by special arrangement with D&B. *Notes:* Values in parentheses above columns indicate the number of establishments in the sample. Data shown are for all companies.

D&B KEY BUSINESS RATIOS: SIC 0851

	1998			1997			1996		
	UQ	MED	LQ	UQ	MED	LQ	UQ	MED	LQ
Solvency									
Quick ratio	3.9	1.7	.7	2.4	1.0	.5	2.0	1.1	.6
Current ratio	6.3	2.1	1.2	4.1	1.9	1.1	4.2	1.6	.8
Current liabilities/Net worth (%)	7.2	30.3	165.1	18.4	62.7	145.1	14.5	54.2	205.1
Current liabilities/Inventory (%)	63.2	116.1	169.0	54.0	100.4	159.2	66.7	126.0	334.2
Total liabilities/Net worth (%)	23.0	88.9	213.5	31.7	119.6	194.8	30.7	108.4	218.1
Fixed assets/Net worth (%)	25.7	72.1	135.3	24.4	69.2	137.4	23.1	51.7	109.0
Efficiency									
Collection period (days)	8.4	15.3	47.8	7.5	20.8	51.7	8.8	29.6	47.5
Sales to Inventory	448.0	219.1	53.3	192.7	8.1	6.3	170.5	9.0	3.1
Assets/Sales (%)	24.1	34.4	56.7	26.5	43.7	68.3	32.1	56.4	90.8
Sales/Net Working Capital	38.9	12.6	5.9	11.7	6.9	4.5	10.7	6.4	2.7
Accounts payable/Sales (%)	.8	4.2	6.5	1.6	2.8	5.2	1.5	3.4	4.6
Profitability									
Return - Sales (%)	8.7	1.1	-3.2	5.6	2.8	.5	15.2	5.1	1.5
Return - Assets (%)	31.2	3.6	-3.8	17.6	6.4	2.0	25.9	9.0	2.9
Return - Net Worth (%)	54.8	6.2	-5.1	46.6	13.2	3.6	75.2	25.6	7.2

Source: Dun & Bradstreet. Data in this table are copyright (c) 1999 of Dun & Bradstreet. Reprinted by special arrangement with D&B. *Note:* UQ stands for "Upper Quartile" and represents the top 25 percent of sample; MED stands for "Median"; and LQ stands for "Lower Quartile" and represents the lowest 25 percent.

D&B INDUSTRY NORMS: SIC 0900 - FISHING, HUNTING & TRAPPING

	1998 (25) Estab.		1997 (43) Estab.		1996 (42) Estab.	
	$	%	$	%	$	%
Cash	778,886	21.7	235,384	14.2	193,941	18.7
Accounts Receivable	276,379	7.7	180,682	10.9	49,782	4.8
Notes Receivable	3,589	.1	81,224	4.9	11,408	1.1
Inventory	294,325	8.2	111,062	6.7	87,118	8.4
Other Current Assets	132,805	3.7	66,305	4.0	108,898	10.5
Total Current Assets	1,485,984	41.4	674,657	40.7	451,147	43.5
Fixed Assets	1,625,969	45.3	795,665	48.0	432,479	41.7
Other Non-current Assets	477,382	13.3	187,313	11.3	153,494	14.8
Total Assets	3,589,335	100.0	1,657,635	100.0	1,037,120	100.0
Accounts Payable	161,520	4.5	104,431	6.3	63,264	6.1
Bank Loans	-	-	-	-	2,074	.2
Notes Payable	39,483	1.1	91,170	5.5	52,893	5.1
Other Current Liabilities	760,939	21.2	319,924	19.3	150,382	14.5
Total Current Liabilities	961,942	26.8	515,525	31.1	268,613	25.9
Other Long Term	757,350	21.1	255,276	15.4	194,979	18.8
Deferred Credits	17,947	.5	1,658	.1	8,297	.8
Net Worth	1,852,097	51.6	885,178	53.4	565,230	54.5
Total Liabilities & Net Worth	3,589,336	100.0	1,657,637	100.0	1,037,119	100.0
Net Sales	2,043,809	100.0	1,681,342	100.0	680,736	100.0
Gross Profits	741,903	36.3	551,480	32.8	297,482	43.7
Net Profit After Tax	143,067	7.0	104,243	6.2	21,784	3.2
Working Capital	524,043	-	159,133	-	182,533	-

Source: Dun & Bradstreet. Data in this table are copyright (c) 1999 of Dun & Bradstreet. Reprinted by special arrangement with D&B. *Notes:* Values in parentheses above columns indicate the number of establishments in the sample. Data shown are for all companies.

D&B KEY BUSINESS RATIOS: SIC 0900

	1998			1997			1996		
	UQ	MED	LQ	UQ	MED	LQ	UQ	MED	LQ
Solvency									
Quick ratio	2.6	1.2	.4	2.0	.7	.3	2.5	.6	.3
Current ratio	4.4	2.3	.7	3.2	2.0	.7	4.8	1.7	.8
Current liabilities/Net worth (%)	15.8	30.1	43.6	20.9	35.9	63.0	10.7	25.7	98.2
Current liabilities/Inventory (%)	73.6	215.2	455.7	92.9	241.5	308.1	123.7	179.5	387.7
Total liabilities/Net worth (%)	30.1	41.5	211.8	30.9	53.5	110.5	26.1	64.8	208.0
Fixed assets/Net worth (%)	28.0	61.7	111.3	40.9	70.1	148.9	34.5	75.8	131.4
Efficiency									
Collection period (days)	10.6	25.9	34.7	6.6	12.1	32.2	8.9	19.5	45.6
Sales to Inventory	26.9	20.5	9.0	25.5	14.4	4.2	23.2	7.5	4.4
Assets/Sales (%)	58.1	73.7	126.3	36.6	63.1	97.3	51.4	71.0	117.9
Sales/Net Working Capital	5.4	2.8	1.5	10.3	7.1	3.6	12.8	5.4	4.2
Accounts payable/Sales (%)	1.2	3.6	6.0	1.7	3.4	8.1	1.5	2.5	5.8
Profitability									
Return - Sales (%)	15.1	4.9	1.6	7.3	3.4	-.1	6.9	3.5	-4.4
Return - Assets (%)	11.6	6.7	3.8	8.4	3.4	-.8	8.3	3.2	-3.6
Return - Net Worth (%)	31.9	10.7	7.3	13.0	4.3	-.6	11.5	6.5	-12.2

Source: Dun & Bradstreet. Data in this table are copyright (c) 1999 of Dun & Bradstreet. Reprinted by special arrangement with D&B. *Note:* UQ stands for "Upper Quartile" and represents the top 25 percent of sample; MED stands for "Median"; and LQ stands for "Lower Quartile" and represents the lowest 25 percent.

D&B INDUSTRY NORMS: SIC 2411 - LOGGING

	1998 (95) Estab.		1997 (154) Estab.		1996 (138) Estab.	
	$	%	$	%	$	%
Cash	88,652	11.8	87,502	10.5	91,657	14.3
Accounts Receivable	39,067	5.2	61,668	7.4	42,944	6.7
Notes Receivable	7,513	1.0	5,833	.7	3,846	.6
Inventory	30,803	4.1	49,168	5.9	37,816	5.9
Other Current Assets	51,088	6.8	47,501	5.7	31,407	4.9
Total Current Assets	217,123	28.9	251,672	30.2	207,670	32.4
Fixed Assets	461,290	61.4	521,676	62.6	389,701	60.8
Other Non-current Assets	72,875	9.7	60,001	7.2	43,585	6.8
Total Assets	751,288	100.0	833,349	100.0	640,956	100.0
Accounts Payable	28,549	3.8	35,001	4.2	33,971	5.3
Bank Loans	3,005	.4	833	.1	2,564	.4
Notes Payable	72,124	9.6	75,835	9.1	42,303	6.6
Other Current Liabilities	107,434	14.3	118,336	14.2	92,938	14.5
Total Current Liabilities	211,112	28.1	230,005	27.6	171,776	26.8
Other Long Term	229,143	30.5	244,171	29.3	167,930	26.2
Deferred Credits	4,508	.6	2,500	.3	1,923	.3
Net Worth	306,525	40.8	356,673	42.8	299,326	46.7
Total Liabilities & Net Worth	751,288	100.0	833,349	100.0	640,955	100.0
Net Sales	1,585,499	100.0	1,484,612	100.0	1,061,280	100.0
Gross Profits	613,588	38.7	592,360	39.9	552,927	52.1
Net Profit After Tax	76,104	4.8	69,777	4.7	58,370	5.5
Working Capital	6,010	-	21,667	-	35,893	-

Source: Dun & Bradstreet. Data in this table are copyright (c) 1999 of Dun & Bradstreet. Reprinted by special arrangement with D&B. *Notes:* Values in parentheses above columns indicate the number of establishments in the sample. Data shown are for all companies.

D&B KEY BUSINESS RATIOS: SIC 2411

	1998			1997			1996		
	UQ	MED	LQ	UQ	MED	LQ	UQ	MED	LQ
Solvency									
Quick ratio	1.5	.6	.3	1.5	.6	.2	1.8	.7	.3
Current ratio	2.4	1.2	.4	2.6	1.1	.4	3.3	1.2	.6
Current liabilities/Net worth (%)	26.9	50.0	112.2	14.7	48.6	133.4	16.8	51.2	116.6
Current liabilities/Inventory (%)	140.9	209.3	317.4	51.6	156.9	491.3	70.8	163.9	345.7
Total liabilities/Net worth (%)	60.8	133.3	240.3	50.5	140.5	260.8	42.5	107.6	235.4
Fixed assets/Net worth (%)	87.7	131.1	205.1	74.4	142.9	266.3	72.4	139.5	247.1
Efficiency									
Collection period (days)	7.7	12.1	26.0	6.9	11.7	23.0	5.8	12.1	21.9
Sales to Inventory	50.0	22.0	8.5	46.2	34.9	10.2	47.2	27.9	8.4
Assets/Sales (%)	36.9	53.0	90.3	33.7	50.3	71.5	33.8	47.6	66.5
Sales/Net Working Capital	19.3	10.8	6.3	32.3	12.3	6.2	23.7	12.1	6.8
Accounts payable/Sales (%)	1.1	2.1	3.2	.7	1.7	3.2	.8	2.1	3.7
Profitability									
Return - Sales (%)	8.2	4.0	.5	6.7	2.6	.8	9.1	3.6	.8
Return - Assets (%)	14.1	6.1	1.4	12.8	5.1	1.4	17.2	6.8	2.0
Return - Net Worth (%)	37.5	13.9	1.9	35.4	14.2	2.6	37.4	20.2	3.0

Source: Dun & Bradstreet. Data in this table are copyright (c) 1999 of Dun & Bradstreet. Reprinted by special arrangement with D&B. *Note:* UQ stands for "Upper Quartile" and represents the top 25 percent of sample; MED stands for "Median"; and LQ stands for "Lower Quartile" and represents the lowest 25 percent.

COMPANY DIRECTORY

This chapter presents brief profiles of 1,000 companies in the Agriculture sector. Companies are public, private, and elements of public companies ("public family members").

Each entry features the *D-U-N-S* access number for the company, the company name, its parent (if applicable), address, telephone, sales, employees, the company's primary SIC classification, a brief description of the company's business activity, and the name and title of its chairman, president, or other high-ranking officer. If the company is an exporter, importer, or both, the fact is indicated by the abbreviations EXP, IMP, and IMP EXP shown facing the *D-U-N-S* number.

Rankings of these companies are shown in Chapter 5. Additional financial data—on an aggregated, industry level—are shown in Chapter 3.

This product includes proprietary data of Dun & Bradstreet, Inc.

D-U-N-S 05-308-8878
21ST CENTURY GENETICS
(*Parent:* Cooperative Resources Intl Inc)
100 Mbc Dr, Shawano, WI 54166
Phone: (715) 526-2141
Sales: $27,071,000   *Employees:* 500
Company Type: Private   *Employees here:* 110
SIC: 0751
    Artificial insemination
Jim Acquistapace, Partner

D-U-N-S 18-347-4568
7TH STANDARD RANCH CO
33374 Lerdo Hwy, Bakersfield, CA 93308
Phone: (661) 399-0376
Sales: $30,000,000   *Employees:* 500
Company Type: Private   *Employees here:* 500
SIC: 0172
    Grape grower & cold storage
Charles Addis, President

D-U-N-S 05-563-5940   EXP
A & D CHRISTOPHER RANCH
305 Bloomfield Ave, Gilroy, CA 95020
Phone: (408) 847-1100
Sales: $83,848,000   *Employees:* 200
Company Type: Private   *Employees here:* 170
SIC: 0161
    Grower of garlic
Donald Christopher, Partner

D-U-N-S 18-930-1880
A & P GROWERS CO-OP INC
(*Parent:* A & P Growers Cooperative Inc)
26487 N Hwy 99, Tulare, CA 93274
Phone: (559) 685-5463
Sales: $20,619,000   *Employees:* 10
Company Type: Private   *Employees here:* NA
SIC: 0174
    Processes almonds and pistachios and farm management
      service
Tom Johnson, President

D-U-N-S 00-695-6429
A D MAKEPEACE CO
158 Tihonet Rd, Wareham, MA
Phone: (508) 295-1000
Sales: $14,738,000   *Employees:* 55
Company Type: Private   *Employees here:* 55
SIC: 0171
    Operates cranberry bogs also operates commercial real estate
      and a sanitary landfill
Christophe Makepeace, President

D-U-N-S 00-692-3262
A DUDA & SONS INC
1975 W State Road 426, Oviedo, FL 32765
Phone: (407) 365-2111
Sales: $297,008,000   *Employees:* 1,600
Company Type: Private   *Employees here:* 110
SIC: 0161
    Vegetable farms/sugar cane farms/citrus groves/whol fresh
      fruits & vegetables & farm mach & equip/sod farms/raises
      beef cattle
Ferdinand S Duda, President

D-U-N-S 06-128-7173
A G S INC
950 Oak Ave, Fillmore, CA 93015
Phone: (805) 524-4091

Sales: $14,200,000   *Employees:* 300
Company Type: Private   *Employees here:* 300
SIC: 0762
    Farm management services/ pruning & harvesting of citrus
      fruits
Virginia A Piedra, President

D-U-N-S 11-839-3149
A J B RANCH
28724 Stockdale Hwy, Bakersfield, CA 93312
Phone: (661) 589-4875
Sales: $11,000,000   *Employees:* 27
Company Type: Private   *Employees here:* 27
SIC: 0241
    Dairy farm
John Bos, Partner

D-U-N-S 10-833-2594
A S P ENTERPRISES INC
2100 NW 99th Ave, Miami, FL 33172
Phone: (305) 593-6958
Sales: $12,240,000   *Employees:* 14
Company Type: Private   *Employees here:* 14
SIC: 0132
    Tobacco dealer
A M Boggs Jr, Partner

D-U-N-S 18-489-6041
ABBYLAND PORK PACK INC
539 Meridian St, Curtiss, WI 54422
Phone: (715) 223-4676
Sales: $28,411,000   *Employees:* 125
Company Type: Private   *Employees here:* 125
SIC: 0751
    Pig slaughtering
Alfredo Perez, President

D-U-N-S 07-740-0034   EXP
ABI ALFALFA INC
(*Parent:* Helena Chemical Co)
6700 Antioch Rd, Shawnee Mission, KS 66204
Phone: (913) 384-4940
Sales: $13,400,000   *Employees:* 300
Company Type: Private   *Employees here:* 35
SIC: 0181
    Seed producer
Roy P Bethel, Partner

D-U-N-S 05-326-0329
ACE TOMATO COMPANY INC
2771 French Camp Rd, Manteca, CA 95336
Phone: (209) 982-5691
Sales: $20,000,000   *Employees:* 50
Company Type: Private   *Employees here:* 50
SIC: 0161
    Green tomato growers & packers
Michael Ginor, President

D-U-N-S 05-974-8152
ADAMS LAND & CATTLE CO INC
1 Mi E & 1/4 N, Broken Bow, NE 68822
Phone: (308) 872-6494
Sales: $12,000,000   *Employees:* 75
Company Type: Private   *Employees here:* 75
SIC: 0211
    Feedlot
Harland Schraufnagel, President

D-U-N-S 14-824-9766
ADAMS LAND CO
N Main St, Leachville, AR 72438
Phone: (870) 539-6314

Sales: $50,000,000   *Employees:* 60
Company Type: Private   *Employees here:* 60
SIC: 0724
     Cotton gin irrigation service whol chemicals fertilizer & seed
        & does land management
Kathleen L Janssen, President

D-U-N-S 05-444-9467
AFFILIATED RICE MILLING INC
     (Parent: Rice Belt Warehouse Inc)
715 S 2nd St, Alvin, TX 77511
Phone: (281) 331-6176
Sales: $20,000,000   *Employees:* 45
Company Type: Private   *Employees here:* 45
SIC: 0723
     Rice dryer & mill
Jerry Adams, President

D-U-N-S 94-395-6151
AG PLANTERS INC
1508 Old 27 N, Lake Harbor, FL 33459
Phone: (561) 996-5873
Sales: $12,400,000   *Employees:* 150
Company Type: Private   *Employees here:* 150
SIC: 0133
     Sugarcane/sugar beet farm
Charles Adams, Chairman of the Board

D-U-N-S 80-593-0450
AG RX INC
751 S Rose Ave, Oxnard, CA 93030
Phone: (805) 487-0696
Sales: $21,000,000   *Employees:* 90
Company Type: Private   *Employees here:* 70
SIC: 0711
     Whol fertilizer
R E Mc Cann Jr, President

D-U-N-S 87-815-9144
AGRESERVES, INC
     (Parent: Deseret Management Corp)
139 E South Temple, Salt Lake City, UT 84111
Phone: (801) 359-1600
Sales: $23,600,000   *Employees:* 500
Company Type: Private   *Employees here:* 10
SIC: 0762
     Farm management
John W Creer, President

D-U-N-S 09-312-2190
AGRI BEEF CO
1555 Shoreline Dr Fl 3, Boise, ID 83702
Phone: (208) 338-2500
Sales: $300,000,000   *Employees:* 515
Company Type: Private   *Employees here:* 40
SIC: 0211
     Cattle feedlot whol veterinary supplies and feed supplements
Robert Rebholtz Jr, President

D-U-N-S 00-691-3545
AGRI-EMPIRE
630 W 7th St, San Jacinto, CA 92583
Phone: (909) 654-7311
Sales: $14,000,000   *Employees:* 200
Company Type: Private   *Employees here:* 20
SIC: 0134
     Grows packs & ships potatoes
Minos Athanassiadis, President

D-U-N-S 18-617-5311
AGRICULTURAL INNOVATION TRADE
3241 Somis Rd, Somis, CA 93066
Phone: (805) 386-5059

Sales: $13,400,000   *Employees:* 130
Company Type: Private   *Employees here:* 10
SIC: 0161
     Vegetable and fruit farm
Larry J Minor, President

D-U-N-S 83-250-6695
AGRINORTHWEST, INC
     (Parent: Deseret Management Corp)
2810 W Clearwater Ave, Kennewick, WA 99336
Phone: (509) 735-6461
Sales: $55,800,000   *Employees:* 100
Company Type: Private   *Employees here:* 100
SIC: 0111
     Farm
Don Sleight, President

D-U-N-S 05-126-1600
AINSWORTH FEED YARDS CO
1 1/2 Mi N of Hwy 20 W, Ainsworth, NE 69210
Phone: (402) 387-2455
Sales: $18,122,000   *Employees:* 25
Company Type: Private   *Employees here:* 25
SIC: 0211
     Beef cattle feedlot
Abel O Maldonado Jr, President

D-U-N-S 61-065-3172
ALASKA OCEAN SEAFOOD LTD
2415 T Ave Anacortes Mari, Anacortes, WA 98221
Phone: (360) 293-6759
Sales: $30,000,000   *Employees:* 170
Company Type: Private   *Employees here:* 170
SIC: 0912
     Commercial fishing
Timothy Voss, Chairman of the Board

D-U-N-S 18-654-0589
ALASKA TRAWL FISHERIES, INC
100 2nd Ave S, Ste 200, Edmonds, WA 98020
Phone: (425) 771-6164
Sales: $40,000,000   *Employees:* 70
Company Type: Private   *Employees here:* 70
SIC: 0912
     Catch & process pollock & whol seafood
Peter Giacomini, Chief Executive Officer

D-U-N-S 02-956-5843
ALEX R THOMAS & CO
290 E Gobbi St, Ukiah, CA 95482
Phone: (707) 462-4716
Sales: $15,000,000   *Employees:* 100
Company Type: Private   *Employees here:* 50
SIC: 0723
     Fresh pear packing
Robert A Sears, President

D-U-N-S 00-948-3447
ALF CHRISTIANSON SEED CO
101 E Section St, Mount Vernon, WA 98273
Phone: (360) 336-9727
Sales: $18,250,000   *Employees:* 86
Company Type: Private   *Employees here:* 84
SIC: 0181
     Vegetable seed breeder grower & marketer
Albert Caviglia, President

D-U-N-S 00-692-1951
ALICO INC
640 S Main St, Labelle, FL 33935
Phone: (941) 675-2966

Sales: $47,433,000   *Employees:* 130
Company Type: Public   *Employees here:* 20
SIC: 0174
    Citrus fruit grove grows sugar cane cattle ranch and real
      estate development sales
Robert C Gibson Jr, President

D-U-N-S 07-004-7105   EXP
ALL ALASKAN SEAFOODS, INC
130 Nickerson St, Ste 307, Seattle, WA 98109
Phone: (206) 285-8200
Sales: $60,000,000   *Employees:* 200
Company Type: Private   *Employees here:* 20
SIC: 0913
    Crab fishing & processing
Jeff Hendricks, General Manager

D-U-N-S 17-703-0418
ALL GREEN CORP
1335 Canton Hwy, Ste G, Marietta, GA 30066
Phone: (770) 973-1600
Sales: $12,500,000   *Employees:* 350
Company Type: Private   *Employees here:* 10
SIC: 0782
    Lawn care service
Craig Cross, President

D-U-N-S 00-797-2169
ALLEN'S HATCHERY INC
126 N Shipley St, Seaford, DE 19973
Phone: (302) 629-9163
Sales: $180,000,000   *Employees:* 300
Company Type: Private   *Employees here:* 125
SIC: 0254
    Poultry hatchery
Alexander R Thomas Iii, President

D-U-N-S 61-683-7068
ALLIANCE DAIRIES
4951 NW 170th St, Trenton, FL 32693
Phone: (352) 463-6613
Sales: $10,000,000   *Employees:* 50
Company Type: Private   *Employees here:* 50
SIC: 0241
    Dairy farm
Kenneth G Christianson, President

D-U-N-S 03-098-7507
ALLSTATE PACKERS INC
6011 E Pine St, Lodi, CA 95240
Phone: (209) 369-3586
Sales: $11,165,000   *Employees:* 30
Company Type: Private   *Employees here:* 30
SIC: 0723
    Fresh fruit & vegetable packing
Alicia Arroyo, President

D-U-N-S 00-527-7132
AMANA SOCIETY, INC
506 39th Ave, Amana, IA 52203
Phone: (319) 622-3051
Sales: $32,045,000   *Employees:* 275
Company Type: Private   *Employees here:* 30
SIC: 0191
    General crop & livestock farming mfg furniture ret general
      stores meat market & mfg woolen goods
Ben H Griffin Iii, Chairman of the Board

D-U-N-S 15-103-1978
AMERICAN FARMS
310 John St, Salinas, CA 93901
Phone: (831) 424-1815

Sales: $12,000,000   *Employees:* 200
Company Type: Private   *Employees here:* 170
SIC: 0161
    Farm
Lloyd Cannon, Chairman of the Board

D-U-N-S 03-270-3969
AMERICAN INTERNATIONAL DAIRIES CORP
1911 Columbia Ave, Franklin, TN 37064
Phone: (615) 790-8141
Sales: $12,000,000   *Employees:* 22
Company Type: Private   *Employees here:* 22
SIC: 0751
    Dairy cattle leasing
Paul R Anderegg, President

D-U-N-S 06-665-6653
AMERICAN LANDSCAPE INC
7949 Deering Ave, Canoga Park, CA 91304
Phone: (818) 999-2041
Sales: $14,525,000   *Employees:* 150
Company Type: Private   *Employees here:* 150
SIC: 0781
    Landscape contractor
Charles C Allen Jr, President

D-U-N-S 94-304-2374
AMERICAN NURSERY PRODUCTS LLC
7010 S Yale Ave, Ste 101, Tulsa, OK 74136
Phone: (918) 523-9665
Sales: $22,757,000   *Employees:* 400
Company Type: Private   *Employees here:* 7
SIC: 0811
    Wholesale distribution and grower of nursery stock
Saints Inc, Managing Partner

D-U-N-S 01-653-4179
AMERICAN PELAGIC FISHING L P
5470 Shilshole Ave NW, Seattle, WA 98107
Phone: (206) 789-5902
Sales: $20,000,000   *Employees:* 60
Company Type: Private   *Employees here:* 60
SIC: 0912
    Finfish fishing
Harvey L Brinton, President

D-U-N-S 07-188-6485
AMERICAN RAISIN PACKERS INC
2335 Chandler St, Selma, CA 93662
Phone: (559) 896-4760
Sales: $11,500,000   *Employees:* 6
Company Type: Private   *Employees here:* 6
SIC: 0723
    Raisin processing/packing
Chiles Wilson, President

D-U-N-S 62-262-5739
AMERICAN WILDERNESS RESOURCES
138 Northwest Rd, Queensbury, NY 12804
Phone: (518) 798-0050
Sales: $12,000,000   *Employees:* 12
Company Type: Private   *Employees here:* 12
SIC: 0811
    Acreage land dealer
Reynold Moessner, President

D-U-N-S 78-249-6913
AMICK PROCESSING INC
Hwy 178, Batesburg, SC 29006
Phone: (803) 532-1400

Sales: $25,400,000   *Employees:* 475
Company Type: Private   *Employees here:* 450
SIC: 0254
    Paultry processing
David Gill, General Partner

D-U-N-S 13-767-2671   EXP
ANDERSON CLAYTON CORP.
    (Parent: Qcus Inc)
3325 W Figarden Dr, Fresno, CA 93711
Phone: (559) 447-1390
Sales: $200,000,000   *Employees:* 250
Company Type: Private   *Employees here:* 250
SIC: 0724
    Cotton ginning/cottonseed oil milling & cotton compresses
Sherry Meek, President

D-U-N-S 18-573-2542
ANDREWS DISTRIBUTION CO
13650 Copus Rd, Bakersfield, CA 93313
Phone: (661) 858-2266
Sales: $15,000,000   *Employees:* 20
Company Type: Private   *Employees here:* 10
SIC: 0723
    Produce packer shipper and broker
Raymond H Mc Anally, President

D-U-N-S 00-250-4256
ANGELICA NURSERIES INC
11129 Locust Grove Rd, Kennedyville, MD 21645
Phone: (410) 928-3111
Sales: $10,000,000   *Employees:* 150
Company Type: Private   *Employees here:* 150
SIC: 0781
    Ornamental horticulture & nursery products
Murray D Strauss, President

D-U-N-S 05-522-9405
ANIMAL MEDICAL CENTER INC
510 E 62nd St, New York, NY 10021
Phone: (212) 838-8100
Sales: $14,024,000   *Employees:* 300
Company Type: Private   *Employees here:* 300
SIC: 0742
    Non-profit animal hospital
J W Fields, Member

D-U-N-S 82-910-3316
ANNETTE ISLAND PACKING CO
PO Box 10, Metlakatla, AK 99926
Phone: (907) 886-4661
Sales: $12,000,000   *Employees:* 8
Company Type: Private   *Employees here:* 8
SIC: 0912
    Fishing & packing
Lisa Torgersen, Partner

D-U-N-S 08-007-0923
ANTHONY VINEYARDS INC
4540 California Ave, Bakersfield, CA 93309
Phone: (805) 631-1871
Sales: $17,420,000   *Employees:* 250
Company Type: Private   *Employees here:* 240
SIC: 0172
    Grape vineyard and citrus fruit groves
John Paboojian Jr, President

D-U-N-S 00-969-8382
ANTON CARATAN & SON
1625 Road 160, Delano, CA 93215
Phone: (661) 725-2575

Sales: $23,477,000   *Employees:* 100
Company Type: Private   *Employees here:* 100
SIC: 0172
    Farms table grapes
Keith Van Buskirk, President

D-U-N-S 03-755-3864   EXP
APIO INC
4575 W Main St, Guadalupe, CA 93434
Phone: (805) 343-2835
Sales: $59,407,000   *Employees:* 75
Company Type: Private   *Employees here:* 60
SIC: 0722
    Crop harvesting and preparation for market
Billy L Amick, President

D-U-N-S 83-625-6669
ARABI GIN CO INC
346 1st St E, Arabi, GA 31712
Phone: (912) 273-2891
Sales: $14,647,000   *Employees:* 9
Company Type: Private   *Employees here:* 9
SIC: 0724
    Cottin gin
Shah Kazemi, President

D-U-N-S 00-691-6852
ARBOR ACRES FARM INC
    (Parent: Booker Holdings Inc)
439 Marlborough Rd, Glastonbury, CT
Phone: (860) 633-4681
Sales: $100,000,000   *Employees:* 750
Company Type: Private   *Employees here:* 236
SIC: 0254
    Chicken hatcheries turkey farm and wholesales lobster
Richard Haire, President

D-U-N-S 04-555-5240
ARBOR TREE SURGERY INC
802 Paso Robles St, Paso Robles, CA 93446
Phone: (805) 239-1239
Sales: $11,135,000   *Employees:* 250
Company Type: Private   *Employees here:* 15
SIC: 0783
    Tree trimming services for public utility lines & ornamental
    tree surgery services
Loyad E Anderson, President

D-U-N-S 06-842-9208
ARIZONA DAIRY CO, L.L.P.
19135 E Elliot Rd, Higley, AZ 85236
Phone: (602) 380-7955
Sales: $18,000,000   *Employees:* 108
Company Type: Private   *Employees here:* 108
SIC: 0241
    Dairy farm
Michael Andrews, Chief Executive Officer

D-U-N-S 02-159-3199
ARMSTRONG FARMS
29550 Cole Grade Rd, Valley Center, CA 92082
Phone: (760) 749-0844
Sales: $10,000,000   *Employees:* 75
Company Type: Private   *Employees here:* 5
SIC: 0252
    Egg production farm
Leverne C Kohl, President

D-U-N-S 04-096-2789
ARTEKA NATURAL GREEN CORP
    (Parent: Landcare USA Inc)
15195 Martin Dr, Eden Prairie, MN 55344
Phone: (612) 934-2000

Sales: $11,000,000
Company Type: Public Family Member
SIC: 0782
   Landscape contractor design planning and management
Robert Rooks, President

Employees: 50
Employees here: 37

D-U-N-S 05-018-8379
ASC FAR EAST INC
2025 1st Ave, Ste 835, Seattle, WA 98121
Phone: (206) 256-2692
Sales: $50,000,000
Company Type: Private
SIC: 0912

Amy Laukaitis, Administrator

Employees: 11
Employees here: 11

D-U-N-S 00-691-7736
ASGROW SEED COMPANY LLC
   (Parent: Monsanto Co)
4140 114th St, Des Moines, IA 50322
Phone: (515) 331-7100
Sales: $394,736,000
Company Type: Public Family Member
SIC: 0181
   Grower of agronomic seeds
Gui Pidgeon, Chief Executive Officer

Employees: 625
Employees here: 60

D-U-N-S 84-897-0893
ASHBRITT, INC.
1280 SW 36th Ave, Ste 201, Pompano Beach, FL 33069
Phone: (954) 973-9200
Sales: $10,530,000
Company Type: Private
SIC: 0782
   Envirnmental contractor
Pat Kelly, General Manager

Employees: 15
Employees here: 15

D-U-N-S 79-468-5024
ASPLUNDH SUBSIDIARY HOLDINGS,
   (Parent: Asplundh Tree Expert Co)
3411 Silverside Rd, Wilmington, DE 19810
Phone: (302) 478-6160
Sales: $175,283,000
Company Type: Private
SIC: 0783
   Holding company
Dominick T Bianco, President

Employees: 2,800
Employees here: 12

D-U-N-S 00-791-1753   EXP
ASPLUNDH TREE EXPERT CO
708 Blair Mill Rd, Willow Grove, PA 19090
Phone: (215) 784-4200
Sales: $1,026,588,000
Company Type: Private
SIC: 0783
   Line clearance for utility industry and municipalities
George Caratan, Partner

Employees: 21,800
Employees here: 400

D-U-N-S 17-721-6074
ATLANTIC SALMON ME LTD LBLTY
66 Western Ave, Fairfield, ME
Phone: (207) 453-7925
Sales: $23,887,000
Company Type: Private
SIC: 0273
   Producer of farm raised atlantic salmon
Tim Murphy, President

Employees: 135
Employees here: 10

D-U-N-S 96-520-4605
AURORA DAIRY FLORIDA LLC
6311 Horizon Ln, Ste 201, Longmont, CO 80503
Phone: (303) 530-8252

Sales: $14,000,000
Company Type: Private
SIC: 0241
   Dairy farm
Eddie Luke, President

Employees: 80
Employees here: 1

D-U-N-S 02-737-5633   EXP
AUVIL FRUIT CO, INC
21902 Sr 97, Orondo, WA 98843
Phone: (509) 784-1711
Sales: $17,880,000
Company Type: Private
SIC: 0175
   Orchard packing & refrigerated warehousing
J D Nelson, Chairman of the Board

Employees: 100
Employees here: 100

D-U-N-S 93-337-8226
AVI HOLDINGS INC
204 W Rosecrans Ave, Gardena, CA 90248
Phone: (310) 538-4980
Sales: $17,800,000
Company Type: Private
SIC: 0742
   Mfg women's misses and junior's outerwear
Marvin Morrison, Partner

Employees: 475
Employees here: 1

D-U-N-S 60-796-1612
AVIAN FARMS INC
1 City Ctr Stop 10, Portland, ME
Phone: (207) 873-0007
Sales: $13,900,000
Company Type: Private
SIC: 0254
   Holding company of primary poultry breeder
Stewart Hanson, President

Employees: 260
Employees here: 4

D-U-N-S 78-662-3355
AVIAN FARMS (KENTUCKY), INC
   (Parent: Avian Farms Inc)
By Pass Hwy 90, Monticello, KY 42633
Phone: (606) 348-3305
Sales: $26,000,000
Company Type: Private
SIC: 0254
   Primary poultry breeder
George W Armstrong, Chairman of the Board

Employees: 170
Employees here: 150

D-U-N-S 60-121-8589
AZCONA HARVESTING
44 El Camino Real Unit A, Greenfield, CA 93927
Phone: (831) 674-2526
Sales: $10,270,000
Company Type: Private
SIC: 0761
   Farm labor contractor
K D Kennedy, President

Employees: 2
Employees here: 2

D-U-N-S 19-070-9600
B & T FARMS
1280 N Melrose Dr, Vista, CA 92083
Phone: (760) 631-4240
Sales: $13,900,000
Company Type: Private
SIC: 0161
   Vegetable farming
Saily Perkins, President

Employees: 135
Employees here: 1

D-U-N-S 04-796-5322
B & W QUALITY GROWERS INC
17825 79th St, Fellsmere, FL 32948
Phone: (561) 571-0800

Sales: $15,000,000   *Employees:* 145
Company Type: Private   *Employees here:* 140
SIC: 0161
    Vegetable farm (watercress farm)
Ashley Payne, Owner

D-U-N-S 09-374-6568
B G MAINTENANCE
1123 Wilkes Blvd, Columbia, MO 65201
Phone: (573) 874-8000
Sales: $14,200,000   *Employees:* 400
Company Type: Private   *Employees here:* 250
SIC: 0782
    Lawn/garden services
Christophe B Asplundh, President

D-U-N-S 08-010-6701
B H HARDAWAY III FARMS INC
945 Broadway, Ste 300, Columbus, GA 31901
Phone: (706) 322-3274
Sales: $34,600,000   *Employees:* 500
Company Type: Private   *Employees here:* 36
SIC: 0139
    General contractor
Christophe B Asplundh, President

D-U-N-S 62-302-6978
B J & E REALTY CO
RR 522, Kreamer, PA 17833
Phone: (570) 374-8148
Sales: $11,089,000   *Employees:* 30
Company Type: Private   *Employees here:* 30
SIC: 0254
    Operates as a chicken farm
Christophe B Asplundh, President

D-U-N-S 18-155-6192
B L T FARMS
5655 Arcturus Ave, Oxnard, CA 93033
Phone: (805) 488-1068
Sales: $16,000,000   *Employees:* 80
Company Type: Private   *Employees here:* 80
SIC: 0161
    Growers of fresh vegetables
Mark Spencer, Chairman of the Board

D-U-N-S 14-838-4977
B T V CROWN EQUITIES, INC
400 Capitol Mall, Ste 2340, Sacramento, CA 95814
Phone: (916) 658-0735
Sales: $18,000,000   *Employees:* 300
Company Type: Private   *Employees here:* 7
SIC: 0172
    Development & operation of vineyard & real estate
        development
S A Galletta, Chairman of the Board

D-U-N-S 18-499-3905
BABE FARMS INC
1485 N Blosser Rd, Santa Maria, CA 93458
Phone: (805) 922-2487
Sales: $13,700,000   *Employees:* 150
Company Type: Private   *Employees here:* 150
SIC: 0161
    Vegetable farm
Thomas Royal, General Manager

D-U-N-S 00-645-3880
BAILEY NURSERIES, INC
1325 Bailey Rd, St. Paul, MN 55119
Phone: (651) 459-9744

Sales: $27,000,000   *Employees:* 470
Company Type: Private   *Employees here:* 200
SIC: 0181
    Whol grower of nursery stock
Marcus Peperzak, President

D-U-N-S 05-615-8637
BAILEY'S NURSERY INC
5401 E Harney Ln, Lodi, CA 95240
Phone: (209) 334-9142
Sales: $10,500,000   *Employees:* 155
Company Type: Private   *Employees here:* 110
SIC: 0181
    Grows & whol nursery stock
Marcus Peperzak, Member

D-U-N-S 02-893-6052
BAIRD-NEECE PACKING CORP
60 S E St, Porterville, CA 93257
Phone: (559) 784-3393
Sales: $13,100,000   *Employees:* 180
Company Type: Private   *Employees here:* 180
SIC: 0723
    Fruit packer
Paul King, President

D-U-N-S 92-646-0957
BAKER FARMING
45499 W Panoche Rd, Firebaugh, CA 93622
Phone: (559) 659-3942
Sales: $12,000,000   *Employees:* 25
Company Type: Private   *Employees here:* 25
SIC: 0172
    Grape vineyard tree nut grove
Dennis Contris, President

D-U-N-S 00-693-6322
BALL HORTICULTURAL CO
622 Town Rd, West Chicago, IL 60185
Phone: (630) 231-3600
Sales: $125,000,000   *Employees:* 2,000
Company Type: Private   *Employees here:* 400
SIC: 0181
    Horticulture product production
Dr John Rappaport, Owner

D-U-N-S 15-082-6303
BALOIAN PACKING CO, INC.
324 N Fruit Ave, Fresno, CA 93706
Phone: (559) 485-9200
Sales: $30,884,000   *Employees:* 300
Company Type: Private   *Employees here:* 300
SIC: 0161
    Vegetable farm
Robert Saglio, President

D-U-N-S 05-087-1706
BARTON COUNTY FEEDERS, INC
1164 SE 40 Rd, Ellinwood, KS 67526
Phone: (316) 564-2200
Sales: $10,000,000   *Employees:* 26
Company Type: Private   *Employees here:* 26
SIC: 0211
    Feed lot
Henry Saglio, Chairman of the Board

D-U-N-S 01-502-6995
BATIZ GREENHOUSES INC
4370 Ljlla Vlg Dr, Ste 610, San Diego, CA 92122
Phone: (619) 824-0433

Sales: $10,000,000
Company Type: Private
SIC: 0182
   Covered food crops farm
Nick Azcona, Partner

Employees: 3
Employees here: 3

    D-U-N-S 80-533-9355
BATSON MILL L. P.
   (Parent: Newpark Resources Inc)
Hwy 770 S, Batson, TX 77519
Phone: (409) 262-8000
Sales: $13,000,000
Company Type: Public Family Member
SIC: 0241
   Sawmill
Milton Allen, President

Employees: 56
Employees here: 56

    D-U-N-S 03-732-3839
BAUMAN LANDSCAPE, INC
115 Brookside Dr, Richmond, CA 94801
Phone: (510) 236-1212
Sales: $19,482,000
Company Type: Private
SIC: 0782
   Landscaping contractor
James A Ballard, President

Employees: 80
Employees here: 80

    D-U-N-S 02-909-1758
BAY CITY FLOWER CO INC
2265 Cabrillo Hwy S, Half Moon Bay, CA 94019
Phone: (650) 726-5535
Sales: $13,400,000
Company Type: Private
SIC: 0181
   Nursery growing potted plants
Bill Bowie, President

Employees: 300
Employees here: 300

    D-U-N-S 07-181-2309
BEAR CREEK CORP
   (Parent: Shaklee Corp)
2518 S Pacific Hwy, Medford, OR 97501
Phone: (541) 776-2362
Sales: $334,713,000
Company Type: Private
SIC: 0175
   Fruit orchard mail order sales whol roses ret orchids
Bill Stokes, President

Employees: 1,100
Employees here: 800

    D-U-N-S 88-479-2094
BEAR CREEK PRODUCTION CO
   (Parent: Bear Creek Corp)
29341 Kimberlina Rd, Wasco, CA 93280
Phone: (661) 758-5186
Sales: $17,800,000
Company Type: Private
SIC: 0181
   Ornamental nursery
Marvin Goodman, President

Employees: 400
Employees here: 250

    D-U-N-S 15-465-4867
BECKER HOLDINGS CORP
660 Beachland Blvd, Vero Beach, FL 32963
Phone: (561) 234-5234
Sales: $40,000,000
Company Type: Private
SIC: 0721
   Through subsidiaries manufactures citrus grove cultivator
    fresh fruit sales & machine harvesting svc
Eldert Van Dam, Owner

Employees: 150
Employees here: 22

    D-U-N-S 05-475-4072
BEEF BELT FEEDERS INC
1350 E Road 70, Scott City, KS 67871

Phone: (316) 872-3059
Sales: $24,400,000
Company Type: Private
SIC: 0211
   Commercial cattle feedlot
Mitch Hirota, President

Employees: 15
Employees here: 15

    D-U-N-S 55-609-5602
BEEF NORTHWEST INC
3455 Victorio Rd, Nyssa, OR 97913
Phone: (541) 372-2101
Sales: $16,700,000
Company Type: Private
SIC: 0211
   Beef cattle feedlot
Richard R Burgoon, President

Employees: 65
Employees here: 45

    D-U-N-S 10-704-9835
BEEF TECH CATTLE FEEDERS, INC.
County Rd 9, Hereford, TX 79045
Phone: (806) 363-6080
Sales: $12,000,000
Company Type: Private
SIC: 0211
   Cattle feedlot
Wavell Robinson, President

Employees: 20
Employees here: 20

    D-U-N-S 19-549-7375
BELAIR PACKING HSE JOINT VENTR
1626 90th Ave, Vero Beach, FL 32966
Phone: (561) 567-1151
Sales: $23,491,000
Company Type: Private
SIC: 0723
   Citrus fruit packing house ret & whol fresh fruits
Gerrit Van Hoven, President

Employees: 60
Employees here: 58

    D-U-N-S 85-851-0688
BELIZE RIVER FRUIT CO., INC
1500 N Big Run Rd, Ashland, KY 41102
Phone: (606) 928-3433
Sales: $10,800,000
Company Type: Private
SIC: 0174
   Citrus fruits grove
Thomas E Atkins Iii, President

Employees: 200
Employees here: 200

    D-U-N-S 16-897-1661
BELK FARMS
57-800 Desert Cactus Dr, Thermal, CA 92274
Phone: (760) 399-5951
Sales: $12,525,000
Company Type: Private
SIC: 0191
   Fresh vegetable farm
Edward Robinson, Partner

Employees: 30
Employees here: 30

    D-U-N-S 00-905-4289
BEN A THOMAS INC
634 S Bailey St, Ste 102, Palmer, AK 99645
Phone: (907) 746-6131
Sales: $14,500,000
Company Type: Private
SIC: 0241
   Logging
Tom Lam, President

Employees: 266
Employees here: 140

    D-U-N-S 18-050-0118
BEREND BROS INC
1116 E Scott Ave, Wichita Falls, TX 76303
Phone: (940) 723-2735

Sales: $24,723,000   *Employees:* 125
Company Type: Private   *Employees here:* 10
SIC: 0213
    Livestock & egg production & retails farm supplies
Jim Turner, President

D-U-N-S 07-057-6665
BEST FRIENDS PET CARE, INC.
520 Main Ave, Norwalk, CT
Phone: (203) 846-3360
Sales: $16,763,000   *Employees:* 800
Company Type: Private   *Employees here:* 40
SIC: 0752
    Pet services
Wilber S Souza, President

D-U-N-S 96-542-5382
BETHEL GRAIN CO
300 S Commercial St, Benton, IL 62812
Phone: (618) 439-7000
Sales: $17,000,000   *Employees:* 50
Company Type: Private   *Employees here:* 50
SIC: 0723
    Dry corn milling
Gordon Bailey Jr, Chairman of the Board

D-U-N-S 05-643-6751
BETTERAVIA FARMS
1850 W Stowell Rd, Santa Maria, CA 93458
Phone: (805) 925-2417
Sales: $31,519,000   *Employees:* 250
Company Type: Private   *Employees here:* 250
SIC: 0161
    Growers of vegetables
Edward J Craig, President

D-U-N-S 87-451-0696
BHB INC
3320 N Buffalo Dr, Ste 103, Las Vegas, NV 89129
Phone: (702) 395-8778
Sales: $14,170,000   *Employees:* 140
Company Type: Private   *Employees here:* 140
SIC: 0782
    Landscaping service
Robert Neece, President

D-U-N-S 87-744-1774
BLACK DOG FARMS OF CALIFORNIA
530 W 6th St, Holtville, CA 92250
Phone: (760) 356-2951
Sales: $32,000,000   *Employees:* 150
Company Type: Private   *Employees here:* 150
SIC: 0161
    General farming produce and fruit grower packer and
      shipper
Otto Geisert, President

D-U-N-S 09-391-2863
BLACK GOLD FARMS
1 Potato Ln, Forest River, ND 58233
Phone: (701) 248-3788
Sales: $11,000,000   *Employees:* 10
Company Type: Private   *Employees here:* 5
SIC: 0134
    Potato farm
Anna C Ball, President

D-U-N-S 93-271-8794
BLAINE LARSEN PROCESSING INC
2379 E 2300 N, Hamer, ID 83425
Phone: (208) 662-5501

Sales: $27,400,000   *Employees:* 400
Company Type: Private   *Employees here:* 400
SIC: 0723
    Potato processing
John Balletto, Owner

D-U-N-S 07-647-8429
BLEDSOE RANCH CO
N of Town Hwy 385, Wray, CO 80758
Phone: (970) 332-4955
Sales: $12,000,000   *Employees:* 20
Company Type: Private   *Employees here:* 20
SIC: 0211
    Beef cattle feedlots & beef cattle except feedlots
Edward Baloian, Chairman of the Board

D-U-N-S 13-147-2011
BLUE NORTH FISHERIES INC
4502 14th Ave NW, Seattle, WA 98107
Phone: (206) 782-3609
Sales: $10,000,000   *Employees:* 3
Company Type: Private   *Employees here:* 3
SIC: 0913
    Operate tenders & crab & finfish fishing boats
Crokett A Profitt, President

D-U-N-S 00-895-7631
BLUEBIRD INC
10135 Mill Rd, Peshastin, WA 98847
Phone: (509) 782-1216
Sales: $16,312,000   *Employees:* 30
Company Type: Private   *Employees here:* 25
SIC: 0723
    Fruit packing
Raul Batiz, President

D-U-N-S 19-410-0921
BOETHING TREELAND FARMS INC
23475 Long Valley Rd, Woodland Hills, CA 91367
Phone: (818) 883-1222
Sales: $17,600,000   *Employees:* 375
Company Type: Private   *Employees here:* 50
SIC: 0811
    Tree farm
C E Doss, President

D-U-N-S 79-917-0543
BONITA NURSERIES INC
    (Parent: Eurofresh Ltd)
13355 W Ashcreek, Willcox, AZ 85643
Phone: (520) 384-4621
Sales: $14,759,000   *Employees:* 230
Company Type: Private   *Employees here:* 230
SIC: 0161
    Tomato farm
Michael Bauman, President

D-U-N-S 80-882-2951
BOOKER HOLDINGS INC
439 Marlborough Rd, Glastonbury, CT
Phone: (860) 633-4681
Sales: $40,200,000   *Employees:* 750
Company Type: Private   *Employees here:* 150
SIC: 0254
    Chicken hatcheries turkey and salmon farm
Harrison Higaki, Chairman of the Board

D-U-N-S 18-281-5647
BORDERS, NOWELL
N Hwy 281 To Fm 490 4 Mi, Edinburg, TX 78539
Phone: (956) 383-0712

Sales: $11,500,000   *Employees:* 15
Company Type: Private   *Employees here:* 15
SIC: 0161
  Watermelon farm
William H Williams, President

D-U-N-S 02-936-0518
BORDIER'S NURSERY INC
7231 Irvine Blvd, Irvine, CA 92618
Phone: (949) 559-4221
Sales: $13,400,000   *Employees:* 300
Company Type: Private   *Employees here:* 300
SIC: 0181
  Growers of nursery stock
William H Williams, President

D-U-N-S 88-386-0397
BORG PAK, INC
1601 E Olympic Blvd 105, Los Angeles, CA 90021
Phone: (213) 688-9388
Sales: $12,000,000   *Employees:* 110
Company Type: Private   *Employees here:* 100
SIC: 0723
  Repacking of produce
Richard Becker, Chairman of the Board

D-U-N-S 05-801-7401   EXP
BOSKOVICH FARMS INC
711 Diaz Ave, Oxnard, CA 93030
Phone: (805) 487-2299
Sales: $85,000,000   *Employees:* 750
Company Type: Private   *Employees here:* 350
SIC: 0161
  Grows and packages vegetables
Richard E Becker, Chairman of the Board

D-U-N-S 82-584-5977
BRACHT FEEDYARDS, INC
1931 I Rd, West Point, NE 68788
Phone: (402) 372-3662
Sales: $25,000,000   *Employees:* 12
Company Type: Private   *Employees here:* 12
SIC: 0211
  Feedlot
Richard E Becker, President

D-U-N-S 02-051-8403
BRANDT CO INC
299 W Main St, Brawley, CA 92227
Phone: (760) 344-3430
Sales: $14,000,000   *Employees:* 60
Company Type: Private   *Employees here:* 7
SIC: 0211
  Cattle feeding & crop farmer
Charles Duff, President

D-U-N-S 14-478-0863
BRICKMAN GROUP LTD
375 S Flowers Mill Rd, Langhorne, PA 19047
Phone: (215) 757-9400
Sales: $130,000,000   *Employees:* 900
Company Type: Private   *Employees here:* 30
SIC: 0781
  Landscape maintenance service
John S Wilson Jr, President

D-U-N-S 09-369-2267
BROETJE ORCHARDS
1111 Fishhook Park Rd, Prescott, WA 99348
Phone: (509) 749-2217

Sales: $36,290,000   *Employees:* 1,200
Company Type: Private   *Employees here:* 1,200
SIC: 0175
  Apple & cherry orchards & fruit packing
Jim Nicholson, Vice-President

D-U-N-S 07-804-0185
BROMM CATTLE CO INC
255 County Road 21, Craig, NE 68019
Phone: (402) 377-2823
Sales: $20,000,000   *Employees:* 11
Company Type: Private   *Employees here:* 11
SIC: 0211
  Beef cattle feedlot corn farm soybean farm
John M Luther, General Partner

D-U-N-S 03-124-2126
BROOKOVER FEED YARDS INC
50 Grandview Dr, Garden City, KS 67846
Phone: (316) 275-9206
Sales: $19,631,000   *Employees:* 78
Company Type: Private   *Employees here:* 3
SIC: 0211
  Cattle feed yard
Larry Addington, President

D-U-N-S 05-134-5239
BROOKS TROPICALS INC
18400 SW 256th St, Homestead, FL 33031
Phone: (305) 247-3544
Sales: $37,455,000   *Employees:* 350
Company Type: Private   *Employees here:* 350
SIC: 0762
  Grove maintenance service & packing house for fresh fruits
    & vegetables & imports fresh fruit
Drew Belk, Partner

D-U-N-S 78-366-2539
BROWN'S OF CAROLINA, INC.
  (Parent: Smithfield Foods Inc)
785 Nc Hwy 24 E, Warsaw, NC 28398
Phone: (910) 296-1800
Sales: $10,790,000   *Employees:* 550
Company Type: Public Family Member   *Employees here:* 100
SIC: 0213
  Hog farming
William Bemus, President

D-U-N-S 02-906-1728
BRUCE CHURCH INC
  (Parent: Fresh International Corp)
1020 Merrill St, Salinas, CA 93901
Phone: (831) 758-4421
Sales: $42,800,000   *Employees:* 502
Company Type: Private   *Employees here:* 150
SIC: 0161
  Growers packers & shippers of produce
Ben A Thomas Jr, President

D-U-N-S 02-335-5951
BRUCE COMPANY OF WISCONSIN INC
2830 W Beltline Hwy, Middleton, WI 53562
Phone: (608) 836-7041
Sales: $26,978,000   *Employees:* 150
Company Type: Private   *Employees here:* 100
SIC: 0782
  Landscape contracting and landscape & golf course
    maintenance and golf course construction
Ben Zehner, Owner

D-U-N-S 83-470-0387
BUCIO LOURDES FARM
1027 Gunner St, Santa Maria, CA 93458

Phone: (805) 349-2884
Sales: $21,200,000
Company Type: Private   *Employees:* 250
SIC: 0161   *Employees here:* 250
    Vegetable/melon farm
John A Mohns, President

D-U-N-S 05-052-1228
BUD ANTLE, INC
    (Parent: Dole Fresh Vegetables Inc)
639 S Sanborn Rd, Salinas, CA 93901
Phone: (831) 422-8871
Sales: $299,900,000   *Employees:* 3,500
Company Type: Public Family Member   *Employees here:* 300
SIC: 0161
    Shipper of vegetables
Donald Berend, President

D-U-N-S 12-383-7221
BURCH FARMS
685 Burch Rd, Faison, NC 28341
Phone: (910) 267-5781
Sales: $14,906,000   *Employees:* 90
Company Type: Private   *Employees here:* 90
SIC: 0161
    Produce farm
Charles A Cocotas, Chairman of the Board

D-U-N-S 00-786-9522
BUURMA FARMS, INC
3909 Kok Rd, Willard, OH 44890
Phone: (419) 935-6411
Sales: $12,390,000   *Employees:* 30
Company Type: Private   *Employees here:* 30
SIC: 0161
    Vegetable farm
Kevin Farrell, Member

D-U-N-S 04-441-5065
BYRD HARVEST INC
192 Guadalupe St, Guadalupe, CA 93434
Phone: (805) 343-2011
Sales: $15,000,000   *Employees:* 300
Company Type: Private   *Employees here:* 300
SIC: 0722
    Vegetable harvester packer and shipper
Henri Ardantz, Partner

D-U-N-S 82-863-5714
C & C FARMS
2107 Porter Pike, Bowling Green, KY 42103
Phone: (502) 843-9228
Sales: $12,000,000   *Employees:* 20
Company Type: Private   *Employees here:* 20
SIC: 0212
    Beef cattle
Mark Brady, President

D-U-N-S 02-756-4728
C & G FARMS INC
25453 Iverson Rd, Chualar, CA 93925
Phone: (831) 679-2978
Sales: $15,000,000   *Employees:* 60
Company Type: Private   *Employees here:* 60
SIC: 0161
    Farm
Kenneth Peterson, President

D-U-N-S 17-549-3634
C & M PACKING INC
29701 River Rd, Gonzales, CA 93926
Phone: (831) 675-1119

Sales: $12,500,000   *Employees:* 250
Company Type: Private   *Employees here:* 250
SIC: 0722
    Produce harvesting
Gregg Halverson, President

D-U-N-S 07-201-2909
C B BUNTING & SONS
Davistown Rd, Pinetops, NC 27864
Phone: (252) 827-4342
Sales: $20,000,000   *Employees:* 30
Company Type: Private   *Employees here:* 30
SIC: 0132
    General crop & hog farm
Leon Ellwell, President

D-U-N-S 00-692-6786   EXP
C BREWER AND COMPANY LTD
26-238 Hawaii Belt Rd, Hilo, HI 96720
Phone: (808) 969-1826
Sales: $100,700,000   *Employees:* 1,600
Company Type: Private   *Employees here:* 40
SIC: 0173
    Macadamia nut and sugar cane grower
Blaine Larsen, President

D-U-N-S 02-071-2113
C R I FEEDERS INC
26 Miles NW Off Hwy 136, Guymon, OK 73942
Phone: (580) 545-3344
Sales: $10,100,000   *Employees:* 57
Company Type: Private   *Employees here:* 57
SIC: 0211
    Cattle feedlot
Henry A Bledsoe, Owner

D-U-N-S 07-166-6614
CACTUS FEEDERS, INC.
2209 W 7th Ave, Ste 200, Amarillo, TX 79106
Phone: (806) 373-2333
Sales: $336,380,000   *Employees:* 365
Company Type: Private   *Employees here:* 73
SIC: 0211
    Operates cattle feedlots
Michael F Burns, President

D-U-N-S 94-950-4427
CACTUS OPERATING, LTD.
2209 W 7th Ave, Ste 200, Amarillo, TX 79106
Phone: (806) 373-2333
Sales: $335,000,000   *Employees:* 50
Company Type: Private   *Employees here:* 50
SIC: 0211
    Operates 5 feedlots
Veryln D Emswiler, President

D-U-N-S 10-571-3333
CADIZ, INC
100 Wilshire Blvd Fl 16, Santa Monica, CA 90401
Phone: (909) 980-2738
Sales: $100,157,000   *Employees:* 985
Company Type: Public   *Employees here:* 25
SIC: 0723
    Fruit & vegetable growers & water related land development
Ken Krueger, President

D-U-N-S 03-367-2312
CAGLE'S FARMS INC
    (Parent: Cagles Inc)
Hwy 41 S, Dalton, GA 30720
Phone: (706) 278-2372

Sales: $16,100,000
Company Type: Public Family Member
SIC: 0254
   Poultry hatchery feed manufacturer and grow out
James C Justice Ii, President

Employees: 300
Employees here: 2

D-U-N-S 00-922-6614
CAGWIN & DORWARD
8001 Binford Rd, Novato, CA 94945
Phone: (415) 892-7710
Sales: $13,667,000
Company Type: Private
SIC: 0782
   Landscape contractor
John E Boething, President

Employees: 220
Employees here: 50

D-U-N-S 05-064-3436
CAL-MAINE FOODS INC
3320 W Woodrow Wilson Ave, Jackson, MS 39209
Phone: (601) 948-6813
Sales: $309,071,000
Company Type: Public
SIC: 0252
   Egg production
David Sullivan, President

Employees: 1,574
Employees here: 35

D-U-N-S 03-058-2894
CALBERI INC
3605 W Pendleton Ave, Santa Ana, CA 92704
Phone: (714) 979-5221
Sales: $15,001,000
Company Type: Private
SIC: 0723
   Packaging shipping & processing of fresh fruit
Wil Van Heyningen, Chairman of the Board

Employees: 14
Employees here: 12

D-U-N-S 04-714-0280
CALGENE INC
   (*Parent:* Monsanto Co)
1920 5th St, Davis, CA 95616
Phone: (530) 753-6313
Sales: $21,700,000
Company Type: Public Family Member
SIC: 0161
   Developing genetically engineered plants & plant pdts
William D Grant, President

IMP EXP

Employees: 256
Employees here: 130

D-U-N-S 00-690-4866
CALIFORNIA ARTICH & VEGE
10855 Cara Mia Pkwy, Castroville, CA 95012
Phone: (831) 633-2144
Sales: $65,272,000
Company Type: Private
SIC: 0723
   Vegetable packer & shipper
James D Nelson, President

Employees: 60
Employees here: 60

D-U-N-S 83-589-2159
CALIFORNIA FAMILY FOODS LLC
6550 Struckmeyer Rd, Arbuckle, CA 95912
Phone: (530) 476-3326
Sales: $30,000,000
Company Type: Private
SIC: 0723
   Crop preparation for market
Mark C Booth, Partner

Employees: 50
Employees here: 50

D-U-N-S 04-660-8097
CALIFORNIA REDI-DATE CO
84675 Ave 60, Thermal, CA 92274
Phone: (760) 399-5111

Sales: $12,800,000
Company Type: Private
SIC: 0723
   Crop preparation for market
Nowell Borders, Owner

Employees: 150
Employees here: 45

D-U-N-S 05-987-2887
CALLERY-JUDGE GROVE LP
4001 Seminole Pratt Whitn, Loxahatchee, FL 33470
Phone: (561) 793-1676
Sales: $10,000,000
Company Type: Private
SIC: 0174
   Citrus fruit groves
Ernest P Bordier Jr, Chairman of the Board

Employees: 55
Employees here: 55

D-U-N-S 04-092-8095
CANADIAN FEEDYARDS, INC.
Hwy 60, Canadian, TX 79014
Phone: (806) 323-5333
Sales: $23,610,000
Company Type: Private
SIC: 0211
   Cattle feed yard
Joseph M Boskovich, Chief Executive Officer

Employees: 4
Employees here: 4

D-U-N-S 06-639-5427
CAPROCK INDUSTRIES
   (*Parent:* Cargill Inc)
905 S Fillmore St, Ste 700, Amarillo, TX 79101
Phone: (806) 371-3700
Sales: $375,000,000
Company Type: Private
SIC: 0211
   Feedlot
Richard Bossen, President

Employees: 213
Employees here: 21

D-U-N-S 80-786-8112
CARIBBEAN AGRICULTURE PROJECTS
81 Smugglers Cove Dr, Gulf Breeze, FL 32561
Phone: (850) 939-3956
Sales: $18,000,000
Company Type: Private
SIC: 0711
   Soil preparation services crops-planting/protecting crop
     harvesting services cotton ginning services
Edward Bracht, President

Employees: 300
Employees here: 200

D-U-N-S 79-337-8324
CARMEL VALLEY PACKING, INC
1910 Penwick Cir, Salinas, CA 93906
Phone: (831) 443-8116
Sales: $13,500,000
Company Type: Private
SIC: 0723
   Vegetable packing service
William L Brandt, President

Employees: 150
Employees here: 150

D-U-N-S 02-484-7444
CARROLL'S FOODS INC
2822 W Nc Hwy 24, Warsaw, NC 28398
Phone: (910) 293-3434
Sales: $500,000,000
Company Type: Private
SIC: 0213
   Hog & turkey production
Ralph Broetje, Owner

Employees: 1,350
Employees here: 250

D-U-N-S 60-977-5770
CARROLL'S FOODS OF VIRGINIA
434 E Main St, Waverly, VA 23890
Phone: (804) 834-2109

Sales: $103,572,000
Company Type: Private
SIC: 0213
    Raises hogs
Don Bromm, President

Employees: 580
Employees here: 580

D-U-N-S 04-632-4554
CARSON COUNTY FEEDYARDS, INC.
Fm 2385, Panhandle, TX 79068
Phone: (806) 537-3531
Sales: $11,060,000
Company Type: Private
SIC: 0211
    Cattle feedlot
Sam E Brookover, President

Employees: 21
Employees here: 21

D-U-N-S 19-467-5310
CASCADE COLUMBIA FOODS LTD
350 N Juniper St, Kennewick, WA 99336
Phone: (509) 586-6749
Sales: $10,000,000
Company Type: Private
SIC: 0723
    Vegetable packing service
William Baxter, President

Employees: 215
Employees here: 215

D-U-N-S 04-507-6655
CATTLCO INC
889 Ridge Lake Blvd, Memphis, TN 38120
Phone: (901) 766-4600
Sales: $31,100,000
Company Type: Private
SIC: 0211
    Cattle feedlot
Paul Brooks, President

Employees: 150
Employees here: 150

D-U-N-S 14-922-7902
CATTLCO
1301 E Burlington Ave, Fort Morgan, CO 80701
Phone: (970) 867-5692
Sales: $31,200,000
Company Type: Private
SIC: 0211
    Cattle feedlot and cattle management service
Ronald G Brown, President

Employees: 140
Employees here: 15

D-U-N-S 03-062-3136
CATTLEMENS INC
(Parent: National Farms Inc)
4 1/2 Mile N of Turon, Turon, KS 67583
Phone: (316) 497-6421
Sales: $42,983,000
Company Type: Private
SIC: 0211
    Cattle feed yard
Steve Taylor, Chairman of the Board

Employees: 100
Employees here: 20

D-U-N-S 18-398-0721
CECELIA PACKING CORP
24780 E South Ave, Orange Cove, CA 93646
Phone: (559) 626-5000
Sales: $20,000,000
Company Type: Private
SIC: 0723
    Crop preparation for market
Leland C Bruce, President

Employees: 150
Employees here: 150

D-U-N-S 17-400-4416
CEDAR BLUFF CATTLE FEEDERS
RR 2 Box 71, Ellis, KS 67637
Phone: (785) 726-3100

Sales: $20,000,000
Company Type: Private
SIC: 0211
    Beef cattle feedlot
Lourdes Bucio, Owner

Employees: 14
Employees here: 14

D-U-N-S 02-866-9638
CENTRAL CAL TMATO GROWERS COOP
500 Thornton Rd, Merced, CA 95340
Phone: (209) 722-8086
Sales: $20,000,000
Company Type: Private
SIC: 0723
    Tomato packing and shipping
Lawrence A Kern, President

Employees: 3
Employees here: 3

D-U-N-S 15-985-9677
CENTRAL FARM OF AMERICA
780 3rd Ave Rm 37, New York, NY 10017
Phone: (212) 891-7810
Sales: $11,600,000
Company Type: Private
SIC: 0254
    Holding company
Richard Betz, President

Employees: 217
Employees here: 3

D-U-N-S 05-394-4112
CHAPEL VALLEY LANDSCAPE CO
3275 Jennings Chapel Rd, Woodbine, MD 21797
Phone: (410) 442-2310
Sales: $13,951,000
Company Type: Private
SIC: 0782
    Landscaping contractor
Bill Burch, Partner

Employees: 90
Employees here: 90

D-U-N-S 06-269-7701
CHAPPELL FARMS INC
166 Boiling Springs Rd, Barnwell, SC 29812
Phone: (803) 584-2565
Sales: $13,700,000
Company Type: Private
SIC: 0213
    Raises hogs & grows peaches wheat and soybeans
Loren Buurma, Secretary

Employees: 185
Employees here: 185

D-U-N-S 05-063-4849
CHARLES DONALD PULPWOOD INC
Anthony St, Port Gibson, MS 39150
Phone: (601) 437-4012
Sales: $36,147,000
Company Type: Private
SIC: 0241
    Contractor
Joe George, President

Employees: 23
Employees here: 23

D-U-N-S 10-210-0070
CHARLES G WATTS INC
308 John St, Salinas, CA 93901
Phone: (831) 757-4955
Sales: $14,300,000
Company Type: Private
SIC: 0723
    Packer & grower of vegetables
Dean Cherry, Owner

Employees: 150
Employees here: 6

D-U-N-S 03-990-1210
CHERRY LAKE FARMS INC
7836 Cherry Lake Rd, Groveland, FL 34736
Phone: (352) 429-2171

Sales: $20,572,000
Employees: 200
Company Type: Private
Employees here: 190
SIC: 0174
Grapefruit & orange groves for export & ornamental tree
farm & nursery
Carlos Amaral, President

D-U-N-S 62-783-6778
CHESAPEAKE FOREST PRODUCTS CO
(Parent: Chesapeake Corp)
19th & Main Sts, West Point, VA 23181
Phone: (804) 843-5000
Sales: $10,000,000
Employees: 196
Company Type: Public Family Member
Employees here: 79
SIC: 0811
Manages timberlands and provides raw materials and mfg
hardwood & pine lumber
Inocente Morales, President

D-U-N-S 86-828-6840
CHIEF MATTAWA ORCHARDS
22139 G Rd Sw, Mattawa, WA 99349
Phone: (509) 932-4227
Sales: $10,000,000
Employees: 5
Company Type: Private
Employees here: 5
SIC: 0175
Fruit tree orchard
C B Bunting Iii, Partner

D-U-N-S 00-794-4036
CHIEF WENATCHEE
1705 N Miller St, Wenatchee, WA 98801
Phone: (509) 662-5197
Sales: $13,118,000
Employees: 130
Company Type: Private
Employees here: 130
SIC: 0723
Contract fruit packing
John W Buyers, Chairman of the Board

D-U-N-S 00-704-9299
CHILDRESS GIN & ELEVATOR CO
3909 County Road 532, Monette, AR 72447
Phone: (870) 486-5476
Sales: $10,000,000
Employees: 15
Company Type: Private
Employees here: 10
SIC: 0724
Cotton gin & agricultural fertilizers & chemicals
Louis Trentman, President

D-U-N-S 05-154-1597
CHIQUITA BRANDS INTERNATIONAL
250 E 5th St, Ste 2400, Cincinnati, OH 45202
Phone: (513) 784-8000
Sales: $2,433,726,000
Employees: 40,000
Company Type: Public
Employees here: 1,000
SIC: 0179
Production & distribution of fresh & prepared fruits
vegetables and fruit juices
Paul Engler, President

D-U-N-S 02-809-3037
CHOOLJIAN & SONS INC
5287 S Del Rey Ave, Del Rey, CA 93616
Phone: (559) 888-2031
Sales: $26,343,000
Employees: 60
Company Type: Private
Employees here: 54
SIC: 0723
Raisin packing
Terry Manz, Chief Financial Officer

D-U-N-S 00-920-2086
CHOOLJIAN BROS PACKING CO INC
3192 S Indianola Ave, Sanger, CA 93657

Phone: (559) 875-5501
Employees: 45
Sales: $26,247,000
Employees here: 45
Company Type: Private
SIC: 0723
Raisin packing
Keith Brackpool, Chief Executive Officer

D-U-N-S 06-152-9400
CHRISTENSEN CATTLE CO
2132 14th Rd, Central City, NE 68826
Phone: (308) 946-3803
Sales: $35,000,000
Employees: 55
Company Type: Private
Employees here: 30
SIC: 0211
Cattle feedlot
J D Cagle, Chairman of the Board

D-U-N-S 87-713-3033
CHRISTENSEN FARM & FEEDLOTS INC
121 1st Ave S, Sleepy Eye, MN 56085
Phone: (507) 794-5310
Sales: $14,200,000
Employees: 150
Company Type: Private
Employees here: 147
SIC: 0213
Hog feedlot
Dennis Dougherty, President

D-U-N-S 83-888-3965
CIRCLE C FARMS
1393 Yates Spring Rd, Brinson, GA 31725
Phone: (912) 246-7090
Sales: $10,000,000
Employees: 25
Company Type: Private
Employees here: 25
SIC: 0131
Farm
Juan Toche, Owner

D-U-N-S 09-770-0215
CIRCLE E FEED LOT INC
2 Miles W on 196 Hwy, Potwin, KS 67123
Phone: (316) 752-3221
Sales: $12,876,000
Employees: 17
Company Type: Private
Employees here: 17
SIC: 0211
Custom cattle feedlot
Fred R Adams Jr, Chief Executive Officer

D-U-N-S 87-283-2563
CIRCLE FOUR FARMS
341 S Main, Milford, UT 84751
Phone: (435) 387-2107
Sales: $70,000,000
Employees: 400
Company Type: Private
Employees here: 400
SIC: 0213
Swine farm
George Murai, President

D-U-N-S 02-509-8096
CLARENCE DAVIDS & CO
22901 Ridgeland Ave, Matteson, IL 60443
Phone: (708) 388-6990
Sales: $11,000,000
Employees: 90
Company Type: Private
Employees here: 45
SIC: 0782
Landscaper & lawn maintenance contractor
Lloyd M Kunimoto, President

D-U-N-S 10-850-2477
CLARK HUTTERIAN BRETHREN INC
41181 179th St, Raymond, SD 57258
Phone: (605) 532-3142

Sales: $10,000,000   *Employees:* 100
Company Type: Private   *Employees here:* 100
SIC: 0191
    Grain & livestock farm & mfg livestock equipment
Edward Boutonnet, President

D-U-N-S 00-305-2990
CLARK'S FEED MILLS INC
RR 61 Box N, Shamokin, PA 17872
Phone: (717) 648-4351
Sales: $15,402,000   *Employees:* 72
Company Type: Private   *Employees here:* 60
SIC: 0251
    Poultry farm mfg feed & ret lawn garden & pet supplies
David Myers, Partner

D-U-N-S 92-877-8356
CLASSIC CATTLE CO L P
I 40 E, Wildorado, TX 79098
Phone: (806) 426-3325
Sales: $20,600,000   *Employees:* 28
Company Type: Private   *Employees here:* 28
SIC: 0211
    Beef cattle feedlot
William M Jeffrey, President

D-U-N-S 17-372-1143
CLEAN CUT INC
    (*Parent:* Landcare USA Inc)
8711 Burnet Rd, Ste F72, Austin, TX 78757
Phone: (512) 458-8873
Sales: $15,000,000   *Employees:* 250
Company Type: Public Family Member   *Employees here:* 150
SIC: 0782
    Lawn/garden services landscape services
James Callery, President

D-U-N-S 04-283-4200
CLEAR SPRINGS FOODS INC
1500 E 4424 N, Buhl, ID 83316
Phone: (208) 543-4316
Sales: $15,400,000   *Employees:* 385
Company Type: Private   *Employees here:* 385
SIC: 0273
    Trout farm
Joe Hathoot, President

D-U-N-S 00-167-7970
CLINTON NURSERIES INC
114 W Main St, Clinton, CT
Phone: (860) 669-8611
Sales: $17,287,000   *Employees:* 127
Company Type: Private   *Employees here:* 77
SIC: 0181
    Grower of nursery stock
Corey Hudson, Executive Director

D-U-N-S 04-933-8700
CLOUDS LANDSCAPING SPRNKLR SERVICE INC
908 Sharp Cir, North Las Vegas, NV 89030
Phone: (702) 649-1330
Sales: $11,418,000   *Employees:* 70
Company Type: Private   *Employees here:* 70
SIC: 0782
    Landscaping contractor
Douglas M Campbell, Chief Operating Officer

D-U-N-S 02-802-6243
COALINGA FEED YARD INC
35244 Oil City Rd, Coalinga, CA 93210
Phone: (559) 935-1681

Sales: $11,838,000   *Employees:* 20
Company Type: Private   *Employees here:* 20
SIC: 0211
    Cattle feed lot
Ray L Brownfield, President

D-U-N-S 14-472-5280   EXP
COBB-VANTRESS, INC.
    (*Parent:* Tyson Foods Inc)
US Hwy 412 E, Siloam Springs, AR 72761
Phone: (501) 524-3166
Sales: $50,000,000   *Employees:* 415
Company Type: Public Family Member   *Employees here:* 70
SIC: 0751
    Poultry breeding
Larry Lewallen, Vice-President

D-U-N-S 36-176-1372
COHARIE FARMS
300 Westover Rd, Clinton, NC 28328
Phone: (910) 592-0105
Sales: $22,000,000   *Employees:* 90
Company Type: Private   *Employees here:* 90
SIC: 0213
    Hog farm
Jon W Sponheimer, President

D-U-N-S 04-956-7688
COLE KING RANCH & FARM
King Cole Dr, Milton, DE 19968
Phone: (302) 684-8555
Sales: $11,000,000   *Employees:* 60
Company Type: Private   *Employees here:* 60
SIC: 0211
    Cattle feedlot
David Carlson, President

D-U-N-S 92-763-2356
COLOR SPOT NURSERIES, INC
    (*Parent:* KCSN Acquisition Co LP)
3478 Buskirk Ave, Ste 260, Pleasant Hill, CA 94523
Phone: (925) 934-4443
Sales: $113,400,000   *Employees:* 1,828
Company Type: Private   *Employees here:* 28
SIC: 0181
    Produces & distributes bedding plants
John Bartch, Member

D-U-N-S 82-466-0039   EXP
COLORADO GREENHOUSE HOLDINGS
1490 W 121st Ave 202, Denver, CO 80234
Phone: (303) 457-7600
Sales: $24,944,000   *Employees:* 563
Company Type: Private   *Employees here:* 30
SIC: 0161
    Produce greenhouse specializing in tomatoes
Oscar Gardea, President

D-U-N-S 00-967-3609   EXP
COLUMBIA HELICOPTERS INC
14452 Arndt Rd NE, Aurora, OR 97002
Phone: (503) 678-1222
Sales: $100,000,000   *Employees:* 775
Company Type: Private   *Employees here:* 320
SIC: 0241
    Logging contractor air cargo services & helicopter repair
    services
James Guy, President

D-U-N-S 78-624-0309
COLUMBIA RIVER SUGAR CO
321 S Beech St A2, Moses Lake, WA 98837
Phone: (509) 766-1933

Sales: $21,000,000

Company Type: Private

SIC: 0191

Employees: 6

Employees here: 6

General crop farm

F J Faison Jr, President

D-U-N-S 78-496-9230

COLUMBIA WEST VIRGINIA CORP

(Parent: Columbia Forest Products Inc)

222 SW Columbia St, Portland, OR 97201

Phone: (503) 224-5300

Sales: $10,000,000

Company Type: Private

SIC: 0241

Employees: 139

Employees here: 4

Mfg veneer

F J Faison Jr, President

D-U-N-S 80-279-6318

CONAGRA-MAPLE LEAF MILLING

1 Conagra Dr, Omaha, NE 68102

Phone: (402) 595-4000

Sales: $14,800,000

Company Type: Private

SIC: 0723

Employees: 180

Employees here: 1

Flour milling

Frank Simms, President

D-U-N-S 00-893-9910

CONARD-PYLE CO INC

372 Rosehill Rd, West Grove, PA 19390

Phone: (610) 869-2426

Sales: $13,400,000

·*Company Type:* Private

SIC: 0181

Employees: 300

Employees here: 190

Shrubbery & rose nursery

Don Kizirian, President

D-U-N-S 04-126-6073

CONFEDERATED TR WRM SPRGS

1233 Veterans St, Warm Springs, OR 97761

Phone: (541) 553-1161

Sales: $52,817,000

Company Type: Private

SIC: 0811

Employees: 1,500

Employees here: 650

Timber tracts hydro-electric generation plants hotels radio
broadcasting

Dan Frost, President

D-U-N-S 01-051-5286

CONOLEY FRUIT HARVESTER INC

931 W Oakland Ave, Oakland, FL 34760

Phone: (407) 656-6900

Sales: $15,080,000

Company Type: Private

SIC: 0722

Employees: 20

Employees here: 20

Crop harvesting services

Shelby Massey, Chairman of the Board

D-U-N-S 07-656-1638

CONTINENTE NUT LLC

112 Sandy Ln, Oakley, CA 94561

Phone: (925) 625-2355

Sales: $10,000,000

Company Type: Private

SIC: 0172

Employees: 25

Employees here: 22

Farmer packer & shipper of produce

Shelby Massey, Principal

D-U-N-S 00-541-6698

COOPER HATCHERY INC

P.O. Box 547, Oakwood, OH 45873

Phone: (419) 594-3325

EXP

Sales: $110,000,000

Company Type: Private

SIC: 0254

Employees: 700

Employees here: 200

Poultry hatchery turkey farm processed turkey & whol grains

Hank Walton, Partner

D-U-N-S 80-935-7486

COOPERATIVE RESOURCES INTERNATIONAL INC

100 Mbc Dr, Shawano, WI 54166

Phone: (715) 526-2141

Sales: $72,013,000

Company Type: Private

SIC: 0751

Employees: 1,200

Employees here: 125

Artificial insemination dairy herd improvement & milk
testing services

C L Haw, President

D-U-N-S 61-345-7126

CORCPORK CO

3922 Avenue 120, Corcoran, CA 93212

Phone: (559) 992-8421

Sales: $10,000,000

Company Type: Private

SIC: 0213

Employees: 100

Employees here: 100

Hog farm

David G Roth, President

D-U-N-S 06-968-3597

CORKSCREW GROWERS INC

27771 Industrial St, Bonita Springs, FL 34135

Phone: (941) 992-1801

Sales: $21,200,000

Company Type: Private

SIC: 0161

Employees: 250

Employees here: 250

Tomato grower

Steven Pierce, President

D-U-N-S 05-285-3884

CORONA COLLEGE HEIGHTS

8000 Lincoln Ave, Riverside, CA 92504

Phone: (909) 351-4944

Sales: $14,300,000

Company Type: Private

SIC: 0723

Employees: 200

Employees here: 200

Crop preparation for market

Mike D Grace, President

D-U-N-S 04-402-5609

COSTA NURSERY FARMS INC

22290 SW 162nd Ave, Goulds, FL 33170

Phone: (305) 247-3248

Sales: $36,458,000

Company Type: Private

SIC: 0181

Employees: 460

Employees here: 460

Growers of nursery stock shrubs and potted plants

Christine Torres, Office Manager

D-U-N-S 08-518-3101

COYOTE LAKE FEEDYARD, INC.

7 Mi S on Hwy 214 & 9, Muleshoe, TX 79347

Phone: (806) 946-3321

Sales: $25,202,000

Company Type: Private

SIC: 0211

Employees: 23

Employees here: 23

Cattle feed lot

Toshio Kama, President

D-U-N-S 62-779-7962

CP MEILLAND INC

620 E St, Ste B, Wasco, CA 93280

Phone: (661) 758-7800

Sales: $10,000,000   *Employees:* 16
Company Type: Private   *Employees here:* 12
SIC: 0181
  Rosebush nursery
J L Reeve Iv, President

D-U-N-S 00-515-9629   EXP
CPC INTERNATIONAL APPLE
909 Naches Ave, Tieton, WA 98947
Phone: (509) 673-3113
Sales: $12,000,000   *Employees:* 30
Company Type: Private   *Employees here:* 30
SIC: 0723
  Fruit packing & cold storage warehousing
H P Chappell, President

D-U-N-S 00-915-3396
CRANE MILLS
22938 South Ave, Corning, CA 96021
Phone: (530) 824-5427
Sales: $12,993,000   *Employees:* 45
Company Type: Private   *Employees here:* 45
SIC: 0241
  Logging operation tree farm almond orchard
Charles Donald Jr, President

D-U-N-S 00-893-9936
CREEKSIDE MUSHROOMS LTD
1 Moonlight Dr, Worthington, PA 16262
Phone: (724) 297-5491
Sales: $20,000,000   *Employees:* 400
Company Type: Private   *Employees here:* 400
SIC: 0182
  Mushroom farm
Charles G Watts, President

D-U-N-S 00-694-0225
CREIGHTON BROTHERS LLC
4217 E Old Road 30, Warsaw, IN 46580
Phone: (219) 267-3101
Sales: $40,000,000   *Employees:* 160
Company Type: Private   *Employees here:* 12
SIC: 0252
  Poultry egg farm mfg egg processing & hog feedlot
Michael Sallin, President

D-U-N-S 18-542-0643
CRIST FEED YARD INC
553 W Road 40, Scott City, KS 67871
Phone: (316) 872-7271
Sales: $19,000,000   *Employees:* 35
Company Type: Private   *Employees here:* 20
SIC: 0211
  Cattle feed yard & farm
Thomas Blackburn, President

D-U-N-S 08-197-5773
CROMAN CORP
146 Mistletoe Rd, Ashland, OR 97520
Phone: (541) 482-1221
Sales: $45,000,000   *Employees:* 220
Company Type: Private   *Employees here:* 10
SIC: 0241
  Lumber mill
Gary W Chavers, Owner

D-U-N-S 05-686-0430
CROSBYTON SEED CO.
306 E Main St, Crosbyton, TX 79322
Phone: (806) 675-2308

Sales: $11,570,000   *Employees:* 45
Company Type: Private   *Employees here:* 23
SIC: 0119
  Grows hybrid sorghum pearl & grain millet and sunflower
  seeds
Brian Birdsall, President

D-U-N-S 80-434-0990
CROWN PACIFIC PARTNERS, LP
121 SW Morrison St, Portland, OR 97204
Phone: (503) 274-2300
Sales: $505,588,000   *Employees:* 1,100
Company Type: Public   *Employees here:* 35
SIC: 0811
  Timber tracts & sawmills
Randy Gibson, President

D-U-N-S 00-349-2592
CRYSTAL FARMS INC
4900 Winder Hwy, Gainesville, GA 30501
Phone: (770) 967-6152
Sales: $65,000,000   *Employees:* 175
Company Type: Private   *Employees here:* 80
SIC: 0252
  Egg production and feed mill
Carl H Lindner, Chairman of the Board

D-U-N-S 96-989-1084
CUBA TIMBER CO
112 Shaw Rd, Cuba, AL 36907
Phone: (205) 392-7496
Sales: $15,381,000   *Employees:* 25
Company Type: Private   *Employees here:* 25
SIC: 0811
  Timber tract operation
Carl Chooljian, President

D-U-N-S 03-051-6223
CUDDY FARMS INC
  (Parent: Cuddy International Corp)
6140 W Marshville Blvd, Marshville, NC 28103
Phone: (704) 624-5055
Sales: $76,000,000   *Employees:* 700
Company Type: Private   *Employees here:* 20
SIC: 0254
  Producer of turkey hatching eggs & pults
Leo Chooljian, President

D-U-N-S 96-676-5828
CUSTOM-PAK INC
318 E New Market Rd, Immokalee, FL 34142
Phone: (941) 657-4421
Sales: $15,100,000   *Employees:* 154
Company Type: Private   *Employees here:* 99
SIC: 0161
  Tomato farm
Carroll Christensen, President

D-U-N-S 17-496-8651
D & D FARMS INC
205 W Dakota Ave, Pierre, SD 57501
Phone: (605) 224-6336
Sales: $20,000,000   *Employees:* 215
Company Type: Private   *Employees here:* 30
SIC: 0213
  Hog confinement
Bob Christenson, President

D-U-N-S 88-367-9649
D BRUCE CUDDY
1528 Hasty Rd, Marshville, NC 28103
Phone: (704) 624-3422

Sales: $10,000,000
Employees: 50
Company Type: Private
Employees here: 50
SIC: 0253
    Turkey farm
Tim Dewey, Partner

D-U-N-S 00-690-4080
D M CAMP & SONS
Hwy 99 & Merced Ave, Bakersfield, CA 93312
Phone: (661) 399-5511
Sales: $24,500,000
Employees: 80
Company Type: Private
Employees here: 20
SIC: 0191
    General crop farming
Gerg Calhoun, Owner

D-U-N-S 00-691-1176
D'ARRIGO BROS CAL A CAL CORP
383 W Market St, Salinas, CA 93901
Phone: (831) 424-3955
Sales: $105,000,000
Employees: 900
Company Type: Private
Employees here: 50
SIC: 0161
    Vegetable grower
Leonard Waldner, President

D-U-N-S 04-437-9998
DALE BONE FARMS INC
6160 S Nc 58, Nashville, NC 27856
Phone: (252) 443-2311
Sales: $10,849,000
Employees: 75
Company Type: Private
Employees here: 75
SIC: 0161
    Cucumber tobacco & sweet potato farm
Jerry Peterson, Manager

D-U-N-S 04-734-9428
DAN SCHANTZ FARM & GREENHOUSES
8025 Spinnerstown Rd, Zionsville, PA 18092
Phone: (610) 967-2361
Sales: $18,000,000
Employees: 60
Company Type: Private
Employees here: 53
SIC: 0181
    Growing of flowers & vegetable farm
Dwight Potter, Controller

D-U-N-S 05-324-0321
DANELL BROS INC
8265 Hanford Armona Rd, Hanford, CA 93230
Phone: (559) 582-1251
Sales: $10,000,000
Employees: 70
Company Type: Private
Employees here: 20
SIC: 0722
    Custom harvesting
Jane Dilday, Treasurer

D-U-N-S 09-956-4759
DANIELSKI HARVESTING & FARMING
1 Mi W on Hwy 20, Valentine, NE 69201
Phone: (402) 376-3039
Sales: $11,113,000
Employees: 15
Company Type: Private
Employees here: 15
SIC: 0191
    General crop farm & trucking
Clarence Davids Sr, Chairman of the Board

D-U-N-S 15-445-6370
DARR FEED LOT INC
42826 Road 759, Cozad, NE 69130
Phone: (308) 324-2363

Sales: $13,576,000
Employees: 33
Company Type: Private
Employees here: 33
SIC: 0211
    Cattle feed lot
Bruce Tomlinson, President

D-U-N-S 06-332-7530
DAVE KINGSTON PRODUCE INC
477 Shoup Ave, Ste 207, Idaho Falls, ID 83402
Phone: (208) 522-2365
Sales: $24,200,000
Employees: 350
Company Type: Private
Employees here: 30
SIC: 0723
    Crop preparation for market
Kenneth A Clark, President

D-U-N-S 00-790-3180
DAVEY TREE EXPERT CO
1500 N Mantua St, Kent, OH 44240
Phone: (330) 673-9511
Sales: $295,079,000
Employees: 5,200
Company Type: Public
Employees here: 120
SIC: 0783
    Tree service
Steve Denny, General Partner

D-U-N-S 02-917-6740
DAVEY TREE SURGERY CO
    (Parent: Davey Tree Expert Co)
2617 S Vasco Rd, Livermore, CA 94550
Phone: (925) 443-1723
Sales: $38,500,000
Employees: 1,200
Company Type: Public Family Member
Employees here: 40
SIC: 0783
    Tree surgery
Rex Gore, President

D-U-N-S 04-802-9110
DAVID J FRANK LANDSCAPE CONTRACTING
N120 W 21350 Freistadt Rd, Germantown, WI 53022
Phone: (414) 255-4888
Sales: $13,500,000
Employees: 225
Company Type: Private
Employees here: 150
SIC: 0782
    Landscape architects & lawn & garden care
J O Eastman, Chairman of the Board

D-U-N-S 04-554-3576
DAYLAY EGG FARMS, INC
11177 Township Road 133, West Mansfield, OH 43358
Phone: (937) 355-6531
Sales: $25,000,000
Employees: 170
Company Type: Private
Employees here: 10
SIC: 0252
    Chicken egg farm
Warren H Richards Jr, President

D-U-N-S 80-780-9884
DEAN CLUCK CATTLE CO
Hc 3 Box 47, Gruver, TX 79040
Phone: (806) 733-5021
Sales: $18,000,000
Employees: 28
Company Type: Private
Employees here: 28
SIC: 0211
    Beef cattle feedlot
James D Cloud, President

D-U-N-S 18-372-1380
DEKALB POULTRY RESEARCH INC
    (Parent: Central Farm Of America)
200 Gurler Rd, Dekalb, IL 60115
Phone: (815) 754-2900

Sales: $11,500,000   *Employees:* 214
Company Type: Private   *Employees here:* 36
SIC: 0254
  Produces markets & distributes white and brown egg parent
    breeding stock
James Anderson, President

D-U-N-S 05-542-9682
DEKALB SWINE BREEDERS INC
  (Parent: Dekalb Genetics Corp Del)
3100 Sycamore Rd, Dekalb, IL 60115
Phone: (815) 758-9152
Sales: $57,000,000   *Employees:* 380
Company Type: Public Family Member   *Employees here:* 60
SIC: 0213
  Hog feedlot & dist of hogs
Roy Chikasawa, President

D-U-N-S 79-063-1311
DEL MONTE FRESH PRODUCE HAWAII
  (Parent: Del Monte Fresh Produce Na)
94-1000 Kunia Rd, Kunia, HI 96759
Phone: (808) 621-1208
Sales: $37,100,000   *Employees:* 650
Company Type: Private   *Employees here:* 650
SIC: 0179
  Pineapple plantation
James Bell, President

D-U-N-S 78-694-3464
DELBERT L WHEELER
1200 N White Swan Rd, White Swan, WA 98952
Phone: (509) 874-2471
Sales: $10,000,000   *Employees:* 30
Company Type: Private   *Employees here:* 30
SIC: 0241
  Logging
W N Waters Jr, Partner

D-U-N-S 03-557-6792
DELTA COTTON CO-OPERATIVE INC
Hwy 34e, Marmaduke, AR 72443
Phone: (870) 597-2741
Sales: $10,000,000   *Employees:* 17
Company Type: Private   *Employees here:* 17
SIC: 0724
  Cotton gin & ret fertilizer & agricultural chemicals & grain
    elevator & crop consultant
Harry Bonk, Owner

D-U-N-S 03-435-8804
DELTA GIN CO INC
805 Verona St, Newellton, LA 71357
Phone: (318) 467-5101
Sales: $12,025,000   *Employees:* 5
Company Type: Private   *Employees here:* 5
SIC: 0724
  Cotton gin
Michael F Vukelich, Chairman of the Board

D-U-N-S 06-012-6067
DELTA PACKING CO OF LODI
5950 E Kettleman Ln, Lodi, CA 95240
Phone: (209) 334-1023
Sales: $26,000,000   *Employees:* 25
Company Type: Private   *Employees here:* 25
SIC: 0723
  Fresh fruit & vegetable packing
Jim Renella, President

D-U-N-S 06-996-9152
DEMLER EGG RANCH
1455 N Warren Rd, San Jacinto, CA 92582

Phone: (909) 654-8166
Sales: $12,000,000   *Employees:* 35
Company Type: Private   *Employees here:* 35
SIC: 0252
  Chicken egg farm
W G Lematta, Chairman of the Board

D-U-N-S 02-593-7848
DESSERAULT RANCH INC
1045 Desmarais Rd, Moxee, WA 98936
Phone: (509) 452-3469
Sales: $17,300,000   *Employees:* 250
Company Type: Private   *Employees here:* 250
SIC: 0139
  Field crop farm
Gary J Curtis, Executive

D-U-N-S 11-941-1189
DETTLE CATTLE CO
301 N Main, Stratford, TX 79084
Phone: (806) 366-3201
Sales: $14,000,000   *Employees:* 18
Company Type: Private   *Employees here:* 18
SIC: 0212
  Beef cattle-except feedlot whol livestock
Crawford Jones, Director

D-U-N-S 02-457-4766
DIAMOND CREEK FARMS INC
State Road 1713, Goldsboro, NC 27530
Phone: (919) 778-3130
Sales: $29,800,000   *Employees:* 265
Company Type: Private   *Employees here:* 265
SIC: 0253
  Produces turkey eggs & turkey breeder
Harry L Demorest, President

D-U-N-S 00-904-1179
DIAMOND FRUIT GROWERS INC
3495 Chevron Dr, Hood River, OR 97031
Phone: (541) 354-5300
Sales: $40,000,000   *Employees:* 80
Company Type: Private   *Employees here:* 40
SIC: 0723
  Fruit packer
Mike Sullivan, Chief Financial Officer

D-U-N-S 10-923-8162
DIESTEL TURKEY RANCH
22200 Lyons Bald Mt Rd, Sonora, CA 95370
Phone: (209) 532-4950
Sales: $10,000,000   *Employees:* 50
Company Type: Private   *Employees here:* 50
SIC: 0253
  Turkey ranch
Steven Hutton, President

D-U-N-S 01-388-1511
DILLON FLORAL CORP
933 New Berwick Hwy, Bloomsburg, PA 17815
Phone: (570) 784-5770
Sales: $10,143,000   *Employees:* 138
Company Type: Private   *Employees here:* 97
SIC: 0181
  Whol florist also growing cut flowers & potted plants
Raymond Calicka Sr, Treasurer

D-U-N-S 10-344-9146
DIMARE ENTERPRISES INC
N & Fresno Sts, Newman, CA 95360
Phone: (209) 862-2872

Sales: $49,000,000   *Employees:* 325
Company Type: Private   *Employees here:* 10
SIC: 0174
    Fruit/vegetable growers packers & shippers
E B Conoley Ii, President

D-U-N-S 09-346-3545   EXP
DIMARE HOMESTEAD, INC
    (Parent: Dimare Brothers Inc)
258 NW 1st Ave, Homestead, FL 33030
Phone: (305) 245-4211
Sales: $56,124,000   *Employees:* 15
Company Type: Private   *Employees here:* 15
SIC: 0161
    Vegetable growers specializing in tomatoes and vegetable
      packing service
John A Continente Sr, Member

D-U-N-S 04-608-4398
DIMARE RUSKIN INC
    (Parent: Dimare Homestead Inc)
5715 US Hwy 41 N, Ruskin, FL 33572
Phone: (813) 645-3241
Sales: $20,246,000   *Employees:* 12
Company Type: Private   *Employees here:* 12
SIC: 0723
    Tomato packaging
Kenneth Gerlack, President

D-U-N-S 06-864-3220
DINKLAGE FEED YARD, INC.
10152 Road 20, Sidney, NE 69162
Phone: (308) 254-5941
Sales: $16,300,000   *Employees:* 90
Company Type: Private   *Employees here:* 30
SIC: 0211
    Feedlot
James R Cooper, President

D-U-N-S 05-025-8698
DIXIE FARMS
State Farmers Market, Plant City, FL 33566
Phone: (813) 754-7652
Sales: $16,088,000   *Employees:* 40
Company Type: Private   *Employees here:* 40
SIC: 0171
    Strawberry and vegetable farm
James Garrity, Personnel-Human Resources

D-U-N-S 95-717-6332
DIXIE LOWER TIMBER COMPAN
Bashi Rd, Thomasville, AL 36784
Phone: (334) 636-1500
Sales: $13,000,000   *Employees:* 30
Company Type: Private   *Employees here:* 30
SIC: 0851
    Forestry services
Thomas Lyon, Chief Executive Officer

D-U-N-S 04-401-0213
DMB PACKING CORP
N & Fresno St, Newman, CA 95360
Phone: (209) 862-2872
Sales: $40,000,000   *Employees:* 320
Company Type: Private   *Employees here:* 150
SIC: 0174
    Grows packs & ships citrus fruits & vegetables
Joseph D Clougherty, Partner

D-U-N-S 18-050-7063
DMB PACKING CORP
82025 Avenue 44, Indio, CA 92201
Phone: (760) 347-3336

Sales: $12,800,000   *Employees:* NA
Company Type: Private   *Employees here:* 200
SIC: 0174
    Citrus fruit grove vegetable/melon farm
William D Grant, Secretary

D-U-N-S 60-284-1934
DOLE BAKERSFIELD INC
    (Parent: Dole Food Company Inc)
10000 Ming Ave, Bakersfield, CA 93311
Phone: (661) 664-6100
Sales: $30,000,000   *Employees:* 500
Company Type: Public Family Member   *Employees here:* 500
SIC: 0172
    Growing packing distributing and marketing of deciduous
      and citrus products
John Demshki, President

D-U-N-S 00-896-5428
DOLE FOOD CO, INC
31365 Oak Crest Dr, Thousand Oaks, CA 91361
Phone: (818) 879-6600
Sales: $4,336,120,000   *Employees:* 44,000
Company Type: Public   *Employees here:* 175
SIC: 0179
    Grower processor and distributor of fruits & vegetables
Jose A Costa Jr, President

D-U-N-S 61-905-4208   EXP
DOLE FRESH VEGETABLES, INC
    (Parent: Dole Food Company Inc)
639 S Sanborn Rd, Salinas, CA 93901
Phone: (831) 422-8871
Sales: $222,700,000   *Employees:* NA
Company Type: Public Family Member   *Employees here:* NA
SIC: 0723
    Packer & shipper of fresh vegetables
E W Williams Jr, Chairman of the Board

D-U-N-S 94-348-6738
DON SMITH CATTLE
620 Fir St, Correctionville, IA 51016
Phone: (712) 372-4107
Sales: $12,230,000   *Employees:* 2
Company Type: Private   *Employees here:* 2
SIC: 0212
    Cattle farm
John Crane, Chairman of the Board

D-U-N-S 00-232-4390
DOROTHY LOUGH
Turkey Ln, Winthrop, ME
Phone: (207) 377-9927
Sales: $13,038,000   *Employees:* 75
Company Type: Private   *Employees here:* 63
SIC: 0252
    Egg farm
Roger Claypoole, President

D-U-N-S 78-366-7116
DOUBLE A FEEDERS INC
Clayton, NM 88415
Phone: (505) 374-2591
Sales: $28,000,000   *Employees:* 18
Company Type: Private   *Employees here:* 18
SIC: 0211
    Cattle feed lot
W E Creighton, Chief Executive Officer

D-U-N-S 10-898-0343
DOUBLE D PROPERTIES INC
28900 Old State Road 80, Belle Glade, FL 33430
Phone: (561) 996-2215

Sales: $18,000,000   *Employees:* 40
Company Type: Private   *Employees here:* 40
SIC: 0133
    Management service for sugarcane and vegetable farms
Richard Crist, Shareholder

D-U-N-S 07-186-1579
DRESICK FARMS, INC
19536 Jayne Ave, Huron, CA 93234
Phone: (559) 945-2513
Sales: $10,100,000   *Employees:* 110
Company Type: Private   *Employees here:* 100
SIC: 0161
    Grows lettuce cantaloupe tomatoes garlic & onions
Bud L Kaufman, President

D-U-N-S 01-140-0108
DU BROW'S NURSERIES INC
251 W Northfield Rd, Livingston, NJ
Phone: (973) 992-0598
Sales: $13,500,000   *Employees:* 76
Company Type: Private   *Employees here:* 40
SIC: 0781
    Landscape architects planning and nursery stock
Nathan R Boardman, President

D-U-N-S 36-168-7080
DUARTE NURSERY INC
1555 Baldwin Rd, Hughson, CA 95326
Phone: (209) 531-0351
Sales: $25,000,000   *Employees:* 150
Company Type: Private   *Employees here:* 150
SIC: 0181
    Production nursery grapes
Peter W Stott, President

D-U-N-S 06-857-7741
DUCKS UNLIMITED INC
1 Waterfowl Way, Memphis, TN 38120
Phone: (901) 758-3825
Sales: $103,547,000   *Employees:* 425
Company Type: Private   *Employees here:* 125
SIC: 0971
    Wildlife management organization
Jim Brock, President

D-U-N-S 00-797-3316
DUNDEE CITRUS GROWERS ASSN
111 1st St S, Dundee, FL 33838
Phone: (941) 439-1574
Sales: $33,363,000   *Employees:* 70
Company Type: Private   *Employees here:* 70
SIC: 0723
    Citrus packing house
Ron Coulfal, President

D-U-N-S 00-796-0263   EXP
DURBIN MARSHALL FOOD CORP
2830 Commerce Blvd, Birmingham, AL 35210
Phone: (205) 956-3505
Sales: $175,000,000   *Employees:* 2,200
Company Type: Private   *Employees here:* 50
SIC: 0252
    Integrated chicken broiler production
Charles S Goodman, Owner

D-U-N-S 01-056-2437
DUTCH COUNTRY EGG FARMS INC
Sunset Dr, Fredericksburg, PA 17026
Phone: (717) 865-6637

Sales: $11,855,000   *Employees:* 30
Company Type: Private   *Employees here:* 25
SIC: 0252
    Egg farm
Peter Widderington, Chief Executive Officer

D-U-N-S 00-190-9464   EXP
E RITTER & CO INC
106 Frisco St, Marked Tree, AR 72365
Phone: (870) 358-2200
Sales: $41,358,000   *Employees:* 145
Company Type: Private   *Employees here:* 60
SIC: 0131
    Cotton & soybean farming cotton gin telephone exchanges
      ret lumber & building materials whol farm implements gas
      & tires
Sheryl Weisinger, President

D-U-N-S 07-182-9543
E W BRANDT & SONS INC
561 Ragan Rd, Wapato, WA 98951
Phone: (509) 877-3193
Sales: $16,000,000   *Employees:* 75
Company Type: Private   *Employees here:* 25
SIC: 0723
    Operates packaging facilities & fruit orchard
Conard C Inc, Shareholder

D-U-N-S 78-726-6311
EAGLE PRODUCE LTD PARTNERSHIP
7332 E Butherus Dr, Scottsdale, AZ 85260
Phone: (602) 998-1444
Sales: $10,000,000   *Employees:* 200
Company Type: Private   *Employees here:* 4
SIC: 0161
    Vegetable & melon farm
Peter Hancock, President

D-U-N-S 13-127-8897   EXP
EARTHRISE FARMS
113 E Hoober Rd, Calipatria, CA 92233
Phone: (760) 348-5027
Sales: $13,219,000   *Employees:* 53
Company Type: Private   *Employees here:* 1
SIC: 0191
    General farm specializing in algae
David W Snyder, President

D-U-N-S 03-999-7911
EASTSIDE NURSERY INC
6723 Lithopolis Rd, Groveport, OH 43125
Phone: (614) 836-9800
Sales: $11,022,000   *Employees:* 35
Company Type: Private   *Employees here:* 35
SIC: 0782
    Landscape & sodding contractor
D B Cuddy, Owner

D-U-N-S 02-242-8486
ECKENBERG FARMS INC
26064 SW Rd L, Mattawa, WA 99349
Phone: (509) 932-4600
Sales: $11,900,000   *Employees:* 30
Company Type: Private   *Employees here:* 30
SIC: 0723
    Hay cubing
D M Camp, Partner

D-U-N-S 94-945-6537
ED SILVA
21 River Rd, Gonzales, CA 93926
Phone: (831) 675-2327

Sales: $18,300,000
Company Type: Private
SIC: 0161
  Vegetable/melon farm
Andrew A D Arrigo, Chairman of the Board

Employees: 200
Employees here: 200

D-U-N-S 07-821-5977
EDALEEN DAIRY PRODUCTS LLC
9593 Guide Meridian Rd, Lynden, WA 98264
Phone: (360) 354-5342
Sales: $13,000,000
Company Type: Private
SIC: 0241
  Dairy farm
Dale C Bone, President

Employees: 56
Employees here: 30

D-U-N-S 04-652-4013   EXP
EDAW INC
753 Davis St, San Francisco, CA 94111
Phone: (415) 433-1484
Sales: $50,429,000
Company Type: Private
SIC: 0781
  Landscape architects
Daniel W Schantz, Partner

Employees: 330
Employees here: 70

D-U-N-S 07-222-5881
EDWARD D STONE JR AND ASSOC
1512 E Broward Blvd, Fort Lauderdale, FL 33301
Phone: (954) 524-3330
Sales: $10,115,000
Company Type: Private
SIC: 0781
  Landscape architects and planners
Danny Danell, President

Employees: 73
Employees here: 60

D-U-N-S 02-087-1786
EDWARD J WOERNER & SONS INC
505 S Flagler Dr, West Palm Beach, FL 33401
Phone: (561) 835-3747
Sales: $50,934,000
Company Type: Private
SIC: 0181
  Sod farm
Clarence Danielski, Partner

Employees: 650
Employees here: 63

D-U-N-S 02-524-5242
EGGS WEST
13610 S Archibald Ave, Ontario, CA 91761
Phone: (909) 947-6207
Sales: $13,700,000
Company Type: Private
SIC: 0252
  Chicken egg production
Craig Uden, Manager

Employees: 150
Employees here: 100

D-U-N-S 00-253-3115
EL MODENO GARDENS INC
11911 Jeffrey Rd, Irvine, CA 92620
Phone: (949) 559-1234
Sales: $25,000,000
Company Type: Private
SIC: 0181
  Grows nursery stock
Darrell Garrett, Owner

Employees: 320
Employees here: 220

D-U-N-S 06-884-6971
ELBOW ENTERPRISES INC
12021 Avenue 328, Visalia, CA 93291
Phone: (559) 734-1177

Sales: $25,000,000
Company Type: Private
SIC: 0724
  Cotton gin
Dave Kingston, President

Employees: 8
Employees here: 8

D-U-N-S 15-420-9613
ELLOREE GIN CO INC
645 Snider St, Elloree, SC 29047
Phone: (803) 897-2141
Sales: $15,107,000
Company Type: Private
SIC: 0724
  Cotton gin and merchandise bale cotton
Robert Woolley, Owner

Employees: 20
Employees here: 20

D-U-N-S 09-803-9852
EMCO HARVESTING CO
P.O. Box 6403, Yuma, AZ 85366
Phone: (520) 344-5045
Sales: $19,700,000
Company Type: Private
SIC: 0761
  Farm labor contractor crop preparation for market farm
    management services
R D Cowan, President

Employees: 562
Employees here: 562

D-U-N-S 06-785-8811   EXP
EMERALD PACKING COMPANY INC
2823 N Orange Blossom Trl, Orlando, FL 32804
Phone: (407) 423-0531
Sales: $10,804,000
Company Type: Private
SIC: 0723
  Fresh citrus fruit packing service
David J Frank, President

Employees: 14
Employees here: 14

D-U-N-S 00-917-5555
ENOCH PACKING CO INC
10715 E American Ave, Del Rey, CA 93616
Phone: (559) 888-2151
Sales: $49,494,000
Company Type: Private
SIC: 0723
  Raisin packing
Susan Petrocco, Treasurer

Employees: 150
Employees here: 150

D-U-N-S 06-625-4509
ENVIRONMENTAL CARE INC
  (Parent: Environmental Industries Inc)
24121 Ventura Blvd, Calabasas, CA 91302
Phone: (818) 223-8500
Sales: $100,000,000
Company Type: Private
SIC: 0781
  Landscape maintenance services
Kurt Lausecker, President

Employees: 2,800
Employees here: 10

D-U-N-S 10-144-0899
ENVIRONMENTAL CONSULTANTS
301 Lakeside Park, Southampton, PA 18966
Phone: (215) 322-4040
Sales: $11,900,000
Company Type: Private
SIC: 0851
  Forestry services
James C De Angelis, President

Employees: 260
Employees here: 251

D-U-N-S 09-712-0471
ENVIRONMENTAL EARTHSCAPES INC
2101 E Grant Rd, Tucson, AZ 85719
Phone: (520) 571-1139

Sales: $19,737,000
Company Type: Private   *Employees: 500*
SIC: 0782   *Employees here: 6*
    Landscape contracting and maintenance
Dean Cluck, General Partner

D-U-N-S 05-079-6176
ENVIRONMENTAL INDUSTRIES INC
24121 Ventura Blvd, Calabasas, CA 91302
Phone: (818) 223-8500
Sales: $351,318,000   *Employees: 5,600*
Company Type: Private   *Employees here: 100*
SIC: 0781
    Landscape service site development golf construction and
      management tree nursury
Dr Larry F Vint, President

D-U-N-S 94-892-8627
ENVIRONMENTRAL CARE INC (EII)
    (Parent: Environmental Industries Inc)
4777 Old Winter Garden Rd, Orlando, FL 32811
Phone: (407) 292-9600
Sales: $351,318,000   *Employees: 750*
Company Type: Private   *Employees here: 750*
SIC: 0782
    Landscape contractors lawn services
Roy L Poage, President

D-U-N-S 09-174-6065
EPPICH GRAIN INC
151 N Canal Blvd, Mesa, WA 99343
Phone: (509) 269-4693
Sales: $20,000,000   *Employees: 20*
Company Type: Private   *Employees here: 20*
SIC: 0723
    Corn drying service & grain storage elevator
Hani Elnaffy, President

D-U-N-S 07-641-4135   EXP
ERICKSON AIR-CRANE CO., LLC
3100 Willow Springs Rd, Central Point, OR 97502
Phone: (541) 664-5544
Sales: $27,200,000   *Employees: 500*
Company Type: Private   *Employees here: 500*
SIC: 0241
    Helicopter logging contractor heavy lift powerline
      construction contractor & helicopter leasing
Delbert L Wheeler, Owner

D-U-N-S 01-031-4607
ERWIN-KEITH INC
1529 Hwy 193, Wynne, AR 72396
Phone: (870) 238-2079
Sales: $38,000,000   *Employees: 43*
Company Type: Private   *Employees here: 28*
SIC: 0119
    Seed cleaning & growing
Jacob Koorneef, President

D-U-N-S 05-440-9685
ESBENSHADE FARMS
220 Eby Chiques Rd, Mount Joy, PA 17552
Phone: (717) 653-8061
Sales: $11,000,000   *Employees: 120*
Company Type: Private   *Employees here: 24*
SIC: 0252
    Chicken egg farms having a total of 1000000 laying hens &
      operates a feed mill
Phillip Williams, Office Manager

D-U-N-S 92-772-5952
EUNICE RICE MILL, LLC
101 E Vine Ave, Eunice, LA 70535

Phone: (318) 457-9294
Sales: $25,000,000   *Employees: 35*
Company Type: Private   *Employees here: 35*
SIC: 0723
    Rice mill
Frank R Burnside Jr, President

D-U-N-S 79-452-6806
EUROFRESH LTD
13355 W Ashcreek Rd, Willcox, AZ 85643
Phone: (520) 384-4621
Sales: $15,003,000   *Employees: 240*
Company Type: Private   *Employees here: 2*
SIC: 0161
    Holding company
Carl Elkins, Finance

D-U-N-S 04-608-3135
EVANS PROPERTIES INC
12833 US Hwy 301, Dade City, FL 33525
Phone: (352) 567-5661
Sales: $20,700,000   *Employees: 350*
Company Type: Private   *Employees here: 50*
SIC: 0174
    Citrus groves
John Demler, Partner

D-U-N-S 08-854-8466
EVERETT ASHURST
1246 W Ross Rd, El Centro, CA 92243
Phone: (760) 352-8860
Sales: $10,000,000   *Employees: 15*
Company Type: Private   *Employees here: 15*
SIC: 0279
    Bee farm honey processing & whol honey
John Denison, President

D-U-N-S 09-274-6551
EXETER PACKERS INC
1250 E Myer Ave, Exeter, CA 93221
Phone: (559) 592-5168
Sales: $130,000,000   *Employees: 585*
Company Type: Private   *Employees here: 230*
SIC: 0723
    Citrus fruit packing
Johnny Deniz, President

D-U-N-S 00-691-8262   EXP
F A BARTLETT TREE EXPERT
1290 E Main St, Stamford, CT
Phone: (203) 323-1131
Sales: $89,910,000   *Employees: 1,700*
Company Type: Private   *Employees here: 45*
SIC: 0783
    Tree and shrub maintenance spraying pruning trimming and
      removal services
Joe A Porter, Chairman of the Board

D-U-N-S 82-567-2579
F F GONSALEZ FARMS
1224 Santa Clara St, Santa Paula, CA 93060
Phone: (805) 525-1828
Sales: $10,000,000   *Employees: 150*
Company Type: Private   *Employees here: 149*
SIC: 0139
    Cilantro farm
Kenneth Desserault, President

D-U-N-S 06-573-6415
FAIRLEIGH CORP
515 Main St, Scott City, KS 67871
Phone: (316) 872-1111

Sales: $24,878,000
Company Type: Private
SIC: 0211
   Beef cattle feedlot
Stephen M Dettle, Partner

Employees: 45
Employees here: 45

D-U-N-S 04-602-3792
FARM-OP, INC
315 E New Market Rd, Immokalee, FL 34142
Phone: (941) 657-4421
Sales: $42,600,000
Company Type: Private
SIC: 0161
   Vegetable farm
Robert W Dillon, President

Employees: 500
Employees here: 25

D-U-N-S 03-628-7279
FARMAX LAND MANAGEMENT INC
11156 E Annadale Ave, Sanger, CA 93657
Phone: (559) 875-7181
Sales: $13,500,000
Company Type: Private
SIC: 0723
   Fresh fruit packing
James L Maxwell Jr, President

Employees: 150
Employees here: 150

D-U-N-S 00-690-2563
FARMERS INVESTMENT CO.
1525 E Sahuarita Rd, Sahuarita, AZ 85629
Phone: (520) 791-2852
Sales: $14,100,000
Company Type: Private
SIC: 0723
   Pecan processing
Ronald K Girardelli, President

Employees: 200
Employees here: 180

D-U-N-S 02-032-4612
FARMING TECHNOLOGY CORP
   (Parent: Smokin-Spuds Inc)
3173 Produce Row, Houston, TX 77023
Phone: (713) 923-5693
Sales: $47,220,000
Company Type: Private
SIC: 0134
   Potato farming and packaging
Dick Dykstra, Partner

Employees: 120
Employees here: 1

D-U-N-S 87-863-4278   EXP
FARMINGTON FRESH
7735 S Rt 99 W Frntage Rd, Stockton, CA 95215
Phone: (209) 983-9700
Sales: $12,000,000
Company Type: Private
SIC: 0175
   Fruit tree orchard freight transportation arrangement
Tim Diestel, Owner

Employees: 6
Employees here: 6

D-U-N-S 06-589-7266
FARRENS TREE SURGEONS INC
   (Parent: Asplundh Subsidary Holdings)
708 Blair Mill Rd, Willow Grove, PA 19090
Phone: (215) 784-4200
Sales: $20,029,000
Company Type: Private
SIC: 0783
   Tree trimming services for public utility lines
Thomas F Dimare, President

Employees: 470
Employees here: 10

D-U-N-S 10-423-8522
FEATHER RIVER FOOD CO INC
1900 Feather River Blvd, Marysville, CA 95901
Phone: (530) 742-7866

Sales: $13,106,000
Company Type: Private
SIC: 0723
   Processes & retorts prunes mfg & packages sweetened
    coconut
Paul Dimare, President

Employees: 35
Employees here: 35

D-U-N-S 00-377-7463
FEDERAL DRYER & STORAGE CO
Hwy 165, England, AR 72046
Phone: (501) 842-2301
Sales: $18,812,000
Company Type: Private
SIC: 0723
   Rice dryer & whol soybeans
Paul Dimare, President

Employees: 8
Employees here: 8

D-U-N-S 03-274-9574
FERNLEA NURSERY INC
3806 SW 96th St, Palm City, FL 34990
Phone: (561) 287-1160
Sales: $10,000,000
Company Type: Private
SIC: 0181
   Ornamental nursery
Thomas O Connel, Chief Executive Officer

Employees: 315
Employees here: 40

D-U-N-S 05-576-6695
FILLMORE-PIRU CITRUS ASSN
743 Sespe Ave, Fillmore, CA 93015
Phone: (805) 524-3551
Sales: $16,200,000
Company Type: Private
SIC: 0723
   Citrus grading sorting & packing
Roy Dinsdale, President

Employees: 200
Employees here: 7

D-U-N-S 07-250-0382   EXP
FISHER RANCH CORP
10600 Ice Plant Rd, Blythe, CA 92225
Phone: (760) 922-4151
Sales: $14,291,000
Company Type: Private
SIC: 0191
   General farming
Charles Lawton, Partner

Employees: 5
Employees here: 5

D-U-N-S 11-982-9232
FIVE CROWNS, INC
551 W Main St, Ste 2, Brawley, CA 92227
Phone: (760) 344-1930
Sales: $23,556,000
Company Type: Private
SIC: 0161
   Growerpacker and shipper of vegetables and fruits
T J Pope, President

Employees: 5
Employees here: 5

D-U-N-S 96-436-5357
FLETCHER CHALLENGE FOREST USA
   (Parent: Fletcher Chllnge Inds USA Ltd)
7458 New Ridge Rd, Hanover, MD 21076
Phone: (410) 850-5433
Sales: $48,000,000
Company Type: Private
SIC: 0851
   Forestry services
Thomas F Dimare, President

Employees: 4
Employees here: 4

D-U-N-S 18-328-2128
FLO SUN INC
316 Royal Poinciana Plz, Palm Beach, FL 33480
Phone: (561) 655-6303

Sales: $40,300,000
Company Type: Private
SIC: 0133
　Sugarcane farm mfg raw sugar cane & sugar grinding
Tony Medeiros, Manager

Employees: 1,110
Employees here: 4

D-U-N-S 14-467-1500
FLORAL PLANT GROWERS, L.L.C.
1133 Ebenezer Church Rd, Rising Sun, MD 21911
Phone: (410) 658-6100
Sales: $10,700,000
Company Type: Private
SIC: 0181
　Ornamental nursery
Carl F Dobler Jr, Partner

Employees: 240
Employees here: 40

D-U-N-S 10-694-8169
FLORIDA GARDINIER CITRUS
10 Sarasota Center Blvd, Sarasota, FL 34240
Phone: (941) 378-1794
Sales: $10,000,000
Company Type: Private
SIC: 0174
　Citrus groves
Hank Doelman, Co-Owner

Employees: 20
Employees here: 4

D-U-N-S 13-358-2262
FLORIDA NORTH HOLSTEINS LC
2740 W County Road 232, Bell, FL 32619
Phone: (352) 463-7174
Sales: $13,636,000
Company Type: Private
SIC: 0241
　Dairy farm
Gregory L Costley, President

Employees: 120
Employees here: 120

D-U-N-S 04-998-6144
FLOWERWOOD NURSERY INC
6470 Dauphin Island Pkwy, Mobile, AL 36605
Phone: (334) 443-6540
Sales: $23,299,000
Company Type: Private
SIC: 0181
　Growing of nursery stock
David H Murdock, Chairman of the Board

Employees: 500
Employees here: 120

D-U-N-S 05-997-1630
FORD COUNTY FEED YARD INC
　(*Parent:* Ford Holding Company Inc)
12466 Hwy 154, Ford, KS 67842
Phone: (316) 369-2252
Sales: $30,549,000
Company Type: Private
SIC: 0211
　Cattle feedlot
Lawrence A Kern, President

Employees: 59
Employees here: 59

D-U-N-S 02-136-8618
FORD HOLDING COMPANY INC
12466 US Hwy 400, Ford, KS 67842
Phone: (316) 369-2252
Sales: $40,749,000
Company Type: Private
SIC: 0211
　Holding company
Don Bartleston, Owner

Employees: 68
Employees here: 3

D-U-N-S 17-327-3269
FORDEL INC
1000 Airport Blvd, Mendota, CA 93640
Phone: (559) 655-3241

Sales: $14,000,000
Company Type: Private
SIC: 0723
　Melon packing
Don Smith, Owner

Employees: 50
Employees here: 50

D-U-N-S 80-112-5816
FORESTRY INTERNATIONAL INC
4640 Poplar Springs Dr, Meridian, MS 39305
Phone: (601) 485-3199
Sales: $12,000,000
Company Type: Public
SIC: 0811
　Integrated forestry company
Dorothy Lough, Owner

Employees: 20
Employees here: 20

D-U-N-S 05-167-5197
FOSTER DAIRY FARMS
1707 Mchenry Ave, Modesto, CA 95350
Phone: (209) 576-3400
Sales: $250,000,000
Company Type: Private
SIC: 0241
　Dairy farm
Gene Atchley, President

Employees: 590
Employees here: 60

D-U-N-S 00-917-8856
FOSTER POULTRY FARMS
1000 Davis St, Livingston, CA 95334
Phone: (209) 394-7901
Sales: $1,000,000,000
Company Type: Private
SIC: 0254
　Poultry farm & poultry processing
David Young, President

Employees: 7,200
Employees here: 3,000

D-U-N-S 08-290-7858
FOUR SEASONS LANDSCAPING & MAINTENANCE CO
951 Edgewater Blvd A200, Foster City, CA 94404
Phone: (650) 372-1500
Sales: $16,500,000
Company Type: Private
SIC: 0781
　Landscape maintenance
Mike Dresick, President

Employees: 450
Employees here: 150

D-U-N-S 84-920-1132
FOUR SEASONS PRODUCE PKG CO
122 Abbott St, Salinas, CA 93901
Phone: (831) 772-8400
Sales: $17,900,000
Company Type: Private
SIC: 0723
　Crop packing
Sheldon Du Brow, President

Employees: 250
Employees here: 250

D-U-N-S 08-706-5850
FOXLEY CATTLE CO
7480 La Jolla Blvd, La Jolla, CA 92037
Phone: (619) 551-6615
Sales: $75,832,000
Company Type: Private
SIC: 0211
　Cattle feedlot & buys & whol grain
Jim Duarte, President

Employees: 110
Employees here: 10

D-U-N-S 02-456-2282
FRANKLIN FARMS INC
931 Route 32, North Franklin, CT
Phone: (860) 642-3000

EXP

Sales: $39,000,000   *Employees:* 590
Company Type: Private   *Employees here:* 550
SIC: 0182
     Mushroom farm mushroom processor (blanched and
       marinated)
E W Dubois, President

D-U-N-S 13-161-1345
FRANSCIONI BROTHERS, INC
335 Pajaro St, Salinas, CA 93901
Phone: (831) 757-9131
Sales: $10,302,000   *Employees:* 20
Company Type: Private   *Employees here:* 20
SIC: 0161
     Vegetable growers
Matthew B Connolly Jr, Executive Vice-President

D-U-N-S 01-379-8657
FRED J JAINDL
3150 Coffeetown Rd, Orefield, PA 18069
Phone: (610) 395-3333
Sales: $20,000,000   *Employees:* 100
Company Type: Private   *Employees here:* 100
SIC: 0253
     Operates a turkey corn and wheat farm & a fruit orchard
William L Raley, Chairman of the Board

D-U-N-S 13-162-0114
FRESH EXPRESS INC
    (Parent: Fresh International Corp)
1020 Merrill St, Salinas, CA 93901
Phone: (831) 422-5917
Sales: $159,700,000   *Employees:* 2,500
Company Type: Private   *Employees here:* 100
SIC: 0723
     Prepares packaged salads
L W Dunson Jr, Vice-President

D-U-N-S 07-631-5829
FRESH INTERNATIONAL CORP
1020 Merrill St, Salinas, CA 93901
Phone: (831) 422-5334
Sales: $191,200,000   *Employees:* 3,000
Company Type: Private   *Employees here:* 5
SIC: 0723
     Operations in growing packing cooling shipping of fresh
       vegetables & fresh vegetable products
Marshall B Durbin Jr, Chairman of the Board

D-U-N-S 05-712-3283   EXP
FRESH WESTERN MARKETING INC
    (Parent: Albert Fisher Holdings Inc)
1156 Abbott St, Salinas, CA 93901
Phone: (831) 758-1390
Sales: $168,000,000   *Employees:* 500
Company Type: Private   *Employees here:* 500
SIC: 0722
     Grower marketer shipper & harvester of produce
Dale L Snader, President

D-U-N-S 01-722-3889
FRIO FEEDERS LLC
RR 4, Hereford, TX 79045
Phone: (806) 276-5899
Sales: $20,000,000   *Employees:* 14
Company Type: Private   *Employees here:* 14
SIC: 0751
     Livestock services
Edward P Frazier, President

D-U-N-S 03-372-0103
FUNSTON GIN CO
161 Sale City Rd, Funston, GA 31753

Phone: (912) 941-2273
Sales: $18,567,000   *Employees:* 11
Company Type: Private   *Employees here:* 11
SIC: 0724
     Cotton gin and wholesales cotton
E R Arnold, President

D-U-N-S 03-613-5283
G & B ENTERPRISES LTD
2026 Greenville Hwy, Liberty, SC 29657
Phone: (864) 843-9465
Sales: $10,000,000   *Employees:* 28
Company Type: Private   *Employees here:* 28
SIC: 0252
     Poultry egg farm
Everette W Brandt, President

D-U-N-S 04-449-9598
G & H SEED CO, INC.
1110 W Mill St, Crowley, LA 70526
Phone: (318) 783-7762
Sales: $47,822,000   *Employees:* 130
Company Type: Private   *Employees here:* 50
SIC: 0723
     Crop preparation for market ret misc merchandise
Stephen A Martori, Limited Partner

D-U-N-S 08-152-9208
G & S LIVESTOCK
4556 E Independence Rd, Attica, IN 47918
Phone: (765) 762-2474
Sales: $23,000,000   *Employees:* 5
Company Type: Private   *Employees here:* 5
SIC: 0119
     Hog and grain farmer
Yoshimichi Ota, President

D-U-N-S 06-134-6060
G & U INC
RR 2, Goshen, NY 10924
Phone: (914) 651-4471
Sales: $10,200,000   *Employees:* 125
Company Type: Private   *Employees here:* 125
SIC: 0161
     Vegetable farm
W L Wilson, President

D-U-N-S 11-332-3760
GADSDEN TOMATO CO
218 Graves St, Quincy, FL 32351
Phone: (850) 627-7696
Sales: $12,400,000   *Employees:* 186
Company Type: Private   *Employees here:* 186
SIC: 0723
     Packs & processes tomatoes
Max Eckley, Partner

D-U-N-S 19-557-1419
GALLO CATTLE CO
10561 US Hwy 140, Atwater, CA 95301
Phone: (209) 394-7984
Sales: $55,000,000   *Employees:* 350
Company Type: Private   *Employees here:* 350
SIC: 0241
     Dairy farms, nsk
Steve Taft, President

D-U-N-S 19-683-0228
GARCIA FARMING & HARVESTING
1518 Moffett St, Ste D, Salinas, CA 93905
Phone: (831) 422-4001

Sales: $12,000,000   *Employees:* 300
Company Type: Private   *Employees here:* 30
SIC: 0161
   Vegetable/melon farm
Ed Silva, Owner

D-U-N-S 93-903-2322
GARDEN CITY FEED YARD, LLC
1805 W Annie Scheer Rd, Garden City, KS 67846
Phone: (316) 275-4191
Sales: $16,349,000   *Employees:* 30
Company Type: Private   *Employees here:* 30
SIC: 0211
   Cattle feed yard
Aileen Brandsma, President

D-U-N-S 80-307-4012
GARDEN DESIGN GROUP INC
11126 Shady Trl, Ste 107, Dallas, TX 75229
Phone: (972) 243-6467
Sales: $11,645,000   *Employees:* 140
Company Type: Private   *Employees here:* 140
SIC: 0781
   Landscape services
Joseph Brown, Chief Executive Officer

D-U-N-S 62-339-5381
GARDNER TURFGRASS INC
1333 W 120th Ave, Ste 111, Denver, CO 80234
Phone: (303) 252-1900
Sales: $11,892,000   *Employees:* 200
Company Type: Private   *Employees here:* 6
SIC: 0181
   Sod farm
Lester Woerner, President

D-U-N-S 80-618-7597
GARGIULO, INC
   (Parent: Monsanto Co)
15000 Old 41 N, Naples, FL 34110
Phone: (941) 597-3131
Sales: $160,000,000   *Employees:* 250
Company Type: Public Family Member   *Employees here:* 25
SIC: 0161
   Vegetable & berry crop farm fruit & vegetable packing whol
     fresh fruit & vegetables
David L Edwards, President

D-U-N-S 02-456-4791
GARLAND FARM SUPPLY INC
250 N Belgrade Ave, Garland, NC 28441
Phone: (910) 529-9731
Sales: $10,209,000   *Employees:* 18
Company Type: Private   *Employees here:* 15
SIC: 0723
   Feed mill
H D Foster, President

D-U-N-S 10-276-1186
GARLIC CO
18602 Zerker Rd, Bakersfield, CA 93312
Phone: (661) 393-4212
Sales: $21,000,000   *Employees:* 85
Company Type: Private   *Employees here:* 85
SIC: 0139
   Field crop farm
Timothy K Hennessy, President

D-U-N-S 19-564-1824
GARROUTTE FARMS INC
739 E Lake Ave, Watsonville, CA 95076
Phone: (831) 722-6965

Sales: $13,800,000   *Employees:* 250
Company Type: Private   *Employees here:* 250
SIC: 0171
   Berry crop farm
Peter N Groot, President

D-U-N-S 10-697-8778
GARY T RAAK & ASSOCIATES INC
10881 E 260th St, Elko, MN 55020
Phone: (612) 461-6548
Sales: $10,000,000   *Employees:* 12
Company Type: Private   *Employees here:* 12
SIC: 0272
   Horses/other equines farm
Robert O Dell, President

D-U-N-S 03-322-6705
GAY & ROBINSON INC
1 Kaumakani Ave, Kaumakani, HI 96747
Phone: (808) 335-3133
Sales: $20,033,000   *Employees:* 280
Company Type: Private   *Employees here:* 280
SIC: 0133
   Sugar cane growers
Bob Faris, President

D-U-N-S 01-165-7889
GEERLINGS GREENHOUSE INC
496 William St, Piscataway, NJ
Phone: (732) 752-2500
Sales: $12,000,000   *Employees:* 50
Company Type: Private   *Employees here:* 50
SIC: 0181
   Grower of potted plants
Robert Elliott, President

D-U-N-S 08-752-8675
GENERAL PRODUCE DISTRS INC
2980 Hart Ct, Franklin Park, IL 60131
Phone: (847) 451-0026
Sales: $12,000,000   *Employees:* 25
Company Type: Private   *Employees here:* 25
SIC: 0723
   Fresh fruit and vegetable packaging
Jerry Eller, President

D-U-N-S 94-422-2983
GENEX COOPERATIVE INC
391 Pine Tree Rd, Ithaca, NY 14850
Phone: (607) 272-2011
Sales: $72,013,000   *Employees:* 400
Company Type: Private   *Employees here:* 100
SIC: 0751
   Cooperative artifical breeding service
J A Dantzler Ii, President

D-U-N-S 00-335-7159
GENTRY'S POULTRY CO INC
Hwy 39 E, Ward, SC 29166
Phone: (864) 445-2161
Sales: $40,000,000   *Employees:* 275
Company Type: Private   *Employees here:* 275
SIC: 0251
   Poultry growing and processing plant
Edward Montiel, Owner

D-U-N-S 79-454-2084
GEORGE AMARAL RANCHES INC
25453 Iversen Rd, Chualar, CA 93925
Phone: (831) 679-2977

Sales: $27,536,000
Company Type: Private
SIC: 0161
   Row crop farm
Harold Arost, President

Employees: 60
Employees here: 60

D-U-N-S 07-187-9506
GERAWAN FARMING, INC
15749 E Ventura Ave, Sanger, CA 93657
Phone: (559) 787-8780
Sales: $10,000,000
Company Type: Private
SIC: 0723
   Fruit packing
Albert L English, Chairman of the Board

Employees: 50
Employees here: 12

D-U-N-S 05-036-0288
GERAWAN RANCHES
15749 E Ventura Ave, Sanger, CA 93657
Phone: (559) 787-8780
Sales: $15,300,000
Company Type: Private
SIC: 0175
   Grows peaches plums nectarines and grapes
Dennis Vartan, President

Employees: 270
Employees here: 40

D-U-N-S 01-655-3484
GERRALDS VDLIA SWEET ONONS INC
17156 Hwy 301 N, Statesboro, GA 30458
Phone: (912) 764-7526
Sales: $21,100,000
Company Type: Private
SIC: 0723
   Vegetable packing
Bruce Wilson, President

Employees: 300
Employees here: 300

D-U-N-S 04-775-6127
G.F. STRUCTURES CORP
4655 W Arthington St, Chicago, IL 60644
Phone: (773) 626-4122
Sales: $32,654,000
Company Type: Private
SIC: 0782
   Contractor specializing in park improvements guard rail and
     fence construction
Ed Eckenberg, President

Employees: 80
Employees here: 80

D-U-N-S 07-078-7577
GILDER TIMBER INC
3rd Ave, Glenwood, GA 30428
Phone: (912) 523-5181
Sales: $13,000,000
Company Type: Private
SIC: 0241
   Logging and pulpwood contractor
Dennis Holewinski, President

Employees: 15
Employees here: 15

D-U-N-S 04-453-6324
GIORGI MUSHROOM CO
Park Rd, Blandon, PA 19510
Phone: (610) 926-8811
Sales: $18,000,000
Company Type: Private
SIC: 0182
   Mushroom farm
John S Hasbrouck Jr, Treasurer

Employees: 450
Employees here: 290

D-U-N-S 05-298-5405
GIROUX'S POULTRY FARM INC
8957 Route 9, Chazy, NY 12921
Phone: (518) 846-7300

Sales: $10,381,000
Company Type: Private
SIC: 0252
   Poultry farm
Burton S Sperber, Chairman of the Board

Employees: 40
Employees here: 40

D-U-N-S 04-309-8896
GIUMARRA VINEYARDS CORP
11220 Edison Hwy, Edison, CA 93220
Phone: (661) 395-7000
Sales: $95,483,000
Company Type: Private
SIC: 0172
   Operates grape vineyards
Bruce Wilson, President

Employees: 500
Employees here: 500

D-U-N-S 00-886-5292
GLACIER FISH CO L.L.C.
1200 Westlake Ave N, Seattle, WA 98109
Phone: (206) 298-1200
Sales: $45,000,000
Company Type: Private
SIC: 0912
   Fish harvesting & processing
Lee Eppich, President

Employees: 250
Employees here: 250

D-U-N-S 03-861-6330
GLASS CORNER GREENHOUSE INC
3525 Bristol Ave NW, Grand Rapids, MI 49544
Phone: (616) 784-0583
Sales: $11,000,000
Company Type: Private
SIC: 0181
   Greenhouse floral products
Dick Foy, President

Employees: 110
Employees here: 110

D-U-N-S 06-138-1174
GLASSCOCK COUNTY COOP
300 Cr Coop, Garden City, TX 79739
Phone: (915) 397-2211
Sales: $10,992,000
Company Type: Private
SIC: 0724
   Cotton ginning services whol farm supplies
Ernest Smith, President

Employees: 15
Employees here: 15

D-U-N-S 10-301-9139
GLENN WALTERS NURSERY INC
7375 NW Roy Rd, Cornelius, OR 97113
Phone: (503) 693-1125
Sales: $20,000,000
Company Type: Private
SIC: 0181
   Grows nursery stock
Harry C Erwin Ii, President

Employees: 300
Employees here: 22

D-U-N-S 04-474-6220
GLENWOOD FOODS LLC
20850 Jackson Ln, Jetersville, VA 23083
Phone: (804) 561-3447
Sales: $10,449,000
Company Type: Private
SIC: 0252
   Egg farm
H G Esbenshade, Owner

Employees: 75
Employees here: 75

D-U-N-S 87-621-8819
GOLD COAST PISTACHIO'S INC
1326 W Herndon Ave, Fresno, CA 93711
Phone: (559) 432-7246

Sales: $12,065,000
Company Type: Private
SIC: 0173
    Tree nut grove
Weston Fuselier, Evp

Employees: 33
Employees here: 7

D-U-N-S 92-617-3774
GOLD COST PISTACHIOS INC
39840 S El Dorado Ave, Coalinga, CA 93210
Phone: (559) 934-1053
Sales: $25,000,000
Company Type: Private
SIC: 0173
    Pistachio processor
Yohan V Berg, President

Employees: 50
Employees here: 50

D-U-N-S 00-327-3554
GOLD KIST INC
244 Perimeter Center Pkwy, Atlanta, GA 30346
Phone: (770) 393-5000
Sales: $1,651,115,000
Company Type: Private
SIC: 0254
    Poultry and pork processing
William Evans, President

Employees: 16,500
Employees here: 400

D-U-N-S 17-677-7845
GOLD STAR MUSHROOM CO
670 Clauss Rd, Lenhartsville, PA 19534
Phone: (610) 562-5200
Sales: $10,000,000
Company Type: Private
SIC: 0182
    Covered food crops farm
James E Evans Jr, Chairman of the Board

Employees: 50
Employees here: 50

D-U-N-S 01-970-3677   EXP
GOLD STAR WHOLESALE NURSERY
1265 Mass Ave, Lexington, MA
Phone: (781) 861-1111
Sales: $14,000,000
Company Type: Private
SIC: 0181
    Grower whol & retials nursery stock
Everett Ashurst, Owner

Employees: 40
Employees here: 25

D-U-N-S 07-094-6132
GOLDEN ACRES FARMS
87770 Avenue 62, Thermal, CA 92274
Phone: (760) 399-5666
Sales: $20,806,000
Company Type: Private
SIC: 0161
    Vegetable farm
Mark Collins, Chairman of the Board

Employees: 20
Employees here: 20

D-U-N-S 87-718-0984
GOLDEN MERGER CORP
    (Parent: Veterinary Centers Of America)
3420 Ocean Park Blvd, Santa Monica, CA 90405
Phone: (310) 392-9599
Sales: $31,100,000
Company Type: Public Family Member
SIC: 0742
    Holding company for veterinary care hospitals & clinics
Peter J Smith, President

Employees: 830
Employees here: 80

D-U-N-S 00-440-1360
GOLDEN ROD BROILERS INC
85 13th St NE, Cullman, AL 35055
Phone: (256) 734-0941

Sales: $50,500,000
Company Type: Private
SIC: 0251
    Poultry farm
Thomas E Mikulastik, President

Employees: 1,010
Employees here: 500

D-U-N-S 96-260-9442
GOLDEN VALLEY PRODUCE LLC
4343 Golden Valley Dr, Buttonwillow, CA 93206
Phone: (661) 587-9445
Sales: $24,200,000
Company Type: Private
SIC: 0723
    Vegetable packing services
Mike Pike, President

Employees: 350
Employees here: 350

D-U-N-S 12-027-3693
GOLDEN WEST NUTS INC
1555 Warren Rd, Ripon, CA 95366
Phone: (209) 599-6193
Sales: $33,591,000
Company Type: Private
SIC: 0723
    Almond processing & farming
Berne H Evans Iii, President

Employees: 40
Employees here: 38

D-U-N-S 09-347-8618
GOSCHIE FARMS INC
7365 Meridian Rd NE, Silverton, OR 97381
Phone: (503) 873-5638
Sales: $250,000,000
Company Type: Private
SIC: 0139
    Farm hops grain hay & seed farm
Salvatore Pipitone Jr, President

Employees: 9
Employees here: 9

D-U-N-S 10-249-1107
GOSSETT'S INC
118 S Maddox Ave, Dumas, TX 79029
Phone: (806) 935-4266
Sales: $15,000,000
Company Type: Private
SIC: 0212
    Beef cattle-except feedlot
Francisco F Gonsalez, Owner

Employees: 10
Employees here: 10

D-U-N-S 07-803-1010
GOTTSCH FEEDING CORP
1015 N 204th Ave, Elkhorn, NE 68022
Phone: (402) 289-4421
Sales: $315,848,000
Company Type: Private
SIC: 0211
    Beef cattle feedlot
John Fairleigh, President

Employees: 56
Employees here: 7

D-U-N-S 16-135-6217
GRAND MESA EGGS, INC
1133 21 Rd, Grand Junction, CO 81505
Phone: (970) 858-7556
Sales: $10,132,000
Company Type: Private
SIC: 0252
    Chicken eggs & started pullet farm
William Lipman, President

Employees: 50
Employees here: 42

D-U-N-S 04-249-1688
GREAT AMERICAN FARMS INC
1287 W Atlantic Blvd, Pompano Beach, FL 33069
Phone: (954) 785-9400

Sales: $30,000,000   *Employees:* 15
Company Type: Private   *Employees here:* 15
SIC: 0191
    Agricultural production and marketing of agricultural
      products
Stanley Shamoom, President

    D-U-N-S 05-810-2831
GREAT BEND FEEDING INC
5 Miles NW on Hwy 96, Great Bend, KS 67530
Phone: (316) 792-2508
Sales: $16,143,000   *Employees:* 33
Company Type: Private   *Employees here:* 33
SIC: 0212
    Cattle feedlot
Richard S Walden, President

    D-U-N-S 02-114-4985
GREAT LAKES PACKERS INC
400 Great Lakes Pkwy, Bellevue, OH 44811
Phone: (419) 483-2956
Sales: $12,500,000   *Employees:* 60
Company Type: Private   *Employees here:* 60
SIC: 0723
    Vegetable & fruit packing service
Ben Goolsby, President

    D-U-N-S 06-203-6884
GREENHEART FARMS INC
902 Zenon Way, Arroyo Grande, CA 93420
Phone: (805) 481-2234
Sales: $12,200,000   *Employees:* 350
Company Type: Private   *Employees here:* 350
SIC: 0182
    Vegetable crops grown under cover
Bob Brocchini, President

    D-U-N-S 03-299-2778
GREENLEAF NURSERY CO
Hwy 82 S, Park Hill, OK 74451
Phone: (918) 457-5172
Sales: $45,183,000   *Employees:* 1,200
Company Type: Private   *Employees here:* 600
SIC: 0181
    Nursery stock growers
Christophe B Asplundh, President

    D-U-N-S 00-408-7284
GRIFFIN, BEN HILL INC
700 Scenic Hwy, Frostproof, FL 33843
Phone: (941) 635-2251
Sales: $61,328,000   *Employees:* 130
Company Type: Private   *Employees here:* 40
SIC: 0174
    Citrus fruit grower & packer fertilizer mixing cattle ranch &
      country club
A P Henderson, President

    D-U-N-S 03-214-3505
GRIFFIN-HOLDER CO
20445 US Hwy 50, Rocky Ford, CO 81067
Phone: (719) 254-3363
Sales: $15,097,000   *Employees:* 300
Company Type: Private   *Employees here:* 200
SIC: 0161
    Onion farm
Joe Howe, President

    D-U-N-S 05-550-7677
GRIFFIN LAND & NURSERIES, INC
1 Rckerfeller Plz 2301, New York, NY 10020
Phone: (212) 218-7910

Sales: $46,288,000   *Employees:* 259
Company Type: Public   *Employees here:* 5
SIC: 0181
    Plant nurseries & whol garden centers real estate developers
      & managers of commercial & industrial buildings
Richard Fassio, President

    D-U-N-S 08-144-5801
GRIFFIN PRODUCE CO INC
1129 Harkins Rd, Salinas, CA 93901
Phone: (831) 757-3033
Sales: $50,807,000   *Employees:* 25
Company Type: Private   *Employees here:* 17
SIC: 0723
    Grower packer & shipper of fresh vegetables
Sumio Kawanabe, President

    D-U-N-S 03-356-0509   EXP
GRIMMWAY ENTERPRISES INC
14141 Di Giorgio Rd, Di Giorgio, CA 93203
Phone: (661) 854-6201
Sales: $280,000,000   *Employees:* 3,000
Company Type: Private   *Employees here:* 35
SIC: 0723
    Carrot packing plant
James Schieferle, President

    D-U-N-S 19-936-2393
GROWERS VEGETABLE EXPRESS
1219 Abbott St, Salinas, CA 93901
Phone: (831) 757-9700
Sales: $143,907,000   *Employees:* 342
Company Type: Private   *Employees here:* 342
SIC: 0161
    Vegetable grower & packing service
Dana B Fisher Sr, President

    D-U-N-S 03-744-6754
GTC-GTC LTD
14574 Weld County Road 64, Greeley, CO 80631
Phone: (970) 351-6000
Sales: $12,000,000   *Employees:* 25
Company Type: Private   *Employees here:* 25
SIC: 0723
    Bean processing
Joseph J Colace Jr, President

    D-U-N-S 08-244-7319
GUIDE DOGS FOR THE BLIND INC
350 Los Ranchitos Rd, San Rafael, CA 94903
Phone: (415) 499-4000
Sales: $50,459,000   *Employees:* 250
Company Type: Private   *Employees here:* 150
SIC: 0752
    Raises and trains guide dogs and trains the individuals that
      utilize the dogs
George Hofer, President

    D-U-N-S 80-900-0508
GULFSTREAM TOMATO GROWERS LTD
21150 SW 167th Ave, Miami, FL 33187
Phone: (305) 235-4161
Sales: $21,100,000   *Employees:* 300
Company Type: Private   *Employees here:* 300
SIC: 0723
    Crop preparation for market vegetable/melon farm
Anthony Johnston, President

    D-U-N-S 00-406-1289
GUSTAFSON'S DAIRY INC
4169 County Road 15a, Green Cove Springs, FL 32043
Phone: (904) 284-3750

Sales: $21,700,000   *Employees:* 325
Company Type: Private   *Employees here:* 210
SIC: 0241
    Dairy farm
Alfonso Fanjul Jr, Chairman of the Board

D-U-N-S 01-842-4978
HAIDA CORP
8th Street Ext, Hydaburg, AK 99922
Phone: (907) 285-3721
Sales: $13,531,000   *Employees:* 10
Company Type: Private   *Employees here:* 7
SIC: 0811
    Timber tract
Bruce Daniel, Chief Financial Officer

D-U-N-S 00-692-1209
HAINES CY CITRUS GROWERS ASSN
8 Railroad Ave, Haines City, FL 33844
Phone: (941) 422-1174
Sales: $14,927,000   *Employees:* 200
Company Type: Private   *Employees here:* 200
SIC: 0723
    Citrus fruit packing house
Xavier Gardinier, Chairman of the Board

D-U-N-S 02-712-4762
HAMILTON COUNTY DAIRY, L.L.C.
P.O. Box 13, Syracuse, KS 67878
Phone: (316) 376-2053
Sales: $13,000,000   *Employees:* 30
Company Type: Private   *Employees here:* 30
SIC: 0241

Donald T Bennink, Manager

D-U-N-S 82-489-3549
HANOR CO INC
E4614 Hwy 14 60, Spring Green, WI 53588
Phone: (608) 588-9170
Sales: $13,100,000   *Employees:* 213
Company Type: Private   *Employees here:* 11
SIC: 0291
    General animal farm
James Joiner, President

D-U-N-S 80-541-2624
HANSEN RANCHES
7124 Whitley Ave, Corcoran, CA 93212
Phone: (559) 992-3111
Sales: $15,000,000   *Employees:* 8
Company Type: Private   *Employees here:* 8
SIC: 0191
    General farm
Gregory L Smith Sr, President

D-U-N-S 00-918-5880
HANSFORD COUNTY FEEDERS LP
10 Miles NE of Gruver, Gruver, TX 79040
Phone: (806) 733-5025
Sales: $15,000,000   *Employees:* 3
Company Type: Private   *Employees here:* 3
SIC: 0211
    Cattle feedlot
Eleanor A Harmon, President

D-U-N-S 00-699-1475
HANSON NORTH AMERICA
581 Main St, Woodbridge, NJ
Phone: (732) 919-9777

Sales: $140,800,000   *Employees:* 3,000
Company Type: Private   *Employees here:* 3,000
SIC: 0811
    Timber tract operation sawmill/planing mill crude
    petroleum/natural gas production
George Herrmann, President

D-U-N-S 01-641-2512
HARLAN SPRAGUE DAWLEY INC
298 S County Line Rd, Indianapolis, IN 46229
Phone: (317) 894-7521
Sales: $40,500,000   *Employees:* 1,350
Company Type: Private   *Employees here:* 185
SIC: 0279
    Laboratory animal production
George Herrmann, Principal

D-U-N-S 04-710-8493
HARLLEE PACKING, INC
2308 US Hwy 301, Palmetto, FL 34221
Phone: (941) 722-7747
Sales: $10,000,000   *Employees:* 15
Company Type: Private   *Employees here:* 15
SIC: 0723
    Tomato packing house
William R Johnston, President

D-U-N-S 83-308-9725
HARLOFF PACKING OF EAST TENN
5424 Enka Hwy, Morristown, TN 37813
Phone: (423) 581-3312
Sales: $21,100,000   *Employees:* 300
Company Type: Private   *Employees here:* 300
SIC: 0723
    Vegetable packing
Louis Turp, President

D-U-N-S 00-690-9634
HARRIS MORAN SEED CO
555 Codoni Ave, Modesto, CA 95357
Phone: (209) 579-7333
Sales: $38,600,000   *Employees:* 275
Company Type: Private   *Employees here:* 120
SIC: 0181
    Grower of vegetable seeds
Tom Foster, Vice-President

D-U-N-S 60-995-2585
HARRIS WOOLF CAL ALMONDS
26060 Fresno Coalinga Rd, Coalinga, CA 93210
Phone: (559) 884-2435
Sales: $266,164,000   *Employees:* 24
Company Type: Private   *Employees here:* 24
SIC: 0723
    Almond preparation service including hulling & shelling
Bob Fox, President

D-U-N-S 00-329-2281
HARRISON POULTRY INC
Star St, Bethlehem, GA 30620
Phone: (770) 867-7511
Sales: $29,700,000   *Employees:* 555
Company Type: Private   *Employees here:* 550
SIC: 0254
    Operates hatchery poultry processor and ret propane gas
James Marcus, Chairman of the Board

D-U-N-S 06-043-8439
HARTUNG BROTHERS INC
6813 Helena Rd, Arena, WI 53503
Phone: (608) 588-2536

Sales: $37,363,000   *Employees:* 85
Company Type: Private   *Employees here:* 35
SIC: 0161
     Vegetable production seed corn production & whol fertilizer
Ramon G Del Real, President

D-U-N-S 08-311-3993
HARVEY BROTHERS FARM INC
900 Logan Blvd N, Naples, FL 34119
Phone: (941) 597-5692
Sales: $11,560,000   *Employees:* 30
Company Type: Private   *Employees here:* 30
SIC: 0161
     Pepper tomato & potato farm
Dennis Parnagian, President

D-U-N-S 07-290-7421
HASTINGS PORK CORP
Hastings Industrial Park, Hastings, NE 68901
Phone: (402) 463-0551
Sales: $12,000,000   *Employees:* 152
Company Type: Private   *Employees here:* 150
SIC: 0213
     Hog feeding
William C Foxley, President

D-U-N-S 62-795-6543
HAWAIIAN SWEET, INC.
Milo St, Keaau, HI 96749
Phone: (808) 966-7435
Sales: $12,000,000   *Employees:* 90
Company Type: Private   *Employees here:* 90
SIC: 0723
     Fresh papaya & guava fruit packing and sorting and
     packaging papaya puree
Frank Pinney, Owner

D-U-N-S 60-433-5968
HAYES FEED YARD INC
RR 1 Box 189, Silver Creek, NE 68663
Phone: (402) 747-2069
Sales: $10,000,000   *Employees:* 6
Company Type: Private   *Employees here:* 6
SIC: 0211
     Beef cattle feedlot
Wilhelm Meya, President

D-U-N-S 11-875-2971
HAZELNUT GROWERS OF OREGON
401 N 26th Ave, Cornelius, OR 97113
Phone: (503) 648-4176
Sales: $31,620,000   *Employees:* 47
Company Type: Private   *Employees here:* 40
SIC: 0723
     Process filberts
Ray Franscioni, President

D-U-N-S 17-758-8159
HEALDS VALLEY FARMS INC
6715 W Monte Cristo St, Edinburg, TX 78539
Phone: (956) 380-0102
Sales: $15,665,000   *Employees:* 250
Company Type: Private   *Employees here:* 125
SIC: 0174
     Citrus fruit grove crops-planting/protecting
Fred J Jaindl, Owner

D-U-N-S 80-230-5334
HEARTLAND FARMS INC
907 3rd Ave, Hancock, WI 54943
Phone: (715) 249-5555

Sales: $16,004,000   *Employees:* 70
Company Type: Private   *Employees here:* 70
SIC: 0161
     Irrigated vegetable farm including potato peas beans and
     sweet corn
Fred Voge, Owner

D-U-N-S 05-769-2600
HELLER BROS PACKING CORP
288 9th St, Winter Garden, FL 34787
Phone: (407) 656-2124
Sales: $76,366,000   *Employees:* 50
Company Type: Private   *Employees here:* 50
SIC: 0174
     Citrus & tomato growers packers & shippers
Mark Drever, President

D-U-N-S 02-814-0234
HENRY AVOCADO PACKING CORP
2355 E Lincoln Ave, Escondido, CA 92027
Phone: (760) 745-6632
Sales: $41,378,000   *Employees:* 70
Company Type: Private   *Employees here:* 70
SIC: 0179
     Avocado growers & shipping
Steve Taylor, Chairman of the Board

D-U-N-S 00-110-4629
HERBERT C HAYNES INC
RR 2, Winn, ME
Phone: (207) 736-3412
Sales: $87,982,000   *Employees:* 100
Company Type: Private   *Employees here:* 99
SIC: 0241
     Mfg pulpwood & wood chips & logging contractor
Steve Church, President

D-U-N-S 05-696-8258
HERMANN ENGELMANN GREENHOUSES
2009 Marden Rd, Apopka, FL 32703
Phone: (407) 886-3434
Sales: $32,800,000   *Employees:* 740
Company Type: Private   *Employees here:* 215
SIC: 0181
     Grows indoor foliage
Stan Gossett, Principal

D-U-N-S 02-599-3536
HERNDON MARINE PRODUCTS INC
322 Huff St, Aransas Pass, TX 78336
Phone: (361) 758-5373
Sales: $95,000,000   *Employees:* 32
Company Type: Private   *Employees here:* 8
SIC: 0913
     Shrimp producer & whol fresh shrimp operates freezers for
     storage brokers shrimp drydock facility mfg & whol ice &
     whol fuel
Ehud Peikes, President

D-U-N-S 17-582-3285
HERRERA PACKING INC
2105 Sinton Rd, Santa Maria, CA 93458
Phone: (805) 349-2237
Sales: $13,000,000   *Employees:* 400
Company Type: Private   *Employees here:* 400
SIC: 0723
     Vegetable packing service
Tom Stallings, President

D-U-N-S 05-789-0675
HI-LO OIL CO, INC
534 S Kansas Ave, Topeka, KS 66603
Phone: (785) 357-6161

Sales: $31,157,000   *Employees:* 3
Company Type: Private   *Employees here:* 3
SIC: 0212
    Cattle ranch
Michael Gallo, General Partner

D-U-N-S 03-586-4263
HICKMAN'S EGG RANCH, INC.
7403 N 91st Ave, Glendale, AZ 85305
Phone: (602) 872-1120
Sales: $34,000,000   *Employees:* 100
Company Type: Private   *Employees here:* 100
SIC: 0252
    Chicken egg farm whol chicken feed & ret eggs
Corrie Fuquay, President

D-U-N-S 83-469-7419
HIGHLAND LIGHT, INC
3600 15th Ave W, Ste 300, Seattle, WA 98119
Phone: (206) 216-0220
Sales: $15,135,000   *Employees:* 100
Company Type: Private   *Employees here:* 100
SIC: 0912
    Fishing vessel
W L Brooks, President

D-U-N-S 05-733-0391
HIJI BROS., INC.
750 Pacific Ave, Oxnard, CA 93030
Phone: (805) 487-0673
Sales: $16,200,000   *Employees:* 175
Company Type: Private   *Employees here:* 6
SIC: 0161
    Vegetable farm
Raymond Hensgens, President

D-U-N-S 09-270-8254
HILLANDALE FARMS INC
US Hwy 41n, Lake City, FL 32055
Phone: (904) 755-1870
Sales: $79,979,000   *Employees:* 268
Company Type: Private   *Employees here:* 16
SIC: 0252
    Chicken egg farm
Paul E Gibson, Owner

D-U-N-S 06-190-7473
HILLANDALE FARMS OF FLORIDA INC
US Hwy 41 N, Lake City, FL 32055
Phone: (904) 755-1870
Sales: $37,701,000   *Employees:* 300
Company Type: Private   *Employees here:* 40
SIC: 0252
    Chicken egg farm
Harold Utter, President

D-U-N-S 09-805-9942
HILLIARD BROTHERS OF FLORIDA,
Flaghole Rd, Clewiston, FL 33440
Phone: (941) 983-5111
Sales: $13,098,000   *Employees:* 70
Company Type: Private   *Employees here:* 70
SIC: 0212
    Cattle ranch sugarcane farm and citrus grove
Richard Crandall Jr, President

D-U-N-S 18-504-4351
HILLTOWN PACKING CO
9 Harris Pl A, Salinas, CA 93901
Phone: (831) 784-1931

Sales: $13,500,000   *Employees:* 300
Company Type: Private   *Employees here:* 300
SIC: 0723
    Vegetable packing service
William Maxwell, President

D-U-N-S 61-925-0665   EXP
HINES HORTICULTURE INC
12621 Jeffrey Rd, Irvine, CA 92620
Phone: (949) 559-4444
Sales: $53,100,000   *Employees:* 1,200
Company Type: Public   *Employees here:* 500
SIC: 0181
    Grower & wholesaler of nursery stock
Enrique Garcia, President

D-U-N-S 00-260-8391
HINES II INC
    (Parent: Hines Horticulture Inc)
12621 Jeffrey Rd, Irvine, CA 92620
Phone: (949) 559-4444
Sales: $17,800,000   *Employees:* 400
Company Type: Public Family Member   *Employees here:* 3
SIC: 0181
    Grower of nursery stock
Odess Lovin, Treasurer

D-U-N-S 07-427-1248
HITCH FEEDERS I INC
    (Parent: Hitch Enterprises Inc)
309 Northridge Cir, Guymon, OK 73942
Phone: (580) 338-8575
Sales: $35,700,000   *Employees:* 200
Company Type: Private   *Employees here:* 25
SIC: 0211
    Beef cattle feedlot
Andrew K Haynes, President

D-U-N-S 05-308-0990
HITCH FEEDERS II, INC
    (Parent: Hitch Enterprises Inc)
20 Mi S & 8 Mi W, Garden City, KS 67846
Phone: (316) 275-6181
Sales: $26,861,000   *Employees:* 50
Company Type: Private   *Employees here:* 50
SIC: 0211
    Cattle feedlot
Alvern Gardner, President

D-U-N-S 02-933-0792
HOLLANDIA DAIRY
622 E Mission Rd, San Marcos, CA 92069
Phone: (760) 744-3222
Sales: $36,000,000   *Employees:* 200
Company Type: Private   *Employees here:* 200
SIC: 0241
    Dairy farm
Christian Leleu, President

D-U-N-S 06-204-0902
HOMA CO
60 E Halsey Rd, Parsippany, NJ
Phone: (973) 887-6500
Sales: $46,356,000   *Employees:* 120
Company Type: Private   *Employees here:* 45
SIC: 0173
    Grows processes wholesales and imports dried nuts and fruits
Christian Leleu, Chairman of the Board

D-U-N-S 04-892-6240
HONDO CO (INC)
410 E College Blvd, Roswell, NM 88201
Phone: (505) 622-3140

Sales: $23,900,000   *Employees:* 478
Company Type: Private   *Employees here:* 80
SIC: 0212
   Beef cattle-except feedlot
Ernest Smith, President

   D-U-N-S 07-708-7328
HOPE LAND FARM
101 E Street Rd, Kennett Square, PA 19348
Phone: (610) 444-3300
Sales: $11,000,000   *Employees:* 170
Company Type: Private   *Employees here:* 170
SIC: 0241
   Dairy farm
John Layous, Partner

   D-U-N-S 14-472-6775
HORNBECK SEED CO INC
210 Drier Rd, De Witt, AR 72042
Phone: (870) 946-2087
Sales: $12,000,000   *Employees:* 30
Company Type: Private   *Employees here:* 30
SIC: 0723
   Mfg seed
Will Garroutte Sr, President

   D-U-N-S 62-393-6788
HORTICULTURAL FARMS INC
Hwy 111 Calvary Rd, Cairo, GA 31728
Phone: (912) 377-3033
Sales: $28,500,000   *Employees:* 650
Company Type: Private   *Employees here:* 66
SIC: 0181
   Growing of shrubberies
Gary T Raak, President

   D-U-N-S 00-142-6063   EXP
HUBBARD FARMS INC
   (Parent: Merck & Co Inc)
Turnpike Rd, Walpole, NH
Phone: (603) 756-3311
Sales: $37,500,000   *Employees:* 700
Company Type: Public Family Member   *Employees here:* 160
SIC: 0254
   Poultry hatchery specializing as a primary poultry breeding
     stock
Kevin Gates, President

   D-U-N-S 05-706-1806
HUDSON FOODS INC
   (Parent: Tyson Foods Inc)
2210 W Oaklawn Dr, Springdale, AR 72762
Phone: (501) 290-4000
Sales: $833,300,000   *Employees:* 10,000
Company Type: Public Family Member   *Employees here:* 12
SIC: 0252
   Chicken eggs, nsk
Warren S Robinson, Chairman of the Board

   D-U-N-S 18-527-8041
HUERTA PACKING INC
425 W 8th St, Yuma, AZ 85364
Phone: (520) 783-2891
Sales: $13,087,000   *Employees:* 25
Company Type: Private   *Employees here:* 25
SIC: 0161
   Crop growing and packing
Peter Jansen, President

   D-U-N-S 14-471-9523
HUGHSON NUT INC
1825 Verduga Rd, Hughson, CA 95326
Phone: (209) 883-0403

Sales: $15,000,000   *Employees:* 30
Company Type: Private   *Employees here:* 30
SIC: 0722
   Processes almonds
David J Mintjal, President

   D-U-N-S 03-242-6454
HUNT BROTHERS COOPERATIVE INC
Hunt Brothers Rd Se, Lake Wales, FL 33853
Phone: (941) 676-9471
Sales: $10,100,000   *Employees:* 150
Company Type: Private   *Employees here:* 150
SIC: 0723
   Citrus crop preparation service
Bruce Bean, Chief Operating Officer

   D-U-N-S 79-312-3795
HUNTCO FARMS, INC
   (Parent: Huntco Inc)
14323 S Outer 40 600, Chesterfield, MO 63017
Phone: (314) 878-0155
Sales: $55,800,000   *Employees:* 600
Company Type: Public Family Member   *Employees here:* 5
SIC: 0213
   Holding company
Wesley M Gentry Jr, President

   D-U-N-S 09-310-0238   EXP
HY-LINE INTERNATIONAL
2929 Westown Pkwy, Ste 101, West Des Moines, IA 50266
Phone: (515) 225-6030
Sales: $70,089,000   *Employees:* 320
Company Type: Private   *Employees here:* 17
SIC: 0254
   Poultry hatchery
George Amaral, President

   D-U-N-S 02-789-4823
ILLY'S SUNNY SLOPE FARM'S INC
9845 Nancy Ave, Beaumont, CA 92223
Phone: (909) 845-1131
Sales: $14,000,000   *Employees:* 30
Company Type: Private   *Employees here:* 30
SIC: 0252
   Egg ranch
Ronnie Smith, President

   D-U-N-S 80-903-5702
IMPERIAL NURSERIES, INC
   (Parent: Griffin Land & Nurseries Inc)
90 Salmon Brook St, Granby, CT
Phone: (860) 653-4541
Sales: $42,000,000   *Employees:* 259
Company Type: Public Family Member   *Employees here:* 25
SIC: 0181
   Grows & whol nursery stock
Daniel J Gerawan, President

   D-U-N-S 02-834-9678
INDEX MUTUAL ASSOCIATION
18184 Slover Ave, Bloomington, CA 92316
Phone: (909) 877-1577
Sales: $14,277,000   *Employees:* 29
Company Type: Private   *Employees here:* 27
SIC: 0723
   Packer & shipper of avocados
Raymond M Gerawan, Owner

   D-U-N-S 03-282-2009
INDIAN RIVER EXCHANGE PACKERS
7355 9th St Sw, Vero Beach, FL 32968
Phone: (561) 562-2252

Sales: $10,858,000   *Employees:* 150
Company Type: Private   *Employees here:* 10
SIC: 0723
  Citrus packing
Terry Gerrald, President

D-U-N-S 02-757-3336
INLAND FRUIT & PRODUCE CO
Frontage Rd, Wapato, WA 98951
Phone: (509) 877-2126
Sales: $13,560,000   *Employees:* 210
Company Type: Private   *Employees here:* 210
SIC: 0723
  Fruit packing & cold storage
R T Gilder Jr, President

D-U-N-S 80-467-0255
IOWA SELECT FARMS
811 S Oak St, Iowa Falls, IA 50126
Phone: (515) 648-4479
Sales: $150,000,000   *Employees:* 700
Company Type: Private   *Employees here:* 697
SIC: 0213
  Hog feedlot
R K Gildersleeve, President

D-U-N-S 00-407-3078
ISE AMERICA INC
33335 Galena Sassafras Rd, Golts, MD 21635
Phone: (410) 755-6300
Sales: $33,900,000   *Employees:* 407
Company Type: Private   *Employees here:* 12
SIC: 0252
  Producer of chicken eggs
David Carroll, President

D-U-N-S 06-592-5554
IVY ACRES INC
1675 Edwards Ave, Calverton, NY 11933
Phone: (516) 727-1980
Sales: $10,249,000   *Employees:* 45
Company Type: Private   *Employees here:* 45
SIC: 0181
  Whol bedding plants
Craig Giroux, President

D-U-N-S 06-914-9920
J & C ENTERPRISES INC
1221 N Venetian Way, Miami, FL 33139
Phone: (305) 856-4230
Sales: $22,755,000   *Employees:* 35
Company Type: Private   *Employees here:* 3
SIC: 0139
  Potato farm & tropical fruit farm
Salvadore Giumarra, President

D-U-N-S 13-024-1003
J & K FARMS INC
791 Wallace Hwy, Harrells, NC 28444
Phone: (910) 532-4729
Sales: $12,400,000   *Employees:* 150
Company Type: Private   *Employees here:* 150
SIC: 0213
  Hog farm
Erik Breivik, Operations-Production-Mfg

D-U-N-S 05-527-8154
J E ESTES WOOD CO INC
101 N Mount Pleasant Ave, Monroeville, AL 36460
Phone: (334) 575-2444

Sales: $12,485,000   *Employees:* 7
Company Type: Private   *Employees here:* 7
SIC: 0241
  Timber dealer
Richard Mast, President

D-U-N-S 05-108-0653
J F C INC
4150 2nd St S, St. Cloud, MN 56301
Phone: (320) 251-3570
Sales: $190,000,000   *Employees:* 1,800
Company Type: Private   *Employees here:* 100
SIC: 0251
  Raises & processes broiler chickens
B J Haulak, General Manager

D-U-N-S 00-823-7505
J G BOSWELL CO
101 W Walnut St, Pasadena, CA 91103
Phone: (626) 583-3000
Sales: $150,000,000   *Employees:* 2,000
Company Type: Private   *Employees here:* 40
SIC: 0131
  Cotton farming & commercial and residential developer
Glenn Walters, President

D-U-N-S 00-318-0080
J H MILES CO INC
Ft of Southampton Ave, Norfolk, VA 23510
Phone: (757) 622-9264
Sales: $12,687,000   *Employees:* 50
Company Type: Private   *Employees here:* 50
SIC: 0913
  Commercial fishing oysters & clams shucks & packs clams
Ronald S Braswell Jr, President

D-U-N-S 09-831-4099
J-M FARMS INC
7001 S 580 Rd, Miami, OK 74354
Phone: (918) 540-1567
Sales: $12,800,000   *Employees:* 320
Company Type: Private   *Employees here:* 320
SIC: 0182
  Grows mushrooms
Herman Goschie, President

D-U-N-S 78-643-4928
J-V FARMS, INC.
3111 E Gila Ridge Rd, Yuma, AZ 85365
Phone: (520) 726-5061
Sales: $20,317,000   *Employees:* 200
Company Type: Private   *Employees here:* 50
SIC: 0161
  General farm
James M Zanger, President

D-U-N-S 02-301-6462
JACK FROST INC
  (Parent: J F C Inc)
4150 2nd St S, St. Cloud, MN 56301
Phone: (320) 251-3570
Sales: $40,000,000   *Employees:* 250
Company Type: Private   *Employees here:* 65
SIC: 0251
  Raises broiler chickens
Wayne Cook, President

D-U-N-S 03-783-0387
JACK M BERRY INC
3655 State Road 80, Alva, FL 33920
Phone: (941) 675-2769

Sales: $10,400,000   *Employees:* 200
Company Type: Private   *Employees here:* 50
SIC: 0762
    Citrus grove caretaking & citrus grove owner
Odes Thompson, President

D-U-N-S 36-174-7041
JACK NEAL & SON INC
360 Lafata St, St. Helena, CA 94574
Phone: (707) 963-7303
Sales: $14,000,000   *Employees:* 150
Company Type: Private   *Employees here:* 150
SIC: 0172
    Vineyard
Otis Thompson, President

D-U-N-S 02-356-6045
JACK SPARROWK
18780 Hwy 88, Clements, CA 95227
Phone: (209) 759-3530
Sales: $12,000,000   *Employees:* 25
Company Type: Private   *Employees here:* 25
SIC: 0212
    Cattle ranch
Gaylord O Coan, Chairman

D-U-N-S 17-323-1788
JAMAR INDUSTRIES
7909 Edith Blvd NE, Albuquerque, NM 87113
Phone: (505) 898-9690
Sales: $12,100,000   *Employees:* 340
Company Type: Private   *Employees here:* 340
SIC: 0782
    Landscape contractor
Bernardo Penturelli, President

D-U-N-S 60-770-0259
JAMES ABBATE INC
4705 N Sonora Ave, Ste 104, Fresno, CA 93722
Phone: (559) 277-2200
Sales: $16,000,000   *Employees:* 5
Company Type: Private   *Employees here:* 5
SIC: 0723
    Fresh fruit packing & whol fresh fruit
Greg Georgaklis, President

D-U-N-S 11-937-9519
JAMES T SMITH
1260 W Wapato Rd, Wapato, WA 98951
Phone: (509) 877-3437
Sales: $11,000,000   *Employees:* 200
Company Type: Private   *Employees here:* 200
SIC: 0175
    Fruit farm
Joe Kitagawa, President

D-U-N-S 01-532-0328
JCM FARMING INC
9303 W Airport Dr, Visalia, CA 93277
Phone: (559) 651-1600
Sales: $10,000,000   *Employees:* 20
Company Type: Private   *Employees here:* 20
SIC: 0172
    Grapes almonds & citrus fruits
Robert Antin, President

D-U-N-S 05-051-2730
JENSEN CORP LANDSCAPE CONTRACTORS
10950 N Blaney Ave, Cupertino, CA 95014
Phone: (408) 446-1118

Sales: $12,000,000   *Employees:* 40
Company Type: Private   *Employees here:* 40
SIC: 0782
    Landscape contractors
Forrest H Ingram, President

D-U-N-S 07-359-7817
JESSE F MINER
630 W 7th St, San Jacinto, CA 92583
Phone: (909) 654-7311
Sales: $10,643,000   *Employees:* 7
Company Type: Private   *Employees here:* 7
SIC: 0212
    Beef cattle-except feedlot irish potato farm
Jacob Wipf, President

D-U-N-S 08-378-0304
JIM HRONIS & SONS RANCH
32555 Cecil Ave, Delano, CA 93215
Phone: (661) 725-2503
Sales: $17,000,000   *Employees:* 20
Company Type: Private   *Employees here:* 20
SIC: 0172
    Farming of table grapes citrus & alfalfa
Randy Clark, Member

D-U-N-S 05-205-4541
JJR INC
    (Parent: Smith Group Inc)
110 Miller Ave, Ann Arbor, MI 48104
Phone: (734) 662-4457
Sales: $11,012,000   *Employees:* 100
Company Type: Private   *Employees here:* 84
SIC: 0781
    Landscape architects & planners & environmental
      engineering
Jon Hoff, President

D-U-N-S 78-318-9343
JLG HARVESTING INC
495 El Camino Real, Ste K, Greenfield, CA 93927
Phone: (831) 674-0267
Sales: $40,000,000   *Employees:* 600
Company Type: Private   *Employees here:* 200
SIC: 0723
    Vegetable harvesting & packing
Kim Gorans, President

D-U-N-S 60-924-7218
JOE HEIDRICK ENTERPRISES INC
36826 County Road 24, Woodland, CA 95695
Phone: (530) 662-3046
Sales: $10,000,000   *Employees:* 40
Company Type: Private   *Employees here:* 40
SIC: 0111
    General farming including tomato sugar beets wheat
      sunflower alfalfa & corn
Byron Gossett, President

D-U-N-S 00-691-9823   EXP
JOHN I HAAS INC
1615 L St NW, Ste 510, Washington, DC 20036
Phone: (202) 223-0005
Sales: $15,800,000   *Employees:* 229
Company Type: Private   *Employees here:* 25
SIC: 0139
    Hops farm & whol hops
Robert Gottsch Sr, President

D-U-N-S 08-181-8627
JOHN KNEVELBAARD DAIRY
6485 Harrison Ave, Corona, CA 91720
Phone: (909) 983-1388

Sales: $10,000,000
Company Type: Private
SIC: 0241
    Dairy farm
Dr Charles Graham, Owner

Employees: 15
Employees here: 15

D-U-N-S 01-903-8678
JOHN LUCAS TREE EXPERT CO
636 Riverside St, Portland, ME
Phone: (207) 797-7294
Sales: $14,275,000
Company Type: Private
SIC: 0783
    Tree trimming service & telephone and powerline service
Peter Olson, Chairman of the Board

Employees: 350
Employees here: 100

D-U-N-S 62-032-7262
JOHN M FOSTER TURF FARMS
41255 Burr St, Indio, CA 92203
Phone: (760) 360-5464
Sales: $18,000,000
Company Type: Private
SIC: 0181
    Sod farm
Alan J Levy, President

Employees: 200
Employees here: 50

D-U-N-S 18-683-6912
JOHNSON FARMS
RR 1 Box 83, St. Francisville, IL 62460
Phone: (618) 948-2739
Sales: $100,000,000
Company Type: Private
SIC: 0191
    General crop farm corn farm soybean farm wheat farm
Kevin Heinen, President

Employees: 5
Employees here: 5

D-U-N-S 05-228-0294
JOHNSTON FARMS
13031 E Packinghouse Rd, Edison, CA 93220
Phone: (661) 366-3201
Sales: $10,000,000
Company Type: Private
SIC: 0174
    Grower & packer of oranges potatoes and bell peppers
Roger Murphy, President

Employees: 40
Employees here: 40

D-U-N-S 07-119-7321
JONES & ASSOCIATES INC
    (Parent: Hershey Creamery Co)
301 S Cameron St, Harrisburg, PA 17101
Phone: (717) 238-8134
Sales: $10,000,000
Company Type: Private
SIC: 0175
    Fruit tree orchard
Jerome Fritz, President

Employees: 160
Employees here: 4

D-U-N-S 04-395-6275
JOSEPH CAMPBELL CO
    (Parent: Campbell Investment Co)
Campbell Pl, Camden, NJ
Phone: (609) 342-4800
Sales: $123,800,000
Company Type: Public Family Member
SIC: 0161
    Processes ingredient spices & vegetables & mfg finished
      products
Thomas Doak, President

Employees: 1,446
Employees here: 9

D-U-N-S 95-786-4119
JUDSON INC
Hwy 114, Pennington, AL 36916
Phone: (205) 654-2707

Sales: $12,000,000
Company Type: Private
SIC: 0811
    Operates timber tracts
Bruce G Goren, Partner

Employees: 5
Employees here: 5

D-U-N-S 08-957-5617
JUNIATA FEED YARDS
4180 N Liberty Ave, Juniata, NE 68955
Phone: (402) 751-2215
Sales: $100,000,000
Company Type: Private
SIC: 0211
    Cattle feedlot
Hoy Buell, President

Employees: 40
Employees here: 40

D-U-N-S 16-086-2744
KALASHIAN PACKING CO INC
1850 S Parallel Ave, Fresno, CA 93702
Phone: (559) 237-3665
Sales: $10,000,000
Company Type: Private
SIC: 0723
    Dried fruit packing
Edgar M Cullman, Chairman of the Board

Employees: 62
Employees here: 62

D-U-N-S 04-454-1019   IMP EXP
KAOLIN MUSHROOM FARMS INC
649 W South St, Kennett Square, PA 19348
Phone: (610) 444-4800
Sales: $26,800,000
Company Type: Private
SIC: 0182
    Mushroom grower
Stephen Griffin, President

Employees: 670
Employees here: 470

D-U-N-S 02-897-2297
KAPRIELIAN BROS PACKING CO
1750 S Buttonwillow Ave, Reedley, CA 93654
Phone: (559) 638-9277
Sales: $14,300,000
Company Type: Private
SIC: 0723
    Fresh fruit packing
J H Holder, President

Employees: 200
Employees here: 200

D-U-N-S 02-932-7707
KARLESKINT-CRUM INC
225 Suburban Rd, San Luis Obispo, CA 93401
Phone: (805) 543-3304
Sales: $12,505,000
Company Type: Private
SIC: 0782
    Landscaping contractor
Ben H Griffin Iii, Chairman of the Board

Employees: 150
Employees here: 15

D-U-N-S 06-013-8252
KATICICH RANCH
9974 E Fairchild Rd, Stockton, CA 95215
Phone: (209) 931-2016
Sales: $14,200,000
Company Type: Private
SIC: 0175
    Fruit tree orchard
Bob Grimm, President

Employees: 250
Employees here: 250

D-U-N-S 19-848-5799
KEARNEY FERTILIZER INC
Camp Grounds Rd, Bonnie, IL 62816
Phone: (618) 242-7154

Sales: $10,000,000
Company Type: Private
SIC: 0711
   Soil preparation services
Mark S Yahn, President

Employees: 60
Employees here: 10

D-U-N-S 04-911-2071
KEARNY COUNTY FEEDERS INC
N Hwy 25, Lakin, KS 67860
Phone: (316) 355-6630
Sales: $10,000,000
Company Type: Private
SIC: 0211
   Cattle feedlot
Joseph A Rodriguez, President

Employees: 34
Employees here: 34

D-U-N-S 06-332-2978
KEEGAN INC
2570 Eldridge Ave, Twin Falls, ID 83301
Phone: (208) 733-5371
Sales: $12,000,000
Company Type: Private
SIC: 0723
   Produce packing
Ronald Frudden, Partner

Employees: 45
Employees here: 45

D-U-N-S 96-252-4385
KENNETH L MINK & SONS INC
3705 Joy Ln, Waldorf, MD 20603
Phone: (301) 645-4978
Sales: $28,000,000
Company Type: Private
SIC: 0271
   Leaseholder for floor covering departments for 60 macy's
    east department stores
Andy Orris, General Partner

Employees: 35
Employees here: 35

D-U-N-S 00-793-3492   EXP
KING RANCH INC
1415 La St, Ste 2300, Houston, TX 77002
Phone: (713) 752-5700
Sales: $54,700,000
Company Type: Private
SIC: 0212
   Cattle ranchers oil and gas producers newspaper publisher
    ret building materials whol agricultural implements
Richard Bobb, President

Employees: 1,094
Employees here: 45

D-U-N-S 15-634-7585
KINGFISH SEAFOOD INC
6059 W Hwy 98, Panama City, FL 32401
Phone: (850) 785-1103
Sales: $15,000,000
Company Type: Private
SIC: 0912
   Commercial fishing and whol seafood
Joseph E Hagan, Partner

Employees: 26
Employees here: 13

D-U-N-S 80-185-6691
KINGSBURG APPLE PACKERS
10363 Davis Ave, Kingsburg, CA 93631
Phone: (559) 897-5132
Sales: $22,000,000
Company Type: Private
SIC: 0723
   Crop preparation for market
Wally Gundrum, President

Employees: 20
Employees here: 20

D-U-N-S 04-681-3713
KIRSCHENMAN PACKING INC
12826 Edison Hwy, Edison, CA 93220
Phone: (661) 366-5736

Sales: $10,600,000
Company Type: Private
SIC: 0723
   Potato packers
Edwin S Gustafson, President

Employees: 120
Employees here: 120

D-U-N-S 11-816-5497
KITAYAMA BROTHERS INC
13239 Weld Cnty Road 4, Brighton, CO 80601
Phone: (303) 659-8000
Sales: $12,000,000
Company Type: Private
SIC: 0181
   Flower nurseries
Charles Skultka, Chairman of the Board

Employees: 307
Employees here: 125

D-U-N-S 60-795-1597
KLEIN FOODS INC
11455 Old Redwood Hwy, Healdsburg, CA 95448
Phone: (707) 433-6511
Sales: $53,682,000
Company Type: Private
SIC: 0172
   Vineyard & winery
Rod Hamrick, Treasurer

Employees: 250
Employees here: 100

D-U-N-S 02-833-2088
KLINK CITRUS ASSOCIATION
32921 Road 159, Ivanhoe, CA 93235
Phone: (559) 798-1881
Sales: $17,396,000
Company Type: Private
SIC: 0723
   Fresh fruit packing service
Brad Hall, President

Employees: 170
Employees here: 170

D-U-N-S 78-389-6467
KNIGHT MANAGEMENT, INC
205 SW 1st St, Belle Glade, FL 33430
Phone: (561) 996-6262
Sales: $15,000,000
Company Type: Private
SIC: 0133
   Sugar cane and sweet corn production
Dennis Rodenbaugh, Manager

Employees: 40
Employees here: 40

D-U-N-S 00-656-1625
KOEN FARMS INC
383 Hwy 174 N, Hope, AR 71801
Phone: (870) 777-4682
Sales: $18,668,000
Company Type: Private
SIC: 0212
   Chicken egg production
Norman Kranseder, President

Employees: 20
Employees here: 20

D-U-N-S 04-510-7125
KOFKOFF EGG FARM LLC
17 Schwartz Rd, Bozrah, CT
Phone: (860) 886-2445
Sales: $16,300,000
Company Type: Private
SIC: 0252
   Egg farm
James Hansen, General Manager

Employees: 175
Employees here: 115

D-U-N-S 01-352-2008
KURT WEISS FLORIST INC
95 Main St, Center Moriches, NY 11934
Phone: (516) 878-2500

Sales: $35,000,000

Employees: 200

Company Type: Private

Employees here: 180

SIC: 0181

Grows and wholesales potted plants

William Kruse, General Manager

D-U-N-S 00-377-9931

L A HEARNE CO

512 Metz Rd, King City, CA 93930

Phone: (831) 385-5441

Sales: $25,355,000

Employees: 74

Company Type: Private

Employees here: 45

SIC: 0723

Processes dry beans small grains & field crop seed & mfg
livestock feed & distributes fertilizer

Blake Whisenant, Chairman

D-U-N-S 86-738-2038

L & C HARVESTING INC

245 Guadalupe St, Guadalupe, CA 93434

Phone: (805) 343-1608

Sales: $15,000,000

Employees: 300

Company Type: Private

Employees here: 300

SIC: 0722

Crop harvesting services

Alan Murray, President

D-U-N-S 07-803-0863

L & J RANCH INC

233 Friend Rd, St. Libory, NE 68872

Phone: (308) 687-6234

Sales: $21,000,000

Employees: 2

Company Type: Private

Employees here: 2

SIC: 0211

Feed lot

Mason H Lampton, President

D-U-N-S 88-349-4577

L & S HARVESTING INC

651 E Main St, El Centro, CA 92243

Phone: (760) 312-5757

Sales: $11,600,000

Employees: 200

Company Type: Private

Employees here: 200

SIC: 0722

Cutom crop harvesting services

Hal P Harlan, Chief Executive Officer

D-U-N-S 03-714-9226

L L MURPHREY CO

RR 1, Farmville, NC 27828

Phone: (252) 753-5361

Sales: $30,000,000

Employees: 90

Company Type: Private

Employees here: 20

SIC: 0213

Hog farm

Roger Harloff, President

D-U-N-S 00-692-4328

LAKE REGION PACKING ASSN

124 S Joanna Ave, Tavares, FL 32778

Phone: (352) 343-3111

Sales: $10,805,000

Employees: 75

Company Type: Private

Employees here: 75

SIC: 0723

Citrus fruit packers

Jean C Ganas, Chief Operating Officer

D-U-N-S 83-933-0024

LAKE SUPERIOR LAND CO

(Parent: Champion International Corp)

101 Red Jacket Rd, Calumet, MI 49913

Phone: (906) 337-0202

Sales: $15,000,000

Employees: 19

Company Type: Public Family Member

Employees here: 19

SIC: 0241

Timber and real estate sales

Bob Cape, Controller

D-U-N-S 02-819-4520

LAMANUZZI & PANTALEO LTD

1726 Railroad Ave, Clovis, CA 93612

Phone: (559) 299-7258

Sales: $26,190,000

Employees: 150

Company Type: Private

Employees here: 7

SIC: 0172

Vineyards

Robert H Harrison, President

D-U-N-S 01-299-5176

LANDCARE USA, INC

2603 Augusta Dr Fl 13, Houston, TX 77057

Phone: (713) 965-0336

Sales: $137,900,000

Employees: 4,300

Company Type: Public

Employees here: 20

SIC: 0783

Commercial & institutional landscape maintenance &
installation services

Dan Hartung, President

D-U-N-S 05-662-1899

LANDSCAPE CONCEPTS INC

31711 N Alleghany Rd, Grayslake, IL 60030

Phone: (847) 223-0900

Sales: $15,330,000

Employees: 25

Company Type: Private

Employees here: 25

SIC: 0781

Landscape and lawn service

Fred R Harvey, President

D-U-N-S 80-402-7282

LANDSCAPE MAINTENANCE SERVICES

(Parent: Canterbury Information Tech)

666 Plainsboro Rd, Ste 525, Plainsboro, NJ

Phone: (609) 897-0200

Sales: $12,000,000

Employees: 326

Company Type: Public Family Member

Employees here: 1

SIC: 0782

Commercial landscaping

Owen Nelson, Finance

D-U-N-S 00-895-8134

LARSON FRUIT CO

109 N Wenas Ave, Selah, WA 98942

Phone: (509) 697-7208

Sales: $12,206,000

Employees: 110

Company Type: Private

Employees here: 110

SIC: 0723

Fruit packing & refrigerated storage

Hayden Thompson, President

D-U-N-S 02-124-1658

LAS UVAS VALLEY DAIRY

Hc 400, Hatch, NM 87937

Phone: (505) 267-3037

Sales: $15,000,000

Employees: 160

Company Type: Private

Employees here: 160

SIC: 0241

Dairy farm

Lecil Cole, President

D-U-N-S 02-790-0489

LASSEN CANYON NURSERY INC

1300 Salmon Creek Rd, Redding, CA 96003

Phone: (530) 223-1075

Sales: $11,594,000
Company Type: Private
SIC: 0171
   Strawberry plant nursery
Daniel Hawkins, President
Employees: 150
Employees here: 150

D-U-N-S 17-680-0621
LATIGO TRADING CO INC
14415 N Loop Dr, Clint, TX 79836
Phone: (915) 851-1195
Sales: $10,000,000
Company Type: Private
SIC: 0751
   Export cattle and cattle by care products
Chris Hayes, President
Employees: 3
Employees here: 3

D-U-N-S 06-982-7020
LEADER DOGS FOR THE BLIND INC
1039 S Rochester Rd, Rochester, MI 48307
Phone: (248) 651-9011
Sales: $13,274,000
Company Type: Private
SIC: 0752
   Guide dog school
Leonard Spesert, President
Employees: 94
Employees here: 94

D-U-N-S 01-458-7984
LEIDY'S INC
266 W Cherry Ln, Souderton, PA 18964
Phone: (215) 723-4606
Sales: $42,760,000
Company Type: Private
SIC: 0751
   Slaughtering and processing of meats for wholesale
    distribution
Carol Marroquin, Secretary
Employees: 242
Employees here: 242

D-U-N-S 06-398-9552
LEISURE LAWN INC
765 Liberty Ln, Dayton, OH 45449
Phone: (937) 866-2402
Sales: $20,000,000
Company Type: Private
SIC: 0782
   Lawn service
Richard Pavelski, President
Employees: 300
Employees here: 20

D-U-N-S 06-792-1775
LEWIS TREE SERVICE INC
225 Ballantyne Rd, Rochester, NY 14623
Phone: (716) 436-3208
Sales: $50,680,000
Company Type: Private
SIC: 0783
   Utility line tree clearance
Ray Childress, President
Employees: 1,000
Employees here: 50

D-U-N-S 02-340-8594
LIED'S NURSERY CO INC
N63w22039 Hwy 74, Sussex, WI 53089
Phone: (414) 246-6901
Sales: $12,228,000
Company Type: Private
SIC: 0782
   Landscape contractor & landscape maintenance
Rod Kvamme, President
Employees: 105
Employees here: 80

D-U-N-S 13-079-7087
LIFESCAPES INC
6644 Hickory Flat Hwy, Canton, GA 30115
Phone: (770) 345-6644

Sales: $10,000,000
Company Type: Private
SIC: 0782
   Landscape contracting grounds management and landscape
    architecture and irrigation
James Heller, Chairman of the Board
Employees: 130
Employees here: 122

D-U-N-S 00-914-5632
LIHUE PLANTATION COMPANY LTD
   (Parent: AMFAC/JMB Hawaii LLC)
2970 Kele St, Lihue, HI 96766
Phone: (808) 245-7325
Sales: $36,200,000
Company Type: Private
SIC: 0133
   Grower and processor of cane sugar
Charles G Henry, President
Employees: 450
Employees here: 450

D-U-N-S 00-691-4105
LIMONEIRA ASSOCIATES
1141 Cummings Rd, Santa Paula, CA 93060
Phone: (805) 525-5541
Sales: $40,000,000
Company Type: Private
SIC: 0723
   Citrus grower & fruit packing services
Herbert C Haynes, President
Employees: 600
Employees here: 600

D-U-N-S 05-324-0701
LINDEMANN PRODUCE INC
300 E 2nd St, Ste 1200, Reno, NV 89501
Phone: (775) 323-2442
Sales: $65,000,000
Company Type: Private
SIC: 0723
   Fresh fruit packing
Stephen Herbruck, President
Employees: 63
Employees here: 40

D-U-N-S 04-601-3306
LION ENTERPRISES INC
3310 E California Ave, Fresno, CA 93702
Phone: (559) 237-6601
Sales: $70,000,000
Company Type: Private
SIC: 0723
   Raisin packing & drying
Heinz C Prechter, Chairman of the Board
Employees: 150
Employees here: 100

D-U-N-S 06-230-3029
LIPINSKI LANDSCAPING IRRGTION CONTRACTORS
180 Elbo Ln, Mount Laurel, NJ
Phone: (609) 234-2221
Sales: $15,000,000
Company Type: Private
SIC: 0782
   Landscape & irrigation contractors & landscape design
    services
Hermann Engelmann, Chief Executive Officer
Employees: 50
Employees here: 50

D-U-N-S 61-566-5551
LIVESTOCK INVESTMENTS, INC
Hwy 60 Sw, Hereford, TX 79045
Phone: (806) 357-2241
Sales: $55,994,000
Company Type: Private
SIC: 0211
   Beef cattle feedlot
Dalton Hermes, President
Employees: 75
Employees here: 75

D-U-N-S 10-248-6784
LIVESTOCK INVESTORS, INC.
Fm 1057, Summerfield, TX 79085
Phone: (806) 357-2241

Sales: $55,365,000
Company Type: Private
SIC: 0211
  Cattle feedlot
Sydney E Herndon, Treasurer

Employees: 75
Employees here: 75

D-U-N-S 10-312-4244
LIVING FREE
54250 Keen Camp Rd, Mountain Center, CA 92561
Phone: (909) 659-4687
Sales: $10,000,000
Company Type: Private
SIC: 0752
  Animal services
Andy Herrera, President

Employees: 28
Employees here: 28

D-U-N-S 10-275-8133
LONE STAR GROWERS, L P
  (Parent: Color Spot Nurseries Inc)
3478 Buskirk Ave, Ste 260, Pleasant Hill, CA 94523
Phone: (925) 934-4443
Sales: $28,800,000
Company Type: Private
SIC: 0181
  Ornamental nursery
Frederick Hess, President

Employees: 650
Employees here: 25

D-U-N-S 00-904-1443   EXP
LONGVIEW FIBRE CO
300 Fibre Way, Longview, WA 98632
Phone: (360) 425-1550
Sales: $753,244,000
Company Type: Public
SIC: 0241
  Mfg corrugated & solid fibre containers bags paper &
    paperboard & timber
Glen M Hickman, President

Employees: 3,700
Employees here: 2,100

D-U-N-S 19-368-3273
LUCICH FARMS
2337 Zacharias Rd, Patterson, CA 95363
Phone: (209) 892-6500
Sales: $13,500,000
Company Type: Private
SIC: 0723
  Fresh fruit packing
Harley Sietsema, President

Employees: 150
Employees here: 150

D-U-N-S 04-584-2101
LUMBER CITY EGG MARKETERS INC
  (Parent: Sutherlands Foodservice Inc)
Hwy 341 N, Lumber City, GA 31549
Phone: (912) 363-4312
Sales: $10,000,000
Company Type: Private
SIC: 0252
  Egg farm & whol eggs & groceries
Robert Ball, President

Employees: 100
Employees here: 100

D-U-N-S 00-409-3472
LYKES BROS INC
400 N Tampa St, Tampa, FL 33602
Phone: (813) 223-3981
Sales: $150,000,000
Company Type: Private
SIC: 0721
  Citrus grove cultivation juice processing and distribution and
    cattle ranch & insurance agency
Alan J Chaffee, President

Employees: 2,500
Employees here: 120

D-U-N-S 06-924-1206
M & M POULTRY FARM
RR 32, North Franklin, CT

Phone: (860) 642-7555
Sales: $10,000,000
Company Type: Private
SIC: 0252
  Chicken farm
Carlva L Jones, President

Employees: 4
Employees here: 4

D-U-N-S 09-248-0748
M S N INC
849 W 26th St, Houston, TX 77008
Phone: (713) 868-8060
Sales: $11,292,000
Company Type: Private
SIC: 0781
  Landscape architecture & contracting & whol nursery
Tsugio Hiji, President

Employees: 125
Employees here: 110

D-U-N-S 08-008-1573   EXP
MAC FARMS OF HAWAII INC
89-406 Mamalahoa Hwy, Captain Cook, HI 96704
Phone: (808) 328-2435
Sales: $27,295,000
Company Type: Private
SIC: 0173
  Macadamia nut farm
Jack Hazen, President

Employees: 70
Employees here: 60

D-U-N-S 19-549-6831
MACMILLAN BLOEDEL TIMBERLANDS
  (Parent: MacMillan Bloedel Packaging)
4001 Carmichael Rd, Montgomery, AL 36106
Phone: (334) 963-4391
Sales: $14,800,000
Company Type: Private
SIC: 0811
  Assets holding company for timber tracts
Jack E Hazen Jr, President

Employees: 11
Employees here: 2

D-U-N-S 11-272-1055
MADDOX DAIRY
3899 W Davis Ave, Riverdale, CA 93656
Phone: (559) 867-3545
Sales: $10,000,000
Company Type: Private
SIC: 0241
  Dairy farm
Donald C Hershey, President

Employees: 66
Employees here: 1

D-U-N-S 60-245-7905
MAINE FRESH PACK CO-OPERATIVE
2 Pleasant Blvd, Machias, ME
Phone: (207) 255-8520
Sales: $12,700,000
Company Type: Private
SIC: 0723
  Fresh fruit packer
Joe A Hilliard, Partner

Employees: 150
Employees here: 150

D-U-N-S 18-787-4649
MALLOY ORCHARDS, INC
925 Koch Ln, Live Oak, CA 95953
Phone: (530) 695-1861
Sales: $11,400,000
Company Type: Private
SIC: 0175
  Grower of peaches prunes & walnuts & commercial
    harvesting services
Chris Huntington, President

Employees: 200
Employees here: 200

D-U-N-S 00-692-4161
MANATEE FRUIT CO
  (Parent: Palmetto Companies Inc)
1320 33rd St W, Palmetto, FL 34221
Phone: (941) 721-0600

Sales: $14,000,000   *Employees:* 185
Company Type: Private   *Employees here:* 5
SIC: 0181
   Grows flowers & potted plants
Doug Allen, Chairman

D-U-N-S 14-168-6089
MANLEY FARMS, INC
2077 Pine Ridge Rd, Naples, FL 34109
Phone: (941) 597-6416
Sales: $12,000,000   *Employees:* 60
Company Type: Private   *Employees here:* 5
SIC: 0161
   Tomato farm
Steve Thigpen, President

D-U-N-S 02-906-5273   EXP
MANN PACKING CO, INC
1250 Hansen St, Salinas, CA 93901
Phone: (831) 422-7405
Sales: $126,824,000   *Employees:* 500
Company Type: Private   *Employees here:* 500
SIC: 0723
   Packer processor & shipper of vegetables
Paul H Hitch, President

D-U-N-S 18-076-9614
MAP INC
19110 S Molalla Ave, Oregon City, OR 97045
Phone: (503) 655-5524
Sales: $10,658,000   *Employees:* 5
Company Type: Private   *Employees here:* 5
SIC: 0851
   Forestry services
Paul Hitch, President

D-U-N-S 01-652-2823
MAPLE LEAF DUCK FARMS INC
   (Parent: Maple Leaf Farms Inc)
9166 N 200 E, Milford, IN 46542
Phone: (219) 658-4121
Sales: $62,000,000   *Employees:* 750
Company Type: Private   *Employees here:* 250
SIC: 0259
   Duck farm and processing
Karl De Jong, President

D-U-N-S 15-342-7885
MAPLE LEAF FARMS INC
9166 N 200 E, Milford, IN 46542
Phone: (219) 658-4121
Sales: $100,000,000   *Employees:* 1,250
Company Type: Private   *Employees here:* 225
SIC: 0259
   Duck farm & poultry processing plant
Clyde Hollingsworth, Executor

D-U-N-S 60-123-1657
MAR JAC POULTRY INC
   (Parent: Mar-Jac Holdings Inc)
1020 Aviation Blvd, Gainesville, GA 30501
Phone: (770) 536-0561
Sales: $90,949,000   *Employees:* 800
Company Type: Private   *Employees here:* 800
SIC: 0254
   Poultry processor poultry hatchery and food broker
Ali A Amin, Chairman of the Board

D-U-N-S 09-253-8586
MARIANI ENTERPRISES INC
300 Rockland Rd, Lake Bluff, IL 60044
Phone: (847) 234-2172

Sales: $11,196,000   *Employees:* 70
Company Type: Private   *Employees here:* 70
SIC: 0781
   Lawn care services & landscape design
Charles J Tosovsky, President

D-U-N-S 00-796-3945
MARIANI PACKING CO INC
320 Jackson St, San Jose, CA 95112
Phone: (408) 288-8300
Sales: $117,000,000   *Employees:* 275
Company Type: Private   *Employees here:* 275
SIC: 0723
   Dried fruit packaging
Robert O Anderson, Chairman of the Board

D-U-N-S 07-621-0293
MARKO ZANINOVICH INC
1998 Road 152, Delano, CA 93215
Phone: (661) 792-3151
Sales: $120,000,000   *Employees:* 2,000
Company Type: Private   *Employees here:* 2,000
SIC: 0172
   Grape grower packer and shipper
W B Stroud Jr, President

D-U-N-S 60-246-5312
MARLIN PACKING CO
1855 E County 16th St, Yuma, AZ 85365
Phone: (520) 341-0500
Sales: $13,800,000   *Employees:* 200
Company Type: Private   *Employees here:* 200
SIC: 0723
   Citrus packing house
Waymon Hornbeck, President

D-U-N-S 05-864-1457
MARSHALL DURBIN FARMS INC
   (Parent: Durbin Marshall Food Corp)
2830 Commerce Blvd, Birmingham, AL 35210
Phone: (205) 870-5800
Sales: $42,500,000   *Employees:* 850
Company Type: Private   *Employees here:* 10
SIC: 0251
   Broiler production
Richard D Vanlandingham, President

D-U-N-S 01-837-5837
MATERIAL PROCESSING INC
1815 F Ave, Dakota City, NE 68731
Phone: (402) 987-3438
Sales: $20,000,000   *Employees:* 6
Company Type: Private   *Employees here:* 6
SIC: 0711
   Soil decontamination
Brad Howard, President

D-U-N-S 00-913-2184   EXP
MAUI LAND & PINEAPPLE CO INC
120 Kane St, Kahului, HI 96732
Phone: (808) 877-3351
Sales: $136,498,000   *Employees:* 2,270
Company Type: Public   *Employees here:* 27
SIC: 0179
   Grows and cans pineapples
S M Hawkins, President

D-U-N-S 82-636-9720
MAXWELL FOODS INC.
938 Millers Chapel Rd, Goldsboro, NC 27534
Phone: (919) 778-3130

Sales: $92,900,000

Employees: 1,000
Employees here: 150

Company Type: Private
SIC: 0213
    Hog farm
Don Tyson, Sr Chb

D-U-N-S 00-146-8651
MAXXAM GROUP INC
    (Parent: Maxxam Inc*)*
5847 San Felipe St, Houston, TX 77057
Phone: (713) 975-7600
Sales: $287,175,000

Employees: NA
Employees here: NA

Company Type: Public Family Member
SIC: 0811
    Forest products operations
Salvador Huerta, President

D-U-N-S 14-458-2418
MAYFIELD TIMBER CO INC
Hwy 17 S, Toxey, AL 36921
Phone: (334) 843-5543
Sales: $10,227,000

Employees: 35
Employees here: 35

Company Type: Private
SIC: 0241
    Logging industries
Martin Pohl, President

D-U-N-S 02-967-4108

EXP

MCANALLY ENTERPRISES INC.
12215 7th St, Yucaipa, CA 92399
Phone: (909) 797-0144
Sales: $40,040,000

Employees: 400
Employees here: 200

Company Type: Private
SIC: 0252
    Egg producer
Frank M Hunt, Executive

D-U-N-S 12-271-8489
MCARTHUR FARMS INC
1550 NE 208th St, Okeechobee, FL 34972
Phone: (941) 763-4719
Sales: $25,000,000

Employees: 165
Employees here: 127

Company Type: Private
SIC: 0241
    Dairy and beef cattle farm and citrus grove
Robert J Marischen, President

D-U-N-S 09-292-7540
MCCLAIN ENTERPRISES, INC.
501 W Wade Ave, Mountain Home, AR 72653
Phone: (870) 425-5125
Sales: $36,927,000

Employees: 50
Employees here: 40

Company Type: Private
SIC: 0253
    Turkey farm trucking of turkeys & feed mill
Corney Waldner, President

D-U-N-S 95-860-0868
MCCLESKEY COTTON COMPANY LLC
Hwy 118 W, Bronwood, GA 31726
Phone: (912) 995-2616
Sales: $10,000,000

Employees: 5
Employees here: 5

Company Type: Private
SIC: 0131
    Cotton gin
Heinz L Gmbh, Partner

D-U-N-S 19-857-8155
MCCLURE PROPERTIES, LTD
530 5th Avenue Dr W, Palmetto, FL 34221
Phone: (941) 722-4545

Sales: $25,000,000

Employees: 150
Employees here: 150

Company Type: Private
SIC: 0161
    Tomato growers
A B Hudson, Chairman of the Board

D-U-N-S 03-358-1430
MCCORKLE NURSERIES INC
4904 Lckeys Bridge Rd Se, Dearing, GA 30808
Phone: (706) 595-3050
Sales: $10,452,000

Employees: 157
Employees here: 150

Company Type: Private
SIC: 0181
    Nursery & landscaping
Stefan Illy, President

D-U-N-S 02-248-2517
MCDONNELL, INC
7460 Conowingo Ave, Jessup, MD 20794
Phone: (410) 799-7966
Sales: $15,000,000

Employees: 25
Employees here: 25

Company Type: Private
SIC: 0174
    Citrus fruit growers & whol produce
Edgar M Cullman, Chairman of the Board

D-U-N-S 09-288-0541
MCDOUGALL & SONS INC
305 Olds Station Rd, Wenatchee, WA 98801
Phone: (509) 662-0859
Sales: $12,852,000

Employees: 200
Employees here: 200

Company Type: Private
SIC: 0723
    Fresh fruit packer & growers
John Grether, Chairman of the Board

D-U-N-S 92-988-5291
MCGEE TIMBER CO INC
3162 Hwy 404, Duck Hill, MS 38925
Phone: (601) 565-9968
Sales: $15,000,000

Employees: 1
Employees here: 1

Company Type: Private
SIC: 0811
    Timber tract operation subdivider/developer
George F Hamner Jr, President

D-U-N-S 06-866-3426
MCGINLEY-SCHILZ CO
675 Road West F S, Brule, NE 69127
Phone: (308) 287-2341
Sales: $18,290,000

Employees: 25
Employees here: 25

Company Type: Private
SIC: 0211
    Beef cattle feedlot & general farm
Ernie Massoth, Controller

D-U-N-S 95-642-2406
MCHUTCHISON & CO LLC
695 Grand Ave, Ridgefield, NJ
Phone: (201) 943-2230
Sales: $17,000,000

Employees: 51
Employees here: 51

Company Type: Private
SIC: 0781
    Horticultural broker
Susan Putman, President

D-U-N-S 80-387-0526
MCLEAN FEEDYARD, INC.
Fm Rd 273, McLean, TX 79057
Phone: (806) 779-2405

Sales: $11,631,000　　　　　　　　　*Employees:* 21
Company Type: Private　　　　　　　*Employees here:* 21
SIC: 0211
　　Cattle feedyard
James K Sartain, Chief Executive Officer

D-U-N-S 06-693-2872
MECCA FARMS INC
7965 Lantana Rd, Lake Worth, FL 33467
Phone: (561) 968-3605
Sales: $37,401,000　　　　　　　　　*Employees:* 50
Company Type: Private　　　　　　　*Employees here:* 50
SIC: 0161
　　Growers and packers of tomatoes peppers beans cucumbers
Ted Miller, President

D-U-N-S 82-722-9493
MEDICAL MANAGEMENT INTERNATIONAL
14333 NE Sandy Blvd, Portland, OR 97230
Phone: (503) 256-7299
Sales: $48,800,000　　　　　　　　　*Employees:* 1,300
Company Type: Private　　　　　　　*Employees here:* 80
SIC: 0742
　　Veterinary services
Jeff Hansen, President

D-U-N-S 13-183-9243
MELKESIAN RANCH INC
84700 Avenue 44, Indio, CA 92203
Phone: (760) 347-6690
Sales: $24,000,000　　　　　　　　　*Employees:* 400
Company Type: Private　　　　　　　*Employees here:* 400
SIC: 0172
　　Grape farm
Andre W Iseli, President

D-U-N-S 00-401-6804
MELROSE TIMBER CO
Hwy 82 W, McShan, AL 35471
Phone: (205) 375-6277
Sales: $15,213,000　　　　　　　　　*Employees:* 76
Company Type: Private　　　　　　　*Employees here:* 8
SIC: 0851
　　Timber growing
James K Ito, President

D-U-N-S 83-115-1238
MENDES CALF RANCH
13356 Avenue 168, Tipton, CA 93272
Phone: (559) 688-4708
Sales: $16,100,000　　　　　　　　　*Employees:* 70
Company Type: Private　　　　　　　*Employees here:* 70
SIC: 0211
　　Beef cattle feedlot
James V De Wetering, President

D-U-N-S 04-748-5610
MERCER RANCHES INC
46 Sonova Rd, Prosser, WA 99350
Phone: (509) 894-4773
Sales: $17,000,000　　　　　　　　　*Employees:* 50
Company Type: Private　　　　　　　*Employees here:* 50
SIC: 0191
　　Diversified farm
N H Ise, Chairman of the Board

D-U-N-S 13-031-7571
MEREX CORP
1120 Saw Mill River Rd, Yonkers, NY 10710
Phone: (914) 376-0202

Sales: $49,026,000　　　　　　　　　*Employees:* 85
Company Type: Private　　　　　　　*Employees here:* 60
SIC: 0161
　　Growers packagers & distributors of perishable foods
N H Ise, President

D-U-N-S 00-796-7474
MERRILL FARMS
1067 Merrill St, Salinas, CA 93901
Phone: (831) 424-7365
Sales: $13,900,000　　　　　　　　　*Employees:* 150
Company Type: Private　　　　　　　*Employees here:* 25
SIC: 0161
　　Vegetable grower & mfg ice
Nibaldo Capote, President

D-U-N-S 07-105-8929
METROLINA GREENHOUSES INC
16400 Hntrsvlle Cncord Rd, Huntersville, NC 28078
Phone: (704) 875-1371
Sales: $19,896,000　　　　　　　　　*Employees:* 175
Company Type: Private　　　　　　　*Employees here:* 175
SIC: 0181
　　Raises plants & flowers
Kenny Moore, President

D-U-N-S 02-833-7145
MEYER TOMATOES
117 N 1st St, King City, CA 93930
Phone: (831) 385-4047
Sales: $75,605,000　　　　　　　　　*Employees:* 87
Company Type: Private　　　　　　　*Employees here:* 30
SIC: 0161
　　Growers & packer of tomatoes
Paul W Jensen, President

D-U-N-S 00-648-1899
MICHAEL FOODS, INC
5353 Wayzata Blvd, Ste 324, Minneapolis, MN 55416
Phone: (612) 546-1500
Sales: $956,223,000　　　　　　　　*Employees:* 3,870
Company Type: Public　　　　　　　*Employees here:* 9
SIC: 0252
　　Produces & wholesales egg products refrigerated grocery
　　　products refrigerated dairy and potato products
Donald P Helgeson, Chairman of the Board

D-U-N-S 14-850-8716
MICHAEL FOODS OF DELAWARE
　　(Parent: Michael Foods Inc)
5353 Wayzata Blvd, Ste 324, Minneapolis, MN 55416
Phone: (612) 546-1500
Sales: $956,223,000　　　　　　　　*Employees:* 3,870
Company Type: Public Family Member　*Employees here:* 9
SIC: 0252
　　Produces & wholesales egg products refrigerated grocery
　　　products refrigerated dairy and potato products
John E Estes, President

D-U-N-S 03-056-6780
MID AMERICAN GROWERS INC
RR 89, Granville, IL 61326
Phone: (815) 339-6831
Sales: $20,000,000　　　　　　　　　*Employees:* 175
Company Type: Private　　　　　　　*Employees here:* 175
SIC: 0181
　　Greenhouse
James W Boswell, President

D-U-N-S 03-686-9522
MID VALLEY PROCESSING INC
130 Santa Fe Grade Rd, Newman, CA 95360
Phone: (209) 862-1449

Sales: $10,000,000   *Employees:* 25
Company Type: Private   *Employees here:* 25
SIC: 0751
    Slaughtering livestock services
John R Miles, President

D-U-N-S 82-567-2371
MIDWEST FEEDERS INC
5013 13 Rd, Ingalls, KS 67853
Phone: (316) 335-5790
Sales: $14,000,000   *Employees:* 20
Company Type: Private   *Employees here:* 20
SIC: 0212
    Cattle feedlot
Virgil Jurgensmeyer, Chairman of the Board

D-U-N-S 04-670-4987
MIDWEST HTCHY & PLTY FARMS INC
Red Rooster Industrial Pa, Dassel, MN 55325
Phone: (320) 275-3351
Sales: $10,000,000   *Employees:* 25
Company Type: Private   *Employees here:* 5
SIC: 0254
    Poultry hatchery
Victor P Smith, President

D-U-N-S 04-899-5484
MIDWEST POULTRY SERVICES LP
9951 State Road 25 W, Mentone, IN 46539
Phone: (219) 353-7651
Sales: $25,000,000   *Employees:* 300
Company Type: Private   *Employees here:* 25
SIC: 0252
    Chicken egg farm and processor
Donald P Helgeson, Chairman of the Board

D-U-N-S 96-198-7088
MILL CREEK COMPANIES
2001 Ross Ave, Ste 3400, Dallas, TX 75201
Phone: (214) 863-3000
Sales: $14,000,000   *Employees:* 300
Company Type: Private   *Employees here:* 8
SIC: 0181
    Ornamental nursery
Tom Klein, Partner

D-U-N-S 19-412-8070
MILLER DIVERSIFIED CORP
23360 Weld County Rd 35, La Salle, CO 80645
Phone: (970) 284-5556
Sales: $11,378,000   *Employees:* 25
Company Type: Public   *Employees here:* 25
SIC: 0211
    Cattle feed lot
Jack Berry Jr, President

D-U-N-S 00-926-7592
MILLER SHINGLE CO INC
20820 102nd St NE, Granite Falls, WA 98252
Phone: (360) 691-7727
Sales: $13,600,000   *Employees:* 250
Company Type: Private   *Employees here:* 190
SIC: 0241
    Logging contractor & lumber broker
Mark J Neal, President

D-U-N-S 04-486-8537   EXP
MILLS DISTRIBUTING CO, INC
375 W Market St, Salinas, CA 93901
Phone: (831) 757-3068

Sales: $78,371,000   *Employees:* 30
Company Type: Private   *Employees here:* 30
SIC: 0161
    Produce grower/shipper & marketing company
Jack Sparrowk, Owner

D-U-N-S 07-238-4993
MINNESOTA VIKINGS VENTURES,
9520 Viking Dr, Eden Prairie, MN 55344
Phone: (612) 828-6500
Sales: $100,000,000   *Employees:* 880
Company Type: Private   *Employees here:* 120
SIC: 0971
    Holding company for professional football team vending
        machines & cafeteria management
Jim Forrester, President

D-U-N-S 18-802-1869
MISSOURI FARMERS ASSOCIATION
201 Ray Young Dr, Columbia, MO 65201
Phone: (573) 874-5111
Sales: $85,100,000   *Employees:* 1,800
Company Type: Private   *Employees here:* 220
SIC: 0762
    Agricultural cooperative
James Abbate, President

D-U-N-S 12-137-4367
MIVCO PACKING CO
375 W Market St, Salinas, CA 93901
Phone: (831) 422-4479
Sales: $60,323,000   *Employees:* 4
Company Type: Private   *Employees here:* 4
SIC: 0161
    Vegetable farm
James T Smith, Owner

D-U-N-S 15-650-6073
ML MACADAMIA ORCHARDS, L.P.
828 Fort Street Mall, Honolulu, HI 96813
Phone: (808) 532-4130
Sales: $12,128,000   *Employees:* 3
Company Type: Public   *Employees here:* 3
SIC: 0173
    Macadamia nut farm
John Marrelli, President

D-U-N-S 15-337-6447
MOBLEY GIN CO INC
1265 Ga Hwy 133 N, Moultrie, GA 31768
Phone: (912) 782-5291
Sales: $20,079,000   *Employees:* 6
Company Type: Private   *Employees here:* 6
SIC: 0724
    Cotton gin
Duane Wasson, Chairman of the Board

D-U-N-S 06-572-5434
MODERN MUSHROOM FARMS INC
Bypass Newark Rd RR 1, Toughkenamon, PA 19374
Phone: (610) 268-3535
Sales: $25,000,000   *Employees:* 350
Company Type: Private   *Employees here:* 300
SIC: 0182
    Mushroom grower
Jesse Minor, Owner

D-U-N-S 04-006-7670
MOET HENNESSY INC
2 Park Ave Rm 1830, New York, NY 10016
Phone: (212) 340-7480

Sales: $415,965,000

Employees: 9,100

Company Type: Private

Employees here: 12

SIC: 0172

Grape vineyard mfg toilet preparations short-term business credit institution whol wine/distilled beverages

Sophia Hronis, Partner

D-U-N-S 00-690-4049   EXP

MONROVIA NURSERY CO

18331 E Foothill Blvd, Azusa, CA 91702

Phone: (626) 334-9321

Sales: $83,641,000

Employees: 1,700

Company Type: Private

Employees here: 567

SIC: 0181

Grower of nursery stock

Jim R Hoagland, Owner

D-U-N-S 14-765-9742

MONSON RANCHES INC

2330 Outlook Rd, Outlook, WA 98938

Phone: (509) 837-4424

Sales: $34,006,000

Employees: 30

Company Type: Private

Employees here: 30

SIC: 0211

Cattle feed lot

George Sass, President

D-U-N-S 08-859-5186   EXP

MONTEREY MUSHROOMS INC

260 Westgate Dr, Watsonville, CA 95076

Phone: (831) 763-5300

Sales: $156,102,000

Employees: 2,000

Company Type: Private

Employees here: 30

SIC: 0182

Grows mushrooms

Jose L Garcia Sr, President

D-U-N-S 11-327-3866

MONTEZUMA FEEDERS INC

Hwy 56, Montezuma, KS 67867

Phone: (316) 846-2226

Sales: $14,899,000

Employees: 36

Company Type: Private

Employees here: 36

SIC: 0211

Cattle feedlot

Edith Heidrick, Chairman of the Board

D-U-N-S 95-742-0730

MOON NURSERIES OF MARYLAND

145 Moon Dr, Chesapeake City, MD 21915

Phone: (410) 755-6600

Sales: $10,000,000

Employees: 250

Company Type: Private

Employees here: 249

SIC: 0181

Grows and wholesales nursery stock

John Callandri, Owner

D-U-N-S 60-521-5987

MORRELL GROUP INC

2375 Pleasantdale Rd, Atlanta, GA 30340

Phone: (770) 662-8775

Sales: $10,000,000

Employees: 185

Company Type: Private

Employees here: 185

SIC: 0782

Landscape design & maintenance

Henry Barth, Chairman of the Board

D-U-N-S 02-012-1398

MORRISON BROS RANCH

11611 S Higley Rd, Higley, AZ 85236

Phone: (602) 892-0053

Sales: $50,000,000

Employees: 125

Company Type: Private

Employees here: 35

SIC: 0212

Beef cattle production

John Knevelbaard, Owner

D-U-N-S 15-454-9414

MORRISON ENTERPRISES

12th & Brentwood, Hastings, NE 68901

Phone: (402) 463-3191

Sales: $75,000,000

Employees: 210

Company Type: Private

Employees here: 25

SIC: 0191

General crop farming cattle feeding & grain storage

Arthur Batson Jr, President

D-U-N-S 06-291-9550

MOSSBERG SANITATION INC

Nations Bank Bldg, Ste 2b, Great Bend, KS 67530

Phone: (316) 792-6570

Sales: $11,745,000

Employees: 3

Company Type: Private

Employees here: 3

SIC: 0751

Cleans packing plants

John M Foster, President

D-U-N-S 15-064-8517

MULHALL'S NURSERY, INC.

3615 N 120th St, Omaha, NE 68164

Phone: (402) 496-0700

Sales: $12,390,000

Employees: 125

Company Type: Private

Employees here: 125

SIC: 0781

Landscaping service & retail lawn supplies

John M Truluck, Owner

D-U-N-S 04-979-4282

MURAKAMI FARMS INC

1431 SE 1st St, Ontario, OR 97914

Phone: (541) 889-3131

Sales: $18,232,000

Employees: 25

Company Type: Private

Employees here: 25

SIC: 0723

Onion packing

Dave Holder, President

D-U-N-S 05-080-6447

MURANAKA FARM, INC

16014 Chatsworth St, Granada Hills, CA 91344

Phone: (818) 894-6984

Sales: $21,200,000

Employees: 250

Company Type: Private

Employees here: 10

SIC: 0161

Vegetable farm

Wayne Johnson, Partner

D-U-N-S 06-529-1981

MURPHY FARMS INC

4134 S US Hwy 117, Rose Hill, NC 28458

Phone: (910) 289-2111

Sales: $499,065,000

Employees: 2,100

Company Type: Private

Employees here: 700

SIC: 0213

Hog farms

Don M Johnston, Partner

D-U-N-S 04-371-3445

N G PURVIS FARMS INC

2504 Spies Rd, Robbins, NC 27325

Phone: (910) 948-2297

Sales: $13,207,000   *Employees:* 113
Company Type: Private   *Employees here:* 12
SIC: 0213
  Hog and turkey farm
George Holder, President

D-U-N-S 02-745-8009
NATIONAL FOOD CORP
16740 Aurora Ave N, Seattle, WA 98133
Phone: (206) 546-6533
Sales: $33,300,000   *Employees:* NA
Company Type: Private   *Employees here:* NA
SIC: 0252
  Chicken egg & poultry farm
Francis A Duvernois, President

D-U-N-S 36-222-5096
NATIONAL HOG FARMS INC
  (Parent: National Farms Inc)
25000 Weld County Rd 69, Kersey, CO 80644
Phone: (970) 353-9960
Sales: $16,300,000   *Employees:* 175
Company Type: Private   *Employees here:* 175
SIC: 0213
  Hog feedlot
Cecil E Martin, President

D-U-N-S 18-194-7037
NATIONAL PETCARE CENTER INC
736 Whalers Way, Ste F250, Fort Collins, CO 80525
Phone: (970) 226-6632
Sales: $22,172,000   *Employees:* 800
Company Type: Private   *Employees here:* 41
SIC: 0742
  Animal hospital
Mike Donehey, Manager

D-U-N-S 85-855-6517
NATURAL SELECTION FOODS LLC
1721 San Juan Hwy, San Juan Bautista, CA 95045
Phone: (831) 623-7880
Sales: $60,000,000   *Employees:* 200
Company Type: Private   *Employees here:* 200
SIC: 0723
  Vegetable packing
Richard Kalashian, President

D-U-N-S 13-180-5707
NATURE'S TREES INC
360 Adams St, Bedford Hills, NY 10507
Phone: (914) 666-8202
Sales: $14,221,000   *Employees:* 170
Company Type: Private   *Employees here:* 80
SIC: 0783
  Tree shrub & lawn care service arborist services landscape
    design & irrigation maintenance & installation
Michael Pia, President

D-U-N-S 00-923-1655   EXP
NATURIPE BERRY GROWERS
305 Industrial Rd, Watsonville, CA 95076
Phone: (831) 722-2430
Sales: $65,412,000   *Employees:* 35
Company Type: Private   *Employees here:* 22
SIC: 0723
  Processor of fruits & vegetables
Bernard L Kapp, President

D-U-N-S 02-768-1485   EXP
NAUMES INC
2 W Barnett St, Medford, OR 97501
Phone: (541) 772-6268

Sales: $39,700,000   *Employees:* 700
Company Type: Private   *Employees here:* 150
SIC: 0175
  Deciduous tree fruit grower & processor & cold storage
    warehouse
Herbert Kaprielian, Partner

D-U-N-S 07-576-0850
NAVAJO AG PDTS INDUST
Hwy 371, Farmington, NM 87401
Phone: (505) 327-5251
Sales: $37,648,000   *Employees:* 440
Company Type: Private   *Employees here:* 40
SIC: 0191
  Farm
Pamela Crum, President

D-U-N-S 05-838-9941
NELSON TREE SERVICE INC
3300 Office Park Dr 205, Dayton, OH 45439
Phone: (937) 294-1313
Sales: $64,100,000   *Employees:* NA
Company Type: Private   *Employees here:* NA
SIC: 0783
  Tree trimming service
Matt P Katicich, Owner

D-U-N-S 60-207-0575
NEW CARRIZO CREEK FEEDERS LTD
7 Miles SE of Texline, Texline, TX 79087
Phone: (806) 362-4212
Sales: $11,000,000   *Employees:* 22
Company Type: Private   *Employees here:* 22
SIC: 0211
  Beef cattle feedlot
David Kawahara, President

D-U-N-S 19-667-4782
NEW MARKET POULTRY PRODUCTS
145 E Old Cross Rd, New Market, VA 22844
Phone: (540) 740-4260
Sales: $12,718,000   *Employees:* 150
Company Type: Private   *Employees here:* 150
SIC: 0751
  Poultry slaughter for further processing
Mike Kearney, President

D-U-N-S 03-813-7543
NEW WEST FOODS
585 Auto Rd, Watsonville, CA 95076
Phone: (831) 728-4261
Sales: $50,000,000   *Employees:* 107
Company Type: Private   *Employees here:* 30
SIC: 0723
  Frozen fruit processor of strawberries
Bradner A Tate, President

D-U-N-S 05-922-5011
NICKEL FAMILY, L.L.C.
2601 Oswell St, Bakersfield, CA 93306
Phone: (661) 872-5050
Sales: $12,000,000   *Employees:* 135
Company Type: Private   *Employees here:* 85
SIC: 0191
  General farming
Bob Keegan, President

D-U-N-S 06-978-0922
NOAH W KREIDER & SON
1461 Lancaster Rd, Manheim, PA 17545
Phone: (717) 665-4415

Sales: $30,000,000   *Employees:* 450
Company Type: Private   *Employees here:* 10
SIC: 0252
  Chicken farm
David A Mink, Chairman of the Board

D-U-N-S 17-323-0426
NOBLESSE OBLIGE INC
2015 Silsbee Rd, El Centro, CA 92243
Phone: (760) 353-3336
Sales: $60,000,000   *Employees:* 1,200
Company Type: Private   *Employees here:* 1,200
SIC: 0722
  Custom farm service
Kenneth Sessions, President

D-U-N-S 00-986-8480
NORCO RANCH INC
1811 Mountain Ave, Norco, CA 91760
Phone: (909) 737-6735
Sales: $94,000,000   *Employees:* 225
Company Type: Private   *Employees here:* 225
SIC: 0252
  Egg ranch
Richard Kent, Chief Executive Officer

D-U-N-S 02-889-9748
NORMAN'S NURSERY INC.
8665 Duarte Rd, San Gabriel, CA 91775
Phone: (626) 795-7895
Sales: $27,000,000   *Employees:* 650
Company Type: Private   *Employees here:* 50
SIC: 0181
  Nursery stock growers and whol nursery
James Icardo, Member

D-U-N-S 60-531-5936
NORTH PLATTE FEEDERS INC
Hwy 83, North Platte, NE 69103
Phone: (308) 963-4386
Sales: $19,000,000   *Employees:* 35
Company Type: Private   *Employees here:* 35
SIC: 0211
  Feedlot
Kerry L Herndon, President

D-U-N-S 00-490-4686
NORTHERN FRUIT CO, INC
220 3rd St NE, East Wenatchee, WA 98802
Phone: (509) 884-6651
Sales: $11,572,000   *Employees:* 30
Company Type: Private   *Employees here:* 30
SIC: 0723
  Packs fruit
Jack Hunt, President

D-U-N-S 17-755-5356
NORTHLAND CRANBERRIES INC
800 1st Ave S, Wisconsin Rapids, WI 54495
Phone: (715) 424-4444
Sales: $47,375,000   *Employees:* 150
Company Type: Public   *Employees here:* 33
SIC: 0171
  Produce & market cranberry & cranberry products
Wayne Andrus, President

D-U-N-S 05-931-7651   EXP
NORTHWESTERN FRUIT & PROD CO
3581 Mapleway Rd, Yakima, WA 98908
Phone: (509) 966-4830

Sales: $12,000,000   *Employees:* 100
Company Type: Private   *Employees here:* 40
SIC: 0175
  Fruit growers
George H Jackson, President

D-U-N-S 02-922-6586   EXP
NURSERYMEN'S EXCHANGE INC
475 6th St, San Francisco, CA 94103
Phone: (415) 392-0078
Sales: $21,500,000   *Employees:* 485
Company Type: Private   *Employees here:* 40
SIC: 0181
  Growing of nursery stock
George H Jackson, General Partner

D-U-N-S 02-652-4777
O P C FARMS INC
5760 Delta Ave, Tracy, CA 95376
Phone: (559) 693-2700
Sales: $10,000,000   *Employees:* 8
Company Type: Private   *Employees here:* 8
SIC: 0191
  Vegetable farm
Perry Kirkland, President

D-U-N-S 07-357-6951
O'CONNELL LANDSCAPE MAINTENANCE
23091 Arroyo Vis, Rcho Sta Marg, CA 92688
Phone: (949) 589-2007
Sales: $11,254,000   *Employees:* 400
Company Type: Private   *Employees here:* 5
SIC: 0782
  Landscape maintenance
Thomas B Klein, President

D-U-N-S 78-589-8982
O'HARA CORP
120 Tillson Ave, Rockland, ME
Phone: (207) 594-4444
Sales: $15,000,000   *Employees:* 75
Company Type: Private   *Employees here:* 75
SIC: 0912
  Commercial fishing marina incl yacht charter whol & ret
    lobster bait whol ice cubes ret fuel oil & lessor of real
    property
Kenneth Knight, President

D-U-N-S 60-356-7140
OAKDELL EGG FARMS INC
7401 N Glade Rd, Pasco, WA 99301
Phone: (509) 547-8665
Sales: $27,939,000   *Employees:* 60
Company Type: Private   *Employees here:* 35
SIC: 0252
  Egg farm
Wayne Kirschenman, President

D-U-N-S 05-751-2204
OAKLEY GROVES INC
101 A B C Rd, Lake Wales, FL 33853
Phone: (941) 638-1435
Sales: $79,282,000   *Employees:* 400
Company Type: Private   *Employees here:* 100
SIC: 0174
  Citrus fruit grove
Dwight Matsuno, President

D-U-N-S 62-297-7791
OCHOA JC FARM MANAGEMENT & FLC
83558 Avenue 45, Ste 4, Indio, CA 92201
Phone: (760) 342-6858

Sales: $10,500,000   *Employees:* 300
Company Type: Private   *Employees here:* 300
SIC: 0761
    Farm laborers
Tom Kitayama, President

D-U-N-S 19-853-2442
OGLEVEE, LTD
152 Oglevee Ln, Connellsville, PA 15425
Phone: (724) 628-8360
Sales: $11,663,000   *Employees:* 200
Company Type: Private   *Employees here:* 100
SIC: 0181
    Grows & whol geraniums begonias regals & bavarian belles
Eric M Meling, Chief Financial Officer

D-U-N-S 14-440-8580
OMEGA ENTERPRISES
801 Pine St Apt 14f, Seattle, WA 98101
Phone: (206) 622-0322
Sales: $50,000,000   *Employees:* NA
Company Type: Private   *Employees here:* NA
SIC: 0912
    Commercial finfishing vessel mail-order house
Steven L Williams, President

D-U-N-S 02-006-7240
OMNI FACILITY RESOURCES INC
1253 New Market Ave, South Plainfield, NJ
Phone: (908) 755-8400
Sales: $100,000,000   *Employees:* 4,400
Company Type: Private   *Employees here:* 4,400
SIC: 0781
    Holding company
Hillman Koen, President

D-U-N-S 11-506-1269
OORD DAIRY
4581 Maple Grove Rd, Sunnyside, WA 98944
Phone: (509) 837-4779
Sales: $10,000,000   *Employees:* 35
Company Type: Private   *Employees here:* 35
SIC: 0241
    Dairy farm
Samuel Kofkoff, Executive

D-U-N-S 09-798-6004
OPPLIGER FAMILY, LTD.
6 Miles E of Clovis, Clovis, NM 88101
Phone: (505) 389-5321
Sales: $50,000,000   *Employees:* 150
Company Type: Private   *Employees here:* 150
SIC: 0212
    Cattle corn wheat produce & dairy farm
Kurt H Kreher, Partner

D-U-N-S 55-687-2570
OPPLIGER FEEDYARD INC
5 Miles E of Clovis, Clovis, NM 88101
Phone: (505) 389-5321
Sales: $22,887,000   *Employees:* 43
Company Type: Private   *Employees here:* 25
SIC: 0211
    Beef cattle feedlot
Russell Weiss, President

D-U-N-S 04-747-0158   EXP
ORANGE-CO INC
2020 Hwy 17 S, Bartow, FL 33830
Phone: (941) 533-0551

Sales: $109,337,000   *Employees:* 250
Company Type: Public   *Employees here:* 90
SIC: 0174
    Citrus grower mfg frozen concentrated juices & beverages
      and grove management
Steven C Glover, President

D-U-N-S 94-426-2765
ORANGE-CO OF FLORIDA INC
    (Parent: Orange-Co Inc)
2020 US Hwy 17 S, Bartow, FL 33830
Phone: (941) 533-0551
Sales: $14,800,000   *Employees:* 250
Company Type: Public Family Member   *Employees here:* 250
SIC: 0174
    Citrus grower & processor
Lourdes Morales, President

D-U-N-S 16-016-1147
ORANGE COUNTY PRODUCE
210 W Walnut Ave, Fullerton, CA 92832
Phone: (949) 651-9106
Sales: $12,100,000   *Employees:* 125
Company Type: Private   *Employees here:* 125
SIC: 0161
    Crop farm
Mary Jorge, President

D-U-N-S 83-729-7902
ORANGEBURG FOODS INC
443 John C Calhoun Dr, Orangeburg, SC 29115
Phone: (803) 534-4905
Sales: $14,366,000   *Employees:* 37
Company Type: Private   *Employees here:* 25
SIC: 0213
    Hog production mfg feed for hog farms
Rosella Mamot, President

D-U-N-S 95-980-3719
ORGANICS MANAGEMENT CO
526 S Wesley Ave, Oak Park, IL 60304
Phone: (708) 445-9431
Sales: $30,000,000   *Employees:* 3
Company Type: Private   *Employees here:* 3
SIC: 0711
    Holding company
L A Hearne, Chairman of the Board

D-U-N-S 07-676-0982
OSCAR ORTEGA
88-200 Ave 58, Thermal, CA 92274
Phone: (760) 398-6458
Sales: $11,516,000   *Employees:* 1
Company Type: Private   *Employees here:* 1
SIC: 0172
    Farming/equipment rentals
Robert Ludekens, President

D-U-N-S 79-377-2617
P F F J, INC
59 E Center St, Snowflake, AZ 85937
Phone: (520) 536-9106
Sales: $24,000,000   *Employees:* 150
Company Type: Private   *Employees here:* 15
SIC: 0213
    Hog producer and ret of feed
Doris H Murphrey, President

D-U-N-S 04-862-2039
P. H. RANCH, INC
6349 Oakdale Rd, Winton, CA 95388
Phone: (209) 358-5111

Sales: $15,000,000   *Employees:* 50
Company Type: Private   *Employees here:* 50
SIC: 0241
   Dairy farm
James Zampini, President

D-U-N-S 05-843-2642
P R FARMS INC
2917 E Shepherd Ave, Clovis, CA 93611
Phone: (559) 299-0201
Sales: $20,000,000   *Employees:* 225
Company Type: Private   *Employees here:* 220
SIC: 0175
   Grows apples peaches nectarines plums & almonds
Frank Lagomarsino, Trustee

D-U-N-S 04-037-8283
PACIFIC EARTH RESOURCES LLC
305 Hueneme Rd, Camarillo, CA 93012
Phone: (805) 987-8456
Sales: $20,000,000   *Employees:* 170
Company Type: Private   *Employees here:* 80
SIC: 0181
   Sod & nursery stock farm
John Veldhuis, General Manager

D-U-N-S 80-747-5314
PACIFIC OYSTER CO
   (Parent: Dulcich Inc)
3220 SW 1st Ave, Portland, OR 97201
Phone: (503) 226-2200
Sales: $15,000,000   *Employees:* 30
Company Type: Private   *Employees here:* 2
SIC: 0913
   Harvests & whol oysters
Don Schwandt, President

D-U-N-S 05-555-7128
PACIFIC TOMATO GROWERS, LTD
503 10th St W, Palmetto, FL 34221
Phone: (941) 722-3291
Sales: $94,301,000   *Employees:* 75
Company Type: Private   *Employees here:* 50
SIC: 0161
   Tomato vegetable melon farm citrus grove & packing house
Frank P Pantaleo, General Partner

D-U-N-S 18-356-5019
PACKERS OF INDIAN RIVER, LTD
5700 W Midway Rd, Fort Pierce, FL 34981
Phone: (561) 468-8835
Sales: $12,000,000   *Employees:* 25
Company Type: Private   *Employees here:* 25
SIC: 0723
   Fresh citrus fruit packing house
William F Murdy, Chairman of the Board

D-U-N-S 62-334-3845
PACO FEEDYARD INC.
12 Miles South on Hwy 214, Friona, TX 79035
Phone: (806) 265-3433
Sales: $15,000,000   *Employees:* 30
Company Type: Private   *Employees here:* 30
SIC: 0211
   Cattle feed yard
Michael Kerton, Treasurer

D-U-N-S 87-979-8858
PADILLA FARM LABOR C
20486 Road 196, Lindsay, CA 93247
Phone: (559) 562-1166

Sales: $12,800,000   *Employees:* 200
Company Type: Private   *Employees here:* 200
SIC: 0174
   Citrus fruit grove
Gary Horton, President

D-U-N-S 79-111-1073
PALMETTO COMPANIES, INC
1320 33rd St W, Palmetto, FL 34221
Phone: (941) 721-0600
Sales: $13,500,000   *Employees:* 300
Company Type: Private   *Employees here:* 5
SIC: 0181
   Grows ornamental flowers & citrus fruit & whol fresh fowers
Stanton M Pikus, Chairman of the Board

D-U-N-S 00-690-5095
PANDOL & SONS
401 Road 192, Delano, CA 93215
Phone: (661) 725-3755
Sales: $25,692,000   *Employees:* 205
Company Type: Private   *Employees here:* 200
SIC: 0723
   Grower & packer of grapes
Dirk G Herrmann, President

D-U-N-S 07-846-8519
PARAGON PRODUCE CORP
315 E New Market Rd, Immokalee, FL 34142
Phone: (941) 657-4421
Sales: $85,500,000   *Employees:* 1,000
Company Type: Private   *Employees here:* 100
SIC: 0161
   Vegetable growers & farming
Randy Lange, President

D-U-N-S 60-127-6959
PARAMOUNT CITRUS ASSOCIATION
36445 Road 172, Visalia, CA 93292
Phone: (559) 798-3100
Sales: $51,000,000   *Employees:* 650
Company Type: Private   *Employees here:* 150
SIC: 0174
   Grows oranges & lemons packing of fresh fruits
Larry Dobbins, Owner

D-U-N-S 18-177-3268
PARAMOUNT FARMING COMPANY, LP
33141 Lerdo Hwy, Bakersfield, CA 93308
Phone: (661) 399-4456
Sales: $120,000,000   *Employees:* 400
Company Type: Private   *Employees here:* 150
SIC: 0173
   Tree nut grove & fruit farm
George Larse, President

D-U-N-S 01-115-4135
PARIS FOODS CORP
1632 Carman St, Camden, NJ
Phone: (609) 964-0915
Sales: $39,796,000   *Employees:* 46
Company Type: Private   *Employees here:* 10
SIC: 0723
   Packer of frozen fruits & vegetables
Keith Larson, President

D-U-N-S 16-153-1116
PARK LANDSCAPE MAINTENANCE
22421 Gilberto, Ste A, Rcho Sta Marg, CA 92688
Phone: (949) 858-7006

Sales: $11,613,000
Company Type: Private
SIC: 0782
   Landscape maintenance contractor
O L Hilburn, Partner

Employees: 400
Employees here: 300

D-U-N-S 06-428-0035
PARKER INTERIOR PLANTSCAPE
1325 Terrill Rd, Scotch Plains, NJ
Phone: (908) 322-5552
Sales: $15,000,000
Company Type: Private
SIC: 0781
   Interior landscaping services
Kenneth Elwood, President

Employees: 200
Employees here: 200

D-U-N-S 03-322-0732
PARKER RANCH FOUNDATION TRUST
67-1435 Mamalahoa Hwy, Kamuela, HI 96743
Phone: (808) 885-7311
Sales: $15,522,000
Company Type: Private
SIC: 0212
   Cattle ranch
Mary A Lynch, President

Employees: 80
Employees here: 10

D-U-N-S 01-172-4309
PARKER WHOLESALE FLORIST INC
1325 Terrill Rd, Scotch Plains, NJ
Phone: (908) 322-5552
Sales: $10,000,000
Company Type: Private
SIC: 0181
   Ornamental nursery
William Hansen, President

Employees: 40
Employees here: 40

D-U-N-S 03-598-9128
PASQUINELLI PRODUCE CO
350 W 16th St, Ste 400, Yuma, AZ 85364
Phone: (520) 783-7813
Sales: $13,050,000
Company Type: Private
SIC: 0191
   Farm of grains melons and produce
Ronald Lehr, President

Employees: 125
Employees here: 10

D-U-N-S 05-308-1998
PAWNEE BEEFBUILDERS, INC
   (Parent: National Farms Inc)
3 Mi S on Hwy 19 5 Mi E, Larned, KS 67550
Phone: (316) 285-2145
Sales: $16,000,000
Company Type: Private
SIC: 0211
   Cattle feedlot
Thomas K Leidy, President

Employees: 24
Employees here: 24

D-U-N-S 78-479-8126
PEACE RIVER CITRUS PRODUCTS
4104 NW US Hwy 72, Arcadia, FL 34266
Phone: (941) 494-0440
Sales: $58,106,000
Company Type: Private
SIC: 0174
   Citrus manufacturing
Edward Ward, President

Employees: NA
Employees here: NA

D-U-N-S 02-994-5524
PEACH ORCHARD GIN CO INC
Hwy 153, Gideon, MO 63848
Phone: (573) 448-3888

Sales: $11,609,000
Company Type: Private
SIC: 0724
   Cotton gin & whol grain
Douglas Baker, President

Employees: 8
Employees here: 8

D-U-N-S 09-884-6116   EXP
PECO FARMS INC
   (Parent: Peco Foods Inc)
2nd Ave, Gordo, AL 35466
Phone: (205) 364-7121
Sales: $85,000,000
Company Type: Private
SIC: 0251
   Broiler growout operation
Herbert Chafin, Chief Executive Officer

Employees: 609
Employees here: 225

D-U-N-S 03-413-0328   EXP
PECO FOODS INC
3701 Kauloosa Ave, Tuscaloosa, AL 35401
Phone: (205) 345-3955
Sales: $260,000,000
Company Type: Private
SIC: 0254
   Broiler production
Scott Lewis, President

Employees: 3,500
Employees here: 600

D-U-N-S 82-504-3789
PECO FOODS OF MISSISSIPPI INC
   (Parent: Peco Foods Inc)
95 Commerce Blvd, Bay Springs, MS 39422
Phone: (601) 764-4392
Sales: $70,000,000
Company Type: Private
SIC: 0254
   Broiler production
Richard C Alt, President

Employees: 600
Employees here: 600

D-U-N-S 83-344-4573
PENCO INC
1705 Abner Creek Rd, Greer, SC 29651
Phone: (864) 848-9462
Sales: $22,000,000
Company Type: Private
SIC: 0752
   Raising of minature horses and retail automobiles
Willard Sparks, Partner

Employees: 24
Employees here: 2

D-U-N-S 05-414-3706
PENNFIELD CORP
711 Rohrerstown Rd, Lancaster, PA 17603
Phone: (717) 299-2561
Sales: $180,000,000
Company Type: Private
SIC: 0213
   Chicken & hog farms poultry slaughtering & dressing mfg
     feed for poultry & livestock & whol poultry & farm supplies
Thomas O Lied, Chief Executive Officer

Employees: 650
Employees here: 155

D-U-N-S 12-174-1037
PENNINK ARRIMOUR
1965 Byberry Rd, Huntingdon Valley, PA 19006
Phone: (215) 659-6411
Sales: $10,548,000
Company Type: Private
SIC: 0782
   Lawn service landscape contractors landscape counseling &
     planning
Josef B Skelton, Chief Operating Officer

Employees: 250
Employees here: 75

D-U-N-S 11-268-8775
PERI & SONS FARMS INC
430 Hwy 339, Yerington, NV 89447

Phone: (775) 463-3640
Sales: $13,979,000
Company Type: Private
SIC: 0161
   Vegetable/melon farm
Gary Grottke, President

     Employees: 24
     Employees here: 19

     D-U-N-S 03-062-7608
PERRIER FEED LOT
Whirlwind Rd, Dodge City, KS 67801
Phone: (316) 225-4555
Sales: $12,000,000
Company Type: Private
SIC: 0211
   Cattle feedlot
Pierre Tada, President

     Employees: 8
     Employees here: 8

     D-U-N-S 05-382-9800
PERRYTON FEEDERS, INC.
Hwy 70, Perryton, TX 79070
Phone: (806) 435-5466
Sales: $21,446,000
Company Type: Private
SIC: 0211
   Cattle feedlot
George Lindemann, President

     Employees: 65
     Employees here: 36

     D-U-N-S 96-579-2450
PET'S CHOICE INC
305 108th Ave NE, Ste 200, Bellevue, WA 98004
Phone: (425) 455-0727
Sales: $12,000,000
Company Type: Private
SIC: 0742
   Veterinary hospital
Robert Lipinski, President

     Employees: 342
     Employees here: 30

     D-U-N-S 11-936-1475
PETERS RUNNELLS CATTLE CO INC
1001 Bristol Rd 152, Laredo, TX 78045
Phone: (956) 724-3637
Sales: $22,000,000
Company Type: Private
SIC: 0211
   Cattle feedlot
Larry Celle, President

     Employees: 15
     Employees here: 15

     D-U-N-S 04-355-6885   EXP
PETERSON FARMS, INC.
250 S Main St, Decatur, AR 72722
Phone: (501) 752-5000
Sales: $173,000,000
Company Type: Private
SIC: 0254
   Chicken hatchery & broiler raising
Alfred Lion Jr, President

     Employees: 1,450
     Employees here: 1,380

     D-U-N-S 17-380-8684
PETSMART, INC.
19601 N 27th Ave, Phoenix, AZ 85027
Phone: (602) 580-6100
Sales: $1,790,599,000
Company Type: Public
SIC: 0742
   Pet food pet supplies tropical fish and birds
Johnny Trotter, President

     Employees: 18,800
     Employees here: 240

     D-U-N-S 00-543-6233
PFISTER HYBRID CORN CO
187 N Fayette Rte 51, El Paso, IL 61738
Phone: (309) 527-6000

Sales: $12,520,000
Company Type: Private
SIC: 0115
   Corn grower-producer
S L Garrison, President

     Employees: 70
     Employees here: 30

     D-U-N-S 02-882-1130
PHELAN & TAYLOR PRODUCE CO
1860 Pacific Coast Hwy, Oceano, CA 93445
Phone: (805) 489-2413
Sales: $11,300,000
Company Type: Private
SIC: 0723
   Vegetable packer growing and shipping
Sunderland W Everstill, President

     Employees: 150
     Employees here: 150

     D-U-N-S 07-115-6616
PIG IMPROVEMENT COMPANY, INC
   (*Parent:* Dalgety Holdings America Inc)
3033 Nashville Rd, Franklin, KY 42134
Phone: (502) 586-9224
Sales: $69,700,000
Company Type: Private
SIC: 0213
   Pig breeding service developing & marketing genetically
     improved breeding stock
Joe Bradberry, Vice-President

     Employees: 750
     Employees here: 180

     D-U-N-S 03-592-5668
PINAL FEEDING CO
   (*Parent:* Hay Northside Company Inc)
13984 W Van Buren St, Goodyear, AZ 85338
Phone: (602) 932-0800
Sales: $19,300,000
Company Type: Private
SIC: 0211
   Cattle feeding
John Martin, President

     Employees: 85
     Employees here: 2

     D-U-N-S 83-500-1132
PINE-BELT INC
   (*Parent:* Timberland Enterprises Inc)
140 Arkansas St, Monticello, AR 71655
Phone: (870) 367-8561
Sales: $11,398,000
Company Type: Private
SIC: 0851
   Herbicide application
Richard P Wollenberg, Chairman of the Board

     Employees: 12
     Employees here: 12

     D-U-N-S 80-788-5876
PIONEER GROWERS COOPERATIVE
227 NW Avenue L, Belle Glade, FL 33430
Phone: (561) 996-3259
Sales: $40,000,000
Company Type: Private
SIC: 0161
   Celery farm
Manuel C Zepeda, President

     Employees: 10
     Employees here: 10

     D-U-N-S 02-882-1155
PISMO-OCEANO VEGETABLE EXCH
1731 Railroad St, Oceano, CA 93445
Phone: (805) 489-5771
Sales: $26,998,000
Company Type: Private
SIC: 0723
   Crop preparation for market
Shirley Weber, President

     Employees: 27
     Employees here: 27

     D-U-N-S 01-304-2460
PLAINVILLE TURKEY FARM INC
7830 Plainville Rd, Plainville, NY 13137

Phone: (315) 635-3427
Sales: $13,000,000   *Employees:* 160
Company Type: Private   *Employees here:* 160
SIC: 0253
    Turkey farm
Duwayne Skaar, President

D-U-N-S 12-590-9218
PLANNING DSIGN CLLBORATIVE INC
3122 W Cary St, Ste 220, Richmond, VA 23221
Phone: (804) 355-4410
Sales: $18,599,000   *Employees:* 5
Company Type: Private   *Employees here:* 5
SIC: 0781
    Landscape architects & land planners architectural services
    and interior design
Peter Lucich, Partner

D-U-N-S 05-716-8577
PLANTATION FOODS, INC
    (*Parent:* Cargill Inc)
2510 E Lake Shore Dr, Waco, TX 76705
Phone: (254) 799-6211
Sales: $180,000,000   *Employees:* 1,600
Company Type: Private   *Employees here:* 1,300
SIC: 0253
    Raises turkeys & whol chicken meat
Robert H Hayes, President

D-U-N-S 00-418-4805
PM BEEF GROUP LLC
    (*Parent:* PM Beef Holdings LLC)
10920 NW Ambassador Dr, Kansas City, MO 64153
Phone: (816) 880-9500
Sales: $85,000,000   *Employees:* 120
Company Type: Private   *Employees here:* 100
SIC: 0211
    Beef operation from beef cow operation to and including
    marketing
James A Scattini, Partner

D-U-N-S 95-721-7698
PONDEROSA DAIRY
G Ranch and Mecca Rd, Amargosa Valley, NV 89020
Phone: (775) 372-1300
Sales: $13,479,000   *Employees:* 60
Company Type: Private   *Employees here:* 60
SIC: 0241
    Dairy farm
James E Sutherland, Chairman of the Board

D-U-N-S 94-194-6923
POPULAR FARMS INC
5331 N Rose Ave, Oxnard, CA 93030
Phone: (805) 485-2377
Sales: $12,800,000   *Employees:* 200
Company Type: Private   *Employees here:* 200
SIC: 0171
    Berry crop farm
M L Pippin, Chief Executive Officer

D-U-N-S 03-562-3602
PORTLAND GIN CO
US Hwy 165 N, Portland, AR 71663
Phone: (870) 737-2231
Sales: $12,000,000   *Employees:* 17
Company Type: Private   *Employees here:* 12
SIC: 0724
    Cotton gin whol cottonseed & fertilizer cotton warehouse &
    grain elevator
David M Wilson, President

D-U-N-S 18-476-0874
POWELL AND POWELL MILLING INC
Hwy 62, Green Forest, AR 72638
Phone: (870) 438-5656
Sales: $10,000,000   *Employees:* 30
Company Type: Private   *Employees here:* 30
SIC: 0723
    Feed milling & turkey & cattle farming
John Lombardi Jr, Partner

D-U-N-S 02-715-2990
POWELL PLANT FARMS INC
Rural Route 3 Box 1058, Troup, TX 75789
Phone: (903) 842-3123
Sales: $15,900,000   *Employees:* 356
Company Type: Private   *Employees here:* 350
SIC: 0181
    Nursery products production
Luis Caratan, President

D-U-N-S 15-221-1793
PRATT FEEDERS L L C
40010 NW 20th, Pratt, KS 67124
Phone: (316) 672-6448
Sales: $25,000,000   *Employees:* 75
Company Type: Private   *Employees here:* 33
SIC: 0211
    Commercial cattle feedlot
Jose E Fernandez, Partner

D-U-N-S 96-156-5603
PREMIER FARMS
P.O. Box 303, Clarion, IA 50525
Phone: (515) 532-6500
Sales: $10,000,000   *Employees:* 100
Company Type: Private   *Employees here:* 100
SIC: 0213
    Hog farm
Michael G George, President

D-U-N-S 82-556-0428
PREMIER MUSHROOMS, INC
573 Rosedale Rd, Kennett Square, PA 19348
Phone: (610) 444-1325
Sales: $10,000,000   *Employees:* 30
Company Type: Private   *Employees here:* 30
SIC: 0723
    Packaging and wholesale of mushrooms
David A Newton, President

D-U-N-S 62-697-3598
PREMIER PACKING, INC
6301 S Zerker Rd, Shafter, CA 93263
Phone: (661) 393-3320
Sales: $15,000,000   *Employees:* 400
Company Type: Private   *Employees here:* 400
SIC: 0723
    Crop preparation for market
Manuel A Silva, President

D-U-N-S 86-735-5299
PREMIER SWINE BREEDING SYSTEMS
1437 N State Road 29, Michigantown, IN 46057
Phone: (765) 249-2385
Sales: $17,000,000   *Employees:* 13
Company Type: Private   *Employees here:* 13
SIC: 0751
    Livestock breeding services
Rick Vidgen, President

D-U-N-S 05-657-6176
PREMIUM FEEDERS INC
Outlying Area Hwy 36, Scandia, KS 66966

Phone: (785) 335-2222
Sales: $22,586,000   *Employees:* 25
Company Type: Private   *Employees here:* 25
SIC: 0211
   Cattle feed lot
Fred Ernst, President

D-U-N-S 01-533-8189
PREMIUM GOLD ANGUS BEEF, INC
6405 Farmdale Ln, Austin, TX 78749
Phone: (512) 288-3319
Sales: $12,000,000   *Employees:* 6
Company Type: Private   *Employees here:* 6
SIC: 0212
   Beef cattle
Douglas Maddox, General Partner

D-U-N-S 10-174-1403
PRESTAGE FARMS INC
4651 Taylors Bridge Hwy, Clinton, NC 28328
Phone: (910) 592-5771
Sales: $83,600,000   *Employees:* 900
Company Type: Private   *Employees here:* 50
SIC: 0213
   Hog & turkey production
John Magarro, Owner

D-U-N-S 07-426-6271
PRIDE FEEDERS I, LTD
23 Miles SE of Town, Hooker, OK 73945
Phone: (580) 253-6381
Sales: $35,410,000   *Employees:* 50
Company Type: Private   *Employees here:* 50
SIC: 0211
   Beef cattle feed lot
Steven Lion, President

D-U-N-S 07-609-4218
PRIDE INDUSTRIES INC
1 Sierra Gate Plz, Roseville, CA 95678
Phone: (916) 783-5266
Sales: $47,986,000   *Employees:* 2,700
Company Type: Private   *Employees here:* 65
SIC: 0782
   Sheltered workshop
Carl P Mc Cord, President

D-U-N-S 92-888-4618
PRIDE OF SAN JUAN, THE INC
1275 San Justo Rd, San Juan Bautista, CA 95045
Phone: (831) 623-4130
Sales: $12,000,000   *Employees:* 100
Company Type: Private   *Employees here:* 100
SIC: 0161
   Farm
Carl P Mc Cord, President

D-U-N-S 09-206-7586
PRIDES CORNER FARMS, INC
122 Waterman Rd, Lebanon, CT
Phone: (860) 642-7535
Sales: $10,200,000   *Employees:* 45
Company Type: Private   *Employees here:* 45
SIC: 0181
   Grower of nursery
Richard W Mallorie, President

D-U-N-S 06-667-7261
PRO-AG INC
32458 Road 236, Lemoncove, CA 93244
Phone: (559) 597-1475

Sales: $19,000,000   *Employees:* 266
Company Type: Private   *Employees here:* 6
SIC: 0723
   Citrus fruit packing
William A Filter Jr, President

D-U-N-S 61-319-7524
PRODUCERS HOLDING CO
  (Parent: Dunavant Holding Inc)
3797 New Getwell Rd, Memphis, TN 38118
Phone: (901) 369-1500
Sales: $20,800,000   *Employees:* 200
Company Type: Private   *Employees here:* 200
SIC: 0724
   Cotton ginning and whol cottonseed
Whiting H Preston Ii, President

D-U-N-S 83-550-2642
PROGRESSIVE DAIRIES HOLDINGS
5201 California Ave, Bakersfield, CA 93309
Phone: (661) 831-2634
Sales: $15,300,000   *Employees:* 175
Company Type: Private   *Employees here:* 4
SIC: 0241
   Dairy farms
Dominic Manfredini, President

D-U-N-S 05-220-3098
PUGLISI EGG FARMS INC
75 Easy St, Howell, NJ
Phone: (732) 938-2373
Sales: $11,500,000   *Employees:* 35
Company Type: Private   *Employees here:* 35
SIC: 0252
   Chicken egg farm
Kent Manley, President

D-U-N-S 80-196-0436
PULEO TREE CO, INC
3630 Kennedy Rd, South Plainfield, NJ
Phone: (908) 754-2626
Sales: $14,000,000   *Employees:* 16
Company Type: Private   *Employees here:* 16
SIC: 0811
   Whol christmas trees
William Ramsey, President

D-U-N-S 80-736-1274
PUREPAK INC
2640 Sturgis Rd, Oxnard, CA 93030
Phone: (805) 485-1127
Sales: $10,000,000   *Employees:* 100
Company Type: Private   *Employees here:* 100
SIC: 0161
   Grower packer & shipper of produce
Ken Everett, President

D-U-N-S 05-259-7853
PURSLEY INC
9049 59th Avenue Cir E, Bradenton, FL 34202
Phone: (941) 753-7851
Sales: $10,000,000   *Employees:* 200
Company Type: Private   *Employees here:* 20
SIC: 0181
   Turf farm ret lawn & garden supplies & real estate developer
Terry L Tucker, Chairman of the Board

D-U-N-S 10-277-5863
QUALITY FARM LABOR INC
21 4th St, Gonzales, CA 93926
Phone: (831) 675-3690

Sales: $17,500,000
Company Type: Private
SIC: 0761
    Farm labor contractor
Terry L Tucker, President

Employees: 500
Employees here: 500

D-U-N-S 61-379-6622
QUALITY GRAIN COMPANY INC
3805 Crestwood Pkwy 175, Atlanta, GA 30396
Phone: (770) 935-5633
Sales: $23,400,000
Company Type: Private
SIC: 0112
    Rice & soybean farmer & whol grain
Jamal Al-Barzinji, President

Employees: 341
Employees here: 341

D-U-N-S 80-957-6952
QUALITY TURF NURSERIES
17502 State Road 672, Lithia, FL 33547
Phone: (813) 634-3326
Sales: $20,000,000
Company Type: Private
SIC: 0181
    Grows turf grasses
Charles Marder, President

Employees: 160
Employees here: 12

D-U-N-S 07-202-4938
QUARTER M FARMS, INC.
4134 S US Hwy 117, Rose Hill, NC 28458
Phone: (910) 289-6415
Sales: $19,000,000
Company Type: Private
SIC: 0213
    Hog farms
Margaret Gonzales, Owner

Employees: 250
Employees here: 250

D-U-N-S 03-802-4303
QUINCY CORP
    (Parent: Sylvan Foods Inc)
Hwy 65, Quincy, FL 32351
Phone: (850) 875-1600
Sales: $28,000,000
Company Type: Public Family Member
SIC: 0182
    Covered food crops farm
Frank Mariani, President

Employees: 575
Employees here: 575

D-U-N-S 09-227-9629
R A RASMUSSEN & SONS INC
1183 Indian Church Rd, Granger, WA 98932
Phone: (509) 854-1365
Sales: $12,200,000
Company Type: Private
SIC: 0161
    Grows vegetables
William Sawyer Sr, President

Employees: 150
Employees here: 150

D-U-N-S 94-936-9672
R & R FARMS, LLC
9050 San Antonio Rd, Santa Maria, CA 93455
Phone: (805) 934-8491
Sales: $18,300,000
Company Type: Private
SIC: 0161
    Vegetable/melon farm
Mark A Mariani, President

Employees: 200
Employees here: 200

D-U-N-S 00-306-3732
R D BOWMAN & SONS INC
107 Englar Rd, Westminster, MD 21157
Phone: (410) 848-3733

Sales: $22,000,000
Company Type: Private
SIC: 0723
    Feed mill ret garden supplies
Marko B Zaninovich, President

Employees: 55
Employees here: 55

D-U-N-S 08-411-2663
R D OFFUTT CO
2829 S University Dr, Fargo, ND 58103
Phone: (701) 237-6062
Sales: $54,500,000
Company Type: Private
SIC: 0134
    Potato farming & french fry processing
William E Chaney, President

Employees: 545
Employees here: 25

D-U-N-S 78-767-3573
R H PHILLIPS INC
26836 County Road 12a, Esparto, CA 95627
Phone: (530) 662-3215
Sales: $17,258,000
Company Type: Public
SIC: 0172
    Vineyard & winery
Marshall Durbin Jr, Chairman of the Board

EXP

Employees: 165
Employees here: 165

D-U-N-S 11-520-7599
R H PHILLIPS VINEYARD INC
26836 County Road 12a, Esparto, CA 95627
Phone: (530) 662-3215
Sales: $17,258,000
Company Type: Private
SIC: 0172
    Vineyard & winery
K W Davis, President

Employees: 102
Employees here: 102

D-U-N-S 12-143-4849
RAFTER 3 FEEDYARD, INC.
Fm 1055, Dimmitt, TX 79027
Phone: (806) 647-5103
Sales: $32,231,000
Company Type: Private
SIC: 0211
    Cattle feedlot
Matthew W Dietz, Owner

Employees: 33
Employees here: 33

D-U-N-S 61-231-8295
RAHAV ENTERPRISES, INC
18047 N Tatum Blvd, Phoenix, AZ 85032
Phone: (602) 788-0300
Sales: $10,000,000
Company Type: Private
SIC: 0781
    Landscape services lawn/garden services
Gary L Gifford, President

Employees: 30
Employees here: 30

D-U-N-S 00-761-0843
RANDALL FARMS, L.L.C.
3867 Second St, Arcadia, LA 71001
Phone: (318) 263-9004
Sales: $20,000,000
Company Type: Private
SIC: 0251
    Fully integrated processing poultry plant
Vincent J Reina Sr, President

Employees: 400
Employees here: 390

D-U-N-S 05-468-6670
RAY WIEGAND NURSERY INC
47747 Romeo Plank Rd, Macomb, MI 48044
Phone: (810) 286-3655

Sales: $11,484,000 *Employees:* 15
Company Type: Private *Employees here:* 15
SIC: 0181
 Ornamental nursery
J L Maxwell Iii, President

D-U-N-S 00-126-5263 EXP
RAYONIER INC.
1177 Summer St, Stamford, CT
Phone: (203) 348-7000
Sales: $1,104,228,000 *Employees:* 2,500
Company Type: Public *Employees here:* 88
SIC: 0241
 Mfg timber and wood products and specialty pulps
Charles Hurwitz, Chairman of the Board

D-U-N-S 11-510-8268
RED ROCK CATTLE COMPANY INC
 (Parent: Red Rock Feeding Co)
35415 W Sasco Rd, Red Rock, AZ 85245
Phone: (520) 682-3448
Sales: $13,000,000 *Employees:* 7
Company Type: Private *Employees here:* 7
SIC: 0212
 Farm
Marlin Lucas, Principal

D-U-N-S 06-326-0467
RED ROCK FEEDING CO
Sasco Rd, Red Rock, AZ 85245
Phone: (520) 682-3448
Sales: $24,000,000 *Employees:* 35
Company Type: Private *Employees here:* 31
SIC: 0211
 Beef cattle feedlot
Nancy J Davis, President

D-U-N-S 11-269-3221
REITER BERRY FARMS INC
1767 San Juan Rd, Watsonville, CA 95076
Phone: (831) 726-3256
Sales: $12,000,000 *Employees:* 200
Company Type: Private *Employees here:* 200
SIC: 0171
 Strawberry & raspberry farm
Larry Rainwater, Treasurer

D-U-N-S 03-152-7682
RESOURCE MANAGEMENT SERVICE
100 Corporate Rdg, Birmingham, AL 35242
Phone: (205) 991-9516
Sales: $15,255,000 *Employees:* 77
Company Type: Private *Employees here:* 33
SIC: 0851
 Forestry management reforestation forest inventories
  appraisals timber and timberland sales and feasibility
  studies
James E Mc Donnell Sr, President

D-U-N-S 07-644-3464
REYNOLDS CATTLE CO
6788 Colorado 66, Longmont, CO 80504
Phone: (970) 535-4271
Sales: $15,000,000 *Employees:* 8
Company Type: Private *Employees here:* 8
SIC: 0211
 Beef cattle feedlot
Mark Mc Fall, President

D-U-N-S 93-763-7304
RICHARD GUMZ FARMS LLC
8905 Gumz Rd, North Judson, IN 46366
Phone: (219) 896-5441

Sales: $16,000,000 *Employees:* 21
Company Type: Private *Employees here:* 21
SIC: 0115
 Corn mint and bean farm
Dennis Schilz, President

D-U-N-S 05-960-9347
RICHARD S BURFORD
1443 W Sample Ave, Fresno, CA 93711
Phone: (559) 431-0902
Sales: $17,375,000 *Employees:* 85
Company Type: Private *Employees here:* 85
SIC: 0191
 General crop farm
Neal Odom, General Manager

D-U-N-S 07-612-3975
RICHARD WILBUR RANCH
1425 Pease Rd, Yuba City, CA 95993
Phone: (530) 671-2800
Sales: $16,200,000 *Employees:* 286
Company Type: Private *Employees here:* 35
SIC: 0175
 Farming of peaches plums almonds & walnuts & fresh fruit
  packing
Carlton R Lofgren, Chairman of the Board

D-U-N-S 09-445-0806
RIO FARMS
1051 Pacific Ave, Oxnard, CA 93030
Phone: (805) 240-1979
Sales: $20,700,000 *Employees:* 200
Company Type: Private *Employees here:* 63
SIC: 0161
 Vegetable/melon farm
Mccleskey I Member, N/A

D-U-N-S 06-643-7898
RIO QUEEN CITRUS FARMS INC
4012 E Goodwin Rd, Mission, TX 78572
Phone: (956) 585-4303
Sales: $20,000,000 *Employees:* 75
Company Type: Private *Employees here:* 75
SIC: 0174
 Citrus fruit grove crop preparation for market
Daniel Mcclure, Partner

D-U-N-S 13-162-4199
RIOS, JJ FARM SERVICES INC
4890 E Acampo Rd, Acampo, CA 95220
Phone: (209) 333-7467
Sales: $11,893,000 *Employees:* 180
Company Type: Private *Employees here:* 180
SIC: 0761
 Farm labor contractor
Donald Mccorkle Sr, President

D-U-N-S 06-147-1058
RITEWOOD INC
3643 S 4000 E, Franklin, ID 83237
Phone: (208) 646-2213
Sales: $11,771,000 *Employees:* 240
Company Type: Private *Employees here:* 158
SIC: 0252
 Chicken egg farm
Stuart Mcdougall, President

D-U-N-S 01-611-5235
RITZ FOOD INTERNATIONAL INC
1801 S Federal Hwy, Delray Beach, FL 33483
Phone: (561) 278-4546

Sales: $15,000,000   *Employees:* 70
Company Type: Private   *Employees here:* 70
SIC: 0161
    Yuka chips mfr & wholesale
Woody Mcgee, President

D-U-N-S 83-611-9073
RIVER RANCH FRESH FOODS, INC
    (Parent: Albert Fisher Holdings Inc)
1075 Abbott St, Salinas, CA 93901
Phone: (831) 758-1390
Sales: $200,000,000   *Employees:* 650
Company Type: Private   *Employees here:* 150
SIC: 0723
    Vegetable packing services specializing in packaging with
    plastic
Steve Huber, Chief Executive Officer

D-U-N-S 03-173-8974
RIVER RANCH SOUTHWEST INC
    (Parent: River Ranch Fresh Foods Inc)
4721 Simonton Rd, Dallas, TX 75244
Phone: (972) 385-5900
Sales: $20,000,000   *Employees:* 160
Company Type: Private   *Employees here:* 160
SIC: 0723
    Food processing
Joseph Mea Jr, President

D-U-N-S 15-078-5848
RIVERA BLAS
78401 US Hwy 111, La Quinta, CA 92253
Phone: (760) 564-0604
Sales: $15,000,000   *Employees:* 20
Company Type: Private   *Employees here:* 20
SIC: 0172
    Vineyard
Leonard Mecca, Treasurer

D-U-N-S 94-398-3221
RIVERVIEW DAIRY INC
RR 3 Box 255, Morris, MN 56267
Phone: (320) 392-5609
Sales: $10,000,000   *Employees:* 42
Company Type: Private   *Employees here:* 42
SIC: 0241
    Dairy farm
Don Spear, President

D-U-N-S 11-445-3285
ROBERTS ENTERPRISES INC
5001 E Washington St, Phoenix, AZ 85034
Phone: (602) 244-1004
Sales: $60,000,000   *Employees:* 8
Company Type: Private   *Employees here:* 8
SIC: 0211
    Custom cattle feeding & livestock broker
Robert A Melkesian Sr, President

D-U-N-S 02-376-4871
ROCCO FARMS INC
    (Parent: Rocco Enterprises Inc)
1 Kratzer Ave, Harrisonburg, VA 22801
Phone: (540) 568-1400
Sales: $150,000,000   *Employees:* 100
Company Type: Private   *Employees here:* 10
SIC: 0253
    Turkey & chicken farm
John T Mc Shan Jr, Chairman of the Board

D-U-N-S 02-758-8771
ROCHE FRUIT CO INC
609 N 1st Ave, Yakima, WA 98902

Phone: (509) 248-7200
Sales: $10,000,000   *Employees:* 140
Company Type: Private   *Employees here:* 140
SIC: 0723
    Pack & cold storage fruit
Victor Mendes, Owner

D-U-N-S 00-329-9302
ROCHE MANUFACTURING CO INC
717 E Jackson St, Dublin, GA 31021
Phone: (912) 272-3340
Sales: $19,159,000   *Employees:* 45
Company Type: Private   *Employees here:* 35
SIC: 0724
    Mfg fertilizer cotton gin whol grain elevators & farm product
    warehousing
Milton Mercer Jr, President

D-U-N-S 07-722-9730   EXP
ROCK & WATERSCAPE SYSTEMS
11 Whatney, Irvine, CA 92618
Phone: (949) 770-1936
Sales: $20,007,000   *Employees:* 350
Company Type: Private   *Employees here:* 40
SIC: 0782
    Landscaping contractor specializing in waterscape systems
David Blumberg, President

D-U-N-S 14-842-1381
ROCKY MOUNTAIN ELK FOUNDATION
2291 W Broadway St, Missoula, MT 59808
Phone: (406) 523-4500
Sales: $18,909,000   *Employees:* 150
Company Type: Private   *Employees here:* 120
SIC: 0971
    Wildlife conservation & management
Thomas M Merrill, President

D-U-N-S 01-624-5896
ROSE ACRE FARMS INC
6874 N Base Rd, Seymour, IN 47274
Phone: (812) 497-2557
Sales: $100,000,000   *Employees:* 1,200
Company Type: Private   *Employees here:* 100
SIC: 0252
    Egg farm
Felipe Irigoyen, Treasurer

D-U-N-S 06-788-6192
ROSS BREEDERS INC
5015 Bradford Dr NW, Huntsville, AL 35805
Phone: (256) 890-3800
Sales: $35,000,000   *Employees:* 350
Company Type: Private   *Employees here:* 70
SIC: 0254
    Poultry hatchery
Tom Van Wingerden, President

D-U-N-S 80-515-6429
ROUSSEAU FARMING CO II
102 S 95th Ave, Tolleson, AZ 85353
Phone: (602) 936-8208
Sales: $28,000,000   *Employees:* 200
Company Type: Private   *Employees here:* 200
SIC: 0161
    Crop farm
Robert L Meyer, Owner

D-U-N-S 02-900-3779   EXP
ROYAL CITRUS CO
3075 10th St, Riverside, CA 92507
Phone: (909) 686-0987

Sales: $17,824,000
Company Type: Private
SIC: 0174
   Citrus fruit growers & packers
Gregg A Ostrander, President

Employees: 300
Employees here: 300

D-U-N-S 80-993-2205
RUNNING W CITRUS LTD PARTNR
8050 US Hwy 27 S, South Bay, FL 33493
Phone: (561) 996-7257
Sales: $24,000,000
Company Type: Private
SIC: 0174
   Citrus fruit grove
Gregg A Ostrander, President

Employees: 200
Employees here: 10

D-U-N-S 15-804-7803
RUSLER PRODUCE, INC
47762 Hwy 96 E, Avondale, CO 81022
Phone: (719) 947-3361
Sales: $11,900,000
Company Type: Private
SIC: 0161
   Vegetable farm
Nick Van Wingerden, President

Employees: 150
Employees here: 150

D-U-N-S 62-193-9305
RYAN LANDSCAPING, INC
2116 Fry Rd, Houston, TX 77084
Phone: (281) 492-1035
Sales: $10,000,000
Company Type: Private
SIC: 0782
   Landscape contractor & ret nursery & garden supplies
James Tanner, President

Employees: 175
Employees here: 135

D-U-N-S 02-859-0339
S & H PACKING AND SALES CO
1899 Sacramento St, Los Angeles, CA 90021
Phone: (213) 627-3055
Sales: $45,000,000
Company Type: Private
SIC: 0161
   Growers of tomatoes whol fruits/vegetables and crop
   preparation services for market
Jeffrey Sternberger, President

EXP

Employees: 381
Employees here: 20

D-U-N-S 05-459-2688
S & J RANCH INC
   (*Parent:* Dole Food Company Inc)
39639 Avenue 10, Madera, CA 93638
Phone: (559) 439-2598
Sales: $30,000,000
Company Type: Public Family Member
SIC: 0762
   Farm management & citrus packing
Peter Orum, Owner

Employees: 400
Employees here: 300

D-U-N-S 96-586-6700
S AND P CATTLE CO LLC
1921 Mockingbird Ln, Moody, TX 76557
Phone: (254) 857-4900
Sales: $10,000,000
Company Type: Private
SIC: 0212
   Cattle company
Austin J De Coster, President

Employees: 4
Employees here: 4

D-U-N-S 03-220-0198
S M JONES & CO INC
508 Lakeshore Dr, Canal Point, FL 33438
Phone: (561) 924-7191

Sales: $11,000,000
Company Type: Private
SIC: 0723
   Vegetable precooling service
Robert Krouse, Managing Partner

Employees: 12
Employees here: 12

D-U-N-S 02-866-4076
S STAMOULES INC
904 S Lyon Ave, Mendota, CA 93640
Phone: (559) 655-4581
Sales: $14,164,000
Company Type: Private
SIC: 0723
   Fruit & vegetable packer
John Nolen, Managing Director

Employees: 10
Employees here: 10

D-U-N-S 18-877-1638
SAHLMAN HOLDING CO INC
1601 Sahlman Dr, Tampa, FL 33605
Phone: (813) 248-5726
Sales: $65,554,000
Company Type: Private
SIC: 0913
   Harvesting and processing shrimp
Norman Dean, Chairman of the Board

Employees: 20
Employees here: 20

D-U-N-S 03-279-9371
SAHLMAN SEAFOODS INC
   (*Parent:* Sahlman Holding Company Inc)
1601 Sahlman Dr, Tampa, FL 33605
Phone: (813) 248-5726
Sales: $65,554,000
Company Type: Private
SIC: 0913
   Shrimp harvesting and processing
Bruce L Miller Ii, President

Employees: 20
Employees here: 20

D-U-N-S 04-867-6886
SAKUMA BROS FARMS INC
17400 Cook Rd, Burlington, WA 98233
Phone: (360) 757-6611
Sales: $12,515,000
Company Type: Private
SIC: 0171
   Strawberry & raspberry farm & nursery
Basil E Mills, President

Employees: 50
Employees here: 44

D-U-N-S 03-950-3719
SAN VAL CORP
75181 Mediterranean, Palm Desert, CA 92211
Phone: (760) 568-5592
Sales: $22,100,000
Company Type: Private
SIC: 0781
   Landscape & burglar & fire alarms
Donald B Stark, President

Employees: 439
Employees here: 425

D-U-N-S 04-131-8577
SANCHEZ DIAZ FARM LABOR CONTRACTORS
20145 Avenue 360, Woodlake, CA 93286
Phone: (559) 564-2464
Sales: $15,800,000
Company Type: Private
SIC: 0761
   Farm labor contractor local trucking operator
Caeser Larson, President

Employees: 450
Employees here: 450

D-U-N-S 60-658-6824
SAND SYSTEMS INC
4860 33rd Ave, Columbus, NE 68601
Phone: (402) 564-9464

Sales: $14,200,000
Company Type: Private
SIC: 0762
  Manage hog operations
Roger Headrick, President
Employees: 300
Employees here: 300

D-U-N-S 09-604-3708
SANDERSON FARMS INC
225 N 13th Ave, Laurel, MS 39440
Phone: (601) 649-4030
Sales: $521,394,000
Company Type: Public
SIC: 0251
  Broiler chickens production & processing
Brad Frew, President
Employees: 6,358
Employees here: 125

D-U-N-S 11-277-4864
SANDERSON FARMS PRODUCTION DIV
  (Parent: Sanderson Farms Inc)
225 N 13th Ave, Laurel, MS 39440
Phone: (601) 425-2552
Sales: $33,800,000
Company Type: Public Family Member
SIC: 0251
  Production of broiler chickens
Roger E Mills, Partner
Employees: 675
Employees here: 2

D-U-N-S 09-944-7377
SANTA BARBARA FARMS LLC
1200 Union Sugar Ave, Lompoc, CA 93436
Phone: (805) 735-3461
Sales: $18,000,000
Company Type: Private
SIC: 0161
  Vegetable farm & nursery products
John Mobley, President
Employees: 250
Employees here: 250

D-U-N-S 00-691-4170
SATICOY LEMON ASSOCIATION INC
103 N Peck Rd, Santa Paula, CA 93060
Phone: (805) 654-6500
Sales: $91,104,000
Company Type: Private
SIC: 0723
  Pack & ship lemons
Charles J Ciarrocchi Jr, President
Employees: 650
Employees here: 250

D-U-N-S 79-987-9325
SAUVAGE GAS CO
4132 S Rainbow Blvd, Las Vegas, NV 89103
Phone: (785) 475-2241
Sales: $10,000,000
Company Type: Private
SIC: 0119
  Grain farming/casino operation
Frank Jarocki, President
Employees: 10
Employees here: 7

D-U-N-S 07-806-1520
SCARBOROUGH FARMS INC
641 W Lynches River Rd, Lamar, SC 29069
Phone: (843) 326-5613
Sales: $10,000,000
Company Type: Private
SIC: 0252
  Chicken egg farm
Evan G Galbraith, Chairman of the Board
Employees: 45
Employees here: 45

D-U-N-S 00-925-2495
SCHAAKE CORP
1180 Umptanum Rd, Ellensburg, WA 98926
Phone: (509) 925-5346

Sales: $71,834,000
Company Type: Private
SIC: 0211
  Beef cattle feedlot
Miles R Rosedale, Chairman of the Board
Employees: 40
Employees here: 20

D-U-N-S 07-722-9557
SCHEID VINEYARDS CAL INC
  (Parent: Scheid Vineyards Inc (del))
13470 Washington Blvd, Marina Del Rey, CA 90292
Phone: (310) 301-1555
Sales: $19,870,000
Company Type: Public
SIC: 0762
  Owner and manager of grape vineyards
Arvid Monson, President
Employees: 100
Employees here: 10

D-U-N-S 15-984-2913
SCHEID VINEYARDS INC (DEL)
13470 Washington Blvd, Marina Del Rey, CA 90292
Phone: (310) 301-1555
Sales: $19,870,000
Company Type: Private
SIC: 0762
  Owner and manager of grape vineyards
Shah Kazemi, President
Employees: 100
Employees here: 10

D-U-N-S 07-116-4164
SCHROEDER MANATEE INC
7550 Lorraine Rd, Bradenton, FL 34202
Phone: (941) 755-1637
Sales: $15,000,000
Company Type: Private
SIC: 0174
  Citrus groves tree & sod farm vegetable farm cattle ranch
    real estate developer & mining
Duane R Ramsey, President
Employees: 75
Employees here: 65

D-U-N-S 78-767-5511   EXP
SCHUDEL ENTERPRISES, L.L.C.
800 NW Cornell Ave, Corvallis, OR 97330
Phone: (541) 753-3236
Sales: $14,000,000
Company Type: Private
SIC: 0811
  Christmas tree farm
John Purcell, President
Employees: 3
Employees here: 3

D-U-N-S 05-601-0986
SCHUMACHER LANDSCAPING INC
17 Electric Ave, Boston, MA
Phone: (508) 655-6651
Sales: $17,500,000
Company Type: Private
SIC: 0782
  Landscape contractor & services & irrigation installation
George Morrell, Chief Executive Officer
Employees: 35
Employees here: 35

D-U-N-S 03-092-4955
SCHWERTNER FARMS INC
4651 E Fm 4587, Schwertner, TX 76573
Phone: (254) 527-3342
Sales: $10,300,000
Company Type: Private
SIC: 0211
  Beef cattle feedlot whol livestock
Marvin Morrison, Partner
Employees: 60
Employees here: 60

D-U-N-S 82-593-6321
SEABOARD FARMS OF OKLAHOMA
  (Parent: Seaboard Corp)
424 N Main St 200, Guymon, OK 73942
Phone: (580) 338-1470

Sales: $79,900,000   *Employees:* 860
Company Type: Private   *Employees here:* 60
SIC: 0213
    Hog farm and processing plant
Kenneth Morrison, Manager/Partner

D-U-N-S 16-170-0778   EXP
SEABROOK ENTERPRISES INC
3755 Mansell Rd, Alpharetta, GA 30022
Phone: (678) 461-9006
Sales: $27,400,000   *Employees:* 400
Company Type: Private   *Employees here:* 25
SIC: 0723
    Shelling blanching roasting and granulation of peanuts and
       manufactures peanut based food products
Phil Mossberg, Chief Executive Officer

D-U-N-S 02-131-1725
SEALASKA TIMBER CORP
    (Parent: Sealaska Corp)
2030 Sea Level Dr, Ste 202, Ketchikan, AK 99901
Phone: (907) 225-9444
Sales: $140,000,000   *Employees:* 48
Company Type: Private   *Employees here:* 22
SIC: 0851
    Forest management
Juan Moya, President

D-U-N-S 19-861-7268
SELECT FARMS, LTD
3808 N Sullivan Rd, Spokane, WA 99216
Phone: (509) 924-2404
Sales: $11,000,000   *Employees:* 100
Company Type: Private   *Employees here:* 100
SIC: 0181
    Ornamental floriculture & nursery products
Sean Mulhall, President

D-U-N-S 06-845-0196
SELLERS FARMS, INC
1433 14th Rd, Lyons, KS 67554
Phone: (316) 257-5144
Sales: $10,203,000   *Employees:* 12
Company Type: Private   *Employees here:* 12
SIC: 0111
    Operates cattle feedlot & grows wheat
Shigeo Murakami, President

D-U-N-S 06-329-3914
SHAMROCK FARMS CO
16516 E Chandler Hts Rd, Chandler, AZ 85249
Phone: (602) 988-1452
Sales: $21,718,000   *Employees:* 75
Company Type: Private   *Employees here:* 65
SIC: 0241
    Dairy farm
Roy Muranaka, President

D-U-N-S 79-826-5872
SHARPE LAND & CATTLE CO
RR 1, La Belle, MO 63447
Phone: (660) 462-3952
Sales: $19,400,000   *Employees:* 120
Company Type: Private   *Employees here:* 120
SIC: 0211
    Beef cattle feedlot corn farm
Wendell H Murphy, Chairman of the Board

D-U-N-S 80-097-3935
SHARYLAND L. P.
Fm 1016 & S Glasscock Rd, Mission, TX 78573
Phone: (956) 585-4761

Sales: $30,000,000   *Employees:* 449
Company Type: Private   *Employees here:* 30
SIC: 0161
    Farm operation
L T Murray Jr, President

D-U-N-S 14-471-4516
SIERRA HILLS PACKING CO INC
4505 N Jack Tone Rd, Stockton, CA 95215
Phone: (209) 931-5157
Sales: $15,000,000   *Employees:* 30
Company Type: Private   *Employees here:* 30
SIC: 0723
    Fresh fruit packing
Jwa Buyers, Chairman of the Board

D-U-N-S 02-948-1801
SILVER TERRACE NURSERIES INTERNATIONAL
850 Mitten Rd, Burlingame, CA 94010
Phone: (650) 259-9444
Sales: $12,000,000   *Employees:* 75
Company Type: Private   *Employees here:* 15
SIC: 0181
    Flower nursery
Melvin G Pruvis, President

D-U-N-S 02-001-4692
SIMONIAN BROTHERS INC
511 N 7th St, Fowler, CA 93625
Phone: (559) 834-5921
Sales: $10,995,000   *Employees:* 15
Company Type: Private   *Employees here:* 15
SIC: 0723
    Fresh fruit packing
Charles R Jaeschke, Treasurer

D-U-N-S 05-951-1170
SIMPLOT LIVESTOCK COMPANY INC
    (Parent: J R Simplot Co)
3 Miles North of Town, Grand View, ID 83624
Phone: (208) 834-2231
Sales: $59,500,000   *Employees:* 280
Company Type: Private   *Employees here:* 100
SIC: 0211
    Beef cattle & range cows feed lot
Mick Anderson, President

D-U-N-S 08-632-3490
SLEEPY CREEK FARMS INC
938 Millers Chapel Rd, Goldsboro, NC 27534
Phone: (919) 778-3130
Sales: $45,000,000   *Employees:* 400
Company Type: Private   *Employees here:* 100
SIC: 0253
    Turkey farms & turkey egg farms
Sampuran S Khalsa, President

D-U-N-S 06-573-8056
SMITH CATTLE INC
3 Miles North on Hwy 27, Tribune, KS 67879
Phone: (316) 376-4210
Sales: $11,000,000   *Employees:* 27
Company Type: Private   *Employees here:* 20
SIC: 0211
    Cattle feedlot
Gerald C Bookkey, President

D-U-N-S 05-492-2158
SMITH FEED SERVICE INC
    (Parent: Vita Plus Corp)
213 E Mill St, Loyal, WI 54446
Phone: (715) 255-8252

Sales: $16,609,000   *Employees:* 100
Company Type: Private   *Employees here:* 87
SIC: 0723
    Custom grinding whol feed seed & fertilizer & trucking
C L Haw, President

D-U-N-S 07-462-7688
SONOMA-CUTRER VINEYARDS INC
4401 Slusser Rd, Windsor, CA 95492
Phone: (707) 528-1177
Sales: $10,600,000   *Employees:* 160
Company Type: Private   *Employees here:* 160
SIC: 0172
    Grape vineyard/mfg wines
Gary D Burge, President

D-U-N-S 62-623-9636
SONORA PACKING CO, INC
1315 Dayton St, Ste H, Salinas, CA 93901
Phone: (831) 757-2443
Sales: $14,000,000   *Employees:* 400
Company Type: Private   *Employees here:* 400
SIC: 0723
    Harvest cut & pack produce
Andrew Goodman, Chief Executive Officer

D-U-N-S 03-217-1977
SORRELLS BROTHERS PACKING CO
1192 NE Livingston St, Arcadia, FL 34266
Phone: (941) 494-3066
Sales: $20,633,000   *Employees:* 20
Company Type: Private   *Employees here:* 20
SIC: 0722
    Fresh fruit harvesting service & whol fresh fruit
Daniel Van Starrenburg, President

D-U-N-S 85-918-8351
SOUTH EASTERN BOLL WEEVIL ERA
2424 E South Blvd B, Montgomery, AL 36116
Phone: (334) 223-7532
Sales: $36,198,000   *Employees:* 210
Company Type: Private   *Employees here:* 12
SIC: 0724
    Cotton service organization specializing in boll weevil
      eradication
Larry Shikuma, President

D-U-N-S 09-472-0398
SOUTH SHRES RSDENTIAL COML DEV
2200 S Fairview St, Santa Ana, CA 92704
Phone: (714) 434-1190
Sales: $11,217,000   *Employees:* 350
Company Type: Private   *Employees here:* 75
SIC: 0782
    Landscape contractor
Michael D Naumes, President

D-U-N-S 00-327-9619
SOUTHERN ORCHARD SUPPLY CO
50 Lane Rd, Fort Valley, GA 31030
Phone: (912) 825-2891
Sales: $27,400,000   *Employees:* 400
Company Type: Private   *Employees here:* 385
SIC: 0723
    Fresh fruit packaging
Duane Yazzie, Chairman of the Board

D-U-N-S 19-417-8588
SOUTHERN POULTRY FARMS INC
1 Kratzer Ave, Harrisonburg, VA 22801
Phone: (540) 568-1400

Sales: $14,000,000   *Employees:* 115
Company Type: Private   *Employees here:* 7
SIC: 0253
    Agricultural production
Fred C Brumbaugh, President

D-U-N-S 09-287-6465
SOUTHERN SE REG AQUCLTRE ASSN
2721 Tongass Ave, Ketchikan, AK 99901
Phone: (907) 225-9605
Sales: $11,590,000   *Employees:* 15
Company Type: Private   *Employees here:* 6
SIC: 0921
    Fish hatchery
James H Neuhoff, Chairman of the Board

D-U-N-S 08-654-5746
SOUTHLAND FOODS INC
    (Parent: Continental Grain Co)
Cty Rd 114, Jack, AL 36346
Phone: (334) 897-3435
Sales: $60,000,000   *Employees:* 950
Company Type: Private   *Employees here:* 800
SIC: 0251
    Broiler production
Thomas F Neumiller, President

D-U-N-S 03-236-2220   EXP
SPEEDLING, INC
4300 Old US 41 S, Sun City, FL 33586
Phone: (813) 645-3221
Sales: $33,598,000   *Employees:* 250
Company Type: Private   *Employees here:* 121
SIC: 0181
    Produces crop & ornamental seedlings & mfg polystyrene
      nursery products
Carrizo M Lc, General Partner

D-U-N-S 79-923-3200
SPENCER FRUIT CO
1500 W Manning Ave, Reedley, CA 93654
Phone: (559) 637-2100
Sales: $42,039,000   *Employees:* 40
Company Type: Private   *Employees here:* 20
SIC: 0723
    Fruit and vegetable packing & sales
Whitt T Carr, President

D-U-N-S 05-465-8232
SPOKANE TRIBE OF INDIANS
Main St, Wellpinit, WA 99040
Phone: (509) 258-4581
Sales: $47,694,000   *Employees:* 325
Company Type: Private   *Employees here:* 300
SIC: 0241
    Indian tribe mfg post & poles ret grocery store credit unions
      & gaming activities
Redick C Bryan Iii, President

D-U-N-S 07-449-9211
STACY'S, INC
2009 US Hwy 321 N, York, SC 29745
Phone: (803) 684-2331
Sales: $10,793,000   *Employees:* 70
Company Type: Private   *Employees here:* 50
SIC: 0181
    Greenhouses & retails garden supplies
Jim Nickel, President

D-U-N-S 00-794-4077
STADELMAN FRUIT, LLC
314 S 2nd Ave, Yakima, WA 98902
Phone: (509) 452-8571

Sales: $13,736,000   *Employees:* 150
Company Type: Private   *Employees here:* 20
SIC: 0723
    Pack fruits & vegetables
Francis F Coppola, Partner

D-U-N-S 00-697-5635
STAHMANN FARMS INC
8 Mi S W State Hwy 28, Las Cruces, NM 88001
Phone: (505) 526-2453
Sales: $14,197,000   *Employees:* 150
Company Type: Private   *Employees here:* 45
SIC: 0173
    Pecan farm
Noah W Kreider Jr, Partner

D-U-N-S 06-113-4193
STALLWORTH & JOHNSON INC
4290 Dallas County Rd 324, Minter, AL 36761
Phone: (334) 872-4852
Sales: $175,000,000   *Employees:* 60
Company Type: Private   *Employees here:* 22
SIC: 0241
    Logging contractor and sawmill
Alex Abatti Jr, President

D-U-N-S 00-696-6634
STARK BROS NRSRIES ORCHRDS CO
    (Parent: Foster & Gallagher Inc)
New Hwy 54, Louisiana, MO 63353
Phone: (573) 754-5511
Sales: $13,400,000   *Employees:* 300
Company Type: Private   *Employees here:* 250
SIC: 0181
    Ornamental nursery
Haslem Naraghi, President

D-U-N-S 02-950-7464
STARK PACKING CORP
22817 Avenue 196, Strathmore, CA 93267
Phone: (559) 568-1114
Sales: $11,269,000   *Employees:* 100
Company Type: Private   *Employees here:* 10
SIC: 0723
    Fresh fruit packing
Harry Eisen, President

D-U-N-S 03-078-0647
STARKER FORESTS INC
7240 SW Philomath Blvd, Corvallis, OR 97333
Phone: (541) 929-2477
Sales: $10,103,000   *Employees:* 15
Company Type: Private   *Employees here:* 15
SIC: 0811
    Operates timber tract
Charles Norman, President

D-U-N-S 02-697-8676
STARR PRODUCE CO
10 Mi E Hwy 83, Rio Grande City, TX 78582
Phone: (956) 487-2571
Sales: $25,000,000   *Employees:* 210
Company Type: Private   *Employees here:* 200
SIC: 0161
    Vegetable/melon farm
Jack Mccaffery, President

D-U-N-S 05-380-7392   EXP
STEMILT GROWERS INC
123 Ohme Garden Rd, Wenatchee, WA 98801
Phone: (509) 663-1451

Sales: $47,867,000   *Employees:* 600
Company Type: Private   *Employees here:* 480
SIC: 0723
    Fruit packers
James Pauly, President

D-U-N-S 95-714-4686
STEMILT MANAGEMENT INC
123 Ohme Rd, Wenatchee, WA 98801
Phone: (509) 665-0735
Sales: $11,300,000   *Employees:* 240
Company Type: Private   *Employees here:* 200
SIC: 0762
    Farm management services
John Swendrowski, Chief Executive Officer

D-U-N-S 05-841-5258
STEPHEN PAVICH & SONS
23745 Avenue 112, Porterville, CA 93257
Phone: (559) 782-8700
Sales: $15,000,000   *Employees:* 250
Company Type: Private   *Employees here:* 125
SIC: 0172
    Vineyard
Richard Keller, President

D-U-N-S 02-965-6691
STEVE HENDERSON LOGGING INC
2604 Seaport Dr, Lewiston, ID 83501
Phone: (208) 746-1627
Sales: $14,000,000   *Employees:* 55
Company Type: Private   *Employees here:* 2
SIC: 0241
    Logging contractor
Jack Pearlstein, President

D-U-N-S 10-723-2068
STOTZ FARMS INC
11111 W Mc Dowell, Avondale, AZ 85323
Phone: (602) 936-6960
Sales: $10,000,000   *Employees:* 35
Company Type: Private   *Employees here:* 35
SIC: 0241
    Dairy and general crop farm
Yahya O Mohamed, President

D-U-N-S 61-925-7736   EXP
SUBCO PACKAGING INC
1150 Commerce Dr, West Chicago, IL 60185
Phone: (630) 231-0003
Sales: $10,000,000   *Employees:* 90
Company Type: Private   *Employees here:* 90
SIC: 0723
    Contract packaging
Ernie Costamagna, President

D-U-N-S 15-409-2381
SUBLETTE ENTERPRISES INC
6 Mi E 1 Mi N on Hwy 56, Sublette, KS 67877
Phone: (316) 668-5501
Sales: $32,883,000   *Employees:* 75
Company Type: Private   *Employees here:* 46
SIC: 0211
    Commercial feed yard & grain elevator
George D O Connell, President

D-U-N-S 03-136-0480
SUBURBAN LAWN & GARDEN, INC
13635 Wyandotte St, Kansas City, MO 64145
Phone: (816) 941-4700

Sales: $15,000,000   *Employees:* 150
Company Type: Private   *Employees here:* 30
SIC: 0181
    Nursery stock lawn care service sprinkler systems installation
    landscaper ret & whol lawn & garden supplies
Francis J O Hara Sr, President

D-U-N-S 04-886-3203
SUGAR FARMS INC
    (Parent: Flo Sun Inc)
316 Royal Poinciana Plz, Palm Beach, FL 33480
Phone: (561) 655-6303
Sales: $15,700,000   *Employees:* 200
Company Type: Private   *Employees here:* 15
SIC: 0133
    Sugarcane farm
Kent Woodward, President

D-U-N-S 04-632-0305
SUGARLAND FEED YARDS, INC.
Fm 2856, Hereford, TX 79045
Phone: (806) 364-0536
Sales: $13,364,000   *Employees:* 35
Company Type: Private   *Employees here:* 35
SIC: 0211
    Cattle feedlot
Thomas E Oakley, President

D-U-N-S 10-198-5182
SUGARLAND HARVESTING CO
Flaghole Rd, Clewiston, FL 33440
Phone: (941) 983-5111
Sales: $10,799,000   *Employees:* 110
Company Type: Private   *Employees here:* 110
SIC: 0722
    Sugarcane harvesting cooperative
Ed Boutonnet, General Manager

D-U-N-S 60-355-8362   EXP
SUMA FRUIT INTERNATIONAL USA
    (Parent: Fresh Del Monte Produce Inc)
1810 S Academy, Sanger, CA 93657
Phone: (559) 875-5000
Sales: $100,000,000   *Employees:* 67
Company Type: Private   *Employees here:* 50
SIC: 0723
    Packaging fresh fruits
Jorge Ochoa, Owner

D-U-N-S 93-359-8559
SUMMIT FARMS INC
13362 Kenowa Ave, Kent City, MI 49330
Phone: (616) 675-5477
Sales: $10,000,000   *Employees:* 7
Company Type: Private   *Employees here:* 7
SIC: 0175
    Fruit farm
Jorge Ochoa, President

D-U-N-S 04-652-6307
SUMNER PECK RANCH, INC.
14354 Road 204, Madera, CA 93638
Phone: (559) 822-2525
Sales: $10,000,000   *Employees:* 32
Company Type: Private   *Employees here:* 10
SIC: 0191
    General farming
James R Oglevee, Chairman of the Board

D-U-N-S 05-407-9181
SUN-AG INC
7735 County Road 512, Fellsmere, FL 32948
Phone: (561) 571-1204

Sales: $11,800,000   *Employees:* 250
Company Type: Private   *Employees here:* 250
SIC: 0762
    Citrus grove management & maintenance
Don Oppliger, President

D-U-N-S 60-712-1506
SUN AND SANDS ENTERPRISES, LLC
86705 Avenue 54, Ste A, Coachella, CA 92236
Phone: (760) 399-4278
Sales: $43,321,000   *Employees:* 65
Company Type: Private   *Employees here:* 65
SIC: 0161
    Crop grower packer and shipper of vegetables & melons
Greg Duffy, Director

D-U-N-S 60-529-9643
SUN CITY LANDSCAPES LAWN MAINT
2081 E Sunset Rd, Las Vegas, NV 89119
Phone: (702) 260-6309
Sales: $10,000,000   *Employees:* 160
Company Type: Private   *Employees here:* 160
SIC: 0782
    Landscape contractor
Constance Olsen, Owner

D-U-N-S 10-341-9891
SUN-LAND PRODUCTS OF CALIFORNIA
    (Parent: Sun-Diamond Growers Of Cal)
5568 Gibralter Dr, Pleasanton, CA 94588
Phone: (925) 463-8200
Sales: $70,700,000   *Employees:* 50
Company Type: Private   *Employees here:* 50
SIC: 0723
    Whol specialty fruits bulk mixes & mixed nuts
Ben Griffin Iii, Chairman of the Board

D-U-N-S 18-052-7665
SUN PACIFIC FARMING CO
1300 E Myer Ave, Exeter, CA 93221
Phone: (559) 592-7121
Sales: $28,400,000   *Employees:* 600
Company Type: Private   *Employees here:* 500
SIC: 0762
    Citrus grove management & maintenance service
Betina Brown, President

D-U-N-S 78-581-3205
SUN VALLEY FLORAL FARMS
3160 Upper Bay Rd, Arcata, CA 95521
Phone: (707) 826-8700
Sales: $20,447,000   *Employees:* 150
Company Type: Private   *Employees here:* 135
SIC: 0181
    Grows cut flowers under cover and in field nurseries
Henry Oord, Partner

D-U-N-S 95-790-0939
SUN WORLD INTERNATIONAL, INC
    (Parent: Cadiz Inc)
16351 Driver Rd, Bakersfield, CA 93308
Phone: (661) 392-5000
Sales: $99,929,000   *Employees:* 905
Company Type: Public Family Member   *Employees here:* 905
SIC: 0723
    Fruit & vegetable growers
Don Oppliger, General Partner

D-U-N-S 79-340-2033
SUNGROW LANDSCAPE SERVICES
1508 Ferguson Ln A, Austin, TX 78754
Phone: (512) 834-0123

Sales: $10,000,000
Company Type: Private
SIC: 0782
　　Lawn/garden services
Matthew Kawamura, Partner

Employees: 100
Employees here: 80

D-U-N-S 06-888-1135
SUNNILAND FRUIT INC
1350 Report Ave, Stockton, CA 95205
Phone: (209) 941-4323
Sales: $12,401,000
Company Type: Private
SIC: 0723
　　Packers of fresh fruits and vegetables
Eugene C Mooney, President

Employees: 10
Employees here: 6

D-U-N-S 08-646-2660
SUNNY GROVE LANDSCAPING INC
9421 Broadway Ave E, Estero, FL 33928
Phone: (941) 992-1818
Sales: $11,000,000
Company Type: Private
SIC: 0781
　　Landscape planning & counseling
Alfred Smith, President

Employees: 120
Employees here: 120

D-U-N-S 02-186-3329
SUNRIDGE NURSERIES, INC
441 Vineland Rd, Bakersfield, CA 93307
Phone: (661) 858-2237
Sales: $20,359,000
Company Type: Private
SIC: 0721
　　Grows grapevine nursery stock
Jane Witheridge, Chief Executive Officer

Employees: 70
Employees here: 70

D-U-N-S 61-615-9612　　　　　　　　　EXP
SUNSEEDS CO
18640 Sutter Blvd, Morgan Hill, CA 95037
Phone: (408) 776-1111
Sales: $40,000,000
Company Type: Private
SIC: 0181
　　Grows & distributes vegetable seeds
Oscar Ortega, Owner

Employees: 240
Employees here: 37

D-U-N-S 04-865-9338
SUNSHINE RAISIN CORP
626 S 5th St, Fowler, CA 93625
Phone: (559) 834-5981
Sales: $60,000,000
Company Type: Private
SIC: 0723
　　Raisin packing
Joseph D Clougherty, President

Employees: 120
Employees here: 70

D-U-N-S 88-337-3482
SUPERIOR LUMBER CO INC
2695 Glendale Valley Rd, Glendale, OR 97442
Phone: (541) 832-2153
Sales: $20,000,000
Company Type: Private
SIC: 0241
　　Timber sales
Pat Ricchiuti, President

Employees: 3
Employees here: 3

D-U-N-S 04-652-0664
SURABIAN PACKING CO INC
18700 E South Ave, Reedley, CA 93654
Phone: (559) 638-9288

Sales: $12,000,000
Company Type: Private
SIC: 0723
　　Fresh fruit packing
Ray Veldhuis, President

Employees: 10
Employees here: 10

D-U-N-S 05-461-4052
SWA GROUP
2200 Bridgeway, Sausalito, CA 94965
Phone: (415) 332-5100
Sales: $11,000,000
Company Type: Private
SIC: 0781
　　Landscape services
Bill Najjar, Owner

Employees: 100
Employees here: 40

D-U-N-S 00-796-9306
SWANSON FARMS
5213 W Main St, Turlock, CA 95380
Phone: (209) 667-2002
Sales: $13,352,000
Company Type: Private
SIC: 0253
　　Turkey breeder
Richard Rogers, Partner

Employees: 85
Employees here: 85

D-U-N-S 79-549-8179
SWINE GRAPHICS ENTERPRISES, LP
1620 Superior St, Webster City, IA 50595
Phone: (515) 832-5481
Sales: $31,751,000
Company Type: Private
SIC: 0213
　　Hog production
Steve Ziubak, Chief Executive Officer

Employees: 49
Employees here: 30

D-U-N-S 11-913-7099
SYLVAN FOODS, INC.
　　(Parent: Sylvan Inc)
333 Main St, Saxonburg, PA 16056
Phone: (724) 352-7520
Sales: $36,000,000
Company Type: Public Family Member
SIC: 0182
　　Mushroom farm & grower of mushroom spawn
Frank D Dulcich, President

Employees: 900
Employees here: 10

D-U-N-S 60-232-3214　　　　　　　　　EXP
SYLVAN INC.
333 Main St, Saxonburg, PA 16056
Phone: (724) 352-7520
Sales: $81,560,000
Company Type: Public
SIC: 0182
　　Mushroom farm & producer of mushroom spawn
Mac Carraway, Chief Financial Officer

Employees: 900
Employees here: 10

D-U-N-S 05-098-4202
SYLVEST FARMS, INC
3500 Western Blvd, Montgomery, AL 36105
Phone: (334) 281-0400
Sales: $55,000,000
Company Type: Private
SIC: 0251
　　Raise broiler chickens and poultry dressing plant
James L Rogers Iii, Managing Partner

Employees: 1,100
Employees here: 600

D-U-N-S 87-273-1211
T D M FARMS INC
Hwy 701 S, Newton Grove, NC 28366
Phone: (910) 594-0219

Sales: $17,519,000
Company Type: Private   *Employees:* 1
SIC: 0213   *Employees here:* 1
    Raises hogs specializing in sows and feeder pigs
James Rogers, General Manager

D-U-N-S 10-754-5147
T T MIYASAKA INC
209 Riverside Rd, Watsonville, CA 95076
Phone: (831) 722-3871
Sales: $19,512,000
Company Type: Private   *Employees:* 75
SIC: 0171   *Employees here:* 75
    Strawberry farm
Ron Davenport, President

D-U-N-S 12-611-0931
TACKETT FISH FARM
23939 County Road 523, Schlater, MS 38952
Phone: (601) 254-6213
Sales: $14,908,000
Company Type: Private   *Employees:* 100
SIC: 0273   *Employees here:* 100
    Farm raising catfish
David Padilla, Owner

D-U-N-S 04-172-2133   EXP
TACONIC FARMS INC
273 Hover Ave, Germantown, NY 12526
Phone: (518) 537-5200
Sales: $22,827,000
Company Type: Private   *Employees:* 210
SIC: 0279   *Employees here:* 210
    Breeder of laboratory animals raising mice & rats
Sam Klein, President

D-U-N-S 06-404-9141
TAGAWA GREENHOUSES INC
17999 Weld Cnty Road 4, Brighton, CO 80601
Phone: (303) 659-1260
Sales: $15,000,000
Company Type: Private   *Employees:* 150
SIC: 0181   *Employees here:* 150
    Greenhouse growing bedded plants & potted plants
Walter L Preston, President

D-U-N-S 05-988-6044
TALISMAN SUGAR CORP
    (Parent: St Joe Co)
1650 Prudential Dr, Jacksonville, FL 32207
Phone: (904) 396-6600
Sales: $11,800,000
Company Type: Public Family Member   *Employees:* 150
SIC: 0133   *Employees here:* 5
    Sugarcane farm
Lucy Pandol, Partner

D-U-N-S 08-905-3128
TALLEY FARMS
2900 Lopez Dr, Arroyo Grande, CA 93420
Phone: (805) 489-2508
Sales: $12,200,000
Company Type: Private   *Employees:* 150
SIC: 0161   *Employees here:* 150
    Vegetable farm vegetable packing service
Larry Rice, Owner

D-U-N-S 06-708-1794
TALLMADGE BROS INC
132 Water St, Norwalk, CT
Phone: (203) 838-0683

Sales: $10,000,000
Company Type: Private   *Employees:* 120
SIC: 0913   *Employees here:* 65
    Oyster beds & catching of clams lobsters and fish
William Lipman, President

D-U-N-S 03-224-9815
TAMPA FARM SERVICE INC
14425 Haynes Rd, Dover, FL 33527
Phone: (813) 659-0605
Sales: $29,000,000
Company Type: Private   *Employees:* 210
SIC: 0252   *Employees here:* 110
    Chicken egg farm
Stewart Resnick, Partner

D-U-N-S 06-476-5654
TANIMURA & ANTLE, INC
1 Harris Rd, Salinas, CA 93908
Phone: (831) 455-2950
Sales: $300,000,000
Company Type: Private   *Employees:* 2,200
SIC: 0161   *Employees here:* 100
    Vegetable grower & packer
Joseph Mac Ilvaine, President

D-U-N-S 02-131-8613
TAPLETT FRUIT PACKING INC
14277 Chelan Hwy, Wenatchee, WA 98807
Phone: (509) 662-5570
Sales: $10,500,000
Company Type: Private   *Employees:* 150
SIC: 0723   *Employees here:* 150
    Fruit packing service
Samuel Rudderow, President

D-U-N-S 79-559-6881
TARA PACKING CO
121 Spreckes Blvd, Spreckels, CA 93962
Phone: (831) 758-2455
Sales: $21,000,000
Company Type: Private   *Employees:* 600
SIC: 0761   *Employees here:* 600
    Farm labor contractors
Robert Morrison, President

D-U-N-S 06-267-3876
TARHEEL TURKEY HATCHERY INC
1140 E Central Ave, Raeford, NC 28376
Phone: (910) 875-2015
Sales: $14,500,000
Company Type: Private   *Employees:* 200
SIC: 0253   *Employees here:* 200
    Turkey/turkey egg farm
Michael Tracy, Chief Executive Officer

D-U-N-S 03-263-8272
TAYLOR & FULTON INC
932 5th Ave W, Palmetto, FL 34221
Phone: (941) 729-3883
Sales: $21,228,000
Company Type: Private   *Employees:* 90
SIC: 0723   *Employees here:* 50
    Tomato & strwaberry farms & packing house
Arnold Reichman, President

D-U-N-S 03-565-1975
TAYLOR & STUCKEY INC
10415 Stuckey Ln, Trumann, AR 72472
Phone: (870) 483-7625

Sales: $12,364,000
Company Type: Private
SIC: 0724
   Cotton gin general store & whol farm supplies
Jim Parker, President

Employees: 40
Employees here: 40

D-U-N-S 87-852-1277
TAYLOR FRESH FOODS INC
911 Blanco Cir, Ste B, Salinas, CA 93901
Phone: (831) 754-1715
Sales: $40,000,000
Company Type: Private
SIC: 0723
   Vegetable processor
Richard Parker, President

Employees: 600
Employees here: 300

D-U-N-S 06-956-3088
TAYLOR UNITED INC
130 SE Lynch Rd, Shelton, WA 98584
Phone: (360) 426-6178
Sales: $19,000,000
Company Type: Private
SIC: 0913
   Oyster beds & clam digging
Warren Gunderson, Trustee

Employees: 270
Employees here: 160

D-U-N-S 05-643-6645
TEIXEIRA FARMS INC
2600 Bonita Lateral Rd, Santa Maria, CA 93458
Phone: (805) 928-3801
Sales: $40,000,000
Company Type: Private
SIC: 0161
   Vegetable farm growing broccoli cabbage cauliflower celery
   and lettuce
Steven Parker, President

Employees: 188
Employees here: 180

D-U-N-S 06-154-9713
TEJAS FEEDERS, LTD.
Hwy 152, Pampa, TX 79066
Phone: (806) 665-2303
Sales: $27,529,000
Company Type: Private
SIC: 0211
   Feedlot
Gary Pasquinelli, President

Employees: 15
Employees here: 15

D-U-N-S 00-690-4189
TEJON RANCH CO
4436 Lebec Rd, Lebec, CA 93243
Phone: (661) 248-6774
Sales: $40,986,000
Company Type: Public
SIC: 0173
   Operates farms and raises cattle
C L Haw, President

Employees: 90
Employees here: 55

D-U-N-S 19-718-1886
TERRANOVA RANCH INC
16729 W Floral, Helm, CA 93627
Phone: (559) 866-5644
Sales: $10,102,000
Company Type: Private
SIC: 0191
   Crop farm
Kenneth Lin, President

Employees: 30
Employees here: 30

D-U-N-S 95-802-4028
TERRATHERM ENVIRONMENTAL SERVICES
   (Parent: Shell Technology Ventures)
19510 Oil Center Blvd, Houston, TX 77073
Phone: (281) 925-0400

Sales: $10,000,000
Company Type: Private
SIC: 0711
   Soil remediation
R W Becker, President

Employees: 4
Employees here: 4

D-U-N-S 55-607-5950
TERRY FARMS INC
   (Parent: Terry Farms Inc)
303 N Baker St, Ste 200, Mount Dora, FL 32757
Phone: (352) 735-5241
Sales: $52,000,000
Company Type: Private
SIC: 0182
   Through subsidiaries & branches grows & sells mushrooms
Fred Jahna, Vice-President

Employees: 900
Employees here: 4

D-U-N-S 10-220-0342
TERRY FARMS, PRINCETON, INC.
   (Parent: Terry Farms Inc)
27268 US Hwy 6, Princeton, IL 61356
Phone: (815) 875-4436
Sales: $30,000,000
Company Type: Private
SIC: 0182
   Covered food crops farm
Denny Hickman, President

Employees: 500
Employees here: 500

D-U-N-S 80-939-6997
TERRY FARMS ZELLWOOD DIVISION
   (Parent: Terry Farms Inc)
5949 Sadler Rd, Zellwood, FL 32798
Phone: (407) 886-0449
Sales: $12,200,000
Company Type: Private
SIC: 0182
   Covered food crops farm
Flake Mc Haney, President

Employees: 304
Employees here: 304

D-U-N-S 62-785-2775
TEXAS A & M UNIVERSITY
301 Tarrow St, Ste 364, College Station, TX 77840
Phone: (409) 845-2601
Sales: $25,935,000
Company Type: Private
SIC: 0851
   Forest service
George D Hickman, Chairman of the Board

Employees: 318
Employees here: 35

D-U-N-S 96-058-1049
TEXAS FARM INC
9 SW 2nd Ave, Perryton, TX 79070
Phone: (806) 435-5935
Sales: $15,700,000
Company Type: Private
SIC: 0213
   Livestock production
George D Hickman, Chairman of the Board

Employees: 190
Employees here: 190

D-U-N-S 83-469-3798
THANKSGIVING POINT MANAGEMENT CO LC
261 E 1200 S, Orem, UT 84058
Phone: (801) 226-1266
Sales: $11,700,000
Company Type: Private
SIC: 0811
   Trees & sod farm petting zoo & ret nursery
Zachary Casey, President

Employees: 250
Employees here: 5

D-U-N-S 82-482-6960
THERMORETEC CORP
   (Parent: Thermo Terratech Inc)
9 Damon Mill Sq, Ste 3a, Concord, MA

Phone: (978) 371-3200
Sales: $128,409,000
Company Type: Public Family Member   *Employees:* 952
SIC: 0711   *Employees here:* 5
   Soil treatment service
Mary Penland, President

D-U-N-S 08-096-6039
THOMAS BROS GRASS LTD
1926 Acton Hwy, Granbury, TX 76049
Phone: (817) 279-8504
Sales: $10,000,000   *Employees:* 110
Company Type: Private   *Employees here:* 8
SIC: 0181
   Sod farm
Donald E Horn Sr, Chairman of the Board

D-U-N-S 13-108-3537
THOMAS CREEK LUMBER & LOG CO
448 N 2nd Ave, Stayton, OR 97383
Phone: (503) 769-6563
Sales: $15,000,000   *Employees:* 10
Company Type: Private   *Employees here:* 10
SIC: 0241
   Logging contractor & lumber mill
Mark Pennink, President

D-U-N-S 18-486-1540
THOMAS PRODUCE CO
9905 Clint Moore Rd, Boca Raton, FL 33496
Phone: (561) 482-1111
Sales: $36,500,000   *Employees:* 15
Company Type: Private   *Employees here:* 15
SIC: 0161
   Vegetable farm
Thomas Hoerr, President

D-U-N-S 06-638-4504
THOMPSON AGRIPLEX, INC.
Fm 988, Hartley, TX 79044
Phone: (806) 365-4111
Sales: $17,510,000   *Employees:* 20
Company Type: Private   *Employees here:* 20
SIC: 0212
   Raises cattle & corn
James J Peri, President

D-U-N-S 07-878-9104
THORKELSON RANCHES
13218 Elm Ave, Patterson, CA 95363
Phone: (209) 892-9111
Sales: $12,200,000   *Employees:* 150
Company Type: Private   *Employees here:* 150
SIC: 0161
   Farm vegetable
John P Perrier Sr, Partner

D-U-N-S 80-208-0309
TIMBERLAND MANAGEMENT SERVICES INC
Hwy 24, Centreville, MS 39631
Phone: (601) 645-6440
Sales: $10,000,000   *Employees:* 14
Company Type: Private   *Employees here:* 7
SIC: 0241
   Logging services & forest services
Virl Lamunyon, President

D-U-N-S 01-993-2771
TIMBERLAND SILVICULTURAL SERVICES
   (Parent: Timberland Enterprises Inc)
140 Arkansas St, Monticello, AR 71655
Phone: (870) 367-8561

Sales: $86,205,000   *Employees:* 5
Company Type: Private   *Employees here:* 1
SIC: 0851
   Mechanical reforistation services
Shane Kelly, Chief Executive Officer

D-U-N-S 36-295-0966
TO-JO MUSHROOMS INC
974 Penn Green Rd, Avondale, PA 19311
Phone: (610) 268-8082
Sales: $18,000,000   *Employees:* 60
Company Type: Private   *Employees here:* 60
SIC: 0182
   Covered food crops farm
James Peters, President

D-U-N-S 08-504-7108
TOM BARBER
1420 E Telegraph Hill Rd, Madison, IN 47250
Phone: (812) 265-2223
Sales: $14,000,000   *Employees:* 7
Company Type: Private   *Employees here:* 7
SIC: 0781
   Landscape services whol flowers/florist supplies
Vic Evans, Vice-Chairman

D-U-N-S 13-905-7004
TONY ABATTI FARMS LLC
1735 Austin Rd, El Centro, CA 92243
Phone: (760) 353-5811
Sales: $14,449,000   *Employees:* 125
Company Type: Private   *Employees here:* 125
SIC: 0139
   Field crop farm
Samuel J Parker, Chairman of the Board

D-U-N-S 08-277-6113
TORRE & BRUGLIO INC
850 Featherstone St, Pontiac, MI 48342
Phone: (248) 452-9292
Sales: $14,000,000   *Employees:* 55
Company Type: Private   *Employees here:* 55
SIC: 0782
   Landscape contractors lawn maintenance & snowplowing
      service
Arthur J Crowley, President

D-U-N-S 07-993-9823
TORREY FARMS INC
Maltby Rd, Elba, NY 14058
Phone: (716) 757-9941
Sales: $10,850,000   *Employees:* 110
Company Type: Private   *Employees here:* 110
SIC: 0161
   Vegetable farm
John Taylor, President

D-U-N-S 96-024-7468
TOSH FARMS
1586 Atlantic Ave, Henry, TN 38231
Phone: (901) 243-4861
Sales: $14,488,000   *Employees:* 23
Company Type: Private   *Employees here:* 23
SIC: 0191
   Hog farm or feedlot & grain farm
Gregg Beviere, President

D-U-N-S 01-654-5519
TOWNSEND TREE SERVICE CO INC
9211 E Jackson St, Selma, IN 47383
Phone: (765) 282-1234

Sales: $24,900,000　　　　　　　　　　　*Employees:* 775
Company Type: Private　　　　　　　　*Employees here:* 30
SIC: 0783
　　Tree trimming services
Earl Petznick, President

D-U-N-S 09-683-7042
TOWNSENDS FARMS, INC
　　(Parent: Townsends Inc)
RR 24, Millsboro, DE 19966
Phone: (302) 934-9221
Sales: $17,500,000　　　　　　　　　　*Employees:* 350
Company Type: Private　　　　　　　　*Employees here:* 160
SIC: 0251
　　Chicken farm
Joey Van Dee, President

D-U-N-S 01-948-3432
TRACY INDUSTRIES INC
22421 Gilberto, Ste A, Rcho Sta Marg, CA 92688
Phone: (949) 858-7002
Sales: $28,200,000　　　　　　　　　　*Employees:* 800
Company Type: Private　　　　　　　　*Employees here:* 3
SIC: 0782
　　Holding company
Gary Booth, Partner

D-U-N-S 01-355-2278
TREE PRESERVATION CO INC
　　(Parent: Asplundh Subsidiary Holdings)
708 Blair Mill Rd, Willow Grove, PA 19090
Phone: (215) 784-4200
Sales: $14,796,000　　　　　　　　　　*Employees:* 340
Company Type: Private　　　　　　　　*Employees here:* 10
SIC: 0783
　　Tree services for public utility lines
L E Duff, General Manager

D-U-N-S 02-666-1116
TREES, INC
　　(Parent: Trees Holding Company Inc)
7020 Stuebner Airline Rd, Houston, TX 77091
Phone: (713) 692-6371
Sales: $32,100,000　　　　　　　　　　*Employees:* 1,000
Company Type: Private　　　　　　　　*Employees here:* 70
SIC: 0783
　　Tree trimming service
Robert Heiserman, President

D-U-N-S 79-819-2910
TRI-B NURSERY, INC.
Hwy 51 5 Mles W of Hlbert, Hulbert, OK 74441
Phone: (918) 772-3428
Sales: $10,616,000　　　　　　　　　　*Employees:* 180
Company Type: Private　　　　　　　　*Employees here:* 180
SIC: 0181
　　Whol nursery
Charles Smoleny, President

D-U-N-S 05-385-9096
TRI DUNCAN A PARTNERSHIP
12000 Main St, Lamont, CA 93241
Phone: (661) 845-2296
Sales: $14,500,000　　　　　　　　　　*Employees:* 200
Company Type: Private　　　　　　　　*Employees here:* 200
SIC: 0131
　　Farming cotton grapes potatoes alfalfa & onions
Vard Ikeda, President

D-U-N-S 02-360-8185
TRI-STATE BREEDERS COOP
E10890 Penny Ln, Baraboo, WI 53913
Phone: (608) 356-8357

Sales: $20,922,000　　　　　　　　　　*Employees:* 260
Company Type: Private　　　　　　　　*Employees here:* 45
SIC: 0751
　　Artificial insemination service
Jonathan Huntington, President

D-U-N-S 17-339-7902
TRI-STATE FEEDERS, INC
3 Miles South on Hwy 83, Turpin, OK 73950
Phone: (580) 778-3600
Sales: $25,610,000　　　　　　　　　　*Employees:* 30
Company Type: Private　　　　　　　　*Employees here:* 30
SIC: 0211
　　Commercial cattle feed yard
Egbert De Grott, President

D-U-N-S 15-508-4973
TRIANGLE FARMS INC
1164 Monroe St, Ste 8, Salinas, CA 93906
Phone: (831) 442-3011
Sales: $11,179,000　　　　　　　　　　*Employees:* 50
Company Type: Private　　　　　　　　*Employees here:* 50
SIC: 0161
　　Vegetable farm
Mark W Bitz, President

D-U-N-S 00-738-0520
TRIANGLE MANUFACTURING CO
1320 E Division St, Slaton, TX 79364
Phone: (806) 828-6573
Sales: $12,000,000　　　　　　　　　　*Employees:* 47
Company Type: Private　　　　　　　　*Employees here:* 32
SIC: 0724
　　Cotton ginning
J C Plaxco, President

D-U-N-S 01-529-3905
TRIPLE A LANDSCAPE
4742 N Romero Rd, Tucson, AZ 85705
Phone: (520) 696-3223
Sales: $15,000,000　　　　　　　　　　*Employees:* 425
Company Type: Private　　　　　　　　*Employees here:* 425
SIC: 0782
　　Lawn/garden services
Chet Wahlen, President

D-U-N-S 06-503-0553
TROPHY INTERNATIONAL INC
4200 W Ursula Ave, McAllen, TX 78503
Phone: (956) 682-6181
Sales: $11,967,000　　　　　　　　　　*Employees:* 92
Company Type: Private　　　　　　　　*Employees here:* 15
SIC: 0723
　　Vegetable processor

D-U-N-S 00-794-2204
TROUT-BLUE CHELAN, INC
5 Howser Rd, Chelan, WA 98816
Phone: (509) 682-2591
Sales: $25,348,000　　　　　　　　　　*Employees:* 150
Company Type: Private　　　　　　　　*Employees here:* 150
SIC: 0723
　　Contract fruit packing & cold storage
Doug Wagner, President

D-U-N-S 62-268-1351
TRU GREEN LP
860 Ridge Lake Blvd, Memphis, TN 38120
Phone: (901) 681-1800

Sales: $454,900,000   *Employees:* 13,000
Company Type: Private   *Employees here:* 120
SIC: 0782
    Lawn care & pest control service
R B Newcome, President

D-U-N-S 11-599-4923
TYSON BREEDERS, INC.
    (Parent: Tyson Foods Inc)
2210 W Oaklawn Dr, Springdale, AR 72762
Phone: (501) 290-4000
Sales: $107,100,000
Company Type: Public Family Member   *Employees:* 2,000
SIC: 0254   *Employees here:* 2,000
    Poultry breeders/hatchery
Daniel K Powell, President

D-U-N-S 18-421-7123   EXP
TYSON SEAFOOD GROUP
    (Parent: Tyson Foods Inc)
Fishermans Ctr, Seattle, WA 98119
Phone: (206) 282-3445
Sales: $60,000,000
Company Type: Public Family Member   *Employees:* 1,200
SIC: 0912   *Employees here:* 130
    Commercial fishing & process frozen fish & crab
Billy J Powell, President

D-U-N-S 08-372-0193
UNDERWOOD BROS INC
3747 E Southern Ave, Phoenix, AZ 85040
Phone: (602) 437-2690
Sales: $14,066,000   *Employees:* 385
Company Type: Private   *Employees here:* 192
SIC: 0782
    Landscaping & garden contractor & maintenance
John Glessner, Owner

D-U-N-S 04-158-2297
UNDERWOOD FRUIT & WAREHOUSE CO
401 N 1st Ave, Yakima, WA 98902
Phone: (509) 457-6177
Sales: $16,200,000   *Employees:* 200
Company Type: Private   *Employees here:* 9
SIC: 0723
    Packs fresh fruit & operates orchard
Michael Fragale, President

D-U-N-S 10-278-0749
UNI-KOOL PARTNERS
710 W Market St, Salinas, CA 93901
Phone: (831) 424-4137
Sales: $18,200,000   *Employees:* 200
Company Type: Private   *Employees here:* 60
SIC: 0723
    Vacuum cooling & mfg ice
Mike Mcfaddin, President

D-U-N-S 80-820-0356
UNION COUNTY FEED LOT, INC
    (Parent: Perryton Feeders Inc)
Hwy 87, Clayton, NM 88415
Phone: (505) 374-2516
Sales: $12,000,000   *Employees:* 20
Company Type: Private   *Employees here:* 20
SIC: 0211
    Cattle feed lot
Dennis Shoup, President

D-U-N-S 00-411-7156
UNITED STATES SUGAR CORP
111 Ponce De Leon Ave, Clewiston, FL 33440
Phone: (941) 983-8121

Sales: $201,400,000   *Employees:* 2,500
Company Type: Private   *Employees here:* 2,500
SIC: 0133
    Sugar cane growers and refining
Jeff Strnad, President

D-U-N-S 96-046-4832
U.S. TMBRLANDS KLAMATH FLS LLC
6400 Hwy 66, Klamath Falls, OR 97601
Phone: (541) 884-2240
Sales: $80,000,000   *Employees:* 30
Company Type: Private   *Employees here:* 27
SIC: 0811
    Timber tracts
Jerry Bohn, Manager

D-U-N-S 14-856-9684
URBAN FARMER, INC
3232 S Platte River Dr, Englewood, CO 80110
Phone: (303) 781-8857
Sales: $13,044,000   *Employees:* 164
Company Type: Private   *Employees here:* 164
SIC: 0781
    Landscape planning
Royce Hartley, President

D-U-N-S 01-298-8911
USEUGI FARMS INC
1020 State Hwy 25, Gilroy, CA 95020
Phone: (408) 842-1294
Sales: $14,800,000   *Employees:* 162
Company Type: Private   *Employees here:* 162
SIC: 0161
    Vegetable farm
Ron Prestage, President

D-U-N-S 82-568-0598
UTRECHT - AMERICA HOLDINGS,
245 Park Ave Fl 39, New York, NY 10167
Phone: (212) 916-7800
Sales: $21,600,000   *Employees:* 460
Company Type: Private   *Employees here:* 460
SIC: 0811
    Tree farm nursery stock truck carrier & brokerage
William H Prestage, President

D-U-N-S 00-990-6017
VALADCO INC
209 N Main St, Renville, MN 56284
Phone: (320) 329-3225
Sales: $20,000,000   *Employees:* 65
Company Type: Private   *Employees here:* 65
SIC: 0213
    Hog farm or feedlot
Stephen Wyrick, President

D-U-N-S 00-959-0873
VALENCIA HARVESTING INC
3665 Bee Ridge Rd, Sarasota, FL 34233
Phone: (941) 923-4551
Sales: $10,700,000   *Employees:* 175
Company Type: Private   *Employees here:* 175
SIC: 0174
    Orange groves
Ralph Grounds Jr, Member

D-U-N-S 83-565-4005
VALL INC
911 Texas St, Texhoma, OK 73949
Phone: (580) 423-1404

Sales: $15,600,000

Company Type: Private

SIC: 0213

Hog producers

Michael Ziegler, President

Employees: 189

Employees here: 189

D-U-N-S 04-115-8981

VALLEY CREST LANDSCAPE, INC

(*Parent:* Environmental Industries Inc)

24121 Ventura Blvd, Calabasas, CA 91302

Phone: (818) 223-8500

Sales: $143,375,000

Company Type: Private

SIC: 0781

Landscape and irrigation construction site development and golf course construction

Everett Hoekstra, Director

Employees: 1,200

Employees here: 10

D-U-N-S 84-900-2332

VALLEY CREST LANDSCAPE INC

(*Parent:* Environmental Industries Inc)

2926 E Illini St, Phoenix, AZ 85040

Phone: (602) 243-1700

Sales: $35,000,000

Company Type: Private

SIC: 0781

Landscape irrigation golf course & commercial building contractor

Mark Sellew, President

Employees: 250

Employees here: 250

D-U-N-S 07-412-0916

VALLEY CREST TREE CO

(*Parent:* Environmental Industries Inc)

24121 Ventura Blvd, Calabasas, CA 91302

Phone: (818) 223-8500

Sales: $14,100,000

Company Type: Private

SIC: 0811

Tree farm

Kenneth Crandall, President

Employees: 300

Employees here: 10

D-U-N-S 04-325-8078

VALLEY FIG GROWERS INC

2028 S 3rd St, Fresno, CA 93702

Phone: (559) 237-3893

Sales: $10,735,000

Company Type: Private

SIC: 0723

Fig packing

W B Dunavant, Chief Executive Officer

Employees: 50

Employees here: 50

D-U-N-S 11-340-7019

VALLEY HARVESTING & PKG INC

101 E Main St, Heber, CA 92249

Phone: (760) 352-2364

Sales: $40,280,000

Company Type: Private

SIC: 0722

Crop harvesting

Michael Rainwater, President

Employees: 8

Employees here: 4

D-U-N-S 07-357-0558

VALLEY HEIGHTS RANCH LTD

651 Douglas Dr, Oceanside, CA 92054

Phone: (760) 757-5914

Sales: $10,600,000

Company Type: Private

SIC: 0161

Cucumber & tomatoe farm strawberry farm

Bob Provine Jr, President

Employees: 130

Employees here: 130

D-U-N-S 04-146-8349

VALLEY ONIONS INC

(*Parent:* A Duda & Sons Inc)

3 Mile N 23rd Trophy Dr, McAllen, TX 78504

Phone: (956) 631-3311

Sales: $11,400,000

Company Type: Private

SIC: 0161

Vegetable/melon farm

John Puglisi, President

Employees: 150

Employees here: 150

D-U-N-S 18-319-7177

VALLEY PRIDE INC

10855 Cara Mia Pkwy, Ste D, Castroville, CA 95012

Phone: (831) 633-5883

Sales: $22,062,000

Company Type: Private

SIC: 0761

Farm labor contractors

Anthony E Puleo, President

Employees: 400

Employees here: 400

D-U-N-S 08-170-6541

VALLEY RAIN CONSTRUCTION CORP

1206 N Stadem Dr, Tempe, AZ 85281

Phone: (602) 894-2835

Sales: $11,518,000

Company Type: Private

SIC: 0782

Irrigation lawn sprinkler & landscape contractor

Dean Walsh, President

Employees: 110

Employees here: 110

D-U-N-S 04-748-6865

VALLEY ROZ ORCHARDS INC

10 E Mead Ave, Yakima, WA 98903

Phone: (509) 457-4153

Sales: $10,000,000

Company Type: Private

SIC: 0175

Fruit orchard

Phillip D Leckey, President

Employees: 2,500

Employees here: 2

D-U-N-S 05-549-5485

VAN DE GRAAF RANCHES INC

EXP

1691 Midvale Rd, Sunnyside, WA 98944

Phone: (509) 837-3151

Sales: $64,179,000

Company Type: Private

SIC: 0211

Cattle feed lot

Fred Van Wingerden, President

Employees: 50

Employees here: 50

D-U-N-S 01-676-7394

VAN SOLKEMA PRODUCE INC

2630 Prescott, Byron Center, MI 49315

Phone: (616) 878-1508

Sales: $12,000,000

Company Type: Private

SIC: 0723

Packs vegetables

Wayde Kirschenman, President

Employees: 30

Employees here: 30

D-U-N-S 06-232-8844

VAN WINGERDEN INTERNATIONAL

556 Jeffress Rd, Fletcher, NC 28732

Phone: (828) 891-4116

Sales: $17,777,000

Company Type: Private

SIC: 0181

Greenhouse

Curry Roberts, President

Employees: 200

Employees here: 200

D-U-N-S 03-999-0163
VAN'S PINE NURSERY, INC
7550 144th Ave, West Olive, MI 49460
Phone: (616) 399-1620
Sales: $26,358,000   *Employees:* 16
Company Type: Private   *Employees here:* 16
SIC: 0181
   Service growing evergreen stock
J R Cotton, President

D-U-N-S 06-501-2254
VANN BROS
2290 E Camp Hankins Rd, Williams, CA 95987
Phone: (530) 473-2607
Sales: $20,000,000   *Employees:* 50
Company Type: Private   *Employees here:* 50
SIC: 0161
   Tomato cotton alfafa seed & wheat farm
Linda De Santiago, President

D-U-N-S 10-843-6239
VELVET RIDGE GREENHOUSES INC
297 Mount Carmel Rd, Asheville, NC 28806
Phone: (828) 254-3376
Sales: $16,000,000   *Employees:* 118
Company Type: Private   *Employees here:* 35
SIC: 0181
   Grows nursery stock
Howard Barnes, Partner

D-U-N-S 55-688-2322
VENTURE MILLING CO
212 S Bradford St, Seaford, DE 19973
Phone: (302) 628-3114
Sales: $22,253,000   *Employees:* 15
Company Type: Private   *Employees here:* 15
SIC: 0723
   Mfg specialty feed products & warehousing
Harry D Murphy, President

D-U-N-S 07-314-8884
VERIBEST CATTLE FEEDERS INC
9502 Hwy 380, San Angelo, TX 76905
Phone: (915) 655-7117
Sales: $10,412,000   *Employees:* 18
Company Type: Private   *Employees here:* 2
SIC: 0211
   Cattle feedlot operates as a wheat cotton & corn farmer and
      whol grain & operates a grain elevator
Stewart Jeffery, President

D-U-N-S 18-171-1672
VETERINARY CENTERS OF AMERICA
3420 Ocean Park Blvd, Santa Monica, CA 90405
Phone: (310) 392-9599
Sales: $239,389,000   *Employees:* 1,200
Company Type: Public   *Employees here:* 15
SIC: 0742
   Animal hospital services
Dennis Zensen, Chairman of the Board

D-U-N-S 96-054-4021
VIA NORTH AMERICA INC
15950 SW Kanner Hwy, Indiantown, FL 34956
Phone: (561) 597-2126
Sales: $30,600,000   *Employees:* 516
Company Type: Private   *Employees here:* 10
SIC: 0174
   Holding company: citrus
Ernesto Ramirez, Executive

D-U-N-S 00-691-4212
VIGNOLO FARMS
Central Vly Hwy, Shafter, CA 93263
Phone: (661) 325-8243
Sales: $12,400,000   *Employees:* 150
Company Type: Private   *Employees here:* 6
SIC: 0131
   Cotton & grape farm
Greg L Rasmussen, President

D-U-N-S 18-676-7737
VILA AND SON LANDSCAPING CORP
20451 SW 216th St, Miami, FL 33170
Phone: (305) 255-9206
Sales: $11,937,000   *Employees:* 136
Company Type: Private   *Employees here:* 60
SIC: 0782
   Lawn/garden services
Dale Bowman, President

D-U-N-S 02-884-1203
VILLA PARK ORCHARDS ASSN INC
544 N Cypress St, Orange, CA 92867
Phone: (714) 639-7610
Sales: $10,342,000   *Employees:* 385
Company Type: Private   *Employees here:* 12
SIC: 0723
   Fruit crop preparation service
Ronald D Offutt, President

D-U-N-S 07-796-4252
VINCENT B ZANINOVICH & SONS
20715 Avenue 8, Richgrove, CA 93261
Phone: (661) 725-2497
Sales: $11,600,000   *Employees:* 200
Company Type: Private   *Employees here:* 200
SIC: 0172
   Grape grower
John Giguiere, Chairman of the Board

D-U-N-S 13-040-2969
VINERY LLC
Weisenberger Mill Rd, Midway, KY 40347
Phone: (606) 846-5214
Sales: $15,000,000   *Employees:* 50
Company Type: Private   *Employees here:* 50
SIC: 0752
   Animal services
John Giguiere, Co-President

D-U-N-S 83-589-2894
VINIFERA INC
4288 Bodega Ave, Petaluma, CA 94952
Phone: (707) 773-4414
Sales: $10,200,000   *Employees:* 130
Company Type: Private   *Employees here:* 130
SIC: 0172
   Grape vine nursery
Rick Delon, President

D-U-N-S 03-772-4093
VIRGINIA BEEF CORP
1215 James Madison Hwy, Haymarket, VA 20169
Phone: (703) 754-8873
Sales: $21,000,000   *Employees:* 50
Company Type: Private   *Employees here:* 50
SIC: 0181
   Agribusiness
Mike Baca, President

D-U-N-S 04-506-7808
VLASIC FOODS INTERNATIONAL
  (Parent: Campbell Soup Co)
Maiden Creek Rd, Blandon, PA 19510
Phone: (610) 926-4101
Sales: $100,000,000   *Employees:* 1,800
Company Type: Public Family Member   *Employees here:* 330
SIC: 0182
  Mushroom farms
Hadar Rahav, President

D-U-N-S 07-411-0339
W J GRIFFIN INC
600 S Patterson Ave, Santa Barbara, CA 93111
Phone: (805) 964-8831
Sales: $11,000,000   *Employees:* 150
Company Type: Private   *Employees here:* 150
SIC: 0181
  Growing of potted plants
Joseph D Plummer, President

D-U-N-S 03-386-1832
W O SASSER SEAFOOD INC
135 Johnny Mercer Dr, Savannah, GA 31410
Phone: (912) 897-1154
Sales: $10,000,000   *Employees:* 18
Company Type: Private   *Employees here:* 18
SIC: 0913
  Commercial fisherman
Dennis Gore, President

D-U-N-S 04-862-7533
WAIALUA SUGAR COMPANY INC
  (Parent: Dole Food Company Inc)
67-202 Kupahu St, Waialua, HI 96791
Phone: (808) 637-6284
Sales: $24,200,000   *Employees:* 300
Company Type: Public Family Member   *Employees here:* 300
SIC: 0133
  Cane sugar grower
Baljit Nanda, President

D-U-N-S 00-910-3649
WAILUKU AGRIBUSINESS CO INC
  (Parent: C Brewer And Company Ltd)
255 E Waiko Rd, Wailuku, HI 96793
Phone: (808) 244-9570
Sales: $10,539,000   *Employees:* 150
Company Type: Private   *Employees here:* 150
SIC: 0173
  Macadamia nut orchard
Stanley Bloom, Executive

D-U-N-S 60-263-7993
WALKER FARMS
638 N 3500 E, Menan, ID 83434
Phone: (208) 754-4696
Sales: $10,000,000   *Employees:* 40
Company Type: Private   *Employees here:* 40
SIC: 0119
  Cash grains farm beef cattle-except feedlot corn farm field
    crop farm
Raymond J Wiegand Jr, President

D-U-N-S 01-746-4884   EXP
WALTERS GARDENS INC
1992 96th Ave, Zeeland, MI 49464
Phone: (616) 772-4697
Sales: $22,564,000   *Employees:* 370
Company Type: Private   *Employees here:* 370
SIC: 0181
  Ornamental nursery
W L Nutter, Chairman of the Board

D-U-N-S 04-306-9723
WARD FEED YARD INC
RR 2, Larned, KS 67550
Phone: (316) 285-2183
Sales: $19,569,000   *Employees:* 40
Company Type: Private   *Employees here:* 40
SIC: 0211
  Cattle feedlot
Carl G Stevenson, President

D-U-N-S 94-801-0632
WARREN'S TURF GROUP INC
  (Parent: Woerner South Inc)
505 S Flagler Dr, Ste 606, West Palm Beach, FL 33401
Phone: (561) 835-3747
Sales: $13,750,000   *Employees:* 150
Company Type: Private   *Employees here:* 1
SIC: 0181
  Sod farm
Carl G Stevenson, President

D-U-N-S 15-147-3378
WASHINGTON LTTUCE VGETABLE CO
3724 78th Ave E, Puyallup, WA 98371
Phone: (253) 922-2110
Sales: $20,000,000   *Employees:* 15
Company Type: Private   *Employees here:* 12
SIC: 0723
  Vegetable & fruit precooling service & whol fresh fruits &
    vegetables
Ray Samuelson, President

D-U-N-S 00-409-1799
WAVERLY GROWERS COOPERATIVE
7000 Waverly Rd, Waverly, FL 33877
Phone: (941) 439-3602
Sales: $10,000,000   *Employees:* 75
Company Type: Private   *Employees here:* 75
SIC: 0723
  Production & marketing of citrus products
J M Reiter Jr, President

D-U-N-S 16-193-4930
WEBORG CATTLE INC
1737 V Rd, Pender, NE 68047
Phone: (402) 385-3441
Sales: $16,000,000   *Employees:* 12
Company Type: Private   *Employees here:* 12
SIC: 0211
  Custom cattle feeding
Renee Godon, President

D-U-N-S 02-883-4331
WEEKS WHOLESALE ROSE GROWERS
430 E 19th St, Upland, CA 91784
Phone: (909) 949-4409
Sales: $10,300,000   *Employees:* 360
Company Type: Private   *Employees here:* 60
SIC: 0181
  Rose grower
Richard Renk, Chief Executive Officer

D-U-N-S 05-721-2029
WEISS LAKE EGG CO INC
Hwy 411, Centre, AL 35960
Phone: (256) 927-5546
Sales: $10,020,000   *Employees:* 44
Company Type: Private   *Employees here:* 44
SIC: 0252
  Egg processing
Bruno Fritschi, President

D-U-N-S 00-794-4010
WELLS AND WADE FRUIT CO
  (Parent: Dole Food Company Inc)
201 S Union Ave, East Wenatchee, WA 98802
Phone: (509) 886-0440
Sales: $12,100,000
Company Type: Public Family Member   *Employees:* 175
SIC: 0175   *Employees here:* 150
  Grow pack & store fruit
George S Reynolds, President

D-U-N-S 03-050-2546
WENDELL TALLEY
6309 Talley Rd, Stanfield, NC 28163
Phone: (704) 888-2819
Sales: $11,000,000
Company Type: Private   *Employees:* 55
SIC: 0253   *Employees here:* 55
  Turkey and beef cattle farm
Max B Rotholz, President

D-U-N-S 18-667-2663
WEST COTTON AG MANAGEMENT
15900 W Dorris, Huron, CA 93234
Phone: (559) 945-2722
Sales: $10,300,000
Company Type: Private   *Employees:* 200
SIC: 0762   *Employees here:* 200
  Farm management service
Jerome E Gumz, Principal

D-U-N-S 00-778-4028
WESTERN FEED YARD INC
548 S Road I, Johnson, KS 67855
Phone: (316) 492-6256
Sales: $24,144,000
Company Type: Private   *Employees:* 40
SIC: 0211   *Employees here:* 40
  Cattle feedlot
Richard S Burford, Owner

D-U-N-S 95-701-3717
WESTERN FRESH FRUIT SALES
86695 Avenue 54, Ste K, Coachella, CA 92236
Phone: (760) 399-4490
Sales: $14,000,000
Company Type: Private   *Employees:* 2
SIC: 0191   *Employees here:* 2
  General crop farm
Richard G Wilbur, Owner

D-U-N-S 04-600-4636
WESTLAKE FARMS INC
23311 Newton Ave, Stratford, CA 93266
Phone: (559) 947-3328
Sales: $11,800,000
Company Type: Private   *Employees:* 175
SIC: 0131   *Employees here:* 175
  Cotton wheat & barley farm
David Gill, Partner

D-U-N-S 00-286-9261
WHEELER BROTHERS GRAIN CO INC
501 Russworm Ave, Watonga, OK 73772
Phone: (580) 623-7223
Sales: $90,069,000
Company Type: Private   *Employees:* 99
SIC: 0211   *Employees here:* 20
  Operates cattle feed lots & grain elevators & whol feed &
    seed & fertilizer & through subsidiary operates short line
    railroad
Kenneth Martin, President

D-U-N-S 04-144-7947
WHITE'S NURSERY & GREENHOUSES
3133 Old Mill Rd, Chesapeake, VA 23323
Phone: (757) 487-2405
Sales: $15,288,000   *Employees:* 150
Company Type: Private   *Employees here:* 150
SIC: 0181
  Greenhouses
Jose J Rios, President

D-U-N-S 08-319-8051
WHITFIELD TIMBER INC
101 Hwy 71, Wewahitchka, FL 32465
Phone: (850) 639-5556
Sales: $20,000,000   *Employees:* 42
Company Type: Private   *Employees here:* 35
SIC: 0241
  Logging
David K Woodward, President

D-U-N-S 00-331-3442
WIGHT NURSERIES INC
  (Parent: Horticultural Farms Inc)
State Hwy 111, Cairo, GA 31728
Phone: (912) 377-3033
Sales: $20,000,000   *Employees:* 525
Company Type: Private   *Employees here:* 525
SIC: 0181
  Growing of shrubberies
Ritthaler Gerald I, President

D-U-N-S 02-707-0135
WILCO PEANUT CO
2 Mi N on US Hwy 281, Pleasanton, TX 78064
Phone: (830) 569-3808
Sales: $20,000,000   *Employees:* 49
Company Type: Private   *Employees here:* 49
SIC: 0723
  Operates a shelling plant
Carlos Ballesteros Sr, President

D-U-N-S 05-393-7983   EXP
WILKINS-ROGERS INC
27 Frederick Rd, Ellicott City, MD 21043
Phone: (410) 465-5800
Sales: $55,000,000   *Employees:* 125
Company Type: Private   *Employees here:* 110
SIC: 0723
  Flour & corn mill & mfg prepared baking mixes
David Morris, President

D-U-N-S 15-747-5112
WILLIAM E MCBRYDE INC
4.5 Mi S Hwy 117, Uvalde, TX 78801
Phone: (830) 278-3358
Sales: $10,000,000   *Employees:* 4
Company Type: Private   *Employees here:* 4
SIC: 0161
  Selling agent for cabbage & watermelons
John Petty, Owner

D-U-N-S 02-311-3442
WILLMAR POULTRY CO INC
3735 County Road 5 Sw, Willmar, MN 56201
Phone: (320) 235-8850
Sales: $78,600,000   *Employees:* 325
Company Type: Private   *Employees here:* 280
SIC: 0253
  Turkey hatchery & whol turkey and hog medications and
    equipment
Blas Rivera, Owner

D-U-N-S 08-611-6282
WILLMAR POULTRY FARMS INC
3735 Cty Rd 5 Sw, Willmar, MN 56201
Phone: (320) 235-8850
Sales: $10,300,000
Company Type: Private
SIC: 0213
   Turkey farm and manufacture prepared feeds
Joe Graziano, Member

Employees: 130
Employees here: 25

D-U-N-S 04-723-3341
WILLOWAY NURSERIES INC
4534 Center Rd, Avon, OH 44011
Phone: (440) 934-4435
Sales: $10,718,000
Company Type: Private
SIC: 0181
   Growers of shrubs nursery stock & foliage
Gary Fehr, President

Employees: 150
Employees here: 150

D-U-N-S 02-220-4361
WILLOWBROOK FOODS INC
   (Parent: Hudson Foods Inc)
2210 W Oaklawn Dr, Springdale, AR 72762
Phone: (501) 290-4000
Sales: $24,400,000
Company Type: Public Family Member
SIC: 0253
   Turkey farm
Roger Hatton, President

Employees: 200
Employees here: 4

D-U-N-S 01-943-4513
WILSON FARMS INC
10 Pleasant St, Lexington, MA
Phone: (781) 862-3900
Sales: $38,364,000
Company Type: Private
SIC: 0161
   Vegetable farm & ret potted plants
Marvin Roberts, President

Employees: 100
Employees here: 100

D-U-N-S 00-797-5931
WINTER HVEN CTRUS GRWERS ASSN
351 Avenue K Sw, Winter Haven, FL 33880
Phone: (941) 294-2959
Sales: $12,476,000
Company Type: Private
SIC: 0723
   Packing & shipping fresh citrus fruit
George Pace, Chief Executive Officer

Employees: 25
Employees here: 25

D-U-N-S 06-292-1101
WISNER MINNOW HATCHERY INC
715 Pete Haring Rd, Wisner, LA 71378
Phone: (318) 724-6133
Sales: $33,229,000
Company Type: Private
SIC: 0273
   Catfish & minnow farm & processing plant
John M Roche, President

Employees: 130
Employees here: 130

D-U-N-S 03-982-5554
WISPIG LLC
301 Scott Dr, Clinton, WI 53525
Phone: (608) 676-5990
Sales: $15,000,000
Company Type: Private
SIC: 0213
   Hog farm or feedlot
Ed Roche, President

Employees: 2
Employees here: 2

D-U-N-S 04-140-8600
WM BOLTHOUSE FARMS INC
7200 E Brundage Ln, Bakersfield, CA 93307
Phone: (661) 366-7205
Sales: $201,800,000
Company Type: Private
SIC: 0161
   Grows and processes carrots
Jerry L Johnson, President

Employees: 1,850
Employees here: 1,800

D-U-N-S 02-356-6888
WM F RENK & SONS CO, INC
6800 Wilburn Rd, Sun Prairie, WI 53590
Phone: (608) 837-7351
Sales: $10,126,000
Company Type: Private
SIC: 0181
   Raises & whol hybrid seed corn
Gary Wolfe, Executive Director

Employees: 35
Employees here: 33

D-U-N-S 04-149-4402
WM G ROE & SONS INC
500 Avenue R Sw, Winter Haven, FL 33880
Phone: (941) 294-3577
Sales: $20,000,000
Company Type: Private
SIC: 0723
   Citrus packers
Jeff Britt, President

Employees: 40
Employees here: 40

D-U-N-S 00-925-1807
WOERNER DEVELOPMENT INC
105 W Camphor Ave, Foley, AL 36535
Phone: (334) 943-3770
Sales: $17,800,000
Company Type: Private
SIC: 0181
   Sod farm
Roger W Harloff, Owner

Employees: 400
Employees here: 400

D-U-N-S 03-217-9913
WOERNER SOUTH INC
   (Parent: Edward J Woerner & Sons Inc)
505 S Flagler Dr, West Palm Beach, FL 33401
Phone: (561) 835-3747
Sales: $18,851,000
Company Type: Private
SIC: 0181
   Sod farm
Paul Mellon, Owner

Employees: 350
Employees here: 20

D-U-N-S 18-815-7812
WOLFSEN INC
1269 W I St, Los Banos, CA 93635
Phone: (209) 827-7700
Sales: $15,200,000
Company Type: Private
SIC: 0139
   Grows alfalfa cotton tomatoes & sugar beets
William A Rood Dvm, President

Employees: 200
Employees here: 20

D-U-N-S 15-552-9662
WOODCREST PARTNERSHIP
1811 Mountain Ave, Norco, CA 91760
Phone: (909) 737-6735
Sales: $18,000,000
Company Type: Private
SIC: 0252
   Chicken ranch
Daniel C Savadove, Chief Executive Officer

Employees: 200
Employees here: 200

D-U-N-S 03-147-8816
WOODLAND SERVICES, INC
17215 3rd Ave NE, Arlington, WA 98223
Phone: (360) 652-0412
Sales: $18,000,000   *Employees:* 4
Company Type: Private   *Employees here:* 4
SIC: 0241
    Logging
Lois Rust, President

D-U-N-S 08-776-5814
WORKINGMAN'S FRIEND OIL, INC
Bank Iv Tower, Ste 1200, Topeka, KS 66603
Phone: (785) 357-6161
Sales: $15,546,000   *Employees:* 8
Company Type: Private   *Employees here:* 3
SIC: 0212
    Cattle ranches
Ian Panton, President

D-U-N-S 93-335-2841
WORTH GIN CO, INC
1137 E Franklin St, Sylvester, GA 31791
Phone: (912) 776-6908
Sales: $16,000,000   *Employees:* 5
Company Type: Private   *Employees here:* 5
SIC: 0131
    Cotton gin
David Rousseau, Partner

D-U-N-S 00-785-8129
WRIGHT TREE SERVICE INC
    (Parent: Wright Service Corp)
139 6th St, West Des Moines, IA 50265
Phone: (515) 277-6291
Sales: $47,000,000   *Employees:* 1,000
Company Type: Private   *Employees here:* 35
SIC: 0783
    Tree trimming service
Lester W Roy, Chairman of the Board

D-U-N-S 07-562-1706
WYFFELS' HYBRIDS INC
RR 6 Box East, Atkinson, IL 61235
Phone: (309) 936-7833
Sales: $16,000,000   *Employees:* 150
Company Type: Private   *Employees here:* 100
SIC: 0115
    Grows hybrid seed corn
Helen Cardey, Chairman of the Board

D-U-N-S 15-337-5274
YEOMANS WOOD & TIMBER INC
616 W Moring St, Swainsboro, GA 30401
Phone: (912) 237-9940
Sales: $14,322,000   *Employees:* 10
Company Type: Private   *Employees here:* 10
SIC: 0241
    Logging contractor
Steve Ryan, Chief Executive Officer

D-U-N-S 00-445-0987
YODER BROTHERS, INC
115 3rd St Se, Barberton, OH 44203
Phone: (330) 745-2143
Sales: $50,000,000   *Employees:* 1,500
Company Type: Private   *Employees here:* 85
SIC: 0181
    Development and production of horticultural products
Tom Rusler, President

D-U-N-S 80-980-1657
YOUNG PECAN CO
1200 Pecan St, Florence, SC 29501
Phone: (843) 664-2330
Sales: $11,100,000   *Employees:* 116
Company Type: Private   *Employees here:* 100
SIC: 0723
    Pecan processing plant
Mary Cimarolli, Vice-President

D-U-N-S 06-139-7212
YOUNG'S PLANT FARM INC
1862 Saugahatchee Rd, Auburn, AL 36830
Phone: (334) 821-3500
Sales: $10,000,000   *Employees:* 100
Company Type: Private   *Employees here:* 65
SIC: 0181
    Plant nursery
Stephen C Horwath, President

D-U-N-S 04-934-5226
ZACKY FARMS INC
2000 Tyler Ave, El Monte, CA 91733
Phone: (626) 443-9351
Sales: $150,000,000   *Employees:* 3,000
Company Type: Private   *Employees here:* 250
SIC: 0251
    Raises poultry & whol poultry fish & meats
Rodger B Jensen, President

D-U-N-S 00-793-3328
ZAPATA CORP
100 Meridian Ctr, Ste 350, Rochester, NY 14618
Phone: (716) 242-2000
Sales: $133,555,000   *Employees:* 1,100
Company Type: Public   *Employees here:* 7
SIC: 0912
    Commercial menhaden fishing
Pagona Stefanopoulos, President

D-U-N-S 01-706-9246   EXP
ZELENKA NURSERY INC
16127 Winans St, Grand Haven, MI 49417
Phone: (616) 842-1367
Sales: $39,431,000   *Employees:* 220
Company Type: Private   *Employees here:* 100
SIC: 0181
    Nursery
Cory Priest, Manager

D-U-N-S 03-286-2906
ZEPHYR EGG CO
4622 Gall Blvd, Zephyrhills, FL 33541
Phone: (813) 782-1521
Sales: $30,000,000   *Employees:* 175
Company Type: Private   *Employees here:* 175
SIC: 0252
    Chicken egg farm
Thomas C Holt, President

The companies presented in Part II, Chapter 4 - Company Directory are arranged in this chapter in rank order: by sales and by number of employees. Each company's name, rank, location, type, sales, employment figure, and primary SIC are shown. Only companies with reported sales data are included in the "rankings by sales" table; similarly, only companies that report employment data are ranked in the "rankings by employment" table.

Company type is either Public, Private, or Public Family Member. The last category is used to label corporate entities that belong to a group of companies, the relationship being that of a subsidiary or element of a parent. The parents of Public Family Member companies can be found in the company's directory entry presented in Chapter 4, Part II.

This product includes proprietary data of Dun & Bradstreet, Inc.

D&B COMPANY RANKINGS BY SALES

Company	Rank	Location	Type	Sales ($ mil.)	Employ-ment	Primary SIC
Dole Food Co, Inc	1	Thousand Oaks, CA	Public	4,336.1	44,000	1799
Chiquita Brands International	2	Cincinnati, OH	Public	2,433.7	40,000	1799
Petsmart, Inc.	3	Phoenix, AZ	Public	1,790.6	18,800	7429
Gold Kist Inc	4	Atlanta, GA	Private	1,651.1	16,500	2549
Rayonier Inc.	5	Stamford, CT	Public	1,104.2	2,500	2411
Asplundh Tree Expert Co	6	Willow Grove, PA	Private	1,026.6	21,800	7830
Foster Poultry Farms	7	Livingston, CA	Private	1,000.0	7,200	2540
Michael Foods of Delaware	8	Minneapolis, MN	Public Family Member	956.2	3,870	2520
Michael Foods, Inc	9	Minneapolis, MN	Public	956.2	3,870	2520
Hudson Foods Inc	10	Springdale, AR	Public Family Member	833.3	10,000	2520
Longview Fibre Co	11	Longview, WA	Public	753.2	3,700	2411
Sanderson Farms Inc	12	Laurel, MS	Public	521.4	6,358	2519
Crown Pacific Partners, LP	13	Portland, OR	Public	505.6	1,100	8110
Carroll's Foods Inc	14	Warsaw, NC	Private	500.0	1,350	2130
Murphy Farms Inc	15	Rose Hill, NC	Private	499.1	2,100	2130
Tru Green LP	16	Memphis, TN	Private	454.9	13,000	7820
Moet Hennessy Inc	17	New York, NY	Private	416.0	9,100	1720
Asgrow Seed Company LLC	18	Des Moines, IA	Public Family Member	394.7	625	1810
Caprock Industries	19	Amarillo, TX	Private	375.0	213	2110
Environmental Industries Inc	20	Calabasas, CA	Private	351.3	5,600	7810
Environmental Care Inc (EII)	21	Orlando, FL	Private	351.3	750	7829
Cactus Feeders, Inc.	22	Amarillo, TX	Private	336.4	365	2110
Cactus Operating, Ltd.	23	Amarillo, TX	Private	335.0	50	2110
Bear Creek Corp	24	Medford, OR	Private	334.7	1,100	1750
Gottsch Feeding Corp	25	Elkhorn, NE	Private	315.8	56	2110
Cal-Maine Foods Inc	26	Jackson, MS	Public	309.1	1,574	2520
Agri Beef Co	27	Boise, ID	Private	300.0	515	2110
Tanimura & Antle, Inc	28	Salinas, CA	Private	300.0	2,200	1610
Bud Antle, Inc	29	Salinas, CA	Public Family Member	299.9	3,500	1610
A Duda & Sons Inc	30	Oviedo, FL	Private	297.0	1,600	1610
Davey Tree Expert Co	31	Kent, OH	Public	295.1	5,200	7830
Maxxam Group Inc	32	Houston, TX	Public Family Member	287.2	NA	8110
Grimmway Enterprises Inc	33	Di Giorgio, CA	Private	280.0	3,000	7230
Harris Woolf Cal Almonds	34	Coalinga, CA	Private	266.2	24	7230
Peco Foods Inc	35	Tuscaloosa, AL	Private	260.0	3,500	2549
Foster Dairy Farms	36	Modesto, CA	Private	250.0	590	2419
Goschie Farms Inc	37	Silverton, OR	Private	250.0	9	1399
Veterinary Centers of America	38	Santa Monica, CA	Public	239.4	1,200	7420
Dole Fresh Vegetables, Inc	39	Salinas, CA	Public Family Member	222.7	NA	7230
Wm Bolthouse Farms Inc	40	Bakersfield, CA	Private	201.8	1,850	1610
United States Sugar Corp	41	Clewiston, FL	Private	201.4	2,500	1339
Anderson Clayton Corp.	42	Fresno, CA	Private	200.0	250	7240
River Ranch Fresh Foods, Inc	43	Salinas, CA	Private	200.0	650	7230
Fresh International Corp	44	Salinas, CA	Private	191.2	3,000	7230
JFC Inc	45	St. Cloud, MN	Private	190.0	1,800	2519
Allen's Hatchery Inc	46	Seaford, DE	Private	180.0	300	2540
Pennfield Corp	47	Lancaster, PA	Private	180.0	650	2130
Plantation Foods, Inc	48	Waco, TX	Private	180.0	1,600	2530
Asplundh Subsidiary Holdings	49	Wilmington, DE	Private	175.3	2,800	7830
Durbin Marshall Food Corp	50	Birmingham, AL	Private	175.0	2,200	2520
Stallworth & Johnson Inc	51	Minter, AL	Private	175.0	60	2411
Peterson Farms, Inc.	52	Decatur, AR	Private	173.0	1,450	2549
Fresh Western Marketing Inc	53	Salinas, CA	Private	168.0	500	7220
Gargiulo, Inc	54	Naples, FL	Public Family Member	160.0	250	1610
Fresh Express Inc	55	Salinas, CA	Private	159.7	2,500	7230
Monterey Mushrooms Inc	56	Watsonville, CA	Private	156.1	2,000	1820
Iowa Select Farms	57	Iowa Falls, IA	Private	150.0	700	2139
J G Boswell Co	58	Pasadena, CA	Private	150.0	2,000	1310
Lykes Bros Inc	59	Tampa, FL	Private	150.0	2,500	7210
Rocco Farms Inc	60	Harrisonburg, VA	Private	150.0	100	2539
Zacky Farms Inc	61	El Monte, CA	Private	150.0	3,000	2510
Growers Vegetable Express	62	Salinas, CA	Private	143.9	342	1610
Valley Crest Landscape, Inc	63	Calabasas, CA	Private	143.4	1,200	7810
Hanson North America	64	Woodbridge, NJ	Private	140.8	3,000	8110
Sealaska Timber Corp	65	Ketchikan, AK	Private	140.0	48	8510
Landcare Usa, Inc	66	Houston, TX	Public	137.9	4,300	7830
Maui Land & Pineapple Co Inc	67	Kahului, HI	Public	136.5	2,270	1799
Zapata Corp	68	Rochester, NY	Public	133.6	1,100	9129
Brickman Group Ltd	69	Langhorne, PA	Private	130.0	900	7810
Exeter Packers Inc	70	Exeter, CA	Private	130.0	585	7230

D&B COMPANY RANKINGS BY SALES

Company	Rank	Location	Type	Sales ($ mil.)	Employment	Primary SIC
Thermoretec Corp	71	Concord, MA	Public Family Member	128.4	952	7110
Mann Packing Co, Inc	72	Salinas, CA	Private	126.8	500	7230
Ball Horticultural Co	73	West Chicago, IL	Private	125.0	2,000	1810
Joseph Campbell Co	74	Camden, NJ	Public Family Member	123.8	1,446	1610
Marko Zaninovich Inc	75	Delano, CA	Private	120.0	2,000	1720
Paramount Farming Company, LP	76	Bakersfield, CA	Private	120.0	400	1739
Mariani Packing Co Inc	77	San Jose, CA	Private	117.0	275	7230
Color Spot Nurseries, Inc	78	Pleasant Hill, CA	Private	113.4	1,828	1810
Cooper Hatchery Inc	79	Oakwood, OH	Private	110.0	700	2540
Orange-Co Inc	80	Bartow, FL	Public	109.3	250	1749
Tyson Breeders, Inc.	81	Springdale, AR	Public Family Member	107.1	2,000	2540
D'arrigo Bros Cal A Cal Corp	82	Salinas, CA	Private	105.0	900	1610
Carroll's Foods of Virginia	83	Waverly, VA	Private	103.6	580	2130
Ducks Unlimited Inc	84	Memphis, TN	Private	103.5	425	9719
C Brewer and Company Ltd	85	Hilo, HI	Private	100.7	1,600	1739
Cadiz, Inc	86	Santa Monica, CA	Public	100.2	985	7230
Arbor Acres Farm Inc	87	Glastonbury, CT	Private	100.0	750	2549
Columbia Helicopters Inc	88	Aurora, OR	Private	100.0	775	2411
Environmental Care Inc	89	Calabasas, CA	Private	100.0	2,800	7810
Johnson Farms	90	St. Francisville, IL	Private	100.0	5	1910
Juniata Feed Yards	91	Juniata, NE	Private	100.0	40	2110
Maple Leaf Farms Inc	92	Milford, IN	Private	100.0	1,250	2599
Minnesota Vikings Ventures	93	Eden Prairie, MN	Private	100.0	880	9710
Omni Facility Resources Inc	94	South Plainfield, NJ	Private	100.0	4,400	7810
Rose Acre Farms Inc	95	Seymour, IN	Private	100.0	1,200	2520
Suma Fruit International Usa	96	Sanger, CA	Private	100.0	67	7230
Vlasic Foods International	97	Blandon, PA	Public Family Member	100.0	1,800	1820
Sun World International, Inc	98	Bakersfield, CA	Public Family Member	99.9	905	7230
Giumarra Vineyards Corp	99	Edison, CA	Private	95.5	500	1720
Herndon Marine Products Inc	100	Aransas Pass, TX	Private	95.0	32	9130
Pacific Tomato Growers, Ltd	101	Palmetto, FL	Private	94.3	75	1619
Norco Ranch Inc	102	Norco, CA	Private	94.0	225	2520
Maxwell Foods Inc.	103	Goldsboro, NC	Private	92.9	1,000	2130
Saticoy Lemon Association Inc	104	Santa Paula, CA	Private	91.1	650	7230
Mar Jac Poultry Inc	105	Gainesville, GA	Private	90.9	800	2540
Wheeler Brothers Grain Co Inc	106	Watonga, OK	Private	90.1	99	2110
F A Bartlett Tree Expert	107	Stamford, CT	Private	89.9	1,700	7839
Herbert C Haynes Inc	108	Winn, ME	Private	88.0	100	2411
Timberland Silvicultural Services	109	Monticello, AR	Private	86.2	5	8510
Paragon Produce Corp	110	Immokalee, FL	Private	85.5	1,000	1619
Missouri Farmers Association	111	Columbia, MO	Private	85.1	1,800	7620
Boskovich Farms Inc	112	Oxnard, CA	Private	85.0	750	1610
Peco Farms Inc	113	Gordo, AL	Private	85.0	609	2519
Pm Beef Group LLC	114	Kansas City, MO	Private	85.0	120	2110
A & D Christopher Ranch	115	Gilroy, CA	Private	83.8	200	1610
Monrovia Nursery Co	116	Azusa, CA	Private	83.6	1,700	1810
Prestage Farms Inc	117	Clinton, NC	Private	83.6	900	2130
Sylvan Inc.	118	Saxonburg, PA	Public	81.6	900	1820
U.S. Tmbrlands Klamath Fls LLC	119	Klamath Falls, OR	Private	80.0	30	8110
Hillandale Farms Inc	120	Lake City, FL	Private	80.0	268	2520
Seaboard Farms of Oklahoma	121	Guymon, OK	Private	79.9	860	2130
Oakley Groves Inc	122	Lake Wales, FL	Private	79.3	400	1740
Willmar Poultry Co Inc	123	Willmar, MN	Private	78.6	325	2539
Mills Distributing Co, Inc	124	Salinas, CA	Private	78.4	30	1610
Heller Bros Packing Corp	125	Winter Garden, FL	Private	76.4	50	1740
Cuddy Farms Inc	126	Marshville, NC	Private	76.0	700	2540
Foxley Cattle Co	127	La Jolla, CA	Private	75.8	110	2110
Meyer Tomatoes	128	King City, CA	Private	75.6	87	1619
Morrison Enterprises	129	Hastings, NE	Private	75.0	210	1910
Cooperative Resources Intl Inc	130	Shawano, WI	Private	72.0	1,200	7510
Genex Cooperative Inc	131	Ithaca, NY	Private	72.0	400	7510
Schaake Corp	132	Ellensburg, WA	Private	71.8	40	2110
Sun-Land Products of California	133	Pleasanton, CA	Private	70.7	50	7230
Hy-Line International	134	West Des Moines, IA	Private	70.1	320	2549
Circle Four Farms	135	Milford, UT	Private	70.0	400	2139
Lion Enterprises Inc	136	Fresno, CA	Private	70.0	150	7230
Peco Foods of Mississippi Inc	137	Bay Springs, MS	Private	70.0	600	2549
Pig Improvement Company, Inc	138	Franklin, KY	Private	69.7	750	2130
Sahlman Holding Co Inc	139	Tampa, FL	Private	65.6	20	9130
Sahlman Seafoods Inc	140	Tampa, FL	Private	65.6	20	9130

D&B COMPANY RANKINGS BY SALES

Company	Rank	Location	Type	Sales ($ mil.)	Employ-ment	Primary SIC
Naturipe Berry Growers	141	Watsonville, CA	Private	65.4	35	7230
California Artich & Vege	142	Castroville, CA	Private	65.3	60	7230
Crystal Farms Inc	143	Gainesville, GA	Private	65.0	175	2520
Lindemann Produce Inc	144	Reno, NV	Private	65.0	63	7230
Van De Graaf Ranches Inc	145	Sunnyside, WA	Private	64.2	50	2110
Nelson Tree Service Inc	146	Dayton, OH	Private	64.1	NA	7830
Maple Leaf Duck Farms Inc	147	Milford, IN	Private	62.0	750	2599
Griffin, Ben Hill Inc	148	Frostproof, FL	Private	61.3	130	1740
Mivco Packing Co	149	Salinas, CA	Private	60.3	4	1610
All Alaskan Seafoods, Inc	150	Seattle, WA	Private	60.0	200	9130
Natural Selection Foods LLC	151	San Juan Bautista, CA	Private	60.0	200	7230
Noblesse Oblige Inc	152	El Centro, CA	Private	60.0	1,200	7220
Roberts Enterprises Inc	153	Phoenix, AZ	Private	60.0	8	2110
Southland Foods Inc	154	Jack, AL	Private	60.0	950	2519
Sunshine Raisin Corp	155	Fowler, CA	Private	60.0	120	7230
Tyson Seafood Group	156	Seattle, WA	Public Family Member	60.0	1,200	9120
Simplot Livestock Company Inc	157	Grand View, ID	Private	59.5	280	2110
Apio Inc	158	Guadalupe, CA	Private	59.4	75	7220
Peace River Citrus Products	159	Arcadia, FL	Private	58.1	NA	1740
Dekalb Swine Breeders Inc	160	Dekalb, IL	Public Family Member	57.0	380	2139
Dimare Homestead, Inc	161	Homestead, FL	Private	56.1	15	1610
Livestock Investments, Inc	162	Hereford, TX	Private	56.0	75	2110
Agrinorthwest, Inc	163	Kennewick, WA	Private	55.8	100	1110
Huntco Farms, Inc	164	Chesterfield, MO	Public Family Member	55.8	600	2130
Livestock Investors, Inc.	165	Summerfield, TX	Private	55.4	75	2110
Gallo Cattle Co	166	Atwater, CA	Private	55.0	350	2410
Sylvest Farms, Inc	167	Montgomery, AL	Private	55.0	1,100	2519
Wilkins-Rogers Inc	168	Ellicott City, MD	Private	55.0	125	7230
King Ranch Inc	169	Houston, TX	Private	54.7	1,094	2120
R D Offutt Co	170	Fargo, ND	Private	54.5	545	1340
Klein Foods Inc	171	Healdsburg, CA	Private	53.7	250	1720
Hines Horticulture Inc	172	Irvine, CA	Public	53.1	1,200	1810
Confederated Tr Wrm Sprgs	173	Warm Springs, OR	Private	52.8	1,500	8110
Terry Farms Inc	174	Mount Dora, FL	Private	52.0	900	1820
Paramount Citrus Association	175	Visalia, CA	Private	51.0	650	1749
Edward J Woerner & Sons Inc	176	West Palm Beach, FL	Private	50.9	650	1819
Griffin Produce Co Inc	177	Salinas, CA	Private	50.8	25	7230
Lewis Tree Service Inc	178	Rochester, NY	Private	50.7	1,000	7830
Golden Rod Broilers Inc	179	Cullman, AL	Private	50.5	1,010	2519
Guide Dogs For The Blind Inc	180	San Rafael, CA	Private	50.5	250	7520
Edaw Inc	181	San Francisco, CA	Private	50.4	330	7810
Adams Land Co	182	Leachville, AR	Private	50.0	60	7240
Asc Far East Inc	183	Seattle, WA	Private	50.0	11	9120
Cobb-Vantress, Inc.	184	Siloam Springs, AR	Public Family Member	50.0	415	7510
Morrison Bros Ranch	185	Higley, AZ	Private	50.0	125	2120
New West Foods	186	Watsonville, CA	Private	50.0	107	7230
Omega Enterprises	187	Seattle, WA	Private	50.0	NA	9120
Oppliger Family, Ltd.	188	Clovis, NM	Private	50.0	150	2120
Yoder Brothers, Inc	189	Barberton, OH	Private	50.0	1,500	1810
Enoch Packing Co Inc	190	Del Rey, CA	Private	49.5	150	7230
Merex Corp	191	Yonkers, NY	Private	49.0	85	1610
Dimare Enterprises Inc	192	Newman, CA	Private	49.0	325	1740
Medical Management International	193	Portland, OR	Private	48.8	1,300	7420
Fletcher Challenge Forest Usa	194	Hanover, MD	Private	48.0	4	8510
Pride Industries Inc	195	Roseville, CA	Private	48.0	2,700	7820
Stemilt Growers Inc	196	Wenatchee, WA	Private	47.9	600	7230
G & H Seed Co, Inc.	197	Crowley, LA	Private	47.8	130	7239
Spokane Tribe of Indians	198	Wellpinit, WA	Private	47.7	325	2411
Alico Inc	199	Labelle, FL	Public	47.4	130	1740
Northland Cranberries Inc	200	Wisconsin Rapids, WI	Public	47.4	150	1719
Farming Technology Corp	201	Houston, TX	Private	47.2	120	1340
Wright Tree Service Inc	202	West Des Moines, IA	Private	47.0	1,000	7830
Homa Co	203	Parsippany, NJ	Private	46.4	120	1730
Griffin Land & Nurseries, Inc	204	New York, NY	Public	46.3	259	1810
Greenleaf Nursery Co	205	Park Hill, OK	Private	45.2	1,200	1810
Croman Corp	206	Ashland, OR	Private	45.0	220	2411
Glacier Fish Co L.L.C.	207	Seattle, WA	Private	45.0	250	9120
S & H Packing and Sales Co	208	Los Angeles, CA	Private	45.0	381	1619
Sleepy Creek Farms Inc	209	Goldsboro, NC	Private	45.0	400	2539
Sun and Sands Enterprises, LLC	210	Coachella, CA	Private	43.3	65	1610

D&B COMPANY RANKINGS BY SALES

Company	Rank	Location	Type	Sales ($ mil.)	Employ-ment	Primary SIC
Cattlemens Inc	211	Turon, KS	Private	43.0	100	2110
Bruce Church Inc	212	Salinas, CA	Private	42.8	502	1610
Leidy's Inc	213	Souderton, PA	Private	42.8	242	7519
Farm-Op, Inc	214	Immokalee, FL	Private	42.6	500	1610
Marshall Durbin Farms Inc	215	Birmingham, AL	Private	42.5	850	2510
Spencer Fruit Co	216	Reedley, CA	Private	42.0	40	7230
Imperial Nurseries, Inc	217	Granby, CT	Public Family Member	42.0	259	1810
Henry Avocado Packing Corp	218	Escondido, CA	Private	41.4	70	1799
E Ritter & Co Inc	219	Marked Tree, AR	Private	41.4	145	1310
Tejon Ranch Co	220	Lebec, CA	Public	41.0	90	1739
Ford Holding Company Inc	221	Ford, KS	Private	40.7	68	2110
Harlan Sprague Dawley Inc	222	Indianapolis, IN	Private	40.5	1,350	2799
Flo Sun Inc	223	Palm Beach, FL	Private	40.3	1,110	1339
Valley Harvesting & Pkg Inc	224	Heber, CA	Private	40.3	8	7229
Booker Holdings Inc	225	Glastonbury, CT	Private	40.2	750	2549
McAnally Enterprises Inc.	226	Yucaipa, CA	Private	40.0	400	2520
Alaska Trawl Fisheries, Inc	227	Edmonds, WA	Private	40.0	70	9120
Becker Holdings Corp	228	Vero Beach, FL	Private	40.0	150	7210
Creighton Brothers LLC	229	Warsaw, IN	Private	40.0	160	2520
Diamond Fruit Growers Inc	230	Hood River, OR	Private	40.0	80	7230
Dmb Packing Corp	231	Newman, CA	Private	40.0	320	1740
Gentry's Poultry Co Inc	232	Ward, SC	Private	40.0	275	2510
Jack Frost Inc	233	St. Cloud, MN	Private	40.0	250	2519
Jlg Harvesting Inc	234	Greenfield, CA	Private	40.0	600	7230
Limoneira Associates	235	Santa Paula, CA	Private	40.0	600	7230
Pioneer Growers Cooperative	236	Belle Glade, FL	Private	40.0	10	1610
Sunseeds Co	237	Morgan Hill, CA	Private	40.0	240	1810
Taylor Fresh Foods Inc	238	Salinas, CA	Private	40.0	600	7230
Teixeira Farms Inc	239	Santa Maria, CA	Private	40.0	188	1610
Paris Foods Corp	240	Camden, NJ	Private	39.8	46	7230
Naumes Inc	241	Medford, OR	Private	39.7	700	1750
Zelenka Nursery Inc	242	Grand Haven, MI	Private	39.4	220	1810
Franklin Farms Inc	243	North Franklin, CT	Private	39.0	590	1820
Harris Moran Seed Co	244	Modesto, CA	Private	38.6	275	1810
Davey Tree Surgery Co	245	Livermore, CA	Public Family Member	38.5	1,200	7830
Wilson Farms Inc	246	Lexington, MA	Private	38.4	100	1610
Erwin-Keith Inc	247	Wynne, AR	Private	38.0	43	1190
Hillandale Farms of Florida Inc	248	Lake City, FL	Private	37.7	300	2529
Navajo Ag Pdts Indust	249	Farmington, NM	Private	37.6	440	1910
Hubbard Farms Inc	250	Walpole, NH	Public Family Member	37.5	700	2540
Brooks Tropicals Inc	251	Homestead, FL	Private	37.5	350	7629
Mecca Farms Inc	252	Lake Worth, FL	Private	37.4	50	1619
Hartung Brothers Inc	253	Arena, WI	Private	37.4	85	1610
Del Monte Fresh Produce Hawaii	254	Kunia, HI	Private	37.1	650	1799
McClain Enterprises, Inc.	255	Mountain Home, AR	Private	36.9	50	2539
Thomas Produce Co	256	Boca Raton, FL	Private	36.5	15	1619
Costa Nursery Farms Inc	257	Goulds, FL	Private	36.5	460	1810
Broetje Orchards	258	Prescott, WA	Private	36.3	1,200	1759
Lihue Plantation Company Ltd	259	Lihue, HI	Private	36.2	450	1339
South Eastern Boll Weevil Era	260	Montgomery, AL	Private	36.2	210	7249
Charles Donald Pulpwood Inc	261	Port Gibson, MS	Private	36.1	23	2411
Hollandia Dairy	262	San Marcos, CA	Private	36.0	200	2410
Sylvan Foods, Inc.	263	Saxonburg, PA	Public Family Member	36.0	900	1820
Hitch Feeders I Inc	264	Guymon, OK	Private	35.7	200	2110
Pride Feeders I, Ltd	265	Hooker, OK	Private	35.4	50	2110
Christensen Cattle Co	266	Central City, NE	Private	35.0	55	2110
Kurt Weiss Florist Inc	267	Center Moriches, NY	Private	35.0	200	1810
Ross Breeders Inc	268	Huntsville, AL	Private	35.0	350	2549
Valley Crest Landscape Inc	269	Phoenix, AZ	Private	35.0	250	7810
B H Hardaway III Farms Inc	270	Columbus, GA	Private	34.6	500	1390
Monson Ranches Inc	271	Outlook, WA	Private	34.0	30	2110
Hickman's Egg Ranch, Inc.	272	Glendale, AZ	Private	34.0	100	2520
Ise America Inc	273	Golts, MD	Private	33.9	407	2520
Sanderson Farms Production Div	274	Laurel, MS	Public Family Member	33.8	675	2519
Speedling, Inc	275	Sun City, FL	Private	33.6	250	1810
Golden West Nuts Inc	276	Ripon, CA	Private	33.6	40	7230
Dundee Citrus Growers Assn	277	Dundee, FL	Private	33.4	70	7230
National Food Corp	278	Seattle, WA	Private	33.3	NA	2520
Wisner Minnow Hatchery Inc	279	Wisner, LA	Private	33.2	130	2730
Sublette Enterprises Inc	280	Sublette, KS	Private	32.9	75	2110

D&B COMPANY RANKINGS BY SALES

Company	Rank	Location	Type	Sales ($ mil.)	Employ-ment	Primary SIC
Hermann Engelmann Greenhouses	281	Apopka, FL	Private	32.8	740	1810
G.F. Structures Corp	282	Chicago, IL	Private	32.7	80	7829
Rafter 3 Feedyard, Inc.	283	Dimmitt, TX	Private	32.2	33	2110
Trees, Inc	284	Houston, TX	Private	32.1	1,000	7830
Amana Society, Inc	285	Amana, IA	Private	32.0	275	1910
Black Dog Farms of California	286	Holtville, CA	Private	32.0	150	1610
Swine Graphics Enterprises, LP	287	Webster City, IA	Private	31.8	49	2130
Hazelnut Growers of Oregon	288	Cornelius, OR	Private	31.6	47	7230
Betteravia Farms	289	Santa Maria, CA	Private	31.5	250	1610
Cattlco	290	Fort Morgan, CO	Private	31.2	140	2110
Hi-Lo Oil Co, Inc	291	Topeka, KS	Private	31.2	3	2120
Cattlco Inc	292	Memphis, TN	Private	31.1	150	2110
Golden Merger Corp	293	Santa Monica, CA	Public Family Member	31.1	830	7420
Baloian Packing Co, Inc.	294	Fresno, CA	Private	30.9	300	1610
Via North America Inc	295	Indiantown, FL	Private	30.6	516	1740
Ford County Feed Yard Inc	296	Ford, KS	Private	30.5	59	2110
7th Standard Ranch Co	297	Bakersfield, CA	Private	30.0	500	1720
Alaska Ocean Seafood Ltd	298	Anacortes, WA	Private	30.0	170	9120
California Family Foods LLC	299	Arbuckle, CA	Private	30.0	50	7230
Dole Bakersfield Inc	300	Bakersfield, CA	Public Family Member	30.0	500	1720
Great American Farms Inc	301	Pompano Beach, FL	Private	30.0	15	1910
L L Murphrey Co	302	Farmville, NC	Private	30.0	90	2130
Noah W Kreider & Son	303	Manheim, PA	Private	30.0	450	2520
Organics Management Co	304	Oak Park, IL	Private	30.0	3	7110
S & J Ranch Inc	305	Madera, CA	Public Family Member	30.0	400	7620
Sharyland LP	306	Mission, TX	Private	30.0	449	1610
Terry Farms, Princeton, Inc.	307	Princeton, IL	Private	30.0	500	1820
Zephyr Egg Co	308	Zephyrhills, FL	Private	30.0	175	2520
Diamond Creek Farms Inc	309	Goldsboro, NC	Private	29.8	265	2539
Harrison Poultry Inc	310	Bethlehem, GA	Private	29.7	555	2549
Tampa Farm Service Inc	311	Dover, FL	Private	29.0	210	2520
Lone Star Growers, L P	312	Pleasant Hill, CA	Private	28.8	650	1810
Horticultural Farms Inc	313	Cairo, GA	Private	28.5	650	1810
Abbyland Pork Pack Inc	314	Curtiss, WI	Private	28.4	125	7519
Sun Pacific Farming Co	315	Exeter, CA	Private	28.4	600	7629
Tracy Industries Inc	316	Rcho Sta Marg, CA	Private	28.2	800	7829
Double A Feeders Inc	317	Clayton, NM	Private	28.0	18	2110
Kenneth L Mink & Sons Inc	318	Waldorf, MD	Private	28.0	35	2719
Quincy Corp	319	Quincy, FL	Public Family Member	28.0	575	1820
Rousseau Farming Co II	320	Tolleson, AZ	Private	28.0	200	1610
Oakdell Egg Farms Inc	321	Pasco, WA	Private	27.9	60	2520
George Amaral Ranches Inc	322	Chualar, CA	Private	27.5	60	1610
Tejas Feeders, Ltd.	323	Pampa, TX	Private	27.5	15	2110
Blaine Larsen Processing Inc	324	Hamer, ID	Private	27.4	400	7230
Seabrook Enterprises Inc	325	Alpharetta, GA	Private	27.4	400	7230
Southern Orchard Supply Co	326	Fort Valley, GA	Private	27.4	400	7230
Mac Farms of Hawaii Inc	327	Captain Cook, HI	Private	27.3	70	1739
Erickson Air-Crane Co., LLC	328	Central Point, OR	Private	27.2	500	2411
21st Century Genetics	329	Shawano, WI	Private	27.1	500	7510
Bailey Nurseries, Inc	330	St. Paul, MN	Private	27.0	470	1810
Norman's Nursery Inc.	331	San Gabriel, CA	Private	27.0	650	1810
Pismo-Oceano Vegetable Exch	332	Oceano, CA	Private	27.0	27	7230
Bruce Company of Wisconsin Inc	333	Middleton, WI	Private	27.0	150	7829
Hitch Feeders II, Inc	334	Garden City, KS	Private	26.9	50	2110
Kaolin Mushroom Farms Inc	335	Kennett Square, PA	Private	26.8	670	1820
Van's Pine Nursery, Inc	336	West Olive, MI	Private	26.4	16	1810
Chooljian & Sons Inc	337	Del Rey, CA	Private	26.3	60	7230
Chooljian Bros Packing Co Inc	338	Sanger, CA	Private	26.2	45	7230
Lamanuzzi & Pantaleo Ltd	339	Clovis, CA	Private	26.2	150	1720
Avian Farms (Kentucky), Inc	340	Monticello, KY	Private	26.0	170	2540
Delta Packing Co of Lodi	341	Lodi, CA	Private	26.0	25	7230
Texas A & M University	342	College Station, TX	Private	25.9	318	8510
Pandol & Sons	343	Delano, CA	Private	25.7	205	7230
Tri-State Feeders, Inc	344	Turpin, OK	Private	25.6	30	2110
Amick Processing Inc	345	Batesburg, SC	Private	25.4	475	2540
L A Hearne Co	346	King City, CA	Private	25.4	74	7230
Trout-Blue Chelan, Inc	347	Chelan, WA	Private	25.3	150	7230
Coyote Lake Feedyard, Inc.	348	Muleshoe, TX	Private	25.2	23	2110
Bracht Feedyards, Inc	349	West Point, NE	Private	25.0	12	2110
Daylay Egg Farms, Inc	350	West Mansfield, OH	Private	25.0	170	2520

D&B COMPANY RANKINGS BY SALES

Company	Rank	Location	Type	Sales ($ mil.)	Employ- ment	Primary SIC
Duarte Nursery Inc	351	Hughson, CA	Private	25.0	150	1810
El Modeno Gardens Inc	352	Irvine, CA	Private	25.0	320	1810
Elbow Enterprises Inc	353	Visalia, CA	Private	25.0	8	7240
Eunice Rice Mill, LLC	354	Eunice, LA	Private	25.0	35	7230
Gold Cost Pistachios Inc	355	Coalinga, CA	Private	25.0	50	1739
McArthur Farms Inc	356	Okeechobee, FL	Private	25.0	165	2419
McClure Properties, Ltd	357	Palmetto, FL	Private	25.0	150	1619
Midwest Poultry Services LP	358	Mentone, IN	Private	25.0	300	2520
Modern Mushroom Farms Inc	359	Toughkenamon, PA	Private	25.0	350	1820
Pratt Feeders L L C	360	Pratt, KS	Private	25.0	75	2110
Starr Produce Co	361	Rio Grande City, TX	Private	25.0	210	1610
Colorado Greenhouse Holdings	362	Denver, CO	Private	24.9	563	1619
Townsend Tree Service Co Inc	363	Selma, IN	Private	24.9	775	7830
Fairleigh Corp	364	Scott City, KS	Private	24.9	45	2110
Berend Bros Inc	365	Wichita Falls, TX	Private	24.7	125	2130
D M Camp & Sons	366	Bakersfield, CA	Private	24.5	80	1910
Beef Belt Feeders Inc	367	Scott City, KS	Private	24.4	15	2110
Willowbrook Foods Inc	368	Springdale, AR	Public Family Member	24.4	200	2539
Dave Kingston Produce Inc	369	Idaho Falls, ID	Private	24.2	350	7230
Golden Valley Produce LLC	370	Buttonwillow, CA	Private	24.2	350	7230
Waialua Sugar Company Inc	371	Waialua, HI	Public Family Member	24.2	300	1339
Western Feed Yard Inc	372	Johnson, KS	Private	24.1	40	2110
Melkesian Ranch Inc	373	Indio, CA	Private	24.0	400	1720
P F F J, Inc	374	Snowflake, AZ	Private	24.0	150	2130
Red Rock Feeding Co	375	Red Rock, AZ	Private	24.0	35	2110
Running W Citrus Ltd Partnr	376	South Bay, FL	Private	24.0	200	1740
Hondo Co (Inc)	377	Roswell, NM	Private	23.9	478	2120
Atlantic Salmon Me Ltd Lblty	378	Fairfield, ME	Private	23.9	135	2730
Canadian Feedyards, Inc.	379	Canadian, TX	Private	23.6	4	2110
Agreserves, Inc	380	Salt Lake City, UT	Private	23.6	500	7620
Five Crowns, Inc	381	Brawley, CA	Private	23.6	5	1610
Belair Packing Hse Joint Ventr	382	Vero Beach, FL	Private	23.5	60	7230
Anton Caratan & Son	383	Delano, CA	Private	23.5	100	1720
Quality Grain Company Inc	384	Atlanta, GA	Private	23.4	341	1120
Flowerwood Nursery Inc	385	Mobile, AL	Private	23.3	500	1810
G & S Livestock	386	Attica, IN	Private	23.0	5	1190
Oppliger Feedyard Inc	387	Clovis, NM	Private	22.9	43	2110
Taconic Farms Inc	388	Germantown, NY	Private	22.8	210	2799
American Nursery Products LLC	389	Tulsa, OK	Private	22.8	400	8119
J & C Enterprises Inc	390	Miami, FL	Private	22.8	35	1390
Premium Feeders Inc	391	Scandia, KS	Private	22.6	25	2110
Walters Gardens Inc	392	Zeeland, MI	Private	22.6	370	1810
Venture Milling Co	393	Seaford, DE	Private	22.3	15	7230
National Petcare Center Inc	394	Fort Collins, CO	Private	22.2	800	7429
San Val Corp	395	Palm Desert, CA	Private	22.1	439	7810
Valley Pride Inc	396	Castroville, CA	Private	22.1	400	7619
Coharie Farms	397	Clinton, NC	Private	22.0	90	2130
Kingsburg Apple Packers	398	Kingsburg, CA	Private	22.0	20	7230
Penco Inc	399	Greer, SC	Private	22.0	24	7520
Peters Runnells Cattle Co Inc	400	Laredo, TX	Private	22.0	15	2110
R D Bowman & Sons Inc	401	Westminster, MD	Private	22.0	55	7230
Shamrock Farms Co	402	Chandler, AZ	Private	21.7	75	2419
Calgene Inc	403	Davis, CA	Public Family Member	21.7	256	1619
Gustafson's Dairy Inc	404	Green Cove Springs, FL	Private	21.7	325	2410
Utrecht - America Holdings	405	New York, NY	Private	21.6	460	8110
Nurserymen's Exchange Inc	406	San Francisco, CA	Private	21.5	485	1810
Perryton Feeders, Inc.	407	Perryton, TX	Private	21.4	65	2110
Taylor & Fulton Inc	408	Palmetto, FL	Private	21.2	90	7230
Bucio Lourdes Farm	409	Santa Maria, CA	Private	21.2	250	1610
Corkscrew Growers Inc	410	Bonita Springs, FL	Private	21.2	250	1619
Muranaka Farm, Inc	411	Granada Hills, CA	Private	21.2	250	1610
Gerralds Vdlia Sweet Onons Inc	412	Statesboro, GA	Private	21.1	300	7230
Gulfstream Tomato Growers Ltd	413	Miami, FL	Private	21.1	300	7230
Harloff Packing of East Tenn	414	Morristown, TN	Private	21.1	300	7230
Ag Rx Inc	415	Oxnard, CA	Private	21.0	90	7119
Columbia River Sugar Co	416	Moses Lake, WA	Private	21.0	6	1910
Garlic Co	417	Bakersfield, CA	Private	21.0	85	1399
L & J Ranch Inc	418	St. Libory, NE	Private	21.0	2	2110
Tara Packing Co	419	Spreckels, CA	Private	21.0	600	7610
Virginia Beef Corp	420	Haymarket, VA	Private	21.0	50	1819

D&B COMPANY RANKINGS BY SALES

Company	Rank	Location	Type	Sales ($ mil.)	Employ-ment	Primary SIC
Tri-State Breeders Coop	421	Baraboo, WI	Private	20.9	260	7510
Golden Acres Farms	422	Thermal, CA	Private	20.8	20	1610
Producers Holding Co	423	Memphis, TN	Private	20.8	200	7240
Evans Properties Inc	424	Dade City, FL	Private	20.7	350	1740
Rio Farms	425	Oxnard, CA	Private	20.7	200	1610
Sorrells Brothers Packing Co	426	Arcadia, FL	Private	20.6	20	7220
A & P Growers Co-Op Inc	427	Tulare, CA	Private	20.6	10	1749
Classic Cattle Co LP	428	Wildorado, TX	Private	20.6	28	2110
Cherry Lake Farms Inc	429	Groveland, FL	Private	20.6	200	1749
Sun Valley Floral Farms	430	Arcata, CA	Private	20.4	150	1810
Sunridge Nurseries, Inc	431	Bakersfield, CA	Private	20.4	70	7210
J-V Farms, Inc.	432	Yuma, AZ	Private	20.3	200	1610
Dimare Ruskin Inc	433	Ruskin, FL	Private	20.2	12	7230
Mobley Gin Co Inc	434	Moultrie, GA	Private	20.1	6	7240
Gay & Robinson Inc	435	Kaumakani, HI	Private	20.0	280	1339
Farrens Tree Surgeons Inc	436	Willow Grove, PA	Private	20.0	470	7830
Rock & Waterscape Systems	437	Irvine, CA	Private	20.0	350	7829
Ace Tomato Company Inc	438	Manteca, CA	Private	20.0	50	1619
Affiliated Rice Milling Inc	439	Alvin, TX	Private	20.0	45	7230
American Pelagic Fishing L P	440	Seattle, WA	Private	20.0	60	9120
Bromm Cattle Co Inc	441	Craig, NE	Private	20.0	11	2110
C B Bunting & Sons	442	Pinetops, NC	Private	20.0	30	1320
Cecelia Packing Corp	443	Orange Cove, CA	Private	20.0	150	7230
Cedar Bluff Cattle Feeders	444	Ellis, KS	Private	20.0	14	2110
Central Cal Tmato Growers Coop	445	Merced, CA	Private	20.0	3	7230
Creekside Mushrooms Ltd	446	Worthington, PA	Private	20.0	400	1820
D & D Farms Inc	447	Pierre, SD	Private	20.0	215	2130
Eppich Grain Inc	448	Mesa, WA	Private	20.0	20	7230
Fred J Jaindl	449	Orefield, PA	Private	20.0	100	2539
Frio Feeders LLC	450	Hereford, TX	Private	20.0	14	7510
Glenn Walters Nursery Inc	451	Cornelius, OR	Private	20.0	300	1810
Leisure Lawn Inc	452	Dayton, OH	Private	20.0	300	7820
Material Processing Inc	453	Dakota City, NE	Private	20.0	6	7119
Mid American Growers Inc	454	Granville, IL	Private	20.0	175	1810
P R Farms Inc	455	Clovis, CA	Private	20.0	225	1759
Pacific Earth Resources LLC	456	Camarillo, CA	Private	20.0	170	1819
Quality Turf Nurseries	457	Lithia, FL	Private	20.0	160	1819
Randall Farms, L.L.C.	458	Arcadia, LA	Private	20.0	400	2519
Rio Queen Citrus Farms Inc	459	Mission, TX	Private	20.0	75	1749
River Ranch Southwest Inc	460	Dallas, TX	Private	20.0	160	7230
Superior Lumber Co Inc	461	Glendale, OR	Private	20.0	3	2411
Valadco Inc	462	Renville, MN	Private	20.0	65	2139
Vann Bros	463	Williams, CA	Private	20.0	50	1619
Washington Lttuce Vgetable Co	464	Puyallup, WA	Private	20.0	15	7230
Whitfield Timber Inc	465	Wewahitchka, FL	Private	20.0	42	2411
Wight Nurseries Inc	466	Cairo, GA	Private	20.0	525	1810
Wilco Peanut Co	467	Pleasanton, TX	Private	20.0	49	7230
Wm G Roe & Sons Inc	468	Winter Haven, FL	Private	20.0	40	7230
Metrolina Greenhouses Inc	469	Huntersville, NC	Private	19.9	175	1810
Scheid Vineyards Cal Inc	470	Marina Del Rey, CA	Public	19.9	100	7629
Scheid Vineyards Inc (Del)	471	Marina Del Rey, CA	Private	19.9	100	7620
Environmental Earthscapes Inc	472	Tucson, AZ	Private	19.7	500	7829
Emco Harvesting Co	473	Yuma, AZ	Private	19.7	562	7610
Brookover Feed Yards Inc	474	Garden City, KS	Private	19.6	78	2110
Ward Feed Yard Inc	475	Larned, KS	Private	19.6	40	2110
T T Miyasaka Inc	476	Watsonville, CA	Private	19.5	75	1719
Bauman Landscape, Inc	477	Richmond, CA	Private	19.5	80	7829
Sharpe Land & Cattle Co	478	La Belle, MO	Private	19.4	120	2110
Pinal Feeding Co	479	Goodyear, AZ	Private	19.3	85	2110
Roche Manufacturing Co Inc	480	Dublin, GA	Private	19.2	45	7240
Crist Feed Yard Inc	481	Scott City, KS	Private	19.0	35	2110
North Platte Feeders Inc	482	North Platte, NE	Private	19.0	35	2110
Pro-Ag Inc	483	Lemoncove, CA	Private	19.0	266	7230
Quarter M Farms, Inc.	484	Rose Hill, NC	Private	19.0	250	2130
Taylor United Inc	485	Shelton, WA	Private	19.0	270	9130
Rocky Mountain Elk Foundation	486	Missoula, MT	Private	18.9	150	9719
Woerner South Inc	487	West Palm Beach, FL	Private	18.9	350	1819
Federal Dryer & Storage Co	488	England, AR	Private	18.8	8	7230
Koen Farms Inc	489	Hope, AR	Private	18.7	20	2120
Planning Dsign Cllborative Inc	490	Richmond, VA	Private	18.6	5	7810

D&B COMPANY RANKINGS BY SALES

Company	Rank	Location	Type	Sales ($ mil.)	Employ- ment	Primary SIC
Funston Gin Co	491	Funston, GA	Private	18.6	11	7240
Ed Silva	492	Gonzales, CA	Private	18.3	200	1610
R & R Farms, LLC	493	Santa Maria, CA	Private	18.3	200	1610
McGinley-Schilz Co	494	Brule, NE	Private	18.3	25	2110
Alf Christianson Seed Co	495	Mount Vernon, WA	Private	18.3	86	1810
Murakami Farms Inc	496	Ontario, OR	Private	18.2	25	7230
Uni-Kool Partners	497	Salinas, CA	Private	18.2	200	7230
Ainsworth Feed Yards Co	498	Ainsworth, NE	Private	18.1	25	2110
Arizona Dairy Co, L.L.P.	499	Higley, AZ	Private	18.0	108	2419
BTV Crown Equities, Inc	500	Sacramento, CA	Private	18.0	300	1720
Caribbean Agriculture Projects	501	Gulf Breeze, FL	Private	18.0	300	7110
Dan Schantz Farm & Greenhouses	502	Zionsville, PA	Private	18.0	60	1810
Dean Cluck Cattle Co	503	Gruver, TX	Private	18.0	28	2110
Double D Properties Inc	504	Belle Glade, FL	Private	18.0	40	1339
Giorgi Mushroom Co	505	Blandon, PA	Private	18.0	450	1820
John M Foster Turf Farms	506	Indio, CA	Private	18.0	200	1819
Santa Barbara Farms LLC	507	Lompoc, CA	Private	18.0	250	1610
To-Jo Mushrooms Inc	508	Avondale, PA	Private	18.0	60	1820
Woodcrest Partnership	509	Norco, CA	Private	18.0	200	2520
Woodland Services, Inc	510	Arlington, WA	Private	18.0	4	2411
Four Seasons Produce Pkg Co	511	Salinas, CA	Private	17.9	250	7230
Auvil Fruit Co, Inc	512	Orondo, WA	Private	17.9	100	1759
Royal Citrus Co	513	Riverside, CA	Private	17.8	300	1740
Avi Holdings Inc	514	Gardena, CA	Private	17.8	475	7420
Bear Creek Production Co	515	Wasco, CA	Private	17.8	400	1810
Hines II Inc	516	Irvine, CA	Public Family Member	17.8	400	1810
Woerner Development Inc	517	Foley, AL	Private	17.8	400	1819
Van Wingerden International	518	Fletcher, NC	Private	17.8	200	1810
Boething Treeland Farms Inc	519	Woodland Hills, CA	Private	17.6	375	8119
TDM Farms Inc	520	Newton Grove, NC	Private	17.5	1	2130
Thompson Agriplex, Inc.	521	Hartley, TX	Private	17.5	20	2120
Quality Farm Labor Inc	522	Gonzales, CA	Private	17.5	500	7619
Schumacher Landscaping Inc	523	Boston, MA	Private	17.5	35	7829
Townsends Farms, Inc	524	Millsboro, DE	Private	17.5	350	2519
Anthony Vineyards Inc	525	Bakersfield, CA	Private	17.4	250	1720
Klink Citrus Association	526	Ivanhoe, CA	Private	17.4	170	7230
Richard S Burford	527	Fresno, CA	Private	17.4	85	1910
Desserault Ranch Inc	528	Moxee, WA	Private	17.3	250	1399
Clinton Nurseries Inc	529	Clinton, CT	Private	17.3	127	1810
R H Phillips Inc	530	Esparto, CA	Public	17.3	165	1720
R H Phillips Vineyard Inc	531	Esparto, CA	Private	17.3	102	1720
Bethel Grain Co	532	Benton, IL	Private	17.0	50	7230
Jim Hronis & Sons Ranch	533	Delano, CA	Private	17.0	20	1720
McHutchison & Co LLC	534	Ridgefield, NJ	Private	17.0	51	7810
Mercer Ranches Inc	535	Prosser, WA	Private	17.0	50	1910
Premier Swine Breeding Systems	536	Michigantown, IN	Private	17.0	13	7510
Best Friends Pet Care, Inc.	537	Norwalk, CT	Private	16.8	800	7520
Beef Northwest Inc	538	Nyssa, OR	Private	16.7	65	2110
Smith Feed Service Inc	539	Loyal, WI	Private	16.6	100	7230
Four Seasons Landscpng & Maint Co	540	Foster City, CA	Private	16.5	450	7810
Garden City Feed Yard, LLC	541	Garden City, KS	Private	16.3	30	2110
Bluebird Inc	542	Peshastin, WA	Private	16.3	30	7230
Dinklage Feed Yard, Inc.	543	Sidney, NE	Private	16.3	90	2110
Kofkoff Egg Farm LLC	544	Bozrah, CT	Private	16.3	175	2520
National Hog Farms Inc	545	Kersey, CO	Private	16.3	175	2139
Fillmore-Piru Citrus Assn	546	Fillmore, CA	Private	16.2	200	7230
Hiji Bros., Inc.	547	Oxnard, CA	Private	16.2	175	1610
Richard Wilbur Ranch	548	Yuba City, CA	Private	16.2	286	1759
Underwood Fruit & Warehouse Co	549	Yakima, WA	Private	16.2	200	7230
Great Bend Feeding Inc	550	Great Bend, KS	Private	16.1	33	2120
Cagle's Farms Inc	551	Dalton, GA	Public Family Member	16.1	300	2540
Mendes Calf Ranch	552	Tipton, CA	Private	16.1	70	2110
Dixie Farms	553	Plant City, FL	Private	16.1	40	1719
Heartland Farms Inc	554	Hancock, WI	Private	16.0	70	1610
BLT Farms	555	Oxnard, CA	Private	16.0	80	1610
E W Brandt & Sons Inc	556	Wapato, WA	Private	16.0	75	7230
James Abbate Inc	557	Fresno, CA	Private	16.0	5	7230
Pawnee Beefbuilders, Inc	558	Larned, KS	Private	16.0	24	2110
Richard Gumz Farms LLC	559	North Judson, IN	Private	16.0	21	1150
Velvet Ridge Greenhouses Inc	560	Asheville, NC	Private	16.0	118	1810

D&B COMPANY RANKINGS BY SALES

Company	Rank	Location	Type	Sales ($ mil.)	Employment	Primary SIC
Weborg Cattle Inc	561	Pender, NE	Private	16.0	12	2110
Worth Gin Co, Inc	562	Sylvester, GA	Private	16.0	5	1310
Wyffels' Hybrids Inc	563	Atkinson, IL	Private	16.0	150	1150
Powell Plant Farms Inc	564	Troup, TX	Private	15.9	356	1810
John I Haas Inc	565	Washington, DC	Private	15.8	229	1399
Sanchez Diaz Farm Labor Contr	566	Woodlake, CA	Private	15.8	450	7619
Sugar Farms Inc	567	Palm Beach, FL	Private	15.7	200	1339
Texas Farm Inc	568	Perryton, TX	Private	15.7	190	2130
Healds Valley Farms Inc	569	Edinburg, TX	Private	15.7	250	1740
Vall Inc	570	Texhoma, OK	Private	15.6	189	2130
Workingman's Friend Oil, Inc	571	Topeka, KS	Private	15.5	8	2120
Parker Ranch Foundation Trust	572	Kamuela, HI	Private	15.5	80	2120
Clark's Feed Mills Inc	573	Shamokin, PA	Private	15.4	72	2510
Clear Springs Foods Inc	574	Buhl, ID	Private	15.4	385	2730
Cuba Timber Co	575	Cuba, AL	Private	15.4	25	8110
Landscape Concepts Inc	576	Grayslake, IL	Private	15.3	25	7810
Gerawan Ranches	577	Sanger, CA	Private	15.3	270	1759
Progressive Dairies Holdings	578	Bakersfield, CA	Private	15.3	175	2410
White's Nursery & Greenhouses	579	Chesapeake, VA	Private	15.3	150	1810
Resource Management Service	580	Birmingham, AL	Private	15.3	77	8510
Melrose Timber Co	581	McShan, AL	Private	15.2	76	8510
Wolfsen Inc	582	Los Banos, CA	Private	15.2	200	1390
Highland Light, Inc	583	Seattle, WA	Private	15.1	100	9120
Elloree Gin Co Inc	584	Elloree, SC	Private	15.1	20	7240
Custom-Pak Inc	585	Immokalee, FL	Private	15.1	154	1619
Griffin-Holder Co	586	Rocky Ford, CO	Private	15.1	300	1610
Conoley Fruit Harvester Inc	587	Oakland, FL	Private	15.1	20	7220
Eurofresh Ltd	588	Willcox, AZ	Private	15.0	240	1619
Calberi Inc	589	Santa Ana, CA	Private	15.0	14	7230
Alex R Thomas & Co	590	Ukiah, CA	Private	15.0	100	7230
Andrews Distribution Co	591	Bakersfield, CA	Private	15.0	20	7230
B & W Quality Growers Inc	592	Fellsmere, FL	Private	15.0	145	1610
Byrd Harvest Inc	593	Guadalupe, CA	Private	15.0	300	7220
C & G Farms Inc	594	Chualar, CA	Private	15.0	60	1610
Clean Cut Inc	595	Austin, TX	Public Family Member	15.0	250	7820
Gossett's Inc	596	Dumas, TX	Private	15.0	10	2120
Hansen Ranches	597	Corcoran, CA	Private	15.0	8	1910
Hansford County Feeders LP	598	Gruver, TX	Private	15.0	3	2110
Hughson Nut Inc	599	Hughson, CA	Private	15.0	30	7220
Kingfish Seafood Inc	600	Panama City, FL	Private	15.0	26	9120
Knight Management, Inc	601	Belle Glade, FL	Private	15.0	40	1339
L & C Harvesting Inc	602	Guadalupe, CA	Private	15.0	300	7220
Lake Superior Land Co	603	Calumet, MI	Public Family Member	15.0	19	2411
Las Uvas Valley Dairy	604	Hatch, NM	Private	15.0	160	2410
Lipinski Landscaping Irrgtion Contr	605	Mount Laurel, NJ	Private	15.0	50	7829
McDonnell, Inc	606	Jessup, MD	Private	15.0	25	1740
McGee Timber Co Inc	607	Duck Hill, MS	Private	15.0	1	8110
O'Hara Corp	608	Rockland, ME	Private	15.0	75	9120
P H Ranch, Inc	609	Winton, CA	Private	15.0	50	2419
Pacific Oyster Co	610	Portland, OR	Private	15.0	30	9130
Paco Feedyard Inc.	611	Friona, TX	Private	15.0	30	2110
Parker Interior Plantscape	612	Scotch Plains, NJ	Private	15.0	200	7810
Premier Packing, Inc	613	Shafter, CA	Private	15.0	400	7230
Reynolds Cattle Co	614	Longmont, CO	Private	15.0	8	2110
Ritz Food International Inc	615	Delray Beach, FL	Private	15.0	70	1610
Rivera Blas	616	La Quinta, CA	Private	15.0	20	1720
Schroeder Manatee Inc	617	Bradenton, FL	Private	15.0	75	1740
Sierra Hills Packing Co Inc	618	Stockton, CA	Private	15.0	30	7230
Stephen Pavich & Sons	619	Porterville, CA	Private	15.0	250	1720
Suburban Lawn & Garden, Inc	620	Kansas City, MO	Private	15.0	150	1810
Tagawa Greenhouses Inc	621	Brighton, CO	Private	15.0	150	1810
Thomas Creek Lumber & Log Co	622	Stayton, OR	Private	15.0	10	2411
Triple A Landscape	623	Tucson, AZ	Private	15.0	425	7829
Vinery LLC	624	Midway, KY	Private	15.0	50	7520
Wispig LLC	625	Clinton, WI	Private	15.0	2	2130
Haines Cy Citrus Growers Assn	626	Haines City, FL	Private	14.9	200	7230
Tackett Fish Farm	627	Schlater, MS	Private	14.9	100	2730
Burch Farms	628	Faison, NC	Private	14.9	90	1610
Montezuma Feeders Inc	629	Montezuma, KS	Private	14.9	36	2110
Conagra-Maple Leaf Milling	630	Omaha, NE	Private	14.8	180	7230

D&B COMPANY RANKINGS BY SALES

Company	Rank	Location	Type	Sales ($ mil.)	Employ- ment	Primary SIC
MacMillan Bloedel Timberlands	631	Montgomery, AL	Private	14.8	11	8110
Orange-Co of Florida Inc	632	Bartow, FL	Public Family Member	14.8	250	1749
Useugi Farms Inc	633	Gilroy, CA	Private	14.8	162	1610
Tree Preservation Co Inc	634	Willow Grove, PA	Private	14.8	340	7830
Bonita Nurseries Inc	635	Willcox, AZ	Private	14.8	230	1619
A D Makepeace Co	636	Wareham, MA	Private	14.7	55	1719
Arabi Gin Co Inc	637	Arabi, GA	Private	14.6	9	7240
American Landscape Inc	638	Canoga Park, CA	Private	14.5	150	7810
Ben A Thomas Inc	639	Palmer, AK	Private	14.5	266	2411
Tarheel Turkey Hatchery Inc	640	Raeford, NC	Private	14.5	200	2539
Tri Duncan A Partnership	641	Lamont, CA	Private	14.5	200	1310
Tosh Farms	642	Henry, TN	Private	14.5	23	1910
Tony Abatti Farms LLC	643	El Centro, CA	Private	14.4	125	1390
Orangeburg Foods Inc	644	Orangeburg, SC	Private	14.4	37	2130
Yeomans Wood & Timber Inc	645	Swainsboro, GA	Private	14.3	10	2411
Charles G Watts Inc	646	Salinas, CA	Private	14.3	150	7230
Corona College Heights	647	Riverside, CA	Private	14.3	200	7230
Kaprielian Bros Packing Co	648	Reedley, CA	Private	14.3	200	7230
Fisher Ranch Corp	649	Blythe, CA	Private	14.3	5	1910
Index Mutual Association	650	Bloomington, CA	Private	14.3	29	7230
John Lucas Tree Expert Co	651	Portland, ME	Private	14.3	350	7830
Nature's Trees Inc	652	Bedford Hills, NY	Private	14.2	170	7830
AGS Inc	653	Fillmore, CA	Private	14.2	300	7629
BG Maintenance	654	Columbia, MO	Private	14.2	400	7820
Christensen Farm & Feedlots Inc	655	Sleepy Eye, MN	Private	14.2	150	2139
Katicich Ranch	656	Stockton, CA	Private	14.2	250	1759
Sand Systems Inc	657	Columbus, NE	Private	14.2	300	7620
Stahmann Farms Inc	658	Las Cruces, NM	Private	14.2	150	1739
Bhb Inc	659	Las Vegas, NV	Private	14.2	140	7820
S Stamoules Inc	660	Mendota, CA	Private	14.2	10	7230
Farmers Investment Co.	661	Sahuarita, AZ	Private	14.1	200	7230
Valley Crest Tree Co	662	Calabasas, CA	Private	14.1	300	8119
Underwood Bros Inc	663	Phoenix, AZ	Private	14.1	385	7829
Animal Medical Center Inc	664	New York, NY	Private	14.0	300	7429
Agri-Empire	665	San Jacinto, CA	Private	14.0	200	1340
Aurora Dairy Florida LLC	666	Longmont, CO	Private	14.0	80	2410
Brandt Co Inc	667	Brawley, CA	Private	14.0	60	2110
Dettle Cattle Co	668	Stratford, TX	Private	14.0	18	2120
Fordel Inc	669	Mendota, CA	Private	14.0	50	7230
Gold Star Wholesale Nursery	670	Lexington, MA	Private	14.0	40	1810
Illy's Sunny Slope Farm's Inc	671	Beaumont, CA	Private	14.0	30	2529
Jack Neal & Son Inc	672	St. Helena, CA	Private	14.0	150	1720
Manatee Fruit Co	673	Palmetto, FL	Private	14.0	185	1810
Midwest Feeders Inc	674	Ingalls, KS	Private	14.0	20	2120
Mill Creek Companies	675	Dallas, TX	Private	14.0	300	1810
Puleo Tree Co, Inc	676	South Plainfield, NJ	Private	14.0	16	8119
Schudel Enterprises, L.L.C.	677	Corvallis, OR	Private	14.0	3	8119
Sonora Packing Co, Inc	678	Salinas, CA	Private	14.0	400	7230
Southern Poultry Farms Inc	679	Harrisonburg, VA	Private	14.0	115	2530
Steve Henderson Logging Inc	680	Lewiston, ID	Private	14.0	55	2411
Tom Barber	681	Madison, IN	Private	14.0	7	7810
Torre & Bruglio Inc	682	Pontiac, MI	Private	14.0	55	7829
Western Fresh Fruit Sales	683	Coachella, CA	Private	14.0	2	1910
Peri & Sons Farms Inc	684	Yerington, NV	Private	14.0	24	1610
Chapel Valley Landscape Co	685	Woodbine, MD	Private	14.0	90	7829
Avian Farms Inc	686	Portland, ME	Private	13.9	260	2540
B & T Farms	687	Vista, CA	Private	13.9	135	1619
Merrill Farms	688	Salinas, CA	Private	13.9	150	1610
Garroutte Farms Inc	689	Watsonville, CA	Private	13.8	250	1719
Marlin Packing Co	690	Yuma, AZ	Private	13.8	200	7230
Warren's Turf Group Inc	691	West Palm Beach, FL	Private	13.8	150	1819
Stadelman Fruit, LLC	692	Yakima, WA	Private	13.7	150	7230
Babe Farms Inc	693	Santa Maria, CA	Private	13.7	150	1610
Chappell Farms Inc	694	Barnwell, SC	Private	13.7	185	2130
Eggs West	695	Ontario, CA	Private	13.7	150	2520
Cagwin & Dorward	696	Novato, CA	Private	13.7	220	7829
Florida North Holsteins LC	697	Bell, FL	Private	13.6	120	2410
Miller Shingle Co Inc	698	Granite Falls, WA	Private	13.6	250	2411
Darr Feed Lot Inc	699	Cozad, NE	Private	13.6	33	2110
Inland Fruit & Produce Co	700	Wapato, WA	Private	13.6	210	7230

D&B COMPANY RANKINGS BY SALES

Company	Rank	Location	Type	Sales ($ mil.)	Employ-ment	Primary SIC
Haida Corp	701	Hydaburg, AK	Private	13.5	10	8110
Carmel Valley Packing, Inc	702	Salinas, CA	Private	13.5	150	7230
David J Frank Landscape Contr	703	Germantown, WI	Private	13.5	225	7829
Du Brow's Nurseries Inc	704	Livingston, NJ	Private	13.5	76	7810
Farmax Land Management Inc	705	Sanger, CA	Private	13.5	150	7230
Hilltown Packing Co	706	Salinas, CA	Private	13.5	300	7230
Lucich Farms	707	Patterson, CA	Private	13.5	150	7230
Palmetto Companies, Inc	708	Palmetto, FL	Private	13.5	300	1810
Ponderosa Dairy	709	Amargosa Valley, NV	Private	13.5	60	2410
Kitayama Bros Inc	710	Brighton, CO	Private	13.4	110	1810
Abi Alfalfa Inc	711	Shawnee Mission, KS	Private	13.4	300	1810
Agricultural Innovation Trade	712	Somis, CA	Private	13.4	130	1610
Bay City Flower Co Inc	713	Half Moon Bay, CA	Private	13.4	300	1810
Bordier's Nursery Inc	714	Irvine, CA	Private	13.4	300	1810
Conard-Pyle Co Inc	715	West Grove, PA	Private	13.4	300	1810
Stark Bros Nrsries Orchrds Co	716	Louisiana, MO	Private	13.4	300	1810
Sugarland Feed Yards, Inc.	717	Hereford, TX	Private	13.4	35	2110
Swanson Farms	718	Turlock, CA	Private	13.4	85	2539
Leader Dogs For The Blind Inc	719	Rochester, MI	Private	13.3	94	7520
Earthrise Farms	720	Calipatria, CA	Private	13.2	53	1910
N G Purvis Farms Inc	721	Robbins, NC	Private	13.2	113	2130
Chief Wenatchee	722	Wenatchee, WA	Private	13.1	130	7230
Feather River Food Co Inc	723	Marysville, CA	Private	13.1	35	7230
Baird-Neece Packing Corp	724	Porterville, CA	Private	13.1	180	7230
Hanor Co Inc	725	Spring Green, WI	Private	13.1	213	2919
Hilliard Brothers of Florida	726	Clewiston, FL	Private	13.1	70	2120
Huerta Packing Inc	727	Yuma, AZ	Private	13.1	25	1610
Pasquinelli Produce Co	728	Yuma, AZ	Private	13.1	125	1910
Urban Farmer, Inc	729	Englewood, CO	Private	13.0	164	7810
Dorothy Lough	730	Winthrop, ME	Private	13.0	75	2520
Batson Mill L. P.	731	Batson, TX	Public Family Member	13.0	56	2411
Dixie Lower Timber Compan	732	Thomasville, AL	Private	13.0	30	8519
Edaleen Dairy Products LLC	733	Lynden, WA	Private	13.0	56	2410
Gilder Timber Inc	734	Glenwood, GA	Private	13.0	15	2411
Hamilton County Dairy, L.L.C.	735	Syracuse, KS	Private	13.0	30	2419
Herrera Packing Inc	736	Santa Maria, CA	Private	13.0	400	7230
Plainville Turkey Farm Inc	737	Plainville, NY	Private	13.0	160	2539
Red Rock Cattle Company Inc	738	Red Rock, AZ	Private	13.0	7	2120
Crane Mills	739	Corning, CA	Private	13.0	45	2411
Circle E Feed Lot Inc	740	Potwin, KS	Private	12.9	17	2110
McDougall & Sons Inc	741	Wenatchee, WA	Private	12.9	200	7230
California Redi-Date Co	742	Thermal, CA	Private	12.8	150	7230
Dmb Packing Corp	743	Indio, CA	Private	12.8	NA	1740
J-M Farms Inc	744	Miami, OK	Private	12.8	320	1820
Padilla Farm Labor C	745	Lindsay, CA	Private	12.8	200	1749
Popular Farms Inc	746	Oxnard, CA	Private	12.8	200	1719
New Market Poultry Products	747	New Market, VA	Private	12.7	150	7519
Maine Fresh Pack Co-Operative	748	Machias, ME	Private	12.7	150	7230
J H Miles Co Inc	749	Norfolk, VA	Private	12.7	50	9130
Belk Farms	750	Thermal, CA	Private	12.5	30	1910
Pfister Hybrid Corn Co	751	El Paso, IL	Private	12.5	70	1150
Sakuma Bros Farms Inc	752	Burlington, WA	Private	12.5	50	1719
Karleskint-Crum Inc	753	San Luis Obispo, CA	Private	12.5	150	7829
All Green Corp	754	Marietta, GA	Private	12.5	350	7820
C & M Packing Inc	755	Gonzales, CA	Private	12.5	250	7220
Great Lakes Packers Inc	756	Bellevue, OH	Private	12.5	60	7230
J E Estes Wood Co Inc	757	Monroeville, AL	Private	12.5	7	2411
Winter Haven Citrus Growers Assn	758	Winter Haven, FL	Private	12.5	25	7230
Sunniland Fruit Inc	759	Stockton, CA	Private	12.4	10	7230
Ag Planters Inc	760	Lake Harbor, FL	Private	12.4	150	1330
Gadsden Tomato Co	761	Quincy, FL	Private	12.4	186	7230
J & K Farms Inc	762	Harrells, NC	Private	12.4	150	2130
Vignolo Farms	763	Shafter, CA	Private	12.4	150	1310
Buurma Farms, Inc	764	Willard, OH	Private	12.4	30	1610
Mulhall's Nursery, Inc.	765	Omaha, NE	Private	12.4	125	7810
Taylor & Stuckey Inc	766	Trumann, AR	Private	12.4	40	7240
ASP Enterprises Inc	767	Miami, FL	Private	12.2	14	1320
Don Smith Cattle	768	Correctionville, IA	Private	12.2	2	2120
Lied's Nursery Co Inc	769	Sussex, WI	Private	12.2	105	7829
Larson Fruit Co	770	Selah, WA	Private	12.2	110	7230

D&B COMPANY RANKINGS BY SALES

Company	Rank	Location	Type	Sales ($ mil.)	Employ- ment	Primary SIC
Greenheart Farms Inc	771	Arroyo Grande, CA	Private	12.2	350	1820
R A Rasmussen & Sons Inc	772	Granger, WA	Private	12.2	150	1610
Talley Farms	773	Arroyo Grande, CA	Private	12.2	150	1610
Terry Farms Zellwood Division	774	Zellwood, FL	Private	12.2	304	1820
Thorkelson Ranches	775	Patterson, CA	Private	12.2	150	1610
Ml Macadamia Orchards, L.P.	776	Honolulu, HI	Public	12.1	3	1730
Jamar Industries	777	Albuquerque, NM	Private	12.1	340	7829
Orange County Produce	778	Fullerton, CA	Private	12.1	125	1610
Wells and Wade Fruit Co	779	East Wenatchee, WA	Public Family Member	12.1	175	1750
Gold Coast Pistachio's Inc	780	Fresno, CA	Private	12.1	33	1739
Delta Gin Co Inc	781	Newellton, LA	Private	12.0	5	7240
Adams Land & Cattle Co Inc	782	Broken Bow, NE	Private	12.0	75	2110
American Farms	783	Salinas, CA	Private	12.0	200	1610
American International Dairies Corp	784	Franklin, TN	Private	12.0	22	7510
American Wilderness Resources	785	Queensbury, NY	Private	12.0	12	8110
Annette Island Packing Co	786	Metlakatla, AK	Private	12.0	8	9120
Baker Farming	787	Firebaugh, CA	Private	12.0	25	1720
Beef Tech Cattle Feeders, Inc.	788	Hereford, TX	Private	12.0	20	2110
Bledsoe Ranch Co	789	Wray, CO	Private	12.0	20	2110
Borg Pak, Inc	790	Los Angeles, CA	Private	12.0	110	7230
C & C Farms	791	Bowling Green, KY	Private	12.0	20	2120
Cpc International Apple	792	Tieton, WA	Private	12.0	30	7230
Demler Egg Ranch	793	San Jacinto, CA	Private	12.0	35	2520
Farmington Fresh	794	Stockton, CA	Private	12.0	6	1759
Forestry International Inc	795	Meridian, MS	Public	12.0	20	8110
Garcia Farming & Harvesting	796	Salinas, CA	Private	12.0	300	1610
Geerlings Greenhouse Inc	797	Piscataway, NJ	Private	12.0	50	1810
General Produce Distrs Inc	798	Franklin Park, IL	Private	12.0	25	7230
Gtc-Gtc Ltd	799	Greeley, CO	Private	12.0	25	7230
Hastings Pork Corp	800	Hastings, NE	Private	12.0	152	2139
Hawaiian Sweet, Inc.	801	Keaau, HI	Private	12.0	90	7230
Hornbeck Seed Co Inc	802	De Witt, AR	Private	12.0	30	7230
Jack Sparrowk	803	Clements, CA	Private	12.0	25	2120
Jensen Corp Landscape Contractors	804	Cupertino, CA	Private	12.0	40	7829
Judson Inc	805	Pennington, AL	Private	12.0	5	8110
Keegan Inc	806	Twin Falls, ID	Private	12.0	45	7230
Kitayama Brothers Inc	807	Brighton, CO	Private	12.0	307	1810
Landscape Maintenance Services	808	Plainsboro, NJ	Public Family Member	12.0	326	7820
Manley Farms, Inc	809	Naples, FL	Private	12.0	60	1619
Nickel Family, L.L.C.	810	Bakersfield, CA	Private	12.0	135	1910
Northwestern Fruit & Prod Co	811	Yakima, WA	Private	12.0	100	1759
Packers of Indian River, Ltd	812	Fort Pierce, FL	Private	12.0	25	7230
Perrier Feed Lot	813	Dodge City, KS	Private	12.0	8	2110
Pet's Choice Inc	814	Bellevue, WA	Private	12.0	342	7429
Portland Gin Co	815	Portland, AR	Private	12.0	17	7240
Premium Gold Angus Beef, Inc	816	Austin, TX	Private	12.0	6	2120
Pride of San Juan, The Inc	817	San Juan Bautista, CA	Private	12.0	100	1610
Reiter Berry Farms Inc	818	Watsonville, CA	Private	12.0	200	1719
Silver Terrace Nurseries Intl	819	Burlingame, CA	Private	12.0	75	1810
Surabian Packing Co Inc	820	Reedley, CA	Private	12.0	10	7230
Triangle Manufacturing Co	821	Slaton, TX	Private	12.0	47	7240
Union County Feed Lot, Inc	822	Clayton, NM	Private	12.0	20	2110
Van Solkema Produce Inc	823	Byron Center, MI	Private	12.0	30	7230
Trophy International Inc	824	McAllen, TX	Private	12.0	92	7230
Vila and Son Landscaping Corp	825	Miami, FL	Private	11.9	136	7829
Eckenberg Farms Inc	826	Mattawa, WA	Private	11.9	30	7230
Environmental Consultants	827	Southampton, PA	Private	11.9	260	8510
Rusler Produce, Inc	828	Avondale, CO	Private	11.9	150	1610
Rios, Jj Farm Services Inc	829	Acampo, CA	Private	11.9	180	7610
Gardner Turfgrass Inc	830	Denver, CO	Private	11.9	200	1819
Dutch Country Egg Farms Inc	831	Fredericksburg, PA	Private	11.9	30	2520
Coalinga Feed Yard Inc	832	Coalinga, CA	Private	11.8	20	2110
Sun-Ag Inc	833	Fellsmere, FL	Private	11.8	250	7629
Talisman Sugar Corp	834	Jacksonville, FL	Public Family Member	11.8	150	1339
Westlake Farms Inc	835	Stratford, CA	Private	11.8	175	1310
Ritewood Inc	836	Franklin, ID	Private	11.8	240	2520
Mossberg Sanitation Inc	837	Great Bend, KS	Private	11.7	3	7510
Thanksgiving Point Mgmt Co LC	838	Orem, UT	Private	11.7	250	8119
Oglevee, Ltd	839	Connellsville, PA	Private	11.7	200	1810
Garden Design Group Inc	840	Dallas, TX	Private	11.6	140	7810

D&B COMPANY RANKINGS BY SALES

Company	Rank	Location	Type	Sales ($ mil.)	Employment	Primary SIC
McLean Feedyard, Inc.	841	McLean, TX	Private	11.6	21	2110
Park Landscape Maintenance	842	Rcho Sta Marg, CA	Private	11.6	400	7820
Peach Orchard Gin Co Inc	843	Gideon, MO	Private	11.6	8	7240
Central Farm of America	844	New York, NY	Private	11.6	217	2540
L & S Harvesting Inc	845	El Centro, CA	Private	11.6	200	7220
Vincent B Zaninovich & Sons	846	Richgrove, CA	Private	11.6	200	1720
Lassen Canyon Nursery Inc	847	Redding, CA	Private	11.6	150	1719
Southern Se Reg Aqucltre Assn	848	Ketchikan, AK	Private	11.6	15	9219
Northern Fruit Co, Inc	849	East Wenatchee, WA	Private	11.6	30	7230
Crosbyton Seed Co.	850	Crosbyton, TX	Private	11.6	45	1190
Harvey Brothers Farm Inc	851	Naples, FL	Private	11.6	30	1619
Valley Rain Construction Corp	852	Tempe, AZ	Private	11.5	110	7829
Oscar Ortega	853	Thermal, CA	Private	11.5	1	1720
American Raisin Packers Inc	854	Selma, CA	Private	11.5	6	7230
Borders, Nowell	855	Edinburg, TX	Private	11.5	15	1610
Dekalb Poultry Research Inc	856	Dekalb, IL	Private	11.5	214	2540
Puglisi Egg Farms Inc	857	Howell, NJ	Private	11.5	35	2520
Ray Wiegand Nursery Inc	858	Macomb, MI	Private	11.5	15	1810
Clouds Landscpng Sprnklr Serv Inc	859	North Las Vegas, NV	Private	11.4	70	7829
Malloy Orchards, Inc	860	Live Oak, CA	Private	11.4	200	1759
Valley Onions Inc	861	McAllen, TX	Private	11.4	150	1610
Pine-Belt Inc	862	Monticello, AR	Private	11.4	12	8519
Miller Diversified Corp	863	La Salle, CO	Public	11.4	25	2110
Phelan & Taylor Produce Co	864	Oceano, CA	Private	11.3	150	7230
Stemilt Management Inc	865	Wenatchee, WA	Private	11.3	240	7620
M S N Inc	866	Houston, TX	Private	11.3	125	7810
Stark Packing Corp	867	Strathmore, CA	Private	11.3	100	7230
O'Connell Landscape Maintenance	868	Rcho Sta Marg, CA	Private	11.3	400	7829
South Shres Rsdential Coml Dev	869	Santa Ana, CA	Private	11.2	350	7829
Mariani Enterprises Inc	870	Lake Bluff, IL	Private	11.2	70	7810
Triangle Farms Inc	871	Salinas, CA	Private	11.2	50	1610
Allstate Packers Inc	872	Lodi, CA	Private	11.2	30	7230
Arbor Tree Surgery Inc	873	Paso Robles, CA	Private	11.1	250	7830
Danielski Harvesting & Farming	874	Valentine, NE	Private	11.1	15	1910
Young Pecan Co	875	Florence, SC	Private	11.1	116	7230
B J & E Realty Co	876	Kreamer, PA	Private	11.1	30	2549
Carson County Feedyards, Inc.	877	Panhandle, TX	Private	11.1	21	2110
Eastside Nursery Inc	878	Groveport, OH	Private	11.0	35	7829
Jjr Inc	879	Ann Arbor, MI	Private	11.0	100	7810
AJB Ranch	880	Bakersfield, CA	Private	11.0	27	2410
Arteka Natural Green Corp	881	Eden Prairie, MN	Public Family Member	11.0	50	7829
Black Gold Farms	882	Forest River, ND	Private	11.0	10	1340
Clarence Davids & Co	883	Matteson, IL	Private	11.0	90	7829
Cole King Ranch & Farm	884	Milton, DE	Private	11.0	60	2110
Esbenshade Farms	885	Mount Joy, PA	Private	11.0	120	2520
Glass Corner Greenhouse Inc	886	Grand Rapids, MI	Private	11.0	110	1810
Hope Land Farm	887	Kennett Square, PA	Private	11.0	170	2419
James T Smith	888	Wapato, WA	Private	11.0	200	1759
New Carrizo Creek Feeders Ltd	889	Texline, TX	Private	11.0	22	2110
S M Jones & Co Inc	890	Canal Point, FL	Private	11.0	12	7230
Select Farms, Ltd	891	Spokane, WA	Private	11.0	100	1810
Smith Cattle Inc	892	Tribune, KS	Private	11.0	27	2110
Sunny Grove Landscaping Inc	893	Estero, FL	Private	11.0	120	7810
Swa Group	894	Sausalito, CA	Private	11.0	100	7810
W J Griffin Inc	895	Santa Barbara, CA	Private	11.0	150	1810
Wendell Talley	896	Stanfield, NC	Private	11.0	55	2539
Simonian Brothers Inc	897	Fowler, CA	Private	11.0	15	7230
Glasscock County Coop	898	Garden City, TX	Private	11.0	15	7240
Indian River Exchange Packers	899	Vero Beach, FL	Private	10.9	150	7230
Torrey Farms Inc	900	Elba, NY	Private	10.9	110	1610
Dale Bone Farms Inc	901	Nashville, NC	Private	10.8	75	1619
Lake Region Packing Assn	902	Tavares, FL	Private	10.8	75	7230
Emerald Packing Company Inc	903	Orlando, FL	Private	10.8	14	7230
Belize River Fruit Co., Inc	904	Ashland, KY	Private	10.8	200	1740
Sugarland Harvesting Co	905	Clewiston, FL	Private	10.8	110	7220
Stacy's, Inc	906	York, SC	Private	10.8	70	1810
Brown's of Carolina, Inc.	907	Warsaw, NC	Public Family Member	10.8	550	2130
Valley Fig Growers Inc	908	Fresno, CA	Private	10.7	50	7230
Willoway Nurseries Inc	909	Avon, OH	Private	10.7	150	1810
Floral Plant Growers, L.L.C.	910	Rising Sun, MD	Private	10.7	240	1810

D&B COMPANY RANKINGS BY SALES

Company	Rank	Location	Type	Sales ($ mil.)	Employ- ment	Primary SIC
Valencia Harvesting Inc	911	Sarasota, FL	Private	10.7	175	1749
Map Inc	912	Oregon City, OR	Private	10.7	5	8510
Jesse F Miner	913	San Jacinto, CA	Private	10.6	7	2120
Tri-B Nursery, Inc.	914	Hulbert, OK	Private	10.6	180	1810
Kirschenman Packing Inc	915	Edison, CA	Private	10.6	120	7230
Sonoma-Cutrer Vineyards Inc	916	Windsor, CA	Private	10.6	160	1720
Valley Heights Ranch Ltd	917	Oceanside, CA	Private	10.6	130	1619
Pennink Arrimour	918	Huntingdon Valley, PA	Private	10.5	250	7820
Wailuku Agribusiness Co Inc	919	Wailuku, HI	Private	10.5	150	1739
Ashbritt, Inc.	920	Pompano Beach, FL	Private	10.5	15	7829
Bailey's Nursery Inc	921	Lodi, CA	Private	10.5	155	1810
Ochoa Jc Farm Management & Flc	922	Indio, CA	Private	10.5	300	7610
Taplett Fruit Packing Inc	923	Wenatchee, WA	Private	10.5	150	7230
McCorkle Nurseries Inc	924	Dearing, GA	Private	10.5	157	1810
Glenwood Foods LLC	925	Jetersville, VA	Private	10.4	75	2520
Veribest Cattle Feeders Inc	926	San Angelo, TX	Private	10.4	18	2110
Jack M Berry Inc	927	Alva, FL	Private	10.4	200	7629
Giroux's Poultry Farm Inc	928	Chazy, NY	Private	10.4	40	2520
Villa Park Orchards Assn Inc	929	Orange, CA	Private	10.3	385	7230
Franscioni Brothers, Inc	930	Salinas, CA	Private	10.3	20	1610
Schwertner Farms Inc	931	Schwertner, TX	Private	10.3	60	2110
Weeks Wholesale Rose Growers	932	Upland, CA	Private	10.3	360	1810
West Cotton Ag Management	933	Huron, CA	Private	10.3	200	7620
Willmar Poultry Farms Inc	934	Willmar, MN	Private	10.3	130	2130
Azcona Harvesting	935	Greenfield, CA	Private	10.3	2	7610
Ivy Acres Inc	936	Calverton, NY	Private	10.2	45	1810
Mayfield Timber Co Inc	937	Toxey, AL	Private	10.2	35	2411
Garland Farm Supply Inc	938	Garland, NC	Private	10.2	18	7230
Sellers Farms, Inc	939	Lyons, KS	Private	10.2	12	1110
G & U Inc	940	Goshen, NY	Private	10.2	125	1610
Prides Corner Farms, Inc	941	Lebanon, CT	Private	10.2	45	1810
Vinifera Inc	942	Petaluma, CA	Private	10.2	130	1720
Dillon Floral Corp	943	Bloomsburg, PA	Private	10.1	138	1810
Grand Mesa Eggs, Inc	944	Grand Junction, CO	Private	10.1	50	2520
Wm F Renk & Sons Co, Inc	945	Sun Prairie, WI	Private	10.1	35	1810
Edward D Stone Jr and Assoc	946	Fort Lauderdale, FL	Private	10.1	73	7810
Starker Forests Inc	947	Corvallis, OR	Private	10.1	15	8110
Terranova Ranch Inc	948	Helm, CA	Private	10.1	30	1910
CRI Feeders Inc	949	Guymon, OK	Private	10.1	57	2110
Dresick Farms, Inc	950	Huron, CA	Private	10.1	110	1610
Hunt Brothers Cooperative Inc	951	Lake Wales, FL	Private	10.1	150	7230
Weiss Lake Egg Co Inc	952	Centre, AL	Private	10.0	44	2520
Alliance Dairies	953	Trenton, FL	Private	10.0	50	2410
Angelica Nurseries Inc	954	Kennedyville, MD	Private	10.0	150	7810
Armstrong Farms	955	Valley Center, CA	Private	10.0	75	2520
Barton County Feeders, Inc	956	Ellinwood, KS	Private	10.0	26	2110
Batiz Greenhouses Inc	957	San Diego, CA	Private	10.0	3	1820
Blue North Fisheries Inc	958	Seattle, WA	Private	10.0	3	9130
Callery-Judge Grove LP	959	Loxahatchee, FL	Private	10.0	55	1740
Cascade Columbia Foods Ltd	960	Kennewick, WA	Private	10.0	215	7230
Chesapeake Forest Products Co	961	West Point, VA	Public Family Member	10.0	196	8110
Chief Mattawa Orchards	962	Mattawa, WA	Private	10.0	5	1750
Childress Gin & Elevator Co	963	Monette, AR	Private	10.0	15	7240
Circle C Farms	964	Brinson, GA	Private	10.0	25	1310
Clark Hutterian Brethren Inc	965	Raymond, SD	Private	10.0	100	1910
Columbia West Virginia Corp	966	Portland, OR	Private	10.0	139	2411
Continente Nut LLC	967	Oakley, CA	Private	10.0	25	1720
Corcpork Co	968	Corcoran, CA	Private	10.0	100	2130
Cp Meilland Inc	969	Wasco, CA	Private	10.0	16	1810
D Bruce Cuddy	970	Marshville, NC	Private	10.0	50	2530
Danell Bros Inc	971	Hanford, CA	Private	10.0	70	7220
Delbert L Wheeler	972	White Swan, WA	Private	10.0	30	2411
Delta Cotton Co-Operative Inc	973	Marmaduke, AR	Private	10.0	17	7240
Diestel Turkey Ranch	974	Sonora, CA	Private	10.0	50	2539
Eagle Produce Ltd Partnership	975	Scottsdale, AZ	Private	10.0	200	1610
Everett Ashurst	976	El Centro, CA	Private	10.0	15	2799
F F Gonsalez Farms	977	Santa Paula, CA	Private	10.0	150	1399
Fernlea Nursery Inc	978	Palm City, FL	Private	10.0	315	1810
Florida Gardinier Citrus	979	Sarasota, FL	Private	10.0	20	1740
G & B Enterprises Ltd	980	Liberty, SC	Private	10.0	28	2520

D&B COMPANY RANKINGS BY SALES

Company	Rank	Location	Type	Sales ($ mil.)	Employ- ment	Primary SIC
Gary T Raak & Associates Inc	981	Elko, MN	Private	10.0	12	2729
Gerawan Farming, Inc	982	Sanger, CA	Private	10.0	50	7230
Gold Star Mushroom Co	983	Lenhartsville, PA	Private	10.0	50	1820
Harllee Packing, Inc	984	Palmetto, FL	Private	10.0	15	7230
Hayes Feed Yard Inc	985	Silver Creek, NE	Private	10.0	6	2110
Jcm Farming Inc	986	Visalia, CA	Private	10.0	20	1720
Joe Heidrick Enterprises Inc	987	Woodland, CA	Private	10.0	40	1110
John Knevelbaard Dairy	988	Corona, CA	Private	10.0	15	2419
Johnston Farms	989	Edison, CA	Private	10.0	40	1749
Jones & Associates Inc	990	Harrisburg, PA	Private	10.0	160	1759
Kalashian Packing Co Inc	991	Fresno, CA	Private	10.0	62	7230
Kearney Fertilizer Inc	992	Bonnie, IL	Private	10.0	60	7119
Kearny County Feeders Inc	993	Lakin, KS	Private	10.0	34	2110
Latigo Trading Co Inc	994	Clint, TX	Private	10.0	3	7510
Lifescapes Inc	995	Canton, GA	Private	10.0	130	7829
Living Free	996	Mountain Center, CA	Private	10.0	28	7520
Lumber City Egg Marketers Inc	997	Lumber City, GA	Private	10.0	100	2520
M & M Poultry Farm	998	North Franklin, CT	Private	10.0	4	2520
Maddox Dairy	999	Riverdale, CA	Private	10.0	66	2419
McCleskey Cotton Company LLC	1000	Bronwood, GA	Private	10.0	5	1310
Mid Valley Processing Inc	1001	Newman, CA	Private	10.0	25	7519
Midwest Htchy & Plty Farms Inc	1002	Dassel, MN	Private	10.0	25	2540
Moon Nurseries of Maryland	1003	Chesapeake City, MD	Private	10.0	250	1810
Morrell Group Inc	1004	Atlanta, GA	Private	10.0	185	7820
O P C Farms Inc	1005	Tracy, CA	Private	10.0	8	1910
Oord Dairy	1006	Sunnyside, WA	Private	10.0	35	2410
Parker Wholesale Florist Inc	1007	Scotch Plains, NJ	Private	10.0	40	1810
Powell and Powell Milling Inc	1008	Green Forest, AR	Private	10.0	30	7230
Premier Farms	1009	Clarion, IA	Private	10.0	100	2130
Premier Mushrooms, Inc	1010	Kennett Square, PA	Private	10.0	30	7230
Purepak Inc	1011	Oxnard, CA	Private	10.0	100	1610
Pursley Inc	1012	Bradenton, FL	Private	10.0	200	1819
Rahav Enterprises, Inc	1013	Phoenix, AZ	Private	10.0	30	7810
Riverview Dairy Inc	1014	Morris, MN	Private	10.0	42	2410
Roche Fruit Co Inc	1015	Yakima, WA	Private	10.0	140	7230
Ryan Landscaping, Inc	1016	Houston, TX	Private	10.0	175	7829
S and P Cattle Co LLC	1017	Moody, TX	Private	10.0	4	2120
Sauvage Gas Co	1018	Las Vegas, NV	Private	10.0	10	1190
Scarborough Farms Inc	1019	Lamar, SC	Private	10.0	45	2520
Stotz Farms Inc	1020	Avondale, AZ	Private	10.0	35	2410
Subco Packaging Inc	1021	West Chicago, IL	Private	10.0	90	7230
Summit Farms Inc	1022	Kent City, MI	Private	10.0	7	1750
Sumner Peck Ranch, Inc.	1023	Madera, CA	Private	10.0	32	1910
Sun City Landscapes Lawn Maint	1024	Las Vegas, NV	Private	10.0	160	7829
Sungrow Landscape Services	1025	Austin, TX	Private	10.0	100	7829
Tallmadge Bros Inc	1026	Norwalk, CT	Private	10.0	120	9130
Terratherm Environmental Services	1027	Houston, TX	Private	10.0	4	7110
Thomas Bros Grass Ltd	1028	Granbury, TX	Private	10.0	110	1819
Timberland Mgmt Services Inc	1029	Centreville, MS	Private	10.0	14	2411
Valley Roz Orchards Inc	1030	Yakima, WA	Private	10.0	2,500	1759
W O Sasser Seafood Inc	1031	Savannah, GA	Private	10.0	18	9130
Walker Farms	1032	Menan, ID	Private	10.0	40	1190
Waverly Growers Cooperative	1033	Waverly, FL	Private	10.0	75	7230
William E Mcbryde Inc	1034	Uvalde, TX	Private	10.0	4	1610
Young's Plant Farm Inc	1035	Auburn, AL	Private	10.0	100	1810

D&B COMPANY RANKINGS BY EMPLOYMENT

Company	Rank	Location	Type	Sales ($ mil.)	Employ-ment	Primary SIC
Dole Food Co, Inc	1	Thousand Oaks, CA	Public	4,336.1	44,000	1799
Chiquita Brands International	2	Cincinnati, OH	Public	2,433.7	40,000	1799
Asplundh Tree Expert Co	3	Willow Grove, PA	Private	1,026.6	21,800	7830
Petsmart, Inc.	4	Phoenix, AZ	Public	1,790.6	18,800	7429
Gold Kist Inc	5	Atlanta, GA	Private	1,651.1	16,500	2549
Tru Green LP	6	Memphis, TN	Private	454.9	13,000	7820
Hudson Foods Inc	7	Springdale, AR	Public Family Member	833.3	10,000	2520
Moet Hennessy Inc	8	New York, NY	Private	416.0	9,100	1720
Foster Poultry Farms	9	Livingston, CA	Private	1,000.0	7,200	2540
Sanderson Farms Inc	10	Laurel, MS	Public	521.4	6,358	2519
Environmental Industries Inc	11	Calabasas, CA	Private	351.3	5,600	7810
Davey Tree Expert Co	12	Kent, OH	Public	295.1	5,200	7830
Omni Facility Resources Inc	13	South Plainfield, NJ	Private	100.0	4,400	7810
Landcare Usa, Inc	14	Houston, TX	Public	137.9	4,300	7830
Michael Foods of Delaware	15	Minneapolis, MN	Public Family Member	956.2	3,870	2520
Michael Foods, Inc	16	Minneapolis, MN	Public	956.2	3,870	2520
Longview Fibre Co	17	Longview, WA	Public	753.2	3,700	2411
Bud Antle, Inc	18	Salinas, CA	Public Family Member	299.9	3,500	1610
Peco Foods Inc	19	Tuscaloosa, AL	Private	260.0	3,500	2549
Fresh International Corp	20	Salinas, CA	Private	191.2	3,000	7230
Grimmway Enterprises Inc	21	Di Giorgio, CA	Private	280.0	3,000	7230
Hanson North America	22	Woodbridge, NJ	Private	140.8	3,000	8110
Zacky Farms Inc	23	El Monte, CA	Private	150.0	3,000	2510
Asplundh Subsidiary Holdings	24	Wilmington, DE	Private	175.3	2,800	7830
Environmental Care Inc	25	Calabasas, CA	Private	100.0	2,800	7810
Pride Industries Inc	26	Roseville, CA	Private	48.0	2,700	7820
Fresh Express Inc	27	Salinas, CA	Private	159.7	2,500	7230
Lykes Bros Inc	28	Tampa, FL	Private	150.0	2,500	7210
Rayonier Inc.	29	Stamford, CT	Public	1,104.2	2,500	2411
United States Sugar Corp	30	Clewiston, FL	Private	201.4	2,500	1339
Valley Roz Orchards Inc	31	Yakima, WA	Private	10.0	2,500	1759
Maui Land & Pineapple Co Inc	32	Kahului, HI	Public	136.5	2,270	1799
Durbin Marshall Food Corp	33	Birmingham, AL	Private	175.0	2,200	2520
Tanimura & Antle, Inc	34	Salinas, CA	Private	300.0	2,200	1610
Murphy Farms Inc	35	Rose Hill, NC	Private	499.1	2,100	2130
Ball Horticultural Co	36	West Chicago, IL	Private	125.0	2,000	1810
J G Boswell Co	37	Pasadena, CA	Private	150.0	2,000	1310
Marko Zaninovich Inc	38	Delano, CA	Private	120.0	2,000	1720
Monterey Mushrooms Inc	39	Watsonville, CA	Private	156.1	2,000	1820
Tyson Breeders, Inc.	40	Springdale, AR	Public Family Member	107.1	2,000	2540
Wm Bolthouse Farms Inc	41	Bakersfield, CA	Private	201.8	1,850	1610
Color Spot Nurseries, Inc	42	Pleasant Hill, CA	Private	113.4	1,828	1810
JFC Inc	43	St. Cloud, MN	Private	190.0	1,800	2519
Missouri Farmers Association	44	Columbia, MO	Private	85.1	1,800	7620
Vlasic Foods International	45	Blandon, PA	Public Family Member	100.0	1,800	1820
F A Bartlett Tree Expert	46	Stamford, CT	Private	89.9	1,700	7839
Monrovia Nursery Co	47	Azusa, CA	Private	83.6	1,700	1810
A Duda & Sons Inc	48	Oviedo, FL	Private	297.0	1,600	1610
C Brewer and Company Ltd	49	Hilo, HI	Private	100.7	1,600	1739
Plantation Foods, Inc	50	Waco, TX	Private	180.0	1,600	2530
Cal-Maine Foods Inc	51	Jackson, MS	Public	309.1	1,574	2520
Confederated Tr Wrm Sprgs	52	Warm Springs, OR	Private	52.8	1,500	8110
Yoder Brothers, Inc	53	Barberton, OH	Private	50.0	1,500	1810
Peterson Farms, Inc.	54	Decatur, AR	Private	173.0	1,450	2549
Joseph Campbell Co	55	Camden, NJ	Public Family Member	123.8	1,446	1610
Carroll's Foods Inc	56	Warsaw, NC	Private	500.0	1,350	2130
Harlan Sprague Dawley Inc	57	Indianapolis, IN	Private	40.5	1,350	2799
Medical Management International	58	Portland, OR	Private	48.8	1,300	7420
Maple Leaf Farms Inc	59	Milford, IN	Private	100.0	1,250	2599
Broetje Orchards	60	Prescott, WA	Private	36.3	1,200	1759
Cooperative Resources Intl Inc	61	Shawano, WI	Private	72.0	1,200	7510
Davey Tree Surgery Co	62	Livermore, CA	Public Family Member	38.5	1,200	7830
Greenleaf Nursery Co	63	Park Hill, OK	Private	45.2	1,200	1810
Hines Horticulture Inc	64	Irvine, CA	Public	53.1	1,200	1810
Noblesse Oblige Inc	65	El Centro, CA	Private	60.0	1,200	7220
Rose Acre Farms Inc	66	Seymour, IN	Private	100.0	1,200	2520
Tyson Seafood Group	67	Seattle, WA	Public Family Member	60.0	1,200	9120
Valley Crest Landscape, Inc	68	Calabasas, CA	Private	143.4	1,200	7810
Veterinary Centers of America	69	Santa Monica, CA	Public	239.4	1,200	7420
Flo Sun Inc	70	Palm Beach, FL	Private	40.3	1,110	1339

D&B COMPANY RANKINGS BY EMPLOYMENT

Company	Rank	Location	Type	Sales ($ mil.)	Employ-ment	Primary SIC
Bear Creek Corp	71	Medford, OR	Private	334.7	1,100	1750
Crown Pacific Partners, LP	72	Portland, OR	Public	505.6	1,100	8110
Sylvest Farms, Inc	73	Montgomery, AL	Private	55.0	1,100	2519
Zapata Corp	74	Rochester, NY	Public	133.6	1,100	9129
King Ranch Inc	75	Houston, TX	Private	54.7	1,094	2120
Golden Rod Broilers Inc	76	Cullman, AL	Private	50.5	1,010	2519
Lewis Tree Service Inc	77	Rochester, NY	Private	50.7	1,000	7830
Maxwell Foods Inc.	78	Goldsboro, NC	Private	92.9	1,000	2130
Paragon Produce Corp	79	Immokalee, FL	Private	85.5	1,000	1619
Trees, Inc	80	Houston, TX	Private	32.1	1,000	7830
Wright Tree Service Inc	81	West Des Moines, IA	Private	47.0	1,000	7830
Cadiz, Inc	82	Santa Monica, CA	Public	100.2	985	7230
Thermoretec Corp	83	Concord, MA	Public Family Member	128.4	952	7110
Southland Foods Inc	84	Jack, AL	Private	60.0	950	2519
Sun World International, Inc	85	Bakersfield, CA	Public Family Member	99.9	905	7230
Brickman Group Ltd	86	Langhorne, PA	Private	130.0	900	7810
D'arrigo Bros Cal A Cal Corp	87	Salinas, CA	Private	105.0	900	1610
Prestage Farms Inc	88	Clinton, NC	Private	83.6	900	2130
Sylvan Foods, Inc.	89	Saxonburg, PA	Public Family Member	36.0	900	1820
Sylvan Inc.	90	Saxonburg, PA	Public	81.6	900	1820
Terry Farms Inc	91	Mount Dora, FL	Private	52.0	900	1820
Minnesota Vikings Ventures	92	Eden Prairie, MN	Private	100.0	880	9710
Seaboard Farms of Oklahoma	93	Guymon, OK	Private	79.9	860	2130
Marshall Durbin Farms Inc	94	Birmingham, AL	Private	42.5	850	2510
Golden Merger Corp	95	Santa Monica, CA	Public Family Member	31.1	830	7420
Best Friends Pet Care, Inc.	96	Norwalk, CT	Private	16.8	800	7520
Mar Jac Poultry Inc	97	Gainesville, GA	Private	90.9	800	2540
National Petcare Center Inc	98	Fort Collins, CO	Private	22.2	800	7429
Tracy Industries Inc	99	Rcho Sta Marg, CA	Private	28.2	800	7829
Columbia Helicopters Inc	100	Aurora, OR	Private	100.0	775	2411
Townsend Tree Service Co Inc	101	Selma, IN	Private	24.9	775	7830
Arbor Acres Farm Inc	102	Glastonbury, CT	Private	100.0	750	2549
Booker Holdings Inc	103	Glastonbury, CT	Private	40.2	750	2549
Boskovich Farms Inc	104	Oxnard, CA	Private	85.0	750	1610
Environmentral Care Inc (EII)	105	Orlando, FL	Private	351.3	750	7829
Maple Leaf Duck Farms Inc	106	Milford, IN	Private	62.0	750	2599
Pig Improvement Company, Inc	107	Franklin, KY	Private	69.7	750	2130
Hermann Engelmann Greenhouses	108	Apopka, FL	Private	32.8	740	1810
Cooper Hatchery Inc	109	Oakwood, OH	Private	110.0	700	2540
Cuddy Farms Inc	110	Marshville, NC	Private	76.0	700	2540
Hubbard Farms Inc	111	Walpole, NH	Public Family Member	37.5	700	2540
Iowa Select Farms	112	Iowa Falls, IA	Private	150.0	700	2139
Naumes Inc	113	Medford, OR	Private	39.7	700	1750
Sanderson Farms Production Div	114	Laurel, MS	Public Family Member	33.8	675	2519
Kaolin Mushroom Farms Inc	115	Kennett Square, PA	Private	26.8	670	1820
Del Monte Fresh Produce Hawaii	116	Kunia, HI	Private	37.1	650	1799
Edward J Woerner & Sons Inc	117	West Palm Beach, FL	Private	50.9	650	1819
Horticultural Farms Inc	118	Cairo, GA	Private	28.5	650	1810
Lone Star Growers, L P	119	Pleasant Hill, CA	Private	28.8	650	1810
Norman's Nursery Inc.	120	San Gabriel, CA	Private	27.0	650	1810
Paramount Citrus Association	121	Visalia, CA	Private	51.0	650	1749
Pennfield Corp	122	Lancaster, PA	Private	180.0	650	2130
River Ranch Fresh Foods, Inc	123	Salinas, CA	Private	200.0	650	7230
Saticoy Lemon Association Inc	124	Santa Paula, CA	Private	91.1	650	7230
Asgrow Seed Company LLC	125	Des Moines, IA	Public Family Member	394.7	625	1810
Peco Farms Inc	126	Gordo, AL	Private	85.0	609	2519
Huntco Farms, Inc	127	Chesterfield, MO	Public Family Member	55.8	600	2130
Jlg Harvesting Inc	128	Greenfield, CA	Private	40.0	600	7230
Limoneira Associates	129	Santa Paula, CA	Private	40.0	600	7230
Peco Foods of Mississippi Inc	130	Bay Springs, MS	Private	70.0	600	2549
Stemilt Growers Inc	131	Wenatchee, WA	Private	47.9	600	7230
Sun Pacific Farming Co	132	Exeter, CA	Private	28.4	600	7629
Tara Packing Co	133	Spreckels, CA	Private	21.0	600	7610
Taylor Fresh Foods Inc	134	Salinas, CA	Private	40.0	600	7230
Foster Dairy Farms	135	Modesto, CA	Private	250.0	590	2419
Franklin Farms Inc	136	North Franklin, CT	Private	39.0	590	1820
Exeter Packers Inc	137	Exeter, CA	Private	130.0	585	7230
Carroll's Foods of Virginia	138	Waverly, VA	Private	103.6	580	2130
Quincy Corp	139	Quincy, FL	Public Family Member	28.0	575	1820
Colorado Greenhouse Holdings	140	Denver, CO	Private	24.9	563	1619

D&B COMPANY RANKINGS BY EMPLOYMENT

Company	Rank	Location	Type	Sales ($ mil.)	Employ- ment	Primary SIC
Emco Harvesting Co	141	Yuma, AZ	Private	19.7	562	7610
Harrison Poultry Inc	142	Bethlehem, GA	Private	29.7	555	2549
Brown's of Carolina, Inc.	143	Warsaw, NC	Public Family Member	10.8	550	2130
R D Offutt Co	144	Fargo, ND	Private	54.5	545	1340
Wight Nurseries Inc	145	Cairo, GA	Private	20.0	525	1810
Via North America Inc	146	Indiantown, FL	Private	30.6	516	1740
Agri Beef Co	147	Boise, ID	Private	300.0	515	2110
Bruce Church Inc	148	Salinas, CA	Private	42.8	502	1610
21st Century Genetics	149	Shawano, WI	Private	27.1	500	7510
7th Standard Ranch Co	150	Bakersfield, CA	Private	30.0	500	1720
Agreserves, Inc	151	Salt Lake City, UT	Private	23.6	500	7620
B H Hardaway III Farms Inc	152	Columbus, GA	Private	34.6	500	1390
Dole Bakersfield Inc	153	Bakersfield, CA	Public Family Member	30.0	500	1720
Environmental Earthscapes Inc	154	Tucson, AZ	Private	19.7	500	7829
Erickson Air-Crane Co., LLC	155	Central Point, OR	Private	27.2	500	2411
Farm-Op, Inc	156	Immokalee, FL	Private	42.6	500	1610
Flowerwood Nursery Inc	157	Mobile, AL	Private	23.3	500	1810
Fresh Western Marketing Inc	158	Salinas, CA	Private	168.0	500	7220
Giumarra Vineyards Corp	159	Edison, CA	Private	95.5	500	1720
Mann Packing Co, Inc	160	Salinas, CA	Private	126.8	500	7230
Quality Farm Labor Inc	161	Gonzales, CA	Private	17.5	500	7619
Terry Farms, Princeton, Inc.	162	Princeton, IL	Private	30.0	500	1820
Nurserymen's Exchange Inc	163	San Francisco, CA	Private	21.5	485	1810
Hondo Co (Inc)	164	Roswell, NM	Private	23.9	478	2120
Amick Processing Inc	165	Batesburg, SC	Private	25.4	475	2540
Avi Holdings Inc	166	Gardena, CA	Private	17.8	475	7420
Bailey Nurseries, Inc	167	St. Paul, MN	Private	27.0	470	1810
Farrens Tree Surgeons Inc	168	Willow Grove, PA	Private	20.0	470	7830
Costa Nursery Farms Inc	169	Goulds, FL	Private	36.5	460	1810
Utrecht - America Holdings	170	New York, NY	Private	21.6	460	8110
Four Seasons Landscpng & Maint Co	171	Foster City, CA	Private	16.5	450	7810
Giorgi Mushroom Co	172	Blandon, PA	Private	18.0	450	1820
Lihue Plantation Company Ltd	173	Lihue, HI	Private	36.2	450	1339
Noah W Kreider & Son	174	Manheim, PA	Private	30.0	450	2520
Sanchez Diaz Farm Labor Contr	175	Woodlake, CA	Private	15.8	450	7619
Sharyland LP	176	Mission, TX	Private	30.0	449	1610
Navajo Ag Pdts Indust	177	Farmington, NM	Private	37.6	440	1910
San Val Corp	178	Palm Desert, CA	Private	22.1	439	7810
Ducks Unlimited Inc	179	Memphis, TN	Private	103.5	425	9719
Triple A Landscape	180	Tucson, AZ	Private	15.0	425	7829
Cobb-Vantress, Inc.	181	Siloam Springs, AR	Public Family Member	50.0	415	7510
Ise America Inc	182	Golts, MD	Private	33.9	407	2520
American Nursery Products LLC	183	Tulsa, OK	Private	22.8	400	8119
Bear Creek Production Co	184	Wasco, CA	Private	17.8	400	1810
BG Maintenance	185	Columbia, MO	Private	14.2	400	7820
Blaine Larsen Processing Inc	186	Hamer, ID	Private	27.4	400	7230
Circle Four Farms	187	Milford, UT	Private	70.0	400	2139
Creekside Mushrooms Ltd	188	Worthington, PA	Private	20.0	400	1820
Genex Cooperative Inc	189	Ithaca, NY	Private	72.0	400	7510
Herrera Packing Inc	190	Santa Maria, CA	Private	13.0	400	7230
Hines II Inc	191	Irvine, CA	Public Family Member	17.8	400	1810
McAnally Enterprises Inc.	192	Yucaipa, CA	Private	40.0	400	2520
Melkesian Ranch Inc	193	Indio, CA	Private	24.0	400	1720
O'Connell Landscape Maintenance	194	Rcho Sta Marg, CA	Private	11.3	400	7829
Oakley Groves Inc	195	Lake Wales, FL	Private	79.3	400	1740
Paramount Farming Company, LP	196	Bakersfield, CA	Private	120.0	400	1739
Park Landscape Maintenance	197	Rcho Sta Marg, CA	Private	11.6	400	7820
Premier Packing, Inc	198	Shafter, CA	Private	15.0	400	7230
Randall Farms, L.L.C.	199	Arcadia, LA	Private	20.0	400	2519
S & J Ranch Inc	200	Madera, CA	Public Family Member	30.0	400	7620
Seabrook Enterprises Inc	201	Alpharetta, GA	Private	27.4	400	7230
Sleepy Creek Farms Inc	202	Goldsboro, NC	Private	45.0	400	2539
Sonora Packing Co, Inc	203	Salinas, CA	Private	14.0	400	7230
Southern Orchard Supply Co	204	Fort Valley, GA	Private	27.4	400	7230
Valley Pride Inc	205	Castroville, CA	Private	22.1	400	7619
Woerner Development Inc	206	Foley, AL	Private	17.8	400	1819
Clear Springs Foods Inc	207	Buhl, ID	Private	15.4	385	2730
Underwood Bros Inc	208	Phoenix, AZ	Private	14.1	385	7829
Villa Park Orchards Assn Inc	209	Orange, CA	Private	10.3	385	7230
S & H Packing and Sales Co	210	Los Angeles, CA	Private	45.0	381	1619

D&B COMPANY RANKINGS BY EMPLOYMENT

Company	Rank	Location	Type	Sales ($ mil.)	Employ-ment	Primary SIC
Dekalb Swine Breeders Inc	211	Dekalb, IL	Public Family Member	57.0	380	2139
Boething Treeland Farms Inc	212	Woodland Hills, CA	Private	17.6	375	8119
Walters Gardens Inc	213	Zeeland, MI	Private	22.6	370	1810
Cactus Feeders, Inc.	214	Amarillo, TX	Private	336.4	365	2110
Weeks Wholesale Rose Growers	215	Upland, CA	Private	10.3	360	1810
Powell Plant Farms Inc	216	Troup, TX	Private	15.9	356	1810
All Green Corp	217	Marietta, GA	Private	12.5	350	7820
Brooks Tropicals Inc	218	Homestead, FL	Private	37.5	350	7629
Dave Kingston Produce Inc	219	Idaho Falls, ID	Private	24.2	350	7230
Evans Properties Inc	220	Dade City, FL	Private	20.7	350	1740
Gallo Cattle Co	221	Atwater, CA	Private	55.0	350	2410
Golden Valley Produce LLC	222	Buttonwillow, CA	Private	24.2	350	7230
Greenheart Farms Inc	223	Arroyo Grande, CA	Private	12.2	350	1820
John Lucas Tree Expert Co	224	Portland, ME	Private	14.3	350	7830
Modern Mushroom Farms Inc	225	Toughkenamon, PA	Private	25.0	350	1820
Rock & Waterscape Systems	226	Irvine, CA	Private	20.0	350	7829
Ross Breeders Inc	227	Huntsville, AL	Private	35.0	350	2549
South Shres Rsdential Coml Dev	228	Santa Ana, CA	Private	11.2	350	7829
Townsends Farms, Inc	229	Millsboro, DE	Private	17.5	350	2519
Woerner South Inc	230	West Palm Beach, FL	Private	18.9	350	1819
Growers Vegetable Express	231	Salinas, CA	Private	143.9	342	1610
Pet's Choice Inc	232	Bellevue, WA	Private	12.0	342	7429
Quality Grain Company Inc	233	Atlanta, GA	Private	23.4	341	1120
Jamar Industries	234	Albuquerque, NM	Private	12.1	340	7829
Tree Preservation Co Inc	235	Willow Grove, PA	Private	14.8	340	7830
Edaw Inc	236	San Francisco, CA	Private	50.4	330	7810
Landscape Maintenance Services	237	Plainsboro, NJ	Public Family Member	12.0	326	7820
Dimare Enterprises Inc	238	Newman, CA	Private	49.0	325	1740
Gustafson's Dairy Inc	239	Green Cove Springs, FL	Private	21.7	325	2410
Spokane Tribe of Indians	240	Wellpinit, WA	Private	47.7	325	2411
Willmar Poultry Co Inc	241	Willmar, MN	Private	78.6	325	2539
Dmb Packing Corp	242	Newman, CA	Private	40.0	320	1740
El Modeno Gardens Inc	243	Irvine, CA	Private	25.0	320	1810
Hy-Line International	244	West Des Moines, IA	Private	70.1	320	2549
J-M Farms Inc	245	Miami, OK	Private	12.8	320	1820
Texas A & M University	246	College Station, TX	Private	25.9	318	8510
Fernlea Nursery Inc	247	Palm City, FL	Private	10.0	315	1810
Kitayama Brothers Inc	248	Brighton, CO	Private	12.0	307	1810
Terry Farms Zellwood Division	249	Zellwood, FL	Private	12.2	304	1820
Abi Alfalfa Inc	250	Shawnee Mission, KS	Private	13.4	300	1810
AGS Inc	251	Fillmore, CA	Private	14.2	300	7629
Allen's Hatchery Inc	252	Seaford, DE	Private	180.0	300	2540
Animal Medical Center Inc	253	New York, NY	Private	14.0	300	7429
Baloian Packing Co, Inc.	254	Fresno, CA	Private	30.9	300	1610
Bay City Flower Co Inc	255	Half Moon Bay, CA	Private	13.4	300	1810
Bordier's Nursery Inc	256	Irvine, CA	Private	13.4	300	1810
BTV Crown Equities, Inc	257	Sacramento, CA	Private	18.0	300	1720
Byrd Harvest Inc	258	Guadalupe, CA	Private	15.0	300	7220
Cagle's Farms Inc	259	Dalton, GA	Public Family Member	16.1	300	2540
Caribbean Agriculture Projects	260	Gulf Breeze, FL	Private	18.0	300	7110
Conard-Pyle Co Inc	261	West Grove, PA	Private	13.4	300	1810
Garcia Farming & Harvesting	262	Salinas, CA	Private	12.0	300	1610
Gerralds Vdlia Sweet Onons Inc	263	Statesboro, GA	Private	21.1	300	7230
Glenn Walters Nursery Inc	264	Cornelius, OR	Private	20.0	300	1810
Griffin-Holder Co	265	Rocky Ford, CO	Private	15.1	300	1610
Gulfstream Tomato Growers Ltd	266	Miami, FL	Private	21.1	300	7230
Harloff Packing of East Tenn	267	Morristown, TN	Private	21.1	300	7230
Hillandale Farms of Florida Inc	268	Lake City, FL	Private	37.7	300	2529
Hilltown Packing Co	269	Salinas, CA	Private	13.5	300	7230
L & C Harvesting Inc	270	Guadalupe, CA	Private	15.0	300	7220
Leisure Lawn Inc	271	Dayton, OH	Private	20.0	300	7820
Midwest Poultry Services LP	272	Mentone, IN	Private	25.0	300	2520
Mill Creek Companies	273	Dallas, TX	Private	14.0	300	1810
Ochoa Jc Farm Management & Flc	274	Indio, CA	Private	10.5	300	7610
Palmetto Companies, Inc	275	Palmetto, FL	Private	13.5	300	1810
Royal Citrus Co	276	Riverside, CA	Private	17.8	300	1740
Sand Systems Inc	277	Columbus, NE	Private	14.2	300	7620
Stark Bros Nrsries Orchrds Co	278	Louisiana, MO	Private	13.4	300	1810
Valley Crest Tree Co	279	Calabasas, CA	Private	14.1	300	8119
Waialua Sugar Company Inc	280	Waialua, HI	Public Family Member	24.2	300	1339

D&B COMPANY RANKINGS BY EMPLOYMENT

Company	Rank	Location	Type	Sales ($ mil.)	Employ-ment	Primary SIC
Richard Wilbur Ranch	281	Yuba City, CA	Private	16.2	286	1759
Gay & Robinson Inc	282	Kaumakani, HI	Private	20.0	280	1339
Simplot Livestock Company Inc	283	Grand View, ID	Private	59.5	280	2110
Amana Society, Inc	284	Amana, IA	Private	32.0	275	1910
Gentry's Poultry Co Inc	285	Ward, SC	Private	40.0	275	2510
Harris Moran Seed Co	286	Modesto, CA	Private	38.6	275	1810
Mariani Packing Co Inc	287	San Jose, CA	Private	117.0	275	7230
Gerawan Ranches	288	Sanger, CA	Private	15.3	270	1759
Taylor United Inc	289	Shelton, WA	Private	19.0	270	9130
Hillandale Farms Inc	290	Lake City, FL	Private	80.0	268	2520
Ben A Thomas Inc	291	Palmer, AK	Private	14.5	266	2411
Pro-Ag Inc	292	Lemoncove, CA	Private	19.0	266	7230
Diamond Creek Farms Inc	293	Goldsboro, NC	Private	29.8	265	2539
Avian Farms Inc	294	Portland, ME	Private	13.9	260	2540
Environmental Consultants	295	Southampton, PA	Private	11.9	260	8510
Tri-State Breeders Coop	296	Baraboo, WI	Private	20.9	260	7510
Griffin Land & Nurseries, Inc	297	New York, NY	Public	46.3	259	1810
Imperial Nurseries, Inc	298	Granby, CT	Public Family Member	42.0	259	1810
Calgene Inc	299	Davis, CA	Public Family Member	21.7	256	1619
Anderson Clayton Corp.	300	Fresno, CA	Private	200.0	250	7240
Anthony Vineyards Inc	301	Bakersfield, CA	Private	17.4	250	1720
Arbor Tree Surgery Inc	302	Paso Robles, CA	Private	11.1	250	7830
Betteravia Farms	303	Santa Maria, CA	Private	31.5	250	1610
Bucio Lourdes Farm	304	Santa Maria, CA	Private	21.2	250	1610
C & M Packing Inc	305	Gonzales, CA	Private	12.5	250	7220
Clean Cut Inc	306	Austin, TX	Public Family Member	15.0	250	7820
Corkscrew Growers Inc	307	Bonita Springs, FL	Private	21.2	250	1619
Desserault Ranch Inc	308	Moxee, WA	Private	17.3	250	1399
Four Seasons Produce Pkg Co	309	Salinas, CA	Private	17.9	250	7230
Gargiulo, Inc	310	Naples, FL	Public Family Member	160.0	250	1610
Garroutte Farms Inc	311	Watsonville, CA	Private	13.8	250	1719
Glacier Fish Co L.L.C.	312	Seattle, WA	Private	45.0	250	9120
Guide Dogs For The Blind Inc	313	San Rafael, CA	Private	50.5	250	7520
Healds Valley Farms Inc	314	Edinburg, TX	Private	15.7	250	1740
Jack Frost Inc	315	St. Cloud, MN	Private	40.0	250	2519
Katicich Ranch	316	Stockton, CA	Private	14.2	250	1759
Klein Foods Inc	317	Healdsburg, CA	Private	53.7	250	1720
Miller Shingle Co Inc	318	Granite Falls, WA	Private	13.6	250	2411
Moon Nurseries of Maryland	319	Chesapeake City, MD	Private	10.0	250	1810
Muranaka Farm, Inc	320	Granada Hills, CA	Private	21.2	250	1610
Orange-Co Inc	321	Bartow, FL	Public	109.3	250	1749
Orange-Co of Florida Inc	322	Bartow, FL	Public Family Member	14.8	250	1749
Pennink Arrimour	323	Huntingdon Valley, PA	Private	10.5	250	7820
Quarter M Farms, Inc.	324	Rose Hill, NC	Private	19.0	250	2130
Santa Barbara Farms LLC	325	Lompoc, CA	Private	18.0	250	1610
Speedling, Inc	326	Sun City, FL	Private	33.6	250	1810
Stephen Pavich & Sons	327	Porterville, CA	Private	15.0	250	1720
Sun-Ag Inc	328	Fellsmere, FL	Private	11.8	250	7629
Thanksgiving Point Mgmt Co LC	329	Orem, UT	Private	11.7	250	8119
Valley Crest Landscape Inc	330	Phoenix, AZ	Private	35.0	250	7810
Leidy's Inc	331	Souderton, PA	Private	42.8	242	7519
Eurofresh Ltd	332	Willcox, AZ	Private	15.0	240	1619
Floral Plant Growers, L.L.C.	333	Rising Sun, MD	Private	10.7	240	1810
Ritewood Inc	334	Franklin, ID	Private	11.8	240	2520
Stemilt Management Inc	335	Wenatchee, WA	Private	11.3	240	7620
Sunseeds Co	336	Morgan Hill, CA	Private	40.0	240	1810
Bonita Nurseries Inc	337	Willcox, AZ	Private	14.8	230	1619
John I Haas Inc	338	Washington, DC	Private	15.8	229	1399
David J Frank Landscape Contr	339	Germantown, WI	Private	13.5	225	7829
Norco Ranch Inc	340	Norco, CA	Private	94.0	225	2520
P R Farms Inc	341	Clovis, CA	Private	20.0	225	1759
Cagwin & Dorward	342	Novato, CA	Private	13.7	220	7829
Croman Corp	343	Ashland, OR	Private	45.0	220	2411
Zelenka Nursery Inc	344	Grand Haven, MI	Private	39.4	220	1810
Central Farm of America	345	New York, NY	Private	11.6	217	2540
Cascade Columbia Foods Ltd	346	Kennewick, WA	Private	10.0	215	7230
D & D Farms Inc	347	Pierre, SD	Private	20.0	215	2130
Dekalb Poultry Research Inc	348	Dekalb, IL	Private	11.5	214	2540
Caprock Industries	349	Amarillo, TX	Private	375.0	213	2110
Hanor Co Inc	350	Spring Green, WI	Private	13.1	213	2919

D&B COMPANY RANKINGS BY EMPLOYMENT

Company	Rank	Location	Type	Sales ($ mil.)	Employ-ment	Primary SIC
Inland Fruit & Produce Co	351	Wapato, WA	Private	13.6	210	7230
Morrison Enterprises	352	Hastings, NE	Private	75.0	210	1910
South Eastern Boll Weevil Era	353	Montgomery, AL	Private	36.2	210	7249
Starr Produce Co	354	Rio Grande City, TX	Private	25.0	210	1610
Taconic Farms Inc	355	Germantown, NY	Private	22.8	210	2799
Tampa Farm Service Inc	356	Dover, FL	Private	29.0	210	2520
Pandol & Sons	357	Delano, CA	Private	25.7	205	7230
A & D Christopher Ranch	358	Gilroy, CA	Private	83.8	200	1610
Agri-Empire	359	San Jacinto, CA	Private	14.0	200	1340
All Alaskan Seafoods, Inc	360	Seattle, WA	Private	60.0	200	9130
American Farms	361	Salinas, CA	Private	12.0	200	1610
Belize River Fruit Co., Inc	362	Ashland, KY	Private	10.8	200	1740
Cherry Lake Farms Inc	363	Groveland, FL	Private	20.6	200	1749
Corona College Heights	364	Riverside, CA	Private	14.3	200	7230
Eagle Produce Ltd Partnership	365	Scottsdale, AZ	Private	10.0	200	1610
Ed Silva	366	Gonzales, CA	Private	18.3	200	1610
Farmers Investment Co.	367	Sahuarita, AZ	Private	14.1	200	7230
Fillmore-Piru Citrus Assn	368	Fillmore, CA	Private	16.2	200	7230
Gardner Turfgrass Inc	369	Denver, CO	Private	11.9	200	1819
Haines Cy Citrus Growers Assn	370	Haines City, FL	Private	14.9	200	7230
Hitch Feeders I Inc	371	Guymon, OK	Private	35.7	200	2110
Hollandia Dairy	372	San Marcos, CA	Private	36.0	200	2410
J-V Farms, Inc.	373	Yuma, AZ	Private	20.3	200	1610
Jack M Berry Inc	374	Alva, FL	Private	10.4	200	7629
James T Smith	375	Wapato, WA	Private	11.0	200	1759
John M Foster Turf Farms	376	Indio, CA	Private	18.0	200	1819
Kaprielian Bros Packing Co	377	Reedley, CA	Private	14.3	200	7230
Kurt Weiss Florist Inc	378	Center Moriches, NY	Private	35.0	200	1810
L & S Harvesting Inc	379	El Centro, CA	Private	11.6	200	7220
Malloy Orchards, Inc	380	Live Oak, CA	Private	11.4	200	1759
Marlin Packing Co	381	Yuma, AZ	Private	13.8	200	7230
McDougall & Sons Inc	382	Wenatchee, WA	Private	12.9	200	7230
Natural Selection Foods LLC	383	San Juan Bautista, CA	Private	60.0	200	7230
Oglevee, Ltd	384	Connellsville, PA	Private	11.7	200	1810
Padilla Farm Labor C	385	Lindsay, CA	Private	12.8	200	1749
Parker Interior Plantscape	386	Scotch Plains, NJ	Private	15.0	200	7810
Popular Farms Inc	387	Oxnard, CA	Private	12.8	200	1719
Producers Holding Co	388	Memphis, TN	Private	20.8	200	7240
Pursley Inc	389	Bradenton, FL	Private	10.0	200	1819
R & R Farms, LLC	390	Santa Maria, CA	Private	18.3	200	1610
Reiter Berry Farms Inc	391	Watsonville, CA	Private	12.0	200	1719
Rio Farms	392	Oxnard, CA	Private	20.7	200	1610
Rousseau Farming Co II	393	Tolleson, AZ	Private	28.0	200	1610
Running W Citrus Ltd Partnr	394	South Bay, FL	Private	24.0	200	1740
Sugar Farms Inc	395	Palm Beach, FL	Private	15.7	200	1339
Tarheel Turkey Hatchery Inc	396	Raeford, NC	Private	14.5	200	2539
Tri Duncan A Partnership	397	Lamont, CA	Private	14.5	200	1310
Underwood Fruit & Warehouse Co	398	Yakima, WA	Private	16.2	200	7230
Uni-Kool Partners	399	Salinas, CA	Private	18.2	200	7230
Van Wingerden International	400	Fletcher, NC	Private	17.8	200	1810
Vincent B Zaninovich & Sons	401	Richgrove, CA	Private	11.6	200	1720
West Cotton Ag Management	402	Huron, CA	Private	10.3	200	7620
Willowbrook Foods Inc	403	Springdale, AR	Public Family Member	24.4	200	2539
Wolfsen Inc	404	Los Banos, CA	Private	15.2	200	1390
Woodcrest Partnership	405	Norco, CA	Private	18.0	200	2520
Chesapeake Forest Products Co	406	West Point, VA	Public Family Member	10.0	196	8110
Texas Farm Inc	407	Perryton, TX	Private	15.7	190	2130
Vall Inc	408	Texhoma, OK	Private	15.6	189	2130
Teixeira Farms Inc	409	Santa Maria, CA	Private	40.0	188	1610
Gadsden Tomato Co	410	Quincy, FL	Private	12.4	186	7230
Chappell Farms Inc	411	Barnwell, SC	Private	13.7	185	2130
Manatee Fruit Co	412	Palmetto, FL	Private	14.0	185	1810
Morrell Group Inc	413	Atlanta, GA	Private	10.0	185	7820
Baird-Neece Packing Corp	414	Porterville, CA	Private	13.1	180	7230
Conagra-Maple Leaf Milling	415	Omaha, NE	Private	14.8	180	7230
Rios, Jj Farm Services Inc	416	Acampo, CA	Private	11.9	180	7610
Tri-B Nursery, Inc.	417	Hulbert, OK	Private	10.6	180	1810
Crystal Farms Inc	418	Gainesville, GA	Private	65.0	175	2520
Hiji Bros., Inc.	419	Oxnard, CA	Private	16.2	175	1610
Kofkoff Egg Farm LLC	420	Bozrah, CT	Private	16.3	175	2520

D&B COMPANY RANKINGS BY EMPLOYMENT

Company	Rank	Location	Type	Sales ($ mil.)	Employ- ment	Primary SIC
Metrolina Greenhouses Inc	421	Huntersville, NC	Private	19.9	175	1810
Mid American Growers Inc	422	Granville, IL	Private	20.0	175	1810
National Hog Farms Inc	423	Kersey, CO	Private	16.3	175	2139
Progressive Dairies Holdings	424	Bakersfield, CA	Private	15.3	175	2410
Ryan Landscaping, Inc	425	Houston, TX	Private	10.0	175	7829
Valencia Harvesting Inc	426	Sarasota, FL	Private	10.7	175	1749
Wells and Wade Fruit Co	427	East Wenatchee, WA	Public Family Member	12.1	175	1750
Westlake Farms Inc	428	Stratford, CA	Private	11.8	175	1310
Zephyr Egg Co	429	Zephyrhills, FL	Private	30.0	175	2520
Alaska Ocean Seafood Ltd	430	Anacortes, WA	Private	30.0	170	9120
Avian Farms (Kentucky), Inc	431	Monticello, KY	Private	26.0	170	2540
Daylay Egg Farms, Inc	432	West Mansfield, OH	Private	25.0	170	2520
Hope Land Farm	433	Kennett Square, PA	Private	11.0	170	2419
Klink Citrus Association	434	Ivanhoe, CA	Private	17.4	170	7230
Nature's Trees Inc	435	Bedford Hills, NY	Private	14.2	170	7830
Pacific Earth Resources LLC	436	Camarillo, CA	Private	20.0	170	1819
McArthur Farms Inc	437	Okeechobee, FL	Private	25.0	165	2419
R H Phillips Inc	438	Esparto, CA	Public	17.3	165	1720
Urban Farmer, Inc	439	Englewood, CO	Private	13.0	164	7810
Useugi Farms Inc	440	Gilroy, CA	Private	14.8	162	1610
Creighton Brothers LLC	441	Warsaw, IN	Private	40.0	160	2520
Jones & Associates Inc	442	Harrisburg, PA	Private	10.0	160	1759
Las Uvas Valley Dairy	443	Hatch, NM	Private	15.0	160	2410
Plainville Turkey Farm Inc	444	Plainville, NY	Private	13.0	160	2539
Quality Turf Nurseries	445	Lithia, FL	Private	20.0	160	1819
River Ranch Southwest Inc	446	Dallas, TX	Private	20.0	160	7230
Sonoma-Cutrer Vineyards Inc	447	Windsor, CA	Private	10.6	160	1720
Sun City Landscapes Lawn Maint	448	Las Vegas, NV	Private	10.0	160	7829
McCorkle Nurseries Inc	449	Dearing, GA	Private	10.5	157	1810
Bailey's Nursery Inc	450	Lodi, CA	Private	10.5	155	1810
Custom-Pak Inc	451	Immokalee, FL	Private	15.1	154	1619
Hastings Pork Corp	452	Hastings, NE	Private	12.0	152	2139
Ag Planters Inc	453	Lake Harbor, FL	Private	12.4	150	1330
American Landscape Inc	454	Canoga Park, CA	Private	14.5	150	7810
Angelica Nurseries Inc	455	Kennedyville, MD	Private	10.0	150	7810
Babe Farms Inc	456	Santa Maria, CA	Private	13.7	150	1610
Becker Holdings Corp	457	Vero Beach, FL	Private	40.0	150	7210
Black Dog Farms of California	458	Holtville, CA	Private	32.0	150	1610
Bruce Company of Wisconsin Inc	459	Middleton, WI	Private	27.0	150	7829
California Redi-Date Co	460	Thermal, CA	Private	12.8	150	7230
Carmel Valley Packing, Inc	461	Salinas, CA	Private	13.5	150	7230
Cattlco Inc	462	Memphis, TN	Private	31.1	150	2110
Cecelia Packing Corp	463	Orange Cove, CA	Private	20.0	150	7230
Charles G Watts Inc	464	Salinas, CA	Private	14.3	150	7230
Christensen Farm & Feedlots Inc	465	Sleepy Eye, MN	Private	14.2	150	2139
Duarte Nursery Inc	466	Hughson, CA	Private	25.0	150	1810
Eggs West	467	Ontario, CA	Private	13.7	150	2520
Enoch Packing Co Inc	468	Del Rey, CA	Private	49.5	150	7230
F F Gonsalez Farms	469	Santa Paula, CA	Private	10.0	150	1399
Farmax Land Management Inc	470	Sanger, CA	Private	13.5	150	7230
Hunt Brothers Cooperative Inc	471	Lake Wales, FL	Private	10.1	150	7230
Indian River Exchange Packers	472	Vero Beach, FL	Private	10.9	150	7230
J & K Farms Inc	473	Harrells, NC	Private	12.4	150	2130
Jack Neal & Son Inc	474	St. Helena, CA	Private	14.0	150	1720
Karleskint-Crum Inc	475	San Luis Obispo, CA	Private	12.5	150	7829
Lamanuzzi & Pantaleo Ltd	476	Clovis, CA	Private	26.2	150	1720
Lassen Canyon Nursery Inc	477	Redding, CA	Private	11.6	150	1719
Lion Enterprises Inc	478	Fresno, CA	Private	70.0	150	7230
Lucich Farms	479	Patterson, CA	Private	13.5	150	7230
Maine Fresh Pack Co-Operative	480	Machias, ME	Private	12.7	150	7230
McClure Properties, Ltd	481	Palmetto, FL	Private	25.0	150	1619
Merrill Farms	482	Salinas, CA	Private	13.9	150	1610
New Market Poultry Products	483	New Market, VA	Private	12.7	150	7519
Northland Cranberries Inc	484	Wisconsin Rapids, WI	Public	47.4	150	1719
Oppliger Family, Ltd.	485	Clovis, NM	Private	50.0	150	2120
P F F J, Inc	486	Snowflake, AZ	Private	24.0	150	2130
Phelan & Taylor Produce Co	487	Oceano, CA	Private	11.3	150	7230
R A Rasmussen & Sons Inc	488	Granger, WA	Private	12.2	150	1610
Rocky Mountain Elk Foundation	489	Missoula, MT	Private	18.9	150	9719
Rusler Produce, Inc	490	Avondale, CO	Private	11.9	150	1610

D&B COMPANY RANKINGS BY EMPLOYMENT

Company	Rank	Location	Type	Sales ($ mil.)	Employ-ment	Primary SIC
Stadelman Fruit, LLC	491	Yakima, WA	Private	13.7	150	7230
Stahmann Farms Inc	492	Las Cruces, NM	Private	14.2	150	1739
Suburban Lawn & Garden, Inc	493	Kansas City, MO	Private	15.0	150	1810
Sun Valley Floral Farms	494	Arcata, CA	Private	20.4	150	1810
Tagawa Greenhouses Inc	495	Brighton, CO	Private	15.0	150	1810
Talisman Sugar Corp	496	Jacksonville, FL	Public Family Member	11.8	150	1339
Talley Farms	497	Arroyo Grande, CA	Private	12.2	150	1610
Taplett Fruit Packing Inc	498	Wenatchee, WA	Private	10.5	150	7230
Thorkelson Ranches	499	Patterson, CA	Private	12.2	150	1610
Trout-Blue Chelan, Inc	500	Chelan, WA	Private	25.3	150	7230
Valley Onions Inc	501	McAllen, TX	Private	11.4	150	1610
Vignolo Farms	502	Shafter, CA	Private	12.4	150	1310
W J Griffin Inc	503	Santa Barbara, CA	Private	11.0	150	1810
Wailuku Agribusiness Co Inc	504	Wailuku, HI	Private	10.5	150	1739
Warren's Turf Group Inc	505	West Palm Beach, FL	Private	13.8	150	1819
White's Nursery & Greenhouses	506	Chesapeake, VA	Private	15.3	150	1810
Willoway Nurseries Inc	507	Avon, OH	Private	10.7	150	1810
Wyffels' Hybrids Inc	508	Atkinson, IL	Private	16.0	150	1150
B & W Quality Growers Inc	509	Fellsmere, FL	Private	15.0	145	1610
E Ritter & Co Inc	510	Marked Tree, AR	Private	41.4	145	1310
Bhb Inc	511	Las Vegas, NV	Private	14.2	140	7820
Cattlco	512	Fort Morgan, CO	Private	31.2	140	2110
Garden Design Group Inc	513	Dallas, TX	Private	11.6	140	7810
Roche Fruit Co Inc	514	Yakima, WA	Private	10.0	140	7230
Columbia West Virginia Corp	515	Portland, OR	Private	10.0	139	2411
Dillon Floral Corp	516	Bloomsburg, PA	Private	10.1	138	1810
Vila and Son Landscaping Corp	517	Miami, FL	Private	11.9	136	7829
Atlantic Salmon Me Ltd Lblty	518	Fairfield, ME	Private	23.9	135	2730
B & T Farms	519	Vista, CA	Private	13.9	135	1619
Nickel Family, L.L.C.	520	Bakersfield, CA	Private	12.0	135	1910
Agricultural Innovation Trade	521	Somis, CA	Private	13.4	130	1610
Alico Inc	522	Labelle, FL	Public	47.4	130	1740
Chief Wenatchee	523	Wenatchee, WA	Private	13.1	130	7230
G & H Seed Co, Inc.	524	Crowley, LA	Private	47.8	130	7239
Griffin, Ben Hill Inc	525	Frostproof, FL	Private	61.3	130	1740
Lifescapes Inc	526	Canton, GA	Private	10.0	130	7829
Valley Heights Ranch Ltd	527	Oceanside, CA	Private	10.6	130	1619
Vinifera Inc	528	Petaluma, CA	Private	10.2	130	1720
Willmar Poultry Farms Inc	529	Willmar, MN	Private	10.3	130	2130
Wisner Minnow Hatchery Inc	530	Wisner, LA	Private	33.2	130	2730
Clinton Nurseries Inc	531	Clinton, CT	Private	17.3	127	1810
Abbyland Pork Pack Inc	532	Curtiss, WI	Private	28.4	125	7519
Berend Bros Inc	533	Wichita Falls, TX	Private	24.7	125	2130
G & U Inc	534	Goshen, NY	Private	10.2	125	1610
M S N Inc	535	Houston, TX	Private	11.3	125	7810
Morrison Bros Ranch	536	Higley, AZ	Private	50.0	125	2120
Mulhall's Nursery, Inc.	537	Omaha, NE	Private	12.4	125	7810
Orange County Produce	538	Fullerton, CA	Private	12.1	125	1610
Pasquinelli Produce Co	539	Yuma, AZ	Private	13.1	125	1910
Tony Abatti Farms LLC	540	El Centro, CA	Private	14.4	125	1390
Wilkins-Rogers Inc	541	Ellicott City, MD	Private	55.0	125	7230
Esbenshade Farms	542	Mount Joy, PA	Private	11.0	120	2520
Farming Technology Corp	543	Houston, TX	Private	47.2	120	1340
Florida North Holsteins LC	544	Bell, FL	Private	13.6	120	2410
Homa Co	545	Parsippany, NJ	Private	46.4	120	1730
Kirschenman Packing Inc	546	Edison, CA	Private	10.6	120	7230
Pm Beef Group LLC	547	Kansas City, MO	Private	85.0	120	2110
Sharpe Land & Cattle Co	548	La Belle, MO	Private	19.4	120	2110
Sunny Grove Landscaping Inc	549	Estero, FL	Private	11.0	120	7810
Sunshine Raisin Corp	550	Fowler, CA	Private	60.0	120	7230
Tallmadge Bros Inc	551	Norwalk, CT	Private	10.0	120	9130
Velvet Ridge Greenhouses Inc	552	Asheville, NC	Private	16.0	118	1810
Young Pecan Co	553	Florence, SC	Private	11.1	116	7230
Southern Poultry Farms Inc	554	Harrisonburg, VA	Private	14.0	115	2530
N G Purvis Farms Inc	555	Robbins, NC	Private	13.2	113	2130
Borg Pak, Inc	556	Los Angeles, CA	Private	12.0	110	7230
Dresick Farms, Inc	557	Huron, CA	Private	10.1	110	1610
Foxley Cattle Co	558	La Jolla, CA	Private	75.8	110	2110
Glass Corner Greenhouse Inc	559	Grand Rapids, MI	Private	11.0	110	1810
Kitayama Bros Inc	560	Brighton, CO	Private	13.4	110	1810

D&B COMPANY RANKINGS BY EMPLOYMENT

Company	Rank	Location	Type	Sales ($ mil.)	Employ- ment	Primary SIC
Larson Fruit Co	561	Selah, WA	Private	12.2	110	7230
Sugarland Harvesting Co	562	Clewiston, FL	Private	10.8	110	7220
Thomas Bros Grass Ltd	563	Granbury, TX	Private	10.0	110	1819
Torrey Farms Inc	564	Elba, NY	Private	10.9	110	1610
Valley Rain Construction Corp	565	Tempe, AZ	Private	11.5	110	7829
Arizona Dairy Co, L.L.P.	566	Higley, AZ	Private	18.0	108	2419
New West Foods	567	Watsonville, CA	Private	50.0	107	7230
Lied's Nursery Co Inc	568	Sussex, WI	Private	12.2	105	7829
R H Phillips Vineyard Inc	569	Esparto, CA	Private	17.3	102	1720
Agrinorthwest, Inc	570	Kennewick, WA	Private	55.8	100	1110
Alex R Thomas & Co	571	Ukiah, CA	Private	15.0	100	7230
Anton Caratan & Son	572	Delano, CA	Private	23.5	100	1720
Auvil Fruit Co, Inc	573	Orondo, WA	Private	17.9	100	1759
Cattlemens Inc	574	Turon, KS	Private	43.0	100	2110
Clark Hutterian Brethren Inc	575	Raymond, SD	Private	10.0	100	1910
Corcpork Co	576	Corcoran, CA	Private	10.0	100	2130
Fred J Jaindl	577	Orefield, PA	Private	20.0	100	2539
Herbert C Haynes Inc	578	Winn, ME	Private	88.0	100	2411
Hickman's Egg Ranch, Inc.	579	Glendale, AZ	Private	34.0	100	2520
Highland Light, Inc	580	Seattle, WA	Private	15.1	100	9120
Jjr Inc	581	Ann Arbor, MI	Private	11.0	100	7810
Lumber City Egg Marketers Inc	582	Lumber City, GA	Private	10.0	100	2520
Northwestern Fruit & Prod Co	583	Yakima, WA	Private	12.0	100	1759
Premier Farms	584	Clarion, IA	Private	10.0	100	2130
Pride of San Juan, The Inc	585	San Juan Bautista, CA	Private	12.0	100	1610
Purepak Inc	586	Oxnard, CA	Private	10.0	100	1610
Rocco Farms Inc	587	Harrisonburg, VA	Private	150.0	100	2539
Scheid Vineyards Cal Inc	588	Marina Del Rey, CA	Public	19.9	100	7629
Scheid Vineyards Inc (Del)	589	Marina Del Rey, CA	Public	19.9	100	7620
Select Farms, Ltd	590	Spokane, WA	Private	11.0	100	1810
Smith Feed Service Inc	591	Loyal, WI	Private	16.6	100	7230
Stark Packing Corp	592	Strathmore, CA	Private	11.3	100	7230
Sungrow Landscape Services	593	Austin, TX	Private	10.0	100	7829
Swa Group	594	Sausalito, CA	Private	11.0	100	7810
Tackett Fish Farm	595	Schlater, MS	Private	14.9	100	2730
Wilson Farms Inc	596	Lexington, MA	Private	38.4	100	1610
Young's Plant Farm Inc	597	Auburn, AL	Private	10.0	100	1810
Wheeler Brothers Grain Co Inc	598	Watonga, OK	Private	90.1	99	2110
Leader Dogs For The Blind Inc	599	Rochester, MI	Private	13.3	94	7520
Trophy International Inc	600	McAllen, TX	Private	12.0	92	7230
Ag Rx Inc	601	Oxnard, CA	Private	21.0	90	7119
Burch Farms	602	Faison, NC	Private	14.9	90	1610
Chapel Valley Landscape Co	603	Woodbine, MD	Private	14.0	90	7829
Clarence Davids & Co	604	Matteson, IL	Private	11.0	90	7829
Coharie Farms	605	Clinton, NC	Private	22.0	90	2130
Dinklage Feed Yard, Inc.	606	Sidney, NE	Private	16.3	90	2110
Hawaiian Sweet, Inc.	607	Keaau, HI	Private	12.0	90	7230
L L Murphrey Co	608	Farmville, NC	Private	30.0	90	2130
Subco Packaging Inc	609	West Chicago, IL	Private	10.0	90	7230
Taylor & Fulton Inc	610	Palmetto, FL	Private	21.2	90	7230
Tejon Ranch Co	611	Lebec, CA	Public	41.0	90	1739
Meyer Tomatoes	612	King City, CA	Private	75.6	87	1619
Alf Christianson Seed Co	613	Mount Vernon, WA	Private	18.3	86	1810
Garlic Co	614	Bakersfield, CA	Private	21.0	85	1399
Hartung Brothers Inc	615	Arena, WI	Private	37.4	85	1610
Merex Corp	616	Yonkers, NY	Private	49.0	85	1610
Pinal Feeding Co	617	Goodyear, AZ	Private	19.3	85	2110
Richard S Burford	618	Fresno, CA	Private	17.4	85	1910
Swanson Farms	619	Turlock, CA	Private	13.4	85	2539
Aurora Dairy Florida LLC	620	Longmont, CO	Private	14.0	80	2410
Bauman Landscape, Inc	621	Richmond, CA	Private	19.5	80	7829
BLT Farms	622	Oxnard, CA	Private	16.0	80	1610
D M Camp & Sons	623	Bakersfield, CA	Private	24.5	80	1910
Diamond Fruit Growers Inc	624	Hood River, OR	Private	40.0	80	7230
G.F. Structures Corp	625	Chicago, IL	Private	32.7	80	7829
Parker Ranch Foundation Trust	626	Kamuela, HI	Private	15.5	80	2120
Brookover Feed Yards Inc	627	Garden City, KS	Private	19.6	78	2110
Resource Management Service	628	Birmingham, AL	Private	15.3	77	8510
Du Brow's Nurseries Inc	629	Livingston, NJ	Private	13.5	76	7810
Melrose Timber Co	630	McShan, AL	Private	15.2	76	8510

D&B COMPANY RANKINGS BY EMPLOYMENT

Company	Rank	Location	Type	Sales ($ mil.)	Employ-ment	Primary SIC
Adams Land & Cattle Co Inc	631	Broken Bow, NE	Private	12.0	75	2110
Apio Inc	632	Guadalupe, CA	Private	59.4	75	7220
Armstrong Farms	633	Valley Center, CA	Private	10.0	75	2520
Dale Bone Farms Inc	634	Nashville, NC	Private	10.8	75	1619
Dorothy Lough	635	Winthrop, ME	Private	13.0	75	2520
E W Brandt & Sons Inc	636	Wapato, WA	Private	16.0	75	7230
Glenwood Foods LLC	637	Jetersville, VA	Private	10.4	75	2520
Lake Region Packing Assn	638	Tavares, FL	Private	10.8	75	7230
Livestock Investments, Inc	639	Hereford, TX	Private	56.0	75	2110
Livestock Investors, Inc.	640	Summerfield, TX	Private	55.4	75	2110
O'Hara Corp	641	Rockland, ME	Private	15.0	75	9120
Pacific Tomato Growers, Ltd	642	Palmetto, FL	Private	94.3	75	1619
Pratt Feeders L L C	643	Pratt, KS	Private	25.0	75	2110
Rio Queen Citrus Farms Inc	644	Mission, TX	Private	20.0	75	1749
Schroeder Manatee Inc	645	Bradenton, FL	Private	15.0	75	1740
Shamrock Farms Co	646	Chandler, AZ	Private	21.7	75	2419
Silver Terrace Nurseries Intl	647	Burlingame, CA	Private	12.0	75	1810
Sublette Enterprises Inc	648	Sublette, KS	Private	32.9	75	2110
T T Miyasaka Inc	649	Watsonville, CA	Private	19.5	75	1719
Waverly Growers Cooperative	650	Waverly, FL	Private	10.0	75	7230
L A Hearne Co	651	King City, CA	Private	25.4	74	7230
Edward D Stone Jr and Assoc	652	Fort Lauderdale, FL	Private	10.1	73	7810
Clark's Feed Mills Inc	653	Shamokin, PA	Private	15.4	72	2510
Alaska Trawl Fisheries, Inc	654	Edmonds, WA	Private	40.0	70	9120
Clouds Landscpng Sprnklr Serv Inc	655	North Las Vegas, NV	Private	11.4	70	7829
Danell Bros Inc	656	Hanford, CA	Private	10.0	70	7220
Dundee Citrus Growers Assn	657	Dundee, FL	Private	33.4	70	7230
Heartland Farms Inc	658	Hancock, WI	Private	16.0	70	1610
Henry Avocado Packing Corp	659	Escondido, CA	Private	41.4	70	1799
Hilliard Brothers of Florida	660	Clewiston, FL	Private	13.1	70	2120
Mac Farms of Hawaii Inc	661	Captain Cook, HI	Private	27.3	70	1739
Mariani Enterprises Inc	662	Lake Bluff, IL	Private	11.2	70	7810
Mendes Calf Ranch	663	Tipton, CA	Private	16.1	70	2110
Pfister Hybrid Corn Co	664	El Paso, IL	Private	12.5	70	1150
Ritz Food International Inc	665	Delray Beach, FL	Private	15.0	70	1610
Stacy's, Inc	666	York, SC	Private	10.8	70	1810
Sunridge Nurseries, Inc	667	Bakersfield, CA	Private	20.4	70	7210
Ford Holding Company Inc	668	Ford, KS	Private	40.7	68	2110
Suma Fruit International Usa	669	Sanger, CA	Private	100.0	67	7230
Maddox Dairy	670	Riverdale, CA	Private	10.0	66	2419
Beef Northwest Inc	671	Nyssa, OR	Private	16.7	65	2110
Perryton Feeders, Inc.	672	Perryton, TX	Private	21.4	65	2110
Sun and Sands Enterprises, LLC	673	Coachella, CA	Private	43.3	65	1610
Valadco Inc	674	Renville, MN	Private	20.0	65	2139
Lindemann Produce Inc	675	Reno, NV	Private	65.0	63	7230
Kalashian Packing Co Inc	676	Fresno, CA	Private	10.0	62	7230
Adams Land Co	677	Leachville, AR	Private	50.0	60	7240
American Pelagic Fishing L P	678	Seattle, WA	Private	20.0	60	9120
Belair Packing Hse Joint Ventr	679	Vero Beach, FL	Private	23.5	60	7230
Brandt Co Inc	680	Brawley, CA	Private	14.0	60	2110
C & G Farms Inc	681	Chualar, CA	Private	15.0	60	1610
California Artich & Vege	682	Castroville, CA	Private	65.3	60	7230
Chooljian & Sons Inc	683	Del Rey, CA	Private	26.3	60	7230
Cole King Ranch & Farm	684	Milton, DE	Private	11.0	60	2110
Dan Schantz Farm & Greenhouses	685	Zionsville, PA	Private	18.0	60	1810
George Amaral Ranches Inc	686	Chualar, CA	Private	27.5	60	1610
Great Lakes Packers Inc	687	Bellevue, OH	Private	12.5	60	7230
Kearney Fertilizer Inc	688	Bonnie, IL	Private	10.0	60	7119
Manley Farms, Inc	689	Naples, FL	Private	12.0	60	1619
Oakdell Egg Farms Inc	690	Pasco, WA	Private	27.9	60	2520
Ponderosa Dairy	691	Amargosa Valley, NV	Private	13.5	60	2410
Schwertner Farms Inc	692	Schwertner, TX	Private	10.3	60	2110
Stallworth & Johnson Inc	693	Minter, AL	Private	175.0	60	2411
To-Jo Mushrooms Inc	694	Avondale, PA	Private	18.0	60	1820
Ford County Feed Yard Inc	695	Ford, KS	Private	30.5	59	2110
CRI Feeders Inc	696	Guymon, OK	Private	10.1	57	2110
Batson Mill L. P.	697	Batson, TX	Public Family Member	13.0	56	2411
Edaleen Dairy Products LLC	698	Lynden, WA	Private	13.0	56	2410
Gottsch Feeding Corp	699	Elkhorn, NE	Private	315.8	56	2110
A D Makepeace Co	700	Wareham, MA	Private	14.7	55	1719

D&B COMPANY RANKINGS BY EMPLOYMENT

Company	Rank	Location	Type	Sales ($ mil.)	Employ-ment	Primary SIC
Callery-Judge Grove LP	701	Loxahatchee, FL	Private	10.0	55	1740
Christensen Cattle Co	702	Central City, NE	Private	35.0	55	2110
R D Bowman & Sons Inc	703	Westminster, MD	Private	22.0	55	7230
Steve Henderson Logging Inc	704	Lewiston, ID	Private	14.0	55	2411
Torre & Bruglio Inc	705	Pontiac, MI	Private	14.0	55	7829
Wendell Talley	706	Stanfield, NC	Private	11.0	55	2539
Earthrise Farms	707	Calipatria, CA	Private	13.2	53	1910
McHutchison & Co LLC	708	Ridgefield, NJ	Private	17.0	51	7810
Ace Tomato Company Inc	709	Manteca, CA	Private	20.0	50	1619
Alliance Dairies	710	Trenton, FL	Private	10.0	50	2410
Arteka Natural Green Corp	711	Eden Prairie, MN	Public Family Member	11.0	50	7829
Bethel Grain Co	712	Benton, IL	Private	17.0	50	7230
Cactus Operating, Ltd.	713	Amarillo, TX	Private	335.0	50	2110
California Family Foods LLC	714	Arbuckle, CA	Private	30.0	50	7230
D Bruce Cuddy	715	Marshville, NC	Private	10.0	50	2530
Diestel Turkey Ranch	716	Sonora, CA	Private	10.0	50	2539
Fordel Inc	717	Mendota, CA	Private	14.0	50	7230
Geerlings Greenhouse Inc	718	Piscataway, NJ	Private	12.0	50	1810
Gerawan Farming, Inc	719	Sanger, CA	Private	10.0	50	7230
Gold Cost Pistachios Inc	720	Coalinga, CA	Private	25.0	50	1739
Gold Star Mushroom Co	721	Lenhartsville, PA	Private	10.0	50	1820
Grand Mesa Eggs, Inc	722	Grand Junction, CO	Private	10.1	50	2520
Heller Bros Packing Corp	723	Winter Garden, FL	Private	76.4	50	1740
Hitch Feeders II, Inc	724	Garden City, KS	Private	26.9	50	2110
J H Miles Co Inc	725	Norfolk, VA	Private	12.7	50	9130
Lipinski Landscaping Irrgtion Contr	726	Mount Laurel, NJ	Private	15.0	50	7829
McClain Enterprises, Inc.	727	Mountain Home, AR	Private	36.9	50	2539
Mecca Farms Inc	728	Lake Worth, FL	Private	37.4	50	1619
Mercer Ranches Inc	729	Prosser, WA	Private	17.0	50	1910
P H Ranch, Inc	730	Winton, CA	Private	15.0	50	2419
Pride Feeders I, Ltd	731	Hooker, OK	Private	35.4	50	2110
Sakuma Bros Farms Inc	732	Burlington, WA	Private	12.5	50	1719
Sun-Land Products of California	733	Pleasanton, CA	Private	70.7	50	7230
Triangle Farms Inc	734	Salinas, CA	Private	11.2	50	1610
Valley Fig Growers Inc	735	Fresno, CA	Private	10.7	50	7230
Van De Graaf Ranches Inc	736	Sunnyside, WA	Private	64.2	50	2110
Vann Bros	737	Williams, CA	Private	20.0	50	1619
Vinery LLC	738	Midway, KY	Private	15.0	50	7520
Virginia Beef Corp	739	Haymarket, VA	Private	21.0	50	1819
Swine Graphics Enterprises, LP	740	Webster City, IA	Private	31.8	49	2130
Wilco Peanut Co	741	Pleasanton, TX	Private	20.0	49	7230
Sealaska Timber Corp	742	Ketchikan, AK	Private	140.0	48	8510
Hazelnut Growers of Oregon	743	Cornelius, OR	Private	31.6	47	7230
Triangle Manufacturing Co	744	Slaton, TX	Private	12.0	47	7240
Paris Foods Corp	745	Camden, NJ	Private	39.8	46	7230
Affiliated Rice Milling Inc	746	Alvin, TX	Private	20.0	45	7230
Chooljian Bros Packing Co Inc	747	Sanger, CA	Private	26.2	45	7230
Crane Mills	748	Corning, CA	Private	13.0	45	2411
Crosbyton Seed Co.	749	Crosbyton, TX	Private	11.6	45	1190
Fairleigh Corp	750	Scott City, KS	Private	24.9	45	2110
Ivy Acres Inc	751	Calverton, NY	Private	10.2	45	1810
Keegan Inc	752	Twin Falls, ID	Private	12.0	45	7230
Prides Corner Farms, Inc	753	Lebanon, CT	Private	10.2	45	1810
Roche Manufacturing Co Inc	754	Dublin, GA	Private	19.2	45	7240
Scarborough Farms Inc	755	Lamar, SC	Private	10.0	45	2520
Weiss Lake Egg Co Inc	756	Centre, AL	Private	10.0	44	2520
Erwin-Keith Inc	757	Wynne, AR	Private	38.0	43	1190
Oppliger Feedyard Inc	758	Clovis, NM	Private	22.9	43	2110
Riverview Dairy Inc	759	Morris, MN	Private	10.0	42	2410
Whitfield Timber Inc	760	Wewahitchka, FL	Private	20.0	42	2411
Dixie Farms	761	Plant City, FL	Private	16.1	40	1719
Double D Properties Inc	762	Belle Glade, FL	Private	18.0	40	1339
Giroux's Poultry Farm Inc	763	Chazy, NY	Private	10.4	40	2520
Gold Star Wholesale Nursery	764	Lexington, MA	Private	14.0	40	1810
Golden West Nuts Inc	765	Ripon, CA	Private	33.6	40	7230
Jensen Corp Landscape Contractors	766	Cupertino, CA	Private	12.0	40	7829
Joe Heidrick Enterprises Inc	767	Woodland, CA	Private	10.0	40	1110
Johnston Farms	768	Edison, CA	Private	10.0	40	1749
Juniata Feed Yards	769	Juniata, NE	Private	100.0	40	2110
Knight Management, Inc	770	Belle Glade, FL	Private	15.0	40	1339

D&B COMPANY RANKINGS BY EMPLOYMENT

Company	Rank	Location	Type	Sales ($ mil.)	Employ-ment	Primary SIC
Parker Wholesale Florist Inc	771	Scotch Plains, NJ	Private	10.0	40	1810
Schaake Corp	772	Ellensburg, WA	Private	71.8	40	2110
Spencer Fruit Co	773	Reedley, CA	Private	42.0	40	7230
Taylor & Stuckey Inc	774	Trumann, AR	Private	12.4	40	7240
Walker Farms	775	Menan, ID	Private	10.0	40	1190
Ward Feed Yard Inc	776	Larned, KS	Private	19.6	40	2110
Western Feed Yard Inc	777	Johnson, KS	Private	24.1	40	2110
Wm G Roe & Sons Inc	778	Winter Haven, FL	Private	20.0	40	7230
Orangeburg Foods Inc	779	Orangeburg, SC	Private	14.4	37	2130
Montezuma Feeders Inc	780	Montezuma, KS	Private	14.9	36	2110
Crist Feed Yard Inc	781	Scott City, KS	Private	19.0	35	2110
Demler Egg Ranch	782	San Jacinto, CA	Private	12.0	35	2520
Eastside Nursery Inc	783	Groveport, OH	Private	11.0	35	7829
Eunice Rice Mill, LLC	784	Eunice, LA	Private	25.0	35	7230
Feather River Food Co Inc	785	Marysville, CA	Private	13.1	35	7230
J & C Enterprises Inc	786	Miami, FL	Private	22.8	35	1390
Kenneth L Mink & Sons Inc	787	Waldorf, MD	Private	28.0	35	2719
Mayfield Timber Co Inc	788	Toxey, AL	Private	10.2	35	2411
Naturipe Berry Growers	789	Watsonville, CA	Private	65.4	35	7230
North Platte Feeders Inc	790	North Platte, NE	Private	19.0	35	2110
Oord Dairy	791	Sunnyside, WA	Private	10.0	35	2410
Puglisi Egg Farms Inc	792	Howell, NJ	Private	11.5	35	2520
Red Rock Feeding Co	793	Red Rock, AZ	Private	24.0	35	2110
Schumacher Landscaping Inc	794	Boston, MA	Private	17.5	35	7829
Stotz Farms Inc	795	Avondale, AZ	Private	10.0	35	2410
Sugarland Feed Yards, Inc.	796	Hereford, TX	Private	13.4	35	2110
Wm F Renk & Sons Co, Inc	797	Sun Prairie, WI	Private	10.1	35	1810
Kearny County Feeders Inc	798	Lakin, KS	Private	10.0	34	2110
Darr Feed Lot Inc	799	Cozad, NE	Private	13.6	33	2110
Gold Coast Pistachio's Inc	800	Fresno, CA	Private	12.1	33	1739
Great Bend Feeding Inc	801	Great Bend, KS	Private	16.1	33	2120
Rafter 3 Feedyard, Inc.	802	Dimmitt, TX	Private	32.2	33	2110
Herndon Marine Products Inc	803	Aransas Pass, TX	Private	95.0	32	9130
Sumner Peck Ranch, Inc.	804	Madera, CA	Private	10.0	32	1910
Allstate Packers Inc	805	Lodi, CA	Private	11.2	30	7230
B J & E Realty Co	806	Kreamer, PA	Private	11.1	30	2549
Belk Farms	807	Thermal, CA	Private	12.5	30	1910
Bluebird Inc	808	Peshastin, WA	Private	16.3	30	7230
Buurma Farms, Inc	809	Willard, OH	Private	12.4	30	1610
C B Bunting & Sons	810	Pinetops, NC	Private	20.0	30	1320
Cpc International Apple	811	Tieton, WA	Private	12.0	30	7230
Delbert L Wheeler	812	White Swan, WA	Private	10.0	30	2411
Dixie Lower Timber Compan	813	Thomasville, AL	Private	13.0	30	8519
Dutch Country Egg Farms Inc	814	Fredericksburg, PA	Private	11.9	30	2520
Eckenberg Farms Inc	815	Mattawa, WA	Private	11.9	30	7230
Garden City Feed Yard, LLC	816	Garden City, KS	Private	16.3	30	2110
Hamilton County Dairy, L.L.C.	817	Syracuse, KS	Private	13.0	30	2419
Harvey Brothers Farm Inc	818	Naples, FL	Private	11.6	30	1619
Hornbeck Seed Co Inc	819	De Witt, AR	Private	12.0	30	7230
Hughson Nut Inc	820	Hughson, CA	Private	15.0	30	7220
Illy's Sunny Slope Farm's Inc	821	Beaumont, CA	Private	14.0	30	2529
Mills Distributing Co, Inc	822	Salinas, CA	Private	78.4	30	1610
Monson Ranches Inc	823	Outlook, WA	Private	34.0	30	2110
Northern Fruit Co, Inc	824	East Wenatchee, WA	Private	11.6	30	7230
Pacific Oyster Co	825	Portland, OR	Private	15.0	30	9130
Paco Feedyard Inc.	826	Friona, TX	Private	15.0	30	2110
Powell and Powell Milling Inc	827	Green Forest, AR	Private	10.0	30	7230
Premier Mushrooms, Inc	828	Kennett Square, PA	Private	10.0	30	7230
Rahav Enterprises, Inc	829	Phoenix, AZ	Private	10.0	30	7810
Sierra Hills Packing Co Inc	830	Stockton, CA	Private	15.0	30	7230
Terranova Ranch Inc	831	Helm, CA	Private	10.1	30	1910
Tri-State Feeders, Inc	832	Turpin, OK	Private	25.6	30	2110
U.S. Tmbrlands Klamath Fls LLC	833	Klamath Falls, OR	Private	80.0	30	8110
Van Solkema Produce Inc	834	Byron Center, MI	Private	12.0	30	7230
Index Mutual Association	835	Bloomington, CA	Private	14.3	29	7230
Classic Cattle Co LP	836	Wildorado, TX	Private	20.6	28	2110
Dean Cluck Cattle Co	837	Gruver, TX	Private	18.0	28	2110
G & B Enterprises Ltd	838	Liberty, SC	Private	10.0	28	2520
Living Free	839	Mountain Center, CA	Private	10.0	28	7520
AJB Ranch	840	Bakersfield, CA	Private	11.0	27	2410

D&B COMPANY RANKINGS BY EMPLOYMENT

Company	Rank	Location	Type	Sales ($ mil.)	Employ-ment	Primary SIC
Pismo-Oceano Vegetable Exch	841	Oceano, CA	Private	27.0	27	7230
Smith Cattle Inc	842	Tribune, KS	Private	11.0	27	2110
Barton County Feeders, Inc	843	Ellinwood, KS	Private	10.0	26	2110
Kingfish Seafood Inc	844	Panama City, FL	Private	15.0	26	9120
Ainsworth Feed Yards Co	845	Ainsworth, NE	Private	18.1	25	2110
Baker Farming	846	Firebaugh, CA	Private	12.0	25	1720
Circle C Farms	847	Brinson, GA	Private	10.0	25	1310
Continente Nut LLC	848	Oakley, CA	Private	10.0	25	1720
Cuba Timber Co	849	Cuba, AL	Private	15.4	25	8110
Delta Packing Co of Lodi	850	Lodi, CA	Private	26.0	25	7230
General Produce Distrs Inc	851	Franklin Park, IL	Private	12.0	25	7230
Griffin Produce Co Inc	852	Salinas, CA	Private	50.8	25	7230
Gtc-Gtc Ltd	853	Greeley, CO	Private	12.0	25	7230
Huerta Packing Inc	854	Yuma, AZ	Private	13.1	25	1610
Jack Sparrowk	855	Clements, CA	Private	12.0	25	2120
Landscape Concepts Inc	856	Grayslake, IL	Private	15.3	25	7810
McDonnell, Inc	857	Jessup, MD	Private	15.0	25	1740
McGinley-Schilz Co	858	Brule, NE	Private	18.3	25	2110
Mid Valley Processing Inc	859	Newman, CA	Private	10.0	25	7519
Midwest Htchy & Plty Farms Inc	860	Dassel, MN	Private	10.0	25	2540
Miller Diversified Corp	861	La Salle, CO	Public	11.4	25	2110
Murakami Farms Inc	862	Ontario, OR	Private	18.2	25	7230
Packers of Indian River, Ltd	863	Fort Pierce, FL	Private	12.0	25	7230
Premium Feeders Inc	864	Scandia, KS	Private	22.6	25	2110
Winter Haven Citrus Growers Assn	865	Winter Haven, FL	Private	12.5	25	7230
Harris Woolf Cal Almonds	866	Coalinga, CA	Private	266.2	24	7230
Pawnee Beefbuilders, Inc	867	Larned, KS	Private	16.0	24	2110
Penco Inc	868	Greer, SC	Private	22.0	24	7520
Peri & Sons Farms Inc	869	Yerington, NV	Private	14.0	24	1610
Charles Donald Pulpwood Inc	870	Port Gibson, MS	Private	36.1	23	2411
Coyote Lake Feedyard, Inc.	871	Muleshoe, TX	Private	25.2	23	2110
Tosh Farms	872	Henry, TN	Private	14.5	23	1910
American International Dairies Corp	873	Franklin, TN	Private	12.0	22	7510
New Carrizo Creek Feeders Ltd	874	Texline, TX	Private	11.0	22	2110
Carson County Feedyards, Inc.	875	Panhandle, TX	Private	11.1	21	2110
McLean Feedyard, Inc.	876	McLean, TX	Private	11.6	21	2110
Richard Gumz Farms LLC	877	North Judson, IN	Private	16.0	21	1150
Andrews Distribution Co	878	Bakersfield, CA	Private	15.0	20	7230
Beef Tech Cattle Feeders, Inc.	879	Hereford, TX	Private	12.0	20	2110
Bledsoe Ranch Co	880	Wray, CO	Private	12.0	20	2110
C & C Farms	881	Bowling Green, KY	Private	12.0	20	2120
Coalinga Feed Yard Inc	882	Coalinga, CA	Private	11.8	20	2110
Conoley Fruit Harvester Inc	883	Oakland, FL	Private	15.1	20	7220
Elloree Gin Co Inc	884	Elloree, SC	Private	15.1	20	7240
Eppich Grain Inc	885	Mesa, WA	Private	20.0	20	7230
Florida Gardinier Citrus	886	Sarasota, FL	Private	10.0	20	1740
Forestry International Inc	887	Meridian, MS	Public	12.0	20	8110
Franscioni Brothers, Inc	888	Salinas, CA	Private	10.3	20	1610
Golden Acres Farms	889	Thermal, CA	Private	20.8	20	1610
Jcm Farming Inc	890	Visalia, CA	Private	10.0	20	1720
Jim Hronis & Sons Ranch	891	Delano, CA	Private	17.0	20	1720
Kingsburg Apple Packers	892	Kingsburg, CA	Private	22.0	20	7230
Koen Farms Inc	893	Hope, AR	Private	18.7	20	2120
Midwest Feeders Inc	894	Ingalls, KS	Private	14.0	20	2120
Rivera Blas	895	La Quinta, CA	Private	15.0	20	1720
Sahlman Holding Co Inc	896	Tampa, FL	Private	65.6	20	9130
Sahlman Seafoods Inc	897	Tampa, FL	Private	65.6	20	9130
Sorrells Brothers Packing Co	898	Arcadia, FL	Private	20.6	20	7220
Thompson Agriplex, Inc.	899	Hartley, TX	Private	17.5	20	2120
Union County Feed Lot, Inc	900	Clayton, NM	Private	12.0	20	2110
Lake Superior Land Co	901	Calumet, MI	Public Family Member	15.0	19	2411
Dettle Cattle Co	902	Stratford, TX	Private	14.0	18	2120
Double A Feeders Inc	903	Clayton, NM	Private	28.0	18	2110
Garland Farm Supply Inc	904	Garland, NC	Private	10.2	18	7230
Veribest Cattle Feeders Inc	905	San Angelo, TX	Private	10.4	18	2110
W O Sasser Seafood Inc	906	Savannah, GA	Private	10.0	18	9130
Circle E Feed Lot Inc	907	Potwin, KS	Private	12.9	17	2110
Delta Cotton Co-Operative Inc	908	Marmaduke, AR	Private	10.0	17	7240
Portland Gin Co	909	Portland, AR	Private	12.0	17	7240
Cp Meilland Inc	910	Wasco, CA	Private	10.0	16	1810

D&B COMPANY RANKINGS BY EMPLOYMENT

Company	Rank	Location	Type	Sales ($ mil.)	Employ-ment	Primary SIC
Puleo Tree Co, Inc	911	South Plainfield, NJ	Private	14.0	16	8119
Van's Pine Nursery, Inc	912	West Olive, MI	Private	26.4	16	1810
Ashbritt, Inc.	913	Pompano Beach, FL	Private	10.5	15	7829
Beef Belt Feeders Inc	914	Scott City, KS	Private	24.4	15	2110
Borders, Nowell	915	Edinburg, TX	Private	11.5	15	1610
Childress Gin & Elevator Co	916	Monette, AR	Private	10.0	15	7240
Danielski Harvesting & Farming	917	Valentine, NE	Private	11.1	15	1910
Dimare Homestead, Inc	918	Homestead, FL	Private	56.1	15	1610
Everett Ashurst	919	El Centro, CA	Private	10.0	15	2799
Gilder Timber Inc	920	Glenwood, GA	Private	13.0	15	2411
Glasscock County Coop	921	Garden City, TX	Private	11.0	15	7240
Great American Farms Inc	922	Pompano Beach, FL	Private	30.0	15	1910
Harllee Packing, Inc	923	Palmetto, FL	Private	10.0	15	7230
John Knevelbaard Dairy	924	Corona, CA	Private	10.0	15	2419
Peters Runnells Cattle Co Inc	925	Laredo, TX	Private	22.0	15	2110
Ray Wiegand Nursery Inc	926	Macomb, MI	Private	11.5	15	1810
Simonian Brothers Inc	927	Fowler, CA	Private	11.0	15	7230
Southern Se Reg Aqucltre Assn	928	Ketchikan, AK	Private	11.6	15	9219
Starker Forests Inc	929	Corvallis, OR	Private	10.1	15	8110
Tejas Feeders, Ltd.	930	Pampa, TX	Private	27.5	15	2110
Thomas Produce Co	931	Boca Raton, FL	Private	36.5	15	1619
Venture Milling Co	932	Seaford, DE	Private	22.3	15	7230
Washington Lttuce Vgetable Co	933	Puyallup, WA	Private	20.0	15	7230
ASP Enterprises Inc	934	Miami, FL	Private	12.2	14	1320
Calberi Inc	935	Santa Ana, CA	Private	15.0	14	7230
Cedar Bluff Cattle Feeders	936	Ellis, KS	Private	20.0	14	2110
Emerald Packing Company Inc	937	Orlando, FL	Private	10.8	14	7230
Frio Feeders LLC	938	Hereford, TX	Private	20.0	14	7510
Timberland Mgmt Services Inc	939	Centreville, MS	Private	10.0	14	2411
Premier Swine Breeding Systems	940	Michigantown, IN	Private	17.0	13	7510
American Wilderness Resources	941	Queensbury, NY	Private	12.0	12	8110
Bracht Feedyards, Inc	942	West Point, NE	Private	25.0	12	2110
Dimare Ruskin Inc	943	Ruskin, FL	Private	20.2	12	7230
Gary T Raak & Associates Inc	944	Elko, MN	Private	10.0	12	2729
Pine-Belt Inc	945	Monticello, AR	Private	11.4	12	8519
S M Jones & Co Inc	946	Canal Point, FL	Private	11.0	12	7230
Sellers Farms, Inc	947	Lyons, KS	Private	10.2	12	1110
Weborg Cattle Inc	948	Pender, NE	Private	16.0	12	2110
Asc Far East Inc	949	Seattle, WA	Private	50.0	11	9120
Bromm Cattle Co Inc	950	Craig, NE	Private	20.0	11	2110
Funston Gin Co	951	Funston, GA	Private	18.6	11	7240
MacMillan Bloedel Timberlands	952	Montgomery, AL	Private	14.8	11	8110
A & P Growers Co-Op Inc	953	Tulare, CA	Private	20.6	10	1749
Black Gold Farms	954	Forest River, ND	Private	11.0	10	1340
Gossett's Inc	955	Dumas, TX	Private	15.0	10	2120
Haida Corp	956	Hydaburg, AK	Private	13.5	10	8110
Pioneer Growers Cooperative	957	Belle Glade, FL	Private	40.0	10	1610
S Stamoules Inc	958	Mendota, CA	Private	14.2	10	7230
Sauvage Gas Co	959	Las Vegas, NV	Private	10.0	10	1190
Sunniland Fruit Inc	960	Stockton, CA	Private	12.4	10	7230
Surabian Packing Co Inc	961	Reedley, CA	Private	12.0	10	7230
Thomas Creek Lumber & Log Co	962	Stayton, OR	Private	15.0	10	2411
Yeomans Wood & Timber Inc	963	Swainsboro, GA	Private	14.3	10	2411
Arabi Gin Co Inc	964	Arabi, GA	Private	14.6	9	7240
Goschie Farms Inc	965	Silverton, OR	Private	250.0	9	1399
Annette Island Packing Co	966	Metlakatla, AK	Private	12.0	8	9120
Elbow Enterprises Inc	967	Visalia, CA	Private	25.0	8	7240
Federal Dryer & Storage Co	968	England, AR	Private	18.8	8	7230
Hansen Ranches	969	Corcoran, CA	Private	15.0	8	1910
O P C Farms Inc	970	Tracy, CA	Private	10.0	8	1910
Peach Orchard Gin Co Inc	971	Gideon, MO	Private	11.6	8	7240
Perrier Feed Lot	972	Dodge City, KS	Private	12.0	8	2110
Reynolds Cattle Co	973	Longmont, CO	Private	15.0	8	2110
Roberts Enterprises Inc	974	Phoenix, AZ	Private	60.0	8	2110
Valley Harvesting & Pkg Inc	975	Heber, CA	Private	40.3	8	7229
Workingman's Friend Oil, Inc	976	Topeka, KS	Private	15.5	8	2120
J E Estes Wood Co Inc	977	Monroeville, AL	Private	12.5	7	2411
Jesse F Miner	978	San Jacinto, CA	Private	10.6	7	2120
Red Rock Cattle Company Inc	979	Red Rock, AZ	Private	13.0	7	2120
Summit Farms Inc	980	Kent City, MI	Private	10.0	7	1750

D&B COMPANY RANKINGS BY EMPLOYMENT

Company	Rank	Location	Type	Sales ($ mil.)	Employ- ment	Primary SIC
Tom Barber	981	Madison, IN	Private	14.0	7	7810
American Raisin Packers Inc	982	Selma, CA	Private	11.5	6	7230
Columbia River Sugar Co	983	Moses Lake, WA	Private	21.0	6	1910
Farmington Fresh	984	Stockton, CA	Private	12.0	6	1759
Hayes Feed Yard Inc	985	Silver Creek, NE	Private	10.0	6	2110
Material Processing Inc	986	Dakota City, NE	Private	20.0	6	7119
Mobley Gin Co Inc	987	Moultrie, GA	Private	20.1	6	7240
Premium Gold Angus Beef, Inc	988	Austin, TX	Private	12.0	6	2120
Chief Mattawa Orchards	989	Mattawa, WA	Private	10.0	5	1750
Delta Gin Co Inc	990	Newellton, LA	Private	12.0	5	7240
Fisher Ranch Corp	991	Blythe, CA	Private	14.3	5	1910
Five Crowns, Inc	992	Brawley, CA	Private	23.6	5	1610
G & S Livestock	993	Attica, IN	Private	23.0	5	1190
James Abbate Inc	994	Fresno, CA	Private	16.0	5	7230
Johnson Farms	995	St. Francisville, IL	Private	100.0	5	1910
Judson Inc	996	Pennington, AL	Private	12.0	5	8110
Map Inc	997	Oregon City, OR	Private	10.7	5	8510
McCleskey Cotton Company LLC	998	Bronwood, GA	Private	10.0	5	1310
Planning Dsign Cllborative Inc	999	Richmond, VA	Private	18.6	5	7810
Timberland Silvicultural Services	1000	Monticello, AR	Private	86.2	5	8510
Worth Gin Co, Inc	1001	Sylvester, GA	Private	16.0	5	1310
Canadian Feedyards, Inc.	1002	Canadian, TX	Private	23.6	4	2110
Fletcher Challenge Forest Usa	1003	Hanover, MD	Private	48.0	4	8510
M & M Poultry Farm	1004	North Franklin, CT	Private	10.0	4	2520
Mivco Packing Co	1005	Salinas, CA	Private	60.3	4	1610
S and P Cattle Co LLC	1006	Moody, TX	Private	10.0	4	2120
Terratherm Environmental Services	1007	Houston, TX	Private	10.0	4	7110
William E Mcbryde Inc	1008	Uvalde, TX	Private	10.0	4	1610
Woodland Services, Inc	1009	Arlington, WA	Private	18.0	4	2411
Batiz Greenhouses Inc	1010	San Diego, CA	Private	10.0	3	1820
Blue North Fisheries Inc	1011	Seattle, WA	Private	10.0	3	9130
Central Cal Tmato Growers Coop	1012	Merced, CA	Private	20.0	3	7230
Hansford County Feeders LP	1013	Gruver, TX	Private	15.0	3	2110
Hi-Lo Oil Co, Inc	1014	Topeka, KS	Private	31.2	3	2120
Latigo Trading Co Inc	1015	Clint, TX	Private	10.0	3	7510
Ml Macadamia Orchards, L.P.	1016	Honolulu, HI	Public	12.1	3	1730
Mossberg Sanitation Inc	1017	Great Bend, KS	Private	11.7	3	7510
Organics Management Co	1018	Oak Park, IL	Private	30.0	3	7110
Schudel Enterprises, L.L.C.	1019	Corvallis, OR	Private	14.0	3	8119
Superior Lumber Co Inc	1020	Glendale, OR	Private	20.0	3	2411
Azcona Harvesting	1021	Greenfield, CA	Private	10.3	2	7610
Don Smith Cattle	1022	Correctionville, IA	Private	12.2	2	2120
L & J Ranch Inc	1023	St. Libory, NE	Private	21.0	2	2110
Western Fresh Fruit Sales	1024	Coachella, CA	Private	14.0	2	1910
Wispig LLC	1025	Clinton, WI	Private	15.0	2	2130
McGee Timber Co Inc	1026	Duck Hill, MS	Private	15.0	1	8110
Oscar Ortega	1027	Thermal, CA	Private	11.5	1	1720
TDM Farms Inc	1028	Newton Grove, NC	Private	17.5	1	2130

MERGERS & ACQUISITIONS

The following essay presents a look at merger and acquisition activity in the Agriculture sector. A general overview of M&A activity is followed by a listing of actual merger and acquisition events. Purchasing companies are listed in alphabetical order, with a paragraph set aside for each acquisition.

This essay discusses recent merger and acquisition activity in the industry and its effect on the industry. The essay is followed by a list of significant acquisitions and mergers.

The agriculture sector continued a long-standing pattern of consolidation between 1997 and 1999. The industry has long been primarily associated with the thousands of small family farms spread across the nation. When one speaks of acquisitions in agriculture, what springs first to mind is the acquisition of small family farms by large corporate farms. Although precise figures for such acquisitions are difficult to come by, this has been the most important trend in American agriculture for a century. The long-term corporatization of farming is evident in U.S. Department of Agriculture (USDA) statistics: The number of American farms dropped from a peak of 6.8 million in 1935 to around 2 million in the mid-1990s, while the amount of land in cultivation remained constant at approximately 1 billion acres. Between 1959 and 1992 the number of farms in the United States declined by 48 percent while the average acreage per farm increased by 62 percent and the average annual sales per farm increased 1,000 percent.

According to information presented to Congress by Mark Drabenstott of the Federal Reserve Bank of Kansas City, 1998 witnessed a surge in farms being auctioned off - similar to the wave of farm failures in the 1980s. In contrast to the 1980s, in the 1990s, small farmers left farming voluntarily, they were not foreclosed. Those sales of farms, according to Drabenstott, had two sources: First, plummeting commodity prices made it necessary for farmers to exist on ever-thinner margins. Furthermore, farmers rushed to be among the first to sell their land, recalling that those who had waited too long in the 1980s took a loss.

The drop in commodity prices was one of the prime engines of the consolidation in agriculture in the late 1990s. Drabenstott described two types of consolidation that resulted. The first he called "cost-savings . . . driven by one simple principle—the low-cost player survives. "Simply put, large farms could be operated at a significantly lower cost per acre than small ones. The second variety, which Drabenstott said had potentially larger implications for the future of agriculture, was "supply chain" consolidation. This form was marked first by the establishment of strategic alliances between producers, suppliers, distributors and retailers, and later by increasing degrees of vertical integration within a single field. By 1998 the broiler industry—chickens—was vertically integrated to a high degree. But consolidation was underway in other livestock sectors as well. By 1999 four beef packers accounted for nearly 80 percent of steer and heifer slaughter.

Hog packing entered a similar phase of concentration in 1997-98. Some analysts attributed that to a collapse in hog prices in late 1998; others say prices fell so much because of industry concentration. From 1996 to 1998 the top four companies in the industry boosted their share of hog slaughter by 10 points to 54 percent of the market total. Hog production, once the domain of the small farmer, is being taken over by large corporations. That trend is evident in the fact that in 1999 some 50 percent of hogs were produced under contract for large supply chains as opposed to just five percent around 1980.

One thing most experts agree on: the concentration of agricultural production in fewer but larger hands has resulted in benefits for consumers. Prices have dropped, yields have increased, and quality—depending on who one talks to—has improved. These advantages are largely the result of rapid improvements in agricultural science, above all biotechnology and genetic engineering. A major trend has been the involvement of the chemical industry in agriculture.

Monsanto has been an important player in this area. In 1996 and early 1997 Monsanto spent over $6 billion on buying seed companies, including $1.02 billion for Holden's Foundation Seed. In June 1998 it purchased the seed operations of Cargill Inc. for $1.4 billion. At the end of 1998 it spent $2.3 billion for DeKalb Genetics Corp. By 1999 Monsanto was in the forefront of the genetic revolution in agriculture, with varieties of genetically-altered corn, soybean, and cotton in wide cultivation. Its main competitor in this area was another company that had first established itself as a powerhouse in chemicals: DuPont. In the fall of 1997 DuPont bought soy protein producer Protein Technologies International for $1.5 billion. In March 1999 it announced the purchase of Pioneer Hi-Bred International, a leading producer of farm seed, for an astounding $7.7 billion. Dow Chemical acquired Mycogen, an agricultural biotech company, in September 1998 for $322 million.

Accompanying their investment in agricultural biotech companies is a gradual divestment of their traditional chemical production facilities. In September 1997, for example, Monsanto initiated a fundamental shift in direction when it divested its core chemicals businesses in order to concentrate on life science, most importantly, the development and production of genetically altered seed. Around the same time, Rhone-Poulenc culminated its transformation from chemicals to life science. The change is taking place for different reasons. Biotech and genetic engineering in agricultural are seen as high-growth industries, both by executives and investors; the growth potential for chemicals is much lower. There is also a perception that the companies that take charge of the sector while the genetic revolution in agriculture is still in its infancy will win control of the field.

The consolidation of this sector of agriculture will result in a fundamental restructuring felt from the top down to the level of individual farmers and consumers. For instance, when Monsanto buys DeKalb Genetics, it is getting far more than production capacity and a customer base. It is acquiring trademarked intellectual property in the form of gene sequences in the seed it sells. It retains all rights over that seed. As in the case of other types of intellectual property, other companies cannot produce seed with those gene sequences without first signing a licensing agreement with Monsanto. Also, farmers who purchase engineered seed are more and more frequently being required to sign an agreement stating that they will not use seed harvested from their genetically-engineered crops. Seed companies seem to retain control of their product and its progeny in perpetuity.

A variety of factors favor the takeover of smaller research companies, like DeKalb, by giants like Monsanto. First, biotech research is capital-intensive. One investment banker estimated that Monsanto spent over $1 billion on research before it was able to market its first genetically-altered seed. Second, larger companies have sales know-how and distribution networks that smaller, research-based companies do not possess. Finally, the intellectual property and licensing issues make legal costs a significant factor for companies active in agricultural biotech. One analyst has gone so far as to say that litigation is the force driving many acquisitions. For example, Mycogen's profits were significantly affected by high litigation costs—costs that for Dow were insignificant.

A number of super mergers and acquisitions were either planned or consummated between 1997 and 1999. DuPont acquired Pioneer Hi-Bred International; Monsanto purchased Delta & Pine Land; Cargill Inc. purchased Continental Grain's grain merchandising business. All raised anti-trust questions and gave rise to fears that American farming, once and for all, would become the domain of conglomerates.

The DuPont/Pioneer deal, first announced in summer 1997, was seen as a spark that induced other agricultural companies to become involved in acquisitions and mergers. Growth and strategic alliances were seen as critical to success in the industry. With a value of more than $7 billion, the deal also offers an idea of the financial stakes. Monsanto's planned purchase of Delta & Pine Land, first announced in the summer of 1998, was still under the scrutiny of the Antitrust Division of the U.S. Department of Justice in mid-1999. Such mergers and acquisitions spurred, in the first half of 1999, a round of Congressional hearings on the effects of consolidation on farming in the United States.

The most concern, however, was caused by Cargill Inc.'s announcement that it was going to acquire the Continental Grain Company. In 1998 Cargill was listed in *Forbes* as the largest private company in the United States; Continental Grain was number five. They are the top two exporters of grain. Both companies are involved in livestock production and feed, as well as grain storage. The merger was seen in many quarters as an antitrust threat, first, because it eliminated Cargill's main competitor and united the significant, strategically located grain storage capacities of the two companies under a single roof. Second, the acquisition created a giant that controlled 35 percent of U.S. corn, soybean and wheat exports. Critics pointed out that the deal could give rise to abuses similar to those of which Microsoft has been accused: exclusive marketing arrangements, products bundled in merchandising arrangements, and penalizing customers for doing business with competitors. Farmers feared that the new company would be able to dictate low grain prices; apologists maintained that it would improve the competitiveness of American farmers in the world market. Both claims, of course, amounted to the same thing: Cargill would keep grain prices low. A study of the acquisition, done at the Department of Economics of Iowa State University, maintained that it would not decrease competition among buyers of grain from farmers. The study also found that the combination of Cargill and Continental's grain storage capacity would not give the company a stranglehold on delivery.

Continental Grain's decision to sell was probably motivated by the sharp reduction in American grain exports—upon which the company had depended—in the 1990s. It was beyond the point of cost-effectively restructuring. Cargill hoped to use Continental Grain's network to expand its global presence and to maintain Continental Grain's volume while holding costs down through economies of scale.

Accompanying Cargill's plans to purchase Continental Grain were its efforts to sell its own seed businesses. In June 1998 Monsanto reached an agreement to pay $1.4 billion for all of Cargill's international seed operations, including seed research, production, testing, and sales and distribution facilities in Latin America, Europe, Asia, and Africa. Monsanto said the acquisition would strengthen its transformation into a biotech company. Cargill hoped it would strengthen its ties to Monsanto—a hope that seemed to come true just weeks later when the two firms announced a joint venture for animal feed and grain processing products.

In September 1998 Cargill agreed to sell its remaining seed divisions to AgrEvo GmbH, a subsidiary of the pharmaceuticals giants Hoechst Marion Roussel (HMR) and Schering GmbH, for $650 million. AgrEvo intended the acquisition to place it in a strategic position in the biotech market. However, AgrEvo called off the deal in February 1999 when Pioneer Hi-Bred International Inc. filed suit, alleging that Cargill had obtained Pioneer genetic material illegally for use in its research.

Nonetheless, AgrEvo is expected to become one of the dominant players in the field, along with DuPont, Monsanto and Dow, over the coming decades. Cargill's sale of its seed operations—which had totaled about four percent of the American market—was seen as an acknowledgment that it wanted no part of the expensive race to genetically engineer new seed varieties.

Another earth-shattering deal-that-wasn't was first publicized in the summer of 1999. An SEC filing made by Pioneer Hi-Bred International Inc. revealed that DuPont had considered a merger with Monsanto. Monsanto had posted a loss of $250 million for 1998 after having spent some $6 billion on buying seed companies. The company reduced some of its debt through a stock offering in November 1998. In the first half of 1999 it sold its Ortho lawn and garden division for $300 million, the Wellbridge fitness operation for an estimated $15 million, NSC Technologies Inc. for $125 million, and was planning to sell Nutrasweet and its Stoneville cotton seed company. Analysts noted that the debt reduction resulting from the sales made Monsanto more attractive as an acquisition. The deal fell through when Pioneer—whose acquisition DuPont was also negotiating—told DuPont that a merger with Monsanto would negatively affect the Pioneer-DuPont relationship.

Mergers & Acquisitions

AgrEvo, the joint venture of **Hoechst AG** and **Schering AG,** acquired **Biogenic Technologies By,** a Dutch company that produces hybrid and non-hybrid seeds in Asia and the Middle East, for an undisclosed sum in February 1999. [*Chemical Market Reporter*, 3/1/99.]

—acquired **Proagro,** India's second largest seed company, for an undisclosed sum, in February 1999. [*Chemical Week*, 3/3/99.]

— the joint venture of Hoechst AG and Schering AG, acquired **Sementes Ribeiral, Sementes Fartura,** and **Mitla Pesquisa Agricola,** three Brazilian hybrid corn seeds producing companies for an undisclosed amount in May 1999. [*South American Business Information*, 6/1/99.]

BGR acquired assets of **West Coast Shellfish** for an undisclosed amount in September 1998. [*Financial Times*, 10/1/98.]

Bowater Inc. sold 1 million acres of Maine timberland, along with the **Pinkham Lumber Co.** sawmill, to for $220 million in November 1998. [*Pulp & Paper*, 12/98.]

Cactus Feeders Inc. acquired three feedlots from Koch Beef Co. for an undisclosed sum in March 1999. The deal made Cactus the company the largest beef cattle feeder in the world. [*Feedstuffs*, 3/8/99.]

Cargill Inc. acquired **Continental Grain Co.'s** grain merchandising business for an undisclosed amount on July 13, 1999 The acquisition created a business that accounted for 35% of U.S. export volumes for corn, soybean and wheat. [*PR Newswire*, 7/13/99.]

Cathlamet Timber Co. acquired 117,000 acres of timberland in southwest Washington from **Willamette Industries Inc.** for $234 million in January 1999. [*Wood Technology*, 3/99.]

Cenex Harvest Sales, a producer to consumer, farmer-owned cooperative, and **Farmland Industries,** the largest farmer owned cooperative in North America, announced a merger on May 6, 1999. The two groups had 1998 revenues of $16.8 billion. The merger was expected to be completed in June 2000 [*Kansas City Star,* 7/7/99.]

Seed producer **Cenex/Land O'Lakes (LOL)** agreed to acquire the retail distribution business of **Terra Industries Inc.** for $361 million in cash and business earnings from Apr 1, 1999 onwards in May 1999. The acquisition was expected to double Cenex's sales. [*Feedstuffs*, 5/10/99.]

ConAgra Inc. and **Tiger Oats Ltd.**, a South-African company, purchased a majority stake in **ITC Agro-Tech Ltd.,** a branded and commodity-edible oil business in Secunderabad, India for an undisclosed price in November 1997. [*Nation's Restaurant News*, 11/10/97.]

The Conservation Fund purchased 300,000 acres of timberlands in the northeastern United States from **Champion International Corp.** for $76.2 million on July 1, 1999. [*Wall Street Journal*, 7/2/99.]

Crown Pacific announced it would purchase 65,000 acres of timberland in northwestern Washington from **Trillium Corp.** for $153 million on September 15, 1997. [*Knight Ridder/Tribune Business News*, 9/16/97.]

Dole Food Co. announced the acquisition **Finesse Farms** and **Four Farmers, Inc.**, both importers of flowers from Ecuador and Columbia for an undisclosed price on August 4, 1998. [*Miami Herald*, 8/4/98.]

Dow Chemical acquired 100 percent ownership of **Mycogen Corp.,** an agricultural biotechnology company, for $322 million. [*Wall Street Journal*, 9/2/98.]

DuPont announced the purchase of **Pioneer Hi-Bred International,** a leader in plant biotechnology and a leading supplier of farm seed for $7.7 billion. [*New York Times*, 3/15/99.]

Emergent Eugenics, an affiliate of Hicks, Muse, Tate & Furst Inc., agreed to purchase **Stoneville Pedigreed Seed Company**, a cotton seed division, from Monsanto Company for an undisclosed amount of cash on August 6, 1999. [*PR Newswire*, 8/6/99.]

Enso Timber and **Schweighofer** announced they would merge in a deal that involved an undisclosed amount of cash and stock on October 13, 1998. [*Wall Street Journal*, 10/2/98.] Europe, Oct 14, 1998.

Farmers Cooperative Association merged with **Pauline Farmers Cooperative Elevator and Supply Association,** an agricultural supply and marketing cooperative with locations in Pauline and Burlingame, Kansas on September 1, 1998. [*Knight-Ridder/Tribune Business News*, 8/15/98.]

Foster & Gallagher, Inc. of Peoria Illinois announced the acquisition of two seed companies, **Gurney's Seed & Nursery Co.** and **Henry Field's Seed & Nursery Co.** for an undisclosed price on July 13, 1999. [*Journal Star,* 7/13/99.]

Genus plc of Crewe, Cheshire, England agreed in principle to acquire **ABS Global, Inc.** of DeForest, Wisconsin for an undisclosed sum in September 1999. Genus is the leader in the UK cattle breeding industry. [*PR Newswire*, 8/3/99.]

Harvest States Cooperatives and **Cenex Inc.** merged forming a new company valued at $10 billion in June 1998. [*Feedstuffs*, 6/9/98.]

Hicks, Muse, Tate & Furst Inc. acquired L. Daehnfeldt A/S, a Danish horticultural seed company, for DKr 305 million in November 1998. [*PR Newswire*, 8/6/99.]

Koch Agriculture, a subsidiary of Koch Industries, purchased Purina Mills, the nation's largest animal feed company, for an undisclosed amount on March 18, 1998. Koch is the second-largest privately-owned company in the United States. [*Knight-Ridder/Tribune Business News*, 3/19/98.]

Marine Genetics Corp. acquired American Proteins Inc.'s US fishing and production assets for an un-disclosed price in November 1997. [*Chemical Market Reporter*, 11/17/97.]

McDonald Investment Co. Inc. of Birmingham, Ala-bama purchased 816,000-acre tract of timberland in Northern Ontario from Algonna Central Corp., Cana-da's largest inland shipping company, for C$60.2 mil-lion in September 1997. [*Wood Technology*, 10/97.]

Michigan Livestock Exchange and Southern States Cooperative Inc. merged on April 1, 1998. [*Feedstuffs*, 3/23/98.]

Minor's Landscape Services Inc. of Dallas-Fort Worth, Texas purchased Graeber & Associates, a landscaping and contracting firm in Plano Texas, for an undisclosed price in December 1997. [*Chemical Market Reporter*, 11/17/97.]

Monsanto Co. acquired DeKalb Genetics Corp. for an estimated $2.3 billion in December 1998. [*Chemical Market Reporter*, 12/7/98.]

—acquired Cargill Inc.'s international seed operations for $1.4 billion June 1998. [*Feedstuffs*, 7/6/98.]

National Fish and Seafood and Pacific Andes merged in April 1998. [*Nation's Restaurant News*, 3/23/98.]

Northland Cranberries, Inc., a cranberry grower and juice maker based in Wisconson Rapids, WI, agreed to acquire Minot Food Packers, a company in Bridgeton, NJ that specializes in cranberry products, for $37.6 million on May 1, 1998. [*Milwaukee Journal Sentinel*, 5/6/98.]

Perdue Farms of Salisbury Maryland acquired DeLuca Inc., a manufacturer of the Ed & Joan DeLuca branded fresh meal components for ??? in June 1998. [*Supermarket News*, 7/6/98.]

Plains Cotton Cooperative Association (PCCA), a farmer-owned cooperative headquartered in Lubbock, Texas purchased Mission Valley Textiles (MVT), a leading producer of yarn-dyed woven fabric for the apparel and home-furnishings markets for $25-million in May 1998. [*Textile World*, 6/98.]

Plum Creek of Seattle Washington agreed to purchase 905,000 acres of timberlands in Maine from the South African company, Saapi for $180 million. The sale was the second largest timberland deal in U.S. history. [*Pulp & Paper*, 12/98.]

Reservoir Capital Group LLC, an investment group, acquired operations including 13,000 acres of citrus groves from Orange-co, Inc. in a deal estimated at $72 million on July 16, 1999. [*St. Petersburg Times*, 7/16/99.]

Salasnek Fisheries LLC of Detroit and Mercy Fish Co. of Minnesota agreed to merge, forming the Mid-west's largest seafood distributor, in February 1998. The new company was to operate under a Chicago-based holding company, Palestra/SFI LLC, which al-ready owned Salasnek Fisheries. [*Crain's Detroit Business*, 2/9/98.]

Simpson Timber Co. acquired over 5000 acres of timberland from Equitable Insurance Co. for an un-disclosed price in September 1997. [*Wood Technology*, 10/97.]

Smithfield Foods Inc. acquired Carroll's Foods Inc. and its affiliated companies for 4.2 million shares of stock and $231 million in debt assumption on May 9, 1999. The deal made Smithfield the largest hog pro-ducer in the world. [*Feedstuffs*, 5/17/99.]

A Southstar Timber Resources LLC affiliate agreed to purchase 529,000 acres of timberland in Alabama, Tennessee and Mississippi from Kimberly-Clark Corp. for an estimated $300 million in January 1999.[*Wood Technology*, 3/99.]

SWA Group and **Slaney Santana Group**, two of Houston's largest architectural landscapers, merged in February 1998 to form the city's largest landscaping firm. [*Houston Business Journal*, 1/30/98.]

Tembec Inc. acquired **Crestbrook Forest Industries** of Cranbrook of British Columbia for C$201 million in debt takeover and C$70.4 million in cash in April 1999. [*Wood Technology*, 3/99.]

Subsidiaries of **TimberWest Timber Trust** and **Doman Industries** announced their intent to purchase **Pacific Forest Products** together for C$573 million in August 1997. [*Wood Technology*, 9/97.]

TT Acquisitions, Inc., a subsidiary of **Trident Seafoods Corp.** in Seattle, Washington acquired seafood assets of **Tyson Foods,** including sea-worthy fishing and processing vessels, associated fishing rights and onshore processing plants, for an undisclosed price in July 1999. Tyson's fishing fleet is one of the largest on the northwestern Pacific Ocean. [*PR Newswire*, 7/19/99.]

US Timberlands purchased a 45,000 tract of old-growth and second-growth ponderosa pine to **Ochoco Lumber Co.,** Prineville, Oregon for a reported $110 million in August 1997. [*Wood Technology*, 9/97.]

U.S. Timberlands Yakima LLC acquired 56,000 Acres of Timberland from **Boise Cascade** for an undisclosed amount in June 1999. [*Wall Street Journal*, 6/10/99.] *New York Times*, June 10, 1999.

USA Floral Products Inc. announced the acquisition of **Florimex Worldwide** from **Dimon Inc.** for an undisclosed amount on August 13, 1998. [*New York Times*, 8/14/98.]

Further Reading

"Dupont and Monsanto discussed merger, filing reveals." *New York Times*, 7/3/99.

Grooms, Lynn. "When companies converge: What does 'from dirt to dinner plate' mean to growers?" *Farm Industry News*, 10/1/98.

Hayenga, Marvin, and Robert Wisner. "Study evaluates Cargill's purchase of Continental Grain's grain business." *Feedstuffs*, 2/8/99.

Hoffman, John. "Monsanto Buys Cargill's Seeds In Biotech Deal." *Chemical Market Reporter*, 7/6/98.

Howie, Michael. "AgrEvo drops bid for Cargill's seed operations." *Feedstuffs*, 2/8/99.

Howie, Michael. "DuPont/Pioneer deal may spur industry reorganization." *Feedstuffs*, 8/18/97.

"In the mill." *Economist*, 3/20/99.

McDonald, Dale. "The high cost of consolidation." *Farm Industry News*, 4/1/99.

"Monsanto: The makings of an agro monopoly?" *ECN-European Chemical News*, 5/25/98.

Muirhead, Sarah. "Farmland, Cenex Harvest States see unification as means to gain value." *Feedstuffs*, 5/10/99.

"Splicing drugs and agriculture: Technology, markets and Wall Street launch a new breed of firms." *Chemical Week*, 10/29/97.

—Gerald E. Brennan

This chapter presents a selection of business and professional associations active in the Agriculture sector. The information shown is adapted from Gale's *Encyclopedia of Associations* series and provides detailed and comprehensive information on nonprofit membership organizations.

Entries are arranged in alphabetical order. Categories included are name, address, contact person, telphone, toll-free number, fax number, E-mail address and web site URL (when provided). A text block shows founding date, staff, number of members, budget, and a general description of activities.

ADOPT RURAL RESTORATION
PO Box B
Sikeston, MO 63801
Peter C. Myers, Sr., Pres. of Bd.
PH: (573)472-4673
TF: (800)472-4674
FX: (573)471-7971
Founded: 1988. **Staff:** 3. **Members:** 1,000. **Budget:** $65,000. Seeks to restore and revitalize rural America to ensure the food supply for future generations. Works to raise public awareness as to the value and dignity of farm and ranch families. Offers personal assistance to farm families. Fosters communication and exchange between members of rural and urban communities. Organizes prayer groups and promotes Christian values.

AG COMMUNICATIONS IN EDUCATION
PO Box 110811
Gainesville, FL 32611-0811
Julia Goaddy, Coordinator
PH: (352)392-9588
FX: (352)392-7902
E-mail: ace@gnv.ifas.ufl.edu
Founded: 1912. **Staff:** 1. **Members:** 700. **Budget:** $80,000. Agricultural technologists and educators. Seeks to increase public awareness of agricultural, natural resources, and human sciences and related topics. Conducts training courses to increase the effectiveness of agricultural educational programs, government agencies, and research projects.

AGRIBUSINESS COUNCIL
1312 18th St. NW, Ste. 300
Washington, DC 20036
Nicholas E. Hollis, Pres.
PH: (202)296-4563
FX: (202)887-9178
E-mail: agenergy@aol.com
Founded: 1967. **Staff:** 3. **Members:** 400. Business organizations, universities and foundations, and individuals interested in stimulating and encouraging agribusiness in cooperation with the public sector, both domestic and international. Seeks to aid in relieving the problems of world food supply. Supports coordinated agribusiness in the developing nations by identifying opportunities for investment of U.S. private-sector technology management and financial resources. Advises agribusiness leaders about selected developing countries with good investment climates; brings potential investment opportunities to the attention of U.S. agribusiness firms; coordinates informal network of state agribusiness councils and grassroots organization; encourages companies to make investment feasibility studies in agribusiness; provides liaison and information exchange between agribusiness firms, governments, international organizations, universities, foundations, and other groups with the objective of identifying areas of cooperation and mutual interest; encourages projects geared to the conversion of subsistence farming to intensive, higher income agriculture in order to bring the world' rural populations, wherever feasible, into the market economy.

AGRICULTURAL RESEARCH INSTITUTE
9650 Rockville Pike
Bethesda, MD 20814
Richard A. Herrett, Exec.Dir.
PH: (301)530-7122
FX: (301)530-7007
E-mail: ari@nalusda.gov
Founded: 1951. **Staff:** 2. **Members:** 125. **Budget:** $250,000. Originally an integral part of the National Academy of Sciences, incorporated separately in 1973. Analyzes agricultural problems and promotes research by its members to solve them. (ARI does not engage in research activities itself.)

AGRICULTURE COUNCIL OF AMERICA
11020 King St., Ste. 205
Overland Park, KS 66210
W. Patrick Nichols, Pres. & CEO

PH: (913)491-1895
FX: (913)491-6502
E-mail: info@agday.org
URL: http://www.agday.org
Founded: 1973. **Staff:** 8. **Members:** 600. **Budget:** $1,200,000. Farm and commodity organizations, local and national agribusiness firms, co-operatives, ranchers, and individual farmers. Promotes sound agricultural policy and provides communication between the farmer and the urban consumer and decision-makers in Washington, DC. Conducts FoodWatch, a public education and awareness program to build public confidence in the food and fiber industry. Maintains the FoodWatch Information Resource Center. Compiles statistics; conducts surveys; develops and produces educational materials. Coordinates National Agriculture Day.

AGRISERVICES FOUNDATION
648 W. Sierra Ave.
Clovis, CA 93612-0151
Dr. Marion Eugene Ensminger, Pres.
PH: (209)299-2263
FX: (209)299-2098
Founded: 1964. Governed by a board of trustees and a board of advisors, whose purposes are to foster and support programs of education, research, and development that will contribute toward wider and more effective application of science and technology to the practice of agriculture. Programs include: alleviating world food hunger and malnutrition; sponsorship of travel-study groups abroad, which are in-depth studies of agriculture in other countries; short courses abroad.

ALLIANCE FOR SUSTAINABILITY
1521 University Ave. SE
Minneapolis, MN 55414
Ksenia Rudensiuk, Exec.Dir.
PH: (612)331-1099
FX: (612)379-1527
E-mail: iasa@mtn.org
URL: http://www.mtn.org/iasa
Founded: 1983. **Staff:** 2. **Members:** 700. **Budget:** $50,000. Development specialists, farmers, researchers, and other individuals; cooperatives and agricultural, consumer, and environmental groups. Purpose is to promote and contribute to the establishment of agricultural systems that are economically viable, ecologically sound, and socially just and humane. Sponsors programs in education, information dissemination, organizational support, network building, and policy. Promotes information sharing and cooperation through conferences, work exchanges, and organized tours. Furnishes technical expertise in farm practices, market development, and financial planning. Operates speakers' bureau; conducts workshops. Maintains resource center providing information on biological pest control, pesticides, and sustainable agriculture. Projects stressing the theme of sustainability include the following: The Natural Step Training Seminars, the Campaign for Alternatives to Petrochemicals, Advocates for Better Health and the Environment, Center for Alternate Development Initiatives, Skiers Ending Hunger, the Kids Earth Chorus, and the Hopi Ancient Terrace Restoration.

ALPACA BREEDERS OF THE ROCKIES
38620 County Rd. 29
Elizabeth, CO 80107-8702
Ronald C. Hines, Pres.
PH: (303)988-3080
E-mail: abr@cria.com
URL: http://www.alpacabreeders.org
Founded: 1994. **Members:** 100. **Budget:** $9,000. Breeders of alpacas (an alpaca is a close relative of the Llama); processors and distributors of alpaca products. Promotes public awareness of alpacas; seeks to advance the alpaca industries. Facilitates communication and cooperation among members; conducts marketing campaigns. Participates in agricultural fairs; sponsors parades and other social activities.

AMERICAN AGRI-WOMEN
Rte. 2, Box 193
Keota, IA 52248-0193
Sandy Greiner, Pres.
Founded: 1974. **Members:** 42. **Budget:** $60,000. Farm and ranch women's organizations representing 35,000 interested persons. Promotes agriculture; seeks to present the real identity of American farmers to the rest of the population and to develop an appreciation of "the interdependence of the components of the agricultural system." Supports a marketing system which makes quality food and fiber available to all on a reasonable cost basis and at a fair profit to the farmer. Believes that the family farm system is the bulwark of the private enterprise system, and as such must be preserved. Works in areas of legislation, regulations, consumer relations, and education. Maintains resource center and speakers' bureau. Is establishing an oral history project of America's farm and ranch women entitled From Mules to Microwaves; conducts research programs.

AMERICAN AGRI-WOMEN RESOURCE CENTER
251 E. Maple Lawn Rd.
New Park, PA 17352-9436
Gail McPherson, Pres.
PH: (717)382-4878
FX: (717)382-4879
E-mail: maplelawn@cyberia.com
URL: http://www.americanagriwomen.com
Founded: 1977. **Members:** 45,000. Farm women concerned with the advancement of agricultural production within the free enterprise system. Objectives are: to formulate and disseminate educational materials which accurately represent agripolitan America for use by teachers and the public; to initiate and promote educational program to advance the interests and welfare of agriculture. Provides training for women in leadership, public relations, and communications. Conducts workshops, seminars, symposia which illustrate, explain, and inform in various subject areas from kindergarten to adult levels. Awards grants & scholarships to further AAWRC mission and purposes.

AMERICAN AGRICULTURE MOVEMENT
PO Box 399
Sunray, TX 79086
V.B. Morris, Nat. Sec.
PH: (806)733-2203
FX: (806)733-2965
URL: http://www.aaminc.org
Founded: 1977. **Staff:** 4. **Budget:** $200,000. Family farmers and ranchers concerned with governmental agricultural policy. Seeks to: establish a mechanism through which farmers can initiate and approve changes in federal agricultural policies; ensure that foreign and domestically produced agricultural products sell for the same price in the U.S. Promotes: political candidates favoring higher prices for agricultural products; borrower's rights as defined in recent farm credit legislation; cooperation among farmers' organizations and between farm and urban interests; worldwide agricultural supply management and higher prices for agricultural products in international markets. Opposes federal subsidies, excise tax increases, and the patenting of genetically-engineered animals. Achievements include: organization of a grass roots lobbying campaign; bringing the views of U.S. farmers to the attention of international agricultural bodies; changes in elevator bankruptcy laws and FmHa foreclosure procedures. Drafts opinions and supplies information to media on federal and international farm policy issues.

AMERICAN ANGUS ASSOCIATION
3201 Frederick Blvd.
St. Joseph, MO 64506
Richard L. Spader, Exec.VP
PH: (816)383-5100
FX: (816)233-9703
E-mail: angus@angus.org
URL: http://www.angus.org
Founded: 1883. **Staff:** 140. **Members:** 30,000. **Budget:** $16,000,000. Breeders and owners of purebred Angus cattle. Maintains registry for purebred Angus cattle. Collects, verifies, and publishes performance information, pedigrees, and transfers of ownership; offers premiums for the public exhibition of cattle. Promotes sale of Angus cattle in the U.S. through advertising, public information programs, and the Certified Angus Beef Program. Sponsors educational programs; offers children's services.

AMERICAN ASSOCIATION OF GRAIN INSPECTION AND WEIGHING AGENCIES
1629 K St. NW, Ste. 1100
Washington, DC 20006
Paul S. Weller, Jr., Exec.Dir.
PH: (202)785-6740
FX: (202)331-4212
E-mail: agriwash@aol.com
Founded: 1946. **Staff:** 4. **Members:** 50. **Budget:** $100,000. Private and public grain inspection agencies; suppliers and groups affiliated with the industry. Provides a forum for the formulation and promotion of policies pertinent to effective grain inspection and weighing services. Promotes cooperation between members and the Federal Grain Inspection Service. Offers professional representation on issues such as training, equipment selection, laboratory monitoring, industry standardization, and new techniques. Sponsors educational programs.

AMERICAN BANTAM ASSOCIATION
PO Box 127
Augusta, NJ 07822
Eleanor Vinhage, Sec.-Treas.
PH: (973)383-6944
FX: (973)383-6944
Founded: 1915. **Members:** 3,400. Breeders, exhibitors, judges, and others interested in bantams (miniature domestic breeds of poultry).

AMERICAN BLONDE D'AQUITAINE ASSOCIATION
PO Box 12341
North Kansas City, MO 64116
James Spawn, Contact
PH: (816)421-1305
FX: (816)421-1991
E-mail: jspawn321@aol.com
Founded: 1973. **Staff:** 3. **Members:** 160. Registers and promotes the blonde d'Aquitaine breed of cattle in the U.S.

AMERICAN BRAHMAN BREEDERS ASSOCIATION
1313 La Concha Ln.
Houston, TX 77054
Jim Reeves, Exec.VP
PH: (713)795-4444
FX: (713)795-4450
E-mail: abba@brahman.org
URL: http://www.brahman.org
Founded: 1924. **Staff:** 8. **Members:** 1,700. **Budget:** $550,000. Breeders of purebred registered Brahman cattle and others interested in Brahmans or their use for crossbreeding. Works to: keep proper records of pedigree and transfer of ownership of Brahman cattle entered in the Herd Register; assist in the sponsorship of cattle exhibitions and shows; aid scientific education concerning the breeding of Brahman cattle.

AMERICAN BRALERS ASSOCIATION
6723 Ashmore Dr.
Houston, TX 77069-2462
Margaret Watkins, Exec.Sec.
PH: (512)782-3098
Founded: 1982. **Staff:** 1. **Members:** 102. **Budget:** $65,000. Breeders and owners of Bralers, Salers, and Brahman cattle; other individuals interested in the Bralers breed. (The Bralers breed of cattle, produced by the crossbreeding of Brahman and Salers cattle, is said to be highly adaptable to adverse weather conditions, and yields lean meat. The first purebred American Bralers were calved in 1985.) Objectives are to: advance the development of the Bralers breed for the modern market through the use of genetically superior Brahman and Salers cattle; promote the traits of Bralers cattle in the commercial and purebred market; encourage the creation of effective

cooperative marketing programs with breeders of progressive and commercial purebred cattle. Maintains records of pedigrees and transfers of ownership of Bralers. Conducts research. Disseminates information on the breeding, marketing, nutritional value, and physical characteristics of Bralers cattle. Assists in the arrangement and sponsorship of cattle exhibitions and shows. Operates special feeding programs.

AMERICAN CHIANINA ASSOCIATION

PO Box 890
Platte City, MO 64079
Terry Atchison, CEO
PH: (816)431-2808
FX: (816)431-5381
E-mail: aca@sound.net
URL: http://www.chicattle.org
Founded: 1972. **Members:** 6,200. Promotes and registers Chianina cattle.

AMERICAN COTTON EXPORTER'S ASSOCIATION

PO Box 3366
Memphis, TN 38173
William E. May, Sec./Treas.
PH: (901)525-2272
FX: (901)527-8303
Founded: 1975. **Members:** 53. Purposes are to protect the financial well-being of exporters of U.S. grown cotton, to foster and improve international trade, and to preserve the principal of the sanctity of contracts.

AMERICAN COTTON SHIPPERS ASSOCIATION

PO Box 3366
Memphis, TN 38173
William E. May, Sr.VP of Foreign & Domestic Operations
PH: (901)525-2272
FX: (901)527-8303
URL: http://www.ACSA-Cotton.org
Founded: 1924. **Staff:** 10. **Members:** 425. Four affiliated regional cotton shippers' associations comprised of firms of merchants and exporters of raw cotton in bales.

AMERICAN CRANBERRY GROWERS ASSOCIATION

126 Moores Meadow Rd.
Tabernacle, NJ 08088
Neva Moore, Sec.-Treas.
PH: (609)268-0641
FX: (609)268-9232
Members: 150. Cranberry farmers; interested others. Promotes propagation, interest, and development of cranberries. Provides information on the status of cranberry crops in New Jersey. Conducts educational programs.

AMERICAN DEHYDRATED ONION AND GARLIC ASSOCIATION

221 Main St.
San Francisco, CA 94105
J. Dennis McQuaid, Sec.-Treas.
PH: (415)905-0200
FX: (415)543-4940
Founded: 1956. **Members:** 3. Dehydrators of onions and garlic products. Seeks to improve the quality of dehydrated onion and garlic products; works to increase product consumption. Establishes grade specifications and consistent nomenclature within the industry. Sponsors research programs in agricultural practices, plant breeding, and methods of analysis and packaging of industry products.

AMERICAN DEXTER CATTLE ASSOCIATION

26804 Ebenezer Rd.
Concordia, MO 64020
Rosemary Fleharty, Sec.
PH: (660)463-7704
Founded: 1912. **Members:** 450. Breeders of purebred Dexter cattle. Dexter cattle were brought to the U.S. from Ireland in 1912; the

breed is America's smallest, weighing 650-1000 lbs. Seeks to ensure the quality of the breed.

AMERICAN EGG BOARD

1460 Renaissance Dr., Ste. 301
Park Ridge, IL 60068
Louis B. Raffel, Pres.
PH: (708)296-7043
FX: (708)296-7007
Founded: 1976. **Staff:** 19. **Members:** 350. **Budget:** $14,000,000. Board of American egg producers appointed by the Secretary of Agriculture. Offers advertising, educational, research, and promotional programs designed to increase consumption of eggs and egg products. Conducts consumer educators and foodservice seminars, and food safety education programs.

AMERICAN FARM BUREAU FEDERATION

225 Touhy Ave.
Park Ridge, IL 60068
Dean R. Kleckner, Pres.
PH: (847)685-8764
FX: (847)685-8969
URL: http://www.fb.com
Founded: 1919. **Staff:** 82. **Members:** 4,800,000. Federation of 50 state farm bureaus and Puerto Rico, with membership on a family basis. Analyzes problems of members and formulates action to achieve educational improvement, economic opportunity, and social advancement. Maintains speakers' bureau; sponsors specialized education program.

AMERICAN FARM BUREAU FOUNDATION FOR AGRICULTURE

225 Touhy Ave.
Park Ridge, IL 60068
Dean R. Kleckner, Pres.
PH: (847)685-8764
TF: (800)GIFT456
FX: (847)685-8969
URL: http://www.agfoundation.org
Founded: 1967. **Staff:** 2. **Budget:** $400,000. Works to improve profit opportunities in the farming business through advancement of scientific knowledge. Initiates and finances agricultural research by contracting work with universities, public research agencies, and private research firms, in such areas as production and marketing, quality and yield improvement, mechanization, farm safety, conservation of natural resources, improved or better use of fertilizers, insecticides, and herbicides, and ways of increasing net farm income.

AMERICAN FARMLAND TRUST

1200 18th St. NW #800
Washington, DC 20036
Ralph E. Grossi, Pres.
PH: (202)331-7300
URL: http://www.farmland.org
Founded: 1980. **Staff:** 32. **Members:** 31,500. **Budget:** $6,000,000. Dedicated to stopping the loss of productive farmland and promoting farming practices which lead to a healthy environment. Disseminates information on safeguarding farmlands, through conservation easements and other voluntary conservation programs. Encourages and assists policy makers to revise federal, state, and local policies on farmland preservation. Conducts policy development assistance, public education, and land project programs. Aids landowners in private conservancy transactions.

AMERICAN GALLOWAY BREEDERS' ASSOCIATION

310 W. Spruce
Missoula, MT 59802
Bob Mullendore, Contact
PH: (406)728-5719
FX: (406)721-6300
Founded: 1888. **Staff:** 1. **Members:** 125. Breeders of registered Galloway cattle. To promote the breed and maintain a registry. Champions steers at major cattle shows.

AMERICAN GELBVIEH ASSOCIATION
10900 Dover St.
Westminster, CO 80021
PH: (303)465-2333
FX: (303)465-2339
URL: http://ops.agsci.colostate.edu/~aga
Founded: 1971. **Staff:** 15. **Members:** 2,200. **Budget:** $1,400,000.
Individuals who breed Gelbvieh cattle. Objectives are the registration of Gelbvieh cattle and the promotion of the breed. Maintains sire evaluation program.

AMERICAN GREENHOUSE VEGETABLE GROWERS ASSOCIATION
526 Brittany Dr.
State College, PA 16802
Patricia Heuser, Contact
Founded: 1983. **Members:** 190. Greenhouse vegetable growers and greenhouse suppliers. Promotes education within the field through the organization of activities and the exchange of information.

AMERICAN GUERNSEY ASSOCIATION
7614 Slate Ridge Blvd.
PO Box 666
Reynoldsburg, OH 43068
Dave Cochard, Exec.Sec.-Treas.
PH: (614)864-2409
FX: (614)864-5614
URL: http://www.usguernsey.com
Founded: 1877. **Staff:** 6. **Members:** 1,500. **Budget:** $500,000.
Breeders of registered Guernsey dairy cattle. Seeks to: conduct research to assist in the development of breeding a more profitable animal; improve marketing strategy for Guernsey milk; develop motivational programs for Guernsey breeders.

AMERICAN HEREFORD ASSOCIATION
1501 Wyandotte
Kansas City, MO 64108
Craig Husshines, Exec.VP
PH: (816)842-3757
E-mail: records@hereford.org
URL: http://www.hereford.org
Founded: 1881. **Staff:** 50. **Members:** 20,000. **Budget:** $3,500,000.
Breeders of purebred Hereford cattle. Maintains registry, pedigree, and performance records; provides fieldman assistance and guidance; operates speakers' bureau; conducts research programs; maintains hall of fame and museum; sponsors competitions; compiles statistics.

AMERICAN HIGHLAND CATTLE ASSOCIATION
200 Livestock Exchange Bldg.
4701 Marion St.
Denver, CO 80216
Ginnah Moses, Operations Mgr.
PH: (303)292-9102
FX: (303)292-9171
E-mail: ahca@envisionet.net
URL: http://www.home.eznet.net/~highland/ahca.htm
Founded: 1948. **Staff:** 2. **Members:** 950. **Budget:** $100,000. Highland cattle producers and enthusiasts. Maintains cattle registry, promotion, research, and education related to this breed.

AMERICAN-INTERNATIONAL CHAROLAIS ASSOCIATION
PO Box 20247
Kansas City, MO 64195
Dr. Bill V. Able, Exec. VP
PH: (816)464-5977
FX: (816)464-5759
E-mail: charusa@sound.net
URL: http://www.charolaisusa.com
Founded: 1957. **Staff:** 23. **Members:** 4,200. **Budget:** $1,300,000.
Breeders of Charolais and Charolais crossbred cattle in Canada, Mexico, South Africa, United Kingdom, and United States. Main-

tains registry and pedigree records. Conducts cattlemen's seminars. Sponsors the International Junior Charolais Association.

AMERICAN JERSEY CATTLE ASSOCIATION
6486 E. Main St.
Reynoldsburg, OH 43068-2362
Calvin Covington, Exec.Sec.
PH: (614)861-3636
FX: (614)861-8040
E-mail: usjersey@iwaynet.net
URL: http://www.usjersey.com
Founded: 1868. **Staff:** 40. **Budget:** $1,800,000. Owners and breeders of Jersey cattle. Promotes sale and use of Jersey milk through National All-Jersey, Inc., an affiliate.

AMERICAN LANGSHAN CLUB
Rte. 5, Box 75
Claremore, OK 74017
Forrest Beauford, Sec.
PH: (918)341-2238
Founded: 1945. **Members:** 80. Breeders of Langshan poultry. Promotes improvement of the breed. Sponsors national, regional, and state meets.

AMERICAN LIVESTOCK BREEDS CONSERVANCY
Box 477
Pittsboro, NC 27312
Don Bixby, Exec.Dir.
PH: (919)542-5704
FX: (919)545-0022
Founded: 1977. **Staff:** 5. **Members:** 4,000. **Budget:** $300,000.
Works to promote and conserve endangered breeds of livestock and poultry in America. Encourages the use of rare breeds in appropriate commercial operations, diversified farms, living history museums, and zoos. Conducts research on breed status and characteristics. Operates semen bank for rare breeds.

AMERICAN MAINE-ANJOU ASSOCIATION
760 Livestock Exchange Bldg.
Kansas City, MO 64102
John Boddicker, Exec.VP
PH: (816)474-9555
FX: (816)474-9556
E-mail: anjou@qni.com
URL: http://www.maine-anjou.org
Founded: 1969. **Staff:** 7. **Members:** 1,400. **Budget:** $300,000. For the promotion and registration of the Maine-Anjou breed of beef cattle. Has registered 117,000 cattle. Compiles statistics.

AMERICAN MILKING DEVON ASSOCIATION
135 Old Bay Rd.
New Durham, NH 03855
Sue Randall, Contact
PH: (603)859-6611
Founded: 1978. **Members:** 85. Breeders working to promote Devon cattle, a rare breed of red dairy cattle from England.

AMERICAN MILKING SHORTHORN SOCIETY
PO Box 449
Beloit, WI 53512-0449
Stuart Rowe, Exec.Sec.
PH: (608)365-3332
Founded: 1920. **Staff:** 2. **Members:** 500. **Budget:** $150,000.
Breeders of registered Milking Shorthorn cattle producing both milk and beef. Maintains the official registration office for Milking Shorthorn cattle in the U.S.

AMERICAN MURRAY GREY ASSOCIATION
PO Box 34590
North Kansas City, MO 64116
Jim Spawn, Exec.Dir.
PH: (816)421-1994
FX: (816)421-1991
E-mail: jspawn321@aol.com

Founded: 1970. **Staff:** 3. **Members:** 200. Livestock breeders. Promotes the Murray Grey breed of cattle.

AMERICAN MUSHROOM INSTITUTE
1 Massachusetts Ave. NW, Ste. 800
Washington, DC 20001
Laura L. Phelps, Pres.
PH: (202)842-4344
FX: (202)408-7763
Founded: 1955. **Staff:** 3. **Members:** 450. Mushroom growers, processors, suppliers, and researchers united to promote the growing and marketing of cultivated mushrooms. Purposes are: to increase cultivated mushroom consumption; to develop better and more economical methods of growing and marketing mushrooms; to collect and disseminate the latest statistics and other information; to foster research programs beneficial to the industry; to aid members with any problems. Supports a short course on mushroom science at Penn State University and an international congress on mushroom science.

AMERICAN NATIONAL CATTLEWOMEN
5420 S. Quebec
PO Box 3881
Englewood, CO 80155
PH: (303)694-0313
FX: (303)694-2390
Founded: 1952. **Staff:** 4. **Members:** 7,000. Individuals who are employed or interested in the cattle industry. Promotes versatility and healthfulness of beef. Conducts promotional and educational programs including National Beef Cook-Off, Beef Ambassador Competition, Ag in the Classroom, National Ag Day, Beef For Father's Day, Beef Gift Certificates, and Cattle Drive for Hunger.

AMERICAN PINZGAUER ASSOCIATION
21555 State Rte. 698
Jenera, OH 45841
Peg Meents, Sec.
PH: (419)326-8711
TF: (800)914-9883
FX: (419)326-5501
E-mail: apinzgauer@aol.com
Founded: 1973. **Staff:** 1. **Members:** 508. **Budget:** $50,000. Cattle breeders. Promotes and develops the Pinzgauer breed and works to ensure that it will make a significant contribution to the cattle industry. Operates systems for the registration, evaluation, and recording of Pinzgauer cattle. Maintains high breeding standards with emphasis on beef production.

AMERICAN POLLED HEREFORD ASSOCIATION
PO Box 14059
Kansas City, MO 64101-0059
Larry J. Heidebrecht, Pres.
Founded: 1901. **Staff:** 40. **Members:** 10,000. **Budget:** $2,400,000. Breeders and owners of registered purebred Polled Hereford beef cattle. Maintains registry.

AMERICAN POLLED SHORTHORN SOCIETY
PO Box 77
Virginia, IL 62691
Cindy Cagwin, Sec.-Treas.
PH: (217)452-3051
Members: 2,500. Breeders of Polled Shorthorn beef cattle that are registered by American Shorthorn Association.

AMERICAN POMOLOGICAL SOCIETY
102 Tyson Bldg.
University Park, PA 16802
Dr. Robert M. Grassweller, Bus.Mgr.
PH: (814)863-6163
FX: (814)863-6139
E-mail: aps@psu.edu
Founded: 1848. **Staff:** 1. **Members:** 1,000. Professional horticulturists, fruit growers, amateur fruit breeders, testers, and individuals in the nursery business devoted to fruit variety improvement.

AMERICAN POULTRY ASSOCIATION
133 Millville St.
Mendon, MA 01756
Lorna F. Rhodes, Sec.-Treas.
PH: (508)473-8769
FX: (508)473-8769
Founded: 1873. **Members:** 3,500. **Budget:** $69,000. Standard-bred poultry breeders and exhibitors; specialty breed clubs; variety sections; fairs and poultry shows. Has established standards for breeding, exhibiting, and judging purebred fowl, and a standard and code of ethics for poultry judges.

AMERICAN POULTRY HISTORICAL SOCIETY
Science Center
PO Box 6108
Morgantown, WV 26506-6108
PH: (304)293-2231
Founded: 1952. **Members:** 240. Locates, collects, and preserves records, pictures, and other materials connected with development of the poultry industry. Committee of 30 individuals selects persons of outstanding achievement for inclusion in the Poultry Industry Hall of Fame, Beltsville, MD. Maintains speakers' bureau.

AMERICAN POULTRY INTERNATIONAL
5420 1-55 N., Ste. B
Jackson, MS 39211
Don Ford, Chair
PH: (601)956-1715
FX: (601)956-1755
Founded: 1978. **Members:** 14. **Budget:** $50,000. Producers and processors of poultry. Works to ensure that sufficient quantities of frozen poultry and poultry products from the U.S. will be available for export. Products exported include whole fryer chickens, broiler parts, hens, and turkeys.

AMERICAN RED BRANGUS ASSOCIATION
3995 E. Highway 290, Dept. C
Dripping Springs, TX 78620-4205
Cheryl Henderson, Ofc.Mgr.
PH: (512)858-7285
FX: (512)858-7084
E-mail: arba@texas.net
URL: http://www.brangusassc.com
Founded: 1956. **Staff:** 3. **Members:** 1,950. Breeders of Red Brangus cattle; interested individuals. To provide for the registration, preservation of blood purity, and improvement of the Red Brangus breed, a crossbreed of purebred Brahman and Angus cattle. Sponsors field programs to aid in furthering the education of members in selecting profitable breeding stock; assists and cooperates with members who sponsor sales. Conducts annual contest in which heifers are judged and sold at auction.

AMERICAN RED POLL ASSOCIATION
PO Box 014096
Kansas City, MO 64101-0096
Homer Carl, Jr., Sec.-Treas.
Founded: 1883. **Staff:** 1. **Members:** 1,069. Breeders of purebred Red Poll cattle. Maintains registry showing ownership, transfers, and pedigree records of Red Poll cattle.

AMERICAN ROMAGNOLA ASSOCIATION
2000 Flagstone Rd.
Reno, NV 89510
Don Hartry, Off.Mgr.
Founded: 1974. **Staff:** 1. **Members:** 100. Cattle breeders. To maintain herd book and promote Romagnola cattle, a breed noted for hardiness and foraging ability, extreme docility, and excellent beef qualities. Compiles statistics.

AMERICAN ROYAL ASSOCIATION
1701 American Royal Ct.
Kansas City, MO 64102
James D. Taylor, Exec.VP

PH: (816)221-9800
FX: (816)221-8189
E-mail: americanroyal@americanroyal.com
URL: http://www.americanroyal.com
Founded: 1899. **Staff:** 8. **Members:** 1,050. **Budget:** $2,400,000. Business firms and individuals are sponsors. Seeks to further livestock breeds and the agricultural industry through the annual American Royal Livestock, Horse Show and Rodeo.

AMERICAN SALERS ASSOCIATION
7383 Alton Way, Ste. 103
Englewood, CO 80112
Sherry B. Doubet, Mgr.
PH: (303)770-9292
FX: (303)770-9302
E-mail: amsalers@aol.com
URL: http://www.salersusa.org
Founded: 1974. **Members:** 2,000. Breeders of Salers, a French breed of cattle introduced into the United States in 1975, and raised for meat products. Promotes interest in the breed throughout the cattle industry. Maintains registry; sanctions livestock shows; sponsors American Salers Junior Association.

AMERICAN SHORTHORN ASSOCIATION
8288 Hascall St.
Omaha, NE 68124
Dr. Roger E. Hunsley, Exec.Sec.-Treas.
PH: (402)393-7200
FX: (402)393-7203
URL: http://www.beefshorthornusa.com
Founded: 1872. **Staff:** 12. **Members:** 2,500. **Budget:** $500,000. Breeders of registered Shorthorn and Polled Shorthorn beef cattle. Seeks to record pedigrees and improve the breed. Sponsors Shorthorn Foundation.

AMERICAN SIMMENTAL ASSOCIATION
c/o Jerry Lipsey
1 Simmental Way
Bozeman, MT 59715
Jerry Lipsey, Exec. V.P.
PH: (406)587-4531
FX: (406)587-9301
E-mail: simmental@simngene.com
Founded: 1969. **Members:** 12,500. **Budget:** $2,350,000. Promotes registration and improvement of the breeds of Simmental and Simbrah cattle in the U.S.

AMERICAN SOCIETY FOR PLASTICULTURE
526 Brittany Dr.
State College, PA 16803-1420
Patricia E. Heuser, Exec.Sec.
PH: (814)238-2893
FX: (814)238-7051
E-mail: peh4@psu.edu
Founded: 1960. **Staff:** 1. **Members:** 200. **Budget:** $50,000. University departments of agriculture, horticulture, vegetable crops and agricultural engineering conducting research, extension, and teaching; industrial sales and product development departments; professional growers of agricultural crops. Advances agriculture through the use of plastics. Conducts research and education programs.

**AMERICAN SOCIETY OF AGRICULTURAL
    CONSULTANTS**
950 S. Cherry St., Ste. 508
Denver, CO 80246-2664
Thomas Lipefzky, Contact
PH: (303)759-5091
FX: (303)758-0190
E-mail: asac@sgri-associations.org
URL: http://www.agri-associations.org/asac
Founded: 1963. **Staff:** 1. **Members:** 225. **Budget:** $120,000. Members are independent, full-time consultants in many specialty areas serving agribusiness interests throughout the world. Strives to maintain high standards of ethics and competence in the consulting field.

Provides referral service to agribusiness interests seeking consultants having specific knowledge, experience, and expertise. Maintains liaison with governmental agencies utilizing consultants and with legislative and administrative acts affecting consultants.

AMERICAN SOCIETY OF AGRONOMY
677 S. Segoe Rd.
Madison, WI 53711
Robert F. Barnes, Exec.VP
PH: (608)273-8080
FX: (608)273-2021
URL: http://www.agronomy.org
Founded: 1907. **Staff:** 37. **Members:** 11,500. **Budget:** $2,500,000. Professional society of agronomists, plant breeders, physiologists, soil scientists, chemists, educators, technicians, and others concerned with crop production and soil management, and conditions affecting them. Sponsors fellowship program and student essay and speech contests. Provides placement service.

AMERICAN STOCK YARDS ASSOCIATION
1716 S. San Marcus
San Antonio, TX 78207
G. C. Hagelstein, Chm.
PH: (210)223-6331
FX: (210)222-2535
Founded: 1932. **Staff:** 1. **Members:** 20. Stockyard owners united to: maintain and preserve a system of sound, competitive, economical, and public livestock markets; seek just and equitable regulatory conditions affecting livestock marketing; promote the welfare of the livestock industry.

AMERICAN SUGAR CANE LEAGUE OF THE U.S.A.
PO Drawer 938
Thibodaux, LA 70302
Charles J. Malancon, Pres./Gen.Mgr.
PH: (504)448-3707
FX: (504)448-3722
Founded: 1922. **Staff:** 6. **Members:** 800. Sugar cane growers and processors.

AMERICAN SUGARBEET GROWERS ASSOCIATION
1156 15th St. NW, Ste. 1101
Washington, DC 20005
Luther Markwart, Exec.VP
PH: (202)833-2398
FX: (202)833-2962
E-mail: asga@aol.com
URL: http://www.hometown.aol.com/asga/sugar.htm
Founded: 1975. **Staff:** 3. **Members:** 23. **Budget:** $450,000. State and regional sugarbeet growers associations engaged in lobbying for the sugarbeet industry.

AMERICAN TARENTAISE ASSOCIATION
PO Box 34705
Kansas City, MO 64116
James Spawn, Contact
PH: (816)421-1993
FX: (816)421-1991
E-mail: jspwan321@aol.com
Founded: 1973. **Staff:** 4. **Members:** 250. **Budget:** $250,000. Cattlemen raising the Tarentaise breed of cattle (originally imported from France into the U.S.) and who are united for the promotion of the breed. Maintains the history, records, and pedigrees of individual animals.

AMERIFAX CATTLE ASSOCIATION
PO Box 149
Hastings, NE 68902
John Quirk, Sec.
PH: (402)463-5289
FX: (402)463-6652
Founded: 1977. **Staff:** 1. **Members:** 150. Breeders of Amerifax cattle (derived from American Friesian-Angus cross). Maintains

purebred herdbooks, promotes the breed, and disseminates information.

ANKOLE-WATUSI INTERNATIONAL REGISTRY

22484 W. 239 St.
Spring Hill, KS 66083-9306
Becky Lundgren, Exec.Sec.
PH: (913)592-4050
E-mail: watusi@aol.com
Founded: 1983. **Staff:** 1. **Members:** 144. Individuals, families, ranches, and corporations interested in promoting and preserving the Ankole-Watusi cattle breed. Works to protect the ancient and unique heritage of the breed which originated in Africa; increase public awareness of Ankole-Watusi cattle as a distinct breed; preserve bloodline purity through proper breed practices; recognize present breeders and encourage new breeders; aid in the study and dissemination of knowledge of the past ancestry and future breeding of the cattle. Collects and disseminates information relative to the Ankole-Watusi breed; issues certificates of breeding; engages in collective advertising and other promotional and publicity campaigns to inform the public of the benefits and advantages of the Watusi breed. Sponsors full blood and cross breeding-up breeding programs. Compiles statistics.

APRICOT PRODUCERS OF CALIFORNIA

2125 Wylie Dr., Ste. 2A
Modesto, CA 95355
William C. Ferriera, Pres.
PH: (209)524-0801
FX: (209)524-3840
E-mail: apricot@producers.com
Founded: 1961. **Members:** 90. **Budget:** $200,000. Represents members (apricot growers) in negotiations with processors (canners, driers, and freezers) over prices, contracts of sale, and harvest conditions. Objectives are to maintain the highest quality of production and to foster meaningful communication. Represents growers' viewpoints before state and federal bodies.

ASSOCIATION FOR EDUCATING AGRICULTURAL LEADERS

PO Box 20326
Montgomery, AL 36120-0326
Gordon Stone, Exec.VP
PH: (334)288-0097
FX: (334)288-0097
Founded: 1982. **Staff:** 3. **Members:** 14,000. **Budget:** $185,000. Farmers and ranchers ages 18 to 40 involved in agricultural production. Seeks to encourage young farmers and to educate members on the latest production, management, and marketing techniques in farming. Promotes good urban-rural relations and provides information on agricultural issues affecting urban consumers. Assists young farmers in developing leadership skills and works with similar organizations to help improve the economic, educational, and social conditions of rural life. Conducts educational programs. Operates speakers' bureau and charitable program.

ASSOCIATION OF DARK LEAF TOBACCO DEALERS AND EXPORTERS

PO Box 638
Springfield, TN 37172
David Kamer, Pres.
PH: (615)384-9576
FX: (615)384-6461
Founded: 1947. **Members:** 22. Dealers and exporters of dark fire-cured and dark air-cured leaf tobacco. To develop, protect, and expand domestic and foreign markets for dark leaf tobacco; to advise growers of leaf tobacco on requirements of the tobacco manufacturing industry in the U.S. and abroad.

ASSOCIATION OF OFFICIAL SEED ANALYSTS

PO Box 81152
Lincoln, NE 68501-1152
Robert Karrfalt, Pres.

PH: (402)476-3852
FX: (402)476-6547
E-mail: assoc@navix.net
Founded: 1908. **Staff:** 2. **Members:** 75. **Budget:** $100,000. Officials of 60 federal, state, and provincial seed testing and research laboratories. Seeks to: develop uniform rules for testing field, vegetable, flower, and tree seeds; encourage the use of high quality seed; promote research; foster the training of seed analysts.

ASSOCIATION OF OFFICIAL SEED CERTIFYING AGENCIES

600 Watertower Ln., Ste. D
Meridian, ID 83642-6286
Greg Lawry, Contact
Founded: 1919. **Members:** 396. State seed certifying agencies. Promotes breeding, production, and distribution of foundation, registered, and certified seed stocks. Establishes and adopts minimum standards for certification of field and vegetable crops.

AYRSHIRE BREEDERS' ASSOCIATION

Box 1608
Brattleboro, VT 05302-1608
Robert Schrull, Gen.Mgr.
PH: (802)254-7460
FX: (802)257-4332
E-mail: ayrshire@gbla.com
URL: http://www.gbla.com/ayrshire
Founded: 1875. **Staff:** 4. **Members:** 1,500. Breeders of Ayrshire cattle. Sponsors competitions and marketing service; compiles statistics; maintains registry of Ayrshire cattle.

BARZONA BREEDERS ASSOCIATION OF AMERICA

PO Box 631
Prescott, AZ 86302
Karen Halford, Exec.Sec.
PH: (602)445-5150
FX: (602)445-5150
Founded: 1968. **Members:** 80. **Budget:** $60,000. Purebred cattle breeders, commercial cattle breeders, colleges, and agribusiness organizations. Promotes the breeding and "breeding up" of Barzona cattle by providing for registration. Compiles statistics on cattle performance.

BEEF PROMOTION AND RESEARCH BOARD

PO Box 3316
Englewood, CO 80155
Monte Reese, Chief Operating Officer
PH: (303)220-9890
TF: (800)388-2333
FX: (303)220-9280
Founded: 1986. **Staff:** 3. **Members:** 111. **Budget:** $45,000,000. Beef producers. Coordinates public relations, marketing, and dissemination of information for the beef industry. Conducts promotional, consumer information, and industry information campaigns; fosters communication among beef producers; sponsors research. Produces television and radio advertisements.

BEEFMASTER BREEDERS UNIVERSAL

680 Park 10 Blvd., Ste. 290 W.
San Antonio, TX 78213
Wendell Schronk, Exec.VP
PH: (210)732-3132
FX: (210)732-7711
URL: http://www.beefmasters.org
Founded: 1961. **Members:** 4,800. Individuals and groups owning Beefmaster cattle. To improve the breed through performance and quality control programs and to provide better marketing through promotion and BBU-approved sales. Conducts advertising and promotional activities.

BEET SUGAR DEVELOPMENT FOUNDATION

800 Grant St., Ste. 500
Denver, CO 80203
Thomas K. Schwartz, Exec. Officer

PH: (303)832-4460
FX: (303)832-4468
E-mail: info@bsdf-assbt.org
Founded: 1945. **Staff:** 30. **Members:** 15. Sugar beet processing companies in the U.S. and Canada and major beet seed producing firms. To conduct and promote research in beet sugar processing and sugar beet improvement.

BELTED GALLOWAY SOCIETY
PO Box 56
Holly Springs, MD 38635
Joanne Huff-Ritts, Sec.
PH: (601)252-5744
URL: http://www.beltie.org
Founded: 1951. **Staff:** 1. **Members:** 700. **Budget:** $75,000. Breeders of Belted Galloway cattle, a minor breed of beef type of Scotch origin.

BIO-DYNAMIC FARMING AND GARDENING ASSOCIATION
PO Box 29135
San Francisco, CA 94129-0135
Charles Beedy, Exec.Dir.
PH: (415)561-7797
TF: (888)516-7797
FX: (415)561-7796
Founded: 1937. **Members:** 1,500. **Budget:** $300,000. Farmers, gardeners, consumers, physicians, and scientists interested in improving nutrition and health through the production of high quality food using bio-dynamic farming. (Bio-dynamic farming stresses restoration of organic matter to the soil, use of special preparations to stimulate biological activity of soil and plant growth, crop rotation, proper cultivation to avoid structural damage to soil, and establishment of beneficial environmental conditions such as forests, wind protection, and water regulation.)

BLUE ANCHOR, INC.
PO Box 367
Dinuba, CA 93618
Patrick Sanguinetti, Pres.
PH: (209)591-6030
FX: (209)531-7181
Founded: 1901. **Staff:** 85. **Members:** 800. **Budget:** $6,500,000. Cooperative marketing organization distributing deciduous tree fruits and table grapes.

BRIGHT BELT WAREHOUSE ASSOCIATION
PO Box 12004
Raleigh, NC 27605
Malcolm L. Dunkley, Mng.Dir.
PH: (919)828-8988
FX: (919)821-2092
Founded: 1945. **Members:** 300. Flue-cured tobacco warehouses. Promotes a more orderly market for the sale of flue-cured tobacco sold at auction; encourages the exportation of tobacco and continued fair and equitable prices.

BROWN SWISS CATTLE BREEDERS ASSOCIATION OF THE U.S.A.
800 Pleasant St.
Beloit, WI 53511-5456
John Meyer, Exec.Sec.
PH: (608)365-4474
FX: (608)365-5577
E-mail: rogernbs@abl.com
Founded: 1880. **Staff:** 14. **Members:** 1,100. **Budget:** $702,000. Breeders of registered Brown Swiss cattle. Sponsors Brown Swiss shows; participates in research programs; maintains records on Brown Swiss cattle.

BURLEY AND DARK LEAF TOBACCO ASSOCIATION
1100 17th St. NW, Ste. 900
Washington, DC 20036
Pam Pfisterer Clark, Mgr. Dir

PH: (202)296-6820
FX: (202)467-6349
Founded: 1947. **Staff:** 2. **Members:** 11. **Budget:** $200,000. Federation of five associations. Purpose is to promote the sale of burley, dark air-cured and fire-cured tobacco in the U.S. and abroad.

BURLEY AUCTION WAREHOUSE ASSOCIATION
620 S. Broadway St.
Lexington, KY 40508-3126
Denny E. Wilson, Exec.Dir.
PH: (606)255-4504
E-mail: bawa@ate.net
Founded: 1946. **Staff:** 2. **Members:** 220. Warehouse companies selling burley tobacco at auction in the eight burley-producing states (Indiana, Kentucky, Missouri, North Carolina, Ohio, Tennessee, Virginia, and West Virginia). Works with farmers to increase exports of tobacco; encourages fair trade practices in the auction system and supports continuation of the production control program.

BURLEY STABILIZATION CORPORATION
PO Box 6447
Knoxville, TN 37914
William O. L. Myers, Mng.Dir.
PH: (423)525-9381
FX: (423)525-8383
E-mail: bscorp@usit.net
Founded: 1953. **Staff:** 3. **Members:** 140,000. Burley tobacco growers' cooperative marketing organization. Coordinates the price support program for burley tobacco in Tennessee, North Carolina, and Virginia under contract with Commodity Credit Corporation.

BURLEY TOBACCO GROWERS COOPERATIVE ASSOCIATION
PO Box 860
Lexington, KY 40588
Danny McKinney, CEO
PH: (606)252-3561
FX: (606)231-9804
Founded: 1922. **Staff:** 10. **Members:** 525,000. Producers of burley tobacco in Kentucky, Indiana, Ohio, West Virginia, and Missouri. Administers government price supports on tobacco for the Commodity Credit Corporation in this area.

CALAVO GROWERS OF CALIFORNIA
2530 Red Hill Ave.
Santa Ana, CA 92705-5542
Allen J. Vangelos, Pres. & CEO
Founded: 1924. **Staff:** 108. **Members:** 1,850. Cooperative marketing organization. Activities include packaging, promotion, and marketing of avocados, other fresh specialty fruits, and fresh frozen avocado products. Conducts research; compiles statistics; offers computerized services.

CALIFORNIA ARTICHOKE ADVISORY BOARD
PO Box 747
Castroville, CA 95012
Mary Comfort, Exec.Dir
PH: (831)633-4411
TF: (800)827-2783
FX: (831)633-0215
Founded: 1960. **Staff:** 1. **Members:** 24. **Budget:** $400,000. Conducts generic promotions for California artichokes.

CALIFORNIA AVOCADO COMMISSION
1251 E. Dyer Rd., No. 200
Santa Ana, CA 92705
Mark Affleck, Pres. & CEO
PH: (714)558-6761
FX: (714)641-7024
E-mail: vweaver@avocad.org
URL: http://www.avocado.org
Founded: 1978. **Staff:** 12. **Members:** 6,000. **Budget:** $9,586,000. Marketing organization for growers and packers of California avocados. Administers promotion program, directs marketing re-

search, and creates and implements national advertising programs for California avocados.

CALIFORNIA AVOCADO SOCIETY

PO Box 4816
Saticoy, CA 93007
Tom Markle, Pres.
PH: (805)644-1184
URL: http://www.west.net/~lsrose/cas/index.html
Founded: 1915. **Members:** 1,600. Seeks to improve the culture and production of avocados; promotes the general welfare of the avocado industry. Supports research.

CALIFORNIA CANNING PEACH ASSOCIATION

3685 Mt. Diablo Blvd., No. 200
PO Box 7001
Lafayette, CA 94549
Ronald A. Schuler, Pres.
PH: (925)284-9171
FX: (925)284-4217
E-mail: ronschuler@worldnet.att.net
Founded: 1922. **Staff:** 13. **Members:** 625. California cling peach growers. Works to market members' production and obtain a reasonable return for cling peach growers' raw product. Conducts research on breeding new varieties of cling peaches. Compiles statistics on the cling peach industry.

CALIFORNIA DATE ADMINISTRATIVE COMMITTEE

PO Box 1736
Indio, CA 92202
Lugene Schmiedchen
PH: (760)347-4510
TF: (800)223-8748
FX: (760)347-6374
E-mail: cadates@aol.com
URL: http://www.californiadates.org
Founded: 1955. **Members:** 18. **Budget:** $350,000. Marketing organization for growers and handlers of 4 varieties of California dates, under a federal marketing order. Members are representatives of various producers and packers within the industry Members and alternates are selected biennially by the U.S. Secretary of Agriculture based on nominations submitted by the industry groups. Financed by assessments per hundredweight of dates, with the rate approved by the Secretary of Agriculture upon recommendation of the committee member. Administers quality regulations. Sponsors generic market promotion programs. Compiles statistics.

CALIFORNIA DRIED FRUIT EXPORT ASSOCIATION

710 Striker Ave.
Sacramento, CA 95834
Richard W. Novy, Pres.
PH: (530)561-5900
FX: (530)561-5906
Founded: 1925. **Members:** 37. Firms engaged in the export of California dried fruit and tree nuts.

CALIFORNIA DRY BEAN ADVISORY BOARD

531-D N. Alta Ave.
Dinuba, CA 93618
Jerry Munson, Bd.Mgr.
PH: (559)591-4866
FX: (559)591-5744
URL: http://www.nal.usda.gov/fnic/foodcomp
Founded: 1970. **Staff:** 3. **Members:** 22. **Budget:** $1,100,000. Growers and handlers of all varieties of dry beans produced in California. Conducts research to improve quality and marketability; carries on limited promotion; may establish quality standards for California dry beans.

CALIFORNIA FIG ADVISORY BOARD

PO Box 709
Fresno, CA 93712
Ron Klamm, Mgr.

PH: (559)445-5626
FX: (559)224-3447
Founded: 1937. **Staff:** 13. **Members:** 200. Commercial fig growers in California. Operates under the State Department of Agriculture for the advertising and merchandising of figs and fig products.

CALIFORNIA FIG INSTITUTE

PO Box 709
Fresno, CA 93712
Ron Klamm, Mng.Dir.
PH: (559)445-5626
FX: (559)224-3447
Founded: 1937. **Staff:** 3. **Members:** 200. Commercial fig growers in California, which is the only U.S. state that produces figs. Conducts research program.

CALIFORNIA GRAPE AND TREE FRUIT LEAGUE

1540 E. Shaw Ave., Ste. 120
Fresno, CA 93710-8000
Richard Matoian, Pres.
PH: (209)226-6330
FX: (209)222-8326
E-mail: cgtfl@ix.netcom.com
Founded: 1949. **Staff:** 8. **Members:** 350. Growers and shippers of fresh deciduous tree fruits and table grapes in California. Offers group insurance programs.

CALIFORNIA KIWIFRUIT COMMISSION

9845 Horn Rd., Ste. 160
Sacramento, CA 95827
E. Scott Horsfall, Pres.
PH: (916)362-7490
FX: (916)362-7993
E-mail: info@kiwifruit.org
URL: http://www.kiwifruit.org
Founded: 1979. **Staff:** 4. **Members:** 490. **Budget:** $2,225,000. California kiwifruit growers. Conducts cultural and market research; promotes use of kiwifruit internationally and in the U.S. Compiles statistics.

CALIFORNIA MELON RESEARCH BOARD

531-D N. Alta Ave.
Dinuba, CA 93618
J.D. Allen, Mgr.
PH: (559)591-0435
FX: (559)591-5744
Founded: 1972. **Staff:** 3. **Budget:** $240,000. Participants are California melon growers. Conducts research into new varieties, pest control management, and disease control for melons grown in California. (California is the leading melon-growing state in the U.S., producing approximately 80-85% of the annual U.S. melon crop.) Provides funding to universities for research programs.

CALIFORNIA PRUNE BOARD

5990 Stoneridge Dr., Ste. 101
Pleasanton, CA 94588-3234
Richard L. Peterson, Exec.Dir.
PH: (925)734-0150
FX: (925)734-0525
Founded: 1952. **Staff:** 7. California prune producers (14), prune packers (7), and one public sector member. The board operates the California Dried Prune Marketing Order, as amended, under the authority of the Secretary of the California Department of Food and Agriculture, and collects assessments on packers and producers. Uses funds for nonbrand advertising and promotion of prunes and prune products. Handles requests for recipes and resource material.

CALIFORNIA RARE FRUIT GROWERS

The Fuller Arboretum
PO Box 6850
Fullerton, CA 92834-6850
David M. Guggenheim, Pres.
E-mail: info@crfg.org
URL: http://www.crfg.org

Founded: 1968. **Members:** 3,000. **Budget:** $40,000. Horticulturists united to transmit information regarding introduction and growing of rare fruit, to upgrade familiar fruits, and to increase the use of less common fruit. Maintains program to discover, register, and propagate superior fruit trees. Is developing rare fruit areas at Quail Garden Arboretum in North San Diego County, CA, and Fullerton Arboretum in Orange County, CA. Conducts research program. Maintains seed, plant, and scion wood exchange.

CALIFORNIA STRAWBERRY COMMISSION
PO Box 269
Watsonville, CA 95077
David R. Riggs, Pres.
PH: (831)724-1301
FX: (831)724-5973
URL: http://www.calstrawberry.com
Founded: 1955. **Staff:** 17. **Members:** 58. Provides information about strawberries and the people who grow them. Answers questions, offers new recipes containing strawberries, and announces the latest news about strawberries.

CALIFORNIA TABLE GRAPE COMMISSION
PO Box 27320
Fresno, CA 93729-7320
Bruce J. Obbink, Pres.
Founded: 1968. **Staff:** 18. **Members:** 1,100. Grape growers united to promote California table grapes. Conducts research on grape production.

CATFISH FARMERS OF AMERICA
1100 Hwy. 82 E. Ste. 202
Indianola, MS 38751
Hugh Warren, Exec.VP
PH: (601)887-2699
FX: (601)887-6857
Founded: 1966. **Staff:** 4. **Members:** 400. **Budget:** $500,000. Farmers who raise catfish commercially. Membership centered primarily in Alabama, Arkansas, Louisiana, and Mississippi.

CATFISH INSTITUTE
PO Box 247
118 Hayden St.
Belzoni, MS 39038
Bill Allen, Jr., Pres.
PH: (601)247-4913
FX: (601)247-2644
URL: http://www.catfishinstitute.com
Founded: 1986. Seeks to increase public awareness and promote the qualities of Mississippi farm-raised catfish. Monitors the industry and acts as liaison among processors and farmers; serves as information and resource center.

CENTER FOR RURAL AFFAIRS
PO Box 406
Walthill, NE 68067
Don Ralston, Adm.Dir.
PH: (402)846-5428
FX: (402)846-5420
E-mail: info@cfra.org
URL: http://www.cfra.org
Founded: 1973. **Staff:** 24. **Budget:** $1,600,000. Participants are farmers, ranchers, businesspersons, and educators concerned with the decline of the family farm. Purpose is to provoke public thought on social, economic, and environmental issues and government policies affecting rural America, especially the Midwest and Plains regions. Is dedicated to agricultural reform which will conserve human and natural resources, communities, and local farm ownership. Works to define rural economic policy. Conducts on-farm research and disseminates findings; compiles statistics.

CHERRY CENTRAL COOPERATIVE
PO Box 988
Traverse City, MI 49685-0988
Richard L. Bogard, Pres.

PH: (616)946-1860
FX: (616)941-4167
Founded: 1973. **Staff:** 47. Fruit and vegetable growers, processors, and marketers.

CHERRY MARKETING INSTITUTE
PO Box 30285
Lansing, MI 48909-7785
Phillip J. Korson, Mng.Dir.
PH: (517)669-4264
FX: (517)669-3354
URL: http://www.cherrymkt.org
Founded: 1988. Growers of tart cherries. Promotes and encourages the consumption of cherries. Conducts research.

COMMITTEE FOR SUSTAINABLE AGRICULTURE
406 Main St., Ste. 313
Watsonville, CA 95076-4623
Lynn Young, Exec.Dir.
PH: (831)763-2111
FX: (831)763-2112
E-mail: csaefc@csa-efc.org
URL: http://www.csa-efc.org
Founded: 1981. **Staff:** 4. **Members:** 2,000. **Budget:** $250,000. Organic farmers; wholesalers and retailers of natural foods; university level researchers and educators; consumers concerned with food safety, environmental, and land use issues. Seeks to promote agricultural practices that are "ecologically sound, economically viable, and socially just." Works to increase the number of growers using sustainable practices and consumers demanding organically-grown foods. Sponsors harvest fairs, farm tours, and ecological farming conference, and other educational events for sustainable agriculture.

COMMUNICATING FOR AGRICULTURE
112 E. Lincoln Ave.
Fergus Falls, MN 56537
M. E. Smedsrud, Founder/Chmn. of the Bd.
PH: (218)739-3241
TF: (800)432-3276
FX: (218)739-3832
URL: http://www.cainc.org/
Founded: 1972. **Members:** 80,000. **Budget:** $2,000,000. Communicating for Agriculture, Inc. (CA) is a rural nonprofit group whose purpose is to promote the general health, well being and advancement of people in agriculture and agribusiness. CA is actively involved in federal and state issues that affect the quality of life in rural America and provides members with a variety of money-saving benefit programs. The Communicating for Agriculture Scholarship and Education Foundation (subsidiary) conducts a scholarships and grants program, research on rural issues, and international exchange programs with an agricultural focus.

CONCORD GRAPE ASSOCIATION
5775 Peachtree-Dunwoody Rd., Ste. 500-G
Atlanta, GA 30342
Pamela A. Chumely, Exec.Dir.
PH: (404)252-3663
FX: (404)252-0774
E-mail: cqa@assnhq.com
Founded: 1966. **Members:** 11. Processors of Concord grape products. Promotes the interests of members, and the welfare of the industry.

CORNS
Rte. 1, Box 32
Turpin, OK 73950
Carl L. Barnes, Exec.Officer
PH: (580)778-3615
Founded: 1958. **Staff:** 2. **Members:** 4,000. Gardeners, seed savers, small- and large-scale farmers, and others interested in and dedicated to the production and preservation of the genetic diversity of open pollinated (without human intervention) corn varieties. Seeks to maintain these varieties by growing them out, keeping records, and

sharing seeds with others members for further distribution. Maintains speakers' bureau and museum.

COTTON COUNCIL INTERNATIONAL

1521 New Hampshire Ave.
Washington, DC 20036
Allen Terhaar, Exec.Dir.
PH: (202)745-7805
FX: (202)483-4040
E-mail: cottonusa@cotton.org
URL: http://www.cottonusa.org
Founded: 1956. **Staff:** 25. **Budget:** $15,000,000. Representatives of all segments of the U.S. cotton industry. International cotton sales promotion organization cooperating with cotton interests in foreign countries.

COTTON FOUNDATION

PO Box 12285
Memphis, TN 38182-0285
Dr. Andrew G. Jordon, Exec. Officer
PH: (901)274-9030
FX: (901)725-0510
Founded: 1955. **Budget:** $1,000,000. Corporations interested in supporting research and educational programs to promote markets for cotton. Makes grants to public and private institutions, and occasionally to industrial firms, for fundamental and applied research pertaining to cotton production and processing.

COTTON INCORPORATED

1370 Ave. of the Americas, 34th fl.
New York, NY 10019
Michael McNamara, Pub. Relations Dir.
PH: (212)586-1070
FX: (212)265-5386
Founded: 1971. Represents 45,000 cotton producers for research and promotion.

CRANBERRY INSTITUTE

266 Main St.
Wareham, MA 02571-2172
Jere Downing, Exec.Dir.
PH: (508)295-4132
FX: (508)291-1511
E-mail: jdd@capecod.net
Founded: 1952. **Staff:** 2. **Members:** 500. Cranberry growers and handlers in the United States and Canada. Gathers and disseminates information and helps members resolve horticultural and environmental issues related to growing cranberries.

CRESTED FOWL FANCIERS' ASSOCIATION

72 Springer Ln.
New Cumberland, PA 17070
Glen Cryar Gobbel, Jr., Sec.-Treas.
Founded: 1935. **Members:** 112. Persons who breed and exhibit crested large fowl bantams and water fowl. Encourages conformity to standards set by the American Poultry Association and the American Bantam Association. Sponsors district, state, and national meets where trophies, cash, and ribbons are awarded for bantams, large fowl, and water fowl. Presents honorary lifetime membership to individuals making outstanding contributions to the association.

CROP SCIENCE SOCIETY OF AMERICA

677 S. Segoe Rd.
Madison, WI 53711
Robert F Barnes, Exec.VP
PH: (608)273-8086
FX: (608)273-2021
E-mail: rbarnes@agronomy.org
URL: http://www.agronomy.org/asa.html
Founded: 1955. **Staff:** 30. **Members:** 5,500. **Budget:** $2,500,000. Plant breeders, physiologists, ecologists, crop production specialists, seed technologists, turf grass specialists, and others interested in improvement, management, and use of field crops. Seeks to advance research, extension, and teaching of all basic and applied phases of

the crop sciences and to cooperate with all other organizations and societies similarly interested in the improvement, production, management, and utilization of field crops. Maintains numerous committees including Coordination of Resident Education Activities, Crop Registration, Crop Science Teaching Improvement, Crop Terminology, Intersociety Committee on Plant Terminology, and Preservation of Genetic Stocks; also supports various intersociety collaboration committees.

DEMETER ASSOCIATION

Britt Rd.
Aurora, NY 13026
Anne Mendenhall, Dir.
PH: (315)364-5617
FX: (315)364-5224
E-mail: demeter@baldcom.net
Founded: 1982. **Staff:** 1. **Budget:** $40,000. Certifies biodynamic farms. (Biodynamic farming predates organic farming and is based on lectures by Austrian philosopher Rudolf Steiner.)

DEVON CATTLE ASSOCIATION

Drawer 628
Uvalde, TX 78801
Dr. Stewart H. Fowler, Exec.Dir.
Founded: 1918. **Staff:** 1. **Members:** 125. Breeders of purebred registered Devon cattle. Maintains registry, pedigree records, and hall of fame. Encourages a program of performance testing for the genetic improvement of the breed. Sponsors competitions; compiles statistics.

DFA OF CALIFORNIA

710 Striker Ave.
Sacramento, CA 95834
Richard W. Novy, Pres.
PH: (530)561-5900
FX: (530)561-5906
Founded: 1908. **Staff:** 30. **Members:** 42. Processors, packers, grower packers, and wholesalers of prunes, raisins, and other dried fruits, and almonds, pistachios, and walnuts. During season, staff expands to approximately 400. Performs inspection and certification, research and development, and traffic and sanitation services.

DISTILLERS GRAINS TECHNOLOGY COUNCIL

University of Louisville
Academic Bldg., Rm. 425
Louisville, KY 40292
Charles Staff, Exec.Dir.
PH: (502)852-1575
TF: (800)759-3448
FX: (502)852-1577
E-mail: chstaf1@ulkyum.louisville.edu
Founded: 1947. **Staff:** 2. **Members:** 8. Distillers who process grain and recover animal feed, pharmaceutical, and other products as by-products.

EASTERN DARK-FIRED TOBACCO GROWERS ASSOCIATION

1109 S. Main St.
PO Box 517
Springfield, TN 37172
Dan Borthick, Pres.
PH: (615)384-4543
FX: (615)384-4545
Founded: 1932. **Staff:** 4. **Members:** 18,000. Dark tobacco growers. Membership concentrated in Kentucky and Tennessee.

FARM AID

334 Broadway, Ste. 5
Cambridge, MA 02139
Carolyn G. Mugar, Exec.Dir.
PH: (617)354-2922
TF: (800)FARM-AID
FX: (617)354-6992
E-mail: farmaid1@aol.com

Founded: 1985. **Staff:** 5. Created to raise public awareness of the plight of the American family farmer and to provide aid to families dependent on agriculture. Provides funds to organizations aiding farmers, and to programs focusing on long-term solutions to problems faced by farmers.

FARM FOUNDATION
1211 W. 22nd St., Ste. 216
Oak Brook, IL 60523
Walter J. Armbruster, Mng. Dir.
PH: (630)571-9393
FX: (630)571-9580
E-mail: ff@farmfoundation.org
URL: http://www.farmfoundation.org
Founded: 1933. **Staff:** 2. Cooperates with existing agencies in stimulating research and educational activities to improve the economic, social, and cultural conditions of rural life. Sponsors regional and national committees, studies, publications, conferences, and training courses.

FARM LABOR RESEARCH PROJECT
1221 Broadway St.
Toledo, OH 43609-2807
Baldemar Velasquez, Pres.
PH: (419)243-7941
FX: (419)243-5655
Founded: 1981. **Staff:** 12. **Budget:** $750,000. Engages in charitable, educational, and scientific activities as they relate to farmworkers, former farmworkers, and their families, who have been deprived of educational opportunities, who are exposed to many occupational hazards, or who have incomes lower than the federal poverty level. Carries on activities in the fields of elimination of sharecropping and implementation of employee status for farmworkers, grassroots leadership and conflict-resolution development, pesticide education, and health education and services.

FLORIDA CITRUS MUTUAL
Citrus Mutual Bldg.
PO Box 89
Lakeland, FL 33801
Bobby F. McKown, Exec.VP/CEO
PH: (813)682-1111
FX: (813)682-1074
URL: http://www.fl-citrus-mutual.com
Founded: 1948. **Staff:** 23. **Members:** 12,000. **Budget:** $2,000,000. Florida citrus growers' organization supplying market and price information to its members. Marketing of fruit is handled by affiliated shippers and processors.

FLORIDA CITRUS NURSERYMEN'S ASSOCIATION
2686 State Rd. 29 North
Immokalee, FL 34142-9515
Chuck Reed, Pres.
PH: (941)658-3400
FX: (941)658-3469
Founded: 1957. **Members:** 77. Florida citrus nurserymen seeking to promote and support research, education, and self-regulation concerning quality citrus nursery stock. Is currently developing greenhouse techniques for containerized nursery plants.

FLORIDA DEPARTMENT OF CITRUS
PO Box 148
Lakeland, FL 33802
Daniel L. Santangelo, Exec.Dir.
PH: (941)499-2500
FX: (941)284-4300
URL: http://www.floridajuice.com
Founded: 1935. **Staff:** 150. **Budget:** $69,000,000. Established by an act of the Florida legislature and governed by the Florida Citrus Commission, a body of 12 citrus industry members appointed by the governor to staggered 3-year terms. Administers the citrus laws of the state; has regulatory authority over the packing, processing, labeling, and handling of citrus fruits and products. Conducts advertising and merchandising activities, and product marketing, scientific,

and economic research. Investigates areas of flavor control, juice yield, mechanical harvesting, shipping, and production. Compiles statistics. The department developed the process used by the industry for producing frozen concentrated orange juice. Operations are financed by an excise tax in Florida on each box of fruit moved in commercial channels.

FLORIDA FRUIT AND VEGETABLE ASSOCIATION
4401 E Colonial Dr.
Orlando, FL 32814-0155
Mike Stewart, Exec.VP
PH: (407)894-1351
FX: (407)894-7840
E-mail: info@ffva.com
URL: http://www.ffva.com
Founded: 1943. **Staff:** 45. **Members:** 4,500. Growers and shippers of Florida vegetables, sugar cane, citrus, and tropical fruits.

FLORIDA GIFT FRUIT SHIPPERS ASSOCIATION
521 N. Kirkman Rd.
Orlando, FL 32808
Joseph E. Ball, Exec.VP
PH: (407)295-1491
TF: (800)432-8607
FX: (407)290-0918
Founded: 1946. **Staff:** 18. **Members:** 138. **Budget:** $12,000,000. Firms packing and shipping gift fruit packages.

FLORIDA LYCHEE GROWERS ASSOCIATION
18595 SW 238th St.
Homestead, FL 33031
Ruth Betty Hall, Sec.Treas.
PH: (305)245-4707
Founded: 1952. **Staff:** 1. **Members:** 10. Marketing organization of growers of lychee fruit, including longans, mangos, avocados, and carambola.

FLORIDA TOMATO EXCHANGE
PO Box 140635
Orlando, FL 32814
Wayne Hawkins, Exec.VP
PH: (407)894-3071
FX: (407)898-4296
URL: http://www.floridatomatoes.org
Founded: 1974. **Staff:** 6. **Members:** 35. Shippers and packagers of fresh Florida tomatoes. (Florida currently produces 50% of the tomatoes grown in the U.S. for the fresh market.) To promote the efficient production, packaging, distribution, and sale of Florida tomatoes. Cosponsors research projects.

FLUE-CURED TOBACCO COOPERATIVE STABILIZATION CORPORATION
1304 Annapolis Dr.
PO Box 12300
Raleigh, NC 27605
Lionel Edwards, Mgr.
PH: (919)821-4560
FX: (919)821-4564
Founded: 1946. **Staff:** 47. **Members:** 750,000. Flue-cured tobacco producers' marketing cooperative for six southern states.

FOOD ANIMAL CONCERNS TRUST
PO Box 14599
Chicago, IL 60614
Robert A. Brown, Pres.
PH: (773)525-4952
FX: (773)525-5226
URL: http://www.fact.cc
Founded: 1982. **Budget:** $400,000. Foundations and individuals opposed to the industrialization of livestock and poultry production. Examines the adverse impact of "factory farming" on farm income, public health, and animal welfare, and promotes new methods of livestock and poultry production. Maintains speakers' bureau.

GELBRAY INTERNATIONAL
Rte. 1, Box 273C
Madill, OK 73446
Don M. Yeager, Sec.
PH: (580)223-5771
FX: (580)226-5773
Founded: 1981. **Members:** 250. Breeders of Gelbray cattle. Promotes and perpetuates the registration and breeding of Gelbray cattle. The Gelbray breed is the result of crossbreeding between the Brahman, Gelbvieh and Angus. Registers Gelbray.

GEODE RESOURCE, CONSERVATION, AND DEVELOPMENT
3002A Winegard Dr.
Burlington, IA 52601
Jeff Tisl, Coord.
PH: (319)752-6395
FX: (319)752-0106
Founded: 1985. **Staff:** 7. **Members:** 12. **Budget:** $500,000. Provides rural development services in natural resources in such areas as water quality, crop diversification, grant writing, community facilities or services, and planning resource economic development projects for an administration cost.

GRAIN ELEVATOR AND PROCESSING SOCIETY
Box 15026
Minneapolis, MN 55415-0026
David Krejci, Exec.VP
PH: (612)339-4625
FX: (612)339-4644
URL: http://www.geaps.com
Founded: 1930. **Staff:** 6. **Members:** 2,800. International professional organization of operations managers of facilities used for receiving, handling, processing, and storing grain and oilseeds; suppliers of equipment and services to the grain handling and processing industries. Promotes innovation, leadership and excellence in safe and efficient grain handling and processing operations.

GREAT LAKES SUGAR BEET GROWERS ASSOCIATION
485 Plaza N
Saginaw, MI 48604
Richard E. Leach, Jr., Exec.VP
PH: (517)792-1531
FX: (517)792-7165
Founded: 1982. **Staff:** 2. **Members:** 1,500. Sugar beet growers in Michigan.

GREAT PLAINS AGRICULTURAL COUNCIL
Department of Agriculture
Fort Collins, CO 80523
Dr. Melvin D. Skold, Exec.Dir.
Founded: 1946. **Staff:** 1. **Members:** 27. **Budget:** $80,000. Representatives from state Agricultural Experiment Stations, Agricultural Extension Services, agencies of the U.S. Department of Agriculture, and the U.S. Department of Interior. Membership drawn from the ten Great Plains states. Seeks to adapt agricultural programs to conditions prevailing in the Great Plains; provides a forum for exchange of ideas to solve agricultural problems in the Great Plains; identifies and evaluates problems important to the agricultural and rural sector of the region.

GROUNDSWELL INC. OF MINNESOTA
Box 338
Wanda, MN 56294
Diane Irlbeck, Office Mgr.
PH: (507)342-5797
Founded: 1974. **Members:** 2,500. **Budget:** $160,000. Farmers and other individuals who seek to preserve the existence of the family farm and to aid the rural economy in Minnesota and the U.S. as a whole. Educates farmers on their legal rights and the availability of assistance programs. Collects and distributes clothing, and other necessities to needy farmers. Supports legal, peaceful actions to improve the rural economy. Informs members of legislative activity and secures media attention for farmers and the rural economy in general. Maintains speakers' bureau.

HAWAII AGRICULTURE RESEARCH CENTER
99-193 Aiea Heights Dr.
Aiea, HI 96701-3911
Stephanie A. Whalen, Pres.
PH: (808)487-5561
FX: (808)486-5020
E-mail: swhalen@harc-hspa.com
Founded: 1882. **Staff:** 120. **Members:** 150. **Budget:** $5,000,000. Sugar companies raising sugarcane and manufacturing sugar; individuals connected with these firms. Seeks to improve and protect the sugar industry of Hawaii; supports experiment station. Conducts training sessions for members of the sugar industry; compiles statistics.

HENRY A. WALLACE INSTITUTE FOR ALTERNATIVE AGRICULTURE
9200 Edmonston Rd., Ste. 117
Greenbelt, MD 20770
I. Garth Youngberg, Ph.D., Exec.Dir.
PH: (301)441-8777
FX: (301)220-0164
E-mail: Hawiaa@access.digex.net
URL: http://www.hawiaa.org
Founded: 1983. **Staff:** 4. **Members:** 2,000. Organic and conventional farmers, agricultural scientists and educators, nutritionists, and consumers. Seeks to advance systems of food and fiber production that are economically viable, resource conserving, environmentally sound, and sustainable through the long-term development and support of educational programs and scientific investigations. Monitors and reports on related governmental activities.

HOLSTEIN ASSOCIATION USA
1 Holstein Pl.
Brattleboro, VT 05302-0808
Steven Kerr, Exec. Officer
PH: (802)254-4551
TF: (800)952-5200
FX: (802)254-8251
URL: http://www.holstein.com
Founded: 1885. **Staff:** 120. **Members:** 30,000. **Budget:** $16,000,000. Breeders of Holstein cattle. Maintains registry showing ownership, transfers, and pedigree records.

HOME ORCHARD SOCIETY
PO Box 230192
Tigard, OR 97281-0192
Joanie Cooper, Pres.
PH: (503)835-5040
Founded: 1975. **Members:** 900. Professional and amateur home orchardists and others interested in the growing of small orchards at home. Promotes the science, culture, and enjoyment of growing fruit-bearing trees, shrubs, vines, and plants in the home landscape. Conducts educational programs on topics such as fruit propagation and disease, identification of fruit, cultural practices, and maintenance procedures. Holds winter care programs, spring scion events, and fall cider squeeze. Maintains arboretum which assists in the development and maintenance of public arboretai; developing a breeding program for science, perpetuation of historic trees, and preservation of pioneer varieties; collecting existing varieties of trees with emphasis on the quality of flavor, texture, aroma, and succession of harvest. Conducts workshop on pruning, grafting, and budding. Plans include: holding public demonstrations, shows, and competitions to encourage amateur pomologists; developing and maintaining a library.

IDAHO POTATO COMMISSION
PO Box 1068
Boise, ID 83701
M. B. Anderson, Dir.

PH: (208)334-2350
FX: (208)334-2274
URL: http://www.idahopotatoes.com
Founded: 1937. **Staff:** 13. **Budget:** $8,500,000. A department of the State of Idaho; commissioners are appointed by the governor. Five commissioners are active potato growers who represent five growers' organizations; two commissioners are shippers or handlers of Idaho potatoes; and two represent the Idaho potato processors and their associations. Commission is charged with the advertising, public relations, and field merchandising of Idaho-grown potatoes. Selects and directs an active research and educational program in co-operation with the University of Idaho extension service and others. Holds the copyrighted "Idaho" and "Grown in Idaho" seal; manages, licenses, and contracts for its use and reproduction in promoting Idaho potato products.

INSTITUTE FOR AGRICULTURE AND TRADE POLICY
2105 1st Ave. S.
Minneapolis, MN 55404
Mark Ritchie, Pres.
PH: (612)870-0453
FX: (612)870-4846
E-mail: iatp@iatp.org
URL: http://www.iatp.org/iatp
Founded: 1986. **Staff:** 25. **Budget:** $1,150,000. Conducts research programs.

INTERNATIONAL ASSOCIATION OF AQUACULTURE ECONOMICS AND MANAGEMENT
Department of Agricultural and Resource Economics
3050 Maile Way, Gilmore 115
Honolulu, HI 96822
Dr. Yung C. Shang, Pres.
PH: (808)956-8533
FX: (808)956-2811
Founded: 1993. **Members:** 180. Economists, biologists, and administrators. Promotes socioeconomic research and information exchange on aquaculture. Encourages worldwide interest in the science of aquaculture.

INTERNATIONAL BANANA ASSOCIATION
1929 39th St. NW
Washington, DC 20007
Robert M. Moore, Pres.
PH: (202)223-1183
FX: (202)223-1194
Founded: 1982. **Staff:** 3. Members involved in the production, acquisition, transportation, and marketing of bananas. Assists all facets of the industry in resolving problems. Collects and disseminates information about the banana industry; compiles statistics.

INTERNATIONAL BRANGUS BREEDERS ASSOCIATION
5750 Epsilon
San Antonio, TX 78269-6020
Neil Orth, Exec.VP
PH: (210)696-8231
FX: (210)696-8718
E-mail: nancyb@int-brangus.org
URL: http://www.int-brangus.org
Founded: 1949. **Staff:** 12. **Members:** 2,000. **Budget:** $1,100,000. Breeders of registered Brangus cattle (a combination of 3/8 Brahman and 5/8 Aberdeen-Angus cattle). Currently register 33,300 head of cattle.

INTERNATIONAL CORNISH BANTAM BREEDERS' ASSOCIATION
Rte. 1, Box 204D
Louisburg, NC 27549
PH: (919)496-6128
Founded: 1946. **Members:** 154. Breeders and exhibitors of Cornish bantam and Cornish large fowl. Sponsors competitions. Maintains small library.

INTERNATIONAL GOLD STAR PIG REGISTRY
PO Box 1478
Pacifica, CA 94044
Kiyoko Hancock, Dir.
PH: (415)738-8659
Founded: 1988. **Members:** 100. Owners of Gold Star pot-belly pigs. Registers pot-belly pigs.

INTERNATIONAL LIVESTOCK IDENTIFICATION ASSOCIATION
4701 Marion St., Ste. 201
Denver, CO 80216
Cara Strain, Sec.-Treas.
PH: (303)294-0895
FX: (303)294-0918
Founded: 1946. **Members:** 33. State and provincial employees engaged in regulatory work; officials of livestock associations. Conducts research, educational, and discussion programs dealing with use of livestock brands, recording and inspection of brands, cattle theft law, and prosecutions. Maintains speakers' bureau.

INTERNATIONAL LIVESTOCK INVESTIGATORS ASSOCIATION
PO Box 202001
Helena, MT 59620
Marc Bridges, Dir.
PH: (406)444-2045
FX: (406)444-2877
Founded: 1978. Law enforcement officers specializing in livestock investigation. Seeks to reduce crimes associated with livestock, such as theft.

INTERNATIONAL PUMPKIN ASSOCIATION
414 Mason St., Ste. 704
San Francisco, CA 94102
Terry Pimsleur, Pres.
PH: (415)346-4446
FX: (415)249-4630
E-mail: sgarcia@tpnco.com
Founded: 1982. Members in 4 countries united to foster interest in growing giant pumpkins and squash. Sponsors annual World Pumpkin Weigh-Off, a competition designed to locate the largest pumpkin and squash in the world. Disseminates information on pumpkins, which are indigenous to the United States, and studies their role in America's history.

INTERNATIONAL SOCIETY OF CITRICULTURE
Department of Botany and Plant Sciences
Riverside, CA 92521
Charles W. Coggins, Jr., Sec.-Treas.
PH: (909)787-4412
FX: (909)787-4437
E-mail: charles.coggins@ucr.edu
Founded: 1970. **Members:** 1,400. Scientists, professors, corporations, and citrus growers and processors. Promotes and encourages research and the exchange of scientific information and education in the production, handling, and distribution of fresh citrus fruits and products.

INTERNATIONAL WEED SCIENCE SOCIETY
Oregon State Univ.
107 Crop Science Bldg.
Corvallis, OR 97331-3002
Carol Mallory-Smith, Sec.-Treas.
PH: (541)737-5883
FX: (541)737-3407
E-mail: carol.mallory-smith@orst.edu
Founded: 1976. **Members:** 630. Individuals (600) and organizations (30) interested in weed science research and training. Objectives are to promote weed control technology and education, training in weed science and technology, and communications among members. Sponsors workshops; stimulates research and regulatory programs. Encourages development of, and maintains liaison with, weed science and related organizations. Provides calendar of events.

IRI RESEARCH INSTITUTE

PO Box 1276
169 Greenwich Ave.
Stamford, CT 06904-1276
Jerome F. Harrington, Pres.
PH: (203)327-5985
FX: (203)359-1595
E-mail: iriresrch@aol.com
Founded: 1950. **Staff:** 15. **Budget:** $1,000,000. International technical specialists working in agricultural and agribusiness development. Projects have included: development and management of pasture seed industry in Venezuela; livestock improvement in Belize; nontraditional crop improvement program in the Dominican Republic; roadside vegetation and rice production in Brazil; food crops extension program in Indonesia; rice production and management in Guyana; a crop diversification program in Peru, including the Amazon region; coffee production, El Salvador feasibility and evaluation studies, most recently in Costa Rica, Ecuador, Egypt, Honduras, Kenya, Paraguay, Guyana, Saudi Arabia, and the Yemen Arab Republic. Most projects incorporate a training program for academic credit or practical on-the-job training.

JOSEPHINE PORTER INSTITUTE FOR APPLIED BIO-DYNAMICS

PO Box 133
Woolwine, VA 24185-0133
Hugh Courtney, Contact
PH: (540)930-2463
FX: (540)930-2463
Founded: 1985. Seeks to produce quality bio-dynamic agricultural applications based on the scientific research of Rudolph Steiner (1861-1925). (Bio-dynamic farming stresses restoration of organic matter to the soil.) Offers educational programs on the preparation of bio-dynamic applications. Conducts research; disseminates information.

LAND INSTITUTE

2440 E. Water Well Rd.
Salina, KS 67401-9051
Wes Jackson, Pres.
PH: (785)823-5376
FX: (785)823-8728
E-mail: landinst_development@midkam.net
Founded: 1976. **Staff:** 15. **Members:** 2,200. **Budget:** $750,000. Natural Systems Agriculture Program of long-term research to develop grains using perennials grown in mixtures mimicking native prairie; the Sunshine Farm 10-year project in energy accounting for a small farm; the Education and Public Policy Program; and the Rural Community Studies project concerned with sustainable human communities and rural education in small towns.

LEAF TOBACCO EXPORTERS ASSOCIATION

3716 National Dr., Ste. 114
Raleigh, NC 27612
J. T. Bunn, Exec.VP
PH: (919)782-5151
FX: (919)781-0915
Founded: 1939. **Staff:** 2. **Members:** 45. Firms engaged in buying, selling, packing, and storing leaf tobacco in unmanufactured forms.

LEAFY GREENS COUNCIL

33 Pheasant Ln.
St. Paul, MN 55127
Ray L. Clark, Exec.Dir.
PH: (651)484-3321
FX: (651)484-1098
Founded: 1976. **Members:** 78. **Budget:** $30,000. Growers, shippers, packers, and terminal agents. Promotes greater consumption of cabbage, celery, escarole, kale, leaf lettuce, parsley, romaine, spinach, swiss chard, and greens. Provides a forum for discussion of common industry problems. Compiles marketing and serving suggestions for products.

LEAGUE OF RURAL VOTERS EDUCATION PROJECT

2105 1st Ave. S.
Minneapolis, MN 55404
Mark Ritchie, Pres.
PH: (612)870-3400
FX: (612)870-4846
E-mail: mritchie@iatp.org
URL: http://www.iatp.org
Founded: 1983. **Members:** 1,000. **Budget:** $350,000. Individuals concerned with the current plight of the small farm in the U.S. Seeks to educate voters about federal farm legislation; conducts research and disseminates information on government farm policies; provides funds for lobbying on farm issues. Promotes adoption of U.S. farm policies that will benefit the international farming community as well as domestic farmers. Maintains speakers' bureau.

LIVESTOCK CONSERVATION INSTITUTE

1910 Lyda Dr.
Bowling Green, KY 42104
Glenn N. Slack, Exec.Dir.
PH: (502)782-9798
FX: (502)782-0188
E-mail: g.slack@primarnet.net
URL: http://www.lcionline.com
Founded: 1916. **Staff:** 5. **Members:** 150. **Budget:** $250,000. Producers, industry professionals, state and federal regulators, and researchers interested in discussing common issues, building consensus, and offering solutions to the challenges facing meat animal production in North America. Produces educational materials. Addresses industry issues including animal health, livestock care and handling, food safety, and uniform livestock identification.

LIVESTOCK INDUSTRY INSTITUTE

PO Box 1212
Shawnee Mission, KS 66222-0212
Robert Campbell, Exec.Dir.
PH: (913)432-4050
Founded: 1970. **Members:** 500. **Budget:** $195,000. Individuals generally recognized as leaders in their segments of the livestock and red meat industry. Objective is to help maintain equitable and stable profits for the livestock and red meat industry by exploring all business concepts and methods relating to the merchandising of livestock and red meat, and to report the findings to the industry. Awards trusteeship for contributions to the advancement of the industry. Maintains speakers' bureau.

MARKY CATTLE ASSOCIATION

Box 198
Walton, KS 67151
Martie Knudsen, Exec.Sec.
PH: (316)837-3303
E-mail: marky@southwind.net
Founded: 1973. **Staff:** 1. **Members:** 50. Breeders or owners of Marchigiana cattle; cattle companies; investors. Seeks to improve the beef industry by encouraging the efficient production of high quality beef. Maintains records on numbers of Marchigiana cattle in the U.S. and their performance data.

MICHIGAN APPLE COMMITTEE

12800 Escanaba Dr., No. B
Dewitt, MI 48820-8626
Mark Arney, Exec.Dir.
Founded: 1965. **Staff:** 6. **Members:** 1,500. Marketing commodity association for Michigan apples and apple products. Offers seminars; sponsors competitions; compiles statistics. Conducts research programs.

MICHIGAN ASSOCIATION OF CHERRY PRODUCERS

PO Box 30285
Lansing, MI 48909-7785
Philip J. Korson, II, Sec.
PH: (517)669-4264
FX: (517)669-3354

Founded: 1938. **Staff:** 5. **Members:** 2,000. Carries out educational and promotional work for Michigan tart and sweet cherry growers.

NATIONAL ALLIANCE OF INDEPENDENT CROP CONSULTANTS
1055 Petersburg Cove
Collierville, TN 38017
Allison Jones, Exec.VP
PH: (901)861-0511
FX: (901)861-0512
E-mail: jonesnaicc@aol.com
URL: http://www.naicc.org
Founded: 1978. **Staff:** 2. **Members:** 500. **Budget:** $225,000. Independent crop consultants and contract researchers united to promote agriculture and professionalism in the field. Seeks to: assist in the formation of state and national policies relating to agricultural production and of crop management philosophies; support agricultural crop producers by the most ecologically sound, environmentally safe, and economical means. Encourages members to expand their knowledge concerning crop management practices and techniques; participates in research in this area. Provides assistance in the formation of state and regional consultant organizations; offers referral system for members. Complies statistics; sponsors educational programs.

NATIONAL AQUACULTURE COUNCIL
1901 N. Foa Myer Dr., Ste. 700
Arlington, VA 22209
Roy E. Martin, Exec.Dir.
PH: (703)524-8883
FX: (703)524-4619
E-mail: office@nfi.org
Companies that grow, process, or distribute aquaculture products. Promotes the aquaculture industry in the U.S.; acts as a regulatory body within the industry. Conducts lobbying activities; operates speakers' bureau.

NATIONAL ASSOCIATION OF AGRICULTURE EMPLOYEES
PO Box 99-7716
Miami, FL 33299-7716
Leo Cross, Sec.
PH: (305)526-7204
Founded: 1954. **Members:** 500. Federal plant protection and quarantine employees, including entomologists, plant pathologists, and agricultural and biological scientists. To protect the agricultural interests and economy of the U.S. by the enforcement of the Federal Plant Pest and Plant Quarantine Acts, and animal health laws. Is recognized as exclusive bargaining agent of federal plant protection and quarantine employees.

NATIONAL ASSOCIATION OF ANIMAL BREEDERS
401 Bernadette Dr.
PO Box 1033
Columbia, MO 65205-1033
Gordon A. Doak, Pres.
PH: (573)445-4406
FX: (573)446-2279
E-mail: naab-css@naab-css.org
URL: http://www.naab-css.org
Founded: 1947. **Staff:** 8. **Members:** 25. Farmer cooperatives and private businesses interested in the improvement of farm livestock in the U.S., Canada, Mexico, and other countries. In the U.S., farmer cooperatives represent 60% of membership; private business, 40%. Approximately $100,000 per year is distributed through a research grant program.

NATIONAL ASSOCIATION OF COUNTY AGRICULTURAL AGENTS
207 W. Tacoma.
Ellensburg, WA 98926
Don Drost, Pres.
PH: (509)962-7507
FX: (509)962-7574

Founded: 1915. **Members:** 7,000. **Budget:** $400,000. County agricultural agents and extension workers. Serves the county agents of 50 state associations.

NATIONAL ASSOCIATION OF FARMER ELECTED COMMITTEEMEN
2030 County Rd. N
Oakland, NE 68045
Verner Magnusson, Pres.
PH: (402)377-2236
Founded: 1965. **Members:** 33,000. Works to: build a sound farm program; promote conservation; preserve the family farm; develop an export market; promote parity for farmers.

NATIONAL ASSOCIATION OF STATE DEPARTMENTS OF AGRICULTURE
1156 15th St. NW, Ste. 1020
Washington, DC 20005
Richard W. Kirchhoff, CEO
PH: (202)296-9680
FX: (202)296-9686
E-mail: nasda@patriot.net
URL: http://www.nasda-hq.org
Founded: 1916. **Staff:** 9. **Members:** 54. **Budget:** $20,000,000. Directors of state and territorial departments of agriculture. To coordinate policies, procedures, laws, and activities between the states and federal agencies and Congress. Conducts research.

NATIONAL CATTLEMAN'S BEEF ASSOCIATION
PO Box 3469
Englewood, CO 80155
Charles P. Schroeder, CEO
PH: (312)467-5520
FX: (312)467-9767
Founded: 1962. A division of the Natural Cattlemen's Beef Association. Companies and individuals engaged in the feeding and production of cattle, or the packing and processing of meat. Seeks to enhance public demand for beef and beef products. Promotes beef as a dietary constituent; disseminates information; conducts research.

NATIONAL CHERRY GROWERS AND INDUSTRIES FOUNDATION
PO Box 946
Hood River, OR 97031
George Ing, Mng.
PH: (541)386-7710
FX: (541)386-1177
Founded: 1954. **Staff:** 2. Growers and processors of brine, canned and frozen cherries. Promotes the cherry industry through research, advertising, and recipes. Promotes market and product development. Provides recipes, point-of-sale materials, and special promotional assistance.

NATIONAL CHICKEN COUNCIL
1015 15th ST. NW, Ste. 930
Washington, DC 20005
George B. Watts, Pres.
PH: (202)296-2622
FX: (202)293-4005
E-mail: wroenigk@chickenusa.org
Founded: 1954. **Staff:** 11. **Members:** 225. **Budget:** $2,500,000. Membership includes producers and processors of broiler chickens; distributors and allied industry. Sponsors National Chicken Cooking Contest and National Chicken Month. Compiles statistics; conducts generic promotion program for chicken; provides government relations services for member companies.

NATIONAL COTTON COUNCIL OF AMERICA
PO Box 820285
Memphis, TN 38182-0285
Phillip C. Burnett, Exec.VP
PH: (901)274-9030
FX: (901)725-0510
E-mail: info@cotton.org

Founded: 1938. **Members:** 21,794. Delegates from 19 cotton producing states, named by their respective producer, ginner, warehousemen, merchant, cooperative, textile manufacturer, and cottonseed crusher organizations in each state. Seeks to increase consumption of U.S. cotton and cottonseed products. Conducts public relations, economic, and technical activities. Represents cotton interests in Washington, DC. Maintains Committee for the Advancement of Cotton as political action arm.

NATIONAL COTTON GINNERS' ASSOCIATION
PO Box 820285
Memphis, TN 38182-0285
Fred Johnson, Exec. Officer
PH: (901)274-9030
FX: (901)725-0510
Founded: 1936. **Staff:** 1. **Members:** 1,500. Cotton ginners. Sponsors short courses on cotton ginning.

NATIONAL COUNCIL OF AGRICULTURAL EMPLOYERS
1112 16th St. NW, Ste. 920
Washington, DC 20036
Sharon M. Hughes, Exec.VP
PH: (202)728-0300
FX: (202)728-0303
E-mail: ncae@erols.com
Founded: 1964. **Staff:** 2. **Members:** 270. **Budget:** $350,000. Growers of agricultural commodities who employ hand labor for field crops; processors and handlers, farm and commodity organizations, and others whose business is related to labor - intensive farming in the U.S.. Aims to improve the position and image of U.S. agriculture as an employer of labor and to facilitate and encourage the establishment and maintenance of an adequate force of agricultural employees. Serves as clearinghouse for exchange of information on labor supply, length of employment, and other conditions of work. Does not engage in recruitment, housing, supplying, or employment of agricultural workers, and does not represent its members or others in negotiating with labor unions or other organizations, or in agreeing to any contract relating to hours, wages, or working conditions. Keeps members abreast of national legislation affecting agricultural labor.

NATIONAL DRY BEAN COUNCIL
6707 Old Dominion Dr., Ste. 315
Mc Lean, VA 22101
Philip Kimball, Exec.Dir.
PH: (703)556-9305
FX: (703)556-9301
Founded: 1950. **Staff:** 5. **Members:** 13. Promotes the interests of dry bean producers and workers.

NATIONAL FAMILY FARM COALITION
110 Maryland Ave. NE, Ste. 307
Washington, DC 20002
Katherine Ozer, Exec.Dir.
PH: (202)543-5675
FX: (202)543-0978
E-mail: nffc@nffc.net
URL: http://www.nffc.net
Founded: 1986. **Staff:** 3. **Members:** 39. Small farm and rural organizations including the Federation of Southern Cooperatives and Land Assistance Fund, Groundswell Inc. of Minnesota, North American Farm Alliance, and the RAFI-USA. Seeks to assure U.S. consumers of ample quantities of domestically-produced food that is affordably priced and of high quality, and to reestablish a stable rural society by preserving economically viable family-owned and operated farms. Strives to increase the political participation and awareness of rural Americans, and works to develop an alliance with supportive urban Americans. Supports sustainable agriculture, the restoration of federal farm price supports and effective supply management, debt restructuring programs, and emergency aid to farm families in need of food, shelter, and health care. Coalition is distinct from group of same name listed in index as defunct.

NATIONAL FARM-CITY COUNCIL
225 Touhy Ave.
Park Ridge, IL 60068
Marsha H. Purcell, Sec.-Treas.
PH: (847)685-8764
FX: (847)685-8896
Founded: 1955. **Budget:** $35,000. Individual and corporate members, including businesses, industries, associations, publications, government agencies, and youth and service groups. American Farm Bureau Federation serves as coordinating agency. Works to bring about better understanding between the rural and urban segments of American and Canadian society and thus strengthen the nations and their free economic society. Sponsors Farm-City Week in November. Distributes educational and consumer-oriented materials. Works through all communications media to "tell the agricultural story to city people and the city business story to farmers."

NATIONAL FARMERS ORGANIZATION
2505 Elwood Dr.
Ames, IA 50010-2000
Eugene F. Paul, National President
PH: (515)292-2000
FX: (515)292-7106
E-mail: info@netins.net
URL: http://www.nfo.org
Founded: 1955. Nonpartisan organization of farmers who bargain collectively to obtain contracts with buyers, processors, and exporters for the sale of farm commodities. Works to continuously improve such contracts. Conducts educational programs; maintains speakers' bureau.

NATIONAL FARMERS UNION
11900 E. Cornell Ave.
Aurora, CO 80014-3194
Leland H. Swenson, Pres.
PH: (303)337-5500
TF: (800)347-1961
FX: (303)368-1390
E-mail: nfu.denver@nfu.org
URL: http://www.nfu.org
Founded: 1902. **Staff:** 20. **Members:** 293,000. Farm families interested in agricultural welfare. Carries on educational, cooperative, and legislative activities. Represents members' interests especially in acquiring a more equitable share of the food dollar. Assists farm families in developing self-help institutions such as cooperatives.

NATIONAL FEDERATION OF MILK HAULER
  ASSOCIATIONS
3112 Kipling Way
Louisville, KY 40205
Mills Kersey, Exec.Sec.
Founded: 1970. Serves as negotiation unit between milk haulers and milk plants in resolving such labor issues as hauling rates, mergers, and unloading times.

NATIONAL GRAIN TRADE COUNCIL
1300 L St. NW, Ste. 925
Washington, DC 20005
Robert Petersen, Pres.
PH: (202)842-0400
FX: (202)789-7223
Founded: 1930. **Staff:** 3. **Members:** 64. **Budget:** $300,000. Federation of grain exchanges and national association of grain merchandisers, distributors, exporters, banks, processors, futures commission brokers, and warehouses.

NATIONAL GRANGE
1616 H St. NW
Washington, DC 20006
Kermit W. Richardson, Master
PH: (202)628-3507
FX: (202)347-1091
E-mail: jcummings@nationalgrange.org
URL: http://www.nationalgrange.org

Founded: 1867. **Staff:** 20. **Members:** 300,000. **Budget:** $1,200,000. Rural family service organization with a special interest in agriculture. Promotes mission and goals through legislative, social, educational, community service, youth, and member services programs. Sponsors needlework and stuffed toy contests.

NATIONAL INSTITUTE FOR SCIENCE, LAW, AND PUBLIC POLICY
1424 16th St. NW, Ste. 105
Washington, DC 20036
James S. Turner, Pres.
PH: (202)462-8800
FX: (202)265-6564
E-mail: firm@swankin-turner.com
URL: http://www.swankin-turner.com
Founded: 1978. **Staff:** 3. Seeks to influence public policies on food production topics, including sustainable agriculture, food safety, and nutrition by uniting individuals working to develop sustainable forms of agriculture and consumers concerned about health and quality food. Promotes agricultural techniques that do not involve the use of chemical fertilizers or pesticides. Monitors federal regulatory practices in the areas of milk pricing, the use of prescription drugs, and interpretation of food and drug law. Operates information clearinghouse on the food additive aspartame (Nutrasweet); maintains Takoma Urban Farm using sustainable agriculture methods. Makes available internships in law, food safety, and publishing; provides training in sustainable agriculture. Disseminates in formation; maintains speakers' bureau.

NATIONAL ONION ASSOCIATION
822 7th St., No. 510
Greeley, CO 80631
Wayne Mininger, Exec.VP
PH: (970)353-5895
FX: (970)353-5897
E-mail: wmininger@weldnet.com
URL: http://www.onions-usa.org
Founded: 1913. **Staff:** 3. **Members:** 700. **Budget:** $400,000. Growers, brokers, grower-shippers, shippers, suppliers, and support professionals engaged in the onion industry. Promotes the onion industry. Compiles monthly statistical report of stocks-on-hand, acreage, yield, and production of onions in the U.S. Lobbies issues of importance to national onion industry.

NATIONAL ORGANIZATION FOR RAW MATERIALS
333 White St.
Florence, MS 39073
Robert S. Norsworthy, Pres.
PH: (601)845-6504
FX: (601)845-6399
Founded: 1971. **Staff:** 1. **Members:** 400. Studies the U.S. and world economies, emphasizing the interaction between agricultural parity prices and general prosperity. Supports the enactment of a National Economic Stability Act which would establish a pricing structure for specific agricultural commodities thereby stabilizing the market prices of similar raw materials. (NESA would, in part, eliminate federal crop subsidies, set the prices of enumerated imported commodities at 110% parity, and equate the minimum wage to the parity price of a bushel of wheat.) Conducts seminars; operates speakers' bureau; compiles statistics.

NATIONAL ORGANIZATION OF POLL-ETTES
PO Box 156
Birnamwood, WI 54414
Sue Beckett, Chm.
PH: (715)449-2197
Founded: 1969. **Members:** 900. Seeks to promote the Polled Hereford cattle breed and industry. Selects national queen to promote beef cattle. Maintains museum.

NATIONAL PLANT BOARD
Bureau of Plant Industry
PO Box 94756
Lincoln, NE 68509-4756
Stephen V. Johnson, Contact
PH: (402)471-2394
FX: (402)471-6892
E-mail: stephenj@agr.state.ne.us
Founded: 1925. **Staff:** 1. **Members:** 51. **Budget:** $8,000. Members represent the states of the U.S. and Puerto Rico in plant inspection, quarantine, and regulatory matters. Seeks to advance and protect agriculture, horticulture, and forestry on state, national, and international levels.

NATIONAL POTATO COUNCIL
5690 DTC Blvd., Ste. 230E
Englewood, CO 80111-3200
A. R. Middaugh, Exec.Dir.
PH: (303)773-9295
FX: (303)773-9296
E-mail: npcspud@ix.netcom.com
URL: http://www.npcspud.com
Founded: 1948. **Staff:** 4. **Members:** 10,500. **Budget:** $600,000. Commercial potato growers. Takes action on national potato legislative, regulatory, and environmental issues.

NATIONAL POTATO PROMOTION BOARD
7555 E. Hampden Ave., Ste. 412
Denver, CO 80231
Tim O'Conner, Pres. & CEO
PH: (303)369-7783
FX: (303)369-7718
Founded: 1972. **Staff:** 13. **Members:** 6,200. **Budget:** $8,000,000. Growers of five or more acres of potatoes. Provides a way to organize and finance a national promotion program for potatoes, to increase consumption, expand markets, and make the growing and marketing of potatoes a better business for all; carries out effective and continuous coordinated marketing research, retail marketing, consumer advertising, public relations, and export programs.

NATIONAL TURKEY FEDERATION
1225 New York Ave. NW, Ste., 400
Washington, DC 20005
Stuart E. Proctor, Jr., Pres.
PH: (202)898-0100
FX: (202)898-0203
E-mail: info@turkeyfed.org
URL: http://www.turkeyfed.org
Founded: 1939. **Staff:** 11. **Members:** 4,000. The national advocate for all segments of the turkey industry, providing services and conducting activities which increase demand for its members' products by protecting and enhancing their ability to profitably provide wholesome, high-quality, nutritious products.

NATIONAL WATERMELON ASSOCIATION
PO Box 38
Morven, GA 31638
Nancy Childers, Exec.Sec.-Treas.
PH: (912)775-2130
FX: (912)775-2344
Founded: 1914. **Staff:** 3. **Members:** 700. **Budget:** $500,000. Individuals involved in the production, marketing, and sales of watermelon. Maintains files of clippings and business records. Maintains speakers bureau and conducts educational programs.

NORTH AMERICAN BLUEBERRY COUNCIL
4995 Golden Foothill Parkway, Ste. 2
El Dorado Hills, CA 95762
Mark Villata, Exec.Dir.
PH: (916)933-9399
FX: (916)985-0666
E-mail: bberry@blueberry.org
URL: http://www.blueberry.org
Founded: 1965. **Members:** 45. State and local commissions of

blueberry growers and marketers in the U.S. and Canada. Formed to act as clearinghouse for research and development activities in blueberry production and to provide a central publicity and promotion agency for all production areas. Conducts research; compiles statistics.

NORTH AMERICAN CORRIENTE ASSOCIATION

1912 Clay St.
North Kansas City, MO 64116
Jim Spawn, Exec. Dir.
PH: (816)421-1992
FX: (816)421-1991
E-mail: jspawn321@aol.com
Founded: 1982. **Staff:** 4. **Members:** 700. **Budget:** $150,000. Breeders of Corriente cattle, a breed developed in Mexico from Spanish cattle and used for team roping and bulldogging because of their endurance and small size. Purposes are to promote the use of Corriente cattle as a rodeo animal and to preserve the purity of the breed by instituting and monitoring a registered breeding program. Has created classification rules for full, half, three-quarter, and seven-eighths blood Corrientes in order to upgrade the status of the breed. Refers buyers to registered Corriente breeders.

NORTH AMERICAN DEER FARMERS ASSOCIATION

9301 Anapolis Rd., No. 206
Lanham, MD 20706
Barbara Ramey Fox, Exec.Dir.
PH: (301)459-7708
FX: (301)459-7864
E-mail: info@nadefa.org
URL: http://www.nadefa.org
Founded: 1983. **Staff:** 1. **Members:** 560. **Budget:** $185,000. Small farmers, farming suppliers, and individuals interested in environmentally-friendly farming alternatives. Promotes the production of venison and other agricultural products. Offers educational programs and research through its Cervid Livestock foundation.

NORTH AMERICAN EXPORT GRAIN ASSOCIATION

1300 L St. NW, Ste. 900
Washington, DC 20005
Daniel G. Amstutz, Pres.
PH: (202)682-4030
FX: (202)682-4033
E-mail: naega@internetmci.com
Founded: 1920. **Staff:** 4. **Members:** 40. **Budget:** $500,000. U.S. and Canadian exporters of grain and oilseeds from the United States.

NORTH AMERICAN LIMOUSIN FOUNDATION

7383 S Alton Way, Ste. 100
Englewood, CO 80112
John Edwards, Exec.VP
PH: (303)220-1693
FX: (303)220-1884
E-mail: jedwards@nalf.org
URL: http://www.nalf.org
Founded: 1968. **Staff:** 19. **Members:** 45,000. Individuals who own and raise Limousin cattle. Purposes are to: promote the Limousin breed; record performance of the cattle; issue registrations and keep the herd book. Sponsors BEEF performance program.

NORTH AMERICAN NORMANDE ASSOCIATION

11538 Spudville Rd.
Hibbing, MN 55746
Brian Toivola, Pres.
PH: (218)262-1933
FX: (218)262-1933
Founded: 1982. **Members:** 206. Cattle breeders interested in importing purebred cattle and participating in a pedigree program for the development of the Normande breed in the U.S. and Canada. Seeks to promote registration of the Normande breed, and to ensure that the Normande breed will make a significant contribution to the improvement of the cattle industry.

NORTH AMERICAN SOUTH DEVON ASSOCIATION

7383 S. Alton Way, Ste. 103
Englewood, CO 80112
Ronda Lanser, Recording Sec.
PH: (303)770-3130
Founded: 1974. **Staff:** 1. **Members:** 185. **Budget:** $100,000. Owners and breeders interested in encouraging the development, registration, and promotion of South Devon cattle. Conducts junior educational and training programs; compiles performance data on breeders' cattle.

NORTHWEST FRUIT EXPORTERS

105 S. 18th St., Ste. 227
Yakima, WA 98901
Tom Mathison, Pres.
PH: (509)576-8004
FX: (509)576-3646
Founded: 1976. **Staff:** 5. **Members:** 98. **Budget:** $1,000,000. Growers and exporters of fresh sweet cherries and apples in the Pacific Northwest. Seeks to overcome Japanese trade barriers that block the importation of foreign agricultural products. Conducts promotional activities.

NORTHWEST HORTICULTURAL COUNCIL

6 So. 2nd St.
PO Box 570
Yakima, WA 98901
Christian Schlect, Pres.
PH: (509)453-3193
FX: (509)457-7615
Founded: 1947. **Staff:** 6. **Members:** 8. To collect and disseminate information for and coordinate activities of Washington, Oregon, and Idaho tree fruit industries.

OF AGRICULTURE

South Bldg., SM-3
Washington, DC 20250
Otis N. Thompson, Exec.Dir.
PH: (202)720-4898
FX: (202)720-2799
Founded: 1929. **Staff:** 3. **Members:** 9,000. Professional, scientific, technical, and administrative personnel of U.S. Department of Agriculture, Farm Credit Administration, Food and Drug Administration, and Environmental Protection Agency in government classified grades.

ORGANIC CROP IMPROVEMENT ASSOCIATION

1001 Y St., Ste. B
Lincoln, NE 68508-1172
Betty Kananen, Exec.Dir.
PH: (402)477-2323
FX: (407)477-4325
E-mail: info@ocia.org
URL: http://www.ocia.org
Founded: 1984. **Members:** 30,000. Certification organization representing growers, processors, and manufacturers worldwide. Seeks to improve credibility of certified products through audit trail and crop improvement.

PACIFIC COAST CANNED PEAR SERVICE

1220 North St., No. A267
Sacramento, CA 95814-5607
Thomas J. Elliott, Gen.Mgr.
Founded: 1959. Nonprofit marketing group representing Bartlett pear growers in Oregon, Washington, and California. Encourages increased consumption of canned pears. Conducts promotional merchandising programs aimed at retailers, consumers, and the foodservice industry; sponsors dealer service and market representative programs; provides educational materials for school home economics classes, school lunch directors, and supermarket operators.

PARK GALLATIN HEREFORD ASSOCIATION
10069 River Rd.
Bozeman, MT 59718
Chuck Colback, Pres.
PH: (406)587-3024
FX: (406)587-3024
E-mail: hereford@montana.campuscw.net
Founded: 1960. **Members:** 40. Breeders of purebred Hereford cattle. Promotes development of the breed; sponsors Hereford shows, tours, and other educational activities.

PAW PAW FOUNDATION
147 Atwood Research Facility
Kentucky State University
Frankfort, KY 40601-2355
Snake C. Jones, Contact
Founded: 1988. **Members:** 350. **Budget:** $7,000. Horticulturists with an interest in the paw paw, the largest fruit indigenous to North America. Promotes commercial farming and sale of paw paws; seeks to improve paw paw strains. Conducts research in areas including paw paw breeding, horticulture, harvesting, and commercial use. Collects and evaluates paw paw germplasm; provides technical assistance to horticulturists working with paw paws; disseminates quality paw paw samples for use by chefs and scientists and in consumer trials and market research.

PEOPLE, FOOD AND LAND FOUNDATION
35751 Oak Springs Dr.
Tollhouse, CA 93667
George Ballis, Coord.
PH: (559)855-3710
FX: (559)855-4774
E-mail: sunmt@psnw.com
URL: http://www.psnw.com/~sunmt
Founded: 1974. **Staff:** 4. **Members:** 500. **Budget:** $40,000. Small farmers, consumers, and individuals concerned with low-water use, arid land crops, organic methods for small farmers and gardeners, and low-tech passive solar models for farm, food processing, and home use. Sponsors Sun Mountain Research Center. Activities include a "Seminar in Reality"; herbal food preparation; floral; medicinal, and culinary uses of native plants; shamanism; self-healing. Operates speakers' bureau; maintains 2500 volume library on agriculture, gardening, land, and irrigation control. Sponsors intern program.

PIEDMONTESE ASSOCIATION OF THE UNITED STATES
108 Livestock Ex. Bldg.
Denver, CO 80216
Kenneth Metcalf, Jr., Pres.
PH: (303)295-7287
FX: (303)295-7935
Founded: 1984. **Staff:** 1. **Members:** 350. Breeders of Piedmontese cattle, which are raised for beef production and are renowned for the low fat content of their meat. Promotes use of Piedmontese cattle by the U.S. beef industry. Conducts research; compiles statistics.

PINEAPPLE GROWERS ASSOCIATION OF HAWAII
1116 Whitmore Ave.
Wahiawa, HI 96786
Jerry D. Vriesenga, Pres.
PH: (808)621-3200
FX: (808)621-7410
Founded: 1943. **Staff:** 1. **Members:** 3. Growers and canners of pineapple in Hawaii. Promotes sale of fresh and canned pineapple products.

POTASH AND PHOSPHATE INSTITUTE
655 Engineering Dr., No. 110
Norcross, GA 30092
D. W. Dibb, Pres.
PH: (770)447-0335
FX: (770)448-0439
Founded: 1935. **Staff:** 30. **Members:** 13. Supports scientific research, particularly in the areas of soil fertility evaluation, soil testing, plant analysis, and tissue testing in state universities and experiment stations; participates in growers' meetings, dealer training courses, crops and soils workshops, and diagnostic clinics. Produces publications for educational use.

POTATO ASSOCIATION OF AMERICA
575 Coburn Hall, Rm. 6
Univ. of Maine
Orono, ME 04469-5715
Creighton Miller, Contact
PH: (207)581-3042
FX: (207)581-3015
Founded: 1913. **Staff:** 3. **Members:** 1,100. **Budget:** $87,000. Breeders, entomologists, horticulturists, plant pathologists, soil and fertilizer specialists, food technologists, producers, and handlers. Publishes research on the Irish (white) potato.

POULTRY BREEDERS OF AMERICA
1530 Cooledge
Tucker, GA 30084
Don Dalton, Sec.-Treas.
PH: (770)493-9401
FX: (770)493-9257
E-mail: ddalton@poultryegg.org
Founded: 1959. **Members:** 30. Breeders of poultry.

POULTRY SCIENCE ASSOCIATION
1111 N. Dunlap Ave.
Savoy, IL 61874
C.L. Sapp, Bus.Mgr.
PH: (217)356-3182
FX: (217)398-4119
E-mail: psa@assochq.org
URL: http://www.psa.uiuc.edu/
Founded: 1908. **Staff:** 4. **Members:** 2,000. **Budget:** $500,000. Members are from academia, industry, and government, with many involved in the research, teaching, or extension of poultry science and related fields.

PRAIRIEFIRE RURAL ACTION
4211 Grand Ave.
Des Moines, IA 50312
PH: (515)274-6468
FX: (515)274-2003
Founded: 1985. **Staff:** 8. **Budget:** $380,000. Purpose is to aid farmers and their families in the midwestern U.S. Provides advocacy on behalf of farmers. Organizes rural communities to keep farmers informed about public policy issues affecting agriculture; also organizes coalitions of rural groups and individuals. Conducts training and educational programs for rural clergy and farm leaders.

PROCESSED APPLES INSTITUTE
5775 Peachtree-Dunwoody Rd., Ste. 500-G
Atlanta, GA 30342
Andrew G. Ebert, Ph.D., Exec.Dir.
PH: (404)252-3663
FX: (404)252-0774
E-mail: pai@assnhq.com
Founded: 1951. **Staff:** 5. **Members:** 70. **Budget:** $170,000,000. Processors of apple products and suppliers to the industry. Conducts program to improve business conditions in the apple products industry and to enable the industry to serve the interests of consumers. Conducts research programs.

PROFESSIONAL FARMERS OF AMERICA
Box 6
219 Parkade
Cedar Falls, IA 50613
Merrill J. Oster, Pres.
PH: (319)277-1271
TF: (800)635-3931
FX: (319)277-7982
E-mail: editors@profarmer.com
URL: http://www.profarmer.com

Founded: 1972. **Members:** 25,000. Provides farmers with marketing strategies, data on market trends, and analyses of market-impacting developments worldwide. Offers seminars and home study courses. Sponsors commercial exhibits.

PROTEIN GRAIN PRODUCTS INTERNATIONAL
600 Maryland Ave. SW, Ste. 305W
Washington, DC 20024
Betsy Faga, Pres.
PH: (202)554-1618
FX: (202)554-1616
E-mail: prograin@aol.com
Founded: 1974. **Staff:** 2. **Members:** 24. **Budget:** $100,000. Grain milling companies that are processors of specially blended corn, wheat, and sorghum foods that are used primarily for overseas feeding programs. Conducts wide range of domestic and overseas marketing activities stressing maximum expansion of existing and potential world markets for members' products.

PUREBRED DAIRY CATTLE ASSOCIATION
PO Box 816
Brattleboro, VT 05302-0816
Kelli Dunklee, Coord.
PH: (802)254-4551
FX: (802)254-8251
Founded: 1940. **Staff:** 1. **Members:** 7. Federation of seven dairy cattle breeders associations: Ayrshire, Brown Swiss, Guernsey, Holstein, Jersey, Milking Shorthorn, and Red and White.

RAFI-USA
PO Box 640
Pittsboro, NC 27312
Betty Bailey, Exec. Dir.
PH: (919)542-1396
FX: (919)542-0069
URL: http://www.rafiusa.org
Founded: 1990. **Staff:** 12. Works for the preservation of family farms, the conservation and sustainable use of agricultural biodiversity, and the socially responsible use of new technologies.

RAISIN ADMINISTRATIVE COMMITTEE
3445 N. 1st St.
Fresno, CA 93726
Terry W. Stark, Mgr.
PH: (209)225-0520
FX: (209)225-0652
E-mail: info@raisins.org
Founded: 1949. **Staff:** 16. **Members:** 47. Producers of grapes that are processed as raisins; processors of raisins. Establishes minimum quality standards; develops and releases industry statistics; works to improve market discipline.

RAISIN BARGAINING ASSOCIATION
3425 N. 1st St., Ste. 209
Fresno, CA 93726
Vaughn Koligian, CEO
PH: (209)221-1925
FX: (209)221-0725
Founded: 1966. **Staff:** 5. **Members:** 2,000. Raisin growers. Acts as bargaining agency between members and raisin packers and processors.

RARE FRUIT COUNCIL INTERNATIONAL
PO Box 561914
Miami, FL 33256-1914
Maurice Kong, Pres.
PH: (305)378-4457
FX: (813)474-6133
E-mail: tfncws@gate.net
URL: http://www.gate.net/~tfnews
Founded: 1955. **Staff:** 5. **Members:** 1,000. **Budget:** $35,000. Individuals in 34 countries interested in propagating and raising tropical fruit plants. Promotes tropical pomology in suitable areas of the world and informs the public of the merits of tropical fruit.

Introduces and distributes new species, improved varieties, mutations, and clones of fruit plants. Conducts research and educational programs.

RED AND WHITE DAIRY CATTLE ASSOCIATION
HC1 Box 71B
Crystal Spring, PA 15536
E-mail: rwdcaone@nb.net
Founded: 1964. **Staff:** 5. **Members:** 1,000. Individuals, partnerships, and corporations with an active interest in Red and White dairy cattle. Objectives are to: encourage and promote the breeding and development of a new breed of Red and White dairy cattle; make adequate provisions for a registry; conduct scientific and statistical studies of the ability of Red and Whites to produce milk efficiently. Promotes the exhibition and public recognition of Red and Whites and encourages breed improvement through artificial insemination.

RED ANGUS ASSOCIATION OF AMERICA
Box 4201, I-35, N.
Denton, TX 76207
Dr. Robert Hough, Exec.Sec.
PH: (817)387-3502
FX: (817)383-4036
Founded: 1954. **Staff:** 15. **Members:** 1,800. **Budget:** $1,500,000. Breeders of purebred Red Angus cattle. Seeks to improve the breed through application of scientific methods of selection. Conducts performance testing program as prerequisite to registry of animals. Sponsors Red Angus divisions in livestock shows; compiles statistics. Issues registration papers for purebred Red Angus cattle.

RED RIVER VALLEY SUGARBEET GROWERS ASSOCIATION
1401 32nd St. SW
Fargo, ND 58103-3430
Mark F. Weber, Exec.Dir.
PH: (701)239-4151
FX: (701)239-4276
Founded: 1926. **Staff:** 2. **Members:** 2,100. **Budget:** $400,000. Sugar beet growers in North Dakota and Minnesota. Promotes the realization of a strong and stable sugar industry, and the well-being of its members. Concerns include: migrant seasonal farm workers, unemployment and workers' compensation, transportation, and highway use laws including truck weight, truck taxes, railroad service, and labor union issues. Favors U.S. participation in an International Sugar Agreement to better stabilize world sugar production, and investigates restrictions and regulations on products containing sugar. Conducts public relations campaign on the "value of sugar as a good food." Lobbies state and national legislators. Sponsors research and education board to aid extension services in Minnesota and North Dakota in developing research; conducts research program on the use of herbicides and fungicides.

SANTA GERTRUDIS BREEDERS INTERNATIONAL
PO Box 1257
Kingsville, TX 78364
Robert Swize, Associate Dir.
PH: (512)592-9357
FX: (512)592-8572
E-mail: truegert@aol.com
URL: http://www.sgbi.org
Founded: 1951. **Staff:** 7. **Members:** 3,000. **Budget:** $650,000. Producers of Santa Gertrudis beef cattle. Seeks to continue and promote Santa Gertrudis cattle. Activities include classification and registration of cattle. Sponsors approved livestock shows and youth endowment fund; maintains individual herd inventory and Total Performance Program.

SILVER WYANDOTTE CLUB OF AMERICA
3534 Tuhce Rd.
Evansville, WI 53536
Todd Kaehler, Exec.Dir.
PH: (608)876-6469
Founded: 1901. **Members:** 100. Breeders of standard-bred and

Bantam Silver Laced Wyandotte poultry. Promotes the exchange of information among members.

SOCIETY FOR THE PRESERVATION OF POULTRY ANTIQUITIES
1878 230th St.
Calamus, IA 52729
Glenn Drowns, Sec.-Treas.
PH: (319)246-2299
Founded: 1971. **Staff:** 2. **Members:** 600. **Budget:** $5,000. Individuals united to preserve poultry antiquities. Sponsors competitions.

SOUTHERN COTTON ASSOCIATION
PO Box 3366
Memphis, TN 38173
Susan A. Braslow, Exec.VP/Sec.
PH: (901)525-2272
FX: (901)527-8303
E-mail: acsa-mem-sbraslow@worldnet.att.net
Founded: 1916. **Staff:** 2. **Members:** 100. Cotton merchants and allied cotton interest groups. Keeps members informed of matters relating to cotton, and represents their views to state and federal government bodies (principally departments of agriculture) regarding legislation and rulings affecting cotton. Maintains ten committees.

SOUTHERN COTTON GINNERS ASSOCIATION
874 Cotton Gin Pl.
Memphis, TN 38106
Lee Todd, Exec.VP
PH: (901)947-3104
FX: (901)947-3103
Founded: 1967. **Staff:** 4. **Members:** 375. **Budget:** $300,000. Cotton ginners; associate members are firms serving the industry, such as oil mills, warehouses, banks, and chemical companies. Offers educational and informational services to cotton gin management, keeping them informed of federal and state regulations. Conducts seminars on safety, insurance, proper record keeping practices, and OSHA air pollution control requirements; also engages in research concerning the disposal of cotton gin waste. Offers placement service; compiles statistics.

SOUTHERN U.S. TRADE ASSOCIATION
World Trade Center, Ste. 1540
2 Canal St.
New Orleans, LA 70130
Jim Ake, Exec.Dir.
PH: (504)568-5986
FX: (504)568-6010
E-mail: susta@susta.org
URL: http://www.susta.org
Founded: 1973. **Staff:** 8. **Members:** 285. **Budget:** $8,000,000. Departments of agriculture of the Southern states; food and agricultural manufacturers and exporters operating in the southern United States. Promotes the export of high-value food and agricultural products of the South. Participates in international trade exhibitions and conducts point of sale promotions in food chains and restaurants worldwide; organizes overseas trade missions and other promotional campaigns; "provides information and assistance with transportation and financing of export sales and works closely on an individual basis with its export company membership to develop and expand their share of agricultural export markets." Operates Market Access Program, which provides financial assistance to members' marketing activities. Sponsors economics and marketing research and educational programs.

SUN GROWERS OF CALIFORNIA
PO Box 9024
Pleasanton, CA 94566
William Beaton, Pres.
PH: (925)463-8200
FX: (925)463-7492
URL: http://www.sungrowers.com
Founded: 1980. **Staff:** 800. Walnut, hazelnut, pecan, Brazil nut, almond, raisin, prune, fig, and dried apricot, peach, pear, and apple marketing organization. Acts as an administrative and marketing service organization for Diamond Walnut Growers, Sun-Maid Growers of California, Sunsweet Growers, Valley Fig Growers, and Sun-Land Products of California.

SUN-MAID GROWERS OF CALIFORNIA
13525 S. Bethel Ave.
Kingsburg, CA 93631
Barry Kriebel, Pres.
PH: (209)896-8000
TF: (800)272-4746
FX: (209)897-2362
E-mail: gmcbee@sunmaid.com
Founded: 1912. **Staff:** 100. **Members:** 1,500. Agricultural processing and marketing cooperative. Processes and markets all types and varieties of raisins in bulk and consumer packages, raisin bread, dried fruits, fruit bits (a mixture of dried fruits), and beverage alcohol.

SUNKIST GROWERS
PO Box 7888
Van Nuys, CA 91409-7888
Vince Lupinacci, Pres. & CEO
PH: (818)986-4800
FX: (818)379-7511
Founded: 1893. **Staff:** 1500. **Members:** 6,500. Citrus fruit marketing cooperative.

SUNSWEET GROWERS
901 N. Walton Ave.
Yuba City, CA 95993
William Haase, Pres./CEO
PH: (530)674-5010
FX: (530)751-5238
Founded: 1917. **Members:** 650. Prune and dried fruit processing organization. Jointly markets and distributes commodities with Sun-Diamond Growers of California, Diamond Walnut Growers, Sun-Maid Growers of California, and Valley Fig Growers.

SWEET POTATO COUNCIL OF THE UNITED STATES
c/o Harold H. Hoecker
PO Box 14
Marsh Hill Rd.
McHenry, MD 21541
Harold H. Hoecker, Exec.Sec.
PH: (301)387-9537
Founded: 1962. **Members:** 2,500. Sweet potato producers, packers, processors, equipment manufacturers and suppliers; research and educational personnel. Conducts educational programs.

TEXAS LONGHORN BREEDERS ASSOCIATION OF AMERICA
2315 N. Main St., Ste. 402
Fort Worth, TX 76106
Don L. King, Exec.Dir.
PH: (817)625-6241
FX: (817)625-1388
E-mail: tblaa@tlbaa.com
Founded: 1964. **Staff:** 8. **Members:** 3,700. **Budget:** $600,000. Individuals, firms, and organizations interested in the Texas Longhorn breed of cattle. Promotes public awareness of the Texas Longhorn, its link with history, and its role in modern beef production. Encourages practices to preserve purity of the breed and recognizes Texas Longhorn cattle breeders. Maintains registry for all purebred Texas Longhorns. Presents awards of recognition; provides speakers on limited basis; sponsors junior competitions; compiles breed and research statistics. Coordinates promotion and research to encourage the use of Longhorns by cattlemen. Operates computerized information services.

TOBACCO ASSOCIATES
1725 K St. NW, Ste. 512
Washington, DC 20006
Kirk Wayne, Pres.
PH: (202)828-9144
FX: (202)828-9149
Founded: 1947. **Staff:** 7. **Members:** 100,000. Producers and warehousemen in the flue-cured producing area. Promotes the export market for flue-cured tobacco.

TOBACCO INDUSTRY LABOR/MANAGEMENT COMMITTEE
c/o Robert Curtis
10401 Connecticut Ave.
Kensington, MD 20895
Robert Curtis, Exec. Officer
PH: (301)933-8600
FX: (301)946-8452
Founded: 1984. **Members:** 6. Unions (5) and management associations (1). Aims to: contribute to greater cooperation among labor and management; improve job security. Conducts public education programs concerning tobacco industry issues.

TOMATO GENETICS COOPERATIVE
Cornell University
252 Emerson Hall
Department of Plant Breeding
Ithaca, NY 14853-1901
Theresa M. Fulton, Managing Editor
FX: (607)255-6683
E-mail: tf12@cornell.edu
Founded: 1950. **Members:** 450. Research geneticists, plant breeders, and individuals interested in tomato genetics and the exchange of research information and stocks. Coordinates international activities; compiles bibliography of papers on tomato genetics. Maintains resource library.

TRANSPORTATION, ELEVATOR AND GRAIN MERCHANTS ASSOCIATION
1300 L St. NW, Ste. 925
Washington, DC 20005
Robert Petersen, Sec.
PH: (202)842-0400
FX: (202)789-7223
Founded: 1918. **Members:** 28. **Budget:** $60,000. Terminal and subterminal grain elevator operators and wholesale grain dealers.

UNITED BRAFORD BREEDERS
422 E. Main, Ste. 218
Nacogdoches, TX 75961
Rodney L. Roberson, Ph.D., Exec.Dir.
PH: (409)569-8200
FX: (409)569-9556
E-mail: ubb@brafords.org
Founded: 1969. **Staff:** 6. **Members:** 500. **Budget:** $175,000. Producers of Braford cattle. Registers pedigrees and records production data. Encourages and assists with field days, auction sales, and promotional activities.

UNITED EGG ASSOCIATION
1 Massachusetts Ave., No. 800
Washington, DC 20001
Albert E. Pope, Pres.
PH: (202)789-2499
FX: (202)682-0775
URL: http://www.unitedegg.org
Founded: 1982. **Staff:** 4. **Members:** 750. Individuals involved in all facets of the egg industry. Promotes the consumption and export of eggs through education and the dissemination of information. Members are involved in such areas as political action, nutrition, and education.

UNITED EGG PRODUCERS
PO Box 170
Eldridge, IN 52748
Albert E. Pope, Pres.
PH: (319)285-9100
FX: (319)285-9109
E-mail: info@unitedegg.org
URL: http://www.unitedegg.org
Founded: 1968. **Staff:** 5. **Members:** 500. **Budget:** $1,000,000. Regional egg marketing cooperatives whose members are independent egg producers. Aids members in improving efficiency in production, distribution, and marketing of eggs. Maintains legislative office in Washington, DC, which serves as congressional liaison. Compiles statistics; provides specialized education programs.

UNITED FARM WORKERS OF AMERICA
19700 Woodford-Tehachapi Rd.
Keene, CA 93531
Arturo S. Rodriguez, Pres.
PH: (805)822-5571
FX: (805)822-6103
Founded: 1962. **Staff:** 130. **Members:** 50,000. **Budget:** $500,000,000. AFL-CIO. Agricultural laborers. Chief purpose is to achieve collective bargaining rights for U.S. farm workers. Seeks to give farm laborers dignity and pride in their work by improving working and safety conditions and wages. Educates farm workers in the political and social arenas. Trains workers in skills needed for work in the fields and in the office of the union; espouses nonviolence. Archives of the union are housed at Wayne State University Labor Archives, Detroit, MI.

UNITED FRESH FRUIT AND VEGETABLE ASSOCIATION
727 N. Washington St.
Alexandria, VA 22314
Thomas E. Stenzel, Pres.
PH: (703)836-3410
FX: (703)836-7745
E-mail: uffva@uffva.org
Founded: 1904. **Staff:** 20. **Members:** 1,500. **Budget:** $3,200,000. "Represents the interests of producers and distributors of commercial quantities of fresh fruits and vegetables. Represents the business interests of growers, shippers, processors, brokers, wholesalers and distributors of produce, working together with our customers at retail and foodservice, our suppliers at every step in the distribution chain, and international partners."

U.S. APPLE ASSOCIATION
6707 Old Dominion Dr., Ste. 320
Mc Lean, VA 22101
Kraig R. Naasz, Pres.
PH: (703)442-8850
FX: (703)790-0845
URL: http://www.usapple.org
Founded: 1970. **Staff:** 8. **Members:** 650. **Budget:** $1,750,000. Represents all segments of the apple industry; over 600 individual firms involved in the apple business, as well as 36 state and regional apple associations representing the 9000 apple growers throughout the country. Seeks to provide the means for all segments of the apple industry to join in appropriate collective efforts to profitably produce and market apples and apple products. Unifies a diverse industry to achieve three primary goals: to represent the entire industry on national issues; to increase demand for apples and apple products; and to provide information on matters pertaining to the apple industry.

UNITED STATES BEEF BREEDS COUNCIL
PO Box 696020
San Antonio, TX 78269
Neil Orth, Pres.
PH: (210)696-8231
FX: (210)696-8718
Founded: 1952. **Members:** 21. Executive officers of purebred cattle associations who meet to discuss and coordinate the activities of the purebred beef industry.

UNITED STATES EGG MARKETERS
4500 Hugh Howell Rd., S-270
Tucker, GA 30084
Jerry Faulkner, Pres.
PH: (770)939-5532
FX: (770)621-0907
E-mail: gfaulk2038.@aol.com
Founded: 1981. **Staff:** 8. **Members:** 26. **Budget:** $750,000. Egg producers and processors. Provides cooperative purchase and sales benefits.

U.S. FARMERS ASSOCIATION
W 2561 Sunset Dr.
Campbellsport, WI 53010
William Gudex, Editor
PH: (920)533-8020
Founded: 1952. **Staff:** 2. **Members:** 500. **Budget:** $10,000. Progressive organizations across the U.S. and Canada interested in parity for farmers, civil rights, and peace.

U.S. POULTRY AND EGG ASSOCIATION
1530 Cooledge Rd.
Tucker, GA 30084
Don Dalton, Pres.
PH: (770)493-9401
FX: (770)493-9257
E-mail: webmaster@poultryegg.org
URL: http://www.poultryegg.org
Founded: 1947. **Staff:** 15. **Members:** 900. Producers, hatcherymen, feed millers, processors, packagers, and manufacturers and suppliers of products and services used in the production cycle of poultry products. Identifies problem areas and needs of the membership and concentrates industry efforts toward solutions. Represents the industry in its relationships with government agencies, members of Congress, and other related industry groups. Coordinates research needs and funding. Current research programs are in the areas of vaccine development, improved diagnostic methodologies, innovative carcass disposal methods, manure utilization, microbiological quality of finished product, further processing, processing, product development, poultry housing and husbandry. Sponsors ongoing research programs on production and animal health.

U.S. TROUT FARMERS ASSOCIATION
111 W. Washington St., Ste. 1
Charles Town, WV 25414-1529
Renee Eckley, Pres.
PH: (304)728-2189
FX: (304)728-2196
E-mail: ustfa@intrepid.net
URL: http://www.ustfa.org
Founded: 1954. **Staff:** 1. **Members:** 300. Trout farmers, suppliers, academics, students, and individuals interested in the trout farming industry. Promotes the trout farming industry and recreational trout fishing. Established a Trout Farmers Quality Assurance Program; monitors legislation related to the aquaculture industry.

U.S.A. PLOWING ORGANIZATION
7660 Burns Rd.
Versailles, OH 45380
William A. Goettemoeller, Sec.-Treas.
PH: (937)526-3525
FX: (937)526-3100
Founded: 1963. **Members:** 225. Current and former plowing competitors; individuals interested in plowing contests. Goal is to promote interest in and understanding of land tillage. Sponsors annual national contest wherein winners may qualify to compete in annual World Ploughing Contest. Conducts seminars and training meetings.

UNIVERSAL PROUTIST FARMERS FEDERATION
PO Box 56466
Washington, DC 20040
A. Mahadevananda, Chief Sec.

PH: (202)829-2278
FX: (202)829-0462
E-mail: proutwdc@prout.org
URL: http://www.prout.org
Founded: 1982. **Staff:** 4. **Members:** 1,000. Farmers involved with small scale organic farming. Advocates the Prout philosophy that resources should be shared in order to guarantee basic human needs, such as food, water, shelter, and education. (Prout is an acronym for Progressive Utilization Theory, a social, economic, and political theory based on the writings of the philosopher P.R. Sarkar.) Seeks government recognition of small farmers' needs, which include proper financing and management training. Provides information on large scale organic farming. Sponsors food distribution slide shows. Offers children's services. Compiles statistics. Plans to form producer cooperatives, seed distribution centers, farmworkers' and credit unions, information resource center on organic and traditional farming, legal information center, and "future farmers" cooperatives made up of urban dwellers.

VALLEY FIG GROWERS
PO Box 1987
Fresno, CA 93718
Mike Emigk, Pres.
PH: (559)237-3893
FX: (559)237-3898
Founded: 1959. **Members:** 47. Growers of dried fruit. Processes and packages dried fruit; jointly markets and distributes commodities with Sun-Diamond Growers of California, Sun-Maid Growers of California, Sunsweet Growers, and Diamond Walnut Growers.

VIRGINIA POULTRY BREEDERS ASSOCIATION
Rte. 3, Box 672
Ashland, VA 23005
Tommy Stanley, Sec.
PH: (804)798-8111
Founded: 1963. **Members:** 272. Individuals interested in the preservation and betterment of purebred poultry. Encourages youth to raise traditional breeds of poultry. Sponsors annual picnic and competitions.

WASHINGTON STATE APPLE COMMISSION
2900 Euclid Ave.
PO Box 18
Wenatchee, WA 98807-0018
Steven L. Lutz, Pres./CEO
PH: (509)663-9600
FX: (509)662-5824
E-mail: jthomas@bestapples.com
URL: http://www.treefruit.com
Founded: 1937. **Staff:** 48. **Members:** 4,500. Apple growers in the state of Washington united for advertising, promotion, and publicity of Washington apples.

WEED SCIENCE SOCIETY OF AMERICA
810 E. 10th St.
Lawrence, KS 66044
John Breithaupt, Exec.Sec.
PH: (785)843-1235
FX: (785)843-1274
E-mail: wssa@allenpress.com
Founded: 1950. **Members:** 2,300. Professional society of biological and chemical scientists and engineers involved in weed control research, extension, teaching, and regulatory activities; research and sales personnel from chemical and equipment industries.

WELSH BLACK CATTLE ASSOCIATION
208 N Hymera East St.
Shelburn, IN 47879
Sue Case, Sec.
PH: (812)383-9233
Founded: 1975. **Members:** 102. Individuals interested in raising and promoting Welsh Black cattle. Objectives are to conduct research on Welsh Black and other breeds of cattle and to improve the

breeding and production of existing cattle herds through the infusion of Welsh Black blood. Provides methods of gathering information on the cross-breeding of Welsh Black cattle; conducts marketing and development programs. Maintains records of performance, bloodlines, ownership, and other information regarding cattle breeds.

WESTERN GROWERS ASSOCIATION
17620 Fitch St.
Irvine, CA 92614
David L. Moore, Pres.
PH: (949)863-1000
TF: (800)949-4704
E-mail: dmoore@wga.com
URL: http://www.wga.com
Founded: 1926. **Staff:** 235. **Members:** 2,600. California and Arizona growers, shippers, and packers of fresh produce; brokers, distributors, jobbers, and members of allied industries. Represents members' concerns in areas including: transportation; legislation; standardization; labor relations; marketing services; public relations; legal services; insurance compensation.

WHEAT FOODS COUNCIL
10841 S. Parker Rd.
No. 105
Parker, CO 80134
Judi Adams, Pres.
PH: (303)840-8787
FX: (303)840-6877
E-mail: wfc@wheatfoods.org
URL: http://www.wheatfoods.org
Founded: 1972. **Staff:** 3. **Members:** 50. **Budget:** $1,340,000. Wheat producers, companies, and associations. Works to increase the domestic demand for wheat foods through nutrition education. Maintains speakers' bureau.

WHITE PARK CATTLE ASSOCIATION OF AMERICA
419 N. Water St.
Madrid, IA 50156
PH: (515)795-2013
Founded: 1975. **Staff:** 1. **Members:** 528. Owners and others interested in White Park cattle. Collects, verifies, records, preserves, and publishes pedigrees of White Park cattle. Goals are to maintain the purity of the breed and to seek identification of the breed as "genetically superior."

WILD BLUEBERRY ASSOCIATION OF NORTH AMERICA
59 Cottage St.
Bar Harbor, ME 04609-0180
John Sauve, Exec. Officer
TF: (800)233-9453
FX: (207)244-0043
E-mail: wildblue@acadia.net
Founded: 1981. **Members:** 50. **Budget:** $800,000. Companies and individuals involved in growing and processing wild blueberries. Seeks to promote the use of wild blueberries throughout North America and overseas.

WINROCK INTERNATIONAL INSTITUTE FOR AGRICULTURAL DEVELOPMENT
38 Winrock Dr.
Morrilton, AR 72110
Frank Tugwell, Pres.CEO
PH: (501)727-5435
FX: (501)727-5242
E-mail: information@winrock.org
URL: http://www.winrock.org
Founded: 1985. Purpose is to provide technical assistance and encouragement to agricultural developments in the U.S. and the Third World. Provides policy analysis services and assistance in increasing agricultural productivity and rural employment while protecting the environment. Focuses efforts on agriculture, forestry and natural resources, rural employment and enterprise development, and leadership and human resource development.

WOMEN IN LIVESTOCK DEVELOPMENT
PO Box 808
Little Rock, AR 72203
Beth A. Miller, Coordinator
PH: (501)376-6836
TF: (800)422-0474
FX: (501)376-8906
E-mail: bamwild@aol.com
URL: http://www.heifer.org/end_hunger/women.htm
Founded: 1990. Seeks to address gender issues in development projects involving livestock. Group maintains that women gain respect in traditional societies if they acquire ownership of livestock, and that such ownership will not upset the existing social structure. Conducts research and educational programs.

WOMEN INVOLVED IN FARM ECONOMICS
PO Box 70
Animas, NM 88020
Sheila Massey, Pres.
PH: (505)548-2705
FX: (505)548-2613
E-mail: masseyfarm@vtc.net
URL: http://www.wifeline.com
Founded: 1976. **Members:** 2,000. **Budget:** $90,000. Committed to improving profitability in production agriculture through educational, legislative, and cooperative programs. Promotes public and governmental awareness of the importance of agriculture in the American economy; maintains that agriculture is the most vital renewable industry and that economic prosperity in the United States is dependent upon economic prosperity in agriculture. Upholds the "family farm" concept for the production of food and fiber in the U.S. Works with governmental agencies and Congress to promote stability in the agricultural industry. Encourages communication regarding agricultural issues. Cooperates with other agricultural organizations and commodity groups in an effort to provide a unified voice for the industry. Conducts educational activities. Sponsors National Ag Day promotions.

WORLD AQUACULTURE SOCIETY
Louisiana State University
143 J. M. Parker Coliseum
Baton Rouge, LA 70806
Juliette L. Massey, Dir.
PH: (225)388-3137
FX: (225)388-3493
E-mail: wasmas@aol.com
URL: http://www.was.org
Founded: 1970. **Staff:** 4. **Members:** 2,400. **Budget:** $150,000. Libraries, institutions, students, interested individuals. Purpose is to secure, evaluate, promote, and distribute educational, scientific, and technological advancement of aquaculture and mariculture throughout the world. Promotes exchange and cooperation between persons interested in aquaculture (the cultivation of plants and animals in both freshwater and marine environments for domestic purposes, especially food.) Provides a forum for the exchange of information among scientists, fish farmers, businesspersons, bureaucrats, and others; promotes and evaluates the educational, scientific, and technological development of aquaculture throughout the world. Advocates the training of aquaculture workers in accredited colleges and universities. Encourages private industry and government agencies to support aquaculture research, development, and educational activities. Disseminates information on the status, potential, and problems of aquaculture. Sponsors competitions and special interest workshops.

WORLD WATUSI ASSOCIATION
PO Box 14
Crawford, NE 69339-0014
Christy Hawk, Exec.Sec.
PH: (303)921-4676
FX: (303)921-3155
Founded: 1985. **Staff:** 1. **Members:** 300. **Budget:** $25,000. Membership in 3 countries includes: enthusiasts of animal novelty breeds; ranchers; members of the rodeo industry; investors; cow or bull

owners. Promotes the Watusi breed of cattle and disseminates information on their uses and value. Conducts periodic cattle shows and sales. (The Watusi breed originated in Africa and is sometimes referred to as the African Longhorn because the cattle possess the largest and longest horns of any cattle in the world.) Registers cattle pedigrees.

WORLD'S POULTRY SCIENCE ASSOCIATION, U.S.A. BRANCH
PO Box 506
Fayetteville, AR 72702
Richard H. Forsythe, Sec.-Treas.
PH: (501)442-3892
FX: (202)401-1602
E-mail: forsythe@comp.uark.edu
Founded: 1965. **Members:** 400. Americans who have a financial interest, through ownership, employment, or avocation, in the poultry industry or allied industries and who are members of the World's Poultry Science Association. Provides for the participation of the U.S. in the quadrennial World's Poultry Congress. Promotes member and industry participation in the meetings. Cooperates with trade associations in promoting better understanding between the poultry industry in the U.S. and in other parts of the world. Works together with the Poultry Science Association in promoting participation of poultry scientists in all international affairs related to poultry science and industry and in providing grants to assist scientists in the participation in World's Poultry Congress. Supports youth poultry training programs.

CONSULTANTS

Consultants and consulting organizations active in the Agriculture sector are featured in this chapter. Entries are adapted from Gale's *Consultants and Consulting Organizations Directory* (*CCOD*). Each entry represents an expertise which may be of interest to business organizations, government agencies, non-profit institutions, and individuals requiring technical and other support. The listees shown are located in the United States and Canada.

In Canada, the use of the term "consultant" is restricted. The use of the word, in this chapter, does not necessarily imply that the firm has been granted the "consultant" designation in Canada.

Entries are arranged in alphabetical order. Categories include contact information (address, phone, fax, web site, E-mail); names and titles of executive officers; founding date, staff, and description.

A & L PLAINS LABORATORIES

PO Box 1590
Lubbock, TX 79408
E.A. Coleman, President
PH: (806)763-4278
FX: (806)763-2762
E-mail: al-labs@juno.com
Founded: 1977. **Staff:** 12. Provides agricultural, environmental and hazardous waste consultation and laboratory analyses. As agricultural consultants, assists the individual grower, grower group, fertilizer and chemical suppliers, and governmental agencies. As environmental and hazardous waste consultants, serves the mining industry, other consultants, concerned groups and governmental agencies, primarily in the areas of soils overburden, and water and wastewater.

A & L WESTERN AGRICULTURAL LABS

1311 Woodland Ave., Ste. 1
Modesto, CA 95351
PH: (209)529-4080
FX: (209)529-4736
E-mail: webmaster@al-labs-west.com
URL: http://www.al-labs-west.com
Founded: 1971. Serves the analytical needs of agricultural clients. Services include analysis of soil, plant, fertilizer, food, metals, and other environmental analysis.

AAS - FOSTER LAKE & POND MANAGEMENT

308 Loop Rd.
PO Box 1294
Garner, NC 27529
John E. Foster, Owner
PH: (919)772-8548
FX: (919)662-0158
E-mail: foster@concentric.net
Founded: 1983. **Staff:** 4. Provides and pond management services.

AB CONSULTING CO., INC.

3939 N. 48th St.
Lincoln, NE 68504
Ronald J. Gaddis, President
PH: (402)464-8021
FX: (402)464-5764
Founded: 1972. **Staff:** 4. Offers agricultural and engineering consulting. Specific services include irrigation pump and well testing, computer-designed sprinkler and spray nozzle packages, forensic engineering, soil and water engineering, tillage systems design, rural development, computer system design and software development, topographical surveying analysis software, surveying, irrigation system design, technical training programs, and field testing for irrigation equipment. Serves private industries as well as government agencies.

ABALONE INTERNATIONAL INC.

PO Box 1640
Crescent City, CA 95531
Chris Van Hook, Contact
PH: (707)464-6913
FX: (707)464-1802
Founded: 1988. **Staff:** 5. Provides abalone to aquaculturists. Also designs aquaculture systems, including aeration.

ABC LABS

7200 E. ABC Ln.
PO Box 1097
Columbia, MO 65205
Dr. Jake Halliday, President and CEO
PH: (573)474-8579
TF: (800)538-5227
FX: (573)443-9089
URL: http://abclabs.com
Founded: 1968. **Staff:** 250. Offers analytical chemical and bioassay services. Industries served: pharmaceutical, agricultural, chemical and consumer products.

ACAESA CO.

1248 Bedford Hwy.
Bedford, NS, Canada B4A 1C6
Johan D. Koppernaes, Chairman/CEO
PH: (902)835-8348
FX: (902)835-0134
Founded: 1992. **Staff:** 60. Offers conceptual designs, feasibility studies, business plans, preparation of construction plans, specifications and contract documents, construction management, construction inspection, and start-up and commissioning of: fish processing plants and fishing vessels, dairies and food processing plants, cold storages and ice making plants, environmental plants—air, water and sewage, mineral resource exploration and evaluation, solid and liquid waste pollution prevention plants, transportation systems shipping, railways, trucking and air, and harbors, wharves, schools, hospitals, and town halls. Industries served: fishing vessel owners, fish plant owners, beverage companies, cheese companies, dairies, railroad companies, ship owners, aquaculture companies, mining and construction, federal, provincial and municipal governments, and governmental infrastructure corporations.

ACUALTEC, CIA. LTDA.

630 E. Second St.
Tucson, AZ 85705
PH: (520)622-5222
FX: (520)622-2256
Provides aquaculture design services.

ADVANCE INTERNATIONAL CO.

16 Canal Run E.
Washington Crossing, PA 18977-1106
Eugene Chen, Dr. of Veterinary Med., President, Owner
PH: (215)493-4428
FX: (215)493-4256
E-mail: aic1987@aol.com
Founded: 1986. **Staff:** 3. Offers international marketing services to agribusinesses, specializing in developing animal feed and health market for concerns in Asia/Pacific region.

ADVANCED AQUACULTURAL TECHNOLOGIES, INC.

PO Box 426
Syracuse, IN 46567
PH: (219)457-5802
FX: (219)457-5887
Provides closed high density growth systems and biofilter design and management. Also involved in aquaculture R&D.

ADVANCED AQUACULTURE SYSTEMS INC.

4509 Hickory Creek Ln.
Brandon, FL 33511
PH: (813)653-2823
FX: (813)684-7773
URL: http://www.advancedaquaculture.com
Develops aquacultural systems, specializing in aeration and biofilter design and management, and closed high density growth systems.

AG RESOURCES INC.

6601 Palacio
Amarillo, TX 79109
Larry Womble, President
PH: (806)358-0395
FX: (806)352-0340
Founded: 1984. **Staff:** 10. An international agribusiness and consulting firm involved in development of turnkey agricultural projects and appropriate technology transfer programs overseas (developed and developing nations). Also manages investment financed livestock operations in the domestic United States as well as being an exporter of various implements, equipment and commodities related to business in the United States and internationally.

AG SERVICES OF TEXAS

Box 590
Wharton, TX 77488
L. Reed Green, President

PH: (409)532-5951
FX: (409)532-8329
Founded: 1975. **Staff:** 5. Agrochemical research consultants providing expertise in quality assurance services. Also offers complete integrated crop management. Serves as expert witness. Industries served: agriculture and forestry, banking and finance, chemical, insurance, and the legal profession.

AG-SYSTEMS INTERNATIONAL, LTD.
89 13th St.
Clintonville, WI 54929
T.J. Tooley, President
PH: (715)823-3242
FX: (715)823-3242
URL: http://www.tjtooley.com
Founded: 1976. **Staff:** 2. Provides specialized planning services for feeding, manure handling, ventilation systems, herd replacement facilities, milk houses or milking parlor complexes.

BEVERLY AGAR
RR 1
Phelpston, ON, Canada L0L 2K0
Beverly Agar, Contact
PH: (705)322-1918
FX: (705)322-0819
Offers land use planning services such as agricultural assessments, impact studies, MDS calculation, and soil surveys.

AGDEVCO
101-320 Gardiner Park Ct.
Regina, SK, Canada S4V 1R9
Bruce Hanson, Contact
PH: (306)721-8077
FX: (306)721-6140
Consultant offering agricultural business management services.

AGLAND INVESTMENT SERVICES
900 Larkspur Landing Cir., Ste. 240
Larkspur, CA 94939
William P. Mott, President
PH: (415)461-5820
FX: (415)461-6803
E-mail: wmott@aglandinvest.com
URL: http://www.aglandinvest.com
Founded: 1976. **Staff:** 8. An agribusiness consulting and investment company which provides a wide range of economic, marketing, technical and investment consultation to agricultural producers, agribusiness companies, and government agencies in the Western United States and in many countries around the world. Agland tends to concentrate on high-value specialty crops, including fruits, vegetables, and cut flowers.

AGMAR INC.
1215 Emerald Crescent
Saskatoon, SK, Canada S7J 4J2
Judith L. Dyck, President
PH: (306)955-5507
FX: (306)955-8151
E-mail: agmar@webster.sk.ca
Founded: 1982. Agricultural consulting services include equipment procurement, litigation support, marketing, appraisal, and farm management.

AGMARK (AGRI-MARKETING CORP.)
9741 James Ave., S.
Bloomington, MN 55431
Jim Wetherbee, President
PH: (612)881-3288
TF: (888)318-8861
FX: (612)881-3289
E-mail: agmark2@aol.com
Founded: 1975. **Staff:** 4. Provides retail agricultural marketing assistance programs, advertising services (newsletters, direct mail and

other types of advertising), and incentive programs to the agricultural industry.

AGPRO, INC.
Rte. 7, Box 100
Paris, TX 75462
D. Joe Gribble, President
PH: (903)785-5531
TF: (800)527-1030
FX: (903)784-7895
E-mail: agpro@neto.com
URL: http://www.agprousa.com
Founded: 1962. **Staff:** 14. Offers agricultural engineering design consultation for animal raising facilities including dairies, beef feedlots, swine operations, and embryo transplant facilities. Services include land utilization, plot plans, building design, equipment selection, integration with other farm and commercial activities, pollution control systems, genetic engineering systems, and computer applications. Also offers computer control and automation consultation, as well as consultation for waste management and control for food processing plants.

AGRESULTS, INC.
11015 SW 69th Ave. Rd.
Miami, FL 33156
Dean W. Wheeler, President
PH: (305)669-9086
FX: (305)669-9234
E-mail: agresults@aol.com
Founded: 1992. **Staff:** 1. Provides agricultural and agribusiness expertise, specializing in the tropics. Advises on agricultural production, fresh produce packing and handling, land use planning, agribusiness development, quality assurance, mechanization, and training. Industries served: agricultural worldwide.

AGRI-BUSINESS CONSULTANTS, INC.
2720 Alpha Access
Lansing, MI 48910
Neil R. Miller, Crop Consultant
PH: (517)482-7506
FX: (517)482-6944
E-mail: 73072.1314@compuserve.com
Founded: 1983. **Staff:** 5. Agricultural consultants providing fertilizer recommendations, crop protection recommendations, soil fertility and crop protection consulting, irrigation scheduling, educational sessions, contract research, and expert witness services. Industries served: farmers and ag-chemical companies.

AGRI BUSINESS GROUP INC.
3905 Vincennes Rd., Ste. 402
Indianapolis, IN 46268
Mike Jackson, President
PH: (317)875-0139
TF: (800)285-8859
FX: (317)875-0507
E-mail: jgoode@abginc.com
URL: http://www.abginc.com
Founded: 1979. **Staff:** 90. Offers contract research in the areas of pesticide efficacy, environmental test, plant interaction, plant breeding, plant growth regulators, plant nutrition, rotation and tillage, demonstration plots, and greenhouse testing. Also offers field project management for clients in five midwestern locations owned by the company and at subcontractor testing sites throughout the United States. Provides custom-designed training programs in the following areas: sales, sales management, coaching, market research, strategic planning, and mergers and acquisition consulting.

AGRI-BUSINESS SERVICES, INC.
PO Box 1237
Lakeville, MN 55044
Michael J. Morrison, President
PH: (612)469-6767
FX: (612)469-6768
E-mail: agribus@spacestar.net

Founded: 1968. **Staff:** 6. Personnel recruiters and executive search consultants in food processing and agribusiness. Includes all aspects of industrial, food service and consumer food manufacturing and marketing. Also includes all aspects of feed, seed, grain, agricultural chemical, animal health and agricultural equipment manufacturing marketing. Specialize in sales, marketing, technical, engineering and manufacturing professionals.

AGRI-CON CORP.
Rte. 3, Box 31
Norton, KS 67654-0301
Leroy S. Atwell, President
PH: (913)877-2918
Founded: 1985. **Staff:** 1. Offers agricultural consulting and farm management for the family farm. Provides financial planning and turnarounds. Specializing in farm feed lot operations and management.

AGRI-MANAGEMENT GROUP, LTD.
2820 Walton Commons W., Ste. 108
Madison, WI 53718
Alton D. Block, President
PH: (608)221-3213
TF: (800)551-9230
FX: (608)221-3263
E-mail: agri-man@requestltd.com
URL: http://www.agri-man.com
Founded: 1977. Farm and agri-business consulting firm providing personnel, financial, and farm management services.

AGRI-NUTRITION SERVICES INC.
1240 E. 3rd Ave., Ste. 1
Shakopee, MN 55379
John H. Goihl, Nutritionist
PH: (612)445-7001
TF: (800)322-0437
FX: (612)445-1911
Founded: 1973. **Staff:** 4. Provides nutritional and purchasing consulting services to small feed manufacturers; suppliers to feed industry; and large livestock producers, primarily of swine.

AGRI-PERSONNEL
5120 Old Bill Cook Rd.
Atlanta, GA 30349
David J. Wicker, Contact
PH: (404)768-5701
FX: (404)768-5705
Founded: 1973. Agribusiness consultants active in executive/ professional/technical recruitment and placement, and in mergers, acquisitions, and divestitures in various industries including dairy, feed, food, fertilizer, farm chemicals, poultry and egg, animal health, and pulp and paper.

AGRIBUSINESS DEVELOPMENT PARTNERS
1570 E. Tomahawk Dr.
Salt Lake City, UT 84103
David C. Hamblin, Managing Director
PH: (801)359-1189
FX: (801)328-1004
E-mail: hamblinm@burgoyne.com
Founded: 1979. **Staff:** 4. Consultancy specializes in the development, management, and financing of modern food and fiber systems throughout the world. Expertise includes knowledge in the organization and growth of private enterprise agribusiness; management of farms and projects, and technology transfer; analysis of business strategy and the competitive environment; and appropriate resources and operating procedures. Works with investors, owners, financial institutions, governments, and agribusiness corporations.

AGRICAPITAL CORP.
135 W. 50th St., Ste. 1820
New York, NY 10020-1201
Douglas G. Sterkel, Vice President

PH: (212)765-7090
FX: (212)765-2595
E-mail: info@agricapital.com
URL: http://www.agricapital.com
Founded: 1983. **Staff:** 5. Provides investment banking services for agribusiness clients in the U.S. and abroad, including financial consulting, debt and equity placements and joint ventures, and mergers and acquisitions. Industries served: agribusiness and food companies.

AGRICULTURAL ASSESSMENTS INTERNATIONAL CORP.
2606 Ritchie-Marlboro Rd.
Upper Marlboro, MD 20772-9208
Jorge Romero, Secretary
PH: (301)336-5229
FX: (301)336-5682
E-mail: wwigton@qqic.net
URL: http://www.qqic.net
Founded: 1983. **Staff:** 10. Provides agricultural and environmental monitoring and generation of statistics.

AGRICULTURAL CONSULTING SERVICES, INC.
159 Caroline St.
Rochester, NY 14620
Richard F. Wildman, President
PH: (716)473-1100
FX: (716)473-1765
Founded: 1983. **Staff:** 10. Provides farm business management services including business and economic analysis, computer hardware and software installation and training, and enterprise budgets and analysis. Also offers crop production management, monitoring, and advises in the areas of crop nutrition, pest management, weed control, tillage practices, and irrigation scheduling. Environmental work includes complete analytical and monitoring services for soil, wastewater, sludge, and groundwater. Serves farms and agribusiness.

AGRICULTURAL ENGINEERING ASSOCIATES
102 E. 2nd St.
Uniontown, KS 66779
John A. George, President
PH: (316)756-4845
TF: (800)499-3893
FX: (316)756-4847
E-mail: georgeaea@ckt.net
URL: http://www.agengineering.com
Founded: 1974. **Staff:** 16. Agricultural engineering consultants offering guidance on the design of swine production facilities, beef feedlots, dairy facilities, waste management systems, soil and water conservation design and resource development including watershed planning, dam design and irrigation supply dam design, grain and feed storage, drying and processing facilities, irrigation system evaluation and design, rural water district system design, land leveling design for irrigation and drainage, and land surveying. Industries served: production and commercial agriculture; research, demonstration and test facilities; government agencies, and in-house materials testing laboratories.

AGRICULTURAL SYSTEMS ENGINEERING
5100 S. 62nd St.
Lincoln, NE 68516-1952
Gerald R. Bodman, Contact
PH: (402)483-1024
FX: (402)466-9397
Founded: 1967. **Staff:** 2. Agricultural engineering consultants offering designs, plans and specifications for farmstead engineering projects, including structural design, environmental control systems, milking systems, extraneous (stray) voltage investigations, materials handling/grain storage, and manure management. Consultant has authored and co-authored numerous articles and papers. List of specific titles or publications may be obtained by contacting firm. Also serves as expert witness.

AGRICULTURAL TECHNOLOGY INC.

656 Ivy Ln.
Solvang, CA 93463
C.J. Elam, President
PH: (805)688-6475
FX: (805)688-6293
E-mail: dnvelam@syv.com
Founded: 1970. **Staff:** 2. Offers livestock nutrition and management consulting.

AGRICULTURAL TRAINING & TECHNOLOGY, INC.

PO Box 7513
Amarillo, TX 79114-7513
Bill C. Clymer, Ph.D., Contact
PH: (806)622-1866
FX: (806)622-3285
E-mail: clymer@arn.net
Founded: 1975. **Staff:** 12. Offers agricultural and livestock services involving crop production, losses, and management; crop and livestock research; expert witness testimony and legal technical counsel; feedlot, livestock, crop, urban, and industrial pest management and control; biological pest management; and pesticide research and development. Crop and livestock laboratory and field research facilities available.

AGRICULTURE INDUSTRIES, INC.

PO Box 1076
West Sacramento, CA 95691
Richard G. Jones, Principal
PH: (916)372-5595
FX: (916)372-5615
URL: http://www.f-a-r-m.com
Founded: 1977. Farm and ranch management and consulting services include hands-on ranch management, ranch real estate and appraisals, financial management, cost analysis, and budgets including line of credit budgets. Properties managed include field and row crops, permanent crops including grapes, almonds and walnuts, and cattle and grazing land.

AGRIDEVELOPMENT CO.

10795 Bryne Ave.
Los Molinos, CA 96055
Richard B. Bahme, President
PH: (916)527-8028
FX: (916)527-6288
Founded: 1967. **Staff:** 4. Provides consulting and advisory services in the following subject areas of specialization: (1) agricultural damage claims investigations (chemicals, fire, water, soil, crops, pests); (2) market surveys and product evaluation-fertilizers and agricultural chemicals; (3) study of natural resources and crop production potential; (4) forest, range, and ecological studies-productivity and environmental impact; (5) farm and forest management plans and programs-growth, yield, and quality improvement practices. Industries served: agricultural (farming, chemicals), fertilizers, plant protection, governmental, insurance, and legal.

AGRIMANAGEMENT, INC.

408 N. First St.
Yakima, WA 98907-0583
Donald L. Jameson, President
PH: (509)453-4851
TF: (800)735-6368
FX: (509)452-6760
E-mail: agrimgt@televar.com
URL: http://www.agrimgt.com
Founded: 1967. **Staff:** 10. Offers field testing and other consulting services for farmers and related agri-business firms. Scheduled services include soil testing, plant tissue testing, irrigation monitoring, and pest management. Also provides insect counting to support chemical efficacy testing, and pre-acquisition site assessments for land purchasers. Professionally trained consultants use scientifically designed tests and data collection procedures to analyze farm and field conditions and to give written recommendations on how to proceed. Experienced at providing expert testimony. Industries served:

dairymen, farmers, chemical manufacturers, food processors, municipalities, attorneys, realtors, developers, and engineering firms.

AGRITECH, INC.

1989 W. 5th Ave., Ste. 6
Columbus, OH 43212
William E. Riddle, President
PH: (614)488-2772
FX: (614)488-0320
E-mail: agritech@iwaynet.net
URL: http://agritechinc.com
Founded: 1985. **Staff:** 2. A consulting research organization dedicated to serving agribusiness; food, beverage, and dairy processing industries; and government agencies. The client's technology base is used to identify new markets, improve existing markets, develop targeted business and technology plans, and improve operational activities. Specializes in market research, value-added market assessments, feasibility studies, and the evaluation of business and technology plans and strategies. In addition, the firm matches agricultural resources with potential markets to identify value-added products that can promote economic growth. Central and South America and the Middle East.

AGRIVISTA

8440 Woodfield Crossing Blvd., Ste. 300
Indianapolis, IN 46240
Robert M. Book, President
PH: (317)818-6025
TF: (800)697-0316
FX: (317)469-2200
Founded: 1991. **Staff:** 6. Offers agricultural and food processing clients comprehensive industry knowledge and contacts, insightful strategies, counsel, sales producing marketing and communications services, and predictable costs at or below clients expectations. As management consultants firm offers defined project management, non-financial problem solving within the corporation, creating joint venture opportunities including shared distribution, long term strategic planning, short term tactical planning and implementation, marketing staffing evaluations-setting performance guidelines, marketing functions evaluation internalize or externalize, and preparation for global marketing. Research capabilities provide clients global marketing opportunities, competitive position and/or image in the marketplace, discovery of unfulfilled customer needs, new product test marketing, customer satisfaction studies, communications efficiency/advertising awareness and communication strategy verification and testing. In the areas of marketing communications, firm offers creative positioning and development of advertising materials (print, broadcast, direct mail, etc.), media analysis and placement-coordination of external service, sales promotion, sales kits, dealer sales aids, collateral materials and point-of-sale, corporate graphic standards, corporate communications to employees and investors, sales training materials, both printed and audio visual, position papers and speech writing, and incentive programs, sales contests, corporate meetings and conventions. Other services include employee recruitment and merger and acquisition activity. Industries served: agribusiness, cooperatives, and food processors.

AGRO CORP.

RR 2, Box 88A
Brighton, IL 62012-9900
E. Allen Lash, President/CEO
PH: (618)372-3000
FX: (618)372-4000
Founded: 1967. **Staff:** 64. Offers a broad range of services in the areas of asset management, consulting, investment acquisition, marketing, planning, financial analysis, resource analysis, accounting, recordkeeping, tax preparation, tax consulting and software. Offers opportunities to all facets of the agricultural spectrum including farmers, non-farm entrepreneurs, financial institutions and agribusinesses. Clients range from local farmers to multinational agribusinesses.

AGRO ENGINEERING INC.
0210 County Rd. 2 SO.
Alamosa, CO 81101-9758
Leroy Salazar, President
PH: (719)852-4957
FX: (719)852-5146
E-mail: agro@agro.com
URL: http://www.agro.com
Founded: 1982. **Staff:** 8. Provides agricultural engineering services including water irrigation systems design, pest control, fertility assessment, and farm management services for clients in Southern Colorado and the San Louis Valley.

AGRO HAWAII INC.
86-365 Kuwale Rd.
Waianae, HI 96792-2710
Donald Takaki, Contact
PH: (808)696-4417
FX: (808)696-8625
Agricultural consulting firm.

AGRO INDUSTRY ADVISORY SERVICES
  INTERNATIONAL
65 Crabtree Rd.
Concord, MA 01742
Erik Kissmeyer-Nielsen, Contact
PH: (978)369-5420
FX: (978)287-0181
E-mail: kissmeyer@aol.com
Founded: 1970. **Staff:** 1. Economic and technical advisor to agricultural and food industry international. Technical, economic and marketing evaluation of existing projects and in-depth feasibility studies of potential projects, particularly fruit and vegetable production and processing. Serves private industries as well as government agencies.

AGRONOMIC & NUTRITIONAL CONSULTANTS, INC.
RR 1, Box 186
Princeton, IN 47670
Steven J. Engels, President
PH: (812)729-6090
FX: (812)724-3008
E-mail: agcon@evansville.net
Founded: 1982. **Staff:** 1. Offers soil, plant and animal production consulting services as follows: soil and feed samples are collected and analyzed; feeding and fertilizing recommendations are made; and troubleshooting of problems in season is available.

AGRONOMIC SERVICES INC.
PO Box 1757
Woodstock, NB, Canada E0J 2B0
David C. Frost, President
PH: (506)328-6534
Provides agricultural consulting services related to potato production and storage management, soil chemistry and plant nutrition.

AGSTAT
6394 Grandview Rd.
Verona, WI 53593
Jon Baldock, Contact
PH: (608)845-7993
FX: (608)845-7993
E-mail: agstat@aol.com
Founded: 1979. **Staff:** 3. Agricultural consultant offering these services: contract research, experimental design/statistical analyses, computer programs to assist in agricultural decisions, soil testing, plant tissue analysis, crop production recommendations, pest scouting/crop monitoring, troubleshooting crop production problems, and agricultural insurance claims investigation.

AGTOPROF INC.
116 E. Heritage Dr.
Tyler, TX 75703
Pierre DeWet, Contact

PH: (903)561-9444
FX: (903)561-9990
E-mail: agtoprof@usac.net
Agricultural consulting firm provides managerial expertise.

AGVISE LABORATORIES INC.
PO Box 510, Hwy. 15
Northwood, ND 58267
Robert Deutsch, President
PH: (701)587-6010
FX: (701)587-6013
E-mail: agvise@polarcomm.com
URL: http://agviselabs.com
Founded: 1976. **Staff:** 55. Offers analytical services to agriculture and related support companies in crop production, and pest management. Other Agvise services include field contract research, and GLP compliant soil and water characterization. Serves private industries as well as government agencies.

AIRSEP CORP.
290 Creekside Dr.
Buffalo, NY 14228-2070
PH: (716)691-0202
TF: (800)874-0202
FX: (716)691-0707
Provides standard and custom designed PSA (pressure swing adsorption) oxygen systems to aquaculture industry.

ALKEN-MURRAY CORP.
417 Canal St.
New York, NY 10013
PH: (212)431-4020
FX: (212)431-4944
Specializes in treatments for water, waste, and fuel; algae cultivation; and analytical chemical services for aquaculturists.

FRANKLIN L. ALLEN, ASSOCIATED FORESTERS
2395 Hwy. 73 S.
Marianna, FL 32447
Franklin L. Allen, Owner
PH: (904)526-3921
FX: (904)482-4547
Founded: 1979. **Staff:** 5. Forestry consultants offering the following: timber marketing, forest management, timber appraisals and inventories, real estate appraisals and brokerage (acreage), timberland investment counseling, urban forestry, game management, and environmental and raw material availability studies.

WALTER ALLISON & ASSOCIATES LTD.
PO Box 175
Florenceville, NB, Canada E0J 1K0
Walter Allison, Owner
PH: (506)392-8372
FX: (506)392-6061
Offers agricultural engineering services such as the design of fruit and vegetable storage facilities, farmland drainage, and soil and water conservation.

ALLTECH
PH: (618)587-2603
FX: (618)587-4803
E-mail: alltech@alltechrandd.com
URL: http://www.alltechrandd.com
An agriculture and horticulture research-based company. Services include professional training and education, research services, marketing development support educational and diagnostic materials.

NOEL ALON
2045 Cheltenham Ln.
Columbia, SC 29223
PH: (803)738-0372
FX: (803)738-0372
E-mail: xmaswave@concentric.net

Advises on breeding crawfish and conducts contract research and development for aquaculturists.

ALTERNATIVE AQUACULTURE ASSOCIATION
PO Box 109
Breinigsville, PA 18031
PH: (610)395-5854
FX: (610)395-8202
Advises aquaculturists in the areas of home aquaculture, custom fish breeding, and biofilter design and management.

JOSEPH F. ALTICK, M.S.
549 Howard St.
Ventura, CA 93003
PH: (805)653-5701
FX: (805)653-0540
Provides aquaculture design and engineering services.

AMERICAN AQUAFARMS INTERNATIONAL INC.
229 Saville Pl.
Prescott, AZ 86303
PH: (520)777-8953
FX: (520)777-8953
Advises on custom fish rearing and investing in aquaculture industry. Also engaged in contract R&D and aquaculture design.

AMERICAN BIOSYSTEMS, INC.
PO Box 21221
Roanoke, VA 24018
Edward M. Goyetle, President
PH: (540)344-6469
TF: (888)344-6469
FX: (540)345-1247
E-mail: info@americanbiosystems.com
URL: http://www.americanbiosystems.com
Founded: 1981. **Staff:** 5. Provide consulting services for water quality management, wastewater and industrial waste treatment, aquaculture system wastewater management. Also sales and marketing of industrial enzymes for cleaning purposes as well as ingredients for animal and aquaculture feeds.

AMERICAN SOCIETY OF AGRICULTURAL
CONSULTANTS
950 S. Cherry St., Ste. 508
Denver, CO 80246-2664
PH: (303)759-5091
FX: (303)758-0190
E-mail: asac@agri-associations.org
URL: http://www.agri-associations.org/asac
Founded: 1963. **Staff:** 2. Association of agricultural consultants. Maintains directory of members who provide a variety of agricultural consulting services.

AMERICAN TECHNOLOGIES, INC.
6029 Stoney Creek Dr.
Fort Wayne, IN 46825
PH: (219)482-1756
FX: (219)482-1756
Advises aquaculture industry on stock, including frog, bass, and crawfish production.

AML INDUSTRIES, INC.
3500 Davisville Rd.
Hatboro, PA 19040
Aaron M. Lavin, President
PH: (215)674-2424
TF: (800)258-4410
FX: (215)674-3252
E-mail: info@lavincentrifuge.com
URL: http://www.lavincentrifuge.com
Founded: 1945. Offers assistance in aquaculture, specializing in algae cultivation, and filtration/purification systems.

ANA LAB CORP.
PO Box 9000
Kilgore, TX 75663-9000
C.H. Whiteside, President
PH: (903)984-0551
FX: (903)984-5914
E-mail: corp@ana-lab.com
URL: http://www.ana-lab.com
Founded: 1965. **Staff:** 175. Offers technical consulting services in environmental pollution, arson investigation, general chemistry, and agricultural problems. Serves private industries as well as government agencies. Geographic areas served: continental United States, Mexico, and Canada.

MARV ANDERSON & ASSOCIATES LTD.
326 Vista Manor
Sherwood Park, AB, Canada T8A 4J7
Marvin S. Anderson, President
PH: (403)464-4020
FX: (403)449-0651
Founded: 1974. Consulting economists and agrologists providing specialized services in natural resource management, agriculture, and economic development. Offers water resource economics, agricultural development, community and regional development, and farm management.

NANCY BROWN ANDISON
1 Robert Speck Pky., Ste. 1100
Mississauga, ON, Canada L4Z 3M3
Nancy Brown Andison, Contact
PH: (905)949-7400
FX: (905)949-7415
Offers agricultural management consulting services such as trade evaluation, marketing, human resources, and computer systems assistance.

ANIMAL BREEDING CONSULTANTS
PO Box 313
Sonoma, CA 95476
Fred T. Shultz, Contact
PH: (707)996-2863
FX: (707)996-3561
E-mail: 105204.3065@compuserve.com
Founded: 1952. **Staff:** 2. Consulting services include development and supervision of agricultural and aquaculture production systems and genetic improvement programs. Animal improvement, feeds and feeding, disease control, husbandry, and economics are integrated into programs adapted to the special needs and circumstances of the client. Expertise with chickens, turkeys, beef cattle, dairy cattle, sheep, swine, horses, algae, fish and shellfish. Serves private industries as well as government agencies.

APPLIED TECHNOLOGY & MANAGEMENT, INC.
400 Australian Ave., Ste. 855
West Palm Beach, FL 33401
PH: (561)659-0041
FX: (561)659-3733
Offers expertise in the areas of aquaculture biofilter design, feasibility studies, environmental issues, lake and stream management, marine aquarium management, and oceanography.

AQUA-BIO CONCEPTS
6121 NE 197th St.
Seattle, WA 98155
PH: (206)483-4155
FX: (206)483-4155
Engaged in aquaculture design, specializing in closed high density growth systems, contract research and development, biofilter design and management, animal nutrition, and feed formulation.

AQUA BIO SERVICES
PO Box 623
Larkspur, CA 94977
Douglas Wilkerson, Owner

PH: (415)924-8305
FX: (415)924-7073
E-mail: aquabio@linex.com
URL: http://www.seacage.com
Founded: 1992. Designs aquacultural environments, specializing in feasibility studies, site evaluations, aquaculture management, and abalone production.

AQUA FISHERIES LTD.
2620 N. Ten
Ocean Springs, MS 39564
PH: (601)875-1866
FX: (601)875-1866
URL: http://www.comexba.com
Involved in lake and stream management, marine aquarium management, biofilter design, and contract research and development. Industries served: aquaculture.

AQUA SIERRA, INC.
8350 S. Mariposa Dr.
Morrison, CO 80465-2418
William J. Logan, President
PH: (303)697-5486
TF: (800)524-3474
FX: (303)697-5069
E-mail: wlogan@aqua-sierra.com
URL: http://www.aqua-sierra.com_water
Founded: 1989. **Staff:** 6. Designs and installs water features including lakes, ponds and artificial streams. Engineering and installation of ozone enhanced bottom diffused aeration systems, continuous bacterial injection technology for lakes, ponds and wastewater systems. Aquaculture engineering and development in closed, high density growth applications. Fisheries evaluation and management. Lake reclamation.

AQUA SPRINGS
19465 200th Ave.
Big Rapids, MI 49307
PH: (616)796-2284
FX: (616)796-2284
Provides aquaculture design for U.S. clients.

AQUA TROPICS
13B Vistaway
Kennewick, WA 99336
PH: (509)735-3474
Counsels on the breeding of crawfish for aquaculture industry.

AQUACARE ENVIRONMENT INC.
1155 N. State St., Ste. 303
Bellingham, WA 98225
Henning Gatz, President
PH: (360)734-7964
FX: (360)734-9407
E-mail: ecologic@aquacare.com
URL: http://www.aquacare.com
Founded: 1987. **Staff:** 3. Provides support services to aquaculture industry. Emphasis on controlled environment aquaculture technology/

AQUACULTURAL RESEARCH CORP.
Chapin Beach Rd.
PO Box 2028
Dennis, MA 02638
PH: (508)385-3933
FX: (508)385-3935
Provides expertise in clam breeding, algae cultivation, and aquaculture design and engineering.

AQUACULTURE BIO-TECHNOLOGIES, INC.
PO Box 6501
South Bend, IN 46660
PH: (219)232-4345
FX: (219)232-5891

Designs aquacultural environments, specializing in closed high density growth systems, contract research and development, animal feed, and feed formulation.

AQUACULTURE BIOENGINEERING CORP.
PO Box 8
Rives Junction, MI 49277
PH: (517)569-3474
FX: (517)569-3474
E-mail: visforel@aol.com
Offers wide variety of services involving aquaculture design and engineering, including feasibility studies, site evaluations, water quality, environmental issues, aeration, feed and feed formulation, and salmon production.

AQUACULTURE ENTERPRISES, INC.
8314 Loring Dr.
Bethesda, MD 20817
Martin Sterenbuch, Esq., Contact
PH: (301)365-5515
FX: (301)365-5644
Offers financial counsel on investing in aquaculture industry, and other start-up business ventures.

AQUACULTURE SERVICES
5425 Boggy Creek Rd.
Orlando, FL 32824
PH: (407)856-8187
FX: (407)856-8377
Specializes in aquaculture design, finfish cultures, polycultures, and air and water filtration and purification expertise.

AQUAFARMS 2000 INC.—EQUIPMENT MANUFACTURING
474 Galtier Plaza 175 E. 5th
St. Paul, MN 55101
TF: (800)293-2963
FX: (612)290-9363
Provides aquaculture design engineering services.

AQUAFAUNA BIO-MARINE, INC.
PO Box 5
Hawthorne, CA 90250
Italo (Bud) Insalata, Director
PH: (310)973-5275
FX: (310)676-9387
E-mail: aquafauna@aquafauna.com
URL: http://www.aquafauna.com
Offers expertise in aquaculture systems and design including aeration pumps, ultraviolet technology, heating and other aquatic applications including genetic marking technology through new subsidiary called ASICo (Aquatic Stock Improvement Co.)

AQUAFOOD BUSINESS ASSOCIATES
PO Box 16190
Charleston, SC 29412
Raymond J. Rhodes, President
PH: (803)795-9506
FX: (803)795-9477
Founded: 1985. **Staff:** 3. Full service business consulting firm specializing in the seafood and aquaculture industries. Services include business-to-business marketing research and development, market assessments, financial feasibility studies, business planning, and venture capital sourcing. Industries served: commercial fishermen, seafood processors, seafood wholesalers/distributors, seafood restaurants, aquaculture producers, aquaculture feed and equipment suppliers, and government agencies.

AQUAGENIX
411 W. Orion St.
Tempe, AZ 85283
PH: (602)820-5900
FX: (602)820-0651
URL: http://www.aquagenix.com
Engaged in recreational fisheries management (lake and stream), and

services in the areas of water quality, weed control, and aeration systems for the aquaculture industry.

AQUANETICS SYSTEMS, INC.
5252 Lovelock St.
San Diego, CA 92110
PH: (619)291-8444
FX: (619)291-8335
E-mail: aquanetics@juno.com
Develops closed high density growth systems for aquaculture industry, specializing in biofiltration design and management.

AQUARESEARCH, LTD.
PO Box 208
North Hatley, PQ, Canada J0B 2C0
PH: (819)842-2494
FX: (819)842-2902
Engaged in lake and stream aquaculture management, weed control, and contract research and development. Also designs closed high density growth systems, including biofilter design and management.

AQUARIUM DESIGNS, INC.
4240 W. 76th St.
Edina, MN 55435
Ronald E. Raasch, President & CEO
PH: (612)831-8575
TF: (800)213-8375
FX: (612)831-8642
Founded: 1978. **Staff:** 11. Designs and manages biofilter systems for aquaculturists, restaurants, and businesses.

AQUARIUS ASSOCIATES
PO Box 662
Port Norris, NJ 08349
W.J. Caneonier, Dir. Research/Development
PH: (609)785-0402
FX: (609)785-1544
Founded: 1984. **Staff:** 3. Engaged in aquaculture design and contract research and development. Also offers services in the areas of shellfish culture, hatchery design, shellfish sanitation, depuration and water quality.

AQUASOURCE
101 Crosby St.
New York, NY 10012
PH: (212)343-2548
FX: (212)343-2548
Provides marketing services and conducts feasibility studies for aquaculture industry.

AQUATEC SYSTEMS, INC.
2780 N. Riverside Dr., Ste. 702
Tampa, FL 33602
PH: (813)223-3883
FX: (813)223-3919
Designs and develops aquaculture environments, including biofilter design and management. Specializes in closed high density growth systems.

AQUATIC & ENVIRONMENTAL ENGINEERING
  SERVICES
5261 Highland Rd., Ste. 313
Baton Rouge, LA 70808
Dr. Thomas B. Lawson, Ph.D., P.E., Founder/Owner
PH: (504)769-7286
FX: (504)766-8455
E-mail: aees94@eatel.net
URL: http://www.explore-br.com/aquatic/
Founded: 1994. **Staff:** 2. Provides aquaculture engineering services, including closed high density growth systems, aeration, and biofilter design and management, compost engineering, backyard compost units, and koi pond design and products.

AQUATIC CONTROL, INC.
PO Box 100
Seymour, IN 47274
Robert L. Johnson, President
PH: (812)497-2410
TF: (800)753-5253
FX: (812)497-2460
Founded: 1966. **Staff:** 12. Provides consulting services in aquatic and terrestrial ecology, including fish and wildlife population management, industrial fish and wildlife enhancement programs, aquatic weed control, fish stocking, management of cooling reservoirs, and lake aeration equipment, consultation installation and maintenance.

AQUATIC DESIGN & CONSTRUCTION LTD.
3450 Meridian Rd.
Okemos, MI 48864
PH: (517)347-5537
FX: (517)347-4999
E-mail: shrimpone@aol.com
Offers services in aquatic design, project planning, engineering, GPS surveying, GIS mapping, feasibility studies, construction management, and CAD design. Specializes in shrimp farming. Fluent in Spanish.

AQUATIC FARMS, LTD.
207 Lawrence St.
Ravenna, OH 44266
PH: (330)239-2929
FX: (330)239-8436
E-mail: officeafl@aol.com
Offers aquaculture design/engineering, including pond engineering, water quality services, aquaculture business management guidance, feasibility studies, prawn and shrimp production, and polyculture expertise.

AQUATIC MANAGEMENT SERVICES (NEW YORK)
318 Church Rd.
Putnam Valley, NY 10579-2512
PH: (914)526-2248
FX: (914)526-2076
Offers services in the areas of fisheries biology and aquaculture management, specializing in aeration systems and weed control.

AQUATIC RESEARCH CO.
2732 Tremont
Dover, OH 44622
PH: (330)364-1951
Offers services in the areas of aquaculture biofilter design and management, fish behavior, polycultures, and management issues.

AQUATIC RESOURCE CONSULTING
R.D. 2
Box 2562
Saylorsburg, PA 18353
PH: (717)992-6443
E-mail: jhartvir@sumlink.net
Provides expertise in the areas of analytical chemical services, electrofishing, fish behavior (ecology research), fisheries biology, lake and stream recreational fisheries management and management guidance, and water quality issues.

AQUATIC RESOURCE MANAGERS
HC 71
Box 172-A
Graysville, TN 37338
James W. Miller, Owner
PH: (615)554-3284
FX: (615)554-3284
E-mail: jimfish@bledsoe.net
Founded: 1980. Offers services in the areas of aquaculture investment, site evaluations, feasibility studies, lake and stream management and management guidance, fisheries biology, tilapia and trout production, and educational programs.

AQUATIC RESOURCES
2610 Meier Rd.
Sebastopol, CA 95472
PH: (707)829-1194
FX: (707)829-0554
Engaged in aquaculture design and management, abalone production, and bioassay services.

AQUAVENTURES
201 Luke St.
Edenton, NC 27932
PH: (919)482-7354
FX: (919)482-3393
Advises aquaculturists in the breeding of crawfish.

ARBEX FOREST DEVELOPMENT CO. LTD.
PO Box 879
Richmond, ON, Canada K0A 2Z0
P.G. Prins, President
PH: (613)838-2047
FX: (613)838-5419
Founded: 1971. **Staff:** 5. Forestry consultants with expertise in silvicultural operations, tree planting, plantation tending, plantation assessment, plantation thinnings, tree pruning, tree marking; forest inventory—sampling design, field sampling, data compilation, preparation of forest cover type maps, land valuation; forest development planning; cartography; forest management planning; forestry components of integrated rural development, transmigration development; regional development; and watershed management.

ARGENT CHEMICAL LABORATORIES
8702 152nd Ave. NE
Redmond, WA 98052
PH: (206)885-3777
TF: (800)426-6258
FX: (206)885-2112
Offers biofilter design and management, aeration systems, and diagnostics services to aquaculture industry.

ASCHEMAN ASSOCIATES CONSULTING
2921 Beverly Dr.
Des Moines, IA 50322
Robert E. Ascheman, President
PH: (515)276-7371
TF: (800)798-7371
FX: (515)276-8707
E-mail: rascheman@aol.com
Founded: 1979. **Staff:** 2. Provides consulting, expert witness and related agribusiness services to agricultural-oriented businesses including: (1) producers, (2) agrochemical, fertilizer, seed and equipment companies, (3) the insurance industry, and (4) the legal profession, as well as government agencies.

JAMES E. ASHER, CONSULTING FORESTER
393 Terrace Rd.
Lake Arrowhead, CA 92352
James E. Asher, Contact
PH: (909)337-2672
FX: (909)336-2910
Founded: 1957. **Staff:** 3. Offers forest resource potential investigation including full-service forestland management (Western softwoods and hardwoods); reforestation tree planting; harvesting engineering and supervision; forest inventory and appraisal; forest products utilization and marketing; urban forestry; and forest and tree damage appraisal (expert witness, litigation, forest and tree valuation erosion control plans). Active throughout Southern California and the West.

ASHMEAD ECONOMIC RESEARCH INC.
4500 16th Ave. NW, Ste. 300
Calgary, AB, Canada T3B 0M6
Ralph Ashmead, Owner
PH: (403)247-9690
FX: (403)247-9915
E-mail: rashmead@igw.ca
Consulting in agricultural finance and farm management is offered. Economic forecasting and alternative energy source services are also available.

ASSET MANAGEMENT CONSULTING GROUP
PO 308
Rossville, IN 46065
PH: (765)379-2449
FX: (765)379-2325
Firm offers extensive knowledge in agriculture.

ASSOCIATES IN RURAL DEVELOPMENT, INC.
PO Box 1397
Burlington, VT 05402
George Burrill, President
PH: (802)658-3890
FX: (802)658-4247
E-mail: dread@ardinc.com
URL: http://www.ardinc.com
Founded: 1977. **Staff:** 100. Privately owned consulting firm that offers a broad range of project planning, design, implementation, evaluation, and applied research services in five sectors: management and institutional development; natural resources and the environment; agriculture and irrigation; water supply, sanitation, and environmental health; and infrastructure and energy resources. Information technology services, including geographic information systems (GIS), global positioning systems (GPS), and computer visualization, are also offered.

ATLANTIC AGRI-FOOD ASSOCIATES INC.
2660 RR 4, Route 560
Centreville, NB, Canada E0J 1H0
Raymond P. Carmichael, Owner
PH: (506)276-3311
FX: (506)276-3311
Provides crop and livestock production consulting services including feasibility analysis, agronomic research, financial planning, debt structuring, project management, and conference planning. Georeferenced crop production management; precision farming support, equipment and service.

MIKE E. AYEWOH, PH.D.
10 Meadow St.
Mansfield, PA 16933
Michael Ehi Ayewoh, Contact
PH: (717)662-0277
FX: (717)662-0277
Areas of consulting include: grants from private and public sources (activities include, but not limited to: prospect research, proposal writing, solicitation of funds, and management (pre and post) of funded projects); strategic and operational planning; assessment/ evaluation studies; youth (to 20 years of age) and adult program initiatives; other alternative sources of funding.

BACKSWATH MANAGEMENT INC.
97 King's Dr.
Winnipeg, MB, Canada R3T 3E8
Terry Betker, President
PH: (204)261-8400
FX: (204)261-8800
E-mail: canstar@escape.ca
URL: http://www.escape/~bmi/
Consultant offering agricultural business management services in the areas of human resources and finance.

COLIN BAGWELL FORESTRY
102 Saralee Dr.
Huntsville, AL 35811
Colin Bagwell, Contact

PH: (205)536-6583
FX: (205)852-1177
E-mail: cojbag@compuserve.com
Founded: 1970. **Staff:** 2. Offers counsel on the management of timberlands for forest products, land appraisal, real estate sales, tree planting, feasibility studies, environmental impact studies, timber trespass, damage appraisal, forest chemical sales, timber sales, biological studies, and urban tree analysis. Also offers services in forest mapping, aerial photography, wildlife management, insect and disease control, and kudzu control. Can serve as expert witness in any of these areas. Industries served: attorneys, accountants, timber companies, banks, private owners, resource companies, and government agencies.

BAHME & ASSOCIATES
10795 Bryne Ave.
Los Molinos, CA 96055
John Beale Bahme, Ph.D., Principal
PH: (916)527-8028
FX: (916)527-6288
E-mail: bahme@snowcrest.net
Specializes in forensic agriculture and horticulture. Provides analysis and appraisal of crop loss. Specializes in tree, vine, field, row, vegetable and ornamental crops.

JOHN D. BAKER & ASSOCIATES
6613 Bradley Blvd.
Bethesda, MD 20817
John D. Baker, President
PH: (301)469-7954
Founded: 1980. **Staff:** 2. Agribusiness management firm offers consulting services to U.S. food processors and others having volatile input costs and also international agribusiness. Specialization is in commodity purchasing organization, business and procurement planning, training in commodity purchasing and general procurement, price and profit risk control, price forecasting methods, market research and project feasibility. Serves the following industries: agriculture, consumer products, food and beverage, manufacturing, nonprofits, and retail and wholesale.

BAKER LAND & TIMBER MANAGEMENT INC.
PO Box 5624
Alexandria, LA 71307
Donald J. Baker, President
PH: (318)473-8751
FX: (318)443-1647
E-mail: blanbake@aol.com
Founded: 1986. **Staff:** 2. Offers general forestry services including forest land management, timber marking and marketing services, timber estimates and appraisals, expert witness testimony in forestry matters, SIP (Stewardship Incentives Program) management plan development, periodic tract inspections for absentee landowners, and detailed forest management plans. Licensed arborist in Louisiana; consultation limited to urban trees, member, Association of Consulting Foresters of America, Inc. Provides forest management work to private, nonindustrial landowners; and consultation to forest industry clients on matters within capacity as expert forester.

BARLOTT CONSULTING LTD.
600 First Edmonton Place
10665 Jasper Ave.
Edmonton, AB, Canada T5J 3S9
Paul J. Barlott, President
PH: (403)448-7471
FX: (403)421-1270
Agricultural services offered include conservation planning, environmental impact assessment, computer applications, decision support systems, feasibility studies, strategic and operational planning, and water management.

BARTEE AGRICHEMICAL CONSULTANTS, INC.
817 E. Northview
Olathe, KS 66061
Sam N. Bartee, President

PH: (913)782-9666
FX: (913)782-9666
Founded: 1982. **Staff:** 2. Agricultural chemical consultant in pesticide research and development. Specialties are herbicides, plant regulators, and product formulations. Performs contract research for performance evaluations of agrichemicals. Serves as expert witness in pesticide complaints and nonperformance investigations. Creates agrichemical project designs and does feasibility studies.

B.C. RESEARCH INC.
3650 Wesbrook Mall
Vancouver, BC, Canada V6S 2L2
Hugh Wynne-Edwards, President
PH: (604)224-4331
FX: (604)224-0540
E-mail: bcri@bcr.bc.ca
URL: http://www.bcr.bc.ca
Founded: 1993. **Staff:** 85. Corporation solves practical industrial problems for clients in both the private and public sectors by performing contract research on a confidential basis. Expertise is offered in the fields of advanced industrial materials, air quality emissions, aquaculture biotechnology, bulk handling, chemical analysis, chemical products and processes, engine systems, extractive metallurgy, fisheries and food products, forest biotechnology, industrial testing, mechanical engineering, natural gas vehicles, occupational health, ocean engineering, redox chemistry, and waste management. Industries served: performs multidisciplinary industrial research in the broad areas of forestry, fisheries, engineering, mining, environmental, and chemical industries. Also serves government agencies.

DONALD S. BELL CONSULTING FORESTER
PO Box 455
Bruce, MS 38915
Donald S. Bell, Contact
PH: (601)983-4903
Founded: 1978. **Staff:** 7. Consulting forester offering the following: timber sales administration (including timber marking, timber marketing and compliance), timber inventory, timber appraisals, forest management plans, long term forest management services, timber and forestland taxation services, estate planning, market and industrial feasibility studies, damage and trespass assessments, forest land litigation, timber resource studies, and environmental impact studies. Also serves government agencies.

BENNETT & PETERS, INC.
8313 O'Hara Ct.
Baton Rouge, LA 70806
PH: (504)927-3500
FX: (504)927-2017
E-mail: info@southerntrees.com
URL: http://www.southerntrees.com/bap
Founded: 1950. Specializes in forest management, inventory and timber sales, geographic information systems (GIS) and computerized forest management planning.

BENTON LABORATORIES, INC.
345 Brookwood Dr.
Athens, GA 30604
J. Benton Jones, Jr., President
PH: (706)546-0425
FX: (706)548-4891
Founded: 1978. **Staff:** 2. Agricultural consultants on crop production management, soil fertility evaluation, soil testing and plant analysis, hydroponic crop production and greenhouse growing, analytical service for soils, plant tissue, water and other biological substances for elemental contents; environmental consulting related to agricultural activity and water pollution. Serves private industries as well as government agencies.

A. H. BESWICK AND ASSOCIATES
19 Revcoe Dr.
North York, ON, Canada M2M 2B9
Alan H. Beswick, Owner

PH: (416)229-0175
FX: (416)229-9639
E-mail: alcla@netside-cafe.on.ca
Provides meat and food industry business analyses, including financial assessments, feasibility studies, strategic planning, and project management services. Also offers livestock marketing assistance.

BIRD FORESTRY SERVICE
Rte. 7, Box 382
Center, TX 75935
Mike Bird, President
PH: (409)598-3053
FX: (409)598-9579
URL: http://www.bfsinc.com
Founded: 1979. Works to maintain an economically productive forest with a healthy natural environment. Management strategies are designed to maximize fiber production and are based on economically sound and environmentally safe methods. Utilizes the latest technology, including custom aerial photography, a computer generated mapping system, and current forestry software programs. Services include endangered species consultation, forest management, habitat analysis and enhancements, timber sales and harvest supervision, wetland determinations and delineations, logging plans, wildlife management, reforestation, resource inventories, appraisals and recommendations, forest herbicide recommendations and applications, resource management plans, prescribed burning, damage appraisals and testimony, and boundary line maintenance.

BLUE MAX HORTICULTURAL CONSULTING
2202 N. Ridge Ave.
Tifton, GA 31794-2835
Dr. Max Austin, Horticulture Consultant
PH: (912)382-0399
E-mail: maustin@surfsouth.com
URL: http://members.surfsouth.com/~maustin
Horticulture consulting. Worldwide participation as a speaker and/or consultant for researchers, extension specialists, and industry representatives.

BLUE RIDGE FORESTRY CONSULTANTS, INC.
11171 Hume Rd.
Hume, VA 22639
Gary Alan Younkin, President
PH: (540)364-1238
FX: (540)364-4177
E-mail: youkin@erols.com
Founded: 1979. **Staff:** 3. Involved in administering timber sales for private landowners and preparing forest product appraisals; activities include timber sale design, advertising, marketing, contract preparation and supervising field activities. Also develops forest management plans. Serves private industries as well as government agencies.

BUD BLUMENSTOCK
5755 Nutting Hall
Orono, ME 04469-5755
Marvin W. (Bud) Blumenstock, Contact
PH: (207)581-3202
FX: (207)581-3207
Founded: 1976. **Staff:** 1. Forest management consultant with experience in the business and financial aspects of tree growing and harvesting including logging and saw mills. Specialty includes chain saw and timber harvesting safety procedures. Industries served: timber, logging, sawmill, pulp and paper.

BOLLYKY ASSOCIATES INC.
31 Strawberry Hill Ave.
Stamford, CT 06902
PH: (203)967-4223
FX: (203)967-4845
E-mail: ljbbai@bai-ozone.com
URL: http://www.bai-ozone.com/
Ozone consultants. Engineering services include acting as specialists in treatment processes and treatment systems such as drinking water treatment, DI water systems, industrial wastewater treatment, toxic and hazardous waste treatment, water recycling, advanced oxidation processes such as, zebra mussel control, aquaculture and aquarium water treatment, industrial process streams, and treatment of air streams for odor and pollutant removal. Designs, tests and evaluates ozone generators, ozone decomposers, ozone contractors, UV-ozone reactors, and specialty treatment systems design. Performs treatability studies, and laboratory and pilot plant testing. Designs full scale ozone treatment systems.

BYRON L. BONDURANT
265 Franklin St.
Dublin, OH 43017
Byron L. Bondurant, Contact
PH: (614)889-2469
Founded: 1964. Offers counsel on agricultural systems and management with emphasis on soil and water, structures, and materials handling equipment. Also advises on agricultural estate and corporation management, land smoothing, water and crop storage, crop drying and processing. Other services include curricula development, research and extension in agriculture and engineering. Industries served: agriculture, educational institutions and government agencies.

H.F. 'HAL' BOWMAN
4000 Hope Ln.
Dunsmuir, CA 96025
H.F. Bowman, Contact
PH: (916)235-2590
FX: (916)235-2590
Founded: 1979. **Staff:** 2. Consulting forester specializing in forest management and valuation. Services include fair market valuations for large forest products companies, and timber cruise and valuations, forest management plans, timber stand improvement, and zoning and land use advice for small land owners. Serves government needs also.

ROBERT S. (BOB) BOYD
1111 Sumter Ave.
Tallahassee, FL 32301
Robert S. Boyd, Owner
PH: (904)877-9493
FX: (904)656-4512
E-mail: Treesno1@aol.com
Founded: 1972. **Staff:** 2. Involved in land and timber management, planning, sales and operations, control burning, game management, tree marking, cruising, appraisals of land and timber, estate planning, urban forestry and environmental studies. Industries served: forest products companies, private and public landowners, real estate, engineering, investment and appraisal companies, power companies, and government agencies.

BRADLEY AGRI-CONSULTING INC.
236 Pomona St., Ste. 100
El Cerrito, CA 94530-1668
Bernard L. Bradley, President
PH: (510)525-0250
FX: (510)525-7818
E-mail: bradac@worldnet.att.net
Founded: 1980. **Staff:** 5. Complete agri-business and food processing industry consultancy serving international clients. Provides marketing and market surveys, product development and introduction, competitive intelligence, regulatory and environmental concerns, acquisitions and licensing, confidential contacts, export/import concerns, foreign negotiations and representation, training, information systems, applications and data transfer and lead management. Serves private industries as well as government and donor agencies.

ED BRAUN & ASSOCIATES
604 1st St. SW, Ste. 375
Calgary, AB, Canada T2P 1M7
Ed Braun, President
PH: (403)266-0660
FX: (403)263-3040

Founded: 1981. **Staff:** 2. Provides services in the following areas: farm appraisals, equipment appraisals, financial consulting, cash flow and budget preparation, credit negotiations, farm business analysis, and farm credit studies. Industries served: Canadian government agencies, banks and lending institutions, and the private Canadian farming industry.

ELDON J. BRICK
Drawer 42
Netherhill, SK, Canada S0L 2M0
Eldon J. Brick, Contact
PH: (306)463-3635
FX: (306)463-3551
E-mail: e.brick@sk.sympatico.ca
Farm business management consultant offering financial planning and analysis and assistance with agricultural computer applications. Also has expertise in surface rights negotiations and expert testimony.

BRUBAKER AGRONOMIC CONSULTING SERVICES, INC.
4340 Oregon Pike
Ephrata, PA 17522-9476
Michael W. Brubaker, Contact
PH: (717)859-3276
TF: (800)840-1711
FX: (717)859-3416
E-mail: bacs@pdt.net
URL: http://www.brubakerag.com
Founded: 1978. **Staff:** 25. Agronomy consultant offering such services as soil testing, plant analysis, field scouting, and complete fertilizer, pesticide, and lime recommendations. Current specialization in nutrient management which encompasses manure, sludge, septage, and commercial fertilizer requirements. Independent of any fertilizer company. Also provides agrichemical contract research to major chemical companies. Industries served: municipalities, farmers, agri-chemical manufacturers, and state and national organizations.

LLOYD B. BULLERMAN
6701 Amhurst Dr.
Lincoln, NE 68510-2306
Lloyd B. Bullerman, Contact
PH: (402)472-2801
FX: (402)472-1693
E-mail: lbullerman@foodsci.unl.edu
Founded: 1985. **Staff:** 1. Agricultural consultant specializing in microbiology, molds, mycotoxins, food-borne bacterial pathogens, and food and feed safety, including preservation and storage of cereal grains.

JOHN BURTON
129 Chisholm Rd.
Regina, SK, Canada S4S 5N9
John Burton, Contact
PH: (306)584-2590
FX: (306)586-1055
E-mail: johnburton@bfsmedia.com
Founded: 1991. **Staff:** 2. Agricultural consulting services include economic and policy planning and special interest in transportation issues. Offers expertise in resource management and policy planning. Experience in agriculture in developing countries.

CALIFORNIA AGRICULTURAL GROUP
Box 774
Esparto, CA 95627
Ronald E. Voss, CEO
PH: (916)787-4463
FX: (916)787-4463
Founded: 1993. **Staff:** 32. Group consists of short- and long-term agricultural production and marketing consultancies, individuals or teams, with a wide range of commodity and scientific expertise. Expertise in sustainable agriculture, appropriate technology, small farms, pest management, rural environmental, and rural/urban interface issues; education, program development, community and rural

development, problem solving services; and women in agriculture, arts/crafts cooperatives, home-based industry. Most consultants are University of California cooperative extension specialists or advisors. Industries served: agricultural production, agricultural marketing, pest management, government agencies, cooperatives, and associations.

CAMPBELL GROUP
1 SW Columbia, Ste. 1720
Portland, OR 97258
PH: (503)275-9675
FX: (503)275-9667
E-mail: info@campbellgroup.com
URL: http://www.campbellgroup.com
Founded: 1981. Provider of timberland investment and management services.

CANADIAN FISHERY CONSULTANTS LTD.
1489 Hollis St.
Halifax, NS, Canada B3J 2R7
Alan Perry, President
PH: (902)422-4698
FX: (902)422-8147
E-mail: cfcl@canfish.com
URL: http://www.canfish.com
Founded: 1980. **Staff:** 7. Natural resources management consultants specialize in supplying professional expertise to sectors within the fishing/aquaculture industry. Offers a range of expertise dealing with the culturing, harvesting, processing, and marketing of fish species. Projects executed have involved financial and technical feasibility studies; design, evaluation, and retrofitting of fish processing facilities; resource analysis; site selection; design of fish culturing facilities; and increasing commercial use of fish processing wastes and by-catch. Industries served: fisheries, resource sector, processing/fish handling industry, government departments, environmental sectors, port authorities, international financing institutions, etc.

VIOLET E. CANDLISH
1702 924-14 Ave. SW
Calgary, AB, Canada T2R 0N7
Dr. Violet E. Candlish, Contact
PH: (403)244-5081
FX: (403)244-5081
E-mail: candlshb@cadvision.com
URL: http://www.cadvision.com/violetbook/index.html
Offers agricultural business consulting services such as research planning, business analysis, policy analysis, and business management. Areas of expertise are animal nutrition and plant biochemistry.

CAROLINA MARKET CONSULTANTS
Rte. 1, Box 356
Johnsonville, SC 29555
Ned L. Huggins, Contact
PH: (843)386-3848
FX: (843)386-3848
Founded: 1973. **Staff:** 2. Provides consulting services on market trading and investing techniques with emphasis on sound money management. Also offers expertise on risk management for all financial and agricultural commodities. Clients include individual investors and traders. Also provides agricultural hedging for farmers and agri-businesses including market strategies and tactics.

C.C. CANADA FORESTRY CO.
819 Mill St.
Camden, SC 29020
C.C. Canada, Contact
PH: (803)432-9780
FX: (803)432-0232
Founded: 1977. **Staff:** 4. Provides consulting services in forest management and appraisal. Services include financial counsel especially in the agricultural field and timberland; and aid in securing loans with major insurance companies for agricultural and agri-business loans. Also advises large corporations, as well as individuals,

on real estate investments and acquisitions. Works with government agencies.

CENTER FOR ANIMAL HEALTH AND PRODUCTIVITY
School of Veterinary Medicine, University of Pennsylvania
382 W. Street Rd.
New Bolton Center
Kennett Square, PA 19348-1692
Dr. Charles Ramberg, Director
PH: (610)444-5800
FX: (610)444-0126
E-mail: admin@cahp.nbc.upenn.edu
URL: http://cahpwww.nbc.upenn.edu/
Founded: 1986. Mission is to develop, communicate and apply knowledge needed for improvement of the health productivity of food animal populations. Implements teaching, research and service programs directed toward the improvement of health and productivity in food animal herds and flocks. Programs involve an integrated approach employing expertise in disciplines such as clinical nutrition, reproduction, health economics, and computer science in addition to conventional specialties in veterinary medicine. Educational activities include instruction of veterinary students in production systems medicine, postgraduate training and continuing education for food animal practitioners. Provides an infrastructure for applied research and directly supports specific research and development projects pertaining to the health management of food animal populations. Provides health management services for animal populations and conducts field investigation of herd and flock problems which pose a threat to the economic productivity of animal agriculture. Constitutes an important line of early defense against the spread of economically important disease among food animal populations.

CENTROL, INC.
714 Atlantic Ave.
Morris, MN 56267
Larry Sax, Contact
PH: (320)589-4293
FX: (320)589-4301
E-mail: sax@centrol.com
URL: http://centrol.com
Founded: 1979. **Staff:** 13. Offers farm management consulting services to improve farmer profitability. Services emphasize crop management: soil fertility, field scouting, field operations, irrigation scheduling and field planning.

CENTROL OF TWIN VALLEY
PO Box 367
Twin Valley, MN 56584-0367
Dennis Berglund, Contact
PH: (218)584-5107
FX: (218)584-5100
Founded: 1981. **Staff:** 22. A farm management company consulting on all agronomic areas (soils, entomology, agronomy, plant pathology) as they relate to agricultural production and management.

CENTURY RAIN AID
31691 Dequindre
Madison Heights, MI 48071
Damian Zawacki, Design Manager
PH: (248)588-2990
TF: (800)347-4272
FX: (248)588-3528
E-mail: brlard@rainaid.com
URL: http://www.rainaid.com
Founded: 1964. **Staff:** 150. Agriculture and landscaping, irrigation and outdoor lighting design, and pond/lake aeration design.

CERES CORP.
424 B 2nd St.
Davis, CA 95616
PH: (530)756-0778
FX: (530)756-0484
E-mail: aginfo@ceresgroup.com
URL: http://www.ceresgroup.com

Business consulting for agribusiness. Provides analysis and planning services to agricultural input suppliers, growers, the food and fiber processing and marketing industries, commodity, associations and agricultural cooperatives. Also provides commodity specific agricultural and market information and customized market research projects to clients.

DEWEY CHANDLER
PO Box 2252
Yakima, WA 98907
Dewey Chandler, Contact
PH: (509)453-3414
FX: (509)577-8782
Founded: 1976. **Staff:** 1. Offers insect and disease pest management consulting for tree fruits (apple, pear, cherry and other stone fruits).

CHARTERED FORESTERS
Hwy. 90 W
PO Drawer 650
Quincy, FL 32353-0650
Norman Kinney, ACf, RF, President
PH: (850)875-4747
FX: (850)627-6280
Founded: 1958. **Staff:** 9. Offers services in timberland management, timber sales, tree planting, brush control, timber cruising and damage appraisals.

CHECCHI AND CO. CONSULTING
1899 L St., N.W., Ste. 800
Washington, DC 20036
Vincent Checchi, President
PH: (202)452-9700
FX: (202)466-9070
E-mail: checchi@checchiconsulting.com
URL: http://www.checchiconsulting.com
Founded: 1951. **Staff:** 45. Offers research, analysis and technical assistance in: economics, finance, agriculture, agricultural credit, agro-industry, development banking, education and training, private enterprise development, and legal reform. Serves private firms, U.S. government agencies, and international organizations.

CHILSON'S MANAGEMENT CONTROLS, INC.
9645 Arrow Rt., Ste. L
Rancho Cucamonga, CA 91730
Richard L. Chilson, President
PH: (909)980-5338
FX: (909)987-3154
E-mail: chilson@chilson.com
URL: http://www.chilson.com
Founded: 1973. **Staff:** 22. Active in egg production, processing, and marketing management consulting. Provides turnkey computer systems for the poultry industry and agribusiness, including hardware, software, installation, training, and continuing support. Software includes flock records, egg processing, perishable distribution, feed mill, and all accounting packages (20 systems). Industries served: poultry, feed, and perishable distribution.

LARRY E. CHRISTENSON AGRICULTURAL ENGINEER
903 10th St.
Kalona, IA 52247
Larry E. Christenson, Contact
PH: (319)656-3380
FX: (319)656-3380
Founded: 1979. **Staff:** 3. Agricultural consultant specializing in agricultural structures and animal environment. Services include facilities evaluation and planning for beef, dairy, poultry, and swine; plans, designs and writes specifications for new livestock production facilities and renovation; animal environment design and waste management planning; grain handling facilities design and farmstead planning; alternate energy systems evaluation and farm energy audits; and loss investigation and expert testimony on product liability.

BRYAN CHUNYK
PO Box 2535
Station M
Calgary, AB, Canada T2P 2N6
Bryan Chunyk, Contact
PH: (403)290-6266
FX: (403)290-5957
Provides agricultural business consulting services.

CLARK CONSULTING INTERNATIONAL, INC.
PO Box 600
Dundee, IL 60118-0600
Warren E. Clark, President
PH: (847)836-5100
FX: (847)836-5140
E-mail: ag-PR@agpr.com
URL: http://www.agPR.com/consulting
Founded: 1986. **Staff:** 3. Multipurpose agrimarketing communications consulting firm including public relations, market research, advertising and direct mail expertise. Serves the seed, chemical, machinery, computer and agricultural futures industries. Internet promotion and product marketing in agriculture.

CMB RESOURCES
PO Box 1488
Fredericksburg, TX 78624
PH: (830)997-3856
TF: (888)759-9051
FX: (830)997-2974
E-mail: blackwel@cmbresources.com
URL: http://www.cmbresources.com
Agricultural products consultants.

COASTAL AG RESEARCH INC.
PO Box KK
East Bernard, TX 77435
David Wilde, President
PH: (409)335-4451
FX: (409)335-4183
E-mail: car@intertex.net
Founded: 1978. **Staff:** 4. Offers services in research involving efficacy, residue, and soil dissipation in all crops grown in Texas. Also provides legal consulting and expert witness services. Industries served: all ag chemical related industries, environmental related industries, government, and any private enterprise seeking research results.

JACK COLLIER, CONSULTING ENGINEER
1512 Bay St.
Santa Cruz, CA 95060-4731
Jack E. Collier, Contact
PH: (831)425-1430
Founded: 1980. Natural systems engineering consulting firm offers counsel on vermicomposting—large scale conversion of organic wastes, including municipal wastewater solids (sludges), into earthworm compost. (Earthworm compost is a highly stabilized, odorless humus.) Primarily serves the horticultural industry and has been involved in research impacting on the work of government agencies.

**MARTY CONNELL AGRICULTURAL & FINANCIAL
  MANAGEMENT, INC.**
10 N. 27th St., Ste. 200
Billings, MT 59103
Martin R. Connell, President
PH: (406)252-4745
FX: (406)252-6424
E-mail: 103507.53@compuserve.com
Founded: 1965. **Staff:** 5. Offers management and financial consulting services in the agricultural and business fields. Specific services include: workouts, negotiations, restructures, and business evaluations. Industries served: agricultural and small business.

JOSEPH F. CONNOR, DVM
34 W. Main
Carthage, IL 62321
Joseph F. Connor, President
PH: (217)357-2811
FX: (217)357-6665
E-mail: cvsltd@hogvet.com
URL: http://hogvet.com
Founded: 1976. **Staff:** 10. Offers swine management services, specializing in segregated production, swine herd management, disease control, nutrition, computerized records analysis, and disease status diagnosis and evaluation. Serves as coordinator in vaccine and pharmaceutical trials.

CONSORTIUM OF INTERNATIONAL CONSULTANTS
8677 Highwood Dr.
San Diego, CA 92119-1410
Guy Hill, Contact Executive
PH: (619)646-2418
FX: (619)464-6573
E-mail: ciconsd@worldnet.att.net
Founded: 1993. Consulting in agriculture, institutional development, financial management and controls, training and technology transfer, environment, irrigation systems, water usage, soil studies, information systems, project design, implementation and evaluation, exports of traditional production, non-traditional agricultural crops export development, agribusiness development, integrated-industrial-commercial operations, marketing and marketing studies, privatization of agricultural development, management, integrated pest control, rural development planning, grain storage and drying, grasses and legumes, livestock and management, credit institutions. Feasibility studies, monitoring and evaluations, project proposals.

CONSULAGR, INC.
2269 DeWindt Rd.
Newark, NY 14513-8803
James R. Peck, President
PH: (315)331-7791
FX: (315)331-1294
Founded: 1965. **Staff:** 5. Offers agricultural consulting in soils, crop production, animal husbandry, farm business management and computer applications. Provides analytical services and interpretation of agricultural chemistry. Prepares production and management plans and programs for farm business. Develops feasibility studies on farm business changes and expansions. Prepares and presents seminars on farm business management with emphasis on tactical and strategic management of the agricultural business.

DENIS COTE
282 Lister-Kaye Crescent
Swift Current, SK, Canada S9H 4J7
Denis Cote, Contact
PH: (306)773-6328
FX: (306)778-7461
E-mail: dcote@t2.net
Offers farm and agribusiness financial and management consulting services including project design, business planning, and financial and credit evaluations.

CREEKSIDE CONSULTING, INC.
67 Creekside Dr.
Harpersville, AL 35078
Robert Gandy, Owner
PH: (205)672-8587
FX: (205)672-8264
E-mail: Postmaster@Creeksideinc.com
URL: http://www.creeksideinc.com
Founded: 1995. Consultants specialize in forest regeneration.

**SHARON E. CREGIER HORSE TRANSPORT
  CONSULTANT**
PO Box 1100
Montague, PE, Canada C0A 1R0
Sharon E. Cregier, F.I.A.S.H., Ph.D., Consultant

PH: (902)838-4017
FX: (902)838-2882
E-mail: scregier@pei.sympatico.ca
Staff: 1. Equine specialist who offers sources of information and latest research findings and projects on factors affecting the transport of the horse. Additional expertise in animal welfare and equine ethology. Provides bibliographic search services and book and article salvage/editing. Industries served: horse breeders, horse transporters, animal welfare organizations, educational institutions, and government agencies.

JEAN-MICHEL CREPIN
9938 67th Ave.
Edmonton, AB, Canada T6E 0P5
Jean-Michel Crepin, Contact
PH: (403)438-5522
FX: (403)434-8586
Agricultural consulting services include soil fertility analysis, soil reclamation assistance, soil-plant relations assessment, and agrochemical research and development.

CROP AID
2806 Western Acres
El Campo, TX 77437
Dan E. Bradshaw, Contact
PH: (409)543-3416
FX: (409)543-7824
E-mail: ricepro@wcnet.net
Founded: 1977. **Staff:** 3. Agricultural consultant offering development of integrated crop production and protection programs, specializing in soil fertility, plant nutrition, variety testing, crop pest management, and agriculture/environmental interactions.

CROP GUARD RESEARCH, INC.
RR 1
Box 41
Colony, OK 73021
Roger R. Musick, Ph.D., President
PH: (405)797-3213
FX: (405)797-3214
E-mail: cgri@itlnet.net
Founded: 1980. **Staff:** 6. Offers agricultural expertise involving contract research (GLP), residue trials (soil dissipation, RAC, efficacy, and environmental fate). Experienced in most agricultural crops including peanuts, pasture/range pecans, cotton, wheat, alfalfa, potatoes, peaches, melons, corn, soy beans, and vegetables.

CROP PRO-TECH, INC.
2019 S. Main
Bloomington, IL 61704-7303
David J. Harms, President
PH: (309)828-2767
FX: (309)827-9091
E-mail: 75774.500@compuserve.com
Founded: 1976. **Staff:** 15. Agricultural consultants offering services in crop monitoring and integrated crop management, and research and development of chemicals, seed and equipment. Serves private industries as well as government agencies.

LORNE S. CROSSON
PO Box 30
Limerick, SK, Canada S0H 2P0
Lorne S. Crosson, Contact
PH: (306)263-4612
FX: (306)263-4612
E-mail: l.crosson@sk.sympatico.ca
Offers soil and terrain analysis, irrigation land classification, environmental impact studies and related agricultural consulting services

**CURRY-WILLE & ASSOCIATES, CONSULTING
  ENGINEERS**
425 S. 2nd St.
Ames, IA 50010
Jerry L. Wille, President

PH: (515)232-9078
FX: (515)232-9083
E-mail: willecsa@aol.com
Founded: 1978. **Staff:** 6. Offers consultation on agricultural experiment stations, commercial and private facilities, livestock and poultry housing, feed processing, seed handling, and storage of grain and fertilizer. Provides building layouts, structural, mechanical and electrical designs, site development and waste management for agricultural facilities. These facilities include agricultural research, livestock, grain, feed, fertilizer, and commercial facilities. Serves private industries as well as government agencies.

CURTIS & TOMPKINS LTD.
2323 5th St.
Berkeley, CA 94710
C. Bruce Godfrey, President
PH: (510)486-0900
FX: (510)486-0532
Founded: 1878. **Staff:** 60. Offers analytical chemistry consulting and testing services to the environmental, agricultural, government agencies, energy, and related industries.

CUSTOM INVENTIONS AGENCY
1015 S. Palomino Rd.
Carthage, MO 64836
Richard E. Diggs, President
PH: (417)358-8173
TF: (800)225-4298
FX: (417)358-0971
Founded: 1975. **Staff:** 2. Independent consultant advises on the following matters: how to invent, new product development, and custom inventing to solve problems. Specific areas of focus include farm and irrigation projects, national planning for maximum production, and strategic weapon systems. Consultant is holder of numerous patents in energy and irrigation systems. Serves private industry as well as government agencies worldwide.

DARGAN & FLOWERS, INC.
PO Box 246
Darlington, SC 29540
William Flowers, President
PH: (803)393-2211
FX: (803)395-0056
E-mail: forester9@earthlink.net
Founded: 1948. **Staff:** 3. Offers consultation and assistance in management of forest properties, including arrangements to assume all, if specified, management responsibilities for extended periods. Services include appraisals, management plans, marking for cutting, complete sales service (forest products and rural land), reforestation, fire protection plans and development, and wildlife management. Industries served: principally small private landowners; occasional jobs for forest industry.

DAVIS AG CONSULTANTS, INC.
PO Drawer D
Leland, MS 38756
L.B. Davis, Contact
PH: (601)686-4200
FX: (601)686-2515
Founded: 1985. **Staff:** 5. Offers expert investigation and evaluation of special agricultural problems, including product liability, chemical drift or misapplication affecting crops, man and animals, and forestry and other plants. Also makes recommendations regarding liability, amount of loss, salvage and/or treatment. Serves as expert witness. Represents attorneys, chemical companies, ag flying services, ag service companies, and farmers. Has also conducted training seminars for State Regulatory Personnel regarding training tracing drift, symptoms of various chemicals on various crops, man, animals, etc.

DAVIS AGRI-SERVICE
PO Box 38
McCool Junction, NE 68401-0038
Rolland L. Davis, President

PH: (402)724-2293
FX: (402)724-2293
Staff: 7. Agricultural consulting firm with experience in crop management, soil management, water management, pest management, and sludge management. Serves as expert witness in crop management. Industries served: farming and government.

DEBONNE RANCH MANAGEMENT, INC.

PO Box 1935
Palm Desert, CA 92261
Bernard J. Debonne, Contact
PH: (760)564-4139
FX: (760)564-4207
Founded: 1966. **Staff:** 20. Offers farm management and farm development for citrus groves, date gardens and table grape vineyards. Specializes in the development and management of extensive agricultural investments on behalf of investors and absentee owners, both foreign and domestic.

WILLIAM H. DEROLF & ASSOCIATES

PO Box 6532
Dothan, AL 36302
William H. DeRolf, Contact
PH: (334)793-2498
FX: (334)712-7747
Founded: 1971. **Staff:** 3. Forestry management consultants with experience in preparation and/or implementation of forest management plans; forestland and timber appraisal for buyers or sellers; appraisal of damage from fire, wind, or vandalism; environmental planning and protection for proposed development programs; game management; timber production for maximum profits; timber marketing; reforestation, including tree planting; prescribed burning; fair market value appraisals; and application of forest chemicals.

DEVELOPMENT ALTERNATIVES, INC.

7250 Woodmont Ave., Ste. 200
Bethesda, MD 20814
Donald R. Mickelwait, CEO
PH: (301)718-8699
FX: (301)718-7968
URL: http://www.dai.com
Founded: 1970. **Staff:** 250. Provides high quality planning, technical assistance, project management, and research services to private and public organizations in developing countries. Specializes in economic policy, agriculture and agribusiness, natural resource management, investment and privatization services, enterprise development, and financial services. Operates branch offices in Manila, Philippines; Bangkok, Thailand; Tashkent, Uzbekistan; and Beijing, China.

DEYHLE VETERINARY SERVICES

PO Box 180
Canyon, TX 79015
Charles E. Deyhle, Jr., Contact
PH: (806)655-5995
FX: (806)655-5995
E-mail: deyhlevet@amaonline.com
Founded: 1951. **Staff:** 3. Offers services in the health management of cattle in intensified production systems. Also offers personnel training in related fields. A small business firm.

DILIGENCE INC.

21241 Ventura Blvd., Ste. 250
Woodland Hills, CA 91364
Vince Croal, President
PH: (818)888-6748
TF: (800)809-8210
FX: (818)888-5370
E-mail: help@diligeninc.com
Litigation support and consulting in consumer, commercial, real estate, dealer, agriculture, specialized lending, standards and practice of bank operations, check processing, security, trust, compliance, liquidation, and administration.

DOANE MARKETING RESEARCH

1807 Park 270 Dr., Ste. 300
St. Louis, MO 63146
Carl E. Block, President
PH: (314)878-7707
TF: (800)753-6263
FX: (314)878-7616
URL: http://www.doanemr.com
Founded: 1984. **Staff:** 60. Provides qualitative and quantitative services as well as analysis for agricultural-oriented industries. Industries served: agricultural chemical manufacturers, animal health manufacturers, hybrid seed, agricultural equipment and supply.

HAROLD G. DODDS

51 Apex St.
Winnipeg, MB, Canada R3R 3A4
Harold G. Dodds, Contact
PH: (204)895-8071
FX: (204)895-8071
E-mail: hdodd@upbiz.net
Agricultural communication services, such as information needs assessment and electronic and print publishing assistance, are offered.

GEORGE DOYLE, INC.

2207 Military Hwy.
Pineville, LA 71360
George D. Screpetis, President
PH: (318)640-3034
FX: (318)640-0369
E-mail: trish@linknet.net
Founded: 1980. **Staff:** 2. Timber utilization and management services include export hardwood log grading, forest land sales, hardwood sawmill training, pine and hardwood sawmill analysis, and hardwood log and lumber grading. Also offers expertise in log grade yield studies, timber marking and sales, timber products marketing, timber cruising and appraisal, and forest land management. Industries served: private landowners, lumber and plywood manufacturers and Mid-South exporters, and government agencies.

DPRA INC.

200 Research Dr.
Manhattan, KS 66505
Richard E. Seltzer, President/CEO
PH: (785)539-3565
FX: (785)539-5353
URL: http://www.dpra.com
Founded: 1960. **Staff:** 190. Consultants on a variety of environmental problems and situations. Experience includes agriculture, agribusiness, water pollution control, and hazardous and municipal waste management. Activities emphasize litigation support, data management, and information services, as well as international programs. Serves private industries as well as government agencies.

BRIAN DUCK

5924 Dewdney Ave.
Regina, SK, Canada S4T 1C8
Brian A. Duck, Contact
PH: (306)949-7892
FX: (306)569-8649
Offers animal production consulting services related to nutrition, breeding, management, marketing, and international extension.

DUNIGAN BROTHERS

PO Box 208
Black Oak, AR 72414
Eddie Dunigan, Contact
PH: (870)486-2870
E-mail: hedunrga@ipa.net
Founded: 1968. **Staff:** 2. Agricultural consultants specializing in insect control and insecticide recommendations.

EAGLESON FARMS
RR 3
Parkhill, ON, Canada N0M 2K0
Gary R. Eagleson, Owner
PH: (519)238-2676
FX: (519)238-8919
Provides agricultural education and training in animal science, farm management, rural economic development, and marketing.

ECO SOIL SYSTEMS, INC.
10740 Thornmint Rd.
San Diego, CA 92127
PH: (619)675-1660
FX: (619)592-7642
E-mail: support@ecosoil.com
URL: http://www.ecosoil.com
Agricultural pest management consultants.

EDEN BIOSCIENCE
11816 N. Creek Pky. N.
Bothell, WA 98011
Jerry Butler, President
PH: (425)806-7300
TF: (800)635-6866
FX: (425)806-7400
E-mail: huntb@edenbio.com
URL: http://www.edenbio.com
Founded: 1977. **Staff:** 45. Offers domestic and foreign consulting in the areas of integrated pest/crop management and problem solving in agriculture, forestry, ornamental and related plant industries. Provides full service lab facilities for diagnosis of plant health problems and preplant soil testing for pathogens and pests. Specialties include plant parasitic nematodes, fungal pathogens, and general plant disease diagnosis. Industries served: agriculture, forestry, small fruit growers, microbreweries, biotechnology, and composting industry.

EDUCATIONAL SERVICES
3762 Messner Rd. E.
Wooster, OH 44691
L.B. Willett, Ph.D., Contact
PH: (330)264-9858
FX: (330)264-9879
E-mail: willett.2@osu.edu
Founded: 1972. **Staff:** 1. Consultation provided on the distribution of environmental contaminants in livestock systems and toxicity in domestic animals, and in the management of dairy cattle. Services frequently provided to chemical, insurance, legal, and feed production organizations.

LARRY ELDER/ASSOCIATES—CONSULTING ENGINEERS
888 Blue Spring Dr.
Westlake Village, CA 91361
Larry Elder, President
PH: (805)496-0907
FX: (805)495-7890
Founded: 1966. **Staff:** 4. Mechanical engineering consultant specializing in agricultural applications: material handling systems for cattle feeds and related installations at cattle feed yards; dehydrating and processing of forage and other roughage feeds for livestock; and reviews of agricultural bulk feed storage problems, such as high moisture, spontaneous heating, dust control, etc. Serves as expert witness in relevant cases. Also offers biomass studies for energy utilization of by-products and crops for energy purposes. Recent emphasis on solid waste handling and processing studies that cover recycling collection, separation, processing, baling, and shipping. Provides services to government.

WENDY ELRICK, BUSINESS EDUCATION CURRICULUM CONSULTANTS
1740 Line 40
New Hamburg, ON, Canada N0B 2G0
Wendy Elrick, Contact
PH: (519)662-6951

Agricultural consultant offering services related to farm management.

EMPLOYMENT PLACE
721 E. 16th St.
Cheyenne, WY 82001
Kenneth D. Andrews, President
PH: (307)632-0534
FX: (307)638-2104
E-mail: agrecruit@aol.com
URL: http://members.aol.com/agrecruit/agrec.htm
Founded: 1987. **Staff:** 2. A twofold placement firm operates as a general employment agency offering services to all areas of employment. Also serves as Ag Recruiters offering services to the agricultural professional. Industries served: all areas including government agencies in the U.S.; also serve fields of plant science, animal science, engineering, agri-business, management, sales and service.

ENERGY ENGINEERING LTD.
PO Box 1837
Sydney, NS, Canada B1S 3B9
K.L. Chrisholm, President
PH: (902)562-6544
FX: (902)539-0699
Founded: 1976. Energy engineering consultancy offers the following: energy cost reduction, furnace design, aquaculture hardware design and construction, industrial engineering and productivity improvement, waste water treatment and environmental studies, aquaculture site evaluation, technical and economic feasibilities, refrigeration systems, and general mechanical and process engineering. Industries served: metallurgical, aquaculture, steel fabrication, clay processing, fisheries, and government agencies.

ENTECH ENVIRONMENTAL CONSULTANTS LTD.
200 - 1285 Pender St.
Vancouver, BC, Canada V6E 4B1
S. Fred Sverre, President
PH: (604)688-6691
FX: (604)688-8915
Founded: 1973. **Staff:** 6. Offers comprehensive environmental consulting services with proven expertise in environmental data collection and interpretation, and in the formulation of appropriate approaches to remediation. Services include: development impact studies (linear, mines, airports, energy, industrial, etc.); biological studies (birds, fisheries, jellyfish, wildlife and vegetation studies, stream inventory, marine benthic studies, etc.); water quality studies; technology development; recycling and remediation; aquaculture (site survey and development, inventory certification, technology transfer); forestry; hydrogeology (saltwater and freshwater, wells and hatchery water supply surveys, groundwater contamination studies); business analysis and development (business plans, market evaluations, longterm forecasts and negotiation mediation); and communications (seminars and brochures). Industries served: private industries, such as mining, energy, forestry, aquaculture, petrochemical, manufacturing, and government agencies.

ENVIRONMENTAL TECHNOLOGIES INSTITUTE, INC.
3224 Wake Forest Hwy.
Durham, NC 27703
Milton Ganyard, Jr., President
PH: (919)598-0289
FX: (919)596-6854
Founded: 1981. **Staff:** 10. Provides applied field research on effects of pesticides in environment for industries meeting EPA registration requirements. Serves private industries as well as government agencies. Geographic areas served: U.S., Canada, and Mexico.

FALL LINE FORESTRY CONSULTANTS, LLC
10800 Alpharetta Hwy., Ste. 208-A8
Roswell, GA 30076
James C. Barnett, Principal
PH: (404)255-7239
E-mail: falline@pop.flash.net
URL: http://www.flash.net/~falline

Founded: 1987. Forestry consultants. Services include forest land acquisition and sales, tax-free exchanges, timberland financing sources, and timber inventory and appraisal.

FARM FOR PROFIT
4345 Hwy. 21
Embarrass, MN 55732
TF: (800)232-7693
FX: (218)984-3212
E-mail: soilplus@northernnet.com
URL: http://www.farmforprofit.com
An agricultural program of proper soil management; good plant nutrition, well-managed chemical rates; and continued education and training.

FARM RESEARCH INSTITUTE
3 College Park Ct.
Savoy, IL 61874
Steve Hofing, President
PH: (217)352-8098
FX: (217)352-1425
E-mail: fri@centrec.com
Founded: 1946. Operates research panels to seek knowledge about attitudes, buying habits and future plans of the farm market for client firms. Helps plan, execute, interpret and report on research projects.

FARM STRATEGY INC.
1119A - 5 Ave. NW
Calgary, AB, Canada T2N 0R7
Rowland W. Davies, Contact
PH: (403)283-1316
FX: (403)283-1316
E-mail: rmdavies@telasplanet.net
Founded: 1989. **Staff:** 1. Offers comprehensive agricultural financial and resource management consulting services.

FARMERS SOFTWARE EXCHANGE ASSOCIATION
PO Box 660
Fort Collins, CO 80522
Neil C. Havermale, President
PH: (970)493-1722
TF: (800)237-4182
FX: (970)493-3938
E-mail: info@farmsoft.com
URL: http://www.farmsoft.com
Founded: 1986. **Staff:** 7. Involved in consulting and training farmers and ranchers, their bankers and associations in the successful installation and/or application of microcomputers to increase productivity. Applies farming systems research methods to define requirements, testing parameters, software maintenance and user support of computerized on-farm record systems.

FARMWARD ENTERPRISES, INC.
365 Surrey Race Rd.
Salley, SC 29137
John A. Bass, President
PH: (803)648-7563
FX: (803)648-7563
Founded: 1984. **Staff:** 2. Provides an unusual combination of scientific and informational services in evaluating and gathering data for pesticides, equipment and entomological needs. Consultants can develop the protocols required for research and development efforts and then conduct that research as described by a protocol. Services include the field tests data gathering and statistical analysis of the results. Services are offered to chemical, PCO, farmers, and resort corporations.

FARMWEST MANAGEMENT LTD.
Drawer 42
Netherhill, SK, Canada S0L 2M0
PH: (306)463-3551
FX: (306)463-3635
E-mail: e.brick@sk.sympatico.ca
Farm business management firm offering fiscal strategy develop-

ment and analysis, as well as technical assistance with agricultural computer applications.

FCM ASSOCIATES, INC.
PO Box 70096, Plaza Sta.
Sunnyvale, CA 94086
Fengchow C. Ma, President
PH: (408)730-4543
FX: (408)733-6275
E-mail: fcmconsult@aol.com
Founded: 1962. Offers services to agricultural industry in the areas of agricultural engineering, implements, and machinery application and evaluation. Provides feasibility studies; planning/design for mechanization of agricultural units and rice production; and research and development of technology for uplift agricultural production in developing regions. Also offers study, assessment, planning, and evaluation of laboratory procedures and handling of hazardous materials. Provides organizational management assessment and productivity analyses.

BEN FELT & ASSOCIATES
3805 Pinnacle Pl.
Escondido, CA 92025
Ben Felt, Contact
PH: (760)789-6455
FX: (619)746-6076
Founded: 1984. **Staff:** 2. Advises lenders, owners and managers of agricultural enterprises on matters of financial administration. Also provides expertise in structuring international merger and acquisition opportunities. Concentrates in the following areas: investment capital; expert witness testimony; general financial management advice; preparation of cash flow projections and budgets; provides problem loan administration and negotiates debt restructure; and analyzes the financial impact that economic and political trends may have upon the enterprise. Geographic areas served: Arizona and California.

FINTRAC INC.
1746 Kalorama Rd. NW
Washington, DC 20009-5162
Claire E. Starkey, President
PH: (202)462-8475
FX: (202)462-8478
E-mail: info@fintrac.com
URL: http://www.fintrac.com
Founded: 1975. **Staff:** 17. Market research, quality assurance and Internet services for agribusiness industry.

FISHERIES WEST, INC.
PO Box 7224
Boise, ID 83707
Barry Ross, President
PH: (208)345-1991
FX: (208)344-6159
Founded: 1986. **Staff:** 7. Offers environmental consulting on fisheries work, their establishment and evaluation, and manufacturing of pontoon boats. Expertise available on riparian habitat improvement. Also provides other water-based environmental consulting.

FITCH & MARSHALL, INC.
408 N. First St.
PO Box 583
Yakima, WA 98907-0583
James B. Fitch, President
PH: (509)453-2354
TF: (800)735-6368
FX: (509)452-6760
E-mail: agrimgt@televar.com
Founded: 1994. **Staff:** 1. Firm provides agricultural economic research, agricultural business management consulting, feasibility studies, market research, and financing proposals. Experienced at providing expert witness services. Firm works with farmers, ranchers, dairymen, chemical manufacturers, food processors, muni-

cipalities, attorneys, realtors, developers, engineering firms, government agencies, and agricultural commissions and associations.

FIVE-G CONSULTING
32854 S. Dryland Rd.
Molalla, OR 97038
D. Joe Gribble, President
PH: (503)829-4844
FX: (503)829-4112
E-mail: fiveg@molalla.net
Founded: 1986. **Staff:** 6. Provides engineering and design services for commercial, agricultural, animal raising, and food processing facilities with strong emphasis on pollution control, reclamation of by-products, protection of the environment, functional efficiency, and regulatory compliance.

FOOD & AGROSYSTEMS, INC.
1289 Mandarin Dr.
Sunnyvale, CA 94087
Thomas R. Parks, Contact
PH: (408)245-8450
FX: (408)245-8450
Founded: 1979. **Staff:** 20. A practical, problem-solving organization working with food and agriculture related industry and offering technical, engineering, economic and management assistance in the following areas individually or as integrated programs: crop harvest and post-harvest handling, storage, transportation and packing; processing of fruits, vegetables, fruit juices and concentrates, sauces, and baby foods; meat, fish, and poultry production and processing; including pet food and by-product processing; estimation of capital investment and operating costs for expansion or new construction; plant startup; identification and analysis of markets; HACCP program training; process engineering; plant design and equipment selection/design, procurement and shipment; packaging, distribution and warehousing; and productivity improvement/reduction of operating costs. Extensive international experience. Industries served: food and agriculture-related industries, and pharmaceutical and biomedical industries.

FOOD & FIBER & ENVIRONMENTAL HORTICULTURE
CONSULTANT
7406 Stanley Park Rd.
Carpinteria, CA 93013-3116
Walter S. Barrows, Sr., Pres., CEO
PH: (805)684-1114
FX: (805)684-5141
E-mail: DRDIRT@lawinfo.com
URL: http://www.lawinfo.com/biz/drdirt
Founded: 1975. **Staff:** 1. Agriculture consulting in encroachment and nuisance, public entities liability, adjacent property liability, pesticides, herbicides, agricultural chemicals, flooding, drainage, irrigation, water damage, eucalyptus tree liability, insurance claims casualty loss evaluation and nursery evaluation.

FORECON, INC.
Crown Bldg.
100 E. 2nd St.
Jamestown, NY 14701
Ronald S. Johnson, President
PH: (716)664-5602
FX: (716)664-6648
E-mail: forecon1@aol.com
URL: http://www.foreconinc.com
Founded: 1954. **Staff:** 30. Offers technical counsel in the following areas: (1) forestry land management, inventories, forest land appraisals, timber sales, feasibility studies; logging road design and layout; (2) recreation park and trail design; (3) ecology—forest environmental impact statements; street tree management and design; and (4) conservation tree planting; timber stand improvement contracting; wildlife habitat improvement. Also maintains Timberland Realty, a forestland real estate brokerage. Serves private industries as well as government agencies.

FORESTRY ASSOCIATES
PO Box 392
Preston, MN 55965
Maynard W. Underbakke, Contact
PH: (507)765-2713
Founded: 1960. **Staff:** 2. Offers counsel and appraisal data to private and public landowners on land evaluation, timber management, timber marketing, tree planting, reforestation, arboriculture, fire and disease prevention, wildlife management, recreational use and related activities.

FORESTRY CONSULTANTS, INC.
PO Box 684
Opelika, AL 36803-0684
Melisa V. (Himel) Love, President
PH: (334)745-7530
FX: (334)742-9775
E-mail: fcinc@mindspring.com
Founded: 1984. **Staff:** 3. Offers general forestry consulting including timber sale preparation and administration, timberland management, management plans, regeneration and silviculture, inventory, appraisals, resource surveys, and feasibility studies. Serves the private landowner, industry, and government agencies.

FORINTEK CANADA CORP.
2665 E. Mall
Vancouver, BC, Canada V6T 1Z4
PH: (604)224-3221
FX: (604)222-5690
URL: http://www.forintek.ca
Dedicated to research for Canada's solid wood products industry. A partnership based on the concept of shared risks, shared costs and shared benefits.

STEVE FRANSON CO.
1234 W. Keats
Fresno, CA 93711
Steve Franson, Contact
PH: (559)225-9111
FX: (559)225-9119
Founded: 1987. Specializes in assisting financially troubled agribusinesses through times of crises. Clients are business owners and lenders who need help resolving problem loans. Provides hands-on crises management and management consulting, as well as interim management for companies in transition.

FRAZIER CONSULTING SERVICE, INC.
PO Drawer 957
Leland, MS 38756
A. Lee Frazier, President
PH: (601)686-7324
FX: (601)686-4446
E-mail: alf@tecinfo.com
Founded: 1978. **Staff:** 6. Agricultural consultants interested in investigation of special agricultural problems-crop damage, chemical drift, products liability, disease, insects, weeds and other problems. Industries served: insurance companies, farmers, attorneys, and chemical companies.

G.W. FULLER ASSOCIATES, LTD.
4207 Old Orchard
Montreal, PQ, Canada H4A 3B3
Gordon W. Fuller, President
PH: (514)481-6814
FX: (514)484-0612
Founded: 1978. **Staff:** 6. Provides consulting expertise on quality control, quality assurance and product integrity systems for food and agribusiness; new product development; legal and expert witness; in-house training programs; product, process and market audits; and crisis management and trouble shooting. Experience offered in food service work, agribusiness, government food legislation and international food legislation, food canning, and frozen foods.

GEE, LAMBERT & COURNEYA
244 Pall Mall St., Ste. 401
London, ON, Canada N6A 5P6
Lloyd R. Davenport, Consulting Partner
PH: (519)673-1421
FX: (519)679-8540
Accounting firm offering financial management services to agricultural organizations.

GEOLOGIC RECOVERY SYSTEMS
2300 Hwy. 60, W.
Mulberry, FL 33860
Ray Alkhatib, Vice President/General Manager
PH: (941)425-1084
FX: (941)425-2692
Founded: 1980. **Staff:** 27. Offers consulting services in soil remediation.

GEORGIA AGRI-SCIENTIFIC, INC.
PO Box 390
Hawkinsville, GA 31036
Matthew T. Henry, Contact
PH: (912)892-2366
FX: (912)783-0525
E-mail: geagsci@cstel.net
Founded: 1975. **Staff:** 5. Offers scientific field research for agrichemical industry; operates under Good Laboratory Practices Standards. Industries served: agricultural chemical and pharmaceutical companies.

GLADES CROP CARE, INC.
949 Turner Quay
Jupiter, FL 33458
Madeline Mellinger, President
PH: (561)746-3740
FX: (561)746-3775
Founded: 1973. **Staff:** 25. Offers customized crop health management programs, development of vegetable IPM programs, professional custom field research of ag chemicals and biotechnology products for residue, efficacy performance studies, and breeding. Crops: vegetables, citrus, sugarcane, turf, rice and ornamentals.

GOLDEN SPREAD INTERNATIONAL SERVICES, INC.
825 S. 10th St.
Memphis, TX 79245
Wayne Sweatt, President
PH: (806)259-2556
TF: (800)776-5129
FX: (806)259-3812
Founded: 1986. **Staff:** 5. International consultants for irrigation equipment and farm machinery requirements. Activities include feasibility studies, analysis and designing of irrigation, technical services and training, as well as implementation and management of agricultural projects. Serves private industries as well as government agencies.

DONALD R. GOOD
1275 Castlehill Crescent
Ottawa, ON, Canada K2C 2B2
Donald R. Good, Contact
PH: (613)225-0226
FX: (613)225-1150
E-mail: bgraham@magi.com
Offers planning and evaluation services for agricultural government and industry operations. Specializes in land and agriculture resource management.

TRENNA GRABOWSKI, CPA, LTD.
12047 St. Rt. 37
Benton, IL 62812
Trenna R. Grabowski, CPA
PH: (618)435-4020
FX: (618)438-9804
E-mail: grabeau@midwest.net

Founded: 1985. **Staff:** 6. Taxation and general business consultant offering financial management, strategic planning, and budgeting for agribusiness and small and family-owned firms. Heavily involved in tax planning and research. Consulting on choosing hardware and software for agribusiness. Related experience in personal financial planning, tax planning, and projections.

WILLIAM W. GRAHAM
1275 Castlehill Crescent
Ottawa, ON, Canada K2C 2B2
William W. Graham, Contact
PH: (613)225-0226
FX: (613)225-1150
E-mail: bgraham@magi.com
Offers research, analysis, and planning for agriculture, resource management, and environmental issues. Specializes in by-product utilization and organic waste processing (from agriculture and food industries).

GRANDIN LIVESTOCK HANDLING SYSTEMS INC.
1205 W. Elizabeth, Ste. E122
Fort Collins, CO 80521
Temple Grandin, President
PH: (303)229-0703
FX: (303)491-5326
Founded: 1977. **Staff:** 1. Designer of livestock handling facilities for cattle, hogs and sheep on ranches, feedlots, slaughter plants and auctions. Also consults on humane slaughter methods, reducing stress on animals to improve meat quality, and transportation problems involving cattle, pigs or sheep. Industries served: cattle ranch, meat packing, cattle feedlots, beef industry, pork industry, sheep industry, as well as government agencies.

GREIG AND ASSOCIATES
PO Box 15862
Tampa, FL 33684
Ian Greig, Senior Partner
PH: (813)935-1583
FX: (813)915-9469
E-mail: iang@juno.com
URL: http://www.members.xoom/igreig/
Founded: 1996. Management and technical services for agriculture; production of tropical and sub-tropical fruits; pineapple specialists; drainage of agricultural lands, soil conservation, land preparation and tillage practices; plantation design and construction; equipment design, testing, and calibration; crop protection, agrichemicals, and fertilizers; application safety, container disposal; management of plantations, orchards, ranches and nurseries; feasibility and marketing studies; research projects.

GSA & ASSOCIATES, INC.
1 Sunrise Point Rd.
Lake Wylie, SC 29710
George S. Appleton, Founder and President
PH: (803)831-7676
FX: (803)831-7709
E-mail: georges@vnet.net
Founded: 1976. **Staff:** 1. Offers consulting services internationally directed toward animal health/animal healthcare products (livestock/poultry), specifically, general business development, executive search in animal pharmaceutical/biologicals industry, strategic planning, market research and acquisition/divestiture. Industries served: human pharmaceutical houses with animal healthcare products interest, animal healthcare firms and biotechnology companies, and allied industries, and government agencies.

J.H. HARE & ASSOCIATES, INC.
PO Box 1470
Stanwood, WA 98292
J.H. Hare, President
PH: (360)387-5555
FX: (360)387-4187
E-mail: nareco@tgi.net
URL: http://www.tgi.netl~hareco

Founded: 1970. **Staff:** 4. Agribusiness management consultants with extensive experience in: animal nutrition and feed formulation, agrimarketing, technical services to agribusiness, agricultural promotion, and sales and sales training. Serves the agriculture and food and beverage industries, as well as government agencies.

HARTEN BUTZI & SON INC.

6488 Jessamine Ct.
Westerville, OH 43081
PH: (614)882-2769
FX: (614)882-2769
Founded: 1984. Feed grinding specialists.

HARVEST FOODS LTD.

201-112 Research Dr.
Saskatoon, SK, Canada S7N 3R3
Garven R. Stuart, Owner
PH: (306)975-0085
FX: (306)975-1075
E-mail: harvest.foods@innovaionplace.com
Management consulting services, including market research, economic feasibility evaluations, and agriculture sector reviews, are provided to the agriculture food and agri-business industries.

HARZA ENGINEERING CO.

Sears Tower
233 S. Wacker Dr.
Chicago, IL 60606-6392
J.E. Lindell, Vice President
PH: (312)831-3000
FX: (312)831-3999
E-mail: info@harza.com
URL: http://www.harza.com
Founded: 1920. **Staff:** 800. An international consulting firm that provides quality engineering, environmental, and architectural services to private enterprises and government agencies in the development of water, energy, and land resources. Specializes in the planning, design, permitting, and construction management of dams and reservoirs; pumped storage projects; hydroelectric facilities; water supply systems; fish hatchery and passage facilities; private power development; electrical power transmission and distribution systems; navigation locks; waterfront facilities; parks and recreational facilities; educational facilities; pharmaceutical facilities; roads, highways, and bridges; tunnels and underground structures; water; and wastewater treatment facilities. Other services include: agriculture and irrigation development; dam inspection and rehabilitation; equipment acquisition management; technology transfer and training; environmental studies and mitigation; flood control; and water quality monitoring.

HAWAII AGRICULTURE RESEARCH CENTER

99-193 Aiea Heights Dr., Ste. 300
Aiea, HI 96701-3911
Stephanie A. Whalen, President and Director
PH: (808)487-5561
FX: (808)486-5020
E-mail: harc@harc-hspa.com
Founded: 1882. **Staff:** 65. Private agricultural research organization offering consultation and research on all phases of sugarcane growing, harvesting, processing, and the production of energy from sugarcane fiber; and field and laboratory studies for any crop pesticide residue registration with the EPA. Advises on operational and agronomic procedures used to develop new varieties, grow, and process sugarcane. Also provides training programs in the above mentioned areas. Services offered to other sugarcane producing industries worldwide. Research and consulting on diversified crops including coffee, forestry, forage, and biomass production.

HAWTHORNE CO.

1351 210th St.
Red Oak, IA 51566
Gerald E. Anderson, President
PH: (712)623-5131
FX: (712)623-5132

Founded: 1984. **Staff:** 1. Agricultural consultant serves commercial banks or lending institutions with loan portfolio analysis. Also helps agricultural entities with business analysis. Emphasis is on cattle and grain to include country elevator management. Serves the agriculture, banking and finance, and real estate industries.

W. KEITH HEAD, P.A.G.

Box 1746
Nipawin, SK, Canada S0E 1E0
W. Keith Head, P.A.G.
PH: (306)862-4355
FX: (306)862-2355
E-mail: wkhead@sk.sympatico.ca
Provides agricultural consulting services related to soil conservation, waste management, pedology, agronomy, and vegetation and landscape mapping.

HERBERT R. HEINICKE

1302 W. Boston Ave.
Indianola, IA 50125
Herbert R. Heinicke, Contact
PH: (515)961-8933
FX: (515)961-8903
Founded: 1971. **Staff:** 1. Technical consultant to pet food, food, and feed industries in such areas as product and ingredient development, quality assurance, nutritional evaluation, government and regulatory compliance, and production trouble shooting services. Serves private industries as well as government agencies.

DIRK H. HELMS INC.

91 Douglas Park Rd.
Winnipeg, MB, Canada R3J 1Z3
Dirk H. Helms, Owner
PH: (204)888-0778
FX: (204)888-0778
URL: http://www.cyberspc.mb.ca/~dhelms
Founded: 1985. **Staff:** 2. Management of non-urban real estate. Management consulting regarding dryland farming: feasibility studies: projects planning, establishment - supervision. Land Management: erosion control, conservation, maintenance. Real Estate Services (Licensed Brokerage): appraisals, management of non-urban properties, procurement and dispersal of real estate. Languages: English, German, some French, Spanish, and Dutch.

HENDRICKSEN, THE CARE OF TREES

2371 S. Foster Ave.
Wheeling, IL 60090-6591
Scott Jamieson, President
PH: (847)394-8002
FX: (847)394-3376
E-mail: +cot@careoftrees.com
Founded: 1946. **Staff:** 400. Provides horticultural services involving casualty loss appraisals, inventory and evaluation, expert witness testimony, design and estimating, horticultural writing and technical editing. Industries served: agriculture, horticulture, arboriculture, landscaping, and government in the U.S.

GUY C. HILL, G H ASSOCIATES

8677 Highwood Dr.
San Diego, CA 92119-1410
Guy C. Hill, Contact
PH: (619)464-2418
FX: (619)464-6573
E-mail: ciconsd@worldnet.att.net
Founded: 1966. International consultant offers expertise in the following areas: agribusiness, agribusiness development and conceptualization, institutional development, and privatization of parastatel agri-enterprises. Additional services include nontraditional agribusiness exports, integrated agricultural/commercial marketing projects, marketing and promotion. Also assists in market development and strategies for penetration. Conducts feasibility studies, specializes in economics and market analysis and development, cooperative organization and diversification. Offers small enterprise development and rural development expertise. Provides financial and

management consulting services, business plans and product profitability studies. Serves private industries as well as government agencies and financial institutions.

HOLMSEN FORESTRY LTD.
540 Shannon Way,
Delta, BC, Canada V4M 2W5
Karsten Holmsen, Principal
PH: (604)943-7784
E-mail: kholmsen@direct.ca
URL: http://www.forestind.com/holmsen/
Founded: 1976. Integrated resources planning, evaluation and appraisals; timberland valuation and marketing; forest management, forest harvesting, engineering and development; logging systems, equipment selection and procurement; international forestry, forest industries, plantations and indigenous forest inventories and management, agroforestry; contract services in thinning, pruning, plantation, weed control, and fertilization (international only); and special projects, research, training and education.

DONALD HOOVER
First Edmonton Place, Ste. 600
Edmonton, AB, Canada T5J 3S9
Donald Hoover, Contact
PH: (780)448-7440
FX: (780)421-1270
E-mail: serecon@compusmart.ab.ca
Offers market research, feasibility studies, investment analysis, and program evaluations for agricultural operations. Real property appraisals, farm financing, and management services are also available.

HOYSLER ASSOCIATES, INC.
1400 Cannon Cir., Ste. 2
Faribault, MN 55021
Stanley L. Burmeister, President
PH: (507)334-3934
FX: (507)334-3936
Founded: 1978. **Staff:** 10. Offers consulting services in the field of agriculture, economic loss evaluation, farm management, rural appraisal, and personal injury actions involving farmers. Industries served: agriculture and government agencies.

CHARLES HOYT CO.
4991 E. McKinley Ste. 116
Fresno, CA 93727-1969
PH: (209)456-2478
FX: (209)456-2463
E-mail: choyt@hoytco.com
URL: http://www.hoytco.com
Founded: 1984. An agricultural management consulting firm that specializes in business assistance to and the operation of agricultural based firms. Services include management of lender relationships reorganizing accounting and management information for proper diagnostic control, financial and operational "work outs," working capital restructuring, forecasting and budgeting, development of operational plans, interim general management, asset sales and purchases, personnel acquisition and training, feasibility studies, and crisis control.

IRVING F. HUMPHREY
7770 Firenze Ave.
Los Angeles, CA 90046
Irving F. Humphrey, President
PH: (213)851-1198
Founded: 1970. **Staff:** 4. Provides expert witness testimony in court cases regarding trees and landscaping. Other services include appraisal for casualty losses in the landscape and diagnosis of tree problems for homeowners. Also inspects and diagnoses individual trees and shrubs to determine source of problems. Industries served: logging and government agencies.

HUNTSMAN MARINE SCIENCE CENTRE
Brandy Cove Rd.
St. Andrews, NB, Canada E0G 2X0
J. M. Anderson, Chair
PH: (506)529-1200
FX: (506)529-1212
E-mail: huntsman@nbnet.nb.ca
URL: http://www.unb.ca/web/huntsman
Founded: 1969. **Staff:** 50. Marine scientists providing consulting services in areas of aquaculture, marine science, systematics, marine education, environmental assessment and benthic ecology. Technical training is offered in applied marine science. Firm also experienced in scientific editing. Primary industry served is the fishery business, but also serves government agencies.

ROBERT S. HYDE
5423 Portage Ave.
Headingley, MB, Canada R4H 1E5
Robert S. Hyde, Contact
PH: (204)987-7703
FX: (204)987-7705
E-mail: wolfe@mb.sympatico.ca
Management consulting services primarily to the agriculture and biotechnology sectors. Functional areas include strategic planning, market assessments, human resource management, organization development, and executive recruitment.

INDUCTIVE ENGINEERING
602 State St.
Cedar Falls, IA 50613
Dale M. Gumz, Owner
PH: (319)266-0476
Founded: 1970. An engineering consultant for agriculture, construction, consumer products, and specialty machines. Forensic and safety services include accident reconstruction, design analysis, human factors, manufacturing processes, mechanical and electrical, occupational safety, product liability, product and machine design. Acts as an expert witness.

INSECT CONTROL & RESEARCH, INC.
1330 Dillon Heights Ave.
Baltimore, MD 21228
Robin G. Todd, Director
PH: (410)747-4500
FX: (410)747-4928
E-mail: icr@erols.com
Founded: 1946. **Staff:** 10. Pesticide registration, testing, and screening specialists offer consulting on vector borne diseases and household and public health pests. Industries served: chemical, pest control, pharmaceutical, and government agencies.

INTERFOREST, LLC
1353 Boston Post Rd., Ste. 7
Madison, CT 06443
PH: (203)245-7436
FX: (203)245-7135
E-mail: interforest@snet.net
URL: http://www.iforest.com
Seeks to increase the value and the liquidity of forest properties for major landowners and investors. Provides sustainable forestry planning and management, timberland investment, and applied research services through a world-wide network of scientists and professionals.

INTERMAP TECHNOLOGIES LTD.
2 Gurdwara Rd., Ste. 200
Nepean, ON, Canada K2E 1A2
Brian L. Bullock, President and CEO
PH: (613)226-5442
TF: (800)836-1213
FX: (613)226-5529
E-mail: info@intermap.ca
URL: http://www.intermaptechnologies.com
Founded: 1972. **Staff:** 25. Offers agricultural consulting services

related to tropical agriculture and irrigation in developing countries, including regional planning, comprehensive river basin studies, project planning, and feasibility studies.

INTERNATIONAL MEAT INSPECTION CONSULTANTS
PO Box 264
Germantown, MD 20875
PH: (301)570-1058
E-mail: imic@ss-inc.com
URL: http://www.ss-inc.com/imic.html
USDA FDA food labeling experts providing consulting services to the meat and poultry food industry.

INTRANCO INC.
1825 Eye St., Ste. 400
Washington, DC 20006
William Lake, President
PH: (202)429-6820
FX: (202)429-9574
Founded: 1980. **Staff:** 37. Provides management consulting for agribusinesses, primarily enterprises in the Third World. Works with private entrepreneurs and government-sponsored institutions. Has experience with livestock, fruits, vegetables, field crops, small animals, fisheries, and poultry. Engages in the international trade of agricultural equipment, machinery and raw products. Industries served: food and feed industries, and government agencies.

IRZ CONSULTING
505 E. Main
Hermiston, OR 97838
PH: (541)567-0252
FX: (541)567-4239
E-mail: irz@eoni.com
URL: http://www.irz.com/IRZ
Founded: 1984. A full-service irrigation engineering and consulting firm. Specializes in large scale irrigation development, design, and construction management.

CAROL JAMES COMMUNICATIONS
888 16th St. NW, Ste. 300
Washington, DC 20006
Carol L. James, Contact
PH: (202)835-7476
FX: (202)296-7047
E-mail: cjcomm@cjcomm.com
Founded: 1984. **Staff:** 1. Communications consultant specializing in issue management, offering issue analysis, identification, monitoring, public affairs campaigns/strategies, and research supportive of public affairs strategies. Industries served: U.S. food system companies and associations from production agriculture to consumer branded marketers and related suppliers such as agribusiness lenders; cooperatives; mutual insurance sector; and government agencies in the U.S.

JMLORD, INC.
267 N. Fulton
Fresno, CA 93701
Joseph M. Lord, Jr., Contact
PH: (209)268-9755
FX: (209)486-6504
E-mail: jmlord@lightspeed.net
URL: http://bizweb.lightspeed.net/~jmlord
Founded: 1979. **Staff:** 9. Consultants with expertise in agronomy, agricultural and civil engineering as well as soil and plant sciences. Provides water and fertility management, irrigation and drainage system design with computer usage, laboratory analysis and weather station use to support day by day management of production agriculture in the Western United States. Serves such industries as agriculture, water districts, federal, state, and county agencies as well as utilities.

JOBS IN HORTICULTURE, INC.
2214 Douglas Dr.
Carlisle, PA 17013
Jack L. Ferrell, President
PH: (717)240-0810
TF: (800)428-2474
FX: (800)884-5198
E-mail: agquest@hortjobs.com
URL: http://www.hortjobs.com
Founded: 1992. **Staff:** 4. Career consulting and career services with emphasis on agriculture and horticulture. A small business providing services in the U.S. and Canada.

LOYD JOHNSON
287 Herman Bailey Rd.
Somerville, AL 35670
Loyd Johnson, Contact
PH: (256)778-7602
E-mail: 71045.1561@compuserve.com
Founded: 1982. **Staff:** 1. Agricultural engineering consultant specializing in tropical land development and food production. Activities include development of irrigation, drainage, roads, bridges, sanitation machine and processing systems for agricultural experiment stations and food production in the lowland tropics. Industries served: national and international research centers and agricultural projects, as well as government agencies.

ARDEN KASHISHIAN
5044 B N. Wishon
Fresno, CA 93704
Arden Kashishian, Contact
PH: (559)226-4253
FX: (559)226-5376
E-mail: ardenkash@aol.com
Founded: 1975. **Staff:** 1. Agricultural consultant offering on-site feasibility and development studies as well as advice on basic farm practices, primarily for production agriculture. Industries served: all agriculture and agricultural exports/imports.

KELLER-BLIESNER ENGINEERING
78 E. Center
Logan, UT 84321
Jack Keller, CEO
PH: (801)753-5651
FX: (801)753-6139
Founded: 1960. **Staff:** 7. Agricultural engineering consultants specializing in irrigation system planning, design, management, analysis, and construction. Services also include agricultural resource engineering, training, and expert witness testimony for legal purposes. Serves private industries as well as government agencies.

KENT SEAFARMS CORP.
11125 Flintkote Ave., Ste. J
San Diego, CA 92121
James M. Carlberg, Exec. Vice President
PH: (619)452-5765
FX: (619)452-0075
Founded: 1979. **Staff:** 70. Specializes in striped bass aquaculture.

KEY AGRICULTURAL SERVICES INC.
114 S. Shady Ln.
Macomb, IL 61455-2610
Dean E. Wesley, President
PH: (309)833-1313
FX: (309)833-3993
E-mail: keyag@maconb.com
URL: http://www.keyaginc.com
Founded: 1977. **Staff:** 8. Firm offers expertise in agronomy, soil science, GIS/GPS consulting.

DAVID W. KIDD
27 Dundurn Pl.
Winnipeg, MB, Canada R3G 1C1
Dr. David W. Kidd, Contact

PH: (204)783-9613
FX: (204)772-6279
E-mail: kiddd@solutions.mb.ca
Founded: 1982. **Staff:** 1. Undertakes short-term assignments in developing countries. Orientation to small holder agriculture and to practical field oriented work. Services include agricultural extension and training, rural development, participatory planning, community owned water supply, and appropriate technology. Works with government agencies, international agencies, and private firms.

ROGER A. KILLINGSWORTH AND ASSOCIATES
816 1st St.
Jonesville, LA 71343
Roger A. Killingsworth, President
PH: (318)339-7613
FX: (318)339-7022
E-mail: kasscola@centuryinter.net
URL: http://www.agri-associations.org
Founded: 1970. **Staff:** 2. Provides agriculture land selection and appraisal for domestic and foreign clients, as well as agricultural consulting including soil and land use studies, training and development, management of farms with absentee owners/investors, and drainage design. Agronomy specialists offering relevant expert witness services. Serves agricultural community, oil industry, and insurance companies, as well as banking, financial institutions, and government agencies.

KING INTERNATIONAL
36 Pine Ave.
Lake Zurich, IL 60047
S.M. King, Ph.D., MBA, Contact
PH: (847)540-0552
FX: (847)540-0552
Founded: 1970. **Staff:** 1. Consultant who performs business and farm analyses, crop production evaluations, agricultural market analysis, market development, and business planning activities. Serves private industries as well as government agencies.

KIRK NURSERY CONSULTANTS
PO Box 96
Chester, SC 29706
Kirk Clark, Contact
PH: (803)377-1213
FX: (803)377-1213
Founded: 1984. Main area of expertise is greenhouse nursery production, with special emphasis on annual and perennial bedding plants, flowering specialty crops, vegetable transplants, and ground cover. Experience in this area includes the production, marketing, sales and delivery of these products. Supplies consulting services in the areas of crop culture, production scheduling, disease and pest control, new product development and packaging, variety selection, and marketing. Has also served as an expert in the resolution of insurance claims, and in the assessment of nursery facilities that have been secured by lending institutions or trusts. Industries served: wholesale nursery, legal, banking, manufacturing, ag chemical, horticulture, floriculture, and agriculture.

WILLIAM KNIPE AND ASSOCIATES
1120 Lewis Ln.
Boise, ID 83712
William B. Knipe, Jr., President
PH: (208)345-3163
FX: (208)344-0936
Founded: 1964. **Staff:** 6. Agriculture, agri-business, general business, real estate, and land consultants. Services include farm and ranch management land appraisal, livestock management and marketing, pasture production and management, market analysis, site analysis, feasibility studies, data processing, farm/ranch investment and related consulting. Clients include banks and other financial institutions, insurance companies, corporations, farmers, ranchers, prospective purchasers of farms and ranches, corporate farms and ranches, government agencies, and investors of all kinds.

KRAFT INC.
7960 Bay Dr.
Pigeon, MI 48755
Lowell E. Kraft, CEO
PH: (517)856-4621
FX: (517)790-2611
Founded: 1926. **Staff:** 8. Agricultural consultants specializing in subsurface drainage engineering.

LAMBERT AGRICULTURAL CONSULTING, INC.
PO Box 1019
Innis, LA 70747
Harold C. Lambert, President
PH: (504)492-2790
FX: (504)492-2789
Founded: 1981. **Staff:** 2. Licensed, certified, independent crop consultant. Primary business activities include insect pest management (survey and consultation) in field crops, soil sampling, soil test interpretations and fertility recommendations provided for grower/ clients.

LAND SYSTEMS INTERNATIONAL INC.
712 Sandpiper Point
Fort Collins, CO 80525
Robert C. Malmgren, Contact
PH: (970)223-3201
Founded: 1979. A consulting firm specializing in waste resource management, soil modification, equine footing on horse arenas and water conservation.

LANDIS INTERNATIONAL INC.
PO Box 5126
Valdosta, GA 31603
Dr. William Ronald Landis, President, CEO
PH: (912)247-6472
TF: (800)624-0436
FX: (912)242-1562
E-mail: landismainel.datasys.net
Founded: 1982. **Staff:** 16. Firm provides a full range of regulatory services to the agricultural industry, specializing in registering agricultural products with the U.S. Environmental Protection Agency.

LAVA NURSERY INC.
PO Box 370
Parkdale, OR 97041
Robert K. Moore, Vice President
PH: (541)352-7303
TF: (800)531-0963
FX: (541)352-7325
Founded: 1976. **Staff:** 3. Reforestation of temperate conifer forests, specializing in severe climate sites, high elevation, and arid, cold climates. Produces over ten million seedlings annually in two nursery sites. Industries served: forest products, forest land management, small woodland owners, and government agencies.

SONNY LEFKOWITZ, RMC
PO Box 520412
Miami, FL 33152-0412
Sonny Lefkowitz, President
PH: (305)829-2990
TF: (800)535-3355
FX: (305)470-9992
Founded: 1989. **Staff:** 1. Offers care and handling techniques to professional retail or wholesale florists and importers to extend life of fresh cut-flowers, increase profits, reduce waste, satisfy customers, and promote repeat business. Also conducts motivational seminars.

B.R. LESLIE AND ASSOCIATES
999 Ogden St.
Coquitlam, BC, Canada V3C 3P2

PH: (604)944-2929
FX: (604)944-9088
E-mail: info@brianleslie.com
URL: http://www.brianleslie.com
Provides services to the solid wood products industry in three areas: consulting, claims and complaints settlement, and technical sales support and trading.

LINDAHL, BROWNING, FERRARI & HELLSTROM, INC.
23550 SW Corporate Pky.
Palm City, FL 34990
Thomas Vokoun, PSM, Vice President
PH: (561)286-3883
TF: (888)USE-LBFH
FX: (561)286-3925
E-mail: lbfh@gate.net
URL: http://lbfh.com
Founded: 1970. **Staff:** 105. Engineers and surveyors provide services to the public sector and large-scale land development and agriculture for water, wastewater, transportation, water resources, and agriculture engineering.

LIVESTOCK NUTRITION AND MANAGEMENT SERVICES
2507 S. Nineo, Ste. 8
Omaha, NE 68124-2065
Willis F. Nickelson, President
PH: (402)397-3798
FX: (402)397-3798
Founded: 1981. **Staff:** 1. Animal scientist/consultant serving agriculture in the area of livestock feeding.

LONG PEST MANAGEMENT, INC.
720 Hwy. 308
Thibodaux, LA 70302
W. Henry Long, President
PH: (504)446-3520
FX: (504)446-3520
Founded: 1965. **Staff:** 5. Agricultural consultants offering pest scouting and recommendations for insect, disease and weed control, soil testing with fertilizer recommendations and other services. Serves growers of sugar cane, soybeans, corn, and wheat.

LORANDA GROUP INC.
40 Adloff Ln., Ste. 5
Springfield, IL 62703
John D. Moss, President
PH: (217)544-4200
FX: (217)544-4213
E-mail: loranda@loranda.com
URL: http://www.loranda.com
Founded: 1995. A farmland appraiser that researches and analyzes farms. Considers soil types, topography, drainage, recent sales of similar properties in the area, location, climate, accessibility, long-term potential, improvements, weighted average crop yield, income potential, potential of dividing the property into multiple tracts for greater value.

LUCAS TREE EXPERT CO.
636 Riverside St.
Portland, ME 04104
Arthur Batson, Jr., President
PH: (207)797-7294
FX: (207)797-0752
E-mail: info@lucastree.com
URL: http://www.lucastree.com
Founded: 1926. **Staff:** 350. In the landscape area provides overall project management, including site analysis, design analysis, cost savings for the client while increasing project quality, maintenance recommendations using Integrated Pest Management to reduce costs and the impact of chemicals on the environment. In forestry, consults on the proper use of chemicals and timber stand improvement reports. In agriculture, provides plant control recommendations and appropriate chemical usages. Serves the utility industry in utility line clearance and maintenance as well as line construction.

MACKEY'S VETERINARY SERVICE
PO Box 57
Greeley, CO 80632
Donald R. Mackey, Contact
PH: (970)353-0995
FX: (970)356-8913
Founded: 1942. **Staff:** 3. Offers counsel on the treatment and prevention of diseases of dairy and feedlot cattle. Serves private industries as well as government agencies.

GIANPAOLO MAESTRONE
4 Sophia Ln.
Staten Island, NY 10304
Gianpaolo Maestrone, Contact
PH: (718)987-5010
Founded: 1987. **Staff:** 2. Professional veterinarian with Board Certification in Veterinary Microbiology, plus twenty-five years experience in human and veterinary pharmaceutical industry. Conducts feasibility studies, development and clearance of animal health products for systemic, topical, anti-mastitic and growth promotion uses. Specializes in selection, evaluation and registration of fish health products. Serves the aquaculture, agriculture, and pharmaceutical industries.

DARIA MAKOTA, CGA, BSA
Box 55
Grand Marais, MB, Canada R0E 0T0
Daria Makota, Principal
PH: (204)754-3314
FX: (204)754-3314
E-mail: cara@cancom.net
Founded: 1988. **Staff:** 1. Provides financial management services and acts as a lecturer, writer, and consultant, with a specialty in finance in agriculture.

MANRIQUE INTERNATIONAL AGROTECH
PO Box 61145
Honolulu, HI 96839
Dr. Luis A. Manrique, Owner
PH: (808)533-0391
FX: (808)734-0561
E-mail: manrique@lava.net
URL: http://www.lava.net/manrique/miat.htm
A consulting company that provides specialized technical services in the areas of soil management, soil conservation, tropical agronomy, crop production, and land and/or environmental assessment.

MARBIL ENGINEERING ASSOCIATES
6910 Furman Pky.
Riverdale, MD 20737
William A. Bailey, Contact
PH: (301)459-1607
FX: (301)459-1607
Founded: 1985. **Staff:** 3. Consulting engineers specializing in livestock transportation with feed and water: air (pens and pallets), sea (pens and containers), and land (rail and truck). Related expertise in design and development of partial or total farm layout including buildings, pens, passageways, cleaning and waste handling, water and electric distribution systems, etc. Emphasis is on humane treatment of all livestock at all times. Also specializes in greenhouse and plant growth chamber design, fabrication and operation as new types of lamps come on the market-new lamp fixtures are designed and tested with growing plants. Serves private industries as well as government agencies worldwide.

S.J. MARSDEN & CO., INC.
Rte. 3, Box 93
Rogersville, MO 65742-9214
Stephen J. Marsden, President
PH: (417)753-4000
TF: (800)753-9199
FX: (417)753-2000
E-mail: herbal@dialnet.net
URL: http://www.herbaladvantage.com

Founded: 1980. **Staff:** 4. Provides counsel, development and management services for domestic and international projects. Specializes in agricultural project design, feasibility studies, and construction supervision for greenhouse projects and related support systems for vegetable, flower, or grass fodder production in soil or hydroponics. Related services include construction supervision, management supervision, project start-up, vegetable packing systems, flower grading systems, selective personnel recruiting, product procurement, systems evaluation, site analysis surveys, and soil testing.

MARUTANI AND ASSOCIATES—PACIFIC BASIN AGRIBUSINESS CONSULTANTS

PO Box 10388
Hilo, HI 96721-5388
Herbert K. Marutani, Contact
PH: (808)969-7488
FX: (808)969-7488
Founded: 1984. **Staff:** 1. Offers services in production economics (feasibility studies and analysis) and marketing (analysis and development) of tropical crops, such as fruits, nuts, vegetables, orchard crops, ornamentals, and exotic plants. Also provides consultation in the development and maintenance of small business and cooperatives. Working knowledge of Japanese and Spanish.

JAMES K. MARYANSKI, MYCOLOGIST

1720 Larch Dr.
Mount Prospect, IL 60056
James K. Maryanski, Contact
PH: (847)390-0810
FX: (847)390-0810
Founded: 1982. **Staff:** 1. Consulting mycologist with special expertise in the detection, isolation and enumeration of molds and yeasts from foods and food products, feedstuffs, cereal grains, forages, cosmetics, paper products, etc. Services include: mold and yeast identification to the species level; interpretation and significance of fungi detected; mold and yeast related consultation and problem solving; fungal-related storage studies; development and supervision of quality control programs; and plant inspections, independent sampling and analysis. Industries served: food, feed, paper, cosmetic, confection and soft drink industries, government agencies, and all independent consultant laboratories.

MASON, BRUCE & GIRARD, INC., CONSULTING FORESTERS

707 SW Washington St., Ste. 1300
Portland, OR 97205
PH: (503)224-3445
FX: (503)224-6524
URL: http://www.masonbruce.com
Founded: 1921. Provides forestry-consulting services to the large and small landowners. Specializes in harvest planning, inventory, GIS, or environmental service needs.

DANIEL F. MAYER

5206 Pear Butte
Yakima, WA 98901
Daniel F. Mayer, Contact
PH: (509)452-6555
Founded: 1980. **Staff:** 5. Provides consultant services dealing with entomology (insects). Activities include providing pest control recommendations, research with new pesticides and chemical testing and expert witness services. Industries served are growers, agribusiness firms, chemical companies developing pesticides for agriculture, government agencies, and attorneys.

MANSEL M. MAYEUX

1980 Woodland Dr.
Baton Rouge, LA 70808
Mansel M. Mayeux, Contact
PH: (504)926-1769
Founded: 1965. **Staff:** 1. Offers consulting and analysis of farm equipment management. Services include analysis of accidents and expert testimony on product liability and safety of farm machinery,

anhydrous ammonia and propane distribution systems to include pressure vessels, safety valves, and hoses.

PATRICK J. MCENTEGART

24-16 Steinway St., Ste. 636
Long Island City, NY 11103
Patrick J. McEntegart, Contact
PH: (718)634-0460
FX: (718)278-1769
Founded: 1987. **Staff:** 8. Firm provides cost engineering, construction management, feasibility studies, and budgeting services. Serves the construction, agriculture, and manufacturing industries worldwide.

MCKINNON, ALLEN & ASSOCIATES, LTD.

1115 46th Ave. SE
Calgary, AB, Canada T2G 2A5
S.D. Allen, President
PH: (403)243-4345
FX: (403)243-4345
Founded: 1960. **Staff:** 6. The firm's multidisciplinary work team provides independent opinions and practical solutions to a variety of problems in the areas of agribusiness, farm and ranch management, agricultural environmental consulting and rural land use. Specific areas of expertise are as follows: financial advisory consulting, agricultural environmental monitoring, general agricultural management consulting, economic evaluation, land use planning, land valuation, surface rights disputes and expropriations, farm management for absentee owners, and damage claims.

MEDALLION LABORATORIES

9000 Plymouth Ave.
Minneapolis, MN 55427
Dr. Michael Baim, Contact
PH: (612)540-4453
TF: (800)245-5615
FX: (612)540-4010
E-mail: medlabs@cis.compuserve.com
URL: http://www.medlabs.com
Founded: 1974. **Staff:** 50. Firm specializes in the fields of analytical testing, microbiological testing, pesticides, and physical testing. Innovative technology, superior customer service, and a staff of over 40 analysts and consultants provide the flexibility and expertise to meet a client's analytical needs.

MORGAN R. MELLETTE CO.

PO Box 435
Gainesville, GA 30503
Morgan R. Mellette, Owner
PH: (770)534-3091
Founded: 1979. **Staff:** 1. Offers timber and land appraisals, timber sales, forest management planning, reforestation, and land surveying for non-industrial private forest landowners.

DWIGHT W. MICHENER

4980 Old State Rte. 73
Waynesville, OH 45068
Dwight W. Michener, Contact
PH: (513)897-7236
Founded: 1970. **Staff:** 2. Agricultural consultant specializing in irrigation and drainage engineering, including tile drains, surface drains, small dams, surface and sprinkler irrigation, land leveling, channels, and rock dams. Also offers income tax preparation. Serves private industries as well as government agencies. Active internationally with experience in Ethiopia, Turkey, Pakistan, Iraq, and Syria.

MICRO-MACRO INTERNATIONAL, INC.

183 Paradise Blvd., Ste. 108
Athens, GA 30607
Harry A. Mills, President

PH: (706)548-4557
TF: (800)837-8664
FX: (706)548-4891
E-mail: micrmacr@aol.com
Founded: 1988. **Staff:** 9. Offers consultation on agricultural production field, container, greenhouse and hydroponic systems. Provides analytical services for the analysis of water, wastewater, soil, plant tissue and other biological substances for their element content. Industries served: agricultural producers, research institutes and individuals, fertilizer manufacturers, and government agencies.

MICROBAC INCORPORATED ELSA SERVICE

517 N. George St.
York, PA 17404
T.F. Lagattuta, Laboratory Director
PH: (717)846-4953
FX: (717)846-4986
Founded: 1959. **Staff:** 10. Provides technical counsel on chemical and microbiological testing, evaluation and quality control services primarily for environmental, agribusiness, feed industry and food manufacturing. Offers consultation, advisory services, research and development on technical problems, new product formulation, and product or process improvement. Also performs general testing of refrigerants, food products, solid waste, water and wastewater for compliance with EPA, DER, FDA and other governmental agencies.

MID-SOUTH AG RESEARCH, INC.

2383 Hinkley Rd.
Proctor, AR 72376
K.E. Savage, President
PH: (870)732-2981
FX: (870)735-7752
E-mail: MSAGRI@aol.com
Founded: 1981. **Staff:** 3. Agricultural research consultants who specialize in custom field research with pesticides on agronomic crops grown in the delta area of Arkansas, Missouri and Tennessee. Residue test conducted under GLP. Serves agricultural/chemical companies, both domestic and international.

MID-STATE LABORATORY, LLC

9410 W. Placer Ave.
Visalia, CA 93291
PH: (209)651-9044
FX: (209)651-9047
E-mail: info@midstatelab.com
URL: http://www.midstatelab.com
Founded: 1979. Agricultural and industrial testing. Specialties include analysis for crop nutrition (soil, agricultural water, and plant tissue) and testing for feed, waste water, pesticides, and microbiological properties. Also provides Grid sampling and GPS services.

MIDWEST LABORATORIES, INC.

13611 B St.
Omaha, NE 68144
Kennard Pohlman, President
PH: (402)334-7770
TF: (800)677-0256
FX: (402)334-9121
E-mail: deboer@midwestlabs.com
URL: http://www.midwestlabs.com
Founded: 1975. **Staff:** 65. Soil sampling and analysis, environmental testing and regulations, including air, water, wastewater, sludge, food testing and labeling requirements.

MILLER AGRICULTURAL CONSULTING SERVICES

10967 County Rd. 19
Lawton, ND 58345
Earl R. Miller, President
PH: (701)655-3591
E-mail: jd7020@polarcomm.com
Founded: 1984. **Staff:** 2. Agricultural consultant works with clients in the area of machine design and safety as it pertains to machines used in the production of agricultural crops. Crops include wheat, barley, corn, sunflowers, sugar beets, and potatoes.

MILLER PUBLISHING CORP.

PO Box 34908
Memphis, TN 38184-0908
PH: (901)372-8280
FX: (901)373-6180
E-mail: mktgsubs@millerpublishing.com
URL: http://www.millerpublishing.com
Founded: 1927. Information source on forest product markets and supply sources.

MITCON INC.

2116 27th Ave. NE, No. 234
Calgary, AB, Canada T2E 7A6
PH: (403)735-1800
FX: (403)735-1803
E-mail: info@mitcon.com
URL: http://www.mitcon.com
A marketing service focusing on risk management; a cash brokerage service offered to grain companies, processors, end-users and exporters; an off-farm cash grain brokerage service offered to grain producers.

HUGH E. MOBLEY

114 Aegean Way
Wetumpka, AL 36093
PH: (334)567-4462
E-mail: hughmobley@aol.com
URL: http://www.pcinc.com/mobley
Specializes in fire behavior, prescribed burning, smoke management, fire control, and litigation.

D. SCOTT MOODY

Rte. 1, Box 409, FM 1118E
Kingsville, TX 78363
D. Scott Moody, Contact
PH: (512)592-6614
FX: (512)592-8958
E-mail: krbogman@interconnect.net
Founded: 1978. **Staff:** 3. Agricultural consultant working primarily with farmers: instructing them on the proper timing, method of application and chemicals to use in the control of agricultural pests. These pests include insects, weeds, and other various pathogens that affect crops. Also performs contract research for the chemical industry that is involved in producing new chemicals for the farming community. This research includes residue sampling, efficacy data, and gathering other data that the company deems appropriate. Industries served: farming, chemical, pesticide, and research.

W.S. MOORE CONSULTING

PO Box 9527
Berkeley, CA 94709
Wayne S. Moore, President
PH: (510)524-1163
FX: (510)524-8085
Founded: 1982. **Staff:** 4. Active in the marketing of horticulture and gardening-related products, including pest-control products.

MSC BUSINESS SERVICES

Box 8736
Camp Hill, PA 17001-8736
Michael W. Evanish, Manager
PH: (717)761-2740
FX: (717)731-3505
E-mail: fms@pfb.com
Founded: 1957. **Staff:** 50. Agricultural consultants specializing in financial management, enterprise analysis, tax planning, loan acquisition, and estate planning for farm and small business enterprises. Leases computers and accounting software through PFA FACCTS program. For Pennsylvania users, PFB Legal Services Plan is also available.

J. STEWART MURRAY
639 Borebank St.
Winnipeg, MB, Canada R3N 1G1
J. Stewart Murray, President
PH: (204)488-3885
FX: (204)489-0129
E-mail: murag@mb.sympatico.ca
Founded: 1989. **Staff:** 1. Marketing and sales consultants for agri-industrial and environmental products. Industries served: agriculture/agribusiness, water and wastewater treatment, environmental technology and industrial supply trades, and government agencies in Canada.

NATURAL PROPERTIES CONSULTING FORESTRY
4120 Clemson Blvd., Ste. E
Anderson, SC 29621-1176
PH: (864)224-5111
E-mail: natural@ww-interlink.net
URL: http://www.ww-interlink.net/natural/forestry
Consulting forestry services to the timberland owners. Offers consulting in land sales, timber sales and forest management activities such as reforestation, forest inventory and taxes.

MICHAEL D. NEAL & ASSOCIATES, INC.
PO Box 37
Colerain, NC 27924
Michael D. Neal, President
PH: (919)356-2747
FX: (919)356-1206
Founded: 1972. **Staff:** 9. Offers complete forest management consulting services including timber estimates and appraisals, damage and trespass appraisals, timber and land sales, and reforestation. NC certified general real estate appraiser. Serves government agencies also.

NEMEC AGRISERVICES INC.
PO Box 467
Snook, TX 77878-0467
Stanley J. Nemec, President
PH: (409)272-8022
FX: (409)272-1636
Founded: 1973. **Staff:** 4. Serves in advisory capacity to agricultural industry. Counsels on crop production practices, emphasizing insect and weed management. Conducts agricultural research, involving laboratory and field testing of new and registered products, and innovative methods for agronomic production. Also performs investigations related to crop/land damage, pollution, and expert testimony for litigation.

JAMES C. NOFZIGER, PH.D.
7252 Remmet Ave., Ste. 208
Canoga Park, CA 91303
James C. Nofziger, Ph.D.
PH: (818)347-3053
FX: (818)347-2401
Founded: 1961. Agricultural consultant specializing in nutrition and management of meat and dairy animals, and in by-product utilization. Feasibility studies, expert witness.

NORTH AMERICAN PUMP CORP.
5026 Belmont Rd.
Grand Forks, ND 58201-8046
George M. Bowman, President
PH: (701)772-1389
FX: (701)772-6427
Founded: 1963. **Staff:** 5. Makes recommendations to individuals, large-scale farming operations, agricultural products processors and government subdivisions on selection of pumping, irrigation, spraying, and pressure cleaning equipment. Serves private industries as well as government agencies.

NORTH COAST RESOURCE MANAGEMENT
PO Box 509
Redwood Valley, CA 95470
Mark D. Edwards, President
PH: (707)485-7211
FX: (707)485-8962
E-mail: gpssales@ncrm.com
URL: http://www.ncrm.com
Provider of Global Positioning System (GPS) equipment, rental, training and education. Resource management division includes registered professional foresters, professional archaeologists, and professional consulting biologists. Services in the areas of forestry, archaeology, and geographic information systems (GIS).

NORTHAMERICAN ENVIRONMENTAL SERVICES, INC.
PO Box 26521
Austin, TX 78755-0521
D. Craig Kissock, President
PH: (512)264-2828
Founded: 1984. **Staff:** 5. A firm of specialized technical and management consultants with expertise in the environmental sciences. Experienced in soil erosion and sediment control, soil classification, and range management. Serves private industries as well as government agencies.

JOHN S. NOTESTINE
4 Mi. N. Hwy. 25
Leoti, KS 67861
PH: (316)375-4733
TF: (800)628-5613
FX: (316)375-2418
Staff: 1. Firm provides numerous agricultural services, including the following: crop scouting for weeds and insects; agricultural consulting regarding chemical use and application by ground and air; irrigation, flood, and sprinkler; and chem-fallow, min-til, and no-til under dryland and irrigation. Serves local farmers in Wichita, Scott, Logan, Greely, and Wallace counties in western Kansas.

RALPH OSTERLING CONSULTANTS, INC.
1650 Borel Pl., Ste. 204
San Mateo, CA 94402
Ralph Osterling, President
PH: (650)573-8733
FX: (650)345-7890
E-mail: rsoc@ix.netcom.com
Founded: 1978. **Staff:** 6. Urban and rural forestry consultants whose activities include appraisal, evaluation, cruising, harvest management, tree management plans (vertical hazards) for golf courses, and reforestation. Erosion control and land reclamation specialty includes site evaluation, specification preparation, construction supervision, monitoring and tree planting.

PACE CONSULTING
1267 Diamond St.
San Diego, CA 92109
Wendy Gelernter, Ph.D.
PH: (619)272-9897
FX: (619)483-6349
E-mail: stowell@pace-ptri.com
URL: http://www.pace-ptri.com
Founded: 1986. **Staff:** 1. Provides cost effective and environmentally compatible solutions to complex agricultural production problems. Conducts accurate weed and insect identification, disease diagnosis, evaluation of nutritional conditions, and application of the principles of integrated pest management. Assesses catastrophic crop loss incidents, including expert investigation, loss estimate, summary reports, and testimony to determine cause and extent of real damages. Also reviews agricultural chemical and biotechnology products/companies and recommends pursuing or terminating further research and development. Industries served: agriculture, golf courses, environmental clean-up/bioremediation, and government in continental U.S., primarily southwestern states; and northern Mexico.

PACE MARKETING, INC.
PO Box 2039
Stuart, FL 34994-2039
K. Bond Pace, President
PH: (561)871-9682
FX: (561)286-9547
Founded: 1976. **Staff:** 3. Assists shrimp producers in design and setup of U.S. and overseas facilities. Industries served: seafood importers/processors, seafood brokers/agents, firearms, and government worldwide.

PACIFIC AGRI-VEST
37-C Sandpiper
Palm Desert, CA 92260
Dale Hibler, President
PH: (760)568-6737
FX: (760)568-0747
E-mail: pacagrVEST@aol.com
Founded: 1982. **Staff:** 1. Provides services in the areas of evaluation, acquisition, mortgage financing, and sale of irrigated farms and associated agribusiness. Prepares agricultural feasibility studies for joint ventures on irrigated farms, and tree and vine crops; agricultural fair market value appraisals; and farm management plans (operations and development). Also appraises machinery and equipment related to agricultural packing and food processing industries. As an accredited rural appraiser (CA certified general appraiser), serves as expert witness on land values and crop losses. Industries served: individuals, insurance, banks, irrigation districts, other public utilities, the military, government, and attorneys in southern California and western Arizona.

PACIFIC FOREST CONSULTANTS, INC.
200 N. Edwards
Newberg, OR 97132
Dennis W. Callegari, Vice President
PH: (503)537-9300
TF: (800)364-6188
FX: (503)537-9320
URL: http://pacific-forest.com
Founded: 1984. **Staff:** 6. Timberland investment and management consultants offer the following services: timberland inventory and appraisal, timberland management and computer software design. Also provides real estate services (forestland) via affiliated brokerage. Serves private, non-industrial land owners and investors, institutional investors, municipal watersheds, utilities, and other forestland owners including foreign investors.

PACIFIC HORTICULTURE/LANDSCAPE AND AGRONOMY CONSULTANTS
1000 Wood Stock Ln.
Ventura, CA 93001
Donald F. Rodrigues, Contact
PH: (805)644-1336
FX: (805)644-1579
Founded: 1972. **Staff:** 3. Horticultural consultants offering services in landscaping, pest management, agronomy, and tree appraisals. Primarily involved with government agencies, landscape architects, developers and others with problem diagnoses as related to horticulture. Also performs site surveys, development inspections and specification writing. Provides expert witness services.

PACIFIC ORGANICS, INC.
255 Richmond St. SE
Salem, OR 97301-6714
Rob Gould, Contact
PH: (503)361-2302
FX: (503)585-6065
E-mail: info@pacorganics.com
URL: http://www.pacorganics.com
Founded: 1992. **Staff:** 2. Specializes in the development and marketing of organic fertilizers and soil amendments derived from organic by-products. Provides technical analysis of a by-product to assess its value in the marketplace. Offers recommendations for the best marketing opportunities for the material. Writes fertilizer labels,

packaging, brochures, and similar technical and marketing materials. Offers guidance through the fertilizer label registration process with state agencies. Serves the food processing, mining, fisheries, and agriculture industries.

PALO DURO CONSULTATION, RESEARCH, AND FEEDLOT, AGRI-RESEARCH CENTER, INC.
Rte. 1, Box 37
Canyon, TX 79015
Dr. David T. Bechtol, President
PH: (806)499-3304
FX: (806)499-3394
E-mail: dbechtol@paloduro-consulting.com
URL: http://paloduro-consulting.com
Founded: 1974. **Staff:** 5. A multi-purpose, multi-man veterinary practice with specialties in feedlot and beef cattle consultation and beef cattle research. Utilizes various management tools that are unique to this practice and they include: customized and comprehensive treatment book; cattle accounting system -computer health evaluation program; regular educational seminars for personnel; post mortem book assist personnel in routine necropsy procedures; regular detailed up-dates on important animal health issues; and comprehensive monthly written reports, covering results and recommendations for the period. Offers training and educating personnel in comprehensive cattle health management procedures. Also advises management to maximize performance and minimize losses. Works closely with cattle order buyers, auction barns, and cow-calf producers to define problem areas and prevent excessive morbidity and mortality in cattle feeding operations. Serves the agriculture, banking and finance, education, the legal profession, government agencies, manufacturing, pharmaceutical, publishing, and service industries.

PAN EARTH DESIGNS
PO Box 1928
Yelm, WA 98597
Bruce Weiskotten, CEO
PH: (360)458-9173
FX: (360)458-9123
Founded: 1990. **Staff:** 2. Provides sustainable, integrated design, consulting and contract management services in architecture, landscape, agriculture, and renewable resource management; wetlands delineation and environmental assessment for real estate, development, community land trusts, wildlife preserves, and private land holders; sustainable community planning and development for municipal and tribal governments, developers, and community land trusts; and non-toxic, energy efficient residential house and landscape design integrating archetypal architecture to produce added value (clean, safe, low maintenance, user-friendly houses, gardens and homesteads).

PAULSEN GROUP, INC.
13411 Tamarack Rd.
Silver Spring, MD 20904-1468
PH: (301)384-1838
E-mail: rpaulsen@interserv.com
URL: http://www.paulsengroup.com
Founded: 1990. An environmental research company dedicated to using applied research to solve environmental problems. Uses GIS, GPS and remote sensing technologies. Also specializes in precision farming, field studies and fate and transport modeling.

PEAR DOCTOR, INC.
4825 Loasa Dr.
Kelseyville, CA 95451
Broc Gerald Zoller, President
PH: (707)279-9773
FX: (707)279-4335
Founded: 1979. **Staff:** 2. Agricultural consultant to deciduous fruit growers offering advice on production methods, loss investigations for insurance and litigation purposes, agricultural property evaluations, and plant disease diagnosis.

PERT LABS
145 Peanut Dr.
Edenton, NC 27932
Stan Bullington, President
PH: (919)482-4456
FX: (919)482-5370
Founded: 1967. **Staff:** 19. Offers consulting in all phases of peanut processing, product development of peanut foods, process systems, stability and shelf life studies, taste panels and quality control programs. Special consulting in the areas of dry roast seasonings and custom peanut butter formulations/processing systems. Also provides microbiological testing and analytical services with special emphasis on aflatoxin testing, extraneous matter and pesticide residue testing.

PEST MANAGEMENT ENTERPRISES, INC.
101 Third St.
Cheneyville, LA 71325
Grady E. Coburn, Ph.D., President
PH: (318)279-2165
FX: (318)279-2165
E-mail: coburname1@aol.com
Founded: 1975. **Staff:** 9. Offers agricultural consulting and contract research (GLP compliant) to the agricultural industry.

PEST PROS INC.
PO Box 188
Plainfield, WI 54966
Randy VanHaren, President
PH: (715)335-4046
FX: (715)335-4746
E-mail: pestpros@unlontel.net
Founded: 1984. **Staff:** 6. Offers agricultural consulting involving fertility and pesticide recommendations, soil microbe assay, contract research, and GLP/efficacy.

PLANT SCIENCES, INC.
342 Green Valley Rd.
Watsonville, CA 95076-1305
Richard D. Nelson, President
PH: (831)728-7771
FX: (831)728-4967
E-mail: plantsci@compuserve.com
Founded: 1985. **Staff:** 50. Agricultural consulting firm offers crop management, contract research, plant tissue culture, plant breeding, and biocontrol. Industries served: agriculture and forestry, chemical, and individuals.

RICKS H. PLUENNEKE AND ASSOCIATES
6155 Dick Price Rd.
Fort Worth, TX 76140-7847
Dr. Ricks Pluenneke, Contact
PH: (817)478-0761
FX: (817)478-0761
E-mail: phyton@aol.com
Founded: 1975. **Staff:** 6. Agricultural/environmental consultant offering services in the plant sciences. Also infrared aerial photography, soil and plant analyses, bioassays, phytotoxic testing and related forensic areas. Clients include farmers, ranchers, attorneys, insurance companies, government agencies, agricultural chemical companies, landscapers, nurseries, colleges, airports, cemeteries, and architects. Geographic areas served: United States and international.

PRAGMA CORP.
116 E. Broad St.
Falls Church, VA 22046-4501
Jacques Defay, Pres.
PH: (703)237-9303
FX: (703)237-9326
E-mail: pragma1@pragmacorp.com
URL: http://www.pragmacorp.com
Founded: 1977. **Staff:** 65. Offers expertise in the fields of finance, corporate governance, agriculture and agribusiness, training and education, health environment and urban development, municipal de-

velopment, systems and technology. Clients include: U.S. and international private firms; development institutions; non-governmental and private voluntary organizations; and academic institutions.

PRO - TECH - AG
Bowling Green Rd.
Lexington, MS 39095
John M. Kimbrough, III, President
PH: (601)834-1318
FX: (601)834-3430
Founded: 1969. **Staff:** 4. Offers crop consulting in entomology, plant health, weed science, and soil analysis. Recent work has also included research and development activities in agricultural chemicals and related equipment for agri-chemical products. Serves private industries as well as government agencies.

PROMAR INTERNATIONAL, INC.
1625 Prince St., Ste. 200
Alexandria, VA 22314
Nicholas A. Young, President & CEO
PH: (703)739-9090
FX: (703)739-9098
E-mail: promar@promarinternational.com
URL: http://www.promarinternational.com
Founded: 1983. **Staff:** 28. Strategic marketing and business consulting firm specializing in serving clients along the entire food chain, from farmer or producer to end consumer. Together with the Produce Studies Group of Newbury, UK, forms one of the world's largest consulting firms specializing in agriculture and food and production, distribution, and marketing of agri-food products. Examples of strategic studies undertaken include: "Functional Foods and Nutraceuticals: The US Opportunity"; "Riding the US Ethnic Food Tide"; "Global Sweetener Markets"; "Value Enhanced Corn and Soybeans"; "The Globalization of Meat Markets"; and "On-line Retailing in the US".

RAINEY COMMODITIES INC.
2810 Summer Oaks Dr.
Memphis, TN 38134
David A. Rainey, Vice President
PH: (901)384-8077
TF: (800)626-9384
FX: (901)384-8072
Founded: 1978. **Staff:** 4. Advises on acquisitions and divestitures of agribusinesses. Also provides commodity brokerage services.

RANCH MANAGEMENT CONSULTANTS
7719 Rio Grande Blvd. NW
Albuquerque, NM 87107
PH: (505)898-7417
FX: (505)898-9368
E-mail: rmcalb@aol.com
URL: http://www.ranchmanagement.com
Subject matter includes business management as well as technical aspects of agriculture, including reproduction, nutrition, grazing management and drought, in addition to people and time management.

RAS ENTERPRISES
Rte. 4, Box 37
Hico, TX 76457
Royce Samford, President
PH: (254)796-4779
FX: (254)796-4779
Founded: 1977. **Staff:** 3. Agricultural consultants in the areas of livestock and crop production, product development, and financial evaluation. Services include business counsel and management of investment for farms and ranches. Serves private industries as well as government agencies.

BARGYLA RATEAVER
9049 Covina St.
San Diego, CA 92126
Bargyla Rateaver, Contact

PH: (619)566-8994
FX: (619)586-1104
E-mail: brateaver@aol.com
Founded: 1965. **Staff:** 1. Promotes the use of biological (sustainable, alternative, organic) methods in agriculture and horticulture, on any scale, worldwide. Offers assistance in the selection of products suitable for biological farming.

J.W. REED, CONSULTANT
ABC Sports Turf
Houston, TX 77077-5719
J.W. Reed, Contact
PH: (281)493-3327
FX: (281)293-0273
E-mail: jwrturf@aol.com
URL: http://abcsportsturf.com
Founded: 1986. **Staff:** 3. Offers services in sports turf management, field construction and renovation, soil amendments, and deep tine aeration. Industries served: college, high school, and sports associations.

RESEARCH PLANNING, INC.
1121 Park St.
Columbia, SC 29202
Linos Cotsapas, Vice President
PH: (803)256-7322
FX: (803)254-6445
E-mail: info@researchplanning.com
Founded: 1990. **Staff:** 25. Consultants in information systems serving the fields of environmental technology and oil spill research, nationally and internationally. Expertise is in information management, including GIS mapping technology. Develops databases for natural resource management for use by a wide variety of clients, with a strong component/need for geographical references. Emphasis is on the synthesis, interpretation, and digitization of information in a manner which allows easy use in decision-making, usually using microcomputers. In addition, services and products are offered in shrimp mariculture, including site selections, hatchery technology, farm management, business plans, and prefabricated hatcheries. Serves private industries as well as government agencies.

RESOURCES INTERNATIONAL—DIVISION OF SORTOR ENGINEERING, INC.
2100 Tulare St., Ste. 402
Fresno, CA 93721-2150
Bill C. Bilbo, President
PH: (209)683-6516
FX: (209)683-6512
Founded: 1969. **Staff:** 6. Agricultural consultants and engineers providing counsel, and management and implementation services to farmers, livestock producers, lending institutions, utilities, attorneys, realtors, developers, investors, industrialists, government agencies and other firms and institutions involved in the development and use of agricultural resources throughout the world.

RL&L ENVIRONMENTAL SERVICES LTD.
17312 106 Ave.
Edmonton, AB, Canada T5S 1H9
C. McLeod, President
PH: (403)483-3499
FX: (403)483-1574
E-mail: edmonton@rll.ca
URL: http://www.rll.ca
Founded: 1977. **Staff:** 34. Specialization areas include: fisheries and aquatic ecosystem research on large rivers and remote environments; impact assessments of hydro power and water management developments; development of project mitigation strategies, environmental protection guidelines and environmental inspection services; assessment of the effects of forest harvesting, mining pipelines, and other land use activities on fisheries resources and aquatic habitat; development, implementation and assessment of fish habitat restoration and enhancement strategies; limnology and water quality sampling; including aquatic invertebrate, dissolved gas and sediment monitoring for regulatory standards; use of radio, ultrasonic,

archival and GPS data acquisition for fish habitat studies; information programs and technology transfer for fisheries and aquatic environmental protection. Firm also offers a variety of standard environmental management services and routinely partners with other firms and professionals to offer inclusive project services in the fields of water quality analysis, environmental engineering and hydrology, and reclamation planning.

F. HERBERT ROBERTSON
1026 W. 8th St.
Panama City, FL 32401
F. Herbert Robertson, Contact
PH: (850)763-5049
Founded: 1959. Functions for and in behalf of persons requiring assistance with their forest properties. Also offers assistance with brokerage of timber and/or timberland, and forest management planning and operation. Specialists in tree nutrition and insect and disease control for shade trees.

ROGERS ENGINEERING INC.
626 47th St. E
Saskatoon, SK, Canada S7X 5X3
R. Barry Rogers, M.Sc., BSAE, President
PH: (306)975-0500
FX: (306)975-0499
E-mail: rogers.ino@sk.sympatico.ca
Founded: 1982. **Staff:** 11. A professional agricultural engineering and agronomy research and development company, offering engineering and agronomic research, management, and specialty equipment manufacturing services to agricultural equipment manufacturers, governments, and individual agriculturalists. These services are concentrated in new product research and development, chemical field and plot research, custom fabricating, research management, funding sourcing, agronomy, market analysis, and patenting assistance.

ROGERS ENTOMOLOGICAL SERVICES, INC.
Box 660
Cleveland, MS 38732
Mills L. Rogers, Jr., President
PH: (601)846-1217
TF: (800)801-2775
FX: (601)846-1236
Founded: 1954. **Staff:** 10. Agricultural consultant offers expertise in entomological matters concerning cotton, rice, and soy beans. Serves private industries as well as government agencies.

RUSH, MARCROFT & ASSOCIATES
28951 Falcon Ridge Rd.
Salinas, CA 93908
Dale W. Rush, Ph.D., Contact
PH: (408)484-4834
FX: (408)484-4837
E-mail: ag4n6@aol.com
Founded: 1971. **Staff:** 5. Agricultural consultants specializing in forensic agronomy-the investigation and field evaluation of crop loss complaints. Clients include insurance companies, growers, potential plaintiffs or defendants, and attorneys.

SALISBURY MANAGEMENT SERVICES, INC.
PO Box 10
Eaton Rapids, MI 48827-0010
Michael H. Salisbury, President
PH: (517)663-5600
FX: (517)663-5608
E-mail: sms@salisbury-management.com
URL: http://www.salisbury-management.com
Founded: 1979. **Staff:** 6. Provides financial and business management consulting to agriculture and agriculture related businesses. Services include preparation of cash flows, credit package applications, financial restructures and turnarounds, and economic loss analysis and expert witness testimony for the legal profession. Designs and implements computer applications and/or systems, generally

turn key computer systems with back-up support and service. Serves private industries as well as government agencies.

SARKIS V. SARABIAN AND ASSOCIATES INC.
2266 S. De Wolf Ave.
Sanger, CA 93657
Sarkis V. Sarabian, President
PH: (209)268-2830
FX: (209)493-2909
E-mail: sffarms@aol.com
Founded: 1966. **Staff:** 4. Provides agricultural consulting specializing in land development, feasibility studies, marketing studies, and farm management evaluation and reorganization. Experienced as expert witness regarding pesticides, herbicides, and agricultural management. Grape and tree fruit culture, packing, storage, and marketing. Has worked in 11 foreign countries.

SCHICK INTERNATIONAL, INC.
3010 First Commerce Center
Salt Lake City, UT 84101-1413
Seth H. Schick, President
PH: (801)359-3012
FX: (801)359-2401
Founded: 1970. **Staff:** 35. Offers engineering, economic and agricultural consulting services on resource development projects around the world. Recent experience in design of dams and irrigation systems and culinary water systems.

SCHRAMM, WILLIAMS & ASSOCIATES INC.
517 C St. NE
Washington, DC 20002
PH: (202)543-4455
FX: (202)543-4586
E-mail: swaconsult@aol.com
Founded: 1984. Agriculture consultants.

JOHN K. SCHUELLER
1410 NW 30th St.
Gainesville, FL 32605
John K. Schueller, Contact
PH: (352)335-6384
Founded: 1983. **Staff:** 1. Consulting engineer with experience in mechanical, industrial, and agricultural engineering to aid mainly construction equipment, agricultural, manufacturing, and automotive industries with design, automation, and the manufacturing process.

SCIENTIFIC AG CO.
1734 D St., Ste. 2
Bakersfield, CA 93301
Joe Traynor, President
PH: (805)327-2631
Founded: 1973. **Staff:** 4. Offers agricultural consulting on entomology in all phases of crop growth and production including soil fertility and plant nutrition, soil evaluation, irrigation, and crop feasibility studies.

SCIENTIFIC AGRICULTURAL SERVICES INC.
3393 Atlas Peak Rd.
Napa, CA 94558
Wayne R. Jones, President
PH: (707)257-0585
FX: (707)257-0109
Founded: 1975. **Staff:** 3. Consulting agronomists specializing in soil amendment and plant nutritional programs.

SEA-ARM CONSULTING ASSOCIATES
640 Line St.
Hollister, CA 95023
Samuel Armstrong, Partner
PH: (831)637-1468
FX: (831)637-4377
E-mail: samarm@aol.com
Founded: 1980. **Staff:** 6. Offers expertise regarding financial restructuring (including start-ups and spin-offs) and technology transfer, relating to agriculture production, processing, and marketing. Special emphasis on cooperatives. Industries served: agriculture, agribusiness, cooperatives, and government.

SHASTA LAND MANAGEMENT CONSULTANTS
1229 South St.
Redding, CA 96001
James Chapin, Contact
PH: (916)225-8900
FX: (916)225-8909
E-mail: RPS130@aol.com
Founded: 1980. **Staff:** 6. Services include forest management, timber appraisal, land appraisal, wildlife management, environmental planning, wetlands surveys, recreation planning, and timber harvest plans. Industries served: timber industry, recreation (resorts and marinas), land development and construction, livestock and ranching, private forest landowner, and government agencies.

PHILIP T. SIARKOWSKI
Lake Shore Rd.
Essex, NY 12936
Philip T. Siarkowski, Contact
PH: (518)962-8936
FX: (518)962-8936
Founded: 1978. **Staff:** 1. Forestry consultant offering the following services: forest inventories, appraisals and mapping; forest management plans, timber marking and timber sales, as agent for forest landowners; wildlife habitat improvement; tree planting; and access road layout. Also performs property inspections for absentee landowners and provides expert testimony in timber trespass and timber theft court cases. Serves government agencies.

SIGMA ONE CORP.
PO Box 12836
Research Triangle Park, NC 27709
David Franklin, Partner
PH: (919)361-9800
FX: (919)361-5858
E-mail: Sigma1@mindspring.com
URL: http://www.sigmaone.com
Develops and analyzes information that enables policy makers and individuals to choose strategies, processes and technologies that enhance well being in profitable and sustainable manners. Applies the economics of labor markets, human capital, goods and services distribution and technology and resource use at the policy level. Applies management sciences to issues of marketing, finance and risk sharing arrangements at the enterprise level.

GEORGE F. SILVER & ASSOCIATES
301 College St.
Burlington, VT 05401
George F. Silver, Contact
PH: (802)658-0460
FX: (802)863-1562
E-mail: gsilver@together.net
Founded: 1970. **Staff:** 4. Offers a wide variety of real estate consulting services (valuation, feasibility analysis, etc.). Intensive background in agricultural real estate.

CAREY B. SINGLETON
4813 Hollywood Rd.
College Park, MD 20740
Carey B. Singleton, Contact
PH: (301)345-4784
Founded: 1976. Consulting agricultural economist experienced with African economic development and other aspects of international economics. Recent research in production and consumption of sugar and sweeteners throughout the world.

LAWRENCE H. SKROMME
2144 Landis Valley Rd.
Lancaster, PA 17601
Lawrence H. Skromme, Contact
PH: (717)392-6127

Founded: 1978. **Staff:** 1. Consulting agricultural engineer specializing in appropriate mechanization and farm operations for developing countries. Emphasis is on farm machinery development and management. Recent expert witness work in farm equipment patent and accident cases. Serves private industries as well as government agencies.

B. BRUCE SNIDER
113 E. Coolidge
Harlingen, TX 78550
B. Bruce Snider, Contact
PH: (956)423-3314
Founded: 1962. **Staff:** 1. Independent entomology consultant to farmers on crops such as cotton, citrus, vegetables, peanuts, melons, and similar crops.

SOBEK ENGINEERING
Rte. 1, Box 7
Edwall, WA 99008
Irvin G. Sobek, Contact
PH: (509)236-2371
FX: (509)236-2426
Founded: 1977. **Staff:** 1. Provides consulting engineering service in the food processing field and associated agribusiness areas. Has served in the frozen food, flour milling, and freeze-drying areas, as well as agricultural and industrial accident investigation. Also conducts noise surveys and noise abatement engineering.

SOUTHERN FISH CULTURISTS, INC.
PO Box 490251
Leesburg, FL 34749-0251
John F. Dequine, President
PH: (352)787-1360
Founded: 1953. **Staff:** 5. Provides counseling services in problems of aquatic ecology: effects of pollution on aquatic organisms, fish kill evaluations, environmental assessments, fish and bait culture, fisheries management, and aquatic weed control. Serves private industries as well as government agencies.

SOUTHERN PLANTATIONS GROUP, INC.
PO Box 70967
Albany, GA 31707
Joseph H. Marshall, President
PH: (912)439-0012
FX: (912)883-8881
E-mail: sps@surfsouth.com
Founded: 1978. **Staff:** 10. Provides appraisal and counseling services for investors and lenders in farm land, timberland and agribusiness projects across the Southern U.S.; and farm planning, budgeting, management, and accounting services for farmers near its area of activity. Specific services include establishing and reviewing investment criteria, investment selection and negotiation, alternative investment analysis and review, management and operations audits, appraisals, problem investments, and management of property investment and divestment. Industries served: investors, lenders, government agencies, agribusinesses in production, agriculture, input, and marketing sectors. U.S., southeast Asia and Latin America.

SOUTHWEST FARM ADVISORS
PO Box 36533
Phoenix, AZ 85067
Pete Morrow, Director
PH: (602)944-9393
TF: (800)666-4155
E-mail: jpmorrow@usdahelp.com
URL: http://www.usdahelp.com
Provides advice and representation to Borrowers in the FSA (FmHA) Farm Loan Programs. Issues include debt restructuring, preventing offsets, new loans, and debt settlement.

SOYPRO INTERNATIONAL, INC.
314 Main St.
Cedar Falls, IA 50613
R. W. Fischer, Chairman/President

PH: (319)277-4700
TF: (800)747-4706
FX: (319)266-8544
E-mail: bjfischer3@aol.com
Founded: 1963. **Staff:** 5. Offers counsel to foreign businesses, institutions and governments in the oilseed and protein industries including planning, organization, crop production, processing, plant construction, product development, marketing and distribution of oilseed products.

SPECIALTY AG SERVICE
5456 Edna Rd.
San Luis Obispo, CA 93401
PH: (805)783-2516
FX: (805)543-4618
E-mail: sas@fix.net
URL: http://www.fix.net/~sas
Performs soil fertility testing services via U.S. mail; soil fertility, water analysis, plant protection, research, and pasture improvement consultation and support services.

H.J. SQUIRES LTD.
122 University Ave.
St. Johns, NF, Canada A1B 1Z5
H.J. Squires, President
PH: (709)895-2757
E-mail: hope.squires@nf.sympatico.ca
Founded: 1984. **Staff:** 3. Offers marine biological research consultation including mariculture of invertebrates. Industries served: fisheries, mariculture, and government agencies.

HARVEY J. STANGEL AND ASSOCIATES
116 Lincoln Ave.
Highland Park, NJ 08904
Harvey J. Stangel, President
PH: (908)846-8886
FX: (908)846-8886
E-mail: hjps.assochp@worldnet.att.net
Founded: 1970. **Staff:** 1. International and domestic marketing consultants offering market studies, evaluation of market trends and marketing problems for fertilizers, ag chemicals, animal nutrition products and related industrial markets, and raw material needs. Extensive experience in market studies for new plants and expansion of facilities. Geographic areas served: U.S. and Canada, outside of U.S. by individual contract.

LARRY STEINBAUER
2389 N. Longwood Dr.
Decatur, IL 62525-3070
Larry Steinbauer, Contact
PH: (217)429-4330
Staff: 12. Provides complete farm management services and consulting that include agricultural land selection and appraisal for domestic and foreign clients.

STEVENS ASSOCIATES
49 Emma St., Ste. 101
Guelph, ON, Canada N1E 6X1
R. William C. Stevens, President
PH: (519)837-3369
FX: (519)837-0729
E-mail: stevens@sentex.net
URL: http://www.agrifood-strategy.com
Founded: 1967. **Staff:** 5. Agri-business strategic plans and alliances, technical audits of livestock and poultry production, forensic investigations, applied R & D, and government relations. Agricultural labor dispute mediation.

STEWART AGRICULTURAL RESEARCH SERVICES, INC.
PO Box 509
Macon, MO 63552
Ellsworth R. Stewart, President

PH: (660)762-4240
FX: (660)762-4295
E-mail: stewart1@marktwain.net
Founded: 1975. **Staff:** 30. Provides research, development, registration, management, and educational services in agriculture. Conducts custom research in applied agronomic sciences and in the creation of new pesticides, crop varieties, biological agents, plant growth regulators, fertilizers, and specialty chemicals. Develops environmental safety and registration studies. Advises on experimental design, research techniques, statistical analysis, and research programs. Performs feasibility studies, training, and all aspects of field crop production. Manages experiment stations, agricultural development, research, extension, and environmental safety. Industries served: agricultural, chemical, genetic, biotechnology, financial, and government.

SUNBELT MARKETING SERVICES INC.
2600 Britt Rd.
Mount Dora, FL 32757-1486
Margaret E. Hensinger, Contact
PH: (352)383-8811
TF: (800)451-4016
FX: (352)735-2688
E-mail: duragreen@aol.com
Founded: 1982. **Staff:** 14. Specialists in horticultural and agricultural product, crop and equipment marketing and advertising. Serves private industries as well as government agencies.

SUSTAINABLE ENVIRONMENTAL SOLUTIONS, INC.
9875 Widmer Rd.
Lenexa, KS 66215
Frank Bryant, President
TF: (800)897-1163
E-mail: info@ses-corp.com
URL: http://www.ses-corp.com
Founded: 1998. An environmental consulting company that provides the agricultural and industrial communities with environmental services. Provides third-party verification of environmental programs as well as traditional environmental services such as regulatory compliance, training, risk management planning, Phase I Environmental Assessments, and environmental monitoring.

TALBOTT ARM
HC 60, Box 5620
Lakeview, OR 97630
Peter Talbott, Contact
PH: (541)635-8587
FX: (503)947-3482
Founded: 1990. Provides agricultural resource management with emphasis on business planning, integrated resource management, marketing, procurement of breeding stock (beef), enterprise analysis, conflict resolution, and analysis of grazing and breeding programs. Industries served: agricultural production units (ranches), financial institutions, real estate firms, and government agencies.

TARALAN CORP.
6 Second St. NE
Buffalo, MN 55313
Brennan Malanaphy, President
TF: (800)776-3823
FX: (612)682-2081
E-mail: f@teralan.com
Founded: 1972. **Staff:** 15. Agricultural consultants offering agronomic services to crop input suppliers and farmer clients in the United States. Services include marketing and agronomic support for suppliers and crop consulting programs for farmers. Industries served: crop producers, crop production input suppliers, farm managers, government agencies, and lenders to agriculture.

TECHNOSERVE, INC.
49 Day St.
Norwalk, CT 06854
Edward Bullard, President

PH: (203)852-0377
TF: (800)999-6757
FX: (203)838-6717
Founded: 1968. **Staff:** 200. Offers management and business advisory services primarily to medium-scale community-based agricultural enterprises and institutions. Firm is nonprofit and services are 90% funded by outside donors. Clients cover about 10% of costs. Purpose is to help low-income people. Serves private industries as well as government agencies.

TEMPLIN FORESTRY, INC.
PO Box 10
Bentley, LA 71407
Steven K. Templin, President
PH: (318)899-3361
FX: (318)899-7382
URL: http://www.templinforestry.com
Founded: 1983. **Staff:** 7. Offers forest management with emphasis on economic and environmental cost-benefit analysis. Conducts forest land appraisals. Provides real estate expertise. Industries served: forest landowners and/or investors interested in acquiring forest land, as well as government agencies.

L. WILLIAM TEWELES & CO.
777 E. Wisconsin Ave., Ste. 3375
Milwaukee, WI 53202
L. William Teweles, President
PH: (414)273-4854
FX: (414)273-8140
E-mail: teweles@aol.com
URL: http://www.teweles.com
Founded: 1973. International specialist in seed and plant sciences. Services include mergers and acquisitions, strategic planning, technology evaluation. Serves private industries as well as government agencies.

TEXAS PLANT & SOIL LAB., INC.
RR 7, Box 213Y
Edinburg, TX 78539-9206
Esper K. Chandler, President
PH: (956)383-0739
FX: (956)383-0730
E-mail: kchandler@txplant-soillab.com
URL: http://www.txplant-soillab.com
Founded: 1938. **Staff:** 9. Provides agricultural expertise specializing in comprehensive programs for soil, water, and plant analysis. Promotes maximum economic production through balanced plant nutrition, using crop logging method of plant analysis for most field, vegetable, and fruit crops. Also specializes in organic testing and recommendation, and soil restoration. President is certified professional agronomist and soil scientist.

THOROUGHBRED CONSULTING SERVICE, INC.
4604 NE 10th Pl.
Ocala, FL 34470
Samuel Lee Hunt, Sr., Contact
PH: (352)236-1142
Founded: 1984. **Staff:** 3. Specialists in the horse industry and horse business in general, such as purchasing horses, horse farms, feed and care of animals. Also provides expertise in money management and cost control. Serves also as a certified appraiser and deals in horse sales. Industries served: horse industry.

THURMOND AND ASSOCIATES
124 Forest Glen Dr.
Piedmont, SC 29673
TF: (800)707-8722
E-mail: info@thurmondinc.com
URL: http://www.thurmondinc.com
Independent forestry consulting and appraisal firm.

TIMBER JACK'S FORESTRY SERVICES
Jack E. Thomas, III, Contact

PH: (908)428-1126
E-mail: timberjack3@hotmail.com
URL: http://www.geocities.com/WallStreet/2789
Serves forest landowners through the application of forest management expertise.

TIMBERLAND RESOURCE SERVICES INC.

PO Box 4956
Dublin, GA 31040
Russell Falk, Contact
PH: (912)275-3579
FX: (912)275-0154
Founded: 1988. **Staff:** 2. A forestry consultant firm specializing in forest investments and basing findings on future market analysis. Services offered to landowners include: timber cruising, stand thinnings, GPS, management plans, marketing assistance, supervision, and site preparation. Serves private industries as well as government agencies.

TIMBERLAND SERVICES, INC.

PO Box 248
Fayette, AL 35555
Harrell Trice, Jr., President
PH: (205)932-6085
FX: (205)932-6085
Founded: 1974. **Staff:** 6. Provides land and/or timber management services to landowners in west Alabama and east Mississippi.

DENNIS L. TOMPKINS

324 Sumner Ave.
Sumner, WA 98390
Dennis L. Tompkins, Contact
PH: (206)863-2186
FX: (206)863-7846
Founded: 1980. **Staff:** 1. Forestry consultant specializing in urban forestry and Christmas tree industry. Services include feasibility studies, plantation inspections, cultural recommendations, pest control recommendations, and related appraisals. As certified arborist will serve as expert witness in courts of law.

TREMBLAY CONSULTING

394 S 335 E
Jerome, ID 83338
Albert J. Hornbacher, Secretary
PH: (208)324-1148
FX: (208)324-1203
Founded: 1969. **Staff:** 6. Agricultural consultants specializing in increased crop quality and quantity through continuous monitoring of major crops for soil moisture and plant nutrients. Crops covered include potatoes, corn, onions, sugarbeets, alfalfa, and grain.

TRIMENSION GROUP

No. 104-110 Research Dr.
Innovation Place, SK, Canada S7N 3R3
Larry Goodfellow, President
PH: (306)668-2560
FX: (306)975-1156
E-mail: trimension@trimension.ca
URL: http://www.trimension.ca
A management consulting firm. Services include leadership training, team building, marketing strategies, strategic planning, project evaluation, feasibility studies, restructuring, and business plans.

TRUETT, INC.

224 Highland Dr.
PO Drawer 1496
Livingston, AL 35470
Earl A. (Bud) Truett, Contact
PH: (205)652-7638
FX: (205)652-7638
Founded: 1985. **Staff:** 1. Provides timber and timberland appraisals, timber and timberland marketing and brokerage, and forest inventory and analysis (financial). Also offers expertise in forest, wildlife and aesthetics management planning and implementation;

silvicultural and logging contract administration and negotiation; and habitat development for target wildlife species. Industries served: forest products industry, nonindustrial private landowners, and government agencies. Geographic areas served: East Mississippi and West Alabama.

UNITED HORTICULTURAL SUPPLY

4429 N. Hwy. Dr.
Tucson, AZ 85705
Jerald E. Wheeler, Ph.D., Plant Pathologist/Agronomist
PH: (520)293-4330
FX: (520)887-5369
E-mail: uhstucxon@theriver.com
Staff: 10. Agricultural chemical consultant with strong background in plant pathology, landscape maintenance, agricultural uses of various chemicals, and in handling cyanide toxicity problems in gold and silver mines.

JAMES M. VARDAMAN & CO., INC.

PO Box 22766
Jackson, MS 39225
PH: (601)354-3123
URL: http://www.vardaman.com
Founded: 1951. Serves as forest management specialists for timberland owners. Also provides appraisals and caretaker services.

VAUGHN AGRICULTURAL RESEARCH SERVICES LTD.

R.R. No. 2
Branchton, ON, Canada N0B 1L0
Fred Vaughn, President
PH: (519)740-8739
FX: (519)740-8857
E-mail: fvaughn@varsl.com
URL: http://www.varsl.com
Founded: 1989. Provides independent research and consulting services to agricultural and biotechnology industry, government and grower organizations.

JOEL R. VINSON

English Rd.
PO Box 1491
5 N. Lee St.
Forsyth, GA 31029
Joel R. Vinson, Contact
PH: (912)994-1078
FX: (912)994-0880
Founded: 1978. **Staff:** 13. Provides general forestry and wildlife management services. Also offers real estate appraisal/investment analysis, forestry litigation assistance, timber marking, timber sales administration, tree planting, site preparation, and prescribe burning. Industries served: utilities, lumber, insurance, and government agencies.

VIRGINIA BRANCH OF F & W FORESTRY SERVICES, INC.

404 8th. NE., Ste. C
Charlottesville, VA 22902
Eley C. Frazer, III, Chm. of the Bd., ACF, ARA
PH: (804)296-1464
TF: (800)362-8497
FX: (804)296-5700
E-mail: gworrell@rlc.net
Founded: 1962. **Staff:** 80. Consultants and managers in forestry, agriculture, and environmental sciences. Specific services include: timber inventory and appraisals, timber sales and logging supervision, forest and wildlife management plans, investment and financial analysis, farm and ranch management services, and environmental and regional studies. Industries served: forestry and agriculture, as well as government agencies.

NEAL WALKER

PO Box 985
Littlefield, TX 79339
Neal Walker, Contact

PH: (806)385-3517
Firm offers consulting services in the areas of agricultural economics, credit, cooperatives, price and sector analysis, food aid logistics, policy, and institution building statistics.

KENNETH D. WEISS
7823 Mystic View Ct.
Derwood, MD 20855-2275
Kenneth D. Weiss, Contact
PH: (301)947-8150
FX: (301)869-8992
E-mail: Plansolv@aol.com
URL: http://www.ronb.com/plansolv
Founded: 1982. International trade and business consultant specializing in agribusiness, organizing import/export businesses, import procurement, export marketing, import/export procedures, international trade policies, and international licensing and investment. Serves small and large clients including American and foreign importers, exporters, investors and governments.

WESTERN RANGE SERVICE
PO Box 1330
Elko, NV 89803
Al Steninger, President
PH: (775)738-4007
FX: (775)753-7900
Founded: 1968. **Staff:** 4. Offers consulting services in range and ranch management, ranch and rural appraisals, and ranch real estate. Serves private industry, primarily cattle ranchers.

WHALEY & ASSOCIATES
1545 E. Calimyrna
Fresno, CA 93710
Julian W. Whaley, Contact
PH: (209)439-4570
FX: (209)439-8507
E-mail: julian_whaley@CSUFresno.edu
Founded: 1972. **Staff:** 2. Investigates crop losses to identify causal factors and evaluate economic significance for insurance agencies, growers, attorneys, government agencies, and irrigation districts.

WHITE COMMERCIAL CORP.
1101 E. Ocean Blvd.
Stuart, FL 34996
PH: (561)283-2420
TF: (800)327-7000
FX: (561)288-1685
URL: http://www.whitecommercial.com
Grain merchandising consultants.

RALPH E. WILLIAMS & ASSOCIATES
PO Box 2652
West Lafayette, IN 47906
Ralph E. Williams, President
PH: (765)742-2529
Founded: 1984. **Staff:** 1. Offers services in forensic entomology, use of insects in crime scene investigations. Serves prosecuting attorneys, law enforcement agencies, state and local coroners and medical examiners. Also provides training and consulting services in livestock and poultry pest control and public health pest control. Serves agribusiness, local and state public health agencies, and individuals.

KARIN WISIOL & ASSOCIATES
614 Indian Rd.
Glenview, IL 60025-3406
Karin Wisiol, Ph.D., President
PH: (708)729-7786
FX: (708)729-7786
Founded: 1981. Consultant in applied plant sciences and resource use for crop, range, and natural resource management. Related expertise in ecology, climatology, mathematical modeling, and publishing. Produces research and analysis, forecasting and estimation models, expert systems and other software, SAS programs and ana-lysis, scientific and technical writing and editing, as well as training aids. Speaks French, German, and Spanish. Industries served: agribusiness, conservation and wildlife organizations, government agencies, and the publishing industry.

WOODLAND MANAGEMENT INC.
Kruse Woods One Bldg., Ste. 468
5285 SW Meadows Rd.
Lake Oswego, OR 97035-3228
Daniel F. Green, President
PH: (503)684-4004
FX: (503)684-4005
E-mail: woodland@teleport.com
Founded: 1953. **Staff:** 3. Specializes in providing management of forest and Christmas tree properties in the western U.S. Specialties include logging supervision, log sales, measurement and valuation of timber stands, management of forests for wildlife and aesthetic resources, and management and sales of Christmas trees. Woodland's staff also has expertise in land purchases by foreign investors, and serving as expert witnesses. Industries served: utilities, aluminum companies, local governments, and individuals.

EDWARD A. YEARY
1318 E. Portals
Fresno, CA 93710
Edward A. Yeary, Contact
PH: (209)439-6535
FX: (209)447-0684
Founded: 1977. **Staff:** 1. Provides assistance with litigation in agricultural production and management concerns. Often involves damage claims, or evaluation of damage claims, for damage caused by chemical or mechanical abuses as well as disease problems. Also provides assistance with or participates in development of environmental impact reports and organization and management of farms. Industries served: production agriculture, agri-business, and the legal profession.

WARREN T. ZITZMANN
117 Tollgate Way
Falls Church, VA 22046
Warren T. Zitzmann, Contact
PH: (703)536-3444
Founded: 1984. **Staff:** 1. Certified planner offering advisory service to small towns and rural areas on land use planning, zoning, and protection of farmland. Serves private industries as well as government agencies. Geographic areas served: Virginia and Delaware.

CHAPTER 9 - PART II

TRADE INFORMATION SOURCES

Adapted from Gale's *Encyclopedia of Business Information Sources* (*EBIS*), the entries featured in this chapter show trade journals and other published sources, including web sites and databases. Entries list the title of the work, the name of the author (where available), name and address of the publisher, frequency or year of publication, prices or fees, and Internet address (in many cases).

AG CONSULTANT
Meister Publishing Co.
37733 Euclid Ave.
Willoughby, OH 44094
PH: (440)942-2000
FX: (440)942-0662
Eight times a year. $14.00 per year. Published for crop consultants and farm managers.

AG EXECUTIVE
Ag Executive, Inc.
PO Box 180
Bushnell, IL 61422
PH: (309)772-2168
FX: (309)772-2167
E-mail: darrellld@aol.com
Monthly. $78.00 per year. Newsletter. Topics include farm taxes, accounting, real estate, and financial planning.

AGEXPORTER
Available from U.S. Government Printing Office
Washington, DC 20402
PH: (202)512-1800
FX: (202)512-2250
E-mail: gpoaccess@gpo.gov
URL: http://www.access.gpo.gov
Monthly. $26.00 per year. Issued by the Foreign Agricultural Service, U.S. Department of Agriculture. Edited for U.S. exporters of farm products. Provides practical information on exporting, including overseas trade opportunities.

AGRI FINANCE
Doane Agricultural Service Co.
11701 Borman Dr.
St. Louis, MO 63146-4199
PH: (314)569-2700
FX: (314)569-1083
Nine times a year. $36.00 per year.

AGRI MARKETING: THE MAGAZINE FOR PROFESSIONALS SELLING TO THE FARM MARKET
Doane Information Service
11701 Borman Dr.
St. Louis, MO 63146
PH: (314)569-2700
FX: (314)564-1083
11 times a year. $30.00 per year.

AGRICOLA
U.S. National Agricultural Library
Beltsville, MD 20705
PH: (301)504-6813
FX: (301)504-7473
Covers worldwide agricultural literature. Over 2.8 million citations, 1970 to present, with monthly updates. Inquire as to online cost and availability.

AGRICOLA ON SILVERPLATTER
Available from SilverPlatter Information, Inc.
100 River Ridge Rd.
Norwood, MA 02062-5026
PH: (800)-343-0064
FX: (781)769-8763
Quarterly. $825.00 per year. Produced by the National Agricultural Library. Provides about three million citations on CD-ROM to the literature of agriculture, agricultural economics, animal sciences, entomology, fertilizer, food, forestry, nutrition, pesticides, plant science, water resources, and other topics. Each quarterly disc covers the past ten years, with archival discs available from 1970.

AGRICULTURAL CREDIT AND RELATED DATA
American Bankers Association
1120 Connecticut Ave., N.W.
Washington, DC 20036-3971

PH: (800)-338-0626
FX: (202)663-7543
URL: http://www.aba.com
Annual.

AGRICULTURAL ECONOMICS AND AGRIBUSINESS
John Wiley & Sons, Inc.
605 Third Ave.
New York, NY 10158
PH: (800)-225-5945
FX: (212)850-6088
Gail L. Cramer and Clarence W. Jensen. 1997. Seventh edition. Price on application.

AGRICULTURAL ENGINEERING ABSTRACTS
Available from CAB International North America
198 Madison Ave.
New York, NY 10016
PH: (800)-528-4841
FX: (212)686-7993
E-mail: cabi@cabi.org
URL: http://www.cabi.org
Monthly. $590.00 per year. Published in England by CAB International, formerly Commonwealth Agricultural Bureaux. Provides worldwide coverage of the literature.

AGRICULTURAL FINANCE
Iowa State University Press
2121 South State Ave.
Ames, IA 50014-8300
PH: (800)-862-6657
FX: (515)292-3348
Warren F. Lee and others. 1988. $39.95. Eighth revised edition.

AGRICULTURAL LAW
Matthew Bender & Co., Inc.
Two Park Ave.
New York, NY 10016
PH: (800)-223-1940
FX: (212)244-3188
E-mail: international@bender.com
URL: http://www.bender.com
15 looseleaf volumes. 1,830.00. Periodic supplementation. Covers all aspects of state and federal law relating to farms, ranches and other agricultural interests. Includes five volumes dealing with agricultural estate, tax and business planning.

AGRICULTURAL LETTER
Federal Reserve Bank of Chicago
PO Box 834
Public Information Center
Chicago, IL 60690
PH: (312)322-5112
Quarterly. Free

AGRICULTURAL MATHEMATICS
The Interstate Publishers, Inc.
PO Box 50
Danville, IL 61834-0050
PH: (800)-843-4774
FX: (217)446-9706
E-mail: info-ipp@ippinc.com
URL: http://www.ippinc.com
Roger Higgs and others. 1981. $33.25. Second edition.

AGRICULTURAL OUTLOOK
Available from U.S. Government Printing Office
Washington, DC 20402
PH: (202)512-1800
FX: (202)512-2250
Monthly. $40.00 per year. Issued by the Economic Research Service of the U.S. Department of Agriculture. Provides analysis of agriculture and the economy.

AGRICULTURAL POLICIES, MARKETS, AND TRADE:
MONITORING AND EVALUATION
Organization for Economic Cooperation and Development
2001 L St., N. W., Ste. 650
Washington, DC 20036-4910
PH: (800)-456-6323
FX: (202)785-0350
E-mail: washington.contact@oecd.org
URL: http://www.oecd.wash.org
Annual. $62.00. A yearly report on agricultural and trade policy developments in the 24 OECD member countries.

AGRICULTURAL PRODUCT PRICES
Cornell University Press
PO Box 250
Ithaca, NY 14851
PH: (800)-666-2211
FX: (800)-688-2877
E-mail: orderbook@cupserv.org
URL: http://www.cornellpress.cornell.edu
William G. Tomek and Kenneth L. Robinson. 1990. $32.50. Third edition.

AGRICULTURAL RESEARCH
Available from U.S. Government Printing Office
Washington, DC 20402
PH: (202)512-1800
FX: (202)512-2250
Monthly. $28.00 per year. Issued by the Agricultural Research Service of the U.S. Department of Agriculture. Presents results of research projects related to a wide variety of farm crops and products.

AGRICULTURAL STATISTICS
Available from U.S. Government Printing Office
Washington, DC 20402
PH: (202)512-1800
FX: (202)512-2250
E-mail: gpoaccess@gpo.gov
URL: http://www.access.gpo.gov
Annual. $25.00. Produced by the National Agricultural Statistics Service, U.S. Department of Agriculture. Provides a wide variety of statistical data relating to agricultural production, supplies, consumption, prices/price-supports, foreign trade, costs, and returns, as well as farm labor, loans, income, and population. In many cases, historical data is shown annually for 10 years. In addition to farm data, includes detailed fishery statistics.

AGRICULTURE, ECONOMICS AND RESOURCE
MANAGEMENT
Prentice Hall
One Lake St.
Upper Saddle River, NJ 07458
PH: (800)-223-1360
FX: (800)-445-6991
URL: http://www.prenhall.com
Milton M. Snodgrass and Luther T. Wallace. 1980. $48.20. Second edition.

AGRICULTURE FACT BOOK
Available from U.S. Government Printing Office
Washington, DC 20402
PH: (202)512-1800
FX: (202)512-2250
E-mail: gpoaccess@gpo.gov
URL: http://www.access.gpo.gov
Annual. $14.00. Issued by the Office of Communications, U.S. Department of Agriculture. Includes data on U.S. agriculture, farmers, food, nutrition, and rural America. Programs of the Department of Agriculture in six areas are described: rural economic development, foreign trade, nutrition, the environment, inspection, and education.

AGRICULTURE AND TRADE REPORT
Available from U.S. Government Printing Office
Washington, DC 20402

PH: (202)512-1800
FX: (202)512-2250
E-mail: gpoaccess@gpo.gov
URL: http://www.access.gpo.gov
Quarterly. $17.00 per year. Issued by the Economic Research Service, U.S. Department of Agriculture. Provides data on agricultural supply, demand, and prices in four regions of the world: China, the former USSR, Europe, and the NAFTA region. (Situation and Outlook Reports.)

AGRONOMY JOURNAL
American Society of Agronomy, Inc.
677 S. Segoe Rd.
Madison, WI 53711
PH: (608)273-8080
FX: (608)273-2021
E-mail: journal@agronomy.org
URL: http://www.agronomy.org/journals/aj.html
Bimonthly. $117.00 per year.

AMERICAN AGRICULTURAL ECONOMICS
ASSOCIATION -HANDBOOK/DIRECTORY
American Agricultural Economics Association
Heady Hall, Room 80
1110 Buckeye Ave.
Ames, IA 50010-8063
PH: (515)233-3202
FX: (515)233-3101
E-mail: lchristo@iastate.com
1995. $20.00.

AMERICAN FRUIT GROWER BUYER'S GUIDE
Meister Publishing Co.
37733 Euclid Ave
Willoughby, OH 44094
PH: (440)942-2000
FX: (440)942-0662
Annual. $5.00.

AMERICAN JOURNAL OF AGRICULTURAL ECONOMICS
American Agricultural Economics Association
110 Buckeye Ave.
Ames, IA 50010-8063
PH: (515)233-3202
FX: (515)233-3101
URL: http://www.aaea.org
Five times a year. Free to members; others, $99.00 per year. Provides a forum for creative and scholarly work in agriculture economics.

AMERICAN POTATO JOURNAL
Potato Association of America
157 Park St., Ste. 23
Bangor, ME 04401
PH: (207)942-9732
FX: (207)942-9733
Monthly. Individuals, $40.00 per year; libraries $65.00 per year. Information relating to production, marketing, processing, storage, disease control, insect control and new variety releases.

AMERICAN VEGETABLE GROWER
Meister Publishing Co.
37733 Euclid Ave.
Willoughby, OH 44094
PH: (440)942-2000
FX: (440)942-0662
Monthly. $15.95 per year.

AMERICAN VEGETABLE GROWER SOURCE BOOK
Meister Publishing Co.
37733 Euclid Ave.
Willoughby, OH 44094
PH: (440)942-2000
FX: (440)942-0662

Annual. $2.75.

AOAC INTERNATIONAL JOURNAL
AOAC International
481 N. Frederick Ave., Ste. 500
Gaithersburg, MD 20877-2917
PH: (301)924-7077
FX: (301)924-7089
Bimonthly. Members $176.00 per year; non-members, $242.00 per year; institutions, $262.00 per year.

BIOLOGICAL AND AGRICULTURAL INDEX
H.W. Wilson Co.
950 University Ave.
Bronx, NY 10452
PH: (800)-367-6770
FX: (718)590-1617
11 times a year. Annual and quarterly cumulations. Service basis.

CAB ABSTRACTS
CAB International North America
845 N. Park Ave.
Tucson, AZ 85719
PH: (800)-528-4841
FX: (520)621-3816
E-mail: cabi-nao@cabi.org
URL: http://www.cabi.org
Contains 46 specialized abstract collections covering over 10,000 journals and monographs in the areas of agriculture, horticulture, forest products, farm products, nutrition, dairy science, poultry, grains, animal health, entomology, etc. Time period is 1972 to date, with monthly updates. Inquire as to online cost and availability. *CAB Abstracts on CD-ROM* also available, with annual updating.

CHICAGO BOARD OF TRADE STATISTICAL ANNUAL
Board of Trade of the City of Chicago
141 W. Jackson Blvd.
Chicago, IL 60604
PH: (312)435-3500
Annual.

COMMERCIAL REVIEW
Oregon Feed and Grain Association
2380 N.W. Roosevelt St.
Portland, OR 97210-2323
PH: (503)226-2758
FX: (503)244-0947
Commercial Review, Inc. Weekly. $30.00 per year.

CONSUMER MAGAZINE AND ADVERTISING SOURCE
SRDS
1700 Higgins Rd.
Des Plaines, IL 60018
PH: (800)-851-7737
FX: (847)375-5001
URL: http://www.srds.com
Monthly. $529.00 per year. Contains advertising rates and other data for U.S. consumer magazines and agricultural publications. Also provides consumer market data for population, households, income, and retail sales.

CORN ANNUAL
Corn Refiners Association, Inc.
1701 Pennsylvania Ave., N.W., Ste. 950
Washington, DC 20006
PH: (202)331-1634
FX: (202)331-2054
E-mail: details@corn.org
URL: http://www.corn.org
Annual. Single copies free.

COST OF DOING BUSINESS: FARM AND POWER EQUIPMENT DEALERS, INDUSTRIAL DEALERS, AND OUTDOOR POWER EQUIPMENT DEALERS
North American Equipment Dealers Association
10877 Watson Rd.
St. Louis, MO 63127-1081
PH: (314)821-7220
FX: (314)821-0674
Annual. $50.00. Provides data on sales, profit margins, expenses, assets, and employee productivity.

COTTON DIGEST INTERNATIONAL
Cotton Digest Co., Inc.
PO Box 820768
Houston, TX 77282-0768
PH: (713)977-1644
FX: (713)783-8658
E-mail: cottonabb@aol.com
Monthly. $40.00 per year.

COTTON FARMING
Vance Publishing Corp.
400 Knightsbridge Parkway
Lincolnshire, IL 60069
PH: (800)-621-2845
FX: (913)438-0695
Monthly. Controlled circulation.

COTTON GROWER
Meister Publishing Co.
37733 Euclid Ave.
Willoughby, OH 44094
PH: (440)942-2000
FX: (440)942-0662
9 times a year. $16.95 per year.

COTTON INTERNATIONAL
Meister Publishing Co.
37733 Euclid Ave.
Willoughby, OH 44094
PH: (440)942-2000
FX: (440)942-0662
Annual. $30.00.

COTTON: PART ONE, BIMONTHLY REVIEW OF THE WORLD SITUATION; PART TWO, WORLD STATISTICS
International Cotton Advisory Committee
1629 K St., N.W., Ste. 702
Washington, DC 20006
PH: (202)463-6660
FX: (202)463-6950
Bimonthly. $135.00 per year. Editions in English, French, German and Spanish.

COTTON PRICE STATISTICS
U.S. Department of Agriculture
Washington, DC 20250
PH: (202)720-2791
Monthly.

COTTON PRODUCTION PROSPECTS FOR THE DECADE TO 2005: A GLOBAL REVIEW
The World Bank, Office of the Publisher
1818 H St., N. W.
Washington, DC 20433
PH: (202)473-1155
FX: (202)522-2627
E-mail: books@worldbank.org
Hamdy M. Eisa and others. 1994. $8.95. Provides information on cotton's key technologies, marketing, consumption, production trends, and price prospects.

COTTON'S WEEK
National Cotton Council of America
PO Box 12285
Memphis, TN 38182-0285
PH: (901)274-9030
FX: (901)725-0510
Weekly. Free to members; non-members, $250.00 per year. Newsletter.

**COUNTY AGENTS DIRECTORY: THE REFERENCE BOOK
FOR AGRICULTURAL EXTENSION WORKERS**
Doane Agricultural Service Co.
11701 Borman St.
St. Louis, MO 63146-4199
PH: (314)569-2700
FX: (314)569-1083
Biennial. $23.95. About 17,000 county agents and university agricultural extension workers.

CROP PROTECTION CHEMICALS REFERENCE
Chemical and Pharmaceutical Press, Inc.
888 Seventh Ave., Ste. 2800
New York, NY 10106
PH: (800)-544-7377
FX: (212)399-1122
1994. $130.00. 10th edition. Contains the complete text of product labels. Indexed by manufacturer, product category, pest use, crop use, chemical name, and brand name.

CROP SCIENCE
Crop Science Society of America
677 S. Segoe Rd.
Madison, WI 53711
PH: (608)273-8080
FX: (608)273-2021
URL: http://www.agronomy.org/journals.cs.html
Bimonthly. $118.00 per year.

**DEALER PROGRESS: FOR FERTILIZER/AG CHEMICAL
RETAILERS**
Clear Window, Inc.
15444 Clayton Rd., Ste. 314
Ballwin, MO 63011
PH: (314)527-4001
FX: (314)527-4010
Bimonthly. $40.00 per year. Published in association with the Fertilizer Institute. Includes information on fertilizers and agricultural chemicals, including farm pesticides.

DERWENT CROP PROTECTION FILE
Derwent, Inc.
1725 Duke St., Ste. 250
Alexandria, VA 22314
PH: (800)-451-3551
FX: (703)519-5829
E-mail: info@derwent.com
URL: http://www.derwent.com
Provides citations to the international journal literature of agricultural chemicals and pesticides from 1968 to date, with updating eight times per year. Inquire as to online cost and availability.

**DICTIONARY OF AGRICULTURE: FROM ABACA TO
ZOONOSIS**
Lynne Rienner Publishers
1800 30th St., Ste. 314
Boulder, CO 80301
PH: (303)444-6684
FX: (303)444-0824
Kathryn L. Lipton. 1995. $75.00. Emphasis is on agricultural economics.

DOANE'S AGRICULTURAL REPORT
Doane Information Services
11701 Borman Dr.
Saint Louis, MO 63146
PH: (314)569-2700
FX: (314)569-1083
Weekly. $98.00 per year. Newsletter. Covers farm marketing and management. Includes telephone hotline.

ECONOMIC ACCOUNTS FOR AGRICULTURE
Organization for Economic Cooperation and Development
2001 L St., N. W., Ste. 650
Washington, DC 20036-4910
PH: (800)-456-6323
FX: (202)785-0350
1996. $51.00. Provides data for 14 years on agricultural output and its components, intermediate consumption, and gross value added to net income and capital formation. Relates to various commodities produced by the 24 OECD member countries.

ENCYCLOPEDIA OF AGRICULTURE SCIENCE
Academic Press, Inc.
525 B St., Ste. 1900
San Diego, CA 92101-4495
PH: (800)-937-8000
FX: (800)-874-6418
E-mail: ap@acad.com
URL: http://academicpress.com/
Charles J. Arntzen and Ellen M. Ritter, editors. 1994. $625.00. Four volumes.

ESTATE PLANNING FOR FARMERS AND RANCHERS
Shepard's
555 Middle Creek Parkway
Colorado Springs, CO 80921
PH: (800)-743-7393
FX: (800)-525-0053
Donald H. Kelley and David A. Ludtke. 1986. $215.00. Two volumes. Second edition.

FAO QUARTERLY BULLETIN OF STATISTICS
Available from UNIPUB
4611-F Assembly Dr.
Lanham, MD 20706-4391
PH: (800)-274-4888
FX: (800)-865-3450
E-mail: query@kraus.com
URL: http://www.unesco.org/publications
Food and Agriculture Organization of the United Nations. Quarterly. $24.00 per year. Provides international data on agricultural production, trade, and prices, covering the major commodities of many countries. Text in English, French, and Spanish.

FARM CHEMICALS
Meister Publishing Co.
37733 Euclid Ave.
Willoughby, OH 44094
PH: (440)942-2000
FX: (440)942-0662
Monthly. $23.00 per year.

FARM CHEMICALS HANDBOOK
Meister Publishing Co.
37733 Euclid Ave.
Willoughby, OH 44094
PH: (440)942-2000
FX: (440)942-0662
Annual. $89.00. Manufacturers and suppliers of fertilizers, pesticides, and related equipment used in agribusiness.

FARM EQUIPMENT
Johnson Hill Press, Inc.
PO Box 803
Fort Atkinson, WI 53538-0803

PH: (800)-547-7377
FX: (414)563-1701
Seven times a year. $40.00 per year.

***FARM EQUIPMENT WHOLESALERS ASSOCIATION
MEMBERSHIP DIRECTORY***
Farm Equipment Wholesalers Association
PO Box 1347
Iowa City, IA 52244
PH: (319)354-5156
FX: (319)354-5157
Annual. $50.00. Lists approximately 100 members.

FARM INDUSTRY NEWS
Intertec Publishing Co., Webb Div.
7900 International Dr., Ste. 300
Minneapolis, MN 55425
PH: (800)-629-9907
FX: (800)-633-6219
E-mail: farmindustrynews@intertec.com
12 times a year. $12.95 per year. Includes new products for farm use.

FARM JOURNAL
Farm Journal, Inc.
1500 Market St.
Philadelphia, PA 19102-2181
PH: (215)557-8900
FX: (215)568-4221
URL: http://www.farmjournal.com
14 times a year. $14.95 per year. Includes supplements.

FARM LABOR
U.S. Department of Agriculture
Washington, DC 20250
PH: (202)447-2791
Monthly.

FARM MANAGEMENT
John Wiley and Sons, Inc.
605 Third Ave.
New York, NY 10158-0012
PH: (800)-526-5368
FX: (212)850-6088
Michael D. Boehlje and Vernon R. Eidman. 1984. $59.95.

FARM MANAGEMENT
McGraw-Hill, Inc.
1221 Ave. of the Americas
New York, NY 10020
PH: (800)-722-4726
FX: (212)512-2821
Ronald D. Kay and W.K. Edwards. 1993. $55.00. Third edition.

FARM MANAGEMENT: PRINCIPLES, PLAN, BUDGETS
Stipes Publishing L.L.C.
10-12 Chester St.
Champaign, IL 61820
PH: (217)356-8391
FX: (217)356-5753
E-mail: stipes@soltec.com
John Herbst and Duane Erickson. 1996. $25.80. 10th edition.

FARM MORTGAGE DEBT
U.S. Department of Agriculture, Economic Research Service
Washington, DC 20250
PH: (301)344-2340
Annual.

FARM POWER AND MACHINERY MANAGEMENT
Iowa State University Press
2121 S. State Ave.
Ames, IA 50014-8300

PH: (800)-862-6657
FX: (515)292-3348
Donnell Hunt. 1995. $52.95. Ninth edition.

FARMER'S DIGEST
Lessiter Publications
PO Box 624
Brookfield, WI 53008-0624
PH: (414)782-4480
FX: (414)782-1252
E-mail: lessub@aol.com
10 times a year. $17.95 per year. Current information on all phases of agriculture.

FEED BULLETIN
Jacobsen Publishing Co.
300 W. Adams St.
Chicago, IL 60606
PH: (312)726-6600
FX: (312)726-6654
Daily. $340.00 per year.

FEED AND FEEDING DIGEST
National Grain and Feed Association
1201 New York Ave., Ste. 830
Washington, DC 20005
PH: (202)289-0873
FX: (202)289-5388
Monthly.

***FEED INDUSTRY RED BOOK: REFERENCE BOOK AND
BUYER'S GUIDE FOR THE MANUFACTURING
INDUSTRY***
ZMAG Publishing, Inc.
500 Pine St., Ste. 202
Chaoka, MN 55318
PH: (612)448-5402
FX: (612)448-6935
Annual. $40.00. List of over 200 firms involved in the large animal and pet food manufacturing and distribution business, including sources of feed ingredients and suppliers of feed materials handling equipment.

FEEDS AND FEEDING
Prentice Hall
One Lake St.
Upper Saddle River, NJ 07458
PH: (800)-223-1360
FX: (800)-445-6991
URL: http://www.prenhall.com
Arthur E. Cullison and Robert S. Lowrey. 1986. $97.00. Fourth edition.

***FEEDSTUFFS: THE WEEKLY NEWSPAPER FOR
AGRIBUSINESS***
ABC, Inc.
PO Box 2400
Minnetonka, MN 55343
PH: (612)931-0211
FX: (612)938-1832
URL: http://ww.feedstuffs.com
Weekly. $109.00 per year.

***FIELD CROP ABSTRACTS: MONTHLY ABSTRACT
JOURNAL ON WORLD ANNUAL CEREAL, LEGUME,
ROOT, OILSEED AND FIBRE CROPS***
Available from CAB International North America
198 Madison Ave.
New York, NY 10016
PH: (800)-528-4841
FX: (212)686-7993
E-mail: cabi@cabi.org
URL: http://www.cabi.org
Monthly. $1,165.00 per year. Published in England by CAB Interna-

tional, formerly Commonwealth Agricultural Bureaux. Provides worldwide coverage of the literature.

FINANCIAL MANAGEMENT IN AGRICULTURE
The Interstate Publishers, Inc.
PO Box 50
Danville, IL 61834-0050
PH: (800)-843-4774
FX: (217)446-9706
E-mail: info-ipp@ippinc.com
URL: http://www.ippinc.com
Peter Barry and others. 1995. $42.95. Fifth edition.

FLOUR MILLING PRODUCTS
U.S. Bureau of the Census
Washington, DC 20233-0800
PH: (301)457-4100
FX: (301)457-3842
URL: http://www.census.gov
Monthly and annual. Covers production, mill stocks, exports, and imports of wheat and rye flour. (Current Industrial Reports, M20A.)

FMRA NEWS
American Society of Farm Managers and Rural Appraisers
950 S. Cherry St., Ste. 508
Denver, CO 80222-2664
PH: (303)758-3513
FX: (303)758-0190
E-mail: asfmra@agri-associations.org
Bimonthly. $24.00.

FOOD DISTRIBUTION MAGAZINE
Phoenix Media Network, Inc.
PO Box 811768
Boca Raton, FL 33481-1768
PH: (561)447-0810
Monthly. $49.00 per year. Edited for marketers and buyers of domestic and imported, specialty or gourmet food products, including ethnic foods, seasonings, and bakery items.

FOOD SCIENCE AND TECHNOLOGY ABSTRACTS [ONLINE]
IFIS North American Desk
6363 Clark Ave.
National Food Laboratory
Dublin, CA 94568
PH: (800)-336-3782
FX: (510)833-8795
URL: http://www.ifis.org
Produced by International Food Information Service. Provides about 500,000 online citations, with abstracts, to the international literature of food science, technology, commodities, engineering, and processing. Approximately 1,800 periodicals are covered. Time period is 1969 to date, with monthly updates. Inquire as to online cost and availability.

FOOD SCIENCE AND TECHNOLOGY ABSTRACTS
International Food Information Service Publishing
Shinfield
Lane End House
Reading RG2 9BB, England
PH: (3 4)88 3895
FX: (173)488 5065
E-mail: ifis@inf.org
Monthly. $1,590.00 per year. Provides worldwide coverage of the literature of food technology and food production.

FOOD SCIENCE AND TECHNOLOGY ABSTRACTS [CD-ROM]
Available from SilverPlatter Information, Inc.
100 River Ridge Rd.
Norwood, MA 02062-0543
PH: (800)-343-0064
FX: (781)769-8763
E-mail: info@silverplatter.com
URL: http://www.silverplatter.com
Quarterly. $3,700 per year. Produced by International Food Information Service (home page is http://www.ifis.org). Provides worldwide coverage on CD-ROM of the literature of food technology and production. Various types of publications are indexed, with abstracts, including about 1,800 periodicals. Time period is 1969 to date.

FOODS ADLIBRA
General Mills, Inc.
9000 Plymouth Ave. N.
Foods Adlibra Publications
Technical Information Services
Minneapolis, MN 55427
PH: (612)540-4759
FX: (612)540-3166
Contains online citations, with abstracts, to the technical and business literature of food processing and packaging. New products and new ingredients are featured. Covers about 250 trade journals and 500 research journals from 1974 to date, with monthly updates. Inquire as to online cost and availability.

FOODS ADLIBRA: KEY TO THE WORLD'S FOOD LITERATURE
Foods Adlibra Publications
9000 Plymouth Ave. N.
Minneapolis, MN 55427
PH: (612)540-4759
FX: (612)540-3166
Semimonthly. $240.00 per year. Provides journal citations and abstracts to the literature of food technology and packaging.

FOODS AND NUTRITION ENCYCLOPEDIA
CRC Press, Inc.
2000 Corporate Blvd., N. W.
Boca Raton, FL 33431
PH: (800)-272-7737
FX: (800)-374-3401
E-mail: order@crcpress.com
URL: http://www.crcpress.com
Audrey H. Ensminger and others. 1993. $382.00. Second edition. Two volumes.

FOREIGN AGRICULTURAL TRADE OF THE UNITED STATES
Available from U.S. Government Printing Office
Washington, DC 20402
PH: (202)512-1800
FX: (202)512-2250
Monthly. $30.00 per year. Issued by the Economic Research Service of the U.S. Department of Agriculture. Provides data on U.S. exports and imports of agricultural commodities.

GRAIN AND FEED MARKET NEWS: WEEKLY SUMMARY AND STATISTICS
U.S. Dept. of Agriculture
PO Box 96456
Agricultural Marketing Service, Livestock and Seed Div.
Washington, DC 20090-6456
PH: (202)720-6231
FX: (202)690-3732
Weekly. $85.00 per year.

GRAINS: PRODUCTION, PROCESSING, MARKETING
Chicago Board of Trade
141 W. Jackson Blvd., Ste. 2210
Chicago, IL 60654-2994
PH: (800)-572-3276
FX: (312)341-3168
E-mail: bw0050@cbot.com
URL: http://www.cbot.com
1992. $12.00. Revised edition.

HANDBOOK OF TRANSPORTATION AND MARKETING IN AGRICULTURE
Franklin Book Co., Inc.
7804 Montgomery Ave.
Elkins Park, PA 19027
PH: (215)635-5252
FX: (215)635-6155
1981. Vol. 1, $252.00; vol. 2, $282.00.

HORTICULTURAL ABSTRACTS: COMPILED FROM WORLD LITERATURE ON TEMPERATE AND TROPICAL FRUITS, VEGETABLES, ORNAMENTS, PLANTATION CROPS
Available from CAB International North America
198 Madison Ave.
New York, NY 10016
PH: (800)-528-4841
FX: (212)686-7993
E-mail: cabi@cabi.org
URL: http://www.cabi.org
Monthly. $1,290.00 per year. Published in England by CAB International, formerly Commonwealth Agricultural Bureaux. Provides worldwide coverage of the literature of fruits, vegetables, flowers, plants, and all aspects of gardens and gardening.

IMPLEMENT AND TRACTOR PRODUCT FILE
Intertec Publishing Corp.
6151 Powers Ferry Rd., N.W., Ste. 200
Atlanta, GA 30339
PH: (800)-621-9907
FX: (800)-633-6219
Annual. $29.95. Supplement to *Implement and Tractor.*

IMPLEMENT AND TRACTOR: THE BUSINESS MAGAZINE OF THE FARM AND INDUSTRIAL EQUIPMENT INDUSTRY
Freiburg Publishing Co., Inc.
PO Box 7
Cedar Falls, IA 50613
PH: (319)277-3599
FX: (319)277-3783
URL: http://www.ag-implement.com
Six times a year. $25.00 per year. Includes annual *Product File* and *Red Book.*

INTERNATIONAL GRAINS COUNCIL WORLD GRAIN STATISTICS
International Wheat Council, Haymarket House
One Canada Sq.
Canary Wharf E14 5AE, England
PH: (171) 513 1122
FX: (4 1)1 712 00
Annual. $125.00. Text in English, French, Russian and Spanish.

INTRODUCTION TO AGRICULTURAL MARKETING
McGraw-Hill, Inc.
1221 Ave of the Americas
New York, NY 10020
PH: (800)-722-4726
FX: (212)512-2821
Robert E. Branson and Douglas G. Norvell. 1983. Price on application.

JOURNAL OF RANGE MANAGEMENT: COVERING THE STUDY, MANAGEMENT, AND USE OF RANGELAND ECOSYSTEMS AND RANGE RESOURCES
Society for Range Management
1839 York St.
Denver, CO 80206-1213
PH: (303)355-7070
Bimonthly. $95.00 per year. Technical articles oriented towards research in range science and management.

JOURNAL OF VEGETABLE CROP PRODUCTION
Haworth Press, Inc.
10 Alice St.
Binghamton, NY 13904-1580
PH: (800)-429-6784
FX: (800)-895-0582
Quarterly. Individuals, $36.00 per year; institutions, $60.00 per year; libraries, $90.00 per year. Covers the production and marketing of vegetables.

KANSAS FARMER
Farm Progress Cos.
191 S. Gary Ave.
Carol Stream, IL 60188
PH: (630)690-5600
FX: (630)462-2869
15 times a year. $19.95 per year.

KNIGHT-RIDDER CRB COMMODITY YEARBOOK
John Wiley and Sons, Inc.
605 Third Ave.
New York, NY 10158-0012
PH: (800)-225-5945
FX: (212)850-6088
E-mail: business@jwiley.com
URL: http://www.wiley.com
Knight-Ridder Financial Publishing Staff. 1995. 75.00

LAND ECONOMICS: A QUARTERLY JOURNAL DEVOTED TO THE STUDY OF ECONOMIC AND SOCIAL INSTITUTIONS
University of Wisconsin Press, Journals Div.
114 N. Murray St.
Madison, WI 53715
PH: (608)262-4952
FX: (608)262-7560
Daniel W. Bromley, editor. Quarterly. Individuals, $40.00 per year; institutions, $83.00 per year.

MAIZE ABSTRACTS
Available from CAB International North America
198 Madison Ave.
New York, NY 10016
PH: (800)-528-4841
FX: (212)686-7993
E-mail: cabi@cabi.org
URL: http://www.cabi.org
Bimonthly. $620.00 per year. Published in England by CAB International, formerly Commonwealth Agricultural Bureaux. Provides worldwide coverage of the literature.

MAJOR STATISTICAL SERIES OF THE UNITED STATES DEPARTMENT OF AGRICULTURE: HOW THEY ARE CONSTRUCTED AND USED
Available from U.S. Government Printing Office
Washington, DC 20402
PH: (202)783-3238
U.S. Department of Agriculture. Irregular.

MARKETING FARM PRODUCTS: ECONOMIC ANALYSIS
Iowa State University Press
2121 S. State Ave.
Ames, IA 50014-8300
PH: (800)-862-6657
FX: (515)292-3348
Geoffrey Shepherd and Gene Futrell. 1982. $39.95. Seventh edition.

MECHANICS IN AGRICULTURE
Interstate Publishers, Inc.
PO Box 50
Danville, IL 61834-0050

PH: (800)-843-4774
FX: (217)446-9706
E-mail: info-ipp@ippinc.com
URL: http://www.ippinc.com
Lloyd J. Phipps and Carl L. Reynolds. 1992. $49.95. Fourth edition.

MILLING AND BAKING NEWS
Sosland Publishing Co.
4800 Main, Ste. 100
Kansas City, MO 64112-2513
PH: (816)756-1000
FX: (816)756-0494
Weekly. $99.00 per year. News magazine for the breadstuffs industry.

MONTANA FARMER
Western Farmer-Stockman Magazines
PO Box 2160
Spokane, WA 99210-1615
PH: (509)459-5361
FX: (509)459-5102
Monthly. $15.00. per year.

NAEDA EQUIPMENT DEALER
North American Equipment Dealers Association
10877 Watson Rd.
St. Louis, MO 63127-1081
PH: (314)821-7220
FX: (314)821-0674
Monthly. $40.00 per year. Covers power equipment for farm, outdoor, and industrial use.

NAEDA EQUIPMENT DEALER BUYER'S GUIDE ISSUE
North American Equipment Dealers Association
10877 Watson Rd.
St. Louis, MO 63127-1081
PH: (314)821-7220
FX: (314)821-0674
Annual. $25.00. List of manufacturers and suppliers of agricultural, lawn and garden, and light industrial machinery.

***NATIONAL GRAIN AND FEED ASSOCIATION
    DIRECTORY***
1201 New York Ave., Ste. 830
Washington, DC 20005
PH: (202)289-0873
FX: (202)289-5388
Annual. Price on application.

NEBRASKA FARMER
Farm Progress Cos.
191 S. Gary Ave.
Carol Stream, IL 60188
PH: (630)690-5600
FX: (630)462-2869
15 times a year. $19.95 per year.

NEWS FOR FAMILY FARMERS AND RURAL AMERICANS
Farmers Educational and Cooperative Union of America
400 Virginia Ave., S.W., Ste. 710
Washington, DC 20024
PH: (202)554-1600
FX: (202)554-1654
Monthly. $10.00 per year.

NORTH AMERICAN GRAIN AND MILLING ANNUAL
Sosland Publishing Co.
4800 Main St., Ste. 100
Kansas City, MO 64112-2513
PH: (816)756-1000
FX: (816)756-0494
E-mail: worldgrain@sosland.com
Annual. $90.00. Features listings of the major grain facilities in the

U.S. and Canada. Provides an annual overview of the U.S. grain industry and a complete reference to equipment and service suppliers.

NTIS ALERTS: AGRICULTURE & FOOD
National Technical Information Service
5285 Port Royal Rd.
Technology Administration
U.S. Department of Commerce
Springfield, VA 22161
PH: (800)-553-6847
FX: (703)321-8547
Semimonthly. $145.00 per year. Provides descriptions of government-sponsored research reports and software, with ordering information. Covers agricultural economics, horticulture, fisheries, veterinary medicine, food technology, and related subjects.

***NUTRITION ABSTRACTS AND REVIEWS, SERIES B:
    LIVESTOCK FEEDS AND FEEDING***
Available from CAB International North America
198 Madison Ave.
New York, NY 10016
PH: (800)-528-4841
FX: (212)686-7993
E-mail: cabi@cabi.org
URL: http://www.cabi.org
Monthly. $760.00 per year. Published in England by CAB International, formerly Commonwealth Agricultural Bureaux. Provides worldwide coverage of the literature.

OFFICIAL GUIDE: TRACTORS AND FARM EQUIPMENT
North American Equipment Dealers Association
10877 Watson Rd.
St. Louis, MO 63127-1081
PH: (314)821-7220
FX: (314)821-0674
Semiannual. $80.90 per year.

OREGON WHEAT
Oregon Wheat Growers League
PO Box 400
Pendleton, OR 97801
PH: (503)276-7330
FX: (503)276-1723
Monthly. Free to members; non-members, $15.00 per year. Deals with planting, weeds, and disease warnings, storage and marketing of wheat and barley. Specifically for Oregon growers.

***OUTLOOK FOR UNITED STATES AGRICULTURAL
    EXPORTS***
Available from U.S. Government Printing Office
Washington, DC 20402
PH: (202)512-1800
FX: (202)512-2250
E-mail: gpoaccess@gpo.gov
URL: http://www.access.gpo.gov
Quarterly. $8.50 per year. Issued by the Economic Research Service, U.S. Department of Agriculture. (Situation and Outlook Reports.)

***THE PACKER: DEVOTED TO THE INTEREST OF
    COMMERCIAL GROWERS, PACKERS, SHIPPERS,
    RECEIVERS AND RETAILERS OF FRUITS,
    VEGETABLES AND OT***
Vance Publishing Corp.
10901 West 84th Terrace
Lenexa, KS 66214-0695
PH: (800)-255-5113
FX: (913)438-0695
E-mail: thepacker@compuserve.com
URL: http://www.thepacker.com
Weekly. $55.00 per year.

POTATO ABSTRACTS
Available from CAB International North America
198 Madison Ave.
New York, NY 10016
PH: (800)-528-4841
FX: (212)686-7993
E-mail: cabi@cabi.org
URL: http://www.cabi.org
Bimonthly. $360.00 per year. Published in England by CAB International, formerly Commonwealth Agricultural Bureaux. Provides worldwide coverage of the literature.

PRODUCE AVAILABILITY AND MERCHANDISING GUIDE
Vance Publishing Corp.
10901 West 84th Terrace
Lenexa, KS 66214-0695
PH: (800)-255-5113
FX: (913)438-0695
E-mail: thepacker@compuserve.com
URL: http://www.thepacker.com
Annual. $35.00. A buyer's directory giving sources of fresh fruits and vegetables. Shippers are listed by location for each commodity.

PRODUCE MERCHANDISING: THE PACKER'S RETAILING AND MERCHANDISING MAGAZINE
Vance Publishing Corp.
10901 West 84th Terrace
Lenexa, KS 66214-0695
PH: (800)-255-5113
E-mail: thepacker@compuserve.com
URL: http://www.thepacker.com

PRODUCE NEWS
Zim-Mer Trade Publications, Inc.
2185 Lemoine Ave.
Fort Lee, NJ 07024
PH: (201)592-9100
FX: (201)592-0809
Weekly. $35.00 per year.

PROGRESSIVE FARMER
Southern Progressive Co.
2100 Lakeshore Dr.
Birmingham, AL 35209
PH: (800)-292-2340
FX: (205)877-6700
URL: http://www.pathfinder.com/pf
Monthly. $16.00 per year. 17 regional editions. Includes supplement *Rural Sportsman*.

QUALITY OF COTTON REPORT
U.S. Department of Agriculture, Agricultural Marketing Service
Washington, DC 20250
PH: (202)720-8999
Weekly.

SOIL SCIENCE: AN INTERDISCIPLINARY APPROACH TO SOILS RESEARCH
Williams and Wilkins Co.
351 W. Camden St.
Baltimore, MD 21202-2436
PH: (800)-527-5597
FX: (410)528-4422
E-mail: custserv@wilkins.com
URL: http://www.wwilkins.com
Monthly. Individuals, $108.00 per year; institutions, $195.00 per year.

SPECIALTY FOOD INDUSTRY DIRECTORY
Phoenix Media Network, Inc.
PO Box 811768
Boca Raton, FL 33481-1768
PH: (561)447-0810
Annual. $20.00. Lists manufacturers and suppliers of specialty foods, and services and equipment for the specialty food industry. Featured food products include legumes, sauces, spices, upscale cheese, specialty beverages, snack foods, baked goods, ethnic foods, and specialty meats.

STATISTICAL ANNUAL: GRAINS, OPTIONS ON AGRICULTURAL FUTURES
Chicago Board of Trade.
141 W. Jackson Blvd., Ste. 2210
Education and Marketing Services Dept.
Chicago, IL 60604-2994
PH: (800)-572-3276
FX: (312)341-3168
E-mail: bw0050@cbot.com
URL: http://www.cbot.com
Annual. Includes historical data on Wheat Futures, Options on Wheat Futures, Corn Futures, Options on Corn Futures, Oats Futures, Soybean Futures, Options on Soybean Futures, Soybean Oil Futures, Soybean Meal Futures.

UNITED STATES CENSUS OF AGRICULTURE
U.S. Bureau of the Census
Washington, DC 20233-0800
PH: (301)457-4100
FX: (301)457-3842
URL: http://www.census.gov
Quinquennial. Results presented in reports, tape, CD-ROM, and Diskette files.

USDA
PH: (202)720-2791
E-mail: agsec@usda.gov
URL: http://www.usda.gov
United States Department of Agriculture. The USDA home page has six sections: News and Information; What's New; About USDA; Agencies; Opportunities; Search and Help. Keyword searching is offered from the USDA home page and from various individual agency home pages. Agencies are the Economic Research Service, Agricultural Marketing Service, National Agricultural Statistics Service, National Agricultural Library, and about 12 others. Updating varies. Fees: Free.

VEGETABLE GROWING HANDBOOK: ORGANIC AND TRADITIONAL METHODS
Chapman and Hall
115 Fifth Ave., 4th Fl.
New York, NY 10003-1004
PH: (800)-842-3636
FX: (212)260-1730
E-mail: info@chaphall.com
URL: http://www.chaphall.com
Walter E. Splittstoesser. 1990. $72.95. Third edition.

VEGETABLES AND SPECIALTIES SITUATION AND OUTLOOK
Available from U.S. Government Printing Office
Washington, DC 20402
PH: (202)512-1800
FX: (202)512-2250
Three times a year. $13.00 per year. Issued by the Economic Research Service of the U.S. Department of Agriculture. Provides current statistical information on supply, demand, and prices.

WACA NEWS
Western Agricultural Chemicals Association
3835 N. Freeway Blvd., Ste. 140
Sacramento, CA 95834
PH: (916)446-9222
FX: (916)565-0113
Quarterly. Free.

WEEKLY COTTON TRADE REPORT
New York Cotton Exchange
Four World Trade Center
New York, NY 10048
PH: (212)938-7909
Weekly. $100.00 per year.

WESTERN GROWERS ASSOCIATION--MEMBERSHIP
   DIRECTORY
Western Growers and Shipper Publishing Co.
PO Box 2130
Newport Beach, CA 92658
PH: (714)863-1000
FX: (714)863-9028
Annual.

WESTERN GROWERS AND SHIPPER: THE BUSINESS
   MAGAZINE OF THE WESTERN PRODUCT INDUSTRY
Western Grower and Shipper Publishing Co.
PO Box 2130
Newport Beach, CA 92658
PH: (714)863-1000
FX: (714)863-9028
Western Growers Association. Monthly. $18.00 per year.

WHEAT, BARLEY, AND TRITICALE ABSTRACTS
Prentice Hall
240 Frisch Ct.
Paramus, NJ 07652-5240
PH: (800)-947-7700
FX: (800)-445-6991
E-mail: cabi@cabi.org
URL: http://www.gopher.prenhall.com:7o/1
Henry Cheeseman. Bimonthly. $710.00 per year. Published in England by CAB International, formerly Commonwealth Agricultural Bureaux. Provides worldwide coverage of the literature.

WHEAT FACTS
National Association of Wheat Growers
415 Second St., N.E., Ste. 300
Washington, DC 20002
PH: (202)547-7800
FX: (202)546-2638
Annual. Price on application.

WHEAT LIFE
Washington Association of Wheat Growers
109 E. First St.
Ritzville, WA 99169-2394
PH: (509)659-0610
11 times a year. $12.00 per year. Covers research, marketing information, and legislative and regulatory news pertinent to the wheat and barley industries of the Pacific Northwest.

WILSONDISC: BIOLOGICAL AND AGRICULTURAL
   INDEX
H. W. Wilson Co.
950 University Ave.
Bronx, NY 10452
PH: (800)-367-6770
FX: (718)590-1617
Monthly. $1,495.00 per year, including unlimited online access to *Biological and Agricultural Index* through WILSONLINE. Provides CD-ROM indexing of over 200 periodicals covering agriculture, agricultural chemicals, biochemistry, biotechnology, entomology, horticulture, and related topics.

WILSONLINE: BIOLOGICAL AND AGRICULTURAL
   INDEX
H. W. Wilson Co.
950 University Ave.
Bronx, NY 10452
PH: (800)-367-6770
FX: (718)590-1617
Indexes a wide variety of agricultural and biological periodicals, 1983 to date. Weekly updates. Inquire as to online cost and availability.

WORLD AGRICULTURAL ECONOMICS AND RURAL
   SOCIOLOGY ABSTRACTS: ABSTRACTS OF WORLD
   LITERATURE
Available from CAB International North America
198 Madison Ave.
New York, NY 10016
PH: (800)-528-4841
FX: (212)686-7993
E-mail: cabi@cabi.org
URL: http://www.cabi.org
Monthly. $905.00 per year. Published in England by CAB International, formerly Commonwealth Agricultural Bureaux. Provides worldwide coverage of the literature.

WORLD AGRICULTURAL SUPPLY AND DEMAND
   ESTIMATES
Available from U.S. Government Printing Office
Washington, DC 20402
PH: (202)512-1800
FX: (202)512-2250
Monthly. $29.00 per year. Issued by the Economics and Statistics Service and the Foreign Agricultural Service of the U.S. Department of Agriculture. Consists mainly of statistical data and tables.

TRADE SHOWS

Information presented in this chapter is adapted from Gale's *Trade Shows Worldwide* (*TSW*). Entries present information needed for all those planning to visit or to participate in trade shows for the Agriculture sector. *TSW* entries include U.S. and Canadian shows and exhibitions.

Entries are arranged in alphabetical order by the name of the event and include the exhibition management company with full contact information, frequency of the event, audience, and principal exhibits.

AAEA ANNUAL MEETING
415 So. Duff Ave., Ste. C
Ames, IA 50010-6600
PH: (515)233-3202
FX: (515)233-3101
URL: http://www.aaea.org
Frequency: Annual. **Audience:** Agricultural Economists. **Principal Exhibits:** Agricultural economics software, hardware, teaching texts, tools, equipment, supplies, and services.

AG EXPO--MICHIGAN AGRICULTURAL EQUIPMENT EXPOSITION
103 Farrall Hall
East Lansing, MI 48824-1323
PH: (517)355-3477
TF: (800)366-7055
FX: (517)432-1563
URL: http://www.egr.msu.edu/AgE/agexpo
Frequency: Annual. **Audience:** Agricultural producers. **Principal Exhibits:** Agricultural equipment, products, and services, including tractors, structures, tilling equipment, grain handling systems, feeding equipment, forage harvesting equipment, and improvement systems, irrigation systems, seeds and fertilizers, livestock equipment, and dairy equipment.

AG-EXPO--NORTH AMERICAN SEED FAIR
3401 S. Parkside Dr. S.
Lethbridge, AB, Canada T1J 4R3
PH: (403)328-4491
FX: (403)320-8139
E-mail: lethexhb@telusplanet.net
URL: http://www.telusplanet.net/public/lethexhb
Frequency: Annual. **Audience:** Farmers, ranchers, and general public. **Principal Exhibits:** Agricultural machinery, agricultural chemicals, seeds and related equipment, supplies, and services.

AG EXPO (SOUTH DAKOTA)
121 N. Grand
Pierre, SD 57501
PH: (605)224-2445
FX: (605)224-9913
Frequency: Annual. **Audience:** Dealers. **Principal Exhibits:** Agricultural equipment, supplies, and services, including agricultural chemicals and machinery.

AG PROGRESS DAYS
College of Agricultural Sciences
420 Agricultural Administration Bldg.
University Park, PA 16802
PH: (814)865-2081
FX: (814)865-1677
E-mail: bah4@psu.edu
URL: http://apd.cas.psu.edu
Frequency: Annual. **Audience:** General public. **Principal Exhibits:** Agricultural equipment, supplies, and services, including machinery, hybrid corn seed field plots, and educational material.

AGRI NEWS FARM SHOW
PO Box 6118
18 1st Ave. SE
Rochester, MN 55903-6118
PH: (507)285-7600
TF: (800)533-1727
FX: (507)281-7436
Frequency: Annual. **Audience:** Farmers and trade professionals. **Principal Exhibits:** Farming equipment, supplies, and services.

AGROTECH
383 Main Ave.
PO Box 6059
Norwalk, CT 06851

PH: (203)840-5358
FX: (203)840-4804
E-mail: inquiry@nepcon.reedexpo.com
URL: http://www.reedexpo.com
Frequency: Biennial. **Principal Exhibits:** Equipment, supplies, and services for agriculture, food and catering.

AMERICAN ASSOCIATION OF BOVINE PRACTITIONERS ANNUAL CONFERENCE
PO Box 218
South Barre, VT 05670
PH: (802)476-6555
FX: (802)479-0147
Frequency: Annual. **Audience:** Veterinarians, related professionals, and exhibitor participants. **Principal Exhibits:** Pharmaceutical and biological manufacturers equipment companies, agricultural related companies, and computer programs and supplies.

AMERICAN FEED INDUSTRY ASSOCIATION FEED INDUSTRIES SHOW
1501 Wilson Blvd., Ste. 1100
Arlington, VA 22209
PH: (703)524-0810
FX: (703)524-1921
E-mail: mailafia@tomco.net
Frequency: Biennial. **Audience:** Feed industry executives, and production, operations, and plant managers. **Principal Exhibits:** Feed equipment, services, and ingredients.

AMERICAN RABBIT BREEDERS ASSOCIATION NATIONAL CONVENTION
8 Westport Ct.
Bloomington, IL 61704-8233
PH: (309)664-7500
FX: (309)664-0941
E-mail: arbamail@aol.com
Frequency: Annual. **Principal Exhibits:** Rabbit breeds exhibition.

AMERICAN ROYAL LIVESTOCK, HORSE SHOW, AND RODEO
1701 American Royal Ct.
Kansas City, MO 64102
PH: (816)221-9800
FX: (816)221-8189
E-mail: amroyal@aol.com
Frequency: Annual. **Audience:** General public, agricultural producers and suppliers, and agriculture-related professionals. **Principal Exhibits:** Equipment, supplies, and services related to livestock and horses and gift items, clothing, jewelry, etc.

AMERICAN SOCIETY OF AGRONOMY MEETING AND EXHIBITS
677 Segoe Rd.
Madison, WI 53711-1086
PH: (608)273-8080
FX: (608)273-2021
URL: http://www.agronomy.org
Frequency: Annual. **Principal Exhibits:** Agricultural equipment, supplies, and services.

AMERICAN SOCIETY OF ANIMAL SCIENCE CONFERENCE
1111 North Dunlap Ave.
Savoy, IL 61874
PH: (217)356-3182
FX: (217)398-4119
E-mail: asas@assohq.org
Frequency: Annual. **Principal Exhibits:** Exhibits related to the investigation, instruction, or extension in animal science and in the production, processing, and dissemination of livestock and livestock products.

AMERICAN SOCIETY OF FARM MANAGERS AND RURAL APPRAISERS ANNUAL CONVENTION
6201 Howard St.
Niles, IL 60714
PH: (708)647-1200
TF: (800)322-5510
FX: (708)647-7055
Frequency: Annual. **Principal Exhibits:** Agricultural equipment, supplies, and services.

AMERICAN SOYBEAN ASSOCIATION ANNUAL CONFERENCE--COMMODITY CLASSIC
12125 Woodcrest Executive Dr., Ste. 100
St. Louis, MO 63141
PH: (314)576-1770
FX: (314)576-2786
URL: http://www.oilseeds.org
Frequency: Annual. **Principal Exhibits:** Soybean industry related equipment, supplies, and services.

ANNUAL MEETINGS OF THE AMERICAN SOCIETY OF AGRONOMY, CROP SCIENCE SOCIETY OF AMERICA, AND SOIL SCIENCE SOCIETY OF AMERICA
677 Segoe Rd.
Madison, WI 53711-1086
PH: (608)273-8080
FX: (608)273-2021
URL: http://www.agronomy.org
Frequency: Annual. **Audience:** Agronomists, crop scientists, and soil scientists. **Principal Exhibits:** Agronomy, crop science, and soil science publications, products, services, and equipment.

ARA CONVENTION & EXPO
11701 Borman Dr., Ste. 110
St. Louis, MO 63146
PH: (314)567-6655
TF: (800)844-4900
FX: (314)567-6808
E-mail: ara@agretailerassn.org
URL: http://www.agretailerassn.org
Frequency: Annual. **Principal Exhibits:** Agricultural chemicals and fertilizers.

ARKANSAS FARM SHOW
c/o Don Freppon
PO Box 551
Little Rock, AR 72203
PH: (501)396-4316
TF: (800)772-5767
FX: (501)396-4330
Frequency: Annual. **Audience:** Trade and general public. **Principal Exhibits:** Farm equipment, agricultural chemicals, and related agricultural equipment, supplies, and services.

ASSOCIATION OF OPERATIVE MILLERS TECHNICAL CONFERENCE AND TRADE SHOW
5001 College Blvd., Ste. 104
Leawood, KS 66211
PH: (913)338-3377
FX: (913)338-3553
Frequency: Annual. **Principal Exhibits:** Cereal milling equipment, ancillary equipment, supplies, and services.

BARRON COUNTY FARM SHOW
PO Box 1
Chippewa Falls, WI 54729
PH: (715)723-5061
FX: (715)723-5061
Frequency: Annual. **Principal Exhibits:** Agricultural equipment, supplies, and services.

BIG IRON FARM SHOW AND EXHIBITION
PO Box 797
West Fargo, ND 58078-0797

PH: (701)282-2200
TF: (800)456-6408
FX: (701)282-6909
Frequency: Annual. **Audience:** Farmers from the upper Midwest. **Principal Exhibits:** Agricultural machinery and related equipment, supplies, and services.

CALIFORNIA FARM EQUIPMENT SHOW
PO Box 1475
4450 S. Laspine St.
Tulare, CA 93275
PH: (209)688-1751
TF: (800)999-9186
FX: (209)686-5065
E-mail: agricenter@worldnet.att.net
URL: http://www.farmshow.org
Frequency: Annual. **Audience:** Farmers, dairymen and international buyers. **Principal Exhibits:** Agricultural equipment, supplies, and services.

CANADIAN INTERNATIONAL FARM EQUIPMENT SHOW
1434 Chemong Rd., Unit 3, RR 1
Peterborough, ON, Canada K9J 6X2
PH: (705)741-2536
FX: (705)741-2539
E-mail: cifes@dawnmorris.on.ca
URL: http://www.dawnmorris.on.ca
Frequency: Annual. **Audience:** Farmers, manufacturers' representatives, and general public. **Principal Exhibits:** Equipment, supplies, and services for farmers, including machinery, material handling equipment, barn buildings, silos, feed, seed, fertilizer, chemicals, and banking services.

CANADIAN WESTERN AGRIBITION
Canada Centre Bldg.
Box 3535
Regina, SK, Canada S4P 3J8
PH: (306)565-0565
FX: (306)787-9963
E-mail: agribition@sk.sympatico.ca
Frequency: Annual. **Audience:** General public; livestock trade personnel; grain farmers; agricultural and commercial trade organizations. **Principal Exhibits:** Eggs; grain; commercial and registered livestock, including beef and dairy cattle, horses, sheep, and swine; innovations in agricultural technology; new developments in Canadian food products; grain and forage equipment; home improvement equipment.

CENTRAL MINNESOTA FARM EXPO
PO Box 1
Chippewa Falls, WI 54729
PH: (715)723-5061
FX: (715)723-5061
Frequency: Annual. **Principal Exhibits:** Agricultural equipment, supplies, and services.

CORN REFINERS ASSOCIATION AND NATIONAL CORN GROWERS ASSOCIATION CORN UTILIZATION AND TECHNOLOGY CONFERENCE
1701 Pennsylvania Ave. NW, Ste. 950
Washington, DC 20006
PH: (202)331-1634
FX: (202)331-2054
Frequency: Biennial. **Principal Exhibits:** Exhibits for corn refining firms that manufacture corn starches, sugars, syrups, oils, feed, and alcohol by wet process. Suppliers to corn wet milling industry and to corn producers.

CROP SCIENCE SOCIETY OF AMERICA MEETING AND EXHIBITS
677 Segoe Rd.
Madison, WI 53711-1086
PH: (608)273-8080
FX: (608)273-2021

Frequency: Annual. **Principal Exhibits:** Agricultural equipment, supplies, and services.

DAKOTA FARM SHOW
PO Box 737
Austin, MN 55912
PH: (507)437-4577
FX: (507)437-7752
Frequency: Annual. **Audience:** Farmers. **Principal Exhibits:** Agricultural equipment, supplies, and services.

EASTERN REGIONAL NURSERYMEN SHOW
15245 Shady Grove Rd., Ste. 130
Rockville, MD 20850
PH: (301)990-8350
TF: (800)376-2463
FX: (301)990-9771
E-mail: erna@mgmtsol.com
URL: http://www.erna.org
Frequency: Annual. **Audience:** Nursery trade. **Principal Exhibits:** Green goods, hard goods, and allied horticultural lines.

EAU CLAIRE FARM SHOW
PO Box 1
Chippewa Falls, WI 54729
PH: (715)723-5061
FX: (715)723-5061
Frequency: Annual. **Audience:** Farmers, agricultural instructors, and students. **Principal Exhibits:** Farm machinery and dairy equipment.

ELECTRIC POWER AND FARM EQUIPMENT SHOW
13 Odana Ct.
PO Box 44364
Madison, WI 53744-4364
PH: (608)276-6700
FX: (608)276-6719
Frequency: Annual. **Audience:** General public, farmers, farm equipment dealers, and other farm industry personnel. **Principal Exhibits:** Farm machinery, including tractors, field equipment, minimum tillage, no-till, harvesting equipment, and farm supplies; lawn, garden, and outdoor power equipment; irrigation equipment; farmstead mechanization equipment; dairy equipment.

EMPIRE FARM DAYS
PO Box 566
Stanley, NY 14561
PH: (716)526-5356
FX: (716)526-6576
E-mail: espcefd@aol.com
Frequency: Annual. **Audience:** Agricultural trade. **Principal Exhibits:** Agricultural equipment, supplies, and services.

FARM CREDIT COUNCIL CONFERENCE
50 F St., N.W., Ste. 900
Washington, DC 20001
PH: (202)626-8710
URL: http://www.fccouncil.com
Frequency: Annual. **Principal Exhibits:** Exhibits of interest to Farm Credit System, a nationwide financial cooperative that makes loans to agricultural producers, rural home buyers, farmer cooperatives, and rural utilities.

FARM PROGRESS SHOW
191 S. Gary Ave.
Carol Stream, IL 60188
PH: (708)462-2892
FX: (708)462-2869
Frequency: Annual. **Audience:** Farmers and agribusiness representatives; general public. **Principal Exhibits:** Farm machinery and equipment, trucks, livestock equipment, buildings, seed, chemicals, computers, and other agricultural products and services.

FARM SCIENCE REVIEW
College of Food, Agricultural, and Env. Sciences
590 Woody Hayes Dr.
Agricultural Engineering Bldg., Rm. 232
Columbus, OH 43210
PH: (614)292-4278
TF: (800)644-6377
FX: (614)292-9448
Frequency: Annual. **Audience:** Producers and other agribusiness professionals; general public. **Principal Exhibits:** Agricultural equipment, supplies, and services.

FARMFAIR INTERNATIONAL
PO Box 1480
Edmonton, AB, Canada T5J 2N5
PH: (403)471-7210
TF: (888)800-7275
FX: (403)471-8176
E-mail: npmarket@planet.eon.net
URL: http://www.northlands.com
Frequency: Annual. **Audience:** Farmers, ranchers, and general public. **Principal Exhibits:** Livestock shows and livestock sales.

FARMFEST
Box 731
Lake Crystal, MN 56055
PH: (507)726-6863
TF: (800)347-5863
FX: (507)726-6750
Frequency: Annual. **Audience:** Livestock and grain farmers and general public. **Principal Exhibits:** Farm equipment and machinery; computers and software products; chemicals, seeds, and crops; and techniques of planting, tillage, and harvesting.

FARWEST NURSERY SHOW
2780 SE Harrison Ave., No. 102
Milwaukie, OR 97222
PH: (503)653-8733
TF: (800)342-6401
FX: (503)653-1528
E-mail: farwest@oan.org
URL: http://www.nurseryguide.com
Frequency: Annual. **Audience:** Northwestern United States and national nurserymen. **Principal Exhibits:** Nursery stock, equipment, machinery, chemicals, and miscellaneous supplies and services for the nursery industry.

FEWA ANNUAL MEETING AND CONVENTION
611 Southgate Ave.
Iowa City, IA 52240
PH: (319)354-5156
FX: (319)354-5157
E-mail: info@FEWA.org
URL: http://www.FEWA.org
Frequency: Annual. **Audience:** Owners and managers. **Principal Exhibits:** Equipment, supplies, and services for independent wholesalers of shortline and specialty farm equipment, light industrial tractors, lawn and garden tractors, turf care equipment, estate and park maintenance equipment, and power vehicles for outdoor recreation and sports.

FFA NATIONAL AGRICULTURAL CAREER SHOW
PO Box 15160
Alexandria, VA 22309
PH: (703)360-3600
FX: (703)360-5524
Frequency: Annual. **Principal Exhibits:** Agricultural equipment, supplies, and services.

FOND DU LAC FARM EXPO
PO Box 1
Chippewa Falls, WI 54729
PH: (715)723-5061
FX: (715)723-5061

Frequency: Annual. **Principal Exhibits:** Agricultural equipment, supplies, and services.

FOODPRO
383 Main Ave.
PO Box 6059
Norwalk, CT 06851
PH: (203)840-5358
FX: (203)840-4804
E-mail: inquiry@nepcon.reedexpo.com
URL: http://www.reedexpo.com
Frequency: Biennial. **Principal Exhibits:** Equipment, supplies, and services for agriculture, food and catering.

FOREST EXPO
3851 18th Ave.
Prince George, BC, Canada V2N 1B1
PH: (604)563-8833
FX: (604)563-8909
Frequency: Biennial. **Audience:** Members of the forestry industry. **Principal Exhibits:** Forestry equipment, supplies, and services.

FOREST PRODUCTS MACHINERY & EQUIPMENT EXPOSITION
2900 Indiana Ave.
Kenner, LA 70065
PH: (504)443-4464
FX: (504)443-6612
Frequency: Biennial. **Audience:** Trade professionals. **Principal Exhibits:** Equipment, supplies, and services for the forest products industry.

FORT WAYNE FARM SHOW
811 Oakland Ave. W.
PO Box 1067
Austin, MN 55912
PH: (507)437-4697
TF: (800)949-3976
FX: (507)437-8917
E-mail: tradexpo@smig.net
URL: http://www.tradexpos.com
Frequency: Annual. **Audience:** Farmers. **Principal Exhibits:** Agricultural equipment, supplies, and services.

GRAIN ELEVATOR AND PROCESSING SOCIETY EXCHANGE
Box 15026
Minneapolis, MN 55415-0026
PH: (612)339-4625
FX: (612)339-4644
E-mail: info@geaps.com
URL: http://www.geaps.com
Frequency: Annual. **Audience:** Grain handling professionals. **Principal Exhibits:** Grain handling and processing equipment, supplies, and services.

GRAND NATIONAL RODEO, HORSE SHOW, AND LIVESTOCK EXPO
PO Box 34206
San Francisco, CA 94134
PH: (415)469-6000
FX: (415)337-0941
Frequency: Annual. **Audience:** General public. **Principal Exhibits:** Livestock equipment, supplies, and services.

GREATER PEORIA FARM SHOW
PO Box 737
Austin, MN 55912
PH: (507)437-7969
FX: (507)437-7752
Frequency: Annual. **Audience:** Farmers. **Principal Exhibits:** Agricultural equipment, supplies, and services.

GROWEREXPO
PO Box 9
335 N. River St.
Batavia, IL 60510
PH: (630)208-9080
TF: (800)456-5380
FX: (630)208-9350
E-mail: GTALKS@xnet.com
URL: http://www.growertalks.com
Frequency: Annual. **Audience:** Greenhouse growers and floral producers. **Principal Exhibits:** Equipment and supplies for greenhouse growers, including seeds, fertilizers, growth media, chemicals, structures, plastics, environmental controls, and computers.

HAWKEYE FARM SHOW
PO Box 737
Austin, MN 55912
PH: (507)437-4577
FX: (507)437-7752
Frequency: Annual. **Audience:** Farmers. **Principal Exhibits:** Agricultural equipment, supplies, and services.

INDIANA AGRI-BUSINESS EXPOSITION
Merchants Plaza
101 W. Washington St., Ste. 1313, E. Tower
Indianapolis, IN 46204
PH: (317)634-6137
FX: (317)687-9650
Frequency: Annual. **Audience:** Agriculture industry professionals. **Principal Exhibits:** Agricultural equipment, supplies, and services, including feed, elevators, mixers, fertilizers, feed and fertilizer ingredients, soybean processors, corn millers, soft wheat millers, chemicals, and domestic and foreign grains.

INDIANA-ILLINOIS FARM EQUIPMENT SHOW
4 Highwater Rd.
Hilton Head, SC 29928
PH: (843)686-5640
FX: (843)686-5640
Frequency: Annual. **Audience:** Farmers. **Principal Exhibits:** Farm equipment, supplies, and services, including seeds and agricultural chemicals.

INTER-AMERICAN ASSOCIATION OF AGRICULTURAL LIBRARIANS AND DOCUMENTALISTS CONFERENCE
c/o IICA
Apartado 55-2200
Coronado, Costa Rica
PH: (506) 2294741
FX: (506) 2294741
E-mail: iicahq@iica.ac.cr
Frequency: Triennial. **Principal Exhibits:** Equipment, supplies, and services for libraries, library schools, and technical institutions in the field of agriculture, animal science, forestry, and related fields.

INTERNATIONAL AGRICULTURAL FAIR--FOOD, AGRICULTURE AND EQUIPMENT
7847 Convoy Ct., Ste. 105
San Diego, CA 92111-1220
PH: (619)277-5580
FX: (619)277-9411
E-mail: vniic@aol.com
Frequency: Annual. **Principal Exhibits:** Agricultural equipment, supplies, and services.

INTERNATIONAL BEDDING PLANT CONFERENCE AND TRADE SHOW
206 6th Ave., Ste. 900
Des Moines, IA 50309
PH: (512)282-8192
TF: (800)647-7742
FX: (512)282-9117
E-mail: bpi@bpint.org
URL: http://www.bpint.org

Frequency: Annual. **Audience:** Greenhouse growers industry. **Principal Exhibits:** Products and services for commercial growers, retailers, and others involved in the bedding and container plant industry.

INTERNATIONAL PLOWING MATCH AND FARM MACHINERY SHOW
367 Woodlawn Rd., Unit 6
Guelph, ON, Canada N1H 7K9
PH: (519)767-2928
TF: (800)661-7569
FX: (519)767-2101
Frequency: Annual. **Audience:** Farmers, buyers, trade professionals, and general public. **Principal Exhibits:** Agricultural exhibits.

IOWA AGRIBUSINESS EXPOSITION
900 Des Moines St., Ste. 150
Des Moines, IA 50309
PH: (515)262-8323
FX: (515)262-8960
Frequency: Annual. **Audience:** Agribusiness retailers. **Principal Exhibits:** Products and services for the agricultural retail industry.

KANSAS AGRI-BUSINESS EXPO
816 SW Tyler
Box 2429
Topeka, KS 66601
PH: (913)234-0461
FX: (913)234-2930
Frequency: Annual. **Audience:** Grain elevator owners and managers, fertilizer and chemical dealers, grain brokers, and commodity merchants. **Principal Exhibits:** Fertilizer and chemical manufacturers equipment, distributors, grain and feed related equipment, related service firms, and agriculture software companies.

KANSAS BEEF EXPO
6031 SW 37th St.
Topeka, KS 66614-5128
PH: (785)273-5115
FX: (785)273-3399
Frequency: Annual. **Audience:** Livestock producers. **Principal Exhibits:** Cattle and cattle industry equipment, supplies, and services.

KANSAS STATE FAIR
2000 N. Poplar
Hutchinson, KS 67502-5598
PH: (316)669-3600
TF: (800)362-FAIR
Frequency: Annual. **Principal Exhibits:** General fair type exhibits, including special programs, attractions, youth, agriculture, livestock, and entertainment.

KFYR RADIO AGRI INTERNATIONAL STOCK & TRADE SHOW
210 N. 4th St.
PO Box 1738
Bismark, ND 58502
PH: (701)255-5555
TF: (800)472-2170
FX: (701)255-8155
E-mail: frontdesk@kfyr.com
URL: http://www.kfyr.com
Frequency: Annual. **Audience:** Farmers and ranchers. **Principal Exhibits:** Agricultural equipment, supplies, and services.

LA AERIAL APPLICATION CONFERENCE
208 Bellewood Dr.
Baton Rouge, LA 70806
PH: (504)925-8897
FX: (504)926-2680
Frequency: Annual. **Principal Exhibits:** Equipment, supplies, and services for agricultural aviation.

LAKE COUNTY FAIR
50 S. U.S. Rte. 45
Box 216
Grayslake, IL 60030-0216
PH: (847)223-2204
FX: (847)223-2260
Frequency: Annual. **Audience:** Professionals, educators, and business persons. **Principal Exhibits:** Business education, service to general public, competitive and agricultural.

LCI ANNUAL MEETING
1910 Lyda Dr.
Bowling Green, KY 42104
PH: (502)782-9798
FX: (502)782-0188
Frequency: Annual. **Principal Exhibits:** Exhibits regarding animal health, livestock care and handling, food safety, and uniform livestock identification.

MAGIE--MIDWEST AGRI INDUSTRIES EXPO
PO Box 186
St. Anne, IL 60964
PH: (815)427-6644
TF: (800)892-7122
FX: (815)427-6573
Frequency: Annual. **Audience:** Agricultural fertilizer and chemical industry retailers. **Principal Exhibits:** Agricultural chemical and fertilizer application equipment, supplies, and services.

MANITOBA AG DAYS
PO Box 214
Oak Bluff, MB, Canada R0G 1N0
PH: (204)275-1424
FX: (204)275-5960
Frequency: Annual. **Audience:** Crop and livestock producers and general public. **Principal Exhibits:** Agricultural equipment, supplies, and services, including pesticides, fertilizers, seed, machinery, computer and financial services, livestock products.

MATE--MONTANA AGRI-TRADE EXPOSITION
208 N. 29th St., Ste. 214
Billings, MT 59101
PH: (406)245-0404
FX: (406)245-3897
E-mail: jerryd@wtp.net
Frequency: Annual. **Audience:** Farmers, ranchers, and general public. **Principal Exhibits:** Agricultural, farming, ranching, hunting, and fishing equipment, supplies, and services.

MICHIGAN AGRI-BUSINESS ANNUAL CONVENTION AND TRADE SHOW
2133 University Dr., Ste. 200
Okemos, MI 48864
PH: (517)349-9420
Frequency: Annual. **Audience:** Wholesale and retail agricultural trade professionals. **Principal Exhibits:** Agribusiness equipment, supplies, and services.

MID-AMERICA FARM SHOW
120 Ash St.
Salina, KS 67401-0586
PH: (785)827-9301
FX: (785)827-9758
Frequency: Annual. **Audience:** Farmers and ranchers, insurance and real estate brokers, and related professionals; general public. **Principal Exhibits:** Agricultural equipment, supplies, and services, including irrigation equipment, fertilizer, farm implements, hybrid seed, agricultural chemicals, tractors, feed, farrowing crates and equipment, silos and bins, storage equipment, and farm buildings.

MID-ATLANTIC NURSERYMEN'S WINTER TRADE SHOW
PO Box 11739
Baltimore, MD 21206

PH: (410)882-5300
TF: (800)431-0066
FX: (410)882-0535
Frequency: Annual. **Audience:** Nurserymen, garden centers, landscape contractors, arborists, greenhouse growers. **Principal Exhibits:** Equipment, supplies, and services relating to all aspects of nursery business.

MID-SOUTH FARM AND GIN SUPPLY EXHIBIT
874 Cotton Gin Pl.
Memphis, TN 38106
PH: (901)947-3104
FX: (901)947-3103
Frequency: Annual. **Audience:** Agribusiness professionals. **Principal Exhibits:** Agricultural equipment, supplies and services.

MID-TEX FARM AND RANCH SHOW
101 S. University Parks Dr.
PO Drawer 1220
Waco, TX 76703-1220
PH: (817)752-6551
FX: (817)752-6618
Frequency: Annual. **Audience:** Agriculture-related trades. **Principal Exhibits:** Agricultural and ranch equipment.

MIDWEST FARM SHOW
PO Box 1
Chippewa Falls, WI 54729
PH: (715)723-5061
FX: (715)723-5061
Frequency: Annual. **Audience:** Farmers. **Principal Exhibits:** Farm materials handling equipment, supplies, and services.

MINNESOTA NURSERY AND LANDSCAPE ASSOCIATION MEETINGS AND TRADE SHOW
PO Box 130307
St. Paul, MN 55425-0003
PH: (612)633-4987
FX: (612)633-4986
Frequency: Annual. **Audience:** Garden center personnel, landscape designers, and landscape contractors. **Principal Exhibits:** Nursery industry equipment, supplies, and services; landscape contracting equipment, supplies, and services.

NATIONAL AGRI-MARKETING ASSOCIATION CONFERENCE
11020 King St., Ste. 205
Overland Park, KS 66210
PH: (913)491-6500
FX: (913)492-6502
E-mail: agrimktg@nama.org
URL: http://www.nama.org
Frequency: Annual. **Audience:** Marketing, sales, and advertising executives representing companies that sell farm and ranch products; advertising agency personnel; farm media. **Principal Exhibits:** Marketing and communication suppliers, including trade publications, radio and television broadcast sales organizations, premium/ incentive manufacturers, printers, marketing research firms, photographers, and related professionals.

NATIONAL AGRICULTURAL BANKERS CONFERENCE
1120 Connecticut Ave. NW
Washington, DC 20036
PH: (202)663-5191
FX: (202)663-5210
Frequency: Annual. **Audience:** Bank CEOs, mainly from community banks in rural areas, executive vice presidents, senior vice presidents, economists, analysts. **Principal Exhibits:** The latest developments in the agricultural lending business, as well as strategies for better market share, profitability and customer service.

NATIONAL AGRICULTURAL PLASTICS CONGRESS AND TRADE SHOW
526 Brittany Dr.
State College, PA 16803-1420
PH: (814)238-7045
FX: (814)238-7051
E-mail: peh4@psu.edu
Frequency: Every 18 mos. **Audience:** Academic researchers and extension professionals, growers, plastics manufacturers and distributors. **Principal Exhibits:** Equipment, supplies, and services relating to use of plastics in agriculture, horticulture, i.e., greenhouse production; mulch film, drip irrigation, etc.

NATIONAL ASSOCIATION OF WHEAT GROWERS CONVENTION
415 2nd St., NE, Ste. 300
Washington, DC 20002
PH: (202)547-7800
FX: (202)546-2638
E-mail: nawgi@aol.com
Frequency: Annual. **Audience:** Wheat producers. **Principal Exhibits:** Agri-chemicals; seed and fertilizers; farm equipment, machinery, and supplies; computers and computer software; communication systems; marketing services; commodity brokerage services.

NATIONAL CATTLEMEN'S BEEF ASSOCIATION ANNUAL CONVENTION AND TRADE SHOW
5420 S. Quebec St.
PO Box 3469
Englewood, CO 80155
PH: (303)694-0305
FX: (303)694-2851
E-mail: cattle@beef.org
URL: http://www.beef.org
Frequency: Annual. **Audience:** Association affiliates, ancillary groups, ranch owners and operators. **Principal Exhibits:** Products and services for the beef cattle industry, including animal health products, pharmaceuticals, biologicals, feed and feed additives, commodities, livestock machinery, computer technology, and related equipment and supplies.

NATIONAL CUSTOM APPLICATOR EXPOSITION
900 Des Moines St., Ste. 150
Des Moines, IA 50309
PH: (515)262-8323
FX: (515)262-8960
Frequency: Annual. **Audience:** Custom applicators of agricultural fertilizers and agrichemicals. **Principal Exhibits:** Agrichemicals, fertilizers, spray equipment tanks, agriplanes, and agricomputer and flotation equipment.

NATIONAL FARM MACHINERY SHOW AND CHAMPIONSHIP TRACTOR PULL
PO Box 37130
Louisville, KY 40233
PH: (502)367-5000
FX: (502)367-5299
Frequency: Annual. **Audience:** Agribusiness trade and general public. **Principal Exhibits:** Agricultural products, equipment, supplies, and services.

NATIONAL POTATO COUNCIL'S ANNUAL MEETING
5690 DTC Blvd., Ste. 230E
Englewood, CO 80111-3200
PH: (303)773-9295
FX: (303)773-9296
E-mail: npcspud@ix.netcom.com
URL: http://www.npcspud.com
Frequency: Annual. **Principal Exhibits:** Potato growing equipment, supplies, and services.

NATIONAL WESTERN STOCK SHOW AND RODEO
4655 Humboldt St.
Denver, CO 80216

PH: (303)297-1166
FX: (303)292-1708
Frequency: Annual. **Audience:** Agricultural and livestock trade; general public. **Principal Exhibits:** Jewelry, apparel, household goods, agricultural products, and service groups.

NCTE--NORTH CENTRAL TURFGRASS EXPOSITION
104 S. Michigan Ave., Ste. 1500
Chicago, IL 60603
PH: (312)201-0101
Frequency: Annual. **Audience:** Turfgrass professionals and grounds care professionals. **Principal Exhibits:** Turfgrass industry equipment, supplies, and services, including chemicals and fertilizers.

NEBRASKA AGRI-BUSINESS EXPOSITION
1111 Lincoln Mall, Ste. 308
Lincoln, NE 68508-2882
PH: (402)476-1528
FX: (402)476-1259
Frequency: Annual. **Audience:** Farmers and grain, feed, fertilizer, and agrichemical dealers. **Principal Exhibits:** Grain, feed, fertilizers, agrichemicals, and related equipment and supplies of the farm industry.

NEBRASKA FARM EXPOSITION
1367 33rd Ave.
Columbus, NE 68601
PH: (402)564-2866
TF: (800)651-5568
FX: (402)564-2867
Frequency: Annual. **Audience:** Farmers and ranchers. **Principal Exhibits:** Farm products, equipment, and services.

NEW ENGLAND EQUIPMENT DEALERS ANNUAL CONVENTION AND TRADE SHOW
PO Box 895
Concord, NH 03302-0895
PH: (603)225-5510
FX: (603)225-5510
Frequency: Annual. **Audience:** Retail equipment dealers. **Principal Exhibits:** Farm, industrial, and outdoor power equipment.

NEW HAMPSHIRE FARM AND FOREST EXPOSITION
PO Box 2042
Concord, NH 03302
PH: (603)271-3552
FX: (603)271-1109
Frequency: Annual. **Audience:** Farmers, foresters, wood processors, landowners, and consumers. **Principal Exhibits:** Agricultural and forest technology, products, and services.

NEW JERSEY ANNUAL VEGETABLE MEETING AND TRADE SHOW
377 N. Locust Ave.
Marlton, NJ 08053
PH: (609)985-4382
FX: (609)985-4382
Frequency: Annual. **Audience:** Vegetable growers, marketers, and handlers, researchers, extension teachers, government agency personnel, and related professionals. **Principal Exhibits:** Pesticides, fertilizers, containers, equipment, machinery, packing house equipment, roadside market products, and allied services, including farm credit.

NEW YORK FARM SHOW
PO Box 3470
Syracuse, NY 13220
PH: (315)457-8205
FX: (315)451-3548
Frequency: Annual. **Audience:** Trade and general public. **Principal Exhibits:** Agricultural equipment, supplies, and services.

NORTH AMERICAN DEER FARMERS ASSOCIATION ANNUAL CONFERENCE AND EXHIBIT
9301 Anapolis Rd., No. 206
Lanham, MD 20706
PH: (301)459-7708
FX: (301)459-7864
E-mail: info@nadefa.org
URL: http://www.nadefa.org
Frequency: Annual. **Principal Exhibits:** Deer farming equipment, supplies, and services.

NORTH AMERICAN FARM AND POWER SHOW
811 Oakland Ave. W.
PO Box 1067
Austin, MN 55912
PH: (507)437-4697
TF: (800)949-3976
FX: (507)437-8917
E-mail: tradexpo@smig.net
URL: http://www.tradexpos.com
Frequency: Annual. **Audience:** Trade and general public. **Principal Exhibits:** Farm equipment, supplies, and services; lawn and garden equipment; industrial equipment. **Held in conjunction with:** Farm Equipment Association Annual Convention.

NORTH AMERICAN INTERNATIONAL LIVESTOCK EXPOSITION
PO Box 36367
Louisville, KY 40233
PH: (502)595-3166
FX: (502)367-5299
Frequency: Annual. **Principal Exhibits:** Livestock related equipment, supplies, and services.

NORTH AMERICAN OUTLOOK CONFERENCE
600 Harrison St.
San Francisco, CA 94107
PH: (415)905-2200
TF: (800)227-4675
FX: (415)905-2232
URL: http://www.mfi.com
Frequency: Annual. **Principal Exhibits:** Exhibits relating to the key economic factors that shape the wood industry.

NORTH DAKOTA FUTURE FARMERS OF AMERICA ASSOCIATION CONFERENCE
State Capitol, 15th Fl.
600 E Blvd.
Bismarck, ND 58505
PH: (701)328-3185
Frequency: Annual. **Principal Exhibits:** Agriculture equipment, supplies, and services.

NORTH DAKOTA STATE FAIR
Box 1796
Minot, ND 58702
PH: (701)857-7620
FX: (701)857-7622
E-mail: ndsf@minot.com
Frequency: Annual. **Audience:** General public. **Principal Exhibits:** Agricultural and home living equipment, supplies, and services.

NORTH DAKOTA WINTER SHOW
Box 846
Valley City, ND 58072
PH: (701)845-1401
FX: (701)845-3914
Frequency: Annual. **Audience:** Farmers and ranchers. **Principal Exhibits:** Agricultural displays and livestock.

NORTHEASTERN FOREST PRODUCTS EQUIPMENT
PO Box 69
Old Forge, NY 13420

PH: (315)369-3078
FX: (315)369-3736
E-mail: nela@telenet.net
Frequency: Annual. **Audience:** Loggers, sawmill personnel, paper company employees, foresters, land owners, and others associated with the harvesting and processing of lumber. **Principal Exhibits:** Forest industry services, equipment, and associated products.

NORTHERN INTERNATIONAL LIVESTOCK EXPOSITION
PO Box 1981
Billings, MT 59103
PH: (406)256-2495
TF: (888)NILE-TIX
FX: (406)256-2494
Frequency: Annual. **Audience:** Farmers, ranchers, related professionals, and general public. **Principal Exhibits:** Agricultural equipment, supplies, and services, and home products crafts.

NORTHWEST AGRICULTURAL SHOW
4672 Drift Creek Rd., SE
Sublimity, OR 97385
PH: (503)769-7120
FX: (503)769-3549
Frequency: Annual. **Audience:** Farmers, other agricultural buyers, and the general public. **Principal Exhibits:** Agricultural equipment and services.

NORTHWEST DAIRY AND FARM EQUIPMENT SHOW
6321 Norman Rd.
Stanwood, WA 98292
PH: (360)652-9781
FX: (360)629-2015
E-mail: equipshow@aol.com
Frequency: Annual. **Audience:** Agriculture equipment, supplies, and services. **Principal Exhibits:** Dairy and farm equipment, supplies, and services.

OHIO BEEF EXPO
10600 US Highway 42
Marysville, OH 43040-9526
PH: (614)873-6736
FX: (614)873-6835
E-mail: ohiobeef@aol.com
Frequency: Annual. **Audience:** Trade professionals and beef producers from East and West. **Principal Exhibits:** Feed, equipment, seed, feeder calves, cattle breed displays, livestock pharmaceuticals, and other general farm supplies and services.

OHIO STATE FAIR
717 East 17th Avenue
Columbus, OH 43211-2698
PH: (614)644-4000
FX: (614)644-4031
URL: http://www.ohioexpocenter.com
Frequency: Annual. **Audience:** General public. **Principal Exhibits:** Agriculture, arts and crafts, commercial sales, state departments, youth groups, animals, utilities, foods, fine arts, and livestock.

OKLAHOMA FARM SHOW
Farm Progress Companies
191 S. Gary Ave.
Carol Stream, IL 60188-2095
PH: (630)462-2956
FX: (630)588-2081
Frequency: Annual. **Audience:** Farmers and ranchers; farm equipment and supply dealers. **Principal Exhibits:** Farm machinery, supplies, and chemicals; seed; feed; farm buildings; and livestock equipment and supplies.

OREGON STATE FAIR
2330 17th St., NE
Salem, OR 97310

PH: (503)378-3247
FX: (503)373-1788
Frequency: Annual. **Audience:** General public. **Principal Exhibits:** General merchandise and products, agricultural products and livestock.

OZARK FALL FARMFEST
PO Box 630
Springfield, MO 65801-0630
PH: (417)833-2660
FX: (417)833-3769
Frequency: Annual. **Audience:** Trade professionals and general public. **Principal Exhibits:** Agricultural products and services, including livestock.

PAN-AMERICAN INTERNATIONAL LIVESTOCK EXPOSITION
PO Box 150009
Dallas, TX 75315
PH: (214)421-8723
FX: (214)421-8710
Frequency: Annual. **Audience:** Agriculture. **Principal Exhibits:** Livestock, livestock equipment, agricultural technology, and consumer products.

PENN-JERSEY EQUIPMENT DEALERS CONVENTION
1203 York Rd.
Mechanicsburg, PA 17055-9769
PH: (717)258-8476
FX: (717)258-8478
Frequency: Annual. **Audience:** Retail equipment trade professionals. **Principal Exhibits:** Farm, light industrial, lawn and garden and outdoor power equipment.

PENNSYLVANIA HORTICULTURAL SOCIETY'S PHILADELPHIA FLOWER SHOW
100 N. 20th St., 5th Fl.
Philadelphia, PA 19103-1495
PH: (215)988-8800
FX: (215)988-8810
E-mail: janeteva@libertynet.org
Frequency: Annual. **Audience:** Landscapers, horticulturists, florists, and general public. **Principal Exhibits:** Horticultural and horticulture education equipment, supplies, and services.

PENNSYLVANIA LANDSCAPE AND NURSERY TRADE SHOW AND CONFERENCE
1924 N. 2nd St.
Harrisburg, PA 17102
PH: (717)238-1673
FX: (717)238-1675
Frequency: Annual. **Audience:** Nursery, landscape, and garden center trade. **Principal Exhibits:** Nursery stock, pesticides, fertilizer, garden center novelties, mulch, and related equipment, supplies, and services.

POWER SHOW OHIO
6124 Avery Rd.
PO Box 68
Dublin, OH 43017
PH: (614)889-1309
FX: (614)889-0463
Frequency: Annual. **Audience:** Trade professionals and general public. **Principal Exhibits:** Construction equipment, agricultural equipment, and outdoor power equipment.

PRAIRIE EAST HORTICULTURAL TRADE SHOW
676 Borebank St.
Winnipeg, MB, Canada R3N 1G2
PH: (204)254-2293
FX: (204)257-5205
E-mail: frontline@escape.ca
URL: http://www.escape.ca/~frontline
Frequency: Annual. **Audience:** Landscape and greenhouse retailers

and staff. **Principal Exhibits:** Products and services relating to the landscape and greenhouse growers industry.

RED AND WHITE DAIRY CATTLE ASSOCIATION ANNUAL MEETING
HC1, Box 71B
Crystal Spring, PA 15536
PH: (814)735-4221
FX: (814)735-3473
E-mail: rwdcaone@nb.net
Frequency: Annual. **Audience:** Cattle breeders, farmers. **Principal Exhibits:** Exhibits related to the milk production capabilities of Red and White cattle.

ST. LOUIS FARM SHOW
10805 Sunset Office Dr., Ste. 202
St. Louis, MO 63127
PH: (314)966-5757
TF: (800)430-6334
FX: (314)966-8438
E-mail: mvea@aol.com
Frequency: Annual. **Audience:** Farmers and farm equipment dealers. **Principal Exhibits:** Farm equipment and supplies and agriculture products.

SIMA--INTERNATIONAL SALON OF FARM MACHINERY/ CANADA
435 De L'Inspecteur
Montreal, PQ, Canada H3C 2K8
PH: (514)861-8241
FX: (514)861-8246
Frequency: Biennial. **Audience:** Farm producers, farm machinery retailers, agrologists, industry wholesalers, and financial and governmental institutions. **Principal Exhibits:** Farm machinery, including trucks and implements, harvesting equipment, seeding and cultivating equipment, dairy and farmstead equipment, lawn and garden equipment, chain saws, seeds and chemicals, and computers and software in agriculture.

SIOUX EMPIRE FARM SHOW
Agri-Business Division
PO Box 1425
Sioux Falls, SD 57101
PH: (605)336-1620
FX: (605)336-6499
Frequency: Annual. **Audience:** Agricultural producers. **Principal Exhibits:** Agricultural equipment, supplies, and services.

SIOUXLAND FARM SHOW
PO Box 737
Austin, MN 55912
PH: (507)437-4577
FX: (507)437-7752
Frequency: Annual. **Audience:** Farmers. **Principal Exhibits:** Agricultural equipment, supplies, and services.

SOCIETY OF AMERICAN FORESTERS NATIONAL CONVENTION
5400 Grosvenor Ln.
Bethesda, MD 20814
PH: (301)897-8720
FX: (301)897-3690
Frequency: Annual. **Audience:** Professional foresters and the general public. **Principal Exhibits:** Forestry equipment, publications, hardware and software, chemicals, machinery, and geographic information systems.

SOCIETY FOR RANGE MANAGEMENT ANNUAL CONFERENCE
1839 York St.
Denver, CO 80206
PH: (303)355-7070
FX: (303)355-5059
URL: http://cnrit.tamu.edu/srm

Frequency: Annual. **Audience:** Range managers and scientists. **Principal Exhibits:** Range management equipment and supplies.

SOIL SCIENCE SOCIETY OF AMERICA MEETING AND EXHIBITS
677 Segoe Rd.
Madison, WI 53711-1086
PH: (608)273-8080
FX: (608)273-2021
URL: http://www.agronomy.org
Frequency: Annual. **Principal Exhibits:** Agricultural equipment, supplies, and services.

SOIL AND WATER CONSERVATION SOCIETY ANNUAL MEETING
7515 NE Ankeny Rd.
Ankeny, IA 50021-9764
PH: (515)289-2331
TF: (800)843-7645
FX: (515)289-1227
E-mail: swcs@swcs.org
URL: http://www.swcs.org
Frequency: Annual. **Audience:** Researchers, administrators, educators, legislators, farmers, and others concerned with soil and water conservation. **Principal Exhibits:** Equipment, supplies, services, and information on soil and water conservation, including publications.

SOUTH DAKOTA GRAIN AND FEED ASSOCIATION ANNUAL CONVENTION
423 Citizens Bldg.
PO Box 579
Aberdeen, SD 57402-0579
PH: (605)225-7845
FX: (605)225-6506
E-mail: cgaabr@dtgnet.com
Frequency: Annual. **Audience:** Grain firms, elevator owners, managers, directors and employees. **Principal Exhibits:** Equipment and supplies related to elevators, grain and feed industry.

SOUTH DAKOTA STATE FAIR
Box 1275
Huron, SD 57350
PH: (605)353-7340
TF: (800)529-0900
FX: (605)353-7348
Frequency: Annual. **Audience:** General public. **Principal Exhibits:** Agricultural-related equipment, supplies, and services.

SOUTHERN FARM SHOW
PO Box 36859
Charlotte, NC 28236
PH: (704)376-6594
TF: (800)849-0248
FX: (704)376-6345
Frequency: Annual. **Audience:** Farmers, landscapers, farm equipment dealers. **Principal Exhibits:** Agriculture equipment, supplies, and chemicals.

SOUTHERN SEEDSMEN'S ASSOCIATION CONVENTION AND TRADE SHOW
624 27th St.
Lubbock, TX 79404-1406
Frequency: Annual. **Principal Exhibits:** Seed, chemicals, equipment, software, bag and sign.

SOUTHWESTERN EXPOSITION AND LIVESTOCK SHOW
PO Box 150
Fort Worth, TX 76101-0150
PH: (817)877-2400
FX: (817)877-2499
Frequency: Annual. **Audience:** General public. **Principal Exhibits:** Livestock and merchandise.

SPOKANE AG EXPO
1020 W. Riverside
Spokane, WA 99210-2147
PH: (509)747-0077
FX: (509)459-4108
Frequency: Annual. **Audience:** Farmers, ranchers, agribusiness professionals, and general public. **Principal Exhibits:** Farm machinery, technology, and services.

STEER
PO Box 1236
Bismarck, ND 58502
PH: (701)258-4911
FX: (701)258-7684
Frequency: Annual. **Principal Exhibits:** Exhibits related to missionary farming.

STOCKTON AG EXPO
445 W. Weber Ave., Ste. 220
Stockton, CA 95203
PH: (209)547-2960
FX: (209)466-5271
URL: http://www.stocktonchamber.org
Frequency: Annual. **Audience:** Farmers. **Principal Exhibits:** Farm production products, services, and equipment.

SUNBELT AG EXPO
PO Box 28
Tifton, GA 31793
PH: (912)387-7088
FX: (912)387-7503
Frequency: Annual. **Audience:** Farmers and agribusiness people. **Principal Exhibits:** Agricultural equipment, seed and chemical products. Crops are harvested and tilled during the show to demonstrate equipment.

TAN-MISSLARK--NURSERY, GARDEN AND LANDSCAPE SUPPLY SHOW
7730 S. IH-35
Austin, TX 78745-6698
PH: (512)280-5182
TF: (800)880-0343
FX: (512)280-3012
E-mail: plantx@onr.com
URL: http://www.growzone/
Frequency: Annual. **Audience:** Nursery and related trades professionals. **Principal Exhibits:** Plant materials including foliage, bedding plants, trees, palms. Allied products including machinery, equipment and supplies for horticulture industry.

TEXAS PECAN GROWERS CONFERENCE & TRADE SHOW
PO Drawer CC
College Station, TX 77841
PH: (409)846-3285
FX: (409)846-1752
E-mail: psouth@tpga.org
URL: http://www.tpga.org
Frequency: Annual. **Audience:** Pecan growers. **Principal Exhibits:** Pecan growing equipment, supplies, and services.

TEXAS AND SOUTHWESTERN CATTLE RAISERS ASSOCIATION ANNUAL TRADE SHOW
1301 W. 7th St.
Fort Worth, TX 76102
PH: (817)332-7155
TF: (800)242-4820
FX: (817)332-5446
Frequency: Annual. **Audience:** Association members and trade. **Principal Exhibits:** Livestock, agricultural products, trucks, implements, southwest/western apparel and home furnishings.

TIMBER
1477 Chain Bridge, Ste. 200
PO Box 7270
McLean, VA 22101
PH: (703)356-8200
FX: (703)790-7237
E-mail: 76631,1703@compuserve.com
Frequency: Biennial. **Audience:** Lumber trade. **Principal Exhibits:** Chain saws, logging equipment, sawmills, firewood processors, computers, pallet equipment, portable band saws, grinders, kilns, and related equipment, supplies, and services.

TOPEKA FARM SHOW
811 Oakland Ave. W.
PO Box 1067
Austin, MN 55912
PH: (507)437-4697
TF: (800)949-3976
FX: (507)437-8917
E-mail: tradexpo@smig.net
URL: http://www.tradexpos.com
Frequency: Annual. **Audience:** Farmers and ranchers. **Principal Exhibits:** Agricultural and ranch equipment, supplies, and services.

TRIUMPH OF AGRICULTURE EXPOSITION--FARM AND RANCH MACHINERY SHOW
1613 Farnam St., Ste. 666
Omaha, NE 68102-2142
PH: (402)346-8003
TF: (800)475-SHOW
FX: (402)346-5412
Frequency: Annual. **Audience:** Farmers and other agricultural trade. **Principal Exhibits:** Farm equipment and supplies.

TRUCK LOGGERS ASSOCIATION CONVENTION AND TRADE SHOW
815 W. Hastings St., Ste. 725
Vancouver, BC, Canada V6C 1B4
PH: (604)684-4291
FX: (604)684-7134
E-mail: office@truckloggers.com
URL: http://www.truckloggers.com
Frequency: Annual. **Audience:** Trade and general public. **Principal Exhibits:** Forestry related products and equipment, supplies, and services.

TURFGRASS
PO Box 223
White Marsh, MD 21162
PH: (410)335-3700
FX: (410)335-0164
Frequency: Annual. **Audience:** Golf course suppliers, landscapers, commercial dealers, and other trade professionals. **Principal Exhibits:** Golf course equipment, chemicals, fertilizers, soil mixes, top dressings, nursery stock and sand.

UNITED FRESH FRUIT AND VEGETABLE ASSOCIATION ANNUAL CONVENTION AND EXPOSITION
727 N. Washington St.
Alexandria, VA 22314
PH: (703)836-3410
FX: (703)836-7745
E-mail: produce@uffva.org
Frequency: Annual. **Audience:** Growers and shippers; brokers; wholesalers; retailers involved in produce operations; owners and corporate officers of produce companies. **Principal Exhibits:** Equipment, supplies, cartons, packaging machinery, computers, sorting and sizing equipment, harvesting equipment, film wrap manufacturing, and commodity organizations.

WALNUT COUNCIL CONFERENCE
260 S. 1st St., Ste. 2
Zionsville, IN 46077

PH: (317)873-8780
FX: (317)873-8788
E-mail: FhvaAwmaWc@CompuServe.Com
Frequency: Annual. **Audience:** Walnut growers, foresters, landowners, wood industry employees, and university representatives. **Principal Exhibits:** Equipment, supplies, and services for walnut growing.

WESTERN CANADA FARM PROGRESS SHOW
Box 167
Regina, SK, Canada S4P 2Z6
PH: (306)781-9200
FX: (306)781-9396
E-mail: wctps@sk.sympatico.ca
Frequency: Annual. **Audience:** Canadian and American agribusiness people, international buyers. **Principal Exhibits:** Farm equipment and associated industry displays.

WESTERN FAIR FARM SHOW
PO Box 4550
London, ON, Canada N5W 5K3
PH: (519)438-7203
FX: (519)679-3124
E-mail: fair.info@westernfair.on
Frequency: Annual. **Audience:** Farmers, trade professionals, and general public. **Principal Exhibits:** Farm equipment and machinery; feed and fertilizer displays; supplies and services for agribusiness.

WESTERN FARM SHOW
638 W. 39th St.
Kansas City, MO 64111
PH: (816)561-5323
FX: (816)561-1249
URL: http://www.westernfarmshow.com
Frequency: Annual. **Audience:** Farmers, retailers and trade professionals. **Principal Exhibits:** equipment, supplies, and services relating to the agricultural industry.

WESTERN FORESTRY CONFERENCE
4033 SW Canyon Rd.
Portland, OR 97221
PH: (503)226-4562
FX: (503)226-2515
E-mail: wfca@teleport.com
Frequency: Annual. **Audience:** Foresters, forestry technicians, and lumber and timber industry personnel. **Principal Exhibits:** Forestry equipment, including firefighting equipment and supplies, remote sensing services, computer hardware and software, safety equipment, nursery supplies and services.

WESTERNER DAYS
4847 A 19th St.
Red Deer, AB, Canada T4R 2N7
PH: (403)309-0203
FX: (403)341-4699
Frequency: Annual. **Audience:** Trade professionals and general public. **Principal Exhibits:** Commercial exhibits include home care products, personal products, information and educational type space, agricultural and urban exhibits, government and commercial exhibitors, concessions and outside exhibits.

WICHITA FARM AND RANCH SHOW
811 Oakland Ave. W.
PO Box 1067
Austin, MN 55912
PH: (507)437-4697
TF: (800)949-3976
FX: (507)437-8917
E-mail: tradexpo@smig.net
URL: http://www.tradexpos.com
Frequency: Annual. **Audience:** Farmers and ranchers. **Principal Exhibits:** Farm and ranch equipment, supplies, and services, distributors and wholesalers.

WISCONSIN FARM PROGRESS DAYS
University of Wisconsin-Madison
1450 Linden Dr.
Madison, WI 53706
PH: (608)262-2966
FX: (608)262-6055
Frequency: Annual. **Audience:** Farmers, consumers, agribusiness and agency personnel, farm families, youth. **Principal Exhibits:** Agricultural equipment, supplies, and services, family living and youth.

WISCONSIN POTATO AND VEGETABLE INDUSTRY SHOW
PO Box 327
Antigo, WI 54409
PH: (715)623-7683
FX: (715)623-3176
E-mail: wpvga@newnorth.net
Frequency: Annual. **Audience:** Potato and vegetable growers. **Principal Exhibits:** Equipment, chemical companies, production services, financial information, and marketing techniques.

WOOD TECHNOLOGY CLINIC AND SHOW
600 Harrison St.
San Francisco, CA 94107
PH: (415)905-2200
TF: (800)227-4675
FX: (415)905-2232
URL: http://www.mfi.com
Frequency: Annual. **Audience:** Forest industry managers, operations supervisors, consultants, and technicians. **Principal Exhibits:** Equipment, supplies, and services related to the wood products industry, including sawmilling panel production and woodworking.

WOOD TECHNOLOGY PAVILION AT EXPOCORMA
600 Harrison St.
San Francisco, CA 94107
PH: (415)905-2200
TF: (800)227-4675
FX: (415)905-2232
URL: http://www.mfi.com
Frequency: Annual. **Principal Exhibits:** A showcase of the latest in equipment for forestry, forestry services and related activities.

WORLD BEEF EXPO
2820 Walton Commons W., Ste. 101
Madison, WI 53704-6785
Frequency: Annual. **Audience:** Beef producers. **Principal Exhibits:** Equipment, supplies, and services for beef producers.

WORLD DAIRY EXPO
2820 Walton Commons W., Ste. 101
Madison, WI 53704-6785
Frequency: Annual. **Audience:** Dairy producers. **Principal Exhibits:** Equipment, supplies, and services for dairy producers, including cattle.

THE WORLD'S SHOWCASE OF HORTICULTURE
1000 Johnson Ferry Rd., Ste. E-130
Marietta, GA 30068-2100
PH: (770)973-9026
FX: (770)973-9097
E-mail: mail@mail.sna.org
URL: http://www.sna.org
Frequency: Annual. **Audience:** Wholesale and retail nurserymen and suppliers. **Principal Exhibits:** Nursery products, including plants, chemicals, machinery and equipment, soil and soil supplements, and plant containers.

WYOMING STOCK GROWERS ASSOCIATION ANNUAL CONVENTION AND TRADE SHOW
113 E. 20th St.
PO Box 206
Cheyenne, WY 82003

PH: (307)638-3942
FX: (307)635-2524
Frequency: Annual. **Audience:** Ranchers, farmers, agribusiness and government personnel, and rural residents. **Principal Exhibits:** Farm and ranch equipment; scales; solar equipment; video equipment; communications equipment; livestock; animal feed and growth stimulants; rodenticide; animal health and nutritional products; computers.

MASTER INDEX

The Master Index presents company and organization names, names of individuals, SIC industry names, and terms. Each entry in the index is followed by one or more page numbers.

Master Index

Master Index

GEOGRAPHICAL COMPANY INDEX

The Geographical Company Index presents company names by state. Page references are to the company's listing in Chapter 4, Company Directory, in both Part I and Part II.

Alabama

Apac-Alabama Inc, p. 87
B E & K Construction Co, p. 89
Brasfield & Gorrie, LLC, p. 93
Brice Building Co Inc, p. 93
Caddell Construction Co Inc, p. 95
Cuba Timber Co, p. 415
Dixie Lower Timber Company, p. 418
Dunn Investment Co, p. 103
Durbin Marshall Food Corp, p. 419
Flowerwood Nursery Inc, p. 423
Golden Rod Broilers Inc, p. 427
Harbert Corp, p. 112
J E Estes Wood Co Inc, p. 433
Judson Inc, p. 435
MacMillan Bloedel Timberlands, p. 439
Marshall Durbin Farms Inc, p. 440
Mayfield Timber Co Inc, p. 441
Melrose Timber Co, p. 442
Myrick, Batson & Gurosky Inc, p. 132
Peco Farms Inc, p. 449
Resource Management Service, p. 454
Robins and Morton Group, pp. 142-43
Ross Breeders Inc, p. 455
Rust Constructors Inc, p. 144
South Eastern Boll Weevil Era, p. 459
Southland Foods Inc, p. 459
Stallworth & Johnson Inc, p. 460
Stewart-Ledlow Inc, p. 148
Superfos Construction (U.S.), p. 149
Sylvest Farms, Inc, pp. 462-63
Weiss Lake Egg Co Inc, pp. 470-71
White-Spunner Construction, p. 156
Woerner Development Inc, p. 472
Young's Plant Farm Inc, p. 473

Alaska

Annette Island Packing Co, p. 403
Arctic Slope Regional Construction Co, p. 88
Ben A Thomas Inc, p. 406
Haida Corp, p. 429
Klukwan Inc, p. 123
Sealaska Timber Corp, p. 458
Southern Se Reg Aqucltre Assn, p. 459

Arizona

American Fence and Sec Co Inc, p. 86
Arizona Dairy Co, L.L.P., p. 403
Beazer Homes Arizona Inc, p. 91
Bonita Nurseries Inc, p. 407
Chas Roberts A/C Inc, p. 98
Conelly Swinerton Construction Inc, p. 100
Continental Homes Inc, p. 100
D L Withers Construction LC, p. 101
Daniel Enterprises, Inc., p. 101
Eagle Produce Ltd Partnership, p. 419
Emco Harvesting Co, p. 420
Environmental Earthscapes Inc, pp. 420-21
Eurofresh Ltd, p. 421
Farmers Investment Co., p. 422
F.N.F. Construction, Inc., p. 107
Fulton Homes Corp, p. 109

Haydon Building Corp, pp. 113-14
Hickman's Egg Ranch, Inc., p. 431
Homes by Dave Brown, p. 115
Huerta Packing Inc, p. 432
Hunter Contracting Co., p. 116
J-V Farms, Inc., p. 433
Jeffrey C Stone Inc, p. 120
Joe E Woods Inc, p. 120
Kenyon Companies, p. 122
Kitchell Corp, p. 123
Linear Construction, Inc., p. 126
Marlin Packing Co, p. 440
Meadow Valley Corp, p. 130
Meritage Corp, p. 130
Morrison Bros Ranch, p. 444
Northern Pipeline Construction Co, p. 134
Opus West Corp, p. 136
P F F J, Inc, pp. 447-48
Paddock Pool Construction Co., p. 137
Pasquinelli Produce Co, p. 449
Petsmart, Inc., p. 450
Pinal Feeding Co, p. 450
Pulice Construction Inc, p. 140
Rahav Enterprises, Inc, p. 453
Red Rock Cattle Company Inc, p. 454
Red Rock Feeding Co, p. 454
Richmond American Homes, Inc., p. 142
Roberts Enterprises Inc, p. 455
Rousseau Farming Co II, pp. 455-56
Schuff Steel Co, p. 145
Shamrock Farms Co, p. 458
Shasta Industries Inc, p. 146
Stotz Farms Inc, p. 460
Target General Inc, p. 150
Triple A Landscape, p. 466
Underwood Bros Inc, p. 467
Valley Crest Landscape Inc, p. 468
Valley Rain Construction Corp, p. 468
W M Grace Companies Inc, p. 153
Webb Del Corp, p. 155
Wilson Electric Co, Inc., p. 157

Arkansas

Adams Land Co, p. 400
CDI Contractors, LLC, p. 96
Childress Gin & Elevator Co, p. 412
Cobb-Vantress, Inc., p. 413
Delta Cotton Co-Operative Inc, p. 417
E Ritter & Co Inc, p. 419
Erwin-Keith Inc, p. 421
Federal Dryer & Storage Co, p. 422
Hornbeck Seed Co Inc, p. 432
Hudson Foods Inc, p. 432
Koen Farms Inc, p. 436
Latco Inc, pp. 124-25
McClain Enterprises, Inc., p. 441
Peterson Farms, Inc., p. 450
Pine-Belt Inc, p. 450
Portland Gin Co, p. 451
Powell and Powell Milling Inc, p. 451
Taylor & Stuckey Inc, pp. 463-64
Timberland Silvicultural Services, p. 465
Tyson Breeders, Inc., p. 467
Vratsinas Construction Co, p. 153

COMPANY INDEX BY SIC

The Company Index by SIC presents company names arranged by Standard Industrial Classification codes. Page references are to the company's listing in Chapter 4, Company Directory, in both Part I and Part II.

SIC Index

SIC Index

0212 - continued
Premium Gold Angus Beef, Inc, p. 452
Red Rock Cattle Company Inc, p. 454
S and P Cattle Co LLC, p. 456
Thompson Agriplex, Inc., p. 465
Workingman's Friend Oil, Inc, p. 473

0213 - Hogs

Berend Bros Inc, p. 406
Brown's of Carolina, Inc., p. 408
Carroll's Foods Inc, p. 410
Carroll's Foods of Virginia, p. 410
Chappell Farms Inc, p. 411
Christensen Farm & Feedlots Inc, p. 412
Circle Four Farms, p. 412
Coharie Farms, p. 413
Corcpork Co, p. 414
D & D Farms Inc, p. 415
Dekalb Swine Breeders Inc, p. 417
Hastings Pork Corp, p. 430
Huntco Farms, Inc, p. 432
Iowa Select Farms, p. 433
J & K Farms Inc, p. 433
L L Murphrey Co, p. 437
Maxwell Foods Inc., p. 441
Murphy Farms Inc, pp. 444-445
N G Purvis Farms Inc, p. 445
National Hog Farms Inc, p. 445
Orangeburg Foods Inc, p. 447
P F F J, Inc, pp. 447-448
Pennfield Corp, p. 449
Pig Improvement Company, Inc, p. 450
Premier Farms, p. 451
Prestage Farms Inc, p. 452
Quarter M Farms, Inc., p. 453
Seaboard Farms of Oklahoma, p. 458
Swine Graphics Enterprises, LP, p. 462
T D M Farms Inc, p. 464
Texas Farm Inc, p. 464
Valadco Inc, p. 467
Vall Inc, p. 468
Willmar Poultry Farms Inc, p. 472
Wispig LLC, p. 472

0241 - Dairy Farms

A J B Ranch, p. 401
Alliance Dairies, p. 402
Arizona Dairy Co, L.L.P., p. 403
Aurora Dairy Florida LLC, p. 404
Batson Mill L. P., p. 405
Ben A Thomas Inc, p. 406
Charles Donald Pulpwood Inc, p. 411
Columbia Helicopters Inc, p. 413
Columbia West Virginia Corp, pp. 413-414
Crane Mills, p. 415
Croman Corp, p. 415
Delbert L Wheeler, p. 417
Edaleen Dairy Products LLC, p. 420
Erickson Air-Crane Co., LLC, p. 421
Florida North Holsteins LC, p. 423
Foster Dairy Farms, p. 423
Gallo Cattle Co, p. 424
Gilder Timber Inc, p. 426

Gustafson's Dairy Inc, pp. 428-429
Hamilton County Dairy, LLC, p. 429
Herbert C Haynes Inc, p. 430
Hollandia Dairy, p. 431
Hope Land Farm, p. 432
J E Estes Wood Co Inc, p. 433
John Knevelbaard Dairy, pp. 434-435
Lake Superior Land Co, p. 437
Las Uvas Valley Dairy, pp. 437-438
Longview Fibre Co, p. 439
Maddox Dairy, p. 439
Mayfield Timber Co Inc, p. 441
McArthur Farms Inc, p. 441
Miller Shingle Co Inc, p. 443
Oord Dairy, p. 447
P. H. Ranch, Inc, p. 448
Ponderosa Dairy, p. 451
Progressive Dairies Holdings, p. 452
Rayonier Inc., p. 454
Riverview Dairy Inc, p. 455
Shamrock Farms Co, p. 458
Spokane Tribe of Indians, p. 459
Stallworth & Johnson Inc, p. 460
Steve Henderson Logging Inc, p. 460
Stotz Farms Inc, p. 460
Superior Lumber Co Inc, p. 462
Thomas Creek Lumber & Log Co, p. 465
Timberland Management Services Inc, p. 465
Whitfield Timber Inc, p. 471
Woodland Services, Inc, p. 473
Yeomans Wood & Timber Inc, p. 473

0251 - Broiler, Fryer, and Roaster Chickens

Clark's Feed Mills Inc, pp. 412-413
Gentry's Poultry Co Inc, p. 425
Golden Rod Broilers Inc, p. 427
J F C Inc, p. 434
Jack Frost Inc, p. 433
Marshall Durbin Farms Inc, p. 440
Peco Farms Inc, p. 449
Randall Farms, LLC, pp. 453-454
Sanderson Farms Inc, p. 457
Sanderson Farms Production Div, p. 457
Southland Foods Inc, p. 459
Sylvest Farms, Inc, pp. 462-463
Townsends Farms, Inc, p. 466
Zacky Farms Inc, p. 473

0252 - Chicken Eggs

Armstrong Farms, p. 403
Cal-Maine Foods Inc, p. 410
Creighton Brothers LLC, p. 415
Crystal Farms Inc, p. 415
Daylay Egg Farms, Inc, p. 416
Demler Egg Ranch, p. 417
Dorothy Lough, p. 418
Durbin Marshall Food Corp, p. 419
Dutch Country Egg Farms Inc, p. 419
Eggs West, p. 420
Esbenshade Farms, p. 421
G & B Enterprises Ltd, p. 424
Giroux's Poultry Farm Inc, p. 426
Glenwood Foods LLC, p. 426

1542 - continued

Faulkner Group, Inc, p. 106

FCI Constructors, Inc, p. 106

Fisher Development Inc, p. 107

Fletcher Construction Co Hawaii Ltd, p. 107

Flint Industries, Inc, p. 107

Florida Mivan Inc, p. 107

Fontaine Bros Inc, p. 108

Fortney & Weygandt, Inc., p. 108

Fowler-Jones Beers Construction, p. 108

Frank Messer & Sons Construction Co, p. 108

FTR International Inc, p. 108

G B I Construction Inc, p. 109

G E Johnson Construction Co, p. 109

G J F Construction Corp, p. 109

G W Murphy Construction Co, p. 109

Gall, Landau Young Construction Co, p. 109

Gamma Construction Co, p. 109

General Pacific Construction, p. 110

Gerald H Phipps Inc, p. 110

Geupel De Mars Inc, p. 110

Giant Construction Co, p. 110

Global Energy Eqp Group LLC, p. 110

Granger Management Corp, p. 111

Granger Northern Inc, p. 111

H B E Corp, p. 112

H J Russell & Co, p. 112

Hagerman Construction Corp, p. 112

Harbert Corp, p. 112

Harbison-Mahony-Higgins Inc, p. 113

Hardaway Group Inc, p. 113

Hardin Construction Group Inc, p. 113

Hathaway Dinwiddie Construction Group, p. 113

Hawkins Construction Co, p. 113

Henegan Construction Co Inc, p. 114

Henry Bros Co, p. 114

Hensel Phelps Construction Co, p. 114

Hitt Contracting Inc, p. 114

Hog Slat Inc, p. 114

Holder Corp, p. 114

Holzmann, Philipp USA Ltd,, p. 115

Horst Group Inc, p. 115

Howa Construction, Inc, p. 116

Howard S Wright Construction Co, p. 116

Huber Hunt & Nichols Inc, p. 116

Hunt Corp, p. 116

ICI Construction Inc, p. 117

Intech Construction Inc, p. 117

International Energy Corp, p. 117

J A Jones Inc, p. 118

J A Tiberti Construction Co, p. 118

J E Dunn Construction Co, p. 118

J H Findorff & Son Inc, p. 119

J H McCormick Inc, p. 119

J P Cullen & Sons Inc, p. 119

J R Austin Co, p. 119

J R Roberts Enterprises, p. 119

James G Kennedy & Co Inc, p. 119

James McHugh Construction Co, p. 119

Jaynes Corp, p. 120

Jeffrey C Stone Inc, p. 120

John Moriarty & Associates, p. 120

John T Callahan & Sons Inc, p. 120

Jones Brothers Construction Corp, p. 121

Kalikow, H. J. & Co., LLC, p. 121

Keenan, Hopkins, p. 122

Keene Construction Co of Central Florida, p. 122

Keller Construction Co Ltd, p. 122

Kitchell Corp, p. 123

Klinger Companies, Inc, p. 123

Koll Co, p. 123

Kraemer Brothers, LLC, p. 123

Kraft Construction Co, p. 123

Kraus-Anderson, Inc, p. 124

Kvaerner Construction Inc, p. 124

L E Wentz Co, p. 124

L F Driscoll Co, p. 124

Landmark Organization, Inc, p. 124

Latco Inc, pp. 124-125

Lathrop Co Inc, p. 125

Law Co Inc, p. 125

Layton Construction Co, p. 125

LCS Holdings, Inc., p. 125

Lechase Construction Services LLC, p. 125

Lee Kennedy Co Inc, p. 125

Lehr Construction Corp, p. 125

Leopardo Companies, Inc., p. 125

Lewis Lease Crutcher, p. 126

Linbeck Corp, p. 126

Lincoln Builders, Inc, p. 126

Loftin Constructors, Inc., p. 126

Louis P Ciminelli Construction Co, p. 126

LP Snyder Langston, pp. 126-127

Lyda Inc, p. 127

M A Mortenson Companies, p. 127

M & H Enterprises Inc, p. 127

M B Kahn Construction Co Inc, p. 127

M J Anderson Inc, p. 127

M W Builders, Inc, p. 127

Macomber Enterprises, Inc, p. 128

Main Street Operating Co Inc, p. 128

Manhattan Construction Co, p. 128

Market & Johnson, Inc, p. 128

Marshall Erdman & Associates, p. 128

Mascaro Construction Co Lp, p. 128

MBK Construction Ltd, p. 129

McCarthy Building Companies, p. 129

McGough Construction Co, Inc, p. 129

McHugh Enterprises, Inc., p. 129

Michael/Curry Companies, Inc, p. 130

Mitchell Construction Co, p. 131

Myler Co Inc, p. 132

Myrick, Batson & Gurosky Inc, p. 132

Nason & Cullen Group Inc, p. 133

Neenan Co, p. 133

Nielsen Dillingham Builders, p. 134

Ninteman Construction Co, p. 134

N.L. Barnes Construction, Inc, p. 134

Nor-Am Construction Co, p. 134

Norwood Co, pp. 134-135

Nova Corp, p. 135

O & G Industries Inc, p. 135

Obayashi U. S. Holdings Inc, p. 135

OC America Construction Inc, p. 135

Okland Construction Co, pp. 135-136

O'Neil Industries, Inc., p. 135

Opus U.S. Corp, p. 136

Opus West Corp, p. 136

Osman Construction Corp, p. 136

Oxford Holdings, Inc, p. 136

SIC Index

SIC Index

SIC TO NAICS AND NAICS TO SIC CONVERSION GUIDE

This appendix presents complete conversion tables from SIC codes to NAICS codes. SIC stands for *Standard Industrial Classification*, the "old" system of classifying economic activities. NAICS stands for *North American Industry Classification System*, the new classification for classifying economic activities in the United States, Canada, and Mexico.

The first part of the appendix presents the SIC to NAICS Conversion Guide. Four-digit SIC codes and names are shown in bold type. NAICS codes and names are shown beneath, indented, each item labelled "NAICS". An SIC industry may convert to one or more NAICS industries.

The second part, starting on page 715, shows the same information but in the reverse format: the NAICS to SIC Conversion Guide. NAICS codes and names are shown in bold type; the equivalent SIC codes, beneath, are shown indented. A NAICS-coded industry may have one, more than one, or no SIC equivalent (two instances).

SIC TO NAICS CONVERSION GUIDE

AGRICULTURE, FORESTRY, & FISHING

0111 Wheat
NAICS 11114   Wheat Farming
0112 Rice
NAICS 11116   Rice Farming
0115 Corn
NAICS 11115   Corn Farming
0116 Soybeans
NAICS 11111   Soybean Farming
0119 Cash Grains, nec
NAICS 11113   Dry Pea & Bean Farming
NAICS 11112   Oilseed Farming
NAICS 11115   Corn Farming
NAICS 111191 Oilseed & Grain Combination Farming
NAICS 111199 All Other Grain Farming
0131 Cotton
NAICS 11192   Cotton Farming
0132 Tobacco
NAICS 11191   Tobacco Farming
0133 Sugarcane & Sugar Beets
NAICS 111991 Sugar Beet Farming
NAICS 11193   Sugarcane Farming
0134 Irish Potatoes
NAICS 111211 Potato Farming
0139 Field Crops, Except Cash Grains, nec
NAICS 11194   Hay Farming
NAICS 111992 Peanut Farming
NAICS 111219 Other Vegetable & Melon Farming
NAICS 111998 All Other Miscellaneous Crop Farming
0161 Vegetables & Melons
NAICS 111219 Other Vegetable & Melon Farming
0171 Berry Crops
NAICS 111333 Strawberry Farming
NAICS 111334 Berry Farming
0172 Grapes
NAICS 111332 Grape Vineyards
0173 Tree Nuts
NAICS 111335 Tree Nut Farming
0174 Citrus Fruits
NAICS 11131   Orange Groves
NAICS 11132   Citrus Groves
0175 Deciduous Tree Fruits
NAICS 111331 Apple Orchards
NAICS 111339 Other Noncitrus Fruit Farming
0179 Fruits & Tree Nuts, nec
NAICS 111336 Fruit & Tree Nut Combination Farming
NAICS 111339 Other Noncitrus Fruit Farming
0181 Ornamental Floriculture & Nursery Products
NAICS 111422 Floriculture Production
NAICS 111421 Nursery & Tree Production
0182 Food Crops Grown under Cover
NAICS 111411 Mushroom Production
NAICS 111419 Other Food Crops Grown under Cover
0191 General Farms, Primarily Crop
NAICS 111998 All Other Miscellaneous Crop Farming
0211 Beef Cattle Feedlots
NAICS 112112 Cattle Feedlots
0212 Beef Cattle, Except Feedlots
NAICS 112111 Beef Cattle Ranching & Farming

0213 Hogs
NAICS 11221   Hog & Pig Farming
0214 Sheep & Goats
NAICS 11241   Sheep Farming
NAICS 11242   Goat Farming
0219 General Livestock, Except Dairy & Poultry
NAICS 11299   All Other Animal Production
0241 Dairy Farms
NAICS 112111 Beef Cattle Ranching & Farming
NAICS 11212   Dairy Cattle & Milk Production
0251 Broiler, Fryers, & Roaster Chickens
NAICS 11232   Broilers & Other Meat-type Chicken
            Production
0252 Chicken Eggs
NAICS 11231   Chicken Egg Production
0253 Turkey & Turkey Eggs
NAICS 11233   Turkey Production
0254 Poultry Hatcheries
NAICS 11234   Poultry Hatcheries
0259 Poultry & Eggs, nec
NAICS 11239   Other Poultry Production
0271 Fur-bearing Animals & Rabbits
NAICS 11293   Fur-bearing Animal & Rabbit Production
0272 Horses & Other Equines
NAICS 11292   Horse & Other Equine Production
0273 Animal Aquaculture
NAICS 112511 Finfish Farming & Fish Hatcheries
NAICS 112512 Shellfish Farming
NAICS 112519 Other Animal Aquaculture
0279 Animal Specialities, nec
NAICS 11291   Apiculture
NAICS 11299   All Other Animal Production
0291 General Farms, Primarily Livestock & Animal Specialties
NAICS 11299   All Other Animal Production
0711 Soil Preparation Services
NAICS 115112 Soil Preparation, Planting & Cultivating
0721 Crop Planting, Cultivating & Protecting
NAICS 48122   Nonscheduled Speciality Air Transportation
NAICS 115112 Soil Preparation, Planting & Cultivating
0722 Crop Harvesting, Primarily by Machine
NAICS 115113 Crop Harvesting, Primarily by Machine
0723 Crop Preparation Services for Market, Except Cotton Ginning
NAICS 115114 Postharvest Crop Activities
0724 Cotton Ginning
NAICS 115111 Cotton Ginning
0741 Veterinary Service for Livestock
NAICS 54194   Veterinary Services
0742 Veterinary Services for Animal Specialties
NAICS 54194   Veterinary Services
0751 Livestock Services, Except Veterinary
NAICS 311611 Animal Slaughtering
NAICS 11521   Support Activities for Animal Production
0752 Animal Specialty Services, Except Veterinary
NAICS 11521   Support Activities for Animal Production
NAICS 81291   Pet Care Services
0761 Farm Labor Contractors & Crew Leaders
NAICS 115115 Farm Labor Contractors & Crew Leaders
0762 Farm Management Services
NAICS 115116 Farm Management Services
0781 Landscape Counseling & Planning
NAICS 54169   Other Scientific & Technical Consulting
            Services
NAICS 54132   Landscape Architectural Services

0782 Lawn & Garden Services
NAICS 56173 Landscaping Services
0783 Ornamental Shrub & Tree Services
NAICS 56173 Landscaping Services
0811 Timber Tracts
NAICS 111421 Nursery & Tree Production
NAICS 11311 Timber Tract Operations
0831 Forest Nurseries & Gathering of Forest Products
NAICS 111998 All Other Miscellaneous Crop
NAICS 11321 Forest Nurseries & Gathering of Forest
Products
0851 Forestry Services
NAICS 11531 Support Activities for Forestry
0912 Finfish
NAICS 114111 Finfish Fishing
0913 Shellfish
NAICS 114112 Shellfish Fishing
0919 Miscellaneous Marine Products
NAICS 114119 Other Marine Fishing
NAICS 111998 All Other Miscellaneous Crop Farming
0921 Fish Hatcheries & Preserves
NAICS 112511 Finfish Farming & Fish Hatcheries
NAICS 112512 Shellfish Farming
0971 Hunting, Trapping, & Game Propagation
NAICS 11421 Hunting & Trapping

MINING INDUSTRIES

1011 Iron Ores
NAICS 21221 Iron Ore Mining
1021 Copper Ores
NAICS 212234 Copper Ore & Nickel Ore Mining
1031 Lead & Zinc Ores
NAICS 212231 Lead Ore & Zinc Ore Mining
1041 Gold Ores
NAICS 212221 Gold Ore Mining
1044 Silver Ores
NAICS 212222 Silver Ore Mining
1061 Ferroalloy Ores, Except Vanadium
NAICS 212234 Copper Ore & Nickel Ore Mining
NAICS 212299 Other Metal Ore Mining
1081 Metal Mining Services
NAICS 213115 Support Activities for Metal Mining
NAICS 54136 Geophysical Surveying & Mapping Services
1094 Uranium-radium-vanadium Ores
NAICS 212291 Uranium-radium-vanadium Ore Mining
1099 Miscellaneous Metal Ores, nec
NAICS 212299 Other Metal Ore Mining
1221 Bituminous Coal & Lignite Surface Mining
NAICS 212111 Bituminous Coal & Lignite Surface Mining
1222 Bituminous Coal Underground Mining
NAICS 212112 Bituminous Coal Underground Mining
1231 Anthracite Mining
NAICS 212113 Anthracite Mining
1241 Coal Mining Services
NAICS 213114 Support Activities for Coal Mining
1311 Crude Petroleum & Natural Gas
NAICS 211111 Crude Petroleum & Natural Gas Extraction
1321 Natural Gas Liquids
NAICS 211112 Natural Gas Liquid Extraction
1381 Drilling Oil & Gas Wells
NAICS 213111 Drilling Oil & Gas Wells

1382 Oil & Gas Field Exploration Services
NAICS 48122 Nonscheduled Speciality Air Transportation
NAICS 54136 Geophysical Surveying & Mapping Services
NAICS 213112 Support Activities for Oil & Gas Field
Operations
1389 Oil & Gas Field Services, nec
NAICS 213113 Other Oil & Gas Field Support Activities
1411 Dimension Stone
NAICS 212311 Dimension Stone Mining & Quarry
1422 Crushed & Broken Limestone
NAICS 212312 Crushed & Broken Limestone Mining &
Quarrying
1423 Crushed & Broken Granite
NAICS 212313 Crushed & Broken Granite Mining &
Quarrying
1429 Crushed & Broken Stone, nec
NAICS 212319 Other Crushed & Broken Stone Mining &
Quarrying
1442 Construction Sand & Gravel
NAICS 212321 Construction Sand & Gravel Mining
1446 Industrial Sand
NAICS 212322 Industrial Sand Mining
1455 Kaolin & Ball Clay
NAICS 212324 Kaolin & Ball Clay Mining
1459 Clay, Ceramic, & Refractory Minerals, nec
NAICS 212325 Clay & Ceramic & Refractory Minerals Mining
1474 Potash, Soda, & Borate Minerals
NAICS 212391 Potash, Soda, & Borate Mineral Mining
1475 Phosphate Rock
NAICS 212392 Phosphate Rock Mining
1479 Chemical & Fertilizer Mineral Mining, nec
NAICS 212393 Other Chemical & Fertilizer Mineral Mining
1481 Nonmetallic Minerals Services Except Fuels
NAICS 213116 Support Activities for Non-metallic Minerals
NAICS 54136 Geophysical Surveying & Mapping Services
1499 Miscellaneous Nonmetallic Minerals, Except Fuels
NAICS 212319 Other Crushed & Broken Stone Mining or
Quarrying
NAICS 212399 All Other Non-metallic Mineral Mining

CONSTRUCTION INDUSTRIES

1521 General Contractors-single-family Houses
NAICS 23321 Single Family Housing Construction
1522 General Contractors-residential Buildings, Other than
Single-family
NAICS 23332 Commercial & Institutional Building
Construction
NAICS 23322 Multifamily Housing Construction
1531 Operative Builders
NAICS 23321 Single Family Housing Construction
NAICS 23322 Multifamily Housing Construction
NAICS 23331 Manufacturing & Industrial Building
Construction
NAICS 23332 Commercial & Institutional Building
Construction
1541 General Contractors-industrial Buildings & Warehouses
NAICS 23332 Commercial & Institutional Building
Construction
NAICS 23331 Manufacturing & Industrial Building
Construction

1542 General Contractors-nonresidential Buildings, Other than Industrial Buildings & Warehouses
NAICS 23332   Commercial & Institutional Building Construction

1611 Highway & Street Construction, Except Elevated Highways
NAICS 23411   Highway & Street Construction

1622 Bridge, Tunnel, & Elevated Highway Construction
NAICS 23412   Bridge & Tunnel Construction

1623 Water, Sewer, Pipeline, & Communications & Power Line Construction
NAICS 23491   Water, Sewer & Pipeline Construction
NAICS 23492   Power & Communication Transmission Line Construction

1629 Heavy Construction, nec
NAICS 23493   Industrial Nonbuilding Structure Construction
NAICS 23499   All Other Heavy Construction

1711 Plumbing, Heating, & Air-conditioning
NAICS 23511   Plumbing, Heating & Air-conditioning Contractors

1721 Painting & Paper Hanging
NAICS 23521   Painting & Wall Covering Contractors

1731 Electrical Work
NAICS 561621 Security Systems Services
NAICS 23531 Electrical Contractors

1741 Masonry, Stone Setting & Other Stone Work
NAICS 23541   Masonry & Stone Contractors

1742 Plastering, Drywall, Acoustical & Insulation Work
NAICS 23542   Drywall, Plastering, Acoustical & Insulation Contractors

1743 Terrazzo, Tile, Marble, & Mosaic Work
NAICS 23542   Drywall, Plastering, Acoustical & Insulation Contractors
NAICS 23543   Tile, Marble, Terrazzo & Mosaic Contractors

1751 Carpentry Work
NAICS 23551   Carpentry Contractors

1752 Floor Laying & Other Floor Work, nec
NAICS 23552   Floor Laying & Other Floor Contractors

1761 Roofing, Siding, & Sheet Metal Work
NAICS 23561   Roofing, Siding, & Sheet Metal Contractors

1771 Concrete Work
NAICS 23542   Drywall, Plastering, Acoustical & Insulation Contractors
NAICS 23571   Concrete Contractors

1781 Water Well Drilling
NAICS 23581   Water Well Drilling Contractors

1791 Structural Steel Erection
NAICS 23591   Structural Steel Erection Contractors

1793 Glass & Glazing Work
NAICS 23592   Glass & Glazing Contractors

1794 Excavation Work
NAICS 23593   Excavation Contractors

1795 Wrecking & Demolition Work
NAICS 23594   Wrecking & Demolition Contractors

1796 Installation or Erection of Building Equipment, nec
NAICS 23595   Building Equipment & Other Machinery Installation Contractors

1799 Special Trade Contractors, nec
NAICS 23521   Painting & Wall Covering Contractors
NAICS 23592   Glass & Glazing Contractors
NAICS 56291   Remediation Services
NAICS 23599   All Other Special Trade Contractors

FOOD & KINDRED PRODUCTS

2011 Meat Packing Plants
NAICS 311611 Animal Slaughtering

2013 Sausages & Other Prepared Meats
NAICS 311612 Meat Processed from Carcasses

2015 Poultry Slaughtering & Processing
NAICS 311615 Poultry Processing
NAICS 311999 All Other Miscellaneous Food Manufacturing

2021 Creamery Butter
NAICS 311512 Creamery Butter Manufacturing

2022 Natural, Processed, & Imitation Cheese
NAICS 311513 Cheese Manufacturing

2023 Dry, Condensed, & Evaporated Dairy Products
NAICS 311514 Dry, Condensed, & Evaporated Milk Manufacturing

2024 Ice Cream & Frozen Desserts
NAICS 31152   Ice Cream & Frozen Dessert Manufacturing

2026 Fluid Milk
NAICS 311511 Fluid Milk Manufacturing

2032 Canned Specialties
NAICS 311422 Specialty Canning
NAICS 311999 All Other Miscellaneous Food Manufacturing

2033 Canned Fruits, Vegetables, Preserves, Jams, & Jellies
NAICS 311421 Fruit & Vegetable Canning

2034 Dried & Dehydrated Fruits, Vegetables, & Soup Mixes
NAICS 311423 Dried & Dehydrated Food Manufacturing
NAICS 311211 Flour Milling

2035 Pickled Fruits & Vegetables, Vegetables Sauces & Seasonings, & Salad Dressings
NAICS 311421 Fruit & Vegetable Canning
NAICS 311941 Mayonnaise, Dressing, & Other Prepared Sauce Manufacturing

2037 Frozen Fruits, Fruit Juices, & Vegetables
NAICS 311411 Frozen Fruit, Juice, & Vegetable Processing

2038 Frozen Specialties, nec
NAICS 311412 Frozen Specialty Food Manufacturing

2041 Flour & Other Grain Mill Products
NAICS 311211 Flour Milling

2043 Cereal Breakfast Foods
NAICS 31192   Coffee & Tea Manufacturing
NAICS 31123   Breakfast Cereal Manufacturing

2044 Rice Milling
NAICS 311212 Rice Milling

2045 Prepared Flour Mixes & Doughs
NAICS 311822 Flour Mixes & Dough Manufacturing from Purchased Flour

2046 Wet Corn Milling
NAICS 311221 Wet Corn Milling

2047 Dog & Cat Food
NAICS 311111 Dog & Cat Food Manufacturing

2048 Prepared Feed & Feed Ingredients for Animals & Fowls, Except Dogs & Cats
NAICS 311611 Animal Slaughtering
NAICS 311119 Other Animal Food Manufacturing

2051 Bread & Other Bakery Products, Except Cookies & Crackers
NAICS 311812 Commercial Bakeries

2052 Cookies & Crackers
NAICS 311821 Cookie & Cracker Manufacturing
NAICS 311919 Other Snack Food Manufacturing
NAICS 311812 Commercial Bakeries

2053 Frozen Bakery Products, Except Bread
NAICS 311813 Frozen Bakery Product Manufacturing
2061 Cane Sugar, Except Refining
NAICS 311311 Sugarcane Mills
2062 Cane Sugar Refining
NAICS 311312 Cane Sugar Refining
2063 Beet Sugar
NAICS 311313 Beet Sugar Manufacturing
2064 Candy & Other Confectionery Products
NAICS 31133   Confectionery Manufacturing from Purchased
Chocolate
NAICS 31134   Non-chocolate Confectionery Manufacturing
2066 Chocolate & Cocoa Products
NAICS 31132   Chocolate & Confectionery Manufacturing from
Cacao Beans
2067 Chewing Gum
NAICS 31134   Non-chocolate Confectionery Manufacturing
2068 Salted & Roasted Nuts & Seeds
NAICS 311911 Roasted Nuts & Peanut Butter Manufacturing
2074 Cottonseed Oil Mills
NAICS 311223 Other Oilseed Processing
NAICS 311225 Fats & Oils Refining & Blending
2075 Soybean Oil Mills
NAICS 311222 Soybean Processing
NAICS 311225 Fats & Oils Refining & Blending
2076 Vegetable Oil Mills, Except Corn, Cottonseed, & Soybeans
NAICS 311223 Other Oilseed Processing
NAICS 311225 Fats & Oils Refining & Blending
2077 Animal & Marine Fats & Oils
NAICS 311613 Rendering & Meat By-product Processing
NAICS 311711 Seafood Canning
NAICS 311712 Fresh & Frozen Seafood Processing
NAICS 311225 Edible Fats & Oils Manufacturing
2079 Shortening, Table Oils, Margarine, & Other Edible Fats &
Oils, nec
NAICS 311225 Edible Fats & Oils Manufacturing
NAICS 311222 Soybean Processing
NAICS 311223 Other Oilseed Processing
2082 Malt Beverages
NAICS 31212   Breweries
2083 Malt
NAICS 311213 Malt Manufacturing
2084 Wines, Brandy, & Brandy Spirits
NAICS 31213   Wineries
2085 Distilled & Blended Liquors
NAICS 31214   Distilleries
2086 Bottled & Canned Soft Drinks & Carbonated Waters
NAICS 312111 Soft Drink Manufacturing
NAICS 312112 Bottled Water Manufacturing
2087 Flavoring Extracts & Flavoring Syrups nec
NAICS 31193   Flavoring Syrup & Concentrate Manufacturing
NAICS 311942 Spice & Extract Manufacturing
NAICS 311999 All Other Miscellaneous Food Manufacturing
2091 Canned & Cured Fish & Seafood
NAICS 311711 Seafood Canning
2092 Prepared Fresh or Frozen Fish & Seafoods
NAICS 311712 Fresh & Frozen Seafood Processing
2095 Roasted Coffee
NAICS 31192   Coffee & Tea Manufacturing
NAICS 311942 Spice & Extract Manufacturing
2096 Potato Chips, Corn Chips, & Similar Snacks
NAICS 311919 Other Snack Food Manufacturing

2097 Manufactured Ice
NAICS 312113 Ice Manufacturing
2098 Macaroni, Spaghetti, Vermicelli, & Noodles
NAICS 311823 Pasta Manufacturing
2099 Food Preparations, nec
NAICS 311423 Dried & Dehydrated Food Manufacturing
NAICS 111998 All Other Miscellaneous Crop Farming
NAICS 31134   Non-chocolate Confectionery Manufacturing
NAICS 311911 Roasted Nuts & Peanut Butter Manufacturing
NAICS 311991 Perishable Prepared Food Manufacturing
NAICS 31183   Tortilla Manufacturing
NAICS 31192   Coffee & Tea Manufacturing
NAICS 311941 Mayonnaise, Dressing, & Other Prepared Sauce
Manufacturing
NAICS 311942 Spice & Extract Manufacturing
NAICS 311999 All Other Miscellaneous Food Manufacturing

TOBACCO PRODUCTS

2111 Cigarettes
NAICS 312221 Cigarette Manufacturing
2121 Cigars
NAICS 312229 Other Tobacco Product Manufacturing
2131 Chewing & Smoking Tobacco & Snuff
NAICS 312229 Other Tobacco Product Manufacturing
2141 Tobacco Stemming & Redrying
NAICS 312229 Other Tobacco Product Manufacturing
NAICS 31221   Tobacco Stemming & Redrying

TEXTILE MILL PRODUCTS

2211 Broadwoven Fabric Mills, Cotton
NAICS 31321   Broadwoven Fabric Mills
2221 Broadwoven Fabric Mills, Manmade Fiber & Silk
NAICS 31321   Broadwoven Fabric Mills
2231 Broadwoven Fabric Mills, Wool
NAICS 31321   Broadwoven Fabric Mills
NAICS 313311 Broadwoven Fabric Finishing Mills
NAICS 313312 Textile & Fabric Finishing Mills
2241 Narrow Fabric & Other Smallware Mills: Cotton, Wool,
Silk, & Manmade Fiber
NAICS 313221 Narrow Fabric Mills
2251 Women's Full-length & Knee-length Hosiery, Except Socks
NAICS 315111 Sheer Hosiery Mills
2252 Hosiery, nec
NAICS 315111 Sheer Hosiery Mills
NAICS 315119 Other Hosiery & Sock Mills
2253 Knit Outerwear Mills
NAICS 315191 Outerwear Knitting Mills
2254 Knit Underwear & Nightwear Mills
NAICS 315192 Underwear & Nightwear Knitting Mills
2257 Weft Knit Fabric Mills
NAICS 313241 Weft Knit Fabric Mills
NAICS 313312 Textile & Fabric Finishing Mills
2258 Lace & Warp Knit Fabric Mills
NAICS 313249 Other Knit Fabric & Lace Mills
NAICS 313312 Textile & Fabric Finishing Mills
2259 Knitting Mills, nec
NAICS 315191 Outerwear Knitting Mills
NAICS 315192 Underwear & Nightwear Knitting Mills
NAICS 313241 Weft Knit Fabric Mills
NAICS 313249 Other Knit Fabric & Lace Mills

2261 Finishers of Broadwoven Fabrics of Cotton
NAICS 313311 Broadwoven Fabric Finishing Mills
2262 Finishers of Broadwoven Fabrics of Manmade Fiber & Silk
NAICS 313311 Broadwoven Fabric Finishing Mills
2269 Finishers of Textiles, nec
NAICS 313311 Broadwoven Fabric Finishing Mills
NAICS 313312 Textile & Fabric Finishing Mills
2273 Carpets & Rugs
NAICS 31411　Carpet & Rug Mills
2281 Yarn Spinning Mills
NAICS 313111 Yarn Spinning Mills
2282 Yarn Texturizing, Throwing, Twisting, & Winding Mills
NAICS 313112 Yarn Texturing, Throwing & Twisting Mills
NAICS 313312 Textile & Fabric Finishing Mills
2284 Thread Mills
NAICS 313113 Thread Mills
NAICS 313312 Textile & Fabric Finishing Mills
2295 Coated Fabrics, Not Rubberized
NAICS 31332　Fabric Coating Mills
2296 Tire Cord & Fabrics
NAICS 314992 Tire Cord & Tire Fabric Mills
2297 Nonwoven Fabrics
NAICS 31323　Nonwoven Fabric Mills
2298 Cordage & Twine
NAICS 314991 Rope, Cordage & Twine Mills
2299 Textile Goods, nec
NAICS 31321　Broadwoven Fabric Mills
NAICS 31323　Nonwoven Fabric Mills
NAICS 313312 Textile & Fabric Finishing Mills
NAICS 313221 Narrow Fabric Mills
NAICS 313113 Thread Mills
NAICS 313111 Yarn Spinning Mills
NAICS 314999 All Other Miscellaneous Textile Product Mills

APPAREL & OTHER FINISHED PRODUCTS MADE FROM FABRICS & SIMILAR MATERIALS

2311 Men's & Boys' Suits, Coats & Overcoats
NAICS 315211 Men's & Boys' Cut & Sew Apparel Contractors
NAICS 315222 Men's & Boys' Cut & Sew Suit, Coat, & Overcoat Manufacturing
2321 Men's & Boys' Shirts, Except Work Shirts
NAICS 315211 Men's & Boys' Cut & Sew Apparel Contractors
NAICS 315223 Men's & Boys' Cut & Sew Shirt, Manufacturing
2322 Men's & Boys' Underwear & Nightwear
NAICS 315211 Men's & Boys' Cut & Sew Apparel Contractors
NAICS 315221 Men's & Boys' Cut & Sew Underwear & Nightwear Manufacturing
2323 Men's & Boys' Neckwear
NAICS 315993 Men's & Boys' Neckwear Manufacturing
2325 Men's & Boys' Trousers & Slacks
NAICS 315211 Men's & Boys' Cut & Sew Apparel Contractors
NAICS 315224 Men's & Boys' Cut & Sew Trouser, Slack, & Jean Manufacturing
2326 Men's & Boys' Work Clothing
NAICS 315211 Men's & Boys' Cut & Sew Apparel Contractors
NAICS 315225 Men's & Boys' Cut & Sew Work Clothing Manufacturing
2329 Men's & Boys' Clothing, nec
NAICS 315211 Men's & Boys' Cut & Sew Apparel Contractors

NAICS 315228 Men's & Boys' Cut & Sew Other Outerwear Manufacturing
NAICS 315299 All Other Cut & Sew Apparel Manufacturing
2331 Women's, Misses', & Juniors' Blouses & Shirts
NAICS 315212 Women's & Girls' Cut & Sew Apparel Contractors
NAICS 315232 Women's & Girls' Cut & Sew Blouse & Shirt Manufacturing
2335 Women's, Misses' & Junior's Dresses
NAICS 315212 Women's & Girls' Cut & Sew Apparel Contractors
NAICS 315233 Women's & Girls' Cut & Sew Dress Manufacturing
2337 Women's, Misses' & Juniors' Suits, Skirts & Coats
NAICS 315212 Women's & Girls' Cut & Sew Apparel Contractors
NAICS 315234 Women's & Girls' Cut & Sew Suit, Coat, Tailored Jacket, & Skirt Manufacturing
2339 Women's, Misses' & Juniors' Outerwear, nec
NAICS 315999 Other Apparel Accessories & Other Apparel Manufacturing
NAICS 315212 Women's & Girls' Cut & Sew Apparel Contractors
NAICS 315299 All Other Cut & Sew Apparel Manufacturing
NAICS 315238 Women's & Girls' Cut & Sew Other Outerwear Manufacturing
2341 Women's, Misses, Children's, & Infants' Underwear & Nightwear
NAICS 315212 Women's & Girls' Cut & Sew Apparel Contractors
NAICS 315211 Men's & Boys' Cut & Sew Apparel Contractors
NAICS 315231 Women's & Girls' Cut & Sew Lingerie, Loungewear, & Nightwear Manufacturing
NAICS 315221 Men's & Boys' Cut & Sew Underwear & Nightwear Manufacturing
NAICS 315291 Infants' Cut & Sew Apparel Manufacturing
2342 Brassieres, Girdles, & Allied Garments
NAICS 315212 Women's & Girls' Cut & Sew Apparel Contractors
NAICS 315231 Women's & Girls' Cut & Sew Lingerie, Loungewear, & Nightwear Manufacturing
2353 Hats, Caps, & Millinery
NAICS 315991 Hat, Cap, & Millinery Manufacturing
2361 Girls', Children's & Infants' Dresses, Blouses & Shirts
NAICS 315291 Infants' Cut & Sew Apparel Manufacturing
NAICS 315223 Men's & Boys' Cut & Sew Shirt, Manufacturing
NAICS 315211 Men's & Boys' Cut & Sew Apparel Contractors
NAICS 315232 Women's & Girls' Cut & Sew Blouse & Shirt Manufacturing
NAICS 315233 Women's & Girls' Cut & Sew Dress Manufacturing
NAICS 315212 Women's & Girls' Cut & Sew Apparel Contractors
2369 Girls', Children's & Infants' Outerwear, nec
NAICS 315291 Infants' Cut & Sew Apparel Manufacturing
NAICS 315222 Men's & Boys' Cut & Sew Suit, Coat, & Overcoat Manufacturing
NAICS 315224 Men's & Boys' Cut & Sew Trouser, Slack, & Jean Manufacturing
NAICS 315228 Men's & Boys' Cut & Sew Other Outerwear Manufacturing
NAICS 315221 Men's & Boys' Cut & Sew Underwear & Nightwear Manufacturing
NAICS 315211 Men's & Boys' Cut & Sew Apparel Contractors

NAICS 315234 Women's & Girls' Cut & Sew Suit, Coat, Tailored Jacket, & Skirt Manufacturing

NAICS 315238 Women's & Girls' Cut & Sew Other Outerwear Manufacturing

NAICS 315231 Women's & Girls' Cut & Sew Lingerie, Loungewear, & Nightwear Manufacturing

NAICS 315212 Women's & Girls' Cut & Sew Apparel Contractors

2371 Fur Goods

NAICS 315292 Fur & Leather Apparel Manufacturing

2381 Dress & Work Gloves, Except Knit & All-leather

NAICS 315992 Glove & Mitten Manufacturing

2384 Robes & Dressing Gowns

NAICS 315231 Women's & Girls' Cut & Sew Lingerie, Loungewear, & Nightwear Manufacturing

NAICS 315221 Men's & Boys' Cut & Sew Underwear & Nightwear Manufacturing

NAICS 315211 Men's & Boys' Cut & Sew Apparel Contractors

NAICS 315212 Women's & Girls' Cut & Sew Apparel Contractors

2385 Waterproof Outerwear

NAICS 315222 Men's & Boys' Cut & Sew Suit, Coat, & Overcoat Manufacturing

NAICS 315234 Women's & Girls' Cut & Sew Suit, Coat, Tailored Jacket, & Skirt Manufacturing

NAICS 315228 Men's & Boys' Cut & Sew Other Outerwear Manufacturing

NAICS 315238 Women's & Girls' Cut & Sew Other Outerwear Manufacturing

NAICS 315291 Infants' Cut & Sew Apparel Manufacturing

NAICS 315999 Other Apparel Accessories & Other Apparel Manufacturing

NAICS 315211 Men's & Boys' Cut & Sew Apparel Contractors

NAICS 315212 Women's & Girls' Cut & Sew Apparel Contractors

2386 Leather & Sheep-lined Clothing

NAICS 315292 Fur & Leather Apparel Manufacturing

2387 Apparel Belts

NAICS 315999 Other Apparel Accessories & Other Apparel Manufacturing

2389 Apparel & Accessories, nec

NAICS 315999 Other Apparel Accessories & Other Apparel Manufacturing

NAICS 315299 All Other Cut & Sew Apparel Manufacturing

NAICS 315231 Women's & Girls' Cut & Sew Lingerie, Loungewear, & Nightwear Manufacturing

NAICS 315212 Women's & Girls' Cut & Sew Apparel Contractors

NAICS 315211 Mens' & Boys' Cut & Sew Apparel Contractors

2391 Curtains & Draperies

NAICS 314121 Curtain & Drapery Mills

2392 Housefurnishings, Except Curtains & Draperies

NAICS 314911 Textile Bag Mills

NAICS 339994 Broom, Brush & Mop Manufacturing

NAICS 314129 Other Household Textile Product Mills

2393 Textile Bags

NAICS 314911 Textile Bag Mills

2394 Canvas & Related Products

NAICS 314912 Canvas & Related Product Mills

2395 Pleating, Decorative & Novelty Stitching, & Tucking for the Trade

NAICS 314999 All Other Miscellaneous Textile Product Mills

NAICS 315211 Mens' & Boys' Cut & Sew Apparel Contractors

NAICS 315212 Women's & Girls' Cut & Sew Apparel Contractors

2396 Automotive Trimmings, Apparel Findings, & Related Products

NAICS 33636 Motor Vehicle Fabric Accessories & Seat Manufacturing

NAICS 315999 Other Apparel Accessories, & Other Apparel Manufacturing

NAICS 323113 Commercial Screen Printing

NAICS 314999 All Other Miscellaneous Textile Product Mills

2397 Schiffli Machine Embroideries

NAICS 313222 Schiffli Machine Embroidery

2399 Fabricated Textile Products, nec

NAICS 33636 Motor Vehicle Fabric Accessories & Seat Manufacturing

NAICS 315999 Other Apparel Accessories & Other Apparel Manufacturing

NAICS 314999 All Other Miscellaneous Textile Product Mills

LUMBER & WOOD PRODUCTS, EXCEPT FURNITURE

2411 Logging

NAICS 11331 Logging

2421 Sawmills & Planing Mills, General

NAICS 321913 Softwood Cut Stock, Resawing Lumber, & Planing

NAICS 321113 Sawmills

NAICS 321914 Other Millwork

NAICS 321999 All Other Miscellaneous Wood Product Manufacturing

2426 Hardwood Dimension & Flooring Mills

NAICS 321914 Other Millwork

NAICS 321999 All Other Miscellaneous Wood Product Manufacturing

NAICS 337139 Other Wood Furniture Manufacturing

NAICS 321912 Hardwood Dimension Mills

2429 Special Product Sawmills, nec

NAICS 321113 Sawmills

NAICS 321913 Softwood Cut Stock, Resawing Lumber, & Planing

NAICS 321999 All Other Miscellaneous Wood Product Manufacturing

2431 Millwork

NAICS 321911 Wood Window & Door Manufacturing

NAICS 321914 Other Millwork

2434 Wood Kitchen Cabinets

NAICS 337131 Wood Kitchen Cabinet & Counter Top Manufacturing

2435 Hardwood Veneer & Plywood

NAICS 321211 Hardwood Veneer & Plywood Manufacturing

2436 Softwood Veneer & Plywood

NAICS 321212 Softwood Veneer & Plywood Manufacturing

2439 Structural Wood Members, nec

NAICS 321913 Softwood Cut Stock, Resawing Lumber, & Planing

NAICS 321214 Truss Manufacturing

NAICS 321213 Engineered Wood Member Manufacturing

2441 Nailed & Lock Corner Wood Boxes & Shook

NAICS 32192 Wood Container & Pallet Manufacturing

2448 Wood Pallets & Skids

NAICS 32192 Wood Container & Pallet Manufacturing

2449 Wood Containers, nec
NAICS 32192   Wood Container & Pallet Manufacturing
2451 Mobile Homes
NAICS 321991 Manufactured Home Manufacturing
2452 Prefabricated Wood Buildings & Components
NAICS 321992 Prefabricated Wood Building Manufacturing
2491 Wood Preserving
NAICS 321114 Wood Preservation
2493 Reconstituted Wood Products
NAICS 321219 Reconstituted Wood Product Manufacturing
2499 Wood Products, nec
NAICS 339999 All Other Miscellaneous Manufacturing
NAICS 337139 Other Wood Furniture Manufacturing
NAICS 337148 Other Nonwood Furniture Manufacturing
NAICS 32192   Wood Container & Pallet Manufacturing
NAICS 321999 All Other Miscellaneous Wood Product
            Manufacturing

FURNITURE & FIXTURES

2511 Wood Household Furniture, Except Upholstered
NAICS 337122 Wood Household Furniture Manufacturing
2512 Wood Household Furniture, Upholstered
NAICS 337121 Upholstered Household Furniture
            Manufacturing
2514 Metal Household Furniture
NAICS 337124 Metal Household Furniture Manufacturing
2515 Mattresses, Foundations, & Convertible Beds
NAICS 33791   Mattress Manufacturing
NAICS 337132 Upholstered Wood Household Furniture
            Manufacturing
2517 Wood Television, Radio, Phonograph & Sewing Machine Cabinets
NAICS 337139 Other Wood Furniture Manufacturing
2519 Household Furniture, nec
NAICS 337143 Household Furniture (except Wood & Metal)
            Manufacturing
2521 Wood Office Furniture
NAICS 337134 Wood Office Furniture Manufacturing
2522 Office Furniture, Except Wood
NAICS 337141 Nonwood Office Furniture Manufacturing
2531 Public Building & Related Furniture
NAICS 33636   Motor Vehicle Fabric Accessories & Seat
            Manufacturing
NAICS 337139 Other Wood Furniture Manufacturing
NAICS 337148 Other Nonwood Furniture Manufacturing
NAICS 339942 Lead Pencil & Art Good Manufacturing
2541 Wood Office & Store Fixtures, Partitions, Shelving, & Lockers
NAICS 337131 Wood Kitchen Cabinet & Counter Top
            Manufacturing
NAICS 337135 Custom Architectural Woodwork, Millwork, &
            Fixtures
NAICS 337139 Other Wood Furniture Manufacturing
2542 Office & Store Fixtures, Partitions Shelving, & Lockers, Except Wood
NAICS 337145 Nonwood Showcase, Partition, Shelving, &
            Locker Manufacturing
2591 Drapery Hardware & Window Blinds & Shades
NAICS 33792   Blind & Shade Manufacturing
2599 Furniture & Fixtures, nec
NAICS 339113 Surgical Appliance & Supplies Manufacturing
NAICS 337139 Other Wood Furniture Manufacturing

NAICS 337148 Other Nonwood Furniture Manufacturing

PAPER & ALLIED PRODUCTS

2611 Pulp Mills
NAICS 32211   Pulp Mills
NAICS 322121 Paper Mills
NAICS 32213   Paperboard Mills
2621 Paper Mills
NAICS 322121 Paper Mills
NAICS 322122 Newsprint Mills
2631 Paperboard Mills
NAICS 32213   Paperboard Mills
2652 Setup Paperboard Boxes
NAICS 322213 Setup Paperboard Box Manufacturing
2653 Corrugated & Solid Fiber Boxes
NAICS 322211 Corrugated & Solid Fiber Box Manufacturing
2655 Fiber Cans, Tubes, Drums, & Similar Products
NAICS 322214 Fiber Can, Tube, Drum, & Similar Products
            Manufacturing
2656 Sanitary Food Containers, Except Folding
NAICS 322215 Non-folding Sanitary Food Container
            Manufacturing
2657 Folding Paperboard Boxes, Including Sanitary
NAICS 322212 Folding Paperboard Box Manufacturing
2671 Packaging Paper & Plastics Film, Coated & Laminated
NAICS 322221 Coated & Laminated Packaging Paper &
            Plastics Film Manufacturing
NAICS 326112 Unsupported Plastics Packaging Film & Sheet
            Manufacturing
2672 Coated & Laminated Paper, nec
NAICS 322222 Coated & Laminated Paper Manufacturing
2673 Plastics, Foil, & Coated Paper Bags
NAICS 322223 Plastics, Foil, & Coated Paper Bag
            Manufacturing
NAICS 326111 Unsupported Plastics Bag Manufacturing
2674 Uncoated Paper & Multiwall Bags
NAICS 322224 Uncoated Paper & Multiwall Bag
            Manufacturing
2675 Die-cut Paper & Paperboard & Cardboard
NAICS 322231 Die-cut Paper & Paperboard Office Supplies
            Manufacturing
NAICS 322292 Surface-coated Paperboard Manufacturing
NAICS 322298 All Other Converted Paper Product
            Manufacturing
2676 Sanitary Paper Products
NAICS 322291 Sanitary Paper Product Manufacturing
2677 Envelopes
NAICS 322232 Envelope Manufacturing
2678 Stationery, Tablets, & Related Products
NAICS 322233 Stationery, Tablet, & Related Product
            Manufacturing
2679 Converted Paper & Paperboard Products, nec
NAICS 322215 Non-folding Sanitary Food Container
            Manufacturing
NAICS 322222 Coated & Laminated Paper Manufacturing
NAICS 322231 Die-cut Paper & Paperboard Office Supplies
            Manufacturing
NAICS 322298 All Other Converted Paper Product
            Manufacturing

PRINTING, PUBLISHING, & ALLIED INDUSTRIES

2711 Newspapers: Publishing, or Publishing & Printing
NAICS 51111   Newspaper Publishers
2721 Periodicals: Publishing, or Publishing & Printing
NAICS 51112   Periodical Publishers
2731 Books: Publishing, or Publishing & Printing
NAICS 51223   Music Publishers
NAICS 51113   Book Publishers
2732 Book Printing
NAICS 323117 Book Printing
2741 Miscellaneous Publishing
NAICS 51114   Database & Directory Publishers
NAICS 51223   Music Publishers
NAICS 511199 All Other Publishers
2752 Commercial Printing, Lithographic
NAICS 323114 Quick Printing
NAICS 323110 Commercial Lithographic Printing
2754 Commercial Printing, Gravure
NAICS 323111 Commercial Gravure Printing
2759 Commercial Printing, nec
NAICS 323113 Commercial Screen Printing
NAICS 323112 Commercial Flexographic Printing
NAICS 323114 Quick Printing
NAICS 323115 Digital Printing
NAICS 323119 Other Commercial Printing
2761 Manifold Business Forms
NAICS 323116 Manifold Business Form Printing
2771 Greeting Cards
NAICS 323110 Commercial Lithographic Printing
NAICS 323111 Commercial Gravure Printing
NAICS 323112 Commercial Flexographic Printing
NAICS 323113 Commercial Screen Printing
NAICS 323119 Other Commercial Printing
NAICS 511191 Greeting Card Publishers
2782 Blankbooks, Loose-leaf Binders & Devices
NAICS 323110 Commercial Lithographic Printing
NAICS 323111 Commercial Gravure Printing
NAICS 323112 Commercial Flexographic Printing
NAICS 323113 Commercial Screen Printing
NAICS 323119 Other Commercial Printing
NAICS 323118 Blankbook, Loose-leaf Binder & Device
         Manufacturing
2789 Bookbinding & Related Work
NAICS 323121 Tradebinding & Related Work
2791 Typesetting
NAICS 323122 Prepress Services
2796 Platemaking & Related Services
NAICS 323122 Prepress Services

CHEMICALS & ALLIED PRODUCTS

2812 Alkalies & Chlorine
NAICS 325181 Alkalies & Chlorine Manufacturing
2813 Industrial Gases
NAICS 32512   Industrial Gas Manufacturing
2816 Inorganic Pigments
NAICS 325131 Inorganic Dye & Pigment Manufacturing
NAICS 325182 Carbon Black Manufacturing
2819 Industrial Inorganic Chemicals, nec
NAICS 325998 All Other Miscellaneous Chemical Product
         Manufacturing

NAICS 331311 Alumina Refining
NAICS 325131 Inorganic Dye & Pigment Manufacturing
NAICS 325188 All Other Basic Inorganic Chemical
         Manufacturing
2821 Plastics Material Synthetic Resins, & Nonvulcanizable Elastomers
NAICS 325211 Plastics Material & Resin Manufacturing
2822 Synthetic Rubber
NAICS 325212 Synthetic Rubber Manufacturing
2823 Cellulosic Manmade Fibers
NAICS 325221 Cellulosic Manmade Fiber Manufacturing
2824 Manmade Organic Fibers, Except Cellulosic
NAICS 325222 Noncellulosic Organic Fiber Manufacturing
2833 Medicinal Chemicals & Botanical Products
NAICS 325411 Medicinal & Botanical Manufacturing
2834 Pharmaceutical Preparations
NAICS 325412 Pharmaceutical Preparation Manufacturing
2835 In Vitro & in Vivo Diagnostic Substances
NAICS 325412 Pharmaceutical Preparation Manufacturing
NAICS 325413 In-vitro Diagnostic Substance Manufacturing
2836 Biological Products, Except Diagnostic Substances
NAICS 325414 Biological Product Manufacturing
2841 Soaps & Other Detergents, Except Speciality Cleaners
NAICS 325611 Soap & Other Detergent Manufacturing
2842 Speciality Cleaning, Polishing, & Sanitary Preparations
NAICS 325612 Polish & Other Sanitation Good Manufacturing
2843 Surface Active Agents, Finishing Agents, Sulfonated Oils, & Assistants
NAICS 325613 Surface Active Agent Manufacturing
2844 Perfumes, Cosmetics, & Other Toilet Preparations
NAICS 32562   Toilet Preparation Manufacturing
NAICS 325611 Soap & Other Detergent Manufacturing
2851 Paints, Varnishes, Lacquers, Enamels, & Allied Products
NAICS 32551   Paint & Coating Manufacturing
2861 Gum & Wood Chemicals
NAICS 325191 Gum & Wood Chemical Manufacturing
2865 Cyclic Organic Crudes & Intermediates, & Organic Dyes & Pigments
NAICS 32511   Petrochemical Manufacturing
NAICS 325132 Organic Dye & Pigment Manufacturing
NAICS 325192 Cyclic Crude & Intermediate Manufacturing
2869 Industrial Organic Chemicals, nec
NAICS 32511   Petrochemical Manufacturing
NAICS 325188 All Other Inorganic Chemical Manufacturing
NAICS 325193 Ethyl Alcohol Manufacturing
NAICS 32512   Industrial Gas Manufacturing
NAICS 325199 All Other Basic Organic Chemical
         Manufacturing
2873 Nitrogenous Fertilizers
NAICS 325311 Nitrogenous Fertilizer Manufacturing
2874 Phosphatic Fertilizers
NAICS 325312 Phosphatic Fertilizer Manufacturing
2875 Fertilizers, Mixing Only
NAICS 325314 Fertilizer Manufacturing
2879 Pesticides & Agricultural Chemicals, nec
NAICS 32532   Pesticide & Other Agricultural Chemical
         Manufacturing
2891 Adhesives & Sealants
NAICS 32552   Adhesive & Sealant Manufacturing
2892 Explosives
NAICS 32592   Explosives Manufacturing
2893 Printing Ink
NAICS 32591   Printing Ink Manufacturing

2895 Carbon Black
NAICS 325182 Carbon Black Manufacturing
2899 Chemicals & Chemical Preparations, nec
NAICS 32551 Paint & Coating Manufacturing
NAICS 311942 Spice & Extract Manufacturing
NAICS 325199 All Other Basic Organic Chemical
　　　　　Manufacturing
NAICS 325998 All Other Miscellaneous Chemical Product
　　　　　Manufacturing

PETROLEUM REFINING & RELATED INDUSTRIES

2911 Petroleum Refining
NAICS 32411 Petroleum Refineries
2951 Asphalt Paving Mixtures & Blocks
NAICS 324121 Asphalt Paving Mixture & Block Manufacturing
2952 Asphalt Felts & Coatings
NAICS 324122 Asphalt Shingle & Coating Materials
　　　　　Manufacturing
2992 Lubricating Oils & Greases
NAICS 324191 Petroleum Lubricating Oil & Grease
　　　　　Manufacturing 2999

RUBBER & MISCELLANEOUS PLASTICS PRODUCTS

3011 Tires & Inner Tubes
NAICS 326211 Tire Manufacturing
3021 Rubber & Plastics Footwear
NAICS 316211 Rubber & Plastics Footwear Manufacturing
3052 Rubber & Plastics Hose & Belting
NAICS 32622 Rubber & Plastics Hoses & Belting
　　　　　Manufacturing
3053 Gaskets, Packing, & Sealing Devices
NAICS 339991 Gasket, Packing, & Sealing Device
　　　　　Manufacturing
**3061 Molded, Extruded, & Lathe-cut Mechanical Rubber
　　　Products**
NAICS 326291 Rubber Product Manufacturing for Mechanical
　　　　　Use
3069 Fabricated Rubber Products, nec
NAICS 31332 Fabric Coating Mills
NAICS 326192 Resilient Floor Covering Manufacturing
NAICS 326299 All Other Rubber Product Manufacturing
3081 Unsupported Plastics Film & Sheet
NAICS 326113 Unsupported Plastics Film & Sheet
　　　　　Manufacturing
3082 Unsupported Plastics Profile Shapes
NAICS 326121 Unsupported Plastics Profile Shape
　　　　　Manufacturing
3083 Laminated Plastics Plate, Sheet, & Profile Shapes
NAICS 32613 Laminated Plastics Plate, Sheet, & Shape
　　　　　Manufacturing
3084 Plastic Pipe
NAICS 326122 Plastic Pipe & Pipe Fitting Manufacturing
3085 Plastics Bottles
NAICS 32616 Plastics Bottle Manufacturing
3086 Plastics Foam Products
NAICS 32615 Urethane & Other Foam Product
　　　　　Manufacturing
NAICS 32614 Polystyrene Foam Product Manufacturing

3087 Custom Compounding of Purchased Plastics Resins
NAICS 325991 Custom Compounding of Purchased Resin
3088 Plastics Plumbing Fixtures
NAICS 326191 Plastics Plumbing Fixtures Manufacturing
3089 Plastics Products, nec
NAICS 326122 Plastics Pipe & Pipe Fitting Manufacturing
NAICS 326121 Unsupported Plastics Profile Shape
　　　　　Manufacturing
NAICS 326199 All Other Plastics Product Manufacturing

LEATHER & LEATHER PRODUCTS

3111 Leather Tanning & Finishing
NAICS 31611 Leather & Hide Tanning & Finishing
3131 Boot & Shoe Cut Stock & Findings
NAICS 321999 All Other Miscellaneous Wood Product
　　　　　Manufacturing
NAICS 339993 Fastener, Button, Needle, & Pin Manufacturing
NAICS 316999 All Other Leather Good Manufacturing
3142 House Slippers
NAICS 316212 House Slipper Manufacturing
3143 Men's Footwear, Except Athletic
NAICS 316213 Men's Footwear Manufacturing
3144 Women's Footwear, Except Athletic
NAICS 316214 Women's Footwear Manufacturing
3149 Footwear, Except Rubber, nec
NAICS 316219 Other Footwear Manufacturing
3151 Leather Gloves & Mittens
NAICS 315992 Glove & Mitten Manufacturing
3161 Luggage
NAICS 316991 Luggage Manufacturing
3171 Women's Handbags & Purses
NAICS 316992 Women's Handbag & Purse Manufacturing
**3172 Personal Leather Goods, Except Women's Handbags &
　　　Purses**
NAICS 316993 Personal Leather Good Manufacturing
3199 Leather Goods, nec
NAICS 316999 All Other Leather Good Manufacturing

STONE, CLAY, GLASS, & CONCRETE PRODUCTS

3211 Flat Glass
NAICS 327211 Flat Glass Manufacturing
3221 Glass Containers
NAICS 327213 Glass Container Manufacturing
3229 Pressed & Blown Glass & Glassware, nec
NAICS 327212 Other Pressed & Blown Glass & Glassware
　　　　　Manufacturing
3231 Glass Products, Made of Purchased Glass
NAICS 327215 Glass Product Manufacturing Made of
　　　　　Purchased Glass
3241 Cement, Hydraulic
NAICS 32731 Hydraulic Cement Manufacturing
3251 Brick & Structural Clay Tile
NAICS 327121 Brick & Structural Clay Tile Manufacturing
3253 Ceramic Wall & Floor Tile
NAICS 327122 Ceramic Wall & Floor Tile Manufacturing
3255 Clay Refractories
NAICS 327124 Clay Refractory Manufacturing

3259 Structural Clay Products, nec
NAICS 327123 Other Structural Clay Product Manufacturing

3261 Vitreous China Plumbing Fixtures & China & Earthenware Fittings & Bathroom Accessories
NAICS 327111 Vitreous China Plumbing Fixture & China & Earthenware Fittings & Bathroom Accessories Manufacturing

3262 Vitreous China Table & Kitchen Articles
NAICS 327112 Vitreous China, Fine Earthenware & Other Pottery Product Manufacturing

3263 Fine Earthenware Table & Kitchen Articles
NAICS 327112 Vitreous China, Fine Earthenware & Other Pottery Product Manufacturing

3264 Porcelain Electrical Supplies
NAICS 327113 Porcelain Electrical Supply Manufacturing

3269 Pottery Products, nec
NAICS 327112 Vitreous China, Fine Earthenware, & Other Pottery Product Manufacturing

3271 Concrete Block & Brick
NAICS 327331 Concrete Block & Brick Manufacturing

3272 Concrete Products, Except Block & Brick
NAICS 327999 All Other Miscellaneous Nonmetallic Mineral Product Manufacturing
NAICS 327332 Concrete Pipe Manufacturing
NAICS 32739 Other Concrete Product Manufacturing

3273 Ready-mixed Concrete
NAICS 32732 Ready-mix Concrete Manufacturing

3274 Lime
NAICS 32741 Lime Manufacturing

3275 Gypsum Products
NAICS 32742 Gypsum & Gypsum Product Manufacturing

3281 Cut Stone & Stone Products
NAICS 327991 Cut Stone & Stone Product Manufacturing

3291 Abrasive Products
NAICS 332999 All Other Miscellaneous Fabricated Metal Product Manufacturing
NAICS 32791 Abrasive Product Manufacturing

3292 Asbestos Products
NAICS 33634 Motor Vehicle Brake System Manufacturing
NAICS 327999 All Other Miscellaneous Nonmetallic Mineral Product Manufacturing

3295 Minerals & Earths, Ground or Otherwise Treated
NAICS 327992 Ground or Treated Mineral & Earth Manufacturing

3296 Mineral Wool
NAICS 327993 Mineral Wool Manufacturing

3297 Nonclay Refractories
NAICS 327125 Nonclay Refractory Manufacturing

3299 Nonmetallic Mineral Products, nec
NAICS 32742 Gypsum & Gypsum Product Manufacturing
NAICS 327999 All Other Miscellaneous Nonmetallic Mineral Product Manufacturing

PRIMARY METALS INDUSTRIES

3312 Steel Works, Blast Furnaces , & Rolling Mills
NAICS 324199 All Other Petroleum & Coal Products Manufacturing
NAICS 331111 Iron & Steel Mills

3313 Electrometallurgical Products, Except Steel
NAICS 331112 Electrometallurgical Ferroalloy Product Manufacturing

NAICS 331492 Secondary Smelting, Refining, & Alloying of Nonferrous Metals

3315 Steel Wiredrawing & Steel Nails & Spikes
NAICS 331222 Steel Wire Drawing
NAICS 332618 Other Fabricated Wire Product Manufacturing

3316 Cold-rolled Steel Sheet, Strip, & Bars
NAICS 331221 Cold-rolled Steel Shape Manufacturing

3317 Steel Pipe & Tubes
NAICS 33121 Iron & Steel Pipes & Tubes Manufacturing from Purchased Steel

3321 Gray & Ductile Iron Foundries
NAICS 331511 Iron Foundries

3322 Malleable Iron Foundries
NAICS 331511 Iron Foundries

3324 Steel Investment Foundries
NAICS 331512 Steel Investment Foundries

3325 Steel Foundries, nec
NAICS 331513 Steel Foundries

3331 Primary Smelting & Refining of Copper
NAICS 331411 Primary Smelting & Refining of Copper

3334 Primary Production of Aluminum
NAICS 331312 Primary Aluminum Production

3339 Primary Smelting & Refining of Nonferrous Metals, Except Copper & Aluminum
NAICS 331419 Primary Smelting & Refining of Nonferrous Metals

3341 Secondary Smelting & Refining of Nonferrous Metals
NAICS 331314 Secondary Smelting & Alloying of Aluminum
NAICS 331423 Secondary Smelting, Refining, & Alloying of Copper
NAICS 331492 Secondary Smelting, Refining, & Alloying of Nonferrous Metals

3351 Rolling, Drawing, & Extruding of Copper
NAICS 331421 Copper Rolling, Drawing, & Extruding

3353 Aluminum Sheet, Plate, & Foil
NAICS 331315 Aluminum Sheet, Plate, & Foil Manufacturing

3354 Aluminum Extruded Products
NAICS 331316 Aluminum Extruded Product Manufacturing

3355 Aluminum Rolling & Drawing, nec
NAICS 331319 Other Aluminum Rolling & Drawing,

3356 Rolling, Drawing, & Extruding of Nonferrous Metals, Except Copper & Aluminum
NAICS 331491 Nonferrous Metal Rolling. Drawing, & Extruding

3357 Drawing & Insulating of Nonferrous Wire
NAICS 331319 Other Aluminum Rolling & Drawing
NAICS 331422 Copper Wire Drawing
NAICS 331491 Nonferrous Metal Rolling, Drawing, & Extruding
NAICS 335921 Fiber Optic Cable Manufacturing
NAICS 335929 Other Communication & Energy Wire Manufacturing

3363 Aluminum Die-castings
NAICS 331521 Aluminum Die-castings

3364 Nonferrous Die-castings, Except Aluminum
NAICS 331522 Nonferrous Die-castings

3365 Aluminum Foundries
NAICS 331524 Aluminum Foundries

3366 Copper Foundries
NAICS 331525 Copper Foundries

3369 Nonferrous Foundries, Except Aluminum & Copper
NAICS 331528 Other Nonferrous Foundries

3398 Metal Heat Treating
NAICS 332811 Metal Heat Treating
3399 Primary Metal Products, nec
NAICS 331111 Iron & Steel Mills
NAICS 331314 Secondary Smelting & Alloying of Aluminum
NAICS 331423 Secondary Smelting, Refining & Alloying of
    Copper
NAICS 331492 Secondary Smelting, Refining, & Alloying of
    Nonferrous Metals
NAICS 332618 Other Fabricated Wire Product Manufacturing
NAICS 332813 Electroplating, Plating, Polishing, Anodizing, &
    Coloring

FABRICATED METAL PRODUCTS, EXCEPT MACHINERY & TRANSPORTATION EQUIPMENT

3411 Metal Cans
NAICS 332431 Metal Can Manufacturing
3412 Metal Shipping Barrels, Drums, Kegs & Pails
NAICS 332439 Other Metal Container Manufacturing
3421 Cutlery
NAICS 332211 Cutlery & Flatware Manufacturing
3423 Hand & Edge Tools, Except Machine Tools & Handsaws
NAICS 332212 Hand & Edge Tool Manufacturing
3425 Saw Blades & Handsaws
NAICS 332213 Saw Blade & Handsaw Manufacturing
3429 Hardware, nec
NAICS 332439 Other Metal Container Manufacturing
NAICS 332919 Other Metal Valve & Pipe Fitting
    Manufacturing
NAICS 33251 Hardware Manufacturing
3431 Enameled Iron & Metal Sanitary Ware
NAICS 332998 Enameled Iron & Metal Sanitary Ware
    Manufacturing
3432 Plumbing Fixture Fittings & Trim
NAICS 332913 Plumbing Fixture Fitting & Trim Manufacturing
NAICS 332999 All Other Miscellaneous Fabricated Metal
    Product Manufacturing
3433 Heating Equipment, Except Electric & Warm Air Furnaces
NAICS 333414 Heating Equipment Manufacturing
3441 Fabricated Structural Metal
NAICS 332312 Fabricated Structural Metal Manufacturing
3442 Metal Doors, Sash, Frames, Molding, & Trim Manufacturing
NAICS 332321 Metal Window & Door Manufacturing
3443 Fabricated Plate Work
NAICS 332313 Plate Work Manufacturing
NAICS 33241 Power Boiler & Heat Exchanger Manufacturing
NAICS 33242 Metal Tank Manufacturing
NAICS 333415 Air-conditioning & Warm Air Heating
    Equipment & Commercial & Industrial
    Refrigeration Equipment Manufacturing
3444 Sheet Metal Work
NAICS 332322 Sheet Metal Work Manufacturing
NAICS 332439 Other Metal Container Manufacturing
3446 Architectural & Ornamental Metal Work
NAICS 332323 Ornamental & Architectural Metal Work
    Manufacturing
3448 Prefabricated Metal Buildings & Components
NAICS 332311 Prefabricated Metal Building & Component
    Manufacturing

3449 Miscellaneous Structural Metal Work
NAICS 332114 Custom Roll Forming
NAICS 332312 Fabricated Structural Metal Manufacturing
NAICS 332321 Metal Window & Door Manufacturing
NAICS 332323 Ornamental & Architectural Metal Work
    Manufacturing
3451 Screw Machine Products
NAICS 332721 Precision Turned Product Manufacturing
3452 Bolts, Nuts, Screws, Rivets, & Washers
NAICS 332722 Bolt, Nut, Screw, Rivet, & Washer
    Manufacturing
3462 Iron & Steel Forgings
NAICS 332111 Iron & Steel Forging
3463 Nonferrous Forgings
NAICS 332112 Nonferrous Forging
3465 Automotive Stamping
NAICS 33637 Motor Vehicle Metal Stamping
3466 Crowns & Closures
NAICS 332115 Crown & Closure Manufacturing
3469 Metal Stamping, nec
NAICS 339911 Jewelry Manufacturing
NAICS 332116 Metal Stamping
NAICS 332214 Kitchen Utensil, Pot & Pan Manufacturing
3471 Electroplating, Plating, Polishing, Anodizing, & Coloring
NAICS 332813 Electroplating, Plating, Polishing, Anodizing, &
    Coloring
3479 Coating, Engraving, & Allied Services, nec
NAICS 339914 Costume Jewelry & Novelty Manufacturing
NAICS 339911 Jewelry Manufacturing
NAICS 339912 Silverware & Plated Ware Manufacturing
NAICS 332812 Metal Coating, Engraving , & Allied Services to
    Manufacturers
3482 Small Arms Ammunition
NAICS 332992 Small Arms Ammunition Manufacturing
3483 Ammunition, Except for Small Arms
NAICS 332993 Ammunition Manufacturing
3484 Small Arms
NAICS 332994 Small Arms Manufacturing
3489 Ordnance & Accessories, nec
NAICS 332995 Other Ordnance & Accessories Manufacturing
3491
3492 Fluid Power Valves & Hose Fittings
NAICS 332912 Fluid Power Valve & Hose Fitting
    Manufacturing
3493 Steel Springs, Except Wire
NAICS 332611 Steel Spring Manufacturing
3494 Valves & Pipe Fittings, nec
NAICS 332919 Other Metal Valve & Pipe Fitting
    Manufacturing
NAICS 332999 All Other Miscellaneous Fabricated Metal
    Product Manufacturing
3495 Wire Springs
NAICS 332612 Wire Spring Manufacturing
NAICS 334518 Watch, Clock, & Part Manufacturing
3496 Miscellaneous Fabricated Wire Products
NAICS 332618 Other Fabricated Wire Product Manufacturing
3497 Metal Foil & Leaf
NAICS 322225 Laminated Aluminum Foil Manufacturing for
    Flexible Packaging Uses
NAICS 332999 All Other Miscellaneous Fabricated Metal
    Product Manufacturing
3498 Fabricated Pipe & Pipe Fittings
NAICS 332996 Fabricated Pipe & Pipe Fitting Manufacturing

3499 Fabricated Metal Products, nec
NAICS 337148 Other Nonwood Furniture Manufacturing
NAICS 332117 Powder Metallurgy Part Manufacturing
NAICS 332439 Other Metal Container Manufacturing
NAICS 33251   Hardware Manufacturing
NAICS 332919 Other Metal Valve & Pipe Fitting
      Manufacturing
NAICS 339914 Costume Jewelry & Novelty Manufacturing
NAICS 332999 All Other Miscellaneous Fabricated Metal
      Product Manufacturing

INDUSTRIAL & COMMERCIAL MACHINERY & COMPUTER EQUIPMENT

3511 Steam, Gas, & Hydraulic Turbines, & Turbine Generator Set Units
NAICS 333611 Turbine & Turbine Generator Set Unit
      Manufacturing
3519 Internal Combustion Engines, nec
NAICS 336399 All Other Motor Vehicle Parts Manufacturing
NAICS 333618 Other Engine Equipment Manufacturing
3523 Farm Machinery & Equipment
NAICS 333111 Farm Machinery & Equipment Manufacturing
NAICS 332323 Ornamental & Architectural Metal Work
      Manufacturing
NAICS 332212 Hand & Edge Tool Manufacturing
NAICS 333922 Conveyor & Conveying Equipment
      Manufacturing
3524 Lawn & Garden Tractors & Home Lawn & Garden Equipment
NAICS 333112 Lawn & Garden Tractor & Home Lawn &
      Garden Equipment Manufacturing
NAICS 332212 Hand & Edge Tool Manufacturing
3531 Construction Machinery & Equipment
NAICS 33651   Railroad Rolling Stock Manufacturing
NAICS 333923 Overhead Traveling Crane, Hoist, & Monorail
      System Manufacturing
NAICS 33312   Construction Machinery Manufacturing
3532 Mining Machinery & Equipment, Except Oil & Gas Field Machinery & Equipment
NAICS 333131 Mining Machinery & Equipment Manufacturing
3533 Oil & Gas Field Machinery & Equipment
NAICS 333132 Oil & Gas Field Machinery & Equipment
      Manufacturing
3534 Elevators & Moving Stairways
NAICS 333921 Elevator & Moving Stairway Manufacturing
3535 Conveyors & Conveying Equipment
NAICS 333922 Conveyor & Conveying Equipment
      Manufacturing
3536 Overhead Traveling Cranes, Hoists & Monorail Systems
NAICS 333923 Overhead Traveling Crane, Hoist & Monorail
      System Manufacturing
3537 Industrial Trucks, Tractors, Trailers, & Stackers
NAICS 333924 Industrial Truck, Tractor, Trailer, & Stacker
      Machinery Manufacturing
NAICS 332999 All Other Miscellaneous Fabricated Metal
      Product Manufacturing
NAICS 332439 Other Metal Container Manufacturing
3541 Machine Tools, Metal Cutting Type
NAICS 333512 Machine Tool Manufacturing
3542 Machine Tools, Metal Forming Type
NAICS 333513 Machine Tool Manufacturing

3543 Industrial Patterns
NAICS 332997 Industrial Pattern Manufacturing
3544 Special Dies & Tools, Die Sets, Jigs & Fixtures, & Industrial Molds
NAICS 333514 Special Die & Tool, Die Set, Jig, & Fixture
      Manufacturing
NAICS 333511 Industrial Mold Manufacturing
3545 Cutting Tools, Machine Tool Accessories, & Machinists' Precision Measuring Devices
NAICS 333515 Cutting Tool & Machine Tool Accessory
      Manufacturing
NAICS 332212 Hand & Edge Tool Manufacturing
3546 Power-driven Handtools
NAICS 333991 Power-driven Hand Tool Manufacturing
3547 Rolling Mill Machinery & Equipment
NAICS 333516 Rolling Mill Machinery & Equipment
      Manufacturing
3548 Electric & Gas Welding & Soldering Equipment
NAICS 333992 Welding & Soldering Equipment Manufacturing
NAICS 335311 Power, Distribution, & Specialty Transformer
      Manufacturing
3549 Metalworking Machinery, nec
NAICS 333518 Other Metalworking Machinery Manufacturing
      3552
3553 Woodworking Machinery
NAICS 33321   Sawmill & Woodworking Machinery
      Manufacturing
3554 Paper Industries Machinery
NAICS 333291 Paper Industry Machinery Manufacturing
3555 Printing Trades Machinery & Equipment
NAICS 333293 Printing Machinery & Equipment
      Manufacturing
3556 Food Products Machinery
NAICS 333294 Food Product Machinery Manufacturing
3559 Special Industry Machinery, nec
NAICS 33322   Rubber & Plastics Industry Machinery
      Manufacturing
NAICS 333319 Other Commercial & Service Industry
      Machinery Manufacturing
NAICS 333295 Semiconductor Manufacturing Machinery
NAICS 333298 All Other Industrial Machinery Manufacturing
3561 Pumps & Pumping Equipment
NAICS 333911 Pump & Pumping Equipment Manufacturing
3562 Ball & Roller Bearings
NAICS 332991 Ball & Roller Bearing Manufacturing
3563 Air & Gas Compressors
NAICS 333912 Air & Gas Compressor Manufacturing
3564 Industrial & Commercial Fans & Blowers & Air Purification Equipment
NAICS 333411 Air Purification Equipment Manufacturing
NAICS 333412 Industrial & Commercial Fan & Blower
      Manufacturing
3565 Packaging Machinery
NAICS 333993 Packaging Machinery Manufacturing
3566 Speed Changers, Industrial High-speed Drives, & Gears
NAICS 333612 Speed Changer, Industrial High-speed Drive, &
      Gear Manufacturing
3567 Industrial Process Furnaces & Ovens
NAICS 333994 Industrial Process Furnace & Oven
      Manufacturing
3568 Mechanical Power Transmission Equipment, nec
NAICS 333613 Mechanical Power Transmission Equipment
      Manufacturing

3569 General Industrial Machinery & Equipment, nec
NAICS 333999 All Other General Purpose Machinery
Manufacturing

3571 Electronic Computers
NAICS 334111 Electronic Computer Manufacturing

3572 Computer Storage Devices
NAICS 334112 Computer Storage Device Manufacturing

3575 Computer Terminals
NAICS 334113 Computer Terminal Manufacturing

3577 Computer Peripheral Equipment, nec
NAICS 334119 Other Computer Peripheral Equipment
Manufacturing

3578 Calculating & Accounting Machines, Except Electronic Computers
NAICS 334119 Other Computer Peripheral Equipment
Manufacturing
NAICS 333313 Office Machinery Manufacturing

3579 Office Machines, nec
NAICS 339942 Lead Pencil & Art Good Manufacturing
NAICS 334518 Watch, Clock, & Part Manufacturing
NAICS 333313 Office Machinery Manufacturing

3581 Automatic Vending Machines
NAICS 333311 Automatic Vending Machine Manufacturing

3582 Commercial Laundry, Drycleaning, & Pressing Machines
NAICS 333312 Commercial Laundry, Drycleaning, & Pressing
Machine Manufacturing

3585 Air-conditioning & Warm Air Heating Equipment & Commercial & Industrial Refrigeration Equipment
NAICS 336391 Motor Vehicle Air Conditioning Manufacturing
NAICS 333415 Air Conditioning & Warm Air Heating
Equipment & Commercial & Industrial
Refrigeration Equipment Manufacturing

3586 Measuring & Dispensing Pumps
NAICS 333913 Measuring & Dispensing Pump Manufacturing

3589 Service Industry Machinery, nec
NAICS 333319 Other Commercial and Service Industry
Machinery Manufacturing

3592 Carburetors, Pistons, Piston Rings & Valves
NAICS 336311 Carburetor, Piston, Piston Ring & Valve
Manufacturing

3593 Fluid Power Cylinders & Actuators
NAICS 333995 Fluid Power Cylinder & Actuator
Manufacturing

3594 Fluid Power Pumps & Motors
NAICS 333996 Fluid Power Pump & Motor Manufacturing

3596 Scales & Balances, Except Laboratory
NAICS 333997 Scale & Balance Manufacturing

3599 Industrial & Commercial Machinery & Equipment, nec
NAICS 336399 All Other Motor Vehicle Part Manufacturing
NAICS 332999 All Other Miscellaneous Fabricated Metal
Product Manufacturing
NAICS 333319 Other Commercial & Service Industry
Machinery Manufacturing
NAICS 33271 Machine Shops
NAICS 333999 All Other General Purpose Machinery
Manufacturing

ELECTRONIC & OTHER ELECTRICAL EQUIPMENT & COMPONENTS, EXCEPT COMPUTER EQUIPMENT

3612 Power, Distribution, & Specialty Transformers
NAICS 335311 Power, Distribution, & Specialty Transformer
Manufacturing

3613 Switchgear & Switchboard Apparatus
NAICS 335313 Switchgear & Switchboard Apparatus
Manufacturing

3621 Motors & Generators
NAICS 335312 Motor & Generator Manufacturing

3624 Carbon & Graphite Products
NAICS 335991 Carbon & Graphite Product Manufacturing

3625 Relays & Industrial Controls
NAICS 335314 Relay & Industrial Control Manufacturing

3629 Electrical Industrial Apparatus, nec
NAICS 335999 All Other Miscellaneous Electrical Equipment
& Component Manufacturing

3631 Household Cooking Equipment
NAICS 335221 Household Cooking Appliance Manufacturing

3632 Household Refrigerators & Home & Farm Freezers
NAICS 335222 Household Refrigerator & Home Freezer
Manufacturing

3633 Household Laundry Equipment
NAICS 335224 Household Laundry Equipment Manufacturing

3634 Electric Housewares & Fans
NAICS 335211 Electric Housewares & Fan Manufacturing

3635 Household Vacuum Cleaners
NAICS 335212 Household Vacuum Cleaner Manufacturing

3639 Household Appliances, nec
NAICS 335212 Household Vacuum Cleaner Manufacturing
NAICS 333298 All Other Industrial Machinery Manufacturing
NAICS 335228 Other Household Appliance Manufacturing

3641 Electric Lamp Bulbs & Tubes
NAICS 33511 Electric Lamp Bulb & Part Manufacturing

3643 Current-carrying Wiring Devices
NAICS 335931 Current-carrying Wiring Device Manufacturing

3644 Noncurrent-carrying Wiring Devices
NAICS 335932 Noncurrent-carrying Wiring Device
Manufacturing

3645 Residential Electric Lighting Fixtures
NAICS 335121 Residential Electric Lighting Fixture
Manufacturing

3646 Commercial, Industrial, & Institutional Electric Lighting Fixtures
NAICS 335122 Commercial, Industrial, & Institutional Electric
Lighting Fixture Manufacturing

3647 Vehicular Lighting Equipment
NAICS 336321 Vehicular Lighting Equipment Manufacturing

3648 Lighting Equipment, nec
NAICS 335129 Other Lighting Equipment Manufacturing

3651 Household Audio & Video Equipment
NAICS 33431 Audio & Video Equipment Manufacturing 3652
NAICS 51222 Integrated Record Production/distribution

3661 Telephone & Telegraph Apparatus
NAICS 33421 Telephone Apparatus Manufacturing
NAICS 334416 Electronic Coil, Transformer, & Other Inductor
Manufacturing
NAICS 334418 Printed Circuit/electronics Assembly
Manufacturing

3663 Radio & Television Broadcasting & Communication Equipment
NAICS 33422   Radio & Television Broadcasting & Wireless Communications Equipment Manufacturing

3669 Communications Equipment, nec
NAICS 33429   Other Communication Equipment Manufacturing

3671 Electron Tubes
NAICS 334411 Electron Tube Manufacturing

3672 Printed Circuit Boards
NAICS 334412 Printed Circuit Board Manufacturing

3674 Semiconductors & Related Devices
NAICS 334413 Semiconductor & Related Device Manufacturing

3675 Electronic Capacitors
NAICS 334414 Electronic Capacitor Manufacturing

3676 Electronic Resistors
NAICS 334415 Electronic Resistor Manufacturing

3677 Electronic Coils, Transformers, & Other Inductors
NAICS 334416 Electronic Coil, Transformer, & Other Inductor Manufacturing

3678 Electronic ConNECtors
NAICS 334417 Electronic ConNECtor Manufacturing

3679 Electronic Components, nec
NAICS 33422   Radio & Television Broadcasting & Wireless Communications Equipment Manufacturing
NAICS 334418 Printed Circuit/electronics Assembly Manufacturing
NAICS 336322 Other Motor Vehicle Electrical & Electronic Equipment Manufacturing
NAICS 334419 Other Electronic Component Manufacturing

3691 Storage Batteries
NAICS 335911 Storage Battery Manufacturing

3692 Primary Batteries, Dry & Wet
NAICS 335912 Dry & Wet Primary Battery Manufacturing

3694 Electrical Equipment for Internal Combustion Engines
NAICS 336322 Other Motor Vehicle Electrical & Electronic Equipment Manufacturing

3695 Magnetic & Optical Recording Media
NAICS 334613 Magnetic & Optical Recording Media Manufacturing

3699 Electrical Machinery, Equipment, & Supplies, nec
NAICS 333319 Other Commercial & Service Industry Machinery Manufacturing
NAICS 333618 Other Engine Equipment Manufacturing
NAICS 334119 Other Computer Peripheral Equipment Manufacturing Classify According to Function
NAICS 335129 Other Lighting Equipment Manufacturing
NAICS 335999 All Other Miscellaneous Electrical Equipment & Component Manufacturing

TRANSPORTATION EQUIPMENT

3711 Motor Vehicles & Passenger Car Bodies
NAICS 336111 Automobile Manufacturing
NAICS 336112 Light Truck & Utility Vehicle Manufacturing
NAICS 33612   Heavy Duty Truck Manufacturing
NAICS 336211 Motor Vehicle Body Manufacturing
NAICS 336992 Military Armored Vehicle, Tank, & Tank Component Manufacturing

3713 Truck & Bus Bodies
NAICS 336211 Motor Vehicle Body Manufacturing

3714 Motor Vehicle Parts & Accessories
NAICS 336211 Motor Vehicle Body Manufacturing
NAICS 336312 Gasoline Engine & Engine Parts Manufacturing
NAICS 336322 Other Motor Vehicle Electrical & Electronic Equipment Manufacturing
NAICS 33633   Motor Vehicle Steering & Suspension Components Manufacturing
NAICS 33634   Motor Vehicle Brake System Manufacturing
NAICS 33635   Motor Vehicle Transmission & Power Train Parts Manufacturing
NAICS 336399 All Other Motor Vehicle Parts Manufacturing

3715 Truck Trailers
NAICS 336212 Truck Trailer Manufacturing

3716 Motor Homes
NAICS 336213 Motor Home Manufacturing

3721 Aircraft
NAICS 336411 Aircraft Manufacturing

3724 Aircraft Engines & Engine Parts
NAICS 336412 Aircraft Engine & Engine Parts Manufacturing
3728
NAICS 336413 Other Aircraft Part & Auxiliary Equipment Manufacturing

3731 Ship Building & Repairing
NAICS 336611 Ship Building & Repairing

3732 Boat Building & Repairing
NAICS 81149   Other Personal & Household Goods Repair & Maintenance
NAICS 336612 Boat Building

3743 Railroad Equipment
NAICS 333911 Pump & Pumping Equipment Manufacturing
NAICS 33651   Railroad Rolling Stock Manufacturing

3751 Motorcycles, Bicycles, & Parts
NAICS 336991 Motorcycle, Bicycle, & Parts Manufacturing

3761 Guided Missiles & Space Vehicles
NAICS 336414 Guided Missile & Space Vehicle Manufacturing
3764

3769 Guided Missile Space Vehicle Parts & Auxiliary Equipment, nec
NAICS 336419 Other Guided Missile & Space Vehicle Parts & Auxiliary Equipment Manufacturing

3792 Travel Trailers & Campers
NAICS 336214 Travel Trailer & Camper Manufacturing

3795 Tanks & Tank Components
NAICS 336992 Military Armored Vehicle, Tank, & Tank Component Manufacturing

3799 Transportation Equipment, nec
NAICS 336214 Travel Trailer & Camper Manufacturing
NAICS 332212 Hand & Edge Tool Manufacturing
NAICS 336999 All Other Transportation Equipment Manufacturing

MEASURING, ANALYZING, & CONTROLLING INSTRUMENTS

3812 Search, Detection, Navigation, Guidance, Aeronautical, & Nautical Systems & Instruments
NAICS 334511 Search, Detection, Navigation, Guidance, Aeronautical, & Nautical System & Instrument Manufacturing

3821 Laboratory Apparatus & Furniture
NAICS 339111 Laboratory Apparatus & Furniture Manufacturing

3822 Automatic Controls for Regulating Residential & Commercial Environments & Appliances
NAICS 334512 Automatic Environmental Control Manufacturing for Regulating Residential, Commercial, & Appliance Use

3823 Industrial Instruments for Measurement, Display, & Control of Process Variables & Related Products
NAICS 334513 Instruments & Related Product Manufacturing for Measuring Displaying, & Controlling Industrial Process Variables

3824 Totalizing Fluid Meters & Counting Devices
NAICS 334514 Totalizing Fluid Meter & Counting Device Manufacturing

3825 Instruments for Measuring & Testing of Electricity & Electrical Signals
NAICS 334416 Electronic Coil, Transformer, & Other Inductor Manufacturing
NAICS 334515 Instrument Manufacturing for Measuring & Testing Electricity & Electrical Signals

3826 Laboratory Analytical Instruments
NAICS 334516 Analytical Laboratory Instrument Manufacturing

3827 Optical Instruments & Lenses
NAICS 333314 Optical Instrument & Lens Manufacturing

3829 Measuring & Controlling Devices, nec
NAICS 339112 Surgical & Medical Instrument Manufacturing
NAICS 334519 Other Measuring & Controlling Device Manufacturing

3841 Surgical & Medical Instruments & Apparatus
NAICS 339112 Surgical & Medical Instrument Manufacturing

3842 Orthopedic, Prosthetic, & Surgical Appliances & Supplies
NAICS 339113 Surgical Appliance & Supplies Manufacturing
NAICS 334510 Electromedical & Electrotherapeutic Apparatus Manufacturing

3843 Dental Equipment & Supplies
NAICS 339114 Dental Equipment & Supplies Manufacturing

3844 X-ray Apparatus & Tubes & Related Irradiation Apparatus
NAICS 334517 Irradiation Apparatus Manufacturing

3845 Electromedical & Electrotherapeutic Apparatus
NAICS 334517 Irradiation Apparatus Manufacturing
NAICS 334510 Electromedical & Electrotherapeutic Apparatus Manufacturing

3851 Ophthalmic Goods
NAICS 339115 Ophthalmic Goods Manufacturing

3861 Photographic Equipment & Supplies
NAICS 333315 Photographic & Photocopying Equipment Manufacturing
NAICS 325992 Photographic Film, Paper, Plate & Chemical Manufacturing

3873 Watches, Clocks, Clockwork Operated Devices & Parts
NAICS 334518 Watch, Clock, & Part Manufacturing

MISCELLANEOUS MANUFACTURING INDUSTRIES

3911 Jewelry, Precious Metal
NAICS 339911 Jewelry Manufacturing

3914 Silverware, Plated Ware, & Stainless Steel Ware
NAICS 332211 Cutlery & Flatware Manufacturing
NAICS 339912 Silverware & Plated Ware Manufacturing

3915 Jewelers' Findings & Materials, & Lapidary Work
NAICS 339913 Jewelers' Material & Lapidary Work Manufacturing

3931 Musical Instruments
NAICS 339992 Musical Instrument Manufacturing

3942 Dolls & Stuffed Toys
NAICS 339931 Doll & Stuffed Toy Manufacturing

3944 Games, Toys, & Children's Vehicles, Except Dolls & Bicycles
NAICS 336991 Motorcycle, Bicycle & Parts Manufacturing
NAICS 339932 Game, Toy, & Children's Vehicle Manufacturing

3949 Sporting & Athletic Goods, nec
NAICS 33992 Sporting & Athletic Good Manufacturing

3951 Pens, Mechanical Pencils & Parts
NAICS 339941 Pen & Mechanical Pencil Manufacturing

3952 Lead Pencils, Crayons, & Artist's Materials
NAICS 337139 Other Wood Furniture Manufacturing
NAICS 337139 Other Wood Furniture Manufacturing
NAICS 325998 All Other Miscellaneous Chemical Manufacturing
NAICS 339942 Lead Pencil & Art Good Manufacturing

3953 Marking Devices
NAICS 339943 Marking Device Manufacturing

3955 Carbon Paper & Inked Ribbons
NAICS 339944 Carbon Paper & Inked Ribbon Manufacturing

3961 Costume Jewelry & Costume Novelties, Except Precious Metals
NAICS 339914 Costume Jewelry & Novelty Manufacturing

3965 Fasteners, Buttons, Needles, & Pins
NAICS 339993 Fastener, Button, Needle & Pin Manufacturing

3991 Brooms & Brushes
NAICS 339994 Broom, Brush & Mop Manufacturing

3993 Signs & Advertising Specialties
NAICS 33995 Sign Manufacturing

3995 Burial Caskets
NAICS 339995 Burial Casket Manufacturing

3996 Linoleum, Asphalted-felt-base, & Other Hard Surface Floor Coverings, nec
NAICS 326192 Resilient Floor Covering Manufacturing

3999 Manufacturing Industries, nec
NAICS 337148 Other Nonwood Furniture Manufacturing
NAICS 321999 All Other Miscellaneous Wood Product Manufacturing
NAICS 31611 Leather & Hide Tanning & Finishing
NAICS 335121 Residential Electric Lighting Fixture Manufacturing
NAICS 325998 All Other Miscellaneous Chemical Product Manufacturing
NAICS 332999 All Other Miscellaneous Fabricated Metal Product Manufacturing
NAICS 326199 All Other Plastics Product Manufacturing
NAICS 323112 Commercial Flexographic Printing
NAICS 323111 Commercial Gravure Printing
NAICS 323110 Commercial Lithographic Printing
NAICS 323113 Commercial Screen Printing
NAICS 323119 Other Commercial Printing
NAICS 332212 Hand & Edge Tool Manufacturing
NAICS 339999 All Other Miscellaneous Manufacturing

TRANSPORTATION, COMMUNICATIONS, ELECTRIC, GAS, & SANITARY SERVICES

4011 Railroads, Line-haul Operating
NAICS 482111 Line-haul Railroads
4013 Railroad Switching & Terminal Establishments
NAICS 482112 Short Line Railroads
NAICS 48821 Support Activities for Rail Transportation
4111 Local & Suburban Transit
NAICS 485111 Mixed Mode Transit Systems
NAICS 485112 Commuter Rail Systems
NAICS 485113 Bus & Motor Vehicle Transit Systems
NAICS 485119 Other Urban Transit Systems
NAICS 485999 All Other Transit & Ground Passenger Transportation
4119 Local Passenger Transportation, nec
NAICS 62191 Ambulance Service
NAICS 48541 School & Employee Bus Transportation
NAICS 48711 Scenic & Sightseeing Transportation , Land
NAICS 485991 Special Needs Transportation
NAICS 485999 All Other Transit & Ground Passenger Transportation
NAICS 48532 Limousine Service
4121 Taxicabs
NAICS 48531 Taxi Service
4131 Intercity & Rural Bus Transportation
NAICS 48521 Interurban & Rural Bus Transportation
4141 Local Bus Charter Service
NAICS 48551 Charter Bus Industry
4142 Bus Charter Service, Except Local
NAICS 48551 Charter Bus Industry
4151 School Buses
NAICS 48541 School & Employee Bus Transportation
4173 Terminal & Service Facilities for Motor Vehicle Passenger Transportation
NAICS 48849 Other Support Activities for Road Transportation
4212 Local Trucking Without Storage
NAICS 562111 Solid Waste Collection
NAICS 562112 Hazardous Waste Collection
NAICS 562119 Other Waste Collection
NAICS 48411 General Freight Trucking, Local
NAICS 48421 Used Household & Office Goods Moving
NAICS 48422 Specialized Freight Trucking, Local
4213 Trucking, Except Local
NAICS 484121 General Freight Trucking, Long-distance, Truckload
NAICS 484122 General Freight Trucking, Long-distance, less than Truckload
NAICS 48421 Used Household & Office Goods Moving
NAICS 48423 Specialized Freight Trucking, Long-distance
4214 Local Trucking with Storage
NAICS 48411 General Freight Trucking, Local
NAICS 48421 Used Household & Office Goods Moving
NAICS 48422 Specialized Freight Trucking, Local
4215 Couriers Services Except by Air
NAICS 49211 Couriers
NAICS 49221 Local Messengers & Local Delivery
4221 Farm Product Warehousing & Storage
NAICS 49313 Farm Product Storage Facilities
4222 Refrigerated Warehousing & Storage
NAICS 49312 Refrigerated Storage Facilities

4225 General Warehousing & Storage
NAICS 49311 General Warehousing & Storage Facilities
NAICS 53113 Lessors of Miniwarehouses & Self Storage Units
4226 Special Warehousing & Storage, nec
NAICS 49312 Refrigerated Warehousing & Storage Facilities
NAICS 49311 General Warehousing & Storage Facilities
NAICS 49319 Other Warehousing & Storage Facilities
4231 Terminal & Joint Terminal Maintenance Facilities for Motor Freight Transportation
NAICS 48849 Other Support Activities for Road Transportation
4311 United States Postal Service
NAICS 49111 Postal Service
4412 Deep Sea Foreign Transportation of Freight
NAICS 483111 Deep Sea Freight Transportation
4424 Deep Sea Domestic Transportation of Freight
NAICS 483113 Coastal & Great Lakes Freight Transportation
4432 Freight Transportation on the Great Lakes - St. Lawrence Seaway
NAICS 483113 Coastal & Great Lakes Freight Transportation
4449 Water Transportation of Freight, nec
NAICS 483211 Inland Water Freight Transportation
4481 Deep Sea Transportation of Passengers, Except by Ferry
NAICS 483112 Deep Sea Passenger Transportation
NAICS 483114 Coastal & Great Lakes Passenger Transportation
4482 Ferries
NAICS 483114 Coastal & Great Lakes Passenger Transportation
NAICS 483212 Inland Water Passenger Transportation
4489 Water Transportation of Passengers, nec
NAICS 483212 Inland Water Passenger Transportation
NAICS 48721 Scenic & Sightseeing Transportation, Water
4491 Marine Cargo Handling
NAICS 48831 Port & Harbor Operations
NAICS 48832 Marine Cargo Handling
4492 Towing & Tugboat Services
NAICS 483113 Coastal & Great Lakes Freight Transportation
NAICS 483211 Inland Water Freight Transportation
NAICS 48833 Navigational Services to Shipping
4493 Marinas
NAICS 71393 Marinas
4499 Water Transportation Services, nec
NAICS 532411 Commercial Air, Rail, & Water Transportation Equipment Rental & Leasing
NAICS 48831 Port & Harbor Operations
NAICS 48833 Navigational Services to Shipping
NAICS 48839 Other Support Activities for Water Transportation
4512 Air Transportation, Scheduled
NAICS 481111 Scheduled Passenger Air Transportation
NAICS 481112 Scheduled Freight Air Transportation
4513 Air Courier Services
NAICS 49211 Couriers
4522 Air Transportation, Nonscheduled
NAICS 62191 Ambulance Services
NAICS 481212 Nonscheduled Chartered Freight Air Transportation
NAICS 481211 Nonscheduled Chartered Passenger Air Transportation
NAICS 48122 Nonscheduled Speciality Air Transportation
NAICS 48799 Scenic & Sightseeing Transportation , Other

4581 Airports, Flying Fields, & Airport Terminal Services
NAICS 488111 Air Traffic Control
NAICS 488112 Airport Operations, Except Air Traffic Control
NAICS 56172 Janitorial Services
NAICS 48819 Other Support Activities for Air Transportation
4612 Crude Petroleum Pipelines
NAICS 48611 Pipeline Transportation of Crude Oil
4613 Refined Petroleum Pipelines
NAICS 48691 Pipeline Transportation of Refined Petroleum
Products
4619 Pipelines, nec
NAICS 48699 All Other Pipeline Transportation
4724 Travel Agencies
NAICS 56151 Travel Agencies
4725 Tour Operators
NAICS 56152 Tour Operators
4729 Arrangement of Passenger Transportation, nec
NAICS 488999 All Other Support Activities for Transportation
NAICS 561599 All Other Travel Arrangement & Reservation
Services
4731 Arrangement of Transportation of Freight & Cargo
NAICS 541618 Other Management Consulting Services
NAICS 48851 Freight Transportation Arrangement
4741 Rental of Railroad Cars
NAICS 532411 Commercial Air, Rail, & Water Transportation
Equipment Rental & Leasing
NAICS 48821 Support Activities for Rail Transportation
4783 Packing & Crating
NAICS 488991 Packing & Crating
**4785 Fixed Facilities & Inspection & Weighing Services for
Motor Vehicle Transportation**
NAICS 48839 Other Support Activities for Water
Transportation
NAICS 48849 Other Support Activities for Road
Transportation
4789 Transportation Services, nec
NAICS 488999 All Other Support Activities for Transportation
NAICS 48711 Scenic & Sightseeing Transportation, Land
NAICS 48821 Support Activities for Rail Transportation
4812 Radiotelephone Communications
NAICS 513321 Paging
NAICS 513322 Cellular & Other Wireless Telecommunications
NAICS 51333 Telecommunications Resellers
4813 Telephone Communications, Except Radiotelephone
NAICS 51331 Wired Telecommunications Carriers
NAICS 51333 Telecommunications Resellers
4822 Telegraph & Other Message Communications
NAICS 51331 Wired Telecommunications Carriers
4832 Radio Broadcasting Stations
NAICS 513111 Radio Networks
NAICS 513112 Radio Stations
4833 Television Broadcasting Stations
NAICS 51312 Television Broadcasting
4841 Cable & Other Pay Television Services
NAICS 51321 Cable Networks
NAICS 51322 Cable & Other Program Distribution
4899 Communications Services, nec
NAICS 513322 Cellular & Other Wireless Telecommunications
NAICS 51334 Satellite Telecommunications
NAICS 51339 Other Telecommunications
4911 Electric Services
NAICS 221111 Hydroelectric Power Generation
NAICS 221112 Fossil Fuel Electric Power Generation
NAICS 221113 Nuclear Electric Power Generation

NAICS 221119 Other Electric Power Generation
NAICS 221121 Electric Bulk Power Transmission & Control
NAICS 221122 Electric Power Distribution
4922 Natural Gas Transmission
NAICS 48621 Pipeline Transportation of Natural Gas
4923 Natural Gas Transmission & Distribution
NAICS 22121 Natural Gas Distribution
NAICS 48621 Pipeline Transportation of Natural Gas
4924 Natural Gas Distribution
NAICS 22121 Natural Gas Distribution
**4925 Mixed, Manufactured, or Liquefied Petroleum Gas
Production And/or Distribution**
NAICS 22121 Natural Gas Distribution
4931 Electric & Other Services Combined
NAICS 221111 Hydroelectric Power Generation
NAICS 221112 Fossil Fuel Electric Power Generation
NAICS 221113 Nuclear Electric Power Generation
NAICS 221119 Other Electric Power Generation
NAICS 221121 Electric Bulk Power Transmission & Control
NAICS 221122 Electric Power Distribution
NAICS 22121 Natural Gas Distribution
4932 Gas & Other Services Combined
NAICS 22121 Natural Gas Distribution
4939 Combination Utilities, nec
NAICS 221111 Hydroelectric Power Generation
NAICS 221112 Fossil Fuel Electric Power Generation
NAICS 221113 Nuclear Electric Power Generation
NAICS 221119 Other Electric Power Generation
NAICS 221121 Electric Bulk Power Transmission & Control
NAICS 221122 Electric Power Distribution
NAICS 22121 Natural Gas Distribution
4941 Water Supply
NAICS 22131 Water Supply & Irrigation Systems
4952 Sewerage Systems
NAICS 22132 Sewage Treatment Facilities
4953 Refuse Systems
NAICS 562111 Solid Waste Collection
NAICS 562112 Hazardous Waste Collection
NAICS 56292 Materials Recovery Facilities
NAICS 562119 Other Waste Collection
NAICS 562211 Hazardous Waste Treatment & Disposal
NAICS 562212 Solid Waste Landfills
NAICS 562213 Solid Waste Combustors & Incinerators
NAICS 562219 Other Nonhazardous Waste Treatment &
Disposal
4959 Sanitary Services, nec
NAICS 488112 Airport Operations, Except Air Traffic Control
NAICS 56291 Remediation Services
NAICS 56171 Exterminating & Pest Control Services
NAICS 562998 All Other Miscellaneous Waste Management
Services
4961 Steam & Air-conditioning Supply
NAICS 22133 Steam & Air-conditioning Supply
4971 Irrigation Systems
NAICS 22131 Water Supply & Irrigation Systems

WHOLESALE TRADE

5012 Automobiles & Other Motor Vehicles
NAICS 42111 Automobile & Other Motor Vehicle
Wholesalers

5013 Motor Vehicle Supplies & New Parts
NAICS 44131   Automotive Parts & Accessories Stores - Retail
NAICS 42112   Motor Vehicle Supplies & New Part Wholesalers

5014 Tires & Tubes
NAICS 44132   Tire Dealers - Retail
NAICS 42113   Tire & Tube Wholesalers

5015 Motor Vehicle Parts, Used
NAICS 42114   Motor Vehicle Part Wholesalers

5021 Furniture
NAICS 44211   Furniture Stores
NAICS 42121   Furniture Wholesalers

5023 Home Furnishings
NAICS 44221   Floor Covering Stores
NAICS 42122   Home Furnishing Wholesalers

5031 Lumber, Plywood, Millwork, & Wood Panels
NAICS 44419   Other Building Material Dealers
NAICS 42131   Lumber, Plywood, Millwork, & Wood Panel Wholesalers

5032 Brick, Stone & Related Construction Materials
NAICS 44419   Other Building Material Dealers
NAICS 42132   Brick, Stone & Related Construction Material Wholesalers

5033 Roofing, Siding, & Insulation Materials
NAICS 42133   Roofing, Siding, & Insulation Material Wholesalers

5039 Construction Materials, nec
NAICS 44419   Other Building Material Dealers
NAICS 42139   Other Construction Material Wholesalers

5043 Photographic Equipment & Supplies
NAICS 42141   Photographic Equipment & Supplies Wholesalers

5044 Office Equipment
NAICS 42142   Office Equipment Wholesalers

5045 Computers & Computer Peripheral Equipment & Software
NAICS 42143   Computer & Computer Peripheral Equipment & Software Wholesalers
NAICS 44312   Computer & Software Stores - Retail

5046 Commercial Equipment, nec
NAICS 42144   Other Commercial Equipment Wholesalers

5047 Medical, Dental, & Hospital Equipment & Supplies
NAICS 42145   Medical, Dental & Hospital Equipment & Supplies Wholesalers
NAICS 446199 All Other Health & Personal Care Stores - Retail

5048 Ophthalmic Goods
NAICS 42146   Ophthalmic Goods Wholesalers

5049 Professional Equipment & Supplies, nec
NAICS 42149   Other Professional Equipment & Supplies Wholesalers
NAICS 45321   Office Supplies & Stationery Stores - Retail

5051 Metals Service Centers & Offices
NAICS 42151   Metals Service Centers & Offices

5052 Coal & Other Minerals & Ores
NAICS 42152   Coal & Other Mineral & Ore Wholesalers

5063 Electrical Apparatus & Equipment Wiring Supplies, & Construction Materials
NAICS 44419   Other Building Material Dealers
NAICS 42161   Electrical Apparatus & Equipment, Wiring Supplies & Construction Material Wholesalers

5064 Electrical Appliances, Television & Radio Sets
NAICS 42162   Electrical Appliance, Television & Radio Set Wholesalers

5065 Electronic Parts & Equipment, Not Elsewhere Classified
NAICS 42169   Other Electronic Parts & Equipment Wholesalers

5072 Hardware
NAICS 42171   Hardware Wholesalers

5074 Plumbing & Heating Equipment & Supplies
NAICS 44419   Other Building Material Dealers
NAICS 42172   Plumbing & Heating Equipment & Supplies Wholesalers

5075 Warm Air Heating & Air-conditioning Equipment & Supplies
NAICS 42173   Warm Air Heating & Air-conditioning Equipment & Supplies Wholesalers

5078 Refrigeration Equipment & Supplies
NAICS 42174   Refrigeration Equipment & Supplies Wholesalers

5082 Construction & Mining Machinery & Equipment
NAICS 42181   Construction & Mining Machinery & Equipment Wholesalers

5083 Farm & Garden Machinery & Equipment
NAICS 42182   Farm & Garden Machinery & Equipment Wholesalers
NAICS 44421   Outdoor Power Equipment Stores - Retail

5084 Industrial Machinery & Equipment
NAICS 42183   Industrial Machinery & Equipment Wholesalers

5085 Industrial Supplies
NAICS 42183   Industrial Machinery & Equipment Wholesalers
NAICS 42184   Industrial Supplies Wholesalers
NAICS 81131   Commercial & Industrial Machinery & Equipment Repair & Maintenance

5087 Service Establishment Equipment & Supplies
NAICS 42185   Service Establishment Equipment & Supplies Wholesalers
NAICS 44612   Cosmetics, Beauty Supplies, & Perfume Stores

5088 Transportation Equipment & Supplies, Except Motor Vehicles
NAICS 42186   Transportation Equipment & Supplies Wholesalers

5091 Sporting & Recreational Goods & Supplies
NAICS 42191   Sporting & Recreational Goods & Supplies Wholesalers

5092 Toys & Hobby Goods & Supplies
NAICS 42192   Toy & Hobby Goods & Supplies Wholesalers

5093 Scrap & Waste Materials
NAICS 42193   Recyclable Material Wholesalers

5094 Jewelry, Watches, Precious Stones, & Precious Metals
NAICS 42194   Jewelry, Watch , Precious Stone, & Precious Metal Wholesalers

5099 Durable Goods, nec
NAICS 42199   Other Miscellaneous Durable Goods Wholesalers

5111 Printing & Writing Paper
NAICS 42211   Printing & Writing Paper Wholesalers

5112 Stationery & Office Supplies
NAICS 45321   Office Supplies & Stationery Stores
NAICS 42212   Stationery & Office Supplies Wholesalers

5113 Industrial & Personal Service Paper
NAICS 42213   Industrial & Personal Service Paper Wholesalers

5122 Drugs, Drug Proprietaries, & Druggists' Sundries
NAICS 42221   Drugs, Drug Proprietaries, & Druggists' Sundries Wholesalers

5131 Piece Goods, Notions, & Other Dry Goods
  NAICS 313311 Broadwoven Fabric Finishing Mills
  NAICS 313312 Textile & Fabric Finishing Mills
  NAICS 42231 Piece Goods, Notions, & Other Dry Goods
        Wholesalers
5136 Men's & Boys' Clothing & Furnishings
  NAICS 42232 Men's & Boys' Clothing & Furnishings
        Wholesalers
5137 Women's Children's & Infants' Clothing & Accessories
  NAICS 42233 Women's, Children's, & Infants' Clothing &
        Accessories Wholesalers
5139 Footwear
  NAICS 42234 Footwear Wholesalers
5141 Groceries, General Line
  NAICS 42241 General Line Grocery Wholesalers
5142 Packaged Frozen Foods
  NAICS 42242 Packaged Frozen Food Wholesalers
5143 Dairy Products, Except Dried or Canned
  NAICS 42243 Dairy Products Wholesalers
5144 Poultry & Poultry Products
  NAICS 42244 Poultry & Poultry Product Wholesalers
5145 Confectionery
  NAICS 42245 Confectionery Wholesalers
5146 Fish & Seafoods
  NAICS 42246 Fish & Seafood Wholesalers
5147 Meats & Meat Products
  NAICS 311612 Meat Processed from Carcasses
  NAICS 42247 Meat & Meat Product Wholesalers
5148 Fresh Fruits & Vegetables
  NAICS 42248 Fresh Fruit & Vegetable Wholesalers
5149 Groceries & Related Products, nec
  NAICS 42249 Other Grocery & Related Product Wholesalers
5153 Grain & Field Beans
  NAICS 42251 Grain & Field Bean Wholesalers
5154 Livestock
  NAICS 42252 Livestock Wholesalers
5159 Farm-product Raw Materials, nec
  NAICS 42259 Other Farm Product Raw Material Wholesalers
5162 Plastics Materials & Basic Forms & Shapes
  NAICS 42261 Plastics Materials & Basic Forms & Shapes
        Wholesalers
5169 Chemicals & Allied Products, nec
  NAICS 42269 Other Chemical & Allied Products Wholesalers
5171 Petroleum Bulk Stations & Terminals
  NAICS 454311 Heating Oil Dealers
  NAICS 454312 Liquefied Petroleum Gas Dealers
  NAICS 42271 Petroleum Bulk Stations & Terminals
**5172 Petroleum & Petroleum Products Wholesalers, Except Bulk
    Stations & Terminals**
  NAICS 42272 Petroleum & Petroleum Products Wholesalers
5181 Beer & Ale
  NAICS 42281 Beer & Ale Wholesalers
5182 Wine & Distilled Alcoholic Beverages
  NAICS 42282 Wine & Distilled Alcoholic Beverage
        Wholesalers
5191 Farm Supplies
  NAICS 44422 Nursery & Garden Centers - Retail
  NAICS 42291 Farm Supplies Wholesalers
5192 Books, Periodicals, & Newspapers
  NAICS 42292 Book, Periodical & Newspaper Wholesalers
5193 Flowers, Nursery Stock, & Florists' Supplies
  NAICS 42293 Flower, Nursery Stock & Florists' Supplies
        Wholesalers
  NAICS 44422 Nursery & Garden Centers - Retail

5194 Tobacco & Tobacco Products
  NAICS 42294 Tobacco & Tobacco Product Wholesalers
5198 Paint, Varnishes, & Supplies
  NAICS 42295 Paint, Varnish & Supplies Wholesalers
  NAICS 44412 Paint & Wallpaper Stores
5199 Nondurable Goods, nec
  NAICS 54189 Other Services Related to Advertising
  NAICS 42299 Other Miscellaneous Nondurable Goods
        Wholesalers

RETAIL TRADE

5211 Lumber & Other Building Materials Dealers
  NAICS 44411 Home Centers
  NAICS 42131 Lumber, Plywood, Millwork & Wood Panel
        Wholesalers
  NAICS 44419 Other Building Material Dealers
5231 Paint, Glass, & Wallpaper Stores
  NAICS 42295 Paint, Varnish & Supplies Wholesalers
  NAICS 44419 Other Building Material Dealers
  NAICS 44412 Paint & Wallpaper Stores
5251 Hardware Stores
  NAICS 44413 Hardware Stores
5261 Retail Nurseries, Lawn & Garden Supply Stores
  NAICS 44422 Nursery & Garden Centers
  NAICS 453998 All Other Miscellaneous Store Retailers
  NAICS 44421 Outdoor Power Equipment Stores
5271 Mobile Home Dealers
  NAICS 45393 Manufactured Home Dealers
5311 Department Stores
  NAICS 45211 Department Stores
5331 Variety Stores
  NAICS 45299 All Other General Merchandise Stores
5399 Miscellaneous General Merchandise Stores
  NAICS 45291 Warehouse Clubs & Superstores
  NAICS 45299 All Other General Merchandise Stores
5411 Grocery Stores
  NAICS 44711 Gasoline Stations with Convenience Stores
  NAICS 44511 Supermarkets & Other Grocery Stores
  NAICS 45291 Warehouse Clubs & Superstores
  NAICS 44512 Convenience Stores
5421 Meat & Fish Markets, Including Freezer Provisioners
  NAICS 45439 Other Direct Selling Establishments
  NAICS 44521 Meat Markets
  NAICS 44522 Fish & Seafood Markets
5431 Fruit & Vegetable Markets
  NAICS 44523 Fruit & Vegetable Markets
5441 Candy, Nut, & Confectionery Stores
  NAICS 445292 Confectionary & Nut Stores
5451 Dairy Products Stores
  NAICS 445299 All Other Specialty Food Stores
5461 Retail Bakeries
  NAICS 722213 Snack & Nonalcoholic Beverage Bars
  NAICS 311811 Retail Bakeries
  NAICS 445291 Baked Goods Stores
5499 Miscellaneous Food Stores
  NAICS 44521 Meat Markets
  NAICS 722211 Limited-service Restaurants
  NAICS 446191 Food Supplement Stores
  NAICS 445299 All Other Specialty Food Stores
5511 Motor Vehicle Dealers
  NAICS 44111 New Car Dealers

5521 Motor Vehicle Dealers
NAICS 44112   Used Car Dealers
5531 Auto & Home Supply Stores
NAICS 44132   Tire Dealers
NAICS 44131   Automotive Parts & Accessories Stores
5541 Gasoline Service Stations
NAICS 44711   Gasoline Stations with Convenience Store
NAICS 44719   Other Gasoline Stations
5551 Boat Dealers
NAICS 441222 Boat Dealers
5561 Recreational Vehicle Dealers
NAICS 44121   Recreational Vehicle Dealers
5571 Motorcycle Dealers
NAICS 441221 Motorcycle Dealers
5599 Automotive Dealers, nec
NAICS 441229 All Other Motor Vehicle Dealers
5611 Men's & Boys' Clothing & Accessory Stores
NAICS 44811   Men's Clothing Stores
NAICS 44815   Clothing Accessories Stores
5621 Women's Clothing Stores
NAICS 44812   Women's Clothing Stores
5632 Women's Accessory & Specialty Stores
NAICS 44819   Other Clothing Stores
NAICS 44815   Clothing Accessories Stores
5641 Children's & Infants' Wear Stores
NAICS 44813   Children's & Infants' Clothing Stores
5651 Family Clothing Stores
NAICS 44814   Family Clothing Stores
5661 Shoe Stores
NAICS 44821   Shoe Stores
5699 Miscellaneous Apparel & Accessory Stores
NAICS 315   Included in Apparel Manufacturing Subsector
                     Based on Type of Garment Produced
NAICS 44819   Other Clothing Stores
NAICS 44815   Clothing Accessories Stores
5712 Furniture Stores
NAICS 337133 Wood Household Furniture, Except
                     Upholstered, Manufacturing
NAICS 337131 Wood Kitchen Cabinet & Counter Top
                     Manufacturing
NAICS 337132 Upholstered Household Furniture
                     Manufacturing
NAICS 44211   Furniture Stores
5713 Floor Covering Stores
NAICS 44221   Floor Covering Stores
5714 Drapery, Curtain, & Upholstery Stores
NAICS 442291 Window Treatment Stores
NAICS 45113   Sewing, Needlework & Piece Goods Stores
NAICS 314121 Curtain & Drapery Mills
5719 Miscellaneous Homefurnishings Stores
NAICS 442291 Window Treatment Stores
NAICS 442299 All Other Home Furnishings Stores
5722 Household Appliance Stores
NAICS 443111 Household Appliance Stores
5731 Radio, Television, & Consumer Electronics Stores
NAICS 443112 Radio, Television, & Other Electronics Stores
NAICS 44131   Automotive Parts & Accessories Stores
5734 Computer & Computer Software Stores
NAICS 44312   Computer & Software Stores
5735 Record & Prerecorded Tape Stores
NAICS 45122   Prerecorded Tape, Compact Disc & Record
                     Stores

5736 Musical Instrument Stores
NAICS 45114   Musical Instrument & Supplies Stores
5812 Eating & Drinking Places
NAICS 72211   Full-service Restaurants
NAICS 722211 Limited-service Restaurants
NAICS 722212 Cafeterias
NAICS 722213 Snack & Nonalcoholic Beverage Bars
NAICS 72231   Foodservice Contractors
NAICS 72232   Caterers
NAICS 71111   Theater Companies & Dinner Theaters
5813 Drinking Places
NAICS 72241   Drinking Places
5912 Drug Stores & Proprietary Stores
NAICS 44611   Pharmacies & Drug Stores
5921 Liquor Stores
NAICS 44531   Beer, Wine & Liquor Stores
5932 Used Merchandise Stores
NAICS 522298 All Other Non-depository Credit
                     Intermediation
NAICS 45331   Used Merchandise Stores
5941 Sporting Goods Stores & Bicycle Shops
NAICS 45111   Sporting Goods Stores
5942 Book Stores
NAICS 451211 Book Stores
5943 Stationery Stores
NAICS 45321   Office Supplies & Stationery Stores
5944 Jewelry Stores
NAICS 44831   Jewelry Stores
5945 Hobby, Toy, & Game Shops
NAICS 45112   Hobby, Toy & Game Stores
5946 Camera & Photographic Supply Stores
NAICS 44313   Camera & Photographic Supplies Stores
5947 Gift, Novelty, & Souvenir Shops
NAICS 45322   Gift, Novelty & Souvenir Stores
5948 Luggage & Leather Goods Stores
NAICS 44832   Luggage & Leather Goods Stores
5949 Sewing, Needlework, & Piece Goods Stores
NAICS 45113   Sewing, Needlework & Piece Goods Stores
5961 Catalog & Mail-order Houses
NAICS 45411   Electronic Shopping & Mail-order Houses
5962 Automatic Merchandising Machine Operator
NAICS 45421   Vending Machine Operators
5963 Direct Selling Establishments
NAICS 72233   Mobile Caterers
NAICS 45439   Other Direct Selling Establishments
5983 Fuel Oil Dealers
NAICS 454311 Heating Oil Dealers
5984 Liquefied Petroleum Gas Dealers
NAICS 454312 Liquefied Petroleum Gas Dealers
5989 Fuel Dealers, nec
NAICS 454319 Other Fuel Dealers
5992 Florists
NAICS 45311   Florists
5993 Tobacco Stores & Stands
NAICS 453991 Tobacco Stores
5994 News Dealers & Newsstands
NAICS 451212 News Dealers & Newsstands
5995 Optical Goods Stores
NAICS 339117 Eyeglass & Contact Lens Manufacturing
NAICS 44613   Optical Goods Stores
5999 Miscellaneous Retail Stores, nec
NAICS 44612   Cosmetics, Beauty Supplies & Perfume Stores
NAICS 446199 All Other Health & Personal Care Stores
NAICS 45391   Pet & Pet Supplies Stores

NAICS 45392 Art Dealers
NAICS 443111 Household Appliance Stores
NAICS 443112 Radio, Television & Other Electronics Stores
NAICS 44831 Jewelry Stores
NAICS 453999 All Other Miscellaneous Store Retailers

FINANCE, INSURANCE, & REAL ESTATE

6011 Federal Reserve Banks
NAICS 52111 Monetary Authorities-central Banks
6019 Central Reserve Depository Institutions, nec
NAICS 52232 Financial Transactions Processing, Reserve, & Clearing House Activities
6021 National Commercial Banks
NAICS 52211 Commercial Banking
NAICS 52221 Credit Card Issuing
NAICS 523991 Trust, Fiduciary & Custody Activities
6022 State Commercial Banks
NAICS 52211 Commercial Banking
NAICS 52221 Credit Card Issuing
NAICS 52219 Other Depository Intermediation
NAICS 523991 Trust, Fiduciary & Custody Activities
6029 Commercial Banks, nec
NAICS 52211 Commercial Banking
6035 Savings Institutions, Federally Chartered
NAICS 52212 Savings Institutions
6036 Savings Institutions, Not Federally Chartered
NAICS 52212 Savings Institutions
6061 Credit Unions, Federally Chartered
NAICS 52213 Credit Unions
6062 Credit Unions, Not Federally Chartered
NAICS 52213 Credit Unions
6081 Branches & Agencies of Foreign Banks
NAICS 522293 International Trade Financing
NAICS 52211 Commercial Banking
NAICS 522298 All Other Non-depository Credit Intermediation
6082 Foreign Trade & International Banking Institutions
NAICS 522293 International Trade Financing
6091 Nondeposit Trust Facilities
NAICS 523991 Trust, Fiduciary, & Custody Activities
6099 Functions Related to Deposit Banking, nec
NAICS 52232 Financial Transactions Processing, Reserve, & Clearing House Activities
NAICS 52313 Commodity Contracts Dealing
NAICS 523991 Trust, Fiduciary, & Custody Activities
NAICS 523999 Miscellaneous Financial Investment Activities
NAICS 52239 Other Activities Related to Credit Intermediation
6111 Federal & Federally Sponsored Credit Agencies
NAICS 522293 International Trade Financing
NAICS 522294 Secondary Market Financing
NAICS 522298 All Other Non-depository Credit Intermediation
6141 Personal Credit Institutions
NAICS 52221 Credit Card Issuing
NAICS 52222 Sales Financing
NAICS 522291 Consumer Lending
6153 Short-term Business Credit Institutions, Except Agricultural
NAICS 52222 Sales Financing
NAICS 52232 Financial Transactions Processing, Reserve, & Clearing House Activities

NAICS 522298 All Other Non-depository Credit Intermediation
6159 Miscellaneous Business Credit Institutions
NAICS 52222 Sales Financing
NAICS 532   Included in Rental & Leasing Services Subsector by Type of Equipment & Method of Operation
NAICS 522293 International Trade Financing
NAICS 522298 All Other Non-depository Credit Intermediation
6162 Mortgage Bankers & Loan Correspondents
NAICS 522292 Real Estate Credit
NAICS 52239 Other Activities Related to Credit Intermediation
6163 Loan Brokers
NAICS 52231 Mortgage & Other Loan Brokers
6211 Security Brokers, Dealers, & Flotation Companies
NAICS 52311 Investment Banking & Securities Dealing
NAICS 52312 Securities Brokerage
NAICS 52391 Miscellaneous Intermediation
NAICS 523999 Miscellaneous Financial Investment Activities
6221 Commodity Contracts Brokers & Dealers
NAICS 52313 Commodity Contracts Dealing
NAICS 52314 Commodity Brokerage
6231 Security & Commodity Exchanges
NAICS 52321 Securities & Commodity Exchanges
6282 Investment Advice
NAICS 52392 Portfolio Management
NAICS 52393 Investment Advice
6289 Services Allied with the Exchange of Securities or Commodities, nec
NAICS 523991 Trust, Fiduciary, & Custody Activities
NAICS 523999 Miscellaneous Financial Investment Activities
6311 Life Insurance
NAICS 524113 Direct Life Insurance Carriers
NAICS 52413 Reinsurance Carriers
6321 Accident & Health Insurance
NAICS 524114 Direct Health & Medical Insurance Carriers
NAICS 52519 Other Insurance Funds
NAICS 52413 Reinsurance Carriers
6324 Hospital & Medical Service Plans
NAICS 524114 Direct Health & Medical Insurance Carriers
NAICS 52519 Other Insurance Funds
NAICS 52413 Reinsurance Carriers
6331 Fire, Marine, & Casualty Insurance
NAICS 524126 Direct Property & Casualty Insurance Carriers
NAICS 52519 Other Insurance Funds
NAICS 52413 Reinsurance Carriers
6351 Surety Insurance
NAICS 524126 Direct Property & Casualty Insurance Carriers
NAICS 52413 Reinsurance Carriers
6361 Title Insurance
NAICS 524127 Direct Title Insurance Carriers
NAICS 52413 Reinsurance Carriers
6371 Pension, Health, & Welfare Funds
NAICS 52392 Portfolio Management
NAICS 524292 Third Party Administration for Insurance & Pension Funds
NAICS 52511 Pension Funds
NAICS 52512 Health & Welfare Funds
6399 Insurance Carriers, nec
NAICS 524128 Other Direct Insurance Carriers

6411 Insurance Agents, Brokers, & Service
NAICS 52421   Insurance Agencies & Brokerages
NAICS 524291 Claims Adjusters
NAICS 524292 Third Party Administrators for Insurance & Pension Funds
NAICS 524298 All Other Insurance Related Activities

6512 Operators of Nonresidential Buildings
NAICS 71131   Promoters of Performing Arts, Sports & Similar Events with Facilities
NAICS 53112   Lessors of Nonresidential Buildings

6513 Operators of Apartment Buildings
NAICS 53111   Lessors of Residential Buildings & Dwellings

6514 Operators of Dwellings Other than Apartment Buildings
NAICS 53111   Lessors of Residential Buildings & Dwellings

6515 Operators of Residential Mobile Home Sites
NAICS 53119   Lessors of Other Real Estate Property

6517 Lessors of Railroad Property
NAICS 53119   Lessors of Other Real Estate Property

6519 Lessors of Real Property, nec
NAICS 53119   Lessors of Other Real Estate Property

6531 Real Estate Agents & Managers
NAICS 53121   Offices of Real Estate Agents & Brokers
NAICS 81399   Other Similar Organizations
NAICS 531311 Residential Property Managers
NAICS 531312 Nonresidential Property Managers
NAICS 53132   Offices of Real Estate Appraisers
NAICS 81222   Cemeteries & Crematories
NAICS 531399 All Other Activities Related to Real Estate

6541 Title Abstract Offices
NAICS 541191 Title Abstract & Settlement Offices

6552 Land Subdividers & Developers, Except Cemeteries
NAICS 23311   Land Subdivision & Land Development

6553 Cemetery Subdividers & Developers
NAICS 81222   Cemeteries & Crematories

6712 Offices of Bank Holding Companies
NAICS 551111 Offices of Bank Holding Companies

6719 Offices of Holding Companies, nec
NAICS 551112 Offices of Other Holding Companies

6722 Management Investment Offices, Open-end
NAICS 52591   Open-end Investment Funds

6726 Unit Investment Trusts, Face-amount Certificate Offices, & Closed-end Management Investment Offices
NAICS 52599   Other Financial Vehicles

6732 Education, Religious, & Charitable Trusts
NAICS 813211 Grantmaking Foundations

6733 Trusts, Except Educational, Religious, & Charitable
NAICS 52392   Portfolio Management
NAICS 523991 Trust, Fiduciary, & Custody Services
NAICS 52519   Other Insurance Funds
NAICS 52592   Trusts, Estates, & Agency Accounts

6792 Oil Royalty Traders
NAICS 523999 Miscellaneous Financial Investment Activities
NAICS 53311   Owners & Lessors of Other Non-financial Assets

6794 Patent Owners & Lessors
NAICS 53311   Owners & Lessors of Other Non-financial Assets

6798 Real Estate Investment Trusts
NAICS 52593   Real Estate Investment Trusts

6799 Investors, nec
NAICS 52391   Miscellaneous Intermediation
NAICS 52392   Portfolio Management
NAICS 52313   Commodity Contracts Dealing
NAICS 523999 Miscellaneous Financial Investment Activities

SERVICE INDUSTRIES

7011 Hotels & Motels
NAICS 72111   Hotels & Motels
NAICS 72112   Casino Hotels
NAICS 721191 Bed & Breakfast Inns
NAICS 721199 All Other Traveler Accommodation

7021 Rooming & Boarding Houses
NAICS 72131   Rooming & Boarding Houses

7032 Sporting & Recreational Camps
NAICS 721214 Recreational & Vacation Camps

7033 Recreational Vehicle Parks & Campsites
NAICS 721211 Rv & Campgrounds

7041 Organization Hotels & Lodging Houses, on Membership Basis
NAICS 72111   Hotels & Motels
NAICS 72131   Rooming & Boarding Houses

7211 Power Laundries, Family & Commercial
NAICS 812321 Laundries, Family & Commercial

7212 Garment Pressing, & Agents for Laundries
NAICS 812391 Garment Pressing & Agents for Laundries

7213 Linen Supply
NAICS 812331 Linen Supply

7215 Coin-operated Laundry & Drycleaning
NAICS 81231   Coin-operated Laundries & Drycleaners

7216 Drycleaning Plants, Except Rug Cleaning
NAICS 812322 Drycleaning Plants

7217 Carpet & Upholstery Cleaning
NAICS 56174   Carpet & Upholstery Cleaning Services

7218 Industrial Launderers
NAICS 812332 Industrial Launderers

7219 Laundry & Garment Services, nec
NAICS 812331 Linen Supply
NAICS 81149   Other Personal & Household Goods Repair & Maintenance
NAICS 812399 All Other Laundry Services

7221 Photographic Studios, Portrait
NAICS 541921 Photographic Studios, Portrait

7231 Beauty Shops
NAICS 812112 Beauty Salons
NAICS 812113 Nail Salons
NAICS 611511 Cosmetology & Barber Schools

7241 Barber Shops
NAICS 812111 Barber Shops
NAICS 611511 Cosmetology & Barber Schools

7251 Shoe Repair Shops & Shoeshine Parlors
NAICS 81143   Footwear & Leather Goods Repair

7261 Funeral Services & Crematories
NAICS 81221   Funeral Homes
NAICS 81222   Cemeteries & Crematories

7291 Tax Return Preparation Services
NAICS 541213 Tax Preparation Services

7299 Miscellaneous Personal Services, nec
NAICS 62441   Child Day Care Services
NAICS 812191 Diet & Weight Reducing Centers
NAICS 53222   Formal Wear & Costume Rental
NAICS 812199 Other Personal Care Services
NAICS 81299   All Other Personal Services

7311 Advertising Agencies
NAICS 54181   Advertising Agencies

7312 Outdoor Advertising Services
NAICS 54185   Display Advertising

7313 Radio, Television, & Publishers' Advertising Representatives
NAICS 54184   Media Representatives
7319 Advertising, nec
NAICS 481219 Other Nonscheduled Air Transportation
NAICS 54183   Media Buying Agencies
NAICS 54185   Display Advertising
NAICS 54187   Advertising Material Distribution Services
NAICS 54189   Other Services Related to Advertising
7322 Adjustment & Collection Services
NAICS 56144   Collection Agencies
NAICS 561491 Repossession Services
7323 Credit Reporting Services
NAICS 56145   Credit Bureaus
7331 Direct Mail Advertising Services
NAICS 54186   Direct Mail Advertising
7334 Photocopying & Duplicating Services
NAICS 561431 Photocopying & Duplicating Services
7335 Commercial Photography
NAICS 48122   Nonscheduled Speciality Air Transportation
NAICS 541922 Commercial Photography
7336 Commercial Art & Graphic Design
NAICS 54143   Commercial Art & Graphic Design Services
7338 Secretarial & Court Reporting Services
NAICS 56141   Document Preparation Services
NAICS 561492 Court Reporting & Stenotype Services
7342 Disinfecting & Pest Control Services
NAICS 56172   Janitorial Services
NAICS 56171   Exterminating & Pest Control Services
7349 Building Cleaning & Maintenance Services, nec
NAICS 56172   Janitorial Services
7352 Medical Equipment Rental & Leasing
NAICS 532291 Home Health Equipment Rental
NAICS 53249   Other Commercial & Industrial Machinery & Equipment Rental & Leasing
7353 Heavy Construction Equipment Rental & Leasing
NAICS 23499   All Other Heavy Construction
NAICS 532412 Construction, Mining & Forestry Machinery & Equipment Rental & Leasing
7359 Equipment Rental & Leasing, nec
NAICS 53221   Consumer Electronics & Appliances Rental
NAICS 53231   General Rental Centers
NAICS 532299 All Other Consumer Goods Rental
NAICS 532412 Construction, Mining & Forestry Machinery & Equipment Rental & Leasing
NAICS 532411 Commercial Air, Rail, & Water Transportation Equipment Rental & Leasing
NAICS 562991 Septic Tank & Related Services
NAICS 53242   Office Machinery & Equipment Rental & Leasing
NAICS 53249   Other Commercial & Industrial Machinery & Equipment Rental & Leasing
7361 Employment Agencies
NAICS 541612 Human Resources & Executive Search Consulting Services
NAICS 56131   Employment Placement Agencies
7363 Help Supply Services
NAICS 56132   Temporary Help Services
NAICS 56133   Employee Leasing Services
7371 Computer Programming Services
NAICS 541511 Custom Computer Programming Services
7372 Prepackaged Software
NAICS 51121   Software Publishers
NAICS 334611 Software Reproducing

7373 Computer Integrated Systems Design
NAICS 541512 Computer Systems Design Services
7374 Computer Processing & Data Preparation & Processing Services
NAICS 51421   Data Processing Services
7375 Information Retrieval Services
NAICS 514191 On-line Information Services
7376 Computer Facilities Management Services
NAICS 541513 Computer Facilities Management Services
7377 Computer Rental & Leasing
NAICS 53242   Office Machinery & Equipment Rental & Leasing
7378 Computer Maintenance & Repair
NAICS 44312   Computer & Software Stores
NAICS 811212 Computer & Office Machine Repair & Maintenance
7379 Computer Related Services, nec
NAICS 541512 Computer Systems Design Services
NAICS 541519 Other Computer Related Services
7381 Detective, Guard, & Armored Car Services
NAICS 561611 Investigation Services
NAICS 561612 Security Guards & Patrol Services
NAICS 561613 Armored Car Services
7382 Security Systems Services
NAICS 561621 Security Systems Services
7383 News Syndicates
NAICS 51411   New Syndicates
7384 Photofinishing Laboratories
NAICS 812921 Photo Finishing Laboratories
NAICS 812922 One-hour Photo Finishing
7389 Business Services, nec
NAICS 51224   Sound Recording Studios
NAICS 51229   Other Sound Recording Industries
NAICS 541199 All Other Legal Services
NAICS 81299   All Other Personal Services
NAICS 54137   Surveying & Mapping Services
NAICS 54141   Interior Design Services
NAICS 54142   Industrial Design Services
NAICS 54134   Drafting Services
NAICS 54149   Other Specialized Design Services
NAICS 54189   Other Services Related to Advertising
NAICS 54193   Translation & Interpretation Services
NAICS 54135   Building Inspection Services
NAICS 54199   All Other Professional, Scientific & Technical Services
NAICS 71141   Agents & Managers for Artists, Athletes, Entertainers & Other Public Figures
NAICS 561422 Telemarketing Bureaus
NAICS 561432 Private Mail Centers
NAICS 561439 Other Business Service Centers
NAICS 561491 Repossession Services
NAICS 56191   Packaging & Labeling Services
NAICS 56179   Other Services to Buildings & Dwellings
NAICS 561599 All Other Travel Arrangement & Reservation Services
NAICS 56192   Convention & Trade Show Organizers
NAICS 561591 Convention & Visitors Bureaus
NAICS 52232   Financial Transactions, Processing, Reserve & Clearing House Activities
NAICS 561499 All Other Business Support Services
NAICS 56199   All Other Support Services
7513 Truck Rental & Leasing, Without Drivers
NAICS 53212   Truck, Utility Trailer & Rv Rental & Leasing

7514 Passenger Car Rental
NAICS 532111 Passenger Cars Rental
7515 Passenger Car Leasing
NAICS 532112 Passenger Cars Leasing
7519 Utility Trailer & Recreational Vehicle Rental
NAICS 53212 Truck, Utility Trailer & Rv Rental & Leasing
7521 Automobile Parking
NAICS 81293 Parking Lots & Garages
7532 Top, Body, & Upholstery Repair Shops & Paint Shops
NAICS 811121 Automotive Body, Paint, & Upholstery Repair
         & Maintenance
7533 Automotive Exhaust System Repair Shops
NAICS 811112 Automotive Exhaust System Repair
7534 Tire Retreading & Repair Shops
NAICS 326212 Tire Retreading
NAICS 811198 All Other Automotive Repair & Maintenance
7536 Automotive Glass Replacement Shops
NAICS 811122 Automotive Glass Replacement Shops
7537 Automotive Transmission Repair Shops
NAICS 811113 Automotive Transmission Repair
7538 General Automotive Repair Shops
NAICS 811111 General Automotive Repair
7539 Automotive Repair Shops, nec
NAICS 811118 Other Automotive Mechanical & Electrical
         Repair & Maintenance
7542 Carwashes
NAICS 811192 Car Washes
7549 Automotive Services, Except Repair & Carwashes
NAICS 811191 Automotive Oil Change & Lubrication Shops
NAICS 48841 Motor Vehicle Towing
NAICS 811198 All Other Automotive Repair & Maintenance
7622 Radio & Television Repair Shops
NAICS 811211 Consumer Electronics Repair & Maintenance
NAICS 443112 Radio, Television & Other Electronics Stores
7623 Refrigeration & Air-conditioning Services & Repair Shops
NAICS 443111 Household Appliance Stores
NAICS 81131 Commercial & Industrial Machinery &
         Equipment Repair & Maintenance
NAICS 811412 Appliance Repair & Maintenance
7629 Electrical & Electronic Repair Shops, nec
NAICS 443111 Household Appliance Stores
NAICS 811212 Computer & Office Machine Repair &
         Maintenance
NAICS 811213 Communication Equipment Repair &
         Maintenance
NAICS 811219 Other Electronic & Precision Equipment
         Repair & Maintenance
NAICS 811412 Appliance Repair & Maintenance
NAICS 811211 Consumer Electronics Repair & Maintenance
7631 Watch, Clock, & Jewelry Repair
NAICS 81149 Other Personal & Household Goods Repair &
         Maintenance
7641 Reupholster & Furniture Repair
NAICS 81142 Reupholstery & Furniture Repair
7692 Welding Repair
NAICS 81149 Other Personal & Household Goods Repair &
         Maintenance
7694 Armature Rewinding Shops
NAICS 81131 Commercial & Industrial Machinery &
         Equipment Repair & Maintenance
NAICS 335312 Motor & Generator Manufacturing
7699 Repair Shops & Related Services, nec
NAICS 561622 Locksmiths
NAICS 562991 Septic Tank & Related Services

NAICS 56179 Other Services to Buildings & Dwellings
NAICS 48839 Other Supporting Activities for Water
         Transportation
NAICS 45111 Sporting Goods Stores
NAICS 81131 Commercial & Industrial Machinery &
         Equipment Repair & Maintenance
NAICS 11521 Support Activities for Animal Production
NAICS 811212 Computer & Office Machine Repair &
         Maintenance
NAICS 811219 Other Electronic & Precision Equipment
         Repair & Maintenance
NAICS 811411 Home & Garden Equipment Repair &
         Maintenance
NAICS 811412 Appliance Repair & Maintenance
NAICS 81143 Footwear & Leather Goods Repair
NAICS 81149 Other Personal & Household Goods Repair &
         Maintenance
7812 Motion Picture & Video Tape Production
NAICS 51211 Motion Picture & Video Production
7819 Services Allied to Motion Picture Production
NAICS 512191 Teleproduction & Other Post-production
         Services
NAICS 56131 Employment Placement Agencies
NAICS 53222 Formal Wear & Costumes Rental
NAICS 53249 Other Commercial & Industrial Machinery &
         Equipment Rental & Leasing
NAICS 541214 Payroll Services
NAICS 71151 Independent Artists, Writers, & Performers
NAICS 334612 Prerecorded Compact Disc , Tape, & Record
         Manufacturing
NAICS 512199 Other Motion Picture & Video Industries
7822 Motion Picture & Video Tape Distribution
NAICS 42199 Other Miscellaneous Durable Goods
         Wholesalers
NAICS 51212 Motion Picture & Video Distribution
7829 Services Allied to Motion Picture Distribution
NAICS 512199 Other Motion Picture & Video Industries
NAICS 51212 Motion Picture & Video Distribution
7832 Motion Picture Theaters, Except Drive-ins.
NAICS 512131 Motion Picture Theaters, Except Drive-in
7833 Drive-in Motion Picture Theaters
NAICS 512132 Drive-in Motion Picture Theaters
7841 Video Tape Rental
NAICS 53223 Video Tapes & Disc Rental
7911 Dance Studios, Schools, & Halls
NAICS 71399 All Other Amusement & Recreation Industries
NAICS 61161 Fine Arts Schools
7922 Theatrical Producers & Miscellaneous Theatrical Services
NAICS 56131 Employment Placement Agencies
NAICS 71111 Theater Companies & Dinner Theaters
NAICS 71141 Agents & Managers for Artists, Athletes,
         Entertainers & Other Public Figures
NAICS 71112 Dance Companies
NAICS 71131 Promoters of Performing Arts, Sports, &
         Similar Events with Facilities
NAICS 71132 Promoters of Performing Arts, Sports, &
         Similar Events Without Facilities
NAICS 51229 Other Sound Recording Industries
NAICS 53249 Other Commercial & Industrial Machinery &
         Equipment Rental & Leasing
**7929 Bands, Orchestras, Actors, & Other Entertainers &
   Entertainment Groups**
NAICS 71113 Musical Groups & Artists
NAICS 71151 Independent Artists, Writers, & Performers

NAICS 71119 Other Performing Arts Companies
7933 Bowling Centers
NAICS 71395 Bowling Centers
7941 Professional Sports Clubs & Promoters
NAICS 711211 Sports Teams & Clubs
NAICS 71141 Agents & Managers for Artists, Athletes, Entertainers , & Other Public Figures
NAICS 71132 Promoters of Arts, Sports & Similar Events Without Facilities
NAICS 71131 Promoters of Arts, Sports, & Similar Events with Facilities
NAICS 711219 Other Spectator Sports
7948 Racing, Including Track Operations
NAICS 711212 Race Tracks
NAICS 711219 Other Spectator Sports
7991 Physical Fitness Facilities
NAICS 71394 Fitness & Recreational Sports Centers
7992 Public Golf Courses
NAICS 71391 Golf Courses & Country Clubs
7993 Coin Operated Amusement Devices
NAICS 71312 Amusement Arcades
NAICS 71329 Other Gambling Industries
NAICS 71399 All Other Amusement & Recreation Industries
7996 Amusement Parks
NAICS 71311 Amusement & Theme Parks
7997 Membership Sports & Recreation Clubs
NAICS 48122 Nonscheduled Speciality Air Transportation
NAICS 71391 Golf Courses & Country Clubs
NAICS 71394 Fitness & Recreational Sports Centers
NAICS 71399 All Other Amusement & Recreation Industries
7999 Amusement & Recreation Services, nec
NAICS 561599 All Other Travel Arrangement & Reservation Services
NAICS 48799 Scenic & Sightseeing Transportation, Other
NAICS 71119 Other Performing Arts Companies
NAICS 711219 Other Spectator Sports
NAICS 71392 Skiing Facilities
NAICS 71394 Fitness & Recreational Sports Centers
NAICS 71321 Casinos
NAICS 71329 Other Gambling Industries
NAICS 71219 Nature Parks & Other Similar Institutions
NAICS 61162 Sports & Recreation Instruction
NAICS 532292 Recreational Goods Rental
NAICS 48711 Scenic & Sightseeing Transportation, Land
NAICS 48721 Scenic & Sightseeing Transportation, Water
NAICS 71399 All Other Amusement & Recreation Industries
8011 Offices & Clinics of Doctors of Medicine
NAICS 621493 Freestanding Ambulatory Surgical & Emergency Centers
NAICS 621491 Hmo Medical Centers
NAICS 621112 Offices of Physicians, Mental Health Specialists
NAICS 621111 Offices of Physicians
8021 Offices & Clinics of Dentists
NAICS 62121 Offices of Dentists
8031 Offices & Clinics of Doctors of Osteopathy
NAICS 621111 Offices of Physicians
NAICS 621112 Offices of Physicians, Mental Health Specialists
8041 Offices & Clinics of Chiropractors
NAICS 62131 Offices of Chiropractors
8042 Offices & Clinics of Optometrists
NAICS 62132 Offices of Optometrists
8043 Offices & Clinics of Podiatrists
NAICS 621391 Offices of Podiatrists

8049 Offices & Clinics of Health Practitioners, nec
NAICS 62133 Offices of Mental Health Practitioners
NAICS 62134 Offices of Physical, Occupational, & Speech Therapists & Audiologists
NAICS 621399 Offices of All Other Miscellaneous Health Practitioners
8051 Skilled Nursing Care Facilities
NAICS 623311 Continuing Care Retirement Communities
NAICS 62311 Nursing Care Facilities
8052 Intermediate Care Facilities
NAICS 623311 Continuing Care Retirement Communities
NAICS 62321 Residential Mental Retardation Facilities
NAICS 62311 Nursing Care Facilities
8059 Nursing & Personal Care Facilities, nec
NAICS 623311 Continuing Care Retirement Communities
NAICS 62311 Nursing Care Facilities
8062 General Medical & Surgical Hospitals
NAICS 62211 General Medical & Surgical Hospitals
8063 Psychiatric Hospitals
NAICS 62221 Psychiatric & Substance Abuse Hospitals
8069 Specialty Hospitals, Except Psychiatric
NAICS 62211 General Medical & Surgical Hospitals
NAICS 62221 Psychiatric & Substance Abuse Hospitals
NAICS 62231 Specialty Hospitals
8071 Medical Laboratories
NAICS 621512 Diagnostic Imaging Centers
NAICS 621511 Medical Laboratories
8072 Dental Laboratories
NAICS 339116 Dental Laboratories
8082 Home Health Care Services
NAICS 62161 Home Health Care Services
8092 Kidney Dialysis Centers
NAICS 621492 Kidney Dialysis Centers
8093 Specialty Outpatient Facilities, nec
NAICS 62141 Family Planning Centers
NAICS 62142 Outpatient Mental Health & Substance Abuse Centers
NAICS 621498 All Other Outpatient Care Facilities
8099 Health & Allied Services, nec
NAICS 621991 Blood & Organ Banks
NAICS 54143 Graphic Design Services
NAICS 541922 Commercial Photography
NAICS 62141 Family Planning Centers
NAICS 621999 All Other Miscellaneous Ambulatory Health Care Services
8111 Legal Services
NAICS 54111 Offices of Lawyers
8211 Elementary & Secondary Schools
NAICS 61111 Elementary & Secondary Schools
8221 Colleges, Universities, & Professional Schools
NAICS 61131 Colleges, Universities & Professional Schools
8222 Junior Colleges & Technical Institutes
NAICS 61121 Junior Colleges
8231 Libraries
NAICS 51412 Libraries & Archives
8243 Data Processing Schools
NAICS 611519 Other Technical & Trade Schools
NAICS 61142 Computer Training
8244 Business & Secretarial Schools
NAICS 61141 Business & Secretarial Schools
8249 Vocational Schools, nec
NAICS 611513 Apprenticeship Training
NAICS 611512 Flight Training
NAICS 611519 Other Technical & Trade Schools

8299 Schools & Educational Services, nec
NAICS 48122 Nonscheduled speciality Air Transportation
NAICS 611512 Flight Training
NAICS 611692 Automobile Driving Schools
NAICS 61171 Educational Support Services
NAICS 611691 Exam Preparation & Tutoring
NAICS 61161 Fine Arts Schools
NAICS 61163 Language Schools
NAICS 61143 Professional & Management Development
         Training Schools
NAICS 611699 All Other Miscellaneous Schools & Instruction
8322 Individual & Family Social Services
NAICS 62411 Child & Youth Services
NAICS 62421 Community Food Services
NAICS 624229 Other Community Housing Services
NAICS 62423 Emergency & Other Relief Services
NAICS 62412 Services for the Elderly & Persons with
         Disabilities
NAICS 624221 Temporary Shelters
NAICS 92215 Parole Offices & Probation Offices
NAICS 62419 Other Individual & Family Services
8331 Job Training & Vocational Rehabilitation Services
NAICS 62431 Vocational Rehabilitation Services
8351 Child Day Care Services
NAICS 62441 Child Day Care Services
8361 Residential Care
NAICS 623312 Homes for the Elderly
NAICS 62322 Residential Mental Health & Substance Abuse
         Facilities
NAICS 62399 Other Residential Care Facilities
8399 Social Services, nec
NAICS 813212 Voluntary Health Organizations
NAICS 813219 Other Grantmaking & Giving Services
NAICS 813311 Human Rights Organizations
NAICS 813312 Environment, Conservation & Wildlife
         Organizations
NAICS 813319 Other Social Advocacy Organizations
8412 Museums & Art Galleries
NAICS 71211 Museums
NAICS 71212 Historical Sites
8422 Arboreta & Botanical or Zoological Gardens
NAICS 71213 Zoos & Botanical Gardens
NAICS 71219 Nature Parks & Other Similar Institutions
8611 Business Associations
NAICS 81391 Business Associations
8621 Professional Membership Organizations
NAICS 81392 Professional Organizations
8631 Labor Unions & Similar Labor Organizations
NAICS 81393 Labor Unions & Similar Labor Organizations
8641 Civic, Social, & Fraternal Associations
NAICS 81341 Civic & Social Organizations
NAICS 81399 Other Similar Organizations
NAICS 92115 American Indian & Alaska Native Tribal
         Governments
NAICS 62411 Child & Youth Services
8651 Political Organizations
NAICS 81394 Political Organizations
8661 Religious Organizations
NAICS 81311 Religious Organizations
8699 Membership Organizations, nec
NAICS 81341 Civic & Social Organizations
NAICS 81391 Business Associations
NAICS 813312 Environment, Conservation, & Wildlife
         Organizations

NAICS 561599 All Other Travel Arrangement & Reservation
         Services
NAICS 81399 Other Similar Organizations
8711 Engineering Services
NAICS 54133 Engineering Services
8712 Architectural Services
NAICS 54131 Architectural Services
8713 Surveying Services
NAICS 48122 Nonscheduled Air Speciality Transportation
NAICS 54136 Geophysical Surveying & Mapping Services
NAICS 54137 Surveying & Mapping Services
8721 Accounting, Auditing, & Bookkeeping Services
NAICS 541211 Offices of Certified Public Accountants
NAICS 541214 Payroll Services
NAICS 541219 Other Accounting Services
8731 Commercial Physical & Biological Research
NAICS 54171 Research & Development in the Physical
         Sciences & Engineering Sciences
NAICS 54172 Research & Development in the Life Sciences
**8732 Commercial Economic, Sociological, & Educational
   Research**
NAICS 54173 Research & Development in the Social Sciences
         & Humanities
NAICS 54191 Marketing Research & Public Opinion Polling
8733 Noncommercial Research Organizations
NAICS 54171 Research & Development in the Physical
         Sciences & Engineering Sciences
NAICS 54172 Research & Development in the Life Sciences
NAICS 54173 Research & Development in the Social Sciences
         & Humanities
8734 Testing Laboratories
NAICS 54194 Veterinary Services
NAICS 54138 Testing Laboratories
8741 Management Services
NAICS 56111 Office Administrative Services
NAICS 23   Included in Construction Sector by Type of
         Construction
8742 Management Consulting Services
NAICS 541611 Administrative Management & General
         Management Consulting Services
NAICS 541612 Human Resources & Executive Search Services
NAICS 541613 Marketing Consulting Services
NAICS 541614 Process, Physical, Distribution & Logistics
         Consulting Services
8743 Public Relations Services
NAICS 54182 Public Relations Agencies
8744 Facilities Support Management Services
NAICS 56121 Facilities Support Services
8748 Business Consulting Services, nec
NAICS 61171 Educational Support Services
NAICS 541618 Other Management Consulting Services
NAICS 54169 Other Scientific & Technical Consulting
         Services
8811 Private Households
NAICS 81411 Private Households
8999 Services, nec
NAICS 71151 Independent Artists, Writers, & Performers
NAICS 51221 Record Production
NAICS 54169 Other Scientific & Technical Consulting
         Services
NAICS 51223 Music Publishers
NAICS 541612 Human Resources & Executive Search
         Consulting Services
NAICS 514199 All Other Information Services

NAICS 54162   Environmental Consulting Services

PUBLIC ADMINISTRATION

9111 Executive Offices
NAICS 92111   Executive Offices
9121 Legislative Bodies
NAICS 92112   Legislative Bodies
9131 Executive & Legislative Offices, Combined
NAICS 92114   Executive & Legislative Offices, Combined
9199 General Government, nec
NAICS 92119   All Other General Government
9211 Courts
NAICS 92211   Courts
9221 Police Protection
NAICS 92212   Police Protection
9222 Legal Counsel & Prosecution
NAICS 92213   Legal Counsel & Prosecution
9223 Correctional Institutions
NAICS 92214   Correctional Institutions
9224 Fire Protection
NAICS 92216   Fire Protection
9229 Public Order & Safety, nec
NAICS 92219   All Other Justice, Public Order, & Safety
9311 Public Finance, Taxation, & Monetary Policy
NAICS 92113   Public Finance
9411 Administration of Educational Programs
NAICS 92311   Administration of Education Programs
9431 Administration of Public Health Programs
NAICS 92312   Administration of Public Health Programs
9441 Administration of Social, Human Resource & Income Maintenance Programs
NAICS 92313   Administration of Social, Human Resource & Income Maintenance Programs
9451 Administration of Veteran's Affairs, Except Health Insurance
NAICS 92314   Administration of Veteran's Affairs
9511 Air & Water Resource & Solid Waste Management
NAICS 92411   Air & Water Resource & Solid Waste Management
9512 Land, Mineral, Wildlife, & Forest Conservation
NAICS 92412   Land, Mineral, Wildlife, & Forest Conservation
9531 Administration of Housing Programs
NAICS 92511   Administration of Housing Programs
9532 Administration of Urban Planning & Community & Rural Development
NAICS 92512   Administration of Urban Planning & Community & Rural Development
9611 Administration of General Economic Programs
NAICS 92611   Administration of General Economic Programs
9621 Regulations & Administration of Transportation Programs
NAICS 488111 Air Traffic Control
NAICS 92612   Regulation & Administration of Transportation Programs
9631 Regulation & Administration of Communications, Electric, Gas, & Other Utilities
NAICS 92613   Regulation & Administration of Communications, Electric, Gas, & Other Utilities
9641 Regulation of Agricultural Marketing & Commodity
NAICS 92614   Regulation of Agricultural Marketing & Commodity

9651 Regulation, Licensing, & Inspection of Miscellaneous Commercial Sectors
NAICS 92615   Regulation, Licensing, & Inspection of Miscellaneous Commercial Sectors
9661 Space Research & Technology
NAICS 92711   Space Research & Technology
9711 National Security
NAICS 92811   National Security
9721 International Affairs
NAICS 92812   International Affairs
9999 Nonclassifiable Establishments
NAICS 99999   Unclassified Establishments

NAICS TO SIC CONVERSION GUIDE

AGRICULTURE, FORESTRY, FISHING, & HUNTING

11111 Soybean Farming
SIC 0116 Soybeans
11112 Oilseed Farming
SIC 0119 Cash Grains, nec
11113 Dry Pea & Bean Farming
SIC 0119 Cash Grains, nec
11114 Wheat Farming
SIC 0111 Wheat
11115 Corn Farming
SIC 0115 Corn
SIC 0119 Cash Grains, nec
11116 Rice Farming
SIC 0112 Rice
111191 Oilseed & Grain Combination Farming
SIC 0119 Cash Grains, nec
111199 All Other Grain Farming
SIC 0119 Cash Grains, nec
111211 Potato Farming
SIC 0134 Irish Potatoes
111219 Other Vegetable & Melon Farming
SIC 0161 Vegetables & Melons
SIC 0139 Field Crops Except Cash Grains
11131 Orange Groves
SIC 0174 Citrus Fruits
11132 Citrus Groves
SIC 0174 Citrus Fruits
111331 Apple Orchards
SIC 0175 Deciduous Tree Fruits
111332 Grape Vineyards
SIC 0172 Grapes
111333 Strawberry Farming
SIC 0171 Berry Crops
111334 Berry Farming
SIC 0171 Berry Crops
111335 Tree Nut Farming
SIC 0173 Tree Nuts
111336 Fruit & Tree Nut Combination Farming
SIC 0179 Fruits & Tree Nuts, nec
111339 Other Noncitrus Fruit Farming
SIC 0175 Deciduous Tree Fruits
SIC 0179 Fruit & Tree Nuts, nec
111411 Mushroom Production
SIC 0182 Food Crops Grown Under Cover
111419 Other Food Crops Grown Under Cover
SIC 0182 Food Crops Grown Under Cover
111421 Nursery & Tree Production
SIC 0181 Ornamental Floriculture & Nursery Products
SIC 0811 Timber Tracts
111422 Floriculture Production
SIC 0181 Ornamental Floriculture & Nursery Products
11191 Tobacco Farming
SIC 0132 Tobacco
11192 Cotton Farming
SIC 0131 Cotton
11193 Sugarcane Farming
SIC 0133 Sugarcane & Sugar Beets

11194 Hay Farming
SIC 0139 Field Crops, Except Cash Grains, nec
111991 Sugar Beet Farming
SIC 0133 Sugarcane & Sugar Beets
111992 Peanut Farming
SIC 0139 Field Crops, Except Cash Grains, nec
111998 All Other Miscellaneous Crop Farming
SIC 0139 Field Crops, Except Cash Grains, nec
SIC 0191 General Farms, Primarily Crop
SIC 0831 Forest Products
SIC 0919 Miscellaneous Marine Products
SIC 2099 Food Preparations, nec
112111 Beef Cattle Ranching & Farming
SIC 0212 Beef Cattle, Except Feedlots
SIC 0241 Dairy Farms
112112 Cattle Feedlots
SIC 0211 Beef Cattle Feedlots
11212 Dairy Cattle & Milk Production
SIC 0241 Dairy Farms
11213 Dual Purpose Cattle Ranching & Farming
No SIC equivalent
11221 Hog & Pig Farming
SIC 0213 Hogs
11231 Chicken Egg Production
SIC 0252 Chicken Eggs
11232 Broilers & Other Meat Type Chicken Production
SIC 0251 Broiler, Fryers, & Roaster Chickens
11233 Turkey Production
SIC 0253 Turkey & Turkey Eggs
11234 Poultry Hatcheries
SIC 0254 Poultry Hatcheries
11239 Other Poultry Production
SIC 0259 Poultry & Eggs, nec
11241 Sheep Farming
SIC 0214 Sheep & Goats
11242 Goat Farming
SIC 0214 Sheep & Goats
112511 Finfish Farming & Fish Hatcheries
SIC 0273 Animal Aquaculture
SIC 0921 Fish Hatcheries & Preserves
112512 Shellfish Farming
SIC 0273 Animal Aquaculture
SIC 0921 Fish Hatcheries & Preserves
112519 Other Animal Aquaculture
SIC 0273 Animal Aquaculture
11291 Apiculture
SIC 0279 Animal Specialties, nec
11292 Horse & Other Equine Production
SIC 0272 Horses & Other Equines
11293 Fur-Bearing Animal & Rabbit Production
SIC 0271 Fur-Bearing Animals & Rabbits
11299 All Other Animal Production
SIC 0219 General Livestock, Except Dairy & Poultry
SIC 0279 Animal Specialties, nec
SIC 0291 General Farms, Primarily Livestock & Animal
    Specialties;
11311 Timber Tract Operations
SIC 0811 Timber Tracts
11321 Forest Nurseries & Gathering of Forest Products
SIC 0831 Forest Nurseries & Gathering of Forest Products
11331 Logging
SIC 2411 Logging

114111 Finfish Fishing
SIC 0912 Finfish
114112 Shellfish Fishing
SIC 0913 Shellfish
114119 Other Marine Fishing
SIC 0919 Miscellaneous Marine Products
11421 Hunting & Trapping
SIC 0971 Hunting & Trapping, & Game Propagation;
115111 Cotton Ginning
SIC 0724 Cotton Ginning
115112 Soil Preparation, Planting, & Cultivating
SIC 0711 Soil Preparation Services
SIC 0721 Crop Planting, Cultivating, & Protecting
115113 Crop Harvesting, Primarily by Machine
SIC 0722 Crop Harvesting, Primarily by Machine
115114 Other Postharvest Crop Activities
SIC 0723 Crop Preparation Services For Market, Except Cotton Ginning
115115 Farm Labor Contractors & Crew Leaders
SIC 0761 Farm Labor Contractors & Crew Leaders
115116 Farm Management Services
SIC 0762 Farm Management Services
11521 Support Activities for Animal Production
SIC 0751 Livestock Services, Except Veterinary
SIC 0752 Animal Specialty Services, Except Veterinary
SIC 7699 Repair Services, nec
11531 Support Activities for Forestry
SIC 0851 Forestry Services

MINING

211111 Crude Petroleum & Natural Gas Extraction
SIC 1311 Crude Petroleum & Natural Gas
211112 Natural Gas Liquid Extraction
SIC 1321 Natural Gas Liquids
212111 Bituminous Coal & Lignite Surface Mining
SIC 1221 Bituminous Coal & Lignite Surface Mining
212112 Bituminous Coal Underground Mining
SIC 1222 Bituminous Coal Underground Mining
212113 Anthracite Mining
SIC 1231 Anthracite Mining
21221 Iron Ore Mining
SIC 1011 Iron Ores
212221 Gold Ore Mining
SIC 1041 Gold Ores
212222 Silver Ore Mining
SIC 1044 Silver Ores
212231 Lead Ore & Zinc Ore Mining
SIC 1031 Lead & Zinc Ores
212234 Copper Ore & Nickel Ore Mining
SIC 1021 Copper Ores
212291 Uranium-Radium-Vanadium Ore Mining
SIC 1094 Uranium-Radium-Vanadium Ores
212299 All Other Metal Ore Mining
SIC 1061 Ferroalloy Ores, Except Vanadium
SIC 1099 Miscellaneous Metal Ores, nec
212311 Dimension Stone Mining & Quarrying
SIC 1411 Dimension Stone
212312 Crushed & Broken Limestone Mining & Quarrying
SIC 1422 Crushed & Broken Limestone
212313 Crushed & Broken Granite Mining & Quarrying
SIC 1423 Crushed & Broken Granite

212319 Other Crushed & Broken Stone Mining & Quarrying
SIC 1429 Crushed & Broken Stone, nec
SIC 1499 Miscellaneous Nonmetallic Minerals, Except Fuels
212321 Construction Sand & Gravel Mining
SIC 1442 Construction Sand & Gravel
212322 Industrial Sand Mining
SIC 1446 Industrial Sand
212324 Kaolin & Ball Clay Mining
SIC 1455 Kaolin & Ball Clay
212325 Clay & Ceramic & Refractory Minerals Mining
SIC 1459 Clay, Ceramic, & Refractory Minerals, nec
212391 Potash, Soda, & Borate Mineral Mining
SIC 1474 Potash, Soda, & Borate Minerals
212392 Phosphate Rock Mining
SIC 1475 Phosphate Rock
212393 Other Chemical & Fertilizer Mineral Mining
SIC 1479 Chemical & Fertilizer Mineral Mining, nec
212399 All Other Nonmetallic Mineral Mining
SIC 1499 Miscellaneous Nonmetallic Minerals, Except Fuels
213111 Drilling Oil & Gas Wells
SIC 1381 Drilling Oil & Gas Wells
213112 Support Activities for Oil & Gas Operations
SIC 1382 Oil & Gas Field Exploration Services
SIC 1389 Oil & Gas Field Services, nec
213113 Other Gas & Field Support Activities
SIC 1389 Oil & Gas Field Services, nec
213114 Support Activities for Coal Mining
SIC 1241 Coal Mining Services
213115 Support Activities for Metal Mining
SIC 1081 Metal Mining Services
213116 Support Activities for Nonmetallic Minerals, Except Fuels
SIC 1481 Nonmetallic Minerals Services, Except Fuels

UTILITIES

221111 Hydroelectric Power Generation
SIC 4911 Electric Services
SIC 4931 Electric & Other Services Combined
SIC 4939 Combination Utilities, nec
221112 Fossil Fuel Electric Power Generation
SIC 4911 Electric Services
SIC 4931 Electric & Other Services Combined
SIC 4939 Combination Utilities, nec
221113 Nuclear Electric Power Generation
SIC 4911 Electric Services
SIC 4931 Electric & Other Services Combined
SIC 4939 Combination Utilities, nec
221119 Other Electric Power Generation
SIC 4911 Electric Services
SIC 4931 Electric & Other Services Combined
SIC 4939 Combination Utilities, nec
221121 Electric Bulk Power Transmission & Control
SIC 4911 Electric Services
SIC 4931 Electric & Other Services Combined
SIC 4939 Combination Utilities, NEC
221122 Electric Power Distribution
SIC 4911 Electric Services
SIC 4931 Electric & Other Services Combined
SIC 4939 Combination Utilities, nec
22121 Natural Gas Distribution
SIC 4923 Natural Gas Transmission & Distribution
SIC 4924 Natural Gas Distribution

SIC 4925 Mixed, Manufactured, or Liquefied Petroleum Gas
Production and/or Distribution
SIC 4931 Electronic & Other Services Combined
SIC 4932 Gas & Other Services Combined
SIC 4939 Combination Utilities, nec

22131 Water Supply & Irrigation Systems
SIC 4941 Water Supply
SIC 4971 Irrigation Systems

22132 Sewage Treatment Facilities
SIC 4952 Sewerage Systems

22133 Steam & Air-Conditioning Supply
SIC 4961 Steam & Air-Conditioning Supply

CONSTRUCTION

23311 Land Subdivision & Land Development
SIC 6552 Land Subdividers & Developers, Except Cemeteries

23321 Single Family Housing Construction
SIC 1521 General contractors-Single-Family Houses
SIC 1531 Operative Builders

23322 Multifamily Housing Construction
SIC 1522 General Contractors-Residential Building, Other
Than Single-Family
SIC 1531 Operative Builders

23331 Manufacturing & Industrial Building Construction
SIC 1531 Operative Builders
SIC 1541 General Contractors-Industrial Buildings &
Warehouses

23332 Commercial & Institutional Building Construction
SIC 1522 General Contractors-Residential Building Other than
Single-Family
SIC 1531 Operative Builders
SIC 1541 General Contractors-Industrial Buildings &
Warehouses
SIC 1542 General Contractor-Nonresidential Buildings, Other
than Industrial Buildings & Warehouses

23411 Highway & Street Construction
SIC 1611 Highway & Street Construction, Except Elevated
Highways

23412 Bridge & Tunnel Construction
SIC 1622 Bridge, Tunnel, & Elevated Highway Construction

2349 Other Heavy Construction

23491 Water, Sewer, & Pipeline Construction
SIC 1623 Water, Sewer, Pipeline, & Communications & Power
Line Construction

**23492 Power & Communication Transmission Line
Construction**
SIC 1623 Water, Sewer, Pipelines, & Communications & Power
Line Construction

23493 Industrial Nonbuilding Structure Construction
SIC 1629 Heavy Construction, nec

23499 All Other Heavy Construction
SIC 1629 Heavy Construction, nec
SIC 7353 Construction Equipment Rental & Leasing

23511 Plumbing, Heating & Air-Conditioning Contractors
SIC 1711 Plumbing, Heating & Air-Conditioning

23521 Painting & Wall Covering Contractors
SIC 1721 Painting & Paper Hanging
SIC 1799 Special Trade Contractors, nec

23531 Electrical Contractors
SIC 1731 Electrical Work

23541 Masonry & Stone Contractors
SIC 1741 Masonry, Stone Setting & Other Stone Work

23542 Drywall, Plastering, Acoustical & Insulation Contractors
SIC 1742 Plastering, Drywall, Acoustical, & Insulation Work
SIC 1743 Terrazzo, Tile, Marble & Mosaic work
SIC 1771 Concrete Work

23543 Tile, Marble, Terrazzo & Mosaic Contractors
SIC 1743 Terrazzo, Tile, Marble, & Mosaic Work

23551 Carpentry Contractors
SIC 1751 Carpentry Work

23552 Floor Laying & Other Floor Contractors
SIC 1752 Floor Laying & Other Floor Work, nec

23561 Roofing, Siding & Sheet Metal Contractors
SIC 1761 Roofing, Siding, & Sheet Metal Work

23571 Concrete Contractors
SIC 1771 Concrete Work

23581 Water Well Drilling Contractors
SIC 1781 Water Well Drilling

23591 Structural Steel Erection Contractors
SIC 1791 Structural Steel Erection

23592 Glass & Glazing Contractors
SIC 1793 Glass & Glazing Work
SIC 1799 Specialty Trade Contractors, nec

23593 Excavation Contractors
SIC 1794 Excavation Work

23594 Wrecking & Demolition Contractors
SIC 1795 Wrecking & Demolition Work

**23595 Building Equipment & Other Machinery Installation
Contractors**
SIC 1796 Installation of Erection of Building Equipment, nec

23599 All Other Special Trade Contractors
SIC 1799 Special Trade Contractors, nec

FOOD MANUFACTURING

311111 Dog & Cat Food Manufacturing
SIC 2047 Dog & Cat Food

311119 Other Animal Food Manufacturing
SIC 2048 Prepared Feeds & Feed Ingredients for Animals &
Fowls, Except Dogs & Cats

311211 Flour Milling
SIC 2034 Dehydrated Fruits, Vegetables & Soup Mixes
SIC 2041 Flour & Other Grain Mill Products

311212 Rice Milling
SIC 2044 Rice Milling

311213 Malt Manufacturing
SIC 2083 Malt

311221 Wet Corn Milling
SIC 2046 Wet Corn Milling

311222 Soybean Processing
SIC 2075 Soybean Oil Mills
SIC 2079 Shortening, Table Oils, Margarine, & Other Edible
Fats & Oils, nec

311223 Other Oilseed Processing
SIC 2074 Cottonseed Oil Mills
SIC 2079 Shortening, Table Oils, Margarine & Other Edible
Fats & Oils, nec
SIC 2076 Vegetable Oil Mills, Except Corn, Cottonseed, &
Soybean

311225 Edible Fats & Oils Manufacturing
SIC 2077 Animal & Marine Fats & Oil, nec
SIC 2074 Cottonseed Oil Mills
SIC 2075 Soybean Oil Mills

SIC 2076 Vegetable Oil Mills, Except Corn, Cottonseed, &
   Soybean
SIC 2079 Shortening, Table Oils, Margarine, & Other Edible
   Fats & Oils, nec

31123   Breakfast Cereal Manufacturing
SIC 2043 Cereal Breakfast Foods

311311 Sugarcane Mills
SIC 2061 Cane Sugar, Except Refining

311312 Cane Sugar Refining
SIC 2062 Cane Sugar Refining

311313 Beet Sugar Manufacturing
SIC 2063 Beet Sugar

**31132   Chocolate & Confectionery Manufacturing from Cacao
   Beans**
SIC 2066 Chocolate & Cocoa Products

31133   Confectionery Manufacturing from Purchased Chocolate
SIC 2064 Candy & Other Confectionery Products

31134   Non-Chocolate Confectionery Manufacturing
SIC 2064 Candy & Other Confectionery Products
SIC 2067 Chewing Gum
SIC 2099 Food Preparations, nec

311411 Frozen Fruit, Juice & Vegetable Processing
SIC 2037 Frozen Fruits, Fruit Juices, & Vegetables

311412 Frozen Specialty Food Manufacturing
SIC 2038 Frozen Specialties, NEC

311421 Fruit & Vegetable Canning
SIC 2033 Canned Fruits, Vegetables, Preserves, Jams, & Jellies
SIC 2035 Pickled Fruits & Vegetables, Vegetable Sauces, &
   Seasonings & Salad Dressings

311422 Specialty Canning
SIC 2032 Canned Specialties

311423 Dried & Dehydrated Food Manufacturing
SIC 2034 Dried & Dehydrated Fruits, Vegetables & Soup
   Mixes
SIC 2099 Food Preparation, nec

311511 Fluid Milk Manufacturing
SIC 2026 Fluid Milk

311512 Creamery Butter Manufacturing
SIC 2021 Creamery Butter

311513 Cheese Manufacturing
SIC 2022 Natural, Processed, & Imitation Cheese

311514 Dry, Condensed, & Evaporated Milk Manufacturing
SIC 2023 Dry, Condensed & Evaporated Dairy Products

31152   Ice Cream & Frozen Dessert Manufacturing
SIC 2024 Ice Cream & Frozen Desserts

311611 Animal Slaughtering
SIC 0751 Livestock Services, Except Veterinary
SIC 2011 Meat Packing Plants
SIC 2048 Prepared Feeds & Feed Ingredients for Animals &
   Fowls, Except Dogs & Cats

311612 Meat Processed from Carcasses
SIC 2013 Sausages & Other Prepared Meats
SIC 5147 Meat & Meat Products

311613 Rendering & Meat By-product Processing
SIC 2077 Animal & Marine Fats & Oils

311615 Poultry Processing
SIC 2015 Poultry Slaughtering & Processing

311711 Seafood Canning
SIC 2077 Animal & Marine Fats & Oils
SIC 2091 Canned & Cured Fish & Seafood

311712 Fresh & Frozen Seafood Processing
SIC 2077 Animal & Marine Fats & Oils
SIC 2092 Prepared Fresh or Frozen Fish & Seafood

311811 Retail Bakeries
SIC 5461 Retail Bakeries

311812 Commercial Bakeries
SIC 2051 Bread & Other Bakery Products, Except Cookies &
   Crackers
SIC 2052 Cookies & Crackers

311813 Frozen Bakery Product Manufacturing
SIC 2053 Frozen Bakery Products, Except Bread

311821 Cookie & Cracker Manufacturing
SIC 2052 Cookies & Crackers

**311822 Flour Mixes & Dough Manufacturing from Purchased
   Flour**
SIC 2045 Prepared Flour Mixes & Doughs

311823 Pasta Manufacturing
SIC 2098 Macaroni, Spaghetti, Vermicelli & Noodles

31183   Tortilla Manufacturing
SIC 2099 Food Preparations, nec

311911 Roasted Nuts & Peanut Butter Manufacturing
SIC 2068 Salted & Roasted Nuts & Seeds
SIC 2099 Food Preparations, nec

311919 Other Snack Food Manufacturing
SIC 2052 Cookies & Crackers
SIC 2096 Potato Chips, Corn Chips, & Similar Snacks

31192   Coffee & Tea Manufacturing
SIC 2043 Cereal Breakfast Foods
SIC 2095 Roasted Coffee
SIC 2099 Food Preparations, nec

31193   Flavoring Syrup & Concentrate Manufacturing
SIC 2087 Flavoring Extracts & Flavoring Syrups

**311941 Mayonnaise, Dressing & Other Prepared Sauce
   Manufacturing**
SIC 2035 Pickled Fruits & Vegetables, Vegetable Seasonings, &
   Sauces & Salad Dressings
SIC 2099 Food Preparations, nec

311942 Spice & Extract Manufacturing
SIC 2087 Flavoring Extracts & Flavoring Syrups
SIC 2095 Roasted Coffee
SIC 2099 Food Preparations, nec
SIC 2899 Chemical Preparations, nec

311991 Perishable Prepared Food Manufacturing
SIC 2099 Food Preparations, nec

311999 All Other Miscellaneous Food Manufacturing
SIC 2015 Poultry Slaughtering & Processing
SIC 2032 Canned Specialties
SIC 2087 Flavoring Extracts & Flavoring Syrups
SIC 2099 Food Preparations, nec

BEVERAGE & TOBACCO PRODUCT MANUFACTURING

312111 Soft Drink Manufacturing
SIC 2086 Bottled & Canned Soft Drinks & Carbonated Water

312112 Bottled Water Manufacturing
SIC 2086 Bottled & Canned Soft Drinks & Carbonated Water

312113 Ice Manufacturing
SIC 2097 Manufactured Ice

31212   Breweries
SIC 2082 Malt Beverages

31213   Wineries
SIC 2084 Wines, Brandy, & Brandy Spirits

31214   Distilleries
SIC 2085 Distilled & Blended Liquors

31221 Tobacco Stemming & Redrying
SIC 2141 Tobacco Stemming & Redrying
312221 Cigarette Manufacturing
SIC 2111 Cigarettes
312229 Other Tobacco Product Manufacturing
SIC 2121 Cigars
SIC 2131 Chewing & Smoking Tobacco & Snuff
SIC 2141 Tobacco Stemming & Redrying

TEXTILE MILLS

313111 Yarn Spinning Mills
SIC 2281 Yarn Spinning Mills
SIC 2299 Textile Goods, nec
313112 Yarn Texturing, Throwing & Twisting Mills
SIC 2282 Yarn Texturing, Throwing, Winding Mills
313113 Thread Mills
SIC 2284 Thread Mills
SIC 2299 Textile Goods, NEC
31321 Broadwoven Fabric Mills
SIC 2211 Broadwoven Fabric Mills, Cotton
SIC 2221 Broadwoven Fabric Mills, Manmade Fiber & Silk
SIC 2231 Broadwoven Fabric Mills, Wool
SIC 2299 Textile Goods, nec
313221 Narrow Fabric Mills
SIC 2241 Narrow Fabric & Other Smallware Mills: Cotton,
          Wool, Silk & Manmade Fiber
SIC 2299 Textile Goods, nec
313222 Schiffli Machine Embroidery
SIC 2397 Schiffli Machine Embroideries
31323 Nonwoven Fabric Mills
SIC 2297 Nonwoven Fabrics
SIC 2299 Textile Goods, nec
313241 Weft Knit Fabric Mills
SIC 2257 Weft Knit Fabric Mills
SIC 2259 Knitting Mills nec
313249 Other Knit Fabric & Lace Mills
SIC 2258 Lace & Warp Knit Fabric Mills
SIC 2259 Knitting Mills nec
313311 Broadwoven Fabric Finishing Mills
SIC 2231 Broadwoven Fabric Mills, Wool
SIC 2261 Finishers of Broadwoven Fabrics of Cotton
SIC 2262 Finishers of Broadwoven Fabrics of Manmade Fiber
          & Silk
SIC 2269 Finishers of Textiles, nec
SIC 5131 Piece Goods & Notions
313312 Textile & Fabric Finishing Mills
SIC 2231 Broadwoven Fabric Mills, Wool
SIC 2257 Weft Knit Fabric Mills
SIC 2258 Lace & Warp Knit Fabric Mills
SIC 2269 Finishers of Textiles, nec
SIC 2282 Yarn Texturizing, Throwing, Twisting, & Winding
          Mills
SIC 2284 Thread Mills
SIC 2299 Textile Goods, nec
SIC 5131 Piece Goods & Notions
31332 Fabric Coating Mills
SIC 2295 Coated Fabrics, Not Rubberized
SIC 3069 Fabricated Rubber Products, nec

TEXTILE PRODUCT MILLS

31411 Carpet & Rug Mills
SIC 2273 Carpets & Rugs
314121 Curtain & Drapery Mills
SIC 2391 Curtains & Draperies
SIC 5714 Drapery, Curtain, & Upholstery Stores
314129 Other Household Textile Product Mills
SIC 2392 Housefurnishings, Except Curtains & Draperies
314911 Textile Bag Mills
SIC 2392 Housefurnishings, Except Curtains & Draperies
SIC 2393 Textile Bags
314912 Canvas & Related Product Mills
SIC 2394 Canvas & Related Products
314991 Rope, Cordage & Twine Mills
SIC 2298 Cordage & Twine
314992 Tire Cord & Tire Fabric Mills
SIC 2296 Tire Cord & Fabrics
314999 All Other Miscellaneous Textile Product Mills
SIC 2299 Textile Goods, nec
SIC 2395 Pleating, Decorative & Novelty Stitching, & Tucking
          for the Trade
SIC 2396 Automotive Trimmings, Apparel Findings, & Related
          Products
SIC 2399 Fabricated Textile Products, nec

APPAREL MANUFACTURING

315111 Sheer Hosiery Mills
SIC 2251 Women's Full-Length & Knee-Length Hosiery,
          Except socks
SIC 2252 Hosiery, nec
315119 Other Hosiery & Sock Mills
SIC 2252 Hosiery, nec
315191 Outerwear Knitting Mills
SIC 2253 Knit Outerwear Mills
SIC 2259 Knitting Mills, nec
315192 Underwear & Nightwear Knitting Mills
SIC 2254 Knit Underwear & Nightwear Mills
SIC 2259 Knitting Mills, nec
315211 Men's & Boys' Cut & Sew Apparel Contractors
SIC 2311 Men's & Boys' Suits, Coats, & Overcoats
SIC 2321 Men's & Boys' Shirts, Except Work Shirts
SIC 2322 Men's & Boys' Underwear & Nightwear
SIC 2325 Men's & Boys' Trousers & Slacks
SIC 2326 Men's & Boys' Work Clothing
SIC 2329 Men's & Boys' Clothing, nec
SIC 2341 Women's, Misses', Children's, & Infants' Underwear
          & Nightwear
SIC 2361 Girls', Children's, & Infants' Dresses, Blouses &
          Shirts
SIC 2369 Girls', Children's, & Infants' Outerwear, nec
SIC 2384 Robes & Dressing Gowns
SIC 2385 Waterproof Outerwear
SIC 2389 Apparel & Accessories, nec
SIC 2395 Pleating, Decorative & Novelty Stitching, & Tucking
          for the Trade
315212 Women's & Girls' Cut & Sew Apparel Contractors
SIC 2331 Women's, Misses', & Juniors' Blouses & Shirts
SIC 2335 Women's, Misses' & Juniors' Dresses
SIC 2337 Women's, Misses', & Juniors' Suits, Skirts, & Coats
SIC 2339 Women's, Misses', & Juniors' Outerwear, nec

SIC 2341 Women's, Misses', Children's, & Infants' Underwear & Nightwear
SIC 2342 Brassieres, Girdles, & Allied Garments
SIC 2361 Girls', Children's, & Infants' Dresses, Blouses, & Shirts
SIC 2369 Girls', Children's, & Infants' Outerwear, nec
SIC 2384 Robes & Dressing Gowns
SIC 2385 Waterproof Outerwear
SIC 2389 Apparel & Accessories, nec
SIC 2395 Pleating, Decorative & Novelty Stitching, & Tucking for the Trade

315221 Men's & Boys' Cut & Sew Underwear & Nightwear Manufacturing
SIC 2322 Men's & Boys' Underwear & Nightwear
SIC 2341 Women's, Misses', Children's, & Infants' Underwear & Nightwear
SIC 2369 Girls', Children's, & Infants' Outerwear, nec
SIC 2384 Robes & Dressing Gowns

315222 Men's & Boys' Cut & Sew Suit, Coat & Overcoat Manufacturing
SIC 2311 Men's & Boys' Suits, Coats, & Overcoats
SIC 2369 Girls', Children's, & Infants' Outerwear, nec
SIC 2385 Waterproof Outerwear

315223 Men's & Boys' Cut & Sew Shirt Manufacturing
SIC 2321 Men's & Boys' Shirts, Except Work Shirts
SIC 2361 Girls', Children's, & Infants' Dresses, Blouses, & Shirts

315224 Men's & Boys' Cut & Sew Trouser, Slack & Jean Manufacturing
SIC 2325 Men's & Boys' Trousers & Slacks
SIC 2369 Girls', Children's, & Infants' Outerwear, NEC

315225 Men's & Boys' Cut & Sew Work Clothing Manufacturing
SIC 2326 Men's & Boys' Work Clothing

315228 Men's & Boys' Cut & Sew Other Outerwear Manufacturing
SIC 2329 Men's & Boys' Clothing, nec
SIC 2369 Girls', Children's, & Infants' Outerwear, nec
SIC 2385 Waterproof Outerwear

315231 Women's & Girls' Cut & Sew Lingerie, Loungewear & Nightwear Manufacturing
SIC 2341 Women's, Misses', Children's, & Infants' Underwear & Nightwear
SIC 2342 Brassieres, Girdles, & Allied Garments
SIC 2369 Girls', Children's, & Infants' Outerwear, nec
SIC 2384 Robes & Dressing Gowns
SIC 2389 Apparel & Accessories, NEC

315232 Women's & Girls' Cut & Sew Blouse & Shirt Manufacturing
SIC 2331 Women's, Misses', & Juniors' Blouses & Shirts
SIC 2361 Girls', Children's, & Infants' Dresses, Blouses & Shirts

315233 Women's & Girls' Cut & Sew Dress Manufacturing
SIC 2335 Women's, Misses', & Juniors' Dresses
SIC 2361 Girls', Children's, & Infants' Dresses, Blouses & Shirts

315234 Women's & Girls' Cut & Sew Suit, Coat, Tailored Jacket & Skirt Manufacturing
SIC 2337 Women's, Misses', & Juniors' Suits, Skirts, & Coats
SIC 2369 Girls', Children's, & Infants' Outerwear, nec
SIC 2385 Waterproof Outerwear

315238 Women's & Girls' Cut & Sew Other Outerwear Manufacturing
SIC 2339 Women's, Misses', & Juniors' Outerwear, nec
SIC 2369 Girls', Children's, & Infants' Outerwear, nec

SIC 2385 Waterproof Outerwear

315291 Infants' Cut & Sew Apparel Manufacturing
SIC 2341 Women's, Misses', Children's, & Infants' Underwear & Nightwear
SIC 2361 Girls', Children's, & Infants' Dresses, Blouses, & Shirts
SIC 2369 Girls', Children's, & Infants' Outerwear, nec
SIC 2385 Waterproof Outerwear

315292 Fur & Leather Apparel Manufacturing
SIC 2371 Fur Goods
SIC 2386 Leather & Sheep-lined Clothing

315299 All Other Cut & Sew Apparel Manufacturing
SIC 2329 Men's & Boys' Outerwear, nec
SIC 2339 Women's, Misses', & Juniors' Outerwear, nec
SIC 2389 Apparel & Accessories, nec

315991 Hat, Cap & Millinery Manufacturing
SIC 2353 Hats, Caps, & Millinery

315992 Glove & Mitten Manufacturing
SIC 2381 Dress & Work Gloves, Except Knit & All-Leather
SIC 3151 Leather Gloves & Mittens

315993 Men's & Boys' Neckwear Manufacturing
SIC 2323 Men's & Boys' Neckwear

315999 Other Apparel Accessories & Other Apparel Manufacturing
SIC 2339 Women's, Misses', & Juniors' Outerwear, nec
SIC 2385 Waterproof Outerwear
SIC 2387 Apparel Belts
SIC 2389 Apparel & Accessories, nec
SIC 2396 Automotive Trimmings, Apparel Findings, & Related Products
SIC 2399 Fabricated Textile Products, nec

LEATHER & ALLIED PRODUCT MANUFACTURING

31611 Leather & Hide Tanning & Finishing
SIC 3111 Leather Tanning & Finishing
SIC 3999 Manufacturing Industries, nec

316211 Rubber & Plastics Footwear Manufacturing
SIC 3021 Rubber & Plastics Footwear

316212 House Slipper Manufacturing
SIC 3142 House Slippers

316213 Men's Footwear Manufacturing
SIC 3143 Men's Footwear, Except Athletic

316214 Women's Footwear Manufacturing
SIC 3144 Women's Footwear, Except Athletic

316219 Other Footwear Manufacturing
SIC 3149 Footwear Except Rubber, NEC

316991 Luggage Manufacturing
SIC 3161 Luggage

316992 Women's Handbag & Purse Manufacturing
SIC 3171 Women's Handbags & Purses

316993 Personal Leather Good Manufacturing
SIC 3172 Personal Leather Goods, Except Women's Handbags & Purses

316999 All Other Leather Good Manufacturing
SIC 3131 Boot & Shoe Cut Stock & Findings
SIC 3199 Leather Goods, nec

WOOD PRODUCT MANUFACTURING

321113 Sawmills
SIC 2421 Sawmills & Planing Mills, General
SIC 2429 Special Product Sawmills, nec
321114 Wood Preservation
SIC 2491 Wood Preserving
321211 Hardwood Veneer & Plywood Manufacturing
SIC 2435 Hardwood Veneer & Plywood
321212 Softwood Veneer & Plywood Manufacturing
SIC 2436 Softwood Veneer & Plywood
321213 Engineered Wood Member Manufacturing
SIC 2439 Structural Wood Members, nec
321214 Truss Manufacturing
SIC 2439 Structural Wood Members, nec
321219 Reconstituted Wood Product Manufacturing
SIC 2493 Reconstituted Wood Products
321911 Wood Window & Door Manufacturing
SIC 2431 Millwork
321912 Hardwood Dimension Mills
SIC 2426 Hardwood Dimension & Flooring Mills
321913 Softwood Cut Stock, Resawing Lumber, & Planing
SIC 2421 Sawmills & Planing Mills, General
SIC 2429 Special Product Sawmills, nec
SIC 2439 Structural Wood Members, nec
321914 Other Millwork
SIC 2421 Sawmills & Planing Mills, General
SIC 2426 Hardwood Dimension & Flooring Mills
SIC 2431 Millwork
32192 Wood Container & Pallet Manufacturing
SIC 2441 Nailed & Lock Corner Wood Boxes & Shook
SIC 2448 Wood Pallets & Skids
SIC 2449 Wood Containers, NEC
SIC 2499 Wood Products, nec
321991 Manufactured Home Manufacturing
SIC 2451 Mobile Homes
321992 Prefabricated Wood Building Manufacturing
SIC 2452 Prefabricated Wood Buildings & Components
321999 All Other Miscellaneous Wood Product Manufacturing
SIC 2426 Hardwood Dimension & Flooring Mills
SIC 2499 Wood Products, nec
SIC 3131 Boot & Shoe Cut Stock & Findings
SIC 3999 Manufacturing Industries, nec
SIC 2421 Sawmills & Planing Mills, General
SIC 2429 Special Product Sawmills, nec

PAPER MANUFACTURING

32211 Pulp Mills
SIC 2611 Pulp Mills
322121 Paper Mills
SIC 2611 Pulp Mills
SIC 2621 Paper Mills
322122 Newsprint Mills
SIC 2621 Paper Mills
32213 Paperboard Mills
SIC 2611 Pulp Mills
SIC 2631 Paperboard Mills
322211 Corrugated & Solid Fiber Box Manufacturing
SIC 2653 Corrugated & Solid Fiber Boxes
322212 Folding Paperboard Box Manufacturing
SIC 2657 Folding Paperboard Boxes, Including Sanitary

322213 Setup Paperboard Box Manufacturing
SIC 2652 Setup Paperboard Boxes
322214 Fiber Can, Tube, Drum, & Similar Products Manufacturing
SIC 2655 Fiber Cans, Tubes, Drums, & Similar Products
322215 Non-Folding Sanitary Food Container Manufacturing
SIC 2656 Sanitary Food Containers, Except Folding
SIC 2679 Converted Paper & Paperboard Products, NEC
322221 Coated & Laminated Packaging Paper & Plastics Film Manufacturing
SIC 2671 Packaging Paper & Plastics Film, Coated & Laminated
322222 Coated & Laminated Paper Manufacturing
SIC 2672 Coated & Laminated Paper, nec
SIC 2679 Converted Paper & Paperboard Products, nec
322223 Plastics, Foil, & Coated Paper Bag Manufacturing
SIC 2673 Plastics, Foil, & Coated Paper Bags
322224 Uncoated Paper & Multiwall Bag Manufacturing
SIC 2674 Uncoated Paper & Multiwall Bags
322225 Laminated Aluminum Foil Manufacturing for Flexible Packaging Uses
SIC 3497 Metal Foil & Leaf
322231 Die-Cut Paper & Paperboard Office Supplies Manufacturing
SIC 2675 Die-Cut Paper & Paperboard & Cardboard
SIC 2679 Converted Paper & Paperboard Products, nec
322232 Envelope Manufacturing
SIC 2677 Envelopes
322233 Stationery, Tablet, & Related Product Manufacturing
SIC 2678 Stationery, Tablets, & Related Products
322291 Sanitary Paper Product Manufacturing
SIC 2676 Sanitary Paper Products
322292 Surface-Coated Paperboard Manufacturing
SIC 2675 Die-Cut Paper & Paperboard & Cardboard
322298 All Other Converted Paper Product Manufacturing
SIC 2675 Die-Cut Paper & Paperboard & Cardboard
SIC 2679 Converted Paper & Paperboard Products, NEC

PRINTING & RELATED SUPPORT ACTIVITIES

323110 Commercial Lithographic Printing
SIC 2752 Commercial Printing, Lithographic
SIC 2771 Greeting Cards
SIC 2782 Blankbooks, Loose-leaf Binders & Devices
SIC 3999 Manufacturing Industries, nec
323111 Commercial Gravure Printing
SIC 2754 Commercial Printing, Gravure
SIC 2771 Greeting Cards
SIC 2782 Blankbooks, Loose-leaf Binders & Devices
SIC 3999 Manufacturing Industries, nec
323112 Commercial Flexographic Printing
SIC 2759 Commercial Printing, NEC
SIC 2771 Greeting Cards
SIC 2782 Blankbooks, Loose-leaf Binders & Devices
SIC 3999 Manufacturing Industries, nec
323113 Commercial Screen Printing
SIC 2396 Automotive Trimmings, Apparel Findings, & Related Products
SIC 2759 Commercial Printing, nec
SIC 2771 Greeting Cards
SIC 2782 Blankbooks, Loose-leaf Binders & Devices
SIC 3999 Manufacturing Industries, nec

323114 Quick Printing
SIC 2752 Commercial Printing, Lithographic
SIC 2759 Commercial Printing, nec
323115 Digital Printing
SIC 2759 Commercial Printing, nec
323116 Manifold Business Form Printing
SIC 2761 Manifold Business Forms
323117 Book Printing
SIC 2732 Book Printing
323118 Blankbook, Loose-leaf Binder & Device Manufacturing
SIC 2782 Blankbooks, Loose-leaf Binders & Devices
323119 Other Commercial Printing
SIC 2759 Commercial Printing, nec
SIC 2771 Greeting Cards
SIC 2782 Blankbooks, Loose-leaf Binders & Devices
SIC 3999 Manufacturing Industries, nec
323121 Tradebinding & Related Work
SIC 2789 Bookbinding & Related Work
323122 Prepress Services
SIC 2791 Typesetting
SIC 2796 Platemaking & Related Services

PETROLEUM & COAL PRODUCTS MANUFACTURING

32411 Petroleum Refineries
SIC 2911 Petroleum Refining
324121 Asphalt Paving Mixture & Block Manufacturing
SIC 2951 Asphalt Paving Mixtures & Blocks
324122 Asphalt Shingle & Coating Materials Manufacturing
SIC 2952 Asphalt Felts & Coatings
324191 Petroleum Lubricating Oil & Grease Manufacturing
SIC 2992 Lubricating Oils & Greases
324199 All Other Petroleum & Coal Products Manufacturing
SIC 2999 Products of Petroleum & Coal, nec
SIC 3312 Blast Furnaces & Steel Mills

CHEMICAL MANUFACTURING

32511 Petrochemical Manufacturing
SIC 2865 Cyclic Organic Crudes & Intermediates, & Organic
   Dyes & Pigments
SIC 2869 Industrial Organic Chemicals, nec
32512 Industrial Gas Manufacturing
SIC 2813 Industrial Gases
SIC 2869 Industrial Organic Chemicals, nec
325131 Inorganic Dye & Pigment Manufacturing
SIC 2816 Inorganic Pigments
SIC 2819 Industrial Inorganic Chemicals, nec
325132 Organic Dye & Pigment Manufacturing
SIC 2865 Cyclic Organic Crudes & Intermediates, & Organic
   Dyes & Pigments
325181 Alkalies & Chlorine Manufacturing
SIC 2812 Alkalies & Chlorine
325182 Carbon Black Manufacturing
SIC 2816 Inorganic pigments
SIC 2895 Carbon Black
325188 All Other Basic Inorganic Chemical Manufacturing
SIC 2819 Industrial Inorganic Chemicals, nec
SIC 2869 Industrial Organic Chemicals, nec

325191 Gum & Wood Chemical Manufacturing
SIC 2861 Gum & Wood Chemicals
325192 Cyclic Crude & Intermediate Manufacturing
SIC 2865 Cyclic Organic Crudes & Intermediates & Organic
   Dyes & Pigments
325193 Ethyl Alcohol Manufacturing
SIC 2869 Industrial Organic Chemicals
325199 All Other Basic Organic Chemical Manufacturing
SIC 2869 Industrial Organic Chemicals, nec
SIC 2899 Chemical & Chemical Preparations, nec
325211 Plastics Material & Resin Manufacturing
SIC 2821 Plastics Materials, Synthetic & Resins, &
   Nonvulcanizable Elastomers
325212 Synthetic Rubber Manufacturing
SIC 2822 Synthetic Rubber
325221 Cellulosic Manmade Fiber Manufacturing
SIC 2823 Cellulosic Manmade Fibers
325222 Noncellulosic Organic Fiber Manufacturing
SIC 2824 Manmade Organic Fibers, Except Cellulosic
325311 Nitrogenous Fertilizer Manufacturing
SIC 2873 Nitrogenous Fertilizers
325312 Phosphatic Fertilizer Manufacturing
SIC 2874 Phosphatic Fertilizers
325314 Fertilizer Manufacturing
SIC 2875 Fertilizers, Mixing Only
32532 Pesticide & Other Agricultural Chemical Manufacturing
SIC 2879 Pesticides & Agricultural Chemicals, nec
325411 Medicinal & Botanical Manufacturing
SIC 2833 Medicinal Chemicals & Botanical Products
325412 Pharmaceutical Preparation Manufacturing
SIC 2834 Pharmaceutical Preparations
SIC 2835 In-Vitro & In-Vivo Diagnostic Substances
325413 In-Vitro Diagnostic Substance Manufacturing
SIC 2835 In-Vitro & In-Vivo Diagnostic Substances
325414 Biological Product Manufacturing
SIC 2836 Biological Products, Except Diagnostic Substance
32551 Paint & Coating Manufacturing
SIC 2851 Paints, Varnishes, Lacquers, Enamels & Allied
   Products
SIC 2899 Chemicals & Chemical Preparations, nec
32552 Adhesive & Sealant Manufacturing
SIC 2891 Adhesives & Sealants
325611 Soap & Other Detergent Manufacturing
SIC 2841 Soaps & Other Detergents, Except Specialty Cleaners
SIC 2844 Toilet Preparations
325612 Polish & Other Sanitation Good Manufacturing
SIC 2842 Specialty Cleaning, Polishing, & Sanitary Preparations
325613 Surface Active Agent Manufacturing
SIC 2843 Surface Active Agents, Finishing Agents, Sulfonated
   Oils, & Assistants
32562 Toilet Preparation Manufacturing
SIC 2844 Perfumes, Cosmetics, & Other Toilet Preparations
32591 Printing Ink Manufacturing
SIC 2893 Printing Ink
32592 Explosives Manufacturing
SIC 2892 Explosives
325991 Custom Compounding of Purchased Resin
SIC 3087 Custom Compounding of Purchased Plastics Resin
**325992 Photographic Film, Paper, Plate & Chemical
   Manufacturing**
SIC 3861 Photographic Equipment & Supplies

325998 All Other Miscellaneous Chemical Product Manufacturing
SIC 2819 Industrial Inorganic Chemicals, nec
SIC 2899 Chemicals & Chemical Preparations, nec
SIC 3952 Lead Pencils & Art Goods
SIC 3999 Manufacturing Industries, nec

PLASTICS & RUBBER PRODUCTS MANUFACTURING

326111 Unsupported Plastics Bag Manufacturing
SIC 2673 Plastics, Foil, & Coated Paper Bags
326112 Unsupported Plastics Packaging Film & Sheet Manufacturing
SIC 2671 Packaging Paper & Plastics Film, Coated, & Laminated
326113 Unsupported Plastics Film & Sheet Manufacturing
SIC 3081 Unsupported Plastics Film & Sheets
326121 Unsupported Plastics Profile Shape Manufacturing
SIC 3082 Unsupported Plastics Profile Shapes
SIC 3089 Plastics Product, nec
326122 Plastics Pipe & Pipe Fitting Manufacturing
SIC 3084 Plastics Pipe
SIC 3089 Plastics Products, nec
32613 Laminated Plastics Plate, Sheet & Shape Manufacturing
SIC 3083 Laminated Plastics Plate, Sheet & Profile Shapes
32614 Polystyrene Foam Product Manufacturing
SIC 3086 Plastics Foam Products
32615 Urethane & Other Foam Product Manufacturing
SIC 3086 Plastics Foam Products
32616 Plastics Bottle Manufacturing
SIC 3085 Plastics Bottles
326191 Plastics Plumbing Fixture Manufacturing
SIC 3088 Plastics Plumbing Fixtures
326192 Resilient Floor Covering Manufacturing
SIC 3069 Fabricated Rubber Products, nec
SIC 3996 Linoleum, Asphalted-Felt-Base, & Other Hard Surface Floor Coverings, nec
326199 All Other Plastics Product Manufacturing
SIC 3089 Plastics Products, nec
SIC 3999 Manufacturing Industries, nec
326211 Tire Manufacturing
SIC 3011 Tires & Inner Tubes
326212 Tire Retreading
SIC 7534 Tire Retreading & Repair Shops
32622 Rubber & Plastics Hoses & Belting Manufacturing
SIC 3052 Rubber & Plastics Hose & Belting
326291 Rubber Product Manufacturing for Mechanical Use
SIC 3061 Molded, Extruded, & Lathe-Cut Mechanical Rubber Goods
326299 All Other Rubber Product Manufacturing
SIC 3069 Fabricated Rubber Products, nec

NONMETALLIC MINERAL PRODUCT MANUFACTURING

327111 Vitreous China Plumbing Fixture & China & Earthenware Fittings & Bathroom Accessories Manufacturing
SIC 3261 Vitreous China Plumbing Fixtures & China & Earthenware Fittings & Bathroom Accessories

327112 Vitreous China, Fine Earthenware & Other Pottery Product Manufacturing
SIC 3262 Vitreous China Table & Kitchen Articles
SIC 3263 Fine Earthenware Table & Kitchen Articles
SIC 3269 Pottery Products, nec
327113 Porcelain Electrical Supply Manufacturing
SIC 3264 Porcelain Electrical Supplies
327121 Brick & Structural Clay Tile Manufacturing
SIC 3251 Brick & Structural Clay Tile
327122 Ceramic Wall & Floor Tile Manufacturing
SIC 3253 Ceramic Wall & Floor Tile
327123 Other Structural Clay Product Manufacturing
SIC 3259 Structural Clay Products, nec
327124 Clay Refractory Manufacturing
SIC 3255 Clay Refractories
327125 Nonclay Refractory Manufacturing
SIC 3297 Nonclay Refractories
327211 Flat Glass Manufacturing
SIC 3211 Flat Glass
327212 Other Pressed & Blown Glass & Glassware Manufacturing
SIC 3229 Pressed & Blown Glass & Glassware, nec
327213 Glass Container Manufacturing
SIC 3221 Glass Containers
327215 Glass Product Manufacturing Made of Purchased Glass
SIC 3231 Glass Products Made of Purchased Glass
32731 Hydraulic Cement Manufacturing
SIC 3241 Cement, Hydraulic
32732 Ready-Mix Concrete Manufacturing
SIC 3273 Ready-Mixed Concrete
327331 Concrete Block & Brick Manufacturing
SIC 3271 Concrete Block & Brick
327332 Concrete Pipe Manufacturing
SIC 3272 Concrete Products, Except Block & Brick
32739 Other Concrete Product Manufacturing
SIC 3272 Concrete Products, Except Block & Brick
32741 Lime Manufacturing
SIC 3274 Lime
32742 Gypsum & Gypsum Product Manufacturing
SIC 3275 Gypsum Products
SIC 3299 Nonmetallic Mineral Products, nec
32791 Abrasive Product Manufacturing
SIC 3291 Abrasive Products
327991 Cut Stone & Stone Product Manufacturing
SIC 3281 Cut Stone & Stone Products
327992 Ground or Treated Mineral & Earth Manufacturing
SIC 3295 Minerals & Earths, Ground or Otherwise Treated
327993 Mineral Wool Manufacturing
SIC 3296 Mineral Wool
327999 All Other Miscellaneous Nonmetallic Mineral Product Manufacturing
SIC 3272 Concrete Products, Except Block & Brick
SIC 3292 Asbestos Products
SIC 3299 Nonmetallic Mineral Products, nec

PRIMARY METAL MANUFACTURING

331111 Iron & Steel Mills
SIC 3312 Steel Works, Blast Furnaces , & Rolling Mills
SIC 3399 Primary Metal Products, nec
331112 Electrometallurgical Ferroalloy Product Manufacturing
SIC 3313 Electrometallurgical Products, Except Steel

33121 Iron & Steel Pipes & Tubes Manufacturing from Purchased Steel
SIC 3317 Steel Pipe & Tubes
331221 Cold-Rolled Steel Shape Manufacturing
SIC 3316 Cold-Rolled Steel Sheet, Strip & Bars
331222 Steel Wire Drawing
SIC 3315 Steel Wiredrawing & Steel Nails & Spikes
331311 Alumina Refining
SIC 2819 Industrial Inorganic Chemicals, nec
331312 Primary Aluminum Production
SIC 3334 Primary Production of Aluminum
331314 Secondary Smelting & Alloying of Aluminum
SIC 3341 Secondary Smelting & Refining of Nonferrous Metals
SIC 3399 Primary Metal Products, nec
331315 Aluminum Sheet, Plate & Foil Manufacturing
SIC 3353 Aluminum Sheet, Plate, & Foil
331316 Aluminum Extruded Product Manufacturing
SIC 3354 Aluminum Extruded Products
331319 Other Aluminum Rolling & Drawing
SIC 3355 Aluminum Rolling & Drawing, nec
SIC 3357 Drawing & Insulating of Nonferrous Wire
331411 Primary Smelting & Refining of Copper
SIC 3331 Primary Smelting & Refining of Copper
331419 Primary Smelting & Refining of Nonferrous Metal
SIC 3339 Primary Smelting & Refining of Nonferrous Metals, Except Copper & Aluminum
331421 Copper Rolling, Drawing & Extruding
SIC 3351 Rolling, Drawing, & Extruding of Copper
331422 Copper Wire Drawing
SIC 3357 Drawing & Insulating of Nonferrous Wire
331423 Secondary Smelting, Refining, & Alloying of Copper
SIC 3341 Secondary Smelting & Refining of Nonferrous Metals
SIC 3399 Primary Metal Products, nec
331491 Nonferrous Metal Rolling, Drawing & Extruding
SIC 3356 Rolling, Drawing & Extruding of Nonferrous Metals, Except Copper & Aluminum
SIC 3357 Drawing & Insulating of Nonferrous Wire
331492 Secondary Smelting, Refining, & Alloying of Nonferrous Metal
SIC 3313 Electrometallurgical Products, Except Steel
SIC 3341 Secondary Smelting & Reining of Nonferrous Metals
SIC 3399 Primary Metal Products, nec
331511 Iron Foundries
SIC 3321 Gray & Ductile Iron Foundries
SIC 3322 Malleable Iron Foundries
331512 Steel Investment Foundries
SIC 3324 Steel Investment Foundries
331513 Steel Foundries,
SIC 3325 Steel Foundries, nec
331521 Aluminum Die-Castings
SIC 3363 Aluminum Die-Castings
331522 Nonferrous Die-Castings
SIC 3364 Nonferrous Die-Castings, Except Aluminum
331524 Aluminum Foundries
SIC 3365 Aluminum Foundries
331525 Copper Foundries
SIC 3366 Copper Foundries
331528 Other Nonferrous Foundries
SIC 3369 Nonferrous Foundries, Except Aluminum & Copper

FABRICATED METAL PRODUCT MANUFACTURING

332111 Iron & Steel Forging
SIC 3462 Iron & Steel Forgings
332112 Nonferrous Forging
SIC 3463 Nonferrous Forgings
332114 Custom Roll Forming
SIC 3449 Miscellaneous Structural Metal Work
332115 Crown & Closure Manufacturing
SIC 3466 Crowns & Closures
332116 Metal Stamping
SIC 3469 Metal Stampings, nec
332117 Powder Metallurgy Part Manufacturing
SIC 3499 Fabricated Metal Products, nec
332211 Cutlery & Flatware Manufacturing
SIC 3421 Cutlery
SIC 3914 Silverware, Plated Ware, & Stainless Steel Ware
332212 Hand & Edge Tool Manufacturing
SIC 3423 Hand & Edge Tools, Except Machine Tools & Handsaws
SIC 3523 Farm Machinery & Equipment
SIC 3524 Lawn & Garden Tractors & Home Lawn & Garden Equipment
SIC 3545 Cutting Tools, Machine Tools Accessories, & Machinist Precision Measuring Devices
SIC 3799 Transportation Equipment, nec
SIC 3999 Manufacturing Industries, nec
332213 Saw Blade & Handsaw Manufacturing
SIC 3425 Saw Blades & Handsaws
332214 Kitchen Utensil, Pot & Pan Manufacturing
SIC 3469 Metal Stampings, nec
332311 Prefabricated Metal Building & Component Manufacturing
SIC 3448 Prefabricated Metal Buildings & Components
332312 Fabricated Structural Metal Manufacturing
SIC 3441 Fabricated Structural Metal
SIC 3449 Miscellaneous Structural Metal Work
332313 Plate Work Manufacturing
SIC 3443 Fabricated Plate Work
332321 Metal Window & Door Manufacturing
SIC 3442 Metal Doors, Sash, Frames, Molding & Trim
SIC 3449 Miscellaneous Structural Metal Work
332322 Sheet Metal Work Manufacturing
SIC 3444 Sheet Metal Work
332323 Ornamental & Architectural Metal Work Manufacturing
SIC 3446 Architectural & Ornamental Metal Work
SIC 3449 Miscellaneous Structural Metal Work
SIC 3523 Farm Machinery & Equipment
33241 Power Boiler & Heat Exchanger Manufacturing
SIC 3443 Fabricated Plate Work
33242 Metal Tank Manufacturing
SIC 3443 Fabricated Plate Work
332431 Metal Can Manufacturing
SIC 3411 Metal Cans
332439 Other Metal Container Manufacturing
SIC 3412 Metal Shipping Barrels, Drums, Kegs, & Pails
SIC 3429 Hardware, nec
SIC 3444 Sheet Metal Work
SIC 3499 Fabricated Metal Products, nec
SIC 3537 Industrial Trucks, Tractors, Trailers, & Stackers
33251 Hardware Manufacturing
SIC 3429 Hardware, nec
SIC 3499 Fabricated Metal Products, nec

332611 Steel Spring Manufacturing
SIC 3493 Steel Springs, Except Wire
332612 Wire Spring Manufacturing
SIC 3495 Wire Springs
332618 Other Fabricated Wire Product Manufacturing
SIC 3315 Steel Wiredrawing & Steel Nails & Spikes
SIC 3399 Primary Metal Products, nec
SIC 3496 Miscellaneous Fabricated Wire Products
33271 Machine Shops
SIC 3599 Industrial & Commercial Machinery & Equipment,
nec
332721 Precision Turned Product Manufacturing
SIC 3451 Screw Machine Products
332722 Bolt, Nut, Screw, Rivet & Washer Manufacturing
SIC 3452 Bolts, Nuts, Screws, Rivets, & Washers
332811 Metal Heat Treating
SIC 3398 Metal Heat Treating
**332812 Metal Coating, Engraving , & Allied Services to
Manufacturers**
SIC 3479 Coating, Engraving, & Allied Services, nec
332813 Electroplating, Plating, Polishing, Anodizing & Coloring
SIC 3399 Primary Metal Products, nec
SIC 3471 Electroplating, Plating, Polishing, Anodizing, &
Coloring
332911 Industrial Valve Manufacturing
SIC 3491 Industrial Valves
332912 Fluid Power Valve & Hose Fitting Manufacturing
SIC 3492 Fluid Power Valves & Hose Fittings
SIC 3728 Aircraft Parts & Auxiliary Equipment, nec
332913 Plumbing Fixture Fitting & Trim Manufacturing
SIC 3432 Plumbing Fixture Fittings & Trim
332919 Other Metal Valve & Pipe Fitting Manufacturing
SIC 3429 Hardware, nec
SIC 3494 Valves & Pipe Fittings, nec
SIC 3499 Fabricated Metal Products, nec
332991 Ball & Roller Bearing Manufacturing
SIC 3562 Ball & Roller Bearings
332992 Small Arms Ammunition Manufacturing
SIC 3482 Small Arms Ammunition
332993 Ammunition Manufacturing
SIC 3483 Ammunition, Except for Small Arms
332994 Small Arms Manufacturing
SIC 3484 Small Arms
332995 Other Ordnance & Accessories Manufacturing
SIC 3489 Ordnance & Accessories, nec
332996 Fabricated Pipe & Pipe Fitting Manufacturing
SIC 3498 Fabricated Pipe & Pipe Fittings
332997 Industrial Pattern Manufacturing
SIC 3543 Industrial Patterns
332998 Enameled Iron & Metal Sanitary Ware Manufacturing
SIC 3431 Enameled Iron & Metal Sanitary Ware
**332999 All Other Miscellaneous Fabricated Metal Product
Manufacturing**
SIC 3291 Abrasive Products
SIC 3432 Plumbing Fixture Fittings & Trim
SIC 3494 Valves & Pipe Fittings, nec
SIC 3497 Metal Foil & Leaf
SIC 3499 Fabricated Metal Products, NEC
SIC 3537 Industrial Trucks, Tractors, Trailers, & Stackers
SIC 3599 Industrial & Commercial Machinery & Equipment,
nec
SIC 3999 Manufacturing Industries, nec

MACHINERY MANUFACTURING

333111 Farm Machinery & Equipment Manufacturing
SIC 3523 Farm Machinery & Equipment
**333112 Lawn & Garden Tractor & Home Lawn & Garden
Equipment Manufacturing**
SIC 3524 Lawn & Garden Tractors & Home Lawn & Garden
Equipment
33312 Construction Machinery Manufacturing
SIC 3531 Construction Machinery & Equipment
333131 Mining Machinery & Equipment Manufacturing
SIC 3532 Mining Machinery & Equipment, Except Oil & Gas
Field Machinery & Equipment
**333132 Oil & Gas Field Machinery & Equipment
Manufacturing**
SIC 3533 Oil & Gas Field Machinery & Equipment
33321 Sawmill & Woodworking Machinery Manufacturing
SIC 3553 Woodworking Machinery
33322 Rubber & Plastics Industry Machinery Manufacturing
SIC 3559 Special Industry Machinery, nec
333291 Paper Industry Machinery Manufacturing
SIC 3554 Paper Industries Machinery
333292 Textile Machinery Manufacturing
SIC 3552 Textile Machinery
333293 Printing Machinery & Equipment Manufacturing
SIC 3555 Printing Trades Machinery & Equipment
333294 Food Product Machinery Manufacturing
SIC 3556 Food Products Machinery
333295 Semiconductor Machinery Manufacturing
SIC 3559 Special Industry Machinery, nec
333298 All Other Industrial Machinery Manufacturing
SIC 3559 Special Industry Machinery, nec
SIC 3639 Household Appliances, nec
333311 Automatic Vending Machine Manufacturing
SIC 3581 Automatic Vending Machines
**333312 Commercial Laundry, Drycleaning & Pressing Machine
Manufacturing**
SIC 3582 Commercial Laundry, Drycleaning & Pressing
Machines
333313 Office Machinery Manufacturing
SIC 3578 Calculating & Accounting Machinery, Except
Electronic Computers
SIC 3579 Office Machines, nec
333314 Optical Instrument & Lens Manufacturing
SIC 3827 Optical Instruments & Lenses
**333315 Photographic & Photocopying Equipment
Manufacturing**
SIC 3861 Photographic Equipment & Supplies
**333319 Other Commercial & Service Industry Machinery
Manufacturing**
SIC 3559 Special Industry Machinery, nec
SIC 3589 Service Industry Machinery, nec
SIC 3599 Industrial & Commercial Machinery & Equipment,
nec
SIC 3699 Electrical Machinery, Equipment & Supplies, nec
333411 Air Purification Equipment Manufacturing
SIC 3564 Industrial & Commercial Fans & Blowers & Air
Purification Equipment
333412 Industrial & Commercial Fan & Blower Manufacturing
SIC 3564 Industrial & Commercial Fans & Blowers & Air
Purification Equipment
333414 Heating Equipment Manufacturing
SIC 3433 Heating Equipment, Except Electric & Warm Air
Furnaces

SIC 3634 Electric Housewares & Fans

333415 Air-Conditioning & Warm Air Heating Equipment & Commercial & Industrial Refrigeration Equipment Manufacturing

SIC 3443 Fabricated Plate Work

SIC 3585 Air-Conditioning & Warm Air Heating Equipment & Commercial & Industrial Refrigeration Equipment

333511 Industrial Mold Manufacturing

SIC 3544 Special Dies & Tools, Die Sets, Jigs & Fixtures, & Industrial Molds

333512 Machine Tool Manufacturing

SIC 3541 Machine Tools, Metal Cutting Type

333513 Machine Tool Manufacturing

SIC 3542 Machine Tools, Metal Forming Type

333514 Special Die & Tool, Die Set, Jig & Fixture Manufacturing

SIC 3544 Special Dies & Tools, Die Sets, Jigs & Fixtures, & Industrial Molds

333515 Cutting Tool & Machine Tool Accessory Manufacturing

SIC 3545 Cutting Tools, Machine Tool Accessories, & Machinists' Precision Measuring Devices

333516 Rolling Mill Machinery & Equipment Manufacturing

SIC 3547 Rolling Mill Machinery & Equipment

333518 Other Metalworking Machinery Manufacturing

SIC 3549 Metalworking Machinery, nec

333611 Turbine & Turbine Generator Set Unit Manufacturing

SIC 3511 Steam, Gas, & Hydraulic Turbines, & Turbine Generator Set Units

333612 Speed Changer, Industrial High-Speed Drive & Gear Manufacturing

SIC 3566 Speed Changers, Industrial High-Speed Drives, & Gears

333613 Mechanical Power Transmission Equipment Manufacturing

SIC 3568 Mechanical Power Transmission Equipment, nec

333618 Other Engine Equipment Manufacturing

SIC 3519 Internal Combustion Engines, nec

SIC 3699 Electrical Machinery, Equipment & Supplies, nec

333911 Pump & Pumping Equipment Manufacturing

SIC 3561 Pumps & Pumping Equipment

SIC 3743 Railroad Equipment

333912 Air & Gas Compressor Manufacturing

SIC 3563 Air & Gas Compressors

333913 Measuring & Dispensing Pump Manufacturing

SIC 3586 Measuring & Dispensing Pumps

333921 Elevator & Moving Stairway Manufacturing

SIC 3534 Elevators & Moving Stairways

333922 Conveyor & Conveying Equipment Manufacturing

SIC 3523 Farm Machinery & Equipment

SIC 3535 Conveyors & Conveying Equipment

333923 Overhead Traveling Crane, Hoist & Monorail System Manufacturing

SIC 3536 Overhead Traveling Cranes, Hoists, & Monorail Systems

SIC 3531 Construction Machinery & Equipment

333924 Industrial Truck, Tractor, Trailer & Stacker Machinery Manufacturing

SIC 3537 Industrial Trucks, Tractors, Trailers, & Stackers

333991 Power-Driven Hand Tool Manufacturing

SIC 3546 Power-Driven Handtools

333992 Welding & Soldering Equipment Manufacturing

SIC 3548 Electric & Gas Welding & Soldering Equipment

333993 Packaging Machinery Manufacturing

SIC 3565 Packaging Machinery

333994 Industrial Process Furnace & Oven Manufacturing

SIC 3567 Industrial Process Furnaces & Ovens

333995 Fluid Power Cylinder & Actuator Manufacturing

SIC 3593 Fluid Power Cylinders & Actuators

333996 Fluid Power Pump & Motor Manufacturing

SIC 3594 Fluid Power Pumps & Motors

333997 Scale & Balance Manufacturing

SIC 3596 Scales & Balances, Except Laboratory

333999 All Other General Purpose Machinery Manufacturing

SIC 3599 Industrial & Commercial Machinery & Equipment, nec

SIC 3569 General Industrial Machinery & Equipment, nec

COMPUTER & ELECTRONIC PRODUCT MANUFACTURING

334111 Electronic Computer Manufacturing

SIC 3571 Electronic Computers

334112 Computer Storage Device Manufacturing

SIC 3572 Computer Storage Devices

334113 Computer Terminal Manufacturing

SIC 3575 Computer Terminals

334119 Other Computer Peripheral Equipment Manufacturing

SIC 3577 Computer Peripheral Equipment, nec

SIC 3578 Calculating & Accounting Machines, Except Electronic Computers

SIC 3699 Electrical Machinery, Equipment & Supplies, nec

33421 Telephone Apparatus Manufacturing

SIC 3661 Telephone & Telegraph Apparatus

33422 Radio & Television Broadcasting & Wireless Communications Equipment Manufacturing

SIC 3663 Radio & Television Broadcasting & Communication Equipment

SIC 3679 Electronic Components, nec

33429 Other Communications Equipment Manufacturing

SIC 3669 Communications Equipment, nec

33431 Audio & Video Equipment Manufacturing

SIC 3651 Household Audio & Video Equipment

334411 Electron Tube Manufacturing

SIC 3671 Electron Tubes

334412 Printed Circuit Board Manufacturing

SIC 3672 Printed Circuit Boards

334413 Semiconductor & Related Device Manufacturing

SIC 3674 Semiconductors & Related Devices

334414 Electronic Capacitor Manufacturing

SIC 3675 Electronic Capacitors

334415 Electronic Resistor Manufacturing

SIC 3676 Electronic Resistors

334416 Electronic Coil, Transformer, & Other Inductor Manufacturing

SIC 3661 Telephone & Telegraph Apparatus

SIC 3677 Electronic Coils, Transformers, & Other Inductors

SIC 3825 Instruments for Measuring & Testing of Electricity & Electrical Signals

334417 Electronic Connector Manufacturing

SIC 3678 Electronic Connectors

334418 Printed Circuit/Electronics Assembly Manufacturing

SIC 3679 Electronic Components, nec

SIC 3661 Telephone & Telegraph Apparatus

334419 Other Electronic Component Manufacturing
SIC 3679 Electronic Components, nec
334510 Electromedical & Electrotherapeutic Apparatus Manufacturing
SIC 3842 Orthopedic, Prosthetic & Surgical Appliances & Supplies
SIC 3845 Electromedical & Electrotherapeutic Apparatus
334511 Search, Detection, Navigation, Guidance, Aeronautical, & Nautical System & Instrument Manufacturing
SIC 3812 Search, Detection, Navigation, Guidance, Aeronautical, & Nautical Systems & Instruments
334512 Automatic Environmental Control Manufacturing for Residential, Commercial & Appliance Use
SIC 3822 Automatic Controls for Regulating Residential & Commercial Environments & Appliances
334513 Instruments & Related Products Manufacturing for Measuring, Displaying, & Controlling Industrial Process Variables
SIC 3823 Industrial Instruments for Measurement, Display, & Control of Process Variables; & Related Products
334514 Totalizing Fluid Meter & Counting Device Manufacturing
SIC 3824 Totalizing Fluid Meters & Counting Devices
334515 Instrument Manufacturing for Measuring & Testing Electricity & Electrical Signals
SIC 3825 Instruments for Measuring & Testing of Electricity & Electrical Signals
334516 Analytical Laboratory Instrument Manufacturing
SIC 3826 Laboratory Analytical Instruments
334517 Irradiation Apparatus Manufacturing
SIC 3844 X-Ray Apparatus & Tubes & Related Irradiation Apparatus
SIC 3845 Electromedical & Electrotherapeutic Apparatus
334518 Watch, Clock, & Part Manufacturing
SIC 3495 Wire Springs
SIC 3579 Office Machines, nec
SIC 3873 Watches, Clocks, Clockwork Operated Devices, & Parts
334519 Other Measuring & Controlling Device Manufacturing
SIC 3829 Measuring & Controlling Devices, nec
334611 Software Reproducing
SIC 7372 Prepackaged Software
334612 Prerecorded Compact Disc , Tape, & Record Reproducing
SIC 3652 Phonograph Records & Prerecorded Audio Tapes & Disks
SIC 7819 Services Allied to Motion Picture Production
334613 Magnetic & Optical Recording Media Manufacturing
SIC 3695 Magnetic & Optical Recording Media

ELECTRICAL EQUIPMENT, APPLIANCE, & COMPONENT MANUFACTURING

33511　Electric Lamp Bulb & Part Manufacturing
SIC 3641 Electric Lamp Bulbs & Tubes
335121 Residential Electric Lighting Fixture Manufacturing
SIC 3645 Residential Electric Lighting Fixtures
SIC 3999 Manufacturing Industries, nec
335122 Commercial, Industrial & Institutional Electric Lighting Fixture Manufacturing
SIC 3646 Commercial, Industrial, & Institutional Electric Lighting Fixtures

335129 Other Lighting Equipment Manufacturing
SIC 3648 Lighting Equipment, nec
SIC 3699 Electrical Machinery, Equipment, & Supplies, nec
335211 Electric Housewares & Fan Manufacturing
SIC 3634 Electric Housewares & Fans
335212 Household Vacuum Cleaner Manufacturing
SIC 3635 Household Vacuum Cleaners
SIC 3639 Household Appliances, nec
335221 Household Cooking Appliance Manufacturing
SIC 3631 Household Cooking Equipment
335222 Household Refrigerator & Home Freezer Manufacturing
SIC 3632 Household Refrigerators & Home & Farm Freezers
335224 Household Laundry Equipment Manufacturing
SIC 3633 Household Laundry Equipment
335228 Other Household Appliance Manufacturing
SIC 3639 Household Appliances, nec
335311 Power, Distribution & Specialty Transformer Manufacturing
SIC 3548 Electric & Gas Welding & Soldering Equipment
SIC 3612 Power, Distribution, & Speciality Transformers
335312 Motor & Generator Manufacturing
SIC 3621 Motors & Generators
SIC 7694 Armature Rewinding Shops
335313 Switchgear & Switchboard Apparatus Manufacturing
SIC 3613 Switchgear & Switchboard Apparatus
335314 Relay & Industrial Control Manufacturing
SIC 3625 Relays & Industrial Controls
335911 Storage Battery Manufacturing
SIC 3691 Storage Batteries
335912 Dry & Wet Primary Battery Manufacturing
SIC 3692 Primary Batteries, Dry & Wet
335921 Fiber-Optic Cable Manufacturing
SIC 3357 Drawing & Insulating of Nonferrous Wire
335929 Other Communication & Energy Wire Manufacturing
SIC 3357 Drawing & Insulating of Nonferrous Wire
335931 Current-Carrying Wiring Device Manufacturing
SIC 3643 Current-Carrying Wiring Devices
335932 Noncurrent-Carrying Wiring Device Manufacturing
SIC 3644 Noncurrent-Carrying Wiring Devices
335991 Carbon & Graphite Product Manufacturing
SIC 3624 Carbon & Graphite Products
335999 All Other Miscellaneous Electrical Equipment & Component Manufacturing
SIC 3629 Electrical Industrial Apparatus, nec
SIC 3699 Electrical Machinery, Equipment, & Supplies, nec

TRANSPORTATION EQUIPMENT MANUFACTURING

336111 Automobile Manufacturing
SIC 3711 Motor Vehicles & Passenger Car Bodies
336112 Light Truck & Utility Vehicle Manufacturing
SIC 3711 Motor Vehicles & Passenger Car Bodies
33612　Heavy Duty Truck Manufacturing
SIC 3711 Motor Vehicles & Passenger Car Bodies
336211 Motor Vehicle Body Manufacturing
SIC 3711 Motor Vehicles & Passenger Car Bodies
SIC 3713 Truck & Bus Bodies
SIC 3714 Motor Vehicle Parts & Accessories
336212 Truck Trailer Manufacturing
SIC 3715 Truck Trailers

336213 Motor Home Manufacturing
SIC 3716 Motor Homes
336214 Travel Trailer & Camper Manufacturing
SIC 3792 Travel Trailers & Campers
SIC 3799 Transportation Equipment, nec
336311 Carburetor, Piston, Piston Ring & Valve Manufacturing
SIC 3592 Carburetors, Pistons, Piston Rings, & Valves
336312 Gasoline Engine & Engine Parts Manufacturing
SIC 3714 Motor Vehicle Parts & Accessories
336321 Vehicular Lighting Equipment Manufacturing
SIC 3647 Vehicular Lighting Equipment
336322 Other Motor Vehicle Electrical & Electronic Equipment Manufacturing
SIC 3679 Electronic Components, nec
SIC 3694 Electrical Equipment for Internal Combustion Engines
SIC 3714 Motor Vehicle Parts & Accessories
33633 Motor Vehicle Steering & Suspension Components Manufacturing
SIC 3714 Motor Vehicle Parts & Accessories
33634 Motor Vehicle Brake System Manufacturing
SIC 3292 Asbestos Products
SIC 3714 Motor Vehicle Parts & Accessories
33635 Motor Vehicle Transmission & Power Train Parts Manufacturing
SIC 3714 Motor Vehicle Parts & Accessories
33636 Motor Vehicle Fabric Accessories & Seat Manufacturing
SIC 2396 Automotive Trimmings, Apparel Findings, & Related Products
SIC 2399 Fabricated Textile Products, nec
SIC 2531 Public Building & Related Furniture
33637 Motor Vehicle Metal Stamping
SIC 3465 Automotive Stampings
336391 Motor Vehicle Air-Conditioning Manufacturing
SIC 3585 Air-Conditioning & Warm Air Heating Equipment & Commercial & Industrial Refrigeration Equipment
336399 All Other Motor Vehicle Parts Manufacturing
SIC 3519 Internal Combustion Engines, nec
SIC 3599 Industrial & Commercial Machinery & Equipment, NEC
SIC 3714 Motor Vehicle Parts & Accessories
336411 Aircraft Manufacturing
SIC 3721 Aircraft
336412 Aircraft Engine & Engine Parts Manufacturing
SIC 3724 Aircraft Engines & Engine Parts
336413 Other Aircraft Part & Auxiliary Equipment Manufacturing
SIC 3728 Aircraft Parts & Auxiliary Equipment, nec
336414 Guided Missile & Space Vehicle Manufacturing
SIC 3761 Guided Missiles & Space Vehicles
336415 Guided Missile & Space Vehicle Propulsion Unit & Propulsion Unit Parts Manufacturing
SIC 3764 Guided Missile & Space Vehicle Propulsion Units & Propulsion Unit Parts
336419 Other Guided Missile & Space Vehicle Parts & Auxiliary Equipment Manufacturing
SIC 3769 Guided Missile & Space Vehicle Parts & Auxiliary Equipment
33651 Railroad Rolling Stock Manufacturing
SIC 3531 Construction Machinery & Equipment
SIC 3743 Railroad Equipment
336611 Ship Building & Repairing
SIC 3731 Ship Building & Repairing

336612 Boat Building
SIC 3732 Boat Building & Repairing
336991 Motorcycle, Bicycle, & Parts Manufacturing
SIC 3944 Games, Toys, & Children's Vehicles, Except Dolls & Bicycles
SIC 3751 Motorcycles, Bicycles & Parts
336992 Military Armored Vehicle, Tank & Tank Component Manufacturing
SIC 3711 Motor Vehicles & Passenger Car Bodies
SIC 3795 Tanks & Tank Components
336999 All Other Transportation Equipment Manufacturing
SIC 3799 Transportation Equipment, nec

FURNITURE & RELATED PRODUCT MANUFACTURING

337121 Upholstered Household Furniture Manufacturing
SIC 2512 Wood Household Furniture, Upholstered
SIC 2515 Mattress, Foundations, & Convertible Beds
SIC 5712 Furniture
337122 Nonupholstered Wood Household Furniture Manufacturing
SIC 2511 Wood Household Furniture, Except Upholstered
SIC 5712 Furniture Stores
337124 Metal Household Furniture Manufacturing
SIC 2514 Metal Household Furniture
337125 Household Furniture Manufacturing
SIC 2519 Household Furniture, NEC
337127 Institutional Furniture Manufacturing
SIC 2531 Public Building & Related Furniture
SIC 2599 Furniture & Fixtures, nec
SIC 3952 Lead Pencils, Crayons, & Artist's Materials
SIC 3999 Manufacturing Industries, nec
337129 Wood Television, Radio, & Sewing Machine Cabinet Manufacturing
SIC 2517 Wood Television, Radio, Phonograph, & Sewing Machine Cabinets
337131 Wood Kitchen & Counter Top Manufacturing
SIC 2434 Wood Kitchen Cabinets
SIC 2541 Wood Office & Store Fixtures, Partitions, Shelving, & Lockers
SIC 5712 Furniture Stores
337132 Upholstered Wood Household Furniture Manufacturing
SIC 2515 Mattresses, Foundations, & Convertible Beds
SIC 5712 Furniture Stores
337133 Wood Household Furniture
SIC 5712 Furniture Stores
337134 Wood Office Furniture Manufacturing
SIC 2521 Wood Office Furniture
337135 Custom Architectural Woodwork, Millwork, & Fixtures
SIC 2541 Wood Office & Store Fixtures, Partitions, Shelving, and Lockers
337139 Other Wood Furniture Manufacturing
SIC 2426 Hardwood Dimension & Flooring Mills
SIC 2499 Wood Products, nec
SIC 2517 Wood Television, Radio, Phonograph, & Sewing Machine Cabinets
SIC 2531 Public Building & Related Furniture
SIC 2541 Wood Office & Store Fixtures, Partitions., Shelving, & Lockers
SIC 2599 Furniture & Fixtures, nec
SIC 3952 Lead Pencils, Crayons, & Artist's Materials

337141 Nonwood Office Furniture Manufacturing
SIC 2522 Office Furniture, Except Wood
337143 Household Furniture Manufacturing
SIC 2519 Household Furniture, NEC
337145 Nonwood Showcase, Partition, Shelving, & Locker Manufacturing
SIC 2542 Office & Store Fixtures, Partitions, Shelving, & Lockers, Except Wood
337148 Other Nonwood Furniture Manufacturing
SIC 2499 Wood Products, NEC
SIC 2531 Public Building & Related Furniture
SIC 2599 Furniture & Fixtures, nec
SIC 3499 Fabricated Metal Products, nec
SIC 3952 Lead Pencils, Crayons, & Artist's Materials
SIC 3999 Manufacturing Industries, nec
337212 Custom Architectural Woodwork & Millwork Manufacturing
SIC 2541 Wood Office & Store Fixtures, Partitions, Shelving, & Lockers
337214 Nonwood Office Furniture Manufacturing
SIC 2522 Office Furniture, Except Wood
337215 Showcase, Partition, Shelving, & Locker Manufacturing
SIC 2542 Office & Store Fixtures, Partitions, Shelving & Lockers, Except Wood
SIC 2541 Wood Office & Store Fixtures, Partitions, Shelving, & Lockers
SIC 2426 Hardwood Dimension & Flooring Mills
SIC 3499 Fabricated Metal Products, nec
33791 Mattress Manufacturing
SIC 2515 Mattresses, Foundations & Convertible Beds
33792 Blind & Shade Manufacturing
SIC 2591 Drapery Hardware & Window Blinds & Shades

MISCELLANEOUS MANUFACTURING

339111 Laboratory Apparatus & Furniture Manufacturing
SIC 3829 Measuring & Controlling Devices, nec
339112 Surgical & Medical Instrument Manufacturing
SIC 3841 Surgical & Medical Instruments & Apparatus
SIC 3829 Measuring & Controlling Devices, nec
339113 Surgical Appliance & Supplies Manufacturing
SIC 2599 Furniture & Fixtures, nec
SIC 3842 Orthopedic, Prosthetic, & Surgical Appliances & Supplies
339114 Dental Equipment & Supplies Manufacturing
SIC 3843 Dental Equipment & Supplies
339115 Ophthalmic Goods Manufacturing
SIC 3851 Opthalmic Goods
SIC 5995 Optical Goods Stores
339116 Dental Laboratories
SIC 8072 Dental Laboratories 339117 Eyeglass & Contact Lens Manufacturing
SIC 5995 Optical Goods Stores
339911 Jewelry Manufacturing
SIC 3469 Metal Stamping, nec
SIC 3479 Coating, Engraving, & Allied Services, nec
SIC 3911 Jewelry, Precious Metal
339912 Silverware & Plated Ware Manufacturing
SIC 3479 Coating, Engraving, & Allied Services, nec
SIC 3914 Silverware, Plated Ware, & Stainless Steel Ware
339913 Jewelers' Material & Lapidary Work Manufacturing
SIC 3915 Jewelers' Findings & Materials, & Lapidary Work

339914 Costume Jewelry & Novelty Manufacturing
SIC 3479 Coating, Engraving, & Allied Services, nec
SIC 3499 Fabricated Metal Products, nec
SIC 3961 Costume Jewelry & Costume Novelties, Except Precious Metal
33992 Sporting & Athletic Goods Manufacturing
SIC 3949 Sporting & Athletic Goods, nec
339931 Doll & Stuffed Toy Manufacturing
SIC 3942 Dolls & Stuffed Toys
339932 Game, Toy, & Children's Vehicle Manufacturing
SIC 3944 Games, Toys, & Children's Vehicles, Except Dolls & Bicycles
339941 Pen & Mechanical Pencil Manufacturing
SIC 3951 Pens, Mechanical Pencils, & Parts
339942 Lead Pencil & Art Good Manufacturing
SIC 2531 Public Buildings & Related Furniture
SIC 3579 Office Machines, nec
SIC 3952 Lead Pencils, Crayons, & Artists' Materials
339943 Marking Device Manufacturing
SIC 3953 Marking Devices
339944 Carbon Paper & Inked Ribbon Manufacturing
SIC 3955 Carbon Paper & Inked Ribbons
33995 Sign Manufacturing
SIC 3993 Signs & Advertising Specialties
339991 Gasket, Packing, & Sealing Device Manufacturing
SIC 3053 Gaskets, Packing, & Sealing Devices
339992 Musical Instrument Manufacturing
SIC 3931 Musical Instruments
339993 Fastener, Button, Needle & Pin Manufacturing
SIC 3965 Fasteners, Buttons, Needles, & Pins
SIC 3131 Boat & Shoe Cut Stock & Findings
339994 Broom, Brush & Mop Manufacturing
SIC 3991 Brooms & Brushes
SIC 2392 Housefurnishings, Except Curtains & Draperies
339995 Burial Casket Manufacturing
SIC 3995 Burial Caskets
339999 All Other Miscellaneous Manufacturing
SIC 2499 Wood Products, NEC
SIC 3999 Manufacturing Industries, nec

WHOLESALE TRADE

42111 Automobile & Other Motor Vehicle Wholesalers
SIC 5012 Automobiles & Other Motor Vehicles
42112 Motor Vehicle Supplies & New Part Wholesalers
SIC 5013 Motor Vehicle Supplies & New Parts
42113 Tire & Tube Wholesalers
SIC 5014 Tires & Tubes
42114 Motor Vehicle Part Wholesalers
SIC 5015 Motor Vehicle Parts, Used
42121 Furniture Wholesalers
SIC 5021 Furniture
42122 Home Furnishing Wholesalers
SIC 5023 Homefurnishings
42131 Lumber, Plywood, Millwork & Wood Panel Wholesalers
SIC 5031 Lumber, Plywood, Millwork, & Wood Panels
SIC 5211 Lumber & Other Building Materials Dealers - Retail
42132 Brick, Stone & Related Construction Material Wholesalers
SIC 5032 Brick, Stone, & Related Construction Materials
42133 Roofing, Siding & Insulation Material Wholesalers
SIC 5033 Roofing, Siding, & Insulation Materials

42139 Other Construction Material Wholesalers
SIC 5039 Construction Materials, nec

42141 Photographic Equipment & Supplies Wholesalers
SIC 5043 Photographic Equipment & Supplies

42142 Office Equipment Wholesalers
SIC 5044 Office Equipment

42143 Computer & Computer Peripheral Equipment & Software Wholesalers
SIC 5045 Computers & Computer Peripherals Equipment & Software

42144 Other Commercial Equipment Wholesalers
SIC 5046 Commercial Equipment, nec

42145 Medical, Dental & Hospital Equipment & Supplies Wholesalers
SIC 5047 Medical, Dental & Hospital Equipment & Supplies

42146 Ophthalmic Goods Wholesalers
SIC 5048 Ophthalmic Goods

42149 Other Professional Equipment & Supplies Wholesalers
SIC 5049 Professional Equipment & Supplies, nec

42151 Metal Service Centers & Offices
SIC 5051 Metals Service Centers & Offices

42152 Coal & Other Mineral & Ore Wholesalers
SIC 5052 Coal & Other Mineral & Ores

42161 Electrical Apparatus & Equipment, Wiring Supplies & Construction Material Wholesalers
SIC 5063 Electrical Apparatus & Equipment, Wiring Supplies & Construction Materials

42162 Electrical Appliance, Television & Radio Set Wholesalers
SIC 5064 Electrical Appliances, Television & Radio Sets

42169 Other Electronic Parts & Equipment Wholesalers
SIC 5065 Electronic Parts & Equipment, nec

42171 Hardware Wholesalers
SIC 5072 Hardware

42172 Plumbing & Heating Equipment & Supplies Wholesalers
SIC 5074 Plumbing & Heating Equipment & Supplies

42173 Warm Air Heating & Air-Conditioning Equipment & Supplies Wholesalers
SIC 5075 Warm Air Heating & Air-Conditioning Equipment & Supplies

42174 Refrigeration Equipment & Supplies Wholesalers
SIC 5078 Refrigeration Equipment & Supplies

42181 Construction & Mining Machinery & Equipment Wholesalers
SIC 5082 Construction & Mining Machinery & Equipment

42182 Farm & Garden Machinery & Equipment Wholesalers
SIC 5083 Farm & Garden Machinery & Equipment

42183 Industrial Machinery & Equipment Wholesalers
SIC 5084 Industrial Machinery & Equipment
SIC 5085 Industrial Supplies

42184 Industrial Supplies Wholesalers
SIC 5085 Industrial Supplies

42185 Service Establishment Equipment & Supplies Wholesalers
SIC 5087 Service Establishment Equipment & Supplies Wholesalers

42186 Transportation Equipment & Supplies Wholesalers
SIC 5088 Transportation Equipment and Supplies, Except Motor Vehicles

42191 Sporting & Recreational Goods & Supplies Wholesalers
SIC 5091 Sporting & Recreational Goods & Supplies

42192 Toy & Hobby Goods & Supplies Wholesalers
SIC 5092 Toys & Hobby Goods & Supplies

42193 Recyclable Material Wholesalers
SIC 5093 Scrap & Waste Materials

42194 Jewelry, Watch, Precious Stone & Precious Metal Wholesalers
SIC 5094 Jewelry, Watches, Precious Stones, & Precious Metals

42199 Other Miscellaneous Durable Goods Wholesalers
SIC 5099 Durable Goods, nec
SIC 7822 Motion Picture & Video Tape Distribution

42211 Printing & Writing Paper Wholesalers
SIC 5111 Printing & Writing Paper

42212 Stationary & Office Supplies Wholesalers
SIC 5112 Stationery & Office Supplies

42213 Industrial & Personal Service Paper Wholesalers
SIC 5113 Industrial & Personal Service Paper

42221 Drug, Drug Proprietaries & Druggists' Sundries Wholesalers
SIC 5122 Drugs, Drug Proprietaries, & Druggists' Sundries

42231 Piece Goods, Notions & Other Dry Goods Wholesalers
SIC 5131 Piece Goods, Notions, & Other Dry Goods

42232 Men's & Boys' Clothing & Furnishings Wholesalers
SIC 5136 Men's & Boys' Clothing & Furnishings

42233 Women's, Children's, & Infants' & Accessories Wholesalers
SIC 5137 Women's, Children's, & Infants' Clothing & Accessories

42234 Footwear Wholesalers
SIC 5139 Footwear

42241 General Line Grocery Wholesalers
SIC 5141 Groceries, General Line

42242 Packaged Frozen Food Wholesalers
SIC 5142 Packaged Frozen Foods

42243 Dairy Product Wholesalers
SIC 5143 Dairy Products, Except Dried or Canned

42244 Poultry & Poultry Product Wholesalers
SIC 5144 Poultry & Poultry Products

42245 Confectionery Wholesalers
SIC 5145 Confectionery

42246 Fish & Seafood Wholesalers
SIC 5146 Fish & Seafoods

42247 Meat & Meat Product Wholesalers
SIC 5147 Meats & Meat Products

42248 Fresh Fruit & Vegetable Wholesalers
SIC 5148 Fresh Fruits & Vegetables

42249 Other Grocery & Related Products Wholesalers
SIC 5149 Groceries & Related Products, nec

42251 Grain & Field Bean Wholesalers
SIC 5153 Grain & Field Beans

42252 Livestock Wholesalers
SIC 5154 Livestock

42259 Other Farm Product Raw Material Wholesalers
SIC 5159 Farm-Product Raw Materials, nec

42261 Plastics Materials & Basic Forms & Shapes Wholesalers
SIC 5162 Plastics Materials & Basic Forms & Shapes

42269 Other Chemical & Allied Products Wholesalers
SIC 5169 Chemicals & Allied Products, nec

42271 Petroleum Bulk Stations & Terminals
SIC 5171 Petroleum Bulk Stations & Terminals

42272 Petroleum & Petroleum Products Wholesalers
SIC 5172 Petroleum & Petroleum Products Wholesalers, Except Bulk Stations & Terminals

42281 Beer & Ale Wholesalers
SIC 5181 Beer & Ale

42282 Wine & Distilled Alcoholic Beverage Wholesalers
SIC 5182 Wine & Distilled Alcoholic Beverages
42291 Farm Supplies Wholesalers
SIC 5191 Farm Supplies
42292 Book, Periodical & Newspaper Wholesalers
SIC 5192 Books, Periodicals, & Newspapers
42293 Flower, Nursery Stock & Florists' Supplies Wholesalers
SIC 5193 Flowers, Nursery Stock, & Florists' Supplies
42294 Tobacco & Tobacco Product Wholesalers
SIC 5194 Tobacco & Tobacco Products
42295 Paint, Varnish & Supplies Wholesalers
SIC 5198 Paints, Varnishes, & Supplies
SIC 5231 Paint, Glass & Wallpaper Stores
42299 Other Miscellaneous Nondurable Goods Wholesalers
SIC 5199 Nondurable Goods, nec

RETAIL TRADE

44111 New Car Dealers
SIC 5511 Motor Vehicle Dealers, New and Used
44112 Used Car Dealers
SIC 5521 Motor Vehicle Dealers, Used Only
44121 Recreational Vehicle Dealers
SIC 5561 Recreational Vehicle Dealers
441221 Motorcycle Dealers
SIC 5571 Motorcycle Dealers
441222 Boat Dealers
SIC 5551 Boat Dealers
441229 All Other Motor Vehicle Dealers
SIC 5599 Automotive Dealers, NEC
44131 Automotive Parts & Accessories Stores
SIC 5013 Motor Vehicle Supplies & New Parts
SIC 5731 Radio, Television, & Consumer Electronics Stores
SIC 5531 Auto & Home Supply Stores
44132 Tire Dealers
SIC 5014 Tires & Tubes
SIC 5531 Auto & Home Supply Stores
44211 Furniture Stores
SIC 5021 Furniture
SIC 5712 Furniture Stores
44221 Floor Covering Stores
SIC 5023 Homefurnishings
SIC 5713 Floor Coverings Stores
442291 Window Treatment Stores
SIC 5714 Drapery, Curtain, & Upholstery Stores
SIC 5719 Miscellaneous Homefurnishings Stores
442299 All Other Home Furnishings Stores
SIC 5719 Miscellaneous Homefurnishings Stores
443111 Household Appliance Stores
SIC 5722 Household Appliance Stores
SIC 5999 Miscellaneous Retail Stores, nec
SIC 7623 Refrigeration & Air-Conditioning Service & Repair Shops
SIC 7629 Electrical & Electronic Repair Shops, nec
443112 Radio, Television & Other Electronics Stores
SIC 5731 Radio, Television, & Consumer Electronics Stores
SIC 5999 Miscellaneous Retail Stores, nec
SIC 7622 Radio & Television Repair Shops
44312 Computer & Software Stores
SIC 5045 Computers & Computer Peripheral Equipment & Software
SIC 7378 Computer Maintenance & Repair '
SIC 5734 Computer & Computer Software Stores

44313 Camera & Photographic Supplies Stores
SIC 5946 Camera & Photographic Supply Stores
44411 Home Centers
SIC 5211 Lumber & Other Building Materials Dealers
44412 Paint & Wallpaper Stores
SIC 5198 Paints, Varnishes, & Supplies
SIC 5231 Paint, Glass, & Wallpaper Stores
44413 Hardware Stores
SIC 5251 Hardware Stores
44419 Other Building Material Dealers
SIC 5031 Lumber, Plywood, Millwork, & Wood Panels
SIC 5032 Brick, Stone, & Related Construction Materials
SIC 5039 Construction Materials, nec
SIC 5063 Electrical Apparatus & Equipment, Wiring Supplies, & Construction Materials
SIC 5074 Plumbing & Heating Equipment & Supplies
SIC 5211 Lumber & Other Building Materials Dealers
SIC 5231 Paint, Glass, & Wallpaper Stores
44421 Outdoor Power Equipment Stores
SIC 5083 Farm & Garden Machinery & Equipment
SIC 5261 Retail Nurseries, Lawn & Garden Supply Stores
44422 Nursery & Garden Centers
SIC 5191 Farm Supplies
SIC 5193 Flowers, Nursery Stock, & Florists' Supplies
SIC 5261 Retail Nurseries, Lawn & Garden Supply Stores
44511 Supermarkets & Other Grocery Stores
SIC 5411 Grocery Stores
44512 Convenience Stores
SIC 5411 Grocery Stores
44521 Meat Markets
SIC 5421 Meat & Fish Markets, Including Freezer Provisioners
SIC 5499 Miscellaneous Food Stores
44522 Fish & Seafood Markets
SIC 5421 Meat & Fish Markets, Including Freezer Provisioners
44523 Fruit & Vegetable Markets
SIC 5431 Fruit & Vegetable Markets
445291 Baked Goods Stores
SIC 5461 Retail Bakeries
445292 Confectionery & Nut Stores
SIC 5441 Candy, Nut & Confectionery Stores
445299 All Other Specialty Food Stores
SIC 5499 Miscellaneous Food Stores
SIC 5451 Dairy Products Stores
44531 Beer, Wine & Liquor Stores
SIC 5921 Liquor Stores
44611 Pharmacies & Drug Stores
SIC 5912 Drug Stores & Proprietary Stores
44612 Cosmetics, Beauty Supplies & Perfume Stores
SIC 5087 Service Establishment Equipment & Supplies
SIC 5999 Miscellaneous Retail Stores, nec
44613 Optical Goods Stores
SIC 5995 Optical Goods Stores
446191 Food Supplement Stores
SIC 5499 Miscellaneous Food Stores
446199 All Other Health & Personal Care Stores
SIC 5047 Medical, Dental, & Hospital Equipment & Supplies
SIC 5999 Miscellaneous Retail Stores, nec
44711 Gasoline Stations with Convenience Stores
SIC 5541 Gasoline Service Station
SIC 5411 Grocery Stores
44719 Other Gasoline Stations
SIC 5541 Gasoline Service Station

44811 Men's Clothing Stores
SIC 5611 Men's & Boys' Clothing & Accessory Stores
44812 Women's Clothing Stores
SIC 5621 Women's Clothing Stores
44813 Children's & Infants' Clothing Stores
SIC 5641 Children's & Infants' Wear Stores
44814 Family Clothing Stores
SIC 5651 Family Clothing Stores
44815 Clothing Accessories Stores
SIC 5611 Men's & Boys' Clothing & Accessory Stores
SIC 5632 Women's Accessory & Specialty Stores
SIC 5699 Miscellaneous Apparel & Accessory Stores
44819 Other Clothing Stores
SIC 5699 Miscellaneous Apparel & Accessory Stores
SIC 5632 Women's Accessory & Specialty Stores
44821 Shoe Stores
SIC 5661 Shoe Stores
44831 Jewelry Stores
SIC 5999 Miscellaneous Retailer, nec
SIC 5944 Jewelry Stores
44832 Luggage & Leather Goods Stores
SIC 5948 Luggage & Leather Goods Stores
45111 Sporting Goods Stores
SIC 7699 Repair Shops & Related Services, NEC
SIC 5941 Sporting Goods Stores & Bicycle Shops
45112 Hobby, Toy & Game Stores
SIC 5945 Hobby, Toy, & Game Stores
45113 Sewing, Needlework & Piece Goods Stores
SIC 5714 Drapery, Curtain, & Upholstery Stores
SIC 5949 Sewing, Needlework, & Piece Goods Stores
45114 Musical Instrument & Supplies Stores
SIC 5736 Musical Instruments Stores
451211 Book Stores
SIC 5942 Book Stores
451212 News Dealers & Newsstands
SIC 5994 News Dealers & Newsstands
45122 Prerecorded Tape, Compact Disc & Record Stores
SIC 5735 Record & Prerecorded Tape Stores
45211 Department Stores
SIC 5311 Department Stores
45291 Warehouse Clubs & Superstores
SIC 5399 Miscellaneous General Merchandise Stores
SIC 5411 Grocery Stores
45299 All Other General Merchandise Stores
SIC 5399 Miscellaneous General Merchandise Stores
SIC 5331 Variety Stores
45311 Florists
SIC 5992 Florists
45321 Office Supplies & Stationery Stores
SIC 5049 Professional Equipment & Supplies, nec
SIC 5112 Stationery & Office Supplies
SIC 5943 Stationery Stores
45322 Gift, Novelty & Souvenir Stores
SIC 5947 Gift, Novelty, & Souvenir Shops
45331 Used Merchandise Stores
SIC 5932 Used Merchandise Stores
45391 Pet & Pet Supplies Stores
SIC 5999 Miscellaneous Retail Stores, NEC
45392 Art Dealers
SIC 5999 Miscellaneous Retail Stores, nec
45393 Manufactured Home Dealers
SIC 5271 Mobile Home Dealers

453991 Tobacco Stores
SIC 5993 Tobacco Stores & Stands
453999 All Other Miscellaneous Store Retailers
SIC 5999 Miscellaneous Retail Stores, nec
SIC 5261 Retail Nurseries, Lawn & Garden Supply Stores
45411 Electronic Shopping & Mail-Order Houses
SIC 5961 Catalog & Mail-Order Houses
45421 Vending Machine Operators
SIC 5962 Automatic Merchandise Machine Operators
454311 Heating Oil Dealers
SIC 5171 Petroleum Bulk Stations & Terminals
SIC 5983 Fuel Oil Dealers
454312 Liquefied Petroleum Gas Dealers
SIC 5171 Petroleum Bulk Stations & Terminals
SIC 5984 Liquefied Petroleum Gas Dealers
454319 Other Fuel Dealers
SIC 5989 Fuel Dealers, nec
45439 Other Direct Selling Establishments
SIC 5421 Meat & Fish Markets, Including Freezer Provisioners
SIC 5963 Direct Selling Establishments

TRANSPORTATION & WAREHOUSING

481111 Scheduled Passenger Air Transportation
SIC 4512 Air Transportation, Scheduled
481112 Scheduled Freight Air Transportation
SIC 4512 Air Transportation, Scheduled
481211 Nonscheduled Chartered Passenger Air Transportation
SIC 4522 Air Transportation, Nonscheduled
481212 Nonscheduled Chartered Freight Air Transportation
SIC 4522 Air Transportation, Nonscheduled
481219 Other Nonscheduled Air Transportation
SIC 7319 Advertising, nec
48122 Nonscheduled Speciality Air Transportation
SIC 0721 Crop Planting, Cultivating, & Protecting
SIC 1382 Oil & Gas Field Exploration Services
SIC 4522 Air Transportation, Nonscheduled
SIC 7335 Commercial Photography
SIC 7997 Membership Sports & Recreation Clubs
SIC 8299 Schools & Educational Services, nec
SIC 8713 Surveying Services
482111 Line-Haul Railroads
SIC 4011 Railroads, Line-Haul Operating
482112 Short Line Railroads
SIC 4013 Railroad Switching & Terminal Establishments
483111 Deep Sea Freight Transportation
SIC 4412 Deep Sea Foreign Transportation of Freight
483112 Deep Sea Passenger Transportation
SIC 4481 Deep Sea Transportation of Passengers, Except by Ferry
483113 Coastal & Great Lakes Freight Transportation
SIC 4424 Deep Sea Domestic Transportation of Freight
SIC 4432 Freight Transportation on the Great Lakes - St. Lawrence Seaway
SIC 4492 Towing & Tugboat Services
483114 Coastal & Great Lakes Passenger Transportation
SIC 4481 Deep Sea Transportation of Passengers, Except by Ferry
SIC 4482 Ferries
483211 Inland Water Freight Transportation
SIC 4449 Water Transportation of Freight, nec
SIC 4492 Towing & Tugboat Services

483212 Inland Water Passenger Transportation
SIC 4482 Ferries
SIC 4489 Water Transportation of Passengers, nec
48411   General Freight Trucking, Local
SIC 4212 Local Trucking without Storage
SIC 4214 Local Trucking with Storage
484121 General Freight Trucking, Long-Distance, Truckload
SIC 4213 Trucking, Except Local
484122 General Freight Trucking, Long-Distance, Less Than Truckload
SIC 4213 Trucking, Except Local
48421   Used Household & Office Goods Moving
SIC 4212 Local Trucking Without Storage
SIC 4213 Trucking, Except Local
SIC 4214 Local Trucking With Storage
48422   Specialized Freight Trucking, Local
SIC 4212 Local Trucking without Storage
SIC 4214 Local Trucking with Storage
48423   Specialized Freight Trucking, Long-Distance
SIC 4213 Trucking, Except Local
485111 Mixed Mode Transit Systems
SIC 4111 Local & Suburban Transit
485112 Commuter Rail Systems
SIC 4111 Local & Suburban Transit
485113 Bus & Motor Vehicle Transit Systems
SIC 4111 Local & Suburban Transit
485119 Other Urban Transit Systems
SIC 4111 Local & Suburban Transit
48521   Interurban & Rural Bus Transportation
SIC 4131 Intercity & Rural Bus Transportation
48531   Taxi Service
SIC 4121 Taxicabs
48532   Limousine Service
SIC 4119 Local Passenger Transportation, nec
48541   School & Employee Bus Transportation
SIC 4151 School Buses
SIC 4119 Local Passenger Transportation, nec
48551   Charter Bus Industry
SIC 4141 Local Charter Bus Service
SIC 4142 Bus Charter Services, Except Local
485991 Special Needs Transportation
SIC 4119 Local Passenger Transportation, nec
485999 All Other Transit & Ground Passenger Transportation
SIC 4111 Local & Suburban Transit
SIC 4119 Local Passenger Transportation, nec
48611   Pipeline Transportation of Crude Oil
SIC 4612 Crude Petroleum Pipelines
48621   Pipeline Transportation of Natural Gas
SIC 4922 Natural Gas Transmission
SIC 4923 Natural Gas Transmission & Distribution
48691   Pipeline Transportation of Refined Petroleum Products
SIC 4613 Refined Petroleum Pipelines
48699   All Other Pipeline Transportation
SIC 4619 Pipelines, nec
48711   Scenic & Sightseeing Transportation, Land
SIC 4119 Local Passenger Transportation, nec
SIC 4789 Transportation Services, nec
SIC 7999 Amusement & Recreation Services, nec
48721   Scenic & Sightseeing Transportation, Water
SIC 4489 Water Transportation of Passengers, nec
SIC 7999 Amusement & Recreation Services, nec
48799   Scenic & Sightseeing Transportation, Other
SIC 4522 Air Transportation, Nonscheduled
SIC 7999 Amusement & Recreation Services, nec

488111 Air Traffic Control
SIC 4581 Airports, Flying Fields, & Airport Terminal Services
SIC 9621 Regulation & Administration of Transportation Programs
488112 Airport Operations, except Air Traffic Control
SIC 4581 Airports, Flying Fields, & Airport Terminal Services
SIC 4959 Sanitary Services, nec
488119 Other Airport Operations
SIC 4581 Airports, Flying Fields, & Airport Terminal Services
SIC 4959 Sanitary Services, nec
48819   Other Support Activities for Air Transportation
SIC 4581 Airports, Flying Fields, & Airport Terminal Services
48821   Support Activities for Rail Transportation
SIC 4013 Railroad Switching & Terminal Establishments
SIC 4741 Rental of Railroad Cars
SIC 4789 Transportation Services, nec
48831   Port & Harbor Operations
SIC 4491 Marine Cargo Handling
SIC 4499 Water Transportation Services, nec
48832   Marine Cargo Handling
SIC 4491 Marine Cargo Handling
48833   Navigational Services to Shipping
SIC 4492 Towing & Tugboat Services
SIC 4499 Water Transportation Services, nec
48839   Other Support Activities for Water Transportation
SIC 4499 Water Transportation Services, nec
SIC 4785 Fixed Facilities & Inspection & Weighing Services for Motor Vehicle Transportation
SIC 7699 Repair Shops & Related Services, nec
48841   Motor Vehicle Towing
SIC 7549 Automotive Services, Except Repair & Carwashes
48849   Other Support Activities for Road Transportation
SIC 4173 Terminal & Service Facilities for Motor Vehicle Passenger Transportation
SIC 4231 Terminal & Joint Terminal Maintenance Facilities for Motor Freight Transportation
SIC 4785 Fixed Facilities & Inspection & Weighing Services for Motor Vehicle Transportation
48851   Freight Transportation Arrangement
SIC 4731 Arrangement of Transportation of Freight & Cargo
488991 Packing & Crating
SIC 4783 Packing & Crating
488999 All Other Support Activities for Transportation
SIC 4729 Arrangement of Passenger Transportation, nec
SIC 4789 Transportation Services, nec
49111   Postal Service
SIC 4311 United States Postal Service
49211   Couriers
SIC 4215 Courier Services, Except by Air
SIC 4513 Air Courier Services
49221   Local Messengers & Local Delivery
SIC 4215 Courier Services, Except by Air
49311   General Warehousing & Storage Facilities
SIC 4225 General Warehousing & Storage
SIC 4226 Special Warehousing & Storage, nec
49312   Refrigerated Storage Facilities
SIC 4222 Refrigerated Warehousing & Storage
SIC 4226 Special Warehousing & Storage, nec
49313   Farm Product Storage Facilities
SIC 4221 Farm Product Warehousing & Storage
49319   Other Warehousing & Storage Facilities
SIC 4226 Special Warehousing & Storage, nec

INFORMATION

51111 Newspaper Publishers
SIC 2711 Newspapers: Publishing or Publishing & Printing
51112 Periodical Publishers
SIC 2721 Periodicals: Publishing or Publishing & Printing
51113 Book Publishers
SIC 2731 Books: Publishing or Publishing & Printing
51114 Database & Directory Publishers
SIC 2741 Miscellaneous Publishing
511191 Greeting Card Publishers
SIC 2771 Greeting Cards
511199 All Other Publishers
SIC 2741 Miscellaneous Publishing
51121 Software Publishers
SIC 7372 Prepackaged Software
51211 Motion Picture & Video Production
SIC 7812 Motion Picture & Video Tape Production
51212 Motion Picture & Video Distribution
SIC 7822 Motion Picture & Video Tape Distribution
SIC 7829 Services Allied to Motion Picture Distribution
512131 Motion Picture Theaters, Except Drive-Ins.
SIC 7832 Motion Picture Theaters, Except Drive-In
512132 Drive-In Motion Picture Theaters
SIC 7833 Drive-In Motion Picture Theaters
512191 Teleproduction & Other Post-Production Services
SIC 7819 Services Allied to Motion Picture Production
512199 Other Motion Picture & Video Industries
SIC 7819 Services Allied to Motion Picture Production
SIC 7829 Services Allied to Motion Picture Distribution
51221 Record Production
SIC 8999 Services, nec
51222 Integrated Record Production/Distribution
SIC 3652 Phonograph Records & Prerecorded Audio Tapes & Disks
51223 Music Publishers
SIC 2731 Books: Publishing or Publishing & Printing
SIC 2741 Miscellaneous Publishing
SIC 8999 Services, nec
51224 Sound Recording Studios
SIC 7389 Business Services, nec
51229 Other Sound Recording Industries
SIC 7389 Business Services, nec
SIC 7922 Theatrical Producers & Miscellaneous Theatrical Services
513111 Radio Networks
SIC 4832 Radio Broadcasting Stations
513112 Radio Stations
SIC 4832 Radio Broadcasting Stations
51312 Television Broadcasting
SIC 4833 Television Broadcasting Stations
51321 Cable Networks
SIC 4841 Cable & Other Pay Television Services
51322 Cable & Other Program Distribution
SIC 4841 Cable & Other Pay Television Services
51331 Wired Telecommunications Carriers
SIC 4813 Telephone Communications, Except Radiotelephone
SIC 4822 Telegraph & Other Message Communications
513321 Paging
SIC 4812 Radiotelephone Communications
513322 Cellular & Other Wireless Telecommunications
SIC 4812 Radiotelephone Communications
SIC 4899 Communications Services, nec

51333 Telecommunications Resellers
SIC 4812 Radio Communications
SIC 4813 Telephone Communications, Except Radiotelephone
51334 Satellite Telecommunications
SIC 4899 Communications Services, NEC
51339 Other Telecommunications
SIC 4899 Communications Services, NEC
51411 News Syndicates
SIC 7383 News Syndicates
51412 Libraries & Archives
SIC 8231 Libraries
514191 On-Line Information Services
SIC 7375 Information Retrieval Services
514199 All Other Information Services
SIC 8999 Services, nec
51421 Data Processing Services
SIC 7374 Computer Processing & Data Preparation & Processing Services

FINANCE & INSURANCE

52111 Monetary Authorities - Central Bank
SIC 6011 Federal Reserve Banks
52211 Commercial Banking
SIC 6021 National Commercial Banks
SIC 6022 State Commercial Banks
SIC 6029 Commercial Banks, nec
SIC 6081 Branches & Agencies of Foreign Banks
52212 Savings Institutions
SIC 6035 Savings Institutions, Federally Chartered
SIC 6036 Savings Institutions, Not Federally Chartered
52213 Credit Unions
SIC 6061 Credit Unions, Federally Chartered
SIC 6062 Credit Unions, Not Federally Chartered
52219 Other Depository Credit Intermediation
SIC 6022 State Commercial Banks
52221 Credit Card Issuing
SIC 6021 National Commercial Banks
SIC 6022 State Commercial Banks
SIC 6141 Personal Credit Institutions
52222 Sales Financing
SIC 6141 Personal Credit Institutions
SIC 6153 Short-Term Business Credit Institutions, Except Agricultural .
SIC 6159 Miscellaneous Business Credit Institutions
522291 Consumer Lending
SIC 6141 Personal Credit Institutions
522292 Real Estate Credit
SIC 6162 Mortgage Bankers & Loan Correspondents
522293 International Trade Financing
SIC 6081 Branches & Agencies of Foreign Banks
SIC 6082 Foreign Trade & International Banking Institutions
SIC 6111 Federal & Federally-Sponsored Credit Agencies
SIC 6159 Miscellaneous Business Credit Institutions
522294 Secondary Market Financing
SIC 6111 Federal & Federally Sponsored Credit Agencies
522298 All Other Nondepository Credit Intermediation
SIC 5932 Used Merchandise Stores
SIC 6081 Branches & Agencies of Foreign Banks
SIC 6111 Federal & Federally-Sponsored Credit Agencies
SIC 6153 Short-Term Business Credit Institutions, Except Agricultural
SIC 6159 Miscellaneous Business Credit Institutions

52231 Mortgage & Other Loan Brokers
SIC 6163 Loan Brokers
52232 Financial Transactions Processing, Reserve, & Clearing House Activities
SIC 6019 Central Reserve Depository Institutions, nec
SIC 6099 Functions Related to Depository Banking, nec
SIC 6153 Short-Term Business Credit Institutions, Except Agricultural
SIC 7389 Business Services, nec
52239 Other Activities Related to Credit Intermediation
SIC 6099 Functions Related to Depository Banking, nec
SIC 6162 Mortgage Bankers & Loan Correspondents
52311 Investment Banking & Securities Dealing
SIC 6211 Security Brokers, Dealers, & Flotation Companies
52312 Securities Brokerage
SIC 6211 Security Brokers, Dealers, & Flotation Companies
52313 Commodity Contracts Dealing
SIC 6099 Functions Related to depository Banking, nec
SIC 6799 Investors, nec
SIC 6221 Commodity Contracts Brokers & Dealers
52314 Commodity Brokerage
SIC 6221 Commodity Contracts Brokers & Dealers
52321 Securities & Commodity Exchanges
SIC 6231 Security & Commodity Exchanges
52391 Miscellaneous Intermediation
SIC 6211 Securities Brokers, Dealers & Flotation Companies
SIC 6799 Investors, nec
52392 Portfolio Management
SIC 6282 Investment Advice
SIC 6371 Pension, Health, & Welfare Funds
SIC 6733 Trust, Except Educational, Religious, & Charitable
SIC 6799 Investors, nec
52393 Investment Advice
SIC 6282 Investment Advice
523991 Trust, Fiduciary & Custody Activities
SIC 6021 National Commercial Banks
SIC 6022 State Commercial Banks
SIC 6091 Nondepository Trust Facilities
SIC 6099 Functions Related to Depository Banking, nec
SIC 6289 Services Allied With the Exchange of Securities or Commodities, nec
SIC 6733 Trusts, Except Educational, Religious, & Charitable
523999 Miscellaneous Financial Investment Activities
SIC 6099 Functions Related to Depository Banking, nec
SIC 6211 Security Brokers, Dealers, & Flotation Companies
SIC 6289 Services Allied With the Exchange of Securities or Commodities, nec
SIC 6799 Investors, nec
SIC 6792 Oil Royalty Traders
524113 Direct Life Insurance Carriers
SIC 6311 Life Insurance
524114 Direct Health & Medical Insurance Carriers
SIC 6324 Hospital & Medical Service Plans
SIC 6321 Accident & Health Insurance
524126 Direct Property & Casualty Insurance Carriers
SIC 6331 Fire, Marine, & Casualty Insurance
SIC 6351 Surety Insurance
524127 Direct Title Insurance Carriers
SIC 6361 Title Insurance
524128 Other Direct Insurance Carriers
SIC 6399 Insurance Carriers, nec
52413 Reinsurance Carriers
SIC 6311 Life Insurance
SIC 6321 Accident & Health Insurance

SIC 6324 Hospital & Medical Service Plans
SIC 6331 Fire, Marine, & Casualty Insurance
SIC 6351 Surety Insurance
SIC 6361 Title Insurance
52421 Insurance Agencies & Brokerages
SIC 6411 Insurance Agents, Brokers & Service
524291 Claims Adjusters
SIC 6411 Insurance Agents, Brokers & Service
524292 Third Party Administration for Insurance & Pension Funds
SIC 6371 Pension, Health, & Welfare Funds
SIC 6411 Insurance Agents, Brokers & Service
524298 All Other Insurance Related Activities
SIC 6411 Insurance Agents, Brokers & Service
52511 Pension Funds
SIC 6371 Pension, Health, & Welfare Funds
52512 Health & Welfare Funds
SIC 6371 Pension, Health, & Welfare Funds
52519 Other Insurance Funds
SIC 6321 Accident & Health Insurance
SIC 6324 Hospital & Medical Service Plans
SIC 6331 Fire, Marine, & Casualty Insurance
SIC 6733 Trusts, Except Educational, Religious, & Charitable
52591 Open-End Investment Funds
SIC 6722 Management Investment Offices, Open-End
52592 Trusts, Estates, & Agency Accounts
SIC 6733 Trusts, Except Educational, Religious, & Charitable
52593 Real Estate Investment Trusts
SIC 6798 Real Estate Investment Trusts
52599 Other Financial Vehicles
SIC 6726 Unit Investment Trusts, Face-Amount Certificate Offices, & Closed-End Management Investment Offices

REAL ESTATE & RENTAL & LEASING

53111 Lessors of Residential Buildings & Dwellings
SIC 6513 Operators of Apartment Buildings
SIC 6514 Operators of Dwellings Other Than Apartment Buildings
53112 Lessors of Nonresidential Buildings
SIC 6512 Operators of Nonresidential Buildings
53113 Lessors of Miniwarehouses & Self Storage Units
SIC 4225 General Warehousing & Storage
53119 Lessors of Other Real Estate Property
SIC 6515 Operators of Residential Mobile Home Sites
SIC 6517 Lessors of Railroad Property
SIC 6519 Lessors of Real Property, nec
53121 Offices of Real Estate Agents & Brokers
SIC 6531 Real Estate Agents Managers
531311 Residential Property Managers
SIC 6531 Real Estate Agents & Managers
531312 Nonresidential Property Managers
SIC 6531 Real Estate Agents & Managers
53132 Offices of Real Estate Appraisers
SIC 6531 Real Estate Agents & Managers
531399 All Other Activities Related to Real Estate
SIC 6531 Real Estate Agents & Managers
532111 Passenger Car Rental
SIC 7514 Passenger Car Rental
532112 Passenger Car Leasing
SIC 7515 Passenger Car Leasing

53212 Truck, Utility Trailer, & RV Rental & Leasing
SIC 7513 Truck Rental & Leasing Without Drivers
SIC 7519 Utility Trailers & Recreational Vehicle Rental
53221 Consumer Electronics & Appliances Rental
SIC 7359 Equipment Rental & Leasing, nec
53222 Formal Wear & Costume Rental
SIC 7299 Miscellaneous Personal Services, nec
SIC 7819 Services Allied to Motion Picture Production
53223 Video Tape & Disc Rental
SIC 7841 Video Tape Rental
532291 Home Health Equipment Rental
SIC 7352 Medical Equipment Rental & Leasing
532292 Recreational Goods Rental
SIC 7999 Amusement & Recreation Services, nec
532299 All Other Consumer Goods Rental
SIC 7359 Equipment Rental & Leasing, nec
53231 General Rental Centers
SIC 7359 Equipment Rental & Leasing, nec
532411 Commercial Air, Rail, & Water Transportation Equipment Rental & Leasing
SIC 4499 Water Transportation Services, nec
SIC 4741 Rental of Railroad Cars
SIC 7359 Equipment Rental & Leasing, nec
532412 Construction, Mining & Forestry Machinery & Equipment Rental & Leasing
SIC 7353 Heavy Construction Equipment Rental & Leasing
SIC 7359 Equipment Rental & Leasing, nec
53242 Office Machinery & Equipment Rental & Leasing
SIC 7359 Equipment Rental & Leasing
SIC 7377 Computer Rental & Leasing
53249 Other Commercial & Industrial Machinery & Equipment Rental & Leasing
SIC 7352 Medical Equipment Rental & Leasing
SIC 7359 Equipment Rental & Leasing, nec
SIC 7819 Services Allied to Motion Picture Production
SIC 7922 Theatrical Producers & Miscellaneous Theatrical Services
53311 Owners & Lessors of Other Nonfinancial Assets
SIC 6792 Oil Royalty Traders
SIC 6794 Patent Owners & Lessors

PROFESSIONAL, SCIENTIFIC, & TECHNICAL SERVICES

54111 Offices of Lawyers
SIC 8111 Legal Services
541191 Title Abstract & Settlement Offices
SIC 6541 Title Abstract Offices
541199 All Other Legal Services
SIC 7389 Business Services, nec
541211 Offices of Certified Public Accountants
SIC 8721 Accounting, Auditing, & Bookkeeping Services
541213 Tax Preparation Services
SIC 7291 Tax Return Preparation Services
541214 Payroll Services
SIC 7819 Services Allied to Motion Picture Production
SIC 8721 Accounting, Auditing, & Bookkeeping Services
541219 Other Accounting Services
SIC 8721 Accounting, Auditing, & Bookkeeping Services
54131 Architectural Services
SIC 8712 Architectural Services

54132 Landscape Architectural Services
SIC 0781 Landscape Counseling & Planning
54133 Engineering Services
SIC 8711 Engineering Services
54134 Drafting Services
SIC 7389 Business Services, nec
54135 Building Inspection Services
SIC 7389 Business Services, nec
54136 Geophysical Surveying & Mapping Services
SIC 8713 Surveying Services
SIC 1081 Metal Mining Services
SIC 1382 Oil & Gas Field Exploration Services
SIC 1481 Nonmetallic Minerals Services, Except Fuels
54137 Surveying & Mapping Services
SIC 7389 Business Services, nec
SIC 8713 Surveying Services
54138 Testing Laboratories
SIC 8734 Testing Laboratories
54141 Interior Design Services
SIC 7389 Business Services, nec
54142 Industrial Design Services
SIC 7389 Business Services, nec
54143 Commercial Art & Graphic Design Services
SIC 7336 Commercial Art & Graphic Design
SIC 8099 Health & Allied Services, nec
54149 Other Specialized Design Services
SIC 7389 Business Services, nec
541511 Custom Computer Programming Services
SIC 7371 Computer Programming Services
541512 Computer Systems Design Services
SIC 7373 Computer Integrated Systems Design
SIC 7379 Computer Related Services, nec
541513 Computer Facilities Management Services
SIC 7376 Computer Facilities Management Services
541519 Other Computer Related Services
SIC 7379 Computer Related Services, nec
541611 Administrative Management & General Management Consulting Services
SIC 8742 Management Consulting Services
541612 Human Resources & Executive Search Consulting Services
SIC 8742 Management Consulting Services
SIC 7361 Employment Agencies
SIC 8999 Services, nec
541613 Marketing Consulting Services
SIC 8742 Management Consulting Services
541614 Process, Physical, Distribution & Logistics Consulting Services
SIC 8742 Management Consulting Services
541618 Other Management Consulting Services
SIC 4731 Arrangement of Transportation of Freight & Cargo
SIC 8748 Business Consulting Services, nec
54162 Environmental Consulting Services
SIC 8999 Services, nec
54169 Other Scientific & Technical Consulting Services
SIC 0781 Landscape Counseling & Planning
SIC 8748 Business Consulting Services, nec
SIC 8999 Services, nec
54171 Research & Development in the Physical Sciences & Engineering Sciences
SIC 8731 Commercial Physical & Biological Research
SIC 8733 Noncommercial Research Organizations

54172 Research & Development in the Life Sciences
SIC 8731 Commercial Physical & Biological Research
SIC 8733 Noncommercial Research Organizations
54173 Research & Development in the Social Sciences & Humanities
SIC 8732 Commercial Economic, Sociological, & Educational Research
SIC 8733 Noncommercial Research Organizations
54181 Advertising Agencies
SIC 7311 Advertising Agencies
54182 Public Relations Agencies
SIC 8743 Public Relations Services
54183 Media Buying Agencies
SIC 7319 Advertising, nec
54184 Media Representatives
SIC 7313 Radio, Television, & Publishers' Advertising Representatives
54185 Display Advertising
SIC 7312 Outdoor Advertising Services
SIC 7319 Advertising, nec
54186 Direct Mail Advertising
SIC 7331 Direct Mail Advertising Services
54187 Advertising Material Distribution Services
SIC 7319 Advertising, NEC
54189 Other Services Related to Advertising
SIC 7319 Advertising, nec
SIC 5199 Nondurable Goods, nec
SIC 7389 Business Services, nec
54191 Marketing Research & Public Opinion Polling
SIC 8732 Commercial Economic, Sociological, & Educational Research
541921 Photography Studios, Portrait
SIC 7221 Photographic Studios, Portrait
541922 Commercial Photography
SIC 7335 Commercial Photography
SIC 8099 Health & Allied Services, nec
54193 Translation & Interpretation Services
SIC 7389 Business Services, NEC
54194 Veterinary Services
SIC 0741 Veterinary Services for Livestock
SIC 0742 Veterinary Services for Animal Specialties
SIC 8734 Testing Laboratories
54199 All Other Professional, Scientific & Technical Services
SIC 7389 Business Services

MANAGEMENT OF COMPANIES & ENTERPRISES

551111 Offices of Bank Holding Companies
SIC 6712 Offices of Bank Holding Companies
551112 Offices of Other Holding Companies
SIC 6719 Offices of Holding Companies, nec
551114 Corporate, Subsidiary, & Regional Managing Offices
No SIC equivalent

ADMINISTRATIVE & SUPPORT, WASTE MANAGEMENT & REMEDIATION SERVICES

56111 Office Administrative Services
SIC 8741 Management Services

56121 Facilities Support Services
SIC 8744 Facilities Support Management Services
56131 Employment Placement Agencies
SIC 7361 Employment Agencies
SIC 7819 Services Allied to Motion Pictures Production
SIC 7922 Theatrical Producers & Miscellaneous Theatrical Services
56132 Temporary Help Services
SIC 7363 Help Supply Services
56133 Employee Leasing Services
SIC 7363 Help Supply Services
56141 Document Preparation Services
SIC 7338 Secretarial & Court Reporting
561421 Telephone Answering Services
SIC 7389 Business Services, nec
561422 Telemarketing Bureaus
SIC 7389 Business Services, nec
561431 Photocopying & Duplicating Services
SIC 7334 Photocopying & Duplicating Services
561432 Private Mail Centers
SIC 7389 Business Services, nec
561439 Other Business Service Centers
SIC 7334 Photocopying & Duplicating Services
SIC 7389 Business Services, nec
56144 Collection Agencies
SIC 7322 Adjustment & Collection Services
56145 Credit Bureaus
SIC 7323 Credit Reporting Services
561491 Repossession Services
SIC 7322 Adjustment & Collection
SIC 7389 Business Services, nec
561492 Court Reporting & Stenotype Services
SIC 7338 Secretarial & Court Reporting
561499 All Other Business Support Services
SIC 7389 Business Services, NEC
56151 Travel Agencies
SIC 4724 Travel Agencies
56152 Tour Operators
SIC 4725 Tour Operators
561591 Convention & Visitors Bureaus
SIC 7389 Business Services, nec
561599 All Other Travel Arrangement & Reservation Services
SIC 4729 Arrangement of Passenger Transportation, nec
SIC 7389 Business Services, nec
SIC 7999 Amusement & Recreation Services, nec
SIC 8699 Membership Organizations, nec
561611 Investigation Services
SIC 7381 Detective, Guard, & Armored Car Services
561612 Security Guards & Patrol Services
SIC 7381 Detective, Guard, & Armored Car Services
561613 Armored Car Services
SIC 7381 Detective, Guard, & Armored Car Services
561621 Security Systems Services
SIC 7382 Security Systems Services
SIC 1731 Electrical Work
561622 Locksmiths
SIC 7699 Repair Shops & Related Services, nec
56171 Exterminating & Pest Control Services
SIC 4959 Sanitary Services, NEC
SIC 7342 Disinfecting & Pest Control Services
56172 Janitorial Services
SIC 7342 Disinfecting & Pest Control Services
SIC 7349 Building Cleaning & Maintenance Services, nec
SIC 4581 Airports, Flying Fields, & Airport Terminal Services

56173 Landscaping Services
SIC 0782 Lawn & Garden Services
SIC 0783 Ornamental Shrub & Tree Services
56174 Carpet & Upholstery Cleaning Services
SIC 7217 Carpet & Upholstery Cleaning
56179 Other Services to Buildings & Dwellings
SIC 7389 Business Services, nec
SIC 7699 Repair Shops & Related Services, nec
56191 Packaging & Labeling Services
SIC 7389 Business Services, nec
56192 Convention & Trade Show Organizers
SIC 7389 Business Services, NEC
56199 All Other Support Services
SIC 7389 Business Services, nec
562111 Solid Waste Collection
SIC 4212 Local Trucking Without Storage
SIC 4953 Refuse Systems
562112 Hazardous Waste Collection
SIC 4212 Local Trucking Without Storage
SIC 4953 Refuse Systems
562119 Other Waste Collection
SIC 4212 Local Trucking Without Storage
SIC 4953 Refuse Systems
562211 Hazardous Waste Treatment & Disposal
SIC 4953 Refuse Systems
562212 Solid Waste Landfill
SIC 4953 Refuse Systems
562213 Solid Waste Combustors & Incinerators
SIC 4953 Refuse Systems
562219 Other Nonhazardous Waste Treatment & Disposal
SIC 4953 Refuse Systems
56291 Remediation Services
SIC 1799 Special Trade Contractors, nec
SIC 4959 Sanitary Services, nec
56292 Materials Recovery Facilities
SIC 4953 Refuse Systems
562991 Septic Tank & Related Services
SIC 7359 Equipment Rental & Leasing, nec
SIC 7699 Repair Shops & Related Services, nec
562998 All Other Miscellaneous Waste Management Services
SIC 4959 Sanitary Services, nec

EDUCATIONAL SERVICES

61111 Elementary & Secondary Schools
SIC 8211 Elementary & Secondary Schools
61121 Junior Colleges
SIC 8222 Junior Colleges & Technical Institutes
61131 Colleges, Universities & Professional Schools
SIC 8221 Colleges, Universities, & Professional Schools
61141 Business & Secretarial Schools
SIC 8244 Business & Secretarial Schools
61142 Computer Training
SIC 8243 Data Processing Schools
61143 Professional & Management Development Training Schools
SIC 8299 Schools & Educational Services, nec
611511 Cosmetology & Barber Schools
SIC 7231 Beauty Shops
SIC 7241 Barber Shops
611512 Flight Training
SIC 8249 Vocational Schools, nec
SIC 8299 Schools & Educational Services, nec

611513 Apprenticeship Training
SIC 8249 Vocational Schools, nec
611519 Other Technical & Trade Schools
SIC 8249 Vocational Schools, NEC
SIC 8243 Data Processing Schools
61161 Fine Arts Schools
SIC 8299 Schools & Educational Services, nec
SIC 7911 Dance Studios, Schools, & Halls
61162 Sports & Recreation Instruction
SIC 7999 Amusement & Recreation Services, nec
61163 Language Schools
SIC 8299 Schools & Educational Services, nec
611691 Exam Preparation & Tutoring
SIC 8299 Schools & Educational Services, nec
611692 Automobile Driving Schools
SIC 8299 Schools & Educational Services, nec
611699 All Other Miscellaneous Schools & Instruction
SIC 8299 Schools & Educational Services, nec
61171 Educational Support Services
SIC 8299 Schools & Educational Services nec
SIC 8748 Business Consulting Services, nec

HEALTH CARE & SOCIAL ASSISTANCE

621111 Offices of Physicians
SIC 8011 Offices & Clinics of Doctors of Medicine
SIC 8031 Offices & Clinics of Doctors of Osteopathy
621112 Offices of Physicians, Mental Health Specialists
SIC 8011 Offices & Clinics of Doctors of Medicine
SIC 8031 Offices & Clinics of Doctors of Osteopathy
62121 Offices of Dentists
SIC 8021 Offices & Clinics of Dentists
62131 Offices of Chiropractors
SIC 8041 Offices & Clinics of Chiropractors
62132 Offices of Optometrists
SIC 8042 Offices & Clinics of Optometrists
62133 Offices of Mental Health Practitioners
SIC 8049 Offices & Clinics of Health Practitioners, nec
62134 Offices of Physical, Occupational & Speech Therapists & Audiologists
SIC 8049 Offices & Clinics of Health Practitioners, nec
621391 Offices of Podiatrists
SIC 8043 Offices & Clinics of Podiatrists
621399 Offices of All Other Miscellaneous Health Practitioners
SIC 8049 Offices & Clinics of Health Practitioners, nec
62141 Family Planning Centers
SIC 8093 Speciality Outpatient Facilities, NEC
SIC 8099 Health & Allied Services, nec
62142 Outpatient Mental Health & Substance Abuse Centers
SIC 8093 Specialty Outpatient Facilities, nec
621491 HMO Medical Centers
SIC 8011 Offices & Clinics of Doctors of Medicine
621492 Kidney Dialysis Centers
SIC 8092 Kidney Dialysis Centers
621493 Freestanding Ambulatory Surgical & Emergency Centers
SIC 8011 Offices & Clinics of Doctors of Medicine
621498 All Other Outpatient Care Centers
SIC 8093 Specialty Outpatient Facilities, nec
621511 Medical Laboratories
SIC 8071 Medical Laboratories
621512 Diagnostic Imaging Centers
SIC 8071 Medical Laboratories

62161   **Home Health Care Services**
SIC 8082 Home Health Care Services
62191   **Ambulance Services**
SIC 4119 Local Passenger Transportation, nec
SIC 4522 Air Transportation, Nonscheduled
621991 **Blood & Organ Banks**
SIC 8099 Health & Allied Services, nec
621999 **All Other Miscellaneous Ambulatory Health Care Services**
SIC 8099 Health & Allied Services, nec
62211   **General Medical & Surgical Hospitals**
SIC 8062 General Medical & Surgical Hospitals
SIC 8069 Specialty Hospitals, Except Psychiatric
62221   **Psychiatric & Substance Abuse Hospitals**
SIC 8063 Psychiatric Hospitals
SIC 8069 Specialty Hospitals, Except Psychiatric
62231   **Specialty Hospitals**
SIC 8069 Specialty Hospitals, Except Psychiatric
62311   **Nursing Care Facilities**
SIC 8051 Skilled Nursing Care Facilities
SIC 8052 Intermediate Care Facilities
SIC 8059 Nursing & Personal Care Facilities, nec
62321   **Residential Mental Retardation Facilities**
SIC 8052 Intermediate Care Facilities
62322   **Residential Mental Health & Substance Abuse Facilities**
SIC 8361 Residential Care
623311 **Continuing Care Retirement Communities**
SIC 8051 Skilled Nursing Care Facilities
SIC 8052 Intermediate Care Facilities
SIC 8059 Nursing & Personal Care Facilities, nec
623312 **Homes for the Elderly**
SIC 8361 Residential Care
62399   **Other Residential Care Facilities**
SIC 8361 Residential Care
62411   **Child & Youth Services**
SIC 8322 Individual & Family Social Services
SIC 8641 Civic, Social, & Fraternal Organizations
62412   **Services for the Elderly & Persons with Disabilities**
SIC 8322 Individual & Family Social Services
62419   **Other Individual & Family Services**
SIC 8322 Individual & Family Social Services
62421   **Community Food Services**
SIC 8322 Individual & Family Social Services
624221 **Temporary Shelters**
SIC 8322 Individual & Family Social Services
624229 **Other Community Housing Services**
SIC 8322 Individual & Family Social Services
62423   **Emergency & Other Relief Services**
SIC 8322 Individual & Family Social Services
62431   **Vocational Rehabilitation Services**
SIC 8331 Job Training & Vocational Rehabilitation Services
62441   **Child Day Care Services**
SIC 8351 Child Day Care Services
SIC 7299 Miscellaneous Personal Services, nec

ARTS, ENTERTAINMENT, & RECREATION

71111   **Theater Companies & Dinner Theaters**
SIC 5812 Eating Places
SIC 7922 Theatrical Producers & Miscellaneous Theatrical Services

71112   **Dance Companies**
SIC 7922 Theatrical Producers & Miscellaneous Theatrical Services
71113   **Musical Groups & Artists**
SIC 7929 Bands, Orchestras, Actors, & Entertainment Groups
71119   **Other Performing Arts Companies**
SIC 7929 Bands, Orchestras, Actors, & Entertainment Groups
SIC 7999 Amusement & Recreation Services, nec
711211 **Sports Teams & Clubs**
SIC 7941 Professional Sports Clubs & Promoters
711212 **Race Tracks**
SIC 7948 Racing, Including Track Operations
711219 **Other Spectator Sports**
SIC 7941 Professional Sports Clubs & Promoters
SIC 7948 Racing, Including Track Operations
SIC 7999 Amusement & Recreation Services, nec
71131   **Promoters of Performing Arts, Sports & Similar Events with Facilities**
SIC 6512 Operators of Nonresidential Buildings
SIC 7922 Theatrical Procedures & Miscellaneous Theatrical Services
SIC 7941 Professional Sports Clubs & Promoters
71132   **Promoters of Performing Arts, Sports & Similar Events without Facilities**
SIC 7922 Theatrical Producers & Miscellaneous Theatrical Services
SIC 7941 Professional Sports Clubs & Promoters
71141   **Agents & Managers for Artists, Athletes, Entertainers & Other Public Figures**
SIC 7389 Business Services, nec
SIC 7922 Theatrical Producers & Miscellaneous Theatrical Services
SIC 7941 Professional Sports Clubs & Promoters
71151   **Independent Artists, Writers, & Performers**
SIC 7819 Services Allied to Motion Picture Production
SIC 7929 Bands, Orchestras, Actors, & Other Entertainers & Entertainment Services
SIC 8999 Services, nec
71211   **Museums**
SIC 8412 Museums & Art Galleries
71212   **Historical Sites**
SIC 8412 Museums & Art Galleries
71213   **Zoos & Botanical Gardens**
SIC 8422 Arboreta & Botanical & Zoological Gardens
71219   **Nature Parks & Other Similar Institutions**
SIC 7999 Amusement & Recreation Services, nec
SIC 8422 Arboreta & Botanical & Zoological Gardens
71311   **Amusement & Theme Parks**
SIC 7996 Amusement Parks
71312   **Amusement Arcades**
SIC 7993 Coin-Operated Amusement Devices
71321   **Casinos**
SIC 7999 Amusement & Recreation Services, nec
71329   **Other Gambling Industries**
SIC 7993 Coin-Operated Amusement Devices
SIC 7999 Amusement & Recreation Services, nec
71391   **Golf Courses & Country Clubs**
SIC 7992 Public Golf Courses
SIC 7997 Membership Sports & Recreation Clubs
71392   **Skiing Facilities**
SIC 7999 Amusement & Recreation Services, nec
71393   **Marinas**
SIC 4493 Marinas

71394 Fitness & Recreational Sports Centers
SIC 7991 Physical Fitness Facilities
SIC 7997 Membership Sports & Recreation Clubs
SIC 7999 Amusement & Recreation Services, nec
71395 Bowling Centers
SIC 7933 Bowling Centers
71399 All Other Amusement & Recreation Industries
SIC 7911 Dance Studios, Schools, & Halls
SIC 7993 Amusement & Recreation Services, nec
SIC 7997 Membership Sports & Recreation Clubs
SIC 7999 Amusement & Recreation Services, nec

ACCOMMODATION & FOODSERVICES

72111 Hotels & Motels
SIC 7011 Hotels & Motels
SIC 7041 Organization Hotels & Lodging Houses, on Membership Basis
72112 Casino Hotels
SIC 7011 Hotels & Motels
721191 Bed & Breakfast Inns
SIC 7011 Hotels & Motels
721199 All Other Traveler Accommodation
SIC 7011 Hotels & Motels
721211 RV Parks & Campgrounds
SIC 7033 Recreational Vehicle Parks & Campgrounds
721214 Recreational & Vacation Camps
SIC 7032 Sporting & Recreational Camps
72131 Rooming & Boarding Houses
SIC 7021 Rooming & Boarding Houses
SIC 7041 Organization Hotels & Lodging Houses, on Membership Basis
72211 Full-Service Restaurants
SIC 5812 Eating Places
722211 Limited-Service Restaurants
SIC 5812 Eating Places
SIC 5499 Miscellaneous Food Stores
722212 Cafeterias
SIC 5812 Eating Places
722213 Snack & Nonalcoholic Beverage Bars
SIC 5812 Eating Places
SIC 5461 Retail Bakeries
72231 Foodservice Contractors
SIC 5812 Eating Places
72232 Caterers
SIC 5812 Eating Places
72233 Mobile Caterers
SIC 5963 Direct Selling Establishments
72241 Drinking Places
SIC 5813 Drinking Places

OTHER SERVICES

811111 General Automotive Repair
SIC 7538 General Automotive Repair Shops
811112 Automotive Exhaust System Repair
SIC 7533 Automotive Exhaust System Repair Shops
811113 Automotive Transmission Repair
SIC 7537 Automotive Transmission Repair Shops

811118 Other Automotive Mechanical & Electrical Repair & Maintenance
SIC 7539 Automotive Repair Shops, nec
811121 Automotive Body, Paint & Upholstery Repair & Maintenance
SIC 7532 Top, Body, & Upholstery Repair Shops & Paint Shops
811122 Automotive Glass Replacement Shops
SIC 7536 Automotive Glass Replacement Shops
811191 Automotive Oil Change & Lubrication Shops
SIC 7549 Automotive Services, Except Repair & Carwashes
811192 Car Washes
SIC 7542 Carwashes
811198 All Other Automotive Repair & Maintenance
SIC 7534 Tire Retreading & Repair Shops
SIC 7549 Automotive Services, Except Repair & Carwashes
811211 Consumer Electronics Repair & Maintenance
SIC 7622 Radio & Television Repair Shops
SIC 7629 Electrical & Electronic Repair Shops, nec
811212 Computer & Office Machine Repair & Maintenance
SIC 7378 Computer Maintenance & Repair
SIC 7629 Electrical & Electronic Repair Shops, nec
SIC 7699 Repair Shops & Related Services, nec
811213 Communication Equipment Repair & Maintenance
SIC 7622 Radio & Television Repair Shops
SIC 7629 Electrical & Electronic Repair Shops, nec
811219 Other Electronic & Precision Equipment Repair & Maintenance
SIC 7629 Electrical & Electronic Repair Shops, nec
SIC 7699 Repair Shops & Related Services, NEC
81131 Commercial & Industrial Machinery & Equipment Repair & Maintenance
SIC 7699 Repair Shops & Related Services, nec
SIC 7623 Refrigerator & Air-Conditioning Service & Repair Shops
SIC 7694 Armature Rewinding Shops
811411 Home & Garden Equipment Repair & Maintenance
SIC 7699 Repair Shops & Related Services, nec
811412 Appliance Repair & Maintenance
SIC 7623 Refrigeration & Air-Conditioning Service & Repair Shops
SIC 7629 Electrical & Electronic Repair Shops, NEC
SIC 7699 Repairs Shops & Related Services, nec
81142 Reupholstery & Furniture Repair
SIC 7641 Reupholstery & Furniture Repair
81143 Footwear & Leather Goods Repair
SIC 7251 Shoe Repair & Shoeshine Parlors
SIC 7699 Repair Shops & Related Services
81149 Other Personal & Household Goods Repair & Maintenance
SIC 3732 Boat Building & Repairing
SIC 7219 Laundry & Garment Services, nec
SIC 7631 Watch, Clock, & Jewelry Repair
SIC 7692 Welding Repair
SIC 7699 Repair Shops & Related Services, nec
812111 Barber Shops
SIC 7241 Barber Shops
812112 Beauty Salons
SIC 7231 Beauty Shops
812113 Nail Salons
SIC 7231 Beauty Shops
812191 Diet & Weight Reducing Centers
SIC 7299 Miscellaneous Personal Services, nec

812199 Other Personal Care Services
SIC 7299 Miscellaneous Personal Services, nec,
81221 Funeral Homes
SIC 7261 Funeral Services & Crematories
81222 Cemeteries & Crematories
SIC 6531 Real Estate Agents & Managers
SIC 6553 Cemetery Subdividers & Developers
SIC 7261 Funeral Services & Crematories
81231 Coin-Operated Laundries & Drycleaners
SIC 7215 Coin-Operated Laundry & Drycleaning
812321 Laundries, Family & Commercial
SIC 7211 Power Laundries, Family & Commercial
812322 Drycleaning Plants
SIC 7216 Drycleaning Plants, Except Rug Cleaning
812331 Linen Supply
SIC 7213 Linen Supply
SIC 7219 Laundry & Garment Services, nec,
812332 Industrial Launderers
SIC 7218 Industrial Launderers
812391 Garment Pressing, & Agents for Laundries
SIC 7212 Garment Pressing & Agents for Laundries
812399 All Other Laundry Services
SIC 7219 Laundry & Garment Services, NEC
81291 Pet Care Services
SIC 0752 Animal Speciality Services, Except Veterinary
812921 Photo Finishing Laboratories
SIC 7384 Photofinishing Laboratories
812922 One-Hour Photo Finishing
SIC 7384 Photofinishing Laboratories
81293 Parking Lots & Garages
SIC 7521 Automobile Parking
81299 All Other Personal Services
SIC 7299 Miscellaneous Personal Services, nec
SIC 7389 Miscellaneous Business Services
81311 Religious Organizations
SIC 8661 Religious Organizations
813211 Grantmaking Foundations
SIC 6732 Educational, Religious, & Charitable Trust
813212 Voluntary Health Organizations
SIC 8399 Social Services, nec
813219 Other Grantmaking & Giving Services
SIC 8399 Social Services, NEC
813311 Human Rights Organizations
SIC 8399 Social Services, nec
813312 Environment, Conservation & Wildlife Organizations
SIC 8399 Social Services, nec
SIC 8699 Membership Organizations, nec
813319 Other Social Advocacy Organizations
SIC 8399 Social Services, NEC
81341 Civic & Social Organizations
SIC 8641 Civic, Social, & Fraternal Organizations
SIC 8699 Membership Organizations, nec
81391 Business Associations
SIC 8611 Business Associations
SIC 8699 Membership Organizations, nec
81392 Professional Organizations
SIC 8621 Professional Membership Organizations
81393 Labor Unions & Similar Labor Organizations
SIC 8631 Labor Unions & Similar Labor Organizations
81394 Political Organizations
SIC 8651 Political Organizations
81399 Other Similar Organizations
SIC 6531 Real Estate Agents & Managers
SIC 8641 Civic, Social, & Fraternal Organizations

SIC 8699 Membership Organizations, nec
81411 Private Households
SIC 8811 Private Households

PUBLIC ADMINISTRATION

92111 Executive Offices
SIC 9111 Executive Offices
92112 Legislative Bodies
SIC 9121 Legislative Bodies
92113 Public Finance
SIC 9311 Public Finance, Taxation, & Monetary Policy
92114 Executive & Legislative Offices, Combined
SIC 9131 Executive & Legislative Offices, Combined
92115 American Indian & Alaska Native Tribal Governments
SIC 8641 Civic, Social, & Fraternal Organizations
92119 All Other General Government
SIC 9199 General Government, nec
92211 Courts
SIC 9211 Courts
92212 Police Protection
SIC 9221 Police Protection
92213 Legal Counsel & Prosecution
SIC 9222 Legal Counsel & Prosecution
92214 Correctional Institutions
SIC 9223 Correctional Institutions
92215 Parole Offices & Probation Offices
SIC 8322 Individual & Family Social Services
92216 Fire Protection
SIC 9224 Fire Protection
92219 All Other Justice, Public Order, & Safety
SIC 9229 Public Order & Safety, nec
92311 Administration of Education Programs
SIC 9411 Administration of Educational Programs
92312 Administration of Public Health Programs
SIC 9431 Administration of Public Health Programs
92313 Administration of Social, Human Resource & Income Maintenance Programs
SIC 9441 Administration of Social, Human Resource & Income Maintenance Programs
92314 Administration of Veteran's Affairs
SIC 9451 Administration of Veteran's Affairs, Except Health Insurance
92411 Air & Water Resource & Solid Waste Management
SIC 9511 Air & Water Resource & Solid Waste Management
92412 Land, Mineral, Wildlife, & Forest Conservation
SIC 9512 Land, Mineral, Wildlife, & Forest Conservation
92511 Administration of Housing Programs
SIC 9531 Administration of Housing Programs
92512 Administration of Urban Planning & Community & Rural Development
SIC 9532 Administration of Urban Planning & Community & Rural Development
92611 Administration of General Economic Programs
SIC 9611 Administration of General Economic Programs
92612 Regulation & Administration of Transportation Programs
SIC 9621 Regulations & Administration of Transportation Programs
92613 Regulation & Administration of Communications, Electric, Gas, & Other Utilities
SIC 9631 Regulation & Administration of Communications, Electric, Gas, & Other Utilities

92614 Regulation of Agricultural Marketing & Commodities
SIC 9641 Regulation of Agricultural Marketing & Commodities
92615 Regulation, Licensing, & Inspection of Miscellaneous Commercial Sectors
SIC 9651 Regulation, Licensing, & Inspection of Miscellaneous Commercial Sectors
92711 Space Research & Technology
SIC 9661 Space Research & Technology
92811 National Security
SIC 9711 National Security
92812 International Affairs
SIC 9721 International Affairs
99999 Unclassified Establishments
SIC 9999 Nonclassifiable Establishments